THE CONTINUUM ENCYCLOPEDIA OF
MODERN CRITICISM AND THEORY

The Continuum Encyclopedia of Modern Criticism and Theory

General Editor: Julian Wolfreys

Editorial Associates: Kenneth Womack, Pennsylvania State University and Ruth Robbins, University College Northampton

The Continuum Encyclopedia of Modern Criticism and Theory offers the student and scholar of literary and cultural studies the most comprehensive, single-volume guide to the history and development of criticism in the humanities.

In a clearly organized format, this major reference work takes the reader through introductions to historically influential philosophers, literary critics, schools of thought and movements from Spinoza and Descartes to phenomenology and Heidegger, before turning to its three principal areas of critical attention: Europe, North America and Great Britain.

Addressing the development of literary criticism and theory within the cultural, ideological, historical and institutional parameters of their growth, this volume provides simultaneously a stimulating introduction to theoretical engagement in the humanities, while also offering lucidly written critical interventions into current theory and criticism. Furthermore, while remaining aware of the importance of various contexts within which criticism has grown, the essays also concern themselves with the cross-fertilization between the various academic and intellectual cultures under consideration.

With more than 100 essays from an internationally renowned body of scholars, all of whom are recognized experts in their respective fields, *The Continuum Encyclopedia of Modern Criticism and Theory* offers student readers, scholars and libraries a unique, challenging and indispensable reference guide.

Julian Wolfreys is Associate Professor of Victorian literary and cultural studies with the Department of English at the University of Florida. The author and editor of numerous books and articles, his most recent publications are *Readings: Acts of Close Reading in Literary Theory* and *Victorian Haunting: Spectrality, Gothic, the Uncanny*.

THE CONTINUUM ENCYCLOPEDIA OF MODERN CRITICISM AND THEORY

General Editor Julian Wolfreys

Editorial Associates Ruth Robbins, Kenneth Womack

Editorial Assistants Kara Kalenius, Matthew Massucci, Brian Niro, Eric Tribunella

CONTINUUM ● NEW YORK

For

ANTONY EASTHOPE

In memoriam

2002

The Continuum International Publishing Group, Inc
370 Lexington Avenue, New York, NY 10017

Typeset in 10 on 12pt Goudy
by Hewer Text Limited, Edinburgh, and
printed and bound in Poland by
OZGraf S. A., Olsztyn, Poland

Library of Congress Cataloging-in-Publication Data

The Continuum encyclopedia of modern criticism and theory / general
editor, Julian Wolfreys ; editorial associates, Ruth Robbins, Kenneth
Womack ; editorial assistants, Kara Kalenius ... [et al.].
    p.cm.
Includes bibliographical references and index.
 ISBN 0-8264-1414-1
1. Criticism--History--20th century--Encyclopedias. I. Wolfreys,
Julian, 1958- II. Robbins, Ruth, 1965- III. Womack, Kenneth. IV.
Kalenius, Kara. V. Continuum (Firm)
PN94.C695 2002
801'.95'03--dc21

Contents

Part III CRITICISM, LITERARY AND CULTURAL STUDIES IN ENGLAND, IRELAND, SCOTLAND AND WALES

Foreword

The *Continuum Encyclopedia of Modern Criticism and Theory* offers the student of literary and cultural studies a comprehensive, single-volume guide to the history and development of criticism in the humanities as the twenty-first century opens. While emphasizing the theory and practice of literary and cultural criticism, it provides extensive coverage of related and contextual discourses, as well as critical overviews of the work and reception of major figures responsible, directly or indirectly, for the development of those discourses in the now-related areas of philosophy, poetics, politics, aesthetics, linguistics and psycho-analysis. It does so acknowledging in the process the cultural, historical, ideological and epistemological specificities of the emergence and subsequent transformation of critical and discursive concerns, debates and transformations. The encyclopaedia takes the reader through introductions to historically influential philosophers, literary critics, schools of thought and movements from Spinoza and Descartes to phenomenology and Heidegger, from Coleridge and Arnold to contemporary debates in the areas of cultural studies and post-marxism, through its three principal areas of critical attention, Europe, the USA and Great Britain. Furthermore, while remaining aware of the importance of various contexts within and out of which criticism has grown, the essays contained herein also concern themselves with the equally important issue of cross-fertilization between the various academic and intellectual cultures under consideration.

Having said this, it has to be acknowledged that all encyclopaedias and guides to criticism, whether literary, cultural or, as in the case of this volume, inter- and trans-disciplinary, invariably fall between two stools: aiming at a kind of universality, they become shaped, often inadvertently, by the cultural contexts within which they are produced, whether they recognize this or not. Comprehending this situation and under-standing that it is impossible to escape what is perhaps the central problematic of developing a project such as the present volume, the essays which comprise this encyclopaedia have been commissioned with the idea of acknowledging matters of historical and cultural specificity, and speaking to the limits, the parameters of both the immediate project and the situation of institutional criticism at the beginning of the twenty-first century, from the outset.

Thus the volume and its contributors attempt to deal with an explicitly limited, yet arguably comprehensive, range of topics, figures, subjects and schools of thought (whether the question of the school comes down to a misperception from some other place in the academy or beyond, or the movement has, on occasion, been consciously generated). The *Continuum Encyclopedia* thus provides the reader with essays which address key issues in the history and development of institutional critical practice as these are principally embedded within particular cultures and as these issues have been translated historically as the study of literature and culture has grown and changed, or from culture to culture. In the main, the volume addresses principally literary and cultural areas of critical study, as already stated, but with the intention of demonstrating that these fields, loosely defined, are marked by a constant hybridization of methodologies, disciplines and interests, as often from within as the result of the critical importation of a discourse or epistemology ostensibly alien to the field in question. The volume therefore, and in addition to the already stated goals, sets out to establish the philosophical and ideological parameters and systems or, perhaps better, structures of thought which have come to inform critical practice, and subsequently, though not without resistance, broadened critical practice from interests in purely formal, philological or historically grounded literary study.

While certain essays in the volume are concerned with schools of thought, others deal with more nebulous and general interests in the history of critical thinking and literary study, at the same time seeking to ground development, challenge, debate and change historically and culturally, albeit in a provisional manner in an effort to provide for the student reader a sense of complexity within given cultural moments. Such a practice is of course open to selectivity, but we recognize the limits and problems from the beginning and choose to try to counter these, albeit partially, rather than carrying on as though such issues were not a problem. This will mean that, inevitably for some readers (particularly those who have strong readings of the history of critical development), there will always be something missing: for example, an entry on a beloved figure, or inadequate coverage of a particular moment or movement. More individual entries might be added, and the table of contents could be expanded endlessly. How though does one gauge such things? Include one person, and someone else immediately springs to mind. Ultimately a balance has to be reached, between specificity, detail, singularity and a comprehension of what might best be described as broad trends, persistences, the genealogy of interests and so on.

The volume's division into loosely assumed cultural areas is in no way an attempt to impose order in a procrustean fashion. Inevitably, again, there will be a perceived sense of exclusivity: all encyclopaedias run this risk and, indeed, might be said to be governed by the effort to negotiate and respond to this risk. The very idea of the encyclopaedia calls its editors and contributors to take responsibility for that risk. As the reader will note, several of the contributors choose to address the very idea of the limit, exposing it as arbitrary and artificial, yet something which it is necessary to consider, as part of their broader response to a particular critical issue. As already suggested, it is the contention of this volume that criticism has been shaped by dominant hegemonies of thought, that thought has a cultural history, if not several, and that the theory and practice of criticism as it has developed in the twentieth century within particular university cultures throughout the English-speaking world has been dominated and shaped in particular ways, specifically in North American (particularly US), French and, to a lesser extent, German and British academic milieus and beyond (although one must recognize immediately that this particular term, 'British', is itself problematic, as the final article on so-called British poststructuralism makes clear).

We might thus suggest that despite the necessity of understanding the biographical and personal historical backgrounds of, say, Jacques Derrida, Hélène Cixous, Julia Kristeva, Edward Said, Gayatri Spivak, among so many others, it is equally if not more significant to understand that thought and the texts which mediate thought do not develop in isolation, but are the historically determined product of specific cultures at particular times. Derrida, for example, not only refers to himself repeatedly as only ever being able to express himself in French, but also interprets and reads Hegel and Heidegger in ways that are arguably marked by what may be schematically defined as certain Parisian intellectual contexts, as those contexts have determined and been determined by the reception of Freud, Hegel, Heidegger (to indicate only the most visible, obvious figures) throughout the twentieth century. Similarly, Gayatri Spivak's work is as much indebted to a certain antagonistic relationship with what American and British critics conventionally term poststructuralism as it is to the North American education system in which she was educated as a postgraduate and in which she has taught for a number of years now.

There is, then, no such thing as a pure discourse. Yet, on the other hand, there is no such thing as a finite context or contexts. One cannot speak of either purely national or universal determinations, and, equally, nor can one ascribe to critical thinking either a finite or unchanging condition. Intellectual cultures, like literary genres, have moments of historical ascendance and hegemonic dominance; it is with such issues that this volume is purposely involved and in which it hopes to engage its readers.

Julian Wolfreys

Note on bibliographical references

Dates in parenthetical references following citation or title often refer to the date of original publication, which is given in the bibliographies in square brackets, while, in the bibliographies, the work in question is listed by date of most recent publication, edition or imprint as referred to by the author of the article.

Part I

Critical Discourse in Europe

René Descartes (1596–1650) and Baruch Spinoza (1632–1677): Beginnings

In his 1949 essay, 'The Mirror Stage' (1966), Jacques Lacan, attempting to take his distance from existentialism, divided philosophy into two camps: those that took the *Cogito* as their starting point and those that did not (this statement was repeated many times after, including by some of France's most important thinkers, among them Foucault and Canguilhem). With such a statement, Lacan located the origins of French or even European philosophy not in Husserl, Hegel or even Kant, but in the conflictual field of seventeenth-century philosophy, specifically in the opposing doctrines of René Descartes and Baruch Spinoza. This may come as a surprise to the Anglo-American reader for whom the only conflict associated with the seventeenth-century is that between rationalism and empiricism and for whom Spinoza is a secondary or even tertiary figure, a minor Cartesian only recently admitted into the canon of philosophers deemed worthy of scholarly attention. Further, while Descartes's *Meditations* is well-known even outside the field of philosophy, his name is primarily associated with his proof of God's existence and, through Locke, the doctrine of innate ideas, neither of which are particularly relevant to the concerns of modern French philosophy and theory. How then are we to understand the sense in which the conflict between these two philosophers (assuming that their relation is one of conflict) constitutes a 'beginning'?

There is no question of identifying a French or even continental reading, or readings, of Descartes and Spinoza which would then become the correct interpretation in counter-position to the Anglo-American. Nor is it a question of simply multiplying readings as if, without any true relation to their object, they can never be any other than projections of the culture or historical moment in which they emerge. Instead, we will argue that specific historical moments impose on philosophical texts a historically determined (and therefore identifiable) grid that in turn determines what in a text is visible or invisible, what is compelling and what devoid of interest. There are thus no readings independent of texts and no texts independent of reading. Both the text and its history are equally real, equally material; both must be explained.

Let us begin with Descartes: what did twentieth-century French philosophy select from Descartes and what determined this selection? The fact that Lacan could use a declension of a Latin verb, *cogito* ('I think'), as a noun, suggests very clearly the importance of the first two Meditations. In a very important sense (and Lacan himself, among others, would later have occasion to comment on this), the first two sections of the *Meditations* were abstracted from the text as a whole and even more importantly from the chain of arguments in which they were simply a preliminary step, the nature of which would be modified in the course of the demonstration. Indeed, the meticulous reconstruction of Descartes's 'order of reasons' by Martial Guéroult in a famous commentary many times the length of the *Meditations* themselves, showed beyond any doubt the impressionistic sketchy quality of such readings. The fact remains, however, that the reduction of the *Meditations*, or even Cartesian philosophy as a whole, to 'the Cogito' was not simply 'false', that is without any relation to the text, and it remains to be seen to what extent such a reading was authorized by the *Meditations* themselves.

One might simply read the first paragraph of the *Meditations* to discover what made Descartes so controversial in his own time and so much a contemporary of the twentieth century: the ubiquity of the first person pronoun 'I'. A work devoted to the establishment of the 'first philosophy', that is to the construction of an adequate foundation for philosophical and scientific inquiry, would customarily have avoided reference to the individuality of the philosopher, his fears, hopes and feelings, for fear of being dismissed as outside the universal. Indeed, a tradition dating from Aristotle, and which includes medieval Christian, Jewish and Islamic philosophy, regarded rationality or truth as necessarily collective in nature, residing in the totality of an ever present archive of authoritative works. An individual, in order to escape the particularity of individual existence, had to accede to and participate in this archive to formulate universally valid propositions. Descartes shocked his contemporaries by declaring the necessity of precisely the opposite course, that is of 'demolishing completely' and rejecting as false everything contained in this archive. Instead of referring to a tradition of inquiries and findings, he would begin his reasoning from a position of absolute certainty, not simply the position agreed upon by a majority as valid or true, but a position that could not be doubted.

What is perhaps even more significant is not merely that Descartes regarded it necessary for him as an individual (and it must be as an individual, since the mere existence of other minds – how does he know that the people he sees are not automatons? – and, at the extreme, anything outside of himself must be regarded as illusory until proven otherwise) to cast off all prior knowledge and learning, but that such an action was even possible. 'I am here quite alone,' he announces at the outset of the *Meditations*, a kind of Robinson Crusoe in philosophy, but who, unlike the hapless sailor, has by an act of will removed himself to an island far from others where he can reconstruct a world of knowledge from zero, sure of the foundations that he himself has built. Here it is necessary to step outside the *Meditations* and refer to a later work, *The Passions of the Soul* (1646), that explains in detail what is presupposed in the *Meditations*, namely the ability of the soul (*l'âme* or *mens*) to free itself from the world that envelopes it. Such a freedom is not easily won: 'my habitual opinions keep coming back, and, despite my wishes, they capture my belief which is, as it were, bound over to them as a result of long occupation and the law of custom' (*Meditations*, 15). In this way, the milieu or context of the philosopher is conceived of as external to him, to be accepted or rejected in part or as a totality by a mind endowed with the proper strength of will. Indeed, there is an ethical and even political dimension to the act by which one frees oneself from comfortable illusions and displays the fortitude necessary to endure the absolute solitude that is the necessary, if temporary, consequence of systematic doubt. This is what might be called the heroic moment in Cartesian philosophy: at least it would be regarded as such by philosophers as important to twentieth-century thought as Husserl and Sartre.

He will undertake to destroy the very foundations that support him, risking, as his critic Pascal noted, falling into an abyss in his attempt to find that one certain point from which adequate knowledge can be constructed and without which all hope of distinguishing truth from falsehood is lost. First, the evidence of the senses: although sometimes faulty, do they not present some indubitable truths? In a passage that occasioned a lively debate between two of France's most important philosophers (Derrida and Foucault), Descartes argues that it would appear 'quite impossible' to doubt 'that I am here, sitting by the fire, wearing a winter dressing-gown, holding this piece of paper in my hands' (*Meditations*, 13). Impossible, unless he entertains the idea that he is one of those madmen who believe that they are kings even as they languish in a dungeon. While such a notion might appear far-fetched, does not everyone, sane and mad alike, experience as real what upon awakening is revealed only to have been a dream? Are we not compelled then to doubt all that we glean from the senses? Fortunately (or so it appears for a brief moment), the subtraction of that which is derived from the senses leaves an important body of truths remaining. Surely, two and two equal four whether I am sane or mad, awake or asleep, just as a square necessarily has four sides? Here, Descartes will call upon God to sustain him in his doubt: if there is an omnipotent God, may it not be possible that He has only made it appear to our philosophical pilgrim that there is an earth, sun, sky, extended things, shapes, lines and places when in fact there are none? And if God in his infinite goodness could not be capable of such deception, is it not equally possible to entertain the idea of an evil genius, as powerful as God, but as evil as He is good? He now finds himself in the midst of a boundless, bottomless sea. Or so he fears: in fact, as is well known, doubt presupposes something that doubts. If I doubt, or think, I must exist. I may not have a body, there may not be an external world, but I nevertheless exist as a thinking thing. Descartes has not only established the priority of the individual over the collective, but of the mind over the body.

There is nothing as revolutionary in Cartesian philosophy as the notion that the knowledge of the soul must precede not only a knowledge of other bodies, but even our own body. From now on, we cannot know anything without accounting for how we know it: how do we know that we know? A study of the physical world must therefore begin with an inquiry into the soul, specifically into how it forms clear and distinct, i.e. adequate, ideas. As we have seen, the soul can know itself only by experiencing its independence from extended substance, Descartes's term for the material world; it must understand itself as a substance essentially free from space and time, and from the determinations proper to physical existence. The universe is thus comprised of two substances, the *res cogitans* and the *res extensa*, thinking substance and extended substance or thought and matter. While Descartes's ecclesiastical adversaries charged him with having thus rendered spirit (and God) irrelevant to the physical world, he argued that this freedom allowed for the possibility of the mind's mastery over itself and the bodily impulses to which it was subject.

These positions proved decisive for European philosophy. No longer was it possible to know the world without first understanding the mind that knows, which thus might appear as either the condition of or impediment to knowledge. As Guéroult has argued, some of the major currents in the subsequent history of philosophy are defined by their response to this problem. Kant argued that we cannot know the things in themselves independently of the mind that knows them; instead we must remain content with the world as it appears to us, the phenomenal world. Husserl's phenomenology 'solved' this problem by means of a 'bracketing' (*epoche*) of the world independent of our knowledge and experience, and positing an original agreement between the world as it is and the world as it appears to us. Further, the idea of a self, the 'I' of the 'I think' (*cogito*), finally separate from the world and free, as spiritual substance (*res cogitans*), from merely material determinations and able thus to direct itself, was central to the development of existentialism, especially that of Sartre.

As one of France's most important Spinoza scholars has argued, from the point of view of the perspective just outlined, Spinoza can be seen as Descartes's other, opposing his philosophy point for point. Unlike Descartes, Spinoza begins his major work, the *Ethics*, not with the I that thinks, but, on the contrary, with a set of propositions designed to prove that thought and extension or spirit and matter cannot be separate substances. The topic of Part I is, significantly, not the individual or even man, but God. Spinoza's arguments, nominally devoted to a proof of God's perfection, struck nearly all his contemporaries as a thinly disguised atheism. Drawing on theological controversies, many of which had their origins in medieval and early modern Judaism (Spinoza was born into the Sephardic community in Amsterdam, was educated in its institutions and was finally excommunicated for heresy in 1656), he argued that the notion of God as spirit, prior to matter, creating the material world and endowing it with meaning, was incompatible with the idea of God's greatness. How could spirit 'create' matter out of itself (especially if matter was regarded as inferior to spirit)? How, indeed, could there have been a moment of creation if God were truly omnipresent and all-powerful, that is a moment prior to which a part of God did not exist? How could what is eternally perfect have been lacking? Referring to a distinction between the actual and the possible, as if the latter were a kind of pre-existence, did nothing to solve the problem. The eternal and infinite has no origin, no beginning; all that can exists does: thus, 'whatever is, is in God and nothing can be or be conceived without God' (*Ethics* I, 15), just as God has no existence prior to or outside of creation. God is, according to Spinoza, an immanent cause, entirely coincident with what exists, his will nothing other than the necessity that governs nature as a whole. At the beginning of Part IV, Spinoza would go so far as to use the phrase that made him infamous: 'God, or nature', (*Ethics* IV, Preface), treating the two terms as interchangeable. It is not difficult to see how Spinoza's numerous critics regarded him as having made God disappear into creation, essence into existence and spirit into matter.

As if this were not enough to earn the enmity of theologians from all faiths, Spinoza, in the Appendix to Part I, seeks to explain the causes of the faulty conception of God that is so common and indeed so powerful that it will likely hinder the comprehension of his argument. People insist on regarding God as a transcendent cause, a cause that existed before the world and which brought the world into being to fulfil a pre-existing purpose. Such an idea is common precisely because it constitutes a projection of human experience on God (or Nature): we tend to imagine God in our own image. Spinoza, however, does not stop at the idea that the nearly universal conception of God is nothing more than an idol of human creation that reflects not the divine but the image of its creator. What philosophers in the latter half of the twentieth century have found so provocative in Spinoza's work is the argument that this projected belief in human beings as creators whose actions are undertaken with an end in view is itself false, an illusion heavy with consequences not simply for philosophy but for political and social life as well. We believe we are the causes of our actions and words, Spinoza argues, only because we are conscious of our desires to do or say something, but ignorant of the causes of our desires. We so need to feel that we are masters of ourselves in the face of a world consisting of an infinite concatenation of causes and effects whose course is indifferent to us, our welfare and happiness, that we imagine ourselves in our supposed freedom and transcendence to be the mirror of our creator who thus functions as the guarantor of our delusions of freedom and self-mastery.

Spinoza takes up these problems in detail in Part III of the *Ethics*, where he begins by denouncing the notion that the human world transcends nature, a spiritual realm of freedom in opposition to the necessity that governs the material world. It is this conception above all that prevents us from understanding our emotions which for Spinoza are governed by the same necessity as nature. Anger, hatred and jealousy, like rain and wind, are no less necessary for being inconvenient. The most common form of the notion that the human is outside of nature is our idea of the relation of body and mind. Spinoza's theory is often referred to as parallelism: mind and body are absolutely parallel and whatever happens in or to one also happens in or to the other. Parallelism, however, is not only a term Spinoza never uses, it also fails to convey the fundamental nature of his rejection of any separation of mind and body. For him they are the same: in the same way that he can write God or Nature, he might have said spirit or matter, mind or body. In a certain sense mind disappears into body and thought into action. We believe that the mind, at least during waking hours, directs the body. We believe that when the body undertakes an action, say writing a book, painting a painting or even something as simple as extending our hand to another person, it realizes an intention that existed outside of and prior to that action. For Spinoza, this is an illusion: nobody knows what the body can do solely determined by other bodies. In fact, he suggests, our bodies are moved by other bodies (and he is very interested in the forms of corporeal social organization, such as rituals and ceremonies both secular and religious), while we imagine, much like a dreamer who believes he is talking when in fact he is silent, that we cause an action over which in fact we have no control.

The political consequences of such a positions are serious. Because mind and body are one, whatever increases or decreases the power of the body to act, simultaneously increases or decreases the power of the mind to think. In this way Spinoza, anticipating Foucault, asks us to investigate the social histories of bodies. As for Foucault, the human body is not the atom of society, a fixed and stable point of origin, but is always an aggregate itself made up of smaller bodies and capable of becoming part of a larger body (a couple, a group, a mass, a society) that is no less real because it is an aggregate. It no longer makes sense to ask whether a people have consented to their ruler (which would thus render his rule, no matter how oppressive, legitimate) or a worker to his employer (which no matter how exacting and constraining the labour would then be a legally and morally binding contract). Instead we must begin by asking whether a given relation renders bodies powerful or weak; does it increase their pleasure or pain? In this way all the justifications of domination and exploitation become untenable. In fact, Spinoza refuses every notion of disembodied right (he argues that right equals power), asking only what people have the power to do with or without legal right. Once we cease to see politics in terms of right and law, and instead focus on power, the individual can no longer be the unit of analysis. The chief political force in any society, democratic or despotic, is what Spinoza calls in his last work the multitude or the masses whose support or at least tolerance is the condition of any regime. It is easy to understand why, beginning in 1968, so many of the great commentators on Spinoza have been connected to one variety or another of marxism.

God or nature, mind or body, right or power: Spinoza's anti-transcendentalism according to which that which is expressed disappears into its expression can only extend to that subtle matter, language. To explore this thesis, Spinoza turned his attention to the model of all texts, the Bible. He begins his discussion with a proposition that has proved oblique to many readers: the method of interpreting nature and scripture is the same. We may understand his meaning by returning to the view of nature that he rejects in the *Ethics*. For the superstitious, nature is a mere expression or reflection of something beyond it, something more real or more true: God, the Forms, etc. According to this model, one does not look at nature itself but beyond it to the ends for which it was created or the meaning that it in attenuated form expresses. Nature, from this perspective, is not primary but secondary; the operation of knowledge would be a reduction or a dispelling of nature as if it were the impediment to its own truth. In opposition, Spinoza posits the irreducibility or materiality of nature.

What does this mean for the understanding of scripture? Theologians have for centuries attributed to scripture a hidden depth, of which the literal text is but a mask. Spinoza argues that the meanings that they claim to have found hidden in its interior have in fact been added to the text. They treat scripture not as a text at all but rather as a pretext for the meanings that they will substitute for it. All their approaches amount to a denial of the text in its materiality, its irreducibility; by exhorting us to look beyond it they prevent us from knowing it. The first step in arriving at an adequate knowledge of scripture, then, is to describe its surface very carefully, even to the point of examining punctuation without assuming either coherence or sense. It may well be that certain passages literally do not make sense or are not written in the dialect or language; there may be obvious gaps and ellipses in the text. It may be the case that the text asserts as truth statements that contradict each other. Such a careful description is impossible for readers who begin by assuming the text's perfection and coherence. Their task will be different: not to describe and explain the heterogeneity, contradiction and absence of meaning that is to be found but to explain it away as mere appearance concealing the essence of the text.

Spinoza will treat it as a material, historical artefact. What are the languages of which it is comprised, from what historical period do they date, how many identifiable parts are there to scripture and who assembled them and under what conditions? If its statements are contradictory, can the contradiction be explained historically (texts written in different periods under different circumstances)? But Spinoza does not stop with these already provocative questions: it is not enough to establish the text once and for all and to explain it historically. The history of scripture is not over: it continues to produce new and different effects in new historical situations; it can even cease to mean anything at all and congeal into an indecipherable mass of paper and ink. Of course, if we follow Spinoza's reasoning to the letter, his method is not restricted to the text of scripture. On the contrary, because he rejects the most common postulates of the unity of any text, namely the notions that works originate in and express the intention of an author or that works reflect something more real than themselves which confers upon them their coherence and meaning, his critique extends to the way we read literary, philosophical and political texts as well.

We can see then that, despite certain similarities in language and some common reference points, Descartes and Spinoza stand in stark opposition: on the one hand, a philosophy of the Cogito (not just thought or even consciousness, but also the 'I' as origin of knowledge), positing the primacy of spirit over matter, of soul over body, at the extreme, a political as well as epistemological individualism; on the other, a materialism so thoroughgoing that spirit in all its forms has disappeared into matter, that the human individual is always part of larger individuals and right and law are immanent in power.

This conflict, although several centuries old, has never been more actual than now at the conclusion of the twentieth-century as the conflict to have passed through the crucible of our time unchanged: indeed, it is so intertwined with our thoughts and efforts that it is difficult to imagine a time when we will have passed beyond it.

Warren Montag

Further reading and works cited

Balibar, E. *Spinoza and Politics*. London, 1998.
Descartes, R. *The Philosophical Writings of Descartes, Volume II*. Cambridge, 1984.
Guéroult, M. *Descartes' Philosophy Interpreted According to the Order of Reasons*, Vols 1–2. Minneapolis, MN, 1984
Husserl, E. *Cartesian Meditations: An Introduction to Phenomenology*. The Hague, 1960.
Lacan, J. *Ecrits*. Paris, 1966.
Montag, W. *Bodies, Masses, Power: Spinoza and his Contemporaries*. London, 1999.
Spinoza, B. *The Collected Works of Spinoza*, Vols 1 and 2. Princeton, NJ, 1985.
—. *Tractatus Theologico-Politicus*. New York, 1991.
— and Stolze, T. (eds) *The New Spinoza*. Minneapolis, MN, 1997.

Immanuel Kant (1724–1804) and Georg Wilhelm Friedrich Hegel (1770–1831)

Few thinkers have cast shadows as long on the terrain of postwar literary criticism and theory as Immanuel Kant and G. W. F. Hegel who separately and together open, exemplify and in some respects close the period of European thought known as the Enlightenment. The figures and the work of Kant and Hegel have directly and indirectly been the material from which disciplines and approaches from psychoanalytic to phenomenological criticism, political philosophy to deconstruction have built their characteristic protocols. The vexed history of their influence, waxing and waning, punctuated with 'returns to . . .' and disavowals of one or the other, makes up in some respects the history of modern literary theory itself.

This is a broad claim, and not self-evidently true. Literary criticism has only recently become explicitly concerned with examining its philosophical presuppositions, in ways that differ markedly from one country to another – and which may, indeed, be coming to a close as the period of 'high theory' wanes. For the greater part of the twentieth century the study of literature, even in settings traditionally more friendly to speculative thought than the US or England, found little of profit in taking stock of its procedures more or less systematically. Nor for that matter is it clear how Kant or Hegel's work might further that stocktaking, once it is under way. Kant has little to say about literature, and Hegel's interpretations of literary works have had an influence often more local than disciplinary (with the signal exception of Hegel's profound reshaping of the theory of tragedy, achieved in part through Bradley's renderings of the *Lectures on Aesthetics*). Very little of the practical work of literary criticism and interpretation has stood or fallen on the great questions posed and answered by German idealism.

As soon as 'criticism' gives way to 'literary theory', however, matters change dramatically. The shift from criticism to theory may in principle occur any time that one writes about texts. As a disciplinary matter, however, establishing the analytical bases of the study of literature only becomes a pressing matter in the immediate postwar period, when changes in material and political circumstances focus attention on the humanistic studies as a profession, and increasingly require of these studies different (economic, social, political) justifications. The forms that these legitimation procedures take are again quite distinct, depending on which cultural and educational tradition is at issue. Not only do the values that 'literature' and 'philosophical inquiry' hold in much of Europe (where the disciplinary border between literature and philosophy has for different reasons been fairly porous) differ from their value in the US (where until recently it has not), so do the social and economic roles played in the US and Europe by the universities where such inquiry most often takes place, though their disciplinary distinctions and pedagogical rationale derive complexly from the Encyclopaedist classificatory practices that are the indirect object of inquiry in Kant, and obviously at issue in the project of Hegel's *Encyclopaedia of the Human Sciences*. Further twisting matters, local critical traditions – whether Leavisite practical criticism, the forms of *explication de texte* in the French and Belgian *lycée* after the First World War, or the techniques of close reading developed and popularized in the US – construe and transform quite differently the various legacies of Enlightenment thought. And these, of course, become more widely available with the population displacements provoked by the Second World War, when exiled thinkers like Adorno, Wellek, Brecht, Arendt, de Man and others sought in various ways to rethink continental cultural traditions under the Cold War's light. Finally, the emergence of the thought of Kant and Hegel in central roles in the project of devising a theory of literature has much to do with the contested cultural value that the idealist tradition assumes in Europe in relation to the war itself. For the 'Enlightenment' defined and exemplified through the Weimar period the ideals of cultural literacy that the European wars so profoundly shook. Philosophical idealism embodies 'after' Verdun and 'after' Auschwitz a cultural fantasy in bitter contrast to the realities of two world wars, and is assessed, lionized or rejected in the postwar period in light of this lived contrast.

But the cultural value assumed at this time in Europe and in the United States by idealism's greatest exemplars is not expressed solely in debates over whether various strands of Enlightenment thought give rise to ideologies that lead to war, or whether a different or identical aspect provides the model for a rational public sphere that European political culture abandoned with the rise of fascism. A scattered number of counter-normative approaches to the idealist tradition are proposed in philosophical, political and literary journals immediately before and during the war and these lay the foundation for the reconsideration of Kant and Hegel's legacy that has marked continental philosophy and literary theory in the past thirty years. These counter-normative readings do not come together into anything resembling a coherent approach to the legacies of German idealism, but in retrospect their influential stress on the discontinuities of the Kantian analytics, or on the contingencies of the dialectic, seems to flow largely from their efforts to understand more precisely the place of the aesthetic in the critical and in the Encyclopaedic projects.

For Kant and Hegel, it emerges, reserve for aesthetic questions most broadly, and for literary ones particularly, a place at the defining edge of the discipline of philosophy. At issue are not only judgements concerning the content of this or that work but also judgements that embed a certain fictionality, indeed a kind of literariness, in propositions having no explicitly aesthetic content. In each case – differently, to be sure, but with considerable and fruitful continuities – the care with which the aesthetic judgement is philosophically confined by supplementary tactics suggests the dangerous stresses its necessary presence places on the understanding: necessary both because reflecting the particularity of the sensorium and because concerned with the characteristics of phenomena that distinguish them from concepts on the one hand and from ideas on the other; confined because the 'reflection of particularity' on the subjective side and the 'concern with the distinguishing character of phenomena' on the objective side have no bounds given *a priori* in either the subject or the object, and if unconfined through one heuristic or another can thus practically consume the faculty of judgement. The resulting, complex interaction between the 'necessary function' and the 'confinement' of aesthetic judgements is played out on the question that these judgements confront before all others, and indeed which gives rise to them in the first instance: the question of the relation between the form of presentation (*stellen*) of representations to thought, and their sensible characteristics – between phenomenality and perception.

The indeterminability of aesthetic judgements contrasts markedly with the seeming historical or conceptual teleology of the *Phenomenology of Spirit* or of the three *Critiques*. Just as markedly does it contrast with the largely unexamined historicism that characterized literary studies of the prewar period, and with the purported scientificity of models of intrinsic aesthetic and cultural analysis (predominantly structuralist in inspiration) that come to prominence after the war – defined by Vincent Descombes as the historicist or culturalist positivism of European thought. The appeal of aesthetic judgements is thus easy to understand. Enlisted as models of unconfined human freedom and of human pleasure at a time when the defining metanarratives of western elite culture are in crisis, they seem at once utopian and indispensable to increasingly heterogenous societies. In keeping with this fantasy of culture's social role, for much of the past quarter-century 'literature' was understood to be the aesthetic domain that most clearly staged the question of the relation between the indeterminability of aesthetic judgement and the seeming necessity of establishing determining, foundational premises for ethical judgements – staged it allegorically, referred to it fictionally, treated it thematically. During these years, and until different forms of materialist criticism (new and old historicism, cultural studies) achieved hegemony, the 'theory' of literature occupied itself broadly with formalizing that question and its various provisional answers (psychoanalytic, culturalist, philosophical, or more traditionally 'literary'). At the close of the twentieth century and in the wake of various formalisms, of 'high theory' and of different historicisms, literary criticism and theory has assumed as the programme of cultural studies the task of re-examining the historical and conceptual legacies of the idealist construction of aesthetic judgement set definingly in the Romantic reception of Kant and Hegel's work.

Kant and the doctrine of relative autonomy

'Two things fill the mind with ever new and increasing admiration and awe', Kant concludes his *Critique of Practical Reason*, 'the oftener and more steadily we reflect on them: the starry heavens above me and the moral law within me. I do not merely conjecture them

... I see them before me, and I associate them directly with the consciousness of my own existence.' This poetical observation sets out the broad architecture of Kant's *critical* philosophy – a term understood to cover the works dating roughly from 1774 to the end of his career. The domain, limits and characteristics of judgements concerning 'the place I occupy in the external world of sense' are the subject treated in the 1781 *Critique of Pure Reason*. Judgements concerning the moral law are the province of the *Critique of Practical Reason* (1788), *Metaphysics of Morals* (1797) and *Groundwork of the Metaphysics of Morals* (1785). The human mind, Kant argues, constitutes for itself the conditions of perception and sense *before* it has any experience of this or that object – hence to make judgements concerning our 'experience' or (to use a particularly Kantian word) our 'intuition' of the 'external world of sense' is in fact to address phenomena, 'objects conforming to our mode of representation' and regulated by this mode of representation, rather than 'things by themselves' or 'in themselves' (1998 B: xviii). The critique of metaphysics built on this is devastating: the boundaries Kant sets to speculative reason are the circumstance of the self-regarding subject rather than the 'external world' of things by themselves. To confuse one with the other is to 'destroy' the 'necessary practical use of pure reason', its *moral* use. For in the domain of *moral* judgement, Kant goes on to explain, the negative task undertaken in the *Critique of Pure Reason* yields a profound, *positive* result with respect to what in the *Critique of Practical Reason* he terms the 'only idea of speculative reason whose possibility we know a priori' (5): the idea of freedom. Our 'ignorance with regard to things by themselves', it turns out, restricts our capacity to understand or to know freedom 'by itself', but not, crucially, to '*think* freedom' (1998 B: xxvii). And the idea of 'freedom' is in this sense privileged not only as the *content* of thought or as the object of speculative reason (we think about the phenomenon of freedom, unable to know freedom by itself), but also as the *form* taken a priori by speculative thought in general and as its functional effect.

Kant's efforts to coordinate the domains of fundamental epistemology and of ethics, of knowledge and of desire, understanding and reason, require of him two related, controversial strategies, with profound methodological as well as thematic consequences. Both come under direct attack in the course of the twentieth century and provide the ground for some of the most far-reaching philosophical and literary-critical debates of the past quarter-century. The first concerns the role assigned in the critique of metaphysics to the notion and characteristics of the subject. The second concerns the subordination of aesthetic judgement to reason and understanding, and its simultaneous elevation to a necessary, analytic moment in the transition from epistemological to moral judgements.

Kant's subjects

Kant's critical system is indeed concerned with the status of human agents and of rational human acts, though he does not make such acts coextensive with human subjectivity or its origin. Instead, the Kantian critique of metaphysics turns upon the notion that acts (physical acts as well as certain acts of thought) originate in 'a transcendental ground of the unity of our consciousness in the synthesis of the manifold of all our intuitions' (1998, A:104). On this understanding, Kant's formulation consolidates an argument for the primacy of self-consciousness made sketchily, and with important flaws, as early as Descartes's *Meditations* – correcting and extending it to the domain of practical reason. Corresponding to the 'transcendental ground of unity' in the acting subject is the principle of the will's autonomy with regard to that act – the postulate that one's duty to moral law is coherent and compelling only if one subjects oneself 'only to laws given by oneself but still universal', laws in which one can have no *particular* interest, and which are in this sense *unconditionally* compelling (*Groundwork*, 40). To give oneself such laws requires crucially, Kant suggests, the intervention of the faculty of the imagination: every decision is submitted to the imaginary test of its *outcome* and of a notional universality (one acts 'as if' the grounds for deciding to act held universally, and 'as if' the outcome of the act were immediately and exhaustively present to thought). The representation of 'outcome' and 'universality' must be radically non-empirical (otherwise every decision would be an interested, hence a conditioned one, and never in Kant's sense a 'free' decision) – presented 'as if' they provided determining grounds for this or that decision, but also 'as if' entirely counter-factual. The immediate consequence of this imaginary test is the de-instrumentalization of human agents: every subject as such is presumed definitionally to be able freely and rationally to test his or her judgements in this way – to be autonomous – and cannot in consequence be construed as the means for another subject's judgements, only (in an abstract sense) as an end.

Different and differently influential treatments of political philosophy and of philosophical ethics flow from the notions of duty and *responsibility* that this foundational description of the imaginary autonomy of the will establishes. The debt to Kant is explicit in some cases, implicit in others. The coordination of the concepts of 'rational community', 'transparent communication' and 'public-sphere interest' in the work of Jürgen Habermas, the influential terms in which the North American ethicist John Rawls describes the hypothetical 'veil of ignorance' necessary to produce just judgements in social environments (1971), the emphasis placed by philosophers like Ronald Dworkin (1977) or Alisdair MacIntyre (1981) on rights-based analyses of legal standing, all suggest the scope of the contemporary return to Kant.

Where Habermas, Rawls, Dworkin and the late Foucault may be imagined to represent a return to a (qualified) Kantian foundationalism, engagement with Kant's critical philosophy has as often sought to provide non-foundational accounts. On the continent Nietzsche (refracted through readings of Freud, Marx and particularly of the work of Martin Heidegger) remained the primary philosophical point of reference, particularly in France and Germany. Heidegger's engagement with Kant is constant and fruitful. For Heidegger, the emergence of the notion of the subject is associated with the epochal forgetting of the authentic relation to Being that obtained before the Cartesian, and more properly Kantian, consolidation of the 'age of the world-picture' – an 'age' (though it is also a philosophical tactic, and a style of writing) that subordinates ontological questions (concerned with the nature of Being) to epistemological ones. What Kant describes as 'the objects' conforming to our mode of representation' Heidegger associates with the aligned distinctions between the apparent and the essential, between, as he puts it in *Being and Time*, the 'outside of me [*Aussenwelt*]' and the 'in me [*in mir*]' (Heidegger 1962, 204–5), between an object's phenomenality, or appearing-for-one, and its noumenality, or being-in-itself. This evasion, he argues, finds its modern crystallization in the emergence of the category of the *subiectus* (Heidegger 1962, 317–22); in the *Critique of Pure Reason* it is tied to the complex status accorded the coming-into-images (*Verbildlichung*) of the transcendental schemata. These, Heidegger argues in *Kant and the Problem of Metaphysics*, are images (*Bilder*) in a special sense: they are *both* removed from the empirical realm (of conditionality), *and* revealed to constitute the finitude of the 'I' as its being-in-time (thus making the pre-conditionality of time a non-empirical predicate of the 'I'). This means, however, that it is no longer possible (as both the *Critique of Practical Reason* and the *Critique of Judgement* propose) to construe the Being of beings under the aspect of the unconditionality of the subject's freedom to *understand* imaginative schemata for grasping the world. Rather, it becomes necessary to pose the question of the Being of beings – and of the emergence of the subject, as well as its autonomy – within the constraint of the *limited* freedom 'I' have to fashion those schemata.

Heidegger's anti-foundationalist re-historicization of the problem of representation and his recasting of conditionality (as Being-in-time) as 'my' pre-subjective condition prove decisive in the continental reception of Kant's critique of metaphysics. The influence is clearest in the general field of ethics, though Derrida's far-reaching influence in literary studies is in fact unthinkable without reference to the works he devotes, precisely, to Heidegger's encounter with Kant. The critique of foundational autonomy is pursued exactingly in the work of Emmanuel Levinas, of Gilles Deleuze and of T. W. Adorno.

Heidegger's encounter with Kant's work does not uniquely shape its postwar reception, of course. In the course of the 1950s and early 1960s the Kantian notion of the autonomy of the subject came under considerable pressure from psychoanalytically inflected work as well. The theorization of 'unconscious' causality dating to Freud's *The Interpretation of Dreams* had dramatically shifted the analytic distinction between 'conditioned' and 'unconditioned' decisions from its Kantian alignment with propositions concerning *empirical* judgements on the one hand and *a priori* intuitions on the other, to a fundamentally empirical frame in which every 'unconditioned' proposition or decision reveals itself to be merely an as-yet-unanalysed but always 'conditioned' proposition or decision. This psychic pre-conditioning, however, could quickly take an oppressively orthodox shape: the Oedipal scenario, archetypal psychoanalysis, even the description of infantile object-relations became not only institutionally but conceptually fixed, assuming in the work of postwar critics and psychoanalysts (in Klein, Winnicott, Erikson and others) the foundational role granted a priori, properly transcendent concepts in Kant. This re-transcendentalization of the psychoanalytic critique of idealism provoked its own powerful reaction. In Jacques Lacan's rendering, and beginning with the epoch-making essay from 1949 on 'The Mirror-Stage as Formative of the I as Revealed in Psychoanalytic Experience' (1966), the pre-conditionality of the human subject is the mark of its primary facticity, a mark of the original non-identity between the little man and the world of objects in which he finds himself cast. And this pre-conditionality of the subject, Lacan strikingly suggests in his 1958–9 Seminar and again in his 1963 *Critique* essay, 'Kant with Sade', (1966) is itself unconditioned: it is the source and form of *desire*, and the *duty* to follow these desires has a form exactly homologous to the Kantian duty to acquiesce to the autonomy of the imperatives of conscience. Gilles Deleuze, writing with Félix Guattari, mounted a devastating attack on the re-transcendentalization of the Oedipal scenario in the institutions and languages of psychoanalysis with *Anti-Oedipus* (1972), a work whose understanding of the resolutely Kantian roots of Oedipalization was to be brought out by two prominent followers, Klaus Theweleit (1977) and Peter Sloterdijk, whose *Critique of Cynical Reason* (1983) turns Deleuze's observation in *Nietzsche and Philosophy* that the Kantian critique of metaphysics finally safeguards the supersensible into a description of the pathology of futility that afflicts the legacy of the enlightenment, able to understand its disenfranchisement, to profit from that diagnosis, but unable to do anything to change it.

The distinction between 'foundationalist' and 'non-foundationalist' responses to Kant's work is rough at best, however. The interrupted arc of Michel Foucault's career provides the remarkable example of a thinker perched between disciplines whose ostensible movement from a philosophical historiography highly critical of the hypostatization of the 'humanist' notion of the subject to an autonomous ethics of 'care' in the final writing can be indexed against his encounters with Kant's work – but whose critique of foundationalism in no way follows the same path. Foucault's 1961 *thèse complémentaire* for the *doctorat ès lettres* was an annotated edition of Kant's *Anthropology from a pragmatic point of view*; his most probing early critiques of 'humanist' theses took direct or indirect aim at the de-historicization of the notion of autonomy and of the category of the subject that Foucault found at work in the Critical project. But Foucault's late pieces, 'The Subject and Power' (1983), 'Kant on Enlightenment and Revolution' (1986) and the posthumously published 'What is Enlightenment?' (1984) (a title borrowed from Kant) seem to qualify this critique of Kant's anthropological bent, in some measure assigning his own earlier positions to what he rather sharply calls the 'facile confusions between humanism and Enlightenment'. In a defining set of exchanges with Habermas, Foucault advocates reconstructing a notion of the Enlightenment on non-transcendental but on practical or *performative* bases, 'conceiving [Enlightenment] as an attitude, an ethos, a philosophical life in which the critique of what we are is at one and the same time the historical analysis of the limits that are imposed on us and an experiment with the possibility of going beyond them' (50). But Foucault's 'return' to Kant is only ostensible, for in crucial ways he never 'leaves' Kant at all: even at his most resolutely Heideggerian Foucault never abandons the highly Kantian notion that reason has an intrinsic, if historicized, relation to 'ethos' and to 'experiment'. Where Foucault differs from Kant – and from Habermas and Sloterdijk's versions of Kant – is in his understanding of the status and domain of that relation: it is not *aesthetics*, as in Kant's work, that provides the crucial hinge between reason and ethics, but what could be called (as in Nietzsche) *dynamics*, the critique of the forms in which power is materially exercised.

Sublime aesthetics

With the signal exceptions of its absorption by Benedetto Croce and its treatment in Cassirer's 1918 *Kant's Life and Thought*, Kant's aesthetic theory remained very much on the sidelines in philosophical circles during the first years of the twentieth century. The works in which it is explored – the precritical *Observations on the Feeling of the Beautiful and Sublime* (1763) and the *Critique of Judgement* of 1790 – are to this day treated by Anglo-American philosophers and by literary critics in the neo-positivist tradition with hardly any patience. In his critical period Kant becomes both surprisingly unclear and, as if by way of compensation, almost excessively scholastic in his treatment of the aesthetic. As to a perceived lack of clarity, the *Critique of Judgement*'s exposition of the immediate pleasure afforded reflective intuition by the beautiful (in art as well as nature) strategically muddies the two senses of 'taste' – the highly subjective expression of particular pleasure and the societal approval granted this or that work or natural object – so as to make the notorious particularity of judgements of taste into a general and teachable principle. This principle, however, is founded in peculiarly unanalysable terms that Kant uses nowhere else: there is, he finds, no 'method' for teaching the 'taste' for or the means of producing beautiful art, only a *modus* or 'manner'; nonetheless, the true propaedeutic for the foundation of taste 'is the development [*die Entwickelung*] of moral ideas and the culture of moral feeling', though the capacity to envision and understand, hence rationally to develop, such moral ideas depends upon the faculty of judgement that derives in part from the foundation of taste.

The work's purported 'technicality' notwithstanding, it is Cassirer's rendering of Kant's aesthetics that prevails in literary-critical circles of the postwar period – a reading stressing the crucial place in the architecture of the three *Critiques* that the aesthetical judgement occupies, and stressing, too, what High Romanticism from Goethe and Schiller to Coleridge would find most compelling in Kant's aesthetic project: the relation between the purposiveness of the aesthetic judgement and the *organicity* of natural objects. For Cassirer, Kant's muddiness concerning the status of taste captures a broader ambivalence present already in the *Critique of Pure Reason* on the subject of aesthetic judgements generally. The empirical function of aesthetics, concerned with *evaluating* the 'material' of representations can be bracketed or ignored, or set aside as a 'vain endeavour' (1998, A 20), or considered merely preliminary: aesthetic propositions set aside the question of ver-idification, and take the form 'these characteristics of the phenomenon *qua* phenomenon please or displease' – but the nature of this 'pleasing' or 'displeasing' is of interest only inasmuch as it represents the 'pleasure' at the discovery in relation to phenomena of a pure concept of the understanding. Important as the faculty of judgement may be in providing hypothetical representations of the outcome or possible universality of acts (on the moral side), or in providing *a posteriori* judgements concerning 'the matter of phenomena' (rather than their form, which in a particularly Aristotelian moment Kant proposes 'is ready for them in the mind': 1998, A 18), it is the consideration of the 'transcendental aesthetic' – the region of judgements concerning the *a priori*, pure form of all sensuous intuitions, and the domain of the 'pleasures' associated with the disclosure of those intuitions – that emerges as fundamental in providing what Kant calls the 'means of combining the two parts of philosophy [the theoretical and the practical] into a whole'. In the *Critique of Judgement* Kant seeks to achieve this combination by drawing an analogy between the 'purposiveness [*Zweckmäßigkeit*]' of nature and the 'purposiveness' of aesthetic objects. This 'purposiveness' is formal and transcendental, in the sense that we recognize from the First Critique – it requires no empirical concept of the body (object, etc.) of which it is predicated. Judgements about aesthetic objects work analogously (this work is beautiful, not for the purpose it concretely serves, but inasmuch as the work allows us to intuit in it an abstract purposiveness that no concrete purpose quite exhausts), and by means of this analogy Kant locates the capacity to produce art, to make propositions concerning the artistic object, and to experience pleasure at the intuition of abstract purposiveness, on the same level as the faculty of producing propositions concerning sensibilia and to make judgements concerning our desires (to accomplish this or that), the transcendental sense of purposiveness in the aesthetical judgement as pertains to nature (and by analogy art) becoming associated with the idea of freedom in the moral scheme. In building this analogy Kant finds it useful to return to the pre-Critical distinction between the beautiful and the sublime. The sidelining of the sublime, he continues, has to do in particular with its uselessness in the construction of the 'teleological judgement' forming the bridge between aesthetic and moral judgement, as 'in the sublime there is nothing at all that leads to particular objective principles and forms of nature corresponding to them'. 'We must seek', he concludes, 'a ground external to ourselves for the beautiful in nature, but seek it for the sublime merely in ourselves' (23).

Kant's influence, and particularly his treatment of the feeling of the *beautiful*, is felt acutely in the privilege that early formalist and new critical approaches granted what William Wimsatt called the poem's 'concrete universality', 'the principle by which the critic can try to keep ... rhetorical analysis of poetry together with evaluation, technique together with worth'. This principle, Wimsatt proposes, should be understood by analogy to Kant's 'telling how the imagination constructs the 'aesthetical normal Idea': 'It is the image for the whole race', he continues, citing from the *Critique of Judgement*, 'which floats among all the variously different intuitions of individuals, which nature takes as archetype in her productions of individuals of the same species, but which seems not to be fully reached in any individual case' (1954, 71–2). The organic relation between 'archetype' and 'individual' becomes the mainstay, not just of Wimsatt's explicitly Kantian conception of criticism, but of a protocol of reading concerned to find how the aesthetic work achieves a formal 'unity' between the pleasure that 'irrelevant concreteness' affords precisely as such, and the 'more than usual relevance' of concrete images to the logic of the work of art. In these particular verbal icons the archetype shines through universally, symbolically, supported philosophically on either side by the strong Kantian bolsters of purposiveness and aesthetic irrelevance, exemplified in the poetical and programmatic work of Coleridge and Schiller, and expressed characteristically by means of the synecdochal symbol.

Absent from the explicitly aesthetic formulation and with a rather different, anthropological-linguistic genealogy, this dynamic arrangement of 'concrete' and 'universal' provided in the late 1950s and early 1960s a philosophy for the human sciences in the shape of structuralism. Covertly indebted to Cassirer's understanding of the 'unity of the rule' in Kant, structuralism in the human sciences, and in literary criticism in particular, there are hypothesized the existence of structural rules governing the production and reception of disparate cultural phenomena. Between the two levels – the 'phenomena' of culture, the deep rules of structure – a methodical, indeed a methodological, path can be drawn, involving procedures taken most often from the field of synchronic linguistics, or, as in the fundamental work of Claude Lévi-Strauss, of social anthropology. The reception of Propp's *Morphology of the Folk Tale*, the work of Jakobson, Todorov, Girard and the European narratological school of the late 1960s and early 1970s, certain uses of Lacan and Althusser's work in the early to middle 1960s – all flow from the conceptualization of the regulative transcendental that Cassirer takes from the Critical project. In its aims and procedures structuralism, like New Criticism, appears to mount a strong attack on some of the most cherished legacies of the Enlightenment, the notion of a transcendent and originary 'human essence', isomorphous or not with the 'subject', being ostensibly incompatible with the existence and regulative dimension of abstract and non-human structures. What remains, to use Paul Ricoeur's characterization in 1963 of the work of Lévi-Strauss, is a 'Kantianism without a transcendental subject', 'structure' having assumed the functional position occupied by the 'subject' in the three *Critiques*.

The end of the structuralist moment in Europe, and of the New Critical moment in the United States, might then reasonably be associated with the exhaustion of the romantic response to idealist aesthetics, and the emergence of what is roughly called poststructural philosophy and literary theory with an explicit critique of the regulative transcendental. In a crucial chapter devoted to Kant, Jean-Paul Sartre's *What is Literature?* (1947) had outlined already the consequences of merely replacing the 'transcendental subject' with an aesthetic counterpart – 'form' or 'structure' or 'purposiveness'. Sartre's thinking, as influentially anti-foundational in its way as Heidegger's contemporaneous reading of Kant's ontology proved, bears two constructions. On the one hand, the resolute 'disinterestedness' of the aesthetic judgement proves to be conditioned already the moment one enters a relation to the aesthetic object. On the other hand, the 'task' under whose aspect the work of art presents itself bears a concrete relation to the world of the work's production and reception: literature, Sartre suggests, engages the reader in battles – battles that *What is Literature?* is at pains to make clear are quite literal ones. Each construction of Sartre's phrase might be understood to correspond to a type of critique of the romantic-formalist response to Kant, the first based on an intrinsic questioning of the transcendentalization of the rules of 'structure' or 'form' in the place of the Kantian subject, the second to a properly historicizing questioning of the founding terms of transcendental aesthetics. Curiously, both avenues of critique – often pursued in the same argument – emerge centrally with the reconsideration of Kant's 'mere appendix to the aesthetical judging of purposiveness', the aesthetic category of the *sublime*.

The notion of the sublime is sparsely attended to in literary studies in the US before the advent of philosophically inflected forms of criticism, in some measure because it is hard to square the concept, even in its uninflected form, with Wimsatt's notion that literary criticism should proceed by analogy to the construction of 'the "aesthetical normal Idea" ' to bring 'rhetorical analysis of poetry together with evaluation, technique together with worth'. Hard upon the ground-breaking 1966 conference devoted to 'The Languages of Criticism and the Sciences of Man', however, philosophical and literary interest in the *Critique of Judgement* increased, both in the US, in England and particularly in France. A number of heterodox interpretations of Kant, in line with the double-edged critique sketched in Sartre's early essay, appeared in the middle to late 1970s, including in the United States a number of topical works treating the theme of the sublime in Keats, Blake and others – the essays of Harold Bloom and the more psychoanalytically inflected work of Thomas Weiskel and Neil Hertz being of particular significance. In France, and coinciding with a retreat from the rather overwhelming Hegelianism of French academic circles since the late 1930s, the middle to late 1970s saw the beginning of a remarkable effort to rethink the place of aesthetic judgement in Kant's critical philosophy. Jacques Derrida's *Truth in Painting* included an extended treatment of the notion of *magnitude* in the *Critique*. And there were others, equally influential (though lack of space does not permit going into detail). By the time that the colloquium on 'judgement' was held at Cerisy-la-Salle (1982) the marginalization of Kant's work on aesthetics and Kant's own discomforts with the category of the sublime were accepted, in France and among literary critics elsewhere interested in French intellectual culture, as symptomatic of a productive incoherence in the *Critique of Judgement* – a term initially set aside as leading 'merely' into ourselves rather than toward a supersensible analogue to natural purposiveness, but yielding what would become for Kant an increasingly disturbing instance of the presentation to thought of the radically unpresentable.

The *Critique of Judgement* describes the experience of the sublime as one of blockage and release, echoing on a conceptual level the physiological account of the experiences of the beautiful and the sublime found in Burke. For Kant, however, the 'pain' and 'pleasure' associated with aesthetic experience have nothing to do with the 'efficient causes' of these sensations – 'an unnatural tension and certain violent emotions of the nerves' in one case, the relaxation of that 'unnatural tension' in the other, as Burke famously puts it. Rather, the blockage described in the *Critique of Judgement* affects the faculty of reason, checked by the immeasurable gulf between its capacity to 'measure' an image that presents itself sensibly to thought, and the actual object of thought. What follows this 'painful' experience is the imaginative reconstitution of reason under the aspect of self-admiration.

But is this 'blockage' effectively overcome in Kant? Not entirely, as Lyotard, Bourdieu,

Derrida, Hertz and others show. Just where the critical project poses the means for making the transcendent analogy between epistemology and ethics, the group of philosophers and literary critics writing in the wake of the structural project finds a colossal 'monster', a 'habitus' or a 'differend' that blocks again the re-emergence of the rational, autonomous subject toward which the *Critique of Judgement* seems destined. Each of these terms – the 'colossal', the 'differend', the 'habitus' – might be seen to reflect the dramatic breach that the notion of the sublime opens in the transcendental aesthetic: the presentation of the 'independence of absolute totality' in nature occurs both as an ostensive, direct *representation* and as an *analogy*. This duplicity embeds the empirical (the analogy is driven by the sensible content of the presentation) within the transcendental, dramatically undercutting the association of aesthetics with the ideology of timeless 'taste', and opening the *Critique of Judgement* to radical re-historicizations in the Sartrean line, Pierre Bourdieu's *Distinction* (1979) and later *Logic of Practice* (1980) providing among the most compelling examples.

The Kantian aesthetic that emerged on the continent in the 1970s and early 1980s found its most striking echo in the USA in the work of literary theorists already reacting against the perceived organicism of New Criticism, and to the formalism of structuralist and narratological criticism. Deconstructive critical approaches in particular – indebted to Derrida's work, though inflected in the main by a more deliberately rhetorical language drawn from the work of Northrop Frye, J. Hillis Miller, Harold Bloom or Paul de Man – on occasion explicitly embraced a programmatic 'impersonality', as an early essay by de Man puts it, drawn partly from the work of Maurice Blanchot, but most consequentially from the politico-philosophical critique of Kantian humanism. The years from 1979 to the late 1980s saw the publication of a number of important literary-critical treatments of the *Critique of Judgement* and of the *Critique of Practical Reason*, ranging from the nuanced pragmatism of Barbara Herrnstein Smith's analysis of Kant's notion of 'taste' (1988), to approaches to the 'ethics of reading' that sought to develop non-foundational accounts of the relation between aesthetical and ethical judgements by means of the concept of 'affirmative deconstruction' (Miller, Brodsky, Caruth), to essays seeking to articulate the de-anthropologization of the Kantian aesthetic scheme with a non-positivist account of material change (Paul de Man's 'Kant's Materialism' and 'Phenomenality and Materiality in Kant').

Hegel: the 'outsides' of dialectical thought

The 'return to Hegel' that begins in earnest in France in the 1930s, and which had already taken root in Germany and Italy, amounts, suggests Althusser, to a selective and deliberate 'resurrection' of themes that serve the bourgeoisie's 'desperate efforts' to consolidate its endangered class position and privileges (1997b, 243, 256–7). Published anonymously and redacted only a few months after he attended Gyorgy Lukács' lecture on 'New Problems in Hegelian Research' at the Sorbonne, Althusser's article on 'The Return to Hegel' excited considerable interest, particularly among thinkers on the political Left like Emile Bottigelli and Henri Lefebvre. The article – along with Althusser's review (1947) of Alexandre Kojève's *Introduction to the Reading of Hegel* (1947) – marked the beginning of a vigorous public assault on the understanding of Hegel that dominated in France and Germany until the mid-1960s, the 'anthropological' or 'humanist' Hegelianism of Jean Wahl, of Kojève and of Althusser's teacher Jean Hyppolite.

For Althusser, writing at the beginning of the Cold War, the debate over Hegel's reception was clearly a matter of consequence – and of some personal urgency as well, as he himself had only two years earlier contributed to the 'Great Return' he strikingly condemns a *diplôme d'études supérieures* on the subject of 'The Notion of "Content" in the Thought of G. W. F. Hegel'. The stakes were surely high in part for the reasons that Althusser gives. The 'return to Hegel' ostensibly took Kantianism as its target, but its *means* of attacking idealism set in place an approach to Hegel, and in particular a means of understanding the mechanism of the dialectic, whose sources, as Kojève had made clear, lay in Heidegger's work rather than in Marx's. The result, Althusser suggests in 'The Notion of "Content" ', is that under the cover of a critique of idealism Hegelianism had been falsely returned to a Kantian, transcendental frame. We owe to Hegel, he proposes, what Kant could not allow himself to think: 'the recognition that the *a priori* is *a posteriori*', and the correlative necessity of 'thinking the reality of a transcendental empirical ... the *a-prioricity* of the *a posteriori*'. Had Kant been able to understand correctly the nature of his own categories – which are 'found' or wrought from the table of judgements – he 'would have been constrained to conceive of history', he would have seen like Hegel that 'totality is the reconciliation of Substance and Subject, coinciding in absolute truth', or, to put it in the slightly starker terms in which Althusser reviews Kojève and Hyppolite's works, Kant would have been constrained to conceive of history along the fundamentally Marxist lines suggested by the contradictory notion of the 'transcendental empirical'.

The Hegelian System – so often accused of excessive 'formalism', of 'totalitarianism' – does indeed turn on the great themes that Althusser's words sketch here: the 'reality' or irreality of the empirical, the 'reconciliation [*Aufhebung*, often translated as "sublation" or "subreption"]' of Substance and Subject, the history of consciousness as the coming-into-being of 'absolute truth' in that 'reconciliation', the role of 'contradiction' in the mechanics of the dialectic. The roots of 'anthropological' Hegelianism lie in Hegel's earliest work, rediscovered and circulated in the first decades of the twentieth century – the so-called Berne years, reflecting the critical influence of the mysticism of Jacob Böhme, and before the mature exchanges in Frankfurt and Jena with the poet Friedrich Hölderlin that so changed Hegel's view of Kant. Hegel, who in early correspondence with Schelling had imagined himself 'completing' Kant's philosophy, 'applying' it and 'popularizing' it, found himself increasingly turning away from the most important doctrines of the Kantian circle at the university town of Jena. For Hölderlin, and increasingly for Hegel also, the immediate positing function of the aesthetic amounted to a fantasy, effectively playing down what in the *Logic* Hegel would come to call the 'identity of Being and Nothing' by making this 'nothing' merely a predicate of the Self. The challenge then became to find a way to retain *both* the autonomy of the Subject *and* the radical externality of Substance with respect to Subjectivity, without resorting to the noumenal 'in- or by-itself-ness' of each to explain their relation.

The publication of the *Phenomenology of Spirit* in 1807 was Hegel's first step in providing such an account, a work still bearing considerable traces of the Jena conflation of Fichtean 'absolute Self' with the empirical figure of the Romantic artist, but also profoundly novel in its approach to the task of philosophical scrutiny: 'the true birthplace and secret' of Hegel's System, in Marx's words. The principal means for accomplishing the 'reconciliation' of Substance and Subject in the *Phenomenology of Spirit* is the complex shuttling motion of the dialectic, a term designating at once a logical and a phenomenological procedure, and hence not easily defined. The work, in fact, might as easily be called an *example* of dialectical thought and an *injunction* to perform such thought, as an exposition of its premises and results: every 'moment' of the argument of the *Phenomenology of Spirit* presents itself as a complete cycle of assertion, negation and elimination or elevation (*Aufhebung*), the 'elevated' or reconciled term manifesting, at a greater level of generality, a contradiction that again gets the cycle under way, the entire, repetitive – or, better, cyclical – set of iterations becoming itself the movement, form and content of consciousness as it sets itself before itself as an object of reflection. To whom, though, does the argument 'present itself'? Who is the 'I' that the *Phenomenology of Spirit* addresses? Here we find Hegel at his most daring: the 'experience' abstractly described in the pages of the *Phenomenology of Spirit* slowly reveals itself to be that of the work's reader, who understands the argument's moments by 'performing' them, and understands them to *be* the performance of the movement that it describes. Each 'moment' in the *Phenomenology of Spirit*, then, presents itself to its reader 'first' immediately, appearing as the immediate shining or appearance (*Erscheinung*) of the truth of a phenomenon – for instance, the 'truth' of sense-certainty with which the work opens, or of the richness of particular experience; the 'truth' of the relation that obtains definitionally between the master and the slave; and so on. But this immediate appearing, Hegel proposes, bears 'truth' only in the most impoverished sense, as it excludes every reflection: the 'immediate' truth of sense certainty, or of the apparent relation between the master and the slave, or of the superiority of 'abstract' to 'concrete' thought (or vice versa), in fact conveys no knowledge other than the merely ostensive, and adds nothing to what was already the sate of affairs – that here and now I am confronted with an object other than myself. But take account, Hegel proceeds, of the peculiar structure of the terms in which this apparently tautologous form of ostension operates – *this* object *here* and *now*, for *me* – and there arises, this time *mediated* by that very taking-account and by the conditions of utterance of the ostensive statement, an entirely different scheme. Every term at issue, Hegel writes, in the 'initial', 'empirical' moment when thought takes account of the experience of the senses, bears not only upon 'my' concrete experience, but on the general possibility of being-experienced of the phenomenon, and on the *abstractness* of the subject experiencing: the 'here' and 'now' of 'my' experience of 'this' object *both* locate and particularize the experience, *and* make it comprehensible beyond that particularism, as 'I' can serve to indicate now one, now another grammatical person, and 'here' and 'now' shift in this or that circumstance. The embedding of this generality within 'my' most private experience of the object brings 'me' before myself as an object, as 'nothing' (from the subjective point of view), or as a member of the logical class of 'concrete universals' – an externalization that makes manifest, or represents, what was already a constitutive division, denying me an immediate knowledge of myself ('I' know 'I' am no longer 'I') but making available to me, as my truth, the *experience* of my consciousness of that failed immediacy.

The break with Fichte's rendering of Kant is sharp, but the *Phenomenology of Spirit* proceeds beyond this first, epistemological moment along a path that Hegel will follow unswervingly for the rest of his career. If 'my' particular experience presents itself to me as also necessarily a general one, then the realm of 'my' relation to and consciousness of the world and myself presents itself also as proper to a class, 'my' historical circumstance as proper to the *condition* of historicity, and the particular shape taken for me by the failure of 'my' immediate *knowledge* of myself as the subject of my own thoughts and deeds as a general form of negation proper to the structure of historicity itself. The second moment in the *Phenomenology of Spirit* extends the initial account of the dialectic of sense-certainty to the sphere of social relations, transferring the dialectical elevation of 'my' weakness as mediate subject to an exceptionally influential description of the Slave's ascendancy over the Master. The synthetical notion of 'work' advanced at this level passes from the realm of ethical substance to the doctrines of State and Religion that seek to formalize and legislate that realm, and concludes at the level of greatest generality with the famous, lyrical description of the 'goal' of the 'slow-moving succession of Spirits [*Geister*, also "minds"]' that constitutes the 'conscious, self-mediating process' of History: *totality*, the mediately identical-with-itself, 'Absolute Knowing, or Spirit that knows itself as Spirit'.

Crucially, Hegel imagines this 'extension' of the first, epistemological moment into the realm of ethical substance, and then the 'slow-moving' and 'self-mediating' procession of consciousness up the scale of generalities, under the aspect of *necessity* (*Notwendigkeit*): once 'my' thought is under way (and to the extent that Hegel imagines 'thought' to be the manifestation of contradiction for itself, 'thought' has always already begun), then the moment 'I' come before myself as the experience of the consciousness of my mediacy, the terms of 'my' thought are *necessarily* 'cancelled' and 'elevated [*aufgehoben*]' to the more general level at which 'I' enter into relation with others in the sphere of my work, that is to the level of social labour. Once at that level (and as Hegel makes much clearer in the sections on 'Taking possession of a Thing [*Sache*]' in the *Elements of the Philosophy of Right*), the definition of work as the transformation of matter for use entails understanding all matter as matter-to-be-appropriated and laboured-over, or as potentially 'my' property. Because this 'my' suffers the familiar and contradictory particular universalism that Hegel's pronouns manifest at the 'first', epistemological level, 'my' work opens necessarily onto the spheres of law and of religion, the domains, Hegel argues in the *Elements of the Philosophy of Right*, where the contradiction intrinsic to a matter that is both particularly 'for me', generally 'for all' and intrinsically 'for itself' must be negotiated. The notion of necessity that the *Phenomenology of Spirit* employs thus furnishes Hegel with a powerful historical heuristic as well, concrete historical events becoming the manifestations of the *necessary* movement of *Geist* through natural history. The profoundly progressivist vision that attends this conception of historical necessity, as well as the notion that the moments of thought that make up its phenomenological counterpart are necessary in relation to the *totality* of thought, prove among the most controversial and abiding elements of Hegel's legacy.

The balance of Hegel's works individually and systematically explore the consequences and foundations, in quite different domains, of these early insights. Hegel's aesthetic theory plays a much smaller part in the various declensions of the System than does the aesthetic judgement in Kant, and his discussions of the sublime a role less prominent yet. The conception of literature that Hegel advances openly is fundamentally a cognitive, thematic one: the literary work can serve to reveal the nature of the world, can help make clear the relationship that obtains between 'world' and 'man' – but in the sensuous form of an *intuition*, which must always remain preliminary and external to the genuine revelation of that relationship in thought as a concept (*Begriff*) or in religion as a figurative representation (*Vorstellung*). Thus his crucial treatment of Sophocles' *Antigone* in the *Phenomenology of Spirit* and in the *Lectures on Aesthetics* – decisive in the development of theories of tragedy, from the work of A. C. Bradley to that of Walter Kaufmann or Northrop Frye, and the more recent work of John Winkler – considers the characters in the work as concretizations or reflections of the experience of conflicting claims, Antigone herself becoming a concrete allegorical representation of the notion of inherent contradiction (she is enjoined to obey the law of the gods requiring appropriate funeral rites, and to obey the public, human law that the gods sanction and that Hegel emblematized in the figure of Creon, a law that in this case forbids the burial of her brother). On this understanding, the play concludes by asserting the necessary emergence of civil society from the concretization of its constitutive contradictions, Antigone's sacrifice presenting physically for the play's audience (hence merely as an intuition) what would become, considered under the aspect of its concrete universality, an object of conceptual reflection (*Begriff*). Both Marx and Engels, and with less nuance early twentieth-century marxist critics like Franc Schiller, Mikhail Lifschitz and especially the Lukács of the period from *History and Class Consciousness* (1923) to his *The Young Hegel* of 1948, take from Hegel the sense that the aesthetic, and literature in particular, constitutes in this way a preliminary (if in some instances also a necessary) moment in the formation of thought or ideology – corresponding to the 'intuitive' certainty afforded by sensuous representation, which yields under the pressure of its excessive abstractness to the mediate experience afforded by conceptual reflection – rather than a concrete or instrumental intervention in a specific historical circumstance.

This, then, is the defining *philosophical* context that frames the 'return to Hegel' in the years immediately preceding and following the Second World War. That 'return' is characterized – especially in France, as Michael Kelly has shown (1983, 1986) – by a tension between two dominant interpretative traditions. The first, centred upon Hegel's earlier works, turns on an *eschatological* interpretation of the Hegelian system that partly captures those works' reliance on Böhme, and partly reflects the religious determinism that runs through Hegel's career. On this account, the form assumed by Absolute Knowledge at the conclusion of the *Phenomenology of Spirit* reflects a philosophically achieved position, 'after' which nothing new can strictly speaking be thought. That Hegel embodied this form in the concrete historical figure of Napoleon (whose battered fortunes might raise some questions about his absoluteness) does not affect the heuristic claim, or the Kantian individualism that can return with it: the position of totality achieved in and by means of the *Phenomenology of Spirit* assumes the shape of an Idea regulating the movement *and content* of 'my' thought. The motor of the dialectic's machinery, under this description, is not so much *contradiction* as it is the triad of *desire, negativity* and *recognition*, the central terms in Kojève's *Introduction to the Reading of Hegel* (1947); the work that this dialectical machine performs is *Bildung*, or education. The second interpretative tradition, centred upon Hegel's later works and of a generally socialist inclination, understands the dialectical method as a means to achieving social change, representations (both broadly cultural and literary in particular) as the reflection or externalization of social contradictions, and philosophy, literary criticism and theory as ways of provoking a reflective understanding or internalization of the social and material conditions of the work's production and reception. The stress remains on the primary contradictions in social relations, and the locus of this 'internalization' of contradictions becomes not man – as in the 'anthropological' or humanistic Hegelianism that flows from Kojève's work – but the broader notion of ideology. The characteristic triad of reflection as externalization, dialectical method and reflective internalization can nonetheless be arranged in ways almost as explicitly deterministic as obtains in eschatological readings of the Hegelian system, as in Lifschitz's work or in the Lukács of *Studies in European Realism*, where it occurs again under the aspect of the *necessary*, 'peculiar' synthesis in what Lukács calls 'the central category and criterion of realist literature', the *type*.

Much of the polemic concerning the 'return to Hegel' in postwar Europe flowed as much from continuities as from the tension between these two approaches. Allegiances were never very stable within the two camps, and in the immediate postwar period certain eccentric figures or texts not easily classified in either proved to be at least as influential in forming Hegel's reception. Such is the case in Germany with Heidegger, whose comments on Hegel in *Being and Time* (on Hegel's 'conception of time', ¶82), in the 1942–43 course Heidegger devoted to the *Phenomenology of Spirit* and in the published essay deriving from that course, the crucial 'Hegel's Concept of Experience', had a significant impact in both Germany and France; with Bertolt Brecht's criticism and plays, whose 'estrangement' effects (*Verfremdungseffekt*) put great pressure on the 'organic' synthesis of realistic representation, and closely correspond to the mode of *irony* and to the logic of *contradiction* in Hegel; so too with thinkers associated with what would come to be called the Frankfurt School, like Walter Benjamin and especially Theodor W. Adorno, already in the middle 1930s sketching out what would become his immensely suggestive account of the 'critical category' of *totality*, in *Negative Dialectics* (1966). For Adorno, the imperative to 'convict' totality or merely mythic thought finds expression methodologically in what could be called a re-literarization or a re-rhetoricization of the dialectic – a procedure that cannot be squarely fitted into either an eschatological or a classically materialist account of Hegel's reception. Adorno's closest followers in Germany and the United States have followed Adorno in seeking to define the nature of the 're-literalized' negative dialectic. Critics and philosophers more evidently in the Frankfurt School tradition – Jürgen Habermas in particular – have in contrast adopted a position on the Hegelian legacy that partly reacts to the mixed terms of Adorno's critique, generally objecting that the role Adorno assigned to aesthetics in his approach to Hegel could more properly be assigned to an explicitly *social, communicative* or *intersubjective* understanding of language use (rather than a literary or a merely rhetorical one).

In France the lines between the 'anthropological' and the materialist receptions of Hegel were no firmer, and Kojève's more immediate influence did little to settle them. Georges Bataille and Jacques Lacan – among the most influential of Kojève's students – would take from Kojève's prewar seminars on Hegel a vocabulary and set of approaches that they developed and changed dramatically and fruitfully in the following decades; Maurice Blanchot, reading Hegel through Kojève as well as Heidegger, would in his novels and criticism provide the most explicitly *literary* extension of this vocabulary. Bataille's early writings dwelt inchoately on themes and terms (the insistence of abjection, sacred terror, genuine thought understood as excremental) that would find formal echoes in Kojève's reading of Hegel a decade later. By the time of *Inner Experience* (1943) and even more pointedly in work from the 1950s, the elaboration of Kojèvian themes and terms had been married to an explicit (if entirely heterodox) marxist engagement, in a combination whose deployment of the term 'transgression' in the place of the Hegelian term 'contradiction' and the Kojèvian term 'desire' fits only obliquely the Kojèvian goals of anthropological 'education' – bringing 'man closer to the idea which he makes for himself'. Maurice Blanchot devoted chapters of *The Work of Fire* (1949) to a critique of Hegel's account of the merely 'external' nature of symbolic art, which is faulty, suggests Hegel, because the exteriority of the image never coincides fully with its spiritual content (a more highly mediated form of art being required to achieve such a coincidence. Likewise, Blanchot's enigmatic concluding essay to *The Work of Fire* turns on an interpretation of the *Phenomenology of Spirit* undertaken explicitly through an encounter with Kojève's *Introduction to the Reading of Hegel*, Blanchot's famous description of the 'two slopes of language' amounting to a rewriting of the dialectic of Hegelian aesthetics, with a node of contra-diction no longer described in the earlier language of 'symbol', 'fault' and 'correspondence'.

So too with Lacan was the idiosyncratic revision of Hegel's vocabulary first adopted, brought into contact with Heidegger's work, and then dramatically shifted. Not only does Lacan's elaboration of the structural function of desire as lack (of a real object) flow directly from Kojève's analysis of the desire for recognition in the *Phenomenology of Spirit*'s dialectic of Master and Slave, much of the development of both the technique and the theory of Lacanian criticism occurs *by means of* readings of Hegel's work, and often in confrontation with thinkers who serve as proxies for Kojève and for Hegel. However firmly he condemned Hegel's residual 'humanism', Lacan's engagement with the philosopher's work lasted till the end of his career. Thus, for example, his addresses on 'Subversion of the Subject and Dialectic of Desire in the Freudian Unconscious' and 'Position of the Unconscious' published in *Ecrits* (1966) bear on the ways in which Freud 'reopens' the term 'desire' to 'the play from which revolutions spring, the hinge between truth and knowledge' that Hegel, Lacan writes, associates with the form of 'desire, *Begierde*, where the . . . minimum connection the subject has to ancient knowledge, is guarded so that truth will be immanent in the realization of knowledge'.

By the time that *Hegel et la pensée moderne* appeared in Paris (1971; collecting essays and presentations from Jean Hyppolite's 1968 Collège de France seminar on Hegel's *Logic*), and in great measure on account of the conceptual and terminological revisions of Kojèvian Hegelianism in the work of Bataille, Adorno, Lacan and Blanchot, the heuristic distinction between programmatically marxist renderings of Hegel and an 'anthropological' or humanist Hegelianism was no longer tenable. What Fredric Jameson announced in 1990 as the 'impending Hegel revival' may be said to have begun in Europe and the United States with the exhaustion of that opposition, with the importation into the field of dialectics of the psychoanalytic concepts of over- and under-determination, and with the rediscovery of the notion of 'hegemony' in the work of Antonio Gramsci.

This incipient 'revival' of Hegel in France, Italy and the US has largely been defined in answer to the dramatic revisions of Hegelianism in the work of Louis Althusser and Jacques Derrida from the middle 1970s forward. The description that Louis Althusser provided in 1967 of the means by which 'individuals' become 'subjects' in given societies – famously phrased as the 'interpellation' by ideology of individuals into an existing subject-position where 'I recognize myself' – bears traces of a determinist approach to the work of Marx and Hegel, the interpellating function of ideology having material means (state apparatuses of different sorts) but in fact a structural status clearly imagined with certain psychoanalytic and Hegelian formulations in mind. Althusser's Hegelianism, however, is qualified. From 1962 onwards he argued both for distinguishing between Hegel's vision of society as a 'totality' and Marx's vision of it as a 'complex whole, structured in dominance', and for understanding that Marx's claim to having 'inverted' the Hegelian dialectic was only a 'metaphor for a real materialist transformation of the figures of the dialectic' (as he puts it in the 1975 *Is it Simple to be a Marxist in Philosophy?* (1990)), a 'real transformation' which Marx never provided explicitly. Coordinating the 'materialist' alternative to the idealist dialectic with the description of a structured society required the development of three concepts intended to clarify the deterministic relation between structure and event still palpable in Althusser's early reading of Hegel. The first two formed an integral part of Althusser's published work in the decade from 1965 to 1975. The concept of 'aleatory materialism', the third and last that Althusser developed in an exploration of the materialist dialectic that would lead him toward what he eventually called a 'philosophy of the encounter', remained inchoate, formulated in interviews and unpublished works. Its debt to Heidegger, and to Althusser's own earliest understanding of Hegel, is palpable: 'A philosophy of the *es gibt*', he writes in 'Le courant souterrain ...' (1994) 'of the "it's given thus" ... "opens" onto a vista that restores a kind of transcendental contingency to the world'. The 'transcendental contingency' of Althusser's conception of matter constitutes his last, perhaps his most controversial contribution to the dismantling of the residual categories of 'necessity' and of 'determination' in the Hegelian legacy.

Like Althusser's, Jacques Derrida's engagement with Hegel is constant, fruitful and resolutely unassimilable to any single tradition of reception. As is also true for much of the *Tel Quel* group, his earliest work on Hegel is firmly Bataillean: the fundamental essay on 'Hegelianism', 'From a Restricted to a General Economy' in *Writing and Difference* (1967), works from Bataille's Kojèvian essays to provide a striking account of a productively 'empty' and analogic use of Hegelian *Aufhebung* to 'designate the transgressive relation linking the world of sense to the world of non-sense'. For Derrida this relation is bi-directional, embedding the 'naive conscience' of philosophy (Absolute Knowledge, the philosophy of reflection, the Book) within the world of non-sense, and the world of non-sense (madness, death, writing construed as *écriture*) within that of sense. The consequences of this 'transgressive' (and no longer simply dialectical) re-description of the relation between sense and non-sense are taken in political terms: the movement between Book and writing can be read 'as a reactionary or as a revolutionary movement, or both at once'. The Bataillean strain, and this early insistence on the necessary 'emptiness' of Hegelian *Aufhebung*, are never far from Derrida's treatments of Hegel.

Beginning in the 1980s, and with increased coherence in the decades since, an 'unfamiliar' Hegel has indeed begun to emerge from the interaction of the Althusserian, Derridean and Lacanian critiques of the Hegelian orthodoxies. In the US, the development of 'American' deconstruction in the late 1970s and early 1980s occurred very much under the aspect of a sympathetic critique of Hegelianism remarkably close to that found in Adorno and in Derrida, though inflected with a different and characteristic interest in the question of the philosophical work's *literariness*. In the work of critics like Paul de Man, Andrzej Warminski, Rodolphe Gasché, Timothy Bahti and others a highly rhetoricized Hegel emerges. More overtly psychoanalytic 'returns' to Hegel have included the work of Henry Sussman and especially of Judith Butler, whose 1987 *Subjects of Desire: Hegelian Reflections in Twentieth-Century France* set out the articulation between the stress on embodiment found in the languages of Husserlian phenomenology, and the legacy of Kojèvian 'desire' in Derrida, Foucault and others. In subsequent work Butler has developed influential descriptions of gender performativity, of materiality and of the Hegelian and Freudian postulation that one comes to 'be' through a dependency on the Other. Most explicitly in chapters on Althusser and on the 'Unhappy Consciousness' section of the *Phenomenology of Spirit* in her *The Psychic Life of Power* (1997), Butler provides an account of the 'vulnerability of strategies of subjection' to the 'capacity of desire to be withdrawn and to reattach' 'blindly', a 'blindness' of desire drawn conceptually from both Lacan's description of the metonymic form of desire, and Althusser's account of the 'aleatory' nature of the event – and in both cases marshalled against a deterministic reading of 'desire' in line with Hegelian eschatology.

Butler and Gasché's recent work on Hegel has often been undertaken in open dialogue with such European philosophers as Rosi Braidotti, Ernesto Laclau and Chantal Mouffe (whose *Hegemony and Socialist Strategy* (1985) brought to the fore the political and philosophical weight of the notion of contingency, and provided a far-reaching critique of the Hegelian notion of social totality in terms drawn from Gramsci rather than from Adorno), and especially with the Slovenian Hegelian-psychoanalyst philosophers Mladen Dolar and Slavoj Žižek. Žižek in particular, arguing against Derrida, Gasché and Warminski in a number of publications, suggests that 'tarrying' with the negative moment in the Hegelian philosophy of reflection makes it possible to avoid understanding the distinction between necessity and contingency by means of the 'category of pure formal conversion', and instead to stress the 'undecidable' logic that governs their relation. It is a sign of the productive 'unfamiliarity' of this returning Hegel that in the most recent literary-theoretical and philosophical work about and inspired by him the parallel notions of 'undecideability' and 'contingency', the Althusserian 'encounter' and what Warminski (following Derrida) calls Hegel's 'writing' emerge as a means of envisioning, in Laclau and Mouffe's terms, a 'radical democratic' politics.

Jacques Lezra

Further reading and works cited

Adorno, T. W. *Negative Dialectics*. New York, 1990.
Althusser, L. *Lenin and Philosophy, and Other Essays*. New York, 1972.
—. *Positions, 1964–1975*. Paris, 1976.
—. *Philosophy and the Spontaneous Philosophy of the Scientists & Other Essays*, ed. and intro. G. Elliot. London, 1990.
—. *Ecrits philosophiques et politiques*, Vol. I. Paris, 1994.
—. *For Marx*. London, 1996.
—. *Reading Capital*. London, 1997a.
—. *The Spectre of Hegel*. London, 1997a.
— and Navarro, F. *Filosofia y marxismo*. Mexico, 1988.
Barnett, S. (ed.) *Hegel After Derrida*. London, 1998.
Bataille, G. *Inner Experience*. Albany, NY, 1988.
Benhabib, S. *Critique, Norm, and Utopia*. New York, 1986.
Blanchot, M. *The Work of Fire*. Stanford, CA, 1995.
Bourdieu, P. *Distinction: A Social Critique of the Judgement of Taste*. Cambridge, MA, 1984.
—. *The Logic of Practice*. Stanford, CA, 1990.
Brod, H. *Hegel's Philosophy of Politics*. Boulder, CO, 1992
Butler, J. *Excitable Speech*. New York, 1997.
—. *The Psychic Life of Power*. Stanford, CA, 1997.
—. *Subjects of Desire*. New York, 1999.
— et al. *Contingency, Hegemony, Universality*. London, 2000.
Cassirer, E. *Kant's Life and Thought*. New Haven, CT, 1981.
Croce, B. *What is Living and What is Dead of the Philosophy of Hegel*. New York, 1969.
Deleuze, G. *Nietzsche and Philosophy*. New York, 1983.
—. *Kant's Critical Philosophy*. Minneapolis, MN, 1984.
— and Guattari, F. *Anti-Oedipus*, preface M. Foucault. Minneapolis, MN, 1983.
—. *A Thousand Plateaus*. Minneapolis, MN, 1987.
de Man, P. *Aesthetic Ideology*. Minneapolis, MN, 1996.
Derrida, J. *Writing and Difference*. Chicago, 1978.
—. *Margins of Philosophy*. Chicago, 1982.

—. *Glas*. Lincoln, NE, 1986.

—. *The Truth in Painting*. Chicago, 1987

Descombes, V. *Modern French Philosophy*. Cambridge, 1980.

Dworkin, R. M. *Taking Rights Seriously*. Cambridge, 1977.

Foucault, M. 'The Subject and Power', in *Michel Foucault: Beyond Structuralism and Hermeneutics*, eds B. Dreyfus and P. Rabinow. Chicago, 1983.

—. 'What is Enlightenment? Was ist Aufklärung?', in *The Foucault Reader*, ed. P. Rabinow. New York, 1984.

—. 'Kant on Enlightenment and Revolution', *Economy and Society*, 15, 1, February 1986.

—. *Mental Illness and Psychology*. Berkeley, CA, 1987.

Guyer, P. (ed.) *The Cambridge Companion to Kant*. Cambridge, 1992.

Hamacher, W. *Pleroma: Reading in Hegel*. Stanford, CA, 1998.

Hegel, G. W. F. *Hegel's Philosophy of Right*. Oxford, 1965.

—. *Hegel's Science of Logic*. London, 1969.

—. *Hegel on Tragedy*, eds and intro. A. and H. Paolucci. New York, 1975.

—. *Aesthetics: Lectures on Fine Art*. Oxford, 1975.

—. *Phenomenology of Spirit*. Oxford, 1977.

—. *Elements of the Philosophy of Right*, ed. A. W. Wood. Cambridge, 1991.

Heidegger, M. *Holzwege*. Frankfurt, 1950.

—. *Being and Time*. New York, 1962.

—. *Kant and the Problem of Metaphysics*. Bloomington, IN, 1962.

—. *What is a Thing?* Chicago, 1968.

—. *Hegel's Concept of Experience*. New York, 1983.

Höffe, O. *Immanuel Kant*. Albany, NY, 1994.

Horkheimer, M. and Adorno, T. W. *Dialectic of Enlightenment*. New York, 1972.

Hyppolite, J. *Studies on Marx and Hegel*. New York, 1969.

—. *Figures de la pensée philosophique*. Paris, 1971.

—. *Genesis and Structure of Hegel's 'Phenomenology of Spirit'*. Evanston, IL, 1974.

—. *Logic and Existence*. Albany, NY, 1997.

Jameson, F. *Late Marxism*. London, 1992.

Kant, I. *Observations on the Feeling of the Beautiful and Sublime*. Berkeley, CA, 1981.

—. *Critique of Judgement*. Indianapolis, IN, 1987.

—. *The Metaphysics of Morals*, trans. and ed. M. Gregor. Cambridge, 1996.

—. *Critique of Practical Reason*. Cambridge, 1997.

—. *Critique of Pure Reason*. Cambridge, 1998a.

—. *Groundwork of the Metaphysics of Morals*. Cambridge, 1998b.

Kelly, M. 'The Post-War Hegel Revival in France: A Bibliographical Essay', *Journal of European Studies*, xiii, 1983.

—. 'Hegel in France Today: A Bibliographical Essay', *Journal of European Studies*, xvi, 1986.

Kojève, A. *Introduction to the Reading of Hegel*. Ithaca, NY, 1980.

Lacan, Jacques. *Ecrits*. Paris, 1966.

—. *Ecrits: A Selection*. New York, 1977.

—. *The Ethics of Psychoanalysis, 1959–1960*. New York, 1992.

Laclau, E. and Mouffe, C. *Hegemony and Socialist Strategy*. London, 1985.

Lefebvre, H. *Dialectical Materialism*. London, 1974.

Levinas, E. *Totality and Infinity*. Pittsburgh, PA, 1969.

Lukács, G. *History and Class Consciousness*. Cambridge, MA, 1971.

—. *Studies in European Realism*. London, 1972.

—. *The Young Hegel*. Cambridge, MA, 1976.

MacIntyre, A. C. *After Virtue*. Notre Dame, IN, 1981.

Pinkard, T. *Hegel: A Biography*. Cambridge, 2000.

Propp, V. *Morphology of the Folk Tale*. Austin, TX, 1968.
Rawls, J. *A Theory of Justice*. Cambridge, MA, 1999.
Ricoeur, P. 'Symbole et temporalité', *Archivio di Filosofia*, 1–2, 1963.
Sartre, J.-P. *What is Literature?* Cambridge, MA, 1988.
Sloterdijk, P. *Critique of Cynical Reason*. Minneapolis, MN, 1987.
Smith, B. Herrnstein. *Contingencies of Value*. Cambridge, MA, 1988.
Stern, R. (ed.) *G. W. F. Hegel: Critical Assessments*. London, 1993.
Sussman, H. *The Hegelian Aftermath*. Baltimore, MD, 1982.
Taylor, C. *Hegel*. Cambridge, 1975.
Theweleit, K. *Male Fantasies*. Minneapolis, MN, 1987.
Warminski, A. *Readings in Interpretation*. Minneapolis, MN, 1987.
Weiskel, T. *The Romantic Sublime*. Baltimore, MD, 1976.
Wimsatt, W. K. and Beardsley, M. C. *The Verbal Icon*. Lexington, KY, 1954.
Žižek, S. *The Sublime Object of Ideology*. London, 1989.
—. *Tarrying With the Negative*. Durham, NC, 1993.
—. *The Indivisible Remainder*. London, 1996.
—. *The Ticklish Subject*. London, 1999.

Johann Christian Friedrich Hölderlin (1770–1843)

During his lifetime, more than half of which (1806–43) was spent in mental illness, Friedrich Hölderlin's work and thought was largely unappreciated. Although his Swabian compatriots sought to reclaim him as a poet of the 'homeland', the critical reaction to his lyric work was overwhelmingly negative, so that a collected edition (incomplete as it was) had to wait until 1846. Furthermore, biographical interest in Hölderlin's personal destiny (fostered by the interpretations of Wilhelm Waiblinger, who began visiting him in 1822) overshadowed engagement with his work for most of the nineteenth century.

However, Hölderlin's novel *Hyperion*, published in two volumes in 1797 and 1799, was widely appreciated, and a second edition appeared in 1822. The Romantic authors Bettina and Ludwig Achim von Arnim (1785–1859 and 1781–1831) and Clemens Brentano (1778–1842) held not only *Hyperion*, but some of Hölderlin's lyric work in highest esteem. Through the editorial efforts of Gustav Schwab (1792–1850) and Ludwig Uhland (1787–1862), an incomplete volume of Hölderlin's collected poetry was published in 1826. Finally, the Young Germans' reception of Hölderlin culminated in Alexander Jung's 1848 monograph *Friedrich Hölderlin und sein Werk*. This book influenced the philosopher Friedrich Nietzsche (1844–1900) whose sustained engagement with Hölderlin can be traced back to 1861. It focused, in particular, on the form of what Bothe calls 'the poetic-philosophical discourse (Bothe 1994, 51) and on Empedocles, a tragic character.

During the second half of the nineteenth century, however, Hölderlin scholarship was largely inspired by a scientific-positivist mentality. The most perceptive interpretation in this spirit is probably Emil Petzold's (Petzold 1986), which gives due weight to Hölderlin's utopian-democratic, if not anarchist, political orientation, and to the originality of his thought, as well as to his interlinking of Hellenism with Christianity. By contrast, the most problematic is the psychopathologically inspired work of Wilhelm Lange-Eichbaum (Lange 1909), whose dubious claim to fame relies on its passing psychiatric criteria of 'normality' off as aesthetic-intellectual valorizations.

It was not Nietzsche's own reception of Hölderlin, but elements of his philosophy of art, of history and of 'life' that entered into the transformation of Hölderlin studies at the beginning of the twentieth century, inaugurated by the work of Wilhelm Dilthey (1833–1911) and Norbert von Hellingrath, who fell at Verdun in 1916. Dilthey's influential study *Das Erlebnis und die Dichtung (Lived Experience and Poetry)*, first published in 1906, exalts Hölderlin's poetic stature in an unprecedented manner, while also idealizing him as a visionary (in keeping with the philosopher's understanding of art as non-rational cognition) and depriving his work of both its speculative and socio-political dimensions.

Hellingrath, who had discovered the manuscripts of Hölderlin's late hymns and of his Pindar translations, brought out a collected edition with commentary, in four volumes, the final one of which was published posthumously in 1917. His key concerns are re-mythologization, a conception of language as functioning autonomously rather than communicatively, together with a focus on its musical-incantatory rather than semantic character, the exaltation of German poetic diction in its supposedly unique relation to the ancient Greek, and a view of Hölderlin's entire work as constituting fundamentally a single poem. The most disturbing aspect of Hellingrath's Hölderlin interpretation, however, is its tacit assimilation of Hölderlin's notion of the 'fatherland' to the nationalist rhetoric of his day, coupling it with the idea of the cultural mission and elect status of Germany – the 'secret Germany' envisaged by the poet Stefan George and his circle, of which latter Hellingrath was a member. These construals prefigured the National Socialist distorted interpretation (which did not shy away from textual alteration) and ideological appropriation of Hölderlin in the 1930s and early 1940s. Moreover, all these strands of thought entered in highly complex ways into the powerful readings of Hölderlin that are central to the thought of Martin Heidegger. So did the poetic engagement with Hölderlin on the part of the Austrian poet Georg Trakl, and of Rainer Maria Rilke, although Heidegger remained unresponsive to the inscription of Hölderlin in the work of Paul Celan.

Heidegger, who devoted three lecture courses to Hölderlin's hymns as well a volume of essays of 1936–68, *Erläuterungen zu Hölderlins Dichtung* (Heidegger 1971), understands his own thought in important ways as an 'interlocution' with Hölderlin who articulates the essential being (*Wesen*) of poetry as bringing language to reveal the being of beings, in a modality of revelation that does not violate being's self-withdrawal. Furthermore, Hölderlin, for him, limns the essential-historical self-understanding of his people and of the West.

Heidegger's thought and the Hölderlin translations by Heidegger scholars such as Jean Beaufret and François Fédier have stimulated and influenced an ongoing tradition of French Heidegger interpretation, ranging from the Catholic theological perspective of Jean-Luc Marion to poststructuralist readings by Maurice Blanchot, Jean-Luc Nancy and Philippe Lacoue-Labarthe. A different approach characterizes the biographically and politically oriented labours of Pierre Bertaux. Given the complexity and vitality of both the French and the German scholarship, Hölderlin reveals himself to be a figure of contemporary theoretical importance rather than a precursor in the usual sense.

Life, work and thought

Hölderlin's birth in Lauffen in the Duchy of Würtemberg placed him squarely in a pietist milieu of introspective religiosity (as well as of bourgeois prosperity) that was suspicious of the arts and remote from the cosmopolitanism of the major academic centres. His twice-widowed mother sought to channel her son's high intellectual, literary and musical gifts into the secure career of a small-town or rural pastor, which he always found uncongenial. He received a theological and classical education, first at the monastic boarding school of Maulbronn, then at the Tübingen theological academy. His master's thesis concerned *The History of the Fine Arts Among the Greeks and Parallels between the Sayings of Solomon and Hesiod's Works and Days*. At the Tübingen academy, he formed a close and lasting friendship with the future philosopher G. W. F. Hegel, which was joined, in 1790, by the younger F. W. J. Schelling. Hölderlin's role in the development of German idealism was formative rather than merely receptive. His friendship with the lawyer and revolutionary activist Isaak von Sinclair, which lasted until the latter's death in 1815, also began in Tübingen.

The odes and hymns of his early poetic creativity show both the strong influence of F. G. Klopstock and Hölderlin's characteristic exalted diction. They are concerned with themes such as freedom, harmony, truth, beauty, humanity and nature – topics too abstract to allow them to be poetically fully successful. They also reveal his deep and lasting sympathy for the ideals of the French Revolution, and a nostalgic self-identification with the culture of ancient Greece.

Philosophically, he had studied Plato, Spinoza, Leibniz and Rousseau, and, beginning in 1790, he immersed himself passionately in a thorough study of Kant, and later of Fichte, whose lectures he attended in Jena in 1795 and whose thought he discussed with Hegel. He understood Kant's philosophy to be fundamentally oriented toward the liberation of reason from any form of heteronomy. It resonated, for him, with his own cultural critique that saw an original order of freedom perverted into an order of legality, and with his understanding of the French Revolution as seeking to bring about 'a reign of love', where the ideal and the real are no longer disjoint. At the same time, he criticized a hegemony of reason that subordinated the senses, feeling and creative imagination. Kant's notion of the 'thing in itself' attested, for him, to the fundamental unknowability of the enigma of reality by reason alone. By contrast, love is understood as the power to institute interrelations, enabling one ultimately to think the whole, which Kant's philosophy appeared to him to be incapable of.

He criticized Fichte's thought for leading to the dead-end of an isolated ego. His argument is that pure being cannot be understood as identity; for identity presupposes separation. The difficulty is how to think being as both divisible and without separation.

These philosophical explorations, as well as investigations of the relationship of antiquity to modernity, of the possibility of a 'mythology of reason', of the relation between poetry and philosophy, and other theoretical topics are articulated in a series of essays that he often wrote for the purpose of clarifying and developing his own thoughts, rather than with the intent of publication.

After the conclusion of his studies, he accepted a post as private tutor to Charlotte von Kalb's son Fritz, which took him first to Waltershausen near Jena, then to Jena and Weimar. The position was mediated by Schiller, whom Hölderlin venerated, and who published a number of Hölderlin's early works in periodicals that he edited. The position did not ultimately prove successful. Soon after its termination (after a stay in Jena and a precipitous retreat to his mother's house in Nürtingen), Hölderlin accepted another position as private tutor with the Gontard family in Frankfurt (1796). Here his educational programme and relationship to his pupil Henri proved successful, but his passionate and reciprocated love for the lady of the house, Susette Gontard, whom he called Diotima, brought his employment to an abrupt and emotionally painful end in 1798. He retreated to Homburg, the home of Sinclair.

His work on *Hyperion*, which had continued over some seven years, came to fruition with the publication of the two volumes in 1797 and 1799. The Frankfurt period also brought an intense philosophical interchange with Hegel, whose own position there as private tutor Hölderlin had mediated. His poetic work during this period is marked by formal innovation. In particular, he adopted and perfected the asclepiad and alcaic strophe forms, developing their expressive potential and writing epigrammatic odes. A number of important lyric works, such as *Stimme des Volks*, *An die Deutschen*, *Die Heimath* and *Diotima* took form during this period. However, the culmination of Hölderlin's lyric creativity was still to come.

Given that *Hyperion* is the one work by which Hölderlin was generally known in the nineteenth century, a brief discussion of it is called for. The novel is composed of letters written by the title character, an eighteenth-century Greek (the subtitle calls him 'a hermit in Greece') to his German friend Bellarmin. The letters are retrospective and reflective, revealing Hyperion's life struggles and their resolution. Although the novel is generally considered to be a *Bildungsroman* or novel of personal formation, this has been disputed on the grounds that it is not fundamentally concerned with a personal itinerary, but with a self-consignment to nature (for Hölderlin nature has Spinozan resonance and is a notion akin to that of Being) which gives one poetic entitlement. Hyperion has lost the spontaneous union with nature characteristic of naive consciousness or of childhood through the separative force of a rational quest; his 'eccentric path' (the centre being union) cannot seek to regain it, but must realize a new and higher form of union out of estrangement. His loving mentor is Adamas, whose pronouncement 'God in us' leads him to envisage a social order of free, autonomous individuals. In his friendship with the freedom fighter Alabanda, he seeks to realize this vision in battle, but he soon encounters the power of violence to become an end in itself, rather than remaining subordinate to a higher purpose. In estrangement from Alabanda, he meets the ideal figure of Diotima who tells him that it is enough to be or to live, and that, in the 'divine world', there can be neither masters nor slaves (1976 XI, 768). Their separation is made necessary by his 'eccentric path', and her subsequent death leads him to become, as she had foreseen, an educator of his people through the written word, and a 'priest' of nature in keeping with Hölderlin's understanding of the sacrality of the poet's vocation.

A key work of Hölderlin's first Homburg period – a time during which he sought in vain to establish himself as an independent writer – is his tragedy *Empedocles*, which he had already begun to work on in Frankfurt. It is extant only in three fragmentary versions, together with the theoretical essay 'Ground for Empedocles'. This body of work leads directly on to the theory of tragedy that Hölderlin developed during his second Homburg period (1804–6). The challenge addressed in the three successive versions is that the title character (whose thought is not that of the pre-Socratic philosopher but Hölderlin's own) cannot just choose to embrace death for reasons of his own. Rather, his death must be called for by 'the destiny of his time', or the historical destiny of his homeland.

Hölderlin follows here his understanding of Greek tragedy as the most severe of poetic forms, constrained to purge the tragic events of any merely accidental factors (it is also for this reason that he chooses temporally and culturally remote protagonists). The action is to show forth no mere human dilemma, but a divine process.

Hölderlin achieves this ideal in the third version, but only at the cost of consigning all action to the past. Empedocles here unifies in his individual person the 'aorgic' element of nature (linked to what Hölderlin calls *Todeslust*, a desire for death) and the 'organic' element of human measure, and he does so at a time of the most acute historical opposition of these principles. Since, however, the unification is purely individual and cannot enter into the life of the people, it must by tragic necessity be destroyed. Tragedy is revealed here as intimately bound up with far-reaching historical changes (*Zeitenwende*).

The first Homburg period yielded some major odes, hymns and elegies. The Pindaric hymn *Wie wenn am Feiertage* (*As on a Holiday*), which opens directly upon Hölderlin's late hymnic work, dates from 1800. However, much of the particular importance of this period lies in its rich harvest of philosophical and poetological essays. These address the relationship between philosophy and poetry (philosophical insight forms the basis of poetic practice but cannot grasp the 'higher interconnection'), between art and nature, ancient and modern poetic practice, and questions of poetic form. A key essay for the theory of tragedy is 'Das Werden im Vergehen' ('Becoming in Perishing'), which concerns the relationship of poetry to history, and the tragic law governing both history and nature.

In June of 1800, Hölderlin left Homburg for a brief stay in Nürtingen, followed by a sojourn of several months with his friend C. Landauer in Stuttgart. This happy period gave rise to serene poetry, such as *Der Gang aufs Land*. Hölderlin was able to support himself in Stuttgart by giving private philosophy lessons, but he nevertheless decided, in January 1801, to accept a new position as tutor in Hauptwil, Switzerland. His employment was terminated after only three months, but his experience of the majestic Swiss alpine landscape was for him (always deeply involved in the study of landscape) of great poetic importance. It is mirrored, for instance, in the late hymn *Der Rhein*. The elegy *Heimkunft. An die Verwandten* reflects his homeward journey across the *Bodensee*.

At the end of 1801, he left Germany once more to take on a position as private tutor with the consul D. C. Meyer in Bordeaux, France. This position was likewise of short duration, but important for him in that it allowed him to experience, in the southern landscape and southern culture, the essential presence of antiquity. In late June 1802, Susette Gontard died of an infectious illness. In the same month, Hölderlin arrived in Germany (first Nürtingen and Stuttgart) in a condition of nervous exhaustion and agitation aggravated by grief. By the autumn, he was nevertheless able to begin intensive work on the hymn *Patmos* (dedicated to Count Hessen-Homburg), initiating a period of intense lyric creativity. Through Sinclair's efforts, Hölderlin's translations of Sophocles's *Oedipus Tyrannos* and *Antigone*, together with two difficult but important theoretical essays, were published in 1804, but their reception was distressingly negative, since their idiosyncrasies were ascribed to the poet's rumoured 'madness'. They were staged only in 1951.

Sinclair also procured (and financed) a nominal position as court librarian for Hölderlin in Homburg, which he held until the autumn of 1806, when his mental condition deteriorated to the point that he was forcibly institutionalized, only to be released the next year as incurable. At this time, the master carpenter Heinrich Zimmer (who admired *Hyperion*) offered to take over the patient's care. Hölderlin remained until his death at

Zimmer's home in Tübingen, where his room in the 'tower' commanded a beautiful view, and where, besides his flute, a gift piano was at his disposal.

Several significant changes are evident in Hölderlin's late poetry, which constitutes his supreme lyric achievement. Firstly, the hymnic form predominates over those of the ode and elegy (the latter predominated in 1800), together with a turn to free verse (still written in strophes). Secondly, philosophical reflection and questioning is now incorporated into the poems themselves, which indicates a privileging of the hermeneutic over the visionary mode. The poet's vocation to mediate the holy and to interpret the sacred (divine and heroic) names of history is not the role of a seer, but of a seeker. Finally, this late period is the time of Hölderlin's 'patriotic turning'; but one must guard against reading the adjective in any nationalistic sense. Hölderlin (who had included a famous invective against the Germans in *Hyperion*) now turns toward his native country envisaged in terms of its 'Hesperian' relationship to 'Oriental' Greece, in keeping with the quasi-dialectical philosophy of history elaborated in his Remarks on Sophoclean tragedy. If Germany is to be the place of a new cultural and spiritual flowering, the reason lies, for Hölderlin, in the thoughtfulness and quietude he found among its people. Significantly, he portrays Germania (in *Germanien*) as a priestess and as unarmed.

Some of the late hymns (notably *Griechenland*) are hermetic, but in others such as *Andenken* or *Mnemosyne*, the hermeticism is tempered by a compelling beauty. Heidegger's Hölderlin essays and lecture courses address chiefly the late hymns, including the great stream hymns.

Apart from developing, as already noted, a philosophy of history and carrying forward the theoretical elucidation of tragedy begun during the first Homburg period, the difficult 'Remarks' on Sophoclean tragedy introduce the notion of a 'categorical turning' through which God and man must part from each other, leading to the tragic perdition of the protagonist. The formal analysis highlights the *caesura* as the inscription of this turning.

Hölderlin continued to write poems during his illness. These are generally short rhymed poems of transparent simplicity, but also of a certain rigidity, showing none of the audacity of thought and diction of the poet's lucid work. Perhaps, however, they realize in their own way Hölderlin's belief that what is most exalted stands revealed in the most inconspicuous.

Theoretical importance

The theoretical issues raised by Hölderlin's work are far-reaching, given not only his original researches in poetics and the theory of tragedy, but also and above all the fact that, far from merely drawing on philosophy, he was a well-trained creative philosopher in his own right. His philosophical thought, moreover, is integral to his poetic achievement.

The key Hegelian motifs of spirit seeking to grasp itself through a self-exteriorization in nature and history, together with a dialectical understanding of historical process, are largely Hölderlinian in their incipience. Hölderlin's insightful articulation of the dialectical bond between the cultures of ancient Greece (and more remotely India or the Orient) and Occidental Hesperia (see his 'Remarks on Antigone') are crucial to Heidegger's own efforts to think the 'historical destiny' of the West and the crisis of his time.

The dialectical structure of Hölderlin's historical analyses also informs his poetics. For instance, his theory of the alternation of tones, formulated around 1800, presupposes the dialectical principle that one's 'ownmost' is what is most difficult to realize. Far from coming naturally, it requires the challenges of opposition and estrangement to achieve fruition. Thus the 'ideal' (intellectual-contemplative) tone fundamental to the tragic mode not only calls for a countervailing tone that constitutes the work's 'art-character' (here the heroic), but the tension between these must be mediated by the previously excluded tone (the naive) if the basic tone is to come into its own convincingly. Moreover, the poetic work can only return, as it must, to its original basic tone at the completion of its progressive development by passing through the 'counter-rhythmic interruption' of the *caesura*.

Spirit and dialectics aside, however, Hölderlin thinks otherwise than Hegel, for reason is not, for him, sovereign and capable of grasping absolute reality, but rather the latter poses an always 'hyperbolic' challenge to human thought. In this fundamental conviction, Hölderlin's thought is, as Heidegger puts it, transgressive of metaphysics. Although he remains committed to intrinsic truth (and willing to formulate the grand narratives that Lyotard regards as defining modernity), he anticipates postmodern insights both by his recognition that metaphysical-systematic knowledge of reality as a whole is inachievable, and by his refusal to grant reason sole or sovereign access to truth. Indeed, the hyperbolic challenge to think reality remains, for him, compelling because, where reason comes up against its limits, the senses and feeling remain receptive to intimations of truth.

Truth is not, for him, fundamentally univocal but pluridimensional, and the challenge to think it is a challenge to cultivate openness to new thought-forms and dimensions of experience. Here, one may note, Hölderlin's trans-metaphysical thought is entirely in harmony with his anarchist political persuasions. It is also this challenge of voicing a non-univocal truth (or, more conventionally expressed, of 'saying the holy') which makes for the intensely self-reflective character of Hölderlin's poetic practice – a self-reflective mode of writing that is, of course, carried forward by poets such as Rilke and Celan. Finally, responding to the hyperbolic challenge of truth is, for Hölderlin, always a matter of exposure and risk. The lightning bolt as which the god reveals himself may leave only ashes, or the visionary poet may find himself 'struck by Apollo'. In contrast to the German idealist paradigm of converting negativity into spiritual gain (a paradigm that fails before the horrors of the twentieth century), Hölderlin's thought can countenance disaster and irrecuperable loss, yet it resolutely repudiates nihilism.

Véronique M. Fóti

Further reading and works cited

Allemann, B. *Hölderlin und Heidegger*. Zürich, 1954.

Beck, A. and Raabe, P. *Hölderlin. Eine Chronik in Text und Bild*. Frankfurt, 1970.

Beyer, U. (ed.) *Neue Wege zu Hölderlin*. Würzburg, 1994.

Binder, E., and Weimar, K. *Friedrich Hölderlin. Studien von Wolfgang Binder*. Frankfurt, 1987.

Böschenstein, B. and Rider, J. le (eds) *Holderlin vu de France*. Tübingen, 1987.

Bothe, H. *'Ein Zeichen sind wir, deutungslos'. Die Rezeption Hölderlins von ihren Anfängen bis zu Stefan George*. Stuttgart, 1992.

—. *Hölderlin: Zurhrung*. Hamburg, 1994.

Courtine, J-F. (ed.) *L'Herne: Hölderlin*. Paris, 1989.

Gaier, U. *Hölderlin*. Tübingen and Basel, 1993.

Heidegger, M. *Erläuterungen zu Hölderlins Dichtung*. Frankfurt, 1971.

—. *Hölderlins Hymne 'Der Ister'*, Sommersemester 1942, GA, vol. 53; *Hölderlins Hymne 'Andenken'*, Wintersemester 1941/2, GA, vol. 52; *Hölderlins Hymnen 'Germanien' und 'Der Rhein'*, Wintersemester 1934/35: all in *Heidegger Gesamtausgabe*. Frankfurt am Main, 1976–.

Henrich, D. *Hegel im Kontext*, 4th rev. edn. Frankfurt, 1988.

Hölderlin, F. *Sämtliche Werke*, Grosse Stuttgarter Ausgabe, eds F. Beissner and A. Beck, 15 vols. Stuttgart, 1943–85.

——. *Sämtliche Werke*, Frankfurter historisch-kritische Ausgabe, eds D. E. Sattleer and W. Greddeck, 20 vols. Frankfurt, 1976.

——. *Friedrich Hölderlin: Poems and Fragments.* Cambridge, 1980.

——. *Hölderlin: Hymns and Fragments.* Princeton, NJ, 1984.

——. *Hölderlin. Essays and Letters on Theory*, ed. T. Pfau. Albany, NY, 1988.

Jamme, C., and Pöggeler, O. (eds) *Hölderlins letzte Homburger Jahre (1904–1906).* Bonn, 1988.

Lacoue-Labarthe, P. *L'Antigone de Sophocle, suivi de La Césure du spéculatif.* Paris, 1978.

Lange, W. *Hölderlin – Eine Pathographie.* Stuttgart, 1909.

Lernout, G. *The Poet as Thinker: Hölderlin in France.* New York, 1994.

Petzold, E. *Hölderlin's Brod und Wein. Ein exegetischer Versuch.* Sambor, 1896.

Szondi, P. *Hölderlin Studien. Mit einem Traktat über philologische Erkenntnis.* Frankfurt, 1967.

Warminski, A. *Readings in Interpretation.* Minneapolis, MN, 1987.

Karl Marx (1818–1883)

Although Karl Marx did not compose any sustained piece of writing on aesthetics or literature, he exerted an enormous influence on literary theory and criticism of the twentieth century. Trained as a philosopher in the left Hegelian tradition, Marx is most noted for his contributions to political economy and for his revolutionary political activities. Because his theories about capitalism and about the history of human development encompass society in its entirety, his thought has relevance for art and literature. Marx was educated in the classical tradition and had a tremendous knowledge of European literature. His observations on authors, literary texts and related matters, when combined with the comments of Friedrich Engels, his lifelong associate and collaborator, comprise two large volumes. But these remarks rarely consist of extended discussions: most often they amount to allusions or casual references, more decorative than substantive in nature. The most frequently cited passages of direct literary concern are the criticism of Eugène Sue's serialized novel *The Mysteries of Paris* in *The Holy Family*, the debate with Ferdinand Lassalle over his drama on Franz von Sickingen, and occasional prescriptive comments in the late letters of Friedrich Engels. But the impact of marxism is only partially related to these discussions. Much more important for subsequent writers was the emphasis on the embeddedness of all culture in social and economic relations. Although critics such as Georg Lukács, Antonio Gramsci, Louis Althusser, Raymond Williams, Theodor Adorno and Fredric Jameson have differed significantly on what Marx meant and how one should apply his insights to literary texts, they all agree on the fertile connection between a socioeconomic realm and the arena of culture. Marx's greatest achievement for literary studies was his insistence that literature is never entirely autonomous, and that it represents a mediated ideological statement about genuine social struggle.

Born in Trier in 1818 into an assimilated Jewish family that soon converted to Protestantism, Marx attended the local Gymnasium (college preparatory high school) and in 1835 the University of Bonn, where he was supposed to follow in the footsteps of his father Heinrich and study law. The following year he secretly became engaged to Jenny von Westphalen, whom he married in 1943; of their four children, only two survived their childhood years. In 1836 Marx transferred to Berlin, where he soon became interested in Hegelian philosophy. After his dissertation on Democritus and Epicurus was accepted at the University of Jena in 1841, he turned to journalism, editing for a time the *Rheinische Zeitung* in Cologne until it was banned in 1843. Radicalized by his tenure as editor, Marx was forced to leave Germany and take up residence in Paris in 1843. Here he met Friedrich Engels, the son of a wealthy north German businessman, who had just returned from an extended stay in England. Marx moved to Brussels in 1845, but returned to Germany briefly during the revolutionary years of 1848–9, when he edited the *Neue Rheinische Zeitung*. Expelled in the aftermath of the unsuccessful revolution in 1849, Marx and his family settled in London, where he spent the rest of his life in poverty researching and writing on various topics, mostly on current events or issues pertaining to political economy, and contributing to the organizational efforts of the communist movement. Adversely affected by the death of his wife Jenny and his oldest daughter in the early 1880s, and already in ill health due to years of hardship, Marx died in 1883.

Marx's earliest writings revolve around a critique of religion, which he initially conceived as the preliminary task of any radical philosophy. In the first and only issue of the *Deutsch-französische Jahrbücher* in 1844, he tackled the thorny issue of Jewish emancipation in the notorious essay 'On the Jewish Question'. Although the essay has been frequently controversial because of Marx's derogatory remarks about Jewish business practices, his central argument is that emancipation is incomplete if it entails only religious or political and not a total human emancipation: for Marx genuine emancipation is not achieved with the extension of rights to certain religious groups, but only with a radical refashioning of the total social order. He argues along the same lines in his famous 'Critique of a Hegelian Philosophy of Right', the second essay he included in the *Deutsch-französische Jahrbücher*. In the celebrated comparison between religion and opium, he claims that our concern with the afterlife diverts our attention from the pursuit of happiness in this world. Religion represents the self-alienation of human beings, and just as the critique of religion reveals the true character of belief, so too philosophy should set itself the task of clarifying the obfuscatory aspects of the real world. The trajectory in this important essay starts from a critique of religion and proceeds through philosophy to politics and revolution. Already at this stage in his development Marx had determined that negation in the realm of thought was insufficient: if historical progress is going to occur, there has to be a real struggle involving a historical agent that will propel history forward. The proletariat, as the only class that could represent society as a whole, is appointed the task of redeeming society. Philosophy and the working class hold the hope for the future: the essential task is not just the interpretation of the world, but its wholesale transformation.

In his writings prior to the *Communist Manifesto* Marx often resorted to concepts adopted from his predecessors in order to analyse the economic predicament of the proletariat. A case in point is the notion of 'alienation', which figures prominently in the *Economic and Philosophic Manuscripts*, composed in Parisian exile in 1844. The term is appropriated from G. W. F. Hegel and Ludwig Feuerbach. Hegel admitted nature into his system as the self-alienation of Spirit; thus he maintains that man as a natural being is the self-alienation of the Absolute or of God. Feuerbach holds precisely the opposite position, with which Marx largely concurred: God is self-alienated man, the essence of man abstracted and made alien or strange. In the 1844 *Manuscripts*, however, Marx conceives alienation as the key to a critique of political economy. The basis for his analysis is the observation that under capitalist forms of production the product of labour does not belong to the labourer. Not only is the product thus alienated from the worker, appearing to him as an object belonging to another, it is also the source of wealth for another (the capitalist) and therefore contributes to the bondage of the worker in the production process. The more the worker produces, the more enslaved he is by the alienated products of his labour. This most general and primary form of alienation is in turn the origin of supplemental types that extend into the anthropological realm: the worker is also alienated from the production process, from the essence of the human species (since its essence lies in production), from nature, from other human beings and from himself. The capitalist mode of production, which deprives the worker of the product of his labour, is thus the root cause of all generalized manifestations of social alienation.

Obviously dissatisfied with the anthropological assumptions contained in his discussion of alienation in the 1844 *Manuscripts*, Marx avoided the term in his subsequent writings, referring at one point derisively to 'alienation' as a term he employs so that philosophers will understand him. The notion of alienated labour, however, survives and becomes a cornerstone of Marx's theory in *Capital*, where it is discussed under a somewhat altered label: the fetishism of commodities. Proceeding from an analysis of the commodity form, Marx argues that the fetishism of commodities arises from a specific social arrangement, when commodities are taken to the marketplace and acquire exchange value. If we can decipher the mysterious notion of value, a social hieroglyph, then we can understand what is occurring under conditions of capitalist production. In exposing the production process, however, Marx does not seek to return us to a pristine state prior to alienation, but rather to provide a general methodological principle for modern social phenomena. His central point is that our reflections on social life are necessarily distorted by the confusion wrought by commodity fetishism. The notion of commodities as natural products of human society and development has led us to confound nature and history. The result is a series of false and misleading starting points for political economists, who repeatedly consider derivative phenomena (money, prices) as essential, while regarding the essential as natural. Fetishism of commodities is thus associated with false consciousness, as well as with epistemological inadequacies in bourgeois ideology, and this field of association contributed to its centrality in Georg Lukács' *History and Class Consciousness*, where it reappears as reification or in the notion of an 'administered society' in the writings of the Frankfurt School.

A second central notion in the early writings of Marx is 'ideology'. At issue in the 1840s was a clarification of Marx's views in contrast to the convictions of other left Hegelians and socialists of the times, and Marx, along with Engels, who began collaborating with Marx during the mid 1840s, devoted two longer treatises to this task: *The Holy Family* and *The German Ideology*. Although these works do not explicitly define ideology, it is apparent that Marx associated this notion in the first instance with the abstraction and idealism that is ultimately derived from Hegelian thought. Marx himself had developed from Hegelian philosophy, so in a sense these writings were both a self-critique and an endeavour to carve out a position different from those of his former associates. Hegelians, he argues, remain in the realm of a religious critique, not because they concentrate solely on religious matters, but because they reduce the various critiques they make – of politics, law, morals – to a religious essence. They want to combat deficiencies in the real world by opposing the phrases associated with these deficiencies, and therein they remain entrapped in a particularly German ideology. They propose changing consciousness, but only in so far as this change entails interpreting reality differently – not, as Marx will suggest, by changing reality. By contrast, Marx advocates in *The German Ideology* a materialist basis for analysis. Eschewing ideological explanations for political and social problems, he explains even consciousness and language as dependent on a material basis. Ideology is thus opposed here and elsewhere to 'science' or to views that originate in a materialist analysis of the social order. Ultimately ideology, ideals and ideas are based in the interests of a class seeking to maintain or to gain hegemony, and to the extent that literature contains ideological material, it too participates in class struggle.

The culmination of Marx's early theoretical development and his practical activities in organization appears in the *Manifesto of the Communist Party*. Commissioned by the Communist League as a set of foundational principles, the *Manifesto* contains much spirited writing, but is an uneven document. The third section incorporates Marx and Engels's criticism of other socialist and communist movements, while the second section, betraying the original catechism form in which Engels sketched the initial draft, answers hypothetical questions and corrects widespread misconceptions about communism. Most interesting is the discussion of the role of the bourgeoisie in the first part of the work. Marx considers the bourgeoisie to be a unique and essentially revolutionary class: all previous ruling classes have taken a conservative stance toward production, attempting to limit it and thereby preserve their hegemonic social position. By contrast, the bourgeoisie needs to revolutionize production constantly, introducing more efficient means to increase productivity. Thus the bourgeoisie, which was once a revolutionary class in the historical sense that it opposed and overthrew the feudal order, retains an aspect of its revolutionary promise even after it has gained power. In imposing a rational order on production, however, the bourgeoisie has also revolutionized the ideological sphere. Gone are the feudal superstitions and traditional notions that fettered individuals to a medieval hierarchy. The bourgeois era has not eliminated exploitation and misery; it has merely lifted the veil of religious and political guises that formerly legitimated oppression of the lower classes, and substituted brute force and the cash nexus. Thus despite its despotic role in contemporary society the bourgeoisie has propelled history forward, simplifying class conflict, introducing a new ideological structure, and paving the way for its own downfall by introducing its own grave-diggers: the proletariat.

By the time of the *Manifesto* the place of culture and literature was defined by its role in class struggle. Marx conceived of cultural phenomena as secondary and dependent on a more basic economic order, and the classical and most concise statement of this relationship is contained in the 'Preface' to *A Contribution to the Critique of Political Economy*, published in 1859. Marx begins by defining what he means by the economic base, introducing two important notions: relations of production and productive forces. In other texts Marx explains that the productive forces consist of raw materials and the instruments of production, which together are called the means of production, as well as labour power. Means of production and labour power exist in any epoch, in any human society; changes in productivity, however, are implemented by modifications of one or more factors: technological advances, for example, may increase productive potential, but production can also be augmented by an increase in the work week. What defines an economic mode of production, however, is not the amount produced, but the relationship human beings have to the productive forces, determined largely by ownership of, or effective control over, the productive forces. In slave-holding societies, for example, the ruling classes own both the means of production and the labour power of individuals, while the slaves own nothing. Under capitalism, the proletariat owns only its labour power, which it is compelled to sell on the marketplace in order to survive. Although there is no precise relationship, certain types of relations of production correspond to the development of productive forces. In general slave-based societies are agricultural, while industrial economies are capitalist.

The real foundation of a society is its economic base. But arising from this base is a superstructure, which Marx defines in terms of legal and political matters: despite the insistence of most commentators, Marx does not connect the superstructure with cultural phenomena; instead it appears to contain institutional elements of governmental and judicial significance. However, corresponding to the economic base are also forms of 'social consciousness': the ideas, ideals and ideologies of a social order, which presumably include its philosophy, religion, literature and art. Marx makes it clear that the mode of production determines the social and intellectual sphere: the real social being is located in the economic structure, while consciousness is an epiphenomenon, dependent on the more fundamental realm of production and the relations of production. The struggles and conflicts that occur in this superstructural realm are ultimately derived from a primary arena of contradictions in the base. We must therefore distinguish carefully between the self-consciousness of a given epoch, what it thinks of itself and how it portrays itself, and what this consciousness really represents in objective terms. With this theoretical perspective Marx advocates what Paul Ricoeur would later call a 'hermeneutics of suspicion': in order to accomplish a Marxist interpretation the critic must recognize that the foregrounded ideology is a subterfuge, and that the real meaning of ideas and forms in literature and art is derived from their role in a more fundamental sphere. While the contradictions in the economic realm can be determined with scientific precision, Marx suggests that the legal, political, religious, philosophical and aesthetic struggles, which are no more than the way in which individuals become conscious of contradictions and fight them out, are often more elusive and ambivalent.

Indeed, Marx recognizes in other writings that the relationship between artistic production and economic production is neither simple nor direct. Progress in the economic sphere, which is easily measured in terms of increased productivity, does not necessarily mean a concomitant advance in art. The times of great art do not necessarily correspond at all to what is occurring at the material foundation of society. What we can say, however, is that certain types of artistic products correspond to definite modes of production. The Greek epics, for example, are obvious products of an undeveloped society. Since they are based on Greek mythology and employ a different relationship to natural phenomena, we cannot imagine the production of similar epics in industrial societies, where we encounter steam engines, trains, and telegraphs. Achilles' heroism cannot be reproduced in the same fashion in an age of gunpowder, and the oral nature of the epic seems in doubt with the advent of the printing press. In short, the conditions under which the heroic epic prospered no longer obtain. Explaining the way in which art belongs to its own times, however, is much easier than trying to understand why we enjoy art from the past. Marx asks why we can still appreciate Greek art, now that we are living under enormously changed circumstances. His tentative answer, that we recognize in the Greeks the childhood of humanity, indicates that Marx was not able to integrate all aspects of aesthetics into his historical schema.

The theoretical considerations that Marx sketched for the history and interpretation of literary texts was supplemented in his work only occasionally by concrete case studies. Although Marx exhibits a thorough knowledge of the classics, of Shakespeare and of modern literature in general, only twice does he comment at any length on a particular novel or play, and in both cases the works are known more for Marx's criticisms than for their own literary merit. The first occasion occurred in the 1840s, when Marx discussed Eugène Sue's popular novel *Mysteries of Paris* in *The Holy Family*. Like most of this polemical text, the sections on Sue's novel deal harshly with a work that seems at first glance very close to the socialist and philosophical concerns of Marx and Engels. The novel champions the working class, and Sue evidences obvious sympathy for the proletarian cause. Marx, however, felt that the work was trite and contrived, and that Sue himself was a sentimental, petty-bourgeois, social fantast. In the extended discussion Marx actually writes less about Sue and his work than he does about a particular piece of criticism of the novel, written under the pseudonym Szeliga (Franz Zychlin von Zychlinski), which praises its artistic and ideological merits. In the context of *The Holy Family* Szeliga is portrayed as the typical speculative idealist of the Hegelian school, who was unable to penetrate to the economic realities of the capitalist world, remaining instead on the level of conceptual abstraction that precluded effective critique.

The second longer commentary occurred in 1859, when Ferdinand Lassalle, a leader of the socialist movement in Germany, composed a historical drama entitled *Franz von Sickingen*. The play was written to capture in literary form the experiences of the failed revolution of 1848, but Lassalle chose to project backward and selected for his hero a knight whose revolutionary aspirations during the peasant revolts had similarly ended in defeat. In a letter to Lassalle Marx notes aesthetic deficiencies in the text: the characters are too abstract and not sketched in as full and interesting a fashion as they could be. But his main criticism involves the inaccuracy in depicting the class struggle. For Marx, Sickingen, a free knight struggling to retain the privileges and rights of his class, represents a declining social order; his failure, although tied to the historical predicament of his age, cannot be separated from his position in the social hierarchy, and his campaign against the emperor and the princes, however much this campaign coincides with the interests of the peasants, is undertaken to restore a reactionary system, not to advance history. The real tragedy of the revolution, therefore, is not represented by Sickingen's demise, but by the defeat of progressive elements in the cities and the peasants, who never play an active role in Lassalle's drama. As a consequence of his misconstrual of the class situation, Marx accuses Lassalle of idealistic representation: Sickingen is a mere mouthpiece for progressive views, which he may have held in reality, but which do not legitimately belong to him historically as a member of a declining class. In Marx's critique we encounter the foundation for class-based criticism: implicit in his remarks is the demand that fictional or fictionalized figures represent the views of their class.

The dominant style of fiction in the nineteenth century was realism, and Marx's theory, as well as his comments on specific works, validates a class-conscious variant of realist portrayal. Among the most important remarks on realism, however, were those made by Engels a few years after Marx's death in letters to the novelists Minna Kautsky and Margaret Harkness. Although Engels praises the work of both writers, he suggests their novels may not be realistic enough. He explains that when he speaks of realism he means typical characters in typical situations, not simply the accurate mirroring of historical detail. In Harkness's novel, for example, Engels criticizes the passivity of the proletariat: all help for the working class comes from above; the workers appear unable to organize themselves, which may have been the case earlier in the century, but now is simply incorrect. With regard to Kautsky's work Engels claims that she has not always succeeded in producing types, which he defines as a figure that retains individuality while representing more general dimensions of social relevance. His main concern, however, is that these engaged novelists do not degenerate into tendentiousness. The question of the appropriateness of 'tendency' in art was a frequently discussed topic among committed writers of the mid and late nineteenth century, and both Marx and Engels seem to advocate that authors refrain from injecting their personal sentiments or ideologies into their fiction. They favoured epic narratives in which the writer and her/his views recede into the background. In his letter to Kautsky Engels states that tendency is not in itself inappropriate, but that it must originate in the situation and plot, and not be something added from the outside. And writing to Harkness, Engels maintains that the true realist, which is synonymous with the genuine artist, may represent a progressive view of reality even if the author him/herself has no sympathy with radical causes. Balzac, a favourite author of both Marx and Engels, is the best illustration of someone whose politics were regressive, but whose adherence to realism compelled him to portray the aristocracy, whose views he shared, with bitter satire, and the republicans, whom he disliked, with admiration. The lesson is that tendentiousness is artistically undesirable and unnecessary if a perspicacious writer comprehends and captures social reality dispassionately.

The legacy of Marx's views on literature parallels to a degree his general reception. Among the social democrats Franz Mehring applied basic tenets from Marx and Engels in his numerous contributions to early socialist literary criticism. In the twentieth century Marx's works were fruitfully developed by various critics. Writers such as Walter Benjamin and Theodor Adorno, associated with the Frankfurt school, emphasized the dialectical and creative quality of literary criticism; they were equally adept at close reading and ideological criticism, but they recognized that Marx had to be brought into play with twentieth-century concerns if he was to be relevant. Structuralist marxists, such as Lucien Goldman, Louis Althusser and Pierre Macherey, focused their attention on ideology and consciousness, advancing our understanding of how form and content unite in an uneasy totality. Georg Lukács, perhaps the most prolific marxist critique of the twentieth century, was influential for philosophically based criticism of the Frankfurt School, but he also contributed many works that advanced a more dogmatic stance toward Marx, especially in Eastern Europe. In the Soviet Union and other Eastern bloc countries, one often encountered a version of marxist criticism that elevated Marx's occasional and historically conditioned remarks to inviolable doctrine. Socialist realism, at its best a continuation of nineteenth-century realism, at its worst an artificial and mechanical application of realist features to socialist content, was promulgated in the 1934 Party Congress of the Soviet Union by Andrey Zhdanov, and thereafter Zhdanovism became synonymous with Stalinist cultural politics. Although the ideological strictures on criticism loosened gradually during the 1970s and 1980s, in many communist circles socialist realism and its attendant restrictions remained official policy until just a few years before the decline of Soviet influence in Eastern Europe.

Robert C. Holub

Further reading and works cited

Althusser, L. *For Marx*. New York, 1969.
Anderson, P. *Considerations on Western Marxism*. London, 1976.
Arvon, H. *Marxist Esthetics*. Ithaca, NY, 1973.
Bakhtin, M. *Rabelais and His World*. Cambridge, 1968.
Baxandall, L. and Morowski, S. (eds) *Karl Marx and Friedrich Engels on Literature and Art*. New York, 1974.
Eagleton, T. *Criticism and Ideology*. London, 1976a.
—. *Marxism and Literary Criticism*. Berkeley, CA, 1976b.
Frow, J. *Marxism and Literary Criticism*. Cambridge, 1986.
Goldman, L. *The Hidden God*. New York, 1964.
Goldstein, P. *The Politics of Literary Theory*. Tallahassee, FL, 1990.
Jameson, F. *Marxism and Form*. Princeton, NJ, 1971.
Lukács, G. *The Historical Novel*. New York, 1962.
—. *History and Class Consciousness*. Cambridge, 1971.
Macherey, P. *A Theory of Literary Production*. London, 1978.
McLellan, D. *Karl Marx: His Life and Thought*. London, 1973.
—. *The Thought of Karl Marx*, 2nd edn. London, 1980.
Marx, K. and Engels, F. *Über Kunst und Literatur*, 2 vols. Berlin, 1967.
—. *Collected Works*, 50 vols. London, 1975–.
Nelson, C. and Grossberg, L. (eds) *Marxism and the Interpretation of Culture*. Urbana, IL, 1988.
Prawer, S. S. *Karl Marx and World Literature*. Oxford, 1976.
Solomon, M. (ed.) *Marxism and Art*. New York, 1973.
Trotsky, L. *Literature and Revolution*. New York, 1925.
Tucker, R. C. *The Marx-Engels Reader*. New York, 1972.
Williams, R. *Marxism and Literature*. Oxford, 1977.

Charles Baudelaire (1821–1867) and Stéphane Mallarmé (1842–1898)

In ways unprecedented in mid- and late-nineteenth-century Europe, both Charles Baudelaire and Stéphane Mallarmé created critical aesthetics of alterity where literature and criticism no longer acted as each other's Other. No longer were literature and criticism, for either writer, to be understood as necessarily opposing or complementary, yet distinct, counterparts to each other. Instead, the two writers practised their respective critical poetics of modernity – all the distinctions notwithstanding – as mixed genres: literature as criticism, and criticism as literature. Their work responded to a sense of cultural, political and epistemological crisis framed by the changes late-nineteenth-century France experienced in moving into modernity. In so doing, Baudelaire and Mallarmé instrumentalized strategies that shifted, and shattered, the modalities hitherto associated with literature and criticism as separate entities. Oxymorons and contradictions functioned as allegorizing dynamics to divide identities from within, *pars pro toto* fragmented and dematerialized wholes, and self-reflexivity foregrounded language's metaphoricity as common to both: these strategies significantly reconfigured the identities of both literature and criticism. Walter Benjamin wrote that Baudelaire's aesthetics 'indicated the price for which the sensation of the modern age may be had: the disintegration of aura in the experience of shock' (1968, 194). It might be said, in turn, that decadence, symbolism, modernism and the avant-garde movements all reverberated with the aesthetic after-shocks of the disintegration of aura. However, they also rebuilt their respective aesthetics with those same tools and experiences: disintegration, shock, fragmentation and a focus on the shared medium of literature and criticism – the language of the other which, paradoxically, was now closer and closer to becoming the same language. Today, Baudelaire's and Mallarmé's work in this area continues to raise crucial questions concerning the identity of literature and criticism. What, or who, defines the literary? Who uses the term, to what purpose and for what audience? Where, when and how can we separate the literary from the non-literary? Equally importantly, their questions challenged the respective relationships both literature and criticism have had, and have today, with institutional identities – academic, aesthetic, pedagogic and political. Finally, and yet perhaps most urgently for us at the start of the twenty-first century, their work prompts a thorough questioning of constitutive and/or critical roles of literature-as-criticism in the ways we understand identity in linguistic, cultural, national or international terms.

Their radical rethinking of criticism as/in/through literature, and vice versa, presents key common elements that we will review before addressing in greater detail their different ways of working with these shared elements. Each poet-critic felt addressed by, and addressed himself to, the particularities of his historical time: both were poet-critics embedded in the space and time of their present. No longer did these poet-critics set themselves apart and above. They had departed from earlier nineteenth-century Romantic aspirations of the poet as privileged seer or visionary. For both Baudelaire and Mallarmé, their contemporary contexts – not past history or mythology – provided the primary materials for their literary-critical projects. In this way, their distinctive aesthetics of modernity were attuned to and responsive to questions posed by their changing times.

In Baudelaire's case, his work was shaped by the political transitions preceding, and during, the 1848 Revolution, and then most profoundly by the culture and politics of the Second Empire and by the loss of Paris as it existed before Haussmannization. These changes constructed a new urban space and new modes of sociality. Forms and norms of relationality (self/other, subject/object, individual/group) were redefined and recreated; conventional aesthetic equations between beauty, morality and the natural world no longer absorbed the shocks, nor echoed the reactions, that a rapidly modernizing capitalist society sent through the subjective experiences of the axes of time and space. Baudelaire addressed the inadequacy of conventional aesthetic, political and ethical answers by sketching out new roles for the artist (the dandy, the *flâneur*, the poet as ragpicker (*le chiffonnier*) who recycles rubbish through literary creation), new aesthetic values (the immediacy of subjective effect, an unsentimental poetics of urban abjection, beauty located in artifice), and new arenas for artistic inspiration (the street, the crowd). Mallarmé, in contrast, is one of the first poet-critics to emerge from what was, in Third Republic France, a new social group of writers: the state-employed teacher-writer, author of *Les mots anglais* (1876). References to Third Republic pedagogic, institutional and cultural contexts for the poet-critic thread their way through his prose writings, particularly *La Musique et les lettres* (1894).

Although the work of both poet-critics played, and plays, a decisive role in the developments within French literature and culture, both were also actively involved in literary-critical endeavours outside of their own national and linguistic literary tradition. In Baudelaire's case, his translations of the works of Edgar Allan Poe, and in Mallarmé's case, his work as teacher/scholar of the English language, gave them both strong contacts with the English language, with English and American literature, and with English and American writers and critics. Most influential, however, on the subsequent nature of their critical work is that the contact went beyond the exchange of ideas: both had first-hand experience of writing in a foreign language. At a time when other French writers and critics were advancing various forms of literary and cultural nationalism – from the benign, to the virulent as was the case with Maurice Barrès – the work of Baudelaire and Mallarmé challenged the ideological assumptions formative of national genealogies, literary heritages and protectionist equations between language and culture. One could say that they were un-French in this conventionally most 'French' of areas: the identification of language and culture. Their experiences working in another language afforded them valuable insights, so to speak, into the ways their own language and culture were, in fact, also foreign or other to themselves. This perspective is one Ruth Robbins and Julian Wolfreys find in Baudelaire's economy of the eye, where 'identity becomes something dependent on the other reflecting the self back to the self' (1999, 27). In the visual realm too, then, our identity, Baudelaire shows us, is constituted through interchanges, necessarily outside of the self, and not primarily through interiority.

Closely related to the last commonality of approach is their eschewal of what Flaubert would call literary-critical *lieux-communs*, or *idées reçues*. Just as their experience of the otherness of their own language provided them with critical perspectives on the ideological risks implicit in overvaluing the Frenchness of literature and culture, they both demon-strated a powerful critical energy of insider-outsiders to shake, if not blast away, the clichés of past literary-critical conventions, and to disabuse their readers of spurious forms of aesthetic consensus. For example, what passed for criticism, or what others idolatrously worshipped as 'art' was never spared in their writings. Rosemary Lloyd puts it well, when commenting on Mallarmé's enthusiasm in *Symphonie Littéraire* (1866) for the innovative poetic strategies of Théodore de Banville, where she refers to Mallarmé's horror of the 'rhetoric of literature' (Lloyd 1999, 82). At a time in French literary criticism where the biography-based approaches of Sainte-Beuve held sway, Mallarmé's elimination of the subjective from poetry forced, and still forces, a rethinking of literary criticism and a critical awareness of excess (biographical) baggage. Likewise, as indicated by the immediate censorship in 1857 of six poems in Baudelaire's *Les Fleurs du Mal*, Baudelaire does not simply voice his hostility to stultifying consensus through his art criticism, as in the *Aux Bourgeois* section of his 1846 Salon (*Curiosités Esthétiques*, 97); his own resolutely modern aesthetics shattered consensus about what counts as art.

Baudelaire's work as poet-critic, and specifically as art-critic, began in the 1840s when two distinct aesthetic legacies of romanticism existed in French culture. First, the influence of Victor Cousin's first complete translation of Plato into French (1822–40), and of his subsequent publication of his Sorbonne lectures – delivered from 1822 onwards under the title *Du Vrai, du Beau, et du Bien* (1853) – flourished in romantic Platonism. The work of Vigny and Lamartine, among others, exemplified this approach: the poet created texts intended to awaken in readers a sense of the Ideal essence, to find analogies between the visible (natural) world, and the invisible (Ideal) one. The natural world was central to this strain of romanticism because poets saw in it a symbolic or hieroglyphic form for the deciphering of the Ideal, and saw poetic language as the tool for such deciphering. While Baudelaire rejected in this the focus on Beauty (in its capitalized, idealized exclusivity), his aesthetic project infused temporality and corporeality into romanticism's poetic analogies and correspondences. From a vertical aesthetics of desired transcendence of the material world, Baudelaire de-sublimates and re-embodies an aesthetics through creating horizontal, sensory, correspondences: synaesthesia, or the verbal translations between the senses. Baudelaire's rejection of an exclusive Ideal of Beauty – Platonic, classical or invariable as any system defines it – found articulation in prose poems such as *Chacun sa chimère* and *Le Fou et la Vénus*, and also in poems from *Les fleurs du mal* such as *La mort des artistes* and *Les Plaintes d'un Icare*. Here, Baudelaire presents the artist self-destructively consuming himself in the impossible creative struggle with immutable Beauty.

The recorporealizing of poetic correspondences that Baudelaire derives, and reroutes, from a Platonic strain of romanticism exists alongside a different approach to beauty found in the work of Stendhal. Unlike Victor Cousin's Platonic yoking together of the triad of Beauty, goodness and the real (of Platonic essences), Stendhal's work in *De l'amour* (1822) and *Racine et Shakespeare* (1823) presents beauty as relative; here, beauty is dependent upon feelings, passions, circumstances, locations (to name but a few variables). Baudelaire's impatience with an exclusive fixation on Platonic approaches to Beauty re-emerges clearly in his article on the *Exposition Universelle* of 1855. Here, he mocks an imaginary contemporary doctrinaire of Beauty whose ways of seeing leave him figuratively blind to all beauty that falls outside of his own aesthetic system: such a critic 'would blaspheme life itself and the natural world' (CE, 213). Baudelaire takes the relativity of beauty several steps further than his Romantic predecessors when he asserts that, 'What is beautiful is always bizarre', (CE, 215). Emphasizing the significance of 'life itself' to beauty, and the importance of the individual particularities that 'see' beauty in the bizarre, Baudelaire's aesthetics promoted the subjective perspective of the artist's imagination to central place. Decidedly non-mimetic and non-descriptive, Baudelaire's aesthetics were defined in his *Salon de 1846* as a way of feeling, a beauty that bears the mark of individual passions. However, despite intimations of Rousseau here, Baudelaire's larger project, elaborated in the series of essays comprising *Le Peintre de la vie moderne* (1863), and specifically *L'Éloge du Maquillage*, exposed Rousseau's equations between idealized pasts, nature and virtue as so much primitivist romanticizing of a fictionalized past. The passing jab at Rousseau, however, serves merely as the conceptual prelude to Baudelaire's central aesthetic argument for the ubiquity of artifice, and, more importantly, not simply for the superiority of artifice over nature – as he is often understood to be arguing. Baudelaire goes further than merely disrupting literary-critical conventions here, since he presents the naturalness of the desire for artifice in all cultures – human and animal – at all times, be they so-called 'primitive', 'civilized', 'natural' or 'decadent' cultures.

What we see here is that just as Baudelaire's title for his collection of poems, *Les Fleurs du Mal* (1857) offers us a dynamic oxymoron framing his aesthetic practices, so too does Baudelaire's argument about artifice take the form of an oxymoron: natural artifice. Indeed, in *De L'Héroïsme de la Vie Moderne* (1846), when he gives a definition of the multiple forms of beauty, he uses the same rhetorical structure: 'All beauties contain ... something eternal and something transitory – something of the absolute and something of the particular' (CE, 195). Baudelaire reinforces and multiplies the dynamic duality to make it the distinctive, and defining, feature of the beauty of modernity in *Le Peintre de la vie moderne*. Baudelaire builds an entire aesthetics resting on such dynamic oxymorons. For example, his practice of writing 'prose poems' deploys the same structure, but transfers it to the re-articulation of conventional categories of genre. This final example makes it clear that the oxymoron is not simply a rhetorical ornament, but performs a structuring function for Baudelaire – it gives form to Baudelaire's critical concepts – and in so doing, unites the literary to the critical, both in methods and goals.

One of the most creative critical approaches to this feature of Baudelaire's work has come in the work of Christine Buci-Glucksmann (1989), who studies this dynamic in Baudelaire's writing – the non-dialectical maintenance of contradictions – which she argues is central to Baudelaire's aesthetic of modernity, but is equally important to the writings of Walter Benjamin in the *Arcades Project* (1935). Through an oxymoron of her own, 'Baroque reason', she emphasizes the un-Reasonable, grotesque and paradoxical logic at work through this literary-critical aesthetic specific to modernity. Pointing to the proliferation of such non-dialectical contraries (i.e. which resist recuperation or hierarchical resolution) in Baudelaire and Benjamin's writing, she contends that they constitute an allegorical figuration of an Other (modernity) not as a directly oppositional nature to the modernity of narratives of progress, but rather as an alterity that sustains the very production of further non-dialectical oppositions. For Buci-Glucksmann, this Baudelairean and Benjaminian aesthetic of modernity combines the critical with the destructive, and hollows out from within the founding, and governing, representations of modernity that are buttressed by linear time, narratives of progress, faith in science and rationality. Doubling and destroying the 'substantial' model of modernity, baroque reason opens, through allegory, onto an alterity whose medium is a theatricalized space of figuration within the frame of representation. Allegory here in Buci-Glucksmann's usage works to destroy and demystify the appearance of completeness adhering to representations of reality, producing it instead as ruins and fragmentation. For Buci-Glucksmann, it is a strategy both writers use to make visible the ambivalences – of history, time or subjectivity – through freezing or neutralizing non-dialectical contradictions.

Buci-Glucksmann's study of the allegorized figuration of a baroque reason offers one of the most helpful paths into theorizing Baudelaire's representations of women, and their relationship to his aesthetics of modernity. This she undertakes by according centrality to Benjamin's work on the prostitute. Benjamin sees nineteenth-century mass prostitution resulting in a hyper-visibility of the prostitute's body, a change that had aesthetic repercussions, Buci-Glucksmann argues, by invalidating the figure of woman as mediator of a divine and immortal love, and representation of ideal feminine beauty. Departing from this analysis, Buci-Glucksmann suggests that the nineteenth-century reconfigurations of the visibility and invisibility of the woman's body inevitably rebounds on masculinity. In any binary organization of socio-sexual space, one term cannot shift without having an impact on the other. The disembodied, masculine observers of feminine bodies, deprived of their idealized, feminized mediators of love, project onto the ubiquity of the prostitute's body the precariousness, if not mortality, of masculinity itself. Baudelaire's poems abound in representations of decaying, ageing or dead feminine bodies, just as they eroticize the dead female body as in *Une Charogne*. Buci-Glucksman's analysis offers a nuanced response to such representations in Baudelaire's work. She considers them both as reactive, misogynist, masculinist counter-projections triggered by an awareness of the mortality of a specific historical formation of masculinity; yet, she argues, they can also seen as potentially 'progressive' literary-critical ways of making visible the effects of the capitalist commodification of bodies.

Buci-Glucksmann is one of many critics who offer readings of the critical work performed by the self-reflexive dynamic doubling so characteristic of Baudelaire's writing. Jean Starobinski's study, *Mélancholie au miroir* (1989), links Baudelairean melancholy to a dynamic doubling of the self. No longer is this the romantic melancholy of solitary contemplation in a stark natural landscape of ruins. Instead, Starobinski shows how Baudelaire's melancholic reflexivity develops out of, and yet transforms, the reflexivity of early nineteenth-century German romantic irony to produce the artist's necessary self-critical duality: the self takes itself as its other, its ironic, self-deriding, double, as we see in the lines of 'Héautontimorouménos' where the poetic subject is both victim and executioner, persecutor and persecuted. When we turn to Mallarmé, such staging, or performing, of intrapsychic dramas – one form of the theatricalizing of a poetics of alterity – moves far away from Baudelaire's subjective impressions on embodied, material subjects. Instead, language takes the stage, and its effect on the reader's imagination takes over.

Mallarmé's theatrical poetics of alterity engaged several interrelated dimensions of spacing (*l'espacement*) – e.g. the white page, blanks, silence and punctuation – all of which destabilized any unquestioned certainties about literature's identity. His work did this through making explicit the process of reading, the work (and role) of the reader, and by switching the focus onto the effect – rather than the meaning – of the poem. To say that Mallarmé's poetry produces its own space is to invoke, first, Mallarmé's notion that the reader produces or stages, the poem. By designating the reading process as a *mise en scène* in the reader's mind, Mallarmé emphasizes that we do not receive the poem as a finished product whose meaning pre-exists either in the poet or in the poem. Mallarmé's dramatizing of poetry demands that readers focus on enunciation, on how, rather than what, the poem means, i.e. on its effect. It demands that the reader's own staging of the poem finds its cues by attending to the poem's placement and spacing on the page (the typography, the typeface, the spacing, the metrics). To struggle with the words as discrete entities, extracted from the configuration of the poem itself, is to remain attached to signification, i.e. to what the poem means. Mallarmé's poetry leads us away from signification, and instead to configuration, to text and paratexts, to what is present as well as to the interdependence of presence and constitutive absences. Implicitly theorized here is that verse exists only because blank spaces separate and join the verses.

Since Mallarmé's poetry and prose is simultaneously creative and critical, as we see above, its material practices simultaneously theorize their practice. As he writes in an 1867 letter to Eugène Lefébure, the modern poet is first and foremost a critic. He uses the tools of his literary art – signs – the twenty-four letters of the alphabet, as he puts it in *La Musique et les lettres* (*Oeuvres Complètes* 1945, 646) the way that other literary critics theorize through reasoning, doctrines, manifestos, argumentation or philosophical concepts. His writings combine verse through spacing with the staging of language as performative. Implicitly theorized here is an understanding of spacing that goes beyond blankness and whiteness on the page. Spacing also designates a wide range of differences and similarities in language – phonological, grammatical, rhythmic, and semantic – that are all equally constitutive of verse. In *La Musique et les lettres*, Mallarmé likens the concept of spacing to the spaces separating the different notes in a musical scale. A piece of music doesn't mean anything as such, and yet its contingency is also absolutely necessary within the terms of its form, be it a performance of a sonata in A minor or of a minuet in C major. Analogously, Mallarmé suggests, a poem doesn't mean any one thing, yet its concrete realizations are both contingent and necessary. Language once estranged (though never entirely severed) from any referential, representational or realist expectations – once put under the theatre lights in its otherness – offers the materials from which the reader stages, or produces, the poem's previously unformulated, and unprogrammable, network of relationships as an 'effect' *in* and *on* the reader's mind (OC, 635–57). Words become dislodged from any 'proper' meanings and perform, as in a musical score, in relation to each other, reflecting each other's multiple facets (OC, 366). In Saussurean terms, Mallarmé's spacing intensifies and multiplies all the potential permutations of effect between signifier and signified within the sign and among signs.

Mallarmé's creative and critical poetic practices, by unpeeling language from the reassuring plasterwork of referential illusions, coax readers to explore language's perfor-mativity and have fostered a wide range of creative and critical responses in the twentieth century. A survey of critics' respective emphases affords a useful comparative analysis of the different critical constructions of Mallarmé that readers encounter today. Maurice Blan-chot, one of the his most rigorous readers, analyses the poet's deliberate erosion of the reader's default position – to rely on language's referentiality – and asks what it can mean, given this effacing of straightforward referentiality, to say that literature 'exists'. For example, if language makes things present by abstracting properties from them – as in metonymy, to take but one of many examples – thereby negating them, and absenting them, what kind of existence does literature have (Blanchot 1955)? For Blanchot, Mallarmé's writings gain their singularity by signalling to us that the only way to establish any relationship with death is through language because its strange mode of 'being' lies in its very un-being, an insight he finds compellingly demonstrated in Mallarmé's *Igitur*. While Jacques Derrida, in *La Double Séance* (1972), continues and develops Blanchot's path, in the intervening years appears the monumental 650-page study by Geneva School phenomenologist, Jean-Pierre Richard, *L'Univers imaginaire de Mallarmé* (1961), a pub-lication which sets the stage for an emblematic intergenerational critical struggle which takes Mallarmé as its text and pretext.

Rather than through approaching Mallarmé's spacing as a bridge concept that recasts epistemology in terms of processes of signification (as does Blanchot), Richard approaches space thematically through an exhaustive analysis of Mallarmé's representational figures of space (i.e. the themes of blankness, death, whiteness, sterility, absence). Undertaking the work as a thematic critic, Richard's phenomenological training leads him, first, to project a 'totalizing' analysis (Richard 1961, 14) of the dominant motifs of Mallarmé's writings (space being only one among them) and then to aspire to a comprehensive understanding of the modes, methods and strategies of the creative consciousness at work. In a phrase, Richard aims to discover the 'sensibility in his [Mallarmé's] logic, and a logic to his sensibility' (Richard 1961, 38) through two critical methods: deciphering (the herme-neutic goal) and assembling the parts (the combinative goal). What is immediately clear from this brief description is that Richard shifts the production of the poetic effect away from the reader and back onto the author. Furthermore, although he tracks Mallarmé's poetic syntax (which implies that relationality is central to his analysis), his selection of motifs and themes contains, and transfers, the dynamic potentiality of performative readings to the static structures of a pre-existing, governing, thematic syntax of a creative consciousness. Richard's inventory of themes constituting the architecture of Mallarmé's poetry is outstandingly meticulous and thorough. For that reason, *L'Univers* stands as an 'incontournable' [Fr. essential reading; a text to be reckoned with or not to be ignored], and controversial, scholarly text for any aspiring scholar of creative critical writing in the wake of Mallarmé. However, just as significant to the trajectory of critical thought, is the response it provoked from the perspective of another rigorous reader of Mallarmé – Jacques Derrida – who considers Richard's analysis a distortion of crucial premises underlying Mallarmé's work.

Derrida's response to Richard (Derrida 1972) marks a critical watershed, and yet not only for an understanding of Mallarmé. The Derrida/Richard differences also present an important and lucid exposition of key explanatory elements underlying poststructuralist readers' 'issues' with, if not disdain for, thematic criticism; this approach bore (and still does) the stigma of critical opprobrium in the US Academy during the late 1980s and early 1990s, before cultural studies reinvigorated and relegitimated thematic approaches through different methodological tools, e.g. new historicism's emphasis on culture as the unit of analysis as opposed to phenomenology's emphasis on the individual's creative consciousness. As a debate triggered by Mallarmé's work, and which bears the mark of a specific intellectual moment in the paths of academic theorizing, it merits close examination.

Taking Gérard Genette's lead (Genette 1962), Derrida faults Richard for psychologism in the latter's mapping of Mallarmé's thematic syntax. That is, he disputes Richard's use of an expressive aesthetic framework to interpret Mallarmé's text, and points out that such a premise runs counter to Mallarmé's stated aesthetic of impersonality in Crise de vers (OC, 366), i.e. the goal of yielding 'initiative' to the words themselves, or rather to a given reader's staging of the web-like interrelationships among the multiple registers of multi-faceted signs. Further distortions are embedded in Richard's approach, Derrida argues, because psychologizing readings remain necessarily oblivious to the play of the signifier (the very materiality of language). To psychologize implies a (Hegelian) dialectical reading which sublates the materiality of the words on the page in the name of a higher meaning (the signified, or what Richard posits that Mallarmé intended). Derrida returns us to Mallarmé's spacing as concept, rather than theme, and by connecting the ways signification spaces and grounds epistemology, Derrida aligns spacing with the differential character of language. Supporting his argument with a reading of Mallarmé's short prose text Mimique, Derrida demonstrates the ways Mallarmé's text undoes Platonic assumptions that mimesis is derivative of Ideal, or True, essential forms. Mimique, Derrida argues, posits that the supposed Ideal forms are always already within representation as imitations which do indeed accrue an essential aspect – i.e. they become naturalized – but are nevertheless imitations of originary imitations, not of Ideas: his reading of Mallarmé, concludes Derrida, shows us that we find copies, not originals, at the supposed source of origination.

Where Derrida finds an undoing of Platonic assumptions in Mallarmé's practices of spacing, Jean-François Lyotard interprets spacing from the standpoint of two related and enduring intellectual passions in his own work: his exploration of the processes and practices of aesthetic avant-gardes ranging from Mark Rothko to Sam Francis, and his tenaciously sensitive probing of discourse for the corporeal gestures or pulses of affect. In Discours, figure (1971), Lyotard views Mallarmé's disruptive reconfigurations of spatiality as, in his terms, 'figural' ruptures where the sensible (form, shape) bursts through discursive meaning. Just as Sam Francis considers that colour in his paintings holds a feeling until it finds articulation in discourse, Lyotard privileges Mallarmé's spatiality as a form holder for the as-yet unarticulated. However, together with Lyotard's work, it is undeniably in Julia Kristeva's doctoral thesis, La Révolution du langage poétique (1974), that we find a sustained argument linking Mallarmé's spacing to non-discursive outlets of affect.

Kristeva offers a firmly psychoanalytically framed, and loosely politically oriented, interpretation of Mallarmé's practice of throwing into relief the functions of spacing. Theorizing the pre-Oedipal chora (the semiotic (*le sémiotique*)) as the space excluded by, yet formative of, the symbolic and social order of language, she interprets Mallarmé's spacing as so many ruptures, interruptions and eruptions which mark the rhythms and corporeal drives of unarticulated affect as it breaks through discursive meaning. By taking the symbolic, social and bourgeois orders as synonyms of each other, Kristeva's case for the 'revolutionary' political force of Mallarmé's semiotic disruptions of language stretches its analytic reach awkwardly and unconvincingly between text and the context of Third Republic France, ultimately getting lost somewhere in between. There is copious critical response to Mallarmé's revolutionary poetics, so the concept of revolution is completely justified here. However, Kristeva's programmatic approach to the overall meaning of spacing keeps the lid on the potentially revolutionary ruptures and reconfigurations of relationships between reader and text, between literature and its others.

In conclusion, it is perhaps important to ask where Baudelaire and Mallarmé seem to be leading criticism in the wake of our recent *fin de siècle*? Taking my lead from Ellen Burt (1999), I would suggest, as I have throughout, that both writers' consciousness of their foreignness to themselves – linguistically, culturally – is an address we cannot afford to ignore if we are to think our way through the dilemmas posed by identity. As Burt comments, '... one of those futures [of the text] is of a political life not bounded by the limits of nationalism and the national language ...' (1999, 125).

Elizabeth Constable

Further reading and works cited

Baudelaire, C. *Curiosités Esthétiques, L'Art romantique et autres oeuvres critiques de Baudelaire* [CE]. Paris, 1990.
Benjamin, W. *Illuminations*. New York, 1968.
Blanchot, M. *L'Espace littéraire*. Paris, 1955.
Buci-Glucksmann, S. *La raison baroque de Benjamin à Baudelaire*. Paris, 1984.
Burt, E. *Poetry's Appeal: Nineteenth-Century French Lyric and the Political Space*. Stanford, CA, 1999.
Derrida, J. *La Dissémination*. Paris, 1972.
—. 'Mallarmé', in *Tableau de la littérature française*. Vol. III. Paris, 1974; 'Mallarmé', in *Jacques Derrida: Acts of Literature*, ed. Derek Attridge. New York, 1992.
Genette, G. 'Bonheur de Mallarmé?', *Tel Quel*, 10, 1962.
Gould, E. *Virtual Theater: Virtual Theater from Diderot to Mallarmé*. Baltimore, MD, 1989.
Johnson, B. *Défigurations du Langage Poétique: La Seconde Révolution Baudelairienne*. Paris, 1979.
—. *The Critical Difference*. Baltimore, MD, 1981.
Kristeva, J. *Révolution du langage poétique*. Paris, 1974.
Lloyd, R. *Mallarmé: The Poet and his Circle*. Ithaca, NY, 1999.
Lyotard, J.-F. *Discours, figure*. Paris, 1971.
Mallarmé, S. *Oeuvres Complètes*, ed. H. Mondor [OC]. Paris, 1945.
Richard, J.-P. *L'Univers imaginaire de Mallarmé*. Paris, 1961.
Robbins, R. and Wolfreys, J. 'In the Wake of ... Baudelaire, Valéry, Derrida', *The French Connections of Jacques Derrida*. New York, 1999.
Starobinski, J. *La mélancholie au miroir*. Paris, 1989.

Friedrich Nietzsche (1844–1900)

Friedrich Nietzsche was perhaps the most original and provocative German writer of the nineteenth century. A classical philologist by training, he held a professorship at the University of Basel from 1869 to 1879 before retiring and becoming a freelance author. His writings, which were composed from the early 1870s until the outbreak of his insanity at the start of 1889, covered a wide range of topics in the fields of aesthetics, art, ethics, religion, psychology, politics and sociology. As a philosopher he broke away from the conventions of traditional philosophical prose, employing various innovative forms and rhetorical strategies to construct arguments. Much of his mature work consists of aphorisms; one of his most important books, *Thus Spoke Zarathustra*, is structured as a parody of the Bible and contains parables and maxims of high symbolic value. During his own lifetime Nietzsche's writings were known to only a small circle of admirers. In the preface to one of his last works, *The Antichrist*, Nietzsche wrote: 'Only the day after tomorrow belongs to me. Some are born posthumously', thus predicting exactly the course of his popularity after his death. During the first decades of the twentieth century Nietzsche rapidly became one of the most influential thinkers. Few European authors or critics of the early twentieth century were unaffected by some aspect of Nietzsche's thought; in philosophical circles he was championed by such celebrated thinkers as Martin Heidegger, Karl Jaspers, Jean-Paul Sartre, Jacques Derrida and Michel Foucault; and although Sigmund Freud would downplay his impact, his insights into the workings of the psyche were obviously seminal for the development of the psychoanalytic movement. Because of his elusive style and the often obscure nature of his philosophical message, Nietzsche's writings have been able to bear a wide variety of interpretations, and although not all of his followers would have been welcome to Nietzsche himself, they attest to the immense vitality of his thought.

Nietzsche's earliest published writings dealt with issues in classical philology and are of interest only for specialists. His first book written for the general public, *The Birth of Tragedy from the Spirit of Music*, can be considered an attempt on Nietzsche's part to combine his academic training with his enthusiasm for the composer Richard Wagner. Nietzsche had met Wagner in 1868, and the two men had quickly become friends, although Nietzsche, who was Wagner's junior by thirty years, was clearly subservient to the already celebrated composer. Nietzsche had much in common with Wagner: as an amateur musician himself – Nietzsche composed and played the piano – he appreciated Wagner's innovations and grandiose musical projects. The two men also shared an admiration for the pessimistic philosophy of Arthur Schopenhauer and a longing for the renaissance of cultural greatness in Europe. Nietzsche imagined that Wagner would be the leader of a vast cultural movement, and their friendship was based to a degree on the common dedication to a sacred artistic cause. At one point Nietzsche even imagined giving up his professorship at Basel in order to devote himself full-time to publicity for Wagner and his opera house, which was constructed at Bayreuth and completed in 1876.

The Birth of Tragedy is thus a work of celebration, enlisting classical studies in order to promote the Wagnerian cause. In his initial arguments Nietzsche explains the origins of Greek tragedy as the confluence of two tendencies or spirits in the ancient world: the Apollonian and the Dionysian. The first of these terms, the Apollonian, is associated first and foremost with dream, but it is also related to illusion, since illusion involves something that appears to us in the mind's eye, something that takes definite and limited form. The Apollonian also entails the *principium individuationis* (principle of individuation), for this principle operates precisely as a limiting of chaos, as a cutting out from the flux of phenomena some limited and individual portion. The Apollonian is thus a representational principle, referring to the artistic and epistemological tendency that allows something else to appear or take form. By contrast the Dionysian is first introduced to us as intoxication in contrast to the Apollonian dream. Like the Apollonian, it encompasses a field of association rather than a precise definition. At times Nietzsche likens it to a frenzied, instinctive, unconscious unity; at other points it is associated with oblivion and self-forgetting; and on occasion it becomes more ominous, reminding us of the cruelty and absurdity of existence, of the suffering of the human being and the torments of life on earth. In the Attic tragedies of Aeschylus and Sophocles the Apollonian and Dionysian are united: the anarchic, inchoate Dionysian force finds expression through the Apollonian form or appearance.

The final sections of the original *Birth of Tragedy* – ten sections addressing the rebirth of the tragic spirit in Wagnerian opera were added after completion of the original text – trace the fall of Greek tragedy. Responsible for the demise are two figures: Euripides and Socrates. Nietzsche accuses Euripides of removing the genuine tragic element by eliminating the tragic chorus, which contains the primeval Dionysian impulse, and by introducing characters from everyday life. Euripides, however, is portrayed as the agent of an even more destructive and powerful force, represented by the figure of Socrates. Indeed, Euripides' dramas are based on an aesthetic Socratism. As the representative of the new rationality, Socrates necessarily opposes the Dionysian mysteries, and henceforth the real opposition in western culture becomes one between Dionysus and Socrates. In art the Socratic principle advocates realism, the copying of appearances, rather than essences, the depiction of the world as it exists for us. But Socratic thinking also extends into the realm of epistemology and ethics, where Socrates promotes the intelligibility of the world and virtuous conduct according to universal tenets. The good, the true, and the beautiful thus come into harmony in the Socratic worldview, destroying the fragile synthesis of Apollonian and Dionysian, the pinnacle of cultural achievement in the western world. Ultimately Nietzsche hopes to regain this synthesis in the nineteenth century, and his advocacy of the Wagnerian project stems from his belief that greatness in art can again be attained in the modern world.

The remaining works from Nietzsche's earliest period, the *Untimely Meditations*, likewise revolve around his relationship to Wagner and his championing of cultural renewal in the recently united Second German Empire. The first of these *Meditations* was directed against the smug philistinism of bourgeois life; the third *Meditation* lauded Schopenhauer, the intellectual bond between Wagner and Nietzsche, as an exemplary 'educator'; and the fourth *Meditation* is devoted entirely to Wagner himself and the celebration of his Bayreuth opera house. But Nietzsche also concerned himself with the pedagogical aspect of cultural renewal, and an unpublished lecture series, as well as the second *Untimely Meditation*, 'On the Advantage and Disadvantage of History for Life', focused on the deficiencies in educational practices in Germany. Nietzsche argues that German youth are receiving too much historical education, and that as a result they are inhibited from action and from great accomplishments. Distinguishing among a monumental, an antiquarian and a critical notion of history, he claims that each has distinct advantages, but that any sort of historical education, if promulgated to an extreme, will be ultimately pernicious. Nietzsche's goal is not universal education or an educated populace, but a pedagogical practice and corresponding institutions that will foster the production of greatness. Eschewing the apparent progress detected by his contemporaries, he writes that the goal for humanity does not lie in an end, but in its highest specimens. *On the Advantage and Disadvantage of History*, like most of his earliest work, is a plea for a fundamental change in culture so that genius and greatness will once again hold sway.

Nietzsche's middle period, which stretches from 1876 until 1882, is marked by three momentous changes. In his personal life he broke off his friendship with Wagner and distanced himself from the intellectual world of the tightly knit Bayreuth circle. He also moved further away from classical studies, and although he continued teaching until 1879, in his last years as a professor he was either on leave or repeating courses previously offered. The second change concerns the predominant themes in his writings. Nietzsche continued to devote some attention to culture, but he was no longer solely or primarily concerned with the renaissance he felt imminent in the earlier part of the 1870s. He began to cover a wider range of themes, influenced by earlier writers, in particular the French moralists of the seventeenth and eighteenth centuries. The change that was most easily detectable was his increased willingness to explore topics from philosophy proper, and the beginning of reflection on moral issues in a more serious fashion. But we also find consideration of other matters: science (especially physiology and biology), society (the question of women's rights and socialism), politics, national character and art. His measured stance in these reflections, his willingness to examine matters from various angles, his rejection of dogmatism and desire to search for deeper truths, are all characteristic of this phase of his writing. The youthful vibrancy of his earliest essays gives way to a more sovereign, thoughtful and pensive tone. A third change involves a new style of writing. The four books he published over this five-year period – *Human, All Too Human* (1878 and 1879), *The Wanderer and His Shadow* (1880), *Dawn* (1881) and *The Gay Science* (1882) – were all written in aphorisms. Nietzsche found his own style in this middle period. He was never comfortable with the essay: it demanded too much sustained writing and logic, too much systematic thought and rigorous method. The aphorism allowed him to develop his strengths, which involved sudden insight rather than sustained reflection, the quick sketch of a problem and its solution rather than the patient elaboration of a thought.

The scepticism characteristic of these middle years, combined with a fascination for natural science, led Nietzsche to a consequentially anti-metaphysical position in which he rejected all absolute values, ideals and dualistic models. Increasingly he came to believe that thoughts, ideas, consciousness, language and values are the means men use to deflect attention from our instinctual, biological life. Within this general criticism of metaphysics Nietzsche articulates one of his most noted hypotheses: the death of God. Formulated first as a parable in *Human, All Too Human*, Nietzsche presents God as a deceased and omniscient prison warder, whose demise has no visible effect on the prisoners he had formerly overseen. In aphorism 125 in *The Gay Science*, the death of God is announced by a madman who claims that God has been murdered. The crowd of unbelievers to whom he delivers his message remains unfazed, and the madman concludes that he has come too early, that the news of such an enormous event travels slowly. Significant for Nietzsche's thought is that he does not advocate a simple atheism. Nietzsche distinguishes between ordinary non-believers, who may be associated with the Philistine population of Germany and Europe in his times, and a select group of non-believers, like himself, who have a premonition of the enormous significance of the death of God. God is not simply a divinity; he stands for the entity that provides ethical substance for one's action, and meaning and purpose for life. At one point in human development God occupied a central position in our existence. But the recognition of his demise in the course of human history must entail more than disbelief in a divinity: if our emancipation is to be complete, the death of God must also liberate us from the epistemological and ethical constraints placed on us by any metaphysical system.

If God is no longer the centre of our universe, then humankind is thrown back upon itself and forced to create its own meaning. In his mature work Nietzsche begins to map out a complex conceptual framework for the philosophy of the future. Its initial and most elusive form occurs in *Thus Spoke Zarathustra*, the four-part work many critics consider his magnum opus. In *Zarathustra* Nietzsche highlighted notions that would become the most controversial in his thought. Among the best known terms he introduced is the 'overman' or 'superman'. The 'overman' is characterized by overcoming; Nietzsche conceives of man as a bridge or tightrope between an animal existence and a being that has yet to appear but that is logically possible. The 'overman' is meant as a conception of what we might become if we can breed a new and superior type of human being, if we can create ourselves anew and rid ourselves of the pernicious traditions that have enslaved us. The notion has obvious evolutionary overtones: Nietzsche describes our path from worm to ape to man, and claims that our current state of affairs is one that will also be surpassed. The human species is not the final development in evolutionary history, but an intermediate stage that will itself cede to a higher order of being. The 'overman', however, does not express Nietzsche's agreement with Darwin's theory of evolution, but rather his answer to it. The creation of a new type will not depend on natural selection, the Darwinian mechanism that Nietzsche felt produced only the mediocrity of 'modern man', but on wilful determination.

Along with the overman the highlight of *Zarathustra* for most philosophical interpretations of Nietzsche's writings is the teaching of eternal recurrence. Although this notion had been introduced already in *The Gay Science*, it is presented as the climax of Zarathustra's wisdom. Sometimes advanced as a daring hypothesis, at other times as a doctrine, eternal recurrence states that all things will happen again and have already happened exactly as they are happening now. From Nietzsche's notebooks it is clear that he believed eternal recurrence to be a scientific truth. Drawing on the first law of thermodynamics, which maintains that energy is conserved and finite, and the infinite nature of time, Nietzsche concluded that all configurations of matter that are now achieved must have occurred before and must occur again. So certain was Nietzsche that eternal recurrence was true that he even argues with the second law of thermodynamics, which postulates the tendency toward a state of equilibrium: if equilibrium were possible, Nietzsche reasoned, then it would have already been attained, and since it has not yet been attained, it is not possible. The importance of Nietzsche's notion of eternal recurrence, albeit based on a superficial understanding of science, lies in the ontological and ethical realm. It describes an unusual state of existence that is finite yet recurring, and demands that we act in such a way that we would welcome a recurrence of our actions. For Nietzsche eternal recurrence thus implies an affirmation of being, an *amor fati* or love of fate, since only by embracing life and its possibilities do we live a fulfilled existence.

The third and perhaps most controversial concept that is seminal for *Zarathustra* is the 'will to power'. The notion came into disrepute in part because after his death Nietzsche's sister Elisabeth published a collection of aphorisms from Nietzsche's literary remains under this provocative title. It lent Nietzsche's philosophy an aggressive profile and brought it into the proximity of politics and nationalist aspirations, both of which Nietzsche himself deplored. At the very least it suggests a ruthlessness that contrasts sharply with the genteel manners of nineteenth-century Europe, and no doubt Nietzsche championed the will to power as a provocation to his contemporaries. It is an ill-defined term, but in most cases it appears as the essence of life itself and the sole principle for all occurrences. It is clearly separate from the will of any individual; it is akin to a life force, a monistic tenet that is the ultimate source of all organic and inorganic activity. Because it is highly speculative and totalizing some commentators have seen the will to power as a metaphysical premise, as a substitute for the God Nietzsche declared deceased. But Nietzsche's radical anti-metaphysical stance suggests he had something else in mind, and various critics have found ways to save him from regressing into a metaphysical trap. Will to power may itself be Nietzsche's anti-metaphysical position; in this view it would be tantamount to an inversion of the metaphysical values that Nietzsche elsewhere opposes. It can also be conceived as a statement derived ultimately from science: given Nietzsche's frequent recourse to physics and physiology, will to power could express something about elemental states of energy that are responsible for all substance and thus for all motion and activity. Finally, some observers have suggested that will to power is simply Nietzsche's perspective on things, his view, no better and no more correct or truthful than any other view, but one that can overlay all phenomena and serve as an explanation. Will to power would be something on the level of psychology, a part of our or Nietzsche's interpretation, but not an objective principle of the world. This notion of will to power fits well with Nietzsche's much heralded 'perspectivism', but it contradicts statements that appear to posit will to power as a cosmological precept.

Zarathustra announced a philosopher of the future, and the conceptual universe Nietzsche creates in this book is meant as a basis for future thought and action. But Nietzsche's writing after *Zarathustra* takes up a task that is just as necessary: the revaluation of values. In order to refashion our current value system, Nietzsche investigates how it came into being. His first major area of concern was morality, in particular the morality associated with the Judeo-Christian tradition. In *Beyond Good and Evil* and *On the Genealogy of Morals*, where he undertakes his most thorough examination of western ethics, Nietzsche posits two different value systems, one based on notions of 'good' and 'bad', another on the binary pair 'good' and 'evil'. At some point in the past the former system of values, which Nietzsche regards as noble or aristocratic, was prevalent. The label 'good' was the result of an affirmation of self, and the designation 'bad' arises out of strength and the recognition of something low or common. In time, however, a priestly caste develops from this noble system of values, and from physical weakness it begins to affirm a quite different system of values. As a means of asserting itself against the nobles the priestly caste invents the notion of evil for those who are more powerful. Thus the original deed of the 'herd or slave morality' is a negation, a symptom of *ressentiment* or rancour, and 'good' is refashioned as the term applied to the powerless, the weak, the sick. Nietzsche's mythologized history of values is meant less as an empirical description of humankind's development than as an explanation of how we have forfeited our original instincts and natural drives for the abstract and debilitating ideals of the civilized, Christian world.

Nietzsche is not an ethical philosopher in that he does not propound a system of ethics or basic moral principles. Rather, he is a historian or 'genealogist' of morals, interested in investigating how we have become what we are. The elements of his genealogical method are historical studies, especially legal history, philology, in particular the examination of etymologies, and psychological intuition. With these tools he seeks to answer questions such as 'how did human beings become creatures entitled to make promises?' His answer is that as a species we have undergone a long history of punishment that eventually made us regular and reliable. Indeed, underlying the veneer of civilization and the moral precepts that facilitate social cohabitation is a legacy of cruelty and torture. Nietzsche argues that part of our moral conscience emanates from the debtor – creditor relationship, where the debtor paid by putting his body at the disposal of the creditor, allowing him to inflict upon him an equivalence in suffering. We should not be deceived into thinking that we have become more civilized today; in our current state of sham and denial we are simply unable to face our true nature. After the fact we have accounted for punishment in different ways, giving it an acceptable rationale, but we thereby ignore its origins and function in creating a moral human being. Guilt and bad conscience, by contrast, do not originate in punishment according to Nietzsche. Instead, they are the result of an internalization of aggressive drives. With the war against the instincts that is part of Christian morality we have gradually developed from happy, adventurous, nomadic semi-animals to the domes-ticated, self-incarcerated, repressed, calculating creatures of the modern world.

Although Christianity was not at the root of our miserable condition – the fall begins, Nietzsche suggests, with Socrates and especially with Plato in the ancient world – it has been the foremost ideology of *ressentiment* in our long history of decline. In the works of his middle period Nietzsche had analysed religion in general as an attempt to reinterpret our experience, and he singled out Christianity in particular for its incompatibility with science and for its fantastic mythology: it is a piece of antiquity that does not fit well in the modern era. In his later works, however, Nietzsche assaults Christianity for placing humanity in an impossible situation. Hypothesizing that religion originates in a debt we owe to our forefathers, which eventually leads to a deification of ancestors, Nietzsche remarks that Christianity presents us with the unique situation in which God himself sacrifices himself for humankind. Christ dispenses our obligation to God himself, but in so doing, he places us only further in his debt. The Christian divinity heightens and exacerbates our bad conscience. We preserve and increase our guilt because we can never live up to the conduct prescribed for us, and exacerbate our guilt further by projecting a perfect creditor, one who even sacrifices himself for us his debtors, and in whose debt we will therefore remain into eternity.

Much of Nietzsche's later work is thus preoccupied with a genealogy of Christianity. What is significant about the Judeo-Christian heritage is that it represents the most drastic and consequential overturning of natural values, of instincts and of aristocratic ethics. In *The Antichrist*, where Nietzsche articulates his most sustained assessment of the Christian tradition, he notes that Judaism initially promulgated the 'correct' and 'natural' relation-ship to things. From its origins as a 'natural religion' Judaism took a decisive turn when it developed a 'denatured' God and the notions of 'sin' and 'blessing'. The turn to a supreme being who makes ethical demands on a people, who is conceived in terms of conscience and abstract morality, initiates a downward path for European civilization. Accompanying this change is the advent of a priestly caste that assumes authority over the people. The hegemony of the priest means that all natural behaviour, everything that formerly emanated from the instincts and contained value in itself, is ritualized and conferred with a new value, an anti-value resulting from a desecration of natural existence. Christianity represents an extension and continuation of the regime of the Jewish priesthood. The difference between Christianity and Judaism is that the former negates the remnants of the older Jewish religion and thus turns religion into an unremitting advocate of self-abnegation. Nietzsche views Christ's rebellion against the Jewish priest-hood as the destruction of the vestiges of natural hierarchy remaining in Judaism. Christ is the original anarchist; his death on the cross is not for our moral guilt, but for his own political guilt in attempting to overturn an established order. In Nietzsche's worldview the Christian religion originates in a revaluation of values that is anti-instinctual, democratic and antithetical to natural hierarchies.

Nietzsche's 'immoral', anti-Christian, anti-democratic and vitalistic message was not received well during his own conscious life. Shortly after his mental breakdown in January of 1889, however, his fame, promoted successfully by the enormous efforts of his sister, began to spread throughout Germany and Europe. By the time of his death in 1900, he was already well known, mostly as a cultural critic, among prominent circles of European intellectuals, and he became a significant figure for the literary and cultural elite for much of the twentieth century. His advocacy of cultural renewal, his hatred of middle-class smugness and his own brilliance as a prose writer were his most attractive features during these years. During the two world wars, however, Nietzsche's reputation became embroiled in political controversy: many Germans championed him as an ultra-nationalist, while many non-Germans believed him to be the spirit of aggression and racism. His bellicose language, especially the easily misunderstood parables in *Zarathustra*, and his remarks on the history of religion became especially important. After the Second World War, Nietzsche was rehabilitated in Germany and the West as a philosopher, a process that was initiated in the 1930s and 1940s with the seminal works of Martin Heidegger and Karl Jaspers. Reinterpreted by each successive generation, Nietzsche has been claimed at times by phenomenology, hermeneutics, existentialism, analytical philosophy, poststructuralism and deconstruction.

Robert C. Holub

Further reading and works cited

Aschheim, S. E. *The Nietzsche Legacy in Germany 1890–1990*. Berkeley, CA, 1992.
Bergmann, P. *Nietzsche: The Last Antipolitical German*. Bloomington, IN, 1987.
Clark, M. *Nietzsche on Truth and Philosophy*. Cambridge, 1990.
Danto, A. C. *Nietzsche as Philosopher*. New York, 1980.
Derrida, J. *Spurs: Nietzsche's Styles*. Chicago, 1978.
Foucault, M. *Language, Counter-Memory, Practice: Selected Essays and Interviews*. Ithaca, NY, 1977.
Gilman, S. L. (ed.) *Conversations with Nietzsche*. New York, 1989.
Hayman, R. *Nietzsche: A Critical Life*. New York, 1980.
Heidegger, M. *Nietzsche*, 4 vols. New York, 1979–84.
Holub, R. C. *Friedrich Nietzsche*. New York, 1995.
Janz, C. P. *Friedrich Nietzsche: Biographie*, 3 vols. Munich, 1978.

Jaspers, K. *Nietzsche: An Introduction to the Understanding of His Philosophical Activity*. Tucson, AZ, 1965.

Kaufmann, W. *Nietzsche: Philosopher, Psychologist, Antichrist*. Princeton, NJ, 1974.

Magnus, B. and Higgins, K. M. (eds) *The Cambridge Companion to Nietzsche*. Cambridge, 1996.

Mittasch, A. *Friedrich Nietzsche als Naturphilosoph*. Stuttgart, 1952.

Nehemas, A. *Nietzsche: Life as Literature*. Cambridge, MA, 1985.

Nietzsche, F. *The Genealogy of Morals*. Garden City, NY, 1956.

—. *The Gay Science*. New York, 1974; trans. as *Joyful Wisdom*. New York, 1960.

—. *Thus Spoke Zarathustra. The Portable Nietzsche*, ed. W. Kaufmann. Harmondsworth, 1961.

—. *The Birth of Tragedy, The Case of Wagner*. New York, 1966.

—. *Kritische Gesamtausgabe: Werke*. eds G. Colli and M. Montinari, 30 vols. Berlin, 1967–.

—. *Twilight of the Idols The Portable Nietzsche*. Harmondsworth, 1968.

—. *Human, All Too Human*. Cambridge, 1986.

—. *Untimely Meditations*. Cambridge, 1983; as *Modern Observations*, ed. W. Arrowsmith. New Haven, CT, 1990.

—. *The Complete Works of Friedrich Nietzsche*. Stanford, CA, 1995–.

—. *The Genealogy of Morals*. Oxford, 1996.

—. *Beyond Good and Evil*. Oxford, 1998.

Nietzsche-Studien. Internationales Jahrboch for die Nietzsche-Forschung. Berlin, 1972–.

Solomon, R. C. (ed.) *Nietzsche: A Collection of Critical Essays*. Notre Dame, IN, 1980.

Strong, T. *Friedrich Nietzsche and the Politics of Transfiguration*. Berkeley, CA, 1988.

Sigmund Freud (1856–1939)

Through his invention of psychoanalysis Sigmund Freud deeply altered how western culture thought about itself. Few as skilled in the art of writing have had so profound an impact on medical, political and other practical discourses as Freud had, and fewer still are the men of science who, like him, have produced so important an effect on philosophical thought and artistic works. Freud's *oeuvre* is large – there are twenty-three volumes in the *Standard Edition* – yet, such is the classical clarity of his prose that in the whole of his *corpus* there seems never to have been a single wasted word.

The subject matter of Freud's essays is, however, anything but classical. An experiential core (and failing that, a textual one) lies at the heart of every bit of Freud's writing – experience that, viewed with Freud's courageously honest eye, refuses to lend itself easily to stock narrative treatments or standard literary contrivances. To honour his own unasserted gaze, Freud had to invent fresh narrative strategies: under his pen *the case history* became a new art. Freud perfects a process of writing 'the case' and in doing so discovers, develops and enriches the two key psychic structures of *neurosis* (hysteria, obsessionalism) and *psychosis* (the paraphrenias: schizophrenia, paranoia). Written between the years 1905 and 1918, these histories are exemplary of Freud's psychoanalytic process and of his virtuoso literary style.

In the 'Dora' case (1905, *SE VII*), Freud demonstrated vividly how the *hysteria* he had studied with Josef Breuer earlier (1893–5, *SE II*) 'speaks' through a young girl's gestures and acts, rather than through her words, and belies her verbal discourse. Along the way Freud also painted an unforgettable portrait of Dora, caught in parental love triangles and sexual intrigues that have left her little way out except the hysteric option. With her, Freud also finds that his analytic procedures stumble: he begins to discover how mysterious woman is.

In the 'Ratman' case (1909, SE X), Freud recounts, in rather horrifying detail, the psychic impulses behind a young man's obsessive fantasies of torture by rats. The young military officer's socially approved behaviours have become unbearable compulsions for him. In the analysis, Freud discovers that guilt toward his dead father (who makes ghostly appearances in which he 'commands' the Ratman to kill himself) is the key.

In the only case where Freud discusses psychosis, 'Psycho-Analytic Notes on an Autobiographical Account of a Case of Paranoia' (1911–12, SE XII), Freud analysed Dr Daniel Paul Schreber, but he did so by reading Schreber's memoirs, not by treating him. Schreber was a prominent jurist in Germany who fell ill with paranoid delusions when he was in his fifties. In the history of his mental illness, Schreber described in vivid and complete detail his psychotic system, in which he was 'called upon' to repair the flawed universe by allowing himself to be ravished by God, becoming God's 'wife' and bearing God's children.

In the 'Wolfman' case ([1914–18] SE XVII) Freud showed – in stunning variety and over many decades – how a repression disrupts the amorous life and physical well-being of a Russian émigré patient. The repression had proceeded, Freud discovered, from an unrecallable 'primal scene' in the patient's infancy, where, Freud hypothesized, he had witnessed his parents making love. That scene is retroactively inferred by the analyst from the patient's dreams (one of which regards a tree where wolves sit) which lead to his unconscious fantasies. The primal scene is thus the single factor that insistently warps and blunts the Wolfman's capacity for enjoyment throughout his life.

The significance of Freud's use of exquisitely shaped prose to portray as well as to analyse the aberrations of the mind (and the body it affects) lies in what it is trying to present: the singular structure of unconscious mental phenomena. Thus it is that Freud's case histories do not merely offer the finished results of an analysis, but also its working through, its process: Freud's narrative style reflects the gradual unfolding of an unconscious *knowledge* that remains only partially revealed, in fits and starts, to both the analyst and the patient. And their respective understandings are rarely in harmony, rendering the task of writing a challenge.

Freud also found his style constrained by the nature of his material. By this is meant less the content than the bizarre form that the mental phenomena he discovered assume. He had found, for example, that 'the mind' interacts and intersects with language and speech. But this language is shaped by formal elements for which literary and philosophical history provide no useful models:

1. by the psyche's aberrant *temporality* (*Nachträglichkeit, unconscious memories, screen memories, repetition*);
2. by the psyche's peculiar relation to *speech* (the *parapraxis* or Freudian slip, the disguised sexual *symbol*, the *symptom*);
3. by the variety and peculiarity of the psyche's tools of *representation* (*Darstellung, Vorstellung, Vorstellungsrepräsentanz, condensation, displacement, the dreamwork*); and
4. by the psyche's deployment of several different kinds of *negation* (Freud distinguishes three kinds: regation [*Verneinung*], denial [*Vernichtung*] and foreclosure [*Verwerfung*]).

Freud had first fully described the origin and operations of these mechanisms in a masterwork, *The Interpretation of Dreams* (1900, *SE IV*). His deciphering of the psyche's strategies of representation through the hieroglyphic character of dreams remains one of Freud's capital achievements, comparable, for some, to the discovery of the Rosetta Stone. Indeed, if we had only three of Freud's works we would have a rich, important and seemingly finished *oeuvre*: *The Interpretation of Dreams* (1900, *SE IV and V*), which demonstrates the astonishing variety of the verbal and pictorial distortions deployed by an unconscious wish that seeks to break through repression and declare itself; *The Psychopathology of Everyday Life* (1901, *SE VII*), which examines the formal mechanisms by which the unconscious disrupts discourse; and the volume on *Jokes and Their Relation to the Unconscious* (1905, *SE VIII*), which completes the main work Freud undertook to demonstrate that language is disturbed by the presence of the unconscious even in the most ordinary, everyday behaviours and events.

Of course, Freud did more. He gave the world of art and letters a shock that went well beyond his disclosing the subterranean machinations of disguised desire. The fact is that Freud outraged many people – and not simply for the 'historicist' reason that he was treating matters that were censored under Victorian 'politeness', since his work continues to stir controversy today. (For example, one might refer to the Jeffrey Masson-Janet Malcolm disputes over his seduction theories, or the public outcry over the Smithsonian Institution's exhibition in honour of the 100th anniversary of the *Interpretation of Dreams*.)

At first glance, Freud seemed mainly bent on shaking up a placid society with the news that it is constantly beseiged by an unwelcome guest, the Unconscious. Freud dramatized its presence and made it all the more shocking by insisting on its *sexual* character: the hidden wishes that formed its substance were not only for forbidden sex, their very sexualization was tied to events that occurred in infancy. In his *Three Essays on the Theory of Sexuality* (1905, *SE VII*) and 'My Views on The Part Played by Sexuality in the Aetiology of the Neuroses' (1905–6, *SE VII*), Freud closely observed infants (who lack the means of verbalization; *in-fans* = without speech) and young children. He discovered there the makings of all subsequent forms of adult sexual behaviours, from fantasies to inhibitions, from homosexuality to perversion. He also studied the effect that tabooing sexual knowledge had on children: he examined the accounts young children, kept in the dark about 'the facts of life', devise to explain away the sexual energy they feel in their bodies (and sense in their parents), not to mention the inexplicable advent of a new baby – see 'On the Sexual Theories of Children' (1907, *SE IX*) and the interesting case of 'Little Hans', which consists of a father's reports to Freud regarding his son's fears and of Freud's return commentaries ('Analysis of a Phobia in a Five-Year-Old Boy', 1909, *SE X*). The father was an early devotee of Freud's, the mother had been Freud's patient, and on the birth of a younger sister Hans developed multiple phobias.

More than Freud's insistence on sexuality, what continues to surprise thinkers everywhere today is that he introduced an unheralded complexity into concepts and words that had previously been more simply understood. He had to: he was describing an indescribable entity – the Unconscious – whose presence, force and operations could only be inferred from the phenomena he was the first to single out for analytic attention. The Unconscious, which 'knows no negation', is not merely a temporarily backgrounded thought or perception; it is a mind-within-the-mind. Yet it is not entirely 'in' us, either. The Unconscious is in fact structured and determined by our intimate links to others – to parents, siblings, social and sexual rivals, *et al.* – and to language. Its presence is only 'given away' through slips of the tongue, unsuitable gestures or compulsive acts. These alone are how the Unconscious indirectly manifests itself.

What is the Unconscious? Its contents are comprised of only one thing: a repressed wish (*Wunsch*) that cannot be resolved through a verbal articulation: a desire that cannot speak its name. Since verbalization is one of the only 'satisfactions' society permits us, a repressed wish (i.e. one lacking the means of verbalization) will adopt a variety of circuitous forms to sustain its energy and psychic force. To counter it, the mind energizes itself to bar the injection of this unspeakable desire into social relations. Such a wish may be for forbidden incest, but also for other unavowable, things like murder; it is mainly, but not exclusively, sexual in character. Forced back, the unavowable wish does not disappear, but crystallizes into a fully staged *fantasy*. Elaborated and re-elaborated in the unconscious this fantasy constitutes what Freud calls the 'other scene' [*andere Schauplatz*].

When Freud developed psychoanalysis, he seemed at first to be answering philosophy's traditional demand for the fully examined life (e.g. Socrates' or Kant's questions, 'What can I know?', 'What must I do?', etc.). But Freud's theory also traced its descent to 'hard' science. He was trained as a neurobiologist and as a physician and he greatly admired the work of his near contemporary, Charles Darwin, to whose books *The Descent of Man* and *The Expression of the Emotions in Man and Animals* Freud referred on numerous occasions.

Freud in fact represented a philosophical conundrum. More than anyone had thought possible, he fulfilled the Delphic oracle's challenge to 'Know thyself', the *Nosce te ipsum*. But his 'answer' managed to question, to an unprecedented degree, the very status of *knowledge* itself. He shook the most fundamental assumptions about the very *language* in which human knowledge is conveyed, and he further shook the presumption that human beings actually *desire* to know themselves. For Freud had found that in the very structure of thought itself lay a necessarily unthought, unknowable portion.

The foundations of his 'scientific' side were also disturbed by Freud. Freud's discovery meant that human *biology* was as much or more subject to the *laws of language* and *culture* as it was to the *laws of nature*. The analysis of the psyche had demonstrated irrefutably that the *organic logic* of the *human* body (its natural, teleological functionality) is supplanted wholesale by another logic: the *logos* of speech or language. It is a logic that ruins natural logic, and therefore makes it possible for the mind (made out of logos – reason, speech) to affect the body and make it ill. As Lacan once put it: 'people feel the weight of words'.

Freud's philosophical and scientific revolution thus had the same root: a mind with an unnatural relation to nature; a body that affected, and was even more fundamentally affected by, the mind. How did this come about?

Freud theorized that human mental life originated in a unique way, and he worked these theses out carefully in two early papers, the unpublished (by him) *Project for a Scientific Psychology* (1895, *SE I*) and the 1911 essay, 'The Two Principles of Mental Functioning' (*SE XII*). He never really deviated from this initial vision.

For Freud, the specifically *human* mind was indebted neither to the 'innate ideas' Cartesian rationalism hypothesized, nor to pure experience, as British empiricism and the neurobiological sciences Freud studied, presumed. Freud believed, instead, that human mental life was initially *driven* into existence by being deprived of its 'nature' in a singular fashion. An animal always finds a way to fulfil its natural needs; if not, it dies. But the *human* mind does not accept this simple split of life from death, of satisfied from unsatisfied needs. Refusing to credit 'necessity', faced with a situation where satisfaction is impossible, the human mind concocts a third solution quite different from the animal's forced choice to eat or to die. Instead it devises an alternate *satisfaction*: Freud calls hallucination or *fantasy* our first acts of mentation. Using the emptied maternal breast as his paradigm, Freud shows that even the smallest infant will construct mental substitutes for the satisfaction – the milk – that has been withdrawn. The breast, which no longer supplies nourishment, is recalled as a 'lost' enjoyment made 'present' again to a mind which enjoys it in fantasy. Thus provisionally satisfied, the infant will stay in that mental space until 'reality' finally intervenes and requires active effort to gain nourishment. According to Freud, once humans substitute mentally fabricated satisfactions of their needs that cannot be actually fulfilled, *mental life* as we know it begins. Necessity, *Ananké*, and thus Death remain the cardinal denial of human mental life, and Freud later says that no ego can really believe it is anything but immortal.

The core of human 'consciousness' is therefore formed by a fundamental discounting of 'reality' in favour of what we might call 'metaphor': the substituting of some *image* for some *thing*, which is also the basis of language itself. Freud came to believe that *mental life* as such was specifically designed to shut out the *knowledge* of brute reality (the real absence or real presence of the satisfying thing). At the same time, however, *another knowledge* – precisely of that brute reality – also persisted underneath its metaphorical replacements. As 'conscious' cultural and mental forms (spurred by the drives, and rooted by metaphor and fantasy) became more complex, unconscious knowledge also flowered secretly in equal measure. This hidden twin of conscious thought took thus the paradoxical form of an 'unknown knowledge': the knowledge we had elected *not* to know for the simple reason that we had also elected to *think*.

When Freud founded the new art and science of psychoanalysis he based it entirely on the desire (his own, primarily) to know and to bring this *unconscious knowledge* to the light of rational discourse. But it could not be *his* desire alone. His desire to know had to be doubled: the *analyst's desire to know* about the patient's unconscious must be matched by the *patient's* desire. This underground knowledge had gone, buried by what Freud calls *repression* (*Unterdrängung*), which finds Freud likening the analytic process to an archaeology.

Psychoanalysis quickly became institutionalized as a healing art, in and out of fashion ever since. But after Freud, the *arts* have rarely dispensed with him. It was, tellingly, Leonard Woolf's Hogarth Press that published Freud's works in English translation as they were being written; his wife, Virginia Woolf, and their Bloomsbury Circle mingled socially and intellectually with the Freudians. Later, the French New Wave (Sarraute, Robbe-Grillet) would have been unthinkable without Freud, likewise film. In Alfred Hitchcock's *Spellbound*, *Marnie* and *The Birds* psychoanalysis is thematized; Fritz Lang's *Secret Beyond the Door* makes direct use of psychoanalytic technique and references psychic temporality, and Marguerite Duras' *Hiroshima, mon amour* has been likened to a case history. In her film *Détruire, dit-elle*, Duras says of a forest a female character is afraid to enter: 'The Forest is Freud'.

Freud's work has intrinsic literary interest: the myriad disguises obscuring the reality of sexuality in human affairs; the mis-steps in the spoken word that betrayed cloaked desires; the intimations of an 'other stage' where repressed scenarios of rivalry and romance are granted fantasy stagings – this is also the stuff of plays, novels and poetry. Freud himself used literature: a Shakespeare play (*The Merchant of Venice* in 'The Theme of the Three Caskets', 1913, *SE XII*; *Hamlet* in Mourning and Melancholia', 1915, *SE XIV*), a Goethe poem (Goethe appears in nearly every volume; one example is 'A Disturbance of Memory on the Acropolis', 1936, *SE XXII*), novels by the Russian Dostoevsky ('Dostoevsky and Parricide', 1928, *SE XXI*) and by the Danish Wilhelm Jensen (*Delusions and Dreams in Jensen's Gradiva*, 1906–7, *SE IX*), a story by John Galsworthy (in *Civilization and its Discontents*, 1929, *SE XXI*), not to mention the plays of Sophocles' *Oedipus* cycle whence Freud formulated the 'Oedipus Complex' as the nucleus of the neuroses ('Further Remarks on the Neuro-psychoses of Defence', 1892, *SE III*). He wrote about 'Psychopathic Characters on Stage' (1905, *SE VII*), and in his 'Creative Writers and Daydreaming' (1907, *SE IX*) he located the *fantasy* art deploys as partially Unconscious and partially social. Unlike *unconscious fantasy*, artistic fictions admit of others' participation in a forbidden enjoyment: for example, fictionalized sex and murder.

To some, literature seems diminished by psychoanalysing it. Freud, however, granted art and literature theoretical importance. Freud updated Aristotle's *catharsis*, wondering just why in art social taboos can be violated with impunity and even socially rewarded. In 'Instincts and Their Vicissitudes' (1915, *SE XIV*) Freud began modelling key psycho-analytic concepts on *aesthetic production*, especially *sublimation*, one of the psychic transformations of *drives* into acceptable mental productions.

With the advent of the First World War in which the venerable Austro-Hungarian Empire lost its cultural dominance to the younger British one, the stable society that Freud had taken for granted disappeared and his work now took a different turn: away from the micro-behavioural toward larger cultural assessments. He was particularly concerned with the impact culture has on the psyche. Culture [*Kultur*] – the English 'civilization' – not only smoothes over brutal reality (which remains 'known' only to the Unconscious and its attendant fantasies) but is itself an ongoing source of fresh dilemmas for human existence.

Around the First World War Freud produces some of his most complex concepts. They blend socially recognizable personality traits and behaviours with analysis of their unconscious roots: narcissism, melancholia, repression. At this time he also elaborates the theory of the *drives* (usually, but incorrectly, translated as 'instincts'). *The Papers on Metapsychology* (*SE XIV*) contain these conceptually rich notions as well as Freud's pensive, haunting 'Thoughts for the Time on War and Death' (1915), an essay whose expression and conception alike continue to interest students of literature (MacCannell 2000).

Freud's original 'cultural critique' had a frankly 'mythic' character: *Totem and Taboo* (1913, *SE XIII*). Later he evolved a more anchored and structured discourse concerning socio-cultural life: in 'Beyond the Pleasure Principle' (1920, *SE XVIII*), *Group Psychology and the Analysis of the Ego* (1921, *SE XVIII*), *The Future of an Illusion* (1927, *SE XXI*), *Civilization and its Discontents* (1928, *SE XXI*) and his final major work in this area, *Moses and Monotheism* (1939, *SE XIII*). Freud systematically pursued the psychology of human groups, from the primal horde (run dictatorially by a ferocious Ur-Father who hates and persecutes his sons) through to modern 'artificial' groups, whose Leaders 'love' and nurture those under their command. Freud, rather chillingly, saw the outlines of the first still present in the second, with guilt for a dead father the key to a group's integrity.

Freud painted vividly our discontents (*Unbehangen*) with group life. While his critique of culture was first taken in the eighteenth-century way, i.e. as a conflict between simple, 'natural' man's 'instincts' and arbitrary social laws that forbid them, Freud was telling a far more complex truth. That the *drives* simply contest the constraints of civilization is an illusion: for, Freud found, the drives are in fact only produced by civilization itself. Conversely, without the spur of the drives, civilization and culture have no incentive for further elaboration, the mind is impelled to no new labours: *Drive* (translated as 'instinct' by Strachey), Freud writes, is 'a measure of the demand made on the mind for work' ('Three Essays on Sexuality', *SE VII*, 168).

In Freud's quite vivid pictures of our anguished relation to other people, he also made it clear that only the *civilization* (*Kultur*) we hold in common grants us *human* status. The sacrifices 'the common work of civilization' demands of us make us *sick*, but it is less because our 'animal' parts rebel against cultural constraints, than because culture produces in us *drives* which by their very nature *must* remain unsatisfied. Culture itself generates the unconscious *excess* that spurs it to further elaborations, just as mentation produces a blank absence of knowledge that it then must work to fill.

For Freud the fundamental and insoluble dilemma of human existence is that our *Drives* demand recognition by civilization, but our civilization commands their misrecognition – because it is itself their source. *Drive*, as *excess* energy, is unique and specific to human being, the by-product of our increasing mental activity and an accelerating metaphoric translation of our raw experience. The more we try to contain drives, the less able we are to recognize that inhibitions only generate more drives. We have to try dissipating or discharging the excess energy of drive without resorting to repressive codes and regulations which only enflame, rather than quell, *drive*. The great self-regulatory principles human life has traditionally devised ('the pleasure principle' and 'the reality principle') go only so far and cannot ultimately attenuate the capital drive in us: *death drive*. *Death drive* is the logical extension of a mental life formed by the denial of biological necessity and reality: human beings will defer the satisfaction of their drives at the expense of life itself.

Thus, when Freud took psychoanalysis past the pleasure and reality principles with the radical concept of the *Death Drive* (which he drew from Sabrina Spielrein, a patient, and systematically formulated in 'Beyond the Pleasure Principle'), he posed a major challenge to Aristotelian and neo-Aristotelian assumptions that 'balance' is inherent to and indispensable for social organization, aesthetic works and individual ethics. The simple fact is that we must live with a certain inherent imbalance, an imbalance that is key to human mental health and illness alike.

Freud's complex picture of our relation to civilization was often given simplified treatment in its applications, sometimes with significant effects. Leslie Fiedler, a professor at the State University of New York, Buffalo (a campus that still has a Center for Psychoanalysis and Culture), was among the first American critics to push literary studies beyond textual analysis toward the broad cultural horizon Freud's work implies. Fiedler's *Love and Death in the American Novel* (1960) was frankly Freudian, and deeply disturbed the then genteel world of literary criticism that leaned heavily on aesthetic philosophy and maintained a near-Victorian decorum. So was American critic Norman O. Brown's *Life Against Death; The Psychoanalytical Meaning of History* (1959) and his *Love's Body* (1966). Europeans, of course, had long taken a similar tack, often blending Freud with Marx: Theodor W. Adorno (1967, 1987), and Herbert Marcuse (1955, 1964) were among those who first used Freud's critiques of 'civilization' to attack capitalist culture.

Marcuse, Max Horkheimer and Adorno promoted the Frankfurt School's unique synthesis of Freud and Marx. Walter Benjamin, their Frankfurt School colleague and Adorno's close friend, became known to the English-speaking world in the 1960s with the translation of some of his essays. While working in the field of culture criticism, Benjamin inflected Freud differently from his friends, and ended by deploying Freud in a highly original and insightful manner. Benjamin's way of reading rivalled Freud's in complexity, but Benjamin rarely took up a Freudian concept without making it his own. His essay 'On Some Motifs in Baudelaire' (1973) makes free, but not inaccurate, use of Freud's 'Beyond the Pleasure Principle' to imply that the material culture surrounding this 'lyric poet in the age of high capitalism' had become much like the primordial brew in which Freud had immersed his pre-mental sentient beings. Benjamin focused on the 'shocks' and 'stimuli' that in Freud's 'BPP' overwhelms primitive creatures. These shocks force them to form consciousness as a shield against, rather than a prolongation of, experience. Benjamin analogized Freud's mythic neurological 'shocks' to the inassimilable horrors of modern capitalism and its advancing technologies.

The use of Freud made by 'ethnic' critics, begun by Leslie Fiedler (1955), turned Freud into a crucial ally against the erasure of social and cultural difference that the New Criticism had made one of its tenets. Fiedler's and Brown's books startled literary studies into awareness of the social as well as sexual dimensions in literature. When they appeared the 'age of conformity' in the United States was drawing to a close (as new cultural movements like the Beats gained momentum) and the politicizing of academic and public discourse was about to begin. Freudianism came to the fore as a natural ally of both movements.

Yet official twentieth-century literary criticism in Anglo-America had, in fact, already incorporated several strains of 'Freudianism' though without ever making Freud's methods and theories a focus of outright debate. There were not yet declared Freudians like Frederick Crews (who later turned against Freud), but certain individualist critics like Kenneth Burke, Lionel Trilling and Leon Edel knew Freud well, and diverted him to their own purposes. Burke, for example, did not necessarily agree with Freud, but he did not reject him entirely; instead, Burke placed grammatical mechanisms and rhetorical under-pinnings beneath 'Freudian' insights.

Stanley Edgar Hyman's influential collections of literary critics (*The Armed Vision*, 1948, and *The Critical Performance*, 1960) were intentionally eclectic. They aimed to introduce the students present at the dawning of *literary theory* to a variety of approaches, ranging from the marxist one of Christopher Caudwell's to the New Critics. Hyman's strongest sympathies lay with Kenneth Burke, who connected rhetorical concerns to contemporary social issues and sought to make literature 'equipment for living', often by adapting Freudian topics and methods to this end. (See Burke's use of Freud's 'On the Antithetical Meaning of Primal Words'.) Hyman also befriended Burke's brilliant student Erving Goffman, who published a respectfully yet playfully deviant remodelling of Freud for social analysis, *The Presentation of Self in Everyday Life* (1959). Goffman's highly modified Freud influenced cultural critics like Dean MacCannell (*The Tourist*, 1976) and Michel de Certeau (*The Practice of Everyday Life*, 1984). In the same era, Canadian theorist Marshall McLuhan's 1951 cultural critique in *The Mechanical Bride* had a distinctly 'Freudian' tinge.

Freud's intensive scrutiny of language, speech and rhetorical devices intrigued literary specialists who might otherwise have seemed incompatible in sensibility with Freud's overt sexual focus and broad cultural scope. Thus it was that Charles Kay Ogden, an aesthetic philosopher, and the eighteenth-century specialist I. A. Richards wrote *The Meaning of*

Meaning; a Study of the Influence of Language Upon Thought and of the Science of Symbolism
(1927) and indirectly encouraged Anglo-American criticism to draw inspiration from
Freud.

Ogden and Richards tapped into two different, though kindred, psychological approaches (Freud's and Will James') to tackle the question of *meaning*. To Ogden and
Richards 'meaning' seemed to have a necessarily subjective as well as an objective side.
Richards had disagreed with his teacher G. E. Moore's thesis that words *can* say what we
mean. (Richards, in despair over his arguments with Moore, at one time intended to
become a psychoanalyst.) Together with Ogden, Richards hoped to make their work on
the 'subjective' side of meaning as rigorously logical and 'scientific' as Moore's on the
'objective' side, an enterprise in the spirit of Freud's inquiry. The pair drew on the *sign*
defined by Charles Sanders Peirce (the American whose philosophy of *Pragmaticism* (sic)
inspired William James, his best friend) to designate the literary sign's way of 'meaning'.
(Incidentally, both Derrida and Lacan elected Peirce's sign over Saussure's, Lacan because
of his friend Roman Jakobson, a Peircean semiolinguist.) At the same time, Ogden and
Richards included essays on the *social meaning* of signs and *symbols* by the Freudian
anthropologist Bronislaw Malinowksi in their influential book.

New Criticism held a firm line against 'Freudian' interpretations of literature and its
authors, as the famous essay on the 'Intentional Fallacy' by William K. Wimsatt and
Monroe C. Beardsley in Wimsatt's *The Verbal Icon* (1954) attests: its New Critical stand
against psychobiographical criticism is quite plain. Yet in some way, even an anti-Freudian
New Criticism prepared the ground for accepting Freudian thought. The New Criticism,
after all, had an immense appetite for the intrinsic ambiguity of verbal expression, for
emotional and moral ambivalence in literary tone, and for hidden ironies in poetic
personae. In some students' minds this translated into a potential tie to Freud's 'unconscious' – although there was in fact no true theoretical basis for making such a connection.

Finally, in France, the linguistic analysis of Freud is deepened in the work of Nicholas
Abraham and Maria Torok, who reanalysed Freud's Wolf Man purely on the basis of the
signifer in *The Wolfman's Magic Word*. American critics Avital Ronell and Laurence
Rickels have used their work.

By the mid-twentieth century Freudian criticism was drawn out of its more or less
comfortable closet by two circumstances that proved fateful for Freud's place in the
subsequent literary critical canon. One was the historic entrance of *women*, as writers,
literature professors and critics, into the growing field of modern language studies. The
other was the development, in France, of Jacques Lacan's Freudian School, which marked
deeply the direction of literary criticism there, and of Derridean deconstruction, which
critiqued but also used Freud's close attention to the operations of language. The
appearance of a 'French Freud' exerted significant pressure on literary theory and criticism
in the United States and the United Kingdom; Freud, for the first time, became the explicit
topic of open and impassioned debate.

The movement of women into the literary profession provided a forum for contesting
from within certain of Freud's views of 'civilization and its discontents'. After all, within
that civilization, Freud granted women an exceedingly minor role: 'Women represent the
interests of the family and of sexual life. The work of civilization has become increasingly
the business of men; it confronts them with ever more difficult tasks and compels them to
carry out instinctual sublimations of which women are little capable' (*Civilization and its*

Discontents, 1929, *SE XXI*, 103–4). This made women themselves into one of the 'discontents' 'civilized' man had to put up with.

Indeed, Freud made so little theoretical room for the woman who might labour productively as a creative writer or as a critic that it seems unlikely for women to follow him – at least not without strong dissent. It is a therefore a perpetual surprise that Freud found as many 'daughters' as he did to continue his line of thought, despite his patently patriarchal attitude. Freud's express misogyny ('an individual woman may be a human being in other [than sexual] respects', 'On Femininity', 1933, *SE XXII*, 119), his focus on fathering, his constitutional resistance to recognizing the female portion in cultural transmission, etc., did not prevent a great many women from finding him fascinating.

For Freud was also exceptional in his sympathy *to* women – he had listened, after all, to the hysterics and had spoken for them when they could not speak for themselves. Significant numbers of his earliest followers were women: H. D., Marie Bonaparte, Joan Riviere, Melanie Klein, Lou Andreas-Salomé and, of course, his daughter Anna (Appignanesi and Forester 1992; and Wright 1992). One of the most intriguing pieces of early 'Freudian' literary criticism is Princess Marie Bonaparte's study of sadism, mourning and necrophilia in the work of Edgar Allan Poe (1933) for which Freud wrote the glowing introduction. Bonaparte, a patient of Freud's and his staunchest French supporter, also authored the first psychoanalytic study of *Female Sexuality* (1953).

By the 1970s, New Zealander Juliet Mitchell had seized upon Freud and his French variant, Jacques Lacan, for the critical study of women *in literature* and of literature *by women*. Her books (1974, 1984), in tandem with her 1982 collaborative translation of (and commentary on) Lacan's and the *école freudienne's Feminine Sexuality* (with Jacqueline Rose) appreciated Lacan's updating of Freud for women. With Mitchell's lead, many British and American women critics entered the field, including Elizabeth Abel, Elizabeth Wright, Naomi Segal, Parveen Adams, Madelon Sprengnether, Teresa Brennan, Alice Jardine and Jane Gallop (along with many men, of course), though they were as often inspired the French Freud of Lacan and the French feminists Hélène Cixous, Luce Irigaray and Julia Kristeva as by Freud himself.

Clearly, it was Freud's translation through Lacan that encouraged a path for Freudian literary criticism *by* women, particularly women drawn to 'cultural critique'. Partly contesting and partly advancing it, they focused on Freud's apparent exclusion of women from culture, ethics, social justice. In 'Femininity' Freud had, for example, claimed that the psychic space reserved for social justice was crowded out in woman by her envy of male power – and of the penis [*penisneid*]. Freud's pithy pronouncements made it seem impossible for women to produce cultural insights: woman was, after all, 'a dark continent' where the reason's light was extinguished; woman had a weak Superego; her psychic make-up evolved not from civilizing *guilt* (the guilt for murdering the father incurred by the brothers in *Totem and Taboo*) but simply from *shame*, by which Freud meant fear of exposing her lack of a penis. If woman's genitalia are exposed, they resemble, Freud said, the Medusa's head (1940, *SE XVIII*) that turns men to stone, (i.e. sexually arouses them, but also petrifies them with forebodings of their own death – the ultimate castration).

Why did women persist in looking to Freud? Freud's preponderant desire was to know *about* women, and this singular, perpetually refreshed desire was part of his irresistibility to them. He famously asked, 'What does a woman want?' in a letter to Marie Bonaparte; he wondered openly why femininity was 'a riddle wrapped up in a mystery inside an enigma'. His sheer interest in women seemed sufficient cause for one female critic after another to pause at the edge of his stream of misogyny for a deeper drink. It was, after all, the hysteric's sadly blunted efforts to break through male imposed limits that inspired Freud to create his theory in the first place. Its keystone, the thesis that language had its 'dark' side, also found women had been culturally forced to occupy that obscure space. Freud's theory proved that that was an accident of history and a problem to be solved. Unlike the 'anatomy' that Freud once called our 'destiny' (by which he meant that our organs of excretion and of procreation were inalterably entwined, not that a biological and mental sex were inevitably matched up), our *language* gives sex a culturally embedded *place*. There is no naturally assigned *fate* for each sex. Once Jacques Lacan's exposition of masculine and feminine positions in language made this crystal clear, everything Freud had said about women could be reassessed. (In his *Encore Seminar* XX (1975) Lacan identified two distinctive logics of *feminine* and *masculine* that relieved both sexes of their biological designations and hence of their anatomical 'destiny' – see Copjec (1994).)

The most recent turns of Freudian criticism by women now combine the practice of Freud's strong 'formalism' and textual precision with the surer footing women have gained in his field of cultural critique, a footing enabled largely by Lacan: Joan Copjec (1994), Juliet Flower MacCannell (1991 and 2000), Renata Salecl (1999), Hélène Cixous and Catherine Clément. Even rhetorical critics like Shoshana Felman (1987) have oriented recent work to cultural criticism via psychoanalysis (1991). Other women have taken up the practice of psychoanalysis, like Michele Montrelay, Monique David-Ménard, Julia Kristeva (1980 and 1989) and Luce Irigaray.

At present, there remains both great hope for and great suspicion of Freud for literary and cultural criticism – in equal doses of committed enthusiasm and staunch anti-Freudianism.

Juliet Flower MacCannell

Further reading and works cited

Abraham, N. and Torok, M. *The Wolf Man's Magic Word*, preface J. Derrida. Minneapolis, MN, 1986.

Adorno, T. W. *Prisms*. London, 1967.

—. *Aesthetic Theory*, eds G. Adorno and R. Tiedemann. London, 1984.

Appignanesi, L. and Forrester, J. *Freud's Women*. New York, 1992.

Benjamin, W. *Charles Baudelaire: A Lyric Poet In The Era Of High Capitalism*. London, 1973.

Bonaparte, M. *Edgar Poe, Étude psychanalytique*. Paris, 1933.

—. *Female Sexuality*. New York, 1953.

Brown, N. *Life Against Death*. Middletown, CT, 1959.

—. *Love's Body*. New York, 1966.

Cixous, H. and Clément, C. *The Newly Born Woman*, intro. S. M. Gilbert. Minneapolis, MN, 1986.

Copjec, J. *Read My Desire*. Cambridge, MA, 1994.

De Certeau, M. *The Practice of Everyday Life*. Berkeley, CA, 1984.

Felman, S. *Jacques Lacan and the Adventure of Insight*. Cambridge, MA, 1987.

Fiedler, L. A. *An End to Innocence*. Boston, 1955.

—. *Love and Death in the American Novel*. New York, 1960.

Freud, S. *The Standard Edition of the Complete Psychological Works of Sigmund Freud*, eds J. Strachey and A. Freud, 24 vols London.

Goffman, E. *The Presentation of Self in Everyday Life*. Garden City, NY, 1959.

Hyman, S. *The Armed Vision*. New York, 1955.
—. *Critical Performance*. New York, 1956.
Kristeva, J. *Desire in Language*. New York, 1980.
—. *Black Sun*. New York, 1989.
Lacan, J. *Le Séminaire. Livre XX. Encore*, ed. J.-A. Miller. Paris, 1975.
— and the école freudienne. *Feminine Sexuality*, eds J. Mitchell and J. Rose. New York, 1982.
MacCannell, D. *The Tourist: A New Theory of the Leisure Class*. New York, 1976.
MacCannell, J. F. 'The Regime of the Brother', in *Opening Out*, ed. T. Brennan. London, 1991.
—. *The Hysteric's Guide to the Future Female Subject*. Minneapolis, MN, 2000.
McLuhan, M. *The Mechanical Bride*. Boston, 1967.
Marcuse, H. *Eros and Civilization*. Boston, 1955.
—. *One Dimensional Man*. Boston, 1964
Mitchell, J. *Psychoanalysis and Feminism*. New York, 1974.
—. *Women: The Longest Revolution*. London, 1984.
Ogden, C. K. and Richards, I. A. *The Meaning of Meaning*. London, 1936.
Salecl, R. *Spoils of Freedom*. London, 1994.
Wimsatt, W. K. Jr. *The Verbal Icon*. Lexington, KY, 1954.
Wright, E. *Psychoanalytic Criticism*. New York, 1992.

Ferdinand de Saussure (1857–1913) and Structural Linguistics

Much of the contemporary theoretical project finds its linguistic origins in the intellectual history of structural linguistics and semiotics. The analysis of the social construction of signs, moreover, has influenced the emergence and direction of various political genres of literary criticism, including feminist criticism and cultural studies, among others. As the study of signs, semiotics refers to the analysis of cultural and social referents, especially regarding their impact upon various modes of human behaviour.

Swiss linguist Ferdinand de Saussure advanced the study of signs further as a form of 'semiology' because of its attention to socially and culturally inscribed codes of human interaction. Often considered to be the founder of modern linguistics, Saussure constructed a theory of language whose intellectual legacy continues to resonate within scholarly circles, as evinced by A. J. Greimas's (1917–92) contemporary achievements in terms of semiotics and discourse theory. In addition to his postulation of a social-semiological metatheory, Saussure's influence includes his identification of the places of *langue* and *parole* in language and literary study.

Saussure's theories of signs recognizes the systemic codes and socialized conventions that characterize languages and the manner in which they become internalized by members of a given culture. Understanding that signs both implicitly and explicitly convey information between members of that culture, Saussurean semiotics addresses the nature of the speech acts and non-verbal gestures that mark human discourse communities. Although it quite obviously intersects with Charles Sanders Peirce's earlier linguistic philosophy of signs and their arbitrariness, Saussure's postulation of the sign attempts to elucidate the signifying system itself, rather than merely interpreting the instance of signification. For Saussure, the sign consists of two inseparable aspects, the signifier and the signified. The signifier refers to a set of speech sounds in language, while the signified functions as the meaning that undergirds the sign itself. Eschewing Peirce's theories regarding the objectivity and subjectivity of language, Saussure's semiology contends that the senses of identity or uniqueness of all aspects of language emerge via the differences inherent in that language's network of linguistic relationships, rather than through a given language's objective features. This concept demonstrates Saussure's paradoxical argument that in a given language system 'there are only differences, with no positive terms' (Culler 1981, 21). The importance of Saussure's discoveries finds its origins in the linguist's anticipation of language, in the words of Bertil Malmberg, as an 'abstract, superindividual system' (1967, 9). As with Peirce's theory of signs, however, Saussure's conceptualization of language recognizes the arbitrariness of speech acts and their invariable historical and cultural contingency.

Saussure's postulation of *langue* and *parole* – and their substantial impact upon language study – also demonstrate his significant contributions to twentieth-century linguistics and literary criticism. Saussure's philosophy of language argues that the fundamental aim of semiotics is to understand the concept of *langue* (language) as a possible result of *parole* ('word'). For Saussure, *langue* refers to the basic system of differentiation and combinational rules that allows for a particular usage of signs; *parole* connotes a single verbal utterance, as well as the employment of a sign or set of signs. 'In separating *langue* from *parole*,' Saussure writes, 'we are separating what is social from what is individual and what is essential from what is ancillary or accidental' (Culler 1981, 24). Saussurean linguistics contends, moreover, that signs lack signification in themselves and only accrue meaning via their relationships with other signs. The inherent differences among a set of given signs share, then, in the creation of their meaning. In Saussure's philosophy, David Holdcroft writes, '*langue* is social because it is the product of face-to-face communicative interchanges between members of a linguistic community, each of whom, as a result of these interchanges, has a similar representation of it' (1991, 27). Saussure's comprehension of language's inherently social particularity reveals its autonomous nature and the ways in which it conforms to the norms and linguistic requirements of a given historical or cultural era.

This latter distinction regarding the central philosophy of Saussurean semiotics necessitates the discussion of two additional aspects of the linguist's system of language study, the notion of the phoneme and Saussure's social-semiological metatheory. As the smallest basic speech sound or unit of pronunciation, Saussure's ground-breaking conceptualization of the phoneme represents a signal moment in the history of linguistics. It allows us to distinguish between two different utterances in terms of their measurable physical differences. According to Jonathan Culler, Saussure's postulation of the phoneme provides us with a means for comprehending the 'social significance of objects and actions' and for registering the 'judgements and perception' that a given speaker evinces, often unconsciously, when using a given language in a given historical instance (1991, 81). Having established his concept of the phoneme, Saussure demonstrated that the linguistic system in its entirety can be understood in terms of a theory of syntagmatic and paradigmatic relationships. The former involves the study of language in relational sequences, while the latter refers to the oppositional relationships that exist between linguistic elements that can replace one another. Saussure employed a similar system for understanding the relationships between phonemes, which he explained in terms of their synchronic and diachronic structures. A phoneme exists in a diachronic, or horizontal, relationship with other phonemes that precede and follow it. Synchronic relationships refer to a phoneme's vertical associations with the entire system of language from which individual utterances – or, in regard to the auspices of literary criticism, narratives – derive their meaning.

Saussure's elucidation of the synchronic and diachronic relationships that exist in language and literary study anticipated a number of later theoretical advances in literary criticism, particularly in terms of the advent of new historicism. They also formed the basis for what many of Saussure's expositors refer to as his social-semiological metatheory. Paul J. Thibault describes this system as a 'unitary or self-consistent, rather than a totalizing, social-semiological metatheory'. In addition to attempting to fashion a theory that addresses languages of all types, Saussure's metatheoretical approach to semiology offers, in Thibault's words, 'a structured system comprising the resources which social agents use to make meanings in systematic and socially recognizable ways in a given culture' (1997, 19). The resources to which Thibault refers include the typical lexicogrammatical patterns and relations of the language system. Perhaps more importantly, these resources also include linguistic systems for making meaning in other semiotic modes such as the visual image, the human body, and music and other non-verbal modes for the social construction of meaning. *Voluntarism*, one of the central concepts in the linguist's social-semiological metatheory, involves the voluntary reduction of language to a kind of social institution that depends, in Saussure's words, 'more of less on our own will' (Thibault 1997, 23). In short, we use language as a transparent and often non-semiotic naming mechanism that affords us with a means for reflecting the extralinguistic realities in which we live. The concept of *voluntarism* underscores the ways in which we both consciously and unconsciously exploit language as a system for constructing our own social realities.

By demonstrating the social dynamics inherent in language via such mechanisms as the social-semiological metatheory, Saussure has influenced generations of linguists and literary critics regarding this significant and ground-breaking facet of language and literary study. The subsequent linguistic achievements of Greimas, for instance, reveal the powerful impact of Saussure's intellectual legacy upon the future course of structuralism and structural linguistics. Using many of Saussure's discoveries as his scholarly points of departure, Greimas derived his theories of language as a mechanism involving what he described as the interdependent, 'reciprocal presupposition' of its elements. For Greimas, structural linguistics finds its origins in Saussure's social-semiological metatheory, a system of thought that Greimas later reconceived in terms of the roles of knowledge and power in the social construction of language. Saussurean linguistics provided Greimas with a mechanism for clarifying semiology as a language system, Schleifer writes, 'marked by double articulation, hierarchy, and neutralization' (1987, 181). Because semiotics offers a valuable paradigm for examining the nature of cultural codes and social conventions, a number of literary critics, structural anthropologists and psychoanalytic theorists have explored semiology's interdisciplinary applications – from Barthes and Lévi-Strauss to Lacan and Kristeva, among a wide range of others. Michel Foucault, for example, developed a form of semiological study for addressing changing medical interpretations of disease systems, treatment methodologies for insanity and our frequently shifting perceptions of human sexuality. Frederic Jameson lauds Saussure's semiological achievements as 'a liberation of intellectual energies'. Saussure's imaginative approach to language study, Jameson adds, 'is that of a series of complete systems succeeding each other in time' and the product of 'a perpetual present, with all the possibilities of meaning implicit in its every moment' (1972, 5–6). As with Peirce before him, Saussure articulated a new vision of semiotics that continues to impact the study of language and literature.

Kenneth Womack

Further reading and works cited

Barthes, R. *Elements of Semiology*. New York, 1967.
Culler, J. *Ferdinand de Saussure*. New York, 1976.
—. *The Pursuit of Signs*. Ithaca, NY, 1981.
Eco, U. *A Theory of Semiotics*. Bloomington, IN, 1976.
Harris, R. *Reading Saussure*. London, 1987.
Hawkes, T. *Structuralism and Semiotics*. London, 1977.
Holdcroft, D. *Saussure: Signs, System, and Arbitrariness*. Cambridge, 1991.
Holland, N. *The Critical I*. New York, 1992.
Jameson, F. *The Prison-House of Language*. Princeton, NJ, 1972.
Koerner, E. F. K. *Ferdinand de Saussure*. Braunschweig, 1973.
Lévi-Strauss, C. *Structural Anthropology*. New York, 1972.
Malmberg, B. *Structural Linguistics and Human Communication*. Berlin, 1967.
Saussure, F. de. *Course in General Linguistics*. New York, 1959.
Schleifer, R. A. J. *Greimas and the Nature of Meaning*. Lincoln, NE, 1987.
Thibault, P. J. *Re-Reading Saussure*. London, 1997.

Edmund Husserl (1859–1938)

Edmund Husserl founded the philosophical movement of phenomenology, a movement that was subsequently extended into two broad traditions of literary criticism: phenomenological criticism and poststructuralism. Husserl began his philosophical career by questioning the origin and possibility of meaning. Husserl's earliest work, including his *Philosophy of Arithmetic* (1891), explained meaning through a theory of psychologism: here, meaning is explained as the mental activity of an actual subject or psyche (Husserl 1970a). (So, the meaning of an arithmetical equation would be nothing more than the process of addition occurring in the mind of an individual.) Husserl's early psychologism was subsequently attacked by Gottlob Frege and as a consequence Husserl went on to formulate his theory of transcendental phenomenology, a theory which rejected both psychologism and historicism (1974). As Husserl argued in his late work, *The Crisis of the European Sciences* ([1936] 1970b), both psychologism and historicism explain meaning by describing the formation of concepts from *within* the world: for psychologism meaning is the act of an individual psyche; for historicism meaning emerges from historical contexts. (On a psychologist account the origin of geometry would be explained by referring to the mental acts of its founder, Euclid. On a historicist account geometry could be explained by referring to the Ancient Greek context from which it emerged.) Against these *explanations* of meaning, Husserl argued that the meaningful activity of consciousness was *absolute*: in order to experience a world we need to constitute that world meaningfully. Meaning is not an activity within the world – within history or mind – for it is only through meaning that any world is possible. Furthermore, for Husserl psychological and historicist explanations of the emergence of meaning could not account for the truth or ideality of meaning. The meaning of ideal entities, such as geometrical formulae or numbers, transcends the mental acts of individuals and the collective contexts of historical epochs. The truth of a mathematical equation is true, regardless of its specific context or its particular mental occurrence. Such ideal entities may initially require a factual or material origin (such as the inscription of formulae by the first geometer). But these factual, empirical or material inscriptions express a *sense* which is infinite (infinite, because $2 + 2 = 4$, for example, is true regardless of historical context, specific language or any finite mental act). Husserl's main task, therefore, was twofold. On the one hand he wanted to acknowledge the ideality of meaning: concepts and numbers have a sense that transcends both their material inscription and specific mental acts. On the other hand, and in contrast with Frege, Husserl wanted to avoid simply positing a separate reality for ideal entities (as in realism where the meaning of numbers and logical formulae exists independently of any subject). Husserl negotiated this problem of meaning through his theory of transcendental phenomenology and transcendental subjectivity, articulated in *Ideas* ([1913] 1982). Ultimately, this required Husserl to question the very concepts of being and existence that underpinned the problems of meaning he was investigating.

Husserl was insistent that we ought not to assume some foundation for meaning – such as the mind, history or logic – for any such foundation would itself have to be founded. Husserl therefore set himself the task of providing a foundation for all domains of meaning. In order to secure the truth of ideal meanings and not rely on already assumed foundations (such as the subject of psychologism or the logic of an already constituted science) Husserl argued that we needed to 'bracket' or 'suspend' all our current explanations and theories about the foundation of existence. This bracketing (or *epoche* as Husserl termed it) has two consequences. First, we need to attend to just what is experienced without assuming some ground or foundation; that is, we should consider only what appears – phenomena – and not posit some origin outside experience. This leaves us with a domain of pure immanence; here, we just attend to what is given and we avoid interpreting that givenness. Immanence is 'pure' in this sense because we do not see experience as the experience *of* an external world or as the experience *of* some psychophysical subject. We just attend to what is given, immanently, without taking this immanence to be the sign of anything other than itself. The second consequence of this bracketing or *epoche*, according to Husserl, demands going back to 'things themselves'. Hussserl described his phenomenology as a positivism. We take our experience as it is given. When we experience a thing, Husserl argued, we don't experience perception or sense data; we experience the thing itself. This means that attention to the pure immanence of experience also includes the experience of things. The task is, therefore, not to explain how we get from mind to world – for this assumes that there is an opposition. We need to explain how experience, taken immanently, is always already experience of a world. When we look to the pure immanence of experience we don't see sensations, data, perceptions or pictures of the world; we experience the world itself. Everyday experience is always experience of a world that we take to be present; it is an error of sceptical philosophy to ask how mind reaches the world.

Husserl begins his approach into the possibility of truth by taking everyday experience (or what he terms the 'natural attitude') as his object of inquiry. Husserl argues that we ought to take experience just as it appears and suspend or bracket any assumptions we might have regarding its ultimate existence, truth or foundation. Husserl begins his critique of the 'natural attitude' by arguing that it already contains certain metaphysical assumptions. In everyday experience we assume that we are subjects who then experience some independent world. We assume that the world exists independently of our experience and that we then discover this world through experience. Furthermore, we also assume that we, as subjects, are also beings within this world. And so, Husserl argues, the natural attitude already has some understanding of existence or being. In the language of phenomenology, there is a transcendence in the very immanence of experience. Experience is already experience *of* what is other than itself, or what transcends (transcendence).

In the natural attitude we assume that there is some real world or being, and that this world includes subjects who then come to know objects. We assume that subjects are a part of the world. Rather than assume that there are two types of beings – subjects and objects – Husserl begins his process of doubt by suspending this natural attitude and just attending to experience or what is given. Phenomenology will just examine experience or phenomena, and we will *then* ask how it is that we experience the world *as objective*. In this process of bracketing (or the *epoche*) Husserl likens his approach to Cartesian doubt. But he argues that Descartes's doubt was not sufficiently radical. For Descartes still assumed some object – the subject or *res cogitans* – which would explain all other objects. When Descartes concludes that 'I think therefore I am' he is right in arguing that the one thing we can't doubt is the stream of experience. But he is wrong to say that this experience is located in a thinking substance or mind. Descartes, according to Husserl, was caught in the natural attitude: the assumption that the world is an object for some experiencing subject.

Against this natural attitude Husserl formulates a theory of transcendental subjectivity. Here, the subject is not an assumed thing or substance *within which* experience of the world is located; nor is the subject a thing within the world. The transcendental subject is not a thing, but a process of constitution or 'synthesis' that then makes the experience of any thing possible. Husserl formulates this theory of the transcendental subject by examining the presuppositions of the natural attitude and the very experience of objective being. How is it possible that we experience something *as existing*? How is something taken to be present or real? When we experience a thing as existing or as present we do so because we have a certain connectedness of appearances. A thing is never given all at once; rather, the very character of the object is that it is experienced through time from a series of perspectives. Immanuel Kant had already argued that the very nature of objectivity relies on the synthesizing activity of an experiencing subject. Where Husserl differs from Kant is over the status of the transcendental subject. For Kant, the subject synthesizes experience into a coherent unity, and the subject is able to do so because there are universal or a priori categories through which the received world is ordered. For Husserl, by contrast, the categories through which the world is synthesized are not located in some prior synthesizing subject. Categories are not imposed by an experiencing subject; categories are constituted within the synthesis of experience. The difference between Husserl and Kant is difficult to grasp, but we could say that for Kant there is a subject who synthesizes the world. For Husserl, by contrast, there is synthesis; and it is from this synthesis that subjectivity and objectivity are then constituted.

It is this refusal to locate synthesis *within the subject* that differentiates phenomenology from Cartesianism and Kantianism. There is not a subject who then comes to know an external world. Rather, there is synthesis, or the temporal connectedness of experience, and it is from this passive synthesis or temporal flow that we then are able to think of experiencing subjects and an experienced world (Husserl [1893–1917] 1991). For Husserl, previous theories of metaphysics had remained within the natural attitude; they had assumed that there were subjects who then cognized an outside world. Against this assumption of a boundary between an interior subject and an outside world, Husserl asks how this distinction between subject and object, or interior and exterior, is constituted. He concludes by arguing that objectivity and exteriority are constituted from within experience. When we take something as an existing thing we constitute it in a coherent series of perceptions (temporally) and locate it outside ourselves (spatially). Husserl referred to this character of experience as *intentional*. Consciousness, he argued, is always consciousness *of* some thing – even if this intended object is ideal (such as number), psychological (such as a feeling) or material (such as a thing). Through his theory of intentionality Husserl radically redefined the nature of subjectivity. It's not that we have a subject who then grasps or comes to know the world; consciousness is not a thing or substance that then relates to an outside or material substance. On the contrary, consciousness is always a relation, or transcendence, to what is beyond itself. If we examine experience without the metaphysical presupposition of a separate subject, then we see that experience is always intentional, always directed toward some object. The very phenomena of experience are not experienced as isolated mental data, but as experiences *of objects*. When I perceive a chair, I perceive the thing itself and not some mental picture or representation.

Objectivity is not something that precedes experience but is given through experience. The condition for the possibility of objectivity is just a certain mode of experiencing; an object remains the same through time, and a material object is located in external space. This means that time and space aren't things we experience but transcendental conditions for experience: the very notion of experience demands that we receive something other than ourselves. And so all experience is intentional, related to some object. Husserl referred to this intended object as a *noema*; in so doing he expanded the notion of possible objects of consciousness beyond material things to ideal objects (such as numbers, logical propositions or geometrical formulae). The natural attitude, by contrast, begins from a highly limited interpretation of being – the spatio-temporal thing – and then asks how consciousness can know such things. Husserl, however, insisted on various modes of givenness which would open up domains of objective being that were not reducible to spatio-temporal being or the psychical being of mental entities. The most important instance of this insistence on the objectivity or transcendence of the *noema* was Husserl's argument for *ideal being*. Numbers, logical forms, geometric formulae and so on are not objects in the material world, nor are they fictions or mental entities imposed by a subject. They are essences that can be intuited by any subject whatsoever. Husserl was insistent on the possibility of the intuition of essences. When the geometer describes a formula for triangularity she is formalizing what she intuits as an essential law for any possible triangle. The same applies to number; these entities are not just psychological, for they are given to experience as essential forms for any possible experience. When I think of the number four, for example, I am directed towards an objectivity that is not reducible to my isolated experience; this ideal object cannot be reduced to a psychological phenomenon. The system of number must have had its original constitution from within experience, and then have been given some material symbol or signifier. But the signifier or written number formalizes a meaning that can always be returned to or intuited by any experiencing subject. The *meaning* of an ideal object has an essence that cannot be reduced to an isolated subjective experience or an arbitrarily imposed system. This is where Husserl differs from psychologism, historicism, structuralism and realism (Tragesser 1984). The ideal object has a worldly genesis; it must have been intuited and constituted at some point in empirical history. But once constituted the ideal object is infinitely repeatable and transcends any worldly context. The truths of Euclidean geometry, for example, have an empirical origin in an inscribing subject and a historical moment. But the truths of geometry are true, and remain true, regardless of this factual origin. And it is always possible for us to retrieve the original sense or meaning of these essences.

What Husserl grapples with, in this constitution of the ideal object, is what Jacques Derrida refers to as the 'opening to infinity' (1973). The ideal object has a finite and contextual genesis, but once constituted it exceeds all finitude. The concept of truth, for example, must be articulated in a specific language and a specific time; but, once inscribed, the very concept of truth enables us to think of that which exceeds any finite context. There is, on the one hand, the original subject event or act and, on the other hand, that towards which the act is directed. Any truth must originate in some act of experience (the *noesis*), but *as true* what is experienced goes beyond the particular act. Husserl therefore distinguished between the *noesis* (the active subjective constitution of this object) and the *noema* (the object intended or aimed at). The *noesis* is the 'really inherent' component of meaning; it is the particular mental act undertaken by the subject. The *noesis* is that aspect of experience that can be attributed to the synthesizing activity of the subject. For any object I can recognize its original constitution by some perceiving subject. When I think of 'four' I have some specific *noesis* (either the signifier 'four' or '4', or four perceived objects), but this specific *noesis* is directed towards an object, the *noema*. This *noema* is more than just the concept of four; it is what is meant or intended in the experience. This means that there can be *noematic* unities prior to concepts. We can perceive or intend some sense, Husserl argues, without yet having a formalized concept of that object. There is still, though, a *noesis* and a *noema*: an act – of perception, imagination, memory – and an intended object – a thing, feeling or essence. Every perceptual act aims at some transcendence or intended object, some *noematic* pole, even if there is not an explicit concept for that *noema*. We may have the general concept of red, but I can also have a *noesis* or perception that aims at this quite specific shade. The *noema* is not just 'redness'. Indeed I can intuit the singular essence of this specific shade of red, such that though I have perceived it once I discern a quality that I could perceive again independent of this experience now. An essence is not a generalization from experiences, nor is it the effect of imposing concepts on experience. Essences are intuitable precisely because experience is always more than a mental act; it aims at something beyond itself, given in presence. Let us imagine that I have an experience of a cat; the *noesis* is just that particular perception, from a certain angle, of this furry animal. (I could also remember or imagine the same cat, but these would be different noetic acts. And so memory or imagination aren't weaker forms of perception; they are quite different kinds of experience.) The *noema* is the objective pole; I take this experience to be the experience *of* a cat. This experience can be confirmed and the *noema* can be fulfilled; I go on having coherent experiences that confirm my first perceptions. Or, the experience can be frustrated; what I took to be a cat was actually a doorstop or a soft toy. What Husserl emphasizes in his theory of perception and its poles of *noesis* and *noema* is that consciousness always intends some object and it does so in a particular way: both from a certain perspective but also with a certain type of regard. I don't just encounter the ideal object four or the material being of the cat; each *noema* is given in this or that particular way, as this specific *noesis* or *noetic* act. I relate to the object as desired, remembered, perceived, imagined, feared or represented.

This distinction between the *noesis* and *noema* challenges the natural attitude's interpretation of the world as some form of objectivity that we then experience. The 'world' includes a number of different modes of givenness, and we need to attend to the way differing *noetic* acts relate to essentially different *noema*. We ought not to privilege one form of *noesis* – such as sense perception – and then see all other forms of experience as derived from that. Nor should we regard sense perception as a weaker or unreliable form of knowledge as opposed to logic or mathematics. Each region within the world, Husserl argues, has its own specific way of being known. It's the nature of perception, for example, to relate to its objects as 'actually existing'; it's the nature of fiction to relate to its objects 'as imagined'; and it's the nature of logic to operate as the synthesis of any possible subject. The *noesis*, the act of experience, already relates to different types of objectivity. And this means that we shouldn't restrict ourselves to one form of entity – the objects of perception – to explain all other forms, such as values, logical truths, concepts or numbers. If we examine the phenomena themselves then we are given all sorts of modes of being, including ideal objects, fictional objects and material things. The material thing, far from being the basis of knowledge and subjectivity, is only one particular mode of experienced objectivity. The very essence of the material thing, if we examine the domain of phenomena, is constituted from a concatenation of coherent appearances. It's not that there is a spatio-temporal world that 'we' only grasp in some partial way through experience. It is the very essence of spatio-temporal being that it is given in a series of perceptions and perspectives. The very meaning of 'object' is something that is located in space and remains through time; it is essential to the *noema* of objectivity that it be grasped in a temporal series of perceptions and from a specific point in space. Even a divine intuition, Husserl insists, could not know an *object* absolutely, for it is the very essence of objectivity to be known and experienced in time and space. The objects of memory, logic, desire and imagination have their specific modes of givenness. A memory is not a weaker version of a perception, and a logical proof is not a stronger form of certainty than a perception. It's not as though we have an experience and then work out whether it's a memory, fiction, perception or logical necessity. Different domains of objects are given in essentially different ways. It would be incoherent or absurd, Husserl argues, to dogmatically assert the existence of two types of thing (subjects and objects) and then ask how one of these things (materiality) appears to the other (subjectivity). Rather, the only coherent manoeuvre is to assume the originary or primordial status of appearing. There is appearance – or phenomena – and from this appearing we then conclude that there is a subject who experiences and a world that then appears. The natural attitude – the assumption of the subject as a being who encounters other beings – occurs *after* the original event of appearance. The natural attitude has already made a decision about being; it has assumed that being is something external that then appears to a subject. But Husserl puts appearance or phenomenality before all such interpretations.

Husserl therefore begins his 'transcendental reduction' as a methodological or epistemological manoeuvre: we must bracket all presuppositions about existence and just examine what appears. But this epistemology then leads to a new ontology: it's not that there is a being or presence that then appears; being or presence is constituted from an *absolute* domain of appearance. Husserl therefore refers all being and existence back to the lifeworld or *Lebenswelt* (Husserl 1970). Through time and history certain meanings, forms and languages are constituted. When we experience the world we do so through these sedimented and formed meaningful unities. But because meaning emerges from the flow of experience it is always possible that we can return to the very genesis of meaning. As an example, Husserl demonstrated how the truths of logic should not just be accepted as a static system, for it must always be possible to see the essential truth of these forms. Philosophy ought to be just this responsibility of reason: not the acceptance of truths as things given to experience but the grounding of truth back in the very possibility of experience.

The consequences of Husserl's phenomenology lie in two broad areas: the theory of the subject and the theory of meaning. If we bracket all previous assumptions and begin philosophy from just that which appears, then we are forced to recognize the primacy of conscious life. Any object or being is the outcome of a series of appearances. In the beginning are the phenomena, or pure immanence, and all objectivity is determined from this original domain. This is why Husserl describes his phenomenology as a transcendental idealism; any reality or being can only be understood as having been constituted in the intentional life of consciousness. A complexity arises when we examine just what this consciousness is. Husserl was critical of both Descartes and Kant for assuming that the subject was a type of thing that then imposed the forms of time and space upon the world. For Husserl time is not ideal – the way in which a pre-temporal subject then constitutes a world – time is transcendental. Time is neither subjective nor objective; it is from the flow of time that subject and object are constituted. If we ask who or what constitutes this flow of time then we are at risk of falling back into the natural attitude. For Husserl, the constituted flow of time is not undertaken *by* a subject; the subject is constituted in this temporal synthesis. Perhaps Husserl's most difficult idea, and one that turned the whole subjectivism of phenomenology on its head, was the idea of passive synthesis. Rather than assuming that there are ideal subjects who then form the world through the medium of time, Husserl argued for the primordiality of time. There just is the transcendental flow of time, a flow within which the subject and object can then be formed or constituted (1991). It's true that if we take any being or thing we see it as the outcome of a synthesis of perceptions, but any thought of a being *who synthesizes* would itself be the result of a synthesis. We might say, then, that consciousness is not a thing that synthesizes; it is the event of synthesis from which all things are then rendered possible. Far from being a self-present and identical ground or basis for the world, Husserl's transcendental subject is just this dynamic, synthesizing and pre-objective power or event of synthesis. This leads the way, of course, for a critique of the very use of the word 'subject' or 'consciousness' to describe this event of synthesis. Both Martin Heidegger and Jacques Derrida radicalized Husserl's theory of synthesis in order to criticize subjectivism. If the subject is nothing other than the event of temporal synthesis then it may be more appropriate to locate time as the original event (Heidegger [1927] 1996) or do away with the possibility of an origin altogether (Derrida 1973).

Husserl's phenomenology not only disrupted the very possibility of an originating or self-present subject, it also redefined the very problem of meaning. Husserl argued that all experience was, in some way, meaningful. I always experience the world *as* this or that specific, or intended, being. Meaning is not something we add on to the world. In order to have a world at all experience must originally intend or aim at some unity. But meaning for

Husserl also opens up a domain of ideality beyond any specific experience, and does so from experience itself. Let's say that I perceive four objects. The number four is more than just this specific mental event. Indeed I can intuit *both* these four specific things *and* the essence of four. Husserl argued that we could intuit essences and that we did so from singular or specific experiences. When the concept of four functions in mathematics it is no longer tied to a specific perception but can now extend beyond any finite perception or sense and be repeated infinitely. For Husserl, this theory of the intuition of essences and the constitution of ideality solved the problem of realism versus psychologism. Ideal objects are intuited in finite and empirical circumstances – such as this particular experience of four things – but we can then constitute a logical system (such as the system of number) which can repeat this essence infinitely and independent of all content and specificity. Husserl therefore recognized that the being of ideal objects exceeded specific mental events; they were more than psychological phenomena. But Husserl also resisted realism. Numbers don't exist in some 'third realm' of forms awaiting their apprehension by experience. They are constituted within experience, but then refer to an object or form of any possible experience. This means that the forms of pure logic are forms of possible experience. They must have a finite and empirical origin; but this empirical origin is just the recognition of a form of experience *in general* – not this or that finite experience but what must be true for any possible experience. The formality and ideality of logic or mathematics is constituted by an intuition of the essence of a specific experience. In non-formal domains of meaning, such as natural and literary language, there is more specific content. Thus Husserl's theory of meaning opens the way to consider concepts in terms of their greater or lesser degrees of idealization and formalization. Certain meanings – such as those of logic – refer to possibilities of experience in general, and they do so by abstracting from particular content. Other meanings, such as the concepts of a particular language, cannot be translated and repeated across languages. They are less capable of formalization. Literary language, particularly poetry, would be the least susceptible to formalization but a literary work still has an ideal content or *noematic* core. The meaning of *Hamlet*, for example, lies above and beyond any particular edition or performance. Each reading and each performance is a specific reactivation of the work's infinitely repeatable ideal content. Certain elements of both the work and performance are at the ideal end of the spectrum of meaning; the work relies on certain essential and necessary logic forms – such as time, space, identity and extension. But there are also other ideal objects in the work – the personality of Hamlet, for example – that cannot be entirely freed from the specific textual determination. And there are also specific and local literary effects that are irreducible to meaning and idealization. The use of rhyme, meter and alliteration would not be capable of translation and formalization. At an even more specific level there would be quite singular effects in any work that are not repeatable or formalizable – the specific material form of this edition or this performance. We might say, then, that Husserl's theory of meaning opens up a spectrum of different levels of formalization and conceptuality. Ideal concepts are true for any possible experience and can be repeated infinitely regardless of context (and here we would include the forms of mathematics and logic). Other meanings are less repeatable. I might experience this particular shade of red in this particular instance. I still perceive an essence, but it is singular. The consequences of Husserl's argument that meaning occurs through a process of formalization that constitutes essences from the finitude of experience have been extended in post-Husserlian phenomenological criticism. Hans-Georg Gadamer argued that literary works have an essential core that is then varied with each activation or performance (1989). Further, this essential core and the original concepts are also reconfigured and added to with each subsequent performance. There is not a strict boundary between the formal concepts of philosophy and the specific meanings of a literary text. In each case meaning is only possible through reactivation of the text. In each reactivation the work is intended or made meaningful according to its specific context or lifeworld. Rather than accept concepts or meanings as static forms that we then apply to experience, Gadamer argued that we needed to see concepts as ongoing syntheses of experience. And experience is not an isolated subjective event. On the contrary, because experience is nothing other than a meaningful relation to the world it already relies on the concepts and forms of language and others. The phenomenological tradition of criticism extended Husserl's location of all meaning and being within experience. Texts do not have meanings that we then uncover; the meaning of a text is nothing other than its continual and possible interpretation. But this does not mean that we have lost all objectivity or ideality of a text; for as Husserl argued, ideal objects are constituted through time and history. The meaning of *Hamlet*, for example, occurs through a series of interpretations but also exceeds any single interpretation. There is now the ideal object of the meaning of Shakespeare's play. This ideal object emerges from the finite fact of the original textual inscription, but the play's meaning exceeds any particular edition, copy or performance and can be reactivated infinitely.

Claire Colebrook

Further reading and works cited

Derrida, J. *Speech and Phenomena, and Other Essays on Husserl's Theory of Signs*. Evanston, IL, 1973.
Fuchs, W. W. *Phenomenology and the Metaphysics of Presence*. The Hague, 1976.
Gadamer, H.-G. *Truth and Method*. New York, 1989.
Heidegger, M. *Being and Time*. Albany, NY, 1996.
Husserl, E. *Cartesian Meditations*. The Hague, 1960.
—. *The Idea of Phenomenology*. Dordrecht, 1964
—. *Phenomenology and the Crisis of Philosophy*. New York, 1965.
—. *The Paris Lectures*. The Hague, 1967.
—. *Philosophie der Arithmetik. Mit ergänzenden Texten*, ed. L. Eley. The Hague, 1970a.
—. *The Crisis of European Sciences and Transcendental Phenomenology*. Evanston, IL 1970b.
—. *Logical Investigations*. London, 1970c.
—. 'Letter to Frege: July 18, 1898', 'The Frege-Husserl Correspondence', *Southwestern Journal of Philosophy*, 5, 1974.
—. *Ideas Pertaining to a Pure Phenomenology and to a Phenomenological Philosophy, First Book: General Introduction to a Pure Phenomenology*. The Hague, 1982.
—. *On the Phenomenology of the Consciousness of Internal Time*. Dordrecht, 1991.
Ingarden, R. *The Cognition of the Literary Work of Art*. Evanston, IL, 1973.
Macann, C. *Four Phenomenological Philosophers*. London, 1993.
Mohanty, J. N. *Husserl and Frege*. Bloomington, IN, 1982.
—. *Phenomenology: Between Essentialism and Transcendental Philosophy*. Evanston, IL, 1997.
Ricoeur, P. *Husserl: An Analysis of his Phenomenology*. Evanston, IL, 1967.
—. *From Text to Action*. Evanston, IL, 1991.
Tragesser, R. S. *Husserl and Realism in Logic and Mathematics*. Cambridge, 1984.

Phenomenology

'Phenomenology' names the most decisive development in philosophical thought since the beginning of the nineteenth century. Its significance is first and foremost philosophical, but in so far as all movements in literary theory and criticism have a basis in philosophical thought, the importance of phenomenology for the understanding of literature cannot be underestimated. This can be seen in the attention that phenomenology pays to aesthetics, but even more so in that phenomenology accomplishes a *linguistic turn*, with all its implications as to a theory of literature. While there are specific strands of literary theory that understand themselves explicitly as belonging to phenomenology – in particular the hermeneutic movement of Hans-Georg Gadamer and Paul Ricoeur – nearly all twentieth-century ideas of literary criticism have been engendered by the phenomenological movement, especially structuralism, poststructuralism and deconstruction.

Indeed, as French phenomenologist Maurice Merleau-Ponty said, phenomenology is either everything or nothing (1964). Consequently, phenomenology seems to be of such breadth and complexity that in the following it is only possible to sketch the basic outlines necessary to understand its importance for modern criticism generally. In the course of this outline phenomenology may appear more homogeneous than it really is.

The first book of phenomenology was written by G. W. F. Hegel under the title *Phenomenology of Spirit*. This book concerns an account of the appearance of human spirit, where 'spirit' designates human reality as a historically and culturally integrated reason sedimenting in human consciousness, in art and in political institutions. But why does this book speak of the 'phenomenon' rather than the 'appearance' of spirit? For the two millennia before Hegel, philosophers have generally tried to make the world intelligible by distinguishing appearances from that which appears in them. For example, when Immanuel Kant separated the transcendental form of subjectivity from the actual existence of any one human being then we see the latter as an appearance of the former. Without such a separation we would have to presuppose that the actually existing human being determines the idea of the human being as such; this is what philosophers call 'psychologism' and regard as one of the worst forms of relativism. In other words, philosophers have always distinguished appearance from the absolute that appears in it and which consequently makes appearances intelligible and the world inhabitable. The 'absolute', then, stands for a reality absolutely independent from any mediation.

From this perspective it might be said that phenomenology is the philosophy that realizes the moment at which, as Friedrich Nietzsche says, the true world, as opposed to the world of appearances, has become a myth. An appearance, on the one hand, is something through which something else appears. A phenomenon, on the other hand, and according to its original Greek meaning, is something that shines through and by itself. Hegel expresses this in his book in the form of a relatively inconspicuous sentence, when he writes that 'the supersensible is appearance *qua* appearance' (1977, 89). What Hegel means is that there is nothing which would give meaning to the world without itself being a part of it. Rather, the world is understood as the temporal constitution of its own meaning – it gives rise to the absolute from within itself. In this respect phenomenology is the movement of the overcoming of metaphysics and the realization that, again in Nietzsche's words, 'with the real world we have also done away with the apparent one' (1998, 20).

What are the consequences of such a thinking? *First*, that all truth becomes historical in so far as essences constitute themselves throughout history. This is to say that both the development of philosophical thought and human sensibility itself are in an essential sense historical. *Second*, phenomenology turns against 'theory' understood as the idea of a thinking independent from what it thinks about; and it consequently turns against representation, that is to say against the idea of truth as a thought corresponding to a piece of reality. *Third*, phenomenology becomes the main opponent of any objectivism and hence an essential critique of the rationalism of the Enlightenment. *Fourth*, phenomenology relinquishes the instrumental idea of thinking: in so far as thinking does not represent a lever that can be applied to the world from the outside, the different modes of thinking are themselves understood as an integral part of that reality. From here phenomenology is led to the concept of *description*. *Fifthly*, if thought and its activity are real elements of the world rather than simple means to represent the world, then language gains a special importance in terms not only of understanding the world, but much more essentially in terms of any actual mode of inhabiting the world. If words can no longer be understood as the mere appearance of an ideal meaning, then our whole conception of the world as grasped through language is affected. As Michel Foucault put this, metaphysics is when one claims that there is first of all a thought and then its expression in language. Yet language, to remain with our terminology, is not the appearance of a thought but its phenomenon; in other words, anti-metaphysics or phenomenology is when one claims that there is first of all language and then, by way of its mediation, the constitution of meaning. Hegel expresses this insight by arguing that language is more truthful than our opinions and conscious intentions. In it we directly contradict what we mean to say. Martin Heidegger formulates this strange insight in its clearest form when he says that 'we do not say what we see, but rather the reverse, we see what *one says* about the matter' (1985, 56). From here one can see that phenomenology, in as much as it makes even the sensibility of the human being subject to the historical codification of language, radicalizes the question of history by making it the sole content of philosophy.

The implications of this for an understanding of literature are not to be underestimated, in so far as philosophical texts themselves are no longer seen as instantiating an ideal meaning, but rather are grasped from out of their historical development, so that we find here the origin of the 'death of the author' as that instance that determines the meaning of the literary work. The literary or philosophical text becomes always, in every age, anew. Its origin has to be sought in history rather than in a 'real' historical writer.

Yet, while these points appear straightforward, they harbour a wealth of contradictions: the stress placed on history seems to contradict that placed on description; the opposition to any objectivist philosophy seems to disagree with its apparent positivism; the claim that the world is just what it is conflicts with the determination of being through becoming, that is with the phenomenological theme of constitution; the turn towards 'the things themselves' stands opposed to the claim that the world is first of all given by language.

And even if we solved these problems, we would still have to confront all the arguments that have led philosophy for the best part of 2,400 years to claim that there has to be something independent from this world of experience in order to explain 'the fact of knowledge', that is to say, the meaningfulness of the world.

But phenomenology does not submit easily to criticisms regarding the incoherence of its concepts. It has to a certain extent left the realm of the principle of non-contradiction behind, not only in as much as Hegel understands contradiction as the primal mover of history, but also in that logical contradiction cannot 'overrule' the perceived world. As Merleau-Ponty points out, contradiction would only be permissible as an argument against phenomenology 'if we could put a system of eternal truths in the place of the perceived world, freed from its contradictions' (Merleau-Ponty 1964).

Phenomenology hence moves between metaphysics and positivism, between idealism and realism, between the modern natural sciences and the humanities, between logic and psychologism, between linguistics and relativism, threatened by each of them and yet without coinciding with any. It is thereby especially concerned with its relation to the modern natural sciences, in so far as these have attempted during the nineteenth and twentieth centuries to dominate the discourse of science generally.

One way to get this problem into focus is by contrasting the 'first beginning' of phenomenology in Hegel and Nietzsche, with its 'real' beginning as a discipline and distinctive strand of philosophy in the work of Edmund Husserl. Husserl is often called the 'father' of phenomenology; yet we never understand a child as a mere expression of its father. As with every child, many of its features were decided long before its father was even born, while it, once born, sets out on its own way.

Having described the development of phenomenology from Hegel onwards, it might come as a surprise that Husserl is led to it from the perspective of the question of pure mathematics and hence from a stance that determines phenomenological investigation in complete abstraction not only from the history of philosophical thought, but from all historical reflection. Husserl understands phenomenology first and foremost as a defence against psychologism and relativism as they arose at the end of the nineteenth century. Yet the problem pursued in his early work is the same as that already described, namely the problem of conceiving an *a priori* that determines all empirical understanding of the actual world, without locating such an idea in a transcendent realm. On the ground of this question he tries to found the possibility of an absolute science or a *mathesis universalis*, which is to say a universally valid teaching, under the title of *Transcendental Phenomenology*.

What is phenomenology? As we said, it is an understanding of the world that does not separate the subjective experience of the world from the experienced objects themselves. How can one experience the world directly, without taking this experience as a mere appearance of the 'real things' behind our experience? Husserl's answer is quite straightforward and similar to Descartes's, in that he refers us to the immediate nature of conscious experience. When we see a door, for example, we neither experience a difference between the actual door and its image that our eyes have let through into our consciousness, nor do we regard this image in our head while suffering from an uncertainty concerning the 'real' door through which we wish to pass. Our experience does not at all suffer from a duality of subject and object, but is rather characterized by a unity of seeing and the seen. This is not to say that I confuse myself with the door, but that the impression of immediacy in my experience arises from a correlation between my seeing and the thing seen at any one moment. In so far as what we mean when we speak of 'seeing' and 'the seen' are first of all processes 'in' consciousness, Husserl calls this correlation by its Greek name, that of *noesis* (the act of thinking) and *noema* (the thing thought). The idea of immediacy breaks up when we think about this correlation: maybe we would have confused ourselves with the door, if it was not the case that we 'see' or intuit a difference between the immediate presence of a thing, on the one hand, and its essence, on the other.

This thought allows Husserl to depart from the naive restriction of thinking to the representation of present ideas, to include the greater part of the life of the human soul: objects that are not given to sight, like music or pain, for example; emotions, like fearing or loving; other conscious activities, like remembering, striving, hoping, etc. Husserl's terminology permits us to consider the world of our experiences in its immanent unity, thereby avoiding the question of how the subject could ever reach out from its inner experience towards a world understood in opposition to it. Phenomenology thus undercuts the 'mind–body problem' which had stifled modern philosophy since Descartes.

Husserl originally stands, alone among the 'great' phenomenologists, on the side of a rationalistic intuition identifying the question of conscious knowing with the constitution of the world. Philosophical thought, as he says, is fully determined through its epistemo-logical position, that is to say, philosophy *is* the theory of knowledge (1973). Husserl pursues, in the best Kantian tradition, the attempt to constitute the world according to a theory of judgement as he had opened it up in his first major work, the *Logical Investigations* (1900). We tend to identify the concept of science with the methodology of the modern natural sciences, but to speak of a rigorous science of phenomenology does not mean that the phenomenologist would begin to experiment with objects and record results, nor that her aim consisted in the manipulation of objects. The idea of science derives from Greek antiquity and has always been an integral part of philosophy. Its idea concerns a systematic questioning and ascertaining of knowledge generally. The modern natural sciences are then only one idea of how such a securing of knowledge is possible. Phenomenology has to remain quite independent from these regional ontologies – that is, from sciences that have a specific subject area and that constitute their methods accordingly, so that these methods depend on a prior unreflected presupposition regarding the nature of the objects to be investigated – in so far as it regards experience by bracketing off any preconceptions about it. That is to say, it undercuts the naive convictions of the natural sciences, sedimented in what Husserl calls the natural attitude or common sense. Phenomenology cannot become a function of the natural sciences as they have determined our worldview through their unrivalled success, rather it ultimately pushes for a radically new foundation of these sciences.

Husserl's investigations are, then, more and more drawn to history and language and, fulfilling their claim to a return to the things themselves, he finally arrives at the conception of the lifeworld as opposed to the objectified world of the natural attitude. A short look at *The Vienna Lecture* (1935) will show that Husserl developed the idea of phenomenology in a direction that, finally, fits comfortably into the lineage turning from Hegel and Nietzsche to the later phenomenological strands of the twentieth century.

The starting point of *The Vienna Lecture* is the acknowledgement that Europe, and that is to say the history of philosophy, is in crisis. What might surprise us today is that, in 1935, during a time pushing towards the Second World War, and a time that forced Husserl, who was Jewish, to flee his home, his analysis of this crisis nonetheless centres on the insight that Europe suffers from a misguided rationalism which first appeared with the Enlightenment. In this lecture he describes phenomenology as always having been concerned with the fight against objectivism and he identifies German idealism, including Hegel, as the philosophical force that had first taken up this struggle. The phenomenological reduction, known as the *epoche*, thus becomes not only an epistemological tool for ascertaining the foundations of objective knowledge, but a method by which Husserl proposes to turn against scientism. Phenomenology cannot be a dependent discipline grounding the validity of the natural sciences: 'it is a mistake for the humanistic disciplines to struggle with the natural sciences for equal rights. As soon as they concede to the latter their objectivity as self-sufficiency, they themselves fall prey to objectivism' (1970, 297). In contrast, transcendental phenomenology sets out to ground the natural sciences, but so that in that process they will change beyond recognition. 'There are only two escapes from the crisis of European existence: the downfall of Europe in its estrangement from its own rational sense of life, its fall into hostility toward the spirit and into barbarity; or the rebirth of Europe from the spirit of philosophy through a heroism of reason that overcomes naturalism once and for all' (299).

Today this sense of a crisis seems to have disappeared and in so far as it was described as a crisis coming from the depths of European history, such a swift dissipation might convey the idea that it never was real. And in fact, what Husserl called a misguided rationalism is often represented by us as a short period of irrationalism, following the destruction of which Europe has re-established the link to its Enlightenment tradition. Taking another look at the twentieth century, this history might appear in a different light. Despite certain developments in the sciences, which have born out the claims of phenomenology, in terms of the 'hostility towards spirit' we have advanced relentlessly. By far the clearest characterization of our age stems from a letter that Martin Heidegger wrote in 1967 to a friend:

> In the 'sciences' today reigns a progressively positive stance towards cybernetics and its possibilities. In 'philosophy' there is 'logical positivism', which by means of its theory of language pushes itself more and more to the fore. All these tendencies have to be countered with a principled re-consideration – although we cannot hope for any short term success. Everywhere there will be 'cells' of resistance, formed against the impetuous power of technology. These cells will inconspicuously keep thinking awake, and they will thus prepare the reversal, for which 'man' will cry, in a day yet to come, when the general devastation will have become insupportable. (Heidegger 1987, 352)

Martin Heidegger's first major work *Being and Time* undertakes to show that the epistemological understanding of the world as constituted by positive, affirmative judgements, that is the identification of truth and knowledge, derives from a practical understanding of our relation to things. He argues that our general idea of action as preceded and motivated by rational deliberation is quite mistaken. Rather we think about something in a theoretical mode only once it has lost its integration within the world of action. Thus we use, for example, a hammer without any reflection up to that moment when its handle breaks and our intentions are 'broken' with it. In this way all theoretical engagement in the world is considered a second order phenomenon. This point might appear rather obvious, so that one might wonder what Heidegger is up to. The admirable analytic of the existential modes of our 'Being-in-the-World' can be misunderstood as a positive philosophical doctrine to a degree that even empiricists have begun to like that work, if it were not for its strange elaboration on 'the question of Being'. This 'question of Being' is, first of all, another attempt at understanding the differentiation between the actual thing in front of me and that which Husserl called an essence. It is indeed only through a consideration of this question that the reader comes to realize that the whole book is, as Heidegger says himself, metaphysical, attempting to show that metaphysics has always understood the idea of Being from out of the everyday concerns with beings. We might even say that metaphysics has kept too close to objects – so that they eventually became blurred. Thus arose the idea that it was too abstract, so that to correct it one consequently attempted to tighten one's grip on reality. In this sense metaphysics concerns the abolition of *action at a distance* in favour of a mechanistic understanding of the world. The point this book demonstrates is that the history of metaphysics ends quite logically with its realization in the objectivism of technology, while phenomenology attempts to understand the difference between Being as such and the being of beings, hence suspending the identification of truth and knowledge. The task of phenomenology, according to Heidegger, is then the *Verwindung* – an overcoming in the sense of mourning – of metaphysics. While many commentators have insisted that Heidegger never tried to criticize objectivism in this early work, but rather tries to ground the traditional notion of truth as the adequation of thought and reality, one only needs to think of the aim of phenomenology to return to 'the things themselves'. In other words, phenomenology cannot restrict itself to founding a new philosophy or to ascertaining the methodological structure of the natural sciences, nor can it afford to indulge in the general quibble about positions and worldviews, which are often taken for the task of philosophers. It does not even take a stance for or against technology or the natural sciences, but rather attempts to respond to the needs of a historical situation.

Phenomenology is then not only a historical science, but also places itself as a historical movement, in so far as it is determined by the attempt to find an answer to the alienation effected by a 'misguided rationalism'. This is again clear already in its 'battle-cry' *back to the things themselves*, in so far as it is only possible to go 'back' to these 'things' in as much as one departs from a prior alienation. Phenomenology is, accordingly, thinking in the 'age of complete meaninglessness', as Heidegger calls our time in the opening pages of his seminal lectures on *Nietzsche* (1961).

It sounds more and more as if phenomenology was a rather pessimistic philosophy. It criticizes our age in the most extreme ways while itself being limited to description. But does phenomenology really only describe what has happened after the fact? Already for Hegel the human being can sustain its spiritual existence only in so far as it grasps its history by way of this philosophical mode of description. As Merleau-Ponty says, left to itself perception is ignorant of its own accomplishments; we are hence not only describing what has happened, i.e. the world understood as fact, rather philosophy concerns itself with that which precedes facts and which thus somehow is involved in their constitution.

One of the major questions after Husserl thus becomes the question of the ontic-ontological difference, i.e. of the relation between the *a priori* and the empirical. Both Husserl and the early Heidegger, in unison with most traditional philosophy and thus the natural sciences as well, refuse to allow any possibility that experience could recoil on the transcendental or ontological level. 'From matters of fact nothing ever follows but matters of fact' as Husserl says in *Ideas I* (1982, 17). As we have seen, Husserl concludes from this point the necessity of a methodological revision of the sciences. Later on, in Heidegger and in Merleau-Ponty, this question turns into the much more radical formulation of a correlation between our experience and its transcendental ground. When Heidegger speaks about the 'co-origin of word and thing' as the basis of a turn within the ontic-ontological difference – away from the formulation of the two distinct levels and the consequent problem of their interaction towards the thought of the difference itself – and when Merleau-Ponty formulates the 'primacy of perception' as a nascent logos, phenomenology turns finally to the abolition of the appearing world, in the sense outlined by Nietzsche. In other words, phenomenology sets out to come to terms with metaphysics by 'dropping' transcendental philosophy. This task Heidegger prepares in the thought of a 'history of Being', in so far as it breaks with the metaphysical understanding of Being as universal and hence eternal. The very idea of eternal truths, as he writes in *Being and Time*, is the last remnant of Christian theology in philosophy (1962, 272). This possibility of experience recoiling onto the *a priori*, we have already seen – if unexpectedly – in the case of metaphysics itself as a determination of Being according to our everyday concern with beings.

It is for this reason that phenomenology is not a new empiricism. To talk about such a recoiling of experience onto the *a priori* seems to imply that reason is determined by sense-perception, while in actual fact we are looking initially at an interaction which finally gives rise to an understanding of an expressed immanence. Merleau-Ponty finds a first approach to such an understanding in the form of Gestalt psychology, which realizes a unity of objective and introspective psychology, in that it avoids the artificial separation of a spiritual inside from a mechanistic outside of the mind. The task of the phenomenologist is then to draw the philosophical conclusions from such an approach. Following Heidegger's existential analytic of *Dasein* – his interpretation of the human being as neither determined by its *ratio* nor by its animal being, but rather in its *being-there* – Ludwig Binswanger similarly develops *Daseinsanalyse* as a novel approach in psychoanalysis that attempts to escape the latter's naturalist assumptions.

In all the concreteness of such a return to the 'perceived world', the radicality with which phenomenology assails our common understanding makes the whole enterprise appear highly paradoxical. And while philosophy has from its inception been understood as paradoxical, we often succumb to common-sense arguments. It is no wonder, then, that in a discussion following Merleau-Ponty's paper on *The Primacy of Perception*, a monsieur Bréhier summarizes his impression of phenomenology by saying that 'I see your ideas as being better expressed in literature and in painting than in philosophy. Your philosophy results in a novel' (Merleau-Ponty 1964, 30).

This criticism, half absurd and half true, leads us to one of the most beautiful texts of the phenomenological tradition – Merleau-Ponty's *Eye and Mind*. In this text Merleau-Ponty attempts to show the way in which our experience of seeing, which is exemplified in the painter's relation to the visible world, structures our general understanding of the world. Departing from an analysis of the impact of the discovery of perspective in Renaissance painting on the development of Descartes's philosophy, he argues that a closer study of painting would lead to another philosophy. Already in *The Phenomenology of Perception* (1945), Merleau-Ponty had linked the question of the body to the question of language itself and we have seen that language and sense-experience are essentially linked. Here Merleau-Ponty carries these insights further to develop the thought of the incarnation of vision in speech, which tries to understand the language of phenomena, arising from the cross-over of the intending body and the flesh of the world. It is in this respect that Merleau-Ponty contrasts the experience of painting with the ideology of cybernetics.

The phenomenologist does not describe language as does a linguist, who investigates language in so far as it is an object of theoretical inquiry. Rather, the phenomenologist realizes that language lies at the root of any questioning. Consequently, Heidegger demands an end to all 'philosophy of language', in so far as such a philosophy, by raising linguistics to the level of philosophy, unwittingly introduces an essentially flawed idea of language.

The discussion of language as predetermining sense-experience had, initially, led Heidegger to the formulation of the hermeneutic circle, that is, to the realization of the circular structure of understanding. This is conceived as follows: the natural attitude proposes that there is first the positive presence of a state of affairs, which the human being then attempts to understand in order to master the world. Once understood, this state of affairs is represented by positive affirmative judgements. The phenomenologist, on the other hand, recognizes that there is always the need for an *a priori* in order to make an actual understanding possible. Yet, this *a priori* is not simply conceived as a universal form determining the way in which the intellect deals with experience. Rather it has to have a 'content' as well, which is to say that I already need to know what I want to find out. Thus the acquisition of knowledge appears impossible. Unless, that is, what one knows about the thing beforehand is quite wrong, in other words is a prejudice. In that sense hermeneutics – that is, the science of interpretation – claims that one has to have an (erroneous) understanding of a thing in order to be able to get to know it. But this is also to say that this path, starting out from error, cannot be teleologically oriented towards any absolute truth. For that very reason the history of Being is characterized by Heidegger as the 'errancy' of the human being.

These ideas show that it is not far from the early Heidegger to the later one, who refers, in *On the Way to Language*, to the poet Stefan George: 'where word breaks off no thing may be' (1982, 141). In the same way as the painter, for Merleau-Ponty, attains the unity of seeing and seen, so the poet, for Heidegger, finally gets in touch with the common origin of word and thing. From here it follows that language does not consist of an ideal unity of empty words endowed with ideal significations. Rather language accrues as a significance of an originary being-in-the-world. To clarify this point, it should by now have become evident that it is impossible to understand the development of Heidegger's reflection on language by making a distinction between 'later Heidegger's questionable view that language *makes possible* significance' and a 'more plausible view defended in *Being and Time*', namely 'that all significance is sayable' (Dreyfus 1991, 354), in so far as Heidegger is, from the early 1920s on, on the way to the former claim, while what is here called the 'more plausible view' describes an intellectualism that Heidegger never defended, certainly not in *Being and Time*.

Hermeneutic theory, especially in the work of Gadamer and Ricoeur, develops from the idea of the ontological essence of language. The idea of hermeneutics derives originally from the interpretation of the scriptures; hermeneutic theory applies this idea of interpretation to literature and life. Like most of twentieth-century philosophy it draws its inspiration from Hegel, Husserl and Heidegger. According to this theory, language is at home in literature and especially poetry. These do not describe particular functions of language, rather they are the natural ground in which language sustains its life. This living language can then be made to signify in the everyday situations of determinate judgement. In relation to the metaphysical idea of language this is quite contradictory. On the basis of metaphysics one would have expected that, first and foremost, language exists in the form of determinate judgements like 'this is a yellow stone' or 'now it rains' before one could use these same sentences in literary works. But already the fact that art stands at the beginning of all civilization grants a hint as to its primordial nature. Likewise Kant had written in his

Critique of Judgement (1790), that aesthetic judgements precede determinate judgements, but here, in the claim of hermeneutics, it is furthermore argued that we can only speak and communicate due to the poetic life of language in poetry and literature.

It is clear, then, that we cannot regard language as originally a means of communication. That is to say, that we cannot understand literature as a means by which an author attempts to 'communicate' with us. In literature, more so than in the everyday use of language, language speaks. In literature, then, language exists as the house of Being, in so far as it is only through language that there can be things and hence a world for us. When Heidegger said, in *Being and Time*, that there is Being only as long as there are human beings, then that is not so much because these humans can summon Being by way of their language; instead the human being is summoned by language to a world. Phenomenology thus counters the modern misinterpretation of Aristotle's determination of the human being as the animal that 'has' language. In so far as this is an essential definition, it cannot signify an animal that first exists and then, as well, 'has' the ability to speak. Instead it is a being that *is* only in so far as in speaking it sustains its bond with language. It then seems that it would be more correct to say that language has or speaks us. From this insight the whole question of subjectivity becomes questionable, as in the order of language the other always precedes me in my being. It is from this perspective that Heidegger turns against the anthropological account of language, which makes of it the symbol of the human being.

On account of this thinking of language we might now understand Sartre's answer to the question *What is Literature?* Sartre speaks, in a text with this title, of *engaged literature* which has often been understood as a version of literature subordinated to ideological ends. But Sartre says 'engaged literature'. In other words, it is literature itself that is engaged, rather than an author, whose idea it might be to sway our moods with beautiful words. This is not to say that writing is not an action and that the writer is not 'engaged' in her writing, but not only does Sartre often use accentuation marks when speaking of an 'engaged' writer, more importantly, the writer can only be engaged when being carried by the essence of literature itself. This engagement of literature cannot even be broken by the author. Sartre claims, accordingly, that it is impossible to write an anti-Semitic novel (1967, 46). The literary work is written by an author but its creation is not accomplished before it is read by its readers. The work thus appeals to the reader, that is it issues an appeal, and it can only appeal to the reader as a human being partaking in the revelation of the world. Yet in so far as author and reader are not 'working together' at it – that is, in so far as this creation does not leap over their separation by way of a prior and conscious intention – the work is created due to the engagement of literary language with the freedom of the human being. That is to say, it becomes impossible to make a novel demand that one should negate the freedom of other human beings, in so far as language is the original bond to these others. Certainly, people can sit down and write novels with the firm intent to stir racial hostility, and somebody who takes up such a book might solely be interested in finding a like-minded writer to reconfirm his prejudice and hatred. But in that case such a reader is reading a pamphlet written in pseudo-literary form. As soon as this reader actually reads such a book and partakes in the revealing of language, the intent breaks itself and the novel effects the opposite of what it was conceived for, namely an insight into the inhumanity of racism and the ethical prevalence of the other. To the act of writing one can then apply Sartre's definition of freedom, according to which real freedom does not consist in being able to do whatever one wishes, but in being able to wish what one can do.

Phenomenologists have, in their attempt to return to the things themselves, rediscovered the world. That is to say they have enabled philosophy to deal with the whole of our life, without having to ostracize our emotional and spiritual life (Husserl); they have introduced a thinking of our Being-in-the-world on account of a thinking of Being (Heidegger); they have uncovered the reality of the other human being (Sartre) and the primordial nature of ethics (Lévinas); they have reintroduced that recalcitrant being, the body, into philosophical thought (Merleau-Ponty); and they have liberated literature from its enslavement to representation (Ingarden, Blanchot).

Ullrich Michael Haase

Further reading and works cited

Bernasconi, R. *The Question of Language in Heidegger's History of Being*. Atlantic Highlands, NJ, 1985.

Bernet, R. et al. *An Introduction to Husserlian Phänomenologie*. Evanston, IL, 1993.

Dreyfus, H. *Being-in-the-World – A Commentary on Heidegger's Being and Time*. Cambridge, MA, 1991.

Embree, L. et al. *Encyclopedia of Phenomenology*. Dordrecht, 1997.

Gadamer, H.-G. *Truth and Method*. London, 1975.

Hegel, G. W. F. *Phenomenology of Spirit*. Oxford, 1977.

Heidegger, M. *Being and Time*. Oxford, 1962.

—. *Poetry, Language, Thought*. New York, 1971.

—. *Nietzsche*. San Francisco, 1979.

—. *On the Way to Language*. New York, 1982.

—. *History of the Concept of Time*. Bloomington, IN, 1985.

—. *Zollikoner Seminare*. Frankfurt, 1987.

Husserl, E. *Cartesian Meditations*. The Hague, 1960.

—. *The Idea of Phenomenology*. The Hague, 1973.

—. *Ideas Pertaining to a Pure Phenomenology and to a Phenomenological Philosophie*, vol. I. The Hague, 1982.

—. *The Crisis of European Sciences and Transcendental Phenomenology: An Introduction to Phenomenological Philosophy*. Evanston, IL, 1987.

Ingarden, R. *The Cognition of the Literary Work of Art*. Evanston, IL, 1973.

Jauss, H. R. *Aesthetic Experience and Literary Hermeneutics*. Minneapolis, MN, 1982.

Lyotard, J.-F. *Phenomenology*. New York, 1991.

Merleau-Ponty, M. *Phénoménologie de la perception*. Paris, 1945.

—. *The Primacy of Perception and other Essays*. Evanston, IL, 1964.

Nietzsche, F. *Twilight of the Idols*. Oxford, 1998.

Ricoeur, P. *The Conflict of Interpretations*. Evanston, IL, 1974.

—. *The Rule of Metaphor*. Toronto, 1977.

Sallis, J. *Delimitations*. Bloomington, IN, 1986.

Sartre, J.-P. *What is Literature?* London, 1967.

—. *Being and Nothingness*. London, 1969.

Gaston Bachelard (1884–1962) and Georges Canguilhem (1904–1995): Epistemology in France

In the English-speaking world the name Gaston Bachelard is associated with an excavation of the phenomenology of the poetic imagination. In texts such as *The Poetics of Space*, *Water and Dreams*, *The Psychoanalysis of Fire* and *The Poetics of Reverie*, Bachelard has established a reputation for a dissection of the poetic imagination that he defines in terms of its distance from the non-phenomenological techniques of modern science (Bachelard 1994, 156). However, in France Bachelard's reputation lies primarily in the field of the history and philosophy of science, and the particular epistemological revolution he inaugurates and which counts among its heirs, such figures as Georges Canguilhem and Michel Foucault. Author of over a dozen substantial works in this latter field, the status of Bachelard's writing and its significance for debates over epistemology in twentieth-century France cannot be overstated.

The coexistence of these different styles of works in the collected oeuvre of Bachelard is remarkable because the material dealt with in the works on the poetic imagination is described in Bachelard's epistemological works as part of the complement of epistemo-logical obstacles that hamper the development of science. It is one of the tasks of the epistemologist to conduct a 'psychoanalysis' of the scientific mind with the aim of identifying and clearing the sedimentations of pre-scientific conceptualizations. The status of phenomenology in each genre of his work is instructive here: for the imagination the relation to the 'given', as for instance the psychic state elicited by an image that conveys intimacy, is of an entirely different order to that of the status of the 'given' in modern science, which is defined as the procedures and techniques under which the 'immediate' must give way to the 'constructed' (Bachelard 1968, 122–3). Rather than a phenomen-ology, science is a 'phenomeno-technics'. For natural observation and the objects which supply it contemporary science substitutes phenomena that are in a radical sense constructs of the equipment and procedures of scientific practice. Scientific concepts, in turn, only win their scientific status if they are able to be realized in their technicality (Bachelard 1938, 61).

This technical character of contemporary science supports Bachelard's insistence on a double differentiation of science from common sense, which gauges truth in terms of the immediacy of sensations (Canguilhem 1979, 179), and from the history and epistemology of science as it has conventionally been practised. Against both forms of understanding which transport to science a false concept of historical continuity, Bachelard argues for the discontinuous nature of contemporary scientific development (Bachelard 1953, 211). The implications for the philosophy of science of the break contemporary science represents with other forms of understanding, as well as the accelerated time of contemporary science in which internal epistemological breaks are the norm, are significant. It is, Bachelard argues, only at the level of particular examples that the philosophy of science can give general lessons (Bachelard 1953, 223). And Bachelard's polemic against philosophy is as a consequence directed to the attachment of philosophy to metaphysical precepts. This attachment obscures the pertinent characteristics of modern science and determines traditional philosophy as part of the armoury of obstacles with which science contends. In this essay we will examine the nature of the relationship between Bachelard's formulation of a historically situated but normative epistemology and the self-consciously revolutionary character of the contemporary hard sciences before turning to examine Canguilhem's modifications of Bachelard's epistemology for his own work in the life sciences.

Twentieth-century physics awards priority to arithmetic over geometry and demotes thereby the spatial measurement assumed by pre-scientific experience. This transformed procedure for scientific method also entails a transformation of the methods of philosophical thought. The latter needs to follow the actual procedures through which the sciences attain knowledge. As a first measure, the dependence of philosophy on scientific development requires discarding the perspectives of idealism and realism: the former for its basis in the faculties of an epistemological subject and the latter for its presumption of a unified texture of reality. These perspectives are irrelevant in the face of the mathematicization of the natural sciences. Indeed it is the primacy of mathematicization which underpins Bachelard's account of the constructions by which contemporary science departs from pre-scientific intuitions and the precepts of traditional metaphysics (Privitera 1995, 8).

Against the traditional philosophical approaches to science that had prevailed in the French university system, Bachelard develops a new doctrine of applied analysis for the historical development of the truth-producing practices of the sciences. Dispensing with the ascription to science of a static universalism, Bachelard's approach stresses the necessary mobility of the sciences, which he views as determinate practices in need of regional epistemologies. Canguilhem, along with Foucault and Bourdieu, follow Bachelard in ascribing a privileged status to science: for each figure, the truths of science are located in the contemporary practices of science and thus considered in terms of their historical provisionality. The key for this new style of epistemology, a style scripted by Bachelard as a philosophy of the 'new scientific mind', is that the qualification of scientific truths as historical is not tantamount to a tolerance for relativism.

Bachelard's method for the new history of the sciences is an applied rationalism whose key features are the constructed nature of the scientific object, the development of science by epistemological breaks and the role of the epistemologist as the dialectician of scientific concepts. The regional areas in which Bachelard develops this applied rationalism are those of the hard sciences.

For Bachelard, reason is transformed by the different processes of regional epistemologies. A given knowledge at a given point in its history covers the processes within which experiments are constructed, previous scientific notions corrected and the formulation of standards of proof undertaken. Even within the disciplines of physics and chemistry different forms of reasoning apply. These differences make any single philosophy inappropriate for any given determinate science and discount the fallacious generic category of the sciences, disclosing the need for a dispersed philosophy of regional sciences. As philosophy is apprised of the need to follow the contemporary development of science, so too reason is not, as it is in Kant, a regulative faculty whose ideas give an external horizon towards which science develops. Rather, reason is formed within the specific practices of determinate scientific knowledges and the normative values that regulate these knowledges are those of their current scientific practice.

Bachelard's epistemology defends itself against the charge of historical relativism through a conception of the development of science by the dialecticization of existing scientific concepts. This process develops over two stages: first, epistemological errors are identified by the emergent scientificity so that a rectified science with an enlarged basis can proceed (Bachelard 1968, 24). The conception of history that underpins this exercise cautions against relativism not just in the obsolete status of the prescientific past but in the sanctioned status of this past as the material for dialecticized concepts through which a particular science is expanded. Despite Bachelard's emphasis on the historical discontinuity under which a determinate present may re-evaluate the past, the reconstructive developmental logic under which science develops attests to the strong normative dimension of his philosophy of science.

In *Le nouvel esprit scientifique* Bachelard argues that the rational experimental methods of contemporary science produce the phenomena they study. Hence it is impossible to separate the methods of science from their theoretical fabric: the establishment of determinate scientific facts is the work of the application of a coherent technique (Bachelard 1934, 176). Scientific method is 'rational' as its very object exists in light of its theoretical justification. A phenomenon such as a transuranian element is not an empirical given but a realization of a theoretically based technique that organizes and structures materials according to a preconceived plan (Tiles 1984, 139–40). It is this aspect of contemporary science that Bachelard's epistemology reflects in his view that it is in the practice of science that its objects and its own norms are produced. Further it is because scientific activity carries its own changing criterion for its existence that epistemology as the study of science deals with a historical process (Lecourt 1975, 26).

In modern science, reality becomes a function of the theoretical technique under which it is realized. And the scientific validity of a theory consequently comes to depend on its realization within its sphere of application. This means both that the norms of scientific practice derive from their terrain of application and that any abstraction of scientific theory from this context of practice extracts science from addressing the problems that make it at all meaningful. Correlatively, the constitution of new axiomatic systems are produced not on an unsubstantiated beginning but via the questions of pre-existing theories with which they effect a structural break or rupture. The primacy of experimental practice and the absence of any efficacious metatheory makes discontinuity a feature of the progress of science as each constitution of a new scientific region always implies an epistemological break (Privitera 1995, 14).

The dialectic that is one of the agents of this break does not entail a reduction of the pre-existing scientific theory to falsehood. Instead of a simple rejection of its predecessor the new scientificity places it in a perspective that allows for the enlargement of the basis of scientific inquiry (Bachelard 1968, 115). For instance, wave theory is a historical rupture in the evolution of modern science. Its synthesis of Newtonian and Frenellian thought determines its status as a historical synthesis, i.e. a synthesis built on past science whose own form depends on an epistemological act (Canguilhem 1979, 182). The norm of rectification that organizes the concept of the epistemological rupture in Bachelard conceives of negation as what supports a new mode of calculation rather than a link between contemporary science and the primordial concepts that it 'deforms' (Canguilhem 1979, 186). As contemporary science is a technical and theoretical construct the dialectical progress of science consists in the transformation of the very principles of existing knowledges (Bachelard 1953, 224). This perpetual process of transformation is also an aspect of the culture of contemporary scientific psychology in which anxiety and doubt are necessary companions of discovery. The philosophy of scientific knowledge, correlatively, is an 'open' one which works on the unknown and seeks in reality 'that which contradicts anterior knowledge' (Bachelard 1968, 9).

The dialectic of science includes the moment of rupture from what is now classed as a pre-existing ideology (obsolete history) and the reorganization of the emergent scientificity along with the determinate past form of science (sanctioned history) that is part of the reorganization. This dialectical history is recurrent because the history of the sciences is continually evaluated from the normative laws of contemporary scientific practices (Canguilhem 1979, 182). It is here that the specific tasks of the new philosophy of science emerge. Epistemology is a historical exercise because its object is the specific history of the discipline it examines. But it is also critical as it aims to separate scientific practice from the ideologies that are obstacles to its progress. As the 'defeat of irrationalism' and 'the most irreversible of all histories', the recurrent history of science is a history that is *able* to be recurrently judged and valued (Bachelard 1951, 27). It is this history, applied by Bachelard to the hard sciences of chemistry and mathematical physics, that Canguilhem will take up in the sciences of life.

It is risky to want to present in the form of general principles either Canguilhem's epistemology or his practice of writing the history of science. Such an enterprise would come across many formidable obstacles. His awareness of the specificity of the object of various sciences, whose operational concepts follow their own specific historical rhythms, turns him away from wanting to frame a general epistemology (Canguilhem 1979, 19). This epistemological prudence is further reinforced by the fact that his chosen area is the philosophy and history of the life sciences whose rigor cannot be modelled in mathematics, which also means that the process of formation and rational purification of their concepts cannot be reduced to logical developments of theories. Canguilhem warns against 'the use of hindsight to bring out the latent implications of a theory [that] risks making history seem straightforward and linear when in reality it was far more complex' (Canguilhem 1988, 105). Still less does he think that the heuristic principles of history of the sciences can be applied indiscriminately. This is true even of the principle of epistemological recursion or that of discontinuity. The former was originally developed for the study of mathematical physics and nuclear chemistry, and while it may be 'broadened' (but not 'generalized') to other 'areas of the history of science', it cannot be so 'without a good deal of reflection about the specific nature of the area to be studied' (Canguilhem 1988, 14). As for the epistemology of discontinuity, it 'is appropriate to a period of accelerated change in science' whereas the 'epistemology of continuity has a natural affinity with periods in which knowledge is just awakening' (Canguilhem 1988, 16). The complex process of scientific progress is underlined by the fact that success in one science does not necessarily cause or even entail progress in another; at times it may actually hinder it: 'the success of medical microbiology delayed the inception of a biochemistry of microbes' (Canguilhem 1988,

115). History can belie the scientific claims of a theory, just as, inversely, it may bestow the dignity of science on a theory that was regarded as ideology by many in its inception time. This is what happened, according to Canguilhem, to Darwin's theory of natural selection which had to wait for population genetics to receive experimental proof and hence properly scientific credentials (Canguilhem 1988, 104–6).

Having made these rather brief cautionary remarks, we must nonetheless take due note of the two fundamental thematics which give orientation to his understanding of the history of science and of the significance of (scientific) knowledge. With regard to the former, we may put forth the idea that for Canguilhem, as for Bachelard, the history of science is an inquiry that 'mimics' the practice of the scientist, notwithstanding the fact that it 'is not a science and its object is not a scientific object' (Canguilhem 1979, 22). As to the latter, Canguilhem consistently maintains throughout his philosophical career that scientific activity in general must finally be grounded in the normative activity that life as such is. This is not to deny the autonomy of the sciences, i.e. to question the truths of science in an external fashion, but to make clear that these truths are preceded by a normative decision in favour of the true, which can only be understood in reference to the normative character of the living's relation with its environment. If it is true that 'there is no other truth but that of science' it is also true for him that the idea of science is not scientific, that is it cannot be scientifically justified (Canguilhem, in Balibar 1993, 58–62).

The study of the progress of the sciences requires that the historian adopt a standpoint within scientific discourse. A history of science that intends to go beyond a mere recounting of pronouncements claiming to state the truth (because sanctioned by their contemporary scientific norms) and reveal 'the order of conceptual progress' in a specific science has to bring to bear on its history a theory of what counts as scientific knowledge. This measure, whose precise formulation is epistemology, is provided by the 'present notion of scientific truth' grounded in 'the present scientific culture' that contains a whole series of norms from those of instruments of experimentation to those of methods of observation and proof, to heuristic principles for formulating problems. The epistemologist proceeds from the present model of science toward the beginnings of a science which is the object of study, so that only a part of what was thought to be science is affirmed to be scientific. On the other hand, the reference of the epistemological notion of scientific truth to the present norms of scientificity makes it clear that for Canguilhem this measure is never more than a 'provisional point of culmination' of a history. Only by being historical is epistemology scientific in the sense that it mimics the scientific discourse in which the claim to truth is precisely governed by the possibility of critical correction, and is thus inherently historical: 'If this discourse has a history whose course the historian believes he can reconstruct, it is because it *is* a history whose meaning the epistemologist must reactivate' (Canguilhem 1988, 4–18). By the same token, the epistemologist's history of a science can never be a definitive history since each new constellation of scientific norms carries with it the possibility of a modification in the trajectory of the conceptual progress that the history of that science must trace. Such modifications range from shifts in emphasis to constructions of new trajectories. The recursive nature of history of the sciences in Canguilhem, which he takes over from Bachelard, sets him apart from the positivist tradition, which views history as a continuous and cumulative progress of the mind determined by 'logical laws', whose stages are thus fixed once and for all (Andreski 1974, 19–64). The history of science is truly a history, that is a series of ruptures and innovations (Canguilhem 1988, 116).

The historical modesty of Canguilhem's idea of epistemology also distinguishes his practice from the 'epistemological inquisition' that he detects in the approach of analytic philosophy to the history of science. The analytic philosopher takes the present standards of scientific theory as a complete doctrine and reduces the task of the historian to a meticulous application of these standards to a past science, thus becoming blind to the fact that the past of a present-day science is not the same as that science in the past. A homogeneous history of science, resting its case on a supposed continuity of intention or the identity of terms, suppresses the radical discontinuity within a science of successive object-constructs which are in fact precipitations of a whole gamut of factors irreducible to theoretical implications. The doctrinal epistemology that guides this history proceeds from an attitude that makes it fall prey in the present to a scientistic realism against which its epistemological scruples were meant to protect it vis-à-vis the realistic claims of a past science. The attitude in question sees scientific truths as statements of fact or definitive expressions of various characteristics of reality rather than provisional results of the constructions of the scientific work.

Scientific truths are not descriptions of a given reality, more sophisticated (because more precise or more penetrating) versions of the common-sensical or sensual knowledge. In a very important sense, a science becomes scientific for Canguilhem no less than for Bachelard because it breaks with its 'prehistory' in which it sought its objects in the sensible world already given. It becomes scientific, in other words, from the moment that it manages to create its own object with its own theories and instruments. 'In sum', writes Canguilhem, 'scientific proof is a work since it reorganises the given, since it produces effects without natural equivalent, since it constructs its organs' (Canguilhem 1979, 192). The historian of science must, here too, follow the lead of scientific practice, must mimic this latter – and on two levels. Firstly, history of science must take its bearings from the epistemological task of reconstructing 'the ways and means by which knowledge is produced' (Canguilhem 1988, 7). Not producing scientific knowledge does not mean that philosophical epistemology has nothing to say in relation to the conditions of production of knowledge. No factor that has had a role in the production of a specific scientific concept – be it the state of contemporary technology, the model of scientificity formulated in an adjunct scientific domain, practical and pragmatic requirements imposed by the economy or political system, or the ideologies and myths and metaphors of the social imaginary – should be left out of the history of that science on the pretext that it is not considered scientifically relevant by the present norms of scientificity. For Canguilhem 'there is no history of science which would be *only* history of science', as Balibar puts it (Balibar 1993, 66), since science is precisely a 'progressive process of purification governed by *norms of verification*' (Canguilhem 1988, 39). Hence, the importance for the history of science, in Canguilhem, of 'scientific ideology' and the care with which he describes its relation with science. On a second level, the historian must make her own the awareness of the scientist that her object is not given but constructed and that the question of knowledge is not that of getting close and seizing hold of the object but rather that of producing consistent results. The historian who views the history of science as a record pure and simple of scientific truth, having failed to recognize the role of 'scientific ideology' in the history of the formation of a scientific concept, ends up producing a 'false consciousness of its object. The closer the historian thinks he comes to his object, the farther he is from the target'. Just like the scientist, 'the historian cannot accurately see any object that he does not actively construct. Ideology is mistaken belief in being close to truth. Critical knowledge knows that it stands at a distance from an operationally constructed object' (Canguilhem 1988, 39–40).

For Canguilhem the history of science is 'one of the functions of philosophical epistemology' (Canguilhem 1979, 23). It is thus never simply a history recounted but first and foremost a history judged. Bachelard sought in mathematics the principle of orientation for this judgement; accordingly, in his thought, the 'axis of epistemological evaluation is in effect provided by the vector of mathematization, which defines the direction in which the rationalist activity of the physical sciences is accomplished' (Fichant 1993, 39). Canguilhem's philosophical epistemology, by contrast, takes its bearings from the question of the 'vital meaning' of knowledge, which one may say constitutes the point of convergence of his reflections on biology and medical sciences and practice. For him, knowledge is fundamentally the activity of forming and deploying concepts; and this latter is itself, as Foucault puts it, 'one way of living', that is one way of exchanging information with the environment (Foucault 1991, 21). The two concepts that in effect allow Canguilhem to question knowledge from the perspective of life, namely normativity and error, are in fact the two that define the manner of the existence of the living.

In *The Normal and the Pathological* Canguilhem defines life as 'polarized activity', or more precisely 'a form of reactivity polarized to the variations of the environment in which it develops' (Canguilhem 1991, 130) or as 'polarity and thereby even an unconscious position of value' (Canguilhem 1991, 126). There is an original form of judgement of value which coincides with life as such. The living beings do not confront their environment as an ensemble of facts but as a structure of vitally meaningful possibilities and demands 'centered on them' (Canguilhem 1991, 284). 'Even for an amoeba, living means preference and exclusion' (Canguilhem 1991, 136). The norm is what determines the normal starting from a normative intention. Being normal means to be normative, that is, being able to transcend the already existing norms toward establishing new ones (Canguilhem 1991, 196–7). This ability marks out a 'margin of tolerance' vis-à-vis the environment's inconstancies and hence a certain degree of independence from it. A normal environment is the one that allows the living to be normative, and accordingly, a 'norm of life is superior to another norm when it includes what the latter permits and what it forbids' (Canguilhem 1991, 182). Physiology's very definition of the normal, in the sense of functional constants of regulation, is derivative of the concrete exchanges which the organism conducts with its environment. If the normal state designates the habitual state of the organs and functions, this habitual state is itself the effect of a dynamic equilibrium between the demands of the environment and those of the organism; it is the precipitation, more or less temporary, of the normalization of the organism's relations with the environment, so that the functional and morphological constants are in the final analysis expressions of a concrete vital order (Canguilhem 1991, 162). In the same vein, disease does not consist in the absence of norms. 'Disease is still a norm of life but it is an inferior norm in the sense that it tolerates no deviation from the conditions in which it is valid ... The sick living being is normalized in well-defined conditions of existence and has lost his normative capacity, the capacity to establish norms in other conditions' (Canguilhem 1991, 183). The definition of life as normative activity constitutes Canguilhem's conceptual point of departure for the redefinition of not only physiological terms but also biological ones such as 'species' (Canguilhem 1991, 143). More importantly, perhaps, he places human technology and through this human knowledge too in the perspective of 'vital normativity' that characterizes life in general. 'All human technique, including that of life, is set within life, within an activity of information and assimilation of material' (Canguilhem 1991, 130). Man's 'desire to dominate the environment' which he pursues by means of technology is in fact the flourishing of the 'organic vitality' (Canguilhem 1991, 200–1). And knowledge is 'an anxious quest for the greatest possible quantity and variety of information' (Canguilhem 1979, 364).

The 'discussion with an environment' for the purpose of stabilization of a vital order, that life is for the living being, is primordially a normative activity (Canguilhem 1991, 198). Living is already a judgement of value, not just a division into positive and negative but also, as normative, a devaluation of what exists in the form of power to transcend it and establish new norms and hence a new normality. The normal is thus 'the norm exhibited in the fact' (Canguilhem 1991, 243) and norms 'refer the real to values, express discriminations of qualities in conformity with the polar opposition of a positive and a negative' (Canguilhem 1991, 240). This is why, as we said, the environment is always already confronted as vitally significant, as meaningful. The 'a prioris' of meaningful experience are given by life and not, as in Kant, by the subject. 'To define life as a meaning inscribed in matter is to acknowledge the existence of an a priori objective that is inherently material and not merely formal' (Canguilhem 1979, 362). But this primordial materiality of meaning also makes human meaning radically contingent – not only because the mutation that is the origin of all species, of the multiplication of life, is in fact nothing other than 'an error of heredity' or a 'misinterpretation of genetic information', but also because, in the case of human being, 'life would by error have produced a living thing capable of making errors'. There is a specifically human error which is, Canguilhem says, 'probably one with human errancy. Man makes mistakes because he does not know where to settle'. Man's way of negotiation with the environment is movement; he gathers information 'by moving around, and by moving objects around, with the aid of various kinds of technology'. Canguilhem places error, human errancy, at the origins of human technology and science. 'Man is the living being separated from life by science and struggling to rejoin life by science' (Canguilhem 1975, 105–6). Does this mean that human being somehow has to be perpetually dissatisfied with the meaning already given, and first of all with the judgement that life is? 'If the a priori is in things, if the concept is in life, then to be a subject of knowledge is simply to be dissatisfied with the meaning one finds ready at hand. Subjectivity is therefore nothing other than dissatisfaction' (Canguilhem 1979, 364). But this also means that human being is the living being that cannot but be normative with regard to meaning itself: she is compelled by life itself, by 'the limitation of life's finality', by the surplus of the possible over the real, to question life; she is driven to a search for reasons to live (Canguilhem 1991, 281). 'But to pursue such a goal is also to discover reasons not to live' (Canguilhem, in Delaporte 1994, 384). Human being is the living being that is capable of living a meaning, a normative judgement, that may turn out to be an absolute devaluation of the fact of living (Canguilhem 1979, 183–6). In this case, one may perhaps say that being human is, for better or worse, a compulsion to meaning.

Alison Ross and *Amir Ahmadi*

Further reading and works cited

Andreski, S. (ed.) *The Essential Comte.* New York, 1974.
Bachelard, G. *Le nouvel esprit scientifique.* Paris, 1934.
—. *La formation de l'esprit scientifique.* Paris, 1938.
—. *L'Activité Rationaliste de la physique contemporaine.* Paris, 1951.

—. *Le matérialisme rationnel.* Paris, 1953.
—. *The Philosophy of No.* New York, 1968.
—. *The Poetics of Space.* Boston, 1994.
Balibar, E. 'Science et vérité dans la philosophie de Georges Canguilhem', *Georges Canguilhem: Philosophe, historien des sciences,* ed. François Delaporte. Paris, 1993.
Canguilhem, G. *La Connaissance de la vie.* Paris, 1975.
—. *Études d'histoire et de philosophie des sciences.* Paris, 1979.
—. *Ideology and Rationality in the History of the Life Sciences.* Cambridge, MA, 1988.
—. *The Normal and the Pathological.* New York, 1991.
—. 'Le cerveau et la pensée', in *Georges Canguilhem: Philosophe, historien des sciences,* ed. François Delaporte. Paris, 1993.
Delaporte, F. (ed.) *A Vital Rationalist.* New York, 1994.
Fichant, M. 'Georges Canguilhem et l'Idée de la philosophie', *Georges Canguilhem: Philosophe, historien des sciences,* ed. François Delaporte. Paris, 1993.
Foucault, M. *The Archeology of Knowledge.* London, 1972.
—. 'Introduction'. *The Normal and the Pathological.* New York, 1991.
Hyppolite, J. 'Gaston Bachelard ou le romantisme de l'intelligence', in *Hommage à Gaston Bachelard.* Paris, 1957.
Latour, B. and Bowker, G. 'A booming discipline short of discipline', *Social Studies of Science,* 17, 1987.
Lecourt, D. *Marxism and Epistemology.* London, 1975.
Markus, G. 'Changing Images of Science', *Thesis Eleven,* 33, 1992.
Privitera, W. *Problems of Style.* Albany, NY, 1995.
Rabinow, P. *Essays on The Anthropology of Reason.* Princeton, NJ, 1996.
Tiles, M. *Bachelard, Science and Objectivity.* Cambridge, 1984.

Jean Paulhan (1884–1969) and/versus Francis Ponge (1899–1988)

Jean Paulhan and Francis Ponge not only share strong biographical and ideological origins in common (both were originally from the South of France (Nîmes), and born into protestant and free-thinking families), they also had an intense personal relationship (too complex to be called simply 'friendship') which lasted their whole lives. A chief editor of the *NRF* (*Nouvelle Revue Française*), the leading literary journal between the two World Wars, Paulhan took the decision to publish Ponge's first book (*Douze petits écrits,* 1926). After this, he functioned for Ponge as a kind of literary and intellectual mentor, and their correspondence spans a period of almost fifty years (1923–68).

Nevertheless, aside from the biographical elements, one might be tempted to insist more heavily on all that separates Paulhan and Ponge. The first is seen as a critic (some readers hardly even know that he also wrote *fiction*). The latter is considered exclusively a poet, and even the poet of one single masterwork, *Le Parti pris des choses* (1942), whereas most of his writings are definitely *anti-poetical* in tone and scope. Furthermore, the first represents much of the very diverse and, perhaps, antagonistic tendencies brought together (and not necessarily reconciled) in the *NRF*, with its typical blending of a rather left-wing political involvement and an almost neoclassical sense of taste and well-written French prose, sharp, clear and witty at the same time. The latter, on the contrary, now appears as one of the greatest French poets of the century, who, together with the Belgian author Henri Michaux, has revolutionized our very conception of poetry (and probably of literature and even language in general). Paulhan is also almost ignored by contemporary readers. His (still very incomplete) *Oeuvres complètes* is long sold out, and many of his books are really hard to find. Ponge, however, has been widely adopted and even cherished by the literary and educational institution. His complete works have entered the *ne plus ultra* of French editorial chic, the 'Pléiade' series, and is taught at all levels, from elementary schools to PhD programmes (in France, these programmes are all fixed by the Ministry of Education, not freely chosen by the schools or faculties). And finally, whereas Paulhan has been at the (invisible) centre of French literary life, making and unmaking books, authors and careers as an almighty but hidden God, Ponge has occupied a small but well lit margin of it, and his work has been claimed by every imaginable literary and philosophical school of the twentieth century.

But do biographical (and ideological) convergences, on the one hand, and literary (and institutional) divergences, on the other, keep both in balance? In fact, one should add here one or two elements which tie together Paulhan's and Ponge's writing and thinking, and which do so in such an inextricable manner that one can really consider these two authors, if not as each other's intellectual *alter ego*, than at least as two perfect examples of what French modernism stands for between, say, 1920 and 1970: the first element is the *metapoetical* turn of their literary and critical practice; the second is the way their poetics has always been defined by the authors themselves in *political* terms.

The literary career of Jean Paulhan merges almost completely with the life of the *NRF*, co-founded by André Gide and some of his friends (Paulhan becomes the journal's first editorial assistant in 1920, running the journal from 1925 on). This merging does not of course imply that Paulhan's biography is monolithic or simple. First, Paulhan's editorial functions (not only at the *NRF*, but very soon at Gallimard, France's most important publisher, and, after the Second World War, in the global literary field) constituted him as a very double personality. A typical go-between, having to defend the interests of writers as well as publishers, he developed an extraordinary sense of diplomacy (or hypocrisy, as his enemies liked to put it). In order to preserve the mutual goodwill of both camps, he became a master of literary, social and political tactics. During the German occupation, he managed for example to keep running the *NRF* under German censorship (he only resigned when the Nazis decided to give the *NRF* to a collaborationist writer, Drieu la Rochelle), while at the same time being very active in clandestine publishing and in political *Résistance*. His incredibly rich correspondence, most of which still remains an unknown continent for copyright reasons, reflects the vastness of his socio-literary networks, and the exceptional human qualities which made him the real 'pope' of French literature during more than forty years (although after the Second World War the prewar *NRF* monopoly was rudely challenged by successful newcomers such as *Les Temps modernes* and *Tel Quel*). For his editorial work, he regularly used pseudonyms, and for many years people believed he was really the author of the pornographic cult-novel *Histoire d'O* (in fact written by his mistress and collaborator, Dominique Aury).

If Paulhan published only small books (and often *very* small ones, as far as size or length is concerned), he never ceased to write fiction and essays. His fiction entails mostly short stories (Paulhan never wrote a full-length novel) and is more or less autobiographical. *Le Guerrier appliqué* (1917), for instance, a very unconventional book on his war experiences, remains key reading on the First World War. His *Guide d'un petit voyage en Suisse* (1947) is a mini-travelogue which is also a wonderful example of 'applied philosophy'. Paulhan's essays display a wide range of topics and themes, yet they have only one major subject: language (occasionally language and art, but often either language or art; however, in any case, the questions raised are comparable). From his very first publication on Madagascar proverbs (*Les Hain-Tenys*, 1913), to the paramount essay-books which are *Les Fleurs de Tarbes* (published in 1941, but prepared and rewritten for more than two decades) and the posthumous *Les Incertitudes du langage* (1970), Paulhan never stops turning around the mystery of language, its use, its meaning, but most of all its beauty. For the study of language, however ambiguous and deceptive its results may be, ends always with a kind of epiphany, Beauty and Truth being the final steps of Paulhan's reflection on these matters (his peculiar sensibility to the mystery of language and life explains also why so many readers discover a touch of Oriental mysticism in his work).

But what is language? Paulhan distinguishes three major elements, which appear to have major consequences for other than strictly linguistic speculations.

First, language is a system, where no element ever has meaning by itself, and where meaning both depends on use and context and is permanently shifting. This was indeed the great lesson of Paulhan's study of the so-called 'hain-tenys', small pieces of oral poetry containing more or less stereotyped proverbs which were used in Madagascar in verbal contests (Paulhan spent some years in that colony, and became very hostile towards French colonialism). Speakers of two camps exchange poems and proverbs until one of them finds a proverb-rich poem so well-formed and well-formulated that it blocks the answer of the other, reducing the opponent to silence. Of course, whether a 'hain-teny' is well-formed and well-formulated or not depends not on the utterance itself, but on the context. An oral contest is not the repetition of a stereotyped set of questions and answers, but an open *performance* always full of surprises.

Second, as the 'hain-tenys' example already makes clear, every language is a strange combination of 'stereotyped' and 'original' utterances. However, this does not imply that the very distinction of the two categories can be established once and for all, since speakers and listeners can have different opinions on the degree of 'frozen-ness' of an expression, or since the very use and re-use of stereotypes can alter the perception of its characteristics, and so on.

Third, language is for Paulhan also much more than just a symbolic human activity among others. It always reveals a certain way of thinking, and should therefore be understood as a synthesis of the human mind – an idea that structuralism will of course exploit on a very large scale in later decades. (Paulhan, however, who always links human life and the universe, resembled more a mystical anthropologist of language than a die-hard structuralist.)

The literary and human consequences of these observations are, at least for Paulhan, easy to understand, and he uses his knowledge of hain-tenys *pragmatics* to end a violent discussion on *literary terrorism* (the subtitle of his *Fleurs de Tarbes* runs: 'La Terreur dans les Lettres'). For the terrorists (whom he calls unhappy rhetoricians) linguistic invention and, perhaps, all language, inevitably become a set of stereotypes preventing the speaker from 'expressing' his or her feelings and experiences in a natural, spontaneous way. Hence, in order to 'free' the subject's speech, the terrorist proposes to 'exclude' all stereotypes, and in fact all rhetorics and all literary devices, from the field of writing, making a plea for 'natural', i.e. non literary speech. Thanks to his experience of the 'hain-tenys', which he considers paradigmatic of all human language, Paulhan manages to explain to what extent the conflict between the terrorists and their antagonists, the rhetoricians, is a false one, since it does not take into account the role of context and the specific use of an utterance.

These linguistic and literary stances are then 'transferred' by Paulhan to other areas, such as ethics and politics. Yet since language and life are not opposed, but mutually comprehensive, such a 'transfer' is not just a language-inspired interpretation of life, but a logical consequence of linguistic analysis itself. After the Second World War, the spirit of tolerance which had always impregnated his literary and artistic writings takes an overtly political dimension. Paulhan's battle against literary terrorism becomes a battle against terrorism and political intolerance *in se*. A very influential leader of the 'patriotic' writers' committee born during the *Résistance*, Paulhan publicly fights the prosecution of collaborationist writers, while at the same time strongly affirming the autonomy of literary speech as an illustration of free speech and anti-terrorist play.

Although the third element of Paulhan's definition of language sounds rather outdated nowadays, the influence of Paulhan's writings and work are widely acknowledged. In an era of political correctness, his efforts to avoid major tensions between those who believe that words are 'just words' and those who are convinced that words are 'anything but words' continue to be, in France at least, regularly mentioned with great approval. And Paulhan's own writing, that never-ending rewriting exceeding the limits of any fixed text, book or genre, has become exemplary of new conceptions of authorship and textuality. In that respect, just as with regard to the relationships between writing and politics, the link with Ponge is not difficult to establish, notwithstanding the many other differences between the personalities and literary achievements of the two authors.

At first sight, and contrary to Paulhan's case, life and writing are separated in the example of Francis Ponge by an almost unbridgeable gap, at least at the anecdotal level. After a surrealist beginning (or is it already an intermezzo?), Ponge was obliged to take a job in order to make a living for his family. His marriage put an end to his economic freedom, and all his life he would have to fight poverty. In later texts, he described himself as 'proletarized' by labour: first due to low wages in the 1930s, then due to periods of unemployment, before and after the Second World War, exemplified by his break with the Communist Party (his membership was maintained from 1936 to 1947, and during the first years after the war he worked for a communist newspaper). At the same time, the very difficult material conditions in which he had to write cannot be separated from what is at stake in his writings (during the period he wrote *Le parti pris des choses*, he was allowed only twenty minutes a day to write, having to work at least twelve hours a day and being too tired to write more). The poetry Ponge wrote is indeed not a form of petit-bourgeois escapism. On the contrary, the way Ponge thinks of poetry and practises it stubbornly signifies an absolute and complete denial of any escapism whatsoever. Poetry is an act of resistance, poetry is politics, and is therefore useful and necessary. However, this act of resistance can only be meaningful if at the same time it is directed towards poetry itself, towards the destruction of ways of writing poetry which maintain the gap between text and life, or literature and politics.

As with so many other angry young men of his generation, Ponge had been seduced by the radicalism of the surrealist movement. Very soon, however, he discarded Breton's vision of language and art, and his vision of their relationship with reality, as false and naive, as inauthentic and unrevolutionary. Indeed, whereas the surrealist revolution tends to despise any given reality and the objects of the given world, favouring instead the world of illogical *trouvailles* and dreams, of the unconscious, of the free association of literary metaphors, Ponge realized that literature must commit itself with the world and its objects, rather than with the subjective feelings of the poet. In order to become truly revolutionary, literature must be real, it must stick to the things themselves, and do everything to serve the world occluded by subjective illusions. Refusing the petit-bourgeois and belle-lettrist vision of writing in a surrealist mode, he then began pursuing an ideal of radically impersonal writing which seems anti-poetic, but which was, for him, the only possible embodiment of revolutionary poetry. This was also the project to which he would remain faithful throughout his life. Despite many variations in tone and political orientation, Ponge wanted his writing to be a revolutionary disclosure of the world itself, the very act of writing being of course also one of its aspects.

While one might distinguish four major steps in his poetic career, it is not possible to establish a real gap between these, each new step being in fact a more explicit version of what was already contained in earlier forms. His second book, *Le parti pris des choses* (1942), a small collection of short pieces of poetic prose, illustrates the more traditional side of his objective poetics. Claiming 'one rhetorics for each object', Ponge reinvents in this book a typically French genre, i.e. the 'poésie en prose'. He cuts it of from its lyrical basis, and replaces it by a 'cold', descriptive mode aiming to do justice to both the materiality of the world and that of the word. When describing, for instance, the 'crate', Ponge not only evokes the referential side (for instance by explaining where you can find such things in Paris), but also mentions some aspects of its own, verbal materiality (for instance by detailing the words which surround it in the dictionary, which is the other place where you can find 'crates' certainly). And, as the example already shows, the very choice of many of the objects described in the book also bear this anti-poetical, materialist attitude (later he will give as a major example the oyster, with a famous comment on the 'accent circonflexe' one finds in the French writing of the word 'huître'). What Ponge wants is to 'say the world (and thus also the words)' in its most humble appearances, not to conceal it by poetical and subjective nonsense.

A new step in his writing is seen in *Proêmes* (1948), an experiment in the blurring of boundaries between the text and its critique, between writing a poem and writing a comment on the poem itself. Of course, many texts of *Le parti pris des choses* already contained such a 'metapoetical' level, but with *Proêmes* Ponges makes a decisive opening towards the fusion of several text-types, and more particularly leaps into the mixing-up of the so-called 'finished' and 'draft' versions of a text. His exceptional familiarity with painting and with the artist's workshop was undoubtedly of great help for the understanding of his own poetical practice.

Le parti pris des choses and *Proêmes* had made Ponge famous, at least in the inner circles of the literary in-crowd. Greater public recognition and honour arrived only in the 1960s. But by the time that people really started reading the books from the 1940s, Ponge was already experimenting with new works, whose importance, although widely and officially acknowledged, was barely understood by many readers. In a book such as *Pour un Malherbe* (1965), the combination of texts, drafts, comments, critiques, quotations, etc., is transformed into a tri-dimensional book-object, which is also a sumptuous masterpiece of typography. (Under the influence of the favourite subjects of his art criticism, such as Braque, Picasso or Fautrier, Ponge's writing had become more and more a scrambling of words inspired by the scrambling of colours on the canvas.) Simultaneously, *Pour un Malherbe* is an autobiography, and also a poetic and political manifesto. Ponge invokes the authority of Malherbe, the Renaissance poet who decisively transformed first French poetry, and afterwards French language itself. As far as poetry is concerned, Ponge thus strongly identifies himself with the man who put an end to the domination of the Ronsardian (in fact Petrarchan, subjective and lyrical) tradition in France and substituted it with a more rational, cold, objective mode of writing. (Ponge was here thinking also of Latin, as a language and as a literature, where texts were carved in stone, and he put an increasing emphasis on the historical and structural continuity between Latin and French.) As far as language is concerned, Ponge elaborates a renewed theory of poetry as civil and political action, of poetry firmly rooted in the institutional organization of both the language and the country itself. Ponge's insistence on the necessary encounter of poet and king, and on their common action in the life of the nation, will later be explained by some as a right-wing 'dérive' [right-wing drift; drift to the right] of his politicization of poetry (these are the years of General de Gaulle and Pompidou), and provoke long-lasting controversy.

In the final phase, then, Ponge released not just the typographic version of a text's adventures, but displayed the whole 'workshop' (once again, the pictorial connotations of this programme are evidently present), and included in books such as *La fabrique du pré* (1971) and *Comment une figue de paroles et pourquoi* (1977). This politics of writing and publishing really accomplishes what Ponge had always asked from poetry: that is, the articulation of an act, a text in action, this act becoming life itself. Writing, performing, living, thinking become a whole.

The reading and interpretation of Ponge follows closely the history of literary and critical theory in the twentieth century. Ponge has been read, as has been claimed, within almost every important critical and political current since the Second World War: communism and marxism, phenomenology, existentialism, structuralism, *Tel Quel* and *TXT* materialism, nationalism, deconstruction and – nowadays – the reborn, strongly psychoanalytically oriented philology called genetic criticism. One should stress, however, that there has always existed a strong tension between the author's intention and his readers' interpretations. From the very beginning of his creative labour, Ponge opposed misreadings of his work. The fear of political recuperation of his writings (for instance by the French Communist Party in the first years after the Second World War) may have been one of the most significant arguments in Ponge's decision to incorporate ever more explicitly in his texts their own 'reader's companion', so that the radical novelty of his anti-poetry would be revealed and misreading blocked as much as possible. That he firmly encouraged during the 1960s the materialist-textualist interpretation of his work by the *Tel Quel* group (the studies conducted by Derrida in later years relied heavily upon the essential insights and preferences of this period) may suggest, and for some even suffices to prove, that this was the ideal reader-response for which the author was looking. In fact, nothing is less sure, since at the same moment he made with Philippe Sollers the interview-book which still today determines the larger public understanding of his work, Ponge had started writing very different texts and inventing new, overtly nationalistic and patriotic auto-interpretations for which there was certainly no room in the 'orthodox' textualist-deconstructionist viewpoint.

Francis Ponge always opposed totalitarianism, fascist as well as communist, while simultaneously always trying to escape from too rigid (or too flattering) criticism. For Ponge, the core business of interpretation is always to be accomplished by the individual reader in a personal encounter with the text, and this encounter has to be renewed in every new reading. Ponge's texts are not objects, but acts, and as such they can never be repeated twice. With him, poetry became performance once again.

Jan Baetens

Further reading and works cited

Badré, F. *Paulhan le juste*. Paris, 1996.
Baetens, J. '– Je m'appelle Jacques Maast', *Poétique*, 78, 1989.
Bersani, J. (ed.) *Colloque de Cerisy, Jean Paulhan le souterrain*. Paris, 1976.
Derrida, J. *Signéponge*. Paris, 1988.
Farasse, G. *L'Ane musicien*. Paris, 1996.
Gleize, J.-M. *Francis Ponge*. Paris, 1988.
Paulhan, J. *Le Guerrier appliqué*. Paris, 1930.
—. *Les Hain-Tenys*. Paris, 1939.
—. *Les Fleurs de Tarbes*. Paris, 1941.
—. *Guide d'un petit voyage en Suisse*. Paris, 1947.
—. *Oeuvres complètes*. 5 vols. Paris, 1966–70.
—. *Les Incertitudes du langage*. Paris, 1970.
—. *Correspondance avec Francis Ponge (1923–68)*. Paris, 1986.
Pérez, C.-P. *Entretiens de Francis Ponge avec Philippe Sollers*. Paris, 1997.
— (ed.) *Le clair et l'obscur*. Paris, 1999.
Ponge, F. *Douze petits écrits*. Paris, 1926.
—. *Le Parti pris des choses*. Paris, 1942.
—. *Proêmes*. Paris, 1948.
—. *Pour un Malherbe*. Paris, 1965.
—. *La Fabrique du pré*. Geneva, 1971.
—. *Comment une figue de paroles et pourquoi*. Paris, 1977.
—. *Oeuvres complètes*. Paris, 1999–.
Syrotinski, M. *Defying Gravity*. Albany, NY, 1998.
Veck, B. *Francis Ponge ou le refus de l'absolu littéraire*. Liège, 1993.
Vouilloux, B. *Un art de la figure*. Lille, 1998.

György Lukács (1885–1971)

Philosopher, political theorist and literary critic, György Lukács was an influential marxist intellectual who made pioneering contributions to the study of literature and culture, in spite of the controversy that often surrounded his work. In literary theory, he took the first decisive steps toward a systematic marxist aesthetics based not only on formal criticism, but also on economic sociological and historical analysis. Particularly influential in this regard have been *The Theory of the Novel* (1916), which Lukács wrote before he joined the Communist Party, and *The Historical Novel* (1937). Inspired largely by the dialectics of Hegel, these two works offer historical typologies of literary forms that have influenced such diverse marxist projects as Lucien Goldmann's *The Hidden God* (1955) and Fredric Jameson's *The Political Unconscious* (1981). An advocate of realism, Lukács also initiated a formative debate for marxist literary theory on the politics of expressionism and modernism in general, eliciting notable if sometimes scathing critical responses from such prominent marxists as Ernst Bloch, Theodor Adorno and Bertolt Brecht (see Bloch et al. 1980). Most importantly, Lukács developed the groundbreaking concept of reification in his celebrated work, *History and Class Consciousness* (1923). An original extension of Karl Marx's theory of commodity fetishism, this seminal concept proved to be a major influence on the critical theorists of the Frankfurt School, including their associate Walter Benjamin. It also shaped the thinking of existential marxists like Maurice Merleau-Ponty as well as the New Left movement of the 1960s, especially in the case of Guy Debord's *The Society of the Spectacle* (1967). In exerting such influence, Lukács has come to be widely regarded as a founding figure of western marxism.

Born into a wealthy Jewish family in Budapest, Lukács began his road to marxism as a young aesthete deeply opposed to the ills of modern society. Overwhelmed by a sense of futility, the young Lukács was primarily preoccupied with the tragic division between art and life, falling under the influence of Søren Kierkegaard, Friedrich Nietzsche, Fyodor Dostoyevsky and Henrik Ibsen. At the universities in Berlin and Heidelberg, where he acquired his lifelong interest in German philosophy, Lukács' already acute sense of the socio-economic problems of modernity was further intensified under the tutelage of three eminent sociologists, Georg Simmel, Emil Lask and Max Weber. With the outbreak of the First World War, Lukács became utterly despondent. His tragic sense of the modern condition confirmed, he wrote his *Theory of the Novel* 'in a mood of permanent despair over the state of the world' (12). In 1918, after the success of the Russian Revolution and the subsequent collapse of the Austro-Hungarian Empire, Lukács joined the Hungarian Communist Party (HCP) formed by Béla Kún. His conversion to Marxism marked the beginning of his hopeful sense of political commitment. Along with this newly acquired optimism came a period of intense political activity spanning most of the 1920s, during which time Lukács set aside his literary and aesthetic concerns. In the short-lived Hungarian Soviet Republic, he served as the Deputy Commissar of Public Education and as the Political Commissar of the Red Army's fifth division. As a political exile in Vienna and Berlin, he also played a significant role in the émigré HCP from 1919 to 1929, becoming deputy leader of the Landler faction. A major political activist, Lukács even attended the 1921 Third World Congress of the Communist International in Moscow, where he met Lenin personally.

Lukács political writings of the time, however, were generally not well-received by Soviet authorities. The most significant expression of his political views appeared in *History and Class Consciousness*, the central essay of which, 'Reification and the Consciousness of the Proletariat', theorizes the revolutionary emergence of the proletarian subject out of the dehumanizing forces of capitalism. The work as a whole was strikingly non-dogmatic, making the claim that what was orthodox about Marxism was not its doctrine, but its method: dialectical materialism. For this reason, among others, *History and Class Consciousness* was immediately condemned as heretical by the Comintern Congress in Moscow (its non-doctrinaire views were ultimately more influential among Western European intellectuals). A similar fate befell Lukács' controversial political document, 'The Blum Theses' (1925), mainly because it urged communists to collaborate with bourgeois politicians in Hungary (see Lukács 1972). Faced with increasing dogmatism in the Party following the death of Lenin in 1924, Lukács eventually was forced to retract many of his political views and finally, in 1929, to retire from active politics, although he returned briefly for the ill-fated 1956 Hungarian uprising led by Imre Nagy, who made Lukács his Minister of Culture.

In the 1930s, Lukács resumed his literary and philosophical pursuits, which were now bound up with countering the unreason of fascism and developing a proper marxist aesthetic. In Berlin (1931–3) and then in Moscow (1933–45), he turned his attention to a systematic critique of expressionism and modernism, portraying them as forms of decadence that paved the way for the rise of fascism by universalizing alienation, relativism and fragmentation, rather than seeing them as effects of capitalism. In his numerous essays written for *Internationale Literature, Das Wort* and *Die Linkskurve*, which later appeared in his *Essays on Realism* (1948), *Studies in European Realism* (1950) and *Writer and Critic* (1970), Lukács opposed such forms with a marxian theory of realism that underscored the importance of objective representation, narrative and humanism, as well as the progressive politics of the anti-fascist Popular Front. He was primarily interested in the novel, hoping that his critical efforts would halt the ongoing dissolution of its classic nineteenth-century form, which Lukács traced out fully in *The Historical Novel*.

To many western intellectuals and artists at the time, most notably Bertolt Brecht, it appeared as if Lukács were defending the narrow party doctrine of socialist realism which was developed by Joseph Stalin and Maxim Gorky and promulgated by A. A. Zhdanov, but Lukács' views were much more tolerant, if not always directly stated. Not only did he argue against the reduction of literature to propaganda, he also defended certain bourgeois writers whom he called 'critical realists', the most well-known contemporaneous example being the German novelist Thomas Mann. Basically, in contrast to the theorists of socialist realism, Lukács was concerned not only with content, but also with form. In his opinion, the two were dialectically related, as they were for Marx. Later, after the death of Stalin, when a more open discussion of literary matters was possible, Lukács more clearly distinguished his dialectical understanding of realism from orthodox socialist realism, first in *The Meaning of Contemporary Realism* (1958), a critique of modernism that also illuminates Lukács' distinction between critical and socialist realism, and then in *The Specificity of the Aesthetic* (1963), a systematic but less well-known codification of his theory of realism.

As a complement to his critique of modern experimental art forms, Lukács also attempted a critique of modern philosophy, which culminated with the publication of his *The Destruction of Reason* (1952), a lengthy critical overview of 'irrationalism' in the history of German philosophy beginning with Friedrich Schelling. For Lukács, post-Enlightenment philosophers such as Arthur Schopenhauer, Nietzsche and Martin Heidegger were as responsible for the rise of Nazism as the expressionists because, in disparaging understanding and objectivity and promoting the idea of an unchanging human condition, they undermined the basis of collective opposition to fascism, serving the interests of capitalism by contributing to the creation of passive subjects. Like the expressionists, they endorsed a mythological vision of the isolated individual, ignoring the socio-historical processes responsible for that distinctive modern development. In Lukács' opinion, the true philosopher, like the realist writer, must attempt to grasp and reflect the objective world, to serve the democratic interests of humanism. Lukács' posthumously published *The Ontology of Social Being* (1976), which he laboured unsuccessfully to complete in his final years, was to have systematized his views on the matter.

Informing the different phases and projects of Lukács' career is a developing interest in holistic methodologies that is motivated by a profound concern with overcoming the alienation of the modern world. At first, in his largely metaphysical and pessimistic pre-marxist work, Lukács tends to deploy a holistic approach that is based on establishing a normative ideal totality by which to judge his subject at hand. Occasioned by the author's own tragic sense of estrangement and nostalgia, the ideal totality typically takes the form of a lost organic community or an absolute literary form, both of which are juxtaposed with the modern dissolution of art and the increasing anarchy and chaos of modernity. The result is often an unusual combination of sociology and metaphysics. The most well-known instance of this peculiar approach appears in *The Theory of the Novel*, a philosophical and historical study of the novel's origin and development. In this intensely lyrical work, Lukács idealizes the Greek epic, from which, he claims, the novel descends. Following the lead of Hegel, he argues that the epic form is the representative genre of an organic and stable world, of an intrinsically meaningful social totality in which individuals feel at home. Without exhibiting a conscious sense of time, change or alienation, it arises out of and gives expression to a closed, homogeneous world of innocence, community and immanent meaning, giving form to a metaphysical totality of being in which there is no conflict between self and world, essence and life, subject and object.

With the onset of the individualism and relativism of modernity, however, the favourable social conditions necessary for the production of the epic are undermined. As a result, the epic is transformed into the novel, the representative form of a world emptied of intrinsic meaning and value, a world of insecurity, contingency and eternal homelessness in which individuals live tragically estranged from one another, painfully aware of the gap between what is and what ought to be. In an elegiac tone, Lukács proceeds to develop a stark contrast between the classical epic and the modern novel, pointing out that the form of the latter is marked by a growing concern with irony, self-reflection, time and individual psychology, especially the sense of disillusionment and unfulfilled desire. Although he dimly sees some hope for a renewed epic in Dostoevsky's works, Lukács finally renders a negative judgement on the novel, 'the epic of an age in which the extensive totality of life is no longer directly given, in which the immanence of meaning in life has become a problem, yet which still thinks in terms of totality' (1971b, 56). Having evaluated the novel's historical development in terms of its increasing inability to grasp and represent the totality of its world, Lukács famously concludes that 'the novel is the epic of a world that has been abandoned by God' (88).

In his first marxist work of political theory, *History and Class Consciousness*, Lukács exchanges such metaphysically tinged views of totality for a more materialist understanding of holism, revealing a new sense of optimism. Inspired by a Hegelianized version of marxism, he argues here that the developing class consciousness of the proletariat is favourably positioned to overcome the alienation of the modern world, which is now more explicitly described as a result of the rise of capitalism. The intellectual means by which it can do so is the dialectical method, a materialist approach to the study of society whose main objectives are to grasp the concrete totality of capitalism, to understand its historical development, and to project the likely course of its future progress. Based on Marx's assumption that the social relations of every society form a whole, it strives for a systematic mediation between all the seemingly autonomous social and material entities of the modern world, working against the superficial empirical sense of fragmentation endemic to capitalist societies, combining theory and practice. In political terms, the dialectical method also discloses the underlying but often obscured fact of capitalism, namely that it is not a natural or necessary state, but a historical condition that is sustained by social relationships. It thus provides the proletariat with the opportunity to realize its full human potential, to become conscious of itself as an active agent in the creation of history.

For Lukács, such a holistic dialectical awareness is the necessary precondition for the revolutionary transformation of society, and the great irony is that the very material conditions of capitalism itself allows for the possibility of this revolutionary development. The key assumption behind this view is that the commodity form is 'the central, structural problem of capitalist society in all its aspects' (1971a, 83). Accompanied by such social phenomena as the division of labour, the rationalization of the work process and extensive bureaucratic control, the commodity form is initially responsible for the alienation of the proletariat because it separates workers from the finished products that they produce. Objectifying the proletariat, it reduces them to the status of commodities, since they are forced to sell their labour to survive. The commodity form also destroys the organic social bonds that characterize pre-capitalist societies because it conceals the labour that goes into its production, transforming human beings into passive consumers. The result is that social relationships become mystified; they take on the appearance of things, assuming a kind of unreal or phantom objectivity (reification). The proletariat, in turn, becomes more and more contemplative, as they are filled with the sense of isolation and detachment. Estranged from themselves, they become subject to the debilitating illusion that capitalism is the natural order of things, their sense of space prevailing over their sense of time. Most importantly, they lose their ability to grasp society as a whole.

For Lukács, however, this condition is only temporary. It is characteristic of societies that are only partially dominated by the problem of commodities. In the modern world, where the commodity form has finally permeated capitalist society in its entirety, the proletariat has a new centralized position because the social structure of capitalism is now completely based on the exploitation of labour. According to Lukács, if the proletariat could only become conscious of itself as a commodity, they would of necessity become conscious of the structure of society as a whole. In doing so, they would overcome reification and regain the conscious sense of freedom and creativity proper to humanity. They would realize, in other words, that capitalism is a set of social relations between people and thus subject to change. If acted upon, such a revolutionary consciousness would make the proletariat both the subject and object of history because, in striving to transform the objective material conditions of capitalism, the workers would be putting theory into practice, overcoming their subjective sense of alienation as they create the classless society.

Although Lukács subsequently critiqued some of the assumptions behind this optimistic portrait of the proletarian revolution, he later indicated that *History and Class Consciousness* at least rightly 'reinstated the category of totality in the central position it had occupied throughout Marx's works' (1971a, xx). Lukács might have also indicated that it re-established the importance of the category of totality for his own work, not, however, as some kind of idealized norm, but as a guiding objective for a flexible materialist methodology concerned with conceptualizing the concrete moment of capitalism. As with Marx's works, this dialectical materialist understanding of totality, which is always linked to furthering the ends of the socialist revolution, occupies a central position in the writings that follow *History and Class Consciousness*. It is the substance of Lukács' more orthodox political work on the thought of Lenin, who 'always saw the problems of the age as a whole' (1997, 10), and it is the implacable standard against which he critiques modern philosophical trends such as existentialism (see Lukács 1948).

More significantly, Lukács' dialectical materialist understanding of totality is also the basis of his approach to aesthetics. As he explains in 'Art and Objective Truth' (1954), a true work of art is a carefully wrought 'reflection of life in its total motion, as process and totality' (1970, 39). In other words, it is an objective representation of society that discloses the underlying laws governing its structure and development. Far from being a mere photographic reproduction of the real world, it is the product of an intellectual and artistic process of selection and arrangement in which content is shaped into a unified form. Consequently, the defining feature of Lukács' realist aesthetic is a distinctive synthesis of the particular and the general, the accidental and the necessary, appearance and reality. As a 'concrete totality', it attempts to present, in compressed form, a microcosm of society as a whole. Its social function, as in the case of the dialectical method, is to combat the alienation and fragmentation of capitalist society by providing 'a truer, more complete, more vivid and more dynamic reflection of reality than the receptant otherwise possesses' (36).

As Lukács more fully explained in two memorable essays, 'Narrate or Describe?' (1936) and 'The Intellectual Physiognomy in Characterization' (1936), a totalizing reflection of reality is dependent on the use of narrative and 'typical' characters. Narration allows for the depiction of the dynamic and contradictory character of reality. At its best, it reveals society to be an ongoing historical process. 'Typicality', on the other hand, allows for the mediation between the general and the particular. When used properly, it combines a regard for the individual traits of characters with a simultaneous recognition of their various class and social positions. Through such a technique, Lukács explains, realist writers manage the difficult task of revealing the stratified totality of society that the reflection of objective reality requires. Taken together, typicality and narration allow for the overall possibility of a complete dialectical presentation of reality in art, which for Lukács is best exemplified in the classic 'historical' novels of Sir Walter Scott and Honoré de Balzac, as well as in the later novels of Leo Tolstoy and Thomas Mann.

To this dialectical theory of realism, Lukács adds a holistic view of literary forms in which the category of totality is equally prominent. Instead of narrowly focusing on literature in-and-of itself, Lukács develops a more comprehensive critical practice in which literary forms are correlated with the historical developments out of which they emerge. The most celebrated example of this materialist approach is *The Historical Novel*, whose ambitious goal, as Lukács states in the Foreword, is 'to show how the historical novel in its origin, development, rise and decline follows inevitably upon the great social transformation of modern times; to demonstrate that its different problems of form are but artistic reflections of these social-historical transformations' (17). In accomplishing his objective, Lukács demonstrates that the origins of the historical novel in Scott and Balzac lie in the revolutionary crises of the early nineteenth century, when people all over Europe suddenly became conscious of the fact that their own existence was historically conditioned (19–30). Lukács' contention is that the novel realistically reflects this general 'historical consciousness' through its concern with narrative development, social conflict and representative characters.

After the failure of the proletarian revolution in 1848, Lukács argues, realism lapses first into naturalism and then into formalism, both of which lose their sense of totality as capitalism regains and extends its control. Like realism, naturalism focuses on objective description, but it does so without a narrative sense, presenting random empirical details, succumbing to what Lukács calls 'description' or 'reportage'. It is further distinguished from realism in that it depicts human beings as victims of cataclysmic forces beyond their control. Formalism, on the other hand, in Lukács' account, is marked by a growing solipsism, as indicated in such movements as symbolism, expressionism and surrealism. Like naturalism and its relative impressionism, it focuses on accidental details, but it adds a greater concern with interiority, with the random flow of consciousness. Its typical technique is montage or some kind of spatial form. In each case, Lukács explains, an alienated vision of humanity is developed. The realistic novel's dialectical understanding of society as continuously shaped by human labour is exchanged for an illusory world of lifeless autonomous things no longer under human control. In place of the objective world of realism stands a subjective world of fragmentation. History becomes a backdrop, time appears to stand still and narrative falls by the wayside. An existential rather than a historical sense of humanity begins to emerge.

To account for these various traits historically, Lukács argues that they are symptoms of reification, once again linking the concerns of *History and Class Consciousness* with his aesthetic theories. In his opinion, both naturalism and formalism are shaped by the logic of commodity fetishism. Just as the mystified appearance of the commodity form conceals its basis in the exploitation of labour, so do naturalistic and formalistic works obscure the underlying reality of their time. For this reason, Lukács condemns both movements, claiming that they capitulate to capitalism through their various efforts to undermine objective representation. For this reason also, in *The Meaning of Contemporary Realism*, Lukács criticizes modernism, noting that its rejection of history and its elevation of style and allegory mark a further breakdown of narrative, as well as a further intensification of subjectivity (see 1963, 17–46). Lukács, in this regard, is no crude determinist. While he links literary forms to historical conditions, he finally accords a great deal of emphasis to the theoretical ability to overcome those conditions, the key to which, in the case of fiction, is the totalizing perspective of narrative, the literary equivalent of the dialectical method. Ultimately, this emphasis on striving for totality, which is linked to a humanist concern with overcoming alienation, is the main theme of Lukács' marxist work.

As persuasive and influential as Lukács' defence of totality may be, many subsequent theorists, directly or indirectly, have attempted to call it into question. In the 1960s, for instance, Louis Althusser's structural approach to marxism opposed the kind of humanism that Lukács advocated, stressing the so-called 'epistemological break' separating the young humanist Marx from the older scientific Marx. In the 1970s, the poststructuralist Jean-François Lyotard critiqued totalizing 'master narratives', even as a more general critical climate questioned whether linguistic reference was possible at all. More recently, with the advent of post-marxism in the 1980s and 1990s, theorists like Chantal Mouffe and Ernesto Laclau have questioned the traditional view of class consciousness on the grounds that it does not do justice to the complexities of culture, gender, race and ethnicity. A further problem discrediting this view in the minds of many is its link to the notion of a Leninist 'vanguard' leading the way of the masses.

Whatever the limitations of his thinking may be, Lukács now occupies an important position in the history of literary theory. Because of his ground-breaking studies on literature and culture, he is a canonized figure in most accounts of the early development of marxist theory. But Lukács is not just a historical relic. He is also important for contemporary theory, especially for the ongoing study of modernism and postmodernism.

Most notable in this regard is Lukács' influence on the wide-ranging work of the leading American marxist critic Fredric Jameson, whose defence of periodization, dialectics, totality, narrative, cognitive mapping and realism is indebted to his study of Lukács (see Bloch 1980, 196–7; Jameson 1971, 160–205; 1981, 13, 50–6; Lukács 1983, 1–8). Through Jameson, Lukács' insights on the relationship between reification and the rise of modern literary forms have had a decisive influence on theoretical attempts to historicize modernist and postmodernist culture. For this reason, Lukács' work is still relevant. In many respects, he has pointed out the way to a materialist assessment of twentieth-century culture.

Mitchell R. Lewis

Further reading and works cited

Bernstein, J. M. *The Philosophy of the Novel*. Minneapolis, MN, 1984.

Bloch, E. et al. *Aesthetics and Politics*. London, 1980.

Corredor, E. L. *György Lukács and the Literary Pretext*. New York, 1987.

— (ed.) *Lukács After Communism*. Durham, NC, 1997.

Goldmann, L. *The Hidden God: A Study of the Tragic Vision in the Pensées of Pascal and the Tragedies of Racine*. New York, 1964.

Jameson, F. *Marxism and Form: Twentieth-Century Dialectical Theories of Literature*. Princeton, NJ, 1971.

—. *The Political Unconscious*. Ithaca, NY, 1981.

Kadarkey, A. *Georg Lukács: Life, Thought, and Politics*. Oxford, 1991.

Királyfalvi, B. *The Aesthetics of György Lukács*. Princeton, NJ, 1975.

Lukács, G. *A modern dráma fejlödésének története*. Budapest, 1911.

—. *Existentialisme ou marxisme?* Paris, 1948.

—. *Studies in European Realism: A Sociological Survey of the Writings of Balzac, Stendhal, Zola, Tolstoy, Gorki and Others*. London, 1950.

—. *The Meaning of Contemporary Realism*. London, 1963.

—. *Writer & Critic and Other Essays*. New York, 1970.

—. *History and Class Consciousness*. Cambridge, MA, 1971a.

—. *The Theory of the Novel*. Cambridge, MA, 1971b.

—. *Tactics and Ethics: Political Essays, 1919–1929*, ed. R. Livingstone. New York, 1972.

—. *Soul and Form*. London, 1974a.

—. *Heidelberger Ästhetik, 1916–18*, eds G. Markus and F. Benseler. Darmstadt, 1974b.

—. *Heidelberger Philosophie der Kunst, 1912–14*, eds G. Markus and F. Benseler. Darmstadt, 1974c.

—. *The Young Hegel*. Cambridge, MA, 1976.

—. *The Ontology of Social Being*. 2 vols. London, 1978.

—. *The Destruction of Reason*. Atlantic Highlands, NJ, 1981a.

—. *Essays on Realism*, ed. R. Livingstone. Cambridge, MA, 1981b.

—. *The Historical Novel*. Lincoln, NE, 1983.

—. *Die Eigenart des Ästhetischen*, 2 vols. Berlin, 1987.

—. *German Realists in the Nineteenth Century*. Cambridge, MA, 1994.

—. *Lenin: A Study in the Unity of His Thought*. London, 1997.

Sim, S. *Georg Lukács*. New York, 1994.

Russian Formalism, the Moscow Linguistics Circle, and Prague Structuralism: Boris Eichenbaum (1886–1959), Jan Mukarovsky (1891–1975), Victor Shklovsky (1893–1984), Yuri Tynyanov (1894–1943), Roman Jakobson (1896–1982)

The historical confluence of Russian formalism, the Moscow Linguistics Circle, and the Prague structuralists in the first three decades of the twentieth century acted as one of the most significant and formative influences upon the direction of literary theory and criticism during the latter half of the century. Their various insights into narratology, linguistics and literary interpretation provided later scholars with the intellectual foundations for the structuralist project. Led by such figures as Victor Shklovsky, Boris Eichenbaum, Jan Mukarovsky, Yuri Tynyanov and Roman Jakobson, among others, Russian formalism resulted from the work of two groups of Russian literary critics and linguists, including the Moscow Linguistics Circle (founded in 1915) and the Society for the Study of Poetic Language (founded in St Petersburg in 1916). Russian formalists eschewed the notion that literature could best be understood in terms of such extra-literary matters as philosophy, history, sociology, biography and autobiography. Initially, they employed formalism as a derogatory term for the analysis of literature's formal structures and technical patterns. As Russian formalism's ideology became more refined, however, the concept began to assume more neutral connotations. Russian formalists – as with the Prague structuralists who would champion Russian formalism's critique after their suppression by the Soviet government in the 1930s – argue that literature functions upon a series of unique features of language that allows it to afford the reader with a mode of experience unavailable via the auspices of ordinary language.

Russian formalists refer to these special features of literature as *literaturnost*, or a particular work's 'literariness'. In a 1921 essay, Jakobson writes that 'the object of literary science is not literature but literariness, i.e. what makes a given work a literary work' (Steiner 1984, 23). A Russian-born linguist, Jakobson was professor at the Higher Dramatic School, Moscow (1920–33) and Masarykova University, Brno, Czechoslovakia (1933–9), before emigrating in 1941 to the United States, where he later assumed posts at Columbia University (1943–9), Harvard University (1950–67), and the Massachusetts Institute of

Technology (1957–67). In addition to founding the Prague school of structural linguistics and phonology, his name would later become nearly synonymous with our universal concepts of structuralism as an intellectual movement of considerable influence upon the nature and direction of the twentieth-century theoretical project. For Jakobson, the concept of *literaturnost* underscores the distinctive features inherent in the various discourses and linguistic forms of literature. More specifically, the notion of literariness refers to the internal relations, within a given literary work, among the linguistic signs and signifiers that comprise such formal features of literary study. In *Russian Formalism* (1984), Peter Steiner writes: 'If all literary works were literary, but some at a given moment were more literary than others, it is not an unchangeable essence but a changeable *relationship* among works that constitute literariness' (114). In short, the concept of literariness resides within the relational spaces established by a text's capacity for utilizing literary or poetic language.

Expositors of Russian formalism often ascribe the relational aspects of the formalist critique to Kantian notions of unity, meaning and the organic structure of art. The Russian symbolist Andrey Bely (1880–1934) based his conception of symbolism on Kant's theories regarding the relationship between art and other modes of human experience. In 'The Symbolization of Meaning', Bely profoundly influenced the course of the formalist methodology through his analyses of 'the unity of form and content' and 'the unity of cognition in the forms of experience' (Thompson 1971, 60). While anti-symbolists such as Shklovsky challenged the arguments of Bely and the other progenitors of Russian symbolism, Shklovsky recognized the interpretative value of understanding a given literary work's form in terms of its relationship with the notions of content and experience. Although terminological battles characterized much of early Russian formalism, Shklovsky's 1916 essay, 'Art as Device', provided formalists with a significant touchstone in their quest to establish their own form of intellectual and theoretical unity. Shklovsky's essay advanced a theory of narrative prose in which the author introduced the concept of *priem*, or 'device'. In addition to distinguishing between the aims of literary scholarship and the empirical sciences, the idea of the device afforded Shklovsky with the means for postulating the textual mechanism responsible for the literary structures and effects that distinguish literary modes of experience from the properties of ordinary language. As Jurij Striedter observes in *Literary Structure, Evolution, and Value* (1989), Shklovsky's ground-breaking study of *priem* resulted in 'the thesis that art is nothing but the consistent application and effect of such devices' (23).

Shklovsky advanced Russian formalism's differentiation between ordinary language and artistic discourse by highlighting art's ability to provide avenues of fresh perception that allow us to recognize new dimensions of reality and aesthetic value. Shklovsky contends that art accomplishes this end through its 'defamiliarization' of the world. In addition to revealing the artistic devices that account for artistic effect, Shklovsky hypothesized that this defamiliarizing concept of *ostranenie*, or the 'making strange' of things, finds its origins in literary, as opposed to ordinary, language. While Jakobson, among others, argued that *ostranenie* neglected to account for the artistic essence of poetic language, Shklovsky's analysis of estrangement acted as a defining moment for incipient Russian formalism because of the manner in which it imbued the movement with a significant and much needed sense of intellectual and artistic relevance. Simply put, *ostranenie* provided literary critics with a means for comprehending Russian formalism's goals for understanding the origins of art's creative and transformative vitality. Shklovsky's concept of defamiliarization involves two distinct concepts, including the idea that estrangement challenges conventional notions of linguistic and social perception, thus forcing the perceiver to reconceive his or her relationship with the world. Secondly, *ostranenie* focuses the perceiver's attention upon the literary work, as well as its contingent possibilities for defamiliarization and for undermining the ordinariness inherent in the extra-textual world. As Striedter notes, the innovative and polemical nature of *ostranenie* is underscored by its ramifications in terms of the literary tradition and the concept of canonicity: 'If literature gains and maintains effectiveness only through defamiliarization, once the newly created forms become canonized and thereby automatic, they, too, must be made strange once again. The theory of defamiliarization', Striedter adds, 'flows into a theory of literary evolution as a "tradition of breaking with tradition"' (24).

As with *ostranenie*, Shklovsky's explorations of *syuzhet* (plot) produced a variety of meaningful revelations regarding the role (or lack thereof) of plot in literary works. In a 1921 essay, 'Literature beyond Plot', Shklovsky devotes particular emphasis to works of 'plotless' literature. Shklovsky demonstrates that the dissolution of traditional plot conventions allows for a kind of literary evolution because of the manner in which it forces writers to experiment with new themes and devices. Shklovsky's article yields two significant conclusions in terms of Russian formalism's methodological aims. First, Shklovsky underscores the various ways in which plot experimentation ultimately serves as a catalyst for a given genre's structural evolution – an important aspect of Russian formalism, particularly in terms of the movement's interest in organicism. Second, Shklovsky challenges the boundaries inherent in our understanding of the concept of genre. Rather than functioning as a fixed canon that operates in terms of a set of firm rules and procedures, genre also exists in Shklovsky's schema as a constantly shifting and evolving mechanism. In his own discussions of plot and their structural role in literary works, Tynyanov takes issue with the latter conclusion, especially regarding Shklovsky's comprehension of literary parody, which he perceives as an automatic and comedic device. In his 1921 article, 'Dostoevsky and Gogol: Toward a Theory of Parody', Tynyanov identifies parody as an organic force that – as with *syuzhet* – operates as an instrument for literary evolution because of the way in which parody simultaneously deconstructs its precursory texts as it constructs new forms of narrative.

As one of the most influential formalists of his era, Vladimir Propp (1895–1970) also formulated a system for understanding the operation of literary works based upon a series of functional elements. A professor of philology at Leningrad University, Propp devoted particular attention to the role of surface detail, literary characters and narratological elements in Russian fairy tales. Recognizing that previous efforts at analysing fairy tales in terms of theme and plot had been intellectually fruitless, Propp opted instead to evaluate the tales via the series of character sequences and narrative tropes that characterize their construction. In *Morphology of the Folktale* (1928), Propp emphasizes the abstract structural elements and their textual function in terms of a given work's artistic and aesthetic whole. Propp's important work on behalf of Russian formalism's critical aims cannot be emphasized enough. As Steiner writes, 'On the most abstract level, he conceived of the fairy tale as a narrative about actions performed by certain characters. And it is the actions, and not the interchangeable characters, that count' (1984, 84). By demonstrating the organic qualities of narrative, Propp succeeded in revealing the nature of the generic, structural components of story. Propp's attention, moreover, to the relational aspects of literature finally afford Russian formalism the capacity to establish general laws regarding the conditions and nature of the structural elements associated with narrative. Propp's achievements in terms of Russian fairy tales also provide formalists with the critical means for articulating their programmatic goals and concerns to other schools and their proponents.

As with *ostranenie*, *syuzhet* and Propp's elucidation of various structural elements, Eichenbaum's conception of *skaz* remains among Russian formalism's most significant contributions to literary criticism. A richly textured narrative technique inherent in nineteenth- and twentieth-century Russian prose, *skaz* refers to literary works in which metaphor, theme and point of view function according to the stylistic requirements of oral narration and folk tales. In a 1918 essay, 'The Illusion of the *Skaz*', Eichenbaum offers a detailed discussion of *skaz* as a literary phenomenon, as well as a vehicle for understanding the fundamental nature of plot as a structural element. In addition to defining plot as the 'interweaving of motifs by the aid of their motivations' (in Striedter 1989, 44), Eichenbaum examines the role of the narrator in establishing the tone of a given plot. In an essay on Nikolai Gogol's 'The Overcoat', for example, Eichenbaum explores the ways in which the narrative serves to create distance between the reader and the plot, as well as between the narrator himself and the story's protagonist. The aesthetics of irony in the story demonstrate the manner in which *skaz*'s structural elements exist in a kind of interrelationship that impinges upon the nature of the reader's textual experience. Eichenbaum's postulation of *skaz* exists as a singular moment within the brief history of Russian formalism precisely because of its illumination of the simultaneous roles of such structural elements as linguistics, stylistics, point of view and plot in our consumption and understanding of narrative.

In one of Russian formalism's most significant instances of narratological innovation, Mukarovsky proposed the concept of 'foregrounding', or the act of placing an idea or element in sharp contrast with the other components of a given work of art. Clearly, estrangement or defamiliarization operates as a kind of foregrounding technique that allows readers to perceive the structural nature of literary language. Jakobson, Tynyanov and other formalists accomplish a similar end in their analysis of such structural matters as metre, alliteration and rhyme. As with such fundamental prose concepts as plot and genre, the notions of metre, alliteration and rhyme function as the organic material via which poetry evolves as a literary tradition. In poetry, metre establishes a kind of progressive force that propels the verse, while alliteration and rhyme, on the other hand, serve as regressive elements because of their reliance upon sound repetition. In other words, formalists such as Tynyanov comprehend poetry in terms of these inherently contradictory forces – the former of which contributes to the organic, evolving nature of poetry as a literary tradition, while the latter operates as a constraining mechanism. Foregrounding various structural elements inherent in verse enables critics such as Tynyanov to isolate these narratological components and identify their role in poetry's textual construction. This process also reveals the unifying mechanisms that undergird works of literary art. For the Russian formalists, unity clearly exists as one of the central principles of literary organization.

As with the Russian formalists, contemporary literary critics and linguists clearly owe a historical and intellectual debt to the efforts of the Prague Linguistic Circle, the group of scholars in the former Czechoslovakia who continued the work of the Russian formalists after their suppression by the Soviet government during the 1930s. Led by such figures as Jakobson, Vilém Mathesius (1882–1945), Lucien Tesnière (1893–1954), and René Wellek (1903–95), the Prague structuralists explored the intersections between linguistics and literary theory. As a group, their examinations of language and other sign systems became more specialized and illuminating after they began to absorb the theories of Ferdinand de Saussure regarding the synchronic analysis of language and its semantic functions. In terms of linguistics, the Prague structuralists' most important achievements include the liberation of phonology from phonetics, as well as Jakobson's work on semantics, Mathesius's revolutionary discoveries regarding syntax and Wellek's theories about literary theory and aesthetics. The advent of the Second World War curtailed their activities, which came to a sudden and precipitous halt after the Nazis closed Czech universities in October 1939. Jakobson continued their work in the interim in the United States; the Prague structuralists resumed their activities in Czechoslovakia in the 1950s, only to be interrupted by the pressures of marxist dogmatism. They reformed during the latter half of the 1950s under the auspices of the Soviet-inspired Czechoslovak Academy of Sciences, an organization that witnessed many linguistic accomplishments in the tradition of the Prague Linguistic Circle, especially the discoveries of such figures as Bohumil Trnka (1895–1984) and Josef Vachek (1909–96), among others. The Prague structuralists enjoyed a revival of sorts during the 1990s after the restoration of democracy in Czechoslovakia.

In an essay commemorating the Prague structuralists' pioneering work in 'Phonology and Graphemics', Vachek attributes one of the group's most enduring achievements to the Praguian conception of the phoneme, which has since become a standard phonological term. Jakobson defines the phoneme as 'a set of those concurrent sound properties which are used in the given language to distinguish words of unlike meaning' (14). By high-lighting the nature and function of the basic unit of phonology, the Prague structuralists were poised to emancipate the study of phonology from the more exclusive terrain of phonetics. Phonology involves the study of speech sounds of a given language and their operation within the sound system of that language. In the contemporary parlance of linguistics, the term refers not only to the field of phonemics but also to the study of sound changes in the history of a given language, i.e. diachronic phonology. The Prague structuralists' innovative research on behalf of phonology resulted in new discoveries regarding the problems of written language and orthography, while also serving as a means for highlighting the interdisciplinary connections between linguistics and narratology. The group's work in the 1930s included similar accomplishments in terms of our larger understanding of semantics and syntax. Through his examination of the Russian case system, Jakobson identified the presence of binary oppositions, a concept that would have an impact on our understanding of morphological units, as well as on the course of structuralism. Mathesius is often credited with having postulated the Prague structuralists' sentence-pattern model of syntax, a morphological mechanism that allows for the analysis of the linguistic signs inherent in every communicative speech act.

While many literary historians acknowledge the Prague structuralists' efforts on behalf of linguistic innovation, the group's significant contributions to our understanding of literature and aesthetics merit attention. Felix Vodichka's (1909–) commentaries on the nature of the literary process and Wellek's attempts at formulating general principles of literary study exemplify this aspect of the Prague structuralists' work. In 'The Con-cretization of the Literary Work: Problems of the Reception of Neruda's Works', Vodichka discusses the role of readerly perception in the literary process, a system that he defines in terms of the authorial subject who generates that artistic text and yet another subjectified other, the reader. Recognizing that the socially produced artistic norms of a given era ultimately share in the construction of literary works, Vodichka demonstrates the ways in which readers perceive narratives based upon their own socially and historically contingent moments of being. A signal moment in the early history of reader response and phenomenological criticism, Vodichka's study of perception theories reveals the manner in which the reading process is encoded by the conditions and structural components inherent in the literary experience. 'The higher structure of the artistic literary tradition is always present as a factor organizing the aesthetic effect of the work if it is to become an aesthetic object', Vodichka writes. 'Therefore the work is understood as a sign whose meaning and aesthetic value are comprehensible only on the basis of the literary conventions of a specific period' (110).

Vodichka's study of readerly perception also established several important inroads into our conception of authorship and its place in the construction of literary works. 'Besides the literary work', Vodichka observes, 'the "author" often becomes related to the developing literary structure. Here, we are concerned with the author not as psychophysical being but, in a metonymical sense, as the unity comprised of the works of a particular author in their entirety' (122). As with the Prague structuralists' Russian formalist precursors, Vodichka's conclusions about the interrelationships between authorship and narrative ultimately demonstrate the significant role of unity in the artistic experience. In his various analyses of the general principles that govern literary study, Wellek acknowledges similar interconnections between a given work's structural elements and its capacity for creating unity. 'The work of art is', Wellek writes in *Theory of Literature* (with Austin Warren, 1942), 'considered as a whole system of signs, or structure of signs, serving a specific aesthetic purpose' (141). By accenting the structural devices that characterize the literary experience, the Russian formalists' and Prague structuralists' critique of literature and language inevitably strives to highlight the roles of linguistic signs, artistic unity and literariness that produce our conceptions of narrative. Their discoveries about the nature of linguistics and literary criticism altered the course of twentieth-century textual scholarship and ushered in a new era marked by an interest in narratology and structuralism. The lingering effects of the Russian formalists and Prague structuralists are evidenced, moreover, by the influential scholarly work of such later figures as Roland Barthes, Mikhail Bakhtin and Fredric Jameson, among a host of others.

Kenneth Womack

Further reading and works cited

Bann, S. and Bowlt, J. E. (eds) *Russian Formalism*. New York, 1973.
Chomsky, N. *Current Issues in Linguistic Theory*. The Hague, 1964.
Erlich, V. *Russian Formalism*. The Hague, 1955.
Fried, V. (ed.) *The Prague School of Linguistics and Language Teaching*. Oxford, 1972.
Jakobson, R. and Halle, M. *Fundamentals of Language*. The Hague, 1956.
Jameson, F. *The Prison-House of Language*. Princeton, NJ, 1972.
Luelsdorff, P. A. (ed.) *The Prague School of Structural and Functional Linguistics*. Amsterdam, 1994.
Pomorska, K. *Russian Formalist Theory and Its Poetic Ambience*. The Hague, 1968.
Propp, V. *Morphology of the Folktale*. Austin, TX, 1968.
Shklovsky, Victor. 'Art as Device', in *Russian Formalist Criticism: Four Essays*, eds L. T. Lemon and M. J. Reis. Lincoln, NE, 1965.
—. *A Sentimental Journey: Memoirs, 1917–1922*. Ithaca, NY, 1970.
—. *Theory of Prose*. Elmwood Park, NJ, 1990.

Steiner, P. (ed.) *The Prague School: Selected Writings, 1929–1946*. Austin, TX, 1982.

—. *Russian Formalism: A Metapoetics*. Ithaca, NY, 1984.

Striedter, J. *Literary Structure, Evolution, and Value*. Cambridge, 1989.

Thompson, E. M. *Russian Formalism and Anglo-American New Criticism*. The Hague, 1971.

Tobin, Y. (ed.) *The Prague School and Its Legacy in Linguistics, Literature, Semiotics, Folklore, and the Arts*. Amsterdam, 1988.

Tynyanov, Y. 'Dostoevsky and Gogol: Toward a Theory of Parody', *Texte*, 1, 1921.

Vachek, J. (ed.) *A Prague School Reader in Linguistics*. Bloomington, IN, 1964.

—. 'Phonology and Graphemics', in *The Prague School of Structural and Functional Linguistics*, ed. P. A. Luelsdorff. Amsterdam, 1994.

Vodichka, F. 'The Concretization of the Literary Work: Problems of the Reception of Neruda's Works', in *The Prague School: Selected Writings, 1929–1946*, ed. P. Steiner. Austin, TX, 1982.

Wellek, R. *The Literary Theory and Aesthetics of the Prague School*. Ann Arbor, MI, 1969.

— and Warren, A. *Theory of Literature*. New York, 1942.

Ludwig Wittgenstein (1889–1951)

Ludwig Wittgenstein is one of the most important philosophers of the twentieth century, and the most radical and daring exponent of two of its central modes of thought. As a young student of Bertrand Russell, with a Viennese education that included Kant and Schopenhauer, Wittgenstein developed a severe and rigorous exposition of the Frege-Russell view of language and its representational function. This project, published as the *Tractatus Logico-philosophicus* in 1921, undertakes an account of ontology and the necessary limits of ontology as grounded on the triple relation of logic to proposition to fact to the world, and how this relation determines how we ought to think about the capacities and limits of language. The rest of Wittgenstein's life might be described as an incessant struggle against the bewitching power of this earlier vision, a struggle in which the sheer variety of the particular is brought to bear upon the categorical and austere uniformity of the vision embodied in the *Tractatus*.

For literary theorists, the *Tractatus* is important in several ways. Of most general use will be the fact that the *Tractatus* is sufficiently idealistic in its account of language to make the differences and critiques which Wittgenstein will later spell out applicable to other idealistic theories of language as well, from Saussure to Heidegger to Derrida. The relevance of some of these critiques is considered below.

More particularly, the *Tractatus* also attempts to treat the bedevilling problem of self-reference in formal logic – a problem that will again be at the heart of deconstructive (and even New Critical) approaches to philosophical, literary and psychoanalytic thinking. Russell had shown that paradoxes arise whenever a logical system has sufficient generality to talk about itself: it could then represent well-formed propositions that had the structure of the liar's paradox, which if true would logically have to be false, and if false would logically have to be true. Logic could never guarantee its own reliability, and indeed always seemed to hit a point where it seemed decidedly *un*reliable. Russell had a sort of jury-rigged system to deal with these problems (the 'theory of types', which disallowed such troubling entities as the set of all sets that do not contain themselves: does that set contain itself or not?). But Wittgenstein saw that such problems might bring us to the heart of subjectivity, since they might be paralleled with Kant's account of the inherent elusiveness of the I, the seat of first-person subjective experience (which he called 'the transcendental unity of apperception'). To try to intuit your own subjectivity is to objectify it, and therefore to miss it. The subjective self cannot refer to itself – to its own subjectivity. (Hegel would use the constantly frustrated, constantly renewed attempt at self-reference as the engine for the dynamic production of subjectivity itself, and thus inaugurate the continental philosophical tradition.) In the *Tractatus* Wittgenstein parallels the thinking subject face to face with the world it finds to the eye and the visual field. The eye sees everything within the visual field, but it cannot see itself – it is outside of the field it commands. The subject is outside of the world it can refer to, and language is outside of the things it can sensibly talk about – anything it says about itself, Wittgenstein says, is strictly speaking nonsense (as is, he says, the entire *Tractatus*).

Why should language be paralleled with subjectivity? Are the linguistic paradoxes of self-referentiality internally related to the phenomenological paradoxes of subjectivity? For Wittgenstein they are, since '*The limits of my language* mean the limits of my world' (5.6) The first of the seven major claims of the Tractatus is: 'The world is all that is the case', and what *being the case* means is being a *fact*, not a thing. The cat is not the case; the *fact* that the cat is on the mat may be. Thus Wittgenstein glosses this by saying that the world is the sum of *facts*, not the sum of things, with the further stipulation that 'the world is determined by the facts, *and* by their being *all* the facts' (1.11: first emphasis mine; cf. 4.52). A fact is something that a proposition pictures, and therefore the interface between language and world is a precise one: on the extreme correspondence theory of truth – the so-called picture-theory of language – that Wittgenstein sets forth in the *Tractatus*, the meaning of the sentence corresponds with the fact of the matter (this is Quine's sceptical formulation), and this attention to facts means not that ontology determines language, but that they both share a more basic substrate, which Wittgenstein calls 'logical space': 'The facts in logical space are the world. The world divides into facts' (1.13–1.2).

Wittgenstein admits, indeed he insists, that a paradox of self-referentiality arises immediately if we add to '*all* the facts' that determine the world the *further* fact that these are all the facts. He is thus led to an extreme account of an isolated and proto-existentialist subjectivity which is an unseizable limit condition to language, the eye or self outside of the world that language pictures and which cannot be pictured because everything that can be pictured can be pictured by language. He thus will end by saying that 'There is no such thing as the subject that thinks or entertains ideas … in an important sense there is no subject' (5.631). But this means finally that subjectivity is the deepest of mysteries ('das Ich, das Ich ist das tief Geheimnisvolle,' he says in a 1916 *Notebook* entry, in the midst of a summer in the trenches in battle) since it is not amenable to any discursive analysis: 'what the solipsist *means* is quite correct, only it cannot be *said* but makes itself manifest' (5.62). Because it cannot be said, Wittgenstein will end the *Tractatus* affirming in his most quoted statement, 'Whereof we cannot speak, thereof we must be silent' (7; I quote the well-known 1922 translation of this aphorism).

The *Tractatus* has been much more influential in the history of literature than in literary theory, and one should mention the important role it plays in both Joyce and Beckett's thinking about language. Beckett's *Watt* with its desperately logical main character depicts a Wittgensteinian hero come face to face with his own subjectivity through his attempts to master logical space. Beckett read the *Tractatus* aloud to Joyce when the latter was writing *Finnegans Wake* and a line in *Watt* is almost a direct quotation from the *Tractatus*: 'Do not come down off the ladder, Ifor, I haf taken it away', Erskine jokes, which alludes to Wittgenstein's conclusion: 'My propositions serve as elucidations in the following way: anyone who understands me eventually recognizes them as nonsensical, when he has used them – as steps – to climb up beyond them. (He must, so to speak, throw away the ladder after he has climbed up it.)' (6.54).

The closest analogue in literary theory to the claims of the *Tractatus* may be found in Blanchot: his sense of the alien alterity of the subject, in literary if not in logical space, is similar to the early Wittgenstein's and his account of 'passivity' and infancy (the subject *infantus*, before or beyond language) in the 1960s and after has much in common with Wittgenstein's sense of the subject as a limit of the world. People have naturally attempted to compare the early Wittgenstein with Heidegger's sense of the relation of being and language, but what Russell called Wittgenstein's mysticism – especially in the ethical passages of the *Tractatus* – is considerably closer to the critiques of Heidegger in Blanchot and Levinas than it is to the mysticism in Heidegger himself.

But Blanchot and also Levinas display far more attention to the subjectivity of the other (of *autrui*) than the emphasis on solipsism in the *Tractatus* might seems to give Wittgenstein title to. His later work justifies the comparison, however, since even as it mounts the most powerful critique ever made of the *Tractatus* and the logicist ambitions it arose from, it continues an exploration into the nature of subjectivity and its relation to language that highlights and clarifies the ethical claims of the *Tractatus*.

The most important work by the later Wittgenstein is *Philosophical Investigations*, an unfinished book published posthumously but which comes closest to Wittgenstein's own vision of how he wished to publish his later thought. The fundamental break that *Philosophical Investigations* represents with the *Tractatus* is in its denial that it is the business of language to picture the world. *Philosophical Investigations* sets forth a powerfully non-representational view of language. Language is used for countless things: there are –

> *countless* kinds [of sentence – *Satz*, translated as 'proposition' in the *Tractatus*]: countless different kinds of use of what we call 'symbols', 'words', 'sentences'. And this multiplicity is not something fixed, given once for all; but new types of language, new language-games, as we may say, come into existence, and others become obsolete and get forgotten. (We can get a *rough picture* of this from the changes in mathematics.)
>
> Here the term 'language-*game*' is meant to bring into prominence the fact that the *speaking* of language is part of an activity, or of a form of life.
>
> Review the multiplicity of language-games in the following examples, and in others:
>
> Giving orders, and obeying them –
> Describing the appearance of an object, or giving its measurements –
> Constructing an object from a description (a drawing) –
> Reporting an event –
> Speculating about an event –
> Forming and testing a hypothesis –
> Presenting the results of an experiment in tables and diagrams –
> Making up a story; and reading it –
> Play-acting –
> Singing catches –

Guessing riddles –

Making a joke; telling it –

Solving a problem in practical arithmetic –

Translating from one language into another –

Asking, thanking, cursing, praying.

– It is interesting to compare the multiplicity of the tools in language and of the ways they are used, the multiplicity of the kinds of words and sentence, with what logicians have said about the structure of language. (Including the author of the *Tractatus Logico-philosophicus*.)

The whole of this passage deserves extended comment. Countless kinds of sentences means that there is no *general* form of sentence, nor single structure of niches for the heterogeneous set of forms. (J. L. Austin objected to this claim, but Wittgenstein, more radically determined against systematicity than Austin, believed in the endless possibility of human and therefore linguistic novelty; many of the items on Wittgenstein's list Austin regarded as 'etiolated' or 'parasitic' uses of language, and Jacques Derrida rightly takes the latter to task on this issue.) Wittgenstein insists on a radical multiplicity of language-games. He says that the multiplicity is not fixed or given once and for all and yet at the same time the world that humans inhabit (at a human level) is the world of their linguistic activities and interactions – of their language games. Thus as in the *Tractatus* there is still something essentially synonymous about living in the world and playing language games – there is still a sense in which my language means my world. But Wittgenstein would no longer say that 'the *limits* of language (of that language which alone I understand) mean the limits of my world' (5.62, my italicization). As he says in recantation in the 1928 lecture on ethics: 'The limits of my language? language is not a cage.' And language is no longer something that alone I understand, nor indeed is it the case that *understanding* is the privileged and natural term for our relation to language-games. (This is a good place to contrast Wittgenstein with Davidson and Quine, who begin with a sense of the radical isolation of the human mind from the world around it – an isolation more in keeping with Wittgenstein's views in the *Tractatus* than in the *Investigations*. Wittgenstein's ideas in the *Tractatus* were highly influential on Carnap who was in turn a major intellectual interlocutor of Davidson's teacher, Quine. By the time Wittgenstein was giving the lectures drafted in the *Blue* and *Brown Books*, he was making striking arguments against the existence of what he called 'private languages', a notion of privacy that still survives in Davidson.)

Thus language and the world it inhabits are radically multiple, mutable and free of determination by any epistemological or ontological centre. (Here, Wittgenstein might be compared to the radical empiricism of William James on the one hand – James was perhaps the later Wittgenstein's most important stimulus to thinking, of which more below – and Deleuze on the other, from *Empiricism and Subjectivity* to *A Thousand Plateaus*.)

In the *Tractatus* Wittgenstein had defined the general form of a proposition (*Satz*): 'this is how things stand' (4.5). Like J. L. Austin's constative or locutionary utterance, the proposition wrongly seems the paradigmatic instance of language: a representation of reality. Austin doubts that pure constatives are anything but rare and extreme cases of language use, and suggests that in normal circumstances they are to be met with perhaps only recently and in scientific or technical books. More radical still, Wittgenstein's parenthetical remark on 'the changes in mathematics' means not that maths gives you at least a rough paradigm for the rest of language (this is the logicist or Tractarian viewpoint he now eschews), but that *even* mathematics belongs to a human practice and is itself liable to the sorts of observations and considerations that apply to the countless different language games. This point deserves emphasis, for one of the most important results in mathematical philosophy during the twentieth century was Gödel's Second Incompleteness Theorem, which was a kind of demonstration of the applicability of Russell's paradoxes of self-referentiality to the whole of mathematics of any generalizing power. Wittgenstein, nearly alone among important philosophers of mathematics, had denied the major significance of Gödel's proof, because he alone among major philosophers of mathematics was a thorough-going anti-Platonist: a thorough-going disbeliever in an immutable realm of mathematical truth or falsehood independent of human activity – despite, or perhaps because of, his results, Gödel remained a Platonist to the end. (Even the mathematical intuitionism that he found congenial, while styling itself anti-Platonic, continues to appeal to a Platonic foundation in truth, denying, however, that there may be a truth beyond the possibilities of human construction.) Anti-Platonism characterizes all Wittgenstein's later work, and what we are to notice here is the refusal of a Platonic view of either language or representation. There is no Platonic form of language: there is no canonical mode of representation. Even the propositions of mathematics have a history, and belong therefore to contingency; that history is one of its involvement with human activity and human use.

Wittgenstein's adjurations against the philosophical interest of self-referentiality – adjurations that set him against even in the apparently rigorous mathematical results of people like Gödel – ought to prevent the common misapprehension of Wittgenstein as a kind of genial champion of common-sense – the Wittgenstein put forward most strenuously and most misleadingly by Richard Rorty. Anti-philosophical he may be, but he is not a-philosophical, and his arguments cut sharply at the deepest and most cherished philosophical beliefs. What in particular they cut at – in mathematics as in language as in psychology – is the notion of a governing paradigm, formula, technique, grammar or structure (variously invoked by science, mathematics, logic, linguistics and anthropology) which might provide the rules whereby particular phenomena would arise.

The later Wittgenstein's importance for literary theory is twofold. On a *negative* side, he will unsettle attentive readers coming from a deconstructive or poststructuralist background just as much as he unsettles the Anglo-American partisans of Frege and Russell. The theory of language which various brands of poststructuralism accept is one that continues to see language as largely representational, whether in its ambitions, illusions or aspirations. To show, following Nietzsche, that language constructs the truths and the templates for the truths that it seems to satisfy is still to accept that the major human investment in language is in its representational function. Wittgenstein's tireless denial of the centrality or privileged position of this function cuts deeper than the claims of deconstruction and related poststructuralist theories of discourse, as it avoids their own critiques. This is to say that Wittgenstein denies the most important (although often tacit) claim of poststructuralist theory: that human subjectivity is constituted through the anxious repression of the primal inadequacy of language to represent the very subjectivity that its failure of representation gives rise to. Such a claim arises out of a Hegelian tradition (made central in France by Alexandre Kojève, whose lectures Derrida, Lacan and many others attended) which Wittgenstein came to reject. The multiplicity and variousness of language-games is at the bottom of his rejection of the hypostasis of 'language' at the heart of poststructuralist thought. For Wittgenstein there is no such thing as language, useful as the term is in many contexts. (Similarly, he vexed Russell by denying that there was any such thing as an 'object', though he never denied that there were, say, ink-spots.)

But Wittgenstein's rejection of the hypostasization of language (and a fortiori of language-as-other, of the symbolic order, for example) arises out of a yet more radical view of mental life, a view adumbrated in the *Tractatus*. The later Wittgenstein strenuously denies the usefulness of the appealing notion of a mental state: a state (a feeling, emotion, disposition, etc.) that a mind might be in, and that would belong to a private world separate from the various inaccessible worlds inhabited individually by other minds. (This denial makes him anathema to cognitive psychologists, from Turing on. Turing was Wittgenstein's student at Cambridge, and transcripts of their mathematical disagreements about Gödel, among other things, survive.) Human life, or human subjectivity isn't at bottom for Wittgenstein a way of being but a way of acting. His arguments against the perspicuity of the invocation of mental states and mental contents (what is the content of a state of expectation? of love? of irritation? of intention? of certainty? of knowledge? of self-consciousness? of following a rule? of hope? of anxiety?) rank among the most bracing and powerful passages of his later work. These passages to some extent read like radicalizations of William James: James gives the most fluid and convincing doctrine of the notion of mental contents and states ever propounded, and Wittgenstein goes farther by rejecting the husks represented by the way James formulates his psychological observations and puzzles. James had characterized the privacy of thought as one of its most notable characteristics, but Wittgenstein is concerned to deny this privacy. In a notorious and central passage in *Philosophical Investigations* he writes:

> I can know what someone else is thinking, not what I am thinking.
> It is correct to say 'I know what you are thinking', and wrong to say 'I know what I am thinking.'
> (A whole cloud of philosophy condensed into a drop of grammar.) . . .
> If I see someone writhing in pain with evident cause I do not think: all the same, his feelings are hidden from me. (222–3)

This passage ought to compared to Austin's account of our knowledge of other minds. Language-games are played with others. To have language is to have others: not to *believe in* or to *assume* or to *presuppose* or to *stipulate* others, but to have them in whatever way we have language. Others are: those we use language to interact with. I am no more certain of the meaning of the word *hand* than I am that others exist whom I can touch with my hand.

The result of Wittgenstein's arguments – which by their nature cannot be well-summarized because there is no general doctrine governing them – is to see something like how robust the human psyche is, and yet how fragile that robustness is. Wittgenstein teaches us that we have certainty, but he also teaches us what certainty is, and whatever it is it's not the metaphysical buttress that philosophers have thought it was. Too many people – both admirers and detractors – stop at Wittgenstein's arguments for the psyche's robustness and do not see the fragility that is its obverse. Belonging to the world in countless ways, there are countless ways that the self may be dispossessed from the world, and not just the handful of ways that anxiety about the capacities of representation would designate. There are countless ways of being dispossessed, and therefore the experience of dispossession may itself become endless.

The influential continental thinkers that the later Wittgenstein is in many ways closest to are Blanchot and Merleau-Ponty (heavily influential as they are on Derrida and Lacan respectively). Like them he has a Proustian sense of the unutterable complexity of human experience and of the correspondingly vast region of potential estrangement from experience within experience. That potential for estrangement is already suggested in the *Tractatus*, when he says that there is no such thing as a thinking subject, that the philosophical self does not belong to the world but is its limit. Even in the *Tractatus* the self has nothing to do with mental states, and the array of experience is everything we possess, and therefore everything from which we are dispossessed. Later this will mean that the world that we live in is the only world we have; the things that we do are all that there is to do, and outside of this is not some Platonic or Kantian world to which the subject belongs, but a place where subjectivity is experienced without being able ever to consolidate itself as an independent entity. This is where Wittgenstein is like Proust, in the heartbreaking sense that he gives of the endless variety of the world which nevertheless is not various enough to cure the final isolation and impoverishment of a self all the more estranged from the world as it belongs all the more wholly to it.

William Flesch

Further reading and works cited

Baker, G. P. and Hacker, P. M. S. *An Analytical Commentary on Wittgenstein's 'Philosophical Investigations'*. Oxford, 1983.

Bouveresse, J. *Wittgenstein Reads Freud*. Princeton, NJ, 1995.

Cavell, S. *Must We Mean What We Say?* Cambridge, MA, 1976.

—. *The Claim of Reason*. Cambridge, MA, 1979.

—. *A Pitch of Philosophy*. Cambridge, MA, 1994.

Crary, A. and Read, R. *The New Wittgenstein*. London, 2000.

Dreben, B. 'Quine and Wittgenstein: the Odd Couple', in *Wittgenstein and Quine*. eds R. Arrington and H. J. Glock. London, 1996.

Floyd, J. 'Wittgenstein on 2, 2, 2 ...', *Synthese*, 87, 1991.

Friedlander, E. 'Heidegger, Carnap and Wittgenstein: Much ado about nothing', in *The Story of Analytic Philosophy*, eds A. Biletzki and A. Matar. London, 1998.

Goldfarb, W. 'Metaphysics and nonsense', *Journal of Philosophical Research*, 22, 1997.

Hallett, G. *A Companion to Wittgenstein's 'Philosophical Investigations'*. Ithaca, NY, 1977.

Kripke, S. *Wittgenstein on Rules and Private Language*. Cambridge, MA, 1982.

McGuinness, B. *Wittgenstein, A Life*. Berkeley, CA, 1988.

Monk, R. *Wittgenstein: The Duty of Genius*. New York, 1991.

Quinney, L. *Literary Power and the Criteria of Truth*. Gainesville, FL, 1995.

Shanker, S. *Wittgenstein and the Turning Point in the Philosophy of Mathematics*. Albany, NY, 1987.

Staten, H. *Wittgenstein and Derrida*. Lincoln, NE, 1984.

Wittgenstein, L. *Tractatus Logico-philosophicus*. London, 1961.

—. *On Certainty*, eds G. E. M. Anscombe and G. H. von Wright. Oxford, 1969.

—. *Philosophical Investigations*. Oxford, 1972.

—. *The Blue and Brown Books*. Oxford, 1975.

—. *Wittgenstein's Lectures on the Foundations of Mathematics: Cambridge, 1939*, ed. C. Diamond. Ithaca, NY, 1976.

—. *Remarks on the Foundations of Mathematics*, eds G. H. von Wright, R. Rhees and G. E. M. Anscombe. Oxford, 1978.

—. *Notebooks, 1914–1916*, eds G. E. M. Anscombe and G. H. von Wright. Oxford, 1979.

—. *Zettel*, eds G. E. M. Anscombe and G. H. von Wright. Oxford, 1981.

Martin Heidegger (1889–1976)

Martin Heidegger succeeded Edmund Husserl as the major philosopher of the phenomenological movement. Both Heidegger and Husserl regarded phenomenology as the very beginning of true philosophical inquiry: attention to phenomena is directed to what appears, to what is given or shows itself. Phenomenology, therefore, tries to approach the question of being without assuming any prior interpretation of what being is. It does not, for example, ask whether there *are* such beings as numbers, essences or meanings, for such questions presuppose that we know what it means to exist. Both Husserl and Heidegger were far more concerned with understanding what it means to say that something exists.

Whereas Husserl regarded his own philosophy as a radical beginning that broke free from all previous philosophies, Heidegger insisted on the necessarily historical location of any metaphysics. Heidegger's work usually divided into two broad periods, although there is much debate about the significance of the divide. The first period, prior to the *Kehre* or 'turn', is dominated by Heidegger's *Being and Time* (1927). The main focus of *Being and Time* is '*Dasein*' (or 'there-being'), a term which resists translation precisely because Heidegger was trying to avoid the language of subjectivity, consciousness or man. Such terms, Heidegger argued, presupposed a starting point. What we need to do is begin our questioning in a more radical manner, and not assume that we know what 'mind', 'subject' or even 'thinking' mean. Heidegger begins *Being and Time*, just as Husserl began his phenomenology, with the very problem of beginning: how is it possible to begin metaphysics without presupposing some founding being? According to Heidegger we ought not begin by asserting the existence of some original *being*. Rather, we should assume nothing more than the *question* of being. This is why Heidegger refers to '*Dasein*' rather than man, consciousness or subjectivity. *Dasein*, or 'there-being' is just that point from which being is questioned. *Dasein* is just that being who is capable of asking the question of being. The problem with the history of metaphysics is that it has traditionally begun by assuming the existence of some founding being – such as matter, or man, or subjectivity. Instead of assuming some foundation, *Being and Time* provides an analysis of the being who questions and lays foundations. The first part of *Being and Time* is therefore taken up with what Heidegger refers to as 'existential analysis'. This existential analysis does not begin with a theory or definition of what *Dasein* is but examines all the ways in which we experience ourselves, and then asks how our existence is possible.

Heidegger is, quite justifiably, included in the tradition of existentialism. Although his work needs to be differentiated from other existential thinkers, notably Jean-Paul Sartre, he does insist on the general existentialist claim that we ought not to assume some founding essence that has certain immutable qualities that are then played out in our actual existence. Sartre insisted that our existence precedes our essence: our being is the outcome of the decisions and events of our life. Heidegger argues that it is our essence to 'ek-sist', or to 'dwell' with being (1998, 248). He rejected the traditional opposition between essence (the pure form) and existence (the actualization of that form). Instead, 'ek-sistence' is the essence of a being who is nothing other than its relation to being. By existence Heidegger refers to all the ways in which we live in the world: our past, the complexity of our present, and our directedness towards a future. This is why he uses the term 'Dasein' rather than 'human'. Humans are usually defined as rational animals – beings within the world who then have reason, beings who have an essence. Dasein, by contrast, is not a being who bears certain qualities (such as reason or humanity); Dasein exists by disclosing a world or being.

Heidegger begins his analysis of Dasein by inquiring into how it is possible to form the question of being. What would be the appropriate point from which to ask the question of being? Heidegger insists that we can't just seize upon any specific thing and then ask what being is in general. Being is not a generalization that we gather from examining a collection of beings, for we need to have some understanding of being beforehand in order to say that any single thing 'is'. So being must have a meaning that cannot be reduced to just collecting all the different uses of the word. We cannot, Heidegger insists, begin the question of being from the beings that we have as present before us. Instead we should begin the question of being by looking at the being who is asking the question. For only if we understand how it is that we form the question of being will we be able to understand just what it is we are questioning. The being who is capable of questioning being is Dasein and examining Dasein is an existential analysis. An analysis of Dasein is existential because unlike other beings or entities Dasein 'is' only in so far as it relates to a world. Dasein is not a self-present substance that then comes to know a world. Dasein is always already being-in-the-world.

It might seem that Heidegger's inquiry is circular: we begin to answer the question of being by asking about the being who is asking the question. But Heidegger insists that this circularity is felicitous. The idea of an argument that would not be circular presupposes that there could be some pure point outside our own existence from which we could begin our inquiry. Against this Heidegger insists on the 'hermeneutic circle' of all questioning: we must assume some starting point for the question, but the course of questioning will also illuminate and redefine the point from which we began. And so against the assertion of Dasein as yet one more founding being Heidegger insists that Dasein is a way of interrogating the formation of philosophical foundations. The history of metaphysics has been dominated by the assertion of some grounding presence – such as mind, God, matter, spirit or man – but what has been forgotten is the question of just how such a grounding presence is possible. Heidegger will, in contrast with this tradition of ground laying, ask about Dasein and how Dasein is capable of questioning presence or being. (How is it possible to interrogate grounds or foundations; how is it that we can move beyond any simple assertion of presence and question being?) The fact that we can ask the question of being tells us something about being and how being is made present. It is only possible to ask the question of being if we are already presented with beings. Initially, then, the question of being always begins from a relation to specific beings. We can only ask about being in general because we already exist in relation to the beings of a world.

Heidegger also insists that the question of being is not some empty category imposed by philosophers upon the world. Our questioning power is crucial to the very possibility of having a world. In order to have a world at all, in an everyday sense, we must already have some understanding of being. We have an implicit, but not theoretical, concept of being.

In our day-to-day lives, however, we live this 'pre-ontological' relation to being in the mode or beings that are *Zuhandenheit* or ready-at-hand. Our relation to the world is not objectified or cognized as a subject–object relation. On the contrary, our world is present in the form of projects, purposes, activities and a totality or horizon of meaningful activity. Before we think of the world as simply 'being', and before we understand ourselves as subjects who *know* a world, our world is a world of projects and purposes. Our original relation to the world is one of care or concern (*Sorge*) and not knowledge. The world is not an object to be known but a totality of involvements and possibilities. Indeed, as Heidegger insists, the very being of the world, the fact that we have a world that we take as existing, is grounded upon a prior purposeful 'projection': an understanding of our world as there for our possible becoming and activity. It's not that we have a world that we then come to care about and add values to. Rather, it is *from care* (or some concerned relation) that our world is given. This is why an existential analysis must be primary. Before we can ask about the being of the world we need to understand the ways in which this world is already given in everyday existence. And the condition for any world being given is the concerned existence of *Dasein*.

Heidegger therefore describes a number of what he refers to as existential categories. These categories describe not this or that particular world or *Dasein*, but the very possibility of any world. These categories are not culturally relative; they are possibilities of existence for any world at all. It would not be possible to exist without the categories of care, mood, being-with-others or 'throwness'. For example, any *Dasein* at all is always 'thrown'. We are not born as individuated subjects who then take on a history, language and culture. On the contrary, we exist only through our specific historical and cultural locale; we are 'thrown'. We are already given a specific set of possibilities for existence. But these are *possibilities* (and not determined attributes). And so alongside the category of throwness, Heidegger also insists on the category of 'care'. We can only have a 'world' at all with the overall category of care. Care is the way in which we are always directed towards a world and our future projects. A world is never a meaningless object or matter but is always this world at this time with these possibilities. (Even the seemingly blank world of scientific description is possible only because of scientific projects and aims.) Our world is not some blank data to which we add values; there is no world other than the one disclosed through our purposes and projects. Care – a concerned relation to what is other than ourselves – is an existential category, something that would structure the existence of any possible *Dasein*. The world of 'reality' or 'theory', Heidegger insists, is only possible once we have abstracted from the world of everyday concerns, and this world that responds to the look of theory is itself the outcome of specific concerns (the projects of epistemology, science or observation). Initially and for the most part, Heidegger insists, we relate to the world, not as objective matter that is there to be known, but as a meaningful totality given through this or that mood. (And so mood or 'attunement' is another existential category.)

The question then arises, of course, as to how we move from this involved and concerned relation to the world, to the objectifying theoretical attitude – such as science or philosophy – where the world is perceived as inert presence (or *Vorhandenheit*) for a disengaged viewing subject. Heidegger has two ways of answering this question. The first way is his description of the emergence of the objectification of the world in its inauthentic manner. For the most part we dwell in the world in a mode of involvement and concern. We are, therefore, not aware of the *being* of the world, for we are always caught up with specific beings. However, it is precisely this everyday involvement with beings that usually comprises an inauthentic understanding. We imagine that the world is simply 'there' quite independent of our relation to it or our existence. Because we are so involved in an object world, we don't see the world as specifically *ours*. More importantly, Heidegger argues, we don't see it as a *world*. We think we just encounter objects, despite the fact that in order to perceive any single object an entire world must be presupposed. Any single thing is understood, Heidegger insists, only from within a totality of meaningful projects. If, for example, I perceive a hammer, then I already have all the meanings of what a tool is, what building is and what activity is. In everyday understanding, then, Heidegger insists that the world – or what is nearest to us – is precisely what we do not see. I see identifiable things only because I live as being-in-the-world, but it's this totality of meanings that makes up my world that I do not see. Philosophy, or the theoretical attitude, has also according to Heidegger 'passed over' the understanding of the world. So if Heidegger insists that everyday existence already bears within it the tendency to objectify its world and forget its constitutive involvement, he also makes this claim regarding philosophy and science. Because these disciplines are concerned with knowing and interrogating the world, they forget that there is a world of meaningful projects and concerns before we come to ask the question of being or 'reality'. When the scientist or philosopher asks about being she isolates a being as a separate object devoid of meaning and purpose. But, this way of looking, Heidegger argues, presupposes a world. For in the theoretical attitude I regard the thing in a particular way, abstracted from its everyday use and meaning. I regard it in the manner of 'mere thing in general'.

This is why, Heidegger insists, philosophy has historically asked the question of being *ontically*. It has always taken a particular being or thing (the ontic) as the beginning of its inquiry, but it has not asked *how* it is that we come to know or experience things. This would be an *ontological* question: not the question of this or that being, but the question of how any being at all can be. When we question the world we have tended to do so from the standpoint of those beings around us. We imagine that consciousness or the subject is just one type of being that must then come to know other types of beings, such as objects. We 'pass over' the *ontological* dimension of the world. Heidegger therefore wants to insist on the difference between the ontic and the ontological: the ontic dimension is that of specific beings; the ontological is what allows any being to appear. If I ask you what being means and you point to an object and say, 'This is a being', you are giving me an ontic definition. You are just offering me another being. But if you try to explain what being is *as such* you give me an ontological definition. You might say that being is spirit, or God, or matter. Now Heidegger insists that these sorts of answers, despite their efforts, are still *ontic*; they still define being by pointing to some particular being. An ontological definition would not just point to a present being, but would account for the very possibility of being or how things become present. How is it that we say that something *is* at all? According to Heidegger it is only when we really question the very possibility of being that we are capable of thinking at an ontological level. In *Being and Time* Heidegger tries to think both *Dasein* and world at an ontological level. *Dasein*, for example, is not a thing but is an *existence* that is directed to what is other than itself. The *world* properly considered is *ontological* – rather than ontic – because it is not some *present* thing but that horizon through which things appear.

The world is what enables any thing to come to presence. In order to experience a thing I must grasp it through some understanding – 'as' this or that specific thing – and from some mood or comportment. This is so even if I relate to the thing in a theoretical manner, for here I take the thing as 'mere object' and my mood is one of 'mere looking'. All being is therefore given from some world, and the question of being is possible only because we exist in a world in the manner of involved concern (being-in-the-world). If we think of the world ontically (as a collection of things) we don't really understand what our world is. For the world is not a set of objects we encounter; the world is a meaningful totality of other persons, history, projects, languages and practices. The world is a totality of understanding that is not itself a thing; it is what makes any thing possible. The world is not just what is immediately seen; it is what is presupposed in any act of looking.

However, it's precisely because our everyday involvement is so concerned with beings that we fail to really ask the question of being or the world properly. We merely take one form of being – the being of objects – and then use this understanding to question being in general. Metaphysics has largely been caught up in this failure of the question of being, for it has always answered the question of being by deciding upon some specific being as always present and grounding – the being of the subject, of God, of matter or the idea. (And the thought of this grounding being has always taken the form of an object: we imagine consciousness to be a type of thing, or God to be the highest being.) But Heidegger also describes an *authentic* emergence of the question of being. In his later work Heidegger had isolated certain moments in the history of philosophy and certain forms of art and poetry that opened the possibility for an authentic question of being, even if these possibilities were not taken up. Kant, for example, asked how metaphysics was possible. In so doing he *almost* disclosed that we are beings capable of questioning our world, and so we are not self-present 'subjects' (Heidegger 1990). Certain poets, such as Hölderlin, also described the emergence of the world through language and concern (Heidegger 1971). And ancient Greek philosophers had not yet reduced being to mere objectivity (Heidegger 1984). But Heidegger nevertheless argued that the authentic question of being had generally been forgotten. In his later work Heidegger spent most of his time rereading the history of metaphysics to see how being had been forgotten. In *Being and Time*, though, Heidegger describes the ways in which the authentic question of being might emerge from everyday existence or being-in-the-world.

Heidegger describes the emergence of the sense of ownness and authenticity through a specific mood or attunement. While all our activity is undertaken in a certain mood, such that we never view the world in an empty and objective gaze – for this would still be a specific mood – there are certain moods that disclose our relation to the world. They enable us to see our world *as a world*. Heidegger looks at anxiety or *Angst* as that mood *within* the world that enables us to becomes aware of the world in general. In anxiety, as opposed to fear, I am in a state of dread but there is no specific object of my anxiety. I may *fear* an earthquake or a plane crash, but in this case my worldly mood is directed to, and caught up in, an object. I am still within the general horizon of life's meaning. In anxiety, however, my concern has no object. Because of the absence of any specific object to which my concern might be directed, I am brought up against my relation to the world in general. I am no longer immediately involved with my world, relating to this or that specific being. I have the sense of a relatedness towards the world – that there is some 'thing' that I dread – but there is also *nothing* as such that I fear; my anxiety has no specific being as its object. In fact, anxiety often occurs when the world breaks down. In everyday existence I accept the meaning of my world, without that world being specifically *mine*: I catch the bus, do my job, go home and pay my taxes. Anxiety might enter my world, however, when such meaning is lost: if on my way home I see a destitute woman whose very existence discloses the 'comfort' of my world, or if there is some natural disaster that disrupts the rhythm of everyday life. In such cases I may no longer 'have' a world unselfconsciously. The world seems no longer mine or homely, but not because I have some other world or object in view. I am no longer caught up in the meaning of my world. I am brought back from being absorbed in the world of everyday things, and so the very specificity or limit of my world is made apparent.

In *Being and Time* Heidegger has three ways of describing the ways in which *Dasein* becomes aware of its existence or becomes authentic. In the mood of anxiety, I feel my difference from the world without relating to any specific object. I don't know *what* I fear. But Heidegger also describes the call of conscience; here I become aware of existence not through the world, as in anxiety, but through my own being. In conscience my 'morality' is silenced and I am called to decide. This occurs when I realise that my world has been decided not by myself but by the 'they'. If, for example, the government I have elected engages in a war I don't approve of, or if I see a film that foregrounds the contingency of my moral codes, then I realize that the world is, or has been, constituted by a meaning that *I* did not decide. The voice of conscience, then, does not repeat internalized values. On the contrary, it silences received values so that we are thrown back on our own decision. The very 'silence' of conscience can disclose my everyday moral axioms as derived, given or empty. Authentic conscience for Heidegger lies in *not* hearing the voice of everyday morality. It is because there is no given and immutable morality that I can hear the silent voice of conscience; in *not* telling me what to do, or in saying nothing, conscience 'calls' me to decide. Finally, *Dasein* can also emerge from inauthenticity – where it merely understands itself as a thing – through being-towards-death. If I truly know that I am going to die then I am forced to confront the specificity and finitude of my lifespan. Inauthentically, I imagine that I will get around to doing things 'some day'; I will give up smoking, donate to charities and quit being unreliable. But if I accept that my death is imminent and truly possible, and that no one can die for me, then I am compelled to decide on my existence. If I am going to act I must do so within this life which is wholly mine. And because my lifespan is finite there are only so many possibilities for me; I must decide and act resolutely.

What Heidegger describes through the three 'existentials' of anxiety, conscience and being-towards-death, is the opening of a world-transcending attitude from within the world. (Heidegger does not just assume that there is a properly transcendental attitude that philosophers ought to adopt. Rather, he shows how any attitude, including the attitude of metaphysics, emerges from a concerned relation to, and understanding of, the world.) For the most part we are concerned with objects, and don't pay attention to the horizon of meanings and purposes that constitute the world in which those objects appear. For an object is only perceivable *as* this or that specific thing because there is a system of meaning and understanding within which it is located (a world). In anxiety, however, this horizon of meaning and the totality of purposes breaks down. Anxiety is that existential mood that discloses the very possibility of existence in general. In anxiety I am no longer caught up in my immediate and purposive existence, and I am brought up against existence in general: that there is a world and that it is not exhausted by the horizon and meaning of my specific existence. In being-towards-death, I am brought back to the specificity of my existence. If I am conscious of myself as one who will die at a certain time, then I am brought up against the particularity and finitude of my existence. Only certain possibilities and projects are open to me. I can act, inauthentically, as if there were no specific limit to my life – as if, all things were open and possible indefinitely. Or, I can act authentically, aware that death inscribes a limit to my life. I live for this amount of time at this point in history, and I must face that limit and undertake my projects accordingly.

Heidegger extended this notion of historical resoluteness and the authenticity of the decision in the work and lectures that followed *Being and Time*. In particular, he suggested that the practice of philosophy and the German university needed to be recalled to its own possibilities (Heidegger 1959). It is this aspect of his work that has attracted criticism from philosophers and political theorists who believe that Heidegger's philosophy bears more than a contingent relation to Nazism. It is an uncontested fact that Heidegger did join the National Socialist movement. The more contentious issue is whether Heidegger's manifestly non-political works, in particular *Being and Time*, are tainted with either Nazi ideology or philosophical tendencies that would support such an ideology. Ostensibly, *Being and Time* and Heidegger's work on this history of philosophy strives to think at a level that is pre-political, not concerned with specific cultural or historical values, but with the essential factors that would make such values possible. The issues surrounding Heidegger's politics and its relation to his philosophy are extremely complex, not least because Heidegger saw his entire philosophical project as disengaged from any anthropologism or any theory of values. He was not, he insisted, offering a moral definition of man, humanity or values. Rather, he was trying to understand how such grounding concepts emerge in the first place. How is it that we have come to think of ourselves as subjects who relate to the world? How is it that we think of ourselves as having a specific and self-present essence? How did the human or subjectivity come to function as a grounding moral and metaphysical concept? For an existential analysis will show that the human cannot be the beginning of a metaphysical inquiry, precisely because the very concept of the human is an effect of the entire history of western metaphysics and a series of embedded decisions. This is why Heidegger insisted that his distinction between authenticity and inauthenticity was not a moral distinction. Moral concepts and values, such as those of humanism, are only possible because we are beings who exist, or who can decide on the meaning of our world. The opposition between authenticity and inauthenticity is not a distinction between values but describes the ways in which we think of the origin of values. And so Heidegger was critical of many of the philosophies of his time that argued that the world is constituted through systems of values. What this left out of account, Heidegger insisted, were the deeper questions of how there is a world in general and how ideal forms, such as values, are presented. And so on the one hand, Heidegger's work is placed *before* any politics, for Heidegger is not concerned with this or that political system of values but how it is that we came to think of the world in terms of valuation, quantification and calculation. On the other hand, this critique of value philosophy and his broader critique of the fall of metaphysics into merely technical questioning do seem to resonate with the conservative philosophies of his time. What characterizes Heidegger's work as a whole is just this difficult relation between the supposedly 'primordial' questions of philosophy and the 'merely' anthropological or political questions that Heidegger sets himself against.

Death and anxiety, with the ownness or authenticity they allow, are explicitly 'existential' themes in Heidegger's *Being and Time* which might seem to have little to do with the vast amount of his later work criticizing the history of metaphysics and the forgetting of the question of being. But a clear distinction between Heidegger's early work on *Dasein*'s existence and his later work on the history of being is not possible. A connection can already be seen in the complex relation between authenticity and inauthenticity. Much of Heidegger's language in *Being and Time* would seem to suggest that there is something lamentable or morally culpable about the 'fall' of *Dasein* into inauthenticity. But a closer look shows that Heidegger sees the inauthentic as an essential possibility of being. His use of moral language therefore raises complex ethical questions. If there is no pure origin and if being is initially given in a 'fallen' and ontic understanding, then the attainment of authenticity will not be a simple retrieval of what is proper. Authenticity requires that we recognize that we are essentially distanced from being, or already fallen. For Heidegger, *Dasein* is initially and originally fallen: that is, we undertake our day to day existence without a consideration of being and without an attention to the horizon of our world that makes any being possible. But this is because of the very character of being. We never perceive or apprehend being in general; we only encounter this or that being with this or that meaning. It is because being never presents itself as such that we tend to answer the question of being with this or that already presented being. In anxiety, however, we are brought up against the very possibility of specific and presented beings. We only have present beings because we have a world – a general horizon of meanings and purposes through which any being is given. If that horizon of meaning is disrupted then we can become aware that any present being is always grounded upon that which is not present: the general comportment or relation to existence that constitutes our world. We only have beings because we anticipate some world within which each specific being can then be located. The condition for a being, then, is some 'fore-having' or anticipation of being in general. Each being is therefore effected through *transcendence*, or a *relation* of existence towards a world. When our 'world' no longer coheres (as in anxiety) then we become distanced or estranged from beings. But this authentic moment of anxiety must emerge from an initial and inauthentic involvement in the world. The 'fall' into the everyday attitude that is oblivious of being is no accident or mishap. We can only ask the question of being because we have already been presented with beings.

The problem with the history of western metaphysics has been that it has not recognized the essential fallenness of *Dasein* or the essential concealedness of Being. Philosophers have defined being as though it were simply present for viewing, like any other object. What we need to recognize, Heidegger argues, is that for any being to be present, it must have been presented. This means (a) that it emerges from non-presence, (b) that this emergence occurs through time and (c) that this presented being will therefore never be fully present. When we ask about being, then, we should not seize upon this or that presented being, but should try to think or disclose the very possibility of presentation in general. In *Being and Time* Heidegger takes this essential possibility to be time. Time is not some subjective form through which we view being (for this would locate time 'in' the subject). Nor is time some objective container, as though beings were located 'in' time. For the very notion of a being – as that which remains present – is already a temporal notion. Time is neither subjective nor objective; it is only through time that the relation between subject and object is possible. Heidegger, therefore, goes one step further than Kant. Kant had argued that in order to think of any being at all we must presuppose time, and that time was therefore an *a priori* condition for the knowledge of being. But Heidegger points out that these terms – *a priori* (what is prior) or condition (what is already given) – are already temporal. It's not that we need to *presuppose* time to think of being; being *is time*. *Dasein* is, therefore, not a subject or consciousness who then temporally constitutes the world, as though *Dasein* 'had' temporality as one of its forms. *Dasein* just is temporality: an existence or projectedness towards a future from some past.

When *Dasein* takes itself as an already presented being, placed within time, it understands itself inauthentically. And this parallels any metaphysics that asks the question of being as though being were a presence to be reached or encountered by a questioning subject. When *Dasein* recognizes that it is nothing other than the temporal movement of its own existence, then *Dasein* has the possibility of acting authentically. Similarly, meta-physics ought to question being with an awareness that being is not something present lying passively in wait for the question. Being will always be determined according to the form of the question. Only in recognizing the constitutive force of the question, as a way of existing towards the world, will metaphysics be authentic or responsible. Being *as such* is not given; being is that which 'gives' beings. To answer the question of being is always to offer some particular understanding of being. And this understanding is also anticipated by the question. If, however, we are brought to the awareness of *Dasein* as just that being who can question being, then we are also brought to the event of ontic-ontological difference. We always begin our inquiry through some specific being (the ontic), but there is one type of being that is capable of relating not just to this or that being, but to being in general (the ontological). For the most part, metaphysics has answered the ontological question (of Being) through an ontic understanding (a specific being). But there is one being (*Dasein*) that offers an opening into the ontological, and this is *Dasein* in so far as *Dasein* can *question* being. If we *can* ask the question of being, then this shows that we have the capacity to think beyond this or that given (ontic) being and think the possibility of being, or how it is that we are given any being at all. In *Being and Time* Heidegger had privileged the questioning power of a *Dasein* aware of its historical locatedness and authentic possibilities.

In his later work, Heidegger focused less on the questioning power of *Dasein* and more on the general movement or history of being. But just as his early existential analyses had stressed that the fall into inauthenticity was no accident, so his critique of western metaphysics acknowledges that there is no pure origin to which thought might return. Metaphysics is at once the question of being, but the very emergence of the question must also have already determined being in a certain way and from a certain world. We can never, then, arrive at some ontological ground that is fully disengaged from its ontic origins. And this means that philosophy is *most fallen* or most blind when it has failed to attend to the essential fall or blindness that renders it possible. Heidegger, therefore, insists that philosophy is never a pure and objective theoretical view from nowhere. When it does understand itself as pure *theoria* this is because it has substituted its own specific relation to the world, for a determination of the world in general. Heidegger therefore sets himself two tasks in his critique of metaphysics. The first is *Destruktion*, which examines the history of metaphysical questions and illuminates their points of blindness, the ways in which they have already decided on the nature of being. The second is his positive task of reformulating the very grammar and logic of metaphysics to allow the question of being. In the phase of *Destruktion* Heidegger will show how the terms of a question or text undermine the explicit aims of that text. The clearest example of this is his attention to the visual metaphors that ground philosophy. Words like *theoria* and *eidos* are tied etymolo-gically to looking. The word 'idea' has come to mean – particularly in idealism – the complete and self-present grasp of identical being. But if we think about looking or appearing more deeply, we realize that we can only look at something that is other than ourselves. Looking is a relational term, and describes a directedness to what is not immediate and already given. Metaphysics, however, has been decided on the determina-tion of a 'look' that is at one with itself, a look that is not relational but is a complete and self-present self-appearing. Heidegger wants to take these terms of presence back to their original world-relatedness. Before the metaphysical look of the self-present idea, there must have been a look directed towards a world. We can only think the pure self-regarding look of theory *after* the look that relates to what is other than itself. Heidegger goes through western philosophy looking at a number of terms – such as logic, the subject, idea or *techne* – and shows how these concepts emerge from an original world-relatedness that becomes objectified and forgets its specificity and locatedness. (*Logos* originally meant a saying-gathering *of the world* but has now become reified into a 'logic' that operates independent of any being; *subjectum* originally referred to the content or foundation of a judgement but has now come to mean the 'subject' that can know and ground himself; *eidos* was originally a look at what was given, now the 'idea' has come to mean that which determines all experience and givenness; and *techne* was originally a practice or art for ordering the world but in modernity has become a technology to which all practices and purposes are subordinate.)

There is a conservative and nostalgic aspect to Heidegger's thought, and this is disclosed in his positive prescriptions for the future of philosophy and thinking. Much of Heidegger's later work was taken up with retrieving the question of being from its history of translation away from its Greek origin. Heidegger imagined that through poetry we could confront the very emergence of our world. While everyday language repeated words as so much adequate and ready-made material, poetry reopened the *relation* between word and world, allowing us to retrieve the very possibility of thinking. But Heidegger also anticipated some of the more radical themes of poststructuralism. If it is the case that we only encounter beings and can never think being in general, then this means that thought is essentially ungrounded. Any attempt to think the origin of being will already be caught up in a world of specific beings. The origin can be thought only after the event. Metaphysics cannot have some proper ground or origin, for any offered ground would be the outcome of philosophical grounding. Metaphysics can only be responsible, then, when it recognizes the 'abyss' of thinking. There is not a ground or presence that is then presented to a knowing subject. Rather, there 'is' presencing, from which being is given and which then enables the possibility of the metaphysical question.

Claire Colebrook

Further reading and works cited

Dreyfus, H. *Being-in-the-World: A Commentary on Heidegger's Being and Time, Division 1*. Cambridge, MA, 1991.
Heidegger, M. *An Introduction to Metaphysics*. New Haven, CT, 1959.
—. *What is a Thing?* Lanham, MD, 1967.
—. *What is Called Thinking?* New York, 1968.
—. *Identity and Difference*. New York, 1969.
—. *Poetry, Language, Thought*. New York, 1971.
—. *The Question Concerning Technology and Other Essays*. New York, 1977.
—. *On the Way to Language*. San Francisco, 1982.
—. *Early Greek Thinking*. New York, 1984.
—. *Kant and the Problem of Metaphysics*. Bloomington, IN, 1990.
—. *Basic Writings*, ed. David Farrell Krell. San Francisco, 1993.
—. *Basic Questions of Philosophy*. Bloomington, IN, 1994.
—. *Being and Time*. Albany, NY, 1996.

—. *Pathmarks*, ed. W. McNeill, Cambridge, 1998.

Macann, C. (ed.) *Critical Heidegger*. London, 1996.

Macomber, W. B. *The Anatomy of Disillusion: Martin Heidegger's Notion of Truth*. Evanston, IL, 1967.

Polt, R. *Heidegger: An Introduction*. Ithaca, NY, 1999.

Sallis, J. (ed.) *Reading Heidegger: Commemorations*. Bloomington, IN, 1993.

Taminiaux, J. *Heidegger and the Project of Fundamental Ontology*. Albany, NY, 1991.

Wolin, R. (ed.) *The Heidegger Controversy: A Critical Reader*. Cambridge, MA, 1993.

Antonio Gramsci (1891–1937)

Antonio Gramsci's significance in critical theory largely rests on *The Prison Notebooks*, which details the politics of culture from within a marxist framework, but one that escapes economic determinism and respects the complex, mobile and contradictory dynamics of social interaction. His writing is a fundamental touchstone for postwar left reconsiderations of culture, particularly those that reject high-low culture distinctions, but Gramsci's widespread influence has often come at the cost of abstracting his terminology from the larger context of his work and historical crises that impelled its shape. Gramsci is frequently called on to authorize new critical trajectories, but rarely comprehensively read in ways that think through the impetus for his work – proletarian revolution. Because *The Prison Notebooks* were written while Gramsci was isolated within a fascist jail, published posthumously and had to wait until 1971 for the first major English translation, this selective reading partly comes as a result of interpretations formed by the post-1960s retreat from class as an integral category and western revolution as a foreseeable outcome. But the degree to which critics quote or interpret Gramsci outside of, or in contravention to, his historical context and concern about the relation of the Communist Party to the disempowered is the extent to which these citations become either ornamental or self-aggrandising.

Born in rural Sardinia to an Albanian-Italian clerk and local mother, Gramsci grew up in poverty after his father was imprisoned for embezzlement. Moving to industrialized Turin on a university scholarship, Gramsci ended his study after ill health, financial distress and increasing involvement in socialist politics and journalism. As part of *L'Ordine Nuovo*'s (*The New Order*) editorial collective, he focused on the labour militancy of the 1919–20 Turin Factory Councils, which organized workers by their workplace rather than trade, and seemed to be an Italian equivalent to the Soviets that helped catalyse the Russian Revolution. When management occupied the factories and the government intervened, the movement was defeated and the Italian Socialist Party split. On one side, Gramsci and others formed the Italian Communist Party (PCI), while, on the other, Mussolini organized the far right Fascist Party, which later occupied the government. During the early 1920s, Gramsci was sent to Moscow and Vienna to represent the PCI in the Communist International (Comintern), where he became actively involved in debates about international left strategy. Returning to Italy in 1924 as head of the PCI, he was elected senator during Mussolini's rise to dictatorship. Arrested shortly thereafter, Gramsci was given a political show trial and sentenced by a fascist judge to twenty years' imprisonment. In jail, he began keeping notebooks on cultural and political issues, the work that his reputation largely depends on. This history is crucial to approaching Gramsci's *Prison Notebooks*, since it contextualizes their motive and form.

Although university trained, Gramsci is perhaps unique among this encyclopaedia's subjects for not writing within or for the academy. Typical of the left autodidactic tradition, Gramsci's writing, in its journalistic and carceral phase, does not look to university debates, readers or protocols of presentation. *The Prison Notebooks* exist to reflect on severe political defeat, the crushed worker's movement that set the stage for the rise of Italian fascism amid an international containment of revolutionary movements. There is little in his writing about economics, since he takes the analysis of capitalism's physics as definitively stated by Marx. Instead, he investigates the relation of culture to politics in order to ask: why did not the revolution spread beyond Russia; what prevents the transition to global socialism; and how does Fascism maintain power? Gramsci's self-critical investigation into his own situated experience and commitment to a 'marxism without guarantees', which abandons the sureties of historical teleology, makes his work especially resonant for progressive critical theories that attempt to address the left's increasing marginalization amid the dominance of insurgent conservatism after the 1960s. Similarly, Gramsci influenced pre-1989 internal critiques of the Eastern Bloc's 'actually existing socialism', like DDR dissident Bahro's *The Alternative* (1981).

The conditions of *The Prison Notebooks*' production pose the challenge of triple encoding for contemporary readers. The foremost difficulty is that Gramsci often resorted to elliptic phrases to confound the prison censors who secured the journals. Sometimes it is easy to reconstitute Gramsci's intention, like the substitution of 'philosopher of action' for 'Marx', but, at other times, it is hard to discern when Gramsci is creating terms to stand in momentarily for traditional marxist concepts or when he is forging new terminology to flesh out concepts that were incompletely or poorly developed in previous marxist writings. A further hurdle is that Gramsci's signposting assumes a reader conversant with nine-teenth-century left writings (not only marxist ones) and Comintern debates of the 1920s and 1930s, many of which were either narrowly circulated or never appeared in print form. Without some familiarity with these debates, it becomes harder to capture Gramsci's intentions and interventions. Finally, *The Prison Notebooks* are just that, draft notebooks. Because Gramsci functionally died in prison (he was released to a guarded hospital shortly before collapsing from a brain haemorrhage), he never came close to assembling an authoritative version for publication. While Gramsci was a precise writer who did redraft some sections, a number of his prescient breakthroughs, like the 'Americanism and Fordism' section that analyses modernization and sexuality, is little more than a sketch. Contemporary readers must almost train themselves to read Gramsci intuitively, a task that has frequently led students to rely on the mediation (and agendas) of secondary criticism. As if these hurdles were not enough, the Anglophone readership has only had a portion of the notebooks translated. Though the most frequently used edition, Hoare and Nowell-Smith's *Selections from the Prison Notebooks* (1971), is masterful, it cannot act as a proper substitute for a complete edition, a project now thankfully underway. Despite these challenges to reading him, Gramsci's vocabulary and concepts ground projects like cultural materialism, 'history from the bottom up', Althusser, Balibar and Poulantzas's work on ideology and classes, Birmingham School Cultural Studies, postmarxism, economic debates about postindustrialism/postfordism, and postcolonialism, such as the writing of Said, Spivak and the Subaltern Studies group.

If one theme animates *The Prison Notebooks*, it is the redefinition of the term 'intellectual'. Gramsci rejects the notion that an intellectual is someone endowed with a greater capacity for thought and freedom from material relations. No one is 'unintellectual' in Gramsci's view because everyone has a 'particular conception of the world' and 'line of moral conduct' (Gramsci 1971, 9) even if this sensibility, what Gramsci calls 'common sense', is vague, incoherent or rife with contradictory attitudes. It is not mental brilliance that makes intellectuals, but how subjects achieve the social function of being an intellectual. 'Because it can happen that everyone at some time fries a couple of eggs or sews up a tear in a jacket, we do not necessarily say that everyone is a cook or tailor' (9). Indeed, Gramsci mainly uses *dirigente*, which is poorly translated as 'intellectual' and is better understood as conductor, organizer or, more simply, activist. A fashion magazine writer about cosmetics is no more or less an intellectual (*dirigente*), in Gramsci's sense, than a philosophy professor, since each promotes confidence in the prestige of their object (commodity beauty or abstract meditation). What distinguishes *dirigente* is their varying organic relation to social formations resulting from class, or class-faction, interests. Gramsci differentiates between what he calls 'traditional' and 'organic' *dirigente*, although his terminology is confusing, since both kinds are organic to their respective formations and the difference cannot simply be captured in terms of left–right categories. The traditional intellectual works out of an already existing institutional matrix and mode of social organization, while the organic intellectual emerges from new, oppositional ones. Marxist professors are not automatically organic intellectuals for Gramsci, despite their commitment to anti-bourgeois strategies, because, whatever the left academic's 'local' message, her or his prestige and authority to speak comes from their credentialization within a traditional structure, the university, that continues to aggravate social divisions through the mental/manual hierarchy created by the awarding of diplomas and academic promotion. If the same professor spoke within a 'people's university', which addressed non-dominant groups in ways that did not mimic the traditional university's values of 'excellence', then the scholar would be more 'organic'. One model might be Gramsci's own involvement with the *The New Order*, which provided the Turin Factory Councils with a forum. A 'traditional' journalist-intellectual writing on the strikes would invoke 'objectivity and neutral reportage', while not questioning the links between the newspaper and the factory's owners, but an organic journalist-intellectual would analyse current events in to help create labour confidence in their new modes of interaction. Gramsci's perception that the agents of knowledge emerge from material sites of truth-production is congruent here with Foucault's writings on discursive formations and the creation of disciplines. A second aspect of the organic-traditional distinction is that the more a set of intellectuals becomes embedded within traditional structures, the more they paradoxically believe themselves to be self-defining, even though their self-declared liberation from class (fraction) simply registers what might be called the secret of the 'intellectual-fetish'. Just as Marx began his analysis of capitalism's system of exploitation with the secret of the 'commodity-fetish', Gramsci uses the traditional intellectual's false autonomy to unpack the larger political economy of cultural power.

While Marx only offers a glimpse of what non-commodity relations might look like, Gramsci uses Machiavelli's *The Prince* to illustrate how an organic intellectual might act. Machiavelli's treatise on power is distinctive because 'it is not a systemic treatment, but a "live" work in which political ideology and political science are fused in the dramatic form of a "myth"' (125). Machiavelli broke from traditional formats by writing neither an idealistic utopia nor dry scholastic review. Instead, he composed an advice notebook, but one for a feudal prince he knew was neither ignorant of power-dynamics nor capable of mastering them. Machiavelli's purpose was to publicize these manoeuvres for 'those not in the know' (135), the proto-bourgeoisie who were not yet capable of enacting these tactics but were beginning to confront a moribund feudal society. Machiavelli's representation of the prince was thus a 'concrete fantasy which acts on a dispersed and shattered people to arouse and organize its collective will', where the populace's spontaneous (unorganized) passions were guided to action. This dialectical exchange provides the example for the 'modern prince', which is no longer be an individual (the favoured subject of bourgeois liberalism) but a 'complex element of society' – the (communist) political party (129). Gramsci's trajectory is always from the individual to collective subjects, and the organic *dirigente* is really about groups, not an individual's choice. The party's role is twofold. First, its collective internal operations offer the first glimpses of potential social alternatives, it is a 'concrete fantasy'. Secondly, it engages with popular 'passions' so that the party does not 'traditionalize' itself through bureaucratic, rather than democratic, centralism, rather than the mass, where it could disastrously mistake itself as the historical agent of change and delegate itself as the gatekeeper for deciding the timing of political action. Gramsci believes the party's self-assured isolation was a major cause in the post-1918 revolutionary failures, and, in prison, he recalls Marx's thesis that the educator himself needs education (the *dirigente* must be directed from below).

The question of intellectuals opens the way to reconsider the relation between state and civil society. Gramsci's axiom is that politics is defined by the 'dual perspective' where power arises out of the varying, yet always present, ratio of coercion and consent, violence and persuasion. Gramsci never believes that liberal democracy excludes raw, physical violence (the police, army, punitive legislation) from its arsenal, it has merely become more economical in its use. Close to Weber's claim that the state has a monopoly of legitimate violence, Gramsci believes that rule by oppression is resource-draining and cannot sustain broad-based power over time. For power to be durable it must also be persuasive, educative and work to promote a consensus typified by the acceptance of a common sense, the implicit, unspoken assumption of the everyday and 'naturalness' of civil society and its hierarchies. Gramsci calls this consensus *hegemony*, which he sees as manifested through a three-phased process of group collectivization and strategic alliances. The first is the 'economic-corporate' moment when 'a tradesman feels *obliged* to stand by another trades-man, a manufacturer by another manufacturer, etc. but the tradesman does not yet feel solidarity with the manufacturer' (181). A second 'economic' step is when there is a 'solidarity of interests among all the members of a social class'. Until this point, rule still mainly relies on coercion, but consensual hegemony is achieved when groups 'transcend the corporate limits' of pure economic self-interest and move to an 'ethical-political' phase so that they 'become the interest of other subordinate groups'. When a class (or class fraction) incorporates other social elements so that subaltern common sense, or 'sponta-neous philosophy', becomes protective of the leading class(es), hegemony is achieved. One kind of hegemony is nationalism, whereby the working class support the local bourgeoisie against the interests of far-away workers.

Hegemony does not 'destroy' antagonistic interests, but, in Raymond Williams's phrase, incorporates them, and the 'ethical-political' moment of hegemony is manifested by the rise of a 'historic bloc'. The historic bloc is more than a codeword for class; a bloc is the coalition of social groups, the networks of alliances that can cross class lines. The model

Gramsci draws from is the *Eighteenth Brumaire of Louis Bonaparte*, where Marx described how the future Napoleon III constructed a historic bloc that enlisted the peasantry against their economic-corporate interests, within a regime that included their historic enemies, the Parisian underclass, and was dominated by financial interests. While one fraction usually dominates a bloc, it is also subject to intrinsic pressures arising from trying to keep the constellation of interests pacified. Blocs have these crises of *cultural capital* because their membership is always restless and internally competes for place of preference and right to command the resources that a bloc garners, but a bloc can protectively adapt to economic and political crises because, like parliamentary cabinet reshuffles, it can swiftly reorganize by rehierarchizing its constituent members, perhaps expelling some or including new ones, to respond to changed conditions.

There are immediate advantages of Gramsci's model of hegemony and historic blocs for cultural theory. First, it frees us from a negative model of ideology as false consciousness where dominated groups are simply overwhelmed by dominant ideology, a vertical suppression akin to what Foucault calls the repressive hypothesis. Because hegemony is the complex product of consensus and coercion, it allows us to understand culture as the product of multiple desires and sources of institutional pressures that are not always easily aligned. Since hegemony is as much about getting subjects not to say 'no' as it is for them to clearly say 'yes' to a historic bloc's rule, hegemony can draw in, or articulate, subjects based on aspects of their allegiances in non pre-determined and often highly ambiguous ways. A further advantage to Gramsci's open conception of culture is that hegemony can also describe the relation between intellectuals and the state, a problem that Althusser specifically followed.

Perry Anderson (1976–7) argues that Gramsci's use of *hegemony* is inconsistent throughout *The Prison Notebooks*, which sometimes seems to oppose civil society hegemony to state violence and then sometimes bundles hegemony as an ideological apparatus of the state's armament, to use Althusser's formula. The confusion arises only if one insists, against Gramsci's method, on a scheme of ahistorical, static binarization. Gramsci dissents from the classical view of the state as simply the instrument of the ruling class. Instead, he views the modern state as the 'unstable equilibria' (182) or field of contestation among classes, which is not simply monopolized by the bourgeoisie. Since the state 'integrates' competing interests, it prevents the expense of dominating through violence. Historically, the state was one of Hobbesian violence as the medieval nobility retained power on the basis of its economic-corporate interests. When a nascent group, like the bourgeoisie, achieved the advanced point of the 'ethical-political', it transformed the state into a hegemonic device by having it 'integrate' competing interests and regulate the historic bloc's internal tensions with the creation of a *dirigente* of *dirigente*, the civil servants who help determine what ought to be a bloc's composition.

The state can act as the bloc's glue because it offers various *dirigente* status by investing them with honorifics or licensing, an act that draws the *dirigente* toward the State as the latter increases the former's status within their original group by making it seem as if the *dirigente* are responsible for preserving a group's inclusion within the bloc, a mystification whereby 'political questions are disguised as cultural ones and as such become insoluble' (149). Because the historic bloc state has various kinds of preferment, it is able to lure a social group's *dirigente* away from their original allegiance by offering greater benefits of security and establishment. Gramsci calls this process *transformism* (or passive revolution), when a bloc reorients itself by fusing oppositional elements in order to contain the open expression of class conflict. A recent example of transformism is the post-Thatcher/Reagan phenomenon of liberal opposition parties assuming governmental office only to further the political agenda of their conservative predecessors, a case where 'what is at stake is a rotation in governmental office . . . not the foundation and organization of a new political society' (160).

With the concepts of hegemony and historic blocs, Gramsci turns to discuss the kinds of counter-hegemonic tactics, such as the *war of movement* and the *war of position*. The *war of movement* is likened to a 'classic revolution', which uses a swift, decisive strike to topple the state. This kind of attack succeeded in Tsarist Russia because the obsolete state, lacking any compensatory civil society, quickly fell when faced with popular resistance. The situation is more complicated in the West, where states have more and more complex kinds of blocs to call on when faced with crisis. This situation calls on a *war of position*, or an attempt to create a counter-hegemony, like an alliance between the city (proletariat) and countryside (peasants) that would give it more organizational option. For these reason, Gramsci argues that cultural hegemony must exist alongside, but not necessarily before, political rule if a counter-hegemony is to last. Otherwise, any labouring-class rule will be short-lived because it can be easily outflanked like the Paris Commune. Worse yet, a precipitous defeat throws the defeated into the arms of charismatic forces who promise stability and protection. This is Gramsci's theory of the rise of fascism, a situation he generically calls *Caesarism*, where a momentary stalemate between exhausted antagonists creates the opportunity for the rise of a group which has the stamina to lead and dictate the terms to all the opponents. Caesarist solutions can either be reactionary, like the fascists, or progressive, like Cromwell's Commonwealth, but all will need to develop a new bloc or otherwise quickly fall.

Yet, Gramsci also fears that too great an emphasis on the war of position can weaken subaltern resolve and make a group's *dirigente* lose patience and switch sides. Like the dual perspective of force and persuasion, movement and position must work in dialectical tension. As new blocs become stronger they can hazard gambits of movement to further desegregate the solidarity of the traditional bloc. A counter-hegemony can delegitimize the traditional state by creating a crisis of confidence by attracting the old bloc's members so that the old bloc implodes because it can no longer maintain the architecture that covers its competing interests. If the new bloc's *dirigente* refuse to continue acting as the regulators in the same way that the old ones did, then we have a picture of how the state may 'wither away' in a socialist regime. *The Prison Notebooks* did not fully investigate this process of deconstruction. The horizon of *The Prison Notebooks* is the illustration of what a socialist society might be like after it has conquered the bourgeois one. But *The Prison Notebooks* remain Gramsci's *Grandsire*, incomplete because he was not allowed a life long enough to revise it. The task of critical theory today is to build on Gramsci's foundations and imagine what a 'post' *Modern Prince* would contain.

Stephen Shapiro

Further reading and works cited

Althusser, L. *Lenin and Philosophy and Other Essays*. London, 1971.
Anderson, P. 'The Antinomies of Antonio Gramsci', *New Left Review*, 100, November 1976–January 1977.
Bahro, R. *The Alternative in Eastern Europe*. London, 1981.

Buci-Glucksmann, C. *Gramsci and the State*. London, 1980.

Cammett, J. *Antonio Gramsci and the Origins of Italian Communism*. Stanford, CA, 1967.

David, J. A. (ed.) *Gramsci and Italy's Passive Revolution*. New York, 1979.

Fiori, G. *Antonio Gramsci*. London, 1970.

Gramsci, A. *Selections from the Prison Notebooks*, eds Q. Hoare and G. Nowell Smith. London, 1971.

—. *Selections from Political Writings, 1910–1920*, ed. Q. Hoare. London, 1977.

—. *Selections from Political Writings, 1921–1926*, ed. Q. Hoare. London, 1978.

—. *Selections from the Cultural Writings*, eds. D. Forgacs and G. Nowell Smith. London, 1985.

—. *Prison Notebooks. Vols 1 and 2*, ed. J. Buttigieg. New York, 1992.

Guha, R. and Chakravorty Spivak, G. (eds) *Selected Subaltern Studies*. Oxford, 1988.

Hall, S. *The Hard Road to Renewal*. London, 1988.

— et al. *Policing the Crisis*. London, 1978.

Hunt, A. *Marxism and Democracy*. London, 1980.

International Gramsci Society. http://www.italnet.nd.edu/gramsci/index.html.

Joll, J. *Gramsci*. London, 1977.

Laclau, E. *Politics and Ideology in Marxist Theory*. London, 1977.

Luxemburg, R. *Rosa Luxemburg Speaks*. New York, 1970.

Marx, K. and Engels, F. *Selected Works in One Volume*. New York, 1968.

Mouffe, C. (ed.) *Gramsci and Marxist Theory*. London, 1979.

Poulantzas, N. *Political Power and Social Classes*. London, 1973.

Sassoon, A. Showstack (ed.) *Approaches to Gramsci*. London, 1982.

Simon, R. *Gramsci's Political Thought: An Introduction*. London, 1991.

Sorel, G. *Reflections On Violence*. Cambridge, 1999.

Williams, R. *Problems in Materialism and Culture*. London, 1980.

Walter Benjamin (1892–1940)

The work of German literary and cultural critic Walter Benjamin is one of the most influential sources for postwar literary, historical and cultural studies. Benjamin studied German literature and philosophy but he also travelled widely in Europe and wrote about European cities, and translated Baudelaire and Proust in the 1920s. Introduced to Zionism in 1912 when he was twenty, this interest was supplemented by a friendship with Gershom Sholem (1897–1982) which he formed three years later and carried on in letter form after Sholem left for Palestine in 1923. Sholem's comments on Benjamin are important (see Smith 1985, 51–89). His marxism was formed by association with the Riga-born communist and theatre director Asja Lacis in 1924 (see Benjamin 1979, 45), who introduced him to Brecht in 1929, for a friendship and influence that lasted the rest of his life. The central event of Benjamin's life was the rejection of his monograph on German tragic drama by the University of Frankfurt when it was submitted as a *Habilitationsschrift* in 1925, which subsequently became his only book published in his lifetime (see Benjamin 1977a). This failure to qualify for university teaching committed him instead to a lifetime of freelance writing and broadcasting, and to being patronized by other members of the Frankfurt Institute of Social Research, such as Adorno and Horkheimer, who nonetheless published his work in the Institute's journal, the *Zeitschrift für Sozialforschung*. It produced work towards a project which Benjamin referred to as the *Passagen-Werk*, which he began working on in 1927, and of which the work on Baudelaire (Benjamin 1973), and the essays 'The Work of Art in the Age of Mechanical Reproduction' (Benjamin 1970), 'Central Park' (Benjamin 1985) and the 'Theses on the Philosophy of History' (Benjamin 1970) are some offcuts.

Benjamin's studies of Goethe, Baudelaire, Kafka, Proust, allegory and surrealism have influenced literary criticism, while his cultural critique has been felt in subsequent work on architectural theory, urban space, photography, technology, film and fashion theory and work on the politics of everyday life and in the concept of 'visual culture'. His work has engaged studies of memory; it has been important for theories of Fascism as a cultural phenomenon; it engaged with the power of war in modern societies in the texts on Jünger (Benjamin 1999, 312–21); his essay on violence (Benjamin 1979, 132–55) has influenced legal theory via Derrida (Derrida 1992). While obviously original, Benjamin's writings can be seen to exist in an active dialogue with Brecht, and with Adorno, who as Benjamin's most important interlocutor had his own positions with regard to committed and autonomous art, and the 'culture industry' most challenged by Benjamin. While attempts have been made to link Benjamin to Heidegger and to deconstruction, the depoliticizing strains of this must not take away from his work's engagement with marxism and the task of thinking culture and politics together. The choice of writers Benjamin commented on as a 'literary historian' aligns him with modernism: his work on the loss of experience and of memory, and on art in the new conditions of 'distraction' identifies him with postmodernist arguments. No contemporary critic working on social or cultural theory has been able to neglect Benjamin, and numerous commentaries and articles – often whole issues of journals such as *diacritics*, *Critical Inquiry* and *New German Critique* – have explicated one aspect or another of a very complex and disparate set of issues.

In what follows, an attempt is made to chart some aspects of his writings – which are still not wholly available in English translation – by looking at the movement in Benjamin between the work on German tragic drama (*Trauerspiel* – 'mourning play', or even 'funeral pageant' – i.e. the Baroque dramas of the German seventeenth century) and the uncompleted work on the nineteenth-century Paris Arcades: in other words, Benjamin's work of the 1920s and of the 1930s. In *The Origin of German Tragic Drama*, Benjamin aligns the concepts of history, allegory and *Trauerspiel* together and reads them in contrast to the dominant literary forms of myth, symbol and tragedy. He takes these as idealizations of destruction, ways of finding imaginary compensations from suffering, and supporting the idea that art has the entitlement to make some total and privileged statement about history and society (Benjamin 1977a, 166, 176). Benjamin's critique of the notion that art can reveal the 'totality' of relationships within society sets him against Lukács. The reading of history in relation to fragmentation that Benjamin works with persists to virtually the last thing he wrote, the 'Theses on the Philosophy of History' (1940), the year of his suicide on the Spanish border to avoid falling into the hands of the Nazis. The 'Theses' are Nietzschean in their aphoristic style and in their subject-matter, which quotes from Nietzsche's 'On the Uses and Disadvantages of History for Life' from the volume *Untimely Meditations*, which is a title with resonances in Benjamin's writing (see Benjamin 1977a, 166). The 'Theses' illuminate the earlier work on the *Trauerspiel*; they also give a rich context for understanding Benjamin.

In these 'Theses', the historian as a 'historical materialist' – working not with any idealist frame of reference, but from a materialist standpoint, but not with the rigidities of

Hegelian-Marxist dialectical materialism – opposes himself to a positivist and idealizing 'historicism'. Historicism effectively devalues the present in favour of a past with which it identifies and feels empathy with, which means it is informed by nostalgia. Its empathy is dangerous because it means siding with the victors – who have, after all, written the history books. (This is Benjamin at his most Brechtian.) Historicism also regards history as a development towards the present in a 'chain of events' so that history is seen as a 'continuum' (Benjamin 1970, 258, 259, 263). Yet the present is also seen, by this token, as transitional, which is again a form of devaluing it (Benjamin 1970, 264). Benjamin resists that narrative of development which degrades both the past, because its function is only to lead towards the present, and the present, because that is inferior to the past and only transitional, by stressing *Jetztzeit* – 'the presence of the now' – which he describes as a moment 'shot through with chips of Messianic time' (Benjamin 1970, 265). The present moment, though one of danger and of crisis, is also marked by what in Derrida's terms might be called *différance* – those elements which do not fit or contribute to the totality, and which also promise a complete reversal of everything, a redemption akin to revolution, breaking with the idea of history as linearity, cause and effect. Benjamin never sees his interest in history as describing historical conditions which have ended. For him 'the great writers . . . [work] . . . in a world that comes after them, just as the Paris streets of Baudelaire's poems, as well as Dostoevsky's characters, only existed after 1900' (Benjamin 1979, 48). Or, to put it in the terms of 1931, in an essay entitled 'Literary History and the Study of Literature':

> 'What is at stake is not to portray literary works in the context of their age, but to represent the age that perceives them – our age – in the age during which they arose. It is this that makes literature into an organon of history; and to achieve this, and not to reduce literature to the material of history, is the task of the literary historian. (1999, 464)

To put these antagonistic things together – the present and the past – is not to conflate but to achieve a new 'constellation', remembering – in a typical Benjamin aphorism, 'ideas are to objects as constellations are to stars' (1977a, 34).

Benjamin replaces historicism's belief in progress and the continuum of history with his vision of the fleeting 'angel of history', who sees not a chain of events but 'one single catastrophe which keeps piling wreckage upon wreckage and hurls it in front of his feet' (1970, 259). Elsewhere Benjamin makes the point 'that things "just go on" *is* the catastrophe' (1985, 50). History under this gaze becomes the record of the usual failures, ruins and fragments, and of the fate of things 'untimely', and allegory, the mode of the *Trauerspiel*, may be most appropriate for it, since allegory, in contrast to the symbol, is the mode which advertizes failed equivalencies and correspondences. Benjamin speaks of the 'majesty of the allegorical intention: destruction of the organic and living – the extinguishing of appearance' (1985, 41). Allegory and melancholy go together; Benjamin discusses Dürer's engraving of Melancholy, where the figure of melancholy sits with unused and unusable fragments at her feet, and where no object possesses a 'natural creative relationship' to the human subject (1977a, 140). Allegory refuses natural relationships; melancholy knows its experience is alienated and that the fragment or ruin is all that survives, and to see history as fragmented, an allegorical and melancholic vision, disallows it from being seen as the march of progress, calls attention to what writing 'history' omits, and allows for the putting together of fragments in a different configuration – a different constellation. 'Melancholy betrays the world for the sake of knowledge', Benjamin writes, meaning that melancholia (like Hamlet's) rejects sensuous immediate knowledge, 'but in its tenacious self-absorption it embraces dead objects in order to redeem them' (1977, 157). Hamlet's interest in skulls will come to mind: this is Benjamin the collector. When Benjamin writes that 'allegories are in the realm of thoughts what ruins are in the realm of things' (1977a, 178) he pairs allegory and ruins and makes thinking allegorical, indirect and committed to hollowing out systems of thought into their opposite, into the non-systematic. The allegorist, then, has a destructive character (see Benjamin 1979, 157–9).

This may be illustrated as when, in correspondence, Sholem told Benjamin that his work, with its Jewish Messianism, would be regarded by marxists as counter-revolutionary and bourgeois, and as simply purveying ambiguities (i.e. as giving no fixed direction). Benjamin replied that his writings, while they might be counter-revolutionary from the Party's point of view, would not, for that reason, be at the disposal of the counter-revolution, but would be 'denatured', 'definitely and reliably unusable for the counter-revolution at the risk that no one will be able to use them' (Sholem 1981, 228–33). Ambiguity and allegory become essential in Benjamin in the effort to 'wrest tradition away from a conformism that is about to overpower it' (1970, 257).

'Untimely' writing will not fit the times, so 'no poem is intended for the reader, no picture for the beholder, no symphony for the listener' (Benjamin 1970, 69). If it did, that would deny the alienated status of the reader and of the author as producer. It would also suggest, considering modern urban space, that it is impossible to find adequate images of the city, when the city itself is nothing but images, and is like nothing but itself. The city becomes Benjamin's topic in a way that shows his indebtedness to the sociologist Georg Simmel, who had written about the new forms of mental life produced by the metropolis, and whose lectures in Berlin Benjamin had attended in 1912 (see also Benjamin 1973, 38). In 'Paris – the Capital of the Nineteenth Century' (1935), often seen as a clue to the unfinished *Passagen-werk*, Benjamin reads Baudelaire, whose poetry shows 'profound duplicity' (1973, 26) as a melancholic and allegorist (1973, 170), as though he inherited from the writers of the *Trauerspiel*, and he emphasizes how (like them) Baudelaire's images possess a calculated disharmony between image and object (1973, 98). Images are no longer expressive; Baudelaire could even say that his goal in poetry was 'the creation of a cliché' (1973, 152). Benjamin sees ambiguity as central to nineteenth century 'high capitalism' and he defines it as 'the figurative appeal of the dialectic, the dialectic at a standstill'. A snapshot arrests time in a standstill: hence Benjamin's interest in photography is symptomatic. 'This standstill is Utopia, and the dialectical image therefore a dream image. The commodity clearly provides such an image: as fetish. The [Paris] arcades, which are both house and stars, provide such an image' (1973, 171). The dialectic appears in an ambiguous figuration, but in the image – which is not the image of one thing – it has been arrested, so that the image can be deciphered (Benjamin recalls how the French revolutionaries of 1830 fired at the church clocks to arrest time in the present (1970, 264)).

The 'dialectical image', which is therefore double, is one of Benjamin's most complex thoughts (Jennings 1987). Adorno who also used the term, thought of the image's doubleness being between its essence and its appearance, which would imply the possibility of making a distinction between the true and the false. Benjamin's method, because it is not caught in Adorno's marxism, is the antithesis of this: it does not imply ideology-critique. It does not work on the basis of presupposing the existence of an empirical truth where criticism frees the mind from illusions. Rather, Benjamin argues that 'sundering truth from falsehood is the goal of the materialist method, not its point of departure ... Its point of departure is the object riddled with error' (Benjamin 1973, 103). The work of art cannot be thought of as something simply to be appreciated for its truth, for, as Benjamin will put it in the 'Theses', 'there is no document of civilization which is not at the same time a document of barbarism' (1970, 258). The image which must be deciphered dialectically is not the image of one thing, but is like a folded fan which can be opened up to reveal something multiple (1979, 75), or, like the photograph, it can, by interrupting a flow of events, show an 'optical unconscious' (1979, 243). As when Benjamin writes that in visiting Moscow one gets to know Berlin (1979, 177), and as with montage the image is overdetermined, revealing both past and present, so this doubleness, being both the marker of present alienated reality as fetish, and its opposite, (something Utopian), can only be seen in the light of redemption. The Paris arcades, nineteenth-century shopping malls, which were made vivid to Benjamin through the 'profane illumination' (1979, 227) provided by the surrealist Louis Aragon's novel *Paysan de Paris*, give an example of a dialectical image: houses and stars together because of the way they are lit (with glass roofs), inside and outside at the same moment. When in the 1920s Aragon saw the Passage de l'Opéra, built in the 1820s, it was as a nearly depopulated human aquarium, the ruins of what Benjamin identified as both a nineteenth-century Utopia and of nineteenth-century capitalism (Benjamin 1973, 157–9; Geist 1983, 117–9). The passages, whose name implies no staying, no lingering, represent unconscious dreams realized in architecture. Commodities viewed in the strange light of the passages possess the reality of being the nineteenth-century's dream-images. The ambiguous status of the commodity appears in its character as fetish: Marx said, discussing fetishism, that in capitalism, relations between people assumed 'the phantasmagoric form of a relation between things' (in Smith, 277). The ambiguous world of the images and of the commodity is for Benjamin the phantasmagoria, possessing 'the sex-appeal of the inorganic' (1973, 166). Benjamin notes how, in Baudelaire, the fetish itself speaks, which, as writing, shows Baudelaire's 'empathy with inorganic things' (1973, 55). There is no getting free of the phantasmagoria, but when the image is at a standstill, within that fetishistic structure may be seen the ruin, like the fragments of the *Trauerspiel* study, to be taken out of the continuum of history, and to be seen in the light of redemption. Indeed, we can recognize 'the monuments of the bourgeoisie as ruins even before they have crumbled' like the Passage de l'Opéra (Benjamin 1973, 176), ruins because they are always phantasmagoric.

Modern experience is the experience of ruins, just as the angel of history sees things as ruins; melancholia works with the ruins of experience, which is a way of implying that experience is now impossible, the thesis developed by Giorgio Agamben, the Italian translator of Benjamin, in his *Infancy and History*. 'Some Motifs in Baudelaire' (Benjamin 1973, 110–21) confronts the loss of experience (*Erfahrung*) in modernity, which includes the loss of a communicable past, the loss of storytelling, and the erasure of memory, all things which threaten or diminish the possibility of a reversal in the present. In urban modernity, under the experience of shock, which Benjamin takes to be definitional for modernity, consciousness is screened so that such experiences do not enter memory, a point Benjamin derived from Freud, so that the experience that dominates is the lived experience of the moment (*Erlebnis*). The overwhelming power of information in newspapers, to comment on which Benjamin turns to Karl Kraus, impoverishes awareness in that it blocks off what happens in the present from possessing a relation to experience.

Storytelling, as opposed to the giving of information, produces a way of thinking that can work allegorically or outside the categories of the continuum of history – a story 'resembles the seeds of grain which have lain for centuries in the chambers of the pyramids shut up air-tight and have retained their germinative powers to this day' (Benjamin 1970, 90). Proust's work recalls the importance of involuntary memory, and the difficulty of its existing in the conditions of modernity, since only 'what has not been experienced explicitly and consciously, what has not happened to the subject as an experience' can become part of involuntary memory (Benjamin 1977a, 114). Benjamin associates the loss of involuntary memory with modernity, and its effect is to produce only silence through the loss of communicable experience (1970, 84). The angel (the messenger) of history is also speechless. A crisis in articulation may be compared with what Benjamin argues about Kafka, whose work reveals the 'sickness of tradition', the power of an inert tradition with, nonetheless, the received authority of truth. The weight of tradition leads to speechlessness, for Kafka belonged, Benjamin says, to a tradition whose truth had lost its transmissibility. 'Kafka's real genius was that he tried something entirely new: he sacrificed truth for the sake of clinging to its transmissibility, its haggadic element. Kafka's writings are by their nature parables. But it is their misery and beauty that they had to become *more* than parables. They do not modestly lie at the feet of the doctrine as the haggadah lies at the feet of the Halakah' (1970, 147). The argument draws on a distinction between the Jewish Halakah as the law, the letter, and the haggadah meaning story, troping, free elaboration. Benjamin's Kafka, who is also autobiographical for Benjamin, is committed to free storytelling at the level of parable – writing 'fairy tales for dialecticians' (1970, 117) – narratives which operate as dialectical images, containing in them the power of the false, the non-true, not narratives illustrating some known doctrine.

In Benjamin the text stands outside its positioning within the historical continuum and memory is not a mechanical recall of something determinate, since through involuntary memory the past comes back in different contexts and can be laid hold of, to be rearticulated with the present. This accounts for so much personal memory in Benjamin, for example his writing of his childhood in Berlin, with the intention to let nothing be lost. Benjamin speaks about drawing a diagram of his life, and thinks in terms of a labyrinth; in another moment he thinks about losing one's way in a city, as though the city (Paris) was a labyrinth (Benjamin 1979, 314, 298). A narrative of personal existence becomes like Borges's 'garden of forking paths', not a linear pattern; memory and the city – both of which confuse temporality – come together as indescribable structures, incapable of conceptualization. While memory becomes more important, it is not clear that it can be memory of anything. This point becomes more and more insistent in Benjamin, as in the 'Theses' he says he 'wishes to retain that image of the past which unexpectedly appears [the power of involuntary memory] to man singled out by history at a moment of danger'. The image is 'the spark of hope in the past' (Benjamin 1977a, 257). Similarly, in what is nearly the last 'Thesis', a fact only becomes historical 'posthumously' (1970, 265), not because it is has a causal relationship to something else. It is born later on, in the present. This power of an afterlife is for Benjamin Messianic.

The need to overcome the power of reactive forces which link tradition – which includes in it involuntary memory – to conformism – thereby making it like Kafka's tradition – motivates Benjamin's most famous essay, 'The Work of Art in the Age of Mechanical Reproduction' ([1936] 1970, 219–53). New technological reproducibility takes art forms out of their placing within a historical continuum. Unless the work of art undergoes reproduction, it can be experienced only as repetition, which is empty; reproduction means change and hence implies singularity, difference.

What withers at this point is the work's 'aura', which gives what Benjamin calls 'the unique phenomenon of a distance'. Bourgeois culture gives to the work of art the appearance of distance – distance in time, distance from the experiences and the situation of people, existing in a world of its own. Although the aura is already disintegrating in urban modernity in the experience of shock (1973, 154), it is kept alive in the concept of the work of art, and it makes visible a mysterious wholeness of objects; it is like a halo, giving to art a cultic authority, or a fetishistic status. Fading of the aura is like the loss of the idealizing symbol within the *Trauerspiel* as the melancholy allegorist reduces everything of the systematic, apparently unified world to rubble. Reproducing the work in different forms and also in different media, in making the aura decay, changes people's reactions towards art, brings them close to it, and compels upon people a new type of attention. Whereas 'art' is supposed to require concentration, to appreciate its aura, now the dominant state in which it can be absorbed is distraction. The art form that best illustrates distraction is architecture, 'the reception of which is consummated by a collectivity [not the single privileged consumer] in a state of distraction'. The modern person now performs certain tasks in a state of distraction, and film is the medium above all which produces the public 'as an examiner, but an absent-minded one'.

The three substantial points here – art coming out of its continuum, the decay of aura and the democratization this implies, and the state of distraction – are reminders of a then contemporary crisis that Benjamin, in 1936, knew he was part of. The work of art which is reproduced endlessly gives the opportunity for a new creation of the spectacle within fascism. It also allows for a new separation of forms of art – into those requiring attention, which can, on account of this, be refetishized, and into those which induce in the spectator or listener only distraction. The 'conservative modernism' that is constitutive of fascism can pretend to be upholding standards and so keep art at a distance, but at the same time fascism makes its appeal by its powers of technological reproducibility (consider the use the Nazis made of the cinema). For Benjamin, the potential of technological reproducibility is to politicize art, not to re-auraticize it, as fascism is likely to do. In the last statement of 'The Work of Art', he accuses fascism of aestheticizing politics and concludes that 'Communism responds by politicizing art' (1970, 244). This gives not only a theory of fascism which connects with Guy Debord's 'society of the spectacle' and makes it clear that fascism is not a cultural as much as a political movement (requiring, for instance, a psychoanalytic inquiry into its appeal), it also at the time led to an engagement with Adorno on the subject of using art (which, for Adorno, meant treating art as though it was something instrumental), and on the differences between committed and autonomous art. Most crucially, Benjamin raises the question of how both art and politics would be moved on if the challenge of the last sentence was taken. Certainly, it implies a redefinition of both contemporary art and politics.

If the aestheticization of the political produces, ultimately, fascism, it is part of a wider aestheticism which is content with surfaces, with phantasmagoria, and finds its apt symbol in the 'flâneur', the nineteenth-century idler in the city, who thinks of himself as separate from the commodity-world, but who is not, for the intellectual is also on sale, and so is also part of commodification (Benjamin 1973, 34). That the flâneur is male has become the subject of studies drawing on Benjamin of women's relationships to the city (Wilson 1991). Benjamin's work probes below surfaces; this goes right back to his essay on Goethe's *Elective Affinities* where he distinguishes 'critique', which he practises, from 'commentary'. The former is concerned with the elusive truth-content, which is not, however, anything determinate, the latter with the subject-matter (Benjamin 1996, 297–8). The flâneur 'who goes botanizing on the asphalt' (1973, 36) in thinking that he can give a taxonomy of city types and of city life, by doing so makes the artificial appear natural – which is the definition not only of what symbolism as opposed to allegory does, but of what ideology does.

Yet the flâneur is also an image for Benjamin himself (1979, 299), for the flâneur also undertakes a trip into the city's past, which is also the city's unconscious, and links, as an idea, to the city's 'passages' as labyrinthine. The flâneur is a figure of melancholy because he can also see the city passages as dead, like a corpse (and he is inside the dead thing), as 'dialectics at a standstill' in the sense that there is no movement there, rather the abolition of movement. 'The devaluation of the world of objects in allegory [the theme of the Trauerspiel book] is outdone within the world of objects itself by the commodity' (1985, 34). It is because the commodity allegorizes and as a dead thing invades everything – Benjamin even calls the souvenir a 'relic' – something dead, hollowed out, a fragment (1985, 48) – that the person who looks can be nothing else than melancholic. The allegorist dealt with fragments which had the status of ruins; Baudelaire is the type, for Benjamin, of the flâneur who sees that the commodity now has that status, and has also performed the work of the allegorist. Since the intellectual is also part of the commodity, the sense of death is everywhere. Yet if the commodity brings about this awareness, then it is also doing what the work of the Trauerspiel does – it reveals things as needing redemption, not as under the phantasmagoria. To return to the argument of 'The Work of Art in the Age of Mechanical Reproduction', the fantasy of the work of art still possessing its aura keeps the notion of everything being the same; it keeps appearances going. Technological reproduction has the possibility of working like the power of allegory; it breaks down the sense that art, like everything else, still works in a continuing tradition.

Jeremy Tambling

Further reading and works cited

Benjamin, W. *Illuminations*, ed. and intro. H. Arendt. London, 1970.
—. *Charles Baudelaire: A Lyric Poet in the Era of High Capitalism*. London, 1973.
—. *The Origin of German Tragic Drama*. London, 1977a.
—. *Understanding Brecht*, intro. S. Mitchell. London, 1977b.
—. *One Way Street and Other Writings*. London, 1979.
—. 'Central Park'. *New German Critique*, 34, 1985.
—. *Selected Writings Vol. 1: 1913–1926*, eds M. Bullock and M.W. Jennings. Cambridge, MA, 1996.
—. *Selected Writings Vol. 2: 1927–1934*, eds M. W. Jennings et al. Cambridge, MA, 1999.
Brodersen, M. *Walter Benjamin: A Biography*, ed. M. Dervis. London, 1996.
Buci-Glucksmann, C. *Baroque Reason: The Aesthetics of Modernity*. London, 1994.
Buck-Morss, S. *The Dialectics of Seeing*. Cambridge, MA, 1989.
Derrida, J. 'Force of Law: The Mystical Foundation of Authority', in *Deconstruction and the Possibility of Justice*, eds D. Cornell et al. London, 1992.
Eagleton, T. *Walter Benjamin Or, Towards a Revolutionary Criticism*. London, 1981.
Frisby, D. *Fragments of Modernity*. Cambridge, 1985.
Geist, J. F. *Arcades: The History of a Building Type*. Cambridge, MA, 1983.
Huyssen, A. *After the Great Divide: Modernism, Mass Culture, Postmodernism*. Bloomington, IN, 1986.
Jennings, M. W. *Dialectical Images*. Ithaca, NY, 1987.

Lunn, E. *Marxism and Modernism*. Berkeley, CA, 1982.

McCole, J. *Walter Benjamin and the Antinomies of Tradition*. Ithaca, NY, 1993.

Roberts, J. *Walter Benjamin*. London, 1982.

Sholem, G. *Walter Benjamin: The Story of a Friendship*. Philadelphia, 1981.

Smith, G. (ed.) *On Walter Benjamin: Critical Essays and Recollections* Cambridge MA, 1988.

Steinberg, M. (ed.) *Walter Benjamin and the Demands of History*. Ithaca, NY, 1996.

Wilson, E. *The Sphinx in the City*. Berkeley, CA, 1991.

Wolin, R. *Walter Benjamin: An Aesthetics of Redemption*. New York, 1982.

Reception Theory: Roman Ingarden (1893–1970), Hans-Georg Gadamer (1900–) and the Geneva School

Reception theory may be defined as reflection on the role of the reader in the constitution of the meaning of texts. The philosophers and literary critics discussed in this essay did not, like later critics, consciously describe their work as 'reception theory', nor did they participate in a comparably collective enterprise. Nevertheless, they can be considered as the first generation of contributors to reception theory, in so far as each gives an account of the act of reading a text in which this act plays an essential role in determining its meaning.

The most influential of these accounts has been that of Hans-Georg Gadamer. In *Truth and Method*, he sets out to describe the kind of knowledge produced in the human sciences, which he argues has been misrepresented since the Enlightenment. The fundamental error, in his view, has been to think of the human sciences as analogous to the natural sciences. Since Descartes, scientific research has been based upon the principle that the discipline of reason by method protects against error. The inductive method of the natural sciences, in which laws are induced from the verified results of controlled experiments and predictions made on the basis of these laws, has therefore been the model with which scholars in the human sciences have, more or less explicitly, conceived of their own procedure. For Gadamer, this is a mistake, as the inconsistency of the best attempts to justify the claim to truth of the human sciences in this way suggests. The truth which emerges in disciplines such as literary criticism, history and philosophy is not attained by the kind of method which characterizes the natural sciences.

In Gadamer's view, the first philosopher clearly to understand this was Heidegger. In *Being and Time*, the latter revolutionized the concept of understanding by describing it not as a kind of method which can be applied to the texts which the human sciences take as their objects but as an essential characteristic of human existence as such. Gadamer sets out to develop the significance of this account of understanding for the process of reading and interpretation. The first consequence is that the ideal which characterized historicist accounts of interpretation, such as those of Schleiermacher and Dilthey, namely a purely objective attitude that avoids interpreting the text in terms of the interpreter's concerns, must be abandoned as a fiction. As Heidegger showed, all understanding has a 'fore-structure', or set of already formed experiences, perceptions and concepts, in whose terms the object to be understood appears as such (Heidegger 1962, 192). This is also true of textual interpretation.

Gadamer traces historicist hermeneutics back to the Enlightenment critique of religious tradition, and in particular to its challenge of the dogmatic interpretation of the Bible. In general, the Enlightenment aims to decide the truth or falsity of historical texts by rational principles alone, and without the prejudice which derives from the acceptance of external authority. Gadamer, however, denies that this is possible. He calls it a 'prejudice against prejudice' (1989, 270), by which he means that the opposition of reason to tradition in such hermeneutics is not a self-evident principle but the result of a specific act of judgement, which determines subsequent interpretations. It is, in short, a pre-judgement, or 'prejudice' (*Vorurteil*). Until the Enlightenment, this term did not only have the negative connotation of an unfounded judgement, Gadamer points out, but also indicated a preliminary judgement which may later prove either true or false. A hermeneutics that seeks to give a proper account of the act of interpretation must reinstate the positive connotation of the concept of prejudice and recognize that no interpretation takes place without it. There are, in short, 'legitimate prejudices' and the fundamental question for hermeneutics is how these are to be distinguished from those which critical reason should oppose (277). This question leads Gadamer to the concept of authority. He accepts the Enlightenment distinction between faith in authority and the individual use of reason, but denies that authority is therefore never a source of truth. The Enlightenment distorted the concept of authority, Gadamer argues. It is not a kind of blind obedience, opposed to the free use of reason, but rather is 'based ... on an act of acknowledgement', namely that the other, in a given case, is better informed or has greater insight than oneself. It is of the essence of authority so conceived, therefore, that what he, she or it says 'can, in principle, be discovered to be true' (280). This is the kind of authority that a layman grants a doctor, for example, or an engineer, or that a student grants a teacher. While the former takes the latter's word as that of one better informed than himself in a particular field, he could, in principle, acquire the information necessary to verify its truth.

The most important source of authority to be discredited in the Enlightenment was that of tradition. This also, in Gadamer's view, is mistakenly opposed to reason, since to preserve a doctrine in a tradition is as much a rational choice as to reject it. Tradition is not an inert body of doctrine that must be passively accepted, but rather 'needs to be affirmed, embraced, cultivated' (281). The important aspect of the concept for Gadamer is that, for the finite and temporal beings that we are, tradition, or discourse that comes to us from the past, never simply constitutes an object of knowledge, over against which we stand as knowing subjects, but rather is the very ground in which we stand. 'We are always situated in traditions', he writes, and therefore study traditional materials not as objects independent of us but as elements of the very same process by which our knowledge of them is determined (282). This is why the human sciences cannot be conceived by analogy with the natural sciences, since the latter's object-in-itself simply does not exist in them. Gadamer describes textual interpretation 'less as a subjective act than as participating in an event of tradition' (290), in which the past and the present mutually determine one another. The prejudices or preconceptions which we bring to our interpretation of a text, that is, are determined by our situation at the conjunction of a series of given traditions, and these traditions themselves are developed and altered by our interpretation.

Gadamer's term for the effect of history in understanding historical material is *Wirkungsgeschichte*, or 'history of effect'. His ideal of a good interpretation, that is of one which attains to the truth possible for our finite and temporal understanding, is one determined by *wirkungsgeschichtliches Bewusstsein*, or 'historically effected consciousness'. He describes this as consciousness of the 'situation' in which one interprets, namely a historically determined present with its specific limits. Gadamer calls these limits, which include the interpreter's prejudices, the 'horizon' of his situation. Historicist hermeneutics aimed to reconstitute the author's past horizon and to determine the meaning of the text within that horizon, and without reference to that of the present interpreter. Not only does this suspend the claim to truth of the text – Gadamer compares it to a conversation in which one listens to one's partner only in order to understanding the meaning of his words – but it also wrongly assumes that the present horizon of the interpreter is closed. In fact, Gadamer argues, 'the horizon of the present is continually in the process of being formed', above all by encounters with those of the past (306). In interpreting historical texts in terms of the prejudices determined by our historical situation, we do not merely confirm these prejudices, but test them. In many cases, we discover that the preconceptions we brought to the text are not justified as we read it. This experience of 'being pulled up short' by the text brings to our attention the challenged prejudices and leads us to question their validity (268). Not only do we interpret a text in a way determined by our present horizon, that is, but the past horizon we reconstruct from it also determines that of the present. Gadamer calls this process the 'fusion of horizons', and argues that properly acknowledging and describing it is the task of hermeneutics (307).

Gadamer's views that prejudice is necessarily a part of interpretation, and that such prejudice derives from the interpreter's situation in tradition, have been criticized by neo-marxist scholars such as Jürgen Habermas. The latter argues that prejudices can become the object of rational reflection and thereby no longer function as prejudices. A student who accepts the views of his teacher on authority can, on reaching maturity, reflect upon those views and, if he sees fit, reject them. Habermas writes, 'Gadamer's prejudice for the rights of prejudices certified by tradition denies the power of reflection' (1990, 237). Not only can tradition be rejected in this way, but it often should be, since it imposes itself upon us by force. This criticism, which would be justified with respect to a conservative view of tradition, cannot be applied to Gadamer's theory of interpretation, however, since the latter takes account of it. Tradition, for Gadamer, is a process of conflict between the past and the present, and the kind of ideology-critique that Habermas has in mind is an example of precisely such conflict. Gadamer writes that 'tradition itself is no proof of validity' and must be accepted or rejected on reflection (1986, 286). His point is simply that such reflection does not occur outside tradition, but is necessarily determined by it and constitutive of it. In fact, Gadamer has constructed a comprehensive descriptive theory of interpretation which applies to every act of literary theory and criticism from Leavis to Derrida. While this theory does lead to a certain relativism, in which no single correct meaning of a text can be isolated, it can equally be argued that there is no supra-historical norm with respect to which historically situated interpretations can be described as relative.

Whereas Gadamer's hermeneutics derives from Heidegger's existential account of understanding, Roman Ingarden came to literary theory in working out his relationship to the phenomenology of Edmund Husserl. It seemed to Ingarden that the literary text was a kind of object that could not be given an adequate phenomenological description in terms of Husserl's transcendental idealism. The literary text is neither an entirely ideal object, like numbers or geometrical figures, since it comes into being at a determinate point in time and is subject to certain changes. Nor is it an entirely real object, existing in space and time, since it is comprised of sentences, which are composites of ideal units of meaning. He describes it as an 'intersubjective intentional object', which means that it derives both from acts of the author's consciousness and from the concepts upon which he draws in these acts (Ingarden 1973a, 14). Since these concepts are ideal, the work is available in identical form to an infinite number of readers, and so transcends the consciousness of its author and readers at the same time as it depends upon them.

Ingarden sets out to expound the specific nature of the literary object so conceived. He argues that it is a 'formation constructed of several heterogeneous strata', each of which determine one another and the work as a whole (1973b, 29). These strata he defines as follows: (1) the word-sounds and the higher-order phonetic formations composed of them; (2) the meaning-units and the higher-order sentences and groups of sentences composed of them; (3) the 'schematized aspects' or the ways in which the objects and actions portrayed by the meaning-units are represented to the reader; (4) the 'represented objectivities' portrayed in this way. The literary text is constituted firstly by the word-sounds, which are apprehended as 'typical phonic forms' rather than as concrete sounds, and which 'carry' the fundamental meaning-content of the work (1973b, 37). Ingarden describes the act of meaning something as an 'intentional' act, which means that it is necessarily an act of meaning something in particular, and describes this meant thing as an 'intentional object' or the 'intentional correlate' of the act. The intentional correlates of sentences, in which nouns typically combine with verbs, he calls 'states of affairs'. When such sentences are combined into higher-order semantic systems, such as a novel or a lyric poem, the states of affairs are combined into the represented 'world' of the text. Ingarden ascribes to such texts a 'borrowed' intentionality, since, once complete, their intentional objects are no longer the direct correlate of the author's acts of meaning them, but are, as it were, the trace of these acts. He writes, 'Of the originally intended purely intentional object, there remains, so to speak, only a skeleton, a schema' (1973b, 127).

This schematic quality characterizes the stratum of the objects and actions represented by the meaning-units of the text. These objects Ingarden calls 'purely' intentional objects, since they have no real existence outside the author's initial act of intending them. The essential difference between real and represented objects is that, whereas the former are fully determined, existing in every respect in this particular way as opposed to that, the represented objects of a literary text are characterized by numerous 'spots of indeterminacy', in which their properties are undescribed in some respect (1973b, 249). In the portrayal of a given character in a novel, for example, we may not be told how tall he is, what his voice sounds like, what he does in between the episodes in which his actions are narrated, and so on. The world represented by the literary text is 'only a schematic formation', whose spots of indeterminacy can be filled out by the reader in an infinite number of ways (251). These indeterminacies are partly removed by the 'aspects' of the represented objects presented to the reader. The aspects of an intentional object are 'that which a perceiving subject experiences' of it, as opposed to the object itself, which is inaccessible in its entirety (1973a, 56). In a literary text, a character may appear acoustically, such as Wilfred Owen's sergeant – ' "I takes 'is name sir?" ' – or visually, like Eliot's Princess Volupine, with her 'meagre, blue-nailed, phthisic hand'. Similarly, a scene may be described in meticulous detail, so that we have the impression that there are no almost gaps in the represented space or time, as in certain realist novels, or we might simply glimpse disconnected moments and events, as in certain modernist poems.

Because of the schematic structure Ingarden ascribes to the literary work, he makes a sharp distinction between the work and its 'concretizations', that is the new intentional objects constituted each time a reader performs the act of reading the work. He writes: 'Every literary work is in principle incomplete' and in need of supplementation by a reader (1973b, 251). This supplementation occurs as the reader actively intends the sentences of the text as the objects of his act of reading, so that their 'borrowed' intentionality becomes real again. As a result of this process, many of the spots of indeterminacy at the level of the represented objectivities are 'filled in' by the reader in acts of imagination. In this 'complementing determination' of the object-stratum of the text, Ingarden writes, the 'co-creative activity of the reader comes into play' (1973b, 53). He regards this activity as an 'art' (1973a, 309). A good reader, that is, will fill in the indeterminate parts of the work in a way that corresponds adequately to those which it has determined. This is true also at the level of the aspect-stratum of the text. 'The reader must perform a vivid representation in reading', Ingarden writes, in order internally to experience, or 'intuit', the text's objects in the multiple ways in which their aspects represent them (1973a, 57). The good reader will not merely understand sentences which represent the text's objects acoustically, that is, but will imaginatively intend the objects of such sentences as heard sounds. Furthermore, he will actualize not just any aspects of the represented objects in this way, but only those suggested by the text. The 'life' of the literary work, for Ingarden, consists in the history of these concretizations, transposed into critical discourse, which can influence and be influenced by both one another and the cultural norms of a given age.

Ingarden's theory of the text has been more favourably received than his theory of reception. His account of the interrelated strata of a literary work, although rarely used in practice, in fact provides a structure for very thorough formal analyses of the ways in which texts construct meanings and achieve effects, both in themselves and in comparison to other texts. His distinction between the text and the reader's concretization has proved to be of lasting value, but needs considerable supplementation. In particular, his concept of the correct concretization demanded by a text is difficult to sustain, since, as Gadamer has shown, reading is a more interactive practice than merely filling in a text's blanks. As Wolfgang Iser writes, Ingarden takes account only of a 'one-way incline from text to reader' rather than a 'two-way relationship', in which the reader both brings his own historically and otherwise determined conceptions to the text and allows these conceptions to be challenged (Iser 1978, 173). He does not, in short, account for the historical situation of the reader. Furthermore, while Ingarden's aesthetic approach deals plausibly with the question of aesthetic value, it limits literary criticism to an account of the constitution of such value, and so also neglects the historical situation of the text.

In contrast to Ingarden's emphasis on the intentional structure of the literary text, the literary critics of the Geneva School aim principally to describe the consciousness itself that the reader encounters there. The school takes its name from the association of many of a group of intellectually and personally associated scholars with the University of Geneva. Most prominent among them are Marcel Raymond (1897–1981), Albert Béguin (1901–57), Georges Poulet (1902–91), Jean Rousset (b. 1910), Jean Starobinski (b.

1920) and Jean-Pierre Richard (b. 1922). Despite significant developments of individual interest, all six of these critics practise what Poulet calls the 'criticism of consciousness' (Richard 1954, 9).

In 'Phenomenology of Reading', Poulet argues that the object which emerges from the book in the act of reading is a consciousness, 'the consciousness of another', which allows the reader to enter into its processes of thought and feeling (Poulet 1969, 54). Like Ingarden, he argues that the objects represented by the signs of a literary text take on a more concrete existence when they are actualized by a reader. Poulet argues that, in reading, these objects lose their materiality and assume a new existence, independent of their basis in signs, in the 'innermost self' of the reader. They become purely 'mental entities' dependent for their existence as such on the mind of the reader in which they exist. This dependence means that the unreal world of a read book has the advantage over the real world of not being opposed to the consciousness of the subject who perceives it. Poulet describes the objects that emerge in reading as 'subjectified objects', whose nature seems to the reader to be consubstantial with that of his own consciousness (55). For Poulet, this is a source of value – it is the 'greatest advantage' of literature that it frees us from our usual sense of the incompatibility between our consciousness and its objects.

It is a further characteristic of the objects of a read book that they do not have the autonomy of real objects but are the thoughts of another subject. In reading, Poulet writes, 'I am thinking the thought of another' (55). I become the subject of another's thoughts and feelings, and his mental world becomes mine. But who is this other? It is not exactly the author himself, Poulet argues, although criticism will benefit from as much historical and biographical detail about him as possible, since his life is 'translated' into the work (58). This translation is 'incomplete', however, and what the reader encounters is an 'analogy' of the author's lived experience. The work has a life of its own – indeed, it is a 'sort of human being' – which it lives in the reader while he gives it existence (59). Criticism is the reader's record of the relationship between the consciousness which emerges in reading the work and his own consciousness. The critic's task, for Poulet, is to describe the characteristic qualities of the consciousness he experiences in a given author's works, and to retrace in them the initial moment of self-consciousness upon which it is based (1972, 48). This is the method of Poulet's own critical studies, such as the *Studies in Human Time*, in which he traces the different experiences of temporal existence expressed in the works of a series of literary and philosophical authors.

In 'The Critical Relation', Jean Starobinski responds to the challenge of structuralism, and, like Poulet, argues that the primary fact of reading is the effect of the 'living world' of the text upon the reader (Starobinski 1989, 11). Structural analysis is necessary in order to demonstrate the derivation of this world from the material signs in which it has its basis. But it must not be forgotten that these signs constitute a 'world within a larger world', in which the structure of the work implies a structuring subject (118). Although the author is inaccessible to the critic except through his own textual works and those of others, nevertheless the critic can and must 'interrogate him *in* his work by asking the question, "Who is speaking?" ' (121). Formal analyses of the text, that is, are not ends in themselves, as in structuralism, but can be used to establish an 'intentional trajectory', or the specific nature of the subjectivity coming to expression in the text. Criticism, for Starobinski, must avoid not only the pitfall of too great a subservience to the text but also that of too close an adherence to a method which does not allow the individuality of the text to appear. The ideal mode of criticism, he argues, combines both the 'methodological rigour' of verifiable analytic techniques, and 'reflective openness' in which the subject of the work is thereby allowed to speak in his individuality (126).

Starobinski exemplifies this dual approach in studies such as *Jean-Jacques Rousseau: Transparency and Obstruction* (1988). Here, through numerous close textual analyses, he traces certain fundamental 'symbols and ideas that structured Rousseau's thought' (xi). He argues that Rousseau's experience is such that he both desires a transparent, or purely present, relationship to himself, others and the world, while also desiring to overcome the obstructions that he constantly finds to interrupt such a relationship. Starobinski traces these motifs in Rousseau's fiction, letters, autobiography, philosophy of history, pedagogy and musical theory, and argues that they constitute a 'constant element in Rousseau's life and imagination' (126).

Without the phenomenological framework in which Ingarden describes the intentionality of literary texts, the Geneva critics' fundamental claim to encounter a consciousness in the text lacks convincing support. As J. Hillis Miller points out, their criticism has its roots in the romantic tradition, and it contains a number of romantic presuppositions whose validity can be questioned (Miller 1966, 305). The concept of a fundamental state of pure consciousness, which precedes interaction with its objects, has been challenged by phenomenology, and the concept of pure self-consciousness has been convincingly criticized by Jacques Derrida. As the latter shows, signs mediate presence to oneself, and it is difficult therefore to imagine either that a literary text expresses a previously formed self-consciousness or that it constitutes the formation of such a state, as the Geneva critics believe. Even those who pay greatest attention to the formal aspects of a text, such as Starobinski and Rousset, relate those forms back to modes of consciousness without addressing the question of their transparency. Since the subjectivity encountered in a text is available in no other way than through the text, there is no way of checking the claims of the Geneva School accurately to have reconstructed it, and in practice their results differ considerably. Nevertheless, the Geneva critics' characterizations of the subjective structures expressed in the works of their authors remain impressive. If one accepts that the objects of their analyses are rhetorical constructions rather than expressions of subjectivity, and that literary criticism is not limited to the analysis of these constructions alone, their work remains illuminating.

Luke Ferretter

Further reading and works cited

Béguin, A. *L'Âme romantique et le rêve*. Paris, 1946.
Falk, E. H. *The Poetics of Roman Ingarden*. Chapel Hill, NC, 1981.
Gadamer, H.-G. 'Rhetoric, Hermeneutics and the Critique of Ideology', in *The Hermeneutics Reader*, ed. K. Mueller-Vollmer. Oxford, 1986a.
—. *The Relevance of the Beautiful and Other Essays*, ed. Robert Bernasconi. Cambridge, 1986b.
—. *Truth and Method*. London, 1989.
—. *Gadamer on Celan*, eds R. Heinemann and B. Krajewski. New York, 1997.
Habermas, J. 'A Review of Gadamer's *Truth and Method*', in *The Hermeneutic Tradition*, eds G. L. Ormiston and A. D. Schrift. Albany, NY, 1990.
Heidegger, M. *Being and Time*. Oxford, 1962.
Holub, R. C. *Reception Theory*. London, 1984.
Ingarden, R. *The Cognition of the Literary Work of Art*. Evanston, IL, 1973a.

—. *The Literary Work of Art*. Evanston, IL, 1973b.
—. *The Ontology of the Work of Art*. Athens, OH, 1989.
Iser, W. *The Act of Reading*. London, 1978.
Lawall, S. N. *Critics of Consciousness*. Cambridge, MA, 1968.
Miller, J. Hillis. 'The Geneva School', *Critical Quarterly*, 8, 1966.
Poulet, G. *Studies in Human Time*. Baltimore, MD, 1956.
—. *The Interior Distance*. Baltimore, MD, 1959.
—. 'Phenomenology of Reading', *New Literary History*, 1, 1969.
—. 'Poulet on Poulet: The Self and the Other in Critical Consciousness', *diacritics*, 2, 1972.
—. *Proustian Space*. Baltimore, MD, 1977.
Raymond, M. *From Baudelaire to Surrealism*. London, 1961.
Richard, J.-P. *Littérature et Sensation*. Paris, 1954.
—. *L'Univers imaginaire de Mallarmé*. Paris, 1961.
Rousset, J. *Forme et signification*. Paris, 1962.
Starobinski, J. *Montaigne in Motion*. Chicago, 1985.
—. *Jean-Jacques Rousseau: Transparency and Obstruction*. Chicago, 1988.
—. *The Living Eye*. Cambridge, MA, 1989.
Weinsheimer, J. *Philosophical Hermeneutics and Literary Theory*. New Haven, CT, 1991.
Wellek, R. *Four Critics*. Seattle, WA, 1981.

The Frankfurt School, the Marxist Tradition, Culture and Critical Thinking: Max Horkheimer (1895–1973), Herbert Marcuse (1898–1979), Theodor Adorno (1903–1969), Jürgen Habermas (1929–)

Beginnings

The *Institut für Sozialforschung* (Institute for Social Research) of Frankfurt University was opened on Sunday, 22 June 1924, thanks to an endowment from the son of a millionaire, the marxist Felix Weil, who wanted to create a German equivalent of the Marx-Engels Institute in Moscow in the hope that a foundation of this kind would be of use to a future German Soviet Republic (Wiggershaus 1994, 24). The Institute was thus unusual among German academic institutions in openly espousing marxism as its paradigm for studying the historical socialist and labour movements, economic history and the history of political economy. Kurt Gerlach was nominated as the first Director of the Institute, but he died before he could assume his duties. His successor, Carl Grünberg, despite his sympathy for 'scientific' marxism as a methodology, did, however, uphold the Institute's official independence of the socialist and communist parties (the original proposed name for the Institute – Institut für Marxismus – had been discarded for this reason), even though most of his colleagues, i.e. the Institute's assistants and doctoral students, happened to belong to Germany's various communist groupings.

Grünberg retired after suffering a stroke in 1927 and was succeeded as Director of the Institute in October 1930 by the thirty-five-year-old Max Horkheimer, who was also given a chair in social philosophy at the university. The choice of Horkheimer, who had studied philosophy under the anti-Kantian Hans Cornelius, was something of a surprise since his involvement with the Institute up to that point had been minimal, and his socialist or communist affiliations not very evident – the suspicion was that he owed his appointment in large part to the fact that he was more acceptable to colleagues at the university than his openly marxist predecessor had been. Horkheimer, who quickly showed himself to be an adroit intellectual entrepreneur, ambitious both for himself and the Institute, prompted a switch of emphasis in the Institute's research programmes from social and economic history to social theory. He also placed more weight on collective and interdisciplinary work and brought psychoanalysis within the purview of the Institute's research interests (primarily by appointing Erich Fromm to the Institute). A further change occurred in 1932 when Horkheimer replaced Grünberg's empirically oriented journal *Archiv für die Geschichte des Sozialismus und der Arbeiterwegung* with the more theoretical and interdisciplinary *Zeitschrift für Sozialforschung*. The Institute's older members remained broadly wedded to Grünberg's version of materialism, i.e. a 'positivistic' materialism inspired by Engels and Kautsky with its stress on the inexorable 'laws' of capitalist development, while younger members followed Horkheimer in moving towards a non-monistic Hegelian marxism that owed its provenance to Lukács's *History and Class Consciousness* (1923). It could in fact be argued, as Martin Jay has, that the intellectual agenda of the Frankfurt School involved a repristination of the concerns of the so-called Left Hegelians of the 1840s, especially in so far as both groups were concerned to formulate a philosophy of social praxis that involved giving the Hegelian dialectic a more materialist cast (Jay 1973, 42). The Frankfurt School was not simply post-Left Hegelian and marxist, because its intellectual agendas under Horkheimer were also inflected by the legacy of Nietzsche (with its emphasis on perspectivalism and the need to acknowledge the irreducible element of invention in thought) and Max Weber (who compelled social thinkers to deal not just with the history of institutions and the history of production and technology, but also the history of rationality and rationalization). These interdisciplinary concerns were notably less evident in the work of the members who had been appointed by Grünberg.

Prominent 'older' members of the Institute included the economic historian Karl August Wittfogel, best-known for his work on 'hydraulic societies' and the so-called Asiatic mode of production; Franz Borkenau, another economic historian, who did most of his work on the ideological transformations associated with capitalist development; and Henryk Grossman, also an economic historian, who worked on a wide range of topics, including the theory of capitalist accumulation and crisis developed in his best-known work *The Laws of Accumulation and Collapse*. All three had Communist Party affiliations (Grossman with the Polish rather than the German party) and were supporters of the Bolshevik Revolution and its aftermath in the USSR (though Borkenau became disenchanted with the USSR and subsequently severed his links with the German Communist Party).

Of the 'younger' members, the most prominent at the inception of the Institute was Horkheimer's close friend and trusted colleague, Friedrich Pollock, who served briefly as interim Director before Horkheimer was permanently appointed to the position. Pollock, an economist like Grossman but with a training that also included studies in philosophy under Hans Cornelius, was, unlike Borkenau, Grossman and Wittfogel, sceptical about the USSR's capacity to realize the ideal of human emancipation it purported to serve. More importantly for the work of the Institute, the ever-loyal Pollock supported Horkheimer in his efforts to press the Institute in new intellectual directions, especially the revision of the theoretical foundations of marxism that began to take shape under the latter's leadership. In time an inner circle devoted to this objective would form itself round Horkheimer, consisting of Pollock, Theodor Adorno, Herbert Marcuse, Leo Lowenthal (who was the *Zeitschrift's* managing editor) and Erich Fromm.

Max Horkheimer

Horkheimer's inaugural lecture on assuming the Directorship of the Institute, 'The Current Condition of Social Philosophy and the Task of an Institute of Social Research' ('Die gegenwärtige Lage der Sozialphilosophie und die Aufgaben eines Institutes für Sozial-forschung'), provided a conspectus of the current state of social philosophy in relation to its historical precursors. Clearly attempting to set out an intellectual framework for the Institute's future research programmes, Horkheimer constructed a narrative of crisis to account for the trajectory of German social philosophy. According to Horkheimer, German idealism had made the individual the basis of social action, while Hegel had in the end subordinated the individual to the state, and Schopenhauer's philosophy, which in this sense was 'ahead' of Hegel's, reflected the decisive breakdown of philosophic confidence in an objective totality (Jay 1973, 25). Later thinkers – including the Marburg neo-Kantians, Scheler, Hartmann and Heidegger – would struggle without real success to restore this lost sense of an objective totality or to compensate for its demise. Turning to the present, Horkheimer saw social philosophy not as a homogeneous endeavour ensuing in an incontrovertible body of truth predicated on the uncompromised availability of the notion of totality (this guiding intuition for future work in philosophy owing a great deal to Nietzsche's intellectual legacy), but as an interdisciplinary materialism, buttressed by empirical analysis, with contemporary social problems as its focus (the inspiration for this being the Hegelianized marxism that was to dominate the Institute's research under Horkheimer's leadership).

Horkheimer sought to retain the key elements of the Hegelian dialectic – its emphasis on the essential constructedness of knowledge, the dynamic movement of history – while rejecting Hegel's idealism, which pushed the dialectic to a premature conclusion by insisting that the unfolding of absolute Spirit culminates in a final abolition of the split between subject and object, so that contradictions not resolved in the world will be resolved in Spirit's higher unity. Hegel, in countering the dogmatisms of scepticism and relativism, had succumbed to his own brand of dogmatism. As Horkheimer says:

> Insofar as [Hegel's] method ... still belongs to an idealist system, he has not freed his thought from the old contradiction. His philosophy too is ultimately characterized by the indifference to particular perceptions, ideas and goals which belong to relativism, as well as by the transformation of conceptual structures into substances and the inability to take theoretical and practical account of the dogmatism and historical genesis of is own thought. (1978, 415)

On the other hand, says Horkheimer, the proponents of 'diamat', the deterministic marxism of the Second and Third Internationals, turn marxism into an equally unacceptable and similarly 'closed' dialectic despite their professed desire to turn Hegel's idealism 'on its head'. Social contradictions will not be abolished by some pre-given historical guarantee or telos, as the 'diamat' marxists thought, but only by the practices of concrete historical subjects. The materialist dialectic is necessarily 'unconcluded', and this because thought can never exhaust reality: social reality is not a totality that is available qua totality to consciousness, and it follows that there 'is no general formula for handling the interaction of the forces which must be taken into account in particular theories; the formula must be searched out in each case' (Horkheimer 1986a, 29). Relations between forces, subjects and objects must be grasped historically, and the particularity of the historical and social must be refracted into thought if thought is to do justice to the singularity of the processes and events that constitute the historico-social domain. The social totality can be posited and knowledge of it can be sought, but its constituents are not fixed and they are not therefore epistemically transparent. This is the necessary starting-point for any theory of the relation of truth to historical and social reality.

Most of Horkheimer's thinking on the question of the relation of truth to social reality occurred in the most intellectually active phase of his life, i.e. the period between 1930 and 1945. Central to his thinking on this subject were the propositions that a properly materialist theory of truth and judgement would be one that had the critique of ideology at its core, that praxis is the basis of the verification of judgement, and that interdisciplinary research, some of it with an empirical emphasis, involving economists, historians, sociologists, philosophers and psychologists is crucial for a marxist critical theory capable of avoiding the Scylla of idealism and the Charybdis of the positivism and determinism of 'diamat' (Held 1980, 183).

Horkheimer's attempt to work out a new dialectical logic along the above-mentioned lines amounted to a version of what we today would probably call standpoint theory. Since reality is complex and dynamic and marked by contradiction among its elements, and its subjects and objects are constantly affected by this dynamism and contradiction, the (marxist) theory of this reality has to relate, at a higher level, the particularities of these elements and the inevitably particularized perceptions and apprehensions of them. In this way an appropriately marxist theoretical knowledge of society is achieved through the creation of ensembles of the knowledges afforded at each particular standpoint (Horkheimer 1978, 432–3).

In two other major essays, 'The Latest Attack on Metaphysics' ('Der neueste Angriff und die Metaphysik') and 'Traditional and Critical Theory' ('Traditionelle und Kritische Theorie'), Horkheimer extended the ideological critique of judgement and truth under capitalism made in his earlier articles to the human sciences (geisteswissenschaften). The former essay (Horkheimer 1937) was largely an attack on the then dominant logical positivism, portrayed by its author as a repristination of the age-old nominalist tendency. The logical positivists, by confining the sphere of reason to what was immediately visible in the natural order, made it impossible for there to be a rational conception of society, since the desire for a better world was taken by them to involve a 'mere evaluation' (and hence ultimately 'meaningless') and therefore beyond the purview of rational inquiry. The restriction of speculative reason to the domain of experience and the split between this reason and value initiated by Kant therefore finds a decisive culmination in logical positivism. The latter essay (Horkheimer 1986b), perhaps Horkheimer's most famous, charges 'traditional theory' with an inability to move beyond liberalism, with its prescription of piecemeal reform and a concomitant refusal to seek a transformation of the social totality, while 'critical theory' by contrast takes such a transformation to be rationally determinable and within the compass of human agency.

Horkheimer's theoretical positions were set by the late 1930s, and his best intellectual work was almost done. He was of course to remain productive: the collaboration with Adorno on *Dialectic of Enlightenment* remained ahead, and the shepherding of the Institute through the travails of exile was a major undertaking calling for resourcefulness and administrative acumen. After the Second World War Horkheimer's thinking veered in a more conservative direction (even if he continued to believe that the human demand for happiness is irreducible), and though lionized by the student radicals of the late 1960s like the other members of the Frankfurt School, he disapproved of their aims and aspirations, and his work took on a politically quietistic and increasingly theological turn. So much so that in 1958 he wanted the young Jürgen Habermas removed from the Institute (which had moved back to Germany in 1950) for an article – 'On the Philosophical Debate over Marx and Marxism' – that argued against an abstract philosophy of history in favour of a practically-oriented philosophy of history aimed at the transformation of society (Wiggershaus 1994, 554).

Herbert Marcuse

Born in Berlin, Herbert Marcuse, like Horkheimer and Adorno, came from a family of affluent middle-class assimilated Jews. He studied with Husserl and Heidegger, preparing his *Habilitationsschrift* (subsequently published as *Hegel's Ontology and the Foundation of a Theory of Historicity*) under the supervision of the latter. Relations between Marcuse and Heidegger became strained during the deteriorating political situation in Nazi Germany, and Marcuse broke with Heidegger before he could be employed as his mentor's assistant at Freiburg. Now without the prospect of a job at Freiburg, Marcuse relied on Husserl's good offices to take up his case with the Rector of Frankfurt University, and after a favourable review by Adorno of *Hegel's Ontology* in the *Zeitschrift für Sozialforschung*, Marcuse was added by Horkheimer to the staff of the Institute in 1933. Like many of the Institute's staff, he went into exile, ending up in the United States, where he became a major intellectual catalyst for the 1960s new left. Unlike Adorno, Horkheimer and Pollock, Marcuse did not return to Germany after the war, though he died there while on a visit in 1979.

Marcuse was more explicitly committed to marxism as a theoretico-practical paradigm than were Horkheimer and Adorno, and in addition to his studies of Hegel, his work encompassed analyses of German fascism and the stages of capitalist development, a study of Soviet marxism, a synthesis of Freud and Marx, and many publications in which he outlined a detailed vision of non-repressed life in a post-capitalist society. He also had a more positive conception of the revolutionary transformation of society than his life-long friends Adorno and Horkheimer, and there was sharp disagreement between them when Marcuse enthusiastically supported the 1960s radical student movement.

Marcuse's best-known work, *One-Dimensional Man*, began by sharing Horkheimer's and Adorno's concerns regarding the viability in capitalist societies of a creative social criticism. Reification nullifies the possibility of such a criticism, says Marcuse, because:

> Technical progress, extended to the whole system of domination and co-ordination, creates forms of life (and of power) which appear to reconcile the forces opposing the system and to defeat or refute all protest in the name of the historical prospects of freedom from toil and domination. Contemporary society seems to be capable of containing social change –

qualitative change which would establish essentially different institutions, a new direction in the productive process, new modes of human existence. (11)

Technology has generated affluence (the Heideggerian resonance is evident), and affluence, by freeing people from wants, has effectively undermined any real impulse to oppose the system: the working classes now identify with the system, which has become a benign totalitarianism in the process, precisely in order to safeguard their opportunities for consumption. If Horkheimer and Adorno were unable to identify a form of revolutionary agency capable of overturning today's totally administered societies, Marcuse thought there was just such a radical force in these societies, namely 'the substratum of the outcasts and outsiders, the exploited and persecuted of other races and other colours, the unemployed and unemployable' (200). These excluded individuals have broken with the culture of the market (or rather the market has broken with them), and while Marcuse depicts them as a potential counter-force to capitalism, he notes with caution that what they proffer 'is nothing but a chance':

> The critical theory of society possesses no concepts which could bridge the gap between present and future; holding no promise and showing no success, it remains negative. Thus it wants to remain loyal to those who, without hope, have given and give their life to the Great Refusal. (201)

Critical theory therefore provides a theoretical underpinning (in the form of a philosophy of consciousness with its concomitant philosophy of society and social forces) for the Great Refusal. Marcuse, like its other first-generation exponents, took a wide-angled look at the social reality of the regnant phase of capitalist development, produced a scintillating and prescient analysis of it, but could in the end only endorse one affiliated political principle: unrelenting negativity.

Theodor W. Adorno

Theodor Wiesengrund Adorno's father came from a prosperous assimilated Jewish mercantile family. His mother, born Maria Calvelli-Adorno della Piana of a Corsican noble family, was a successful professional singer before her marriage (Wiesengrund, his father's name, would be dropped after Adorno left Germany in 1934 to go into exile). A precocious talent in both musical aesthetics and philosophy, Adorno had known Horkheimer since 1922, when they were both members of Hans Cornelius's seminar on Husserl. Having obtained his doctorate on Husserl's philosophy under Cornelius, Adorno went to Vienna in 1925 to study musical composition with Alban Berg. His talent for composition not matching his gift for philosophy, Adorno returned to philosophy and took his *Habilitation* under Paul Tillich (Horkheimer was one of the other examiners) in 1931 with a thesis titled 'The Construction of the Aesthetic in Kierkegaard' that was published two years later.

In his 1931 inaugural lecture 'The Actuality of Philosophy' ('Die Aktualität der Philosophie'), Adorno presented an overview of philosophy whose lineaments were to feature consistently in his thinking for the rest of his life. Equating idealist philosophy with Hegelianism (with Husserl's thought constituting a final reduction of the Hegelian system), Adorno rejected this philosophy's 'pretension of totality' in ways that strikingly parallel the similar rejection of the idealist versions of totality that was to be found in Horkheimer's social philosophy:

> Whoever chooses philosophy as a profession today must first reject the illusion that earlier philosophical enterprises began with: that the power of thought is sufficient to grasp the totality of the real ... Philosophy which presents reality as such today only veils reality and eternalises the present condition. (1977, 120)

Finding idealism to be in disarray by the 1930s, Adorno further characterized it as a highly abstract reductive system beset by internal contradictions and antinomies. Though he took issue with Hegel, Adorno and Hegel shared the conviction that philosophy's thought-forms were those of culture and society as well. For both the history of philosophy is coextensive with the history of consciousness. The breakdown of classical idealism made it necessary to recast philosophy, and the prolegomenon to this was an immanent and systematic critique of idealism's propensity for 'identity thinking' (i.e. its positing of a constitutive homology between subject and object and thought and reality). Only a truly dialectical philosophy could overcome the old problems, and a path be paved for philosophy that was neither trivial nor contradictory (1977, 130). Adorno proposed that the immanent critique of philosophy take the form of a critical hermeneutics: while the task of science (*Wissenschaft*) is research, 'that of philosophy is interpretation', so that (and here the influence on Adorno of Walter Benjamin's work on German tragic drama and Goethe's *Elective Affinities* is very evident):

> philosophy persistently and with the claim of truth, must proceed interpretatively without ever possessing a sure key to interpretation; nothing more is given to it than fleeting, disappearing traces within the riddle figures of that which exists and their astonishing entwinings. The history of philosophy is nothing other than the history of such entwinings. (126)

Adorno also maintained that sociology is the basis of this critical hermeneutics, since cultural and intellectual objects express, in mediated form, the existing modes of production in society. Philosophy's basis is thus irreducibly materialist and historical – ideas arise from history, and classical idealism disintegrated because it overlooked this truth (128–9). The task of a materialist philosophy is to show how idealism is destroyed by the social contradictions it expresses and effaces in a simultaneous movement, and to 'demystify' the bourgeois thinker's pretensions to totality and completeness. Influenced as much by Freud (who had already been used by Adorno in his doctoral thesis) as by Marx in this view of philosophy as a form of demystification, Adorno's 'logic of disintegration' sought to pave the way for an emancipatory philosophy that eschewed the 'identity thinking' of the classical philosophical systems. The critical theorist cannot change reality – only the labour of human subjects to change material and social conditions can do this. But by destroying, internally, the hold of conceptual systems on reality, critical theory makes possible the discovery of potentially liberating possibilities that are inherent in humans and things. By freeing objects from our deadening hold, and sustaining a sense of possibility, 'immanent criticism' preserves a place for utopian impulses. In the following years Adorno used this method of an 'immanent criticism' to undertake rigorous technical examinations of Kant, Hegel, Husserl and Heidegger (this was in addition to the study of Kierkegaard that constituted his *Habilitationsschrift*).

As was the case with Horkheimer, changing historical circumstances affected Adorno's own estimation of the possibility of a utopian transformation of society. Stalinism made him sceptical of the utopian possibilities afforded by an 'official' marxism, and Auschwitz and Hiroshima condemned the past that had led up to them and placed the future under the shadow of total catastrophe. Hence, says Adorno, 'life has changed into a timeless succession of shocks, interspersed with, empty, paralysed intervals' (1974, 54). Those who survived Auschwitz are burdened by the guilt of having survived:

> The only responsible course of action is to deny oneself the ideological misuse of one's existence, and for the rest to conduct oneself in private as modestly, unobtrusively and unpretentiously as is required, no longer by good upbringing, but by the shame of still having air to breathe, in hell. (1974, 28; see also 1973, 362–3)

In such a hell, 'our perspective of life has passed into an ideology which conceals the fact that there is life no longer' (1974, 15). Contemporary culture has become completely reified, because it is now so dominated by the exchange mechanism that the social and political forces which underlie our society are no longer fully comprehensible: 'no society which contradicts its very notion – that of mankind – can have full consciousness of itself' (1967, 26). Life is inescapably ideological – 'Things have come to pass where lying sounds like truth, truth like lying' (1974, 108). However, while truth may be difficult, even impossible, to determine, we should not allow ourselves to be terrorized by this fact (1974, 69). Human consciousness no longer has a purchase on the absolute, but truth is still possible, even in a totally reified society. These are seemingly contradictory assertions, and Adorno freely admits to being guilty of this contradiction:

> After everything, the only responsible philosophy is one that no longer imagines it had the Absolute at its command; indeed philosophy must forbid the thought of it in order not to betray that thought, and yet it must not bargain away anything of the emphatic concept of truth. This contradiction is philosophy's element. (1998, 7)

Only when alienation is overcome will it be possible for men and women to think the absolute. But 'the emphatic concepts of truth' cannot be relinquished since they are the only things which contradict the heteronomous reality of the present. Distorted social arrangements can be revealed for what they are – the untruth – only when these distortions are confronted by an ideal which makes apparent the gap between the ideal (or 'concept', to use Adorno's terminology) and reality (or the 'object'). Truth is therefore to be sought in the act of negating existing social reality, and so for Adorno the desire for truth is equivalent to desiring utopia: 'To want substance in cognition is to want a utopia' (1973, 56). Truth is also to be identified with that which enables us to live with oppressing others:

> A new categorical imperative has been imposed by Hitler upon unfree mankind: to arrange their thoughts and actions so that Auschwitz will not repeat itself, so that nothing similar will happen. (1973, 365)

Critical thinking is quintessentially negative and dialectical; it aspires to call continually by their names, instance by instance, all the expressions of alienation which imperceptibly dominate human thought and existing institutions. His unremitting brilliance notwithstanding, Adorno was sometimes too slapdash in his use of such key notions as *alienation*, *truth*, *reconciliation*, etc., and though he did refer in several of his essays to the class struggle, it is not clear what exactly he took this struggle to entail or what he considered its possible outcomes to be. This reluctance or reticence brought him into conflict with the student radicals of the 1960s, and by the time of his death (1969) he had been repudiated by the student movement.

Adorno's intellectual range was astonishing, and little or nothing in the human sciences escaped its compass: philosophy, musicology and musical aesthetics, social psychology, political theory, sociology, literature, art, film theory and educational theory are significantly represented in his oeuvre. Unlike Horkheimer and Herbert Marcuse, who are hardly read today, his writings (along with those of Walter Benjamin) seems somehow to be ahead of us, to have a future beyond their current reception, and even as one acknowledges their problems, Adorno's texts constitute at the same time a salutary and dazzling provocation for those wanting to reflect on the characters of our times.

Jürgen Habermas

Jürgen Habermas was Adorno's assistant, and is widely regarded as the most distinguished of the 'second generation' of the Frankfurt School. Other members of this generation include Oskar Negt, Klaus Offe and Albrecht Wellmer, though none has been as prominent as Habermas, the author of over twenty books and several dozen major articles and reviews.

Habermas's first major philosophical work, *Knowledge and Human Interests* (*Erkenntnis und Intresse*), took from Kant the notion that reason has universal presuppositions, and from Hegel the notion that reason undergoes historical development, to provide a theory of the conditions of possibility for our emancipation from the structures of power and ideology. Three significant departures from the First Frankfurt School soon showed themselves in Habermas's writings: (a) an interest in the theory of rationality, and in particular its *reconstruction* (some have argued that Kant is more important for Habermas than Hegel and Marx); (b) an interest in language, especially the speech-act theory of Austin and Searle, as opposed to consciousness; and (c) a willingness to engage with Anglo-American philosophy, in particular Pierce and G. H. Mead (in addition to Austin and Searle). Commonalities do exist of course, in two areas especially: (a) the shared interest in emancipation; and (b) the conviction that the human lifeworld is to be safeguarded from the depredations of technology and its accompanying instrumental rationality.

Habermas's magnum opus *Theory of Communicative Action* (*Theorie des kommunikativen Handelns*) views society as a multi-tiered amalgam of symbolic structures open to 'communicative understanding', that is as a totality bound by a system of rules of discourse and action that are shared by its participants. These rules constitute a 'discourse ethics', the basis of which is a practical procedure for achieving a non-coercive rational discourse involving free and equal protagonists. In this procedure, each member of society is required to take the perspective of all the others, generating a complex of perspectives that ensues in an overarching 'we-perspective' from which all can test their norms to see if these norms can constitute the basis of a genuinely shared practice. In this way a pragmatic ideal is established, an ideal that has to be embodied in actual speech-situations if democratic arrangements are to be implemented and sustained. Habermas has achieved a blend of the utopian and rational that some have nonetheless found unconvincing (is a very slightly less than ideal procedure still capable of generating norms that can be accepted as valid?). Horkheimer's idea of an interdisciplinary theory of social emancipation is given a kind of realization in Habermas's delineation of this 'universal pragmatics', but Habermas's staunch commitment to a universal rationality would not be shared by the first generation of the Frankfurt School. In fact, a case can be made for suggesting that the intellectual legacy of Horkheimer and Adorno has crossed the Atlantic and found its current stopping point in the work of Fredric Jameson, who in addition to producing exemplary commentary on Adorno, has, among other things, extended the latter's extraordinary insights into late capitalism as a totality inhering in our cultural forms (an insight not much to be found in the Habermasian organon) in ways that Adorno himself could scarcely have anticipated. (Jameson's use of the Althusserian notion of a structural totality gives his account of late capitalism a scope and pertinacity not available to Adorno, who invoked the notion of totality, but only negatively, as a heuristic device in his immanent critique of capitalism. Totality for Adorno is the source of utopian counter-images bespeaking the reconciled life that can be pitted against the distorted life we are compelled to live under capitalist dispensations. It is precisely that – utopian – whereas for Jameson, even as he remains faithful to Adorno, totality is indispensably involved in any attempt to map (and mapping is always a practico-theoretical operation) the cultural and political operations that are constitutive of capitalism.)

The Frankfurt School has given the present-day theorist of culture a powerful meta-language for grasping and comprehending the innumerable forms, and ensembles of forms, through which historicity, temporality and the present coalesce with the capitalist mode of production to produce social and cultural reality. Elements of this metalanguage appear dated or are no longer serviceable for some of us today. But its productive scope has been substantial, its influence immense and salutary.

Kenneth Surin

Further reading and works cited

Adorno, T. W. 'Cultural Criticism and Society', in *Prisms*. London, 1967.
—. *Negative Dialectics*. London, 1973.
—. *Minima Moralia*. London, 1974.
—. 'The Actuality of Philosophy', delivered in 1931. *Telos*, 31, 1977.
—. 'Why Still Philosophy', in *Critical Models*. New York, 1998.
Arato, A. and Gebhardt, E. (eds) *The Essential Frankfurt School Reader*. Oxford, 1978.
Connerton, P. (ed.) *Critical Sociology*. Harmondsworth, 1976.
Habermas, J. *Knowledge and Human Interests*. Boston, 1971.
—. *Theory of Communicative Action. Volume One. Reason and the Rationalization of Society*. Boston, 1984.
Held, D. *Introduction to Critical Theory*. London, 1980.
Horkheimer, M. 'Der neueste Angriff und die Metaphysik', *Zeitschrift für Sozialforschung*, 6, 1, 1937.
—. 'On the Problem of Truth', in *The Essential Frankfurt School Reader*, eds A. Arato and E. Gebhardt. Oxford, 1978.
—. 'Materialism and Metaphysics', in *Critical Theory: Selected Essays*. New York, 1986a.
—. 'Traditional and Critical Theory', in *Critical Theory: Selected Essays*. New York, 1986b.
— and Adorno, T. W. *Dialectic of Enlightenment*. London, 1979.
Jay, M. *The Dialectical Imagination*. London, 1973.
Marcuse, H. *One Dimensional Man*. London, 1968.
Wiggershaus, R. *The Frankfurt School*. Cambridge, MA, 1994.

Mikhail Bakhtin (1895–1975)

Mikhail Bakhtin has been hailed by Tzvetan Todorov as 'the most important Soviet thinker in the human sciences and the greatest theoretician of literature in the twentieth century' (1984, ix), and has had a serious impact on the thinking of literary critics as diverse and distinguished as Roman Jakobson, Wayne Booth, David Lodge and Julia Kristeva. By any standards he is a stunningly original thinker, whose work has implications for philology, semiotics, philosophy (especially ethics and aesthetics), psychology and cultural anthropology as well as for literary history and criticism. Yet virtually his entire life passed in obscurity, not only from the viewpoint of the West but within the Soviet Union as well. The son of a bank manager, Bakhtin was born in Orel, south of Moscow, and like his older brother Nikolai studied classics at Petersburg University (1913–17). He and his family moved to Nevel to avoid some of the hardships of the Civil War in Petersburg, where Bakhtin dominated a group of intellectuals, the first 'Bakhtin circle', including the linguist and musicologist Valentin Voloshinov, the Jewish philosopher M. I. Kagan and the philosopher and literary scholar Lev Pumpiansky. Soon much of the group moved to Vitebsk, where they were joined by Pavel M. Medvedev, a critic who had some official standing with the government.

In 1920 Bakhtin married Elena Okolovich, who would be his lifetime caretaker. During this period he suffered from osteomyelitis of the left leg as well as a typhoid infection of the right; eventually that leg would be amputated and his health always remained precarious. Still, throughout the mid-1920s Bakhtin was quite productive, working on a number of essays and monographs in aesthetics and moral philosophy (some of which has been translated under the title *Art and Answerability*) as well as an early version of his book on Dostoevsky; the surviving notebooks show him moving away from the neo-Kantianism of Ernst Cassirer and Hermann Cohen which had been an important influence. In 1924 he returned to Leningrad, where he was granted a small medical pension but lived in relative obscurity; his friends' involvement in religious questions tended to isolate them, and indeed in 1929 Bakhtin was arrested, apparently for his questionable religious affiliations, and sentenced to ten years in the Solovetsky Islands camp. Meanwhile, *Problems of Dostoevsky's Creative Works* had been published to some acclaim, and some of his influential friends, including Gorky, managed to have his sentence commuted to six years' 'internal exile' in Kazakhstan, probably saving his life. During the early 1930s he held a variety of menial jobs, occasionally lecturing and drafting essays, until in 1936 Medvedev found him a position teaching at the Mordovia Pedagogical Institute in Saransk, about four hundred miles west of Moscow.

In the late 1930s, fearing a purge of the faculty, Bakhtin moved to Savelovo. He published some reviews and finished a book on the novel of education, the publication of which was stopped by the war. Only fragments of it survive. Meanwhile several of his circle, including Medvedev, were executed or died in camps. By 1940 he had prepared a doctoral dissertation for the Gorky Institute on 'Rabelais in the History of Realism' but the war postponed his defence. After teaching in secondary schools awhile, in 1945 he returned to the Pedagogical Institute, eventually becoming Chairman of the Department of General Literature. In 1946 his defence was rescheduled but increasing ideological repression during the Zhdanov period postponed his degree until 1952. And then – probably because of the politically dubious nature of his writing – he was awarded only a candidate's degree.

During the late 1950s his old formalist antagonist Shklovsky mentioned the Dostoevsky work respectfully, as did Jakobson, and by 1960 several young Russian scholars, believing him dead, were making efforts to republish that book. Bakhtin was persuaded to revise the book and the final years of his life were marked by increasing recognition and many more material comforts. Both the surviving formalists and the Tartu semioticians (on the left) celebrated him, as did a young group of Russian Orthodox scholars (on the right). Bakhtin's ability to appeal simultaneously to thinkers of widely divergent positions has continued to characterize his work during its reception in Europe and the Americas. Meanwhile, during his last years he worked on the Rabelais manuscript (which was published in 1965), his notebooks and a host of earlier manuscripts he wished to revise. In 1973 the semiotician Vyacheslav Ivanov claimed that Medvedev's book *The Formal Method in Literary Scholarship*, a critique of formalism published in 1928, was actually written by Bakhtin, as were *Freudianism: A Critical Sketch* (1927) and *Marxism and the Philosophy of Language* (1929), both signed by Voloshinov, and several essays published under Voloshinov's name. Bakhtin did not conclusively either affirm or deny these assertions, and by 1975 he was dead. His final words were 'I go to thee' – perhaps addressed to his beloved wife, who had died in 1971, or perhaps not.

Bakhtin has been claimed by formalists and their successors the structuralists as one of their own, and he shares with both of them the conviction that language must be the fundamental key to analysing and evaluating art and experience. Poststructuralists, beginning with Julia Kristeva (1980), often claim him as a precursor because his attack on the notion of a unified speaking subject as the guarantor of *logos* and his vision of language as inevitably a patchwork of citations anticipates poststructuralist positions. Marxists have claimed him because of his conviction that language is always already ideological and his championing of the dispossessed and admiration for 'the people'. Anti-marxists often see him as a religious thinker, pointing out the parallels between his work and that of Martin Buber, with its highlighting of the 'I–Thou' relation. He is a hero to a neo-Aristotelian like Wayne Booth because he proposes analytic categories for thinking about narration, like a formalist, but also clearly sees literary issues as ethical.

The question of the disputed texts exacerbates some of these issues, since the Voloshinov and Medvedev works are much closer to conventionally marxist thought than are the works published under Bakhtin's name. At this point, though, it is probably the consensus of scholars that while the disputed texts may indeed incorporate many of Bakhtin's ideas, they are not directly his work. But although Bakhtin is not a conventional marxist, neither are most of the western marxists such as Althusser, Adorno or Benjamin. His approach and values are certainly more 'sociological' and anti-idealist than was the work of most Anglo-American literary critics up until the last twenty years. But he is unlike both marxists and many contemporary theorists in his opposition to 'theoretism', the explanation of human phenomena by invoking a set of abstract rules, norms or analytic categories. He is not himself a wholly systematic thinker, and the state of being 'unfinished' or 'unfinalizable' is in fact one of his highest values and is basic to his definition of humanity.

Bakhtin's idea of the self is radically dependent upon others; the self, for him, is an act of grace, the gift of the other. Human consciousness is formed only in a process of perpetual negotiation with other selves by way of their 'languages'. Selfhood is supremely social, and a person who grew up without ever having been exposed to speech would not be fully human for Bakhtin. For Bakhtin, in a way, intersubjectivity precedes subjectivity. Paradoxically, while consciousness is where Bakhtin locates selfhood, consciousness for him is fundamentally linguistic, and thus in his terms an extraterritorial part of the organism. As he remarks, language 'lies on the border between oneself and the other' (Bakhtin 1981, 293). In his early writings on self and other Bakhtin points out that every person benefits from the 'surplus of vision' that others enjoy in looking at him or her and incorporate that vision into their vision of themselves even while opposing or partially assenting to it. So by definition one's finalizing vision of another is never adequate; people, like successful characters in novels, 'do not coincide with themselves'. Bakhtin has little interest in the unconscious, and ascribes to consciousness most of the conflicts, contradictions and complexities that Freudians see in the interaction of conscious and unconscious minds.

Language, the semiotic system that most interests Bakhtin, is not an abstraction for him. He is always concerned with *parole* – the individual instance of speech – rather than *langue* – the system that orders speech. From Bakhtin's perspective, formal study of language systems is useless – and the early Formalists were essentially wrong-headed – because it ignores the way in which speech is always rooted in a particular material situation that contributes a significant part of its meaning. The 'sentence' is objective and can be reiterated, but the 'utterance' is unique and unrepeatable. Further, language is always, in Bakhtin's terms, ideological: that is, each utterance carries with it the aura of a particular idea-system (which may be more or less explicitly political) out of which it was spoken. The most significant aspect of an utterance for Bakhtin is what he terms its addressivity, its quality of being in some respect spoken *toward* someone. Bakhtin calls for a 'metalinguistics' or a 'translinguistics' which would investigate not merely the forms of language but the kinds of material situations in which speech occurs, because each speech act involves not only a theme but at least two interlocutors plus an invisible 'third', a 'superaddressee' providing an imagined absolutely just response – God, human conscience, 'the people', science, etc. (Bakhtin 1986, 126). Bakhtin uses the term 'heteroglossia' to refer to the fact that speech, in so far as it is always embodied in a particular situation, is always multiple, always a mixture of languages which themselves can be further reduced. Everyone participates in numerous 'languages of heteroglossia', each of them claiming privilege. Obviously one of the problems of such a system is to establish any sort of final typology, but Bakhtin was happy to generalize about language types in a strictly provisory way. Toward the end of his life he was wrestling with the problem of what he termed 'speech genres', 'whole utterances belonging to particular generic types' (Bakhtin 1986, 89).

The key to understanding language for Bakhtin is that 'our speech, that is, all our utterances (including creative works) is filled with others' words, varying degrees of otherness or varying degrees of "our own-ness", varying degrees of awareness and detachment. These words of others carry with them their own expression, their own evaluative tone, which we assimilate, re-work, and re-accentuate' (Bakhtin 1986, 89). Thus language is always 'double-voiced', embodying both the language of the speaker (itself an amalgam of that speaker's important interlocutors such as parents, lovers, intellectual influences and so forth) and any immediate or anticipated addressee, towards whom the speaker may linguistically assume a great variety of postures. To a remarkable degree, Bakhtin's theories of self – other relations, of language and consciousness, of ethics and of literature interpenetrate and support one another, so that Gary Saul Morson and Caryl Emerson have offered the term 'prosaics' to suggest both the way Bakhtin's thought is always rooted in the ordinary, the everyday and the immediate and the way his literary system elevates the prose genres over the poetic ones (Morson and Emerson 1990). To a great extent, the 'actor' or 'performer' of Bakhtin's philosophical and ethical writings is the same as the 'author' of his later specifically literary ones, and both groups of writings celebrate the confrontation with alterity.

For literary criticism, Bakhtin's most important essays are probably 'Epic and Novel', 'From the Prehistory of Novelistic Discourse' and 'Discourse in the Novel', all collected in *The Dialogic Imagination* (1981). In an unsystematic but highly suggestive way he lays out a theory of literature that inverts most of the classical assumptions about the hierarchies of writing and what constitutes formal excellence. First, he opposes the novel and its earliest hellenic forms, such as the dialogue, the symposium or Menippean satire, to epic and lyric poetry (and, less convincingly, drama too), arguing that the prose forms are superior in that they are dialogic – founded upon and constituted by dialogue – whereas poetry always tends toward the monologic, the state of a single, authoritative voice. In his book on Dostoevsky, Bakhtin argues that that novelist most fully realized the potential of the form and that his aesthetic process is best described as polyphonic, referring to the interplay between the author's own language and the fully realized languages of his protagonists. While in one sense no real speech or writing can be truly monologic, Bakhtin uses the term to refer to patriarchal, authoritarian, consciously ideological speech that reifies and totalizes; the authorial speech of Tolstoy seems this way to Bakhtin, as opposed to the polyphonic speech of Dostoevsky, in which we can easily find dialogized heteroglossia, a living dialogue of worldviews. In the genuine novel, Bakhtin claims, 'the "depicting" authorial language now lies on the same plane as the "depicted" language of the hero, and may enter into dialogic relations and hybrid combinations with it' (1981, 27–8). Indeed, it can be said that in the fully realized novel the 'author participates in the novel (he is omnipresent in it) *with almost no direct language of his own. The language of the novel is a system of languages that mutually and ideologically interanimate each other*' (1981, 47).

Bakhtin is at his most formalist in categorizing dialogical relations in the novel, although he does so very differently in different works. He talks of the enormous number of ways in which language is stratified – by genres and sub-genres of literature (lyric, oratorical, penny-dreadful), by social professions (lawyers, businessmen, politicians), by social differentiations among groups, by artistic circles, journals and even particular artistic works, all 'capable of stratifying language, in proportion to their social significance' (1981, 290). But his main interest is reserved for different ways in which the language of the author may interact with other languages in the novel. For example, he explores what he terms 'character zones' in novels, areas of the text in which the authorial language changes to reflect the consciousness of a character even when that character is merely mentioned by the author and no direct attempt is being made to represent his or her thoughts. Much later and independently, the critic Hugh Kenner described this as the 'Uncle Charles effect', in reference to a passage in James Joyce's *Portrait of the Artist as a Young Man* where Stephen Dedalus's Uncle Charles 'repairs' to the outhouse, where he finds the air 'salubrious' – a passage that Wyndham Lewis, missing the point, attacked as inflated late-Victorian prose. A character zone is a clear example of heteroglossia; another is the way the novel form uses incorporated genres – short stories, songs, poems, newspaper stories, scholarly or religious genres, for example, as well as the familiar confession, letter, diary and so forth. This is another strength of the novel for Bakhtin, and shows how it is not simply another genre of literature but a 'super-genre', capable of assimilating all the others.

In *Problems of Dostoevsky's Poetics* Bakhtin gives his most elaborate schema for classifying novelistic discourse (1984, 199). His first category is direct, unmediated discourse directed exclusively toward its referential object – essentially, the monologism of the author (and thus something not found in a true novel). The second category is objectified discourse – in other words, a character's speech. Bakhtin notes that this can be more or less 'typed', and in so far as it is *not* typed, the relationship between author's and character's speech approaches dialogue. Double-voiced discourse, or discourse with an orientation toward someone else's discourse, is the third category, and the one that Bakhtin finds crucial. There are several sub-types of double-voiced discourse, the first of which he terms 'unidirectional' and 'convergent'. Examples of this type include stylization, the narration of an independent narrator, the unobjectified discourse of a character who is in part an authorial spokes-person, and first-person narration. One might note that the author is fundamentally sympathetic to all these voice-types. The reverse is the case with 'vari-directional double-voiced discourse' (where the voices are 'divergent'), including parody, the discourse of a character being parodied and 'any transmission of someone else's words with a shift in accent'. The last sort of double-voiced discourse is the reflected discourse of another in which the other discourse exerts influence from without, including the 'hidden internal polemic' (where another's language is being contested without ever being explicitly identified), the discourse 'with a sideward glance' toward someone else's discourse (which is never directly addressed but is indirectly highly influential in producing the speaker's language), or a rejoinder of a dialogue (either explicit or hidden). Elsewhere, Bakhtin deploys very different paradigms, but his main areas of interest remain.

A second characteristic of the novel which is not derivable from his concept of dialogism is the form's participation in a sense of life Bakhtin labels carnival, from the medieval ritual celebration. It is a simplification but perhaps helpful to say that if dialogism is the novel's proper form, carnival underlies its optimal content; the true novel is *carnivalized*. Carnival is probably Bakhtin's most influential formulation, and unsurprisingly it is also the most easily susceptible to abuse. As he develops the notion, principally in *Rabelais and His World* (1968) and *Problems of Dostoevsky's Poetics*, carnival embodies a kind of folk wisdom that celebrates the body and opposes all forms of authority. It is 'a pageant without footlights and without a division into performers and spectators' (Bakhtin 1984, 122). Bakhtin derives his utopian notion of carnival from various medieval celebrations in which a sort of 'licensed misrule' was practised, usually through mockery directed toward the Church and the town's established hierarchy. Often the mighty were ridiculed and a fool was crowned and uncrowned and there was general indulgence in 'base' pleasures of the body. Bakhtin emphasizes the free and familiar contact among people in carnival without regard to hierarchies, in 'carnival mésalliances', as well as the free indulgence in blasphemy and profanation. For Bakhtin carnival expresses the 'joyful relativity' of all structure and order, and through its celebration of the 'bodily lower stratum' affirms a perpetual organic process of birth and death, nourishment and decay, that is wholly transindividual. Although Bakhtin interprets carnival as almost entirely oppositional, it should be noted that many historians view this officially tolerated ritual as a mere 'safety valve' whose effect is to reaffirm the dominant power.

Most kinds of symbolic expression associated with carnival Bakhtin finds in 'carniva-lized' literature, including the all-important carnival laughter, the ritual exchange of insults, parody, creative blasphemy, crowning and decrowning, the highlighting of base bodily functions, including sex, ingestion, defecation and urination, drunkenness, flatu-lence and a host of material appetites. Carnival levels all pretence, and in literary formulation tends toward a 'grotesque realism' that Bakhtin celebrates as the natural form of 'unofficial culture'. Rabelais's works are for Bakhtin the best examples of the tendency of the novel toward carnivalization, though he finds many traces of carnival in Dostoevsky as well. Indeed, Bakhtin traces two separate stylistic lines of development for the novel. One of them originates in the relatively monological language of the 'Sophistic novels' and runs through the medieval novels of gallantry, the Baroque novel and the fictions of Voltaire; the other is rooted in the dialogues and in Menippean satire, the works of Apuleis and Petronius and runs through the uncategorizable works of writers like Rabelais, Sterne and Dostoevsky. The Second Line, as Bakhtin calls it (1981, 371–88), shows the novel's fundamentally dialogized relationship to heteroglossia, while the First Line tends toward objectification and monologism. And as it happens, where the First Line usually strikes a serious tone and involves itself in idealizations, the Second Line is more or less carnivalized from the beginning. Bakhtin's implication is that the traditional genealogy of the novel culminating in the social realism of Stendhal, Austen, Trollope, Balzac, Thackeray and James is actually a diversion from the more anarchic and fertile line running through Rabelais, Cervantes, the picaresque novelists, Goethe, Hugo, Dickens, Sterne – and perhaps, in the twentieth century, writers like Joyce, John Barth and Thomas Pynchon.

A final term of Bakhtin's that has found some currency in contemporary literary criticism is the chronotope, a coinage that literally means 'time-space' and that Bakhtin uses to refer to the characteristic qualities of these parameters within any given fictional genre. Unusually, Bakhtin gives primacy to neither, and is particularly interested in their interaction. His discussion of the chronotope of the Greek 'adventure novel of the ordeal' (200–600 AD) and of the 'adventure novel of everyday life' – Apuleius's *Golden Ass* and Petronius's *Satyricon* – somewhat resembles European phenomenological criticism of the 1960s in its attempt to give the 'inner sense' of a literary universe, in which both time, space, causality, selfhood and other fundamental categories of experience can be deployed in a variety of ways (1981, 86–129). Bakhtin may well have been forced to develop the idea of the chronotope because he is determined to trace the origins of the amorphous form of the novel through its ancient precursors, including locations (such as Menippean satire) where few critics had looked for pre-novelistic traces. But because Bakhtin's idea of the destiny of the novel is something very different from social realism, he re-maps the literary past in radical ways, highlighting texts ignored by most literary historians of the novel.

R. Brandon Kershner

Further reading and works cited

Bakhtin, M. M. *Rabelais and His World*. Cambridge, MA, 1968.
—. *The Dialogic Imagination: Four Essays*. ed. M. Holquist. Austin, TX, 1981.
—. *Problems of Dostoevsky's Poetics*, ed. and trans. C. Emerson. Minneapolis, MN, 1984.
—. *Speech Genres and Other Late Essays*, eds C. Emerson and M. Holquist. Austin, TX, 1986.

—. *Art and Answerability: Early Philosophical Essays by M. M. Bakhtin*, eds M. Holquist and V. Liapunov. Austin, TX, 1990.
Bakhtin, M. M. Medvedev, P. N. *The Formal Method in Literary Scholarship*, Cambridge, MA, 1985.
Clark, K. and Holquist, M. *Mikhail Bakhtin*. Cambridge, MA, 1984.
Kristeva, J. *Desire in Language: A Semiotic Approach to Literature and Art*. New York, 1980.
Lodge, D. *After Bakhtin*. New York, 1990.
Morson, G. S. (ed.) *Bakhtin: Essays and Dialogues on His Work*. Chicago, 1986.
— and Emerson, C. (eds) *Rethinking Bakhtin*. Evanston, IL, 1989.
—. *Mikhail Bakhtin: Creation of a Prosaics*. Stanford, CA, 1990.
Todorov, T. *Mikhail Bakhtin: The Dialogical Principle*. Minneapolis, MN, 1984.
Voloshinov, V. N. *Marxism and the Philosophy of Language*. Cambridge, MA, 1986.
—. *Freudianism: A Critical Sketch*, eds I. R. Titunik and N. R. Bruss. Bloomington, IN, 1987.

Georges Bataille (1897–1962) and Maurice Blanchot (1907–)

Georges Bataille's collected works comprise twelve volumes and Maurice Blanchot's available record of publication indicates a similar output. This output and the overall quality of this production are extraordinary, although, remarkably, more of a rule than an exception in the intellectual landscape to which both belong (one can mention, among others, Levinas, Lacan, Foucault, Barthes, Deleuze and Derrida). One ought to pause further to contemplate an even more extraordinary fact – namely, what kind of writing these thousands upon thousands of pages of Bataille's and Blanchot's writing (and those of other figures just mentioned) contain. Consider, for example, the passage closing Blanchot's short essay on serial music via Thomas Mann's *Doctor Faustus*, 'Ars Nova', included in *L'Entretien infini* (*The Infinite Conversation*). In the space of six pages, the essay itself traverses an immense array of themes, ideas, works and authors – Mann, Schönberg, Lukács, Adorno, Benjamin and Paul Klee, among them (1993, 345–50). It would be difficult to give a full list, since many themes and authors, while implicitly addressed, are not explicitly named, for example Kant, Hegel, Nietzsche and Derrida. Having accomplished this already remarkable feat, Blanchot, in closing, brings into consideration Georges Poulet's *The Metamorphoses of the Circle*, to open yet another set of trajectories. These trajectories traverse just about the richest conceptual space imaginable, even though and because this richness is made possible by that which is irreducibly inaccessible to any knowledge, however encompassing or deep. As will be seen, an analogous epistemology emerges in and defines Bataille's vision as well. Ultimately, this space is defined as, in Blanchot's famous title phrase, 'the space of literature'. Blanchot writes:

> I ask myself why, along with this book the whole history of criticism and culture closed and why, with a melancholy serenity, it seemed at the same time to send us off and to authorize us to enter a new space. What space? Not to answer such a question, certainly, but to show the difficulty of approaching it, I would like to invoke a metaphor. It is nearly understood that the Universe is curved, and it has often been supposed that this curvature has to be positive: hence the image of

a finite and limited sphere. But nothing permits one to exclude the hypothesis of an unfigurable Universe (a term henceforth deceptive); a Universe escaping every optical exigency and also escaping consideration of the whole – essentially non-finite, disunified, discontinuous. What about such a Universe? Let us leave this question here and instead ask another: what about man the day he accepts confronting the idea that the curvature of the world, and even of this world, is to be assigned a negative sign? But will he ever be ready to receive such a thought, a thought that, freeing him from fascination with unity, for the first time risks summoning him to take the measure of an exteriority that is not divine, of a space entirely in question, and even excluding the possibility of an answer, since every response would necessarily fall anew under the jurisdiction of the figure of figures? This amounts perhaps to asking ourselves: is man capable of a radical interrogation? That is, finally, is he capable of literature, if literature turns aside and towards the absence of the book? A question the Ars Nova, in its neutral violence, has already addressed to him. And in this it was indeed a diabolical art: Thomas Mann was finally right. (1993, 350)

It would not be possible to offer a reading of this passage here. Indeed, the question is how one can possibly approach a text, such as Bataille's and Blanchot's, that such passages paradigmatically represent. Extending the trajectories indicated above, the passage con-joins modernist art with modern mathematics and science: the key references include non-Euclidean geometry (here of negative curvature); Einstein's general relativity, in part based on this geometry; and modern cosmology, based on both. This network is further extended to modern philosophy and, in particular, the radical epistemology that defined twentieth-century thought. Thus, even leaving aside the pre-Socratics, especially Heraclitus (whom Blanchot considers in this context in The Infinite Conversation), the notion of the unfigurable has its genealogy in the ideas of, among others, Kant, Hegel, Nietzsche, Heidegger, Bataille, Lacan, Levinas and Derrida. Blanchot also draws upon legal philo-sophy and theology. The combination is remarkable both in range and in bringing these subjects into a complex, irreducibly non-simple, yet cohesive, arrangement. In question is not even so much the intertextuality of Blanchot's text but a richly interlinked conceptual work, which is primarily responsible for this extraordinary density. Arguably, the most remarkable quality of Blanchot's, or Bataille's, thought is that of discerning proximities, one might say radical proximities, between what appears to be so heterogeneous and distant. Far from being exceptional, passages of that kind are found in the immediate vicinity of virtually every point of Bataille's and Blanchot's writing. How, then, is one to approach such works, even if one could leave aside the incessant reciprocity of the relationships between Bataille's and Blanchot's work, further enriching and complicating both texts?

In confronting this task here, I have decided (the possibilities are as abyssal as the impossibilities) to offer a discussion of the architecture of some among their major concepts and/in their networked interrelationships within and between their texts. I understand the term concept itself in the sense that Gilles Deleuze and Felix Guattari give it in their What is Philosophy?, rather than, as is more customary, as an entity established by a generalization from particulars, or indeed 'any general or abstract idea', as they argue, via Hegel, a key figure for both Blanchot and, especially, Bataille, and one of the inspirations for the present approach as well (Deleuze and Guattari 1994, 11–12, 24). A philosophical concept in this sense is an irreducibly complex, multi-layered structure – a multi-component conglomerate of concepts (in their conventional sense), figures, metaphors, particular (ungeneralized) elements and so forth. This view allows one to absorb Bataille's and Blanchot's conceptual entities, or those, such as 'différance', introduced by Derrida under the heading of 'neither terms nor concepts'. (Bataille's and Blanchot's concepts are often entities of this type as well.) Philosophy itself is defined by Deleuze and Guattari as the creation of new concepts in this sense, and even 'concepts that are always new' (1994, 5). Nietzsche would speak of philosophy and philosophers of the future, which view defines as much Bataille's and Blanchot's thought as Nietzsche's own. Both Bataille's and, especially, Blanchot's fiction or, in their own terms, literature can be, and here will be, correlated with this conceptual-philosophical view, in part because their conceptual architecture is defined by both in terms of and through work(s) of literature.

Bataille

If one could *sum up* Bataille's experience, thought and writing in a single phrase (it is crucial that in fact one cannot), it would be his own phrase, 'encounter with the impossible', 'the impossible' itself eventually (in one of his last published works) used by Bataille as his title (1991 – see 'Preface to the Second Edition', 9). This statement must be understood not so much in the sense that these are shaped by an encounter with the impossible, but instead in the sense that they *constitute* this encounter or are reciprocal with it. Nor can one say that Bataille's experience or thought precede and are then (re)presented in his writing; these relationships, too, are defined by a more complex and interactive reciprocity. Accordingly (in parallel with Derrida's 'neither a term nor a concept' of writing) I shall here speak of Bataille's writing as designating this multi-reciprocal field. This multi-reciprocity is one of the effects of the efficacity to which Bataille's 'encounter with the impossible' aims to relate in an irreducibly oblique fashion, or, in Blanchot's terms, in the form of non-relation, for it cannot be done otherwise. This encounter would also constitute a form of, as Bataille calls it, 'sovereign' practice, even though and because the impossible itself in question cannot be *mastered* by any knowledge (in particular, in Hegel's dialectical sense of mastery (*Herrschaft*)). It is irreducibly 'unknowable', the term correlatively employed by Bataille. Bataille terms the relevant aspect of the sovereign practice itself as 'unknowledge (*nonsavoir*)'. Thus Bataille's writing *is* his experience – the experience of existing at 'the (extreme) limit of the possible' and on the threshold of the impossible (the phrase recurs throughout *L'Expérience intérieure*). This, however, can only be said if one uses the term 'experience' in Bataille's sense of 'interior experience' (*expérience intérieure* – sometimes translated as 'inner experience'), in juxtaposition to the classical concept of experience, understood as the experience of presence and particularly of consciousness. As Derrida points out:

> 'that which *indicates itself* as interior experience [in Bataille] is not an experience, because it is related to [no consciousness], no presence, no plenitude, but only to the 'impossible' that it 'undergoes' in torment. This experience above all is not interior; and if it seems to be such because it is related to nothing else, to no exterior (except in the mode of nonrelation, secrecy, and rupture), it is also completely *exposed* to torment – naked; open to an exterior; with no interior reserve or feeling; profoundly superficial. (1980, 272; translation modified)

The phrase 'encounter with the impossible' occurs in *Inner Experience* (*L'Expérience Intérieure*), where the concept is developed via Blanchot's *Thomas the Obscure*. The book is an instalment, along with *Guilty* (*Le coupable*) (1988a), and *On Nietzsche* (*Sur Nietzsche*) (1990), of what was originally conceived of as *La somme athéologique* – both a quasi-autobiographical 'summing-up' of this encounter and a conceptualization, or philosophy, of interior experience. At the same time, the atheological or, more generally, a-ontotheological nature of this encounter and of this summing-up makes them rigorously unsummable. (Following Heidegger and Derrida, ontotheology here designates any form of determination, idealist or materialist, equivalent to the theological determination in positing a single fundamental agency, overt or hidden, which would uniquely or unconditionally govern or control nature, history, interpretation and so forth.) Thus Bataille's writings 'de-cohere', as it were, away from any *attempt* to link them to classical, for example, dialectical, or indeed any conceivable wholeness (understood as an unambiguously determinable arrangement of parts). I stress 'attempt' because one cannot here think in terms of some (logically or ontologically) pre-existing coherence from which one then 'decoheres'. Bataille's practice is defined by un-totalizable but mutually engaging – heterogeneously interacting and interactively heterogeneous – relationships among various problematics, terms, concepts, fragments and other elements of Bataille's text or genres (essays, theoretical treatises, fictions and so forth). One encounters a very different form of organization, which is a consequence of Bataille's radical epistemology, here at work in and deployed by his own writing. (The same argument would apply to the work of Blanchot and a number of other figures mentioned above.)

It may be useful to give a summary of the key features of this epistemology in this context. The particular elements involved interact and are organized: that is, we may meaningfully consider collective configurations of them as having structure. This organization, however, does not fully govern the functioning of each of these elements in their particularity, thus allowing them to assume independent significance – ultimately to the point of defying any attempt to define them by any denomination. Bataille's writings continuously enact configurations of that type, which is essential to what he calls 'sovereign' discursive and conceptual practice, sovereign writing, and necessary for the writing (in the above sense) of sovereignty itself. They do so even as, and by virtue of the fact that, they equally submit and pursue (sovereignty being impossible otherwise) that which escapes even these far-reaching dynamics, or indeed anything; Bataille's writings, in their contigorations, figure that which is irreducibly inaccessible, ultimately inaccessible even as inaccessible, or as 'that'. For, the efficacity itself of the interplay of the (organized) collective and (singular) particular elements, or of either type of 'effects', to begin with, appears to be irreducibly inaccessible, and hence cannot be 'mastered' by any means. It cannot be assigned any available or conceivable terms, such as 'underlying', which makes Bataille appeal to the (irreducibly) 'unknowable' and, in conceiving of this (ultimately in turn inconceivable) process itself, to 'unknowledge'. Nor, however, can (the alterity of) this efficacity be postulated as existing in itself and by itself, as anything to which inaccessible properties can be assigned. Accordingly, the unknowable is not something excluded from the domain or the configuration governed by the logic in question, as an *absolute* other of it, which would return the situation to a classical regime, by enabling one to master the unknowable by exclusion (sovereignty is never mastery). Instead it is irreducibly linked to this configuration and made the efficacity of the effects that define it. It may be added that it is even more the necessary (non)relation to this alterity-efficacity than the fragmentary multiplicity of writing (which is merely one of its effects) that Blanchot refers to (via 'the neutral' and 'the fragmentary') by 'the absence of the book', or Derrida by 'the end of the book and the beginning of writing' (1974).

The situation may appear paradoxical, even impossible, which in part makes Bataille speak of 'the encounter with the impossible', while, however, making the encounter itself with this impossible possible. Indeed it does lead to an epistemology that is complex and difficult, and for some impossible to accept. What is experientially or otherwise intolerable to some, but would be affirmed by and is a necessary condition of interior experience and sovereignty, is that this irreducible loss of meaning is in fact the *efficacity* of meaning, ultimately of all possible meaning. Emerging at the limit of the possible and at the threshold of the impossible, sovereignty accepts and welcomes this type of knowledge or (or accompanied by) unknowledge, defined by Bataille as the process of relating to this unknowable. In other words, in question is not merely a renunciation of a further analysis but the recognition that, at a certain point, any further analysis is in principle excluded. This impossibility, however, does not preclude, but instead enables, a rigorous analysis of the effects of this unknowable efficacity. Hence, according to Bataille, 'it would be impossible to speak of unknowledge [for example, as 'unknowledge'] as such, while we can speak of its effects' (this sentence is omitted from the text published in 'Conférences 1951–1953'). Conversely, 'it would not be possible to seriously speak of unknowledge independently of its effects' (1962, 5; *Oeuvres Complères*, VIII, 219).

The conception just outlined is remarkable, even if not altogether unprecedented (it is found in Blanchot and several other figures mentioned here). It is equally remarkable that this 'calculus', formulated in a rather scientific, almost mathematical mode by Bataille himself, is used and indeed developed by Bataille in considering such ordinary human effects as laughter and tears, which are specifically in question in the elaborations just cited. That is, except that these are neither ordinary nor even 'human' in any classical sense we can give to this word. Indeed they are joined with, and coupled to, such (more conventionally) extraordinary effects as sexual excitation, poetic emotion, the sense of the sacred, ecstasy, sacrifice and the death of God (OC, VIII, 567–8, 592). The conjunction itself of a rigorously formal theoretical framework and something that is, at every level, outside any formalization (in any conceivable sense) is characteristic of Bataille. Now, however, this conjunction itself is given a rigorous epistemological justification by virtue of the fact that these effects, the absolute uniqueness of each occurrence of such phenomena, are formalized as irreducibly unformalizable, while *accessible*. By contrast the efficacity of all effects involved, manifest in 'the sum of all these effects' (OC, VIII, 592), is irreducibly inaccessible, unknowable. How such effects conspire to form, as they sometimes do, rich and complex orders is itself mysterious. By the same token, it cannot be seen as mystical, in the sense that one of the rigorous consequences of the sum of these effects is that no single, omnipotent agency behind them can be postulated. One can speak here of the death of God, in the broad sense of theological-like thinking wherever it is found.

Bataille's own writing becomes a particular case of this epistemology and logic, which would define the epistemology and logic of reading accordingly. This epistemology would never allow (Bataille himself or his readers) a rigorous 'summing-up' of Bataille's (interior) experience and writing under a single non-provisional rubric such as 'encounter with the impossible' or 'encounter' and 'the impossible', however effective it may be conceptually, rhetorically or strategically. The impossible and unknowable in question entails and is the efficacity of these impossibilities as well. It is, however, also the efficacity of the immense possibilities offered to and enacted by Bataille's writing, or offered to his readers, even if 'insurmountable possibilities'. Bataille himself speaks of 'the abyss of possibilities' (*Inner Experience*, 1988b, 103). A seemingly paradoxical but in fact logical consequence of

Bataille's epistemology is that impoverishment and abundance, loss and excess, the impossible and the possible, the unknowable and the richness of knowledge, or a suspension of logic and its most rigorous use all reinforce and enable each other.

It follows that, in approaching Bataille's 'encounter with the impossible', one cannot bypass other major concepts introduced by Bataille and/in their irreducible interactions anymore than Bataille himself could avoid multiplying his concepts, strategies, textual styles and so forth. It would not be possible to properly explain here all of these concepts or the connections among them, even leaving aside that the considerations just given would make it an interminable process. I shall, accordingly, only delineate some of them, which are arguably the most crucial from the concept-oriented perspective here adopted. Beyond those already indicated, in particular interior experience, they include unknowledge, sovereignty, restricted and general economy, chance, and literature and poetry. As follows from the preceding discussion, one can (always provisionally) centre, and some readers have, one's treatment otherwise – on sacrifice, gift, eroticism, ecstasy, expenditure, heterology or literature. I shall comment on some of these as I proceed.

The concept of unknowledge defines the nature and structure of our knowledge in relation to the epistemological situation here outlined. The ultimate nature of unknowledge is itself inaccessible: we cannot know how we ultimately know anymore than what is ultimately responsible for the things (objects of knowledge) that we can know. As I have stressed, however, even though unknowledge places an irreducible limit upon all knowledge, it brings into play the limits of the known and the unknown, the knowable and the unknowable, the possible and the impossible, and of the relationships between them and their limits. Other terms, such as the representable and the unrepresentable, the thinkable and the unthinkable, and so forth would be considered within the same conceptual field.

By analogy with the science of political economy, 'general economy' is defined as the science (theory) of sovereignty. Bataille juxtaposes general economy to classical or 'restricted' economies, such as that of Hegel's philosophy or Marx's political economy. Restricted economies would claim or aim to contain or compensate for irreducible indeterminacy, loss and non-selective – excessive – accumulation within the systems they describe, at least in principle, if not in practice, thus making all expenditure in principle productive. Both fundamentally base their analysis of human practices on the idea of consumption or productive (or at least accountable) expenditure, rather than on (also) taking into account sovereign practices. The latter are assumed to be irreducible by general economy and the engagement with them defines sovereignty, the primary concern of general economy, defined as the science of sovereignty, in whatever domain the latter emerges. As Bataille writes:

> The science of relating the object of thought to sovereign moments in fact is only a *general economy* which envisages the meaning of these objects in relation to each other and finally in relation to the loss of meaning. The question of this *general economy* is situated on the level of *political economy*, but the science designated by this name is only a restricted economy – restricted to commercial values. In question is the essential problem for the science dealing with the use of wealth. The *general economy*, in the first place, makes apparent that *excesses of energy are produced, which by definition cannot be utilized. The excessive energy can only be lost without the slightest aim, consequently without any meaning.* This useless, senseless loss *is* sovereignty. (OC, V, 215–16, emphases added)

Sovereignty, thus, relates to the radical irreducible loss of meaning, which is by the same token also always excessive, in particular with respect to its containment within the experience of presence, consciousness and meaning. It is primarily as such that sovereignty is juxtaposed to the Hegelian mastery or lordship, always linked to meaning, in particular in giving meaning to the loss of meaning, even though Hegel's analysis of death and sacrifice also brings them into a close, almost infinitesimal proximity as well (although the subject is crucial throughout Bataille's work – see especially 'Hegel, la mort, et le sacrifice' (OC, XII, 326–45)). The practice of a general-economic theory may be 'sovereign' or a form of interior experience. Conversely, a given case of interior experience, such as Bataille's, may acquire aspects of scientific investigation, even though his works presenting it, such as *Inner Experience*, are quite different from the more conventionally theoretical genre of, say, *The Accursed Share, Theory of Religion* and related works.

It is crucial that general economy always entails a rigorous deployment of restricted economy. These relationships are irreducible in so far as general economy is the science of the relationships between that which can be accessible by restricted-economic means (which may be the only means of accessibility we possess) and that which is inaccessible by any means, whether those of restricted or those of general economy. Sovereignty, too, must be understood as an ultimately inaccessible part of interior experience. It is experienced or felt (in unknowledge) as unmanifest and unmanifestable in and through the force of its manifest effects, of which we can speak. Short of engaging with these efficacious dynamics and the resulting interactions, one always ends up with a restricted economy, even if in the name of excess, indeterminacy, loss of meaning and so forth. According to Bataille: 'It is regrettable that the notions of "productive expenditure" and "nonproductive expenditure" have a basic value in all the developments of my book. But real life, composed of all sorts of expenditures, knows nothing of *purely* productive expenditure; in actuality it knows nothing of purely unproductive expenditure either' (1989b, 12). This point is often missed by Bataille's critics and admirers alike, which leads to significant misunderstandings of Bataille's works, specifically by assuming him to (uncritically) privilege or idealize expenditure, loss and so forth.

One of the inevitable consequences or correlatives of these considerations is a radical concept of chance, which Bataille argues to be inaccessible to 'the calculus of probability' (1988a, 76). In accordance with the preceding discussion, it would be inaccessible to any conceivable form of calculus, human or divine, which rigorously suspends all theological determination. In other words, this chance is irreducible not only in practice (which may be the case classically as well) but also in principle. There is no knowledge, in practice or in principle, that is or will ever be, or could in principle be, available to us and that would allow us to eliminate chance and replace it with the picture of necessity behind it. Nor, however, can one postulate such a (causal/lawful) economy as unknowable (to any being, individual or collective, human or even divine), but existing, in and by itself, outside our engagement with it. This qualification is crucial. For, some forms of the classical understanding of chance allow for and are indeed defined by this type of assumption. In part proceeding via Blanchot's *Aminadab, Guilty* develops this concept of chance especially powerfully (1988a, 69–86), although Bataille's remarkable notes to 'Conférences 1951–1953' (OC, VIII, 562–3, 564–7) offer a necessary supplement.

Bataille's work may appear to be and has often been associated with and even defined by elements that are traditionally seen as counterparts of (philosophical) rigour – such as poetry, chance, play, eroticism, ecstasy, laughter and other, from the classical or traditional perspective, non-philosophical or counter-philosophical elements. Bataille's writing, however, is rigorous, as well as productive of knowledge. Indeed, for the reasons explained above, it rigorously requires the utmost intellectual, philosophical and logical rigour, even a rigour comparable (although of course not identical) to that of mathematics and the natural or exact sciences. Moreover, they refigure the non-philosophical elements listed above, by relating them, as effects, to (the efficacity of) the unknowable and unknowledge.

Accordingly, Bataille's concept of literature or poetry, including as practiced in his own writing, must be seen as bringing together that which is rigorously scientific or formal, and that which is rigorously (scientifically) outside any scientific treatment or formalization. Thus it conjoins the knowable and the unknowable, classical knowledge and sovereign unknowledge, and so forth. For Bataille, literature or poetry is, in our culture, the highest or the most intense form of the encounter with the impossible and/as of the writing of sovereignty, and, reciprocally, the sovereign writing of inner experience. Naturally, the terms themselves 'literature' and 'poetry' are given a special sense, although this sense manifests itself more readily in some conventional practice of both. (Literature and poetry are not always the same in Bataille, but I shall here suspend the difference between and nuances of these two terms in his work.) As Bataille writes, 'poetry, laughter, ecstasy are not the means for other things', especially not the means for knowledge, as, say, philosophy would require. 'In the [Hegelian] "system", poetry, laughter, ecstasy are nothing. Hegel gets rid of them in a hurry: he knows of no other end than knowledge' (1988b, 111). However, this hidden, subterranean, subversive, Dionysian invasion of poetry, laughter and ecstasy into philosophy is not only inevitable but opens new possibilities for philosophy itself, even if philosophy, as it has constituted – or instituted – itself so far may not want or cannot pursue these possibilities.

Both in relation to his own practice and in general, the association of experience and writing at the extreme limit with poetry or literature is found throughout Bataille's works. He often has in mind more conventionally literary works (as in the essays assembled in *Literature and Evil*), but far from exclusively so, especially in his own case. For poetic experience and writing define Bataille's non-fictional and overtly theoretical works – indeed, one might argue, more so than his fiction. I refer again especially to *Inner Experience*, *Guilty* and *On Nietzsche*. These works must also serve here as paradigmatic examples of Bataille's style. I cannot here consider, beyond the discussion given earlier, specific aspects of writing that result – their ruptured, fragmented structure, their multiple genres, their autobiographical or auto-eroto-biographical aspects, or their engagements with chance – defined by the sovereign epistemology. The possibility of such works, however, is a crucial point that allows one to rethink the possibilities of both literary and philosophical writing.

Bataille describes his own (interior) experience and writing as follows: 'in the desire for an inaccessible unknown, which at all cost we must situate beyond reach, I arrive at this feverish contestation of poetry' (*Inner Experience*, 1988a, 137). Bataille's interior experience and writing fundamentally reflect – indeed, as I said, they are – this experience, they are this chance and this necessity. Moving towards and opening, and then unfolding the unknown and, finally, the unknowable, they reflect and are necessitated by vertiginous – abyssal – oscillations between the known and the unknown, the knowable and the unknowable, the possible and the impossible. One is almost tempted to speak, paying well-deserved homage to Hegel's grand conception (and with Hölderlin in mind), of the vertigo – 'the abyss above' – of oscillations between absolute knowledge and absolute unknowledge. The radical – but never absolute – unknowable at stake in Bataille, however, would, in the same vertiginous abyss, suspend all absolutes, positive and negative, the very absoluteness of the absolute. 'Non-knowledge attained, absolute knowledge is no longer anything but one knowledge among others' (1988b, 55). One cannot quite speak of attaining non-knowledge either. For it is defined by anguish. It is anguish, the uneliminable anguish of the unknowable.

Blanchot

Blanchot summed up his life and writing for us himself, when he said in an autobiographical statement, indeed a micro-autobiography: 'born in 1907 and dedicated his life to literature'. (Naturally, this statement requires caution, for example, given the right-wing political journalism of the 1930s, and the fragmentary nature of Blanchot's autobiographical writing (in the present sense) need not only involve epistemological complexities here considered (although these continue to play a key role). By and large, however, the statement is true from about 1938 on.) The unsummable nature of this summing up (of both Blanchot's experience and work and of literature) is analogous to that of Bataille's 'encounter with the impossible', in part because what is at some point called 'the space of literature' and, then, 'speech' ('plural speech') and 'writing' (including his own) are structured analogously to the spaces of Bataille's unknowable and unknowledge. Ultimately the very possibility of literature, as writing and as reading, may be imperiled. Blanchot will speak of 'the death of reading, the death of writing'. This ultimate abandonment even of literature itself rather than only of culture (both high and low cultures, whose complicity in both directions Blanchot understood so penetratingly) may well be a culmination of Blanchot's lifelong dedication to literature and his most radical insight. This insight is helped by the key literary figures he considers, perhaps especially Hölderlin, Mallarmé and Kafka (although many others considered by Blanchot may be mentioned, Beckett, Woolf and Duras among them). *The Space of Literature* (1951) defines the epistemology of this space in its radical terms perhaps for the first time. *L'Entretien Infini* (*The Infinite Conversation*) (1969), where the 'construction' of this space proceeds by joining Levinas and Bataille (although Hegel, Nietzsche and Heidegger remain as crucial here as elsewhere in Blanchot), and then *The Writing of the Disaster* (1980) takes this epistemology to its ultimate limit just indicated, to 'the death of reading, the death of writing', the culmination of Blanchot's lifelong meditation on the relationships between death and literature or/as all writing. These works will here serve as the main signposts (admittedly too few and far between) in navigating through Blanchot's immense oeuvre.

I am speaking of the 'spaces' analogous to rather than identical to those of Bataille, in part because, while the epistemology is fundamentally parallel and while an often parallel network of concepts is at work, often somewhat different aesthetic, cultural and political aspects of literature itself are stressed. First of all, Blanchot's concept of literature is defined primarily against the background of literature in its more conventional sense, often by selecting a particular set of authors and reading them accordingly. In this respect, a writer of fiction and philosopher (again, in Deleuze and Guattari's sense of a creator of concepts) as he is, Blanchot remains a literary critic, arguably the most philosophical critic of this century. (He does have competition in such figures as Walter Benjamin, Mikhail Bakhtin and Paul de Man.) As a result, there emerges a somewhat different (from Bataille's) cluster of concepts and relations to 'the unknowable' (the latter concept is shifted as well). The very concept of the *space* of literature is specifically Blanchot's, too. It must be kept in mind, however, that, following, among other things, Heidegger's concepts of spatiality (specifically, the spatiality of *Dasein*) and consistently with the radical epistemology in question, space in this sense may not be conceivable and especially visualizable. Hence, in a certain sense it is not spatial in any sense available to us. The enactment of this 'space' in his own work, by and large, takes place more in his fictional works, in contrast to Bataille's (non-fictional) autobiographical writing, although some of Bataille's fictions can be read in this way as well. (Nor are these works scientific, or quasi-scientific, treatises of the type of *The Accursed Share*.) Some non-fictional works, critical and philosophical, contain elements of such an enactment and a few, such as *The Writing of the Disaster* and, to some degree, the earlier *Le Pas Au-Delà* (*The Step Not Beyond*) (1973) could be seen in these terms throughout, while others in more fragmentary ways, which, however, is part of the unsummability in question. (Conversely, some of Bataille's fiction functions similarly as well.) From *Thomas the Obscure* and (its quasi-sequel) *Aminadab*, his fictions become massive allegories of, to stay for the moment with Bataille's terms, the unknowable and unknowledge, and are used as such by both Bataille and later on by Derrida. I here use the term allegory also in de Man's sense, in turn entailing an analogous radical epistemology, which also makes these works allegories of allegory itself.

The political and ethical dimensions of these allegories remain crucial. In general, one would be mistaken to identify Blanchot's criticism or philosophy, let alone his fiction, with any form of, to use de Man's term, aesthetic ideology. As has been rightly stressed by a number of recent commentators, just as, and reciprocally with, philosophical-epistemo-logical ones, the political and ethical dimensions are crucial, and indeed irreducible, in Blanchot's work, in particular proceeding via Bataille (the political) and Levinas (the ethical). Derrida's recent works, such as *The Politics of Friendship* and *The Specters of Marx*, or Deleuze's commentary on and usage of Blanchot's concept of friendship, or of course Bataille's work, may serve as significant examples of deploying these aspects of Blanchot's (as well as Levinas's and, more implicitly, Bataille's) work. In short, as is Bataille's, Blanchot's work is defined by complex heterogeneously interactive reciprocities between all these dimensions, as they invade and pass into each other.

I shall, then, here consider Blanchot's key concepts by traversing, with the preceding discussion of Bataille in mind, this space of reciprocities, proximities and difference between Bataille and Blanchot themselves. I shall use Blanchot's passage with which I began here as a guide, for it contains in a condensed form arguably the most crucial and most radical elements of Blanchot's epistemology and of his conception of literature. Accordingly, although Blanchot is compelled to engage with the network of terms whose multiplicity or dissemination cannot in turn be contained, as does Bataille, I shall here focus on the unfigurable and literature. The latter itself is conceived as a 'radical interrogation' of the unfigurable, or more accurately (we cannot interrogate the unfigurable 'itself' but only its effects), is shaped by an engagement with the unfigurable. Literature, thus, involves processes similar to Bataille's unknowledge as relating to the unfigurable/ unknowable by means of, returning to Blanchot's terms, non-relation. In *The Infinite Conversation* Blanchot ultimately questions the adequacy of interrogation itself, however radical, he questions the very form of 'questioning', which appears to define all of our intellectual history. These conceptions and this agenda are intimated already in such earlier works as *The Space of Literature* and *La livre à venir* (*The Book to Come*) which already intimate the *death* of the book to come or, as will be seen, perhaps even of literature to come.

I shall, again, bypass the immense thicket of Blanchot's concepts and metaphors, and his brilliant usage of the epistemology of modern science (which is found in Bataille as well), specifically geometries of negative curvatures and modern cosmology based on Einstein's general relativity. Here, cutting though this thicket of concepts, is Blanchot's 'definition' of the unfigurable:

> Nothing permits one to exclude the hypothesis of an unfigurable Universe (a term henceforth deceptive); a Universe escaping every optical exigency and also escaping consideration of the whole – essentially non-finite, disunified, discontinuous. What about such a Universe? . . . But will he ever be ready to receive such a thought, a thought that, freeing him from fascination with unity, for the first time risks summoning him to take the measure of an exteriority that is not divine, of a space entirely in question, and even excluding the possibility of an answer, since every response would necessarily fall anew under the jurisdiction of the figure of figures? But will he ever be ready to receive such a thought, a thought that, freeing him from fascination with unity, for the first time risks summoning him to take the measure of an exteriority that is not divine, of a space entirely in question, and even excluding the possibility of an answer, since every response would necessarily fall anew under the jurisdiction of the figure of figures?

The radical exteriority or alterity at stake in these propositions takes on a role analogous to the unknowable in Bataille, as considered earlier. As we recall, Blanchot adds, however: 'This amounts perhaps to asking ourselves: is man capable of a radical interrogation? That is, finally, is he capable of literature, if literature turns aside and towards the absence of the book?'

Blanchot, thus, associates both radical interrogation and the radical unfigurability with literature, even uniquely with literature, even when other fields of human endeavour are at stake, such as serialist music, discussed in 'Ars Nova', or perhaps even modern mathematics and science. That literature would assume for Blanchot the primary role in essentially and radically structuring the space of all art and even culture (or/as counter-culture) is not surprising. That radical interrogation, as conceived by him, signals the ultimate departure from literature – the death of literature, both of writing and of reading – rather than (this could be expected) only from culture, is more remarkable. As I said, *The Writing of the Disaster* will invoke both the death of writing and the death of reading more directly. Accordingly, literature itself (in any way we know it or even can conceive of it) may have to be sacrificed in the process, or rather it may no longer be possible at this limit. That is, such an interrogation may no longer function as literature in any conceivable sense that is meaningful or even definable within our culture, even though the latter appears to permit (including in legal terms) us to apply this term to virtually anything. To begin with, again, analogously to Bataille's unknowledge, at stake here is a process to which no name can apply. Secondly, 'literature' cannot be seen as a 'neutral' name, free of cultural or politico-ideological appurtenances, specifically aesthetic ideology. Blanchot's concept of the 'neutral', a key element of the epistemology and conceptual architecture under discussion here (and, again, of the reciprocity of Bataille's and Blanchot's thought), is designed with these complexities in view.

Once this type of space, the space defined by its relation to the unfigurable (or the unknowable), is introduced, two particular aspects of inhabiting this space, of practice within it, emerge. The first is the exploration (or more generally, knowledge) and productive deployment of whatever is possible under the conditions of the irreducibly unfigurable, and, as we have seen, much and, in a certain sense, everything is possible under these conditions, the best classical knowledge included. Accordingly, new and extraordinarily rich and productive possibilities of knowledge, philosophy, culture, literature or politics do emerge – but, again, *under these conditions*. The second aspect, on the other hand, is the exploration or, to begin with, the experience (interior experience) of existence at the threshold of or in relation to the unfigurable itself, and, as Nietzsche understood, the circumference of knowledge has many such boundary points (Nietzsche 1967, 97–8). Besides, by definition, this exploration is interminable, at least at some of such points, such as those where Blanchot's (*The Space of Literature* and *Le Pas Au-Delà* are perhaps especially graphic examples here, as the latter title indicates) and Bataille's work takes us. Blanchot's (or, again, Bataille's, or other figures' here mentioned) writing is defined and made possible by the complex interplay of both of these aspects. It is, however, especially the second that defines the existence in the space of literature, defines literature, for Blanchot and Bataille, or de Man (but, for a contrast, not necessarily or not in the same way for Derrida or Deleuze).

It may be useful to comment from this vantage point on Blanchot's earlier reading of Beckett in 'Where now, Who now?' Blanchot sees Beckett's *The Unnamable* as 'a decentered book deliberately deprived of every support'. 'It elects to begin precisely where there is no possibility of going on and persists stubbornly in staying there, without resorting to trickery or subterfuge, and stumbles on for three hundred pages'. It follows, first, that 'aesthetic considerations are out of place' in this case. Ultimately, as I said, it may not be possible to speak about literature any longer, certainly in any sense hitherto available. Alluding to Mallarmé's idea of the book, which will contain the whole world (Blanchot has written on the subject extensively), Blanchot suggests that 'what we have before us in *The Unnamable* is not a book because it is more than a book'. I would add, it is not literature because it is more than literature. Or rather, it is both more and less than a book, more and less than literature. 'It is a direct confrontation with the process from which all books derive – with the original point at which the work is inevitably lost, that always destroys the work, but with which an ever more primal relationship has to be established'. Accordingly, 'The unnamable is indeed condemned to drain the cup of infinity' (Blanchot 1982b, 192–4). 'Infinity', however, is here used in (or close to) Levinas's sense in *Totality and Infinity*, as connoting the radically unfigurable, designated by Levinas himself as Autrui – an absolute alterity, exteriority, otherness – which also links, especially for Blanchot, Levinas and Bataille. This infinity (un-finity may be a better name or un-name) unnamably names the radically unnamable, unfigurable, unknowable – in the black space which Beckett invokes and in which everything, all light and all enlightenment, are as inescapably Beckett's 'caged beasts born of caged beasts born of caged beasts born of caged beasts', as we ourselves are (1958, 386). These themes, developed in full measure later in Blanchot, lead to the complex relationships between the ethical and the literary, as indicated earlier. Art, most particularly literature – this is, for Blanchot, the message of Beckett's work, or of other key figures he considers – 'requires that he who practices it should be immolated by art, should become other, not another, not transformed from the human being he was into an artist [like, say, Thomas Mann], with artistic duties, satisfactions and interests, but into nobody, the empty, animated space where art's summons are heard', and ultimately the summons of the death of art. The answer to the question 'why art should require this metamorphosis' is to be 'found in the process by which the work of art, seeking its realization, constantly reverts to the point where it is confronted with failure. ... It is this exploration ... that makes artistic creation such a risky undertaking – both for the artist and for art', especially since one must risk and sacrifice art or literature itself – that is, try to make sure that it ultimately dies as a result (*The Sirens' Song*, 1982a, 196). Naturally, this would worry 'men of culture', 'men of taste', as Blanchot calls them, such writers as Thomas Mann or such critics as Georg Lukács among them, in contrast to Kafka, Beckett or Duras, or the composer Adrian Leverkühn, Mann's protagonist in *Doctor Faustus*. According to Blanchot, however, this is also the one thing, ultimately the only thing, that makes art an important activity. 'It is because *The Unnamable* makes us realize this in the bluntest possible way that it is more important than most of the [so-called] "successful" books published'. Blanchot concludes: 'Let us *try* to hear this voice ... And let us try to go down to the world into which sinks, henceforth condemned to speak, he who in order that he may write dwells in a timelessness where he must die in an endless dying' (197–8). This is this voiceless voice, the unwriteable writing of literature as a non-relational relation to the unfigurable, ultimately unfigurable even as unfigurable, in all of its aspects and implications (artistic, philosophical and political) that becomes or, again, has always been the lifelong dedication of Blanchot's work and that culminates in the death of writing, the death of reading of *The Writing of the Disaster*.

And yet, most disturbingly to the men of culture and taste, such as Mann or Lukács, it is the engagement with the radical unfigurability that appears to make possible all conceivable figuration, and the best figurations, old and new, have in fact or in effect always drawn on this radical unfigurability. Whether in this picture the unfigurable is seen as ultimately defeating figuration, in particular as 'literature', or giving it a chance, however small, is a complex question. As I said, there are significant differences on this point between different thinkers – such as Heidegger, Benjamin, Bataille, Adorno, Blanchot, Barthes, Derrida and de Man, with Blanchot, and de Man, arguably, offering us the least hope here. One might argue that Heidegger, Bataille, Derrida, Barthes and Deleuze are still enamoured with literature as a particular and even privileged form of intellectual practice. By contrast, Blanchot and de Man (especially in their late works) would see literature as crucial but ultimately secondary to the radical interrogation of the radically unfigurable. This view may also be seen as a complex and ambivalent reading of Hegel's famous announcement of 'the death of art' in his *Aesthetics* in 1830.

Whether it is possible as literature, or possible at all, radical interrogation compels us to explore as yet unimagined curvatures of thought, literature and culture, or of the physical universe, and to ask very radical questions concerning them. When, however, as in *The Writing of the Disaster*, at stake become the death of writing, the death of reading, the death of literature, the question is no longer only whether we are capable of literature or writing, if writing becomes the absence of the book or transgresses other currently available forms of it (say, hypertext or other computerized forms of it). Instead the question is whether we are capable of writing if writing itself becomes the absence or the death of writing. Radical interrogations in literature or elsewhere, for example in modern science, may extend the limits of both knowledge and the unknowable well beyond those of which we can conceive now, to forever more complex forms of both figuration and the impossibility of figuration. A truly radical interrogation may or may not be ultimately possible. Either as possible or as impossible, it appears to be ever more necessary, even though and because it may lead us to the death of reading, the death of writing, the death of literature, even the death of interrogation – perhaps to the beginning of something else in this unfigurable ununiverse, in the ununiverse of the unfigurable. If we are lucky, if – 'caged beasts born of caged beast born of caged beasts born of caged beast' – we can ever be so lucky. For Blanchot's *The Writing or the Disaster* also reminds us – indeed this is what the *writing* of the disaster would 'be', if one could assign any ontology (or 'itself-ness') to either this writing or disaster itself –

that it is even more difficult to forget than to figure, or unfigure, the darkness that inhabits and surrounds all these figures – Dante, Hölderlin, Nietzsche or Leverkühn (or Marlow's, if perhaps not Goethe's, Faust), the universe, or innumerable others amid still darker disasters of modernity that defeat silence and speech, or writing – disasters unwriteable and unspeakable, but also unsilenceable. This is a darker, more tragic message of Blanchot's work, but it cannot stop this work itself, the work of writing, the work of reading.

Arkady Plotnitsky

Further reading and works cited

Bataille, G. 'Conférences sur le Non-Savoir', *Tel Quel*, 10, 1962.
—. *Oeuvres Complètes* [OC], 12 vols. Paris 1970–88.
—. *Visions of Excess*, ed. A Stoeckl. Minneapolis, MN, 1985.
—. *Guilty*. New York, 1988a.
—. *Inner Experience*. Albany, NY, 1988b.
—. *Theory of Religion*. New York, 1989a.
—. *The Accursed Share*. New York, 1989b.
—. *On Nietzsche*. New York, 1990.
—. *The Impossible*. San Francisco, 1991.
—. 'Hegel, la mort, et le sacrifice', OC, XII.
Beckett, S. *The Unnamable*. New York, 1958.
Bident, C. *Partenaire invisible*. Editions Champ Vallon, 1998.
Blanchot, M. *The Sirens' Song*. Bloomington, IN, 1982a.
—. *The Space of Literature*. Lincoln, NE, 1982b.
—. *The Writing of the Disaster*. Lincoln, NE, 1986.
—. *The Infinite Conversation*. Minneapolis, MN, 1993.
—. *The Blanchot Reader*, ed. G. Quasha. New York, 1999.
Botting, F. and Wilson, S. (eds) *The Bataille Reader*. Oxford, 1997.
— (eds) *Bataille: A Critical Reader*. Oxford, 1998.
Deleuze, G. and Guattari, F. *What is Philosophy?* London, 1994.
Derrida, J. *Of Grammatology*. Baltimore, MD, 1974.
—. 'From Restricted to General Economy: Hegelianism without Reserve', in *Writing and Difference*. Chicago, 1980.
Gill, C. B. (ed.) *Blanchot: the Demand of Literature*. London, 1996.
Hill, L. *Blanchot: Extreme Contemporary*. London, 1997.
Holland, M. *The Blanchot Reader*. Oxford, 1995.
Levinas, E. *Totality and Infinity*. Pittsburgh, PA, 1969.
Nietzsche, F. *The Birth of Tragedy and the Case of Wagner*. New York, 1967.
Poulet, G. *The Metamorphoses of the Circle* [1961]. Baltimore, MD, 1967.
http://lists.village.virginia.edu/~spoons/blanchot/mb_french_chronological.html.
Stoekl, A. (ed.) 'On Bataille', *Yale French Studies*, 78, 1990.

Bertolt Brecht (1898–1956)

Bertolt Brecht is not generally known as a theorist – at least not to English-speakers with access only to his poetry, some of his plays and limited, if serviceable, translations of a fraction of the critical and theoretical essays (Brecht 1965, 1977, 1992). The view of Brecht as a theatre artist corrupted by politics, who allegedly dismissed the audience's empathetic response to emotion on stage, in the name of reason and alienation in the theatre and out, still prevails in Britain and North America in publications like *The New York Times* or *The Economist* as well as in writing by some academics. This view not only misses Brecht's contribution to theatre and film from Canada to the Philippines, Finland to South Africa, and the impact of his example on renowned directors such as Peter Brook and Jean-Luc Godard, as well as on activists using performance for politics. It also obscures the intensity of the interaction between Brecht and mid-century theorists of *modernity*, modernism, realism and the relationship between aesthetics and politics, especially Ernst Bloch, György Lukács, T. W. Adorno and Walter Benjamin, as well as his impact on the political and cultural theory of younger intellectuals, from those associated with the Frankfurt School in Germany, especially Alexander Kluge, to marxists and others in France, from Roland Barthes to *Cahiers du Cinéma*, and on materialist critics in Britain identified with cultural studies or the film theory of *Screen*. In the United States, Brecht's theory has had a more modest impact outside the purview of Brecht specialists, although feminists as well as marxists have found his work useful including, very recently, Fredric Jameson.

This essay will focus on key critical terms developed by Brecht out of theatre and film practice in Weimar Berlin (1920s–1932) and in the German Democratic Republic (GDR–1948–56) and reflection in exile in Scandinavia and the United States (1933–47). It will also examine the appropriation of these terms by his contemporaries and successors and explore the theoretical implications of methodological differences. Like his contemporary Benjamin, but unlike the professional academics Lukács and Adorno, Brecht wrote experimentally rather than systematically, and published 'creative' and 'critical' texts together in collections called *Versuche* (essays or experiments). Many of Brecht's theoretical insights appear in dramatic form – such as the *Messingkauf* (lit. buying brass; fig. acquiring material for use; Brecht 1965; 1998, v. 22), a dialogue among philosopher, actor, dramaturge and a worker, probably the stage electrician, about the value of art, play and instruction in the theatre. They also appear in parables, such as *Me-ti, Buch der Wendungen* (Brecht 1998, v. 18), whose playful subtitle, meaning 'book of changes' or 'turns of phrase', appropriates the example of Mo-ti (Chinese philosopher; ca. 480–400 BCE) to represent not a system of thought but a series of encounters among a commentator (Me-ti), a Brechtian poet (Kin-jeh) and figures representing the marxist classics, Marx (Ka-me) and

Lenin (Mien-Leh), and their successors from Trotsky (To-tsi) to Stalin (Nien) to the dissidents, Rosa Luxemburg (Sa) and Karl Korsch (Ka-osch), the exiled philosopher Brecht called his 'Marxist teacher' (Brecht 1998, 22, 45; Knopf 1996, 2, 447–76; Gross, in Mews 1997, 168–77). Even his most systematic theoretical statement, the *Short Organum for the Theatre*, first published in 1949 (Brecht 1998, 23, 65–97, 289–97; 1992, 179–205, 276–81) and named after the Renaissance thinker Francis Bacon's *New Organon for the Sciences*, is a series of aphoristic observations.

As 'organum' or 'tool' implies, Brecht used his own terms and those of others as tools for investigating and refunctioning (*Umfunktionieren*) the world as well as the stage, page or screen. This does not mean that in his hands ideas became merely instruments (although critics like Adorno argue as much) but rather that ideas, as Marx argued, are determined by social being and political struggle; they emerge out of material practice and should be tested against it. Although he admired Lenin's revolutionary example, Brecht borrowed most directly from the teaching of dissident marxist and ex-Party member, Karl Korsch, who, like Antonio Gramsci, favoured a philosophy of practice with critical attention to the specific relations of economic and cultural phenomena rather than a generalized theory of economic determinism (Kellner, in Mews 1997, 284). Brecht's marxism was neither doctrinaire nor opportunist, but rather a practical and playful engagement with Marx's 11th thesis on Feuerbach: 'The philosophers have always sought to understand the world; the point, however, is to change it'. His artistry was likewise pragmatic; although he continually experimented with new forms and techniques of performance – from gestic acting and Verfremdung (critical *estrangement*) of character and action in epic – or, more precisely, *epicizing (episierend)* – theatre to the pleasurable and instructive representation of social contradiction in dialectical theatre – he always returned to the question of function. He was thus critical of those, such as Lukács, who remained attached to an apparently immutable form of realism represented by the nineteenth-century novel, and willing to discard techniques that become reified and absorbed as commodities by capitalism (as estrangement and montage have been absorbed by advertising) and thus no longer facilitate a realistic critique of same.

The central, often mistranslated term of Brecht's critical practice is *Verfremdung*. Brecht himself began using the term in an essay written in 1935, 'Alienation Effects in Chinese Acting' (1992, 91–9) in response directly to the estrangement effect – as least for European spectators – of the Chinese opera star and female impersonator Mei Lanfang and indirectly to the theory and practice of the Russian formalists, especially the radical left faction represented by playwrights Vladimir Mayakovski and Brecht's friend, Sergei Tretyakov (1992, 99) rather than the literary theorist Victor Shklovski, who developed the concept of *ostranenie* (defamiliarization). Although John Willett's mistranslation 'alienation' has stuck, the first English translation (published in 1936 as 'The Effects of Disillusion in Chinese Acting'; Brecht 1998, 22, 960) better captures the original sense: undoing theatrical illusion so as to encourage the audience to understand and thus critique the world off as well as onstage (1998, 22, 401). A decade before he coined the term, however, Brecht and his contemporaries in the fertile experimental theatre of 1920s Berlin, such as director Erwin Piscator, designer Caspar Neher and composers Kurt Weill, Hanns Eisler and Paul Hindemith developed the theory out of practice work with techniques that they associated with epic rather than dramatic theatre. Although Brecht called epic theatre 'non-Aristotelian', his antagonist was not so much Aristotle as the sentimental operetta or the Wagnerian *Gesamtkunstwerk*, whose elaborate stage machinery, plaster sets and rousing music enveloped the audience in illusions and fake emotion. In Brecht's most program-matic opposition between epic and dramatic theatre, published in the first volume of *Versuche* (1931), 'epic' signifies narrative voice and point of view, shown in discrete scenes linked by montage rather than the 'dramatic' manipulation of suspense and sudden reversals of bourgeois theatre; in acting by quotation and representation of the gest of the actor towards the character rather than unrestrained emotional embodiment and identification; in separation of the elements such as music and scene design rather the sentimental harmonizing of music and emotion (1992, 37–46; 1998, 24, 78–85). Although this programmatic statement opposed 'sensations' and 'emotions' to 'recognition' and 'decisions', Brecht went on to argue, in 'Theatre for Pleasure and Theatre for Instruction' (written in exile in 1935) that he was not against emotional identification (and in fact recommended it to actors studying their roles) or against pleasure in art for all involved, but rather against the manipulation of emotion, in art as in politics; where the 'dramatic theatre spectator' sees 'nature', 'great art' and 'inescapable' suffering, the 'epic theatre spectator' should see both the art of the representation and the critical exposure of the causes of suffering (1992, 71; 1998, 22, 110). Estrangement in Brecht's usage is thus precisely *not* the 'alienation' of labour, which the early Marx borrows from Hegel's master–slave dialectic, but, as the marxist philosopher Ernst Bloch suggests, the critique of that alienation (Bloch 1972, 3–9).

Although *Verfremdung* has been closely associated with the specific stage techniques mentioned above, Brecht continually renegotiated this association, refunctioning tech-niques for critical representation and for thinking *as* intervention (*eingreifendes Denken*). *Verfremdung* depended on commitment and on opinions and objectives (*Ansichten und Absichten*), without which, he writes in the Short Organum, 'we can represent nothing at all' (1992, 196; 1998, 23, 86). His understanding of commitment was, however, always concrete. Where Jean-Paul Sartre's *engagement* remains a romantic notion of the author's appeal to the reader's 'feeling for freedom' (1949, 40), Brecht focuses on the enactment of critique. The gest, in Willett's archaic translation of Brecht's *Gestus*, carries the original's associations of gist and gesture, meaning and bearing (Brecht 1992, 42). In carriage, tone of voice and interaction, as well as in gesture, the gest conveys the actor's attitude to and social engagement with her action (1998, 22, 329–30; 1992, 104). More broadly, it applies to the producers (director, designer, composer as well as actor) and the means (material and apparatus) used to represent the 'socially significant gest' of the production as a whole, as well as those of its constituent parts (1998, 22, 158; 1992, 86), without, however, losing sight of the representation of contradiction (1998, 23, 288; 1992, 277). Faced with audiences that happily ducked contradictions (as did the enthusiastic bourgeois audience humming 'Mack the Knife' from *The Threepenny Opera*, his most popular and profitable play), Brecht proposed the *Lehrstück* (learning play), which dispensed with audiences and even with the theatre apparatus. Scripts like *The Exception and the Rule* and *He who says yes/He who says no*, accompanied by several options for performance and discussion, offered non-professional players such as workers or students a model for learning through performing controversial action without the pressure of aesthetic standards so as to test the implications of that action hypothetically as well as realistically (1998, 22, 351; see Schoeps in Mews 1997). It is this model, used by communists and youth groups in 1920s Germany, which informs political enactments from workers' agitprop in 1930s America to the role-playing of social conflict of the forum theatre pioneered by Augusto Boal for non-professional groups with limited resources since the 1960s and modified for local performance from the American inner city to Southern African rural slums.

Faced with the complexity of the culture industry in advanced capitalism, however, critique has to use more craft. As Brecht argues, telling the truth about society requires art and cunning as well as courage (1998, 22, 74–79). Showing the act of production and the institutions that sustain capitalist productive relations is key because the act of showing makes visible the social relations otherwise reified in the commodity formation that, as Marx reminds us, treats social relations as relations between things. However clear the picture, on stage, screen or photographic image, the picture alone will not ensure a realistic representation of capitalist society or serve the radical functional transformation (*Funktionswechsel*) of art in society (1998, 21, 439; 22, 265). The workings of the apparatus should be made visible. Noting that 'a photograph of the Krupp factory or of AEG says almost nothing about these institutions', Brecht argues that the 'reification [*Verdinglichung* or thingification] of human relations' and the commodification of art renders obsolete mimetic notions of realistic representation in photographic reproduction and makes imperative the analysis of all levels of production, from the actor's gestic repertoire and the photographic apparatus to the construction and funding of theatres and the publishing and film industries (21, 469).

Some of Brecht's most trenchant comments on the commodification of art, the culture industry and the challenge of critique in areas other than theatre (especially film, photography and radio) appear, like the preceding remark, in *The Threepenny Lawsuit*, which he wrote as part of the action against the Nero film company for softening the film treatment of *The Threepenny Opera* in 1930. Although not apparent from the fragment published in English (1992, 47–50), this essay plays a fundamental role not only in Brecht's theoretical development but also in his influence on contemporaries such as Benjamin, successors such as Enzensberger and Kluge, and antagonists such as Adorno (Giles 1997). Tracking the 'deconstruction' (*Demontierung*) of the author's work (especially the critique in the play of the capitalist as criminal) and its reconstruction, like some second-hand car (1998, 488), as a commodity standardized to the demands of a mass-market audience for films about glamorous outlaws, Brecht anticipates Adorno's argument about the commodification of art under the culture industry (see Adorno 1997, 16–18, 225–61). Arguing that no work of art, however transcendentally universal, is untouched by the apparatus (*apparatfrei*) and that even the autonomy of art, its apparent lack of effect or consequence (*Folgenlosigkeit*) (Brecht 1998, 21, 512), is not untouched, Brecht anticipates the work of Herbert Marcuse (Adorno's colleague at the Frankfurt School) and his comments on the social function of this apparent functionlessness of art: the representation of a beautiful illusion of happiness in a world of oppression (Marcuse 1968, 95–101). Brecht's analysis of the penetration of art by the apparatus and thus the transformation of mystery into commodity reappears in Benjamin's 1936 essay on the 'work of art in the age of its technical reproducibility' (Benjamin 1980, 2, 437–507), whose original title emphasizes the standardization of art by technological (*not* mechanical) reproduction. Benjamin's idea of the aura, the authority and authenticity of art, destroyed by capitalist conditions of reproducibility and replaced by the 'rotten – in the sense of decaying – spell' (*fauligen Zauber*) of the commodity (Benjamin 1980, 2, 477, 492) and the assertion that the reality of photographic representation only appears to transcend the apparatus (458, 495) echo Brecht's analysis of the transformation of art's autonomy or 'functionlessness' into a commodity.

The troubled relationship between art and apparatus, autonomy and *engagement* exercises Brecht, Benjamin and Adorno, but in different ways. Although Benjamin repeatedly praises Brecht's formal innovations, such as the gest, the separation of the elements and the relaxed audience (Benjamin 1973, 3, 21, 15), the last of which reappears in his argument (drawing on film critic Siegfried Kracauer as well as Brecht) for the distracted audience (1980, 465, 504), it is this insistence on the institutional determination of art, including the apparent autonomy of art from the institution, that brings Benjamin closer to Brecht than Adorno. To be sure, Adorno recognizes that autonomy is a 'social fact' (1997, 1) and a response to commodification rather than a complete escape from it (2), but he rejects Brecht's 'abolition of aesthetics' (1992, 20; 1998, 21, 202) and Benjamin's destruction of aura, arguing instead that art can critique society only when it is autonomous and exercises critique only by its autonomy, by 'merely existing' as an art work (Adorno 1997, 226) rather than overtly criticizing existence. In his theory, explicit commitment compromises autonomy because it amounts to advertising and therefore complete commodification. This ideal of the uniqueness and the disinterestedness of the autonomous work links Adorno to the idealist aesthetics of Kant and Hegel; his insistence that the work match an autonomous *idea* does not allow a theory of the institution mediating between the antinomy of 'art' and 'society' and therefore leaves no room for the pragmatic negotiation at different levels of mediation that characterizes Brechtian theoretical and theatrical practice. Although the sharp rejection of Brecht's tendentious 'message in art' as a 'clandestine accommodation with the world' (Adorno 1977b, 193) that characterized Adorno's essay on 'Commitment' (initially published in *Der Monat*, funded by the Cold War institution, the Congress on Cultural Freedom (Willett 1998, 227), in 1962, just after the erection by the GDR of the Berlin Wall had inspired renewed anti-communist attacks on Brecht) gives way in his *Aesthetic Theory* (1970) to the possibility that 'commitment is a higher level of reflection than tendency; it is not just out to correct unpleasant situations . . . [but] aims at the transformation of the preconditions of situations' (1997, 246), Adorno remains committed to form rather than function, rather than, as Brecht has it, refunctioning different forms to different occasions of resistance.

Brecht did not live to read Adorno's critique but his case against the formalist and therefore *unrealistic* tendency of Lukács's theory of realism has some relevance for Adorno as well. To be sure, Adorno attacks Lukács for dogmatically dismissing all modern art as 'decadent' and thus for relapsing into a reactionary defence of immutable tradition rather than the critical realism he claims to advocate (Adorno 1977a, 154–5) and argues instead that the truly modern work of art resists society by refusing to represent it: 'art's asociality is the determinate negation of a determinate society' (1997, 226). But, from Brecht's point of view, both would be idealists to the extent that they insist that art conform to an ideal form, whether that ideal is represented by Balzac's 'realist' depictions of nineteenth-century Paris or Joyce's and Beckett's 'modernist' resistance to linear narratives and transparent reflection. Both also invited Brecht's pragmatic protest, in that they claimed that only art conforming to their respective models would offer an effective critique of actually existing capitalist society.

It is against creeping idealism in modernist and realist critical theory that Brecht defines realistic cultural practice. Lukács's assertion, published in 1938 in *Das Wort* (which included Brecht among the editors but was published in Moscow under the shadow of the show trials against dissident communists), that 'so-called avant-garde literature' was 'anti-realist' (Lukács 1977, 29) because it remained at the level of 'immediacy' (37), apparently refusing 'to mirror objective reality . . . to shape the highly complex mediations in all their unity and diversity' (43), reiterates the orthodox opposition between capitalist decadence and socialist realism, defined by its 'representation of the achievements of socialism and the socialist individual in the present and future' (Zhdanov 1981, 21). Brecht's response, which neither *Das Wort* nor the Comintern-funded *International Literature* would publish, hints at this political pressure by arguing that Lukács's notion of realism was not only unrealistic but also *alienated* from reality (*Wirklichkeitsfremd*) (Brecht 1998, 22, 456; 1977, 70; trans. modified). Lukács's insistence on the normative status of the nineteenth-century novel was thus formalist not only in fixing on a single form to the exclusion of others but also in denying the undeniable reality of modern life that would not fit in outdated forms. The totalizing narratives of so-called socialist realist novels were politically as well as aesthetically unrealistic, in that they offered formal rather than real solutions to the social problems they depicted (1998, 458; 1977, 72). In the GDR of the 1950s, Brecht returned to this problem, objecting to the heroic novel of 'socialist arrival' that provided only fictional solutions to real problems (1998, 23, 259; 1992, 267) and arguing instead that socialist artists should show not only 'victories' but also 'the threat of defeat or else [they would give rise to] the error that victories were easy' (1998, 25, 422; Kruger 1994). Realistic representations are therefore risky; their realistic character depends not only on their accuracy, but also on their capacity to test existing models and means of representation against the pressing demands of a changing reality while maintaining a sense of humour and invention (1998, 22; 409; 1992, 109; 1977, 82). 'Fighting realism' is serious business, but it requires a light rather than a heavy hand: 'The world is certainly out of joint and it will take powerful movements to put it together again, but among the instruments that might serve, there is one, delicate, breakable, which requires handling with ease [*leichte Handhabung beansprucht*]' (1998, 22, 817; 1965, 94; trans. modified).

This articulation of a necessary and delicate balance between the serious business of transforming reality and the light hand needed to represent that transformation artfully and critically is Brecht's signal contribution to contemporary and present-day debates on the art of politics and the politics of art, but it has also been the source of conflicting interpretations of his work. While Lukács and his successors among the GDR bureaucrats and Communist Party officials in France and elsewhere attacked Brecht for an allegedly formalist and anti-realist attachment to avant-garde experiments, structuralists found in *Verfremdung* a semiotic imperative, a self-reflexive attention to the arbitrariness of signs, and poststructuralists or deconstructionists a deferral rather than a consolidation of meaning. Louis Althusser, maverick member of the French Communist Party (PCF), finds Brecht's theatre materialist to the extent that it makes visible the latent structures of recognition in and of the audience rather than simply dishing up an ideologically correct story (1969, 142–51). Roland Barthes, influenced by marxism but no PCF member, praised Brecht in 1957, a few years after the Berliner Ensemble astonished French audiences for 'breaking the Zhdanovian impasse' by 'separating ideology and semiology' (1972, 71). He argues that Brecht's formalism is semiotic, ' a protest against the confines of . .. false Nature; ... in a still alienated society, art must be critical ... the sign must be partially arbitrary' (75). Writing for the poststructuralist magazine *Tel Quel* in 1963, he hailed Brecht as a deconstructionist *avant la lettre*, who 'affirmed meaning but did not fulfil it' in a theatre that did not 'transmit a positive meaning (this is not a theatre of the signified) but show[s] that the world is an object to be deciphered (this is a theatre of the signifier)' (1972, 263). A decade later, in his more reflective memoir, Barthes acknowledged that a radical semiotic reading of Brecht dodges his commitment to fighting realism in the name, perhaps, of the play of the signifier. Noting that he would prefer to 'live with little politics', he quotes Brecht's meditation on the choice between being the 'object' or the 'subject' of 'politics' (Brecht 1998, 22, 304) as though it were Brecht's reproach to Barthes himself (Barthes 1977, 70–1) but also notes that Brecht never quite solved the problem of representation that he posed in the case of the Krupp photograph. In Barthes's view, 'time, history ... the political ... resist copying' or at least the imitation that can be rendered visible in the gest of an actor (1977, 154).

This tension that Barthes notes between Brecht's committed and semiotic moments, between the imperative to render history visible and the arbitrariness of the signs to do so, reappears especially in cinematic appropriations of Brecht to craft what might be called a self-reflexive or cunning realism. In Jean-Luc Godard's 1967 film La Chinoise, one of several of his films to use techniques borrowed from Brecht, Maoist students debate the power of the names of their forebears; Brecht's name remains on the classroom board and the screen as others are erased. While the kind of play and pleasure evoked by the street slogans of May 1968 owed more to the situationists' inheritance of dada and to the erotic liberation theory of Marcuse, then based in California, the writing of Godard and his fellows in Cahiers du Cinéma (especially 1968–72) reflected Brecht's influence. Radicalized by May 1968, Cahiers shifted from celebrations of the classical American cinema to politically charged analyses of cinematic sign systems. Collectively written articles such as 'La Vie est à nous [by Jean Renoir]: A Militant Film' (Browne 1990, 68–88) drew on Brecht's practical example – here his film, Kuhle Wampe (1932), made with composer Eisler and director Slatan Dudow – as well as his theoretical imperatives, especially those of refunctioning form and institution and of the necessary light touch of the instrument of analysis (characteristic of the director Renoir). The English appropriation of Cahiers' example and with it a 'new' cinematic Brecht appeared in Screen magazine from 1974. Where Cahiers in this period consistently emphasized Brecht's 'fighting realism', articles in Screen's first special issue on Brecht played out a tension between celebrations of a poststructuralist Brecht as advocate for the play of the signifier (by the Barthes scholar, Stephen Heath) and a more militant defence of realism (Colin MacCabe; both in Screen 1974), reflecting not only the absence of anything approaching the revolutionary turmoil of May 1968 (and equivalents in Germany and Italy) but also local academic battles about 'Continental theory'. Where Heath and MacCabe used Brecht's example as a way of arguing for forms that could be both realistic and avant-garde, the older marxist critic, Raymond Williams, retained a certain scepticism about the claims for radical form, arguing that 'certain techniques . . . once experimental and actual shocks. .. have become the working conventions of . . . commercial art' (Williams 1989, 62).

In West Germany during the 1960s and 1970s, the growth of the student movement and the extra-parliamentary opposition to what was seen as the erasure and therefore normalization of the Nazi past and the ongoing undemocratic character of the West German state provided the occasion for a revival of the leftist cultural and political theory of the Weimar Republic, including Brecht, whose fighting realism challenged the political quietism and cultural elitism of the Frankfurt School, represented above all by Adorno in his role as professor and director of the institute until 1969. After years of Cold War repression, Brecht reappeared not only as the subject of influential scholarly studies of his most radical theatre and political work (Brüggemann, Steinweg) but also as the inspiration for programmes for the critical refunctioning of the media. Critic Hans Magnus Enzensberger drew on Brecht's utopian formulation of two-way radio as well as Adorno's condemnation of the culture industry in his discussion of community-based alternatives to the 'consciousness industry'. Sociologist Oskar Negt and film-maker and Frankfurt scholar Alexander Kluge developed the idea of the *proletarian* public sphere, the sphere of working-class experience and aspirations which excluded or marginalized the legitimate or bourgeois public sphere by drawing on Brecht's critical reflections on the transformation of media institutions to challenge the concept of the bourgeois public sphere developed by another Frankfurt scholar, Jürgen Habermas. If in the 1970s the name as much as the example of Brecht offered the German New Left a touchstone for revival, twenty years later after the centenary of his birth (1998) Brecht is still the subject of debate in the united Germany, even if some dismiss him as a dead classic.

While Brecht and Brechtian terms entered the general intellectual culture of Europe more than a generation ago, his name resonates almost exclusively in academic circles in the United States, and then usually among Germanists and theatre scholars. His theoretical writings lack the prestige (and syllabus space) granted his contemporaries Benjamin and Adorno or his successors from Barthes to Kluge, although they have been recently picked up by feminists (e.g. Diamond) as well as the doyen of marxist criticism in the United States, Fredric Jameson. Yet even this brief review of Brecht demonstrates his original and lasting contribution to the debates of his day, on the aesthetics and politics of realism and modernism, and his anticipation of many current critical preoccupations, especially the interest in performance and performativity as terms of theoretical and not just theatrical analysis. Rereading Brecht as theorist now not only revitalizes the historic connection debates about aesthetics and politics; it also reminds us that the performative character of the enactment of critique was theorized long before the current Anglophone fashion generated belatedly by readings of J. L. Austin and Judith Butler.

Loren Kruger

Further reading and works cited

Adorno, T. W. *Aesthetic Theory*. Minneapolis, 1997.
Althusser, L. *For Marx*. London, 1969.
Barthes, R. *Critical Essays*. Evanston, IL, 1972.
—. *Roland Barthes by Roland Barthes*. New York, 1977.
Benjamin, W. *Understanding Brecht*. London, 1973.
—. *Gesammelte Schriften*, ed. R. Tiedemann, 12 vols. Frankfurt, 1980.
Bloch, E. '*Entfremdung, Verfremdung*: Alienation, Estrangement', in *Brecht*, ed. E. Munk. New York, 1972.
— et al. *Aesthetics and Politics*, ed. R. Taylor, afterword, F. Jameson. London, 1977. Includes: Adorno 1977a: 'Reconciliation under Duress'; Adorno 1977b: 'Commitment'; Bloch 1977: 'Discussing Expressionism'; Brecht 1977: 'Against Georg Lukács'; Lukács 1977: 'Realism in the Balance'.
Brecht, B. *The Messingkauf Dialogues*. London, 1965.
—. *Werke: Grosse Kommentierte Berliner und Frankfurter Ausgabe*, eds W. Hecht et al., 30 vols. Frankfurt, 1988–98 (cited as Brecht 1998).
—. *Brecht on Theatre: The Development of an Aesthetic*, ed. and trans. J. Willett. New York, 1992.
Browne, N. (ed.) *Cahiers du Cinéma, 1969–1972: The Politics of Representation*. Cambridge, MA, 1990. Includes: Narboni, Pierre and Rivette 1990: 'Montage'; Comolli and Narboni 1990: 'Cinema/Ideology/Criticism'; Bonitzer et al. 1990: '*La Vie est à nous*: A Militant Film'.
Brüggemann, H. *Literarische Technik und soziale Revolution*. Hamburg, 1973.
Diamond, E. *Unmaking Mimesis*. London, 1997.

Enzensberger, H. M. *The Consciousness Industry.* New York, 1974.

Giles, S. *Bertolt Brecht and Critical Theory.* Bern, 1997.

Hecht, W. *Brecht-Chronik.* Frankfurt, 1996.

Knopf, J. (ed.) *Brecht Handbuch: Vol. 1: Theater, Vol. 2: Lyrik, Prosa, Schriften.* Stuttgart, 1996.

Kruger, L. '*Stories from the Production Line*: Modernism and Modernization in the GDR Production Play', *Theatre Journal*, 46, 1994.

Marcuse, H. *Negations.* Boston, 1968.

Mews, S. (ed.) *A Bertolt Brecht Reference Companion.* Westport, CT, 1997. Including: Mews 1997: 'Introduction'; Grimm 1997: 'Alienation in Context: On the Theory and Practice of Brechtian Theater'; Schoeps 1997: 'Brecht's *Lehrstücke*'; Gross, 'Dialectics and Reader Response: Bertolt Brecht's Prose Cycles'; Kellner 1997: 'Brecht's Marxist Aesthetic'; Mews 1997: 'Annotated Bibliography'.

Negt, O. and Kluge, A. *Public Sphere and Experience: Towards an Analysis of the Bourgeois and Proletarian Public Spheres.* Minneapolis, MN, 1993.

Sartre, J.-P. *What is Literature?* New York, 1949.

Screen, special issue on Brecht, 15, 2, 1974. Includes: MacCabe, 1974: 'Realism in the Cinema: Notes on Some Brechtian Theses'; Barthes, 1974: 'Diderot/Brecht/Eisenstein'; Mitchell, 1974: 'From Shklovsky to Brecht'; Brewster 1974: 'A Reply': Heath 1974: 'Lessons from Brecht'.

Steinweg, R. *Das Lehrstück: Bertolt Brechts Theorie einer politisch-ästhetischen Erziehung.* Stuttgart, 1972.

Suvin, D. *To Brecht and Beyond.* Totowa, NJ, 1984.

Völker, K. *Brecht: A Biography.* New York, 1978.

Willett, J. *Brecht in Context.* London, 1998.

Williams, R. *The Politics of Modernism.* London, 1989.

Zhdanov, A. A. 'Soviet Literature: The Richest in Ideas, the Most Advanced Literature', in *Problems in Soviet Literature. Reports and Speeches of the First Soviet Writers Congress*, ed. H. G. Scott. Westport, CT, 1981.

Jacques Lacan (1901–1981)

Psychoanalyst Jacques Lacan was one of the most influential thinkers of his time. The linguistic, philosophical and political scope of his *theory of the subject* stirred intellectuals and artists in his native France and all over the world. He was a faithful interpreter of Freud, but he freely incorporated artistic, mathematical and philosophical insights into his own psychoanalysis without subordinating the Freudian field to any of them. It has been said with reason that Freud took root in France mainly through Lacan. Though he published relatively little in his lifetime, Lacan drew fascinated critical attention whenever his writing made its rare appearance. As his yearly seminars began being transcribed, edited (by his son-in-law, analyst Jacques-Alain Miller) and disseminated in French (1975–98) and English (1978–98), a number of Freudian schools modelled on Lacan's also began training clinicians, in France and out (e.g. Québec, Italy, Spain and Latin America). In 1980 Lacan dissolved the École Freudienne de Paris that he had founded in 1964, and refounded it in its current form, the *École de la Cause Freudienne*. It is not, however, the only Lacanian school extant in Paris.

The Lacanian path into literary criticism is an indirect one. Lacanianism came in fits and starts like the Freudianism to which it strictly (if creatively) adheres. In the United States, a flurry of initial interest was sparked by Lacan's rare American visits to literature and humanities programmes at Johns Hopkins University in 1966 and to MIT and Yale University in 1973. In contrast, by the late 1970s in France Lacan's name had spread beyond the clinic to appear in the broadest spectrum of critical orientations: structuralism, deconstruction, feminism, philosophy, film studies and cultural critique.

A good example of how Lacan's French influence intersected with literary study and criss-crossed the Channel and the Atlantic is Hélène Cixous. Cixous is a James Joyce specialist, poet, playwright and literary theorist who founded *Etudes féminines* in France and promoted the critical concept of *écriture féminine*. In her ground-breaking book on hysteria, *The Newly Born Woman* (co-authored by Clément) Cixous cited Lacan to contest Freud's narrower views of women (1975, 9, 19, 29, 35–6).

If Lacan's work nourished a certain feminist thought, supporting its objections to Freud's patriarchal evaluation of woman, feminist Luce Irigaray resisted what she saw as Lacan's own 'phallogocentricism' (to use Derrida's term). Irigaray viewed Lacan's emphasis on the crucial role language plays in subject formation as lending undue aid and comfort to culture's traditional repression of the feminine. In a series of highly innovative texts Irigaray protested what she felt was Lacan's support for the primacy of a phallic linguistic model that structurally consigned woman to cultural inferiority. If, as Lacan believed, language is the indelible foundation of human being, to Irigaray its very grammatical structure excludes the feminine. Human society, life in common, conceptually depends on the existence of a grammatical 'third person' – always 'It' or 'He' and never 'She'. To Irigaray, an analyst and a trained philosopher, Lacan's *big O Other* was too close to this 'third' person that conceded nothing to woman, and she broke with Lacan. Still, unlike other deconstructive theorists of gender (e.g. Judith Butler) Irigaray appreciated Lacan's attention to sexuality as indispensable for feminist politics. Lacan's logic of *sexuation* (see Copjec 1994, 201–36) remained necessary to support all 'difference' and crucial for any theory of rights. Irigaray writes: 'Equality between men and women cannot be achieved without a *theory of gender as sexed* and a rewriting of the rights and obligations of each sex, *qua different*, in social rights and obligations' (1993, 13).

Leading French theorists viewed Lacan as a systematic thinker whose theses demanded recognition and, often, contestation. Philosopher Gilles Deleuze, with Félix Guattari, is often presumed to include Lacan in his attack on traditional psychiatry. Yet Deleuze and Guattari found Lacan fruitful for their schizoanalysis, particularly his radical reorientation of psychoanalysis toward psychosis, femininity and the passing of the Oedipus complex (i.e. the advent of the superego) and away from Oedipal neurosis. In *Anti-Oedipus*, their 1972 study of capitalism and schizophrenia, Deleuze and Guattari recognized the importance of Lacan's *objet a* (1977, 27n). In 1980 their *1000 Plateaux* echoed Lacan's attention to courtly love, *desire*, *lack* and *jouissance* (1987, 154–6).

However multiple the points of Lacanian insertion into literary criticism – through feminism, the clinic, film studies and political analysis – it was the French *philosophical* battles *over* Lacan that first captured Anglophone literary attention. In these debates the great bone of contention was always the status of *literature* in Lacan's work. The question of literature-and-psychoanalysis had more than literary significance for philosophy. Since these intra-French philosophical arguments eventually exercised great influence in England and North America (largely through comparative literature and critical theory programmes) and set many terms of theoretical debates still ongoing, they demand more than passing mention.

By 1973, French philosophy began to engage Lacan over specifically literary issues. In that year two young philosophers who had embraced Jacques Derrida's critique of Ferdinand de Saussure mounted an attack on Lacan from a similar angle. Saussure, and the structuralists who followed his semiological method, were said by Derrida (1967) to have overvalued *speech* to the detriment of the material, *written sign* that merely 'recorded' it. Lacan was linked to structural linguistics through his invocation of Saussure's semiotic sign (an image plus a concept, a signifier and signified) and by virtue of his close friendship with Peircean semiolinguist Roman Jakobson. Jakobson had linked the metaphoric/metonymic axes of speech to both mental problematics (aphasia) and literary ones: for Jakobson, the interplay between the two tropes formed the respective axes of poetry and realist prose. His discovery paralleled Gregory Bateson's thesis on the genesis of schizophrenia as a linguistic 'double bind' between metaphoric and literal. When Lacan's translator Anthony Wilden linked Lacan to Bateson in his 1972 *System and Structure*, Lacan's 'structuralist' identity seemed confirmed.

Speech was the crucial focus of Saussurean and Jakobsonian linguistics. In his *De La Grammatology* Derrida called attention to the fact that the material conveyance of the sign (by what he called *écriture* – writing) had been overlooked by semiolinguists, and he argued that it was the actual support of any signifying force in speech. Writing was more than the 'writing down' of speech events (*paroles*); *écriture* was the very condition of possibility of speech, the sine qua non of the arbitrariness and free play of even oral signifiers.

With an eye on Derrida's critique, Philippe Lacoue-Labarthe and Jean-Luc Nancy trained their sights on Lacan, for whom speech *and* the material mark ('letter') were both key analytic concepts. In a short book, *Le Titre de la lettre* (1973) they investigated Lacan's thesis that the subject is a *'parlêtre'*, a pun-word meaning both *par lettres* (i.e. through or by means of letters or literature) and *parle être* (speaking being). In their book the pair contended that despite Lacan's attention to 'the letter' his interpretive method remained locked into the letter as inferior handmaiden to 'authentic' voice and 'original' speech. Speech, the analytical medium (the talking cure of 'free association' in the presence of an analyst), exemplified the Saussurean error locating authentic 'truth' only in speech. According to them, Lacan refuses the 'strategy of the signifier' (1992, 135–6) wherein truth is never one and final. Indeed, the oral signifier is structured so that speech itself is always already 'written' in a polysemic, plurivocal 'text' in which meaning is deferred and irreducible to a singular 'truth'. For them Lacan has misplaced confidence in the revelation of truth through authentic or 'full' speech (1992, 83–9).

Lacan was a clinician and not a philosopher or a literary critic but the two philosophers responded so strongly with good reason. By the late twentieth century literature and philosophy had come to be intensely implicated in each other's fate. After Nietzsche (and Heidegger) philosophy was enmeshed in literature and vice versa. Poetry especially was regarded as a unique attention to logos and to the non-prosaic being it produced. To modern thinkers interpreting literary texts it had great philosophical significance. Lacoue-Labarthe and Nancy saw Lacan's interpretative method as a function of a reductive truth that threatened to obscure literature as a source of primary philosophical insight.

In his recent responses to Lacoue-Labarthe philosopher Alain Badiou, critic and sometime playwright, argued that, to the contrary, Lacan was never caught inside the paradigm of literary-philosophy, and that Lacan instead adumbrated a philosophy for *after* the era of anti-philosophy opened by Nietzsche. Philosophy, for Badiou, does not find its 'end' in literature, its fulfilment in poetry as the Heideggerian 'age of poets' asserts. That age is drawing to a close permitting poetry to be relieved of the ethical burdens philosophy has laid on it; for Badiou, Lacan's role in preparing the new stage of philosophy will have been crucial. Lacan advanced philosophy's cause by radicalizing, undercutting and reframing one of its conditions of possibility (1999, 43–4, 81–4, 88–91). To Badiou, Lacan's singular contribution to philosophy's renewal is his refurbishing of the conceptual grounds of *love*, one of Badiou's four fundamental 'conditions' of philosophy (politics, love, the matheme and art).

To adopt either Badiou's or Lacoue-Labarthe and Nancy's evaluation would be, however, to relieve Lacan of any *serious* literary or critical consequence. Thus it is somewhat ironic that it was philosopher Jacques Derrida's critique of Lacan that assured the analyst his place in literary critical history. Derrida opened the question of Lacan's insistent *letter* in the unconscious on specifically *literary* grounds informed by but not ruled by philosophical problematics.

Derrida was institutionally linked to the university space carved out for 'practitioners of the unconscious' at the University of Paris VIII-Vincennes, where he, Foucault, Deleuze, de Certeau, Serge Leclaire, Georges Canguilhem, Jacques-Alain Miller and Hélène Cixous all taught (Roudinesco 1990, 553). Derrida, along with Deleuze, lent political support to Lacan's continued teaching at the *École Normale Supérieure* when Lacan was threatened with expulsion in 1969 (Roudinesco 1990, 539). Yet, when Derrida's reproach to Lacan's 'applied' literary criticism of Poe's *Purloined Letter* in his 1954 seminar (Lacan 1988, 175–205) appeared in *Critique* (and then in *Yale French Studies*) in 1975, it was regarded as an attack that turned many away from using Lacan for literary criticism. Derrida nevertheless rendered an oblique homage to Lacan, transforming Lacan's 'practice of the letter' into his own expanded concept of *écriture*, a homage later made explicit in his essay, 'For the Love of Lacan' (Derrida [1990] 1998, 39–69).

Derrida's complaint in his 1975 article, 'The Purveyor of Truth', is related to Lacoue-Labarthe and Nancy's: that Lacan chiefly relies on extra-textual truth – the 'clinical' truth of the (phallicly organized) unconscious – to bolster the act of interpretation. Derrida notes that the 'truth' of the Lacanian unconscious is manifested in the *letter*, a letter that, as Lacan quipped, always 'arrives at its destination'. Derrida takes this to mean that the analyst 'reads' a subject's unconscious truth rather than the play of textuality that constitutes it. For Derrida, Lacan thereby invokes the presence of some 'thing', some transcendental signified, without adequate attention to the textual dimensionality into which the letter is woven. Literary texts have only truth-effects; to overlook how these effects are produced is a monumental error. To Derrida, Lacan's literary approach is modelled too much on an analyst–patient model, which prizes 'full' speech, and even that model, for Derrida, ignores the 'dead' letter always already conditioning speech acts. Despite Lacan's focus on the *letter*, to Derrida Lacan's critical method remains trapped in a true-speech model.

Yet a closer look at the 'literariness' of the letter Derrida delineates in 'The Purveyor [literally, the postman] of Truth' situates why Lacan's letter-object is inspiring new uses for Lacan in literary criticism. Derrida takes Lacan's 'letter' on three levels: literal (the letters the text is composed of), metaphorical (the missive addressed to an other) and metonymic (it stands for 'letters' or literature, the body of which it is a fragment). For Derrida, Lacan's letter is insufficiently literary. Derrida takes Lacan's dictum concerning the letter's 'destination' to mean its *proper* destination, i.e. that Lacan believes the letter will always find its 'true' or proper 'meaning'; that its message is always received by the proper addressee (the analyst); and that a letter always finds its appropriate location, its proper place, in the body of a text and in the body of texts (literature). Such destining of the letter constitutes a closed circuit that is simply untenable for literary works, since writing can neither predict nor limit its addressees nor claim to possess a singular, transmissible meaning. Meaning, Derrida reminds us, is created solely by relaying a *promise* of meaning from signifier to signifier: it is found neither as offstage obscenity nor as truth buried in the unconscious. A missing or out-of-place letter (like the '*a*' Derrida inserted into *différance*) is 'symptomatic' only of a purely *textual* unconscious, readable on the surface.

Derrida's second complaint is that the transcendental signified or singular truth lies in the Lacanian unconscious and that Lacan sees all textual symptoms (letters) referring to it – the *phallus*: 'indivisible and indestructible ... like the letter which takes its place ... indispensable to the circulation of propriety' (Johnson 1980, 124). If the phallus is *the* 'truth', *the* meaning of a literary text, Derrida rightly concludes that reading as such would cease, and that therefore Lacan and psychoanalysis are wrong for literature. Gayatri Spivak succinctly posed the problem another way: 'All precautions taken, literary criticism *must* operate as if the critic is responsible for the interpretation, and, to a lesser extent, as if the writer is responsible for the text' (1977, 224) To put the unconscious (and Lacan's 'letter' is frankly 'in' the unconscious) at the centre of literary interpretation reduces *meaning* to the *phallus* and blocks the consciousness and 'responsibility' Spivak says are criticism's crucial and necessary fiction.

Was Lacan's *letter* really about elevating phallic truth over 'secondary' representation, however? Did Lacan genially ignore the way texts generate both truth and meaning as *textual effects*? Did the inevitable 'arrival' of Lacan's letter at its 'destination' mean that the *letter* bore a 'full' meaning, and successfully closed an open communication circuit? It would be difficult to comprehend Lacan's critical resurgence if this were the case. A different perspective on the letter for Lacan finds his '*letter*' precisely *not* the representative of the *phallus*, but its *opponent*.

In Lacan's system, the *phallus* is purely symbolic. It is indeed the centre of a centred unconscious (the Symbolic Order), the point where all four coordinates of the subject (the self, the self-image, the subject and the big O Other) are balanced (see Lacan's 'L Schema'). Phallic centrality accrues its merely virtual but dominating psychic power by repressing the Real. The letter, on the other hand, emerges *in* the very Real that the Symbolic represses. Derrida's sympathies with the letter were thus correctly Lacanian, though to him Lacan appeared a phallocrat. Clinically, symbolic balance is the goal, but culturally and literarily the 'feminine' letter gains a crucial ascendancy.

Interestingly, when Lacan responded to critiques of his 'letter' he did so not to Derrida but to Philippe Lacoue-Labarthe and Jean-Luc Nancy, sending the two a 'Love Letter' in his 1972–3 seminar on feminine sexuality, *Encore*. Once this 'love letter' appeared in English (in Mitchell and Rose 1982) it touched off a wave of critical interest in Lacan that concurred with Derrida's resistance to the phallus. Feminist criticism in particular intuited something rebellious at work in the *letter* that precluded its standing-in for the phallus. Instead (and despite his mischievous pronouncements regarding feminine sexuality in it) Lacan's *Encore* (*Seminar* XX) showed the *letter against* the phallus. For Lacan the agency of the letter in the unconscious was *not* 'phallogocentric', but feminine and literary.

Kant had put non-purposive enjoyment at the heart of aesthetic feeling. Lacan, too, analysed *enjoyment* (*jouissance*) by closely attending to the letter. He discovered varieties of enjoyment – feminine, perverse, abusive, phallic – but negatively. He saw these varieties of *jouissance* as all forms of an excess that is specifically excised from all the discourses. Discourses are precisely woven to exclude, shield or disavow this excess *jouissance*.

To Lacan, all traditional ethics and aesthetics deal with excess by weaving 'discourses' as fictions of harmony (which always fails). In contemporary life, the accent has now fallen on transgression, disruption and imbalance. Modern life, that is, highlights the presence of excess and as such it throws the aesthetic principles of Aristotle and the ideals of Kant into question. *Sublimation* and *perversion* are for Lacan characterized by excess (they both *overestimate* their object), and they thus have come to the fore in modernity. Sublimation elevates the excess to dignified heights (e.g. the Lady in Courtly Love); perversion's passion is for the object's overwhelming *jouissance* (e.g. the fetish).

Contrary to Derrida's assumption, then, Lacan's *subject* is not the sociological or political subject of structuralism, or the subject of positive law. For Lacan, the *subject* is nothing except a pure function of its *object*. In other words, the Lacanian *subject* is not a conscious rational, philosophical subject. Nor is the object that defines it empirical in character, for it is pure excess.

Significantly, Lacan's 'overvalued' object at the core of the subject is nothing more nor less than a *letter*, the 'object *little letter* a' (*objet petit a*). By means of this psychic 'object-letter', the *subject* becomes the subject of *unconscious* fantasy as well as of the Symbolic-phallic unconscious. The subject is subject of the unconscious *because* its object is the 'object *little letter* a', the hinge point of the *unconscious fantasy*. This fantasy is what conflicts with and contests the phallically centred, symbolically organized unconscious.

The *letter* traces a Lacanian path for psychoanalytic theory and practice. Lacan calls '*letter*' the mark or imprint left on the *body* by *jouissance*, a *jouissance* that is repressed by language. Against its repression the letter rebels by *stamping* itself on the subject's body. Moreover, the 'body' it inscribes itself on is no ordinary, organic body. It is a 'body' already shaped by language – and that language has banished *jouissance* from its domain. Lacan put it thus: the symbol is the murder of the Thing.

For Lacan, *a subject's symbolic body* is not a *biological* body; it is a body that no longer follows organic logic but instead the logic of the signifier. Language rips the body from its animal niche and deports it into a force field and system of logic entirely distinct from those ruling animate organic life. This violent imposition of language (or symbolic law) denatures the subject and opens it to its specifically human dimensions: reason, thought, social relations. Lacan writes: '[Man] thinks as a consequence of the fact that a structure, that of language – the word implies it – carves up his body, a structure that has nothing to do with anatomy' (1990, 6). The effect of language, whose avatar is the (phallic) *signifier*, is thus to reconstitute the body through words that substitute for what they displace: *metaphors* (see *Seminar I*, 1953–4, and *Seminar III* on psychosis, 1955–6).

Language thus divides a *subject* from its 'being', replacing the body ruled by natural law with one that complies only with the laws of language. Lacan formulated this as *alienation* – or the 'castration of the subject by the signifier'. The phallus, a merely symbolic form of an animal organ (the penis), in this context becomes the very signifier of the entire process of signification: a master *signifier* S_1, the absent centre around which the Symbolic Order is arrayed, the cardinal element 'responsible' for the *orderly* reconfiguration of the body as a logical body. It civilizes the subject, and undertakes the stewardship of society under the rule of chiefly male elders that it silently authorizes and 'guarantees'. The Father, and his Name, 'represent' this S_1.

A deceptively simple set-up like this is, however, not long to be believed. The *phallus* is by no means the sole factor in the formation of the subject nor of the social order for Lacan. While language (etymologically, tongue and blade), makes the subject's body into a *body-without-organs*, what it 'carves' off is something that only its action produces (and that is never fully lost): *jouissance*. That is, the 'phallic signifier' banishes enjoyment (*jouissance*) from the body that is under its sway – and that *body* protests the expulsion much the same way those oppressed by civilization may silently and, at length, openly rebel against the constraints and discontents they endure. (Deleuze had a horror of domestic animals because they are subject to symbolic laws with no means of contesting them.)

In Lacan, what comes directly up against the phallus is the *letter*. How? Non-empirical, *jouissance* is the after-effect of the 'carving' action of the signifier, whose cut produces a material loss of raw energy. This 'lost' energy returns as *drive* (*pulsion*), i.e. not as physical energy, but as energy *psychically represented*. *Jouissance* is thus a complex concept. What is expelled by language is not real 'enjoyment' in the ordinary sense, but a *psychic* discharge modelled on a *neurotic* one. In the *organic* body, discharge is release, fulfilment, brute enjoyment. It is relief from the pressure of the excess energy of external and internal stimuli. In the *logical* body, *jouissance* is only *fantasied* discharge, only a fantasm of *satisfaction* and *need*.

Psychic energy, as drive, latches onto the body wherever the body is not fully under the (phallic) signifier's sway, e.g. primarily in the genital zones, where it appears as 'sex drive'. But it can pop up anywhere in the logicized/language-made body, for like that body, drive is only the after-effect of the *word*. The 'excess' psychic energy (*jouissance*) cumulates, Lacan observes, and when it does it tends to stamp itself on bodily *orifices* and their *rims* (lips, eyelids, anal rings and vaginal labia, etc.) – wherever the continuity of the logical-body encounters an interruption or gap (*Seminar XI*, 1978, 200).

It is crucial to note how Lacan's thesis regarding the constitutive effect of language differs markedly from that of *structuralism*. *Structuralism* sees language as a *positive force*, like Foucault's discursive practices that coercively shape the subject and imprint its arbitrary social character. Lacan took the *opposite* position. For him, the subject is *hollowed out* by language; the crucial impact of the symbol lies not in what it actively *marks on* the subject, but in what it *takes from it*. Language subtracts *being* from the subject: the *signifier* replaces the *jouissance* of being with a promise of meaning. And its spectral companion, the *letter*, hollows out a void into which psychic *jouissance* floods.

In his 1964 seminar Lacan made a diagram of *alienation* that illustrates the 'subject' as ontological *lack* (*manque-à-être*), produced by a double linguistic-ontological lapse. The diagram consists of two overlapping circles (Lacan [1964] 1994, 211). Lacan labels one circle 'meaning' and the other circle 'being'. The *subject* emerges in the concrete gap between two signifiers ('being' and 'meaning') where the circles intersect and overlap, i.e. from 'the superimposition of two lacks'. So does *desire* (1978, 214). As its 'being' disappears into 'meaning', the subject is born *as* desire (*libido*). A lozenge-shaped area of 'non-meaning' lies where the two circles intersect and overlap: Lacan calls this the *lamella*, the *libido* or indestructible life-force that surges forth where *meaning* and *being* lapse equally for the subject.

The fact that language requires a leap to produce its twinned fictions of *being* and of *meaning* inaugurates a specific bridging called '*metaphor*'. Interpreters have been quick to assume that the Lacanian subject of *desire* is thus of purely metaphoric confection. True, metaphoric desire is 'the essence of man' for Lacan, as for Spinoza (1978, 275). But this desire (psychic longing, not empirical need) is 'impure', Lacan tells us: it is not *only* symbolic or metaphoric in character. The desiring subject is rather, Lacan says, a *metonymy*.

Why *metonymy*? Metonymy is the trope that evokes *contiguity with* what it stands for ('need', 'hunger') rather than metaphoric *distance from* its referent (e.g. 'hunger-like'). The distinction is extremely significant for Lacan. It means that *desire* remains surreptitiously linked to those real Things that the symbol seemed to have displaced definitively – to have 'murdered'. But, for Lacan, some *real* object of longing, some material residue, some scrap or remnant of the displaced Thing remains at the heart of all desire – as if, for example, a fragment of the satisfying maternal breast (from which everyone must separate) had remained in the unconscious and continued exerting a force of attraction not fully under the control of reason and social rules.

Of course this internal object is not *really* Real. But it is not *only* symbolic. It has psychic density – *jouissance*. Lacan's pronouncement that the Symbolic makes a 'hole in the Real' is thus counterbalanced by the obverse: in every Symbol there remains a (psychic) kernel of the Real; in every Desire lies a fragment of Drive; and in every social Symbolic Order lies a nucleus that contains some Thing, some event, some deed, some group, that can never be symbolically recognized or assimilated.

Through its constitutive signifiers (symbols, metaphors, the phallus) language thus 'organizes' the subject, but it also *disorganizes* the subject: its after-effects produce a strange, inexplicable energy – *libido* – that issues from what is now a *body-without-organs*, not from hormones or natural urges. *Libido* is a powerful (if negative) force whose field is that of *Drive*. The 'object' of satisfaction of *drive* is not empirical: i.e. it is not the *apple* that sates a psychic hunger but the *enjoyment in it*, an enjoyment retrospectively imagined or prospectively projected as inhering in that apple rather than in the mind. Yet in human desire, it is *jouissance* of the apple that counts, not the nutritive and aesthetic elements of the physical apple. The 'emptiness' of the desiring subject (produced by the signifier's repression of the Real) is in fact filled with half-real, half-hallucinated objects of longing, lodged there where the *letter* has opened a space for them, the space of the Drive that undergirds *desire*.

The *objet a* is thus the kernel of Desire, an 'extra-*jouissance*' that is equally desired but avoided. *Drive* overshoots its target; it 'aims' at the *jouissance* in the *object a* but fails to arrive at its destination: complete satisfaction is lethal *for the subject* (1978, 174–86). All drives therefore represent death drive, but never more than *partially*. Their 'circuit' (joining life to death) is unclosed, or an open loop, or an internal 8, or an invagination, such as diagrammed by Lacan throughout *Seminar XI* (1978, 178).

For Lacan, the *subject* forms around the hollow left by the *object a*'s stamp, around the lesion where *jouissance* cumulates. Lacan goes further, calling *letters* (*objects a*) the very *subjects* of the unconscious (1978, 242). In 'Kant avec Sade' (1989) Lacan formulated a-phallic subject-formation as $ \lozenge a$, which translates roughly as 'the language-divided subject stamped by the *object a*'. (This is his '*formula of fantasy*'.) Recognizing the Fantasy support of Desire (1978, 185) is what inclined Lacan (from the 1960s on) toward scrutiny of the 'envers' (or obscene underside) of the phallic-Symbolic order, and paved the way for new avenues for clinical and literary application. In his clinic, as in his aesthetics, Lacan's *object a*, *jouissance* and *fantasy* began to take conceptual precedence over his *Symbolic Order*, *phallic primacy* and the *signifier*.

This move accelerated a critical encounter between literature and the clinic that Lacan did not so much produce as reproduce. In France, after all, the first important entrée for Freud had come through literature: the Freudian clinic surged following the fanfare with which Surrealism touted the Freudian unconscious. Lacan, through his studies with Gaëtan de Clerambault (who discovered 'mental automatism' in the criminally insane), found parallels between surrealist procedures, which dramatized the unconscious as automatic writing and bizarre metaphors, and psychoanalysis as a clinical procedure. Poet André Breton, painters Salvador Dali and André Masson (Lacan's brother-in-law), writers Sollers, Camus, Sartre, Leiris and Bataille, among others, facilitated Lacan's freedom to move away from the organic logic that had, up till then, dominated the clinic.

Lacan's personal acquaintance with poets, novelists and theorists of aesthetics accustomed him, from the beginning, to engage aesthetics in his clinical work; the seminars he gave to clinicians include meditations on Claudel, Gide, courtly love and Baroque poetry, James Joyce and E. A. Poe. Social scientists and philosophers assisted Lacan part of the way on his route: Lévi-Strauss, Jakobson, Merleau-Ponty. But artists were crucial to his thinking. Once, in his 'Homage to Marguerite Duras', (1987), Lacan invoked Freud's belief that artists were out ahead of analysts and cut the path for them.

The Lacanian 'clinic' tracks the *letter a* that has been traced on the logical body. The analyst, attentive to the patient's signifiers, finds them knotted around a *jouissance* in (and of) the *symptom*. Patiently locating the signifying chain that encrypts or walls off this *jouissance* like a cyst that interrupts the flowing of the signifier, the analyst's process is one of unknotting. Its goal is to free the patient to function effectively in the Symbolic; to lift off the subject's unconscious domination by the commands of an abusive internal Other ('the Other's *Jouissance*'), and by fantasies of seduction or castration by that 'big O' Other. Analysis cannot fully erase the letter-*object a* the subject has crystallized around; it only brings it to knowledge (*savoir*).

In an artistic and literary context, the structure of the subject remains the same: it is a precipitate of *object a, jouissance* and *fantasy*. But here Lacan's emphasis shifts from *symptom* to *sinthome*. Lacan's most elaborate literary analysis was *Le Sinthome, Seminar XXIII* in which he intersected a clinical diagnosis of James Joyce with an analysis of Joyce's aesthetic production: *writing*. For Joyce, whose 'psychical structure' was psychotic (according to Lacan), writing was prophylactic against the threat of psychopathology. How? The answer lies in the structure of the *sinthome*.

In the *symptom* signifiers knot themselves around a hollow left by the letter's stamp, a hollow filled with a threatening *jouissance*. The symptom is a damming-up of jouissance that also provisionally halts the freeplay of signification. The *sinthome*, too, is a place of accumulated psychic excess (surplus *jouissance*). But here excess *jouissance* is bound *to* a signifying formation, one that permits signification – but also dammed-up *jouissance* – to flow again. The *sinthome*-signifier is penetrated with a *jouissance* that the *signifier* a priori excludes, only here pathological *jouissance* is transformed into *jouis-sens* ('enjoy-meant'). For Lacan, the *sinthome* is the signifying face of fantasy, not of the Symbol.

Derrida and Lacan come together and apart once more here. Writing, for Derrida, circulates infinitely, combining the virtues of the signifier (commonality with other subjects, avoidance of lethal *jouissance*) with the aesthetic pleasure of literary art. For Lacan, literature's 'letters' are also those *object a*-letters that retain their connection to the Real, to experience and to a *jouissance* otherwise unattainable. Literature, for Lacan, is thus partly signifier (but a signifier frozen up by the *jouissance* it normally excludes) and partly object (but an object made entirely of the 'letters' of its subject's logical body, which nonetheless leave the body to circulate as freely as signifiers).

Lacan's *sinthome* updates and puts a keener edge on Freud's essay on the creative writer's relation to phantasy, wherein art is prized for furnishing a purely fictional, non-threatening satisfaction of censored (because lethal) drives. For Lacan, art is an even more uniquely crucial entity in the story of the subject-as-written-by-language. Lacan's own inimitable writing style has an 'irreducibly literary dimension', says Shoshana Felman comparing him to Stéphane Mallarmé (Clément 1974, 1). For Lacan, art refills the void left by language – but it 'fills' it only with a second void. Lacan's fable of art is the vase: a potter makes a hole in what is already a hole in the Real (1986, 119–21).

Juliet Flower MacCannell

Further reading and works cited

Apollon, W. and Feldstein, R. (eds) *Lacan, Politics, Aesthetics*. Albany, NY, 1996.
Badiou, A. *Manifesto for Philosophy*. Albany, NY, 1999.
Cantin, L. 'The Letter Against the Phallus', *American Journal of Semiotics*, VII, 3, 1990.
Copjec, J. *Read My Desire*. Cambridge, MA, 1994.
Deleuze, G. and Guattari, F. *Anti-Oedipus*. Minneapolis, MN, 1977.
—. *A Thousand Plateaus*. Minneapolis, MN, 1987.
Derrida, J. *De La Grammatologie*. Paris, 1967.
—. 'The Purveyor of Truth', *Yale French Studies*, 52, 1975.
—. *Resistances of Psychoanalysis*. Stanford, CA, 1998.
Irigaray, L. *Speculum de l'autre femme*. Paris, 1974.
—. *Ce sexe qui n'en est pas un*. Paris, 1977.
Johnson, B. *The Critical Difference*. Baltimore, MD, 1980.
Lacan, J. *Le Séminaire. Livre XX*, ed. J.-A. Miller. Paris, 1975.
—. *Le Séminaire. Livre VII. L'Ethique de la Psychanalyse*, ed. J.-A. Miller. Paris, 1986.
—. 'Homage to Marguerite Duras', in *Duras by Duras*. San Francisco, 1987, pp. 122–9.
—. *The Seminar of Jacques Lacan Book II*, ed. J.-A. Miller. New York, 1988.
—. *Television*, ed. J. Copjec. New York, 1990.
—. *The Four Fundamental Concepts of Psycho-Analysis* (Seminar XI), intro. David Macey. London, 1994.
Lacoue-Labarthe, P. and Nancy, J.-L. *The Title of the Letter*. Albany, NY, 1992.
MacCannell, J. Flower. *Figuring Lacan*. Lincoln, NE, 1986.
Miller, J.-A. 'Extimité', in *Lacanian Theory of Discourse*, eds M. Bracher et al. London, 1994.
Millot, C. *Nobodaddy*. Paris, 1988.
Mitchell, J. *Women: The longest Revolution*. London, 1984.
— and Rose, J. (eds) *Feminine Sexuality*. New York, 1982.
Ragland-Sullivan, E. and Bracher, M. (eds) *Lacan and the Subject of Language*. New York, 1991.
Roudinesco, E. *Jacques Lacan & Co*. Chicago, 1990.
Spivak, G. Chakravorty. 'The Letter as Cutting Edge', *Yale French Studies*, 55/56, 1977.
Walden, A. *System and Structure*. London, 1972.
Wright, E. et al. (eds) *Feminism and Psychoanalysis: A Critical Dictionary*. Oxford, 1991.
Žižek, S. *The Sublime Object of Ideology*. London, 1989.
—. *For They Know Not What They Do*. London 1991.
—. *Looking Awry*. Cambridge, MA, 1992.

The Reception of Hegel and Heidegger in France: Alexandre Kojève (1902–1968), Jean Hyppolite (1907–1968), Maurice Merleau-Ponty (1908–1961)

The reception of Hegel and of Heidegger in France has followed a somewhat similar curve at a century's distance, oscillating between enthusiastic acceptance based on severe misunderstandings, serious scholarship accompanied by new translations of certain works selected from the abundant productions of both philosophers, and a stubborn rejection, quite often proffered in the name of the traditional virtues of French thought, defined since Descartes by clarity of expression and linguistic transparency. Even if there never was a 'Hegel scandal' in the late nineteenth century as there was a 'Heidegger affair' in the 1980s, constant suspicion dogged the thought of Hegel who was accused and still is – although without real foundation – of having provided Bismarck with a model of imperialist and totalitarian doctrine. Since the reception of Heidegger in France is still a burning issue, entailing not only endless political and ethical discussions but also the whole question of translation, and since most canonical texts by Heidegger are almost unreadable in their current French 'versions' – which has had the advantage of forcing readers to go back to the German text – I will start by following the thread provided by Hegel as a surer guide.

Victor Cousin was the first French philosopher who actually met Hegel: he immediately acknowledged the genius of his interlocutor, admired the force and breadth of his vast syntheses, while remaining a little mystified by a 'scholastic language that was entirely his own'. Their meeting in 1816 in Heidelberg (Cousin explains how a first conversation with Hegel made him miss his coach, and decide to come back to be enlightened) is based on the old mixture of seduction, incomprehension and reciprocal projections that has characterized the Franco-German intellectual dialogue. In a typically French about-face, the glimpse of Hegel's system led Cousin to name his own philosophy 'eclectism'! It was left to the French philosophers of history such as Michelet and Quinet to salute their noble German precursor from a safe distance, without wishing to engage with the dense riddles of the text.

The first serious Hegelian philosopher writing in French was, curiously, Italian, more precisely, the Neapolitan Giambattista Vico. Augusto Vera, who had been Hegel's student in Berlin during the last years of the latter's life (Hegel died in 1831), started translating his works into French between 1855 and 1878. His translations are precise and rigorous, and are accompanied by long personal footnotes often quoting Hegel's extemporized remarks during his lectures or his correspondence. What is the most striking feature of these translations for us now is that one does not find the *Phenomenology of Spirit* among them: what interests Vera is to reconstruct the Hegelian system, moving gradually from the *Logic* (trans. 1859), the *Philosophy of Nature* (1863–6), the *Philosophy of Spirit* (1867–70) and finally the *Philosophy of Religion* (1876–8). These translations have been completely forgotten and it is a pity, since they allow one to reconstruct the deep impact of Hegel less on the French philosophy of the time than on poets like Stéphane Mallarmé, Villiers de l'Isle-Adam, Jules Laforgue and last but not least André Breton. André Breton, who had read Hegel's *Philosophy of Nature* very closely, found there many crucial images (his meditations on the crystal, or his use of the phrase 'the magnetic fields' are entirely in debt to Vera's Hegel). Vera chose to translate Hegel's concept (*Begriff*) by '*la notion*', in a somewhat weakened version, but one can still see it echo from Mallarmé to the early Breton. But here was perhaps the original sin of the French reception of Hegel: the omission of the phenomenological 'beginning' of the system, an omission that was repaired with a vengeance by Kojève in the 1930s, when Hegel's system can be read entirely from a few key-terms contained in the *Phenomenology*. By that time, the influence of Heidegger's revised Husserlian phenomenology will have contributed a new tone to philosophy.

Surrealism was a key factor in the rediscovery of Hegel, which led to wholesale embracing of the three Hs (Hegel, Husserl and Heidegger) as the new sources of philosophical thinking in France in the 1930s. If Heidegger's philosophy was not perceived in itself at first – at least as a spectacular break with Husserl's rational phenomenology – the rediscovery of Hegel in the 1930s corresponded with both a discovery of history (that is, of elaborating a discourse about contemporary history, which explains the long flirtation of French Hegelianism with Marxism) and a rediscovery of the concrete, of the world out there, at hand's reach as it were. In this general drift, there was a general agreement between the Hs and their various conceptions of what phenomenology can bring to philosophy.

This is why, after a relatively long eclipse, since, despite Vera's efforts, French philosophy at the end of the nineteenth century and in the first decades of the twentieth century took very different paths (Comte's positivistic religion of science led gradually to the institutional domination of a form of epistemological neo-Kantism, both generating the romantic reaction of Bergson's philosophy of intuition and duration), and the late 1920s and early 1930s were marked by a reawakening of an interest in Hegel. Jean Wahl, who had devoted a brilliant thesis to *The Pluralist Philosophers of Britain and the United States* (1920) and several books on Plato and Descartes, did not look like a typical 'Hegelian' when he published *The Unhappiness of Consciousness in Hegel's Philosophy* in 1929. This book was ground-breaking in that it not only returned to the *Phenomenology of Spirit* but also made extensive use of Hegel's early theological writings such as 'The Positivity of the Christian Religion' and 'The Spirit of Christianity', and the fragments on 'Love' and the 'Idea of a System', texts that had only been published in 1905 by Dilthey. Jean Wahl's originality was to take into account Kierkegaard's critique of Hegelian scholasticism, which led him to stress the role of alienation and desire in Hegel's early works, and presents Hegel as a budding existentialist. For Wahl, there is no historical progress without a dialectics of separation between the consciousness and the object it desires: the tragedy of separation and endless longing is experienced by every subject who will have to pass willy-nilly through stages of alienation and despair before regaining hope. Hope is granted above all by the belief that history will continue in its open-ended progress. This version of Hegel calls up more Bloch's 'principle of hope' than Vera's notion of a strict scientific systematicity, while history introduces a process that is unbounded. Later, Wahl was to stress that this historical path led 'toward the concrete' (as in *Toward the Concrete*, 1932), a concrete that would be processed by consciousness as it progressed along, in terms suggestive of a Husserlian influence.

Like Wahl, the second important commentator of that decade, the Russian born Alexandre Koyré, would stress the importance of the earliest texts, but without opposing them to the repressive nature of the System. What matters for Koyré, in a gesture that anticipates Hyppolite's, is to reconcile the subjective dialectics of separation, unhappiness and striving for reunification with the logical aspect of the doctrine. Koyré stresses the originality of Hegel's conception of time, a time that is dominated by the future. This time nevertheless contains a knowledge that will develop itself by establishing links between the future and the past – even if the present is experienced as contradictory and in conflict. Koyré also stresses the anti-theological and rationalistic aspect of Hegel's philosophy: his system aims not at creating another ontology but an anthropology. All these elements would be soon emphasized and even systematically exaggerated by Koyré's friend and disciple, Alexandre Kojève.

Coming like Koyré from Russia, Alexandre Kojevnikoff suddenly made Hegel not only accessible but indispensable to a whole generation. His famous seminars at the École Pratique des Hautes Études delivered yearly between 1933 and 1940 gathered people as diverse and famous as Raymond Queneau, Georges Bataille, Jacques Lacan, Raymond Aron, Maurice Merleau-Ponty, Jean Desanti and Jean Hyppolite. Kojève's wonderful appeal, his intellectual 'sexiness' one might say, lay in his uncanny ability to transform Hegel's abstract prose into a lively philosophical novel, to give blood and vigour to the notion of a 'gallery of images' traversed by the Spirit in the famous simile provided by Hegel on the penultimate page of his *Phenomenology*. Like Koyré, Kojève dismisses the religious element and stresses the anthropological element: 'According to Hegel – to use the Marxist terminology – Religion is only an ideological superstructure ...' (1969, 32). His own starting point is the famous dialectic of the Master and Slave, a key passage in the original text indeed, which nevertheless takes up less than ten pages out of the 600 pages or so of the whole work. But it is a crucial turning point in the analysis of the discovery of reciprocity by consciousness, and the subsequent need to be acknowledged by a consciousness that will also be free that Kojève can bring both Marx and Heidegger to bear on the Hegelian dialectic. Starting from the central insight that the meeting of Hegel and Napoléon in Jena embodies 'absolute knowledge' at the time of the writing of the *Phenomenology*, Kojève reopens the philosophical interpretation of the old historical scandal, well noted by Hegel, that Greek democracies never abolished slavery. This scandal is then linked with the dynamic function of Desire. If Man is ready to sacrifice his biological self in order to satisfy his desire for recognition in the struggle for death that marked the early times of civilization, one would always find certain individuals who accepted servitude rather than lose their life. Thus, after Speech, Desire and Reciprocity, Slavery is the fourth dominant concept in Hegel's anthropology: '... the possibility of a difference between the *future* Master and the *future* Slave is the fourth and last premise of the *Phenomenology*' (Kojève 1969, 42). History thus begins with this difference between Masters and Slaves, and conversely it will end only when this difference is abolished.

The analysis is well known: since the master has risked death in what might appear as a more authentic relationship to his *Dasein* (with echoes of Heidegger's *Being and Time*, the slave is determined by his 'fear of death'), after his victory, the master can bask in his superiority and leave everything vulgar and material to his slave: he will be content with enjoying the benefits of another's labours. The slave, who owns nothing, not even his desires, since he toils to satisfy the master's least whims, nevertheless discovers another kind of authenticity through a work which slowly transforms nature, whereas the master has to satisfy himself with the more and more empty recognition of his peers. The 'truth' of the master is then the slave, since he is the only one who can reconcile work and knowledge, leaving desire for later, when he can reach the end of the cycle leading to Absolute Knowledge. 'The Master appears only for the sake of engendering the Slave who "overcomes" [*aufhebt*] him as Master, while thereby "overcoming" himself as Slave. And this Slave who has been "overcome" is the one who is satisfied by what he *is* and will understand that he is satisfied in and by Hegel's philosophy, in and by the *Phenomenology*' (Kojève 1969, 47).

The second original element brought by Kojève's reading has been recently revived by Francis Fukuyama, and it is perhaps the most shocking for common sense: it is the thesis of the 'end of history'. For someone who had stressed from the start an anthropological reading while never losing sight of the problem concretely posed by the realization of Absolute Knowledge posed as the last stage of the progression of Spirit through Time, it seemed almost inevitable to assert that the attainment of Absolute Knowledge would result in the elimination of anthropology qua anthropology – that is, in the 'end of man'. A long footnote to the 1938–9 seminar begins by stating almost off-handedly that this is not an apocalyptic vision, but quite the contrary:

> The disappearance of Man at the end of History, therefore, is not a cosmic catastrophe: the natural World remains what it had been from all eternity. And therefore, it is not a biological catastrophe either: Man remains alive as animal in *harmony* with Nature or given Being. What disappears is Man properly so-called – that is, Action negating the given, and Error, or in general, the Subject *opposed* to the object. (Kojève 1969, 158–9)

In this Edenic reverie, wars and revolutions will have disappeared, along with Philosophy as the discourse that accompanied them, while all the arts, passions and the elements of superfluity much needed to fill in an empty time will remain in high demand, since we will be in an endless 'Sunday of Life' (to quote Queneau's witty title). No doubt that snobbism and the 'Japanese' model will play an exemplary role in such a scheme.

It would be idle to try to prove that Hegel never intended this: the 'end of history' belongs to the Hegelian legends skilfully examined by Jon Steward and his collaborators. But as Kojève says in a 1948 letter to the marxist critic Tran-Duc-Thao, his aim was not to find out what Hegel himself meant in his book, but to think with him and from him; he acknowledges that he has unduly stressed the role of the Master and Slave dialectic because he wanted to 'strike people's minds' and offer a new 'propaganda'. As Lacan and many others who have approached Kojève testify, he had only contempt for those who were satisfied with the role of pure intellectuals; he refused all academic honours, and spent most of his life as a high civil servant working on international relations between European states and their former colonies, devising and implementing an original system of aid and compensation. He indeed saw the looming conflict between North and South or between the first and the third world as more fundamental than the issues raised by marxism in terms of industrialization and infrastructure versus superstructure. For him, indeed, the Chinese revolution was only the 'alignment of the provinces' on the scheme already provided by the development of the System.

There was clearly the need for a more scholarly examination of Hegel, and this was to be provided by Hyppolite, who gave the first complete French translation of the *Phenomenology*, then added a systematic commentary, before attempting a synthesis between the earlier and the later Hegel in *Logic and Existence*. One could observe, for instance, how Jacques Lacan slowly moved from a Kojèvian version of Hegel that stressed desire, mirror images and aggressivity, to an ongoing discussion with Hyppolite who was a regular participant in his Seminar in 1954–6. When Lacan states that 'Man's desire is desire of the Other', he is in fact glossing Hyppolite's use of 'The Other' for the object of desire understood as pure alterity or just 'Life'. Unlike Kojève, however, Hyppolite does not take Desire (*Begierde*) for one of the most fundamental concepts in Hegel. And of course, very early in his commentary, he refuses the idea that history might have an end. This would be a 'naive' belief that the system freezes history, and according to him Hegel never fell into that trap. When Hegel famously asserts in the Preface to his *Philosophy of Right* that it is 'just as absurd to fancy that a philosophy can transcend its contemporary world as it is to fancy that an individual can overleap his own age', Hyppolite adds that what matters is the experience of joy and pain in the present, and the awareness that the consciousness seen progressing through various stages in the *Phenomenology* is both a singular and a universal consciousness.

This is the place in which Hyppolite inserts his most systematic and recurrent questioning: if Hegel's thought forms indeed a system, what is the function of this introduction to knowledge constituted by the *Phenomenology*? Why do we have to follow all the divisions and illusions of a consciousness on its way to absolute knowledge, if absolute knowledge is presupposed from the start? He notes that while the *Phenomenology* is the most literary of Hegel's treatises, it is caught up between strong opposites that he names 'panlogicism' on the one hand and 'pantragicism' on the other. We have seen how Wahl had chosen to stress the tragic – even pathetic – elements, in a way that would no doubt impress Georges Bataille: Hegel is indeed the philosopher of the encounter with death and pure negativity, but he also looks at real history and its 'slaughter-bench' without flinching. Hyppolite makes a lot, for instance, of Hegel's interpretation of 'Terror' in revolutionary France. Unlike the first French Hegelians who looked to the German philosopher as someone who helps them go back to history so as to find a meaning in it, Hyppolite is aware of the danger of any philosophy of history that identifies the Real and the Rational: one risks falling into a history of the legitimization of political power, the tragedy of negativity being quickly subsumed by the patience of an overarching concept.

A new tone is therefore sounded just after the Second World War, when Hyppolite published *Logic and Existence* in 1952, an essay that tackles the same problem of the relationship between the 'genesis' of consciousness in the *Phenomenology* and the 'structure' of the concept contained in the *Logic*, but with a different emphasis. This text marks a break with the anthropological readings of Hegel that dominated before the war, and opts resolutely for a quasi-Heideggerian version: if the Logic presupposes the experience of the phenomenon, and if the phenomenology presupposes the concept, none can be reduced to the other, but both are related to the fact that Man is 'the dwelling of the Universal and of the Logos of Being, and thus becomes capable of Truth' (Hyppolite 1997, 187, modified). Curiously, this is Hyppolite's most Heideggerian text, and it sounds very close to Heidegger's 1930–1 lectures on *Hegel's Phenomenology of Spirit*. For instance, Hyppolite writes: 'The Logic's dialectical discourse will be the very discourse of Being, the *Phenomenology* having shown the possibility of bracketing man as natural Dasein' (1997, 42). The

Logic bequeaths us with a fundamental insight into the function of sense: Being is thought absolutely, but only through our existence. An essential difference will therefore constitute the very core of Being: Being projects constantly its own Other, unfolds and generates an inner self-differing. Alert as he was to the Nietzschean and Heideggerian echoes of this thesis, Hyppolite can be said to pave the way to Derrida's and Deleuze's philosophies of Difference – a good decade in advance. Deleuze had noted this point in a famous review of Hyppolite's work, in which he claims that, for Hyppolite, 'Being it not *essence* but *sense*' which allows him to see how Hegel 'transforms metaphysics into logics, and logics into a logics of sense' (Hyppolite 1997, 193), and which entails that the Absolute is *here*, or in other words, that there is 'no secret'. Deleuze points out some difficulties in this Hegelian programme (how can one avoid falling back into the anthropology that has been denounced?) and he suggests that Nietzsche would have been a better guide. At least, it is fascinating to observe how the meeting between Hegel and Heidegger, half-way as it were, predetermines the evolution of French philosophy in the second half of the twentieth century.

This is clearly a far cry from what was at the time felt to be the dominant mode of French phenomenology, a mixture of Husserlian anthropology and existentialism. In 1943, Sartre could still think he was being a true Heideggerian when he merely translated into his own vocabulary two key terms of Hegelian phenomenology, the *Insich* and the *Fürsich* that were readily transformed into *l'en-soi* and *le pour-soi*. By a wilful distortion (since for Hegel what matters is the discrepancy between the way things can be 'in fact' and how they are perceived for a consciousness at a given stage), Sartre returns in fact to a neo-Cartesian dualism opposing the world as positivity (which is in itself) and consciousness as its inverse negativity (since it is always for itself). Sartre's genius is evident in his concrete analyses (of the gaze, of facticity) as if he had borrowed from Hegel and from Hegel only the right to transform philosophy into a novelistic series of vignettes – which would situate him as Kojève's unexpected heir! However, Sartre clearly criticizes what he calls Hegel's 'onto-logical optimism', a logical optimism which would make him trust the truth of the Totality too easily. According to Sartre, there is constantly a sleight of hand by which Hegel thinks he can overcome the singularity of individual consciousness to reach the Whole because the Whole had already been given at the outset. Sartre adds, in a phrase that sounds tantalizing: 'But if Hegel forgets himself, we cannot forget Hegel' (1943, 300). Alas, it is only to add: 'Which means that we are sent back to the cogito.'

Merleau-Ponty will have no difficulty in disentangling several levels of confusion in Sartre's essay, a book he admires in spite of its many shortcuts. The texts he collected in *Sense and Non-Sense* all date from the postwar years, the heady discussions with Sartre and marxist thinkers, and their joint foundation of *Les Temps Modernes*. In a piece on 'Hegel's Existentialism', Merleau-Ponty closes the entire circle of French existentialist variations on Hegel's *Phenomenology*: he first pays homage to Hyppolite's translation and commentary, then moves on to connections with Sartre's *Being and Nothingness* before engaging more decisively with Heidegger's influence. Merleau-Ponty notes that the conclusion of Hegel's major essay could lead one either to join the Communist Party or the Church, and is clearly not a philosophy of the individual choice. In the same way, Heidegger's philosophy has been misconstrued, according to him, as being a-historical, whereas the last part of *Being and Time* contains a philosophy of history. Clearly, in this short piece, Merleau-Ponty is busy pushing existentialism away from its individualistic limitations, so as to confront it with Hegel and Heidegger.

This is what dominates in later texts by Merleau-Ponty, who although he could reproach Sartre for not being marxist enough in the early 1950s, nevertheless kept criticizing the Stalinist doctrine of the French Party. In his posthumous *Notes de Cours 1959–1961* as well as in his unpublished essay that he meant to call '*An Introduction to the Prose of the World*', one can see that Merleau-Ponty's initial debt to Husserl gradually leaves room to a systematic confrontation with Hegel (the very title of 'prose of the world' is borrowed from Hegel) and Heidegger: for both pose the question that was probably still unsolved in Husserl of the links between language and historicity. His last lecture notes on 'the state of philosophy today' sketch an interesting philosophical genealogy: they begin with Husserl, continue with Heidegger and then branch off into Heidegger's reading of Hegel, finally concluding with a confrontation between Hegel and Marx. It looks as if Husserl and Heidegger had been indispensable mediators who would help Merleau-Ponty find 'Hegel and his negativity having descended into the Flesh of the World' (1996, 348). But by that time, the shift in French marxism due to Althusser had started rejecting any trace of Hegelianism in Marx's 'scientific' thought. Whereas Althusser could remark rather positively (in a 1947 review of Kojève) that Kojève's merit had been to show that 'without Heidegger . . . we would never have understood the *Phenomenology of Spirit*' (1997, 171), the later recurrent coupling of both Hs was enough to brand them as idealist and unfit to come into contact with real 'theory'.

Jean-Michel Rabaté

Further reading and works cited

Althusser, L. *Early Writings: The Spectre of Hegel*. London, 1997.
Butler, J. *Subjects of Desire*. New York, 1999.
Descombes, V. *Modern French Philosophy*. Cambridge, 1980.
Fukuyama, F. *The End of History and the Last Man*. New York, 1992.
Heidegger, M. *Hegel's Phenomenology of Spirit*. Bloomington, IN, 1988.
Hyppolite, J. *Logic and Existence*. Albany, NY, 1997.
Jarczyk, G. and Labarrière, P.-J. *De Kojève à Hegel*. Paris, 1996.
Kojève, A. *Introduction to the Reading of Hegel*, ed. A. Bloom. Ithaca, NY, 1969.
Matthews, E. *Twentieth-Century French Philosophy*. Oxford, 1996.
Merleau-Ponty, M. *Sense and Non-Sense*. Evanston, IL, 1964.
—. *Notes de Cours 1959–1961*, ed. C. Lefort. Paris, 1996.
Nancy, J.-L. *Hegel: L'inquiétude du négatif*. Paris, 1997.
Roth, M. S. *Knowing and History*. Ithaca, NY, 1988.
Sartre, J.-P. *L'Etre et le Néant*. Paris, 1943.
Stewart, J. (ed.) *The Hegel Myths and Legends*. Evanston, IL, 1996.
Wahl, J. *The Phirolist Philosophies of Britain and the United States*. London, 1925.
—. *Vers la concret*. Paris, 1932.
—. *Le Malheur de la conscience dans la philosophie de Hegel*. Paris, 1951.
Wolin, R. *Labyrinths*. Amherst, MA, 1995.

Jean-Paul Sartre (1905–1980), Albert Camus (1913–1960) and Existentialism

Albert Camus would probably turn, once again, in his grave at the allegation that he was an existentialist. But his disquiet is better understood through the uneasiness of his personal relationship with Jean-Paul Sartre, who is more obviously associated with the term, than any genuine incommensurability between their beliefs. It is probably the word *absurdity* that is responsible for the persistence with which commentators have linked Camus and existentialism, and the subsequent connection, for which we might hold Martin Esslin at least partly responsible, between absurdity and the ideas about *being* and *freedom* to which Sartre devoted so much intellectual energy. But the idea of absurdity, of which Camus was so fond, was not plucked from the air. Whatever new inflections Camus might have added to it, the notion of the absurd was integral to the philosophical tradition that most informed the work of Camus and Sartre, and can be found, if not always by name, in the work of Kierkegaard, Nietzsche, Heidegger, Husserl and Jaspers. Camus may have refused the label existentialist, but it is difficult to see his thought as anything other than a celebration of this tradition of existentialist and phenomenological philosophy.

Camus's elaboration of the absurd had much in common with Nietzsche and Kierkegaard for its sense of exhilaration about the collapse of metaphysics: a recognition that philosophy and religion were incapable of formulating a universal logic which might render human experience intelligible as a whole. Like Nietzsche, Camus had a sense that the absurdity of the universe entailed the freedom of the human being, and that from the negative realization of Godlessness might emerge a positive philosophy of personal existence. This is the movement of his most philosophical collection of essays *The Myth of Sisyphus*, which takes as its starting point the proposition that suicide is the only serious philosophical question. For Camus, the recognition of a total lack of hope, of life's ultimate meaninglessness and of the finality of death is a kind of liberation into an adventure to be experienced exactly by sustaining the recognition of absurdity. Suicide therefore comes to represent a response to misplaced hope, and it is only by liberating oneself from this kind of hope that life becomes an affirmative adventure. Living absurdity, then, is riding on the back of negativity in the full knowledge of life's absence of meaning. From the twenty-first century this can seem like a rather banal recognition, or a kind of nihilism that affirms no particular course of action. But for Camus, the core of absurdity does not lie in the affirmation of any particular programme of action but in the recognition of choice which results from the advantage of having given up all hope. In *The Myth of Sisyphus*, this condition is expressed through a selection of literary examples, of absurd heroes such as Don Juan and Captain Ahab in Moby Dick, who are taken as emblems of strength in the face of pointlessness. Sisyphus himself, who has been condemned by the gods to the perpetual labour of rolling a stone uphill, is an absurd hero who should be understood not as the subject of irresistible divine malice, but as someone who chooses to strive continuously in the knowledge that he can never succeed. For Camus, Sisyphus represents a happier condition than any misplaced hope of success exactly because he proceeds in the knowledge that his labour is fruitless.

Camus's resort to literary examples throughout *The Myth of Sisyphus* is revealing. There is a clear preference for the emblematic literary example over philosophical reason which could be said to characterize his mode of philosophizing in general terms. Existentialism emerges from a suspicion of philosophical reason that invests literary discourse with a new philosophical importance exactly because literature deals with concrete situations and personal experience without the burden of formulating the general laws to which metaphysics aspired. For H. J. Blackham, the preference for the concrete situation over theoretical reason, or for a philosophy of personal existence over metaphysics, is at the heart of existentialism:

> We are given a world whose pretensions must be broken, a world to be both accepted and refused, a life to be built on the further side of despair; knowledge being irremediably incomplete and uncertain throws the weight of responsibility upon personal decision; reason alone can limit reason, and its present duty is to restore the concrete and thus to eliminate the false theoretical problems which have haunted philosophy and illumine the real problems for which there are no theoretical solutions. As each aspect of the human situation is lit up, the light is reflected upon the personal isolation and responsibility of the existing individual at the centre. (1952, 150)

Blackham doesn't quite say so here, but this tenet that the duty of philosophy is to discard unsolveable theoretical problems and turn instead to the illumination of real problems in concrete situations underlies what might be called the existentialist valorization of literature. It is clear in Camus's writing that the novel is a form that allows the exploration of his thinking on the absurd a concrete, situation-based expression that is more appropriate to existentialist themes than the rigours of the philosophical essay. The impact of Camus's notion of the absurd was undoubtedly enhanced as a result of its elaboration not only in the philosophical essays of *The Myth of Sisyphus* (1942), but in his novel *L'Etranger* (1942) and the earlier drama *Caligula* (1939), both of which seemed to set philosophical ideas about absurdity into concrete situations, in modes of writing which forsake reason for what Martin Esslin would later call a direct experiential validity. This relationship between philosophy and literature is one of the preoccupations that most clearly links Camus to Sartre, and in which the themes of existential philosophy can be most directly linked to concerns of literary theory. *The Myth of Sisyphus* is preoccupied with the critique of reason, with the departure from a pure philosophy of reason into a more paradoxical kind of philosophy capable of apprehending the absurd. This paradoxical philosophy lies somewhere between philosophy and literature, so that the writings of philosophers such as Nietzsche, Heidegger, Jaspers and Husserl are understood to have given up the pursuit of universal truths through pure reason and embraced the absurd through an admission of irrationality: hence, for Camus, absurd reasoning is a kind of composite of art and reason which he describes as a 'confrontation of the irrational and the wild longing for clarity' (1942, 26). Reciprocally, Camus claims that 'the great novelists are philosophical novelists, that is the contrary of thesis-writers' and cites Balzac, Sade, Melville, Stendhal, Dostoevsky, Proust, Mallard and Kafka as examples. This tension between the depiction of concrete situations and the kind of philosophical hope that these situations can be rendered intelligible by reason lies at the heart of existentialism. It is the sense of incompletion of one without the other that seems to lie behind Camus's formulation:

> But if in fact, the preference they have shown for writing in images rather than in reasoned arguments is revelatory of a certain thought that is common to [all the great novelists], convinced of the uselessness of any principle of explanation and sure of the educative message of perceptible appearance. They consider the work of art both as an end and as a beginning. It is the outcome of an often expressed philosophy, its illustration and its consummation. But it is complete only through the implications of that philosophy. It justifies at last the variant of an old theme that a little thought estranges from life whereas much thought reconciles to life. Incapable of refining the real, thought pauses to mimic it. (1942, 93)

This is interesting for several reasons. The sense of tension between thought and image helps to explain the place of fiction and drama for existentialist thinkers like Camus and Sartre as a kind return of thought to mimic the real. By this formulation it is the borderline between philosophy and fiction that contains the most energy for what Camus calls absurd creation. From this point of view, existentialism can be seen as an important pre-history to poststructuralist attitudes to fiction and philosophy in so far as they characteristically challenge any rigid line between the two, and celebrate instead a kind of reason pervaded by creativity and a kind of creativity characterized by critical self-consciousness. Derrida's writing, for example, shows the same oscillation between a kind of playful creativity and the rigours of philosophy, the same doubleness of acceptance and suspicion of the possibility of a philosophical or critical metalanguage.

The productive tension between philosophy and fiction seems to operate for both Camus and Sartre, not only as a guiding principle in their own writings, not only as a choice between writing theoretically and writing fictionally, but as a basis for the critical assessment of other writers. We have already touched on this in Camus, who uses the notion of absurdity, and the absurd hero, as a measure of the greatness of other writers. Similarly in the case of Sartre, his own philosophical frameworks are never distant from his critical writings. Sartre's study of Baudelaire (1946) is a well-known example, where the philosophical perspectives of *Being and Nothingness*, Sartre's most influential philosophical tract, are applied to the life of Baudelaire in a process that he called *existential psychoanalysis*. *Baudelaire* is not so much a work of criticism as an account of the writer's failure to live an authentic existence as a result of the death of his father and the remarriage of his mother to a man that he rejected. Refusing the Freudian account of this scenario in the Oedipus complex, Sartre attempts to establish an interpretation which rejects the idea that humans act according to unconscious motives, and turns instead to his own concept of *bad faith*. In *Being and Nothingness*, Sartre sets out a programme for authentic living which consists in the apprehension of one's freedom and the recognition of choice as the determining factor in the existence of any individual. Baudelaire's bitterness towards his father-in-law is seen by Sartre as a special kind of bad faith that he called Being-for-Others. This is a kind of self-absolution from the responsibility that comes with freedom, in which one blames the condition of one's existence on other people, or in which one chooses to see oneself as if someone else. In addition to being a principle for the assessment of Baudelaire as a writer, there are two important aspects of this analysis. The first is that it distances Sartre's thought from Freud, who sees early childhood as the crucial stage of an individual's formation, which then determines the unconscious desires and motives of the adult. To preserve the idea of freedom, Sartre focuses on an event in Baudelaire's life that took place at the age of eight, at which free individual choices become possible, and any evasion of them through the inauthenticity of Being-for-Others is a failure of responsibility. The second is that it distances Sartre from the marxist tradition, which had always refused the idea of the individual as a sovereign or transcendent realm of free choice, and preferred to subordinate questions of the individual to the social system which determined all aspects of inner life.

There is a strange reciprocity here between Sartre's dealings with a writer and the deployment of his philosophical ideas which I think is characteristic of his work in general. There is a feeling that Sartre's life, his philosophical writings, his views on literature, his evaluation of other writings and his politics are all facets of a unified project. In his dealings with Baudelaire there is a cross-contamination between critic and philosopher (also to be found in his 1952 study of Genet and of Flaubert in 1966) that seems to uphold the values of Sartre's own life and work as he describes it in his autobiography. In *Words*, Sartre makes it clear that the fall into bad faith he describes in Baudelaire contrasts with his own eight-year-old moment of authentic responsibility when he decided irreversibly, and against the will of others, to be a writer. And when he returns to Baudelaire in that text, he adds another account of Baudelaire's fall into bad faith, this time in relation to his uncritical acceptance of the romantic myth of a poet in isolation from society and therefore doomed to unhappiness. Again, the contrast with Sartre's own life is difficult to miss. In *What is Literature*, Sartre's well known polemic in favour of a committed literature, a literature whose worth is measured by its oppositional power and its orientation towards social action, the romantic myth of the poet in social isolation is not sufficiently *engagé*. Indeed, *What is Literature* argues that being a poet at all is something of an obstacle to commitment by the very nature of the poetic language:

> The poet is outside language. He sees words inside out as if he did not share the human condition, and as if he were first meeting the word as a barrier as he comes towards men. Instead of first knowing things by their name, it seems that first he has a silent contact with them, since, turning towards that other species of thing which for him is the word, touching them, testing them, fingering them, he discovers in them a slight luminosity of their own and particular affinities with the earth, the sky, the water, and all created things. (1993, 6)

Commitment is the preserve of prose, in which language is capable of transparency to the world, and particularly when the writer's own world is visible beyond the materiality of language. 'You explain this world to me with an image', says Camus in a similar spirit. 'I realize that you have been reduced to poetry. .. So that science that was to teach me everything ends up in a hypothesis, that lucidity founders in metaphor, that uncertainty is resolved in a work of art' (1942, 25). There is a critical attitude at work here that values philosophical lucidity above the excesses of metaphor, and yet at the same time doubts the ability of that philosophical lucidity to describe existence in its concrete quiddity. It is as if good writing must forsake reason, and yet not err so far into literariness that it becomes poetic. There is a kind of self-endorsement in these views, that philosophy should not venture too far from literature, and that literature should stay within the orbit of philosophy.

Sartre's early philosophy describes the condition of freedom as if it were a simple fact, and the concept of bad faith as a flight from that freedom. Literature is often described as existentialist when it represents the condition of existence against a backdrop of absurdity, or where various forms of bad faith seem to fill the meaningless void in an attempt to push back the anguish of responsibility and freedom. Beckett's drama, also much to his chagrin, is often seen in this way. A backdrop of silence is filled by characters whose habitual actions prevent them from apprehending their freedom. Chief among these habits is the meaningless exchange of apparently unscripted dialogue, the main purpose of which is to give characters the impression of existence through interaction with others. The importance of the mutually dependent pair in early Beckett drama seemed to many to be speaking directly to Sartre's description of the bad faith of Being-for-Others, in which one character's existence is affirmed by the perception of the other. But communication is never a very successful or meaningful business for Beckett's characters, who seem to express only the need to continue trying to express in the knowledge that they will continue to fail. It is easy to understand why critics of the mid-century were eager to read Vladimir and Estragon, Hamm and Clov or Winnie and Willie as allegories of Sartre's descriptions of Being-for-Others, and many of Beckett's own pronouncements seemed to indicate the validity of the approach. Characters who are free to leave fail to do so because they believe their existence to be dependant on another (Vladimir and Estragon), characters who think their existence will end if the other leaves (Hamm and Clov), characters whose primary need is the perception, however negligible, of another (Winnie in relation to Willie) or characters who see themselves as another person (Krapp) seem to be advancing a negative view of the absurdity of interaction with others. The negativity here relates more closely to Sartre's rather gloomy analysis of freedom in *Being and Nothingness* rather than to the optimistic affirmation of the absurd that we get in Camus's *The Myth of Sisyphus*. And Beckett's own hostility to the critical interpretation seems if anything to affirm rather than to deny the link with existential categories, communicating as it does with the suspicion of meta-languages and the valorization of literature as a philosophical mode. As he constantly asserted, his plays were mere existents attesting to the ineffability of knowledge, and yet clearly aimed at the representation of an existential condition which defied and mocked the attempts of reason to render it intelligible.

The importance of existentialism for literature and literary theory might then be summarized in the following categories. (1) Fiction and drama were adopted as suitable discourses for the representation of existential themes by Camus and Sartre. (2) The boundary between philosophy and literature became a source of energy for both, valorizing philosophical fiction and literariness in philosophy. (3) The idea of absurdity developed as a philosophical account of the absence of meaning in the universe, and provided a backdrop for fictional and dramatic explorations of bad faith, freedom and the quest for meaning in Sartre and Camus's own writing. (4) Sartre's philosophical writings provided perspectives on language, especially the role of language as a mode of Being-for-Others, and the demotion of poetic language in relation to political commitment. (5) Sartre's existential psychoanalysis was a form of diagnosis which, against Freud and Marx, sought to reveal a moment of fundamental choice, within or outside fiction, which might, really or hypothetically, be consciously changed. (6) Camus's and Sartre's philosophy provides a critical vocabulary beyond existential psychoanalysis for the description of apparently purposeless and futile fictional and dramatic actions. Perhaps most significantly, if we cast forward to contemporary literary criticism and theory, existentialism can be seen as a set of foundations for the reciprocity between theory and fiction that has characterized postmodernism, and particularly the extent to which literary practice and criticism have aspired to forms of social action and political engagement in the aftermath of the more scientific and formalist concerns of the Anglo-American tradition in the mid-twentieth century.

Mark Currie

Further reading and works cited

Beckett, S. *Waiting for Godot*. London, 1956.
—. *Endgame*. London, 1958.
—. *Krapp's Last Tape*. London, 1959.
—. *Happy Days*. London, 1965.
Blackham, H. J. *Six Existentialist Thinkers*. London, 1952.
Camus, A. *The Myth of Sisyphus*. Harmondsworth, 1942.
—. *The Outsider*. Harmondsworth, 1961.
Danto, A. C. *Sartre*. London, 1975.
Macquarrie, J. *Existentialism*. London, 1972.
Patrik, L. *Existential Literature*. London, 2000.
Poster, M. *Existential Marxism in Postwar France*. Princeton, NJ, 1975.
Sartre, J.-P. *Being and Nothingness*. London, 1957.
—. *Baudelaire*. [1946]. London, 1964.
—. *Words*. London, 1964.
—. *Nausea*. London, 1965.
—. *What is Literature?* London, 1993.

Emmanuel Levinas (1906–1995)

Anyone interested in literature who decides to read Emmanuel Levinas for the first time will very likely experience an awkward tension that will accompany him or her for book after book. On the one hand, in his philosophical writings especially, Levinas refers to a wide range of canonical dramatists, novelists and poets, most of them French, German and Russian. He affirms that he came to philosophy by reading Russian fiction, and observes that 'it sometimes seems to me that the whole of philosophy is only a meditation on Shakespeare' (Levinas 1987a, 72). His major work, *Totalité et infini* (1961), begins with a line from one of Arthur Rimbaud's prose poems and ends with a line from one of Charles Baudelaire's. He devotes a little book to his oldest friend, Maurice Blanchot, for whose novels and *récits* he has the greatest respect, and he consecrates short, admiring texts to Paul Celan, Edmond Jabès, Roger Laporte, Michel Leiris and Marcel Proust. Simply reading his books will reveal that Levinas can write in a lyrical manner when it suits his purposes, and one may even come to find that in general his prose has unique attractions. Scarcely inattentive to Levinas's philosophical originality or the subtlety of his arguments, Jacques Derrida nonetheless notes that '*Totality and Infinity* is a work of art and not a treatise' (1978, 312, n. 7).

On the other hand, before one has gone very far into Levinas's works it will become sharply evident that he launches one of the most virulent attacks on art since Plato composed *The Republic*. In 'Reality and its Shadow' (1948) we are told that art is 'the very event of obscuring, a descent of the night, an invasion of shadow', that it consists 'in substituting an image for being', that every image is '*already a caricature*' and that 'There is something wicked and egoist and cowardly in artistic enjoyment' (Levinas 1987b, 3, 5, 9, 12). Criticism is to be valued over art, we are advised in the same essay, while in *Totality and Infinity* prose is opposed to poetry, leaving us in no doubt that this is to the former's advantage because prose breaks the 'rhythm which enraptures and transports the inter-locutors' (Levinas 1979, 203). In that same work, Rimbaud who summarily informed his former teacher Georges Izambard that 'I is another [*Je est un autre*]' is given a slap over the wrist: 'The alterity of the I that takes itself for another may strike the imagination of the poet precisely because it is but the play of the same' (Levinas 1979, 37). Since Levinas's ethics, as we shall see, turn on elevating the other over the self this can only be received as a harsh judgement on the French poet and the schools of poetics that draw on his revolutionary statement about the 'I'. Yet Levinas can be even more blunt. In another place he speaks of the 'violence' to be found in 'poetic delirium and enthusiasm displayed when we merely offer our mouths to the muse who speaks through us' (Levinas 1990a, 7).

Quite reasonably, anyone with a literary bent who has taken the trouble to read Levinas will ask whether this tension can be resolved and, if so, how. Although art is a peripheral matter for Levinas, the questions he raises with regard to it lead us directly to the centre of his thought, and so we shall follow them. To begin with, one might think that the tension between admiring and condemning art can be explained by appealing to empirical events in Levinas's life, such as his son's decision to pursue a career in music. (Michael Levinas became a composer, concert pianist and teacher of musical analysis at the Conservatoire de Paris.) At no time, however, does the philosopher change his mind about what he criticizes in the arts. And yet when he writes about art he does not always focus on what he finds most worrying about it. 'Reality and its Shadow' (1948) complains that art is not socially committed, so it is odd to look back only a year before and find in 'The Other in Proust' (1947) an author who recognizes that 'Proust is the poet of the social' (Levinas 1996, 102). 'We distrust poetry' we are told in a 1950 essay on Paul Claudel only to hear in a 1969 essay on the same poet that what 'makes language possible' is in all likelihood 'the very definition of poetry' (Levinas 1990a, 121, 132). In 'The Servant and Her Master' (1966) the Blanchot of *Awaiting Oblivion* is praised for his language 'of pure transcendence without correlation … a language going from one singularity to another without their having anything in common' (Levinas 1996, 148). And, later, in 'Paul Celan: From Being to the Other' (1972), the philosopher lauds the poet in terms he elsewhere reserves for ethics: 'The poem goes toward the other' (Levinas 1996, 41). If Levinas has not changed his mind about art, we must ask whether Blanchot, Celan, Claudel and Proust produce something other than art, as Levinas understands the word, or whether they incorporate a criticism of art in what they produce.

Before we can turn our attention to this matter, though, we must consider another attempt to explain Levinas's ambiguous relation to art by way of his biography. For it is sometimes proposed that the strictures in 'Reality and its Shadow' and elsewhere can be explained satisfactorily by noting that Levinas is a Jew and that therefore he feels bound, at one level or another, to respect the divine prohibition against the making of 'graven images' (Exodus 20: 4). Before evaluating this explanation, we need to grasp the scope of the prohibition in question. The commandment is debated in the Babylonian Talmud (Tractate Rosh Hashanah, ch. 2, 24 a–b), and the conclusion reached there is that that images may be made for public display but only when there is no chance they can be worshipped as idols, and that images may be used for purposes of instruction. Levinas is well aware of this. In Lithuania, as a child of observant Jews, he learned to read the Hebrew Bible in its original language. Then, after a period in which religious studies played little or no part in his life, he returned to them but in a new way. From 1947 to 1951 he devoted himself to studying the Talmud under the strict guidance of M. Chouchani, and starting in 1957 gave papers at the annual Colloquium of Jewish Intellectuals that meets in Paris. So one would expect him to have an informed and nuanced understanding of Torah, including Exodus 20: 4. In fact, Levinas is less interested in the prohibition against images as a religious rule than in something that the rule perhaps bespeaks. He wonders if beneath the commandment there is not 'a denunciation, in the structures of signifying and the meaningful, of a certain favoring of representation over other possible modes of thought' (Levinas 1999, 122).

In the sentence I have just quoted Levinas modulates from religion to philosophy, and it needs to be pointed out that he distinguishes his philosophical from his confessional texts. The five collections of his Talmudic readings, from *Quatre lectures talmudiques* (1968) to the posthumous *Nouvelles lectures talmudiques* (1996), are published by Les Éditions de Minuit, while his main philosophical works, *Totalité et infini* (1961) and *Autrement qu'être* (1974), first appeared with Martinus Nijhoff. This empirical division of his labours sends a clear signal to readers. Even so, the line between the two sorts of writing is hardly continuous or straight. Although he does not cite the Talmud in order to establish a philosophical position, he does not hesitate to quote Scripture in order to amplify or clarify points in his non-confessional writings. As his reflections on Exodus 20: 4 suggest, his philosophical thinking sometimes converges with his reflections on Torah and Talmud. Yet these reflections are not confessions of religious belief. As Levinas observes, his Talmudic readings are neither dogmatic nor theological but are in search 'of problems and truths', a discipline he believes to be necessary 'for an Israel wishing to preserve its self-consciousness in the modern world' (Levinas 1990b, 9). 'Israel', for this Jew, denotes an intellectual as well as a political and religious reality, and the former must not be obscured by the latter.

Philosophy derives from the ancient Greeks, Levinas maintains, but in saying that he is not merely endorsing Alfred North Whitehead's *bon mot* that all philosophy is a series of footnotes to Plato. Rather, he is suggesting that intelligibility itself is underwritten by fundamental Greek concepts: '*morphe* (form), *ousia* (substance), *nous* (reason), *logos* (thought) or *telos* (goal), etc.' (Cohen 1986, 19). Thus understood, intelligibility yields a notion of truth as presence. What is true is present or presentable, and it follows that the present moment, the now, is able to hold very different elements together in a relation of sameness. These elements are 'englobed in a history which totalizes time into a beginning or an end, or both, which is presence' (Cohen 1986, 19). A quite different notion of truth may be found in the Hebrew Bible, Levinas reminds us, one that answers to infinity rather than totality. Biblical truth is a matter of the proximity of God; it turns on a call for justice, a concern for the other person. In contemplating this Hebraic sense of truth, Levinas affirms that '*The other qua other is the Other*' [*L'Autre en tant qu'autre est Autrui*]' and consequently that 'The Other alone eludes thematization' (Levinas 1979, 71, 86). Immediately, though, a difficulty appears, one that Derrida was quick to indicate in his reading of *Totality and Infinity*. Can one coherently affirm the Other as infinitely other? 'The other cannot be what it is, infinitely other, except in finitude and mortality (mine *and* its). It is such as soon as it comes into language, of course, and only then, and only if the word *other* has a meaning – but has not Levinas taught us that there is no thought before language?' (Derrida 1978, 114–15). Levinas saw the point of the objection, which perhaps nudged him toward distinguishing the Saying from the Said in *Otherwise than Being* and its satellite essays.

Derrida had pointed out that Levinas was seeking to question philosophy at its deepest level. His was 'a question which can be stated only by being forgotten in the language of the Greeks; and a question which can be stated, as forgotten, only in the language of the Greeks' (Derrida 1978, 133). Plato had spoken of the 'good beyond being' in *The Republic* 509b, and thereby evoked a goodness that does not answer to presence, and Levinas has devoted himself to a radical reinterpretation of Plato's expression. As he says as early as the preface to the first edition of *De l'existence à l'existant* (1947), 'The Platonic formula that situates the Good beyond Being serves as the general guideline for this research – but does not make up its content. It signifies that the movement which leads an existent toward the Good is not a transcendence by which that existent raises itself up to a higher existence, but a departure from Being ...' (Levinas 1988, 15). The issue, then, is how we are to understand transcendence. Levinas condemns the 'false and cruel transcendence' implicit in Greek religion (Bergo, Bergo and Perpich 1998, 9). Transcendence for Hesiod and Homer is conceived as a spatial ascent, and it amounts to idolatry. For all their elevation, the gods are commensurate with humans. To the extent that western knowledge bases itself on the Greeks, it is a secularization of idolatry and a commitment to the value of the same over the other. And to the extent that Christian mysticism is a longing to be taken into the ineffable unity of the Godhead, it too derives from Greek religion. We escape idolatry only when we embark on a transcendence that is not spatial, one that occurs within immanence and disturbs it.

How can one transcend being without understanding the good to be or to confer a higher kind of being? Or, in the words that Levinas will come to use, how can one pass from 'being otherwise' to 'otherwise than being'? Two of the rationalists provide clues, one positive and one negative. René Descartes argued in the third of his *Meditations* that the infinite is not the negation of the finite; on the contrary, since there is more reality in infinite than finite substance, the idea of infinity must precede the idea of the finite. For Levinas, the infinite is the absolutely other, a transcendence that does not generate mystical theologies but that passes in the other's face. Benedict de Spinoza provides the negative clue in his *Ethics*, Book III, proposition six: '*Each thing, in so far as it is in itself, endeavors to persevere in its being*' (Spinoza 1949, 135). Taking Descartes and Spinoza in tandem, Levinas affirms that transcendence consists precisely in yielding one's *conatus essendi*, or self-maintenance in being, in favour of the other person, and this movement from being to the other *is* the good. The 'good beyond being' is thereby wrested from both Platonic metaphysics and religion and is reinterpreted as ethics.

This is not an ethics that depends on choice, for the other person has always and already made a claim on me. At no time did I contract to answer for the other. My responsibility for him or her comes from an immemorial past which has never been present. Levinas's entire thought, in all its density and difficulty, is contained in this original rethinking of Plato's thought about the good. Once formulated, it is tirelessly explored, so that Levinas's mature work can be regarded as so many variations on a theme, although some of these variations are themselves breathtaking in their daring. There is a considerable distance between *Totality and Infinity* and *Otherwise than Being*, to cite only the most dramatic and important instance, but before we can understand either the drama or the importance we must retrace our steps and go back to the beginning, as Levinas himself does in essay after essay.

A philosopher has many beginnings, and Levinas is no exception. One could cite the Plato who broaches 'the good beyond being', the Descartes who writes of the idea of the infinite, the Spinoza who formulates the *conatus essendi*, the Rosenzweig who criticizes totality, or the Bergson who conceives time as duration. More often than not, though, Levinas begins by returning to Edmund Husserl. There is a biographical as well as a philosophical reason for this. After studying at the University of Strasbourg, where he became close friends with Blanchot, Levinas went to the University of Freiburg for the summer semester of 1928 and the winter semester of 1928–9. Husserl had retired from his chair just before Levinas arrived, although he continued teaching throughout the winter semester of 1928–9 until his successor, Martin Heidegger, arrived from the University of Marburg. As it happened, Levinas gave a paper in the last meeting of Husserl's final seminar, which had been devoted to the constitution of intersubjectivity. Levinas's first publications were a review essay on Husserl's *Ideas I* in *Revue Philosophique de la France et de l'Etranger* in 1929, and his doctoral dissertation *The Theory of Intuition in Husserl's Phenomenology* (1930) which led French philosophers, including Jean-Paul Sartre, to German phenomenology. Several further expositions of Husserl's thought followed, along with introductions to Heidegger's bold rethinking of phenomenology in *Being and Time* (1927).

Although Levinas offered patient and thorough explanations of Husserl's phenomenology, which still serve as excellent guides to the subject, he expressed reservations about the master's prizing of theoretical consciousness. In the fifth of the *Logical Investigations* (1899–1901) Husserl had followed Franz Brentano in arguing that intentional experience is either a representation or based on a representation. With *Ideas I* (1913) this thesis is modified, although not sufficiently to concede that non-objectifying acts, such as affection, desire and will, help to constitute objects as meaningful. To be sure, other Husserlian notions – non-theoretical intentionality, the lifeworld, and the lived body – provide ways in which the pertinence of these acts can be acknowledged. But the Husserl of *Ideas I* and beyond holds fast to the view that all non-objectifying acts must ultimately refer to a representation. In other words, perceiving, judging and knowing are granted priority in experience, despite Husserl's claim that being *is* what is experienced. 'This is why the Husserlian concept of intuition is tainted with intellectualism and is possibly too narrow' (Levinas 1973, 94). Over the years Levinas becomes less cautious than that 'possibly' suggests. In the vocabulary of phenomenology, 'intuition' denotes experience in a wider sense than that allowed by empiricists; it includes categories and essences, and makes no presumption about how something exists. (After all, the same thing may be given in a dream, a memory, a perception, or whatever.) Under the influence of Heidegger, which can be detected as early as *The Theory of Intuition*, Levinas releases intuition from the grip of epistemology, and attends to our ways of being in the world rather than human nature. After the Second World War, however, Levinas distances himself from Heidegger for a mixture of philosophical and political reasons, and develops intriguing phenomenologies of fatigue and insomnia that exceed the frame of *Being and Time*. And in the decades to follow, he focuses on what precedes representation and interrupts it: what calls 'the face' or 'infinity' or 'the Other'.

Although Levinas never abandons phenomenology as a method, he unfolds it in his own way. Husserl heavily underlined the importance of the *epoché* or phenomenological reduction. It must come first, he says, and it must be prepared for with the greatest care. In the reduction the thesis of the natural standpoint – that reality is simply objective – is suspended. We shake off the unexamined metaphysics that we habitually absorb from science, and are left instead with experience as concretely lived. This experience can then be examined in all its originality and richness. For Levinas, Husserl's endless refining of the reduction from *Ideas I* to *The Crisis of European Sciences* (completed in 1937) leads more surely to a sterile methodology than to 'the things themselves' as promised in the *Logical Investigations*. The freedom of the reduction is the freedom of theory. Misled by granting representation pride of place in intentional life, Husserl offers no account of how the reduction is based in life as it is lived, and the reduction ends up looking uncomfortably like the natural attitude it seeks to suspend. According to *The Theory of Intuition*, the reduction is hampered by 'the intellectualist character of intuition' (Levinas 1973, 158). Later, in *Totality and Infinity*, we are told more magisterially that the 'very possibility' of the reduction 'defines representation' (Levinas 1979, 125).

It follows that the reduction will always have the effect of objectifying the other person, making a vulnerable singular individual into a representation. Consequently, the *epoche*, as formulated by Husserl, plays little role in Levinas's philosophy. What is alive in phenomenology, he thinks, is the invitation for 'consciousness to understand its own preoccupations, to reflect upon itself and thus discover all the hidden or neglected horizons of its intentionality' (Cohen 1986, 14). Intentionality, the thesis that consciousness is always consciousness of something, is of the greatest importance for him for two reasons. First, intentionality is not an attribute of consciousness but is subjectivity itself. No one is imprisoned in their minds or their selves. And second, because it is outwardly directed, intentionality contains the thought of otherness. In phenomenology, an object is not only given to consciousness but also modified according to the many horizons of intentionality. In no way is this a fall from the objective to the subjective, for the thought that constitutes the object as meaningful has already been solicited by that object. Phenomenology involves a passage from asking *what* we are thinking about to *how* we are thinking about it, and in making that move we find ourselves inquiring how an object has been positioned in and by consciousness. Here, then, at the very centre of phenomenology, Levinas finds what will destroy the hegemony of representation. For 'representation already finds itself placed within horizons that it somehow had not willed, but with which it cannot dispense' and so 'an ethical *Sinngebung*', a bestowing of meaning that is ethical not epistemological, 'becomes possible' (Levinas 1998a, 121).

It is one thing to become possible, another to be realized. The ethical *Sinngebung* occurs not with objects, which can be grasped by consciousness, but with faces which cannot be mastered. When I encounter the other as other, Levinas argues, my act of perception is interrupted thereby preventing any correlation of other and self. An ethical event occurs in a social space that is curved upward in favour of the other. So it is a non-theoretical intentionality that is operative here, although even that will be disturbed by the face. Without having to say a word, this absolutely singular individual addresses me in the mode of command: the face says, 'Thou shalt not kill' and (so Levinas adds in his last writings) 'Do not leave me to die alone'. At first one might think of the critical philosophy, and indeed Levinas can sound very Kantian when he remarks, 'The kingdom of heaven is ethical' (Levinas 1981, 183). Unlike Kant, however, Levinas focuses on the call from the singular other to the singular self, and does not venerate a universal moral law. The silent address is received by me alone, and I alone can accept responsibility for this other person. I respond by saying, as Samuel did, 'Here I am' and in doing so accept responsibility for the other, testifying not to the truth of a representation but to the glory of the infinite. Mortality is therefore witnessed in terms of the *other*'s finitude and weakness, not mine; and this marks what Levinas came to regard as a vast gulf between himself and Heidegger. As Heidegger brilliantly argues in *Being and Time* § 53, death is always my ownmost possibility, indeed the possibility of the impossibility of my existence. I am individuated by anticipating my end. Confronted by the nothingness that awaits me, I experience anxiety: not as a psychological state but as an ontological attunement.

For Levinas, the ultimate question is not 'To be or not to be' but how things stand with the other person. It is not nothingness that is truly frightening but the sheer impersonality of being, what Levinas dubs the *il y a* or 'there is'. We see Levinas emerge as an independent thinker when he titles his 1947 volume *De l'existence à l'existant*. The crucial movement imagined here is from the priority of anonymous being, which interests Heidegger, to the priority of the other person. On Levinas's analysis, the other confronts me in my enjoyment of being, and in recognizing that I am responsible for this other person I cede my place in being and become being-for-the-other. This is the way we escape the horror of the *il y a*. Levinas calls the move from being to being-for-the-other holiness, which for him is an ethical rather than a religious value. The phased counterpart of holiness is the sacred, which he understands by way of institutional religious practice. One can of course be holy within the world of the sacred, yet the sacred can easily lead one away from authentic holiness. It can even involve us in what Lucien Lévy-Bruhl calls 'participation', a state in which emotional experience gains us access to the supernatural. Levinas views this state with increasing distrust and comes to associate it with poetry as much as religion.

The passage to authentic holiness is more heavily marked in *Otherwise than Being* than in *Totality and Infinity*. 'The soul is the other in me', we are told in the later work (Levinas 1981, 191, n. 3), and indeed the whole treatise is a radical attempt to reformulate subjectivity by way of relations with the other person. If Levinas is a humanist, his is a 'humanism of the other man', as the title of one of his books puts it. Responsibility, here, does not relate to the consequences of one's free choices but indicates a state to which one has been elected by the other. 'The word *I* means *here I am*', Levinas ventures, and adds that 'The self is a *sub-jectum*; it is under the weight of the universe, responsible for everything' (Levinas 1981, 114, 115). The asymmetry between self and other which was everywhere apparent in *Totality and Infinity* is pushed to an extreme in *Otherwise than Being*, so that the self is 'obsessed' with the other, 'persecuted' by him or her and held 'hostage'.

If one is tempted to object to Levinas that his ethics are utopian, he would be the first to agree. First, they are utopian in the literal sense that I am required, in responding to the other, to yield my place in being. I thereby create 'a profound utopia' (Levinas 1998b, 145). Second, it needs to be stressed that Levinas is not describing or prescribing normative moral behaviour but merely seeking to show that the ethical has a meaning that is irreducible to representation. Ethics is not morality: the distinction between the two is sharp though not complete. Were there only I and the other in the world, I would owe everything to the other, but as soon as a third party appears, this asymmetry cannot hold sway. There is a call for justice by the third person, which brings reciprocity into play. And yet the fundamental asymmetry between the Other and the Self is supremely important, Levinas thinks. Without it, society would be in danger of becoming totalitarian. Even a small gesture such as saying 'After you' before a doorway indicates that ethical asymmetry interrupts the symmetry of morality.

In *Otherwise than Being*, communication is held to be complete only when one assumes responsibility for the other person. Levinas redraws communication from the perspective of ethics, rather than from social linguistics. In the same move he thoroughly reinterprets the phenomenological reduction. Distinguishing the Saying from the Said, he observes that the true reduction, 'the going back to the hither side of being', is none other than going back 'to the hither side of the said' (Levinas 1981, 45). It should be noted that Saying (*le dire*), should not be confused with Martin Buber's notion of dialogue, which presumes the self and other to stand on the same level. Still less should it be confused with Heidegger's *Sage*, which is also translated as 'Saying' and which the German philosopher regards as 'the being of language in its totality' (Heidegger 1982, 123). On the contrary, Saying for Levinas is an escape from being and totality; it is an addressing of oneself to another, an interruption of a settled or settling state of affairs. Inescapable as it may seem, the language of action is nonetheless misleading here, for Levinas stresses that one is *already* the hostage of the other person and so, strictly speaking, Saying bespeaks a passivity beyond the well-known dialectical duo of activity and passivity.

What is said in an address to the other is less important than that the self responds to a trace of the infinite there, and takes responsibility for this person. Inevitably, even the most naked and vulnerable Saying eventually becomes deposited in a Said: the transcendence of ethical openness becomes mired in ontological immanence. This very text is an example. The hesitations, doublings and unsayings that characterize Levinas's prose end up being smoothed out in a short encyclopaedia article. And yet the Said can be unsaid: Levinas prizes philosophy in this regard, trusting in its untiring ability to start from scratch and rethink a problem. By way of contrast, theology cannot do this, he suggests, although he seems to regard the Queen of the Sciences very narrowly, as a thematizing of a Said and a destruction of true transcendence. Theologians will object, and with reason; it is hard to recognize Karl Barth, Karl Rahner or Jürgen Moltmann – to name only a handful of the French philosopher's contemporaries – from this perspective. Levinas is more favourably disposed toward poetry than theology, for poetry can unsay itself, although in different ways than those practised by the philosophers.

Thinking of Blanchot, Levinas notes that 'the word poetry, to me, means the rupture of the immanence to which language is condemned, imprisoning itself. I do not think that this rupture is a purely aesthetic event. But the word poetry does not, after all, designate a species, the genus of which would be art' (Levinas 1996, 185, n. 4). That Blanchot writes prose, not verse, does not matter in the slightest. 'Poetry', for Levinas, is taken to interrupt representation, the image or ontology, and to be a response to the fleeting trace of the infinite in the face of the other. Poetry is not merely one of the arts, and verse has no monopoly on poetry. It is a name for that which disturbs representation. Where art freezes the other in an image, or indulges itself in the delights of incantation, poetry is by contrast a saying and an unsaying; it is therefore coordinate with transcendence, as understood ethically rather than religiously. Or to say the same thing in slightly different words, poetry interrupts art. This is not an apology for the avant garde; on the contrary, it is an elevation of ethics over aesthetics. What interests Levinas in avant-garde poetics – Blanchot, Celan, Jabès and Leiris, for instance – is that their work follows a trace and does not present a mimetic image. Presumably, though, this response to the trace could also be seen in other writers, in people as different as Jonathan Swift and Samuel Johnson, William Wordsworth and John Keats, Roberto Juarroz and Eugenio Montale.

Kevin Hart

Further reading and works cited

Bergo, B. and Perpich, D. (eds) 'Levinas's Contribution to Contemporary Philosophy', Graduate Faculty
    Philosophy Journal, 20, 2–21, 1, 1998.
Bernasconi, R. and Critchley, S. (eds) Re-Reading Levinas. Bloomington, IN, 1991.
Chalier, C. and Abensour, M. (eds) Emmanuel Lévinas. Paris, 1991.
Cohen, R. A. (ed.) Face to Face with Levinas. Albany, NY, 1986.
Davis, C. Levinas. Cambridge, 1996.
De Boer, T. The Rationality of Transcendence. Amsterdam, 1997.
Derrida, J. Writing and Difference. London, 1978.
—. Adieu to Emmanuel Levinas. Stanford, CA, 1999.
Eaglestone, R. Ethical Criticism. Edinburgh, 1997.
Gibbs, R. Correlations in Rosenzweig and Levinas. Princeton, NJ, 1992.
Heidegger, M. On the Way to Language. New York, 1982.
Lescourret, M.-A. Emmanuel Levinas. Paris, 1994.
Levinas, E. The Theory of Intuition in Husserl's Phenomenology. Evanston, IL, 1973.
—. Totality and Infinity. The Hague, 1979.
—. Otherwise than Being or Beyond Essence. The Hague, 1981.
—. Time and the Other. Pittsburgh, 1987a.
—. Collected Philosophical Papers. The Hague, 1987b.
—. Existence and Existents. Boston, 1988.
—. Difficult Freedom. Baltimore, MD, 1990a.
—. Nine Talmudic Readings. Bloomington, IN, 1990b.
—. Proper Names. Stanford, CA, 1996.
—. Discovering Existence with Husserl. Evanston, IL, 1998a.
—. Entre Nous. New York, 1998b.
—. Alterity and Transcendence. London, 1999.
Llewelyn, J. Emmanuel Levinas. London, 1995.
Peperzak, A. To the Other. West Lafayette, IN, 1993.
Poirié, F. Emmanuel Lévinas: Qui êtes-vous? Lyon, 1987.
Robbins, J. Altered Reading: Levinas and Literature. Chicago, 1999.
Spinoza, B. de. Ethics preceded by On the Improvement of the Understanding, ed. J. Gutman. New York,
    1949.

Simone de Beauvoir (1908–1986) and French Feminism

Simone de Beauvoir set the agenda for late twentieth-century feminism with her essay on the situation of women, *The Second Sex* (1949). In this work she framed many of the concepts, presuppositions and problems that have engaged feminists in the last three decades of the century. Yet her importance for the reading of feminism on both sides of the Atlantic has not always been fully acknowledged. Like Sartre, with whom she was closely associated throughout her life, she, for a time, tended to be dismissed, in the light of the triumph of Lévi-Strauss' structuralism and its appropriation by Lacanian psychoanalysis, as an adherent of an outdated existentialism which was excessively individualistic and which took too little account of the determinations of language and the forces of the unconscious. Her status as the canonical twentieth-century feminist was further undermined by various feminist critiques of Sartre's philosophy. These critiques have posed something of a difficulty for feminists, since de Beauvoir often claimed to have been philosophically unoriginal and to have applied Sartre's philosophical system in her works. From the time in 1928, when de Beauvoir began her affair with Sartre, until his death in 1980, the lives of this couple were closely linked. Despite the intense affairs which each of them had with others, they chose to make their relationship with each other essential to their jointly forged identity. They commented on, and corrected, each other's work, saw each other nearly daily when both in Paris, and corresponded regularly while apart. Given that de Beauvoir was so closely associated with a philosophy that began from a Cartesian subjective questioning, she has, from the point of view of postmodernist and poststructuralist feminists, appeared outdated. In an early and very influential paper, Michele Le Doeuff both acknowledged the importance of de Beauvoir as a feminist precursor, but criticized her adoption of existentialist categories (Le Doeuff 1980). In a later book-length discussion, Le Doeuff stressed de Beauvoir's differences from Sartre, and argued that despite her claims to the contrary, de Beauvoir transformed existentialism (1991). The project of saving de Beauvoir for feminism by asserting her originality and independence from Sartre has been taken up by a significant number of English and American feminists during the 1990s (Simons 1995). This is partly in reaction to the earlier tendency, associated with postmodernism and the emergence of feminisms of difference in the 1980s, to cast de Beauvoir as a male-identified, egalitarian feminist, who, despite her importance for the feminist movement, was philosophically misguided.

Both the treatment of de Beauvoir as completely male identified and the depiction of her as quite independent of Sartre involve distortion. The first gives de Beauvoir too little credit for having recognized and developed an account of the situation of women which both related it to, and differentiated it from, the situation of other oppressed groups. The second gives Sartre too little credit for the role he played in the postwar emergence in France of a left-wing critique of oppression which was both anti-Stalinist and anti-capitalist. The version of existentialist marxism that was developed by this couple during the 1940s and 1950s, had a widespread influence. It was disseminated through the journal Les Temps Modernes and in the plays and novels written by both authors, which constituted their contribution to a committed literature that they consciously used for political ends.

Late twentieth-century feminism would not have had the character it has had had de Beauvoir not provided her account of woman's oppression. Even those feminists who reject her existentialist presuppositions use concepts that she introduced to explain woman's situation. In particular, the idea that woman is man's other and the observation that woman is always defined in relation to man were original to de Beauvoir and have been constantly repeated. De Beauvoir did not produce an independent philosophical system. Her background, philosophical training and interests were sufficiently close to Sartre's that she was happy to influence the development of his philosophical system through discussion, and through the revisions that she made to his major philosophical works. In general she adopted a very similar philosophical outlook to his, although she was early on more sensitive to the constraints on freedom that arise from social circumstance than he was. The influence on their philosophy of the phenomenology of Husserl and Heidegger led them to take a particular interest in le veçu, the lived experience of a particular concrete situation, and from the 1940s onwards, they did much to illuminate the way in which this lived experience emerges out of the constraints of a social situation. The richness of the description of woman's situation in *The Second Sex* owes much to this involvement with capturing *le vécu*, and is one of its great strengths. It has meant, however, that the work has been able to exert an enormous influence, without its philosophical underpinnings being much discussed or very fully appreciated.

This is particularly true in the US, where Betty Friedan, Kate Millett, Shulamith Firestone and Anne Oakley were all more or less inspired by *The Second Sex*, but had read it in the philosophically illiterate Parshley translation and tended to ignore its philosophical commitments. French feminists have also sometimes adopted de Beauvoir's conclusions, while rejecting or ignoring her philosophical premises. Luce Irigaray's *Speculum of the Other Woman* (1974), announces in its title a debt to de Beauvoir's proposition that woman has been man's other. However, its presuppositions are very different to de Beauvoir's existentialism. Irigaray is indebted to Lacanian psychoanalysis, and so she seeks to transform the symbolic order. She accepts the existence of the unconscious, and accepts as a descriptive truth Lacan's claim that the language of consciousness is dominated by the law of the father and a single sexual signifier, the *phallus*. In Sartre's existentialism, by contrast, the unconscious had been replaced by the notion of bad faith. De Beauvoir also rejected the determinism and flight from responsibility that are implicit in Freud's, or Lacan's, psychoanalysis. This allowed her to criticize those elements of psychoanalysis which imply that there is no human freedom while exploiting some of its observations in order to explain women's experience. Irigaray also criticizes Lacan's version of Freudian psychoanalysis, but accepts a basically psychoanalytic framework. In some of her writings the de Beauvoirian idea that woman is other becomes transformed into the idea that there is a feminine language that is other to the masculine symbolic and which can only express itself in ambiguity and madness.

Monique Wittig takes up a different aspect of de Beauvoir's thought. Her influential paper, 'One is Not Born a Woman' (1981), reprinted in *The Straight Mind and Other Essays* (1992), echoes the first sentence of the second volume of de Beauvoir's work. Yet her separatist tendency diverges a great deal from de Beauvoir's ideal, which was for the establishment of a genuine reciprocity between the sexes, in which each would recognize the other as both sovereign subject as well as inessential object. Like some American interpreters of de Beauvoir, in particular, Judith Butler, Wittig seizes on the idea that what woman is has been defined by men, and assumes that a free choice can result in the creation of new genders which do not involve being a woman. This way of reading de Beauvoir comes very close to ascribing to her the nominalism that she rejected in the introduction of *The Second Sex*, and it underplays her emphasis on the real difference in the concrete physical situation of men and women through which they live out their existence.

During the 1950s and early 1960s, de Beauvoir saw the struggle for women's emancipa-tion as part of the wider struggle for the overthrow of capitalist and bourgeois domination. In the early 1970s she was invited to participate in the campaigns of the emerging women's liberation movement in France, and she came to recognize the need for an independent feminist struggle. This was partly due to the recognition that socialism had not brought with it genuine equality between women and men. In 1974 *Les Temps Modernes* published a special issue on the women's movement with the title, 'Les femmes s'entete', and in 1977 the journal *Questions féministes* began, with de Beauvoir as editor. During this period of involvement in the feminist movement, de Beauvoir criticized the emerging emphasis on difference and *écriture feminine* as falling back into essentialist myths, and this no doubt contributed to her being characterized as outdated and male oriented.

Simone de Beauvoir, belonged to a singularly fortunate generation of French women who were able to compete for the *agrégation* in philosophy on almost equal terms with men. This was possible for a short period during the 1920s and 1930s, and has only fairly recently become possible again (Moi 1994, 38–52). She attended lectures at the Sorbonne, and although she was not able to enrol at the prestigious *École Normale* with her male contemporaries, Sartre, Maurice Merleau-Ponty, René Maheu, Raymond Aron and Paul Nizan, she attended lectures there and was included in their discussions as they prepared for the competitive exam. In 1929, de Beauvoir came second in this exam to Sartre, who had failed in the previous year. In doing so she was the youngest person ever to have completed the *agrégation*. Her diaries from this period show her already asking the big 'existential' questions, nostalgic for the certainties of a childhood belief in an Absolute that had been provided by her Catholic background, tending towards despair at the futility of life, uncertain of her own identity and tempted by the immersion of her self in the being of some superior other (Simons 1999, 185–243). The collection of stories *When Things of the Spirit Come First*, which was rejected for publication in the 1930s and finally appeared in 1979, presents, in a fictionalized form, her experiences as a philosophy teacher, and the choices then available to educated bourgeois women of her class, as she conceived them. It also gives a fictionalized account of the death of Zaza, subject of an intense childhood friendship, who was to have married the young Merleau-Ponty, but who died tragically while involved in a conflict with her parents over his suitability as a husband (Francis and Gontier 1987, 83–8). This period of de Beauvoir's life is also recounted in the first volume of her memoirs.

The initiation of de Beauvoir's relationship with Sartre was an important turning point in her life. She says in her memoirs that she felt intellectually dominated by him, despite the fact that all the evidence points to her having been his philosophical equal. And although de Beauvoir claims that she never felt her sex to be a disadvantage while she was young, one can see operating in her life some of the forces of our construction by others that she was later to detail in *The Second Sex*. Comparing her account of her childhood with Sartre's *Les Mots* (1964), one sees that from the beginning his family represented him as a genius, whereas hers recognized her intelligence, but found it a pity that she had not been born a boy (de Beauvoir 1974, 177–8). In the second volume of the memoirs she explains that she did not see herself as a philosopher; she did not aspire to join the elite who attempt 'that conscious venture into lunacy known as a "philosophical system" from which they derive that obsessional attitude which endows their tentative patterns with universal insight and applicability.' She comments: 'As I have remarked before, women are not by nature prone to obsessions of this type' (1965, 221). Unfortunately, this translation obscures de Beauvoir's intentions. In the French text there is no reference to woman's nature, but only to 'la condition féminine' (de Beauvoir 1960, 229). What de Beauvoir is indicating is that, in the light of her upbringing as a girl in a sexist society which did not anticipate and promote female genius, she, like other women, was not prone to the level of arrogance required in order to believe that she would be able to solve philosophical conundrums on which so many great minds have foundered. Whatever the explanation, the 1930s – a period during which Sartre went to Berlin to study Husserl and Heidegger, published *Nausea* (1938) and the philosophical essays that laid the groundwork for *Being and Nothingness* (1943) – were years of relative lack of professional success for de Beauvoir.

Her first attempts at fiction were not published, and it was not until the first years of the war, when she wrote *She Came to Stay* (1943), that she found her literary and philosophical voice. This novel is a fictionalized version of a triangular relationship which existed between Sartre, de Beauvoir and her student Olga Kosakievicz, to whom the book is dedicated. The discussion of the conflict between the consciousness of reality of the protagonist of this novel, Françoise, and the other members of the triangular relationship, Xaviere and Pierre, may well have influenced Sartre's discussion of concrete relations with others in *Being and Nothingness*. If this is the case, then there is every reason to conclude that, without denying de Beauvoir's originality or importance as an influence on Sartre, one can adopt the traditional attitude of reading her novels as applications of many of the schemata outlined in Sartre's work.

The late 1940s were a period of extreme philosophical and literary productivity for de Beauvoir. In 1945, with Sartre, Merleau-Ponty, Aron, Camus, Lieris, Queneau and Olivier, she set up *Les Temps Modernes*, in which she regularly published political, literary and philosophical essays, many of which are only now appearing in English translation. She published her two most obviously philosophical works, *Pyrrhus and Cinéas* and *The Ethics of Ambiguity* in 1944 and 1947 respectively. This period culminated in her two most widely read works, *The Second Sex* (1949) and the novel, *The Mandarins* (1954), for which she received the Prix Goncourt. De Beauvoir's status as a thinker who has shaped the philosophical vocabulary and presuppositions of the late twentieth century is partly obscured by the method that she chose to use, and which she outlined in her essay, 'Littérature et Métaphysique' (1946). There she explains that when young she was torn between the abstract universality of philosophy and the concrete realities of the novel. In order to overcome this conflict she proposes a literature which is concrete, but metaphysically informed. Just as psychology can be treated theoretically, or can inform a novel which deals with concrete events, so too at least some metaphysical outlooks lend themselves to both forms of development (Fullbrook and Fullbrook 1998, 37–51). Following this statement of her desire to illuminate the universal through the concrete she chose to concentrate her efforts on her literary output, and later on her memoirs. Although she does not theorize them as such, the vehicle of the memoir is a perfect means for concretizing a philosophical outlook by locating it in a particular social milieu. De Beauvoir constructs her life story carefully as the story of the emergence of an independent consciousness, its early apprehension of death, its tendency to allow itself to be submerged by others, and its final blossoming as a socially committed, political consciousness devoted to the abolition of oppression and the establishment of an egalitarian world that conforms to the humanist marxism that Sartre expounded in *Critique of Dialectical Reason* (1960). She has been accused of having constructed her biography too carefully, and of having glossed over the moral dubiousness, and emotional cost, of her 'open' relationship with Sartre, in which they remained 'essential' to each other while engaging in other 'contingent' relationships (Bair 1990, 17–18). But this overlooks the philosophical aspect of de Beauvoir's autobiographical enterprise. In *The Second Sex*, she observes that there have been 'sincere and engaging feminine autobiographies but [she says] none can compare with Rousseau's *Confessions* and Stendhal's *Souvenirs d'egotisme*.' She attributes this to the fact that while women have explored the phenomena of the world, they have not attempted to discover meanings, and she asserts that they 'lack metaphysical resonances' (de Beauvoir 1983a, 718–21). In terms of the duality discussed in

'Littérature et Métaphysique', one might say that they have described the concrete and particular, but without attempting to draw from it its metaphysical significance. Her own biography, by contrast, is clearly constructed as a metaphysical journey first towards transcendence and engagement and then into the disturbing realms of old age, which closes off the avenues of transcendent activity and in which the body becomes an obstacle to, instead of an instrument of, transcendent activity. Because of her conscious choice of literature and autobiography as the vehicle for exploring the metaphysical dimensions of existence, her status as a philosopher has been under-estimated. But in taking this approach to the development of metaphysical themes she has been followed by many other French feminists, even those who see themselves as belonging to opposed philosophical traditions. Cixous and Kristeva, in particular, have continued along a path which refuses to choose between literature and metaphysics and have written metaphysical novels, as well as theorizing the psychological and meta-physical elements within literature. In the blurring of the boundary between philosophy and literature which has been characteristic of late twentieth-century literary theory, de Beauvoir emerges as a little acknowledged precursor.

De Beauvoir's philosophical contribution has also been overlooked for the reasons outlined above: the inadequacies of the English text of *The Second Sex*, and the fact that the blossoming of feminism in the 1970s coincided with a widespread rejection of existentialism by a new generation of thinkers intent on establishing their difference from what had gone before. Nevertheless, it is impossible to understand the complex-ities and the limitations of the account of women's oppression that is offered in *The Second Sex* unless one takes into account the philosophical context in which it was produced.

Black, indigenous and third-world women have sometimes criticized the western feminist movement for its elitist and bourgeois orientation. It is important to recognize, however, that at least some of de Beauvoir's thinking in relation to the situation of women was influenced by her exposure to Black American literature, her friendship with Richard Wright and her belief that there were parallels, as well as differences, between the situations of various oppressed groups, blacks, the working class, Jews and women (Simons 1999, 167–84). Sartre, in *Being and Nothingness*, had argued that human free will is the source of value, but that people flee the responsibility that is implied by their freedom and fall into various forms of bad faith. One of these is the spirit of seriousness: the widespread tendency to treat values as givens that have to be obeyed, and as rooted in the essences of things, rather than as residing in the choices of the people who recognize them. A particular form of this spirit of seriousness is Manicheanism, which treats some people as essentially bad and others (usually one's own kind) as essentially good. In her travelogue, *America Day by Day* (1948), de Beauvoir muses on the tendency of the Americans to see the world in terms of good and evil (de Beauvoir 1999, 65–6). In his 1946 essay, 'Anti-Semite and Jew', Sartre had also argued that the anti-Semite takes a Manichean attitude to the world and sets up the Jew as the incarnation of evil, assuming that this evil is an objective reality that justifies his passion rather than a freely adopted passionate attitude. This tendency to structure the world into a pair of opposites is, de Beauvoir thinks, the result of a fundamental feature of consciousness, and she takes from Hegel the idea that 'subject can be posed only in being opposed', an idea which she had already developed in her novel, *She Came to Stay*. The philosophical theory which explains this conflict between consciousness is given its fullest development in *Being and Nothingness*, in the sections on 'The Look' and 'Concrete Relations with Others'.

Sartre begins his mammoth tome with an account of two irreducible regions of being, being for-itself, consciousness, and being in-itself, the material things which are objects for consciousness. Consciousness is defined via the Husserlian dictum that consciousness is always consciousness of something, and from this Sartre concludes that consciousness is never an object of consciousness. This implies that the ego, the self as an object of consciousness, is different from consciousness. Consciousness is transcendent, in the sense that it cannot be identified with any idea or thing in the world. The ego is a thing in the world, an empirical self with a value and meaning derived from free consciousness. The transcendence, or nothingness, of consciousness is the foundation of human freedom. It is often overlooked by feminist interpreters of Sartre that in the middle of his major book Sartre introduces a third irreducible ontological moment, being for-others. In his early essay, 'The Transcendence of the Ego' (1937), Sartre claimed that his theory of being in-itself could solve the problem of solipsism. By the time he was writing *Being and Nothingness*, he had decided that this was a mistake. It seems that it was at this point that his reading of a draft of de Beauvoir's novel, *She Came to Stay*, provided him with a solution to this problem (Simons 1995). In the look of the other I have an immediate apprehension of the existence of others, and feel myself reduced to an object for others. Thus my ego, the object that is myself, is an object for others as well as an object for my consciousness. The fact that I experience the look of the other as a threat to the sovereignty of my evaluation of the world sets up a conflict between consciousnesses not unlike Hegel's, although Sartre refuses to believe that any automatic dialectic of history will resolve the conflict. Sartre then describes two fundamental attitudes to the other consciousness which arise out of this conflict. The attitude of indifference, desire, sadism and hate involves denying the transcendent consciousness of the other, taking one's own consciousness as sovereign and objectifying the other. The attitude of love, language and masochism involves attempting to incorporate the transcendence of the other, accepting one's objectification and adopting an attitude of dependence towards the other's transcendence which is assumed to provide an objective ground of value outside the self. Both of these fundamental attitudes are manifestations of bad faith. In a short section on the Us-object, Sartre suggests that an individual can be objectified as a member of a class and that this is the origin of class consciousness. In 'Anti-Semite and Jew', he uses these schemata to explain the concrete situation of the Jews who find themselves hated by the anti-Semite. There he claims that it is the anti-Semite who creates the Jew.

It is illuminating to read de Beauvoir's *The Second Sex* in the light of this schematic representation of concrete relations with others. If we do so we find that her claim that woman is other amounts to the assertion that women find themselves in a concrete situation in which they are objectified by men. Unlike Jews and blacks, however, who are also objectified as a class, women are scattered among the male population, and this makes them particularly prone to adopt versions of the attitudes of love and masochism, to which de Beauvoir adds narcissism and mysticism. These are all forms of what she calls the fall into immanence in which a conscious subject fails to recognize its transcendence and behaves as though it were a mere thing in-itself, dependent for its meaning on some exterior transcendence.

While I have here emphasized the validity of interpreting de Beauvoir's most influential essay as incorporating structures to be found in *Being and Nothingness*, it should also be recognized that there are differences of detail and of emphasis in the way these schema are developed by Sartre and de Beauvoir. The relationship between their philosophies is currently hotly contested, and a consensus is unlikely to emerge until de Beauvoir's early philosophy becomes more widely available, and until feminists overcome their widespread aversion to taking Sartre seriously. Reading de Beauvoir's early essays, it seems fair to say that one feature which characterizes her method, and differentiates it from Sartre's, is her emphasis on ambiguity. Faced with the choice between the moralism of clean hands and the effectiveness of political expediency in 'Idéalism Moral et Réalism Politique' (1945) she asserts the need for an effective morality. Faced with the choice between the concreteness of literature and the universality of metaphysics in 'Litérature et Métaphysique' (1946) she adopts a method of discovering the universal through the concrete situation. Setting up the situation of humanity in *An Ethics of Ambiguity* (1947), she emphasizes the ambiguity of a consciousness that is flesh, neither determined like a mere material object nor absolutely free like a disembodied spirit. Although she does not consciously develop the theme of ambiguity in *The Second Sex*, there is a sense in which it also haunts this text. Describing the fall into immanence, which she claims has been characteristic of woman's reaction to her situation, she says that this represents a moral fault if the subject consents to it, and if it is inflicted on the subject it spells frustration and oppression. Two incompatible themes seem to war throughout the text. On the one hand woman's situation is one of oppression in which freedom is curtailed. On the other hand women freely submit to the temptations of a situation in which they are able to flee the anguish of moral responsibility. They alienate their freedom in narcissism or love or mystical devotion, rather than consciously taking the responsibility for the world on their shoulders. It is perhaps this ambiguity, which de Beauvoir consciously emphasized, which has allowed so many divergent feminist developments of her text. This may seem to be a fault. But her insistence on not oversimplifying for the sake of a metaphysical system was conscious. And in the light of this emphasis on ambiguity we can see that her resistance to calling herself a philosopher was itself a philosophical stance. She relates that she had no confidence that words could really capture the plenitude of things. Here she is quite at odds with more recent feminists who have tended to reject the idea of a reality beyond words which is only partly represented by them. From de Beauvoir's point of view, words already universalize experience, categorizing different concrete totalities in terms of their shared general features. The philosopher who sets out an abstract system arrogantly universalizes a particular point of view. De Beauvoir resisted this, wanting rather to describe a concrete situation so that others could take from it as many generalities as were still relevant. She succeeded mightily in *The Second Sex*, in which many women of her generation and of later generations have recognized their own conflicts and the outlines of a situation that they share, and which allowed women to come to a fuller consciousness of the concrete realities of their situation. But the subtlety of her philosophical position has been overlooked, and her descendants have tended to adopt one or other of the attitudes which she held in ambiguous tension. The materialist feminists and social constructionists are her most conscious descendants, but they discount the little place that there still exists for freedom and agency in her philosophy of ambiguity. Judith Butler takes the opposite stance, making gender, which is identified with the sexed body, into a free act of performativity and under-emphasizing the constraints of situation. Essentialist feminists of difference are furthest from de Beauvoir's explicit pronouncements, but even they show, in their interest in dualities within the history of philosophy, the marks of her analysis. No contemporary French feminist, has been a completely faithful daughter of de Beauvoir, reproducing her mother's text. Most have repudiated what they take to be her errors. And yet, just as with daughters of flesh and blood who assert their difference from their mothers while reproducing so many of their features, none of the debates within feminism would have developed in the way that they have if de Beauvoir had not set the questions that she did, and had not provided us with the conflicting wealth of observations that make up her most influential text.

Karen Green

Further reading and works cited

Bair, D. *Simone de Beauvoir. A Biography*. London, 1990.

Barnes, H. 'Self-Encounter in *She Came to Stay*', in *The Literature of Possibility*. London, 1961.

Bergoffen, D. *The Philosophy of Simone de Beauvoir*. Albany, NY, 1997.

de Beauvoir, S. *Pyrrhus and Cinéas*, Paris, 1944.

—. 'Idéalism Moral et Réalism Politique', *Les Temps Modernes*, 1, 1945.

—. 'Littérature et Métaphysique', *Les Temps Modernes*, 1, 1946.

—. *The Mandarins*. London, 1960.

—. *Ethics of Ambiguity*. New York, 1962.

—. *The Prime of Life*. Harmondsworth, 1965a.

—. *She Came to Stay*. London, 1965b.

—. *Memoirs of a Dutiful Daughter*. New York, 1974.

—. *The Second Sex*. Harmondsworth, 1983a.

—. *When Things of the Spirit Come First: Five Early Tales*. London, 1983b.

—. *America Day by Day*. Berkeley, CA, 1999.

Francis, C. and Gontier, F. *Simone de Beauvoir: A Life A Love Story*. New York, 1987.

Fullbrook, E. and Fullbrook, K. *Simone de Beauvoir and Jean-Paul Sartre*. London, 1993.

—. *Simone de Beauvoir: A Critical Introduction*. Cambridge, 1998.

Irigaray, L. *Speculum of the Other Woman*. Ithaca, NY, 1984.

Le Doeuff, M. 'Simone de Beauvoir and Existentialism', *Feminist Studies*, 6, 1980.

—. *Hipparchia's Choice*. Oxford, 1991.

Lundgren-Gothlin, E. *Sex and Existence*. Hanover, NH, 1996.

Moi, T. *Feminist Theory and Simone de Beauvoir*. Oxford, 1990.

—. *Simone de Beauvoir: The Making of an Intellectual Woman*. Oxford, 1994.

Pilardi, J. *Simone de Beauvoir Writing the Self*. Westport, CT, 1999.

Sartre, J.-P. *Les Mots*. Paris, 1964.

—. *Being and Nothingness*. London, 1995.

Schwarzer, A. *After the Second Sex*. New York, 1984.

Simons, M. (ed.) *Feminist Interpretations of Simone de Beauvoir*. University Park, PA, 1995.

—. *Beauvoir and the Second Sex*. Lanham, MA, 1999.

Vintges, K. *Philosophy as Passion*. Bloomington, IN, 1996.

Wenzel, H. '*Simone de Beauvoir Witness to a Century*', *Yale French Studies*, 72, 1986.

Wittig, M. 'One is Not Born a Woman', in *The Straight Mind and Other Essays*. Boston, 1992.

Claude Lévi-Strauss (1908–)

Claude Lévi-Strauss is the inventor of structural anthropology, which derives its name from one of its major sources of inspiration, structural linguistics. His ideas and theories have provided new ways of approaching many fundamental anthropological problems, such as the nature of kinship ties, the significance of totemism, the purpose of classification or the meaning of so-called primitive myths. As a writer and a thinker, however, his influence extends beyond the field of anthropology. His writings have had an impact, in particular, on French philosophy (even if the impact, here, is most evident in the form of a conflict between anthropology and philosophy), psychoanalysis and literary criticism. He was also, albeit unwittingly, at the origin of what became in the Paris of the 1960s, the intellectual fashion of structuralism.

Lévi-Strauss's first major book was *The Elementary Structures of Kinship*. It immediately attracted the attention not only of anthropologists but also the broader intellectual community. Simone de Beauvoir, who at the time was writing *The Second Sex*, and the novelist and philosopher of the erotic Georges Bataille, were among the first to review it.

Lévi-Strauss wrote most of *The Elementary Structures* (1949) in New York during the Second World War. He had travelled there as a Jewish refugee fleeing occupied France. Once in New York, he attended the lectures of the Prague School linguist Roman Jakobson where he discovered for the first time structural linguistics. The event was to be a decisive one for the history of structuralism. It was the assimilation of this body of thought into anthropology that was to enable Lévi-Strauss to assemble the various half-formulated ideas and intuitions that he had had so far – including meditations brought about by the contemplation of wild flowers on the border of Luxembourg in 1940 – into the fundamental tenets of structuralism. One aspect of linguistic theory that was particularly important to Lévi-Strauss was the emphasis that it placed on the unconscious activity of the mind.

Structural linguistics, as developed by Swiss linguist Ferdinand de Saussure, showed that language, as a social institution, is governed by rules that are unconscious. When we speak with one another, when we string together sequences of sounds into meaningful sentences, we are not normally aware of the organizing rules that govern what we are doing. Lévi-Strauss proposed that other kinds of social institutions, such as the institution of marriage, for example, are governed by unconscious rules of a similar kind.

Just as the role of linguistics is to discover and analyse what determines, at an unconscious level, our use of language, the role of anthropology, for Lévi-Strauss, is to uncover, beyond empirically observed reality, the unconscious structures and schemas that are the basis of social institutions. And, for Lévi-Strauss, access to the level of the unconscious is what guarantees the objectivity of the anthropologist's observations, since it enables him or her to bypass the potentially misleading secondary interpretations of those involved in the phenomena being studied.

How does the recourse to the unconscious apply to Lévi-Strauss's kinship theory? Different cultures have very different ideas about what constitutes a family. Lévi-Strauss shows, however, that the many different types of kinship systems observed by anthropologists are reducible to a small number of recurring elementary structures. Influenced by the seminal essay *The Gift* by French sociologist Marcel Mauss, Lévi-Strauss proposed that marital alliances between groups took the classic form of reciprocal gift exchanges, the gifts in this case being women. He hypothesized that the hidden, *unconscious,* function of kinship systems was to regulate the exchange of women between groups and ensure the continuity of these exchanges. Thus, what Lévi-Strauss terms 'elementary structures of kinship' corresponds to the basic patterns of the exchange of women between social groups.

He distinguished two basic forms of exchange, which he labelled 'restricted' and 'generalized' (the latter is also referred to as 'marriage in a circle'). The model of the first type of exchange is that of a straight swap between two groups. In the second type, 'generalized' exchange, the schema involves at least three groups related so that A gives to B, who gives to C, who gives back to A. Exchange in this case is indirect and hence more risky, but also potentially more rewarding since it involves a larger number of groups.

Another aspect of linguistic theory that has had a major impact on Lévi-Strauss's thought is the discovery that the sound system of a language does not consist of an aggregation of isolated sounds (phonemes) but in the relationships between those sounds. Phonemes have no value of their own; they are negative entities that exist in and through their opposition to other sounds: the sound [p] is only [p] because it is not [b]. Lévi-Strauss's kinship theory adapts this basic insight to anthropology. Previously, anthropologists, such as the great British anthropologist Sir Alfred Radcliffe-Brown, had assumed that the unit of structure from which kinship systems are built is the elementary family, consisting of a man and his wife and their child or children. For Lévi-Strauss, on the contrary, what is elementary is not families, which are isolated units, but the relationships between those units, in other words the systems of affinal alliances brought about by the movement of reciprocity.

The social rule that brings about the exchange of women is the incest taboo. Lévi-Strauss relates the incest taboo to rules of exogamy, which are rules that require marriage outside of a particular group or category of individuals. His conception is that the primary function of the incest taboo is to oblige individuals to marry out. The incest taboo forces the kin group to make alliances with strangers and thereby create a community. The emergence of the incest taboo – the first social rule – is therefore associated with the emergence of human society itself.

Here, too, Lévi-Strauss's understanding is inspired by linguistic theory, in particular the theory of the phoneme. As purely differential units, phonemes are the means by which two domains are articulated: sound and meaning. In a similar way, although at another level, the incest taboo may also be seen as the means by which two domains are articulated, in this case the domains of nature and culture. And, in a similar way that linguistic rules ensure the communication and circulation of words, the rules of exogamy ensure the communication and circulation of women. In the Lévi-Straussian paradigm, the exchange of words and the exchange of women are similar kinds of phenomena.

One of the reasons why Lévi-Strauss turned to linguistics for inspiration was that it had reached, in its recent developments, a degree of scientific rigour that did not exist in other social sciences. Lévi-Strauss hoped that, by using the methods of linguistics, anthropology might be able to work towards a similar level of scientificity. It is this project that often defines the way in which structuralism is portrayed. It is true that, according to his own stated aims, Lévi-Strauss turned to linguistic theory to help him lay down the foundations of scientifically rigorous methods of analysis in anthropology. However, to see Lévi-Strauss's works exclusively in these terms is reductionist, and conceals the overdetermined nature of his writings, and the often speculative and hazardous nature of his interpretations.

It would be misleading to see Lévi-Strauss's work simply as an application of the methods of structural linguistics to anthropology. Often, as is the case with the kinship theory that I have outlined above, linguistics is brought to bear on anthropology by way of extended analogies. Metaphorical thinking is fundamental to Lévi-Strauss's works, as one can see in his invention of such notions as 'bricolage' – a term he used to describe the kind of intellectual DIY used by myths to create new narratives out of the fragments and debris of old narratives – or in his choice of a book title such as *La Pensée sauvage* (the title relies on a pun: 'pensées' are 'thoughts', but 'la pensée sauvage' is also a wild flower, the Viola Tricolor, the implication being that his book is concerned with 'wild' as opposed to 'domesticated' thinking).

Lévi-Strauss's work on primitive myths illustrates even more clearly the duality that opposes the scientist to the imaginative thinker. On the one hand, using linguistic theory, Lévi-Strauss develops a complex methodology for the analysis of myths, which enables a quasi mathematical formalization of their hidden structures. He decomposes myths into the 'codes' that they use (a code is something like a concealed extended metaphor), their 'armature' (the structural schema underlying a myth or group of myths) and their 'message' (what the myth means). But these concepts are themselves metaphors of a kind, approximations, which Lévi-Strauss is the first to admit possess a degree of indeterminacy and even vagueness. The term 'armature', for example, is borrowed from musicology. It comes from the French for a key signature, the symbols placed at the beginning of each stave which indicate the tonality or key of a composition. By analogy, an armature, in mythology, is the hidden schema that provides the underlying principle of structural unity of a myth.

That Lévi-Strauss should have borrowed from musicology is not coincidental. One of the fundamental themes of the *Mythologiques* – Lévi-Strauss's tetralogy on Amerindian mythology which was published between 1964 and 1971 – is the close affinity that exists between myth and music. In the 'Overture' (the parts of this book are named after various musical forms) to the first volume, *The Raw and the Cooked*, it is not Saussure or Jakobson whom Lévi-Strauss identifies as the founding father of the structural analysis of myths but Wagner. One reason for this is that the recurrence of certain musical themes in Wagner's operas, such as the theme of the renunciation of love in the *Rhinegold*, link episodes in the story which appear to be unrelated but which Lévi-Strauss sees as constituting structural variations of one another.

What motivated Lévi-Strauss in his interpretations of myths was to uncover an order behind what, at first, may appear arbitrary or even absurd (he saw Freud's interpretations of dreams as a model in this respect). Amerindian myths constitute surreal narratives that, at first, do not seem to make much sense. And, as in dreams, their content is uncensored. The Amazonian Tucuna myth M354, which serves as the starting point and guiding thread of volume 3 of the *Mythologiques*, *The Origin of Table Manners*, tells the story of the hunter Monmanéki's quest for a wife. After several unsuccessful marriages with various animals, including a frog which he impregnates by urinating in the hole in which it was hiding, Monmanéki marries a fellow human being. This is how the myth concludes. In order to fish, Monmanéki's wife, who possessed magical powers, would separate into two at the waist. Leaving the lower half of her body behind, the torso would swim into a river where the smell of flesh would attract many fish which it would then catch. Through various twists in the narrative, the torso eventually becomes affixed to Monmanéki's back. It begins to starve Monmanéki to death by stealing his food, then defecates all over him. Monmanéki finally escapes and his wife transforms into a parrot and flies away. (See below for an interpretation of this myth.)

The basic hypothesis underlying the *Mythologiques* is that myths come into being by a process of transformation of one myth into another. For Lévi-Strauss myths do not have any meaning in themselves but only in relation to each other and therefore have to be studied in the course of their transformation from one into another in order to unlock their meanings. To illustrate Lévi-Strauss's method is always problematic because wherever one starts one is always breaking into a chain, or even several chains, of transformations. Equally, wherever one stops will always fall short of arriving at a final interpretation, since it is in the very nature of myths to always be in the process of becoming other myths, none of which contains the final meaning.

Each myth is submitted to an analysis which reveals its connections to other myths. These are progressively brought into the picture and in turn analysed. Lévi-Strauss follows step by step the paths indicated by the myths themselves and which correspond to the paths of their coming into being, drawing something like a map of the lines of mythical descent.

For example, in *The Raw and the Cooked*, Lévi-Strauss shows that a Bororo myth (the 'reference myth' M1), which tells the story of the origin of rainwater, is in fact an inversion of another myth (M7–12) told by a neighbouring population, the Gé, which tells the story of how humans first obtained fire from a jaguar. M1 is a myth about the origin of fire metamorphosed into a myth about the origin of water.

As the reader follows these transformations she is taken on a journey from the tropical forests of central Brazil to the state of Oregon on the Pacific Coast of North America. In the process, series of affiliated myths are integrated into broader units and gradually the picture of a total system – compared by Lévi-Strauss to a nebula – emerges.

The underlying theme with which the whole of Amerindian mythology is concerned, according to Lévi-Strauss, is that of the creation of human culture as an order separate from nature. The purpose of Amerindian myths is to try to explain this founding division, and the numerous other divisions that come in its wake, such as that between day and night, land and sea, man and woman, all the way down to those affecting daily life, such as the distinction between edible and non-edible plants. Lévi-Strauss shows that different populations express the theme of the passage from nature to culture using different symbolic 'codes'. In the South American corpus, it is symbolized by cooking, the transformation of raw food (nature) into food that is ready for human consumption (culture). This explains the symbolic importance of fire, the means of cooking, which is seen as a mediating term between earth and the sky, nature and culture. In the myths of the North American corpus, the symbols which are used to encode the opposition between nature and culture change. What marks the passage from nature to culture is no longer the mediation of cooking, but the invention of costumes, ornaments and the institution of commercial exchanges. Where South American myths oppose the raw to the cooked,

North American myths oppose the naked to the clothed, each opposition being in a relationship of transformation to the other.

The *Mythologiques* rest on what constitutes, in effect, a theory of intertextuality (although the word did not yet exist at the time that Lévi-Strauss was writing). Each myth is defined and understood in terms of its intertextual relationships to other myths (one can see, here again, the influence of the linguistic idea that phonemes are purely negative entities, defined entirely in terms of their relationship to other phonemes).

And Lévi-Strauss's role, as mythographer, is to decipher the hidden logic that explains the transformation of one element in one myth into another element in another. The character of the female torso in the Tucuna myth that I have already cited is explained in this way (*Mythologiques*, vol. 3, 'The Mystery of the Woman Cut into Pieces'). She is not an original creation but the South American version of a character that occurs in North American mythology, a woman-frog. Lévi-Strauss's explanation is that the character of the woman-frog expresses *metaphorically* the idea of a woman who in French would be described, also metaphorically, as 'collante' (she won't let go). The female torso affixed to her husband's back expresses the same idea, but literally. Seen differently, one might say that whereas the North American myth relies on metaphor (a relationship of resemblance) to convey its message, the South American myth relies on *metonymy* (a relationship of contiguity). Hence, Lévi-Strauss argues that as we pass from one hemisphere to the other, metaphor converts into metonymy. And it is this rhetorical manipulation that brings about the simultaneous transformation of one mythological character into another.

The myths that are linked in a series of transformations are treated as a cognate group. Each myth in the group, however dissimilar it appears to be from other myths in the group, is related to a common armature, a logico-sensible schema that is the matrix of that transformational group. The schema has no concrete existence. It is a system of interrelated categories or concepts underlying each group of myths and whose features are deduced by the mythographer. It is, as Lévi-Strauss puts it, the virtual chess board on which the myths of a given transformational series play out their respective games.

Myths use such schemas as logical tools to resolve various formally similar problems by linking them together and treating them as one. In *The Origin of Table Manners* (1968), for example, Lévi-Strauss analyses the schema of the canoe journey, to which many of the myths, including the above Tucuna myth, are said to be related. Myths that draw on this schema are all fundamentally concerned with the problem of distance: geographical distance, but also the distance between celestial bodies and the distance between human beings.

The occupants of the canoe are the moon and the sun. In astronomical terms, the problem that the schema enables mythical thought to tackle is: at what distance should the moon be from the sun in order to guarantee the regular alternation of night and day? If the moon and sun become too far apart, says Amerindian mythology, there is a danger that a total disjunction between night and day will occur, resulting in either eternal night or eternal day (in mythology, a common state of affairs prior to the institution of human culture). If they are too close, there is an equally dangerous risk of a conjunction of night and day (resulting in such disruptions as eclipses).

The schema of the canoe journey maps these astronomical concerns onto the social problem of marriage, and the need for human beings to invent the right social institutions for them to live at the correct distance from one another – like the moon and the sun, neither too far nor too close. In this way, the schema establishes a formal homology between the opposition, on the one hand, between night and day, disjunction and conjunction, and on the other, between the two kinds of marriages against which society must guard itself in order to continue functioning properly: an excessively 'distant' marriage, such as the ones that Monmanéki contracts with animal species rather than fellow human beings, and excessively 'close' marriages, such as an endogamous or incestuous marriage, the dangers of which are dramatized by the story of the female torso affixed to her husband's back.

Life in the canoe, at the mid-point in its journey, represents a cosmological and social ideal where moon and sun, husband and wife, each at their own end of the boat, are kept at exactly the right distance from one another to guarantee a harmonious life.

Lévi-Strauss's analyses of myths as transformations of other myths provide him with a general theory of aesthetic creation which, elsewhere in his works, he has applied to other kinds of creations. *The Way of the Masks*, a study of the masks made by the North American Salish and Kwakiutl, is a book about how populations comes to acquire their own distinctive aesthetic style. It shows that different types of masks, belonging to neighbouring populations, form part of an overarching system of transformations within which the style of each mask may be interpreted as a negation of the style of another. Each population borrows stylistic features which it then transforms to make its own. In *The View from Afar*, Lévi-Strauss traces the myth-like transformations that, from Chrétien de Troyes's medieval romance to Wagner's opera, have affected the Perceval legend. And in *Regarder Écouter Lire*, he applies the logic of mythical transformations to classical painting. He identifies transformations in three versions of *The Arcadian Shepherds*, two painted by Nicholas Poussin in the 1630s and one earlier version by Guercino. Lévi-Strauss argues that the three paintings correspond to three stages in a sequence of transformations in the course of which Guercino's original composition is gradually assimilated by Poussin to be reborn as Poussin's *Arcadian Shepherds*. Lévi-Strauss traces, in particular, the transformation of the skull which occupies a prominent position in the earliest version of the painting, is reduced in the second, then disappears in the last, to be replaced by a mysterious female figure whom Lévi-Strauss interprets as the embodiment of death.

The *Mythologiques* has concerned the literary critic perhaps more than any other work by Lévi-Strauss. In it, Lévi-Strauss formulates one of the key twentieth-century theories of myth, providing new hypotheses about the nature of mythical discourse, the processes of creation behind it and its place and function in human society. The *Mythologiques* also demonstrate the application, to over a thousand myths, of an original method of analysis, whose value and limits Lévi-Strauss constantly comments upon at the same time as he puts it into practice.

There is, however, another quite different explanation of why the *Mythologiques* are particularly relevant to critical theory. As both Roland Barthes and Jacques Derrida have remarked about this text, one of its distinguishing features lies in the unusual status of Lévi-Srauss's critical discourse. Derrida describes it as 'mythomorphic' because it has 'the shape of that about which it speaks' (1978, 286). Barthes sees it as partaking in the cultural revolution that has seen the transformation of critical discourse into a literary genre (Barthes 1987). It corresponds to Barthes's ideal of the 'writerly' text, which weaves together many discourses and codes and involves the reader in an active role of production rather than a passive role of consumption.

These views reflect Lévi-Strauss's own concept that if all myths are transformations of other myths, his own interpretations of Amerindian mythology are themselves simply another version of it, its latest transformation to date. And, in this respect, the *Mythologiques* may be seen as a form of literary creation in their own right, a postmodern text made up of a collage of fragments.

Lévi-Strauss's conception of his relationship to the myths that he studies involves, at its very heart, the notion of a playful and creative interaction between myth and mythographer. In *Histoire de Lynx*, the second of two additions to the *Mythologiques*, Lévi-Strauss uses a chess metaphor to describe the mythographer's task. Myths are the opponent, and the aim of the analyst is to guess his opponent's strategy – in the present case, the hidden rules of transformation that connect, like so many moves in the mythical game, one myth to another. And, each time that a myth is told or read (retold, reread) a new game is played, each one revealing new networks of structural relations and hence generating new versions of the myth in question.

Boris Wiseman

Further reading and works cited

Barthes, R. *Critcism and Truth*. London, 1987.
Derrida, J. *Writing and Difference*. London, 1978.
Hénaff, M. *Claude Lévi-Strauss and the Making of Structural Anthropology*. Minneapolis, MN, 1998.
Lévi-Strauss, C. *The Savage Mind*. London, 1966.
—. *The Elementary Structures of Kinship*. London, 1968.
—. *Mythologiques*, 4 vols. London, 1970–81.
—. *Tristes tropiques*. Harmondsworth, 1976.
—. *Structural Anthropology*. Harmondsworth, 1977.
—. *The Origin of Table Manners*. New York, 1978a.
—. 'Preface'. R. Jakobson, in *Six Lectures on Sound and Meaning*. Hassocks, 1978b.
—. *Myth and Meaning*. London, 1978c.
—. *The Way of the Masks*. London, 1983.
—. *The View from Afar*. New York, 1985.
—. *Histoire de Lynx*. Paris, 1991a.
—. *De Près et de Loin: Conversations with Claude Lévi-Strauss*. Chicago, 1991b.
—. *Regarder Écouter Lire*. Paris, 1993.
Mauss, M. *The Gift*. London, 1990.
Paz, O. *Claude Lévi-Strauss: An Introduction*. London, 1971.

Jean Genet (1910–1986)

Jean Genet is rare among twentieth-century French authors for the speed with which his reputation became established. The author's personal dramas, his 'canonization' by Jean-Paul Sartre and Jean Cocteau, the *succes-de-scandale* which still helps to sell his books, all contributed to an immense celebrity and large numbers of readers, from very early in his career. Genet's works, the most celebrated are his five novels and five dramatic texts, are marked by his simultaneous criticism of, and participation in, radical politics, as well as his obsession with role-playing and identity; as such they anticipate postmodern apprehensions and techniques. The postmodernism in his works is established, as it were, by an avant-garde writing style, a style which often prompts structuralist or deconstructionist modes of reading because of its inherent difficulty and lack of transparency. As Genet himself said of his own works in an essay in *Tel Quel*, his texts resist simple meanings and dramatize the impossibility of pinning down interpretation (Genet 1967).

One of the most important aspects of Genet's writing is the ways in which it requires a rethinking of the boundaries between art and reality, the aesthetic and the political. Thus, far from erasing the irreducible existence of the real (most often blemished by multifaceted evil, the suffering, the isolation and the marginality of the alienated beings whom he obsessively represents in his texts), Genet instead highlights the boundaries that separate fiction from reality. His aestheticism metamorphoses, one might say, the wounds of humanity: the spiritual misery, principally, and its physical abscesses generated by the division of humanity between those who are hand in glove with the reigning order and those who are excluded or who deliberately exclude themselves (Malgron 1988, 34). Genet's writing, beyond the perverse denial of the castration that it constantly betrays, in its taste for misrepresentation, in its games of veils and mirrors, appears, on the one hand, as an attempt at identity recovery or, if one likes, as a defence mechanism (Derrida 1981). His fiction, an epic which tells of internal suffering, corresponds on the other hand to a double postulation: to declare oneself in order to approach the image which hides within us, all the while constantly dissimulating behind a fictional image reflected in a mirror of illusion (Brook and Halpern 1979, 12).

Autobiographical in scope, his novels and plays illuminate the possibilities of survival among men, and sometimes women, bound together by fierce, unrelenting erotic desire that illuminates and transfigures the 'margins' (Foucault 1994, 119–20). As a chronicler of outcasts, lost causes and the underworld, Genet carefully scrutinizes homosexual, black or Palestinian reality. Though his novels are intricate explorations of the questions of identity, primarily of Genet and the men he loves, his plays are, on the other hand, ritualized means for staging and demolishing identity. Throughout his work, he combines crimes and innocence, obscenities and tenderness, blasphemies and mysticism, and seeks to exhaust his creative desire in an excess of scandalous images and of identity quests which incessantly speak to us of imprisoned and suffering beings (Genet 1991, 41).

Genet's narrative works took six years to write, at the frenetic pace of a novel per year. From 1944 to 1949 they succeeded one another very quickly, *Notre-Dame-des-Fleurs* (1944) (*Our Lady of the Flowers*, 1963), *Miracle de la rose* (1946) (*Miracle of the Rose*, 1965), *Pompes funèbres* (1948) (*Funeral Rites*, 1970), *Querelle de Brest* (1944) (*Querelle*, 1974) and *Journal du voleur* (1949) (*The Thief's Journal*, 1965). In these five texts, which all integrate, more or less directly, autobiographical elements, Genet varied the models successively, using three different versions of the novel form: the autobiographical novel, the novel written in the third person and the journal.

The first quasi-autobiographical novel, *Notre-Dame-des-Fleurs*, was written in jail over an extended time as his manuscripts were constantly confiscated by prison officials. The very circumstances of the story highlight in fact Genet's sexual identity. The story is narrated by a masturbating prisoner, Louis Culafroy, alias Divine, who tells us that the characters he/she describes are products of his/her erotic fantasies conceived under the hot wool blanket of his/her bed. At once man and woman, as a transvestite provided with a double designation, this narrator, cast under the sign of a hybrid nature, excessive and beyond limiting definition (Dollimore 1991, 314), has no intention of settling for only one identity, sexual or otherwise. The story is filled with sexually explicit descriptions of male prostitution, through which Divine transforms him/herself into an uncanny being, neither male nor female, whose dynamics lie in the double negation of sexualized identity that has no stable sex/gender. All the characters created in this work are masturbatory fantasies, characters chosen for that evening's delight. Genet thus defined throughout this first novel the psychological nature of fantasy; the characters themselves often 'dream' their sexual encounters with each other (Genet 1979, 33).

Genet's second novel, *Miracle de la rose*, amounts to a hymn to Harcamone, a French criminal of the 1930s whom Genet would have met at Fontevrault Prison. The author describes his fascination for this murderer, while recalling the years he spent in Mettray prison. This complex, often mystical novel is structured around the development of the author's gay passions. In fact, as Edmund White has suggested, the book's scrutiny of prison life is plotted as the development of a mounting gay passion and the exploration of alternative gay identities in which Genet moves from passive relations with prisoners to assuming butch roles (1993, 75). It explores the tendency of lovers to leave men for more 'masculine' prisoners as well as the nuances of sexual relations between older men and young boys. What stands out above all is the miraculous world in which the action takes place, since Harcamone transforms, in his writing, the hard cold prison in which he lives into a world of gentleness and flowers. The work is presented as a long series of love scenes in which mutual affection between men is revealed, in its own time, as a series of transformations and connections.

In contrast to the two preceding novels, where his protagonists are only mental constructs – even if Harcamone was born of a real individual – in his third autobiographical novel entitled *Pompes funèbres*, Genet presents someone whose existence he has shared. Dedicated to Jean Decarnin, a twenty-year-old communist militant killed on the barricades at the time of the Paris liberation, this work is a direct response to real-life events. The author started it less than a month after the death of his lover, at the height of grief. The book proceeds through a series of impersonations; for instance, Genet and Decarnin become a young German (Erik) and his lover, the burly public executioner of Berlin. Hatred becomes love: the dead inhabit the bodies of the living, as when a survivor eats the dead body of his enemy, believing that by his act of cannibalism, he might simultaneously ingest the virtues of the defeated dead man (cannibals are said to steal the virtues of the defeated through eating their noble organs) (Moraly 1988, 54). The novel can be understood as 'incantatory' (or as literary critics say, performative) in two senses: as a ritual to resuscitate Decarnin (Derrida 1981, 92), and as an exorcism through the profanation of Genet's grief and mourning (Malgron 1988, 71–2).

Genet's fourth novel, *Querelle de Brest*, is narrated in the third person as an episode in the life of a sailor, Georges Querelle, a man without faith or morality, who kills in all his ports of call, and manages neither to be pursued nor even suspected. Through the behaviour and choices of this hero, Genet shows us that the prejudice that makes gays 'unnatural' beings responds to the need that most homophobic individuals have to deny their own homosexual urges. Thus, instead of protesting against this absurd prejudice, Genet accentuates the absurdity of it in his novel, while at the same time representing Querelle's sexual delights as the pleasures of an intellectual nature. This aspect of the novel has made many critics regard *Querelle de Brest* as Genet's strongest book. Its dual themes are repressed homosexual desire and violence (Moraly 1988, 86). Sexual attraction to men is rigidly, bitterly denied, while emerging as a form of hero-worship, a substitute for denied heterosexual desire, or as an expiation for guilt. Because this work is Genet's only non-autobiographical novel, he is paradoxically able to be more personal, if less intimate, than he usually is (White 1993, 290).

Finally, *Journal du voleur*, one of Genet's most accessible novels (Simont 1989, 117), deals with the problem of sanctity and the inversion of values. While explicitly referring to Jean Genet's 'career as a thief', this book is filled with portrayals of his lovers and their strengths and foibles. In his depiction of the criminal underworld and the survival tactics it demands of its inhabitants, the author explores the possibilities of 'camp' and outlines the parameters of a criminal subculture that is openly gay. This personal journal has often been perceived by the critics as a loving recreation of criminal style and language, specifically a representation of the charms of the men Genet loves. For some, however, Genet's glorification of homosexuality-as-revolt leads him to equate it with crime in a manner that the bourgeois world he vilifies understands all too readily (Malgron 1988). A difficulty that his book presents to contemporary readers, say others, is one that besets many of his early novels. He is unwilling to consider specific differences between sexuality and crime, instead focusing obsessively on the links between them (Davis 1994). Despite his minute exploration of a milieu excluded from the social order, Genet neglects to define his sexuality in terms other than those provided by the dominant class: as monstrous, criminal and deviant (Bergen 1993).

Through the constant mix of realism, autobiographical elements, fiction and the stylization which permeates all his narrative works, Genet gives the appearance of having written social novels with postmodern tendencies. Notable instances of realism that are entwined with postmodernity include: the diverse shady settings of *Querelle de Brest* (the realistically portrayed lives of the sailors who stop over in Brest, their communal life in the shipyard, La Feria, the brothel where all the men meet, which function as both real and as symbolic settings); the treatment of war crimes in *Pompes funèbres*, representations which fuse horror and pleasure; and *Notre-Dame-des-Fleurs* with its realistic and yet symbolically colourful setting of the 'little queers of the Pigalle' in Paris between the two world wars. As for the descriptions of the prison world in *Miracle de la rose* and *Journal du voleur*, they are so minutely detailed that Michel Foucault asked Genet to co-author a chapter about Mettray prison for his work on punishment and prisons, *Surveiller et punir* (*Discipline and Punish*) (1975).

Having completed his fifth novel, Genet felt that he had had enough of writing. He had already embarked on a new adventure of addressing theatregoers. 'It was essential', he said, 'to change mindsets and to know that I was writing for an audience that is visible and numerous each time, whereas the reader of novels, especially of mine, is invisible and sometimes hidden' (Malgron 1988, 165). The shift to the stage served as a *processus dénegatif* for the author. Genet gives his characters a voice and no longer speaks in his own name, which gives the impression that he is no longer referring to himself. In the shift to drama Genet does not seek the acceptance of polite society but rather recognition from a growing theatrical audience (Aslan 1973, 28).

His first two plays, *Haute Surveillance* (1949) (*Deathwatch*, 1954), and *Les Bonnes* (1954) (*The Maids*, 1954), which were steeped in tragedy and revealed the sombre spectacle of funerary ritual, together constitute a sort of 'chamber play' or *théâtre intime* – in the sense intended by Strindberg – a theatre in which the action, cut off from the outside world, is centred exclusively on the hero as well as on the quest for an image that leads him inevitably to his death. In these two plays, Genet brought to the stage the socially marginalized figures he had also portrayed in his novels: domestic employees, gangsters, prisoners, as well as prison guards and police officers. The theatre thus extends, at the beginning of Genet's dramatic career, the novelistic universe of the author, where the world of the incarcerated continues to exert a strong influence on him. In *Haute Surveillance*, for example, three ordinary prisoners rot in jail. One of them, Yeux-Verts, is condemned to death. The other two (Maurice and Lefranc) vie for his attention, as though the enormity of his crime and the imminence of his death make him a sacred figure. In this gloomy cage, from which none can escape, Lefranc murders Maurice in the hope of impressing Yeux-Verts and to win his attention away from Maurice. However, Lefranc realizes that he is the victim of Yeux-Verts's betrayal – Yeux-Verts turns him in to the guard. This highly symbolic climax emphasizes here Genet's preoccupation with evil, betrayal and martyrdom.

Similarly, but now within a 'rituel à deux', the play *Les Bonnes* highlights another funerary ritual, which can be summarized as follows. In the opening scene, one of the maids, Claire, impersonates the mistress of the house, Madame, and the other maid, Solange, in turn plays her sister, Claire. In the exchanges between the two sisters, the audience discovers that they have anonymously denounced Madame's lover, Monsieur, as a criminal. The maids in their madness waver between wanting to murder Madame, the real person, and wanting to murder Madame-impersonated-by-Claire. A phone call reveals that Monsieur has just been released from jail. When Madame arrives, Claire prepares a poisoned cup of herbal tea for her. However, Madame discovers Monsieur is free and that he awaits her. She neglects her tea and gaily rushes off into the night. The maids, knowing that the anonymous letter of denunciation will be soon traced to them, begin to plan their own deaths. Claire dresses as Madame and drinks the tea, so that her sister Solange will know a kind of infamy and be denounced as a murderer.

In *Les Bonnes* Genet explores the two sisters' quest for an image and questions the social roles they are assigned as a result of their class status. In his next play, *Le Balcon* (1956) (*The Balcony*, 1958), the scene expands and offers a critique of a whole society; his themes finally open out into the world at large in *Les Nègres* (1958) (*The Blacks: A Clown Show*, 1960) and *Les Paravents* (1961) (*The Screens*, 1962), texts in which racial antagonisms are brought to the fore. Through them, the dramatist reflects on, among other things, the way in which the power at the heart of a social group manipulates the image of the group (which the group projects or wishes to project) to achieve its aim, the absolute quest being, according to the playwright (Genet 1991, 102), the most pernicious form of alienation there is. In *Le Balcon*, perhaps the best known of Genet's dramatic works, the action is set in a brothel, or 'house of illusions', in an undisclosed country. Madame Irma's house is a place where plumbers, bank clerks and chiefs of police come to act out their sexual fantasies as judges, bishops, generals and so on. The illusions must be erotic, complete and undisturbed. When the illusion is broken, when one of the prostitutes breaks his or her role as a criminal or a penitent, the illusion is destroyed. However, while the revolution rages in the city, the clients of the 'Grand Balcony' play out their perverse scenarios. Although they are hidden behind closed doors in the brothel, they feel threatened. Their world and their identities – illusory or real – are on the verge of collapsing. Moreover, power will manipulate, in a clandestine manner, their perverse fantasies and exploit their fear in order to turn them into agents of a well-orchestrated repression.

Whereas the quest for an image is here directly linked to the question of exclusion, it is presented in *Les Nègres* and *Les Paravents* in terms of racial identity and takes a definite political turn. Certain socio-political facts – such as the French colonization in Africa, racism and apartheid – are openly called into question. Written as a vehicle for an all-black cast, Les Nègres consists of three complex intrigues all centring on the murder of a white woman, whose coffin remains in the centre of the stage as a symbol of the Blacks' reaction to white domination. The first intrigue recreates, through a ritual, the rape and murder of the woman. The second is far more obscure. In the course of this intrigue, a series of actions which occur off-stage are revealed to the audience by the character St Nazaire. The third intrigue introduces two characters (Village, the murderer, and a prostitute called Virtue) who, in a discussion, allude to the 'New World' dominated by the Blacks. Perched on a balcony are three 'white' members of the court (a queen, a judge and a governor), while beneath them, black actors theatrically recreate the crime to be judged by the dignitaries. The main action of the play – this reconstruction of the crime before the court – takes the form of a *mise en abyme* or a play within a play, thereby accentuating the process of division that occurs between the dominant (white) and the dominated (black). In addition to this, the play, which centres on a mock trial on-stage while a real trial takes place off-stage, is imbued with an intense sexuality as well as an easy-going transvestism (Blacks play Whites, men play women). Not only are men played against women and Blacks against Whites, but the dead are also constantly contrasted to the living.

Finally, Les Paravents – Genet's response to the Algerian war (1954–62) – is literally a work of epic proportions containing nearly a hundred characters. This play details both the war and the relationship between an Arab mother and son – one of the most sophisticated characterizations of a woman in all of Genet's works – in this simple story. Saïd Nettle, a poor worker in an unnamed colony, has a wife, Leila. They both live with his mother and three other members of the Nettle family. Saïd does not get along with his fellow workers on Sir Harold's estate; they ridicule him because his wife is ugly, which leads to fistfights which he always loses. One day, the villagers mock Saïd's mother because her son is an outcast. Then slowly things erode in a sort of moral entropy. The Europeans lose their power and take refuge in self-intoxicating rhetoric. Saïd's mother, almost unintentionally, strangles a French soldier. More and more of the characters die. At the end of the play a trial scene takes place. As with the finale of Les Nègres, Genet reminds us that the real danger is that the revolutionaries will all too successfully emulate their ex-masters, that instead of inventing or rediscovering their own culture and values they will simply retain the European system but fill in the blanks with new Arab – or Black – names.

Some critics (Laroche 1997; Malgron 1988; Read and Birchall 1997; Webb 1982) have reckoned that through these plays Genet, oriented towards international politics, applauds the collapse of the colonial system. For example, when he was writing Les Nègres, France, with the 1954 defeat of Dien Bien Phu still in mind, finally recognized the independence of Laos, Cambodia and Vietnam. Furthermore, while Nasser organized the Arab League and as the Algerian war got under way, Genet wrote Les Paravents, a text which he reworked for years. His theatrical works, following the example of his narrative texts, therefore draw on reality without, however, adopting the principle extolling the virtues of realism. Thus the author only grasps the illusion – fictional and theatrical – to celebrate its deconstruction, or destruction in a flamboyant carnival, celebration and sacrifice of the artificial where the values advocated by the dominant system (linked, amongst other things, to 'norms', to justice and to religion) seem to be subjected to the monotonous wish for power by alienated individuals who, in the work of Genet, wander between life and death (Goldmann 1970, 299).

This Genetian universe, composed of the fringe elements of society, crooks and criminals, in addition to disconcerting many, caused much grinding of pens by commentators, such as Georges Bataille (1957), who wished to solve the 'case of Genet' by denouncing as inadmissible the literary use of Evil and crime made by the author throughout his work. Bataille develops a curious denunciation, which he pursues by taking up the principal elements of the Sartrean argument in *Saint Genet, comédien et martyr* (1952). Keeping in mind that, according to Sartre, the works of Jean Genet consist essentially in depicting Evil up to the point of its own destruction, to the point of annihilating Good, if necessary, the author thereby transforms the outcasts of 'polite society' into a chosen people (Sartre 1952, 55); this task, according to the philosopher, consists in denying the normative universe and its values and in placing this negation as the object in the Genetian hero's quest (1952, 117). However, for Bataille, Genet's will, as with the content of his texts, refers, on the contrary, to a generalized negation of the 'forbidden', to a search for Evil pursued without limitation, until the moment when, all barriers broken, man – represented by the author in his fiction – goes into total decline. Judging that he is constantly infringing on the taboos during their transgression, and that he takes refuge in betrayal and in the negation of his readers' expectations (l'horizon d'attente) – ruining any chance of effective 'communication' (1957, 240) with them – the author of *La Littérature et le mal* concludes that Genet can be the 'sovereign' only in Evil and that Evil is never more evil than when it is punished (Bataille 1957, 207). This point of view is refuted, in the early 1980s, by Jacques Derrida in a work entitled *Glas*, in which the critic pursues his research project on the difference of meaning, annular movement, auto-annulation, through which meaning continually differs and is ultimately deferred.

In *Glas*, Derrida shows that the difference between sexes is transformed into opposition by a dialectical movement (1981, 157), which is what a number of critics in *gay and lesbian studies* have been attempting to illustrate over the last few years. *Glas* constitutes a reflection on sexual difference – notably in Genet's work – and at the same time shows how Jean Genet's fiction offers its readers a long series of living antitheses that toll the bell for the Hegelian dialectic, as with the most scathing of Bataille's commentaries. Derrida also reassesses many of the statements in *Saint Genet, comédien et martyr*. For example, while Sartre asserts that Genet's work reverses the hierarchy of traditional oppositions which structure western thought, and says that the world the author invents represents the opposite of 'reality' inasmuch as it is Evil – rather than Good – that constitutes the privileged term (1952, 119), Derrida tends to prove that the imaginary world of Genet is 'different' from the real world without simply being its opposite, thereby maintaining a relationship of displacement with it and not of negation (1981, 92).

Other works by Jean Genet include numerous poems (*Treasures of the Night: Collected Poems of Jean Genet*, 1981), another novel (*Un captif amoureux* (1986), *Prisoner of Love*, 1992), a treatise on ballet (*Madame Miroir*, 1949) and three more plays (*Elle*, 1989; *Splendid's*, 1993; *Le Bagne*, 1994), works that have only begun to be explored.

Alain-Michel Rocheleau

Further reading and works cited

Aslan, O. *Jean Genet*. Paris, 1973.
Barthes, R. *Essais critiques*. Paris, 1964.
Bataille, G. *La Littérature et le mal*. Paris, 1957.
Bergen, V. *Jean Genet: entre mythe et réalité*. Brussels, 1993.

Brook, P. and Halpern, J. (eds) *Genet: A Collection of Critical Essays*. Englewood Cliffs, NJ, 1979.

Cixous, H. *Three Steps on the Ladder of Writing*. New York, 1993.

Davis, C. 'Genet's *Journal du voleur* and the Ethics of Reading', *French Studies*, 48, 1994.

de Man, P. *Allegories of Reading*. New Haven, CT, 1979.

Derrida, J. *Glas*. Paris, 1981.

Dollimore, J. *Sexual Dissidence*. Oxford, 1991.

Foucault, M. *Surveiller et punir*. Paris, 1975.

—. *Dits et écrits. 1954–1988*. Paris, 1994.

Genet, J. 'L'Étrange mot d' ...' *Tel quel*, 30, 1967.

—. 'Le Secret de Rembrandt', in *Oeuvres complètes*. Paris, 1979.

—. *L'Ennemi déclaré: textes et entretiens*. Paris, 1991.

Goldmann, L. 'Le Théâtre de Genet. Essai d'étude sociologique', in *Structures mentales et création culturelle*. Paris, 1970.

Laroche, H. *Le Dernier Genet*. Paris, 1997.

Mahuzier, B. et al. (eds) 'Same Sex/Different Text. Gay and Lesbian Writing in French', *Yale French Studies*, 90, 1996.

Malgron, A. *Jean Genet*. Lyon, 1988.

Moraly, J.-B. *Jean Genet. La vie écrite. Biographie*. Paris, 1988.

Naish, C. *A Genetic Approach to Structures in the Work of Jean Genet*. Cambridge, 1978.

Oswald, L. *Jean Genet and the Semiotics of Performance*. Indianapolis, IN, 1989.

Read, B. and Birchall, I. *Jean Genet: Ten Years After*. Haomondsworth, 1997.

Sartre, J.-P. *Saint Genet, comédien et martyr*. Paris, 1952.

Simont, J. 'Bel effet d'où jaillissent les roses ... (à propos du *Saint Genet* de Sartre et du *Glas* de Derrida)', *Les Temps modernes*, 510, 1989.

Todd, J. M. 'Autobiography and the Case of the Signature: Reading Derrida's *Glas*', *Comparative Literature*, 38, 1986.

Webb, R. C. *Jean Genet and his Critics: An Annotated Bibliography*. London, 1982.

White, E. *Genet. A Biography*. New York, 1993.

Paul Ricoeur (1913–)

An encyclopaedia of criticism and theory would not be complete without an entry for Paul Ricoeur. However, Ricoeur does not fit easily into the category of 'theory'. His position as a 'poststructuralist' is in doubt and his few forays into literature seem to gesture toward the sort of textual exegesis which theory has largely displaced. Ricoeur is a classically trained phenomenologist, in the tradition of Husserl and Heidegger, who happens to work at the interface of philosophy and literature. Undoubtedly, his work is part of a wider postwar, cultural shift towards an aesthetic, rather than scientific, paradigm for human knowledge, but he would have little time for many of the more rococo claims of literary theory. However, as a professional philosopher working in the French academy he is perhaps closer to Jacques Derrida (they taught a phenomenology seminar together at the Sorbonne) than any other thinker. Their proximity and difference is revealed in a brief exchange between the two. In *The Rule of Metaphor* Ricoeur criticizes Derrida's essay 'White Mythologies' (Derrida 1982). Derrida replies to this in his essay 'The *Retrait* of Metaphor', suggesting that 'it is because I sometimes subscribe to some of Ricoeur's propositions that I am tempted to protest when I see him turn them back against me as if they were not already evident in what I have written' (1978, 12). In other words, Ricoeur's published objection to Derrida is in fact a point of agreement. However, Ricoeur remains an 'un-deconstructed' Heideggerian and as such his philosophy is of interest to critical theory because it is predicated on the double axis of time and language.

Mario J. Valdés describes Ricoeur and Derrida as the 'the two philosophers whose work has given poststructuralism its two faces of hermeneutics and deconstruction' (Valdés 1991, 22). Derrida and Ricoeur share a Heideggerian view of human activity, which rules out the possibility of an errorless reliable origin. The related positions of Ricoeur and Derrida mean that their work shares a number of philosophical and cultural influences. First, they rely on an understanding of the critical 'hermeneutics of suspicion' advanced by Hegelian Marxism, Nietzsche and Freud. Secondly, both Ricoeur and Derrida's thought is informed by the structural linguistics of Saussure, Jakobson and Lévi-Strauss. However, their work is most importantly characterized by its attention to the phenomenological and existentialist theories developed by Husserl, Heidegger, Marcel, Jaspers, Sartre and Merleau-Ponty. Ricoeur and Derrida separate on the question of a shared intentionality in meaning. Valdés calls Ricoeur a poststructuralist – despite this difference to Derrida in their understanding of meaning – because Ricoeur's work 'has developed over the last two decades and not only has taken structuralism and semiotics into full consideration and responded to them but, most significantly, has built on this debate' (Valdés 1991, 39). Valdés's comments are instructive in two ways. First, he makes clear Ricoeur's debt to structuralism in *Time and Narrative* and so positions his work within the field of narrative theory. Second, it identifies *Time and Narrative* as a site of struggle in the inheritance and development of the phenomenological tradition, particularly in relation to Derrida's project of the deconstruction of philosophy. Ricoeur's hermeneutics and Derrida's deconstruction are not in fact radical opposites but rather possible alternative directions within continental phenomenology, which inform and complement one another. Derrida's philosophical inquiry follows Ricoeur's exemplary studies in the larger economy of European phenomenology, both Derrida and Ricoeur are involved in the same reassessment of the phenomenological heritage since Kant and Hegel. Their work is part of a history of ideas which exceeds the narrow limits of the historical periodization of, what the Anglo-Saxon academy calls, poststructuralism. Ricoeur has identified this project as 'the work of mourning' (Ricoeur 1988, 206) for Hegelian thought, while Derrida's own consideration of the phenomenological tradition constitutes a major preoccupation in his writing.

Ricoeur's early work, such as *History and Truth* and *Political and Social Essays*, encourages a rapprochement between Christian theology (of a distinctly Protestant kind) and socialism (of a decidedly Hegelian variety). These texts are an engagement with the ethical, political and social concerns of their historical moment. They are also spirited defences of humanism, which may account for the relative lack of attention paid to early Ricoeur by critical theory. Even within his mature philosophy Ricoeur will always privilege Being over, say, language or narrative. He suggests an ontological sequence starting from our experience of being in the world and in time – preceding and preunderstood outside of language – and proceeding from this condition towards linguistic expression. Ricoeur's work has tended to find favour with those who have sought an alternative to the displacements proposed by postmodernism. His three volumes, *Freud and Philosophy,*

Interpretation Theory and *Hermeneutics and the Human Sciences*, have been key texts for hermeneutics – sometimes thought of as a conservative reflex within critical theory which wishes to adopt the insights of poststructuralist textual analysis while retaining an idea of stability between text and reader. In *Freud and Philosophy* Ricoeur places Freud in a philosophical tradition of interpretation, providing a well-founded if less energetic counterpoint to psychoanalytic criticism. Similarly, in *The Rule of Metaphor* Ricoeur's analysis of figurative language follows a philosophical genealogy and might be said to be more rigorous if less dazzling than Paul de Man's *Allegories of Reading*, written at the same time. Perhaps Ricoeur's most significant contribution to critical theory is the three volumes of *Time and Narrative*, which provide a sustained meditation on the philosophical tradition, history, literature, aporia and temporality. The rest of this entry will discuss the architecture of *Time and Narrative* as a way of outlining some of Ricoeur's key concerns.

Paul Ricoeur outlines the project of *Time and Narrative* in his interview with Richard Kearney:

> My chief concern in this analysis is to discover how the act of *raconter*, of telling a story, can transmute *natural* time into a specifically *human* time, irreducible to mathematical, chronological 'clock time'. How is narrativity, as the construction or deconstruction of paradigms of story-telling, a perpetual search for new ways of expressing time, a production or creation of meaning? That is my question. (1984, 17)

For Ricoeur narrativity is the means by which time can be transformed from a universal constant into an activity of human production. In other words, narrativity is the operation that relates temporality to the production of meaning. However, as the title *Time and Narrative* suggests Ricoeur is well aware of the aporetic relationship that exists between these two concepts. This aporetic relation, in which the conditions of possibility of one figure depend upon the impossible conditions of the other, is outlined by Ricoeur at the opening of Volume 1:

> One presupposition commands all the others, namely, that what is ultimately at stake in the case of the structural identity of the narrative function as well as in that of the truth claim of every narrative work, is the temporal character of human experience. The world unfolded by every narrative work is always a temporal world. Or, as will often be repeated in the course of this study: time becomes human time to the extent that it is organised after the manner of a narrative; narrative, in turn, is meaningful to the extent that it portrays the features of temporal experience. (1984, 3)

The interdependence of time and narrative is complete. Time becomes an activity of human production because it is structured in the form of a narrative, while narrative produces meaning because it represents the structures of time. By 'human time' Ricoeur means, as he tells Kearney:

> The formulation of two opposing forms of time: public time and private time. Private time is mortal time, for, as Heidegger says, to exist is to be a being-towards-death [*Sein-zum-Tode*], a being whose future is closed off by death. As soon as we understand our existence as this mortal time, we are already involved in a form of private narrativity or history; as soon as the individual comes up against the finite limits of its own existence, it is obliged to recollect itself and to make time its *own*. On the other hand, there exists public time. Now I do not mean public in the sense of physical or natural (clock time), but the time of language itself, which continues on after the individual's death. To live in human time is to live between the private time of our mortality and the public time of language. (1984, 20)

This is another aporia that Ricoeur relies upon in his mediation between time and narrative. The 'human time' which narrative both constructs and depends upon is the aporetic consequence of the relation between 'private' time (the mortality of the body) and 'public' time (the temporal experience of the social use of language). This 'public' time is a necessity of the mortality of the body and this 'private' time is made meaningful through the communal use of language. The key issue which Ricoeur's work on narrativity and temporality touches upon in this instance is the relation between language and death (see Vol. 2, 27 and Vol. 3, 270).

Ricoeur's assertion that 'one presupposition commands all the others, namely, that what is ultimately at stake in the case of the structural identity of the narrative function as well as in that of the truth claim of every narrative work, is the temporal character of human experience' may suggest that he is working within the classic phenomenological assumption that narrative is an intentionality of subjective consciousness, rather than the view of narrative suggested by (post)structuralism, that it is a discursive structure which predetermines the subjective operations of consciousness. However, as he explains to Kearney, this is not the case:

> It is both at once. The invaluable contribution made by structuralism was to offer an exact scientific description of the codes and paradigms of language. But I do not believe that this excludes the creative expression of consciousness. The creation of meaning in language comes from the specifically human production of new ways of expressing the objective paradigms and codes made available by language. (1984, 19)

Here Ricoeur is suggesting that another aporetic relation exists within the construction of narrative. Narrative simultaneously represents the structures that determine the possibility of communal linguistic action and is itself constituted by this linguistic action. That is to say, narrative is both constituted by, and constitutive of, the intersubjective process. Ricoeur tells Kearney, 'I would say, borrowing Wittgenstein's term, that the "language game" of narration ultimately reveals that the meaning of human existence is itself narrative' (1984, 17). In this way Ricoeur provides a powerful theory of narrative related to both poststructuralist representations of the subject and a reassessment of the phenomenological tradition.

Having identified the processes of narrativity as aporetic in nature, Ricoeur uses the strategy of aporia to guide his study. He identifies another aporetic figure in the relation between 'fiction' and 'history.' In Volume 3 of the study Ricoeur overlays the two chapters of Section 1, 'The Aporetics of Temporality', and the first two chapters of Section 2, 'Poetics of Narrative: History, Fiction, Time', in order to identify this relation:

> The task of the following five chapters will be to reduce the gap between the respective ontological intentions of history and fiction in order to make sense of what, in Volume 1, I was still calling the interweaving reference of history and fiction, an operation that I take to be a major stake, although not the only one, in the refiguration of time by narrative. (1988, 6)

The avowed aim of this investigation (to demonstrate the shared narrative characteristics of history and literary fiction) comes from Ricoeur's proposal that history and fiction are dependent upon each other in much the same way as time and narrative are interrelated. The structure of literary fiction defines the nature of 'human' time which history describes, while the representation of 'human' time in history provides the material from which literary fictions are constructed. Ricoeur writes in conclusion to Volume 2:

Only after a theory of reading has been proposed in one of the concluding chapters of Volume 3 will fictional narrative be able to assert its claims to truth, at the cost of a radical reformulation of the problem of truth. This will involve the capacity of the work of art to indicate and to transform human action. In the same way, only once the theory of reading has been presented will the contribution of the fictional narrative to the refiguration of time enter into opposition to and into composition with the capacity of historical narrative to speak of the actual past. If my thesis about the highly controversial problem of reference in the order of fiction possesses any originality, it is to the extent that it does not separate the claim to truth asserted by fictional narrative from that made by historical narrative but attempts to understand each in relation to the other. (1985, 160)

For Ricoeur, history and fiction form an aporetic figure in which the nature of the two halves of that figure can only be understood by a determination of their interrelation and the influence one half, continually, simultaneously and irreducibly, plays upon the other:

From these intimate exchanges between the historicization of fictional narrative and the fictionalization of the historical narrative is born what we call human time, which is nothing other than narrated time ... these two interweaving movements mutually belong to each other. (1985, 102)

In order to investigate this mutually dependent figuration between history and literary fiction it is necessary for Ricoeur to adopt a strategy of paradox and to follow the impossible logic of both sides of the figure simultaneously. This is his concern in the first five chapters of Volume 3:

To put this question in more familiar terms, how are we to interpret history's claim, when it constructs a narrative, to reconstruct something from the past? What authorises us to think of this construction as a reconstruction? It is by joining this question with that of the 'unreality' of fictive entities that we hope to make progress simultaneously in the two problems of 'reality' and 'unreality' in narration. (1988, 5)

Only by addressing both halves of the mutually dependent figure simultaneously can progress be made in connection with the problem. In other words, the aporia must be thought through as a whole rather than as the sum of discrete parts. The relation between the two halves of the figure is not merely a question of analytic method but is, says Ricoeur, a question of ontology:

By the interweaving of history and fiction I mean the fundamental structure, ontological as well as epistemological, by virtue of which history and fiction each concretise their respective intentionalities only by borrowing from the intentionality of the other... I am now going to show [in the introduction to Volume 3, Chapter 8, 'The Interweaving of History and Fiction'] that this concretization is obtained only insofar as, on the one hand, history in some way makes use of fiction to refigure time and, on the other hand, fiction makes use of history for the same ends. (1988, 181)

This aporetic relation between history and fiction is important to Ricoeur because it 'refigures' time to produce what he terms 'human time'.

Ricoeur resists effacing the difference between historical and fictional narratives. Simultaneously, Ricoeur insists that, 'the ultimately narrative character of history ... is in no way to be confused with a defence of narrative history' (1988, 154). What is at stake in this study, and in his suggestion that the production of temporality in a narrative form makes any human experience or understanding of history narrative in nature, is the epistemological status of the question of 'truth' and its relation to narrative. This ultimately suggests that all human understanding is narrative in character. In terms of the question of truth, Ricoeur offers a patient argument that depends upon the aporetic necessity of the interrelation of historical and fictional discourse and their irreducibility. Ricoeur does not imagine historical 'truth' to be a matter of accession to events through the undecideability of textual representation (as a certain poststructuralist materialism might). Rather, he sees it as the determination of events that are themselves cast in the form of a narrative, as a consequence of their relation to temporality. Any poststructuralist discussion of the determination of history necessarily involves an investigation of the question of 'truth'. Ricoeur's hermeneutic Heideggereanism is no different. The difficulty involved in Ricoeur's position is not necessarily the acceptance of this description of the effects of narrativity, but rather the problem of squaring this description with Ricoeur's discussion of meaning and language.

For Ricoeur, the question of 'truth' is not merely a matter of the identification of a disjuncture between real events and their culturally and ideologically specific narrative, or linguistic, representation. Rather, having identified 'truth' as an issue within narrative theory (as it relates to a reassessment, which is also a continuation, of the phenomenological tradition) the value of Ricoeur's work is his determination to realign what Gibson calls 'the narratological imaginary' (Gibson 1996, 3). Ricoeur is not concerned with an absolute imposition of an objective truth. Instead he moves the discussion of 'truth' and its relation to narrative away from a simplistic equation between so-called realist narrative, ideological conservatism and an objective truth, as opposed to a modernist or postmodernist narrative, radical subversion and relativism. He identifies the process of narrativity as offering a 'poetic' strategy (and therefore a productive but ultimately ambiguous one) for the discussion of the aporetic conditions of 'truth' claims. The determination of 'truth' is not an opposition between event and representation but an identification of the aporetic relation between event and narrative production of the event, involved in the possibility of human understanding.

For example, Ricoeur considers the aporetic nature of temporal experience (the opening chapter of Volume 1 would be a case in point). Part of Ricoeur's interest in narrative derives from the inability of a 'purely phenomenological' account of temporal experience to avoid becoming bogged down in the aporias it both discovers and generates. The textual practice of narrative offers a means of working through the paralysis of the aporia. Ricoeur comments in Volume 3:

> The hypothesis that has oriented this work from its very beginning, namely, that temporality cannot be spoken of in the direct discourse of phenomenology, but rather requires the mediation of the indirect discourse of narration. The negative half of this demonstration lies in our assertion that the most exemplary attempts to express the lived experience of time in its immediacy result in the multiplication of aporias, as the instrument of analysis becomes ever more precise. It is these aporias that the poetics of narrative deals with as so many knots to be untied. In its schematic form, our working hypothesis thus amounts to taking narrative as a guardian of time, insofar as there can be no thought about time without narrated time. (1988, 241)

It is Ricoeur's assertion that 'there has never been a phenomenology of temporality free of every aporia, and that in principle there can never be one' (1988, 3). In order to produce solutions to the questions posed by temporal experience Ricoeur considers it necessary to discuss these questions in relation to the narrative structure they constitute and by which they themselves are constituted. He writes, 'our study rests on the thesis that narrative composition, taken in its broadest sense, constitutes a riposte to the aporetic character of speculation on time' (Ricoeur 1988, 11). This is a complicated and detailed strategy inhabited by the figure of aporia. The project of *Time and Narrative* faces the 'difficulty that the aporetics of temporality will reveal, namely, the irreducibility of one to the other.' That is to say, the aporias which Ricoeur investigates are pre-existing concepts within phenomenological inquiry and will thus be approached by a narrative mediation in an already irreducibly complex form. However, *Time and Narrative* also depends upon the intervention of phenomenology to explain the narrative discourse it generates.

The introduction to Volume 3 finds Ricoeur's strategy embracing this paradox:

> We must assume the much greater risks of a specifically philosophical discussion, whose stake is whether – and how – the narrative operation, taken in its full scope, offers a 'solution' – not a speculative, but a poetic one – to the aporias that seemed inseparable from the Augustinian analysis of time. (1988, 4)

This is an inevitable consequence of the route Ricoeur chooses to take in relation to the aporias of temporal experience. He comments in conclusion to the penultimate section of his study:

> Let us first say that, if the phenomenology of time can become one privileged interlocutor in the three-way conversation we are about to undertake among phenomenology, historiography, and literary narratology, this is a result not just of its discoveries but also of the aporias it gives rise to, which increase in proportion to its advances. (1988, 96)

While narrative is a means by which to resolve the aporias of phenomenological inquiry, phenomenology is the necessary means by which to explain the narrative solutions. In this way the very action of Ricoeur's project takes on an aporetic form. The interdependence of the narrative modes of history and literature, and the relation of narratology to phenomenology within Ricoeur's work, as Hans Kellner has pointed out (regarding the two components of the study's title): 'lean upon each other like the two parts of the Christian Bible, the latter part of which is proven true because it fulfils the former, the former part of which is proven true because it prefigures the latter' (Kellner 1990, 229). The value of such a strategy is the challenge and support it presents to other theories of narrative which attempt to examine the impossible simultaneity of aporetic conditions.

One of the difficulties in reading Ricoeur is – as a consequence of his Heideggerian training – his ability to accommodate two contradictory positions within an argument. In this way he allows that argument to unfold by the double logic of these contradictions. When Ricoeur seems at his most contradictory he is also at his most rigorously philosophical. Ricoeur's use of the figure of aporia requires expansion. The analytic technology of *Time and Narrative* most frequently involves a dialectical synthesis of two juxtaposed arguments to produce a third concept. This dialectical third is aporetically figured but not necessarily as a result of the creation of a paradox out of the original two arguments. For example, the dialectical synthesis of Aristotle and Augustine gives rise to the concept of 'human time'. However, the aporia of human time's refiguration in narrative is not a result of an aporetic relation between Aristotle's *muthos* and Augustine's *distentio*. The structure of Ricoeur's three volumes is determined by the logic of this argument. Volume 1 of *Time and Narrative* is divided into two sections 'The Circle of Narrative and Temporality' and 'History and Narrative'. The first section acts as a general introduction to the entire argument of the three volumes; each section is divided into three chapters. In Part 1, Chapter 1 presents a reading of the aporetic experience of time, which is in a dialectical relationship with the concepts of emplotment in Chapter 2; Chapter 3 presents this relationship. Thus, Ricoeur places Augustine in dialectic encounter with Aristotle, and this juxtaposition produces the threefold mimesis outlined in Chapter 3.

Similarly, in Part 3, Chapter 4, 'The Eclipse of Narrative', is related to Chapter 5, 'Defences of Narrative', and this dialectic exchange brings about chapter 6, 'Historical Intentionality'. This logical method applies to the entire three-volume project. Thus, Part 1 of *Time and Narrative* is the introduction to the entire argument, whereas Part 2, on historical narrative, is directly countered by Volume 2 on fictional narrative, with Volume 2 serving as the synthesis to the initial problem of human time created through narrativity. Volumes 1 and 2 find their discussions of historiography and literary fiction dialectically synthesized into Volume 3's preoccupation with phenomenological temporality. Phenomenology is described – in contrast to the aporetic pertinence Ricoeur demonstrates elsewhere – as a 'privileged interlocutor in the three-way conversation' (Ricoeur 1988, 96). The work is characterized by an interest in groupings of three: threefold mimesis, three measurements of time, three interlocutors and, of course, its three volumes. This repeated ternary movement within the work can be identified as Ricoeur's formulation of Hegelian culmination in the sign of the analogue as a methodological dynamic which enacts Ricoeur's 'work of mourning' for Hegel.

It is necessary for the project of *Time and Narrative* to subsume a representative selection of all narrative knowledge into the mediation of its argument. Ricoeur's project is to show that all human experience in the lived world is made temporal (and so understandable) when it is refigured into narrative, fictional or historical. In order to demonstrate this *Time and Narrative* requires a strict methodology, which will draw every heterogeneous aspect of this vast object of study under the singular, ordered (or to use Ricoeur's own term concerning the action of narrative, 'concordant') form of the particular model of narrative Ricoeur appropriates. As a result Ricoeur must take those elements of inquiry which do not fit neatly into a narratologically defined category and demonstrate that they are narrative in character. Ricoeur does this by likening them, by analogy, to a trope from narrative theory. In his own words he 'quasifies' them:

> The concepts of quasi-plot, quasi-character, and quasi-event that I had to construct in order to respect the very indirect form of filiation by which the history that is the least narrative in its style of writing nevertheless continues to rely on narrative understanding. (1984, 230)

Hans Kellner comments upon this method:

> All of this quasi-ness reminds us that the Sign of the Analogue, under which the ship sails, certifies the figurative process, which is the life-blood of *Time and Narrative*; its destination, after all, is a refiguration of time by narrative. Each step of the way involves a turn, a tropological allegorization, by which apparently different pieces of reality (the Sign of Same and Other) are resolved provisionally, into analogues, quasis. In this phenomenological strategy, narrative acts as a middle-level tropological process, mediating parts into wholes, without looking over either shoulder at the lower and higher level protocols of language. Narrative is thus the quintessence of Ricoeur's vision of humanity. (1990, 233)

The 'figurative process' that Kellner identifies as 'the life-blood' of Ricoeur's argument is a figuration of language different from that imagined by deconstruction. For Ricoeur and hermeneutics – as Kellner indicates – the figurative process takes place at a structural level within the unit of the textual whole (character, event) rather than at the level of the signifier or trace.

Ricoeur's use of analogue is not so much a description of the mediating power of the tropological process of narrative but rather a narrative approach to the Hegelian dialectic. Ricoeur's description of the narrative characteristics of historiography, and his attempt to breach the impasse of the aporias of phenomenological temporality, can be thought of as a narrativistic approach to the use of Hegelian thought on issues within contemporary hermeneutics. This use of the analogue can be said to be narrativistic or narrativizing because it translates one tropological operation into another. So, Ricoeur's analogue is a radicalization of Hegel. The problem it ultimately poses for Ricoeur's thematization of the aporia is that the apparent resolution of the signs of the Same and the Other must negate the fundamental irreducibility of both halves of the figure of aporia. In other words, Ricoeur's dialectical ontologizing is in tension with the hauntological process of aporia as Derrida understands it (see Derrida 1993). This mediation denies the radical alterity which constitutes the figure it seeks to describe. While Ricoeur may be fascinated by the figure of aporia, his argument is ultimately at odds with the alterity implied by the aporetic. Ricoeur's mediation of the narrative function as an analogue, by means of the process of analogue, is itself a narrative because it is an imaginary resolution of real contradictions. However, this is not necessarily an argument against Ricoeur, it is merely to identify Ricoeur's position as narrativistic. This is an inevitable consequence of Ricoeur's own argument regarding the necessary expression of temporal experience (and so all textuality) in the form of a narrative. Rather this description of Ricoeur's dialectic methodology may just be a further demonstration of Ricoeur's relation to Hegel and the phenomenological tradition.

Martin McQuillan

Further reading and works cited

Clark, S. H. *Paul Ricoeur*. London, 1990.
Dauenhauser, B. P. *Paul Ricoeur*. New York, 1999.
Derrida, J. 'The *Retrait* of Metaphor', *Enclitic*, 2, 1978.
—. *Margins of Philosophy*. Brighton, 1982.
—. *Aporias*. Stanford, CA, 1993.
Gibson, A. *Towards a Postmodern Theory of Narrative*. Edinburgh, 1996.
Hahn, L. E. (ed.) *The Philosophy of Paul Ricoeur*. Chicago, 1995.
Kearney, R. *Dialogues with Contemporary Continental Thinkers*. Manchester, 1984.
—. *Paul Ricoeur*. London, 1996.
Kellner, H. ' "As Real as it Gets ...": Ricoeur and Narrativity', *Philosophy Today*, 34, 3, 1990.
—. 'Narrativity in History: Post-structuralism and Since', *History and Theory*, 26, 1987.
Kemp, T. P. and Ransmussa, D. (eds) *The Narrative Path*. New York, 1989.
Lawlor, L. *Imagination and Chance*. Albany, NY, 1992.
Miller, J. Hillis. 'But are things as we think they are?', *Times Literary Supplement*, 9–15 October 1987.
Reagan, C. E. *Paul Ricoeur*. Chicago, 1998.
Ricoeur, P. *History and Truth*. Evanston, IL, 1965.
—. *Husserl*. Chicago, 1967.
—. *Freud and Philosophy*. New Haven, CT, 1970.
—. *Paul Ricoeur: Political and Social Essays*, eds D. Stewart and J. Bien. Athens, OH, 1974.
—. *Interpretation Theory*. Fort Worth, TX, 1976.

—. *The Rule of Metaphor*. London, 1978.
—. *Hermeneutics and the Human Sciences*, ed. J. Thompson. Cambridge, 1981.
—. *Time and Narrative*, Vol. 1. Chicago, 1984.
—. *Time and Narrative*, Vol. 2. Chicago, 1985.
—. *Fallible Man*. New York, 1986.
—. *Time and Narrative*, Vol. 3. Chicago, 1988.
—. *The Conflict of Interpretations*. London, 1989.
—. *From Text to Action*. London, 1991.
—. *Oneself as Another*. Chicago, 1992.
—. *Figuring the Sacred*. New York, 1995.
—. *Critique and Conviction*. Cambridge, 1997.
—. *The Just*. Chicago, 2000.
Valdés, M. J. (ed.) *Reflection and Imagination*. London, 1991.
Wood, D. (ed.) *On Paul Ricoeur*. London, 1992.

Roland Barthes (1915–1980)

None of the theoreticians who has contributed to the radical transformation of literary and cultural studies since the 1960s has a higher profile than Roland Barthes. His name is associated with controversies about the status of literature and the nature of authorship that represent the public face of the postmodern revolution in literary theory. Yet, despite some famous and hard-fought debates, and a strong connection to major movements and practices – such as semiotics, structuralism and poststructuralism – Barthes cannot be identified with a strict or canonical set of principles, methods or ideas, in the same way as Lacan, Derrida or even Foucault. Barthes's career is remarkable for the breadth of the material that he has been able to deal with, from popular culture to the 'high' literary, from music to film and photography, from public textual conventions to the intense and solipsistic space of the purely subjective, even bodily or perverse, experience of reading.

Despite this eclecticism, Barthes's output revolves around a consistent set of issues. Rather than isolating or preferring a single methodology, his work is marked by the subtle adaptation of or exemplary enthusiasm for a range of theoretical terminologies, lifted variously from Saussurean linguistics, Russian formalism, marxism, Lacanian psychoanalysis, Derridean deconstruction and even Nietzschean perspectivism. The project, which these different terminologies needed to serve, was not the derivation of truth or theoretical finitude, but the attempt to enact a kind of avant-gardism of reading, a social and historical practice of which Barthes was the most subtle and articulate practitioner. The issue that defines Barthes's engagement with reading is the subjective value of the slippage between meaning and meaninglessness *as an experience*. At the communal level, shared conventions of meaning-making exhibit a simultaneous political brutality and historical fragility, exemplifying pressure-points in public culture where orthodox groups and values attempt to disguise or naturalize unresolved conflicts or unrepresented tensions. At the subjective level, textual codes and practices position us in a network of conditioned meanings that can only be evaded by the very instability and breakdown that haunts, indeed defines, them. All this is not understood in Barthes as a philosophy of language or even a theory of subjectivity, but as a narratable experience, touching on issues of class, the body and affectivity.

Barthes's first book-length work *Writing Degree Zero* (1953), a compilation of previously published essays, proposes that the problem of the relationship between language and meaning is not only the main subject of modern literature, but the form of its proper engagement with history. Literature must be seen as a historical phenomenon, not transcending it to form a trans-historical institution of unshakeable human or cultural values. It is this engagement with the 'problematics of language' (1967b, 3) that allows literature to renew its purpose by challenging the limitations of inherited conventions and forms. Literary form, like language itself, is imbued with the rich and unknowable traces of all the uses to which it has already been put. It is thus always already radically historicized, grounded in the tradition of previous practices in which the writer has no choice but to work. There is thus no simple free choice for writers of the mode of their creativity, nor are there any forms – like realism – which can convincingly claim to transcend linguistic conventions to produce an unadulterated engagement with the real world. Each literary form is implicated in the society which produces it, and writers inevitably exemplify social meanings outside of and beyond their own specific needs and intentions. The problematizing of language undertaken by writers from Flaubert onwards insistently reminds us that literary conventions can thus no longer be seen as pragmatic or functional options manipulated by writers seeking an outlet for their already existing ideas by way of free invention or free choice. Writing is itself a 'compromise between freedom and remembrance' (Barthes 1967b, 16), in which the new appears only as a complication or transformation of already located conventions. In modern poetry, this disruption of the inherited takes the form of a stripping away of the normal functions of language, till words appear in their most neutral form, their degree zero. In this way 'the consumer of poetry, deprived of the guide of selective connections, encounters the word frontally, and receives it as an absolute quantity, accompanied by all its possible associations' (Barthes 1967b, 48). In prose, the exemplary case is Camus' *The Outsider*, where 'the social or mythical characters of language are abolished in favour of a neutral and inert state of form' (77), which separates the writing from the dictates of 'a History not its own'. The aim here is to create a rupture in the texture of inherited language use, which confronts the reader with both the limitations of socially situated conventions and the possibility of a language expanding beyond them. Readers or 'consumers', as Barthes sometimes calls them, are thus announced as the possible site of a radical disjunction between conditioned meaning and its disruption.

In the mid-1960s, Barthes's work on literature provoked an attack from the more traditional practitioners of literary criticism, largely as a result of his *On Racine* (1960). This book is made up of three essays. The first and longest is an attempt at defining the Racinian 'type', the second a critique of contemporary Racinian theatre production and the third a polemical statement about the value of literary studies entitled 'History or Literature'. The opening essay is indebted to Lacan and Lévi-Strauss, and rests on the premise that the purpose of literary study is not to transmit moral meaning nor advance national culture, but rather to disinter an author's own dynamic and unresolved anthropology. Barthes's Racine presents a world, not of moral enlightenment nor psychological insight, but unresolved violence, intra-familial rivalry and sexual obsession. The role of literature is not to resolve nor evaluate this world, but to present it in its raw state to an audience who must experience it as a provocation. It is no wonder that this view, accompanied by the polemical statements in the book's final essay, constituted a challenge to the conventional role of criticism and literary study. Sorbonne-based Racine scholar Raymond Picard challenged Barthes in a pamphlet *Nouvelle critique ou nouvelle imposture* [*New Criticism or New Fraud*] (1965), which accused the new styles of criticism of being destructive, irrational, cynical and perverse. Barthes's reply in *Criticism and Truth* (1966) endures as one of the most lucid statements of the inadequacies of traditional criticism and the need for an alternative. It rigorously attacks the naivety and pseudo-objectivity of conventional criticism and its untheorized attitudes to signification. In the end, the book restates the key theme of *Writing Degree Zero* that 'a writer is someone for whom language constitutes a problem' (1987, 64), and links it with what will become a central idea in Barthes's thinking: that plurality is the defining quality of literary language. This plurality allows for meaning, but denies its univocity, insisting that any meaning discernible in a text is inevitably accompanied by a variety of other possible meanings that always destabilize its authority. The experience of meaning must also be an experience of that meaning's precariousness.

Although the material analysed is from another dimension of culture altogether – the inadvertent daily practices of the mass media – Barthes's semiotics repeats many of the same understandings of the relation between text and history that were also developed in *Writing Degree Zero*. Most famously assembled into the collection *Mythologies* (1957) and theorized in its appendix 'Myth Today' and the later *Elements of Semiology* (1964), Barthes's analyses of popular culture also attempt to restore to apparently naive communicative processes the complex function that belies their ostensibly transparent and simple motivation. The aim of these pithy and stylish pieces is to undermine 'the 'naturalness' with which newspapers, art and common sense constantly dress up a reality which, even though it is the one we live in, is undoubtedly determined by history' (Barthes 1973, 11). An example is the analysis of the use of language in the trial of peasant Gaston Dominici for the murder of a family of English tourists camped on his farm. The language of the court and the press conspire together to present Dominici's language as alien, and therefore outside of the logic of common sense and social consensus. The result is that the accused is subject to the narrative reconstruction and platitudinous psychology that underprops this common sense, a psychology based on the clichés of popular realist literature. The function of language therefore is not simply to represent Dominici and his supposed crime, but to confirm a whole petty bourgeois worldview as natural and unquestionable, and us all as subject to its logic. This is the primary function of the myths that Barthes identifies, to transform 'history into nature' (1973, 129), to take the specific and contingent logic of a certain historical social system and present it as unquestionable and inevitable, in short as natural.

In 'Myth Today', Barthes analyses this process as a double movement of signification. The simplest model of language use detects a stable signified beneath the material signifier. Beneath the prosecutor's language in the Dominici case lies the apparently simple attempt to reconstitute a sequence of events that clarify and explain a murder. Yet in this speech, both signifier and signified combine to become together a new signifier, this time of a signified with much broader social resonance, the confirmation of a view of psychology that reassures and rationalizes a whole social order. In this double movement from simple transparent sign to complex myth, signification is appropriated from its apparent function into a political historical function. In this way, the artificiality of sign systems becomes apparent: meaning only appears to be natural. It is in fact thoroughly staged to serve complex political and social needs. Myth is thus 'speech stolen and restored' (1973, 125), Barthes writes. It appears to perform a simple communicative function, but this simplicity is contrived. Another set of meanings has intervened which complicate signification by subsuming it into the needs of more elaborate social processes. This complex multi-layering in turn creates the opportunity for the analyst to perform a sceptical reading. Naive language use, if there is such a thing, can be described. Its logic can be endorsed or rejected, but purely on its own terms. The complex double structure of mythical semiotic systems, on the other hand, allows the analyst access to whole historical and social processes that expose not the truth or falsity of single statements, but the logic and culture of whole realities: semiotics is not a way of assessing the truth or falsehood of statements. It is a way of reading a society. There is 'no semiology which cannot, in the last analysis, be acknowledged as *semioclasm*' (1973, 9), Barthes writes. Meaning is thus not the purpose of signifying systems, but merely one of their artifices. The aim of the active reader is to draw attention to such artifices in order to defy the ruse of meaning and reveal the politics of signification.

Elements of Semiology (1964) represents an attempt to give semiotic analysis a more rigorous basis. The book is built around an explanation of four fundamental binary oppositions: *langue* and *parole*; signifier and signified; syntagm and system; and, finally, denotation and connotation. According to the opposition between *langue* (language) and *parole* (speech act), each individual language event is allowed, even predetermined, by the existence of a 'systematized set of conventions necessary to communication' (1967a, 13), that we conventionally call a language. Because speech can only occur within the context of language, yet we only know language by way of speech, the two are in a genuinely dialectical relationship. This distinction allows the analyst to detect the general principles and possibilities behind each act of signification, and also to see how these principles and possibilities are actualized. The second distinction in *Elements* is the conventional and familiar Saussurian one between the two things that constitute the sign, its material substance (signifier) and 'mental representation' (42) or signified. Thirdly, Barthes distinguishes between system (paradigm in more conventional structuralism) and syntagm. The paradigm represents the various options that can be substituted for one another in a cultural practice, and the syntagm the logical sequence which combines them in order. Various words may substitute for one another in the same position in a sentence, and are thus in a paradigmatic relationship to one another within the same system. The order in which they appear in that sentence betrays their syntagmatic relationship. In a famous example, Barthes proposes that the menu in a restaurant replicates the same logic: the alternative dishes within a course are a system; the logical sequence in which they appear (entrées before main course, main course before dessert) is their syntagm. The final binary opposition Barthes outlines is between denotation and connotation, announcing that 'the future probably belongs to a linguistics of connotation' (1967a, 90). This claim exhibits the contradiction at the heart of this semiotic enterprise. Connotation is seen as 'general, global and diffuse' (91), yet Barthes calls connotation a system (91). This paradox foreshadows how attempts at the rigorous constitution of binary oppositions as rock-hard theoretical principles would soon come undone in Derridean deconstruction, a process of which Barthes would become perhaps one of the less philosophically rigorous but more rhetorically influential fellow-travellers. The most severe version of Barthes's semiotic analysis appears in his treatment of the language of the fashion industry in *The Fashion*

System (1967). His next works represent (especially *S/Z* and *Empire of Signs*) an inversion, even parody of this approach, even though the scepticism they imply towards a putatively scientific methodology always respects and relies on the semioclastic will to read across signs and texts for their unconfessed meanings.

Elements ends with a call for a synchronic approach to language, to present not the unfolding meaning of history in process, but 'a cross-section of history' (Barthes 1967a, 98). This ahistorical approach may defy the traditional marxist imperative to always historicize that haunts much of Barthes's early collection *Critical Essays* (1964) and its celebration of Brecht, yet it foreshadows another model of textual politics, one that would become increasingly important and one with which Barthes is strongly identified: the idea that the instability and plurality of signification resist the homogenization on which all author-itarian systems (political, social and intellectual) depend, thus allowing for the contra-diction, inconclusiveness and ambiguity that can be experienced as at least an image of freedom. It is this idea that Barthes now develops into a fully-fledged understanding of textuality, and the horizons of pleasure, and in turn, subjectivity itself.

Barthes's most famous single piece of writing is the short essay 'The Death of the Author' (1968). More than any other piece, this essay has become notorious among those opposed to the poststructuralist influence on literary studies. Here Barthes argues that the under-standing of a literary text in terms of the biography, psychology or historical context of its author is reductive and limiting, and is a misconstruction of the nature of literary language. 'To give a text an Author is to impose a limit on that text, to furnish it with a final signified, to close the writing' (Barthes 1977a, 147). This closure, in turn, collaborates with all authoritarian systems of meaning-making. A style of reading that engages with the plurality of textuality as 'a multi-dimensional space in which a variety of writings, none of them original, blend and clash' (146) challenges such authority, becoming 'an anti-theological activity, an activity that is truly revolutionary since to refuse to fix meanings is, in the end, to refuse God and his hypostases – reason, science, law' (147). Here, reading against meaning liberates us from the constraints of traditional reading institutions, the academy in particular, and allows us to animate the incommensurability, contradiction and difference implicit in textuality. Here is the most succinct version of Barthes's understanding of reading as an avant-garde activity. The later essay 'From Work to Text' (1971) develops many of these same ideas into a comparison between the traditional model of, on the one hand, the closed work located in fixed and knowable sequences of literary filiation and meaning, and the open text, on the other, which expects and inspires an active reading, 'play, activity, production, practice' (Barthes 1977a, 162). This article is largely an attempt to assimilate Julia Kristeva's idea of the 'intertextual', that texts produce their meaning not from their own internal structures and intentions, but from their relationship with other texts. Reading is seen not as an act of consumption, but of collaboration (Barthes 1977a, 163).

Barthes's most sustained piece of literary criticism *S/Z* (1970) brings together many of the themes of these essays and others, such as the influential essay on narratology 'Introduction to the Structural Analysis of Narrative' (1966). *S/Z* is simultaneously the highest version, and a parody of, structural analysis. It is a book-length treatment of Balzac's story 'Sarrasine', breaking the narrative into 561 units, most of which are a few words or sentences long. These units are then analysed in terms of five functional codes: the hermeneutic, which reveals how enigmas are proposed and then dealt with; the semiotic, which reads semes in terms of their simple denotative function; the symbolic, where meanings operate in a polyvalent or reversible form; the code of actions, which plots the sequence of episodes; and, finally, the referential code, which alludes to culturally sanctioned bodies of knowledge. The story is shown to be built around the interrelationship of these codes. Barthes writes: 'to depict is to unroll the carpet of the codes, to refer not from a language to a referent but from one code to another' (Barthes 1974, 55). The illusion of animation in the realist narrative is the result of the simultaneous function of different codes 'according to unequal wavelengths' (61). The slight disjunction between the codes gives the sense of accident and movement we read as the real. *S/Z* is probably most famous for the argument that realism as a literary genre does not present an open window on the world, but is highly structured around codes and conventions of narrative, an argument enlarged in the book's conclusion to become the general credo of postmodern metafiction (a rising literary style of the time) that 'narrative concerns only itself' (Barthes 1974, 213). This view of realism as highly conventionalized appears in Barthes's work as early as *Writing Degree Zero* (see Barthes 1967b, 67).

Systematic structuralist analysis is also a victim of Barthes's method, despite the latter's apparently mathematical order. It is clearly shown that the operation of the text can be broken into constitutive elements, but these function not as impersonal laws or as universal narrative ingredients, but rather as latent textual experiences that only achieve value when read. Reading is itself an active and open-ended process, a 'nomination in the course of becoming, a tireless approximation, a metonymic labour' (1974, 11). Reading then does not aim for the isolation of a fixed set of meanings, nor does it rely on the architectonics of a rigid, closed system of codes that plot scientifically the horizons of the text and limit the possible values it can produce. In Barthes's words, 'reading does not consist in stopping the chain of systems, in establishing a truth, a legality of the text . . . it consists in coupling these systems, not according to their finite quantity, but according to their plurality' (1974, 11). Here we find an early statement of a theme that would become important in Barthes's later work: readers engage and involve themselves with the plurality and dynamism of the textual experience because they themselves are textual. 'This "I" which approaches the text is already itself a plurality of other texts' (10).

This relationship between subjectivity and textuality is developed fully in Barthes's next major theoretical work *The Pleasure of the Text* (1973). What is discernible here is the influence of Lacanian psychoanalysis and its understanding of the relationship between subjectivity and language, though as he asserts in *Roland Barthes by Roland Barthes*, Barthes's use of other systems of thought is never systematic or 'scrupulous', but allusive, impressionistic and 'undecided' (1977b, 150). *The Pleasure of the Text* picks up on many of the themes that had dominated Barthes's work since 1968, especially the image of the text as defined by plurality. Here, however, the focus of this plurality is the subjectivity of the reader, an idea that had been foreshadowed without being thoroughly developed in the conclusion of 'The Death of the Author'. The experience of the text is to be seen as erotic even perverse, and divided between two collaborating types of affective experience: pleasure, which confirms the reader's sense of self and his culture on the one hand, and *jouissance*, or bliss, that flirts with the loss of self on the other. (It is worth noting that this distinction echoes Nietzsche's bifurcation of Greek literature into Apollonian and Dionysian modes. Nietzsche's influence also emerges in Barthes's aphoristic style here.) These two experiences of textuality are always in some kind of contradiction with one another, but it is this very incommensurability that releases the text's erotic potential. Barthes writes 'neither culture nor its destruction is erotic; it is the seam between them, the fault, the flaw, which becomes so' (Barthes 1975, 7). What is crucial to grasp here is the slippage between the possible sites of these different affects. They are both to be understood, of course, as emotional experiences released in the reader. Yet, the 'text of pleasure' and the 'text of *jouissance*' are discussed as qualitatively different kinds of texts. The text of pleasure 'comes from culture and does not break with it, is linked to a *comfortable* practice of reading' (14). The text of bliss, on the other hand, 'imposes a state of loss' and 'discomforts' (14). Texts thus are agents of affectivity. The spontaneity and freedom of the reader's experience is, if not constrained, at least defined by a putative typology of textuality, though Barthes refrains from offering a list of ingredients of each type of text beyond the kind of impressions captured here. Indeed, the source of any such typology is no longer to be objectified in the text itself, but in its reading. The texts are qualitatively different, but this difference is not to be known in their structure nor in their production, but in their consumption. The nature of the text is radically *subjectivized*, and the ideal reading subject is imagined, who 'keeps the two texts in his field and in his hands the reins of pleasure and bliss', who 'simultaneously and contradictorily participates in the profound hedonism of all culture . . . and in the destruction of that culture: he enjoys the consistency of his selfhood (that is his pleasure) and seeks its loss (that is his bliss)' (Barthes 1975, 14).

From at least *Mythologies* on, Barthes had identified the text, not only as an object to analyse, but also as a site of experience, whether this experience was understood as consumption, mere reading or as the 'doubly perverse' (1975, 14) entwining of bliss and pleasure. The constant challenge of his career had been to work out exactly how the objective nature of the text and the subjective nature of a reader's experience of it could be qualified and quantified together. It would be naïve to announce that this problem's final and absolute destiny was the model we find here of textual object and reading subject as a kind of chiasmus, a mirror-like sharing of a fundamental linguistic nature. Yet this does seem to represent a point of clarification in Barthes's relationship to this issue that earlier alternatives did not. This is especially true of semiology, the objective potential of which Barthes never seemed to fully believe in, perhaps because it never provided a satisfactory account of the motility and active nature of reading.

Two works which followed *The Pleasure of the Text*, *Roland Barthes by Roland Barthes* (1975) and *A Lover's Discourse: Fragments* (1977), commit themselves to the model of the subject as text. The epigraph to *Roland Barthes* says of the fragmented account of the author's life which follows: 'it must all be considered as if spoken by a character in a novel' (Barthes 1977b, 1). A comparable statement opens *A Lover's Discourse*: 'The description of the lover's discourse has been replaced by its simulation, and to that discourse has been restored its fundamental person, the *I*, in order to stage an utterance, not an analysis' (Barthes 1990, 3). In both these texts, the subject is not something to be analysed or even described, but something to be produced out of the heart of the languages and texts that make subjectivity possible. It is not an entity, but an enactment, and it is not to be known but experienced.

Two important statements in *Roland Barthes* reinforce this point, and it is important to recognize how grounded both these sophisticated and generalizable theoretical remarks are in the intensity of, not just anyone's, but Roland Barthes's own idiosyncratic self-identification. First, Barthes defines his relationship to his own time:

> I am only the imaginary contemporary of my own present: contemporary of its languages, its utopias, its systems (i.e. of its fictions), in short, of its mythology or of its philosophy but not of its history, of which I inhabit only the shimmering reflection: the *phantasmagoria*. (1977b, 59)

Here, subjectivity is only conceivable within the horizons of a thoroughly textualized culture. The tone here, however, is not one of loss, or of limitation, but of stimulation, open-endedness and plurality. If we recall the distant yet resonant argument from *Writing Degree Zero*, that modern literature confronted history by problematizing language, we can see how this statement reconfigures subjectivity as an implicit engagement with the social and intersubjective, even if Barthes is no longer confident in describing it as the historical.

The second statement of interest here links the theorist of subjectivity with the contradictory politics of meaning. Speaking of himself in the third person, Barthes writes:

> Evidently he dreams of a world which would be *exempt from meaning* . . . yet for him, it is not a question of recovering a pre-meaning, an origin of the world, of life, of facts, anterior to meaning, but rather to imagine a post-meaning: one must traverse, as though the length of an initiatic way, the whole meaning, in order to be able to extenuate it, to exempt it. (1977b, 87)

The value of the plurality of the text that Barthes had done so much to advertise in the second half of his writing career emerges as the slippage between an encumbering meaning and an imagined post-meaning. It is in the surprise and disorientation that the eruption of meaninglessness into meaning provides that one attains a sense of selfhood.

This argument is developed in Barthes's last major work, his study of photography, *Camera Lucida* (1980). The key theoretical achievement here is the distinction between *studium* and *punctum*, a definition of textual experience not very far from the distinction between the text of pleasure and the text of bliss. The *studium* is an experience of interest in an image, even enthusiasm for it. The *punctum*, on the other hand, thrills and destabilizes, surprises and reveals the subject to itself. Again, the *punctum* is only known as part of the viewer's affective experience, yet it is also an attribute of the text itself. Barthes is able to identify the *punctum* in various of the photos he discusses. The most important example is a photo he does not reproduce of his mother as a child (which he calls the Winter Garden Photograph). This photo which he discovers going through her effects after she has died captures something about her that he is able to recognize and that he had forgotten. The experience is a kind of Proustian epiphany, where one is surprised by a feeling of one's own fleeting authenticity as it emerges from a material re-embodiment of the past. It is this disruption of his normal conception of himself and his mother by a seemingly more real experience of her that revives in Barthes a sense of the 'real', a term that has fascinated and lured him throughout his career. In an argument seemingly oblivious to the image-manipulation that photography has always been subject to, and now of course rendered obsolete by digitalization, Barthes argues for the status of the photographic image as the record of what has literally been. Debate over the veracity of this claim aside, it does provide a useful insight into Barthes's thinking. More than a naive assumption about the deterministic power of the real, Barthes is again asserting that the real is simply an effect. Like subjectivity, reality does not impinge upon us, but is enacted as that location where the text seems to come undone, where the seam between meaning and meaninglessness is under most pressure. Here we experience an intensification of both the sense of the self and of the real. This intensification makes clear the textual nature of both subjectivity and reality. This is not because of the inevitability of textual mediation in our culturally enclosed experience of the world. Texts do not constitute a uniform and unbroken field that wraps us around with representations instead of things. The field of textuality is highly fraught, and ruptured by what we experience as a hypothetical outside that we can never know or validate. Almost invariably these sites of imagined rupture occur where our conventional practices of meaning reach their limit, break down and allow for the meaninglessness that inevitably shadows them. It is this experience of imagined rupture that Barthes sometimes saw as the possibility of a kind of politico-cultural disruption, but that at the end of his career produced not self-consciousness in the traditional humanist sense, but an understanding of textuality as a kind of perpetual re-subjectification.

Nick Mansfield

Further reading and works cited

Barthes, R. *Elements of Semiology*. New York, 1967a.
—. *Writing Degree Zero*. New York, 1967b.
—. *Critical Essays*. Evanston, IL, 1972.
—. *Mythologies*. ed. A. Lavers. London, 1973.
—. *S/Z*. New York, 1974.
—. *The Pleasure of the Text*. New York, 1975.
—. *Image-Music-Text*, ed. S. Heath, Glasgow, 1977a.
—. *Roland Barthes by Roland Barthes*. London, 1977b.
—. *On Racine*. New York, 1983a.
—. *The Fashion System*. New York, 1983b.
—. *The Empire of Signs*. London, 1983c.
—. *Camera Lucida*. London, 1984.
—. *Criticism and Truth*, ed. K. Pilcher Keuneman. Minneapolis, MN, 1987.
—. *A Lover's Discourse: Fragments*. Harmondsworth, 1990.
Calvet, L.-J. *Roland Barthes*. Cambridge, 1994.
Culler, J. *Barthes*. London, 1983.
Hill, L. 'Barthes's Body', *Paragraph, 11*, 1988.
Lavers, A. *Roland Barthes*. London, 1982.
Moriarty, M. *Roland Barthes*. Cambridge, 1991.
Picard, R. *Nouvelle critique ou nouvelle imposture*. Paris, 1965.
Rylance, R. *Roland Barthes*. Hemel Hempstead, 1994.
Ungar, S. *Roland Barthes*. London, 1983.
— and McGraw, B. R. (eds) *Signs in Culture*. Iowa City, IA, 1989.
Wiseman, M. B. *The Ecstasies of Roland Barthes*. London, 1989.

French Structuralism: A. J. Greimas (1917–1992), Tzvetan Todorov (1939–) and Gérard Genette (1930–)

This essay will attempt to give a general synthesis of French structuralist thinking from the 1960s onwards. Yet its focus lies not in a sketch of the historical background of structuralism, however useful (if not indispensable) such a frame of reference may be; the impressive two-volume study by François Dosse offers extensive information regarding the complex networks of relations, persons and influences on the Parisian scene. Rather, I would like to concentrate my discussion on the theoretical and the methodological presuppositions of structuralist thinking, by focusing on the work of three major literary scholars working in (and sometimes against) this productive paradigm in literary studies.

This article consists of two closely interrelated parts. First of all, I will describe the general principles that underlie structuralist thinking. To this end, I will concentrate on three seminal texts: *Sémantique structurale* (1966) by Algirdas Julien Greimas, *Grammaire du Décaméron* (1969) by Tzvetan Todorov, and *Discours du récit* (1972) by Gérard Genette. In the second part, the scholarly career of these three protagonists will be sketched in order to grasp the complexity of their attitude towards structuralist thinking in later years. Thus I hope to demonstrate how the 'structuralists' have gradually come to broaden the scope of their research – in an obvious attempt to cope with the acknowledged limitations of the structuralist project – without, however, having taken recourse to a radical 'poststructuralist' reorientation.

I will indeed argue that, although structuralism may be seen as a historical current in literary studies (roughly situated in the 1960s and 1970s, with its main manifestation in France), its premises still continue to exert a profound influence on our contemporary thinking about literature and culture. Some dreams of structuralism may be declared obsolete or dead; however, structuralism as such, as an ambitious project in the humanities, definitely cannot.

The emergence of structuralism, which can be situated around 1955–60, is related to an important shift in the humanities, which may be roughly characterized as a move from a 'pre-scientific' towards an explicitly 'scientific' approach. In the specific case of literary studies, some younger scholars opposed vehemently the impressionistic and strongly subjective way in which canonized literature was considered. In fact, the analysis of a literary text hardly amounted to anything but a mere paraphrase of its content in a quasi-literary style, clearly intended to enhance its canonized status and its aesthetic merits. This scholarly discourse on literature was severely dismissed as impressionistic (versus systematic) and subjective (versus objective), of local and anecdotal importance only (versus generally valid), as highly normative (versus descriptive-analytical), and finally as literary (versus scientific).

This overall critique, combined with a passionate plea for an entirely new discourse on and method of study of literature, gave rise to an innovative, productive intellectual movement during the 1960s in Paris, which was very soon associated with the name of 'structuralism'. Though controversial in some respects, structuralism almost immediately gained popularity and status among younger scholars. In this respect, it is symptomatic that Greimas' essay on semantics was titled *Sémantique structurale* because the editor thought that adding this fashionable adjective would contribute to its success.

Structuralism coincides with a strong interdisciplinary orientation, in which the pilot-function of modern linguistics was generally acknowledged as a decisive impetus for the scientific reorientation of the humanities in general, and of the discipline of literary studies in particular. Linguistics was supposed to provide not only the theoretical premises but also the concrete methodological tools and the specific concepts for the analysis of numerous phenomena. In this respect, the ideas of Ferdinand de Saussure and Louis Hjelmslev, and, in addition, the paradigm of transformational-generative linguistics primarily associated with the name of Noam Chomsky, proved extremely influential frames of reference.

A supplementary catalysing factor for literary studies was provided by the work of Roman

Jakobson and the anthropologist Claude Lévi-Strauss. In his analysis of social behaviour, Lévi-Strauss endeavoured to go beyond the mere detailed description of empirical data when he set out to seize the mechanisms underlying family relations, myths, rituals and other semiotic practices. He postulated a limited number of fundamental categories (mostly oppositions and homologies), which could be put into practice, modified or combined by means of given transformational principles in order to account fully for the anthropological phenomena. The similarities between this project and the generative model advocated by Chomsky in his *Syntactic Structures* (1957) are striking; the linguist also starts from a limited number of elements and rules in order to generate all possible sentences of a language.

When analysing the classic myth of Oedipus, for instance, Lévi-Strauss (in his *Anthropologie structurale*, 1958) does not restrict himself to one particular textual version. Rather, he constructs his version of the myth as an abstract basic structure from which all particular instances may subsequently be derived. Diversity and specificity thus become secondary to unity and coherence. Moreover, this constructed, 'immanent' level of the 'text' is further rewritten as a fundamental homology of two basic oppositions. One of these oppositions thematizes family relations (underrating vs. overrating of blood relations), the other is related to the origin of mankind (chthonic vs. autochthonic origin). This deep structure analysis results in a paradigmatic interpretation, which reveals the fundamental oppositions at stake in the mythic structure, as well as in a syntagmatic reading, which displays the (chrono-)logical chain of events constituting the mythical plot.

From these preliminary remarks, some basic principles of structuralist thinking may be derived. First of all, structuralists strongly believe in a 'pure', scientific point of view, which is most apparent in their construction of a general theoretical and conceptual framework and, complementarily, in their polemical anti-humanistic attitude. To achieve this ideal, the scholar 'constructs' his object of research, which is subsequently analysed by means of a priori scientific procedures (which are stated to possess universal validity). This analysis resorts to a restricted number of basic categories and oppositions, a set of relations and combinatory principles in order to arrive at more complex and more dynamic structures, and separate, if not hierarchically structured, levels of analysis. Finally, an unambiguously defined conceptual apparatus is considered indispensable to guarantee and to maximize the scientific status of the structuralist enterprise.

A structuralist fascination seems hardly surprising in the case of Algirdas Julien Greimas, since he was, as a professional linguist, first and foremost interested in the construction of a semantic theory destined to analyse linguistic significations. Greimas started as a lexicographer – which accounts for his interest in meaning, in contrast to the almost exclusively syntactic orientation of his fellow-linguists – but gradually he became interested in the way in which isolated word meanings might be combined into larger semantic wholes. In his seminal essay *Sémantique structurale* (1966), Greimas introduces to this end the concept of isotopy, which designates the repetition of certain semantic features in order to enhance the coherence and the homogeneity of syntagms, sentences and, ultimately, of texts in their entirety. Semantic incongruity is subsequently analysed in terms of consecutive isotopies, or else in terms of a clash between different isotopies (e.g. in the case of metaphorical expressions).

In the final chapter of his book, Greimas tries to account for a macro-structural semantics. Relying on Lévi-Strauss's concept of homology and Vladimir Propp's formalist analysis of folktales, he proposes his famous actantial scheme. In fact, the apparent multitude of characters and plots may be reduced to a restricted number of functional roles (or 'actants', in contrast to the actors which operate in a particular narrative) and predicates. First of all, there is the central relation between a subject and an object, a relationship characterized as 'desire'. Next, there is the axis of communication, which relates the sender (the actant provoking the subject's desire, e.g. by expressing a wish or formulating a certain task) to the eventual receiver of the object. Finally, there is the actantial pair of the helper versus the opponent, thematized as the axis of struggle.

In his *Sémantique structurale*, Greimas also proposes – rather succinctly – a syntagmatic model for the analysis of narrative events by postulating a series of tests which the subject has to succeed in completing in a fixed logical order. Later on, this idea is further elaborated and specified. Narratives may be defined as a logical sequence of four phases, which may or may not be realized explicitly in the course of a particular story. First of all, in the Manipulation phase, the virtual subject receives his task through the mediation of the sender. Next, the emerging subject has to obtain the necessary qualifications (knowledge and power) during the Competence phase, before he can really confront and defeat his opponent successfully during the Performance phase. Eventually, the realized subject has to deliver the achieved object to the right receiver in order to get acknowledged as the only true subject. This occurs during the Sanction phase, in which good and evil are separated definitively and the incarnation of the good is rewarded.

A similar fascination for modern linguistics is to be found in Tzvetan Todorov's *Grammaire du Décaméron*, published in 1969. In the programmatic introduction to his study, Todorov pleads for a new science, 'narratology', which would study the essential characteristics of narratives, regardless of their origin and their medium. Although Todorov takes Boccaccio's collection of stories, *Decamerone*, as his main topic of research, the 'grammar' he proposes has obviously far more general (if not universal) pretensions. In this respect, it is not a coincidence that Todorov's text grammar is entirely modelled on Chomskyan linguistic theory.

Todorov takes the 'proposition' (defined as a 'non-decomposable action') as the basic unit of narrative. On a syntactic level, propositions consist of agents and predicates; on a semantic level, they can be analysed in terms of proper names, substantives, adjectives and verbs. Moreover, they may be modified by means of negation and comparatives.

After this first-level analysis, Todorov proposes a theoretical model for the integration of individual propositions into larger sequences. Narratological theory thus takes the form of a structured algorithm: starting from a few basic elements, complex narrative structures are gradually generated by means of combinations, transformations and hierarchical levels. Although the linguistic orientation is dominant on the level of both general argumentation and detailed textual analysis, Todorov's book, however, displays a fundamental ambivalence, which may be considered symptomatic for literary structuralism in general. Indeed, there is a discrepancy between, on the one hand, the detailed (if not exhaustive) analysis of a particular literary text and, on the other hand, the intended level of an abstract (even universalistic) text grammar.

The same holds true for Gérard Genette's *Discours du récit* (1972), which was originally part of a collection of essays, *Figures III*. Taking one particular literary text as his starting point – Proust's *A la recherche du temps perdu*, a masterpiece of literary modernism – Genette presents a general theoretical frame for the analysis of narratives. Once again, linguistic categories seem perfectly suited for describing literary texts as well. Genette borrows the terms 'tense', 'mood' and 'voice' to constitute the basic categories of narrative discourse.

Yet, unlike Todorov, Genette does not entirely resort to linguistics in order to construct his theory. Rather, he integrates the theoretical concepts and the methodological tools developed by traditional literary studies. The specific 'structuralist' dimension of his research lies in Genette's search for conceptual categories that may be applicable to a huge variety of texts. In this respect, he explores the various strategies used to represent the various aspects of temporality: order (chronological versus anachronistic), speed (from ellipsis and summary to descriptive pauses) and frequency (singular versus iterative narration). The chapter on 'Mood' introduces the distinction between the narrator (who tells) and the focalizer (who sees). In his analysis of 'Voice', Genette discusses the various instances of narrative enunciation, in relation to their qualitative position and the level on which they function. Hence, Genette is less interested in the logic of events constituting a plot (in contrast to Todorov) than in the specific modalities of the process of narration itself. In this respect, the influence of Proust's novel of consciousness, which is Genette's exemplary narrative, on his narratological model can hardly be underestimated.

In spite of the at times violent criticism that Genette's proposals have met – a criticism with which the author has endeavoured to cope in his *Nouveaux discours du récit* (1983) – his model undoubtedly remains a stimulating landmark in narratology to the present day.

After the heydays of structuralism, the oeuvres of Greimas, Genette and Todorov have manifested interesting evolutions, in which, perhaps predictably, continuity and discontinuity are precariously balanced. However, one cannot state that, in the cases of these scholars, a major shift of 'structuralism' towards 'poststructuralism' can be witnessed. The protagonists of French structuralist poetics have never drastically deconstructed their initial structuralist project, even though the rather naive dreams of a truly objectivist science of meaning have been largely abandoned. Instead of taking recourse to a deconstructionist or rhetorical stand – as the later Barthes and the members of the *Tel Quel* group have successfully done – Greimas, Genette and Todorov have, each in their own way, tried to compensate for the recognized limitations of structuralism in two ways. On the one hand, they have considerably broadened their field of interest; on the other hand, they refrained from certain structuralist premises and pretensions.

In general, Greimas remains the most typical representative of 'orthodox' structuralist thinking. In fact, he never gave up his dream of constructing a major semiotic theory which would encompass all meaningful phenomena in society: various kinds of texts, but also rituals, human behaviour, emotions, etc. To this end, he continually tried to formulate an adequate metalanguage that would guarantee the scientific character of his enterprise. The landmark for this variant of semiotic research remains the invaluable two-volume *Sémiotique. Dictionnaire raisonné de la théorie du langage*, written/edited in close collaboration with J. Courtés (1979). In fact, Greimas's theory is constructed as a set of hierarchically related metalanguages: the level of 'descriptive' metalanguage is needed to analyse 'objects', but it has also to be validated on the superior levels of a 'methodological' and eventually of an 'epistemological' metalanguage. In the case of Greimas and his followers, theoretical conceptualization and meticulous analysis are thus closely related, since they are intended to sustain and to stimulate one another. In the two volumes *Du Sens* (1970) and *Du Sens II* (1983), Greimas broadens the field of application of his semiotics considerably. He convincingly argues the semantic and narrative dimension at work in all kinds of semiotic constructs: social conventions, a story, a description, as well as fragments from a scholarly essay or a cookbook.

On the other hand, the theory has undergone substantial modifications as well.

Gradually, a shift is noticeable from textual analysis towards the analysis of subjectivity and human experience. Modalities have come to fulfil a decisive role in the discursive construction of narrative sequences and of the rhetoric of subjectivity. Complementary to the level of the enunciated (the story as it is), Greimas stresses the importance of the level of enunciation, i.e. the basic contract between sender and receiver which ought to optimize communication.

From this point of view *Sémiotique des passions. Des états de choses aux états d'âme* (1991) is of crucial importance. In this book, written in close collaboration with Jacques Fontanille, traditionally philosophical subject matter, human passions and emotions, are considered from a semiotic point of view. As a consequence, in order to investigate a passion such as jealousy, the authors start from daily intuitions and their codification in dictionaries in order to describe the actantial and narrative construction of the passion. Next, they reconsider its manifestation in diverse discursive contexts, thus demonstrating both the homogeneity and the crucial variations that are at stake.

In contrast to this thoroughly scientific approach, the short essay *De l'imperfection* (1987) tries to deal with the aesthetic experience in a much more fragmentary, literary style. Taking semiotics as an axiology, Greimas pleads in favour of the so-called 'small ontologies': the delights of secrets and seductions, passion and bodily sensations. The strong scientific rhetoric of his other texts is here replaced by a more frivolous diction, in which examples taken from literature play a central role. Yet, it is not a coincidence that this text was published by a rather obscure publishing house, and that Greimas refrained from referring to it in his other, 'more serious' writings. The same denial (or is it mere ignorance?) is to be found in overviews of French structuralism as well.

Gérard Genette handles the problematic aspects of structuralism in a different way. Like Greimas, most of his work remains largely within the boundaries of the structuralist paradigm. However, at the same time, Genette has managed to establish his own authoritative position, despite the ongoing debates regarding structuralism, owing to his undogmatic position.

In retrospect, one is indeed struck by the fact that Genette has, almost from his early start as a literary scholar, never confined his research to the text as an autonomous, closed universe of meaning. Quite on the contrary, he has taken into account a much broader dimension of textuality. His *Introduction à l'architexte* (1979) studies the problematic relation between individual texts and the categorial concepts of genre and mode. *Palimpsestes* (1982) complicates matters even further, focusing on the crucial question of intertextuality. Genette limits himself in this book to the study of explicit forms of intertextual rewriting (in his terminology the subcategory of 'transtextuality'). Relying on a large variety of examples, taken from different historical periods and different national literatures, he explores a number of transformational relations, ranging from mere imitation to parodies, pastiches and more complex forms of textual transposition. *Seuils* (1987) treats the 'paratextual' elements, which tend to surround a text without constituting an integrated part of it: preface, footnotes, titles, mottoes, blurbs ... This paratextual information, which symbolizes the problematic borders of a text, may fulfil several functions, either in a constructive (affirmative) or in a more deconstructive (ironic or polemic) way.

These publications indicate how Genette tries to account for a large variety of textual phenomena in a deliberate attempt to overcome the limitations of classic structuralism. On the other hand, they still display a major 'structuralist' concern. Instead of drastically deconstructing the concept of text altogether, Genette prefers to explore the marginal zones of inter- and paratextuality in a systematic, coherent and encompassing way. Even the boundaries of texts are thus scrutinized, systematically classified and accordingly analysed. So, in the end, the ideal of a taxonomic structure remains fundamentally unaltered, even though the author frequently underlines the hazardous dimension of his own enterprise. Similarly, his analysis of literary examples pays hardly any attention to their textual and contextual specificity.

Genette's latest publications – the two volumes of L'oeuvre de l'Art, Immanence et transcendance (1994) and La relation esthétique (1997a) – offer a very broad philosophical view on general aesthetics. The first volume considers art as a fascinating combination of immanence (art as a specific object in its own right) and transcendence. The latter term refers to the various ways in which a work of art transcends its own material status: works of art may be copied, transformed and reconsidered throughout history. In this respect, Genette's ideas may be seen as a non-deconstructionist answer to Derrida's concept of iterability and his critique on the logic of origin. The second volume considers the different relation between the work of art and the consumer of art. As such, it complements the rather 'intrinsic' approach of the first book by taking into account the psychological aspects of the aesthetic attention, the aesthetic judgement and, ultimately, the artistic function.

Finally, there is the influential work by Tzvetan Todorov. Although his earliest books were largely consistent with the expectations of structuralism as a scientific framework, Todorov's work was already at that time characterized by an enormous diversity. Instead of opting for a lifelong realization of one and the same theoretical and methodological project (like Greimas did), Todorov prefers to demonstrate the applicability of structuralist thinking to a large variety of literary and cultural phenomena. This very broad field of interest results in a large number of fascinating essays, which formulate a certain problem in a perspicuous yet sometimes rather suggestive manner, rather than analysing it extensively.

Perhaps Todorov's most central text – and obviously one which has become a 'classic' in its own right – is his Introduction à la littérature fantastique (1970). In this brilliant essay, Todorov tackles a major problem in modern Western literature, i.e. the genre of 'fantastic literature'. To this end, several dimensions of literary research are combined in a highly original manner, resulting in the first systematic approach to the genre. First of all, Todorov tries to reconstruct, in accordance with the principles of structuralist narratology at that time, the underlying patterns that yield this 'fantastic effect'. On the level of syntax, the specific concatenation of events contributes strongly to the effect of suspense. On the level of the semantic and thematic organization, Todorov discriminates between themes of the I (e.g. metamorphosis or the multiple personality) and themes of the other (e.g. sexuality, cruelty and death). This apparently intrinsic approach of the genre is, however, supplemented by an analysis of the reading experience. Indeed, fantastic literature leads to a fundamental 'hesitation' in the reader, since he/she cannot decide whether the story is to be believed or not. Hence, the fantastic is situated on the borderline between the marvellous and the uncanny. Finally, Todorov's essay also considers the historical evolution of the genre, an interest that is marginal in most structuralist texts. In fact, Todorov claims that, in our times, the main function of the fantastic, i.e. talking about 'forbidden' taboos, has largely been taken over by psychoanalysis.

In his recent research, Todorov has explored fully these various trajectories. In his work, he has succeeded in demonstrating brilliantly the advantages of a structuralist perspective, while at the same time he transcends the limitations of classic structuralist thinking by taking into account historical components and the experience of the reader as well.

From the 1980s onwards, the growing resonance of Bakhtin's ideas on polyphony and dialogicity has definitely become a major impetus in Todorov's work. Instead of adopting a strictly 'objectivist' point of view, Todorov starts to explore the intricate tension between alterity and identity in various contexts. Several books deal with the images strategically constructed and legitimized by subjects (groups, cultures ...) in dealing with the both seductive and threatening presence of a radical otherness. However, in reverse, this conception of the other fundamentally influences the conception of one's own identity as well. *La conquête de l'Amérique. La question de l'autre* (1982) investigates the coming into being of the 'new' world in the discourse of the Spanish conquistadores, whereas in *Face à l'extrême* (1991) the western trauma of Auschwitz and the excesses of totalitarian societies is discussed.

Nous et les autres (1989) reconstructs the self-image (and the image of otherness) in the history of French civilization. Here as well, the scholarly analysis gradually moves into a more committed strategy of writing, in which the subjectivity of the author and the constructive character of his own narrative are deliberately exploited. In fact, Todorov's recent publications are clearly marked by an important 'ethical turn'. The former anti-individualistic structuralist has become a genuine 'man of letters' who explicitly argues for a new, non-naive form of existential and ethical humanism, in close dialogue with the ideas of French philosophers such as Montaigne and Rousseau. According to Todorov, we have to learn how to cultivate our 'imperfect garden' (*Le jardin imparfait*, 1998): the expression stems from Montaigne. The fact that he recently published an intellectual biography of Benjamin Constant – a narrative of an individual, in his specific socio-historical constellation – is, in view of this humanistic reorientation, hardly a coincidence, nor a surprise.

Dirk de Geest

Further reading and works cited

Culler, J. *Structuralist Poetics*. London, 1975.
Dosse, F. *History of Structuralism*, 2 vols. Minneapolis, MN, 1997.
Genette, G. *Introduction à l'architexte*. Paris, 1979.
—. *Narrative Discourse*. Ithaca, NY, 1980.
—. *Palimpsestes*. Paris, 1982.
—. *Nouveau discours du récit*. Paris, 1983.
—. *L'Oeuvre de l'Art I: Immanence et transcendance*. Paris, 1994.
—. *L'Oeuvre de l'Art II. La relation esthétique*. Paris, 1997a.
—. *Seuils. Paratexts*. Cambridge, 1997b.
Greimas, A. J. *Sémantique structurale*. Paris, 1966.
—. *Du Sens. Essais sémiotiques*. Paris, 1970.
—. *Du Sens II. Essais sémiotiques*. Paris, 1983.
—. *De l'Imperfection*. Périgueux, 1987.
— and Courtés, J. *Sémiotique. Dictionnaire raisonné de la théorie du langage*. Paris, 1986.
— and Fontanille. J. *The Semiotics of Passions*. Minneapolis, 1992.
Scholes, R. E. *Structuralism in Literature*. New Haven, CT, 1974.
Todorov, T. *Qu'est-ce que le structuralisme. 2: Poétique*. Paris, 1968.
—. *Grammaire du Décaméron*. The Hague, 1969.

—. *Introduction à la littérature fantastique*. Paris, 1970.
—. *Mikhail Bakhtine. Le principe dialogique*. Paris, 1981.
—. *La Conquête de l'Amérique*. Paris, 1982.
—. *Nous et les autres*. Paris, 1989.
—. *Face à l'extrême*. Paris, 1991.
—. *Benjamin Constant: la passion démocratique*. Paris, 1997.
—. *Le Jardin imparfait. La pensée humaniste en France*. Paris, 1998.

Louis Althusser (1918–1990) and his Circle

Louis Althusser and the more notable members of the circle of students and colleagues that worked closely with him during most of the 1960s (especially Etienne Balibar and Pierre Macherey) are commonly regarded as structural marxists, that is as marxists who adopted the language and general aims of structuralism. The problem with such a categorization is not merely that it remains too general, but rather that it was categorically false. A careful reader of the texts published during Althusser's lifetime could see the ways in which his concerns were not only different from but opposed to those of the structuralist movement of the time. Now, with the posthumous publication of thousands of pages of essays and books, Althusser's very critical and even hostile view of structuralism from the early 1960s has been made very clear. This is not simply a matter of taxonomy: it is impossible to understand Althusser's approach to literature and philosophy without seeing the way in which his major texts were designed as critiques of the fundamental tenets of the structuralist activity.

Perhaps the best way to measure Althusser's distance from and opposition to the structuralist method of textual interpretation is simply to turn to the theory of reading that he proposes in the introduction to what remains his best-known work, *Reading Capital*. The intervention that Althusser intended the work to be, of course, can only be understood in relation to the precise historical and philosophical moment or conjuncture that Althusser hoped to modify. In 1965 structuralism neared the height of its influence. The following year would see the publication of two special issues of important journals devoted to the topic of structuralism. Roland Barthes's manifesto 'For a Structural Analysis of Narratives' was the introductory essay for an issue of *Communications* on structuralism that included such figures as Gérard Genette, Claude Bremond, Tzvetan Todorov and Umberto Eco. A number of Jean-Paul Sartre's *Les Temps Modernes* included essays on the notion of structure by Pierre Bourdieu and Maurice Godelier, as well as an essay extremely critical of structuralism by a member of Althusser's circle Pierre Macherey.

What explained the interest structuralism inspired at this time? It seemed to herald a new scientific understanding of literature whose scientificity was guaranteed by its close relation to linguistics, the sole social science that was thought to deserve the name. According to this method, literature was no longer a realm of original creations by uniquely endowed men and women that concealed hidden meanings and exhibited a beauty that required long experience to perceive, let alone fully to appreciate. Instead, literature was nothing more than a formal system of possibilities, a rule-governed combination of elements into complex entities. An author had no more control over the emergence of these complex entities than a speaker in everyday life has over grammar. Indeed, to speak a sentence or to write a novel is to submit to a set of rules and to enter into a system of which the 'agent' is almost always unaware. Further, if linguistics has discovered the rules governing the combination of phonemes into morphemes and morphemes into words and words into sentences, we have yet to identify the rules governing the combination of sentences into a still higher unity called discourse. To read a text would be to account for the function of every one of its elements in the structure of the whole, as well as to discover the rules governing the combinations of elements into a coherent whole.

Althusser, of course, was a philosopher, not a literary critic. But structuralism had entered the field of philosophy as well, through such figures as Martial Gueroult) who sought to reconstruct the architectonic unity of the statements that comprised a given philosophical text. To a certain extent, Althusser and his circle regarded such an approach as an open rejection of the impressionistic and careless readings that were all too typical of much pre-Second World War French philosophy. In another sense, however, it seemed merely to be an intensification of a traditional reading of philosophical texts as more or less coherently organized wholes. Literary and philosophical structuralism were for Althusser intimately related and both had their origins in Aristotle's notion of literature as the most philosophical of the modes in which reality might be represented. Both sought to demonstrate the existence of internal orders whose sequences followed a chain of cause and effect or argument and conclusion that moved from a logical starting point to an end. It is not surprising, then, that by the mid-1960s at the latest, Althusser viewed structuralism as a variant of a traditional idealism or metaphysics.

It was not that Althusser rejected the idea that previously non-scientific areas of inquiry, especially in the so-called human sciences, could attain scientific knowledge; on the contrary, he felt very strongly especially at this time that marxism represented an epistemological break or revolution that, if permitted, could be set on the road to scientific knowledge of historical phenomenon. His notion of science, however, drawn from such figures as Bachelard and Canguilhem, precluded the notion that a scientific approach to literature or culture would resemble physics or biology or would necessarily entail the use of mathematical models or even quantitative techniques. Such notions could only result from the imposition of *a priori* principles on a field that might well demand different principles, the rationalism proper to it or the region of which it was a part which remained to be formulated in the process of and not before knowing it. Such a regional rationality, to use Bachelard's expression, could by elaborated on the condition that one would identify and reject the concepts whose application appeared 'obvious' or inescapable.

A scientific understanding of the history of human societies, Althusser announced at the beginning of *Reading Capital*, would necessarily begin with 'the most dramatic and difficult trial of all, the discovery of and training in the meaning of the "simplest" acts of existence: seeing, listening, speaking, reading – the acts which relate men to their works, and to those works thrown in their faces, their "absences of works"' (1975, 16). Althusser himself will begin with the question, 'what is it to read' (1975, 15). Rather than attempt to answer this question immediately, as if one could reason and think in a social, historical and philosophical vacuum, or at least could create such a vacuum through a simple will to objectivity, Althusser first examines the notions that govern reading as it is actually practised. Such an examination is far from easy in that its object is among the apparently 'simplest', most obvious acts, the nature of which appears to be an unquestionable given. Althusser, in an assertion that is at least as relevant to the study of literature as to the study of philosophy, argues that our notion of reading is dominated by 'a religious myth' (17). The model of all texts is the Bible; the practice of reading follows the tradition of scriptural interpretation. The Bible is the word of God and as such is the expression of the Divine Logos. If it appears internally inconsistent or contradictory, if certain of its narratives appear incomplete, fragmented or even incomprehensible, the fault is necessarily that of the interpreter. The inspired reader of scripture knows that the text as a whole is an 'expressive totality in which every part is a pars totalis, immediately expressing the whole that it inhabits in person' (1975, 17). In this way reading is an act of reduction of the surface of the text, which presents the appearance of disorder, to the unity beneath the surface.

The relevance of the 'religious myth of reading' (1975, 17) to the study of literature from Aristotle to structuralism is striking. The intelligibility of a text is a function of its internal coherence; a reading consists of showing the way in which every phrase, word and image expresses a central meaning or theme, or alternately, of showing the way in which the smallest identifiable element (even to the letters of which words are composed) possesses a necessary function in the structure of the whole. In fact, this model so dominates our thinking that to merely to question it seems destined to lead to its inverse, the idea that texts are indeterminate and can (be made to) mean anything. To guide him between the extremes of a religious dogmatism (which can masquerade as a science of the text inspired by linguistics) and an empty scepticism that rejoins religion to the extent that it declares texts, like sacred objects, unknowable and ineffable, Althusser turned to 'the first man ever to have posed the problem of reading and, in consequence of writing': Spinoza (Althusser 1975, 16). Althusser read the *Tractatus Theologico-Politicus* with great care, noting Spinoza's argument that all previous interpreters of scripture had negated and denied the text in its actual state. They approached what was composite, fragmentary and contradictory in the Bible not to explain these, its real characteristics, but to explain them away. Two opposing approaches to texts thus emerged: do we carefully describe and then explain the text as it is in what will inevitably be its real disorder? Or do we reduce this disorder to a more primary order, dividing the text into the essential and necessary and the inessential and the accidental?

Althusser carefully studied the way Marx read the texts of classical political economy and found that he read by drawing a line of demarcation through these texts (although not always and not consciously). The function of this line was to make visible the specific contradiction that these texts exhibited without resolution or even acknowledgement. In the course of their arguments, these works produced conclusions or even in some cases merely evidence that did not support but actually undermined their conclusion but without these discrepancies ever being noted. To describe these phenomena Althusser uses the language of vision: every text is divided between what is visible and what is invisible within it and to it. How can what a text manifests or shows be called invisible? Althusser at this point takes his leave of Spinoza and turns to psychoanalysis, a discipline whose importance in his thought can hardly be overestimated. In saying that what is invisible in a text is not hidden, Althusser refers to the language of psychic defences: the text not only represses, but denies, isolates and splits off those incompatible elements it produces. Althusser calls a reading that seeks precisely to understand a text as much by what it represses as by what it intends to show or say a 'symptomatic reading' (1975, 28).

The use of this language, however, is bound to raise questions. Freud used the language of the defences to describe the forms of conflict proper to human individuals. Does Althusser then hope to trace the defences proper to a given text back to the psyche of its author? We inevitably want to ask, 'whose conflicts are they, anyway?' To the immense chagrin of his numerous and loquacious Anglo-American critics, Althusser dismissed such questions (who makes history, whose actions create social structures) as variants of the model of such questions: who created the universe? To answer such a question is to accept the theological notion of a Creator; Althusser preferred instead to answer the question with another question: what leads us to ask who? The false question (whose conflicts does a text manifest?) can be replaced with a more productive one: what is the cause, or causes of the conflicts proper to texts? Althusser's answer will fortuitously explain not only the causes of textual contradiction, but even of the impulse to ask 'who', that is to know historical phenomena by reducing them to an origin or creator, not God, of course, but Man. To explain the antagonisms that divide every text (including Marx's and his own) he will refer to the existence of something else: ideology.

In the works of the mid-1960s Althusser defined ideology very much in the spirit of Marx's famous discussion of base and superstructure in the *Preface to the Critique of Political Economy*. On the base of a given society (the technological means of production and the relations of production) arises a corresponding system of ideas, culture, religion and law (which often in different and even opposing ways justifies or gives an air of inevitability to the existing order). Ideology is 'the lived relation between men and their world' (Althusser 1970, 213), but one which is primarily unconscious, determining individuals' actions without their being aware of this determination. Following Spinoza, Althusser called this an 'imaginary' relation that is simultaneously illusion and allusion. Individuals' beliefs are not strictly speaking false; it is rather that they invert the relations between cause and effect. (Marx used the figure of the camera obscura which turns the scene viewed through its apparatus upside down to illustrate this notion.) Most commonly individuals believe that they are free, free to work or not to work, free to succeed or fail, to become a garment worker or the chief executive officer of a multinational corporation, depending on whether they have the strength of character or the determination. As Marx put it in *Capital*, they view themselves as 'determined only by their own free will' (1977, 280) and hence remain unaware of the causes external to them that determine them to will and to act as they do. And in the same way that Galileo's discovery of an infinite and thus decentred universe threatened the Roman Church and the doctrines that justified its domination, so a scientific knowledge of history, which would explain events by their causes, could only upset the dominant ideology, that is the ideology that justified the domination of the ruling class. Therefore what Althusser regarded as Marx's scientific discovery of the forms of determination proper to human societies could only be threatening to a host of ideologies which would work tirelessly to discredit and defeat marxism, attempting to obscure by any means necessary a knowledge of social phenomena through their causes.

Few areas were as invested with ideological 'meanings' as art in general and literature specifically. Pierre Macherey's A *Theory of Literary Production*, a work written in the context of the seminars Althusser organized among his students between 1961 and 1968, critically examines the notions that have dominated the study of literature. Macherey treats these notions as 'epistemological obstacles', to use Bachelard's phrase, that block the development of an adequate knowledge of the phenomenon we provisionally refer to as literature. Again, as was the case with Althusser, there can be no question of simply returning to an absolute starting point free of all preconceptions from which we might construct a coherent theory. In *Spontaneous Philosophy* Althusser wrote, 'every space is always already occupied and one can take a position against the adversary who already occupies that position' (1990, 144). Accordingly, the first half of A *Theory of Literary Production* is devoted to the identification and deconstruction of the theories that occupy the field of literary criticism and interpretation. Macherey finds that although these theories may differ significantly in their conceptualization of the nature and causes of literature, they are, despite their vastly different origins and orientations, united around a single ideological objective. The history of literary criticism is nothing less than the history of attempts to deny the material and historical nature of what we now call literature. To begin with, for a good part of its history, literary criticism, as the name implies, was less concerned about the knowledge than the judgement of works of art. For Macherey, it was not simply that critics used 'timeless' criteria to dismiss and reject popular and even avant-garde forms of literature and thereby preserve the canon that appeared to justify bourgeois civilization. It was even more that the operation of judgement, whether its verdict in a given case was positive or negative, told us nothing about the work in question, only whether or not, or to what extent, it conformed to an ideal norm by definition situated outside literature in its actual existence. For Macherey, the notion that the object of criticism is to discriminate between good and bad literary texts, and then to 'appreciate' the former while dismissing the latter is as absurd as the botanist insisting that only beautiful flowers are worthy objects of study.

It is true, of course, that with the critique of the very idea of a canon, such an approach to literature has fallen into disrepute and now appears only at the margins of academic literary studies. Other means of rejecting the objective existence of literary texts and thus of rendering them unknowable, however, continue to flourish. They claim to seek to make possible a knowledge of literary texts, but they do so only by negating the work in its actual existence, reducing to something other than itself. One of the most common and enduring forms of interpretation that explains a text by reducing it to a truth outside of it is that which views literature as the creation of an author. The very idea of creation betrays the theological origins of the notion of author. Like God, the author creates something out of nothing, an original before which there was nothing. The author begins with an idea and proceeds to realize (if, that is, the individual in question has the proper strength of will) that idea in a work of art or literature. The work of art takes shape in and is the work of a single individual who is its origin and agent. As such, in our societies at least, the author is also owner of the intellectual property that he or she creates. This legal fact alone compels us to recognize that if the world outside the author has any role in the creative process, it is a purely secondary or incidental role; it is present, if at all, as the influences that form the background to creation. If we truly seek the meaning of the work, from this perspective, we had better seek it in the mind of its creator: the intention behind it, of course, but also the secret sorrows and dimly remembered childhood traumas that the author might have transmuted through the alchemy of creation into a genuine work of art.

These ideas, so dominant even now that students can be persuaded to question them only with difficulty, are among the most tenacious obstacles to the study of literature. The notion of creation offers a mystical explanation for the existence of literary works: we seek the causes of a work in an author, as if it already existed and needed only to be translated into speech, colour or sound. But when we seek the causes of this cause, the origin of the origin, we are forced to take refuge in (to paraphrase Spinoza) the sanctuary of ignorance:

genius, talent, spontaneity. For Macherey, these notions are not simply myths that replace a real problem with an insoluble mystery, but are logical consequences of the legal ideology that assigns to every act an actor to be credited or held responsible, that addresses or, as Althusser would later say, 'interpellates' individuals as subjects, that is as actors and owners of themselves who are 'determined by their own free will alone' (1977, 280). Instead Macherey argues that the author is not a creator at all but a producer who neither makes the 'raw material' with which he works nor controls the 'means of production' which allow him to write anything at all. Writing becomes a collective, not individual, process in which authors are constrained to produce according to historical determinations. Literary works thus do not express the intentions or even the mind of their author which, even if they are inscribed in the work, do not control it: they are not made in their creator's image.

There are numerous theories of literature, however, that deny a central role to the author and in doing so might appear to recognize the material existence of the literary work. Marxism is often associated with the position, for example, that literature 'reflects' or 'represents' the reality of its historical moment, apart from which it cannot be understood. In the light of the marxism of Althusser and Macherey, however, this position appears inadequate. While they agree that no work can be understood outside of its relation to the historical determinations that make it what it is, neither the concept of 'reflection' nor that of 'representation' allow us to understand this determination. In fact, such notions rob the work of its material existence by arguing that it 'reflects' a reality external to it as if it were merely a shadow or a dim, fleeting image of what is real. The work, according to such theories, yields its meaning only when it is exchanged for or disappears into the history outside of itself which is its truth. There is something paradoxical about a Marxism that makes literature intelligible only by regarding it as insubstantial (immaterial?), reducible to something more primary beyond itself.

Of course, in opposition, twentieth-century versions of formalism and structuralism (in many cases, explicitly invoking Aristotle) have argued that the meaning of a work derives from the necessity of its form rather than from the author's intentions or psychology (the New Critics in the US even identified an 'intentional fallacy') or from its historical context. The model of a great work was one in which every incident, character and image conspired together to produce the harmony of the whole. Often, especially in the English-speaking world, this view rendered the literary work independent of historical and political determinations, a self-enclosed, self-sufficient whole that stood outside (and usually above) social struggles. But there were other, more complex versions of formalism. György Lukács, steeped in Hegel, argued that in understanding a given historical epoch 'the truth is the whole' (Hegel 1977, 11) (which bourgeois thought artificially divides into separate factors each of which must be studied in isolation). Invoking Aristotle, Lukács sought to show that the architectonic unity of the work of art was nothing less than a recreation of the repressed totality. He cited the particular case of Balzac, a reactionary author who, because he surrendered to the demands of formal unity, produced a body of work that, by revealing the hidden totality of his historical moment, was objectively revolutionary.

From Macherey's perspective, such approaches also refused the materiality or irreducibility of the text. Formalism was by no means incompatible with a normative theory that judges works (in this case according to their degree of internal coherence): Lukács, for example, found Thomas Mann's novels 'superior' to those of Kafka or Joyce. Even more importantly, however, formalism in all its variants itself rejects the objective existence of the text precisely by declaring it to be a totality, each of whose parts contributes to the structure of the whole. Such an approach must distort the text into coherence, rejecting as inessential all that does not contribute to the harmony of the whole, fictively resolving and reconciling the conflicts that disturb every work. For even the most sophisticated formalists, those identified with the structuralist movement, literary works only seem disordered and contradictory on the surface; hidden within them (and texts are thus endowed with a 'depth') is the unity that must be uncovered. Again, Macherey draws on Spinoza's denunciation of biblical interpretation as it was practised before him: commentators have not explained scripture as it is in its disorder, with its discrepancies and inconsistencies, but have explained it away, substituting for it a text of their own device.

For Macherey and Althusser, the literary work and the process of literary production are real, material and historical. Works are neither expressions of a mind nor reflections of a history external to them; they are not coherent totalities and they are all surface, concealing nothing. The disorder and conflict that texts exhibit are the inescapable consequences of their historical existence; how might they escape the struggles that traverse the history of which they are a part?

In opposition to Brecht, whom Althusser admired and wrote about, the alienation effect is not one possible dramatic narrative among others from which it would be distinguished by raising problems without resolving them and by preventing any suspension of disbelief on the part of the spectator. It is instead the effect proper to literature as such in that every text, including Brecht's, says more than it wants to say, exhibits more than it knows or desires, and thereby makes visible the contradictions of the ideology it dramatizes. This does not make art or literature subversive; it merely means that a symptomatic reading of literary texts, among many other realities, may yield a raw material that can be shaped into historical knowledge

Through the 1960s, Althusser's discussion of literature and art, as well as Macherey's work, focused on the problem of reading literature, particularly the 'internal relations' of texts as specific transformation of ideology. With his essay, 'Ideology and Ideological State Apparatuses', his concerns shifted somewhat. Althusser went to great lengths to show that ideology was not a matter of ideas or even representations but of material practices that existed in the form of apparatuses and institutions. Thus literature and art could no longer be understood at the level of the text; one instead had to inquire into the institutions, legal, educational and cultural, in which literary texts were produced and 'read' (interpreted and taught at various levels). Further, Althusser's essay compels us to ask not how individuals come to write or read a text, but how the institution of literature 'interpellates' (that is, constitutes or positions) individuals as authors or readers. Althusser's essay on ideology had an enormous influence (although he himself had little more to say in this vein); its effects may be seen in Foucault's *Discipline and Punish* (which is simultaneously a continuation and a critique of Althusser's notion of ideology), as well as in the field of cultural studies, for which Althusser's text is a kind of founding document.

Warren Montag

Further reading and works cited

Althusser, L. *For Marx*. New York, 1970.
—. *Lenin and Philosophy*. New York, 1971.
—. *Reading Capital*. London, 1975.
—. *Philosophy and the Spontaneous Philosophy of the Scientists*. New York, 1990.

Elliott, G. *Althusser*. London, 1987.
Foucault, M. *Discipline and Punish*. New York, 1995.
Hegel, G. W. F. *Phenomenology of Spirit*. London, 1977.
Macherey, P. *A Theory of Literary Production*. Boston, 1978.
—. *The Object of Literature*. Cambridge, 1995.
—. *In a Materialist Way*, ed. W. Montag. London, 1998.
Marx, K. *Capital, Volume 1*. New York, 1977.
Sartre, J.-P. *Les Temps Modernes*, no. 246. Paris, 1945–.
Spinoza, B. *Tractatus Theologico-Politicus*. New York, 1991.

Reception Theory and Reader-Response (I): Hans-Robert Jauss (1922–1997), Wolfgang Iser (1926–) and the School of Konstanz

The Konstanz School is named after the university founded in the early 1960s in southern Germany on the shore of the Bodensee, or Lake of Konstanz, and it denotes the group of scholars and critics who established in the late 1960s and developed through to the late 1980s the critical orientation known variously as the aesthetics of reception (*Rezeptionsästhetik*), the aesthetics of literary response and effect (*Wirkungsästhetik*), or more broadly as reader-response theory. As a fairly loosely affiliated and liberal academic community, it drew together researchers from various German universities and also formed international links, especially with France and the USA. Its ongoing work was published in a series of volumes, largely untranslated, from 1964 until the early 1980s, under the general title *Poetik und Hermeneutik* (*Poetics and Hermeneutics*). As Paul de Man has observed, the linkage of these two terms indicates the ambition of the project: to unite the formalistic and rhetorical approaches to literature with the interpretative – to understand at once how the literary work is made, how it works and takes effect, how it signifies and what it means. All these approaches are to be incorporated under the aegis of a theory of reception or response. The two most celebrated members of the Konstanz School are Hans-Robert Jauss and Wolfgang Iser, and their work will be the focus of this essay.

   A range of philosophical and theoretical influences bear upon the critical positions of Jauss and Iser, which are importantly different from each other, though both centrally affirm the crucial function of reception in the constitution of the work of art, specifically the literary text. Both critics are situated, notwithstanding their claims to radical positions, in firm relation to the major German philosophical tradition that emanates from Kant, and – that major late current deriving from, even as it seeks to reorient, Kantian thought – provides the philosophical grounding for their theorizing. The filiation is from the phenomenology of Edmund Husserl through its development in the reception theory of Hans-Georg Gadamer, Roman Ingarden and the Geneva School, but other approaches – psychoanalytic, sociological and historical – are employed where they are felt to be productive. Reader-response theory seeks to be both eclectic and syncretic.

The Konstanz School is a major tributary, then, to that current of literary criticism which has been generally characterized as the 'turn to' or 'return of the reader' (Freund 1987) and which emphasizes the primacy, or at least the co-primacy, of reception – in particular, reading – in the constitution of the literary text. The reader and the act of reading assume centre stage for this criticism, which seeks to theorize the activity of reading literature, to explore its dynamics, to define its elements and to exemplify and analyse its workings with regard to specific texts. The reader – more abstractly, the process of reading – produces the text as a living entity, an aesthetic object – unread, the text is inert, without effect or value. The literary text is, moreover, a highly complex and special form of language and its reception is equally complex – it is not simply a message issued from an author to be received and deciphered by a reader. Rather, it stimulates both response and interpretation, and these together constitute the activity of reading which, rather than the author alone, creates the literary *work* – something much more than the mere or literal *text*.

In its emphasis on the role of the reader, reception theory clearly, and at times explicitly, counters the assumption of the primacy of the text propounded in New Criticism, which was the dominant critical persuasion when the Konstanz School began to form itself. The New Critical privileging of the textual object, assumed to be largely autonomous – the individual lyric being the most usual, because most convenient, example – is challenged by an approach that seeks to give equal or greater importance and attention to the reader as subject, whose response is understood to be in part directed or stimulated by the text but also to be an exercise of the reader's own imagination, based on knowledge and experience. What has been described as the 'traditional, rigidly hierarchical, view of the text-reader relationship' (Freund 1987, 4) in New Criticism, with the text dominant, and both reader and context firmly subordinated to it, gives way to a theory of the mutuality of text, reader and context in the constitution of the literary work or aesthetic object. Accordingly, reader-response theory (particularly in the work of Jauss and Iser) engages with other critical currents, marxist theory, structuralism, psychoanalytic theory, communications theory and others, since they emphasize variously these different constitutive forces: text, reader, context. It finds in them valuable insights but also, by and large, a restrictive and distorting emphasis on one or other of the constituents. It might be objected that reader-response theory itself gives, by definition, undue precedence to the reader, but its own claim is that it redresses the balance of previous critical theories which have tended toward merely formalist or ideologically motivated models, as in the case of New Criticism and marxism respectively.

Within this general position there are, as I have said, important differences between the two major representatives of the Konstanz School, Jauss and Iser. In part, these derive from their differing academic and intellectual orientations – Jauss a scholar of French literature, with interests covering a wide and diverse historical range, from medieval genre study to the work of Baudelaire and Valéry, but mainly engaged with poetry; Iser a professor of English, whose area of concern is principally located in the more restricted and homogeneous, but also more popular and accessible area of the English novel from its eighteenth-century beginnings to the present day. Iser has clearly been more user-friendly, so to speak, so far as the Anglophone world of literary studies is concerned. More of Iser's work has been translated into English (largely by the author) and Iser has more frequently and consistently been the point of reference in the dissemination of *Rezeptionsästhetik* in Anglophone (and principally American) criticism. In the view of some, though, Jauss has remained the more important and substantial theorist of the two.

A crucial feature of Jauss's development of reader response theory is his emphasis upon the diachronic – the dynamics of literary history. His aim has been to elaborate a historical approach to literature which will replace the assumption of tradition (particularly a national tradition) and the canonical frame established in the nineteenth century with an interrogation of them, drawing on evidence of the historical reception of literature and, more generally, on theorizing the critical and dialectical function of reading in relating and mediating earlier and current understandings of the literary work. This project is polemically adumbrated in Jauss's celebrated essay 'Literary History as a Challenge to Literary Theory', which was his inaugural lecture at Konstanz in 1967, and formed the first chapter of his book *Toward an Aesthetic of Reception*, published in America together with his other major work in English translation, *Aesthetic Experience and Literary Hermeneutics*, both in 1982 (Jauss 1982a, 1982b). In this essay, Jauss challenges views of literary history as given, as a canonically established body of texts, in favour of a conception of that history as dynamic, a continual process of formation, in which the ceaseless interaction between the already received and established and the new and unprecedented in literature ensures an open, ultimately indeterminable though not indefinable dynamic of change and by the same token refuses any teleological idealism. The conception can be interestingly compared to T. S. Eliot's famous pronouncement in 'Tradition and the Individual Talent' that each 'really new' work of art alters the whole structure of the cultural tradition (Eliot 1951, 15). While Eliot's concern is with artistic *creation*, though, Jauss is engaged in theorizing the process of artistic and cultural *reception* – the ways in which the new artwork enters the domain of the already received. As he puts it, 'literature and art only obtain a history that has the character of a process when the succession of works is mediated not only through the producing subject but also through the consuming subject – through the interaction of author and public' (Jauss, 1982a, 15).

Accordingly, historical, social and cultural contexts are all highly important but not, as in the model of literary marxism relayed by Jauss, reducible to crudely determining or determined functions. Nor is the artistic function to be confined to history (Lukács is Jauss's target here), for the formal and rhetorical elements of the work are crucially active determinants and stimuli affecting, indeed producing, its reception and, more largely, inflecting the history of which it is part. (The concept of defamiliarization propounded in Russian formalism is important here.) However, formalist criticism's tendency to dehistoricize the artwork, or to internalize its history as specifically artistic evolution, must in turn be questioned by opening up much further the issue of how the formal qualities of the work stimulate its reception and consequently its impact on a wider social, cultural and historical situation. Jauss sees his project therefore as the 'attempt to bridge the gap between literature and history, between historical and aesthetic functions' (Jauss 1982a, 18), overcoming the limitations of both materialist and formalist approaches, the former viewed as giving undue attention to context, the historical determinations of literary production, the latter seen as overvaluing the text, the formal and aesthetic composition of the literary work, insufficiently related to conditions of historical change. Neither approach pays adequate attention to the reception of the text, the reader or audience or public, whose role for Jauss is crucial. That reception, moreover, is far from being a merely passive process – on the contrary, it is an active determinant in the continual process of historical and cultural formation, a dialectical process of mediation in which new encounters old and both undergo change. Moreover, this dialectic operates no less within the process of reception itself – habits of reading encounter the challenge of new and unprecedented literary works, responses are altered accordingly, and those changed responses work back in turn upon already received work, reformulating the whole literary-historical model. This implies the rejection of an established, positivistically based and purportedly objective canon of literature in favour of a more labile process of canon formation which acknowledges that the individual literary text and relations among texts, past and present, are not fixed but subject to the changes that their renewed reception (or lack of reception) produces. There is a residual conservatism here: Jauss is not seeking to do away with the process of canonization but rather to render it more dynamic, in conformity with what he terms the 'dialogical and at once processlike relationship between work, audience, and new work', forming an 'ongoing totalization' (Jauss 1982a, 19).

The essay concludes with the formulation of seven theses, elaborating further Jauss's new, reception-based model of literary history. Broadly, these seek to ensure that the theory steers a careful middle course between restrictive alternatives – more exactly, that it enables a balance of interests among these alternatives to be sustained. Thus, it must avoid 'the prejudices of historical objectivism' (Jauss 1982a, 20) and enable a conception of canon formation (thesis 1) but also avoid 'the threatening pitfalls of psychology' (Jauss 1982a, 22), that is the dangers of subjectivity, by holding to an 'objectifiable system of expectations', historically verifiable and culturally established (thesis 2). It must recognize the process of historical change but also acknowledge the force of the text's own appearance as new and contemporary (theses 3 and 4); attend to the patterns of evolution within the literary domain and also recognize the individual text's autonomy, giving both diachronic and synchronic analysis their due (theses 5 and 6); and, finally, register the text's relation to history in general but also more specifically to the history of literature in its bearing upon that wider history (thesis 7). These are large ambitions, and reflect perhaps the German tradition of synthetic inclusiveness which finds its apotheosis in Hegel, though Jauss is of course critical of Hegelian idealism. What one might call the 'both-and' tendency is, however, well represented in his theory.

The essay is seminal: most of Jauss's work can be viewed as an extension and elaboration of the theses set out there, applied and developed with reference to a range of areas – art history, genre criticism, medieval and modern French poetry. His other major translated work, *Aesthetic Experience and Literary Hermeneutics*, extends his thinking in broader philosophical terms and, as its title indicates, shifts the concern more toward a generalized and largely abstract elaboration of the relations between aesthetics and hermeneutics – put simply, between literary effect and meaning, respectively. He begins by taking issue with Adorno's aesthetic theory, which he sees as enforcing a view of art as effectual only in its critical and negative functions. Against this, Jauss seeks to endorse the positive pleasure that art provides, a pleasure which involves both an initial surrender of the recipient to the work of art and a process of aesthetic distancing – the Kantian shadow falls across much of Jauss's thinking here. Three 'fundamental categories' of aesthetic pleasure are distinguished and examined in their historical development through the western tradition, from classical antiquity through the medieval period to modernity. They are given Greek names: *poiesis* (the pleasure of making, of artistic creation or recreation), *aisthesis* (the pleasure in the reception of the artwork) and *catharsis* (the pleasure in the emotional communication effected in the artwork).

For Jauss, pleasure – more broadly, aesthetic experience – is important as the primary category of art and its reception, but it is no less important to consider its succession and outcome in understanding, which is where reflection, Jauss's other key term, applies. The two aspects or stages, experience and reflection, are phenomenologically distinct but yet related and both ineluctably embedded in history – here Jauss's debt to Gadamer is explicit. The hermeneutic or interpretative activity of the reader is examined not so much in general and abstract terms, in the way that aesthetic experience was analysed, as through more specific, though still fairly broadly conceived, instances, which occupy the later part of Jauss's study. These include identification with the hero and responses to the comic hero, as well as more closely focused discussions of French lyric, especially Baudelaire. It may be fair to say, however, that Jauss's treatment of aesthetic experience is more substantial and coherent than his discussion of hermeneutics, which tends to take on a more subsidiary and even incidental role in his theory.

The other major representative of the Konstanz School's theory of reception, Wolfgang Iser, may be seen as occupying a contrasting but also complementary position in relation to Jauss – Jauss himself, at least, has viewed Iser's concept of the 'implied reader' as productively partnering his own theorizing of the 'historical reader'. Iser's relatively more narrow focus, very largely limited to the English novel tradition, certainly contrasts with, and perhaps complements, Jauss's much broader ambit. Robert Holub has defined the difference nicely, seeing Jauss as occupied with 'the macrocosm of reception', Iser with 'the microcosm of response' (Holub 1984, 83). Iser's approach, correspondingly more text-based, has been seen as more in accordance therefore with Anglo-American critical traditions, which is why he has proved the more congenial theorist outside the German intellectual arena (Holub 1984, 1992). Iser's concern is with a phenomenology of reading and his most important intellectual debt is to the philosopher and aesthetician Roman Ingarden, while Jauss is engaged with the relation of aesthetics and hermeneutics and owes much in this respect to his teacher Hans-Georg Gadamer.

In his first major work of criticism (Iser 1974), Iser considers an extensive range of English narrative (from Bunyan to Beckett, as his subtitle announces) from the perspective of a phenomenological conception of the reading process. He coins the term 'implied reader' – derived, it is generally agreed, from Wayne Booth's celebrated conception of the 'implied author' (Booth 1961) – to personify a model of this process, in which meaning is established through the interaction of text and reader. Neither text nor reader has autonomy: the text depends on the reader for its meaning to be realized, and the meaning produced by the reader is controlled by the text. Iser's laudable efforts to explicate and theorize this balance of power, so to speak, in the act of reading tend, however, to produce and sustain a fundamental ambiguity and an uncertainty about the status of this 'reader', for which his theory has been criticized. The 'reader' tends at crucial points to become little more than a function of the text and the text in turn more or less simply the articulation of its reading, each pole of the reading relation apt to lose its vaunted polarity.

What is involved, then, in the 'act of reading' as understood phenomenologically in Iser's theory? Firstly, the literary text is viewed, not as an independent or autonomous object, but as an entity constituted in and by its reading, as an 'intentional' or 'hetero-nomous' object, to use Ingarden's terms (1973a, 1973b). Secondly, the text is indeterminate, in the sense that the 'reality' it describes or evokes is incomplete and requires the imaginative and ideational activity of the reader to develop and extend it, to 'realize' it, in effect. Unlike a real object, which is 'all there', so to speak, despite the partiality of any perception of it, the text, though in an elementary sense defined as a real object, a literary structure composed of a certain number of words, is only active and significant as a stimulus to the construction of a virtual world, which is open to any number of realizations ('concretizations', another of Ingarden's terms). On the basis of these fundamental conceptions, derived from phenomenology, Iser formulates a view of literary meaning which resides neither in the text (*qua* object) nor in the reader (*qua* subject) but in the interaction of the two, an interaction which is conditioned by its context. There are then three inseparable though distinguishable elements or aspects to the act of reading: the *text*, which directs its own reading but is also subject to indeterminacy; the *reader*, or more exactly the *reading process*, which realizes the text as the production of meaning through modes of concretization, involving progressive synthesizing of responses and information in order to obtain a coherent and significant result; and the *context* conditioning both text and reading, that is the social and historical norms and assumptions governing both production and reception of any text.

For Iser, though, it is the notion of indeterminacy that is most active and powerful in his scheme of the reading process so far as fiction is concerned, and it carries an evaluative charge. Any text is both available for and worth reading to the extent that it contains 'gaps' or 'blanks' (*Leerstellen*, literally 'empty places') which invite or stimulate the reader to undertake ideational activity in order to fill in these gaps, thus producing a meaning. Such gaps enable and indeed require the reader to contribute to the eventual literary *work*, which is the combination of both textual and reading process, but they do not open the text to the whim of purely subjective interpretation, since they are themselves constructed by the text and in a manner controlled and directed by it. (Here again a certain ambiguity in the apportioning of authority between text and reader is evident.) Ultimately, for Iser this process is valuable in that it promotes a kind of intersubjectivity, or more precisely a displacement of subjectivity, as the subject-reader engages with the object-text and the limits of the self are transcended through relation to the other. The text in its paradoxically limited indeterminacy stimulates the reader's freedom of imagination but resists the arbitrary licence of fantasy; conversely, the reader's ability to activate the text frees it from the illusion of dogmatic completeness and mobilizes its capacity for potentially infinite but, again paradoxically, not undetermined interpretation.

In its sustainedly careful balance and its thoughtful syncretism, Iser's theory merits our respect, but these very qualities are also perhaps what render it ultimately somewhat bland. Its very capaciousness becomes in a way suspect and its even and rather dry tenor give the impression of a slightly stultifying uniformity. Stanley Fish's notorious attack (Fish 1981) in which Iser's theory is denigrated as both uncontroversial and ultimately self-justifying – established not on fundamental epistemological grounds but on agreed protocols of reading which are essentially those of the liberal, cultured and educated European – is perhaps intemperate but also searching, and Iser does not fully engage with it in his response (Iser 1981). Also, while Iser marshals an impressive range of theoretical back-up, so to speak, in support of his theory – he refers to Laingian psychology, communications and speech-act theory, Gestalt psychology, all placed within the basic phenomenological frame – this has the effect of a slightly numbing insistence, a theoretical 'overkill' (Freund 1987, 164), as does the rather repetitious use of exemplification from a limited number of literary texts, the novels of Fielding, Joyce's *Ulysses* and Beckett's trilogy.

Nonetheless, German reception theory, associated with the Konstanz School and with Jauss and Iser in particular, occupies an important and honourable place in the development of literary theory in the second half of the twentieth century. The rather dry academic tone, and the careful, perhaps somewhat ponderous elaboration of argument, together with the syncretic determination of its major exponents make it distinctly less controversial and glamorous than other movements in theory – deconstructionism, poststructuralism – which begin in the mid-1970s to enjoy considerably more attention in the Anglo-American intellectual sphere, so that reception theory on the Konstanz model is quite quickly upstaged. Moreover, the determined elaboration of the theory seems to have ensured a determinate period for its flourishing – roughly, the twenty years or so from its inception in 1967 with the inaugural contributions from both Jauss and Iser. Its subsequent development or transmutation into a 'literary anthropology', as Iser has termed it (Iser 1989), has involved a theoretical diffusing and broadening of concern. As for its provenance, for all its initial situation within the German version of the radicalizing movement of the late 1960s, it does not come out of the blue – like other critical positions which emphasize the role of the reader, it draws upon the phenomenological tradition which stretches back to the early part of the century, and there are significant precursors in the discipline of literary criticism. It is a substantial tributary to a wide and various current of thinking and theory about the importance of reception to the constitution of the literary work – the work of art in general – which has been a major feature of literary theory and criticism in recent years (a selection of works in this area is included in the further reading bibliography to this article).

Jeremy Lane

Further reading and works cited

Amacher, R. E., and Lange, V. (eds) *New Perspectives in German Literary Criticism*. Princeton, NJ, 1979.
Bennett, A. (ed.) *Readers and Reading*. London, 1995.
Booth, W. C. *The Rhetoric of Fiction*. Chicago, 1961.
Eco, U. *The Role of the Reader*. Bloomington, IN, 1979.
Eliot, T. S. *Selected Essays*. London, 1951.
Fish, S. 'Why No One's Afraid of Wolfgang Iser', *diacritics*, 11, 3, 1981.
Freund, E. *The Return of the Reader*. London, 1987.
Garvin, H. R. (ed.) *Theories of Reading, Looking, Listening*. Lewisburg, PA, 1981.
Glowinski, M. 'Reading, Interpretation, Reception', *New Literary History*, 11, Autumn 1978.
Holub, R. C. *Reception Theory*. London, 1984.
—. *Crossing Borders*. Madison, WI, 1992.
Ingarden, R. *The Cognition of the Literary Work of Art*. Evanston, IL, 1973a.
—. *The Literary Work of Art*. Evanston, IL, 1973b.
Iser, W. 'Indeterminacy and the Reader's Response in Prose Fiction', *Aspects of Narrative*, ed. J. Hillis Miller. New York, 1971.
—. *The Implied Reader*. Baltimore, MD, 1974.
—. *The Act of Reading*. Baltimore, MD, 1978.
—. 'Talk Like Whales', *diacritics*, 11, 3, 1981.
—. *Prospecting: from Reader Response to Literary Anthropology*. Baltimore, MD, 1989.
Jauss, H. R. 'Literary History as a Challenge to Literary Theory', *New Literary History*, 2, Autumn 1970.
—. *Toward an Aesthetic of Reception*. Minneapolis, MN, 1982a.
—. *Aesthetic Experience and Literary Hermeneutics*. Minneapolis, MN, 1982b.
Purves, A. C. and Beach, R. *Literature and the Reader*. Urbana, IL, 1972.
Richards, I. A. *Practical Criticism*. New York, 1935.
Rosenblatt, L. *Literature as Exploration*. New York, 1937.

Segers, R. T. 'Readers, Text, and Author: Some Implications of *Rezeptionsästhetik*', *Yearbook of Comparative and General Literature*, 24, 1975.

Slatoff, W. *With Respect to Readers*. Ithaca, NY, 1970.

Suleiman, S. R. and Crosman, I. (eds) *The Reader in the Text*. Princeton, NJ, 1980.

Tompkins, J. P. (ed.) *Reader-Response Criticism*. Baltimore, MD, 1980.

Jean-François Lyotard (1925–1998) and Jean Baudrillard (1929–): The Suspicion of Metanarratives

Any thinker who announces the end of an old epoch and the beginning of a new, if they should do so persuasively, will attract special attention above and beyond the relative merits of their argument. In the case of Jean Baudrillard and Jean-François Lyotard both announce, with different rationales for doing so, the end of modernism and the onset of postmodernism. Neither would speak of the 'beginning' of the postmodern, because a central feature of postmodernism is that it reveals all teleology as an organizational myth. Origin is a construction designed to lend legitimacy and a sense of inevitability to a present-day reality. For Lyotard, this 'reality' will be dictated by the general organization of knowledge, as such knowledge is constituted by computer databases, mass media and the Internet. For Baudrillard, too, there is a crisis of legitimacy, and it is also traceable to the rise of mass media. He, however, is more interested in the use of images to construct 'reality', than the gathering and dissemination of knowledge. Both Lyotard and Baudrillard would agree key reference points of an earlier time – morality, proof, history, even reality – no longer function as communal markers for the 'truth'.

As a result, for Baudrillard, 'reality' is what he calls a 'hyper-reality', one where various representations of 'reality' masquerade as 'simulations' of what is real when, in fact, the unauthorized, illegitimate interplay of these simulations *is* our reality, and the myth there is a 'real' reality behind it just another example of the self-legitimating myth of origin no longer viable or believable in postmodernity. Where Baudrillard would point to the interplay of image-generated 'simulations', Lyotard would point to a similar dynamic of word-generated 'play' in various 'language games'. For Lyotard, various language games translate what is in fact undecidable into what is apparently incontrovertible. If images pose as simulations in order to preserve the myth of a reality available to be simulated, language games allow words to constitute themselves into configurative 'proof' of a truth presumed to underwrite them. Whether image or word-based, both theorists demonstrate a profound suspicion about any narrative purporting to explain or represent.

While Lyotard is most explicit in this, declaring that the postmodern can be virtually defined as the 'death' of any 'master narrative' offering to explain everything, Baudrillard makes a similar grand claim when he argues all simulations, in one way or another, exist in order to posit the illusion of a reality that is elsewhere. Disney World, for example, is, according to Baudrillard, an aggressively 'simulated' world serving to help make the rest of 'America' seem real. Lyotard, also, sees the reality of social fragmentation made more palatable by the emphasis on 'globalization'. Although their emphasis is quite different, both Baudrillard and Lyotard seem to argue for a postmodern dynamic where false oppositions are set up between an assumed 'reality' and a reproducible version of it. This reproduction – or simulacrum, or language game – then paradoxically serves as a guarantor of a 'reality' that is, in fact, only posited by the reproduction itself to give the image (Baudrillard) or the word (Lyotard) a semblance of authority and legitimacy.

Baudrillard's early work in the 1970s begins with Marx and Henri Lefebvre in order to re-examine the notion of 'everyday life'. If, for modernism, the 'everyday' was marked by a self-conscious awareness of the passage of time (T. S. Eliot's 'I measure out my life with coffee spoons'), the postmodern 'everyday' is not so much generated by subjecivity as generative *of* subjectivity. Marx talks about the self-alienation brought on by early capitalism. The worker was reduced to his function. Inner potential is ignored in favour of productivity; modes of production become the infrastructure which controls the superstructure of ideology. Baudrillard's advance is to see Marx as outdated: modes of consumption have replaced production as the dominant infrastructure. As an advertised commodity, an object's function is now not what it does or fails to do, but its relative place in the collective meaning generated by all objects. The key theme of this early work is to stop imagining the subject determines the meaning or relative worth of objects, and understand, instead, how objects and the mass-produced advertising discourse surrounding them produces an inescapable network of signification (what Lacan might call 'The Symbolic Order') which configures, and reconfigures, subjectivity.

With a bow toward Roland Barthes, Baudrillard also insists what is to be analysed is the various fields of mass-produced objects and the discourse of mass-media designed to accompany them. The subject has become a consumer, and the 'consumer' is not an autonomous entity, as the subject was once presumed to be, but a nexus point of consumer goods circulating as 'signs'. Instead of Marx's distinction of use value and exchange value, Baudrillard does away with both terms in favour of 'sign value'. While Marx's theories might continue to be relevant to the study of an earlier era of capitalism, one where modes of production were dominant, the 'sign' now operates independently of the social codes of a class system, or the dominant discourse of an institution, or the hegemony of any given political economy. Here we can see Baudrillard's debt to Saussure, but whereas Saussure posited the signifier cannot fully represent the signified, Baudrillard aligns himself with Lacan in arguing that the 'signified' itself is a myth, just as Marx's description of an earlier time where objects had 'use value' is more nostalgia on his part than economic history.

It is the visual Baudrillard privileges in the spectacle of consumption, not the apparent monetary worth of this or that commodity. A window display does not illustrate the function of the object, nor does it, in and of itself, try to persuade the consumer of its exchange value. Instead it takes its place in what Baudrillard describes as a 'calculus of signs'. The economic 'value' of the object is unimportant; it is its value in what Baudrillard terms the 'ambience' of all other consumer signs that generates value. In this sense, Baudrillard can argue capital accumulates until it becomes visual, and becomes an image taking its place in the ambience of the spectacle of consumption. Marx's emphasis on function and production, rather than the symbol and consumption, actually provides capitalism with a sort of 'alibi' where it can continue to operate, undisturbed, because of Marx's enlightenment-influenced teleology promising the eventual rise of the proletariat and the destruction of the class system. The dynamic Baudrillard uses to expose 'use value' as an invention of the economic system – not something that preceded it – is similar to Derrida's 'metaphysics of presence' where certain metaphysical assumptions are allowed to operate undetected in order to grant a given philosophy the appearance of an authoritative logic.

In *Simulations*, Baudrillard effaces not only use-value but 'nature' as well, arguing everything is cultural in the sense that everything we know as 'reality' is, in fact, a reality effect produced by the ambience of signs in the modern-day spectacle of consumption. 'Culture' is not something pre-existing consumer culture, culture is the production and consumption of signs. Thus commodity culture is not a sub-culture, but rather produces an illusion of a prior 'culture', which it then refers to to legitimate itself. In works translated in the late 1980s, Baudrillard goes on to argue if use value and exchange value represent a self-legitimating rhetorical device rather than an implicit economic history, and if value only circulates symbolically, then in what way does ideology 'reflect' reality? Or, to ask the same question in another way, where is the 'line' between the supposedly 'real' economic infrastructure of production and the supposedly ideological superstructure of religion, art, law, etc.?

In Marx, ideology is a discourse that translates the 'reality' of the system of production and the class system into the accepted 'meaning' promoted by various social institutions. But if use value and exchange value are an 'alibi' for the circulation of Symbolic value, 'reality' and 'meaning' also operate, in tandem, as a sort of alibi that allows signs to circulate in a way independent of a conjectured 'reality' and its corresponding 'meaning'. Once again, in a sort of modernization of Saussure, Baudrillard insists the circulating sign is not related to some exterior reality; its value lies in its capacity to repress ambivalence and obscure the inevitable non-resolution of meaning. In this sense, what the sign appears to refer to is, to borrow Derrida's term, 'always already' a reflection of the sign that poses, with a sort of false humility, as representing it.

In *Fatal Strategies*, Baudrillard regards data as a new form of 'nature'. It seems to legitimate representation, when, in fact, representation creates a simulacrum of a real that does not exist beyond the presumption of its existence as the basis of the representation. Baudrillard turns his attention away from things as signs producing a 'reality-effect', or a simulacrum, and looks to see how this has changed our subjective experience of social practice. He sees 'a universe emptied of event' (1990, 25) and a 'malicious curvature that puts an end to the horizon of meaning' (25). The result is 'the transpolitical' which is the passage from organic equilibria to cancerous metastases' (25). Even seeing this as a crisis is too teleological, so Baudrillard characterizes it as a catastrophe; 'things rush into it' without reference to reality, history or destiny, even though we continue to impose these markers wherever possible. Baudrillard's much publicized declaration that history is at an end is perhaps less radical than his more quiet declaration there are no longer any secrets, everything is transparent and without depth. There is no history because an 'event' is no longer possible once the relative importance of one distinguishable phenomenon is indistinguishable from another.

In what we might regard as Baudrillard's current phase, through the remainder of the 1990s, he seems to heed his own distrust of signs as conveyors of reality, and effects an aphoristic style deliberately fragmented, mixing anecdotes from his past with accounts of travel, interladen with reassertions of his earlier, more theorized positions. In looking over the body of his work thus far, one is struck by his steadfast obsession with the contemporary and the 'everyday'. In a world of every increasing information exchange and symbolic production, Baudrillard's own high-velocity style of observation seems to keep pace in a way traditional philosophical discourse could not hope to imitate.

Perhaps the greatest affinity between Lyotard and Baudrillard is their respect for irresolution and their disdain – even contempt – for conclusion. Lyotard's famous declaration 'I define postmodern as incredulity toward metanarratives' is really declaring incredulity toward any teleological progression appearing to lead to an inevitable conclusion. Knowledge itself is not conclusive, but compensatory; it 'reinforces our ability to tolerate the incommensurable' (1984, xxv). Lyotard has no interest in what is thought, only in what happens in order for a thought to be constituted. He looks over philosophy like a referee of the intellectual, studying the rules, but remaining indifferent to the outcome of any particular game. He would seem to agree with Marx that the philosopher has an obligation to change the world, but he is interested in an infrastructure far more basic and radical than the infrastructure of the modes of production: he wants to understand the rule governing modes of coherence.

Political intervention must occur at the level of the gamesmanship that produces syntax. He tries to give voice to why avant-garde artists like Duchamp and others are political revolutionaries whether they are interested in politics or not. Avant-garde art is revolutionary because it uncouples sense, and therefore does not have to try and derail it. Lyotard redefines the concept of 'action' by disregarding its physical component and evaluating instead its capacity to produce rules of comprehensibility that can compete with, and overwhelm, other rules of comprehensibility from other discourses. If Baudrillard hovers above language, seeing it as a sign system that produces a reality-effect, Lyotard delves way beneath it, seeing 'language games' in competition with one another for the ability to produce meaning at the expense of other, competing, language games. He privileges art, especially the avant-garde, because artists alone, in any medium, create in the interstitial area between language games and meaning. For this reason, they alone draw attention to limits and inconsistencies in 'reality' by drawing attention to which competing language game is dominant in any given version of common sense or political decision-making.

Unlike Baudrillard who analyses obsessively, Lyotard analyses nothing because his interest in language games commits him to a cataloguing and a critique of styles of analysis, rather than the result of this or that analysis. Lyotard also shares Baudrillard's disenchantment with Marx's enlightenment-style dialectic, though his scepticism is based on the practical experience of political journalism and an interest in the struggle for Algerian independence. If Baudrillard is concerned with the invisibly corrosive quality of the status quo and the mundane, Lyotard reserves his ire for failed radicalism, most significantly Soviet marxism as well as what he saw as the shameful failure of marxist pragmatics in Algeria. It is perhaps here he began to prefer the primal activism of the avant-garde artist over the apparently more involved political activist. Action that does not take account of how language games form intention cannot succeed as intervention.

Not surprisingly, then, Lyotard's early work, *Discours, Figure* and *The Libidinal Economy*, turned to the field of aesthetics with the same enthusiasm previously reserved for the field of politics. Aesthetic theory attempts to offer a bridge between form and content, but aesthetic practice itself – the actual production of art – defines and explores this gap between the two, seeing it as a permanent chaos at the base of any construction of truth and desire. By positing the libidinal as an 'economy', Lyotard is insisting desire is a material process, rather than an abstract or merely emotional one. He is less concerned with what desire 'is' than in how it functions. He sees desire as the energy of society, but it is an unstable energy, unpredictably connecting the psychological to the economical in a type of feeling and desire Lyotard calls an 'intensity'. Narrative, broadly defined as a poem or an advertisement, binds these moments of intensities into an apparently coherent pattern in order to exploit the power residing there.

Instead of exploring these intensities, narrative dilutes them in order to 'explain' something else – something always beside the point, since 'the point' is always the intensity that has been exploited. In saying postmodernism expresses an incredulity toward master narratives, Lyotard is directing us away from the comfort of narrative to the more important task of understanding what provides it with its interpretive, totalizing force. The libidinal economy is always about practice, and narrative about theory. But theory for Lyotard does not translate into practice – an opinion held over from his days as a political activist. It may translate into goal-directed action, as it did for Marx, but such action promotes a self-deluding myth of cause and effect which leads to an illusion of progress, and the work of understanding the unrepresentable intensities which underlie intention goes undone. In as much as we can consider Lyotard a political thinker, it is a glaring irony in his argument that his dismissal of master narratives does not permit any grounding of argument, and therefore no criteria for judging or justice.

In other words, Lyotard's abiding suspicion of rhetoric leaves us no way to judge the relative merits of arguments, thereby giving rhetoric more sway over our feelings and actions. Both Lyotard and Baudrillard disallow cause and effect. Lyotard turns to what he calls 'gaming' and Baudrillard to what he calls 'seduction'. For Baudrillard, 'a seductive connection is one that avoids the promiscuity of cause and effect' (1990b, 172). In *Just Gaming*, Lyotard points out different discourses have different rules for playing 'the game'. Even apparently similar concepts like 'justice' and 'truth' call for a different sort of 'gaming'. The fragmentation of the postmodern, then, is an inevitable result of the incommensurability of 'language games'. In a curious parallel, Baudrillard also emphasizes the dynamic of play in his concept of seduction. Rather than interpreting in terms of repression, the conscious or the unconscious, these oppositions give way to a universe that 'must be interpreted in the terms of play, challenges, duels, the strategy of appearances – that is, the terms of seduction' (1990b, 7). As in Lyotard, there is a gamesmanship, 'a seductive reversibility' which undoes the binary oppositions underlying traditional rhetorical strategies with their presumption of access to universal truth.

Beckett's remark that his work consists of 'a stain on silence' also seems to characterize the late work of Baudrillard and Lyotard. In his attempt to find a place for 'justice' in his schema of fragmentation and 'intensities', Lyotard explores the concept of 'the sublime', especially in terms of Kant's definition of it as an attempt to represent the unrepresentable. What Lyotard appreciates the most about the sublime is that it is a feeling and not a theory; or, it is a theory about a feeling, but a feeling that nonetheless exceeds all attempts to theorize it. When a phrase or a work of art evokes a feeling of the sublime, something beyond representation or its subsequent interpretation is demanding our attention. Both Edmund Burke and Kant make it clear the sublime is a paradoxical feeling, terror and delight for Burke, pleasure and pain for Kant. Lyotard's version of this paradox is that the sublime calls for an interpretation from us in such a way as to underline our inability to supply one. Likewise, it seems to announce itself as part of the representation in a manner that can be felt, but not evaluated. In as much as the sublime draws attention to irresolution and lack of integration, it would seem to be a prelude to insight, but, uniquely among feelings, it gives notice of difference in a way that makes it clear the difference is absolute.

It is at this point, in essays gathered in *The Inhuman*, that Lyotard modernizes the debate over the sublime by linking it directly to the avant-garde. We might expect Lyotard to appreciate the goals of avant-garde art because if language is gamesmanship, and the rules of the game dictate and control meaning, than art that sets out to break the rules might, in a sense, ambush the sublime by forcing unexpected ways of thinking brought on by often unwelcome flaunting of the rules of representation. If the sublime is a feeling of 'beyond', the avant-garde produces an excess that cannot be contained and converts unacknow-ledged impossibility into startling possibility. Aesthetic criteria make interpretation easier, but only by curtailing thought. Meaning is an effect of the limits of representation as policed by the rules of the game. The avant-garde is a playfulness that is prior to the rules, and therefore exceeds them. As soon as the avant-garde is aware of its own rules, it is no longer the avant-garde.

By connecting the sublime to the avant-garde, Lyotard connects philosophy to art – perhaps his greatest contribution. The avant-garde accesses the sublime in such a way that an action is called for that can lead only to questions and away from answers. And yet this is not a sneaky return to rules of cause and effect because the avant-garde break with established rules does not operate on the axis of 'success' or 'failure', but on the strictly experimental level of playfulness, a level of play outside the rules, and therefore only aware of pleasure and pain as palpable coordinates. By insisting the sublime is the only aesthetic of the avant-garde, Lyotard is able to see art as without future, as independent of the future. The teleological machine of traditional western aesthetics blows up, assuring the destruc-tion of modernism's late-Enlightenment project of totalization – a project inspired in the first place by capitalism's obsession with quantity and quantification, and therefore something to be resisted at every turn.

Baudrillard locates his later work around the issue of the subject and the object rather than language games, but there is an equally apocalyptic air to his musings. His style grows increasingly aphoristic in his attempt to further defy any illusion of accretion, accumulation or the myth of progress. As he says: 'In the last analysis, object and subject are one. We can only grasp the essence of the world if we can grasp, in all its irony, the truth of this radical equivalence' (1996a). Where Lyotard urges dismantling, Baudrillard is content to point out inevitable dissolution: 'In the past, we had objects to believe in – objects of belief. These have disappeared' (1996a, 142). With the loss of transcendental certitude, any event is much like another, and this is the basis of Baudrillard's notorious claim about 'the end of history'. What we have instead of events is information, since information always presents itself as neither more nor less important than other information.

This belief in information is no more than 'a reflex action of collective credulity' and 'we no more believe in information by divine right than serfs ever believed they were serfs by divine right, but we act as though we do' (142). So we have the impossibility of belief within a system that continues to necessitate it, despite the fact that 'behind this facade, a gigantic principle of incredulity is growing up, a principle of disaffection and the denial of any social bond' (142). It is no longer about the destruction of meaning, or even its rearrangement by the avant-garde, as Lyotard might argue, but simply its disappearance. Where Lyotard is a strategist, planning his next move, securing himself against gamesman-ship and manipulation, Baudrillard is a survivalist, eschewing the comfort of context or meaning in order to stay focused on the reality of absence and alienation at the heart of the unprecedented proliferation of information, meaning and imagery in the mass-media of modernity. The passion for illusion, whether it comes from master narratives or mythologies of accumulation, is something both Lyotard and Baudrillard frankly acknowledge, but they point out that this passion for illusion has taken refuge in our modern passion for information.

Data, for Lyotard, has become 'nature' in postmodern culture, just as the idea of 'nature' has become the alibi for the world of simulation in Baudrillard. And presiding over this nostalgia that reality is not what it once was is theory itself. Theory is a secular religion for Baudrillard. It purports to explain the universal property of things, but in fact it helps organize them so the particular appears connected to the universal. In this sense, theory operates like ceremony: 'both are produced to prevent things and concepts from touching indiscriminately, to create discrimination, and remake emptiness, to re-distinguish what has been confused' (Baudrillard 1990a, 178). Theorists who warn against theory, Lyotard and Baudrillard are master narrativists who declare the death of transcendental certitude; they are masters of reality who insist what we believe to be reality is just the effect of the magician's language act, the illusionist's image projection. The final paradox, fittingly postmodern in its self-effacing self-reflexivity, is that these two thinkers, each insisting on their own status as false prophets, have emerged as among our most valuable commentators on the perpetual 'now' of postmodernity.

Garry Leonard

Further reading and works cited

Baudrillard, J. *The Mirror of Production.* St Louis, 1975.
—. *In the Shadow of the Silent Majorities.* New York, 1983a.
—. *Simulations.* New York, 1983b.
—. *Forget Foucault.* New York, 1988a.
—. *The Ecstasy of Communication.* New York, 1988b.
—. *Fatal Strategies.* New York, 1990a.
—. *Seduction.* New York, 1990b.
—. *Cool Memories.* London, 1990c.
—. *The Perfect Crime.* New York, 1996a.
—. *The System of Objects.* London, 1996b.
Benjamin, A. (ed.) *Judging Lyotard.* London, 1992.
Carroll, D. *Paraesthetics.* London, 1987.
Kellner, D. *Jean Baudrillard.* Oxford, 1989.
Kroker, A. *The Possessed Individual.* Basingstoke, 1992.
Lyotard, J.-F. *Discours, Figure.* Paris, 1971.
—. *The Postmodern Condition.* Manchester, 1984.
—. *Just Gaming.* Manchester, 1985.
—. *The Differend.* Manchester, 1988.
—. *Duchamp's Trans/Formers.* Venice, CA, 1990.
—. *The Inhuman.* Cambridge, 1991.
—. *Libidinal Economy.* London, 1993.

The Social and the Cultural: Michel de Certeau (1925–1986), Pierre Bourdieu (1930–) and Louis Marin (1931–1992)

Considered together, Pierre Bourdieu, Michel de Certeau and Louis Marin correspond to a line of discourse which attempts, through multiple disciplines, to articulate the processes of social and cultural interaction. While it remains impossible to create a totalizing and definitive discourse which could then be read across the various and varied writings of all three of these authors, any comparison and contrast of their respective work invites a number of considerations. It must be noted from the outset, however, that the writing of each of these authors (either explicitly or implicitly) resists attempts to place its subject within singularly literary and/or theoretical enclosures. Instead, these three authors each deliver a facet of ongoing, relational discussion which reflexively posits the creation of the individual in social and cultural spheres; the production and consumption of forms of representation in those spheres; and the relation between the individual and the official discourses created by those forms of representation. It is through the efforts of each author to express and account for these social and cultural forms of representation, and the production/consumption thereof, that a reader of Bourdieu, de Certeau and Marin comes to appreciate the impact of their discourse on methods of thinking through literary theory.

Generally speaking, Bourdieu is a philosophical sociologist, de Certeau a religious historian with an interest in French psychoanalysis, and Marin is an art historian. Bourdieu and de Certeau have, at times, been credited with assistance in creating a 'French model' of socialization which amounts to a form of or an account of the social fabrication of knowledge. These two authors explore the viability of such terms as culture, and the relationship between the individuals who both compromise and compose the very concept of culture. As such, a primary polemic in their writing revolves around the role of the individual who is both exemplary and exceptional in his/her own cultural context. Marin departs from the abstracted construction of social models and is at once situated between the divergent responses of Bourdieu and de Certeau to socially organizing forms of representation.

As suggested by the variety in their critical dispositions, a significant common concern between these authors can be located in (as with many postwar theorists) their growing anxiety with regard to the received authority and autonomy of official discourses. The very nature of their writing invariably resists ambitious actions of correlation, accumulation and generalization. Bourdieu, de Certeau and Marin tend to work both within and against traditional modes of philosophical discourse and, paradoxically, represent (or theorize) the non-theorizable through the incorporative complexity of their interests. Moreover, any proper creation and consideration of their overall oeuvre must realize the potential shortcomings of such an undertaking, as well as the incomplete nature of the individual (and therefore also the cumulative) effect of their writings. Tragically, the death of both Michel de Certeau and Louis Marin (1986 and 1992) cut short not only the work of these writers, leaving many ideas underdeveloped and in want of greater attention, but also the ongoing intercommunication and exchange of ideas between these reflexively influential figures.

Of the three authors discussed, Pierre Bourdieu stands as the most widely disseminated in the English speaking world. Bourdieu's supporters and detractors alike credit Bourdieu with the expansion and realignment of the traditional barriers of philosophy, sociology, anthropology and ethnography, through both his extension of the boundaries of socio-logical questioning and his questioning of the validity of autonomous intellectual and social domains. His ongoing endeavour to create new ways of thinking through cultural phenomena, the concept of culture itself and fundamental systems of symbolic exchange contribute significantly to both marxist and structuralist philosophies. However, the content and character of the exegesis pertaining to Bourdieu and his work, as such, tend to reside in sociological, anthropological or (only more recently) philosophical applica-tions. True to the incorporative nature of Bourdieu's programme, therefore, the explication of his work as either sociological or literary, etc., significantly diminishes and misrepresents a basic characteristic of his writing. In part, the inadequacy of much of the analysis of Bourdieu can be linked to the fact that he was initially trained as a philosopher but began his career primarily as a sociologist. A subsequent explanation of this critical frustration can be traced to the rather paradoxical relationship Bourdieu entertains with his own work. Despite the seemingly contrary evidence to be found in both the traditional rigor of his intellectual training and his election to the chair of Sociology at the bastion of intellectual institutionalism, the Collège de France, in 1982, Bourdieu has repeatedly insisted upon the non-theoretical, anti-philosophical and anti-intellectual position of his work. Any reading of Bourdieu, insists Bourdieu, must first consider both the 'scientific' nature of his argument and the practical nature of his analytical strategy. Of primary concern in his commentary, therefore, is the necessary creation of 'a theory of practice as practice ... as an activity premised upon cognitive operations involving a mode of knowledge that is not that of theory, logic, or concept' (Calhoun et al. 1993, 267). Bourdieu continues, stating 'hundreds of times' that he has 'always been immersed in empirical research projects, and the theoretical instruments [he] was able to produce in the course of these endeavours were intended not for theoretical commentary and exegesis, but to be put to use in new research' (Calhoun et al. 1993, 271). It is within this notion of scientific practicality that Bourdieu negotiates his somewhat tenuous position as the intellectual anti-intellectual, and turns the critical gaze of sociology into the subject of a sociological investigation.

Although trained as a philosopher, Bourdieu began his career as a sociologist in Algeria during the late 1950s. Concurrently, his first major works, Sociologie de L'Algérie (1958) and Travail et travailleurs en Algérie (1963) are both predominantly sociological in orientation. These early moments of sociological study in Bourdieu's career influence a great deal of the anthro-philosophical disposition through the entirety of his work. The observations made of marriage strategies, family organization, conceptualizations of honour and gift giving rituals (particularly of the Kabyle), during an extremely harsh period in the history of Algeria, return throughout his writing as a means of forming the basis of Bourdieu's sustained inquiry of social practice. In Bourdieu's own words, it was 'the gap between the views of the French intellectuals about this war and how it should be brought to an end, and [his] own experiences' which became indicative of his relationship to the intellectual elite and that first prompted him to assume his anthropological-sociological-philosophical mission (Jenkins 1992, 14). Bourdieu's early work, however, failed to earn him any notable critical attention until his book *Les hériteurs, les étudiants et la culture* (1964). Here, Bourdieu announces a major (but retrospectively obvious) shift in the subject of his analytical programme. In *The Inheritors* (the English title), Bourdieu focuses on the way in which the French education system (particularly universities), despite its claims toward a progressive and egalitarian meritocracy, tends to reproduce systems of privilege. Bourdieu suggests, rather scandalously, that those who succeed in the academic world are not necessarily those best suited for fulfilling the stated public goals of the academy. Instead, success and privilege tend to be delegated to those who either explicitly or intuitively understand how to demonstrate an 'unconditional respect for the fundamental principles of the established order' (Bourdieu 1988, 87). Because of the exchange of a strain of commerce, predominantly social and symbolic in value (i.e. cultural capital), privilege tends to statistically support the maintenance of privilege. In both of his most antagonistic writings concerning intellectual institutions, *The Inheritors* and *Homo Academicus* (1984), Bourdieu turns the sociologist's attention, traditionally directed toward the exterior and foreign, upon its very own social structure, thereby implicitly questioning the validity of its own sociological agenda. In other words, Bourdieu manipulates philosophical and socio-logical discourses to examine philosophy and sociology. What emerges, therefore, is an investigation into how that which is traditionally considered common sense serves to reproduce privilege simply because it disguises itself as completely obvious, orthodox and natural.

Through his unwillingness to accept the obvious as such, Bourdieu subsequently announces a secondary departure from the traditional object of philosophical contempla-tion. In Bourdieu's configuration, the miniscule practices of everyday life represent an observable and quantifiable body of information which demonstrates an underlying consistency in human behaviour. As a result, in the investigation of everyday practice, the heretofore banal becomes the sight of an unearthing of the hidden and fundamental structures of social organization. More than merely observing the manner in which these orthodox and natural dispositions perpetuate their own validity within a culture, Bourdieu attempts to unearth the organizing structural relationships which seemingly guide the basic actions of the individual within the symbolic network of a culture. As Bourdieu states, 'I can say that all my thinking started from this point: how can behaviour be regulated without being the product of obedience to set rules?' (Bourdieu 1990, 64). Bourdieu, in other words, hopes to find a middle ground, or balance, between the specifics of individual choice with the determinism of social structures.

As an integral aspect of his method for the analysis of individual practices, Bourdieu delivers (developed from Aristotle, Aquinas and, most recently, Émile Durkheim) the concept of habitus as the means through which an agent negotiates the polarity of structuralist and phenomenological models of social interaction. Bourdieu deploys the habitus in order to describe events as neither systematically predetermined (as structuralism often suggests), thereby devastating the possibility of individual agency outside the determined social order, nor completely produced within, and contingent upon, the individual. The concept of the habitus, therefore, responds to 'the dual need to con-

ceptualize the subject's practice as such, and as having an origin that lay outside itself
(Dosse 1997, 304) How, in other words, can an agent apply learned rules without
recognizing them as such? Put simply, the dual function of the habitus, in theory, facilitates
the mediation of conscious and subconscious forms of decision-making.

To understand better what is suggested in the negotiative potential of the habitus it is
worthwhile to note that Bourdieu himself most often provides the simple term 'disposition'
as the nearest equivalent to the habitus. Disposition allows an agent to simultaneously be
the source of her actions and also permits the foundation of these actions to stem from a
more intuitive level. The operative mobility of habitus closely resembles, to adopt
Bourdieu's analogy, the athlete who has a deep understanding or 'feel for the game'. A
well-trained and skilled athlete does not need to programmatically learn the rules, in this
analogy, to every conceivable contingency possible in a game situation. Likewise, the
individual within a social game need not adhere to the imposition of structural social codes
to be able to work toward the end of his/her social advantage within a cultural dynamic.
Instead, action becomes an intuitive process where the agent actually embodies social rules.
The immediate repercussion of this embodiment formulates the cultural as both within and
extraneous to the individual who may therefore negotiate his/her position within that
culture on varied levels of awareness. In this sense, individual 'social agents who have a feel
for the game, who have embodied a host of practical schemes of perception and
appreciation functioning as instruments of reality construction ... do not need to pose
the objectives of their practice as ends' (Bourdieu, 1998, 80) Thus the individual
demonstrates a practised understanding of social rules and structures to an extent that
they arrive but are not imposed from an exterior structure. Hence the 'natural' and
culturally obvious condition of social structures as the subject becomes (both literally and
figuratively) the embodiment of a cultural paradigm.

Significantly, Bourdieu conceptualizes the habitus as only operating in relation to an
individual field. A field, simply, is a 'structured system of social positions – occupied either
by individuals or institutions – the nature of which defines the situation for their
occupants' (Jenkins 1992, 85). The field both defines and is defined by what is at stake
in, the currency of, social actions. Fields, however, are not always entirely autonomous but
occasionally do interconnect. Because of this, the same habitus is capable of informing a
tremendous variety of practices depending upon the field(s) in which it acts. While this is
to say simply that a single behavioural trait is not always as appropriate in, say, the
workplace as it may be at home, it is also in the nature of dominant fields to impose their
logic upon those less formidable. According to Bourdieu, this explains the reason why the
social organization of the factory may resemble that of the family (or vice versa) while the
two remain relatively distinct social fields.

Here, it becomes worthwhile, particularly for the analysis of Bourdieu's response to literary
and artistic fields, to return to the notion of cultural capital. In his book titled, *La distinction.
Critique sociale du jugement* (1979), Bourdieu advances one of his most significant contributions to marxism through his re-evaluation of what is at stake in the social game. While
traditional marxism posits the desire for economic gain as the primary currency and drive in
class conflict, Bourdieu suggests, instead, that symbolic capital inserts a secondary dimension
to the plotting of a social graph. Noting that Marx actually creates the class which also acts as
his subject ('workers of the world unite'), Bourdieu demonstrates that symbolic currency,
operating in the form of education, the arts and social 'taste', etc., often works counter-
intuitively to marxist thought. Instead, the introduction and exchange of cultural capital

allows cultural fields to isolate and dictate the fundamental basis of their existence. The world of art, for example, tends to posit economic success as the antithesis of genuine artistic achievement. In other words, the counter-economic gains its own form of value. In this sense, Bourdieu notes that the evolution of 'societies tends to make universes (which I call fields) emerge which are autonomous and have their own laws. Their fundamental laws are often tautologies' (Bourdieu 1998, 83). Thus 'the literary field is the economic world reversed; that is, the fundamental law of this specific universe . . . which establishes a negative correlation between temporal (notably financial) success and properly artistic value, is the inverse of the law of economic exchange. The artistic field is a *universe of belief* (Bourdieu 1993, 164). And so, the expression 'art for art's sake' comes to represent the interior logic exclusive to the field of art. That is, the exchange of a currency non-economic in nature creates a situation in which the field of art acts as the source of its own legitimacy. It is an end of, and in, itself. An analysis of art, by Bourdieu's reasoning, is an analysis of the circumstances and contingencies which appear in a cultural interplay that allows an artist his/her artistic validity and value.

There remains, however, a slippery residue in the trace of Bourdieu's position. Bourdieu attempts to avoid a possible conundrum in both the overstated recognition of his cultural (i.e. contaminated, subjective) complicity and the scientific nature of his argument. Put most simply, Bourdieu fails in his attempt to completely break from the determinism found in structuralist models of social control. Instead, the habitus (particularly when employed as the producer of social practice – see Jenkins 1992, 77) tends to simply replace the rigid determinism found in structuralist models. While Bourdieu allows that not all social actions can be accounted for in advance, they all at least appear accounted for within the 'space of possibles' permitted by the habitus (1993, 177). Radical innovation and resistance, therefore, are an impossibility to anyone with an understanding of the habitus and field in which any resistance occurs. And so, as the concept of the habitus appears to open a radical interpretative space, it simultaneously closes down that space by insisting on the prevalence of its overwhelming dogmatic aggression and the prominence allotted for a kind of divine spectator, or symbolic master, the sociologist. It is with this in mind that some critics have charged Bourdieu as existing in a state of radical denial with his object. One must simply locate another's habitus to be able to explain the complexity of that person's behaviour. In this, the sociologist emerges as the master symbolist who, through his superior understanding of symbolic exchange, can account for the behaviour of all others while this very action must remain unrecognized and subconscious to those actually in, embodying, the habitus. Most significantly, however, in the logical conclusion of the sociologist's symbolic dominance, Bourdieu fails in his analysis to account for the action which is conceivably devoid of symbolic value. There is, simply, no action or event which becomes truly subversive or resistant to the dominating discourse. It is in response to the rigidity of this interpretative model, then, that Michel de Certeau works to create a space outside the field of cultural production.

To a certain extent, Bourdieu and de Certeau were contemporaries. As such, there is an expected exchange of ideas which permeate moments of their parallel streams of thought. In terms of their intercommunication and reflexive influence, it is difficult to understate the significance of the fact that Bourdieu's *The Logic of Practice* and de Certeau's *The Practice of Everyday Life* were originally published in the same year (1980). As with Bourdieu, de Certeau finds a rich body of information in the events of common everyday experience. Perhaps in the spirit of Bourdieu's expansionist programme, de Certeau approaches the everyday from a dramatically different direction. In most general terms, de Certeau can be seen as representative of a shift that François Dosse describes as 'the taste for history in the seventies [which] was in some sense a continuation of the interest in anthropology in the sixties' (Dosse 1997, 266). Thus de Certeau, trained as a historian, expands many of the arguments put forth by Bourdieu (as well as Michel Foucault) by staging his arguments within the context(s) of traditionally separate forms of discourse. More than merely rotating the facets of an intellectual vogue, however, this loose shift from anthropology to history announces the continued fracturing of traditionally coherent and autonomous conceptual fields. So, while Bourdieu begins to dismantle the borders of sociology, anthropology and philosophy, de Certeau not only rethinks the external boundaries of history, but also the internal coherency and cohesion of concepts like history and culture. Like Bourdieu, de Certeau does not merely limit his analytic object or aims to the field of his initial training, but instead works through a prismatic array of disciplines to redirect the momentum of, in de Certeau's instance, methods of thinking through philosophy, psychoanalysis and history.

De Certeau takes for his beginning a mixture of his own two predominant interests. Trained as both a Jesuit and a historian, de Certeau begins with early modern religious history. In addition, de Certeau sustains an interesting relation to the French reception of Freud as a founding member of Jacques Lacan's *Ecole freudienne*. De Certeau's early writing focuses most notably on Pierre Favre (a follower of Ignatius) and Jean-Joseph Surin (a seventeenth-century mystic). Not until the 'symbolic revolution' of May 1968, however, does de Certeau begin to open the interpretative spectrum of his research. The seminal *La prise de parole. Pour une nouvelle culture* (1968) announces the redirection of de Certeau's thought. This redirection is confirmed, oddly, by de Certeau's subsequent publication, *La possession de Loudun* (1970), which simultaneously returns to the compass of de Certeau's earlier writing (religious history and mysticism) but with a noted inclusion of poignant heterogeneous social, political and social dimensions. As one might expect, and in the spirit of this expanding and increasingly unclassifiable critical approach, de Certeau's conceptualization of history remains significantly resistant to absolutism. Moreover, the work of Michel de Certeau does not simply continue the programmatic repositioning of Bourdieu's thought. Instead, de Certeau suggests that the 'interpretive mastery, which Bourdieu denies both to other interpreters and to the practitioners themselves, is itself best seen as part of a strategy of intellectual bluff and counter-bluff' (Ahearne 1995, 153). In this sense, de Certeau engages this double-bluff and adopts the critical disposition of Bourdieu, applying it not only to Bourdieu, but also to the writing of history.

And so, de Certeau works toward an understanding of history as a performative act or event which cannot possibly remain uncontaminated (in a similar manner to Bourdieu's complicit and reflexive sociology) by the practices and social structures which have made the production of history possible. Noting, for example, that a 'literary' approach to history tends to treat ideas as simply that, (while the sociological interpreter tends to treat a social artefact as indicative, or a symptom, of a larger social structure), de Certeau argues that 'historians and literary critics were employing "literary" procedures to interpret those texts which in sociological terms most resembled their own – in other words those of a cultural elite' (Ahearne 1995, 19). As such, history is made, examined and sustained by a statistical minority, the cultural elite. De Certeau, in other words, sceptically approaches the role of historian and the history that he fabricates. Instead, de Certeau turns to the margins of these official narratives, stating that:

> A society is thus composed of certain foregrounded practices organizing its normative institu-
> tion and of innumerable other practices that remain 'minor' ... It is in this multifarious and
> silent 'reserve' of procedures that we should look for 'consumer' practices having the double
> characteristic, pointed out by Foucault, of being able to organize both spaces and languages,
> whether on minute or vast scale. (1984, 48)

Furthermore, the history produced by official forms of discourse tends to grossly misrepresent the experiences of a statistical majority supposedly involved, but unaccounted
for, in the upper echelons of cultural exchange. It is in this conflict, between the masses
and the dominant classes, that de Certeau seeks out a method for the theorization of
individual practices, practices which are not represented in official discourse and are, as
such, culturally invisible. De Certeau describes these multitudinous practices as a 'silence'
which disrupts representation. It is this silence which 'indicates a need to think the other of
theory' (Colebrook 1997, 137).

De Certeau's strategy stems from dissatisfaction with both Pierre Bourdieu's and Michel
Foucault's 'use of a single principle – power or production – to account for culture'
(Colebrook 1997, 111). Bourdieu's failure to account for an event devoid of symbolic
value also fails to note, in the same manner as the official historical discourses, the silent
representations of those outside the field of cultural production. Instead, de Certeau
heralds the critical potential of the untheorized, specific, practices of the common and
everyday. De Certeau posits, for example, that 'the modern city is becoming a labyrinth of
images ... A landscape of posters and billboards organizes our reality. It is a mural
language with the repertory of its immediate objects of happiness.' In this landscape,
'commercial discourse continues to tie desire to reality without ever marrying one to the
other. It exposes communication without being able to sustain it' (de Certeau 1994, 20–
1). The fact that the representation, described by de Certeau as both bombarding and
organizing 'our reality', operates solely in a single direction, signifies a gap in the symbolic
exchange. Perhaps best noted in the fact that 'communication' and 'community' share a
common root, de Certeau's description of the city thus organizes a community, but fails to
sustain the communication needed to impose this organization. Here, the experience of
an individual in an urban environment exposes a secondary necessity if official modes of
communication and representation are 'in reality' to shape an individual's actions; that is,
they control also the reception of those modes of discourse. De Certeau argues that this is
simply not the case. Thus the simple activity of walking in the city becomes 'one way in
which the controls and rigidities of urban planning [are] dynamically rewritten' (Haslett
2000, 147). With this in mind, de Certeau then argues (in a vein more optimistic than
that allotted by Bourdieu) that the consuming subject is, in fact, the site of a 'secondary
production' (1984, xiii).

This concern with the aberrant productions of consumers shapes a particular aspect of de
Certeau's writing. To establish this heterology, de Certeau incorporates a spectrum of travel-
writing, historiography and scientific theory in order to demonstrate the way in which
western rationality is shadowed by the concept of the other. The other comes to represent a
site for the elusive alterity that de Certeau covets, but also recognizes must remain, by
definition, defiant to theorization. Significantly, de Certeau produces the notion of 'tactics'
in order to open a space of resistance by the individual consumer who works in opposition to
standard strategies. In de Certeau's conception, 'strategy' represents the manner in which
dominant social structures, rules and norms formulate themselves. De Certeau's use of the
term 'tactics', contrarily, signifies individual practices which appropriate, 'pervert, or use

those rules in opposition to the strategy'. Thus tactics represent the other to the logic of rational strategy. For the obedient subject the 'other is memory – other times which can disrupt the logic of the present. For historiography, the "other" is the past; for reason the "other" is narrative metaphor; for theology the "other" is mysticism; while for travel-writing the "other" is figured through different cultures' (Colebrook, 1997, 124, 128–9). Thus the silence posited by de Certeau simultaneously announces the need to think of the other and, by doing so, articulates the presence of the other.

De Certeau situates culture as a dynamic and fluid network of events, strategies and tactics. Rather than isolate the cultural field, therefore, de Certeau attempts to open spaces of discourse, spaces in which one can articulate the silent margins of culture, spaces in which one can theorize the untheorizable. For this reason, one of the tropes which return throughout de Certeau's writing is the observation of the manner in which individual practices tend not to mimic the official discourses of the cultural self-representation. 'This cultural activity of the non-producers of culture, an activity that is unsigned, unreadable, and unsymbolized, remains the only one possible for all those who nevertheless buy and pay for the showy products through which a productivist economy articulates itself. Marginality is becoming universal' (de Certeau 1984, xvii). Subsequently, de Certeau announces, 'we are witnessing a *multiplicity of cultural places*. It is becoming possible to maintain several kinds of cultural references' (de Certeau 1994, 66).

So, both de Certeau and Bourdieu reposition (albeit separately and with different conclusions) the potential offered in the articulation of culture. For Bourdieu the interpretation of an artistic field, say literature, revolves around the identification of the symbolic (or perhaps economic) currency at stake in that field. Analysis, as such, then focuses on the subtle, disguised contingency that validates the artistic endeavour. De Certeau places a greater significance on the aberrant in order to describe a field of effects produced by consumers (in the case of textual analysis, the readers of a given work) rather than uncovering the intended design (or meaning) of the product. Louis Marin, for his part, embraces modes of representation as the fundamental origins of social control. The observation, reading, of art, therefore, also constitutes a recognition and participation in its effects. In some sense, Louis Marin represents both the middle ground and an advancement of the streams of thought prepared by Pierre Bourdieu and Michel de Certeau. Returning to Bourdieu's aforementioned desire not to theorize but to create a concept of 'practice *as practice*', Marin can be read as only implicitly theoretical. Rather, Marin engages the performative practical response only contemplated by Bourdieu. In a more tangible manner, however, Louis Marin relates most readily to the work of Michel de Certeau in the object of his analysis, specifically art history, and his willingness to enter into a field of tactics.

In *Portrait of the King* (a reference to a seventeenth-century portrait of Louis XIV), Marin activates de Certeau's secondary production through his resistance to consumer passivity, and through his atypical form of reading history, which is devoid of many of the standard features of historical discourse. Instead, Marin's historical account remains conventionally non-historic. As noted by Tom Conley in his foreword to that text, 'scholars might balk at Marin's attempt to write a history with a minimum of events, of dates, names, or of places' (Marin 1988, xiv). In exchange, Marin allots an increasingly prominent role to the production of his specific readings, to the performance of his interpretation and the interplay of his ideas. Thus Marin prepares an archaeology of the way in which paradigms of social control have been passed through the age of Louis XIV to the modern age. Central to these paradigms of power are the arts of representation. Here, Marin studies an identical topic to that of de Certeau in his *Writing of History* (Chapters 2–4), that is the utilization of religious doctrine to organize and justify a central bureaucratic policy. Marin, however, operates from within purely aesthetic confines, and his tactics, therefore, are tactics of play and pleasure.

Marin takes as his primary subject a series of utterances, 'L'état, c'est moi,' 'Le portrait de César, c'est César' and 'Ceçi est Mon corps' ('the state, it is me,' 'the portrait of Caesar is Caesar' and 'this is my body'). Marin contemplates the reciprocity involved in the relationship between king and country, the representation of a king and that king, and the transfiguration of the flesh to food and text. The tautology of each of these statements echoes the self-validating fields of Bourdieu. Their legitimacy perpetuates itself precisely because they are enclosed circuits of logic. For Marin, however, there exists a larger complicity between these expressions. As the king, who embodies the state, encounters a representation of the king, which embodies the king, we, as observers, are witnesses to the transfiguration of the individual into the apparatus of the society itself. By placing these utterances into a discussion of a portrait of Louis XIV, Marin suggests that 'the 'effects' of Louis XIV's aesthetic productions are extensions of our own relations with television, magazines, the fine arts in our best museum, and other phenomena that embody the range of popular and elite culture' (Marin 1988, vii). It is thus within the effects of representations that Marin situates the individual's complicity in allowing 'representation to be perfect in its self-representation' by breathing the life into the entire affair (Marin 1988, 178).

The life that a spectator breathes into representation is a reflexive exchange, for in that representation the observer must ultimately confront himself. As Marin writes, 'I am interested in the painting as representation, but also in the irresistible pull, and stupefying effects, of what *I see in the mirror* it creates. Although what I see is intolerable, everything else seems trifling and childish in comparison' (Marin 1995, 104, emphasis added). To observe painting is, therefore, to enact the transfiguration of the self in painting. For Marin, however, there is also a spatial and textual dimension to the processes of this representation. Aware that he dramatically reshapes the quality of painting by re-representing that event in writing, Marin discusses the textual complexity inherent in the discussion of painting, the transfiguration of painting into text, and the text which is then consumed by the reader ('this is my body'). In Marin's *Sublime Poussin*, Marin posits the act of 'reading' a painting. With regard to the interplay of the text and the image of painting, Marin states that 'put on stage as a viewer of the picture, the reader of the letter is . . . introduced onto the stage of history as a metafigurative figure (if I may use such a term) who . . . gives the viewer – that is, himself – the exact key to the true reading of all that the picture represents' (Marin 1999, 27). Again, Marin argues against any distinction between the reader of an event and the event itself.

Thus Marin contemplates another circuitous logic which permeates all forms of representation. Here, Marin returns to the theorization of the untheorizable mentioned above. How does one contemplate and represent culture that is, in itself, composed entirely of representation? In part, Pierre Bourdieu, Michel de Certeau and Louis Marin, each in his own singular fashion, offer a reflexive recognition that the performer and the performance of a culture cannot be separated. With this in mind, then, each author must operate individually (and with relative degrees of success) to open a space of discourse for the articulation of a cultural phenomenon both shared and singular. It is, simply, the representation of the self through the discourse of the social and the cultural.

Brian Niro

Further reading and works cited

Ahearne, J. *Michel de Certeau*. Stanford, CA, 1995.

Bourdieu, P. *Sociologie de L'Algérie*. Paris, 1958.

—. *Travail et travailleurs en Algérie*. Paris, 1963.

—. *Les hériteurs, les étudiants et la culture* [*The Inheritors*]. Chicago, 1979.

—. *Distinction*. Cambridge, 1984.

—. *Homo Academicus*. London, 1988.

—. *In Other Words*. Cambridge, 1990.

—. *The Field of Cultural Production*, ed. R. Johnson. Cambridge, 1993.

—. *Practical Reason: On the Theory of Action*. Stanford, CA, 1998.

— and Wacquant, L. J. D. *An Invitation to Reflexive Sociology*. Chicago, 1997.

Calhoun, C. et al. (eds) *Bourdieu: Critical Perspectives*. Chicago, 1993.

Colebrook, C. *New Literary Histories*. Manchester, 1997.

de Certeau, M. *The Practice of Everyday Life*. Berkeley, CA, 1984.

—. *Heterologies*. Minneapolis, MN, 1986.

—. *The Writing of History*. New York, 1988.

—. *Culture in the Plural*. Minneapolis, MN, 1994.

—. *The Capture of Speech and Other Political Writings*. Minneapolis, MN, 1997.

—. *The Possession at Loudun*. Chicago, 1999.

Dosse, F. *History of Structuralism vol. 2*. Minneapolis, MN, 1997.

During, S. (ed.) *The Cultural Studies Reader*. London, 1993.

Haslett, M. *Marxist Literary and Cultural Theories*. London, 2000.

Jenkins, R. *Pierre Bourdieu*. London, 1992.

Marin, L. *Utopics*. Highland Park, NJ, 1984.

—. *Portrait of the King*. Minneapolis, MN, 1988.

—. *Food for Thought*. Baltimore, MD, 1989.

—. *To Destroy Painting*. Chicago, 1995.

—. *Sublime Poussin*. Stanford, CA, 1999.

Swartz, D. *Culture and Power*. Chicago, 1997.

Gilles Deleuze (1925–1995) and Félix Guattari (1930–1992)

Both Gilles Deleuze and Félix Guattari pursued their own authorial careers, with Deleuze's work focusing on the history of philosophy and Guattari's work concerned with the institution and politics of psychoanalysis. Their individual interests intersect in their best known jointly authored works *Anti-Oedipus* (Fr. 1972), *A Thousand Plateaus* (1980), *Kafka* (1975) and *What is Philosophy?* (1991).

Deleuze and Guattari's philosophical project is best characterized through the aim of achieving immanence: no 'transcendent' (or external) object can provide a foundation for experience. Any attempt to think of some ultimate explanatory horizon or 'plane' that would account for experience would itself be an object of experience (Deleuze and Guattari

1994, 45). This affirmation of immanence and the rejection of any transcendent ground for experience leads to a theory of 'transcendental empiricism'. If empiricism is an attention to what is given or experienced, then a *transcendental* empiricism insists that there is nothing outside the given, no point from which the given could be explained or 'justified'. But Deleuze and Guattari also expand the notions of the given, perception or experience beyond its traditional (human) boundaries. We tend to think of experience as located within the mind of a perceiving subject. But to do this, they argue, would be to locate experience *within* some plane. Rather than having some 'plane of transcendence' within which experience or the given would be located, they suggest that we should see the given as having no transcendent ground or foundation. It follows, then, that if experience or the given cannot be located within mind or the subject, then we need to think of perception, experience or givenness that extends beyond the human subject. This is why, in *A Thousand Plateaus*, they theorize a 'becoming-animal', and this is also why they consider the movements of machines, particles, genes and a desire that exceeds bounded organisms. In *What is Philosophy?* they describe science as the creation of 'observers' that are neither human nor subjective (129) and they describe art as the creation of 'percepts' that are freed from acts of perceivers. The subject, for Deleuze and Guattari, is an *effect* of a more general observation and perception that exceeds humans.

Philosophy has traditionally regarded the world as a static and inert being, while the human subject is seen to be the privileged experiencer or representer of that world. The given is located within a plane, and this plane has been constructed as an 'image of thought'. Philosophy has assumed that experience is given to a pre-experiential universal subject. Indeed, in *Difference and Repetition* (1994; published in French in 1968) Deleuze argues that western thought is dominated by two prejudices: good sense and common sense. Good sense assumes that there is some general and proper object or truth to which thought must be directed. Common sense assumes that there is a proper mode of thinking which philosophy ought to recognize. Against this traditional project of recognition, Deleuze and Guattari insist that philosophy ought to extend thought beyond any of its present recognisable forms (1994, 140). Rather than have some world correctly repeated in human representation, philosophy should free thought from dogma, preconceived images and limited notions of what constitutes experience. What differentiates philosophical concepts from science is just this 'ascension' into the virtual: whereas science concerns itself with organizing states of affairs, philosophy creates concepts that are events. Unlike the extended objects of science, events are not located within a spatially and temporally delimited field; events are a 'between-time' or *un entre-temps* (Deleuze and Guattari 1994, 148). A science works practically, by taking the *virtual* whole of all that is given and limiting its point of view to an actual field of extended objects. (Think of the way in which geometry fixes the always moving experience of space into determined extended boundaries.) Philosophical concepts move in the other direction, not organizing experience into extended actualities, but expanding the point of view in order to think the virtual whole of experience. Think, for example, of how philosophical concepts express, not this or that object, but the objectivity of being in general. A philosophical concept is not directed to extended things but to an intensity: when a philosopher defines being as expression or spirit or 'eternal return' they create an event, a way of thinking or confronting the very intensity of experience.

In Deleuze's own work, and in Deleuze and Guattari's *What is Philosophy?*, this attempt to free experience from its enclosure within the image of the human subject led to a particular way of reading texts: when we read a philosopher we need to pay attention to the unique problems and questions they create (Deleuze and Guattari 1994, 139). Doing philosophy is not about correcting errors or tidying up ambiguities; it is about creating new possibilities for thinking. Nietzsche is Deleuze's exemplary philosopher in this regard, for it was Nietzsche who enabled us to think of a givenness or experience that exceeds the human subject (Deleuze 1983). For Deleuze, Nietzsche discovered a domain of pre-personal 'singularities' or forces that could not be located within any being, but were forms of positive becoming; not the becoming *of* some identity, but a becoming *from which* any identity might then be effected. There is not one single form of becoming or affirmation but irreducible and divergent modes or 'series' of becoming. Becoming can only truly be affirmed, Deleuze argues, when we embrace empiricism and begin to experience differently. If there is nothing other than becoming, then becoming cannot be located within being or the subject. Thought, therefore, is itself a mode of becoming alongside – and in confrontation with – various other becomings. Not only is thought a form of creation, it also creates or becomes in different modes. Art, for example, is the creation and becoming of affects and percepts (Deleuze and Guattari 1994, 24), while science is the creation of functions and prospects (157). Philosophy is the creation of concepts. Neither art nor philosophy nor science are representations of the real. Deleuze and Guattari reject the idea that there is a real/actual world that then has a virtual copy. Rather, the real includes the actual and the virtual. Concepts and affects are virtual events, no more lacking in reality than actual extended beings.

If we accept this positive character of the virtual then we come close to achieving immanence and transcendental empiricism: for now the actual and the virtual are affirmed within the single and 'univocal' realm of the given. And this means that we no longer separate what *is* (matter) from some higher forming power (form or mind). It is not as though there is some inert undifferentiated being that is then differentiated by mind (dualism). On the contrary, univocal being is a plurality of singularly differentiating forces; no form of difference or becoming is privileged over any other. This was the error of structuralism; it assumed that language was a differentiating power that differentiated the undifferentiated. Against this, Deleuze and Guattari argue that difference is the whole of being. There are the differences of genetic codes, viruses, plant and animal becomings, and various other 'machinic' or inhuman series of difference. Difference is *singular*; in each case difference itself is different. The difference of each work of art is different from each work of philosophy, and each work of philosophy is itself differently different: Kant differs from Hume in a way quite different from Hume's difference from Locke. This means that difference is immanent: not the differentiation *of* some grounding being or identity. Difference itself is all that is affirmed, and to *repeat* difference is to differentiate with a maximum power. Deleuze therefore draws upon Nietzsche's concept of eternal return: difference is eternal, not grounded in a beginning or end outside difference. And difference *returns*, affirming itself over and over again, not in the repetition *of* some being, but in the repetition of difference itself. To truly repeat is to maximize difference.

An affirmative philosophy tries to live up to this challenge of eternal return by creating concepts that produce the maximum difference of thinking. Deleuze and Guattari produce a whole series of concepts. A concept, they argue, does not name some pre-given being. A concept, at its most philosophical and affirmative, dislodges our categories of being. Certain concepts carry the possibility of thought to its 'nth' degree; others, however, weaken the very power of conceptuality. Nietzsche's concept of 'eternal return', for example, affirms the very force of existence: each singular moment should, over and over again, be a radical beginning. The return or recurrence is *eternal* precisely because no moment is subordinated to any other. Without beginning and without end – without an origin and without a goal – each singular moment of existence can bear its own maximum force. But if Nietzsche has created concepts that affirm the very possibility of existence, there are also concepts that are *reactive*: capable of taking the eternal becoming of life and subordinating it to some far off goal or distant origin. The concept of 'man' or the 'human', for example, is just such a concept of 'common sense'. For it is the very nature of our concepts of 'man' or the 'human' to (a) act as an explanatory ground for other concepts; (b) prescribe a good image of thought; and (c) provide a moral foundation. A philosophical concept, by contrast, disrupts recognition and foundations. The concept of eternal return challenges us to think that unbounded force from which concepts are drawn. Leibniz's concept of the 'monad' suggests that we think a world of perceptions that are located beyond the human point of view (Deleuze 1993). Spinoza's notion of 'expression' tries to articulate a univocal being that is not subordinated to anything other than its own becoming (Deleuze 1988).

But philosophy, as the creation of concepts, is not the only domain of affirmative becoming – and *thought* is not the only domain of the givenness of existence. Deleuze and Guattari's work is also concerned with the forms of thought that exceed philosophical conceptuality and forms of experience or givenness that extend beyond thinking. In *What is Philosophy?* Deleuze and Guattari define the other two domains of thought that exist alongside philosophy as art (the creation of affects and percepts) and science (as the creation of functions and prospects). Their main contribution here is the insistence on a difference *in kind* between these domains. Philosophers, for example, aren't scientists and so their task isn't that of formalizing experience into functions; this is the scientist's task. Nor is art philosophy; art isn't about meaning and concepts. Even less is art science; art is not a picturing of the world for a certain purpose. If philosophers create concepts and scientists create functions, artists create affects. It is this emphasis on creation – rather than concepts or description – in art, which leads to Deleuze and Guattari's unique way of approaching literary texts. The most well known example is their work on Kafka (Deleuze and Guattari 1986). Kafka's texts, they argue, are not signs, allegories or metaphors for something outside the text. Indeed Kafka takes all the well-known images of meaning – the law, the father, the book – and shows these images to be the outcome of becomings. Rather than read the castle as an image of passageways directed to a law that always recedes, Deleuze and Guattari argue that it is the positive proliferation of passages and paths that multiplies the events of existence well in excess of any law. Kafka, they argue, is an author of positive becomings, and not of negative law. We should read Kafka for what his texts do and how they work, and not for what they *mean*.

Deleuze and Guattari's approach towards literature and philosophy is an affirmation of their theory of territorialization, deterritorialization and reterritorialization as described in *A Thousand Plateaus*. From an infinite and univocal becoming, always in movement and infinitely divisible, certain territories or identities are formed. And once these territories are formed they can be deterritorialized. Once an image is created, for example, it can free itself from its origin and circulate widely. *Reterritorialization* occurs when the image is then re-grounded. Take for example the formation of a language. First there is a marking out of boundaries, a *territorialization* whereby sounds are organized into phonemes, or lines are formed into script. But there is a movement of *deterritorialization* whereby such sounds can circulate and function independent of any speaker or origin. A language is essentially deterritorialization, the detachment from any ground or origin through general circulation and reference. Reterritorialization occurs when this free movement is subjected, or falls back on, one of its own components as a grounding territory. The 'I' or 'subject' is produced as a sign that grounds all other signs. Once territories are created – such as the image of the subject or the image of the law – it is possible to make the mistake of interpreting such territories as the origin of creation. Traditional readings of Kafka make just this error. They take one of the points in Kafka's castle – the centre of Law – to be the grounding origin from which all other points flow. The text has been 'overcoded' – read through the image of a single signifier. In this reterritorialization, Kafka is read as a writer who laments the ways in which Law recedes from every one of its single instances. Against this, Deleuze and Guattari read Kafka as an instance of minor literature. The major code of law, the father and meaning is deterritorialized, dispersed into movements, passages, flights and wanderings. If read affirmatively we can see Kafka as a writer who shows that any law or ground is the effect of a 'machinic' production: machinic because law is the effect of a movement that is not located within any deciding subject but is the outcome of a network or 'assemblage' of movements. To read Kafka in this way is to deterritorialize the law, to show that law is not the ground of our being but the result of a series of events. Kafka's literature creates affects: the movements and wanderings through the castle, the sounds and rhythms of his writing, and the creation of animal personae. This is why Deleuze and Guattari describe desiring production as *literally* a machine: there is just the proliferation of connections and codings, without an organizing centre (organism) or function (mechanism). Against the idea of force as issuing from a law, father or territory, Deleuze and Guattari assert the creative and affirmative nature of force. Only weak forces subject themselves to a law; active forces, by contrast, are nomadic, deterritorializing and in perpetual flight, not requiring an identity to act as a ground or justification for their becoming.

This is where Deleuze and Guattari's theory of desire comes in. Desire is not the desire *of* a subject. There is just desire, as a flow of energy, and it is from this general and immanent flow that subjects *and* transcendencies are formed. This can be made clear through Deleuze and Guattari's critique of the Oedipus complex and their embrace of a more radical Freud in *Anti-Oedipus* (1983). The Oedipus complex, they argue, is the *effect* of a certain flow of desire. It is a mistake to see the Oedipus story as a way of interpreting all other stories; to do so would be to locate the Oedipal narrative *outside* (or transcendent to) desire. By contrast, Deleuze and Guattari show that the Oedipal narrative is itself a fantasy. The father/analyst imagines that all acts of desire take place as substitutions for the lacking phallus. All desire is explained according to an original object – the full presence of the phallus – which is lost and for which all other objects stand in as signs. For Deleuze and Guattari this places psychoanalysis within a long history of *reactive* or subjectivist theories. In reactivism or subjectivism we see an action or event and then set out to describe its cause or foundation. In so doing we subordinate actions to some prior acting subject. In the case of the Oedipus complex, we assume that all specific acts of desire stand in for some original and unfulfillable desire for a complete and closed origin. But if we understand the flow of desire as existing well beyond any of its subsequent formations, then we will not take one unit of desire – the phallus – as the measure of desire in general. And this is how the critiques of psychoanalysis and capitalism are conjoined. Capital takes the flow of desire and, through a single axiom, measures all flow according to quantifiable and calculable units: the value of labour and the value of property. Similarly, psychoanalysis measures all desire in relation to one of its objects, the phallus. In this manner difference is subordinated to an identifiable measure of the same. Against this restriction of desire and capital to one of its part objects, Deleuze and Guattari insist on singularities and intensities. Desire does not pursue objects in compensation for an original lost object, and societies do not interact through the exchange of a single value. Desire is connective, continually creating new objects. And politics is not just the distribution of power and property; it also concerns the investments that create interests. The micropolitics of *Anti-Oedipus* demands that we look at how capital is created as the object of modern desire, how the subject or ego is produced as the measure for experience. Politics needs to be taken back to the ways in which the flows of desire – intensities – have been reduced to recognizable and exchangeable extended units. What Deleuze and Guattari refer to as 'schizoanalysis' is just this investigation into the 'schiz' or splitting and difference that cuts into the pure flow of desire and encloses its infinite differences into finite units, such as the phallus, the ego, the family, money, labour or property.

Ostensibly, Deleuze and Guattari's two volumes of *Capitalism and Schizophrenia* (*Anti-Oedipus* and *A Thousand Plateaus*) provide a critique of psychoanalysis and Marxism. But the word critique has to be taken seriously here. Deleuze and Guattari use the radical insights of Freud and Marx to reinvigorate the orthodox ossification of psychoanalysis and marxism. What they retrieve from Freud is the positivity of desire: prior to any subject, any 'complex' or any opposition between the actual and the virtual there is just the immanent and eternally recurring flow of desire. These flows of desire produce regularities or territories or codes. The problem comes in when certain territories or codes take themselves as being outside the flow of desire. This happens for example, when one code – the story of Oedipus – regards itself as the interpreter of all other codes. Or, when one territory – the subject, bourgeois man – locates itself as the ground for all other territories.

It is through their radical marxism that their critical theory of desire gains its truly political edge. On the one hand, Deleuze and Guattari have to remain critical of any normalizing theory of marxism. They cannot locate a subject or subject group (the proletariat) as some proper foundation for emancipation. This means also that their critique of capitalism cannot proceed as demystification of ideology to reveal the truth of, or for, some grounding subject or consciousness. Indeed, their criticism of capitalism turns on a quite unique reversal. The standard opposition to capitalism is that it has turned the world into so much quantifiable exchange, such that even the human subject becomes subjected to the flow of an impersonal market. Rather than argue that the flow of exchange should be relocated within the autonomy of the human subject, Deleuze and Guattari argue that capitalism precludes a truly radical flow of desire. Capital *deterritorializes* by subjecting everything to the flow and exchange of capital, but it then effects a massive *reterritor-ialization* by measuring this flow through a single axiom: the units of capital. The very notion of exchange is, in capitalism, grounded in the exchange *of* some value (capital) and *for* some end (profit). At the surface capitalism presents itself as a free flow of exchange without interference, imposed system or foundation. But in actual fact capitalism has measured and restricted flow according to the units of the monetary system. Deleuze and Guattari therefore argue for a properly dialectical extension of the force of capitalism. The flow of exchange should not be restricted to the code of labour and profit (just as the flow of desire in psychoanalysis ought not to be restricted to the signifier of the phallus). When one object locates itself as the explanation of all other objects then the pure and immanent flow of desire and exchange subordinates itself to one of its productions. If, however, we see desire as positive and productive we reverse the political and metaphysical reactions – such as psychoanalysis and capitalism – that try to explain or ground desire. It's not that there is a subject *who* desires. Rather, from certain regular flows of desire, subject effects are formed. It's not that exchange solidifies into a system; the very idea of 'exchange' is the effect of systematizing all units into quantities of capital. The response of Deleuze and Guattari is not to interpret desire, or regain control of the system, but to intensify desire beyond any single interpretation and extend the flow of capital beyond the fixed units of the system.

The political project of *Anti-Oedipus* is therefore intimately tied to the philosophical project of *What is Philosophy?* Both works are united by what Deleuze and Guattari argue to be *the* ethics of philosophy: *amor fati*. Rather than posit some value or redemption beyond or outside of existence – as though this world needed to be justified by some higher goal – the task of philosophy is to joyfully affirm what is. For the most part metaphysics has failed to be affirmative, and this is because it has posited some transcendent plane (or metaphysical ground) outside existence that will give existence its meaning. (The subject, being, God, humanity: all these operate as grounds from which the becoming of existence is explained.) If we see philosophy as metaphysics – the inquiry into some ultimate Being or ground – then we locate our cause and justification beyond existence. A more radical or superior transcendentalism, by contrast, refuses to locate existence within any plane. But this also means that philosophy and politics need to be eternally affirmative. Here, Deleuze and Guattari draw on Nietzsche's philosophy of eternal return. If we accept that there are just active desires, events or flows of force and that it is *from* these events that identifiable beings are constituted, then it is a mistake or *reaction* to take one of these beings as the ground or cause of all others. Philosophy's task is, therefore, to eternally and affirmatively *activate* thought. If some of our created concepts start to look like explanatory foundations or grounding beings, then philosophers need to create new concepts. This means that we need to think philosophy as a process of radical difference and repetition. As soon as an effected identity is taken as a transcendent origin or cause, then philosophy needs to *repeat* the creative force that formed this grounding concept. For example, to truly repeat Plato's *Republic* would not be to write a commentary on the text, but to produce a philosophical event that had the same force today as the original *Republic*. This means that true repetition of an event also creates maximum difference. What philosophy repeats is not theorems, opinions and dogmas but the *force* of philosophy, creating concepts over and over again. It is when philosophy falls into recognition that it becomes metaphysical and reactive: if philosophers see themselves as providing a faithful picture of the human subject then they have belied the active and affirmative event of philosophy. Immanence, therefore, is an eternal project; as soon as one concept operates as the transcendent foundation for all other concepts, then philosophy needs to renew its creative power.

But this project of immanence and eternal return also has a political dimension, as both *Anti-Oedipus* and *A Thousand Plateaus* make clear. It is in these volumes that Deleuze and Guattari demonstrate the concrete significance of a philosophy of immanence. Their invocation of 'becoming-woman', for example, ties the philosophical project of affirmation both to a politics and to a celebration of literature. Thought becomes reactive, they argue, when one of its effects – the image of man or the subject – is then taken as an origin. Against this reactive movement Deleuze and Guattari affirm the event of virtual becoming. The virtual is not a pale copy of the real, nor can the virtual be reduced to a set of possibilities derived from the actual; the virtual itself is real. Fantasies, images, concepts are at one with a univocal realm of being. If being is univocal then no part of being – neither mind, nor matter, nor the human – can act as the privileged ground of all other beings. The problem with the concept of man is that it is a virtual production that takes itself to be the actual foundation for all other productions. The only way to move beyond the reactive concept of man, who is that *being* through which all *becoming* is measured, is to affirm becoming-woman. What is other than the *being* of man would be becoming. Becoming-woman would be the first step in thinking an affirmative becoming capable of maximizing its own difference rather than shoring up its own identity. Becoming-woman is therefore the opening of becoming: not a woman who then becomes, but a becoming that is truly other than the *being* of man. For man's becoming has always been his *own*, a becoming that is the fulfilment or extension of what he is. Becoming-woman, on the other hand – if it is to be more than just an opposition to man – would be at one with becomings beyond thought, identity, decision and the self. Becoming-woman is not the becoming *of being*; it is other than being. This becoming can only be other than the becoming of being if it is a becoming not subordinated to an end outside itself. Molecular becomings are movements of difference that have no end other than themselves; they are neither becoming towards or from identity. Molar becomings, by contrast, are grounded in a being *who becomes*. This understanding of becoming-woman enables a whole new political theory of movements. Micropolitics attends to all those movements of difference that precede and exceed the intentions and identities of subjects. This is why, for Deleuze and Guattari, 'minor' literature is always political. Minor literature frees language from a speaking subject, and shows the ways in which subjects are effects of 'collective' ways of speaking. Politics is not the affirmation or emancipation of identity; if it were so then affirmation would be in the name of some being, and affirmation would be subordinated to one of its effects. Politics is the continual deterritorialization of identity, a 'molecular' process that exposes any 'molar' law to be the outcome of desire and not the ground of desire.

If we take literature to be the expression of some human spirit then literature is subordinated to something other than itself and is located within a historical trajectory of human becoming. But if literature is *literary* then it must be a minor literature, not the continuation or expression of an already existing identity but an event of *style*. Great texts, such as those of Joyce and Kafka, can be described as minor precisely because they are written in such a way that what they say is not located within a speaking subject. Consider the first lines of 'A Painful Case' from Joyce's *Dubliners*. The story begins in the voice of uptight bourgeois moralism: 'Mr James Duffy lived in Chapelizod because he wished to live as far as possible from the city of which he was a citizen and because he found all the other suburbs of Dublin mean, modern and pretentious.' As so often in *Dubliners*, although the sentence is not actually quoted, the way of speaking is already typical of a place rather than a subject. To use the words 'mean, modern and pretentious' or to speak of 'citizens' is to show the ways in which Dublin is already a certain lexicon. The sentence is written in the 'voice' of Dublin. This is why all minor literature is directly political: not because it expresses a political message but because its mode of articulation takes voice away from the speaking subject to an anonymous or pre-personal saying. Joyce's style, for example, is less the expression of an individual subject than it is the articulation of what Deleuze and Guattari refer to as a 'collective assemblage'. Joyce's literature is minor because it takes voice and the saying beyond any meaning, law or proper ground. And the response to such a minor literature should not be its canonization but its repetition. To affirm the event of a great work of literature, for example, is not to copy, mimic or imitate; it is to create another 'great' text. But to be truly great we must repeat all the newness, difference and stylistic divergence of the precursor. True fidelity to a major text is a becoming-minor, affirming a style that does not yet exist, that is not yet recognized and is not yet the style *of* some identifiable movement. For it is in literature that style is not presented as the ornament or overlay of an otherwise coherent content; it is not that there is a sense that is then expressed *through style*. Literature is style itself, the production of affects, masks, personae and voices – a continual affirmation of a becoming that is not the becoming *of* some prior identity. This is what sets literature, when read affirmatively, against the reactive concept of the human. It is not that there is a speaking being – the human – who then deploys style. Rather, the human is an effect of a certain way of speaking. The subject – predicate structure of our sentences, for example, leads us to think of a being who then acts, a speaker who then speaks. Against this subject – predicate structure of the proposition, Deleuze and Guattari affirm forms of literature capable of enacting a grammar of becoming. Their most well-known example is that of free-indirect style. In free-indirect style – as we have seen in the example from Joyce – it is not that there are general human characters who then speak; rather, character is effected from ways of speaking.

Deleuze and Guattari also carry the question of style through to their own philosophy. Their own work, particularly A *Thousand Plateaus*, is written in a manner that demands new ways of reading, thinking and response. Composed in a series of 'plateaus', their work uses intervening voices, oscillates between the tone of a manifesto and the tone of exegesis, wanders through observations on science, literature, politics and philosophy, and concludes not with a proposition but a created concept: 'mechanosphere'. If, as they argue, thought is a response to existence and life, and if life itself is eternal response, then philosophy will be a dynamic event. A *Thousand Plateaus* is, therefore, not a series of propositions whose truth-value can be assessed by some pre-existing logic. It is the creation of a new logic and a new synthesis. The response that such a text invites is less one of interpretation than affirmation. If we ask how A *Thousand Plateaus* works, and not what it means, then we might also be compelled to think of new ways in which texts might work. In the case of A *Thousand Plateaus* its construction or 'working' is rhizomatic or nomadic: not centred around an authorial voice and subject matter but creating new voices and inventing new questions. The challenge of this work lies in the possibility of its *repetition*: to repeat the event of A *Thousand Plateaus* would not be to write and think rhizomatically, but to think (over again) one more way in which we could think and write differently.

Claire Colebrook

Further reading and works cited

Buchanan, I. *Deleuzism*. Edinburgh, 2000.
Deleuze, G. *Nietzsche and Philosophy*. London, 1983.
—. *Spinoza*. San Francisco, 1988.
—. *The Fold*. Minneapolis, MN, 1993.
—. *Difference and Repetition*. New York, 1994.
—. *Negotiations: 1972–1990*. New York, 1995.
—. *Essays: Critical and Clinical*. Minneapolis, MN, 1997.
— and Guattari, F. *Anti-Oedipus*. Minneapolis, MN, 1983.
—. *Kafka*. Minneapolis, MN, 1986a.
—. *Nomadology: The War Machine*. New York, 1986b.
—. *A Thousand Plateaus*. Minneapolis, MN, 1987.

—. *What is Philosophy?* London, 1994.
— and Parnet, C. *Dialogues.* London, 1987.
Hardt, M. *Gilles Deleuze.* Minneapolis, MN, 1993.
Massumi, B. *A User's Guide to Capitalism and Schizophrenia.* Cambridge, MA, 1992.
Stivale, C. *The Two-Fold Thought of Deleuze and Guattari.* New York, 1988.

Michel Foucault (1926–1984)

Michel Foucault began his academic career in the discipline of psychology, obtaining a diploma in 1952 and working in psychiatric hospitals in the early 1950s. But apart from his first book, *Mental Illness and Psychology* (1954), his work extends across the disciplines of history, philosophy, critical theory and literary and cultural studies, as well as psychology and semiotics. His early work does indicate a persistent concern of his later writings, however, in focusing on the systems of human behaviour and thought, and in seeking to identify the reasons and motivations for particular human rituals or actions. Arguably, no other theorist since Freud has had such an impact on contemporary notions of human subjectivity and agency. His influence on the arts and social sciences in general has been both pervasive and incisive, and has had a major impact on the direction of literary and cultural studies in particular.

Along with Jacques Derrida and Roland Barthes, Foucault was perhaps the most significant intellectual responsible for the emergence of poststructuralist theories, and devised several key concepts which are common currency in contemporary critical theory, such as 'discourse', 'technology', 'power', 'epistemé' and 'archaeology'. These concepts were linked for Foucault in his methods of analysing systems of practices and ideas, and tracing these systems through history. Foucault identified sets of associated practices and rituals as indicative of systems of belief and thought. The emergence in the seventeenth century of the ritual of banishing and confining 'insane' people, for example, marked a shift for Foucault in the ways in which people of that time conceived of the relationship between 'reason' and 'madness', and thus a shift in what constituted 'normal' human behaviour. Foucault's historical methods involved identifying epistemic or epochal changes from the evidence of new terminologies, new practices and new institutions. These methods were based on the notion that we could detect that certain human actions were not accidental but occurred within frameworks of repetition, so that we can trace the emergence of specific 'technologies' in a regularity of actions. The systematic confinement of the 'insane' to a specific institution constitutes one example of the 'technologies' which Foucault analyses. Similarly, his argument that modern methods of penal correction and reform could be traced to the eighteenth century was predicated on the evidence of a new type of prison as well as associated changes in the treatment and containment of those found breaking the law. For Foucault, such changes were not isolated from wider shifts in power relations in society, and usually entailed the transformation of prevailing notions of subjectivity.

Foucault called these historical methods 'archaeology', and argued that they differed substantially from 'history' as it was then commonly practised. The 'historian's history', in Foucault's terms, was constructed to seem like a neutral, unbiased narrative of events, which traced historical continuities in order to represent disparate events as parts of the same evolutionary pattern (Foucault 1977a, 152). Foucault modelled his 'archaeological' historical practice, however, on Nietzsche's genealogies, which he discusses in his essay 'Nietzsche, Genealogy, History' (1977a). According to Foucault, genealogy searches for hidden structures of regulation and association, a method of tracing etymological, psychological and ideological ancestors of modern social, cultural or political practices 'in the most unpromising places' (Foucault 1977a, 139). Genealogy was interested in ruptures as well as continuities, contradiction as well as coherence. The genealogist, moreover, is aware of the provisional nature of her/his own subject position in relation to interpretations of the past, in contrast to the historian's pretence of neutrality.

Foucault's 'archaeology' differs only slightly from Nietzsche's genealogy in placing more emphasis on the search for origins or decisive transformations. Foucault argued that there were distinct 'epistemés', or epochs, of history, and that each epistemé contained its own particular ideas of subjectivity, power and history. In practice, this meant that there was a 'well-defined regularity' to different disciplines and modes of thought. Foucault posed the possibility that very different kinds of practices – science, literature, economics, language, anthropology, medicine, history and so on – collaborated implicitly in a self-regulating system of representations. He asks us to believe that connections between disciplines, and shared assumptions between different kinds of thought, are not coincidental. 'What if empirical knowledge, at a given time and in a given culture, *did* possess a well-defined regularity? If the very possibility of recording facts, of allowing oneself to be convinced by them, of distorting them in traditions or of making purely speculative use of them, if even this was not at the mercy of chance?' (Foucault 1974, ix). The associations between different discourses and disciplines, Foucault goes on to argue, reveal not coincidence, but instead an order regulated by powerful ideological conditions.

Foucault's work identifies the points at which new collaborations of this sort emerge and become dominant. This is evident in his 'histories' or 'archaeologies'. In *Madness and Civilization*, he traces the emergence of modern categories and concepts of insanity. In *The Birth of the Clinic*, he analyses the beginnings of modern ideas of medical care and of the care for the health of the human subject. *Discipline and Punish* examined the emergence of modern modes of penal correction, punishment and containment. His last works, the three volumes on *The History of Sexuality*, continued this work by exploring the birth of modern notions of sexual identity and practice, while also marking a return to his early interests in psychology by focusing even more intensely on human subjectivity and the 'technologies of the self'. Each of these works take as their subject different discourses or 'discursive formations', by which Foucault means the powerful collaborations of texts, images, disciplines and practices which make up the prevailing knowledge of distinct areas, such as sexuality, penality or insanity.

This has been an important dimension of Foucault's work for literary and cultural studies. According to his notions of 'discursive formations', literary texts would collaborate with texts of various different kinds – medical, juridical, penal, philosophical, psychological, etc. – to form particular kinds of knowledge and understanding. This means that we can analyse literary texts for the function which they perform in relation to different kinds of knowledge. For example, we might analyse European literary texts to see to what degree and how they collaborate with other texts and images in representing Africa as a savage, uncivilized place, and thereby identify how literary texts might collude with the politics of imperialism. Equally, we might analyse how literary texts represent women in a given time, to explore the relationship between literary representations of women and practices of misogyny. This type of analysis, which treats literary texts as agents which construct and shape the ideologies and practices of a given society or culture, borrows from Foucault's arguments that the connections between different kinds of representation are indications of a powerful discursive formation.

There is a direct correlation for Foucault between the representation of a particular concept and the situation of that concept within a field of power relations. The category of 'insanity', for example, emerges as a defined and distinct object of study at the same time as it is constituted as a site of otherness and abnormality. The production of knowledge about 'insanity' leads to the formation of institutions and technologies to treat it as a condition, and, in turn, the establishment of such institutions and technologies means that there is a new power relationship between the insane and the sane. The insane are, according to this system of representations and relationships, deemed incapable of knowing or caring for themselves, and the sane are correspondingly deemed responsible for treating the insane. This is the argument of Foucault's first major work, *Madness and Civilization* (1961). He begins that book by charting the process whereby the marginalized figures of the medieval world, lepers, were replaced by those of the modern world, the insane. This process, according to Foucault, takes place initially at the level of representations, 'first, a whole literature of tales and moral fables ... [then] in farces and *soties*, the character of the Madman, the Fool, or the Simpleton assumes more and more importance. He is no longer simply a ridiculous and familiar silhouette in the wings: he stands center stage as the guardian of truth' (Foucault 1967, 14). Gradually, the modern world develops methods and practices for dealing with insanity, confining the insane to institutions which serve to police the difference between the mad who are held within the walls of the asylum, and the 'normal' who are free to live in society unaffected. There is a direct relationship between prevailing definitions of normality, and the institutional confinement of the mad, as well as the criminal and the rebel, of course. Foucault's argument suggests that modern societies spin out a dialectic of self and other in which the stability and normality of the self can only be proved by demonizing and estranging the other.

It is important to stress that Foucault's analysis of such power relations recognizes that power is not at the control of individual subjects or groups but is instead a general force which is only visible in particular events and actions. If Nietzsche claimed to be working in a God-less universe, Foucault took this further by appearing to work in a world absent of human agency either. Power operates for Foucault in a structural and systemic way, not as an instrument mastered by human subjects. Foucault defines power relations most clearly, but perhaps also most crudely, in his later works, principally in *Histoire de la sexualité: La volonté de Savoir* [The History of Sexuality, Volume 1, 1990], first published in 1976. Here, Foucault argues that in taking sexuality as an object of study, and in particular addressing the repression of sexuality in the Victorian period, we ought to look not at the individuals or even the particular laws or institutions instrumental in the censorship of sexuality. Instead, Foucault asks us to conceive of the whole discourse of sexuality and its repression becoming prominent in a particular form as a result of the emergence of certain power relations. Sexuality only becomes a prominent discourse during this time, he argues, 'because relations of power established it as a possible object; and conversely, if power was able to take it as a target, this was because techniques of knowledge and procedures of discourse were capable of investigating it' (1981, 98). This makes the relationship between power and discourse seem to be confusingly tautological, but Foucault is emphasizing the ways in which no individual, group, class or sex is responsible for deciding to repress certain aspects of sexuality. Instead, sexuality manifested itself in its particular forms and concepts in any given time because of 'a complex, strategical situation in a particular society' (Foucault 1981, 93). For Foucault, human subjectivity and agency was as much the product of particular discursive formations and power relations as sexuality, penality, insanity or any other concept, and the human belief in the individual ability to affect the society around them consciously and decisively was the effect of a system of beliefs and discourses.

Foucault's theories, like other poststructuralist ideas, are characteristically post-humanist in the sense that they ascribe very little power or responsibility to individual human agency. In a much quoted phrase in the preface to *The Order of Things*, Foucault writes 'it is comforting . . . and a source of profound relief to think that man is only a recent invention, a figure not yet two centuries old, a new wrinkle in our knowledge, and that he will disappear again as soon as that knowledge has discovered a new form' (1974, xxiii). Like Barthes and Derrida, Foucault anticipates the 'death of the subject', in which 'man' is no longer the privileged locus of sovereignty and power. His antipathy towards human sovereignty is the product of a widespread belief among postwar European and American intellectuals that the events of the Second World War revealed the dark side of Enlightenment modernity. The Enlightenment ideal that humankind would evolve progressively towards greater harmony and civilization was severely undermined in the twentieth century by the wars of mass destruction. This led postwar thinkers to argue that the Enlightenment went hand in hand with dark tendencies, which included from the beginning the destructive forces of colonialism, capitalism, poverty, war and famine. These forces were not the product of individual human agency, but were instead the logical consequences of modern social and political systems. This is what Foucault shows in his 'archaeologies', that the dark forces of sexual repression, penality and insanity are not aberrations within modern society – they are not, for example, the residual traces of pre-Enlightenment civilization – but are necessary functions in the production of modern notions of normality. Social and cultural change occurs for poststructuralist thinkers through specific structures or discourses of representation, in which human actions, thoughts and practices are produced as effects. History for Foucault is not the product of human behaviour, but of structural relations.

Some critics of Foucault's thinking have argued that this notion of power relations determining human subjectivity is too gloomy. Frank Lentricchia sees Foucault's account of the archaeologies of power as 'a totalitarian narrative' with a 'depressing message' (Lentricchia, in Veeser 1989, 235). 'Power is everywhere', writes Foucault in *The History of Sexuality*, 'not because it embraces everything, but because it comes from everywhere' (1990, 93). The implication of this notion of the omnipresence of power is that there is no possibility for the emergence of effective resistance or even escape, and indeed this appears to be Foucault's legacy for new historicist critics, particularly Stephen Greenblatt, who argues that subversion only ends up serving the interests of power (Greenblatt 1981). Because power functions by justifying itself in relation to demonized others, opposition to it can only serve to reinforce its modes of operation. Power is thus believed to be ineluctable, which Lentricchia argues, leaves us apathetic and submissive. This emphasis on the omnipresence of power, however, is a feature mostly of Foucault's later work, and perhaps is unfair to his work as a whole. Jon Simons argues that Foucault is caught between two moods, one in which he is 'a prophet of entrapment who induces despair by indicating that there is no way out of our subjection', the other in which he is attracted to the notion of 'untrammelled freedom and an escape from all limitations' (Simons 1995, 3).

The latter optimism is certainly evident in *Madness and Civilization*, for example, in which Foucault reserves a special status for art as a vehicle for freedom. Art and writing, he argues in the conclusion to *Madness and Civilization*, are outside and critical of the discourse of madness. This means that art and writing are privileged as spaces outside of the operation of power. Derrida criticized Foucault's attempt to sustain the illusion of freedom or resistance in the face of a totalitarian concept of discourse as 'the most audacious and seductive aspect of his venture', and 'with all seriousness, the *maddest* aspect of his project' (Derrida 1978, 34). Foucault seemed caught between the desire to maintain a space of freedom and yet at the same time to insist that freedom was impossible within an omnipotent system of discursive formations.

He attempted to resolve this tension in his later work by defining more clearly what he meant by 'power', particularly in arguing that power was not to be understood solely as an instrument of repression or punishment. Power could also produce pleasure, he argued:

> If power were never anything but repressive, if it never did anything but to say no, do you really think one would be brought to obey it? What makes power hold good, what makes it accepted, is simply the fact that it doesn't weigh on us as a force that says no, but that it traverses and produces things, it induces pleasure, forms knowledge, produces discourse. It needs to be considered as a productive network which runs throughout the whole social body. (Foucault 1980, 119)

The force which Foucault calls power certainly produces repression, incarceration, pain and the subjugation and exclusion of marginal peoples, and maintains a vast array of technologies and weapons in its support. But it is not, Foucault argues, an external force which is imposed on us – it is in fact the name of our own repressions, inhibitions and exclusions. It is our own process of self-fashioning and self-policing, which produces our loyalty and obedience, our conformity and unconscious submission in the act of producing us. Power is the term Foucault uses to describe the repressive apparatus of the state. It is our own repressive apparatus, and as such it allows us the pleasure of our own illusions and self-images. This is the major argument of *The History of Sexuality*, in particular, which focuses more clearly than in any other of Foucault's works on the productive and positive aspects of modern discourses on sexuality.

Foucault died in 1984, but his work has had a profound impact on the theoretical foundations of modern literary and cultural studies. In the late 1970s, Foucault conducted seminars at the University of California at Berkeley, and influenced a generation of critics who defined and practised what became known as the new historicism. Critics such as Stephen Greenblatt, Louis Montrose, Catherine Gallagher and D. A. Miller have analysed literary texts from perspectives which are broadly Foucauldian. His later work has been a major influence on the methods and arguments of gender studies too, in the work of Eve Kosofsky Sedgwick and Alan Sinfield, in particular. He has also been influential to the emergence of contemporary postcolonial studies, especially in the work of Edward Said, whose pioneering study of discourses of imperialism, *Orientalism*, borrowed from Foucauldian ideas and concepts. His pervasive impact on a wide range of academic disciplines is testimony to the breadth of thought in his work, which could not be confined to one discipline in particular. Maurice Blanchot asked 'do we know who he is, since he doesn't call himself ... either a sociologist or a historian or a thinker or a metaphysician?' (Blanchot 1990, 93). It is the virtue and also perhaps the problem of Foucault's legacy that he attempted to encompass all these roles in fashioning his structural analyses of modern civilization.

John Brannigan

Further reading and works cited

Blanchot, M. 'Michel Foucault as I imagine him', in M. Foucault and M. Blanchot, *Foucault/Blanchot*. New York, 1990.
Derrida, J. *Writing and Difference*. London, 1978.
Foucault, M. *Raymond Roussel*. Paris, 1963.
—. *Madness and Civilization*. London, 1967.
—. *The Archaeology of Knowledge*. London, 1972.
—. *The Order of Things*. London, 1974.
—. *The Birth of the Clinic*. New York, 1975.
—. *Mental Illness and Psychology*. New York, 1976.
—. *Language, Counter-Memory, Practice*, ed. D. F. Bouchard. Ithaca, NY, 1977a.
—. *Discipline and Punish*. London, 1977b.
—. *Power/Knowledge*, ed. C. Gordon. London, 1980.
—. *The History of Sexuality, Volume 2*. New York, 1985.
—. *The History of Sexuality, Volume 3*. New York, 1986.
—. *The History of Sexuality, Volume 1*. London, 1990.
Greenblatt, S. 'Invisible Bullets: Renaissance Authority and its Subversion', *Glyph*, 8, 1981.
Lentricchia, F. 'Foucault's Legacy: A New Historicism?', in *The New Historicism*, ed. H. Aram Veeser. London, 1989.
McNay, L. *Foucault*. Cambridge, 1994.
Rabinow, P. (ed.) *The Foucault Reader*. London, 1986.
Said, E. *Orientalism: Western Conceptions of the Orient*. London, 1985.
Simons, J. *Foucault and the Political*. London, 1995.
Visker, R. *Michel Foucault*. London, 1995.

Jacques Derrida (1930–)

Jackie Derrida was born in El-Biar, near Algiers, and moved to Paris in 1949, where he studied at the Lycée Louis-le-Grand before being admitted to the École Normale Supérieur. His teachers included Jean Hyppolite and Michel Foucault, and he met fellow Algerian Louis Althusser on the first day he attended rue d'Ulm. He taught at the ENS as *maître-assistant* until 1984 when he took up the position of *directeur d'études* at the École des Hautes Études en Sciences Sociales. On the verge of publishing his first paper, he signed himself 'Jacques Derrida' and has thereafter been known by that name. Derrida's earliest scholarly work was on Edmund Husserl – his 1954 Mémoire, supervised by Maurice de Gandillac, *Le problème de la genèse dans la philosophie de Husserl*, was eventually published in

1990 – and a respect for the rigour of phenomenology marks all his thought, even though his originality depends on a swerve away from Husserl.

From early on, Derrida was impressed by Martin Heidegger's dialogue with and departure from phenomenology. In particular, he was influenced by Heidegger's claim that all metaphysics is at heart a metaphysics of presence. Within western philosophy, as Heidegger reads it, being is construed as presence (an object is present or presentable) or as self-presence (divine or human consciousness). With *Of Grammatology* Derrida was to argue that the border of metaphysics is divided, so that assumptions of presence overtly or covertly structure all sorts of writings, not only those we conventionally identify as philosophy. It follows that the sciences as well as the humanities answer to metaphysics. 'Philosophy can teach science that it is ultimately an element of language, that the limits of its formalization reveal its belonging to a language in which it continues to operate despite its attempts to justify itself as an exclusively "objective" or "instrumental" discourse' (Derrida 1984a, 115). This is not a wholly negative lesson, for Derrida seeks to indicate ways of refiguring our relations to ideas and the institutions that house them. His interpretations are, he insists, affirmative. An open network of words and concepts – including 'différance', 'dissemination', 'spacing' and 'trace' – was patiently established to inaugurate and advance this discourse, although, to Derrida's surprise, his work has become known by just one of the words he put to use: *deconstruction*.

In 1983, when explaining 'deconstruction' in a letter to his Japanese translator, Derrida recalled how it imposed itself on him while writing *Of Grammatology*. 'Among other things', he says, 'I wished to translate and adapt to my own ends the Heideggerian word *Destruktion* or *Abbau*' (Derrida 1991, 270). Both words designate an operation of destructuring or unbuilding, the purpose of which is to reveal how the fundamental concepts of western philosophy have been constructed, and over the years Derrida has taken pains to distance deconstruction, as he practises it, from the instrumental and mechanical overtones of both German words. The word 'deconstruction' is not used in Derrida's first major work, *Edmund Husserl's 'Origin of Geometry': An Introduction* (1962), five years before the better known *Of Grammatology*. Indeed, the interesting metaphor in the earlier text is not 'construction' but 'sedimentation'. The term is Husserl's, and it was used to suggest how a discipline such as geometry develops by researchers building on the assumptions, methods and results of those who came before. More in harmony with Husserl than in disharmony with him, Derrida writes of 'de-sedimentation', of questioning back through history to see how meanings have been formed, reformed or deformed while being transmitted through history. It is in reading the *Introduction* that we see how carefully Derrida follows phenomenology and precisely where and why he leaves it.

Husserl argues that no sharp line can be drawn between the constitution of an ideal object – Pythagoras's theorem, for example – and its historical transmission. His reason: language preserves the sense of an ideal object and allows other people to gain access to it. Derrida agrees with Husserl that language helps to compose ideal objects; however, he disagrees with him on how language establishes itself. Husserl is especially interested in writing, which he believes preserves ideal objects in an exemplary way, and it is over the status of writing that the two philosophers fundamentally differ. For Husserl, the contingency and materiality of writing, *Verkörperung*, can be bracketed, leaving only the pure possibility of embodiment, *Verleiblichung*. Yet, as Derrida argues, *Verleiblichung* and *Verkörperung* cannot be separated in language (1978, 92). An author's pure intentional act can never be protected from the dangers of contingency and catastrophe. A manuscript can always be burned, lost, quoted out of context or delivered to the wrong address. At this point it needs to be stressed that 'writing' for Derrida denotes inscription in general, not merely ideographical marks. Cinema, cybernetics, dance, music, sculpture: all are constituted by acts of inscription, even those that do not answer to voice. The presumption that writing derives from speech, and represents a fall from a natural state of unmediated presence to a speaker or listener, is named phonocentrism. It is a general state of affairs, Derrida thinks, as prevelant in the East as in the West. Logocentrism is a European response to phonocentrism; it is the systematic tendency to locate intelligibility in a self-grounding *Logos*: God, Logic, Reason, Spirit, Will, or any of the other contenders for pride of place in the western philosophical tradition.

Derrida maintains, then, that self-expression is never pure, never fully present to either author or reader, but is always bound to its material mark. Writing is therefore always and already exposed to accidents. Even geometrical figures can be cited out of context, as the lyrics of Eugène Guillevic's *Euclidiennes* charmingly testify. Note that Derrida is not merely pointing out, as an empirical fact, that unexpected events can befall a piece of writing. Rather, he is arguing that the possibility of catastrophe is a structural component of a text. This textual structure is sometimes called destinerrance, a neologism that combines 'destination' (or even 'destiny') and 'errance' (from the Latin *errare*, to wander). A text has a destination, even perhaps a unique addressee, and yet it can always go astray and find other readers to whom it will appear as though sent to them. Beguiling in its simplicity, this formulation nevertheless guides some of Derrida's most sophisticated and subtle readings. For example, consider 'Le facteur de la vérité', his study of Lacan's celebrated seminar on Poe's short story 'The Purloined Letter'. In the original story Minister D – steals a *billet doux* from the royal boudoir with the intention of blackmail, and the brilliant detective C. Auguste Dupin eventually finds the letter in a card-rack in the Minister's rooms. For Lacan, the stolen letter *means* that 'a letter always arrives at its destination'. Derrida takes this concluding remark to be an allegory of Lacan's unconscious hopes for psychoanalysis: 'The deciphering (Dupin's, the Seminar's), uncovered via a meaning (the truth), as a hermeneutic process, itself arrives at its destination' (Derrida 1987, 444). This tacit acknowledgement of the analyst's sense of truth as presence is undone by the counter-claim that 'a letter can always not arrive at its destination' (Derrida 1987, 443–4). No transcendental structure can protect a letter from being misdelivered or not being delivered at all. On the contrary, there is an irreducible possibility of error in textual transmission that is transcendentally inscribed in the text itself.

So from the very beginning of his writing life, Derrida distances himself from transcendental philosophy while rejecting empiricism as an alternative. Instead, he elaborates the meaning and pertinance of what he comes to call 'quasi transcendental' structures (Derrida 1986, 151a–162a, trans. modified). The condition of a mark's possibility to be singular is also, and at the same time, the condition of its possibility to be repeated and thereby to lose any title to absolute singularity. (Incidentally, this clarifies what Derrida means by *la trace*: a singularity erases itself in the very act of being inscribed, leaving only a trace of what has never been able to present itself as such.) In the Parisian intellectual world in which he began to publish and teach, Derrida's discovery of a third position between transcendental philosophy and empiricism meant that he had found a place or, better, a non-place from which to criticize and reformulate both phenomenology and semiology, two of the most important discourses of the time, not least of all because they were opening up new ways of reading Freud and Marx. Derrida used this position both to criticize hasty moves away from philosophy and to affirm the archive of philosophy. On the one hand, contemporary attempts to find a way beyond philosophy (Bataille, Foucault, Lacan, Levinas, Lévi-Strauss) are shown to rely on a venerable metaphysical notion of presence. And on the other hand, the great philosophers (Plato and Hegel, above all) are revealed not to be in fee to metaphysics in any simple or straightforward way. In the *Phaedrus* Plato both fears writing that is removed from its source and affirms the writing in the soul, while Hegel is 'the last philosopher of the book and the first thinker of writing' (Derrida 1976, 26).

Thus far there seems to be no very good reason to link Derrida to literature. In his first writings he appears as a philosopher writing with other philosophers in mind. Later, he will argue that he is not practising philosophy as narrowly understood but trying to find a place or non-place, which as we have seen he calls *la différance* or *la trace*, from which he can question the grounding assumptions of philosophy (Derrida 1984a, 107). It would be a mistake to think that an interest in literature and poetry derives from his years of informal association with *Tel Quel* in the late 1960s, or from his time as a visiting professor at Johns Hopkins University, where he went first in 1968, or from his sojourn at Yale University where he taught regularly for part of each year from 1975 to 1986. To be sure, at Yale he became friends with several eminent literary critics – Harold Bloom, Geoffrey Hartman, Paul de Man and J. Hillis Miller – but while de Man's work in particular would become very important to Derrida, his interest in literature precedes his years of teaching in the United States. While defending his *thèse d'état* in 1980 he reminded the jury that 'my most constant interest, coming even before my philosophical interest I should say, if this is possible, has been directed towards literature, that writing which is called literary' (Derrida 1983, 37). That latter distinction is important. Derrida is less interested in literature understood by way of aesthetic qualities, fictionality or the pleasures of form, than in the acts of inscription which literature allows and encourages. An inscription of the singular, as we have seen, introduces a trace of what cannot be presented; and in considering this trace one uncovers *aporias* – unavoidable and irreconcilable forks encountered in a path of reasoning – that introduce differences and thereby dislodge the metaphysics of presence.

Yet had Derrida spoken only of inscription and never said anything about literature or poetry, one can still imagine authors and critics being intrigued by his work, beginning with his early commentary on Husserl. The *Introduction* develops a phenomenologically exact description of the death of the author (Derrida 1978, 88), which Maurice Blanchot had proposed in a more essayistic manner in the early 1950s and which Roland Barthes was to popularize in the late 1960s. It also gives philosophical justification to the theme of misprision that Harold Bloom was to establish, with Emerson and Freud mainly in mind, in the 1970s. For Derrida argues that 'non-communication and misunderstanding' are 'the very horizon of culture and language' (Derrida 1978, 82). More generally, in its attention to the historicity of ideal objects, the *Introduction* invites us to rethink the meanings and functions of archives and literary histories. After all, the class of ideal objects includes literary texts as well as mathematical theorems. Derrida was of course well aware of that in 1957 when, with Hyppolite as his supervisor, he registered as a thesis topic, 'The ideality of the literary object' (Derrida 1983, 36).

It is no surprise then to find literature itself evoked at the very centre of the *Introduction*. A 'choice of two endeavours' (Derrida 1978, 102) is proposed there, the one associated with Husserl and the other with James Joyce. Here philosophy and literature are seen to offer competing ways of gaining access to the past. Where the Husserl of 'The Origin of

Geometry' tries to render language clear and unequivocal so that a tradition can be passed on without impediment, the Joyce of *Finnegans Wake* seeks to maximize equivocity and thereby to encode the past, in all its variety, in the languages of his text. Husserl aims for complete translatability; Joyce stymies translation in each and every sentence. To choose between these alternatives is impossible. Univocity must remain a horizon for Joyce if he is to remain intelligible, while Husserl must admit that were equivocity completely reduced and expunged from historicity no unique event would be legible. Needless to say, this contrast between Husserl and Joyce is unable to support all that Derrida has said about literature. However, we see from early on that literature is considered in terms of a discussion of philosophy, that no strict and final distinction between the two is countenanced, and that although literature, like philosophy, preserves the past, the possibility of error in transmission cannot be eliminated *a priori*. None of these thoughts supplies any firm leads about the value of Derrida's writings for literary criticism, but taken together they allow us to track him more closely as a reader of literature.

Two ways of following the question of literature in Derrida immediately present themselves. *First*, one could isolate and read his accounts of dramatists, novelists and poets. There are, as one would imagine, a number of French authors on or about whom he writes – Antonin Artaud, Charles Baudelaire, Maurice Blanchot, Gustave Flaubert, Jean Genet, Michel Leiris, Stéphane Mallarmé, Francis Ponge, Philippe Sollers and Paul Valéry – along with people who compose in languages other than his own: Paul Celan, James Joyce, Franz Kafka, Edgar Allen Poe, William Shakespeare, P. B. Shelley and Sophocles. The disparity in size between the two groups could be taken to indicate the greater influence of imaginative writing in his mother tongue, although that could well turn out to be a hasty induction. Joyce impinges on him at least as forcefully as Mallarmé, and we have no reason to suppose that Derrida has written on all the authors whose work is important to him professionally or personally. *Second*, one could seek out Derrida's general remarks on literature. Here we would quickly find ourselves entangled in discussions of literature and ethics, literature and law, literature and metaphysics, literature and politics, literature and psychoanalysis, assuming that we could isolate such pure strains to begin with. We would also find ourselves pondering distinctions between literature, poetry and *belles lettres*, and in the process reflecting on borderline cases excluded from the list of authors with which we started, writers such as Friedrich Nietzsche and Jean-Jacques Rousseau. (The pressure of other borders can be felt now and then: for instance, when Derrida comes to write on André Gide, an important figure in his adolescence, it is not until 1995 and then he writes not on his stories but on a travel narrative, *Retour de l'URSS*.) Passing to more familiar topics of literary criticism, we would discover Derrida's thoughts on autobiography and testimony, genre and the letter, literacy and orality, metaphor and catachresis, mimesis and representation, signs and translation.

To follow the question of literature in Derrida with any sensitivity one must combine the two alternatives. It is by no means easy to do so, since Derrida uses literary writings in very different ways and to very different ends. Sometimes there is very extensive discussion of a writer: in *Glas*, for instance, printed in two side-by-side columns, an entire column is devoted to Genet as well as Hegel. Even so, while the relations between literature and philosophy are discussed from time to time in each column they do not dominate the entire text. Indeed, it is hard to say whether a stretch of text on either side is commentary, criticism, interpretation or paraphrase; it involves all four while not being limited to any. At other times Derrida will evoke a writer with little or no direct acknowledgement of the text. 'Tympan' quotes a passage from Leiris's *La Règle du jeu* in the right-hand margin and, without examining it, lets it resonate with his meditations on borders and limits (Derrida 1982, x–xxix). Always, though, he is concerned with the interrelations of the singular and the general. There are no absolute singularities, he argues, or if there are they cannot be identified. Even an apparently pure singular mark can be repeated outside its original context, and although repetition leads to difference the trait of singularity will be legible in any of the repetitions.

It is this relation of uniqueness and iterability that Derrida calls *idiom*. This is not a style that one can learn, let alone perfect (in the sense that people talk of John Henry Newman as 'a great stylist'); it is 'an intersection of singularities, habitats, voices, graphism, what moves with you and what your body never leaves' (Derrida 1995, 119). No writer can discern his or her idiom, but an acute reader can identify it in another's work. A strong reading would take stock of both an idiom in a lyric, say, as well as the contexts – formal, historical, political, religious, social, and so forth – in which the poem participates. Derrida is no formalist: he insists that 'no meaning can be determined out of context, but no context permits saturation' (Derrida 1979b, 81). Nor is he committed in Arnoldian fashion to a hierarchical distinction between literature and criticism. A strong reading might itself cross a text in a singular fashion, and thereby generate its own idiom. In this way we could talk about the idiom of a critic like Samuel Johnson, S. T. Coleridge or T. S. Eliot, and to the extent that we can and do talk in just that way their critical writings can be considered literature. This is not to say that there are no distinctions whatsoever between literature and literary criticism, only that in their highest reaches they generate similar effects.

Not only does Derrida discuss the relations of the singular and the general but also he performs them by leaguing a particular text with a general question or set of questions. In 1971, while engaging with J. L. Austin's theory of speech acts, Derrida turned his attention to the status and function of signatures. As Austin conceives matters, a signature bespeaks the absence of the singular human being who has signed a document while nonetheless presuming that he or she had been present while signing. His or her proper intentions are in principle needed to be presentable for the signing to be a felicitous performative act. For Derrida, though, this 'signature effect' is underwritten by an aporia: 'the condition of possibility of those effects is simultaneously ... the condition of their impossibility, of the impossibility of their rigorous purity' (1982, 328). To sign one's name is necessarily to allow it to be contaminated by all manner of impurities. A signature can in principle, if not always in fact, be forged, cut into pieces or quoted out of context. Strictly speaking, it is neither inside nor outside a text; it traces an equivocal limit between life and death, subject and work. More surprisingly, Derrida suggests, a signature is not completed when an author appends his or her name to what has been written but when a reader, who may have been quite unforeseen by the author, receives what has been communicated in the signed text. This countersignature, as it is called, is not accidental but constitutive of a text; and those texts which are frequently countersigned, often in different ways, are precisely those whose force we experience. Inevitably, part of this force comes from the passion and insight with which the text in question is a countersignature of other texts.

Derrida's most sustained exploration of signing a work of literature is *Signsponge*, the revised text of his paper at the 1975 Cérisy colloquium on Ponge. A question immediately comes to mind. What relation is there between Derrida's general ideas about signatures and this, or any other, particular body of work? Certainly one cannot rightly speak of applying deconstruction to literature, for it 'is not a doctrine; it's not a method, nor is it a set of rules or tools; it cannot be separated from performatives, from signatures, from a given language' (1996, 217). And yet precisely because deconstruction is not a self-contained theory 'the only thing it can do is apply, to be applied, to something else' (1996, 218). One would therefore expect that when Derrida considers Ponge's signature the earlier remarks on Austin's theory of speech acts will be reset and redirected by the poems he reads. This is indeed what happens. When examining the author of Le parti pris des choses, Derrida shows how signification overruns nomination: a proper name such as 'Ponge' can be turned into a common noun such as 'tissu-éponge' (sponge-cloth) or 'serviette-éponge' (sponge-towel). Plainly, one would not expect to find the same thing in a discussion of Genet's signature in Glas or Blanchot's in Parages.

Even so, it is reasonable to ask why Derrida countersigns some literary texts and not others. The first thing to say, by way of preparation, is that he seems to write on literary authors for somewhat different reasons than those that ground his selection of philosophers. As we have seen, he shows that Plato and Hegel are not committed to a metaphysics of presence in a simple or straightforward way, and he reads his older contemporaries, the Foucault of Madness and Civilisation and the Levinas of Totality and Infinity, in order to indicate, among other things, that they cannot escape metaphysics as readily as they might think they can. Rousseau is chosen for close discussion in Of Grammatology because his age is granted an ' "exemplary" value ... between Plato's Phaedrus and Hegel's Encyclopaedia' (Derrida 1976, 97). And Husserl is inspected partly because of the rigour of the phenomenological method and partly because of his covert dependence on the metaphysics of presence. A good deal more could be said about other philosophers on whom Derrida has written, and of course one could cite seminal thinkers about whom he has said little or nothing. Perhaps given world enough and time he would write about Thomas Aquinas, David Hume or Karl Rahner in a way that would surprise even his most devoted readers.

It is sometimes said that when Derrida writes on literary works he does not seek to uncover strata of presence in the writing but rather affirms the work under consideration. This resolves his writing too readily into a duality of literature and philosophy, and attention to his texts on philosophers he admires such as Le toucher, Jean-Luc Nancy will show that his interest is in following a guiding thread through a complicated fabric of ideas. Literature plays no one role in his writing. At times Derrida turns to a poem or story because of its ability to unsettle the effects of a metaphysical assumption: thus in 'The Double Session' Mallarmé's 'Mimique' is inscribed in a passage of Plato's 'Phaedrus', while in 'Le facteur de la vérité', as we have seen, Poe's story 'The Purloined Letter' is read even more closely than was done in the seminar that Lacan consecrated to it. At other times a literary corpus is scrutinized without being paired with a philosophical text, although philosophical issues are never far away. Questions and themes from the long sequence 'philosophy' can, and often are, tightly folded into the shorter sequence called 'literature' where their provenance will not always be apparent. One thing that attracts Derrida to some literary texts rather than others is a critical relationship with their literariness. 'They bear within themselves, or we could also say in their literary act they put to work, a question, the same one, but each time singular and put to work otherwise: "What is literature?" or "Where does literature come from?" "What should we do with literature?"' (1992, 41).

This helps to explain why Derrida's interest in literature converges on writing of the nineteenth and twentieth centuries. For it is there more than anywhere else that literary works tend to contest their presumed literariness. That said, we should be wary of extending the concept of literature into the indefinite past in order to make an appropriate backdrop for what critics often call, all too quickly, modernist and postmodernist writing. 'Only under the conditions of law does the work have an existence and a substance, and it becomes "literature" only at a certain period of the law that regulates problems involving property rights over works' (Derrida 1992, 215). With the development of copyright laws in Europe from the late seventeenth to the early nineteenth centuries, the meaning of the word 'literature' slowly shifts from 'polite learning' to 'imaginative writing chiefly in the drama, poetry and prose fiction'. The reference to Europe is not accidental since 'literature' is a Latin word, and 'to take account of the latinity in the modern institution of literature' would involve a consideration of 'Christendom as the Roman Church, of Roman law and the Roman concept of the State, indeed of Europe' (Derrida 2000, 21). Literature is an institution not only because it is taught in schools and universities and is regulated by positive laws but also because it is a part of what he calls globalatinization, a covert leaguing of Christianity and capitalism. Latinity is being extended across the world, mainly in and through Anglo-American speech and writing, and the institution of literature plays highly complicated roles in this process.

Enshrined in the notion of literature, as determined before the law, is what Derrida calls 'the right to say everything' (Derrida 1992, 36). The very idea of literature is coordinate with a freedom from political and religious censorship. On Derrida's reasoning, this comes to mean that literature is positively and essentially related to the modern idea of democracy or, more exactly, what in any democratic state is promised about democracy. At any given time, no state coincides perfectly with itself, and from the gap between what is promised and what it is actually performed one can always draw bypassed, repressed or unthought possibilities that can be recombined and reaffirmed. It is these unrealized possibilities, not a future state or a utopia, that constitute what Derrida calls 'a democracy to come'. Derrida himself stresses the importance of forgotten and untried possibilities in Marx and, more generally, has supported an 'open marxism' in France.

An emphasis upon the historical formation of literature, and on the political character of what is formed should not be taken as a sign that literarity has no effects in poems, stories or plays. Although Derrida rejects Husserl's 'principle of principles' because it leads to the fullness of an intuition, and hence to presence, he does not thereby abandon the protocols of phenomenology. And so, while he never posits a literary essence, he credits literarity: 'It is the correlative of an intentional relation to the text, an intentional relation which integrates in itself, as a component or an intentional layer, the more or less implicit consciousness of rules which are conventional or institutional – social, in any case' (Derrida 1992, 44). A poem by Celan, for instance, will encode a good deal of the history and institutions of poetry, and this will be legible for an attentive and well-informed reader.

Not all of Derrida's attention to literature is taken up with archives and traditions, however. He is equally concerned with imagination and invention, about which he has original things to say. In a study of Étienne Bonnot de Condillac's *Essay on the Origin of Human Knowledge*, Derrida observes that all Condillac's problems gather around the two senses of the word 'imagination': 'the reproductive imagination which retraces ... and the productive imagination which, in order to supply, adds something more' (1980, 76). For Derrida, the imagination does not work in the present. Rather, the act of writing introduces a detour which the author follows, and only after the fact is the deviation from the norm perceived and understood, by which stage something new has been added in and through the writing. This approach to the imagination is taken up later by Derrida under the less romantic rubric of invention. Strictly speaking, no invention can abide wholly within the possible, understood by way of conventions, forms and rules; it must also draw on what, from the perspective of the possible, seems quite impossible. 'The interest of deconstruction', we are told, 'is a certain experience of the impossible' (1992, 328). This should not be taken to affirm that a poem, for example, should simply flout all conventions, forms and rules, such as one is sometimes led to believe by the surrealists. On the contrary, a lyric such as Celan's 'Psalm' involves a singular negotiation of German grammar, the poetics of psalms and an understanding of negative theologies, on the one hand, and Celan's experience of the impossible, on the other.

'Nor must we forget', Derrida tells us, 'that deconstruction is itself a form of literature' (1984, 125). Certainly the writings of Jacques Derrida offer their readers a highly distinctive idiom, one that has been heard in all manner of places and with regard to all manner of topics for the last forty years. His influence can be recognized in literature and philosophy, history and politics, theology and the visual arts. If his arguments about inscription have generated controversy inside and outside the university, they have also subtly changed what is studied and how it is studied.

Kevin Hart

Further reading and works cited

Bennington, G. and Derrida, J. *Jacques Derrida*. Chicago, 1993.
Caputo, J. D. (ed.) *Deconstruction in a Nutshell*. New York, 1997.
Clark, T. *Derrida: Heidegger, Blanchot*. Cambridge, 1992.
Culler, J. *On Deconstruction*. Ithaca, NY, 1982.
Derrida, J. *Of Grammatology*. Baltimore, MD, 1976.
—. *Edmund Husserl's 'Origin of Geometry': An Introduction*, preface J. P. Leavey, Jr, ed. D. B. Allison. Stony Brook, NY, 1978.
—. 'Living On', in Harold Bloom et al., *Deconstruction and Criticism*. London, 1979a.
—. *Writing and Difference*. London, 1979b.
—. *The Archeology of the Frivolous*, intro. J. P. Leavey, Jr. Pittsburgh, 1980.
—. *Dissemination*. London, 1981.
—. *Margins of Philosophy*. Chicago, 1982.
—. 'The Time of a Thesis: Punctuations', in *Philosophy in France Today*, ed. A. Montefiore. Cambridge, 1983.
—. 'Deconstruction and the Other'. in *Dialogues with Contemporary Continental Thinkers*, ed. R. Kearney. Manchester, 1984a.
—. *Signéponge/Signsponge*. New York, 1984b.
—. *The Ear of the Other*, ed. C. V. McDonald. New York, 1985.
—. *Glas*. Lincoln, NE, 1986.
—. *The Post Card*. Chicago, 1987.
—. 'Letter to a Japanese Friend', in *A Derrida Reader*, ed. P. Kamuf. New York, 1991.
—. *Acts of Literature*, ed. D. Attridge. London, 1992.
—. *Specters of Marx*, intro. B. Magnus and S. Cullenberg. New York, 1994.
—. *Points: Interviews, 1974–1994*, ed. E. Weber. Stanford, CA, 1995.
—. '"As if I were Dead": An Interview with Jacques Derrida', in *Applying: To Derrida*, eds J. Brannigan et al. Basingstoke, 1996.
— and Blanchot, M. *The Instant of My Death/Demeure*. Stanford, CA, 2000.

Gasché, R. *The Tain of the Mirror*. Cambridge, MA, 1986.
Hart, K. *The Trespass of the Sign*. New York, 2000.
Kamuf, P. (ed.) *A Derrida Reader*. New York, 1991.
Norris, C. *Derrida*. London, 1987.
Schultz, W. R. and Fried, L. L. B. *Jacques Derrida*. New York, 1992.
Wood, D. (ed.) *Derrida*. Oxford, 1992.

Luce Irigaray (1930–)

Feminist philosopher, psychoanalyst, linguist, political thinker and activist, Luce Irigaray is best known for her theory of sexual difference as the horizon of political justice and the ethical paradigm of intersubjective relations. These multiple interdisciplinary affiliations and the centrality of sexual difference in her work have produced many controversies and misunderstandings, ranging from the early charges of essentialism to the more recent critiques that the privileging of sexual difference either ignores other forms of difference, such as race, class and sexuality, or reduces multiple modalities of alterity to the heterosexual model. Despite the growing body of excellent interpretations of Irigaray's thought (Whitford, Chanter, Grosz, Cornell, Butler, Deutscher), the reception of Irigaray has often been often characterized, according to Margaret Whitford, by 'a simultaneous attraction and rejection' (1991, 4) or, according to Penelope Deutscher, by 'Irigaray anxiety' (1996, 6).

To facilitate what Whitford calls critical '*engagement* with Irigaray' in place of 'the alternatives of dismissal or apotheosis' (1991, 25), I would like, first, to sketch out briefly the changing style and emphasis of Irigaray's research, and second, to map out the diverse and often seemingly antinomic connotations of sexual difference in her writings. In a 1995 interview in *Hypatia*, Irigaray describes the three 'phases' of her work on sexual difference. Even though these phases cannot be understood in a linear chronological fashion because they often coexist in her work, Irigaray identifies the first with 'a critique, you might say of the auto-monocentrism of the western subject', the second with an attempt to recover and redefine female subjectivity, and the third with an invention of 'a new model of possible relations between man and woman' (1995, 96). As she writes:

> The third phase of my work thus corresponds ... to the construction of an intersubjectivity respecting sexual difference. This is something, a task, that no one has yet done, I think, something that's completely new. The second phase of my work was to define those mediations that could permit the existence of a feminine subjectivity – that is to say – another subject – and the first phase was the most critical one ... It was a phase in which I showed how a single subject, traditionally the masculine subject, had constructed the world and interpreted the world according to a single perspective. (1995, 96–7)

Associated primarily with *Speculum of the Other Woman* (1974) and *This Sex Which Is Not One* (1977), the first stage of Irigaray's research diagnoses the erasure of sexual difference in the discourses of philosophy, sciences, linguistics and politics. In her critical engagement with key philosophical figures ranging from Aristotle, Plato, Descartes and

Hegel to Nietzsche, Freud, Marx, Heidegger, Levinas and Lacan, Irigaray provides the most sustained critique of the monologism and indifference of the western philosophy, which is incapable of acknowledging the sexed other otherwise than as a deficient copy, a negation, or the atrophied version of the masculine subject. Anticipating the arguments of Eve Kosofsky Sedgwick, Irigaray argues that the regime of the compulsory heterosexuality represents in fact a masculine homosocial order (what she calls 'the reign of masculine hom(m)o-sexuality'), supported by the traffic in women, on the one hand, and the prohibition of homosexual practices, on the other: 'Reigning everywhere, although prohibited in practice, hom(m)o-sexuality is played out through the bodies of women, matter, or sign, and heterosexuality has been up to now just an alibi for the smooth workings of man's relations with himself, of relations among men' (1985, 172).

In her critique of the homosocial order, Irigaray focuses not on the way femininity is represented but on the paradoxical logic of exclusion behind these representations. As she points out, 'the rejection, the exclusion of a female imaginary certainly puts woman in the position of experiencing herself only fragmentarily, in the little-structured margins of a dominant ideology, as waste, or excess, what is left of a mirror invested by the (masculine) 'subject' to reflect himself ... (1985, 30). In particular, Irigaray contests a confinement of time to the interiority of the male subject and the corresponding association of the female body with the exteriority of the space – a set of distinctions, as her work on Aristotle and Plato shows, deeply entrenched in the western philosophical tradition. As she famously writes, in this philosophical imaginary – the imaginary characterized by the unity of form, the predominance of the visual, and 'rather too narrowly focused' on the masculine economy of sameness (1985, 28) – woman and her sex appear as the negative space, abyss, the obverse of God (1993, 7), as 'a horror of nothing to see', or as a nostalgic fantasy of the first and ultimate dwelling associated with the maternal body. What is original in this stage of Irigaray's work is the diagnosis of the numerous symptoms of this sexual indifference, which manifests itself not only in the disregard for the specificity of feminine embodiment, desires and genealogies but also in the disembodied character of linguistic analyses, in the erasure of the drama of enunciation, in the separation of the subject of knowledge from carnality and desire, in the infatuation with formalism and with it the obverse side, the crippling nostalgia for the maternal body, in the rigid separation between the immanence of flesh and the transcendence of the spirit, and, finally, in the nihilism of western culture.

In the second phase of her work, Irigaray is concerned with the recovery and the symbolic reinscription of the 'second sex'. It is important to stress that for Irigaray the work of recovery is inextricably intertwined, first, with the strategic mode of reading – what she calls 'mimicry' (*mimétisme*) – and, second, with the construction of the alternative 'mediations that could permit the existence of a feminine subjectivity' (1995, 96) such as the formation of the maternal genealogy, resymbolizing the mother/daughter relation-ship, the rethinking of the way space and time has been gendered, the rearticulation of the Divine, or the institution of sexuate rights. As this double emphasis on mimicry and mediation suggests, Irigaray is not concerned with the immediacy of the female experience, the affirmation of embodiment or, as some critics have argued, the regression to the pre-Oedipal period. According to Whitford, at stake here is not a recovery of the unmediated female experience, subjectivity or embodiment but a reconstruction of their linguistic and cultural conditions of possibility – that is, the formation of the alternative female imaginary and symbolic orders (1991, 42, 89–97).

The exclusion of femininity means that the female imaginary and the symbolic has to be reconstructed out of the 'remains' which the homosocial economy cannot accommodate and which historically 'have been abandoned to the feminine' (1985, 111, 116). An important first step in this reconstruction is the rhetorical strategy of mimicry. Opposed to masquerade (*la mascarade*), that is, to the unconscious identification with the feminine position in the masculine symbolic, mimicry for Irigaray is a strategic move of a deliberate yet playful repetition, which, by defamiliarizing and denaturalizing the homosocial logic, reveals the historical mechanisms of the exploitation of the feminine and thus opens up the possibility of their reinscription. As she famously writes:

> To play with mimesis is thus, for a woman, to try to recover the place of her exploitation by discourse, without allowing herself to be simply reduced to it. It means to resubmit herself – inasmuch as she is on the side of the 'perceptible', 'matter' – to 'ideas', in particular to ideas about herself, that are elaborated in/by a masculine logic, but so as to make 'visible', by an effect of playful repetition, what was supposed to remain invisible: the cover-up of a possible operation of the feminine in language. (1985, 76)

In Irigaray's later work the strategy of mimicry is supplemented with the reconstruction of the alternative structures of mediation enabling the symbolic and cultural inscription of the female subjectivity. Drawing on a variety of sources – Merleau-Ponty, Levinas, Lacan, Castoriadis – Irigaray offers an alternative paradigm illustrating the intersection between the female imaginary and the symbolic in the figure of the two sets of lips: 'Two sets of lips that, moreover, cross over each other like the arms of the cross, the prototype of the crossroads *between*. The mouth lips and the genital lips do not point in the same direction' (1993, 18). As this chiasmic structure formed by the intersection of the imaginary and the symbolic suggests, Irigaray stresses the inseparability of embodiment and speech, language and subjectivity. Another important feature of Irigaray's articulation of the female symbolic and imaginary is her emphasis on temporality, which displaces the concept of femininity from the negation of essence, expressed in the famous statement by Lacan that the Woman does not exist (1998, 72–3), to the affirmation of becoming. As I argue in 'Toward a Radical Female Imaginary: Temporality and Embodiment in Irigaray's Ethics' (*diacritics*, 1988, 61–7), the discontinuous temporality of becoming is what is at stake in the often misunderstood concept of 'the "mechanics" of fluids' obfuscated on the imaginary level by the structure of the specular image and on the symbolic level by the privilege given to closed sets and to the 'symbol of universality' (1985, 108). According to Drucilla Cornell, the temporal structure of the female imaginary in Irigaray's writings is intertwined with 'the uneraseable trace of utopianism' (1991, 169), a term which does not imply some specific goal outside culture, but, as Elizabeth Weed and Judith Butler similarly argue, a mode of reading 'something other than the already known, the already legible' (1997, 285). By refusing what Butler calls 'the conflation of the social with what is socially given' (1997, 23), Irigaray's emphasis on the futurity of the imaginary and the symbolic structures suggests that 'femininity' is irreducible to its current definitions and representations and thus open to resignfication and contestation.

As the protracted debate on essentialism suggests, many readers of Irigaray have ignored not only her strategic mode of reading based on mimicry but also her twin emphasis on temporality and mediation. As a result, it has often been assumed that the reconstruction of the feminine subjectivity is based on unmediated experience or embodiment existing outside culture. According to Christine Holmlund, where Irigaray seems problematic to her readers is not in her critique of phallocentrism but in 'her visionary re-creations of an undefinable, non-unitary female identity based on difference' (1991, 296). For Mary Ann Doane such a project leads to 'a kind of ghetto politics which maintains and applauds women's exclusion from language and symbolic order' (1987, 12). In the context of such misreadings, it is important to recall that Irigaray consistently criticizes the lure of immediacy on many levels ranging from the mystification of the pre-oedipal sexuality ('extolling the pre-oedipal as a liberation from the norm of genital sexuality entails all the caprice and immaturity of desire' (1996, 27)) to intuitive knowledge of experience, from the historical empiricism to the utopian dream of the immediate community among women. Consequently, the recovery of femininity cannot be confused with 'immediate affect, with self-certainty, mimetic or recapitulative intuitive truth, with historical narrative, etc.' (1996, 62). In response to these lures, she flatly proclaims that 'there is no ... "natural immediacy"' (1996, 107). In fact, it is Irigaray who criticizes women's liberation movements based on 'the fetish' of the unmediated personal experience or on the politics of voice:

> Many women have understood ... that liberation for them was simply to say I ... then they fight among themselves to see who says 'I' the loudest: your 'I' versus my 'I' ...
>
> Thus, if you like, I think that the purely narrative, autobiographical 'I', or the 'I' that expresses only affect, risks being an 'I' that collapses back into a role traditionally granted to woman: an 'I' of pathos ... It seems to me important to accede to a different cultural 'I' – that is, to construct a new objectivity that corresponds not to an indifferent 'I' but to an 'I' that's sexed feminine. It is necessary to remain both objective and subjective. And to remain within a dialectic between the two. (1995, 103)

And she adds, 'I can't myself, all alone, affirm my own experience, since this is something I know only after the fact ... I can't affirm that this is always already the experience of a woman. It must be a dialectic between subjectivity and objectivity' (1995, 104).

Irigaray's emphasis on the reconstruction of the linguistic, cultural and political mediations enabling the existence of the second sex culminates in her work on citizenship and sexuate rights, such as the prohibition of the exploitation of motherhood by religious and civil power, the right of women to civil identities and to the control of their public representations, and finally the right to equal wages and equal share of economic goods. Growing out of her engagement in social liberation movements, this conception of sexuate rights advocates political and institutional changes addressing oppression of women in western democracies, for instance changes in the status of the family (in order to challenge its institutional functions of the accumulation of property and reproduction), in the structures of law and religion (since, as Irigaray insists, religion remains a civil power despite Enlightenment's secularism), and finally in the economic distribution of goods. Irigaray's notion of sexuate rights implies a notion of justice based on an equivalent exchange for both sexes in the economic and the symbolic registers. According to Drucilla Cornell, Irigaray's sexuate rights are an expression of equivalence within the larger horizon of sexual difference:

> The political struggle against *dereliction* in the name of equality of well-being involves the recognition of feminine difference in those circumstances when we are different, as in our relationship to pregnancy, while simultaneously not reinforcing the stereotypes through which patriarchy attempted to make sense of this difference ... These rights are equivalent because they allow difference to be recognized and equally valued without women having to show that they are like men for legal purposes. (1992, 293)

Irigaray's conception of sexuate rights suggests a revision of democratic citizenship in the context of sexual difference. In the late 1980s Irigaray argues for complementing the economic justice (this argument has to be considered in the context of her involvement with the Italian Communist Party) with the constitution of women's political identities as women: for the 'social justice to be possible, women must obtain a civil identity simultaneously' (1994, 63). Without a mediation between economic equality and political identity, women, according to Irigaray, are caught in a double bind between 'the minimum of social rights they can obtain . . . and the psychological or physical price they have to pay for that minimum' (1991, 207). As she argues:

> Women must obtain the right to work and to earn wages, as civil persons, not as men with a few inconvenient attributes: menstrual periods, pregnancy, child rearing, etc. Women must not beg for or usurp a small place in patriarchal society by passing themselves off as half-formed men. (1994, 63)

By providing new modes of mediation between the subjective and the objective, between the private and the public, the economic and the symbolic, the inscription of sexual difference into democratic citizenship creates an alternative 'political ethics that refuses to sacrifice desire for death, power, or money' (1996, 33).

Irigaray's work on sexuate rights and citizenship overlaps with the third and the most controversial stage of her work devoted to the construction of a culture of sexual difference: 'The third phase of my work thus corresponds, as I said, to the construction of an intersubjectivity respecting sexual difference' (1995, 103). In her later works, such as *Je, Tu, Nous: Toward a Culture of Difference* (1990), *Thinking the Difference: For A Peaceful Revolution* (1989), *I Love to You: For a Sketch of a Possible Felicity in History* (1992) and *Être Deux* (1997), Irigaray makes a shift from the genealogical (mother/daughter) and horizontal (women to women sociality) relations among women to 'a new model of possible relations between man and woman' (1995, 103). In place of the single individual or collective subject, her concept of a culture of sexual difference stresses the relational model of subjectivity and utterance – the paradigm of being two (*être deux*). On the basis of sexual difference, she hopes to elaborate a culture of intersubjective relations based on respect for all forms of alterity and diversity.

In order to understand Irigaray's claim that a culture of sexual difference fosters respect for all forms of alterity, it is necessary to engage two crucial concepts in her later work: the labour of the negative and the work of 'disappropriation'. Irigaray associates sexual difference not with a positive identity but with the labour of the negative – with what she calls 'taking the negative upon oneself' (1993, 120) – which produces the internal division and self-limitation of the subject. By redefining and negotiating between the Freudian (castration and the judgement based on negation) and the Hegelian (determinate negation) concepts of negativity, Irigaray argues that the labour of self-limitation in sexual difference leads to a refusal of any identity – individual or collective – based on wholeness and unity:

> The mine of the subject is always already marked by disappropriation [*désappropriation*]: gender [*le genre*]. Being a man or a woman means not being the whole of the subject or of the community or of spirit, as well as not being entirely one's self. The famous *I is another*, the cause of which is sometimes attributed to the unconscious, can be understood in a different way. I is never simply mine in that it belongs to a gender. Therefore, I am not the whole [*je ne suis pas tout*]. (1996, 106; 1992, 166)

Consequently, if Irigaray seems to privilege sexual difference it is because this difference foregrounds disappropriation, alterity and negativity 'in the self and for the self [ce négatif en soi et pour soi], (1996, 106; 1992, 166) as a condition of desire.

Because the identification with either side of sexual divide entails the labour of self-limitation and disappropriation – that is, the acknowledgement of 'not being the whole of the subject or of the community' – sexual difference, Irigaray argues, provides a model of the non-appropriative ethical relation to the Other. Since the negative turned upon the subject no longer posits the Other as the negation or alienation of the subject, sexual difference preserves the irreducible alterity of the Other while at the same time maintaining the insistence of the subject. By stressing the ethical respect for alterity, Irigaray dissociates the labour of the negative in sexual difference from the Hegelian alienation in the master/slave dialectic: 'The asceticism of the negative thus seemed necessary to me but more out of consideration for the other and from collective good sense than as a process of consciousness that would lead to a more accomplished spirituality . . . Hegel knew nothing of the negative like that' (1996, 13). For Irigaray the Other is not a hostile freedom blocking my own, but the very source of my becoming: 'Who are thou? I am and I become thanks to this question' (1993, 74). This reformulation of the negative through sexual difference transforms, according to Irigaray, the Hegelian desire for recognition into an ethical acknowledgement of the alterity of the Other.

As Tina Chanter (1995, 190–224), Drucilla Cornell (1991, 183–6), and Krzysztof Ziarek (1999) have argued, Irigaray's interpretation of the asymmetrical sexual relation in terms of the ethical acknowledgement of the 'unavoidable alterity of the other' is influenced by both Levinas's ethics and the Heideggerian concept of nearness. Unlike the different modalities of the erasure of alterity through domination, knowledge or narcissistic love, the non-symmetrical relation to the Other interrupts the ego's narcissism by calling the subject to responsibility. As her phrase 'I love to you' suggests, Irigaray defines the ethical relation to the Other in terms of indirection and intransitivity – that is, as a an oblique 'relation without a relation' that does not reduce the Other to the order of the same or the narcissistic projection of the subject: 'I cannot completely identify you, even less identify with you . . . I recognize you goes hand in hand with: you are irreducible to me just as I am to you' (1996, 103). As a trace of an oblique address and a radical disconnection, the type of relation implied by the neologism 'I love to you' marks the exposure to the Other and, and at the same time, constitutes a barrier preventing her assimilation – an assimilation that turns love into an act of 'cultural cannibalism' (1996, 110).

By promoting ethical respect for alterity, the creation of a culture of sexual difference, Irigaray argues, 'would allow us to check the many forms that destruction takes in our world, to counteract a nihilism that merely affirms the reversal of the repetitive proliferation of the status quo values – whether you call them the consumer society, the circularity of discourse . . . scientific or technical imperialism' (1993, 5). If her critics charge that this primacy given to sexual difference as the model of ethical and political relations erases other forms of difference, Irigaray responds that the acknowledgement of the irreducibility of sexual difference – of that negative that cannot be sublated into unity – makes it possible 'to respect differences everywhere: differences between the other races, differences between the generations, and so on. Because I've placed a limit on my horizon, on my power' (1995, 110). In response to the charges of heterosexism, she points out that 'it is important not to confuse sexual choice with sexual difference. For me sexual difference is a fundamental parameter of the socio-cultural order; sexual choice is secondary. Even if one chooses to remain among women, it's necessary to resolve the problem of sexual difference' (1995, 112). As Pheng Cheah and Elizabeth Grosz argue in their polemics with Butler and Cornell, Irigaray's ethical and political paradigm of sexual difference does not necessarily lead to compulsory heterosexuality: 'neither *respect for* the other sex nor *fidelity to* one's own sex necessarily implies obligatory *desire for* the other sex' (1998, 13).

Nonetheless, Irigaray's claim that the culture of sexual difference fosters respect for other differences, in particular those of race and sexual orientation, not only remains disappointingly vague and undeveloped but is sometimes undercut by her own comments that 'the problem of race is, in fact, a secondary problem ... and the same goes for other cultural diversities – religious, economic and political ones' (1996, 47). As Butler writes:

> Irigaray does not always help matters here, for she fails to follow through the metonymic link between women and these other Others, idealizing and appropriating the 'elsewhere' as the feminine ... If the feminine is not the only or primary kind of being that is excluded ... what and who is excluded in the course of Irigaray's analysis? (1993, 49)

Butler repeats here Gayatri Chakravorty Spivak's criticism that French feminism fails to address the other articulations of differences among women (1988, 150). One could only wish Irigaray paid more attention to the pertinent intersections between sexual and racial differences in her work: for instance, the critical revisions of the Hegelian master/slave dialectic by black and feminist scholars would be a productive beginning of such a project. Moreover, despite her claims to the contrary, Irigaray herself does not always distinguish carefully enough between sexual difference and sexual orientation, for instance when she refers to the couple as a model not only of sexual difference but also of the ethical relation in love.

Even this cursive survey of the different stages and emphases of Irigaray's research conveys the complexity of her theory of sexual difference. In fact, I would argue that to engage critically the limitations and the possibilities of Irigaray's work, one cannot unify sexual difference into a single concept but, rather, one has to treat it as a heterogeneous configuration consisting of diverse and often seemingly antinomic formulations. Like Derrida's 'différance' or Walter Benjamin's allegorical 'constellation', Irigaray's sexual difference keeps disseminating and subdividing its own textual inscription. In order to trace this diverse configuration, I would like to propose the following seven 'theses on the philosophy of sexual difference':

1. For Irigaray sexual difference does not yet exist. The affirmations of sexual difference cannot, therefore, correspond to the acceptance of the past and present cultural formulations of femininity and masculinity, since this would amount to the reinscription of the sexual indifference, of homosociality. Hence the emphasis in Irigaray's work is on the ongoing invention of sexual difference, on what she calls in the opening pages of An *Ethics of Sexual Difference* 'the production of a new age of though, art, poetry, and language: the creation of a new poetics' (1993, 5).
2. The possibility of such an invention conveys the irreducible futurity of sexual difference. To articulate the temporality of sexual difference, it is necessary, Irigaray argues, to change our conception of becoming from a mere 'survival' to the Nietzschean intensification of living and to disclose a future no longer 'measured by the transcendence of death but by the call to birth of the self and the other' (1993, 186). In the context of feminism, the temporal character of sexual

difference affirms, according to Drucilla Cornell, the revolutionary potential of 'the feminine to be Other than the limits imposed on her' (1991, 102). As I argue in my discussion of temporality in Irigaray's work (Ziarek 1998, 60–71), the thought of sexual difference is inseparable from, to borrow Ernesto Laclau's phrase, 'new reflections on the revolution of our time'. That is why Irigaray proclaims that 'a revolution in thought and ethics is needed if the work of sexual difference is to take place' (1993, 6).

3. Irigaray refuses to define sexual difference in positive (even if only utopian) terms but stresses instead the labour of the negative. Based on a labour of the negative and a work of 'disappropriation', Irigaray's conception of sexual difference, like Lacan's, investigates the limits of the symbolic order rather than an identification with a positive identity. Rather like Joan Copjec's emphasis on the antinomies of sexual difference (1994, 201–36), Irigaray argues that sexual difference produces the internal splitting and division of the subject.

4. Although Irigaray grants the sexual difference the status of the universal, she argues that the only meaning of this paradoxical universality is that it splits the universal into two and thus renders the ideal of the ethical totality of the polis impossible: 'The particularity of this universal is that is it divided into two' (1996, 50). By positing sexual difference as this universal 'which is not one', Irigaray argues that sexual difference not only fractures the ethical totality of the Hegelian Spirit but also contests the models of political association conceived on the basis of the collective subjectivity.

5. The dialectical formulation of sexual difference as the labour of the negative not only necessitates a rethinking of universality but also of negativity. In particular, Irigaray contests the Hegelian and the Sartrean association of immediacy and facticity with nature and the body and the work of the negative with the transcendence of the spirit, culture or concept. By rejecting this model of transcendence, she reformulates the labour of the negative as 'the *sensible transcendental*' – 'as that which confounds the opposition between immanence and transcendence' (1993, 33).

6. The labour of self-limitation in sexual difference does not sublate the Other into a new totality but enables an ethical respect for the Other. In her work, Irigaray reinterprets the absence of sexual relation in Lacan's theory as the possibility of the ethical affirmation of the irreducible alterity of the Other.

7. As mode of an ethical relation to the Other, sexual difference, according to Irigaray, has also to be inscribed in democratic citizenship in order to transform the asymmetrical ethics of Eros into collective justice and to prevent the construction of sexuality either as natural immediacy or as economic commodity. This inscription of sexual difference in democratic politics constitutes another paradox in Irigaray's thought: on the one hand, it calls for the specific institutional changes enabling the legal constitution of women's civil identities as women, but, on the other hand, it foregrounds '*the impossible*' in the formation of all political identities, preventing in this way the reification of existing gender stereotypes into political norms. Penelope Deutscher interprets this paradox in terms of a shift from a 'politics of recognition' to a 'politics of the impossible' – to 'the politics which "recognizes" that which it actually "establishes"' (1995, 154). As Irigaray suggests in *I Love to You*, another important aspect of the politics of the 'impossible' is the

emphasis on the temporal deferral and the structural indetermination of collective identities: 'I am, therefore, a political militant of the impossible (*une militante politique de l'impossible*), which is not to say a utopian. Rather, I want what is yet to be as the only possibility of a future' (1996, 10). To be a political militant of the impossible is to engage in a continuous struggle to displace the frontiers between the possible and the impossible, between the present and the future, between the socially constructed identities and their transformation.

By foregrounding the heterogenous configuration of sexual difference in Irigaray's work, I want, on the one hand, to prevent the interpretation of any of the above statements in isolation from other competing formulations, and, on the other, to frustrate the desire for the impossible unification of her theory, which sometimes can take the form of the coherent chronological narrative with which I started this essay. It is precisely the heterogeneity of sexual difference that constitutes the openness to alterity and futurity. To end I would like to suggest that despite a certain increasing simplification of style in Irigaray's later texts, a similar heterogeneity characterizes the ethical and the aesthetic mode of her writing. Speaking of the counterpoint in her texts between speech and silence, between 'logical formalization' and aesthetic composition, Irigaray suggests that her way of writing leaves the text 'always open onto a new sense, and onto a future sense, and I would also say onto a potential "You" [*Tu*], a potential interlocutor' (1995, 102). Reading Irigaray critically, entering her writings as 'a potential interlocutor' for whom a place has been reserved from the start, means, among other things, respecting this fundamental openness of her texts.

Ewa Ziarek

Further reading and works cited

Burke, C. et al. (eds) *Engaging with Irigaray*. New York, 1994.
Butler, J. *Bodies that Matter*. New York, 1993.
—. 'Against Proper Objects', in *Feminism Meets Queer Theory*, eds E. Weed and N. Schor. Bloomington, IN, 1997.
Chanter, T. *Ethics of Eros*. New York, 1995.
Cheah, P. and Grosz, E. 'Irigaray and the Political Future of Sexual Difference', *diacritics*, 28, 1998.
Copjec, J. *Read My Desire*. Cambridge, MA, 1994.
Cornell, D. *Beyond Accommodation*. New York, 1991.
—. 'Gender, Sex, and Equivalent Rights', in *Feminists Theorize the Political*, eds J. Butler and J. Wallach Scott. New York, 1992.
Deutscher, P. 'Luce Irigaray and her "Politics of the Impossible"', in *Forms of Commitment*, ed. B. Nelson. Melbourne, 1995.
—. 'Irigaray's Anxiety'. *Radical Philosophy*, 80, 1996.
Doane, M. A. *The Desire to Desire*. Bloomington, IN, 1987.
Grosz, E. 'The Hetero and the Homo: The Sexual Ethics of Luce Irigaray', in *Engaging with Irigary*, eds Burke et al. New York, 1994.
Holmlund, C. 'The Lesbian, the Mother, and the Heterosexual Lover'. *Feminist Studies*, 17, 1991.
Irigary, L. *Speculum of the Other Woman*. Ithaca, NY, 1974.
—. *This Sex Which is Not One*. Ithaca, NY, 1985.
—. *An Ethics of Sexual Difference*. Ithaca, NY, 1993.
—. *The Irigary Reader*, ed. M. Whitford. Oxford, 1991.

—. *Thinking the Difference*. New York, 1994.

—. 'Je-Luce Irigaray: A Meeting with Luce Irigaray', *Hypatia*, 19, 1995.

—. *I Love to You*. New York, 1996.

Lacan, J. *The Seminar of Jacques Lacan Book XX*. New York, 1998.

Laclau, E. *New Reflections on the Revolution of our Time*. London, 1990.

Sedgwick, E. Kosofsky. *Between Men*. New York, 1985.

Spivak, G. Chakravorty. *In Other Worlds*. New York, 1988.

Weed, E. 'The More Things Change', in *Feminism Meets Queer Theory*, eds F. Weed and N. Schor. Bloomington IN, 1997.

Whitford, M. *Luce Irigaray*. London, 1991.

Ziarek, E. 'Toward a Radical Female Imaginary: Temporality and Embodiment in Irigaray's Ethics', *diacritics*, 28, 1998.

Ziarek, K. 'Love and the Debasement of Being', *Postmodern Culture*, 10, 1999.

—. 'Proximities', *Continental Philosophy Review* (forthcoming).

Christian Metz (1931–1993)

Contemporary film theory as we know it today could not have developed without Christian Metz. Initially trained in 1960s structural linguistics, Metz used research methods from the emerging 'human sciences' to pursue an understanding of cinema. His work had immense influence among scholars and students for whom the new epistemologies demanded new academic disciplines. In Paul Willemen's assessment, Metz formulated 'the most systematic account of the location of language in cinema within a semiological model' (Heath and Mellencamp 1983, 147). Much of 1970s psychoanalytic film theory responded to Metz's ideas about the cinema's 'imaginary signifier' and the various psychic processes organized by the film text. Metzian tools crafted detailed or 'close textual' analyses of popular narrative movies such as Hitchcock's *The Birds* or Welles's *Touch of Evil* (Heath 1975). And the institutionalization of film studies as a university discipline (and model of interdisciplinary inquiry) is also part of Metz's considerable legacy.

He was himself the first full-fledged film academic in France, taking the first *doctorat d'état* granted for a dissertation on cinema and holding a position as *directeur d'études* in his field at the École des Hautes Études en Sciences Sociales. Metz could certainly claim a vital legacy in postwar French film culture: in André Bazin, *Cahiers du cinéma*, the filmmaker-critics of the New Wave, and new national institutions such as the Cinematheque française and the French national film school (IDHEC). French cultural critics had long taken film seriously in journalistic criticism and aesthetic philosophy. But Metz was not concerned with explaining cinema's past, evaluating its achievements, or prescribing its future. He instead devoted himself to utterly fundamental questions about the intelligibility of movies. Was there a basic 'language system' (*langue*) of film as in verbal communication? What devices might define the user or 'subject' of film language, as do personal pronouns, time and location adverbs, and verb tenses in verbal discourse? Or did the film image differ from the verbal sign? If films made information seem so 'present', so 'obvious', so 'easy to understand', as Metz asked in *Film Language*, why were they so difficult to explain (1974a,

69)? Metz's scrupulous, tenacious approach to these issues set standards that enabled film studies to emerge in many universities in the late 1960s, and to flourish there subsequently as a theoretically sophisticated activity of considerable influence on broader academic studies of culture.

Recently, film studies has undergone several significant crises, including the introduction of digital audio-visual media and the critique of 'Grand Theory' research paradigms (including the subject-position theory of Metz's *Imaginary Signifier*). While Metz is so embedded in the field that any major paradigm shift would inevitably be an occasion to review his work, the present circumstance is an unusually interesting one. This is because post-Theory researchers can value the early Metz's linguistic semiology (while nonetheless rejecting his later psychoanalytic semiotics) and make connections between Metz's 'first semiology' and recent work in film pragmatics and in film narratology (Bordwell and Carroll 1996; Buckland 1995b). The purpose of this essay is to provide a perspective on this recent reactivation of Metz by reviewing the evolution of his work and by observing its effect on current conditions of the field.

Metz was really the first 'modern' film theorist, strategically defining film studies as much by his manner of scholarly communication as by his ideas on cinematic discourse itself. Metz's essays attest to being works-in-progress, more like modern scientific papers than traditional cultural criticism. Footnotes calmly explain earlier versions' imprecisions or flaws in reasoning, and pragmatically acknowledge that ongoing research has entailed reconsideration of earlier findings (Andrew 1976, 214–15). With an overlapping publication schedule for the articles, books and their translations, and with a penchant for dialog with his contemporaries (by means of international colloquia, but also through a style of writing which cites and converses with others' work), Metz became widely known in Europe, Britain and the Americas.

From the early 1960s until his death in 1993, Metz published a series of major essays on the semiology of cinema. His work first appeared in its original French in a variety of Paris-based journals including *Communications*, *La Linguistique*, *Revue d'esthetique*, *Cahiers du cinéma* and *Image et Son*. He was interviewed by *Cinéthique and Ca/Cinéma*, and participated in international scholarly colloquia as well as film festivals such as the Mostra Internazionale del Nuovo Cinema in Pesaro, Italy. Metz long maintained a dialogue with Italian semioticians Umberto Eco, Gianfranco Bettettini and Francesco Casetti. Through these activities and through translations, Metz rapidly became internationally known.

In the 1970s, the British journal *Screen* regularly presented English translations of Metz's work, prefaced by substantial editorials. In the US, *Semiotica* and *New Literary History* published Metz's essays. Moreover, Metz systematically revised his articles and published the revisions, plus new work, in the form of book-length collections: the two-volume *Essais sur la signification au cinéma* (1968, 1972), *Langage et cinéma* (1972), *Le Signifiant imaginaire: Psychanalyse et cinéma* (1977) and *L'Énonciation impersonelle ou le site du film* (1991). Again, translations quickly followed. The principal works known to English-speaking readers are *Film Language: A Semiotics of the Cinema* (1974a), a collection of revised essays drawn from *Essais sur la signification au cinéma*, *Langage et cinéma* and other journal articles, and *The Imaginary Signifier: Psychoanalysis and the Cinema* (1977b), a translation of *Le Signifiant imaginaire*.

Metz's work appears to comprehend three phases. His earliest work was closely tied to structural thought. In the early 1960s, Metz was part of a vanguard semiology research group led by Algirdas Julien Greimas at the Collège de France in Paris (De Behar, in De

Behar and Block 1996, 49). By the mid-1970s, Metz had become interested in explaining the effects of the classical fiction film on the spectator. He expanded the theoretical base of his research by incorporating current psychoanalytic theory, specifically Jacques Lacan's interpretations of Freud (Easthope 79). Metz's later work dealt with enunciation in film. At the time of his death, Metz was working on a study of humour in verbal language.

The linguistic agenda

In his initial semiotic studies, Metz was chiefly concerned with providing a new *logical* account of the medium's specificity. This account would supersede the prescriptive stylistic arguments of prior film theory (namely the debate between advocates of montage and the realists) by deploying the ideas of structural linguists including Saussure, Hjelmslev, Martinet, Jakobson and Halle. Comparable to the goal of Saussurean linguistics, Metz's aim was 'to identify film's specific system of articulation, which should in turn transform film theory into an autonomous, scientific paradigm' (Buckland 1991, 205).

The view that film operated like a language had of course been important to film theory's past. Between the two world wars, for example, the Russian formalist literary theorists and the Soviet montage filmmaker-theorists proposed detailed comparisons between film and language (Bordwell 1985, 17). Their film-language analogy was more complex than the slogan favoured by silent film apologists for whom cinema was a visual Esperanto (Metz 1974a, 31–44). But the conceptual framework of film semiology would claim an even greater rigour, albeit a rigour that was straitjacketed by methodology. Metz's initial film semiotics reasoned that if film possessed features of verbal language as divulged by structural linguistics (such as a relatively autonomous system of articulation), it could be said to resemble verbal language (Buckland 1991, 200). In this Metz used Saussure somewhat opportunistically. Instead of following Saussure's notion that linguistics was a branch of semiology, Metz observed Roland Barthes's reversal of this hierarchy (which meant Metz would overly adhere to Saussurean concepts of verbal signification and look for them in film). By so 'empowering' structural linguistics, Metz had the advantage of promoting systematic, prudently scaled inquiry, but also the drawbacks of negative results. Not only would Metz decide that cinema did not have an autonomous language system or *langue*, but he would also conclude that the film medium lacked the feature of intercommunication necessary to the definition of a language.

Metz nonetheless continued to try to define the specificity of film from the epistemo-logical position of linguistics. But instead of attempting to look for commutable paradigms at the level of the individual image, he now considered the syntagmatic relations between images as the locus of a semiology of film. Deducing eight kinds of space-time relationships between events depicted in narrative films, Metz identified eight syntactic units that, accordingly, articulated such relationships. He presented them in a hierarchic typology he called the *grande syntagmatique*, and applied the whole scheme to an individual film from the French New Wave (Metz 1974a, 92–182). The *alternating syntagm*, for example, signified events occurring in two different spaces (A-B) but simultaneously (A1-B1) or quasi-simultaneously (A1-B1-A2-B2): the heroine detects the fire and runs from the building for help (A1); the firemen are sleeping at the station (B1); smoke thickens at the burning building (A2); the snoring firemen smell smoke and wake up (B2).

Many (including Metz) acknowledged the model's several problems: some syntagms were more successfully isolated than others; all eight syntagms were derived from only one type of film form (narrative); the soundtrack was ignored. Moreover, the phenomenologist in Metz maintained a realist position on the individual image as well as on the existence of a pro-filmic world. According to Thomas Elsaesser, the *grande syntagmatique* suggested that 'filmic syntax corresponds to the rhetorical trope of *dispositio* (determined ordering of undetermined elements – in this case images) rather than to a grammar' (Buckland 1995b, 12). *Language and Cinema* eventually shows Metz's adaptation of Umberto Eco's theory of codes (Heath 1975) and Metz's followers would thus make the ensuing critical trend (textual analysis of classical Hollywood film) a demonstration of rhetorical devices comprising filmic discourse.

From linguistic to psychoanalytic semiotics

In the 1970s, propelled by poststructuralist trends, Metz incorporated Freudian/Lacanian psychoanalysis into his film semiology. In this so-called 'second semiotics', Metz exploited a broader cultural understanding of cinema as a technological, institutional and psychical machine, a conception that had been recently introduced into film theory by Jean-Louis Baudry's articles on the ideological effects of this machine or 'apparatus'. In Constance Penley's words, Baudry saw the cinema as a 'faultless technological simulation' of the psyche while Metz considered cinema more as the psyche's 'extension or prosthesis' (Penley 1989, 61). Hence, Metz's contribution to this trend in film theory is distinct in that his primary goal remained that of realizing a rigorously semiological approach to cinema as a phenomenon that was both imaginary *and* symbolic.

The four essays collected in *The Imaginary Signifier* methodically engage psychoanalytic concepts and classifications to specify (1) the part of fantasy in cinematic signification and (2) the subject implied by the cinema's high quotient of 'imaginariness'. By 'imaginary', Metz meant 'to emphasize the perceptual base of filmic signification, to stress the profoundly fictive nature of the cinematic spectacle, and – most importantly – to align film with Lacan's imaginary register, the register within which identifications are sustained' (Silverman 1983, 288). Actually, Metz invokes Lacan's mirror stage only to describe one of several ways that cinematic discourse configures the subject of the discourse. Metz also conceptualizes the production of the subject (through identification) in terms of the dream-work, the scopic drives (voyeurism, fetishism, exhibitionism), disavowal, primary and secondary processes, etc.

Nonetheless, the principal critique of Metz's psychoanalytic semiotics was aimed at the emphasis he placed on 'primary identification', or the spectator-subject's identification with his own act of vision (via the camera) in experiencing a film. Feminist film theorists took issue with the unacknowledged masculinity of Metz's transcendent and coherent subject (Rose 1980; Doane 1980). They proposed different interpretations of Freudian-Lacanian psychoanalysis and advocated its explicitly political use in gender-specific film theory and practice (Mulvey 1986). Other theorists moved to challenge Metz's reductive account of social, economic and film history (Elsaesser 1986; Nowell-Smith 1985). Still others raised objections to Metz's exclusion of avant-garde, non-narrative and other non-dominant cinematic forms (Penley 1989).

A return to language analysis

On the first page of *The Imaginary Signifier*, Metz asked what psychoanalysis could contribute to the study of cinema. His answer is that it would effect a shift from structural to 'operational' analysis of cinema. But he was not abandoning his original research agenda. 'The psychoanalytic itinerary is from the outset a semiological one, even (above all) if in comparison with a more classical semiology it shifts from attention to the *énonce* to concern for the enunciation' (Metz 1982, 3). Even as he raises the lid on his Pandora's box of the imaginary, Metz remains committed to particular *linguistic* concepts (*énonce*, the utterance; enunciation, the speech act). By then Metz had acknowledged the importance of notions of textuality and subjectivity in a theory of cinematic signification. Psychoanalysis clearly represents an extension of Metz's first semiotics (Rosen 1986, 170), rather than a radical break or a rejection of earlier work (Silverman 1983, 288).

Nonetheless, compared to *Language and Cinema*, *The Imaginary Signifier* reads as a different sort of theoretic investigation. Perhaps the psychoanalytic paradigm proves *too* adequate a basis for analogical reasoning about film, in contrast to Metz's prior experience with the logical reasoning of structural linguistics. As Charles Altman observes, the psychoanalytic paradigm's 'constitutive metaphor (the cinema apparatus equals the psychic apparatus)' confers a unity on the cinematic experience 'it would otherwise lack'. (1985, 530).

But just as Metz had concluded that a structural-linguistic definition of cinema would fail because cinema had no abstract language system or *langue*, he was similarly aware that the question of how film is understood could only be resolved partially by a psychoanalytic methodology. The latter had offered a way to acknowledge and describe the subject in cinematic discourse. But, disseminated in film studies as 'a polemical tool and didactic shorthand' (Elsaesser, in Buckland 1995b, 10), Metz's psycho-semiotics became identified with an amalgam of several other distinct theoretic concerns (apparatus theory, Louis Althusser's notion of interpellation, etc.). In the process, some of the careful discriminations of Metz's linguistic agenda were obscured, notably his definition of the subject as an immanent linguistic entity. He did not equate the subject or 'user' with the actual spectator, but others in the field did, 'adding to the confusion by attributing to this "spectator" a set of constraints and limiting conditions known as subject-positioning, which in turn were said to determine the way films were read by actual spectators' (Elsaesser, in Buckland 1995b, 13).

Towards the end of his life, Metz returned to linguistics, to the work of his teachers, Algirdas Julien Greimas and Roland Barthes, and to the enunciation theory of Emile Benveniste. In the second essay of *The Imaginary Signifier*, 'Story/Discourse: A Note on Two Voyeurisms', Metz had already used Benveniste's distinction between two kinds of utterance (*histoire* and *discours*), here to describe two scopic drives mobilized by cinema (voyeurism and exhibitionism). The merger of linguistic and psychoanalytic paradigms facilitated his thesis: the traditional narrative cinema is primarily voyeuristic and it is an instance of historic utterance. Through techniques such as continuity editing or actors' avoidance of looking directly at the camera, traditional or 'classical' cinema hides or minimizes its discursive markers, its status as speech – just as the voyeur conceals his gaze. This was just the kind of idea that would be used in 'subject-positioning' studies of film spectatorship.

Metz's agenda, though, was not the ideological criticism which developed around issues of subject-positioning. Nor did he attempt a logical or grammatical account of film enunciation. Indeed, in his last published work, *The Impersonal Enunciation, or the Site of Film*, Metz argues that films typically do not 'grammaticalize' enunciator and addressee through deictic terms like personal pronouns. Yet Metz's 'second semiotics' had convinced him of the importance of explaining subjectivity in filmic discourse, and that meant sticking with enunciation theories. This was no minor dilemma, as Warren Buckland and Jan Simons point out, because enunciation was an ambiguous concept in poststructural semiotics (in Buckland 1995b, 113). Sometimes it was construed as an instance of communication, but more often it designated something more immanent, a linguistic instance, that of an abstract subject's discursive competence). In continuing the latter line of reasoning, *The Impersonal Enunciation* was, characteristically, both scrupulous and bold. Enunciation in cinema was reflexive, Metz argued, not deictic. Instead of grammatical categories, rhetorical terms (anaphora, metalanguage) were more adequate to the task of describing a film text's metadiscursive markers–markers, that is, of enunciation.

Metz always remained concerned with film as text rather than as communication. With this last work, though, his more explicit interest in spectatorial competence suggests he may have been reconsidering a communication framework, but was unable to take its broader view of language. That recent cognitive-theoretic studies of narrative film comprehension (Bordwell 1985; Branigan 1992) and a new film semiology (Buckland 1995b) *can* surely attests to Metz's enormous and lasting influence.

Marcia Butzel

Further reading and works cited

Altman, C. F. 'Psychoanalysis and Cinema: The Imaginary Discourse', in *Movies and Methods II*, ed. B. Nichols. Berkeley, CA, 1985.

Andrew, J. D. *The Major Film Theories*. New York, 1976.

Augst, B. 'The Lure of Psychoanalysis in Film Theory', *Cinematographic Apparatus*, ed. T. Hak Kyung Cha. New York, 1980.

Bordwell, D. *Narration in the Fiction Film*. Madison, WI, 1985.

— and Carroll, N. (eds) *Post-Theory*. Madison, WI, 1996.

Branigan, E. *Narrative Comprehension and Film*. London, 1992.

Buckland, W. 'The Structural Linguistic Foundation of Film Semiology', *Language and Communication*, 11, 3, 1991.

—. 'Michel Colin and the Psychological Reality of Film Semiology', *Semiotica*, 107, 1995a.

— (ed.) *The Film Spectator: From Sign to Mind*. Amsterdam, 1995b.

Cook, P. (ed.) *The Cinema Book*. London, 1985.

De Behar and Block, L. (ed.) *Semiotica*, 112, 1996.

De Lauretis, T. *Alice Doesn't: Feminism, Semiotics, Cinema*. Bloomington, IN, 1984.

Doane, M. A. 'Misrecognition and Identity', *Cine-tracts*, 3, 3, Fall 1980.

du Pasquier, S. 'Buster Keaton's Gags', *Journal of Modern Literature*, 3, 2, April, 1973.

Easthope, A. 'Classical Film Theory and Semiotics', *The Oxford Guide to Film Studies*, eds J. Hill and P. Church Gibson. Oxford, 1998.

Elsaesser, T. 'Primary Identification and the Historical Subject: Fassbinder and Germany', in *Narrative Apparatus, Ideology*, ed. P. Rosen. New York, 1986.

Heath, S. 'Film and System', *Screen*, 16, 1, Spring 1975; 16, 2, Summer 1975.

—. *Questions of Cinema*. Bloomington, IN, 1981.

— and Mellencamp, P. (eds) *Cinema and Language*. Frederick, MD, 1983.

Marie, M. and Vernet, M. (eds) *Christian Metz et la théorie du cinéma*. Paris, 1990.

Metz, C. *Essais sur la signification au cinéma* [1968]. Paris, 1972.

—. *Film Language*. New York, 1974a.

—. *Language and Cinema*. The Hague, 1974b.

—. 'The Imaginary Signifier', *Screen*, 16, 2, Summer, 1975.

—. 'History/Discourse: Note on Two Voyeurisms', *Edinburgh 76 Magazine*, 1976.

—. *Essais semiotiques*. Paris, 1977a.

—. *The Imaginary Signifier: Psychoanalysis and Cinema*. Basingstoke, 1977b.

—. 'The Cinematic Apparatus as Social Institution: An Interview', *Discourse*, Fall, 1979.

—. *The Imaginary Signifier*. Bloomington, IN, 1982.

—. *L'Énonciation impersonelle ou le site du film*. Paris, 1991.

—. 'The Impersonal Enunciation, or the Site of Film', in *The Film Spectator: From Sign to Mind*, ed. W. Buckland. Amsterdam, 1995.

Mulvey, L. 'Visual Pleasure and Narrative Cinema', in *Narrative, Apparatus, Ideology*, ed. P. Rosen. New York, 1986.

Nichols, B. 'Style, Grammar, and the Movies', *Movies and Methods I*. Berkeley, CA, 1976.

— (ed.) *Movies and Methods II*. Berkeley, CA, 1985.

Nowell-Smith, G. 'A Note on Story/Discourse', in *Movies and Methods II*, ed. B. Nichols, Berkeley, CA, 1985.

Penley, C. *The Future of an Illusion*. Minneapolis, MN, 1989.

Rose, J. 'The Cinematic Apparatus: Problems in Current Theory', *The Cinematic Apparatus*, eds T. de Lauretis and S. Heath. New York, 1980.

Rosen, P. (ed.) *Narrative, Apparatus, Ideology*. New York, 1986.

Sandro, P. 'Signification in the Cinema', in *Movies and Methods II*, ed. B. Nichols. Berkeley, CA, 1985.

Silverman, K. *The Subject of Semiotics*. New York, 1983.

Stam, R. et al. *New Vocabularies in Film Semiotics*. London, 1992.

Guy Debord (1931–1994) and the Situationist International

Drawing on previous artistic and political avant-gardes, the Situationist movement emerged in the early postwar period. Its membership included writers, painters, film-makers, architects and journalists who saw art as a political intervention capable of providing both an analysis of society's ills and the means to remedy them. The Situationist International (*L'Internationale situationiste*) came into official existence in 1957. Its various small national groups – in France, Algeria, Belgium, Denmark, England, Germany, Holland, Italy, Sweden and the United States – were held loosely together by annual conferences and by the twelve issues of the underground journal *L'Internationale situationiste* that appeared between 1958 and 1969. The movement attained a brief moment of notoriety, even cult status, in the aftermath of May 1968, to which it had made significant theoretical contributions and whose revolts are marked by the Situationists' slogans and their ludic style. The Situationist focus became increasingly sociological and political over time, with members taking outspoken stands on such issues as racial conflict in the United States, the Chinese Cultural Revolution and the war in Indochina. The movement was officially dissolved in 1972. While their names, writings and art works remain virtually unknown, the Situationists had a lasting though largely unacknowledged impact on the terms of debate in French intellectual and cultural life.

Guy Debord – agitator, film-maker, writer, publisher and social critic – was born in Paris and raised in Nice, Pau and Cannes. Unassiduous at school, he spent his childhood reading – Rimbaud, Lautréamont and the Surrealists were among his favourites – and developing a passion for the cinema. In 1951, he moved back to Paris to continue his studies but immediately began to frequent intellectuals seeking to distance themselves from the Saint-Germain-des-Près crowd. Chronic alcoholism and illness made him physically and mentally fragile and would contribute to his suicide on 30 November 1994.

The Situationist movement's dominant spirit and only continuous member, Debord authored most of the articles in *L'Internationale situationiste*, publishing them either signed or anonymously. His originality, his energy and his tenacity held the movement together and account for its lasting importance. It is therefore not implausible to read the imprint of his own psychology in the movement's personality. Orphaned by his father's early death and the indifference of his mother and stepfather, and raised by an over-attentive grandmother, he became the irascible and volatile chief guru of a movement known for its tendency to engulf and then to expel its members without rhyme or reason. Very early, he manifested strong ambivalence about bourgeois values: he denounced all social institutions and disregarded civil authorities yet nevertheless completed his baccalaureate, announcing his brilliant success in the 1951 exams by sending a black-bordered note to his friends. He mocked marriage and defended sexual freedom, yet he was twice married: to Michèle Bernstein from 1954 to 1972 and to Alice Becker-Ho from 1972 to his death. He never held a regular job, insisting on the debilitating effects of paid labour. He thus remained financially dependent most of his life: first on his grandmother, then on Bernstein, who worked at menial jobs and wrote two novels in order to subsidize the Situationist group, in which she nevertheless remained a subordinate member (see Bourseiller, 1999). Further study will hopefully reveal to what extent Bernstein, Becker-Ho, and other women contributed to the elaboration of Situationist positions.

Debord rejected the concept of private property and eschewed copyrights, yet he accused his one-time friend and mentor, Henri Lefebvre, of plagiarism. Frustrated by public resistance to his analyses of the evils of consumer capitalism, he was equally ferocious in his own resistance to fame, realizing that his own positions could too easily be commodified into a fad. Without doubt, Guy Debord was a troubled individual. It is equally clear that he was a genius. He understood the role of culture in society with a prescient clarity that ultimately became so thoroughly absorbed by both mainstream and intelligentsia that his signature remains largely invisible.

Situationist ideas arose in a postwar society characterized by prosperity, material comfort and a growing emphasis on consumer goods. The invention of artificial fibres and building materials provoked an awareness of the threat to the environment posed by excessive consumption. New technologies reduced labour at work and home, turning attention toward leisure activities. At the same time, suburbs sprouted around cities which were increasingly plagued by crime, housing and transportation problems. Decolonization was a preoccupation, as was the enigma of an alienated youth generation, described by Françoise Giroud in her book, *La Nouvelle Vague; Portrait de la jeunesse* (1958). Situationists saw both prosperity and its drawbacks as signalling a crisis in civilization. As early as 1953, Ivan Chtcheglov (a.k.a. Gilles Ivain), a member of the Lettrists, declared that 'A mental disease has swept the planet: banalization. Everyone is hypnotised by production and conveniences – sewage system, elevator, bathroom, washing machine' (Knabb 1981, 2). By 1957, Debord was arguing that modern life had reduced free individuals to the status of cogs in a

capitalist machine. No longer active participants, people had become hypnotized spectators of their own lives. What was needed was a revolution in everyday life (*la vie
quotidienne*).

Situationists were motivated by a desire to oppose capitalism while avoiding orthodox
communist (socialist realist) and surrealist (psychoanalytic) conceptions of art. The
intellectual climate in which they developed their critique was already attuned to the
problems of modernity. Claude Lévi-Strauss had published his work on the structures of
kinship and exchange in traditional societies. Jean Baudrillard was examining the role of
consumer objects in urban France, while Roland Barthes was studying its modern
mythologies. Sociologists and historians of the *Annales* school were developing social
science paradigms for the study of collective 'mentalities', Michel Foucault was pursuing his
historical studies of discourses and material culture, and Louis Althusser had launched his
neo-marxist analysis of ideology and representation. In the United States, David Reisman,
Herbert Marcuse, Marshall McLuhan and Vance Packard were describing the alienated
individual in relation to the communications media and the city.

The Situationist project of transforming consciousness by changing everyday life harks
back to Rimbaud and Lautréamont, to be sure, but its most immediate intellectual
precursor was Henri Lefebvre, whose *Critique de la vie quotidienne* (1947) was an important
influence on the evolution of Debord's thinking, and the two men were for a short time
close friends. Bringing a marxist perspective to the study of daily life, Lefebvre applied the
concepts of alienation and mystification to leisure. Before Debord, he observed that
bourgeois society has separated work from leisure; capitalism sells activities, objects and
images that fail to produce relaxation, creating instead passive attitudes and artificial
desires that cannot be satisfied. Before the Situationists, he decried the complicity of
culture (movies, advertising, commercial eroticism) in this process.

Previous avant-gardes also influenced the early Situationist movement. At the 1951
Cannes film festival, Debord viewed an unsettling film by Isidore Isou. Entitled *Traité de
Bave et d'Éternité*, the film was characterized by disconnection of sound and image,
sequences composed entirely of quotations, and deliberately scratched and distorted
filmstock. Arriving in Paris that autumn, Debord began to frequent Isou and his friends,
who called themselves *Lettrists* to signal their interest in materialist conceptions of art.
Other Lettrists were Jean-Louis and Eliane Brau, Gil Wolman and Maurice Rajsfus. Debord
and Bernstein joined and then soon created a splinter group, the Lettrist International, that
in turn became the founding kernel of the Situationist movement.

The Lettrists favourite strategy was to disrupt and provoke, and their carefully staged
public scandals resulted in memorable notoriety. For example, they invaded the 1950
Notre Dame Easter mass in order to proclaim the death of God. A 1952 press conference
with Charlie Chaplin, in Paris to promote his new film *Limelight*, was interrupted by Lettrist
agitators, including Debord, distributing tracts and shouting offensive though nonsensical
accusations (Bourseiller 1999, 60). Although the declared purpose of both incidents was to
raise public consciousness and demystify institutions and icons, one also detects a youthful
rambunctiousness reminiscent of the Dadaists. Debord retained from these experiences a
conception of art as performance and direct intervention in (or assault on) spectators'
complacency.

Also committed to cultural revolt and contributing to the Situationists' evolution was
the *International Movement for an Imaginist Bauhaus* (MiBi), which included most notably
painters Asger Jorn (from Denmark) and Giuseppe Pinot-Gallizio (Italy). These two artists

had also participated in the short-lived COBRA group (short for Copenhagen-Brussels-Amsterdam) and were in communication with small groups in Germany, Holland and England, each with its own journal and agenda. These groups shared an emphasis on the material basis of cultural production and a commitment to using art to promote class struggle. Other artists who were at some point associated with the Situationists included Jôrgen Nash, Ralph Rumney and Jacqueline De Jong. Three writers were also already active at this stage of the movement's development and later made important contributions to the journal, *L'Internationale situationiste*, Attila Kotányi, Raoul Vaneigem and René Viénet. Along with Debord's *La Société du Spectacle* (1967), Vaneigem's *Traité de savoir-vivre à l'usage des jeunes générations* (1967) and Viénet's *Enragés et situationnistes dans le mouvement des occupations* (1968) played an important role in shaping and interpreting the events of May 1968.

Surrealism was also, of course, an important precursor. The first issue of *L'Internationale situationiste* acknowledged this debt while proclaiming the intention of applying a more resolutely materialist analysis of culture and of avoiding the recuperation to which the earlier movement had fallen victim. The Situationists remained faithful to the surrealist project of gaining access to repressed creativity, spontaneity and a sense of play. At the same time, they conceived of 'repression' in terms more political than psychoanalytical. Peter Wollen goes so far as to say that 'In many ways [the Situationist] project was that of relaunching surrealism on a new foundation, stripped of some of its elements (emphasis on the unconscious, quasi-mystical and occultist thinking, cult of irrationalism) and enhanced by others, within the framework of cultural revolution' (1989, 22).

In the summer of 1957, a meeting in Cosio d'Arroscia in Northern Italy brought together representatives of various European experimental movements. Present at the gathering were Ralph Rumney (for the London Psychogeographic Committee), Asger Jorn and Giuseppe Pinot-Gallizio, along with several fellow artists from the Italian section of MiBi: Walter Olmo, Elena Verrone and Piero Simondo. Michèle Bernstein and Guy Debord represented the French Lettrist International. On 27 July, those assembled voted the Situationist International into existence. Debord presented a theoretical document entitled 'Report on the construction of Situations and on the International Situationist Tendency's Conditions of Organization and Action' (Knabb 1981, 17–25). The essay sets out the basic premise that a complete transformation of society is imperative, and that change can be brought about by means of 'revolutionary experiments in culture'.

Debord's most sustained exposition of the strategies that must be deployed to achieve this goal is to be found in his 1967 book, *The Society of the Spectacle*. The volume consists of 221 numbered propositions redefining consumer capitalism and the class struggle in terms of the *spectacle*, Debord's term for a mode of social relations mediated by representations. As he saw it, capitalism harnesses our imagination for use by the consumer market. Our lived experience and even our desires are transformed into media images and then sold back to us in the form of consumer goods. We thus become the passive spectators or consumers rather than the creators of our lives. Spectacle has become the new religion or opiate that keeps consciousness asleep.

Debord thus moves away from Marx's focus on production toward an emphasis on consumption and leisure. Vacations and television place 'play' in a pseudo-cyclical alternation with 'work', producing only an alienating parody of life. Similarly, separating homes from work and suburbs from cities necessitates networks of automobiles, parking lots, freeways and bypass roads, resulting in a vicious circle of isolation and passivity.

Families remain isolated in their homes, where television saturates them with 'pseudo-needs'. Capitalist spectacle offers an illusion of diversity, but no real choices. This is as true of modes of production as of politicians, movie stars, self-images and soap powder. Because domination is not only economic but also spectacular, the idea of competing economic systems is illusory. Capitalism will not be overthrown by economic revolution. The proletariat will only be liberated by a revolution in consciousness.

With few exceptions (Marguerite Duras's and Alain Resnais's *Hiroshima mon amour*, for example), contemporaneous experimental fiction in cinema and novel were subjected to harsh Situationist criticism for insufficient disruption of existing values. Situationists sought instead to instigate cultural revolution by deploying anarchistic and utopian strategies that we might call genres of living art. They would break rules and wrench objects, images, phrases, the city, desires, leisure activities, human interactions and the self out of their institutionalized meanings. The practices outlined below are all modes of 'constructed situations'. Implicitly indebted to Sartre, these are defined in the first issue of *L'Internationale situationiste* as 'A moment of life concretely and deliberately constructed by the collective organization of a unitary ambience and a game of events'. Their purpose was to produce new social realities by means of (somewhat) controlled experimentation: participants begin by 'setting up, on the basis of more or less clearly recognized desires, a temporary field of activity favourable to these desires'. This leads to 'clarification of these primitive desires' and to the emergence of new desires, which will in turn reveal a 'new reality engendered by the situationist constructions' (Knabb 1921, 43–5).

The most direct of the 'revolutionary experiments in culture' invoked at the 1957 founding meeting involved subverting the market value of the art object. This could be accomplished by mass production, as in Pinot-Gallizio's 'industrial paintings', drawn on rolls of paper to be sold by the metre. The art object's value as private property could also be disrupted through the systematic practice of plagiarism. Each issue of *L'Internationale situationiste* disclaims copyright, declaring that 'All the texts published in *L'Internationale situationiste* may be freely copied, translated or adapted, even without indication as to their origin'. The cultural object as commodity emanating from a (preferably famous) signature could be abolished through *détournement* or diversion: the recycling of texts and images in new contexts. Recalling Duchamp's ready-mades, Warhol's paintings and the surrealists' playfully moustached Mona Lisa, this strategy demonstrates that art involves creating new meanings for existing material. Putting into practice Lautréamont's axiom that 'Plagiarism is necessary; civilization demands it', painter Asger Jorn systematically painted over works by others, appropriating their vision. Debord made films whose soundtrack consisted of quotations, sometimes unaccompanied by images.

Other practices redefined art as an activity without material support. Since desires have been most successfully harnessed for the uses of capital in leisure activities, this is where Situationists invest their efforts. Since they conceived their revolution in *urban* terms, the city served as their laboratory. Prefiguring studies of what was later known as 'social space', Debord and his colleagues posited that psychological states, and thus social relations among individuals, were a function of physical environment. To explore modalities of 'psycho-geography', or the affective dimension of environment, they cultivated *la dérive*, a fashionable French leisure activity defined as 'a mode of experimental behaviour linked to the conditions of urban society: a technique of transient passage through varied ambiences' (Knabb 1981, 45), the Situationist *dérive* consisted of drifting through urban landscapes and becoming attuned to the auras of locales and neighbourhoods. This made it possible to take possession of the city and overcome its alienating fragmentation, rather than mindlessly passing through to a pre-chosen destination. Recalling the surrealists' automatic writing, the *dérive* is thus a kind of automatic walking, whose goal was to bring people into affective harmony with their surroundings. This practice would eventually contribute to the creation of new cities ('unitary urbanism') adapted to human needs – for play and freedom, for example.

Concepts of play and constructed situations are keys to understanding the Situationists' role in the Events of May 1968. Situationists were influential at the earliest stages of the revolts, which began in Strasbourg in 1966, where student anarchist groups came close to resembling the 'workers' councils' the Situationists felt would be the vanguard of the revolution. These groups protested the regimentation and restrictions imposed on student life, outdated styles of teaching, and the alienated nature of student work in a bourgeois university that privileged consumer values over discovery and knowledge. Inspired by Situationists, they created scandals and provoked incidents, distributed 'detourned' comic strips and posters, and published a pamphlet ponderously entitled 'De la misère en milieu étudiant considérée sous ses aspects économique, psychologique, politique, sexuel et notamment intellectuel, et de quelques moyens pour y rémédier'. The pamphlet was written by Mustapha Khayati, a Tunisian Situationist living in Strasbourg, with Guy Debord's editorial support. The brochure ends with a paean to proletarian revolution, conceived as a celebration of unalienated time and unmediated enjoyment of life (1966, 223–5). In the fall of 1967, in the midst of protests against United States, policy in Vietnam, the 'Enragés de Nanterre'e demanded changed living conditions at the Cité universitaire, while *L'Internationale situationiste* called once again for a 'decolonization of daily life'. The liberation of creativity and imagination as forces for social change were central to the student revolts. From Berkeley to Paris, freedom of expression was an act of participatory democracy. Debord himself could be found among the 'students' occupying the Sorbonne and in ad hoc committees attempting to spread the revolts into the factories. Although the Situationists' agenda was only imperfectly understood by the student protesters, their techniques and their spirit of liberation through play were prominent in the revolts.

The first issue of the *Internationale situationiste* (1958) had been categorical: 'There is no such thing as situationism, which would mean a doctrine of interpretation of existing facts. The notion of situationism is obviously devised by antisituationists'. It had been the Situationists' intention to remain in the shadows. Virtually unknown before the Events of May, Debord was in danger of becoming a media star. Imitators and admirers multiplied, but Debord and his colleagues continued to refuse interviews and resist commodification of their positions as just another bourgeois fad. But the tide was against them. The pressure of being idolized from the outside combined with the usual internal conflicts caused the movement to disintegrate. The last issue of *L'Internationale situationiste* appeared in 1969, and the group disbanded early in 1972. It could almost be said that the movement was killed by its own success.

Debord nevertheless continued to militate by returning to his original film-making career. In 1971, he became the protégé of film agent, producer and distributor, Gérard Lebovici. Lebovici, whose sympathies were with the radical Left and the insurgents of May, had also created the publishing house 'Champ Libre', with the editorial support of writer Jorge Semprun. Lebovici agreed to publish a new edition of *La Société du spectacle* and in 1974 produced its film adaptation, a collage of archives, texts, and images, accompanied by a soundtrack of Debord reading from his book. Lebovici subsequently produced several more of Debord's films, including his autobiographical *In girum imus nocte et consumimur igni* (1977). Debord continued to write and translate revolutionary pamphlets, and Lebovici, at the head of his distribution company Artmedia, became one of the French cinema industry's most powerful figures. In March of 1984, Lebovici was assassinated for reasons and by perpetrators unknown. Although not implicated, Debord suffered a media trial by innuendo in connection with the affair. The case was never solved. Although he continued to publish books, notably his 1988 *Commentaires sur la société du spectacle*, after Lebovici's death, he withdrew his films from circulation.

The Situationist movement appeared at the intersection of many artistic and political currents, and it embodied a certain spirit of the times. Consequently, the Situationist legacy is difficult to circumscribe. Some commentators maintain that it remains most visible in a style of thinking and writing that includes, among other features, the typical rhetorical figure of the reversed genitive (as in 'Let's put an end to the spectacle of contestation and move on to the contestation of the spectacle'). Slogans of this sort were so common in public discourse, and the Situationists were so unconcerned with claiming authorship, that their influence dissolved into the larger cultural landscape. Other more significant and lasting contributions can nevertheless be discerned:

- The Situationists exerted an obvious impact on subsequent avant-gardes. For example, Greil Marcus (1989) traces Situationist influence on punk and especially on Jamie Reid, Johnny Rotten and the Sex Pistols, whose irreverent record jackets, posters and performance style recall Situationist provocations.
- The Situationists refused all orthodoxies, and Debord was consistently against totalitarianisms of all stripes. In the face of widespread infatuation with Mao among the intelligentsia, Debord was outspokenly critical of the Chinese Cultural Revolution. He also remained resolutely anti-colonialist. Situationist positions helped to legitimize a diversity of thought in a French Left dominated by the Communist Party. History and a post-Cold War perspective have retrospectively enhanced Situationist credibility.
- If May 1968 placed art closer to the centre of the political map, this is largely attributable to the Situationist movement, which a decade earlier had begun to challenge assumptions about the social functions of culture. The 1960s and 1970s saw a convergence of social and cultural theory, with the result that art was increasingly seen as political. The Chinese Cultural Revolution of course also contributed to the increasing conviction that culture was as important as economics in the political debate. If not displaced, marxist economism was enhanced by the belief that a better world could be imagined and even brought into reality by liberating art and creativity.
- Like earlier cultural figures in the tradition of social and political *engagement* that included Zola, Breton, and Sartre, Situationists signed petitions, penned manifestos and manned barricades. They also went farther than other avant-garde movements in joining revolutionary theory to artistic praxis. The notion that art itself, independent of its creator, can be militant contributed to postmodern conceptions of art as object and as process. Situationists conducted valuable experiments with forms of cultural production that remain indigestible, that resist being bought or sold, kept as an investment or displayed on coffee tables. Contemporary explorations of the aesthetics of everyday experience, of urbanism, and of performance art are indebted to Situationist precursors. The Situationists' success in deconstructing the opposition of highbrow and popular

culture, in creating collective art, and in artistic practices drawing on anthropological conceptions of festival, play, gift, waste and excess contributed to the contemporary discipline of cultural studies.

- In France, the Women's Movement became a significant social force after 1968. Although members of the Situationist International failed to alter power relations between the sexes in their own behaviour, and in fact L'Internationale situationiste reproduces the dominant culture's tradition of representing women as spectacle, they did establish a critique of gender roles that helped shape feminist analyses. Their emphasis on everyday life as it is determined by institutions, including marriage and the family, contributed to contemporary understandings of the private as political. These ideas also notably influenced the cinema of Jean-Luc Godard. For example, in Tout va bien (1974), Godard foregrounds the inseparability of public and private spheres, complicating his representation of class with an analysis of gender relations. Here and elsewhere, Godard uses Lettrist and Situationist techniques of détournement, dissociation of soundtrack and image, altering the material nature of film-stock, and thematizing the material nature of film-making.

The Situationist experiment retains its vitality of the 1960s and 1970s. Now that everything from love to information and from medical care to legal protection is no longer conceived in terms of rights and responsibilities but as consumer goods, and now that education and political leadership have turned into spectacle, Situationist insights seem more pertinent than ever.

Lynn A. Higgins

Further reading and works cited

Althusser, L. Pour Marx. Paris, 1965.
Barthes, R. Mythologies. Paris, 1957.
Baudrillard, J. Le Système des objets. Paris, 1968.
Bourseiller, C. Vie et Mort de Guy Debord, 1931–1994. Paris, 1999.
Debord, G. Oeuvres cinématographiques complètes, 1952–78. Paris, 1978.
—. The Society of the Spectacle New York, 1994.
Giroud, F. La Nouvelle Vague: Portrait de la jeunesse. Paris, 1958.
Internationale situationiste, 1958–69. Amsterdam, 1970.
Khayati, M. De La Misère en milieu étudiant. Strasbourg, 1966.
Knabb, K. (ed.) Situationis International Anthology. Berkeley, CA, 1981.
Lefebvre, H. Critique de la Vie Quotidienne, 2 vols, Paris, 1958.
Lévi-Strauss, C. Les Structures élémentaires de la parenté. Paris, 1949.
Marcus, G. Lipstick Traces; A Secret History of the Twentieth Century. Cambridge, MA, 1989.
McLuhan, M. The Medium Is the Message. New York, 1967.
October 79, Winter 1997.
Riesman, D. et al. The Lonely Crowd. New Haven, CT, 1950.
Sussman, E. (ed.) On the Passage of a Few People Through a Rather Brief Moment in Time: The Situationist International, 1957–1972. Cambridge, MA, 1989.
Vaneigem, R. The Revolution of Everyday Life. London, 1983.
Viénet, R. Enragés et situationniste S dans le mouvement des occupations. Paris, 1968.
Wollen, P. 'Bitter Victory: The Art and Politics of the Situationist International', in On the Passage of a Few People Through a Rather Brief Moment in Time: The Situationist International, 1957–1972, ed. E. Sussman. Boston, 1989.

Umberto Eco (1932–)

Sul finire del primo secolo della nostra era, nell'Isola di Patmos, l'apostolo Giovanni ebbe una visione. Se non fu Giovanni, se non ebbe la visione e semplicemente scrisse un testo sul genere letterario 'visione' (o *Apokalypsis*, Rivelazione), poca conta. Perché quello di cui ci stiamo occupando è un testo (e il modo in cui fu letto). Ora un testo, quando è scritto, non ha più nessuno alle spalle: ha invece...migliaia di interpreti di fronte. La lettura che essi ne danno genera altri testi, che ne sono parafrasi, commento, spregiudicata utilizzazione, traduzione in altri segni, parole, immagini, persino musica.

Un testo è una sfilata di forme significanti che attendono di essere riempite (che la storia, dice Barthes, passa il tempo a riempire): i risultati di questi 'riempimenti' sono quasi sempre altri testi. Peirce avrebbe detto: gli *interpretanti* del primo testo ... [Q]uesto volume verte su alcuni 'interpretanti' del testo detto *Apocalisse* ... [I]l presente volume li ha scelti come punto di partenza e non come punto di arrivo ... [H]anno generato altri testi, di cui quello che ora si legge, su pagine azzurre e rilegato in nero, è ancora uno degli interpretanti, non l'ultimo.

[At the end of the first century of our era, on the island of Patmos, the apostle John had a vision. If it hadn't been John, or if he didn't have the vision and simply wrote a text in the literary genre, 'vision' (or Apocalypse, Revelations), no big deal. Because that which interests us is a text (and the way in which it was read). Now a text, when it is written, no longer has anyone to help it; instead, it has ... thousands of interpretations facing it. The reading these give it generates other texts, which are paraphrases of it, commentaries, open-minded uses, translations into other signs, words, images, even music.

A text is a procession of significant forms that wait to be filled (that the story, says Barthes, passes the time to fill): the results of this 'filling out' are almost always other texts. Peirce would have said, the *interpretants* of the first text ... (T)his volume is concerned with some 'interpretants' from the text called *Apocalypse* ... (T)he present volume has chosen them as the point of departure and not as a point of arrival ... (T)hey have generated other texts, of which this one you now read, on blue pages and re-bound in black, is another one of the interpretants, not the last.]

I've taken the space to cite from the first two paragraphs of Umberto Eco's introduction to the *Beato di Liébana* (1973, 23), mainly because they convey the major aspects of his work I'd like to introduce here: an attraction to multimedia and communication, a preoccupation with the subject of reading, a concern with authority, a recourse to medieval texts as well as to Charles Sanders Peirce, and finally, his narrative voice.

'traduzione in altri segni, parole, immagini, persino musica': multimedia and communication

At first, it may seem odd to cite the *Beato di Liébana* as an example of Umberto Eco's fascination with multimedial modalities, since the text he edits and comments upon stems from a medieval manuscript, hardly the latest in communication technology. Nonetheless, as his self-conscious attention to the blue pages and to the black-bound volume suggests, Eco is just as interested in the medium as in the message. Indeed, Eco's self-reflexive commentary on the *Beato*'s commentaries on the last book of the New Testament, *Revelations*, highlights the edition's reproductions of the original manuscript's striking illuminations. Likewise, at the end of the volume, attention is drawn to the interplay between medieval and modern book production itself through a facsimile copy of Eco's handwritten response to the publisher's request for a biographical statement.

Actually, this edition's self-conscious and self-reflexive attention to the medium mirrors that of the genre known as *Beatus* – after Beatus of Liébana, who composed his commentary on the Apocalypse in ca. 776. Indeed, by the late Middle Ages, vivid and elaborate illuminations had become a characteristic marker of the *Beatus*. Moreover, the term *apocalypse*, as evidenced still today in films and television series, has come to function as a dark and evocative touchstone for the visionary, for scenarios of death and destruction racing alongside the four final horsemen. Replete with such associations, both the genre and the more widely-spread term almost require articulation in diverse media.

Yet, ironically, although the apocalypse evokes and inspires creation in various media, its message is concomitantly concerned with the single event that will end all mortal communication. Medium and message rival each other in the attempt to express such inexpressibles, thereby creating the kind of paradox fomenting at the centre of mystery, of secrecy, the kind of paradox that has intrigued Eco for decades, as evidenced by two of his most popular, 'genre-bending' novels. Thus, generating the action of *The Name of the Rose* (1983) is a monk's poisoning of an Aristotelian manuscript in order to prevent others from being (in his view) destroyed by its persuasive pagan ideas, thereby mirroring the text's deadly message in its murderous medium. Likewise, *Foucault's Pendulum* (1989) narrates an occult society's sinister attempts to define and control the message conveyed by their canonical texts. Secrecy, mystery, paradox – these entice readers to decode, to gain control of, to escape, to create.

Such alluring invitations occupy Eco and prove critical to his semiotic theory. Looking at how western European readers, for example, confront interpretation historically, Eco arrives at two philosophical strains. In his terms, hermeticism transforms the world into an allegory whose codes can be cracked, while gnosticism positions the enlightened individual as able to free humanity from original error. He argues, '[b]oth together, the Hermetic and the Gnostic heritage produce the syndrome of the secret . . . the initiated is someone who understands the cosmic secret' (Eco et al. 1992, 38). Importantly, the reduction of the universe into an allegory and the individual into someone who can decode it not only underscores the reader's role in the grand scheme of things, it also transforms all media, everything, into a text to be interpreted correctly.

While not accepting such interpretative constraints in their entirety, Eco probes various contexts and media, undoubtedly propelled in part by his own voracious appetite for enigmas, puzzles, and all forms of communication. Indeed, in addition to his novels and short stories, Eco has conducted semiotic analyses not only of literary texts, but also of computer culture, books *per se*, comic books, films and architecture. Likewise, Eco has participated in multimedial enterprises: he has collaborated on children's books as well as on WWW and CD-Rom projects, worked for Italian television, lectured widely, been involved in education and pedagogical projects at various levels, and written for print media, including a weekly column for a prominent Italian weekly, *L'Espresso*.

In thus focusing both theory and practice on various instances of communication, Eco conducts semiotic analyses in a quintessentially rhetorical framework. Simply defined, and along classical lines, rhetoric is the art of persuasion which makes an author's attempt to reach an audience its primary aim. And effectively complementing rhetoric's aim is semiotics' concern with signs, how they're made, how they're received, and how they communicate.

Thus, in Eco's approach, the endless possibilities of semiotics are filtered through typically rhetorical concerns, such as accounting for contexts as well as the codes that an author plays against in order to communicate with her or his audience. As Eco puts it:

> The existence of various codes and subcodes, the variety of sociocultural circumstances in which a message is emitted (where the codes of the addressee can be different from those of the sender), and the rate of initiative displayed by the addressee in making presuppositions and abductions – all result in making a message (insofar as it is received and transformed into the *content* of an *expressionn*) an empty form to which possible senses can be attributed. Moreover, what one calls 'message' is usually a *text*, that is, a network of different messages depending on different codes and working at different levels of signification. (1979, 5)

With rhetorically framed semiotic theory, Eco theorizes and practises in various media. And since his subject is often communication, Eco's theory, fiction, and forays into the public circle about the possibilities and limits of communication (as made perhaps most obvious by the secretive, the paradoxical, the mysterious).

La lettura . . . genera altri testi: reading

Although Eco's semiotic framework is rhetorical, his approach differs from that of classical instruction in so far as he minimizes the author's concern with how to cajole audiences into accepting a certain point. Instead, Eco starts from the reader's position in order to explore how readers react to texts and in the process create new ones: 'every reception of a work of art is both an *interpretation* and a *performance* of it, because in every reception the work takes on a fresh perspective for itself' (1979, 49).

It is from this reader's perspective that Eco classifies texts as *open* and *closed*, although pure forms of either type do not exist (1962, 33–5). According to Eco, closed texts, such as Superman comics or Ian Fleming's James Bond novels, attract specific audiences and elicit specific readings. In contrast, open texts, such as James Joyce's *Finnegans Wake*, attract readers who dwell on structure and don't demand a simple message. Whether open or closed, Eco argues that a text (not the author) selects or attracts its own kind of reader, which he calls its Model Reader (1979, 7–10).

This description of how the reader functions, it seems to me, draws upon the same kind of paradox impelling mystery. Readers are *selected* by a text which will either entice them into believing they understand the secret completely or lead them to generate other texts in the attempt to come to terms with its paradoxes. Although a productive approach, at times it also limits the author – audience axis a bit too snugly. For example, while replicating (perhaps) how many readers experience a text, this approach makes the author vanish from view, a marginalization that concomitantly creates slippage. Thus the text seems to transform into a completely unified, almost organic, independent entity: 'any interpretation given of a certain portion of a text can be accepted if it is confirmed by, and must be rejected if it is challenged by, another portion of the same text' (Eco et al. 1992, 65).

Perhaps given Eco's emphases and approach, the diminishing of the author in favour of the text and the location of authorial activity in the reader are inevitable, since highlighting the reader in a rhetorical framework brings interpretation, the semiotic enterprise, to the foreground. Bridging the gap and critical to Eco's approach is the context which both readers and authors share – the unhierarchically arranged, open, culturally coded knowledge and intertextual frames that Eco calls an encyclopaedia, and within which *all* interrelated properties of any given sememe, or potential text, are stored (1986, 68–84).

Eco's concept of the encyclopedia nuances while underlining the importance of contexts. It accounts for the same sign meaning different, or simply differently received, things, and suggests that reading involves a series of operations. For example, texts reveal their topics by means of isotopies, a term Eco borrows from A. J. Greimas to designate the different semantic strategies that allow a text to generate interpretative coherence (1986, 189–201). By means of isotopies, the reader is called upon to implement what Eco calls semantic disclosures. 'Semantic disclosures have a double role: they *blow up* certain properties (making them textually relevant or pertinent) and *narcotize* some others' (1979, 23). So, when readers can forecast what will occur in a narrative, they are led to do so by isotopies, which in effect narrow down the plethora of information provided by intertextual frames, the encyclopedia.

Interpretation, then, involves the ability to negotiate detail and a series of frameworks, which Eco describes as a somewhat circular process: 'the text is an object that the interpretation builds up in the course of the circular effort of validating itself on the basis of what it makes up as its result' (Eco et al. 1992, 64). Recognizing that this description in effect defines the hermeneutic circle, Eco coins a pair of terms: the intention of the text (*intentio operis*) and the intention of the reader (*intentio lectoris*). In doing so, not only is the author marginalized, the text has essentially become a sign for both author and writer: it *stands for* the author to the reader while it concomitantly *stands for* the reader to the author.

I italicized 'stands for' in the last sentence because these words form the defining marker of the sign most used in semiotic theory. As Charles Sanders Pierce defines it, 'A sign, or *representamen*, is something which stands to somebody for something in some respect or capacity.' Peirce goes on to describe the sign's *interpretant*, that sign which is created in the mind of the addressee and which stands for the *object* to be read against a *ground* (Peirce 1960, 135). It is this definition of the sign, and particularly the role of the interpretant, that fuels Eco's approach, so much so that he can identify the *Beato* as an interpretant of *Revelations*.

'Se non fu Giovanni . . .': authority

Over time, the *Beato* had become just such a sign for a certain type of commentary. Part of its credibility as a sign stemmed from Beatus' inclusion of writings by earlier canonical thinkers, such as St Augustine, who too commented on *Revelations*.

Church authorities like Augustine frequently generated commentaries on sacred texts that later themselves became authoritative and were cited to signal, among other things, a conceptual framework. Likewise, Eco cites Barthes and Peirce to situate this *Beato* in a semiotic framework. Such allusions to authority cajole the reader to play text against literary contexts. Yet, once a narrative has widely spread authority – even one as subject to multiple commentaries and interpretative problems as the Bible – ensuing reader-generated narratives tend to conform to it:

...in 1699 we see John Webb...making a different hypothesis: after the Flood, Noah and his Ark did not land on top of Mount Ararat in Armenia but instead in China. Thus the Chinese language is the purest version of Adamic Hebrew, and only the Chinese, having lived for millennia without suffering foreign invasions, preserved it in its original purity. (Eco 1998, 64)

Although inviting readers to engage in literary encyclopaedias, authority curtails the extent of that engagement. Nonetheless, unexpected uses of encyclopaedias, such as Webb's, give life to authoritative narratives, shifting mystery from the message or medium to *how* a reader reads.

'*come punto di partenza e non come punto di arrivo*': Recourse to Medieval Texts

Although Eco's training in medieval textual culture is most widely known through *The Name of the Rose* (1983), as his preoccupation with authority demonstrates, medieval influence on his work goes beyond his first novel. Indeed, Eco's writings are peppered with references to Dante, speculative grammar, and various medieval theologians as well as with medievally derived terms, such as *intentio operis* and *intentio lectoris*. In addition, Eco has explored and applied the scholastic thought of Thomas Aquinas, whose work he has characterized as structuralist, in *Il Problema estetico in Tommaso d'Aquino* (1970) and in his *Arte e bellezza nell'estetica medievale* (1987). Moreover, Eco relies on medieval rhetorical schemes, such as the *ars combinatoria* (the art of generating various combinations from a set of certain givens), which serves him to explain not only how encyclopedias work but also James Bond novels (1979, 155).

At the foundation of Eco's approach to and application of medieval textuality is his fascination with language. Thus *The Search for the Perfect Language* (1995) also reflects medieval preoccupation with Edenic, fallen, and redeemed language, categories that in the Middle Ages defined humanity as well as mortals' relationships to the divine (Colish 1968, 8–81; Gellrich, 1985). Further, Eco's semiotic thought is reflected in the Middle Ages' tripartite approach to language, the *trivium* or the arts of grammar, rhetoric and logic. Indeed, as already stated, Eco's work has similarities with the second art of the *trivium*, rhetoric (Baldwin 1972). Most importantly, since rhetoric only recommends and has no hard and fast rules, it has no signposts to inform users they have erred. Thus its practitioners must be able to read audiences – to read readers – while writing texts that are not delimited by subject matter or scope. Moreover, they should be able to pick out the most appropriate *topoi*, or commonplaces, in order to establish a 'meeting place' for both audience and author. In Eco's terminology, the author must know how to make effective use of shared encyclopaedias.

'*è ancora uno degli interpretanti, non l'ultimo*': Charles S. Peirce

Influenced by medieval foci on language, Eco's semiotic work was foreshadowed in *Opera aperta* (1976a) and *La struttura assente* (1968) and developed in two key texts, *A Theory of Semiotics* (1976b) and *Semiotics and the Philosophy of Language* (1986). Importantly, Peirce's logic-trained language and analyses percolate throughout Eco's rhetorically-framed semiotic approach, as for example seen in Eco's attention to abduction (1976a, *Theory*, 131–3) and to the theory of possible worlds (1994, 65–82).

Abduction is the process by which a conclusion is drawn from a single example, a reader-centred process that depends heavily on contexts and encyclopaedias to fill in gaps. Fitting into this process is Peirce's analysis of two kinds of object, the *dynamic object* (or the object *per se*) and the *immediate object* (or the object as represented through its sign), whereby Peirce argues that we know reality through signs and not through the actual objects themselves. Encyclopedias, however, reveal that signs have multiple meanings. Faced with the numerous possible meanings a sign can have, we can nonetheless understand texts since they are contextualized in a ground and limited by a linear process – that is, according to Eco's reading of Peirce, 'a sign establishes step by step a *habit*, a regularity of behaviour in the interpreter or user of that sign, a habit being 'a tendency . . . to behave in a similar way under similar circumstances' . . . a cosmological regularity' (1979, 192). And abduction-framed, habitually perceived immediate objects allow readers to enter fictional worlds, 'worlds' which readers furnish from encyclopedias to approximate possible scenarios that reference our 'dynamic' world.

This type of channelling of the myriad possibilities invited by an encyclopaedia is critical to Eco's semiotic theory. Rejecting the propensity of some readers to see in every text a world of infinite possibilities along with the attempt of others to find the original intent of an author, Eco argues that texts may have multiple, but not infinite, meanings. He bases this approach in Peirce's notion of unlimited semiosis, whereby each interpretant, in itself constituting a sign, can infinitely produce others. In Peirce's system, however, the interpretants become more and more determined, not loosely associative (1994, 38–41). In theoretical circles, Eco is probably most well known for this position, which he often sets against that of deconstructionists whom he characterizes as more or less libertine readers.

By considering sociocultural contexts in the isotopic framework of possible worlds, Eco is able to explore multiple media, place the reader at the centre of the semiotic enterprise, and bring the reader's creative abilities to the foreground. In doing so, Eco emphasizes that what we know we understand through representations that are grounded in encyclopedias.

'Ora un testo, quando è scritto, non ha più nessuno alle spalle': narrative voice

At the end of a discussion of *Un Drame bien parisien*, Eco writes:

> *Drame* is only a metatext speaking about the co-operative principle in narrativity and at the same time challenging our yearning for co-operation by gracefully punishing our pushiness. It asks us – to prove our penitence – to extrapolate from it the rules of the textual discipline it suggests.

> Which I humbly did. And so should you, and maybe further, gentle reader. (1979, 256)

Thus Eco gives this text a voice and a will, thereby figuratively transforming it into a conversational partner that does its best to elicit its Model Reader.

In this manner, Eco replicates tensions found in Plato's *Phaedrus*, a dialogue depicting Socrates conversing on the topics of love, myths, memory and language. Important here, Socrates contrasts the inferiority of written to oral language. Written language, he complains, cannot interactively respond to different readers' needs nor further the talent of memory (Plato 1993, 274e–275a). Thus, on the literal level, Plato has Socrates prefer the virtues of reasoned conversation over writing. Yet, Socrates' critique must be read with care since, most obviously, his dialogue is conveyed by Plato through writing. Indeed, by building on such ironies, Plato is able to make the dialogue 'spea[k] about the co-operative principle in narrativity and . . . challeng[e] our yearning for co-operation . . . [and] asks us . . . to extrapolate from it the rules of the textual discipline it suggests.'

Eco's often ironic tone and recording of ironies work somewhat like Plato's condemnation of writing in writing. There is truth in the message, but the medium – or in Eco's case, the narrative voice – creates a rival. As such, writing can also function both as an antidote to and as an enhancer of mystery, paradox, language, myth, and thereby create the type of dialogue with readers, perhaps Model Readers, who will contribute to the conversation with other texts.

SunHee Kim Gertz

Further reading and works cited

Baldwin, C. S. *Medieval Rhetoric and Poetic to 1400*. St Clair Shores, MI, 1972.
Barthes, R. *Elements of Semiology*. New York, 1967.
—. *A Barthes Reader*, ed. S. Sontag. New York, 1982.
Bondanella, P. *Umberto Eco and the Open Text*. Cambridge, 1997.
Bouchard, N. and Pravadelli, V. (eds) *Umberto Eco's Alternative*. New York, 1998.
Colish, M. L. *The Mirror of Language*. New Haven, CT, 1968.
Deely, J. *Introducing Semiotic*. Bloomington, IN, 1982.
Eco, U. *La struttura assente*. Milan, 1968.
—. *Il problema estetico in Tommaso d'Aquino*. Milan, 1970.
—, text and commentary, and L. Vázquez de Parga Iglesias, intro. and bibliographical entries. *Beato di Liébana: Miniature del Beato de Fernando I y Sancha (Codice B. N. Madrid Vit. 14–2)*. Parma, 1973.
—. *Opera aperta*. Milano, 1976a.
—. *A Theory of Semiotics*. Bloomington, IN, 1976b.
—. *The Role of the Reader*. Bloomington, IN, 1979.
—. *The Name of the Rose*. New York, 1983.
—. *Semiotics and the Philosophy of Language*. Bloomington, IN, 1986.
—. *Arte e bellezza nell'estetica medievale*. Milan, 1987.
—. *Foucault's Pendulum*. New York, 1989.
—. *The Limits of Interpretation*. Bloomington, IN, 1994.
—. *The Search for the Perfect Language*. Oxford, 1995.
—. *Serendipities*. New York, 1998.
— et al. *Interpretation and Overinterpretation*, ed. S. Collini. Cambridge, 1992.
Elam, K. *The Semiotics of Theatre and Drama*. London, 1980.
Gellrich, J. M. *The Idea of the Book in the Middle Ages*. Ithaca, NY, 1985.
Innis, R. E. (ed.) *Semiotics: An Introductory Anthology*. Bloomington, IN, 1985.
Jakobson, R. *On Language*, ed. L. R. Waugh. Cambridge, MA, 1990.
Peirce, C. S. *Collected Papers of Charles Sanders Peirce*, eds C. Hartshorne and P. Weiss. Cambridge, MA, 1960.
Plato. *The Symposium and The Phaedrus: Plato's Erotic Dialogues*. Albany, NY, 1993.
Scholes, R. *Semiotics and Interpretation*. New Haven, CT, 1982.
Sebeok, T. A. *Signs: An Introduction to Semiotics*. Toronto, 1994.

Modernities: Paul Virilio (1932–), Gianni Vattimo (1936–), Giorgio Agamben (1942–)

Modernity has been and remains a vexed term in the field of recent cultural and philosophical thinking. It is possible, for example, to conceive of a 'modernity' that has existed and developed in the West since the Renaissance, centred around specific notions of sovereignty and subjectivity; it is possible to think modernity as a more specifically 'Enlightenment' project, stemming from a set of beliefs about the inevitability of progress; it is possible to become more all-encompassing and to set a date for the invention of 'history' and the consequent destabilization of 'traditional' cultures, a date that has been set at many points between ancient Rome and the 'industrial revolution'; or it is possible to think modernity as an identifiably twentieth-century project, in which case it comes into uneasy relation with notions of the 'postmodern'.

If we were, however, to name the major terrain on which this definitional conflict has been taking place in the West over the last several decades, it would be one decisively marked by the two great figures of Nietzsche and Heidegger; the principal continental theorists of modernity return again and again to these pillars of the temple with an insistence that borders on the idolatrous, thereby neatly encapsulating the thought that modernity, whatever else it might be, is inevitably striated and fissured by its own forebears. These particular forebears, of course, could be said to be united specifically around their scepticism towards 'enlightenment' and the general forward movement of culture; we thus have within the theory of modernity a continual undertow, a movement backwards that seldom fails to invoke a past, 'pre-modern' model even as it denies the very philosophical ground on which such a fantasy construct might be produced. The theory of modernity, then, is of necessity locked into the cyclical, the circular; even as it asserts the irremediable gap, the unbridgeable difference between present and past, so the past reappears once more as the constitutive feature of its own horizon, as the essential enabling reactive force against which modernity seeks to achieve its own novel velocities.

We need to point too to a further major constituent feature of theories of modernity, inherited again from Heidegger and also from Walter Benjamin, which is the attempt to locate and deal with technology. Again we find ourselves involved here in a play of difference; we might emblematically rediscover it in Baudrillard's joyful pessimism, his exultant castigations, his hallucinated rebuttals of precisely the simulacra that he reproduces time and time again in his work; we will find it, certainly, in the work of the three thinkers to whom I shall attend in this essay: Paul Virilio, Giorgio Agamben and Gianni Vattimo. What we also find in their work is a series of breakings of the boundaries: however modernity is described, it is constantly predicated on the assumption that the old cultural and disciplinary boundaries are impossible to sustain, that what is needed is not merely new methods of approach to cope with the plethora of novelty that characterizes the contemporary West but also a demarcation of the terrain that will set radically new boundaries between disciplines: from which, as would also be the case with Deleuze and Guattari, one might approach, or at the very least gesture towards, a 'disciplinary state' within which there are no boundaries at all, a field and mode of inquiry characterized not by the dogmatic exigencies of subject and object but rather by flux and intensity, by mergings and separations, by slogans and instructions, by language in a condition of essential contortion.

Virilio, for example, is a military historian, architect, urban planner, photographer, cultural theorist, philosopher, film critic and peace strategist. In this mix of skills and disciplines one can simultaneously glimpse the outlines of the field of knowledge as it appears in the guise of modernity, a field principally characterized – and this is to become Virilio's most (paradoxically) enduring theme – by the evanescence consequent upon acceleration and speed:

> – With acceleration there is no more here and there, only the mental confusion of near and far, present and future, real and unreal – a mix of history, stories, and the hallucinatory utopia of communication technologies. (1995, 35)

Such a perspective, such a shattering of lineally conceived times and spaces, is essentially for Virilio a matter of nothing short of a revolution in information, and principally in the media, both those media apparently dedicated to information itself and those aspiring to entertainment:

> – Speed guarantees the secret and thus the value of all information. Liberating the media therefore means not only annihilating the duration of information – of the image and its path – but with these all that endures or persists. What the mass media attack in other institutions (democracy, justice, science, the arts, religion, morality, culture) is not the institutions themselves but the instinct of self-preservation that lies behind them. That is, what they still retain of bygone civilizations for whom everything was a material and spiritual preparation directed against disappearance and death, and in which communicating meant to survive, to remain. (1995, 53)

In Virilio, as we see here, there is a continuing enactment of a play between depth and surface; it is as though Freudian insights about the prevalence of the thanatic can be gestured towards, but to move too deeply into them would mean, as it were, to lose one's footing, to risk one's own critical disappearance before the flood of information, the mesmerizing flow of culture that has replaced or overturned the old boundaries. What Virilio conjures, especially in his best-known text Speed and Politics, in order to capture this new economy of sight and sound is the term 'dromology'. What is at stake here has its origins on the site of the urban revolution; the book opens with Engels' remark of 1848 that 'the first assemblies take place on the large boulevards, where Parisian life circulates with the greatest intensity' (1986, 3), and proceeds through a series of analyses of transitions and transformations in the relative speeds of life in city and countryside, paying particular attention to the military implications of various modulations of speed, from the 'time of the siege' to the era of mass mobilizations. Virilio offers an intrinsic connection between military development, urban planning and the fate of socialism, culminating in an assertion that

> today many people are discovering, somewhat late in the game, that once the 'first public transport' of the revolution has passed, socialism suddenly empties of its contents – except, perhaps, military (national defence) and police (security, incrimination, detention camps). (1986, 18)

It is difficult to say whether Virilio, a writer notable more for a certain stridency of tone than for subtlety of wit, meant to plant this ambiguity about 'public transport'; but certainly the equation thus proposed between *jouissance* and the mode of transport and communication, be it military road or suburban boulevard, would emblematize the inseparability he proposes between desire and movement, the inadequacy of any assessment of the political or sociocultural situation that fails to take into account the simple but all-important facts of access, travel, circulation and destination.

War is, for Virilio, both the enduring emblem and also the machinic driver behind these developments, which tend toward a wholly 'different' distribution of spaces, mobilities, even scales:

> ... in the modern arsenal, everything moves faster and faster; differences between one means and another fade away. A homogenising process is under way in the contemporary military structure, even inside the three arms specifications: ground, sea, and air is diminishing in the wake of an *aeronautical coalescence*, which clearly reduces the specificity of the land forces. But this homogenising movement of combat techniques and instruments of warfare is coupled to one last movement. This is, with the 'weapon-vehicle' *contraction* and the cybernetisation of the system, the volumetric reduction of military objects: *miniaturisation*. (1994a, 18)

I quote this passage as an example of how Virilio's military-historical analyses come to have a clear bearing on a contemporary phase of modernity, in this case of, to take a few re-localized instances, the 'style-cluster' of the 'urban combatant' on the streets of Brixton or Maryhill, the advent of the pseudo-militarized four-wheel-drive as vehicle/ weapon of choice for drug dealers and country vets, and the advent of the WAP-mobile phone.

Speed goes hand in hand with the development and exorbitation of the simulacrum, and the representation here which has always fascinated Virilio (with all the force, we might say, of a forbidden love) is the cinema. But the submersion of the subject in an undecidable play of simulacric forces goes deeper than this and exerts greater pressure on the key issue of technologization:

> Man, fascinated with himself, constructs his double, his intelligent spectre, and entrusts the keeping of his knowledge to a reflection. We're still here in the domain of cinematic illusion, of the mirage of information precipitated on the computer screen – what is given is exactly the information but not the sensation; it is *apatheia*, this scientific impassability which makes it so that the more informed man is the more the desert of the world expands around him, the more the repetition of information (already known) upsets the stimuli of observation, overtaking them automatically, not only in memory (interior light) but first of all in the look, to the point that from now on it's the speed of light itself which limits the reading of information and the important thing in electronic-information is no longer the storage but the display. (1991a, 46)

In modernity, wherever it might be situated against an uncertain background of a perhaps already disappeared realm of 'history', there is a constant emptying out, a demonic *kenosis* that paradoxically encloses desire and replaces its object with a – ghosts on the screen, spectral urban enemies who can never be caught, the shades of absent machines, 'motor-souls' passing invisibly in the night at unimaginable speeds. We might speak here, as Virilio does in *The Lost Dimension*, of the impossible ubiquity of the distant, of that which has already been (telekinetically) 'transported' – the telecommunicative, the 'tele-labourer', the 'tele-spectator', 'tele-local' machinery that is inevitably accompanied by the equipment of 'tele-informatics' (Virilio 1991b, 73–6).

In *Open Sky* Virilio will add to this armoury, this catalogue of the disappeared, a new term from the environs of the cinema and the VDU:

> After 'anthropocentrism' and 'geocentrism', our contemporary *savants* seem now to be in the grip of a new kind of illuminism, or rather **luminocentrism**, capable of hoodwinking them about the profound nature of space and time, the old perspective of the real space of the Quattrocento once again blocking the perspective of the real time of a horizonless cosmos. (1997, 5)

But in this depiction it is surely impossible to miss the tone of nostalgia, the longing for a 'real time' to appear somehow, mysteriously, within the emptied horizon of a cosmos become indeterminately lit, objectless. Onto this scenario comes the ghost of a long-past historical desire–

> According to Epicurus, *time is the accident to end all accidents*. If this is so, then with the teletechnologies of general interactivity we are entering the age of the **accident of the present**, this overhyped remote telepresence being only ever the sudden catastrophe of the reality of the present moment that is our sole entry into duration – but also, as everyone knows since Einstein, our entry into the expanse of the real world.

> After this, the real time of telecommunications would no longer refer only to delayed time, but also to an *ultra-chronology*. Hence my repeatedly reiterated proposal to round off the chronological (before, during, after) with the **dromological** or, if you like, the **chronoscopic** (underexposed, exposed, overexposed). (1997, 14–15)

Thus we return full circle to a dromology, to a science, or perhaps better practice, of speed and relativity; and to a field that is both populated with delights (everything available at the same time, sex while shopping) and yet simultaneously the abandoned site of the concentration camps and military defences that bulk so large – in *Bunker Archeology*, for example – in Virilio's war-conditioned imagination. What has happened, we might say, is that modernity has renounced its hauntings by the past, even if it has had to run so fast in order to do so that the world through which it speeds is reduced to flickers of ambiguous colour on an empty (cinema) screen; the fear is that were the motion to stop it would be to find other spectres, spectres of the present, crowding around the opaque windows of the protected carriage, demanding global redress for their exclusion from the last redoubt.

To turn from Virilio to Giorgio Agamben is to turn from city to study, from a hyperbolic repertoire of public gestures to a medieval intricacy of recourse. The scope of Agamben's work is similarly encyclopaedic, but his reference points are to be found in philology, linguistics, medieval poetics, the psychoanalysis of objects, the psychology of infancy, political theory. *Stanzas: Word and Phantasm in Western Culture*, for example, touches on medieval *acedia*; on Eros, mourning and melancholia; on the theory of fetishism; on Marx and the mystical character of labour; on Benjamin, Baudelaire and Beau Brummell; on the logos and the phantasm; on Narcissus and Pygmalion; on Oedipus and the Sphinx; and on Saussure and Derrida. The book reflects a pure myth of the Fall: the poetic sign, according to Agamben, achieved a fullness of representation in the thirteenth century, following which came an emptying of the sign's supposed plenitude. This structure of a fall from grace runs also through *Infancy and History: Essays on the Destruction of Experience*, from which I will quote a representative passage:

> The question of experience can be approached nowadays only with an acknowledgement that it is no longer accessible to us. For just as modern man has been deprived of his biography, his

experience has likewise been expropriated ... Today, however, we know that the destruction of experience no longer necessitates a catastrophe, and that humdrum daily life in any city will suffice. (Agamben 1993a, 13)

In tones reminiscent of Benjamin, whom he quotes, Agamben goes on to detail the quotidian effects of that negativity which he will elsewhere explore at a philosophical level. None of this, he claims, constitutes 'experience' for the modern man:

> Neither reading the newspaper, with its abundance of news that is irretrievably remote from his life, nor sitting for minutes on end at the wheel of his car in a traffic jam. Neither the journey through the nether world of the subway, nor the demonstration that suddenly blocks the street. Neither the cloud of tear gas slowly dispersing between the buildings of the city centre, nor the rapid blasts of gunfire from who knows where; nor queuing up at a business counter, nor visiting the Land of Cockayne at the supermarket, nor those eternal moments of dumb promiscuity among strangers in lifts and buses. (1993a, 13–14)

Thus far we may not seem too far from Virilio, although Agamben's prose is notably less hiatic, less hysterical, more sombre, more measured: we are in an apparently 'public' world, albeit one from which the meaning of 'public' has drained away, one based on an impossible, phantasmatic notion of plenitude from which we 'measure' (even if through an unavoidable disavowal) the curiously enclosed negativities of the present.

It might well be said that, if we put this together with Virilio, what we unearth from a difficult (bunkered) archaeology is the 'founding conundrum' of the discourse of modernity: namely, that we shall only consider modernity, in its technological fixations, its obsessive renunciations under the guise of pleasure, to have achieved its trajectory when we find ourselves *no longer able to write about it*; for the very act of our inscriptions inevitably recapitulates the mnemic trace, the obliteration of which is, according to these thinkers, modernity's destiny (and 'destiny', in its Nietzschean and Heideggerian articulations, is a repeated textualizing master-code).

Modern poetry, according to Agamben, is 'founded not on new experience, but on an unprecedented lack of experience' (Agamben 1993a, 41). What experience, we may fairly ask, is it that is textually absent, and how may we know its trace? It would seem possible, turning to *Language and Death: The Place of Negativity*, to reassign the epistemic break, for here it is the transcendentalist discourse signalled by Hegel and Hölderlin (and Kojève's laconic and urgent Hegel) that seems to serve to remind of the world we have lost. If the 'mute foundation' of a 'Voice' is

> the mystical foundation for our entire culture (its logic as well as its ethics, its theology as well as its politics, its wisdom as well as its madness) then the mystical is not something that can provide the foundation for another thought – attempting to think beyond the horizon of metaphysics, at the extreme confine of which, at the point of nihilism, we are still moving. The mystical is nothing but the unspeakable foundation; that is, the negative foundation of onto-theology. Only a liquidation of the mystical can open up the field to a thought (or language) that thinks (speaks) beyond the Voice and its *sigetics*; that dwells, that is, not on an unspeakable foundation, but in the infancy (*in-fari*) of man. (1991, 91)

How, though, does this critique link with modernity? In part, perhaps (and in the fuller articulation of this analysis the Jewish roots of Agamben's thought are important) in the figure of the modern student, whose prototype sits 'in a low-ceilinged room "in all things like a tomb", his elbows on his knees and his head in his hands', and whose 'most extreme exemplar is Bartleby, the scrivener who has ceased to write' (Agamben 1995, 65). Or only at the point of an extreme alteration in the concept of history, for

> History as we know it up to now has been no more than its own incessant putting off, and only at the point in which its pulsation is brought to a halt is there any hope of grasping the opportunity enclosed within it, before it gets betrayed into becoming one more historical/epochal adjournment. (1995, 88)

Or in, perhaps, the 'coming politics', the novelty of which will be '*that it will no longer be a struggle for the conquest or control of the State, but a struggle between the State and the non-State (humanity), an insurmountable disjunction between whatever singularity and the State organisation*' (1993b, 85, emphasis in original). The word 'whatever' is talismanic for Agamben, signifying a collaborative refusal, at the extreme limit of state power, by critic and actant to name and thus demolish their own activity; it is, one might like to say, the inscription on the tomb of the unknown thinker; and if it also seems to stand for precisely a conventional defeat of discursive specificity, a kind of high-school signing-off without content, then this would precisely redouble its symbolic force, as well as reminding us of one of Agamben's major works, *The Man without Content*.

The Man without Content is a book about art and aesthetics which points to the absence of art, the destructive power of aesthetics. It looks, as usual in Agamben, to a prior principle of unity, in this case the *Wunderkammer* wherein the 'work of art' would be displayed and thus achieve its meaning in the context of 'natural' curiosities, monsters, bizarrely represented perversions, aberrancies of all kinds; art not as mimesis of the norm but as a marginal representation of the impossible, a curiosity at a level with *trompe d'oeuil*.

> The interruption of tradition, which is for us now a *fait accompli*, opens an era in which no link is possible between old and new, if not the infinite accumulation of the old in a sort of monstrous archive or the alienation effected by the very means that is supposed to help with the transmission of the old ... Suspended in the void between old and new, past and future, man is projected into time as into something alien that incessantly eludes him and still drags him forward, but without allowing him to find his ground in it. (Agamben 1999a, 108)

Perhaps between Virilio's deluges, his drowning speeds and the painful struggles of Benjamin's Angel of History to keep his feet before the blowing gale, we might see Agamben's subject as dragged unwillingly, as into a mire, a swamp, an image of modernity as an obliterating, obscuring force, a further cover for emptiness.

The final words to the Introduction to *Homo Sacer* leave us with the flavour of this willy-nilly tug that can obliterate our best attempts at understanding: 'This book', Agamben says,

> which was originally conceived as a response to the bloody mystification of a new planetary order, therefore had to reckon with problems – first of all that of the sacredness of life – which the author had not, in the beginning, foreseen. In the course of the undertaking. . . it became clear that one cannot . . . accept as a guarantee any of the notions that the social sciences (from jurisprudence to anthropology) thought they had defined or presupposed as evident, and that many of these notions demanded – in the urgency of catastrophe – to be revised without reserve. (1998, 12)

Perhaps what is most surprising about this statement is that any theorist of modernity could have supposed at all the possibility of accepting 'guarantees' from the deeply compromised fields of jurisprudence or anthropology; we might also want to 'reckon with' Kristeva's linkage of the sacred with the schizophrenic, and with the whole question of what it might mean for an 'author' (of modernity) to 'in the beginning' *foresee*.

However, this inscription of revision is perhaps an essential (if unforeseen) feature of the texts of modernity and requires its own recourses: if Virilio's has been to the urban space, and Agamben's to a lost cultural infancy, that of Gianni Vattimo has increasingly been to the cloister and, eventually, to the bosom of Holy Mother Church. Such a trajectory, however, can be shown to have its origins in a by now predictable scenario, namely in an encounter with Nietzsche and Heidegger. *The Adventure of Difference: Philosophy after Nietzsche and Heidegger* touches upon modernity, perhaps, only through Vattimo's dealings with issues of *Überwindung* and *Verwindung* in relation to Heidegger's pronouncements on technology, and in particular with the nature of thinking as:

> The relation between deployed technology and the possibility that thinking may be able to put itself into a position of *Andenken* cannot be direct: *andenkend* thinking is not to be identified with technological thinking, nor is it prepared for by technological thinking, in the sense of being the dialectical outcome of technological thinking. The relation between *Andenken* and technology can only be oblique. (1993, 133)

In later works, however, Vattimo has addressed the consequences of this obliquity for modernity with considerable force. In, to take a major and well-known example, *The End of Modernity* he takes up the complex of issues surrounding the contested rhetorics of 'modernity' and the 'postmodern' and speaks unequivocally of modernity as

> dominated by the idea that the history of thought is a progressive 'enlightenment' which develops through an ever more complete appropriation and reappropriation of its own 'foundations'. These are often also understood to be 'origins', so that the theoretical and practical revolutions of Western history are presented and legitimated for the most part as 'recoveries', rebirths, or returns. (1988, 2)

What becomes immediately apparent at this point is that whatever it is that Vattimo is taking to be 'modernity', it is far more closely aligned with the problematics of western 'modernism' than with the notions espoused by either Virilio or Agamben. 'Modernity', he says later in the book,

> is primarily the era in which the increased circulation of goods ... and ideas, and increased social mobility ... bring into focus the value of the new and predispose the conditions for the identification of value (the value of Being itself) with the new. (1988, 100)

Vattimo's authorities here are Simmel and Gehlen; the focus is evidently on a certain phase of material and ideological production, the mobility of which, for example, has nothing whatever to do with Virilio's hectic history of speeds, nor with Agamben's deep (if weirdly belated) mistrust of the *méconnaissances* of jurisprudence or anthropology. What Vattimo is more concerned with is a detailed interrogation of the 'modern moment': in such a moment, he notices, 'progress seems to show a tendency to dissolve itself, and with it the value of the new as well', and 'this dissolution is the event that enables us to distance ourselves from the mechanism of modernity' (Vattimo 1988, 104). What, here, would constitute 'ourselves'? It would seem that Vattimo is speaking of a historically distanced scenario, rather than one that can be reduced to the mere simulacra of tele-distance.

In accordance with such a historicist, or pragmatic, turn Vattimo provides us with at least the beginning of a way in which the thus far unspoken 'foundation' of modernity (as a westernizing imperative, as the name of global free trade, as the excuse for US neo-imperialism, as the structure underpinning the unequal 'exchange' of 'goods' – in both senses – across the world) might be brought on stage, although it is couched in a further encounter with the Heideggerian and in a re-encounter with anthropology that seems rather after the fact. He says that

> the experience of the anthropologist who wishes to reject both the (Euro- or ethnocentric) evolutionary perspective and the illusion of a possible dialogue or interplay between different cultures is itself a deeply ambiguous one ... The ideal of an anthropology which would be the locus of an authentic encounter with the other – in accordance with a model which, in an over-simplistic and optimistic fashion, would make anthropology the rightful heir to philosophy after the end of the metaphysical epoch, when the hermeneutic perspective predominates – cannot be set in opposition to the notion of anthropology as a scientific description of the constants of all cultures, a notion that has been deeply conditioned by the metaphysical idea of science and, at a practical level, by Western domination of the planet. (1988, 157)

Although this inconclusive reflection might at first glance seem marginal to the 'project of modernity' (by which I mean to designate not a historical or cultural 'fact' but the constructed object of the discourses we are here discussing), I suggest that it is 'in fact' (by an essential postcolonial logic) central, for if there is the prospect of a discourse that is obliterated by modernity, then that discourse would be one that would inspect modernity's promises from a 'different' perspective – the perspective, for example, of China, within which context the modernizing project presents itself with a totally different force.

Vattimo does not pursue these insights, but what he does do, in *The Transparent Society*, and in particular in the chapter 'Utopia, Counter-Utopia, Irony', is provide us with an essential link, on the perhaps unlikely terrain of the film *Blade Runner* and its clones, between technology and the ruin. 'Paradoxically', he says,

> the post-apocalyptic condition these works describe is in some sense a happy one; that is, at least the atomic catastrophe that weighs upon us as a constant threat is imagined to have happened already, and for the survivors this somehow amounts to a form of liberation. A sense of liberation – albeit, as ever, paradoxical – also cloaks the retreat from technology and its products within the post-apocalyptic genre. (1992, 84)

Although he does not go on to discuss it in detail, what Vattimo here touches on is both an essential dialectic of expectation and also a reappraisal of the role of the ruin – the ruins of previous philosophical 'systems', the ruins of the city, the ruins of progressive thought swamped by the vicious divisions of that form of capitalism which is conventionally referred to as 'late', as though its succession by some unimaginably different form, some unimaginable form of difference, were somehow already on the (already foreclosed) global horizon.

But perhaps it is in *Beyond Interpretation: The Meaning of Hermeneutics for Philosophy* that Vattimo most clearly shows both the promise and the defeat of the circular Heideggerian approach to the sacred – and fatal – triptych of metaphysics, modernity and technology:

> The relation of hermeneutics to modern techno-science breaks with all metaphysical and humanist associations when hermeneutics, taking science seriously as a determinant factor in the configuration of Being in modernity, grasps the essential nihilistic meaning of science which is at the same time constitutive of its own destiny. The world as a conflict of interpretations and nothing more is not an image of the world that has to be defended against the realism and positivism of science. It is modern science, heir and completion of metaphysics, that turns the world into a place where there are no (longer) facts, only interpretations. (1997, 26)

The fatal hinge here is 'destiny', the notion that in the hypostasized motion beyond all human control that characterizes the 'progress' of modernism – or perhaps of 'techno-science', whatever that might be – there remains the ineradicable shade of a transcendental meaning towards which culture continues to move, even if that destiny be one of disaster. It is at this point, I would say, that the radicalism derivable from the Nietzschean and Heideggerian models decisively reveals its 'other', the way in which such anti-metaphysical moves, such anti-technological scepticisms, can be automatically – somnambulistically – inverted to provide a further lock on the door to the future.

Modernity, to conclude, may be seen to appear in the works of Virilio, Agamben and Vattimo as a doubly constructed object, constructed first on the site of a global westernizing project and second in the complexly dialectical discourse of theorists who would seek both to espouse – or emulate – the rapidity of its motion and to halt its flow through the appropriation of technological anxieties. What gets ignored in this process is, among other things, the violence which is masked by the smooth flow of 'the modern'. The shades of Nietzsche and Heidegger (even when accompanied by a Japanese interlocutor) serve further to embed the discourse of modernity within a Eurocentric frame, from which the wider consequences of modernization – global warming, the destruction of the environment, the perpetuation of inequities in the international division of labour – are ever more permanently exiled.

In thinking about Virilio, Agamben and Vattimo, perhaps the most salient approach would be through a new (postal) geography. To what addresses are these messages sent? Through what customs points, what passport control, do they pass in their claim on a 'planetary' interpretation of technology? Perhaps even more saliently: what is accomplished by the continuing reduction of the plethora of burgeoning technologies to a single, unitary category of 'techno-science'? It might be suggested that the era in which such a concept could adequately represent such a multiplicity is long gone: Virilio's deployment of weapons science, Agamben's understanding of medieval physics, Vattimo's dealings with the techno, which serves, as it turns out, to be a prelude to a re-espousal of Catholicism – how far do these go in outstripping the complexities of techno-insertion into the heart of the disasters of the global economy, the disavowals and violences signified in the notion of a modernizing 'new world order'?

David Punter

Further reading and works cited

Agamben, G. *Language and Death*. Minneapolis, IN, 1991.
—. *Infancy and History*. London, 1993a.
—. *The Coming Community*. Minneapolis, IN, 1993b.
—. *Stanzas*. Minneapolis, IN, 1993c.
—. *Idea of Prose*. Albany, NY, 1995.
—. *Homo Sacer*. Stanford, CA, 1998.
—. *The Man without Content*. Stanford, CA, 1999a.
—. *The End of the Poem*. Stanford, CA, 1999b.
Der Derian, J. (ed.) *The Virilio Reader*. Oxford, 1998.
Derrida, J. and Vattimo, G. (eds) *Religion*. Cambridge, 1998.
Vattimo, G. *The Transparent Society*. Cambridge, 1992.
—. *The Adventure of Difference*. Cambridge, 1993.
—. *Beyond Interpretation*. Cambridge, 1997.
—. *Belief*. Cambridge, 1999.

Virlio, P. *Speed and Politics*. New York, 1986.
—. *War and Cinema*. London, 1989.
—. *The Aesthetics of Disappearance*. New York, 1991a.
—. *The Lost Dimension*. New York, 1991b.
—. *Bunker Archeology*. New York, 1994a.
—. *The Vision Machine*. Bloomington, 1994b.
—. *The Art of the Motor*. Minneapolis, IN, 1995.
—. *Open Sky*. London, 1997.
—. *The End of Modernity*. Cambridge, 1998.
—. *Polar Inertia*. London, 2000.

Hélène Cixous (1938–)

Hélène Cixous, critic, poet, playwright, novelist, academic innovator, has bent her work in all domains of her activity toward recognizing and exploring *sexual difference* in language and literature. She has insisted unyieldingly on *woman* – a stance that has proved as enigmatic as it is controversial. Because of it, she early came into conflict with a French feminism that had adopted a militant stance regarding the sexes as absolutely equal and interchangeable (e.g., Monique Wittig). In Anglo-American feminist and critical culture Cixous was quickly labelled an 'idealist', 'uneasy about the power of words to hold out against the power of opposition' (Schiach 1991, 33). Her peculiar way of moving back and forth among 'text, performance, unconscious, and biography' (33) has also puzzled many of her readers: but this is Cixous' way of holding out against the inevitable hierarchies that oppositions always bring in their wake. She has indeed baffled critical categories, yet this is also her point: Cixous has held out for the recognition of sexual difference and of 'woman' and made them essentially into non-negotiable demands for critical theory and literary practice with a view to impeding the rigid and false categorizations that arise with sexual opposition. For her, woman is something 'more' than her subjection to the phallic signifier, but in this more, some of her critics have labelled her an 'essentialist'. Yet, no one but Shakespeare, perhaps, has had so fluid a sense that both sexes may at once occupy one body, at least in the 'country of literature'. In an age, she says, where *inscription* has displaced the older literary forms of *representation* and *expression*, we need to acknowledge sexuality in art in order to transcend it. If she has, at times, described herself as 'a woman made of women' (in Cixous 1990, 203), at others, she paints her artistic process as a playwright by claiming that she not only can but that she must reach a way to identify herself with 'man' in order to write:

> I write as a woman ... I can use my body to inscribe the body of a woman. But I can't do that for a man [in prose] ... There are plenty of men in my plays. But that is because the theater is not the scene of sexual pleasure ... in the theater it's the heart that sings. And the human heart has no sex. Sexually, I cannot identify with a male character. Yet the heart feels the same way in man's breast as in a woman's.

Cixous' reasons for her stance on sexual difference have, moreover, a sound philosophical, analytic and literary grounding that has nothing to do with 'biologism', 'essentialism' or anti-equalitarianism. They do, however, have a great deal to do with her alliance with the anti-Hegelian strain in French thinking, a position common to her fellow theorists Jacques Derrida, Michel Foucault and Jean-François Lyotard, not to mention Jacques Lacan. In standing firm for the recognition of sexual difference, Cixous has intended to strike a blow against the 'metaphysics' of opposition in which any difference tends inevitably toward becoming binarily opposed concepts where one always yields to the dominion of the other, à la Hegel. The case of sex is egregious in this respect: the domination of feminine by masculine in western culture is long-standing. An anti-Hegelian stance was, of course, also adopted by the leading male philosophers and critical theorists of Cixous' Parisian circle, but in her hands it is modified in a unique way. Cixous took it upon herself to work out, through the very language that fosters metaphysical skewing, new strategies for 'righting' the system, correcting the imbalance, and providing for what been silenced, engulfed or incorporated by its opposite to have its 'say.' That is why her first major theoretical statements take a poetic, hysterical form: as poetry is repressed by prose, a hysteric's sexual ambivalence is repressed by the prevailing order of binary sexual oppositions.

Cixous' theory often has a militant tone, but it is the tone of someone who takes language as the most serious means of combat: her 'Sorties' of 1975 (in Cixous and Clément 1988) means both 'exits' or the 'way out' and the excursive raids made by a garrison under siege to lift it. Like her fellow émigré to France, Julia Kristeva, Cixous designates the 'way out' of the impasses of contemporary culture and politics as existing in the nether side of language. Unlike Kristeva, Cixous sees human being entirely made of language, so that the raids made by the underside of language are at the same time the same as those made by what Kristeva would call 'the body' or 'the woman'. For Cixous, both body and woman are linguistic effects, but that very fact makes them capable of subverting the language that oppresses them. Where Kristeva's 'revolution in poetic language' locates a choric reserve of 'semiotic' rhythms that disrupt surface discourse but do not overthrow it, however, Cixous is determined to have the feminine rewrite and re-invent that 'surface'.

When Cixous founded the first programme of doctoral studies in Études Féminines in France at Paris VIII (Vincennes) in 1974, she had been Chair of the English Department at the University of Paris at Nanterre since 1967. Even as head of the new programme she continued to direct English doctoral studies: she was, after all, an internationally acclaimed Joyce scholar, and, at age 40, the youngest holder of the doctorat d'état in France, having published her major thesis on Joyce (The Exile of James Joyce) and written a minor thesis on Robinson Jeffers. Within the university system, the emphasis on women in Études féminines was most radical politically. Cixous has, however, claimed that, at the time, she would have greatly preferred to title the new doctoral programme 'Studies in Sexual Difference' (Calle-Gruber 1994, 211). If she was not simply after the 'study of women', what then did Cixous seemingly have in mind in pursuing the politics of feminine studies, the practices of feminine writing and the strategies of feminine reading (see Schiach 1991, 38ff.)? What did 'sexual difference' really mean to Cixous?

It meant that there are two different logical positions that can be taken within language (language being what defines human being as such) and that these go by the name of masculine and feminine. The two perspectives do not fully overlap nor do they diverge completely; they hold a common, vacuous centre – the phallic signifier – but they appropriate or resist it in different ways. In short, they specify two distinctive ways of apprehending and reflecting certain universal human predicaments.

Cixous' commitment to the problematic of difference is linked to her more or less absolute commitment to *literary* language. It is a commitment that has clearly shaped her institutional practices (she insisted on hiring mainly leading creative writers at Vincennes: Butor, Cortazar, and 'poetic' literary critics like Jean-Pierre Richard and Tzvetan Todorov to teach there). It has also deeply informed her theories of feminine writing (*écriture féminine*) and shaped her literary criticism into a uniquely poetic prose. It is crucial to note that her procedure as critic, writer and reader is to force sexual difference to the surface of writing – be it theoretical, dramatic, political, or poetic in nature – so that the writing at last comes to mirror the schism of language, the internal limit that each 'sex' poses to the other within the 'same' language. The goal is not to achieve a Hegelian *sublation*; it is, rather, to accomplish its aesthetic *sublimation* by the 'emptying of the subject' of sex: its capacity for enjoyment is unlocked, but only – and this seems to be crucial for understanding Cixous – at the literary level. She does not seem inclined to bring the programme into everyday life except where life itself has attained poetic insight.

It is thus entirely legitimate, in Cixous' critical theory, to tie literary language to the particular biography and elective theoretical alliances and affective political allegiances of its author. The theme of exile in language, for example, has often informed her theory of poetry. It has drawn her to write about poets like Osip Mandelstam (whom she pairs, unexpectedly, with Nelson Mandela on the basis of the common part-signifier in their names (Cixous 1988)), Anna Akhmatova and Tasso, playwrights like Kleist and Shakespeare, and novelists like Kafka and Joyce, whose language bears the indelible mark of an internal exile. At the same time, Cixous conscientiously admits that her critical predilection for such authors is rooted in her own sense of the linguistic exile she felt as a child of Jewish parents (one of Spanish descent whose family had lived in Morocco, the other an Austro-Hungarian who emigrated from *Mitteleuropa* in 1933) in largely French and Arab speaking Algeria.

Cixous depicts her own particular 'coming to language' as shaping her poetic as well as her critical practice. Her earliest discussion of her artistic process (*La Venue à l'Écriture*, 1977) links it to the fact that, as a child in her peculiar circumstances, she found herself opened to the heteroglossic light that different tongues shed upon each other. For her a language exists beyond languages, something like Benjamin's *reine Sprache* that is 'universal' to human being, but it is a *concrete* universal that she calls different 'countries' in language: the country of poetry, the country of theatre. This 'universal' face is always particularized by reference to her own familial biography: she looks to her father (and his premature death when she was eleven) as crucial for bending her toward poetry in her earliest reflections, but by her 1994 book, Hélène Cixous, *photos de racines* (Calle-Gruber and Cixous), Cixous also begins to track part of the history of her own poetic language to her maternal language, German, with its particular resonances and rhythms.

The authors toward whom Cixous has been drawn in her criticism, from Lispector to Joyce, are generally those who most intensely mark the dramatic rise of a repressed side of language to the surface of discourse. That this 'repressed' or deeply alienated part of language more often than not bears a feminine figure (like Molly Bloom) may account for another aspect of her focus on *woman*. Cixous sees the direct effect of poetic and literary language as having greater power than political engagement or a social choice to grant a voice to what has been unable to speak for itself. When Cixous restaged Sophocles, for example, in her opera, *Le nom d'Oedipe* (1978), she focused on Jocasta, the mother-wife that the ancient playwright all but overlooks as a dramatic presence. When she wrote her first play, *Portrait de Dora* (1976a) (a great success), she dramatized Freud's 'Case of

Hysteria' from the point of view of the analysand, young Dora, and not from that of the good doctor.

Cixous' closest theoretical ally thus seems to be Jacques Derrida (with whom she began discussing Joyce in 1962). His *Glas* influenced her take on Hegel more than a little, as did his work on the critical role of *écriture* in his 'Freud and the Scene of Writing', and his *De la grammatologie*. Cixous' political engagements, always passionate, found expression in close work with Michel Foucault, with whom she examined (and protested through a kind of guerrilla theatre) prison conditions in France. Psychoanalytically – although this is not generally recognized in Anglo-American circles – she is also linked to Jacques Lacan, to whom, of course, most critics assume she is strictly 'opposed' (Sellers 1996, 6, 47). But Cixous's resistance to oppositional thinking should already indicate that her relation to the body of Lacan's work is not simple.

Even if we wished to speak about Cixous purely as a critic (which, given the enormous corpus of her critical work, would be entirely legitimate) it would not be possible to separate her theory from her life entirely; in her theory, no clear demarcation between them is possible. Thus interjecting some of the biographical record may clarify her relation to the thought of Lacan. Lacan was interested in James Joyce, about whom he would eventually write in his seminar on *Le Sinthome*. Because of her great knowledge of Joyce, Cixous' thesis director, Jean-Jacques Mayoux, introduced her to Lacan, and she and Lacan worked together for two years, from 1963 to 1965. Her long-time partner Antoinette Fouque, a political activist in the *Mouvement des femmes* and co-founder of the publishing house, Éditions des femmes, was analysed by Lacan, creating another tie between Cixous' sensibilities and the French teacher of Freud.

In terms of theory, we can say that, like Lacan, Cixous sees human 'life' as an effect of a signifier that excises *jouissance* from reason and from a social life that is ruled by the Law (of language). From Lacan and from Freud both, Cixous learned to appreciate the degree to which language *is* the essence of human life, and that when woman's speech (or anyone else's speech, for that matter) is radically impeded, cut off by cultural limits, that life becomes the object of unleashed, irrational forces of repression as well as the return of the anguishing presence Lacan termed *jouissance*. In the place of a *vouloir-dire* (literally, a 'meaning', but also etymologically, 'a wanting-to-say'), the repressed subject produces only stifled gestures, awkward jerks inconsonant with verbal expression – the kind of verbal expression that grants masculine speakers social rewards and assures them their social place and psychological balance.

Those in command of the word can hide behind it – behind the mask that speech provides (recall Stendhal's dictum that 'words were made to hide men's thoughts'). The hysteric's unbidden gesture is, by contrast, all too visible – to the point that it becomes a 'writing' that can never stop writing itself, even and especially when all avenues of speech are cut off to it. Cixous's aim, in 'The Laugh of the Medusa' and in 'Sorties', is to read the *writing* in hysteria, to read its proto-*écriture féminine*.

In her best-known longer critical work, *The Newly Born Woman* (1975, with Catherine Clément), Cixous and Clément use quotations from Lacan to contest Freud's too narrow view of women. Lacan's own work on sexual difference, *Encore*, appeared the same year (having been offered by him as his seminar of 1972–3). Freud's view of women inspires them to bring out the most subversive feminine positions to challenge male-dominant 'rational' culture – positions that, because they threaten male dominance, have long been severely repressed. One such energetic resource is sorcery and witchcraft.

It is difficult not to read Cixous' criticism and her creative work, especially the 'history plays' she has written, without thinking of hers as an activist social stance. She has resisted the political repression of artists and, more generally, of those, like Nelson Mandela, 'whose word has not been heard for twenty six years' (1990, 196). Yet it cannot be said that her activism has a social as much as it has a literary basis. Her interest in the work of Mauss on 'the gift' and her disdain for consumerism (Schiach 1991, 20ff.) are tied less to an organized political positions than they are to her sense that masculine-based cultures and economies are deeply weakened by a failure to recognize 'the other sex', and that in every domain culture stands in strong need of supplementation not only by a feminine perspective, but by the kind of irrepressible disruption that alone allows the unspoken to be said.

In her life and work Cixous can thus be said to exemplify the comprehensiveness, scope and uniqueness that she believes 'woman' as the revenge of the repressed can bring to bear on those cultural domains traditionally foreclosed to her. But not only 'woman'. For Cixous, woman is more or less the emblem of a power, an energy in language that has been prematurely stifled by a culture of the (phallic) signifier. The hallmark of her own critical prose is its singular power to compress grand philosophical, political and psychoanalytic theories into tellingly pithy, epigrammatic formulations that communicate explosively their critical stance as much through their handling of the signifier – language, sound, rhythm, style – as through systematic exposition and, at times, bitter irony. For example, for her critiques of Freud in La Jeune née [The Newly Born Woman, 1975] and in Le rire de la Méduse ['The Laugh of the Medusa', 1981] Cixous consciously adopts a 'hysterical' persona and tone that become no small part of the criticism she launches. Her way of responding to Hegel's overbearing metaphysical oppositions is to penetrate one side by the other, and to take the most abstract metaphysical concepts and imbue them with familiar objects – especially sex and feminine jouissance ('Sorties', in Cixous and Clément, 1988). Cixous' critical reproaches of Hegel are worthy of Kierkegaard and made in the same spirit, but Cixous' texts could never have been written by the Danish male philosopher in the special feminine way central to Cixous' language. Nor does her prose resemble that of Kristeva, who is equally informed in linguistic and philosophical theory, but whose highly theoretical prose could never be mistaken for Cixous poetically condensed formulations.

It is important to return once more to Cixous' double insistence on woman and on sexual difference. It is a stance that distinguishes her markedly from Judith Butler who, like Cixous, is allied with Derridean deconstruction, but whose fundamental orientation remains Hegelian. Butler, too, contests the 'Hegelian' binary opposition between masculine and feminine (in which one must succumb to the other); her technique is to 'subvert' gender repressions by undermining and loosening the cultural codings of gender, detaching gender from any necessary biological or any linguistic tie to the subject. Cixous' approach sounds superficially similar, but it is really quite different, for she is committed to the struggle within language as such; to wresting the subject free from language by means of language itself. Cixous' argument with the feminist position of egalitarianism is that it is premature and may too quickly override what of 'woman' still needs to be explored, what woman may yield for the arsenal needed to combat language's insistent categorizations. Cixous does not work at the level of shifting surface personae, or masks, like Butler. She instead works her way through language and its laws to the surface: for Cixous, it is the moment of surfacing that counts. Liberation must be constantly re-secured through intimate linguistic struggle that takes the full measure of its opponent's force and dominance.

The critical distinction to be drawn between Cixous's adherence to the principle of sexual difference and that of Lacan is that, for Lacan, sexual difference as such is *the* response of the subject to the effect of the signifier. Cixous has, by using psychoanalytic thought 'creatively', placed herself more in the Derridean deconstructive camp than in the scientific rigour of Freudian-Lacanian thought, to which she (and Derrida) remain, of course, also indebted. For Lacan, the sexualized response to the traumatic alienation of the subject by the signifier dates from the subject's very first encounter with the signifier, with language, with the phallus coming to the rescue and organizing the disarray the signifier introduces into the subject. This encounter structures the logic of the psyche and thus of sex for each subject. For Cixous, in contrast, *writing* – the fact of inscription – voids such unconscious structuring. Writing empties out the subject and makes it available for adopting either masculine or feminine postures – or even a mix of both. This is a mixing that psychoanalysis reserves only for hysteria and to perversion. Cixous appropriates hysteria's unique writing for her dramatic art. Dramatic art sustains (and may even require) the sublimation of sex. Poetry and novel – which operate in the intimate sphere – can, however, never dispense with a sexuality, for sexuality is what defines one's subjective being.

For Cixous, 'masculine' and 'feminine' are nothing more than orientations toward language and its logic – orientations that affect the body and soul alike and are the source of sexual energy. As a creative artist, Cixous has made full use of this energy, derived from an original principle of clivage in much the same way that Hazlitt said Shakespeare did: she works her way toward the emptying out of its cultural remainders, the restrictions produced by the metaphysics of oppositional thinking, but she does so only in order to be able to inhabit other subjects that she *artfully* produces as linguistic effects. At the level of art, sexual difference is neither a given, nor an eternal opposition, but a fundamental principle of insight. In her essay, 'The Two Countries of Writing', Cixous says:

> 'I'm mostly composed of 'women' – quite by chance. I have no trace of my grandfathers except as being wiped out of life. And neither of my grandmothers had traces of grandfathers . . . So I am mostly peopled with 'women.' And it's probably made me write the way I write. I might have been composed of 'men;' and I would have written differently. But then, what are 'men' or 'women' composed of? (Cixous 1990, 197)

The implication is that men and women are composed of language, of effects of the signifier, as Lacan put it.

If one were to make a global assessment of Cixous' critical stance, one would have to place it in the line of German critical romanticism, from Schlegel to Benjamin, in which the transcendence of traditional oppositions opens up the critical beauty of *Kunstprosa*. It is in this context that Cixous' theory and her politics of writing come together in what is perhaps her most interesting *Gesammtwerk* – her 'history plays'. In her collaborations with Ariane Mnouchkine at the Théâtre du Soleil in Paris – on *The Terrible but Unfinished Story of Norodom Sihanouk, King of Cambodia* (1985) and her very popular *L'Indiade* (1987) – all of Cixous' major poetic, theoretical and political practices join together to produce major literary works.

Juliet Flower MacCannell

Further reading and works cited

Calle-Gruber, M. and Cixous, H. 'Portrait de l'écriture' and 'Générique', in *Hélène Cixous, photos de racines*. Paris, 1994.

Cixous, H. *Portrait de Dora*. Paris, 1976a.

—. *The Exile of James Joyce*. London, 1976b.

—. 'The Laugh of the Medusa', in *The Signs Reader*, eds E. Abel and E. K. Abel. Chicago, 1983.

—. *Le Nom d'Oedipe: Chant du corps interdit*. Paris, 1978.

—. *L'Indiade, ou, l'Inde de leurs rêves: et quelques écrits sur le théâtre*. Paris, 1987.

—. *Manne aux Mandelstams aux Mandelas*. Paris, 1988.

—. 'The Two Countries of Writing: Theater and Poetical Fiction', in *The Other Perspective in Gender and Culture*, ed. J. Flower MacCannell. New York, 1990.

—. *The Terrible but Unfinished Story of Norodom Sihanouk, King of Cambodia*. Lincoln, NR, 1994.

—. *Rootprints*. London, 1997.

— and Clément, C. *The Newly Born Woman*, intro. S. Gilbert. Minneapolis, MN, 1975.

Conley, V. Andermatt. *Hélène Cixous: Writing the Feminine*. Lincoln, NE, 1984.

—. *Hélène Cixous*. Toronto, 1992.

Derrida, J. *De la grammatologie*. Paris, 1967.

Foucault, M. and Cixous, H. '"A propos de Marguerite Duras", par Michel Foucault et Cixous', *Cahiers Renaud-Barrault*, 89 (1975).

Sellers, S. *Hélène Cixous*. Cambridge, 1996.

Shiach, M. *Hélène Cixous*. London, 1991.

Philippe Lacoue-Labarthe (1940–) and Jean-Luc Nancy (1940–)

Philippe Lacoue-Labarthe and Jean-Luc Nancy have co-authored important commentaries on some of the decisive texts of our modernity. In 1980, they assembled a conference called 'Les Fins de l'homme: à partir du travail de Jacques Derrida' and, in December of the same year, they co-founded the 'Center for Philosophical Research on the Political', which ran until 1984 and produced two volumes of collected writings (*Rejouer le politique*, 1981 and *Le retrait du politique*, 1982). Their individual publications are not only impressively numerous (far outnumbering their co-authored work), but also impressively diverse, ranging from learned discussions of painting, poetry and music to intricate meditations on freedom and community, subjectivity and mimesis.

Most readers of Lacoue-Labarthe's and Nancy's work will attest to both its usefulness and its difficulty. For over thirty years, their writings and lectures have proved a fecund and indispensable resource for students and scholars interested in literary theory. This necessity is dictated not only by the formidable consensus of academic response (both favourable *and* unfavourable) to their work, but also by the highly instructive nature of the work itself. Studying a text or a question Lacoue-Labarthe and Nancy have treated without consulting what they have said is like missing a crucial lecture.

Perhaps the best testimony to their pedagogical exemplarity as readers comes from those they have submitted to close reading. One, Jacques Lacan, started a 1973 seminar by strongly urging his students to read *The Title of the Letter*. Not usually disposed to praising his commentators, Lacan continued:

> I can say, in a way, it is a question of reading, that I have never been read so well – with so much love . . . We shall say, then, that this is a model of good reading, so much so that I am able to say that I regret never having obtained anything close to it from my followers. (Lacoue-Labarthe and Nancy 1992, vii)

Whether their object is Plato or Aristotle, Descartes or Kant, Schlegel or Schelling, Nietzsche or Heidegger, Blanchot or Bataille, Derrida or Girard, Lacoue-Labarthe and Nancy give us models of good reading – so good, in fact, rarely does anything else come close.

On the other hand, their texts are exceptionally difficult. I would like to dwell for a moment on this difficulty in order to accentuate the constitutive and irreducible role difficulty itself plays in their thinking. One of the first difficulties a new reader will encounter in coming to Lacoue-Labarthe and Nancy, especially one unfamiliar with continental philosophy, is the presupposition of a certain philosophical knowledge. This is itself a familiar objection lodged against 'high theory': theory's assumption that we are already well versed in the concepts, arguments and idioms of an immense and difficult philosophical tradition. It is true that Lacoue-Labarthe and Nancy undertake, for the most part, philosophical readings of (diverse) texts. Their readings mobilize various terms and concepts which are weighted with a specialized and frequently quite complicated meaning; in the movement of their commentary, in their attempt to get from one point to the next, these items are not always unpacked for the 'lay' reader. To be fair, however, Lacoue-Labarthe and Nancy never attempt to burden one with verbal jargon. They use technical-theoretical terminology only in so far as it facilitates their travel. Moreover, they frequently circle back on their language. In the manner of good teachers and translators, they take time to explicate the sense of key words or phrases, remind us of their provenance and descent, their valence and limitations. See, for example, the carefully layered, historical delineation of the term romanticism which prefaces *The Literary Absolute*; or, in their study of Lacan, the helpful explanation of the slippery materiality of the letter and of the crucial role it plays in his constitution (or de-constitution) of the subject (Lacoue-Labarthe and Nancy 1992, 27–32); or the patient tracing of Freud's axiomatic (but unfinished) theory of *identification*, a theory which both grounds and shakes his construction of sociality (Lacoue-Labarthe and Nancy 1989, 1991 and 1997, 1–31).

But there is a more fundamental, and more fundamentally difficult, philosophical presupposition at work in Lacoue-Labarthe's and Nancy's readings. This 'given' which shapes the mode of their inquiry does not involve (at least not primarily) the marshalling of a philosophical vocabulary, tone or posture. Rather, it concerns what the two call *the philosophical*. The generalized tenor of this term seeks to distinguish it from this or that philosophical system, literature, practice or tradition. In 'The "Retreat" of the Political', Lacoue-Labarthe and Nancy define the philosophical as 'a general historico-systematic structure – which, up until recently, one could have called the West – of which philosophy is each time the thematisation, the prefiguration or the anticipation, the reflection (critical or not), the contestation, etc., but which largely overflows the basically restricted field of operations of actual philosophising' (1997, 124).

I call this philosophical premise of their work difficult for several reasons. Difficult, first of all, in the sense of hard to understand and easy to misconstrue. Lacoue-Labarthe and Nancy set up shop in the work space hollowed out by Heidegger's *Destruktion* ('destructuring', 'dismantling') of western metaphysics. This project of destructuring metaphysics follows from the recognition that metaphysics is closed or finished. This critical movement – philosophy is closed, therefore we must dismantle it – would be a non sequitur if the close of philosophy were (mis)taken to mean that philosophy is simply over and out, ineffectual and irrelevant. On the contrary, as Lacoue-Labarthe and Nancy put it, ' "closure" indicates, first of all, the completion of a program ... *and* the constraint of a programming' (Lacoue-Labarthe and Nancy 1997, 125). The exigency of deconstruction emerges from the recognition of philosophy's programmatic endgame, its deathgrip on our modernity.

A related and widely spread misunderstanding which arises from Heidegger's thesis about the end of metaphysics is the notion that if we really want to end metaphysics all we need to do is stop talking about it and move on to something else. A good deal of the politically well-intentioned impatience or hostility towards 'French Heideggereanism' derives, I think, from just this commonsensical view that the endless chatter about the end of philosophy is basically disingenuous. Certainly, when Heidegger says 'Metaphysics cannot be abolished like an opinion' (1993, 67) we do not have to take him at his word; that is, he might only be expressing an opinion. But the least we can do as readers, as Lacoue-Labarthe and Nancy do with equal measures of fidelity and resistance, is to take Heidegger at his word, taking seriously the premise of metaphysics (in both turns of the genitive).

Nowhere is this difficulty more clearly inscribed than in the opening to Lacoue-Labarthe's *Heidegger, Art and Politics*. Echoing the line from Heidegger cited above, Lacoue-Labarthe writes: 'We cannot pass beyond the limit, or what Heidegger called the "closure". We are still living on philosophical ground and we cannot just go and live somewhere else' (1990, 3). Perhaps we need to read these lines in context to hear that they are not spoken in a self-satisfied tone. Terry Eagleton reminds us that for Marx social class is not just an empty metaphysical category, but a form of social alienation. It cannot simply be wished away; 'to undo this alienation you [have] to go, not around class, but somehow all the way through it and out the other side' (1990, 23). Marxists do not dwell on class in order to indulge in the identity it confers or the symbolic distinction it brings, but rather to get out of it. There is a comparable predicament in Lacoue-Labarthe's (and Nancy's) relation to the philosophical. The tone of 'we cannot just go and live somewhere else' is not only sober and severe, but is tinged with a certain anguish or melancholy, a rigorously negated desire to do just that, to 'go and live somewhere else'. The difference between being constrained by metaphysics and being constrained by class, however, is that there is no way of getting out of the former. This places the philosopher in a truly difficult situation. For Lacoue-Labarthe the difficulty of dwelling on this side of philosophy's limit gives rise to a paradoxical imperative: that we no longer desire philosophy and yet desire nothing else, 'that we let philosophy collapse within ourselves and that we open ourselves up to that diminishing, that exhaustion of philosophy, today' (1990, 5). Such a frankly conflicted relationship to philosophy's exhaustion can hardly be deciphered as a calculated recovery of philosophical discourse. Rather, it describes the obligation of a thinker who finds himself enfolded in the unending 'today' of metaphysics.

This difficult, paradoxical experience of his own philosophical orientation relates to another, more spectacular difficulty – namely, the problem of 'Heidegger'. Some chroniclers of the 'Heidegger affair' have contended that the publication of Victor Farias's book

Heidegger et le Nazisme (1987) forced 'French Heideggereans' to awaken from their dogmatic slumber and retreat into a defensive posture. Whatever the accuracy of such a claim, a few things need to be underscored in the case of Lacoue-Labarthe and Nancy. First, the dreadful correspondence between Heidegger's engagement with Nazism and certain aspects of his thought does not come as a surprise to them in 1987. On the contrary, the question of the relation between Heidegger and Nazism in particular, and philosophy and politics in general, animates their teaching and writing since at least the mid–1970s. Second, their paradoxical relationship to the philosophical can only be fully understood in this highly *political* context. For them, it is not a question of 'salvaging' Heidegger but of asking: *given* that Heidegger was the greatest thinker of his century, the one who gave us the most to think, what was it in his thinking that allowed for, or was not sufficiently vigilant to prevent, its (and his) affiliation with the very worst. Finally, taking such a critical stance towards Heidegger presupposes they do not identify what they are doing with any 'Heideggereanism' – for if such a thing exists *in* Heidegger it would be found in those moments of his thought where he abandons the ceaseless interrogation of philosophy for philosophy proper.

Years before the 'Heidegger affair' broke in France, Lacoue-Labarthe and Nancy had begun to bend their philosophical commentary in a political direction. Indeed, the 'Center for Philosophical Research on the Political' was founded in order to enable a serious philosophical questioning of politics – or rather, not politics (*la politique*), but the political (*le politique*); not an analysis of political positions, struggles and ideologies (the domain of political science), nor a reflection on the *specificity* of the political (the domain of political theory), but an inquiry about what constitutes the '*essence* of the political'. Taking their cue from Jacques Derrida's essay 'The Ends of Man', Lacoue-Labarthe and Nancy note in their opening address to the Center:

> What today appears to us necessary, and hence urgent, is rigorously to account for what we are calling the essential (and not accidental or simply historical) co-belonging of the philosophical and the political. In other words, to account for the political as a philosophical determination, and vice versa. (1997, 109)

Of these two research aims, they place special emphasis on the latter: re-examining the philosophical *as* the political. This does not mean excavating the politics of philosophy, probing philosophy's practical agendas, ideological ramifications, or political conse-quences. Rather, it means treating 'western' thought as essentially political from its very beginnings.

Rethinking metaphysics *politically* marks a significant and productive swerve from the path Heidegger lays down. Much of what is stirring and original in Lacoue-Labarthe's and Nancy's later, single-authored work develops out of their collective investigations of the political. But what do they mean by the political? If their understanding of the philo-sophical is deeply indebted to Heidegger's understanding of western metaphysics, then it follows that the political might just as well be thought under Heidegger's rubric of *der Technik* (technology or, more accurately, *technics*, on this latter translation, see, Weber 1996, 59–60). But while the political shadows (follows and retraces) the rich critical motifs which cluster around the theme of technology – including the operationalization of knowledge, the anthropological valorization of work, the globalization of techno-econo-mies, the reduction of the public sphere to opinion management and more – it can't simply be absorbed into Heidegger's framework. Why not?

A brief detour is necessary here. For Heidegger, technology is the 'basic form of appearance in which the will to will arranges and calculates itself in the unhistorical element of the world of completed metaphysics' (1993, 74). In other words, it is merely the outward form and mundane name for some more essential metaphysical operation – namely, what he calls the *Gestell* (usually translated as 'enframing', Lacoue-Labarthe proposes 'installation' or 'erection' (1989, 64–71) and Weber 'emplacement' (1996, 71–2)). *Ge-stell* semantically umbrellas a host of terms that share the root verb *stellen*, meaning to put or to stand or to emplace. Heidegger asks us to hear in *stellen* (and this is important for grasping the tie between the essence of technology and 'the will to will' of modern metaphysics) the overtones of provocation and demand (1977, 14). Technology besets nature as a provocation, a demand to stand by as raw material and energy. This characterization of technology is often interpreted as a critique of instrumental reason. But the critical point for Heidegger is not that technology as an instrument of man winds up instrumentalizing and dehumanizing him (in fact he objects to this instrumental and anthropological conception of technology). Rather, the problem with technological production is that it forgets or ignores a more originary experience of *techne* (art, craft, know-how, knowledge). The decisive meaning of pro-duction (*poiesis*) is not provocation (*Herausfordern*), but bringing-forth (*Hervorbringen*). For Heidegger, the essence of technology is poetic production in the Greek sense of bringing-forth into presence, bringing 'hither out of concealment forth into unconcealment' (1977, 11) – production in the sense, then, of revealing, of *aletheia*. Only in light of this definition can we take full measure of the distortion technology suffers in its metaphysical and modern guises.

Lacoue-Labarthe's and Nancy's analyses of the political cannot be collapsed into Heidegger's questioning of technology because, to put this very schematically, they find something amiss both in his philosophical premise (the staging of *aletheia*) and in his characterization of technology's provocation (the dismantling of *Gestell*). In a minute, patient reading of the *stellen*-words which interlace with *Gestell* across several of Heidegger's texts, Lacoue-Labarthe detects how one of these words goes, effectively, missing: namely *Darstellung* (1989, 43–138). *Darstellung* covers several meanings – portrayal, depiction, exposition, *mise-en-scène*, representation – each of which may be referred (this is essential for Lacoue-Labarthe and Nancy) to the idea of *presenting* in the literary or fictive sense. Tracing how *Darstellung* drops, here and there, out of Heidegger's theoretical view, enables Lacoue-Labarthe to profile a kind of blind spot in his thought. This blind spot marks the formative role fiction or, as he puts it, '*fictioning*' plays in the ontological definition of being itself. For Lacoue-Labarthe, fictioning does not only play a role on the stage of metaphysics, for example, in the form of what Heidegger calls 'the poetizing essence of reason', Kantian reason's 'forming force' (*die bildende Kraft*); fictioning takes part in, or in fact 'is', the *staging* of metaphysics. It is constitutive of metaphysical programming itself. In perhaps the most important vector of his work, Lacoue-Labarthe develops this concept of the fictioning essence of philosophy (what he calls 'onto-typo-logy') in relation to the ancient question of mimesis. Another way he describes Heidegger's blind spot, then, is by pointing to an 'original' or productive mimesis (a 'mimetology') at work in his thought which, because of his Platonic depreciation of mimesis as imitation, he fails to see (1989, 297). Relatedly, Nancy observes that Heidegger's privileged concept of *aletheia* presupposes *Darstellung*. What was supposed to evade the provocations of a frontal set-up, what was supposed to take place outside the metaphysical staging of truth, cannot avoid *exhibiting* itself. Regardless of how philosophy conceives of truth, it always remains something which must be made to appear *as such*. Thus, in *The Sense of the World*, Nancy states a certain reservation in regards to Heidegger's thinking of truth: 'This reservation concerns the degree to which truth as *aletheia* ("veiling/unveiling"), like all other types of truth, continues to operate in terms of presentation, placing-in-view, exhibition, and manifestation' (1997, 16).

But why dwell on something Heidegger misses (especially since his thought enables us to see it)? For this reason: the 'missed' thing – mimesis, fictioning, fashioning, staging, manifestation, presentation, and so forth – is *the political itself*. In other words, Heidegger's disregard of philosophy's foundational fictioning goes hand in hand with his unwillingness to think the essential co-belonging of the philosophical and the political. This inattention to the 'literary' at work in the machinery of philosophy is furthermore inseparable from what Lacoue-Labarthe calls Heidegger's 'overvaluation of the philosophical' – an overvaluation most visible in his 'fundamental reduction of existence to philosophizing' (1989, 288). This is precisely why Lacoue-Labarthe and Nancy provisionally favour the term 'the philosophical' over 'metaphysics'. Heidegger's critical delimitation of metaphysics serves to shield some more authentic philosophizing (the privilege given to *questioning*, for instance) from dismantling. By (re)designating *metaphysics* as *the philosophical*, Lacoue-Labarthe and Nancy leave no margin of philosophy free from deconstruction.

In his introduction to *Retreating the Political*, Simon Sparks proposes that the literary-presentational motifs partially listed above (mimesis, fictioning, fashioning and so forth) be gathered under the heading of the *figure*. Lacoue-Labarthe's and Nancy's theoretical originality lies in their accentuation of the figurative essence of the philosophical – a figurative essence, a will-to-figure, which yokes the philosophical indissociably with the political. According to Sparks the figure is the dominant theme of both their work. Why do they place such theoretical importance on the figure? Sparks writes:

> Because, for them, metaphysics in the process of completing itself, is historically and *essentially* committed to mobilising figures in order to represent itself. Responding to the constraint of an originary programmation...the epoch of onto-theology, what Lacoue-Labarthe and Nancy call the epoch of philosophy 'actualising' itself as the political (and vice versa), is nothing other than the epoch of the bestowal of (the) meaning (of being, of existing) through figures.

Sparks goes on to note that this metaphysical mobilization of figures occurs 'most decisively, through the figure of man, the figure of a human *tupos* determined as the *subjectum* or as the Subject of meaning' (Lacoue-Labarthe and Nancy 1997, xxii). Following Heidegger in this respect, modern metaphysics for Lacoue-Labarthe and Nancy installs the reign of the subject. But for them this subject is above all figurative – or rather, auto-figurative, auto-fictioning.

But where is this metaphysical determination of our modernity, this will-to-figure, figured? Where in the world does it appear? It appears most spectacularly in or as *totalitarianism*. For Lacoue-Labarthe and Nancy, totalitarianism represents, adapting a phrase from Sartre, 'the unsurpassable horizon of our times' (1997, 126). By totalitarianism they refer, of course, to the recent historical examples of the phenomenon: Stalinism, Fascism and, perhaps especially, Nazism. Following the influential analyses of Hannah Arendt and Claude Lefort, they characterize totalitarianism as 'the attempt at a frenzied re-substantialization – a re-incorporation, a *re-organization* in the strongest and most differentiated sense – of the "social body"' (1997, 127).

But Lacoue-Labarthe and Nancy also use totalitarianism to index a more generalized phenomenon, one which extends the frenzy of the recent past into the unending present. This afterlife of totalitarianism is diffuse. It takes the form of the banal and unquestioned view that 'everything is political'. Unlike fascist or soviet totalitarianism, wherein the total domination of the political presented itself quite clearly as terror, today the global ubiquity of such total domination allows it to disappear from view. Total domination goes without saying. Arendt describes total domination as the attempt 'to organize the infinite plurality and differentiation of human beings as if all of humanity were just one individual' (Arendt 1973, 438). In philosophical terms, the total domination of the political denotes the completed installation of the Subject. What goes utterly unchallenged in totalitarianism is the subordination of human beings, of human singularities (but perhaps the talk of the 'human' has always given itself over to such subordination), to the self-actualizing thrust of a heroic humanity. Today this undivided reign of the will-to-figure does not present itself in the figure of a leader, nation, class, or people. Rather it appears as a sort of figurative drive without a figurehead, a headless auto-organization driven by the banal rule of what Jean-François Lyotard has called 'the logic of maximum performance' (1984, xxiv). What Arendt impeccably discerned as total domination continues unabated in the assimilation of all public and human life to the logic of maximal operativity and production. In this insidious form, the political holds total sway by its (almost) total withdrawal or retreat ('retrait').

Useful and urgent as Lacoue-Labarthe's and Nancy's philosophical diagnostic is, their work does not stop here. In addition to its descriptive sense, their catch-phrase 'le retrait du politique' carries also a prescriptive force: to retreat the political in the sense of re-treating it, treating it again, tracing it in a new way. This retreatment is, they acknowledge, an extraordinarily difficult task. It entails, first of all, trying to withdraw the political from its ubiquitous withdrawal. The ethico-political exigency of Lacoue-Labarthe's and Nancy's more recent works issues from their attempt to free the political. Freeing the political means, to put it less heroically, taking the political to its philosophical limit or breaking-point (and vice versa); looking for fissures and openings in its metaphysical foundation; unsettling the grounding of the subject and interrupting its auto-figurative impulsion. How is any of this possible? For Lacoue-Labarthe and Nancy the crux of the matter lies in re-examining the borders of the subject, there where it greets or fails to greet the other (or others). In other words, 'the question of the political evokes the necessity of dwelling on what makes the social relation possible as such' (1997, 180).

Their collective research on the making of the social tie begins, of all places, with psychoanalysis. In some brilliant readings of Freud's socio-cultural texts, Lacoue-Labarthe and Nancy draw our attention to an irresolvable tension between his theoretical assertion of an identity principle at the root of all sociality and a logical unravelling of this principle set in motion by his own attempts to *account* for identity, that is give an account of identity formation (the process of 'identification') that does not presuppose the very thing it is trying to account for (identity). To abbreviate rather brusquely here, they discover at the logical origin of the Freudian subject not a simple relation to others (which would presuppose subjects coming into the social sphere fully constituted, that is, already socialized), but rather a constitutive social alterity, an original dis-connection. 'At its extreme', they write, 'the question of identity is, for Freud, the question of *the identity of a dissociation*' (1991, 39). This question is again foregrounded towards the close of 'The "Retreat" of the Political': 'The so-called question of relation remains, to our mind, *the* central question ... In a general way, one can suggest that this question intervened with the insistence of a theme ... the theme of *desertion* or *dissociation* ...' (1997, 133).

As singular and differentiated as Lacoue-Labarthe's and Nancy's own writings are, we might say that, following their collective interrogation of the political, the difficult obligation to rearticulate the social tie *as* dissociation informs both of their numerous publications. We might even say the motif of dissociated identity is something they share in common with other 'French Heideggereans' (Derrida, Levinas, Blanchot) – were it not for the fact that, as Derrida points out, their thought of dissociation ('the condition of my relation to others') marks a decisive departure from Heidegger's philosophical and political privileging of 'gathering' (*Versammlung*) (Derrida 1997, 14). In order to flesh out this idea of a constitutive dis-association – the '*rapport sans rapport*, the relationless relation' (Derrida 1997, 14) – so central to each of their concerns, I will close with a sketch of Nancy's work on 'being-in-common'.

The text of Nancy's which has received perhaps the most extensive commentary and response is 'The Inoperative Community' (see, for example, Miami Theory Collective (MTC) 1991, Blanchot 1988, and above all Agamben 1993). Towards the beginning of this essay, he notes: 'Until this day history has been thought on the basis of a lost community – one to be regained or reconstituted' (1991, 9). Nancy himself does not conceive community on this traditional humanist model of a lost or broken immanence that must be reworked and restored. Instead he steers the communitarian interrogation of community's substantive identity towards the question of community's very condition of possibility. He asks: before fashioning this or that idea of community, what does it mean to be-in-common? For Nancy, this question is, like the question of being itself, presupposed in our daily being-there in the world. Being-in-common is not a predicate added on to an essentially solitary being. Rather, being-there (*Da-sein*) is none other than being-with (*Mit-sein*). As Christopher Fynsk puts it, '*Mitsein* and *Dasein* are co-originary; Dasein must be thought in its very possibility as being-together' (Nancy 1991, xvi–xvii). Indeed, my feeling lonely or being alone depends for its possibility on a prior ontological potential – a built-in inclination – to share my existence.

Nancy accents Heidegger's relational definition of *Dasein* in order to set us thinking about being-in-common as an enabling rift or partition in our ontological fabric. But where does this being-in-common come into play? 'Community is revealed in the death of others', Nancy says (1991, 15); being-in-common bears an essential relation to death. Human finitude relates to community in both a negative and a positive way. First, the death of the other reveals to me the radical alterity of the experience, the impossibility of fusing the other into some meaningful whole, some larger corporate body. The dying of the other exposes the absolute unavailability of communal immanence. Second, the other's death touches me to acknowledge what we share in common. It is important to discern the precise nature of the pathos in this death scene. The death of the other – be it a loved one, lover, friend or some other – does not bring the inexorable truth of death 'home' to me in the sense of a specular recognition. I do not share the experience of the other's death as an intense imaginative empathy wherein I see myself in the other's place and thereby arrive at a fuller, more appreciative sense of my own. In other words, what I experience in the other's death is not myself, nor myself in the other's place, but the other as such. And in experiencing the alterity of the other at this most altered of moments, I am altered myself – that is, exposed to the alterity 'in' 'me'. In an early text entitled 'Obliteration', Lacoue-Labarthe speaks of this alterity as:

that which, in the subject, deserts (has always already deserted) the subject *itself* and which, prior to any 'self-possession' (and in a mode other than that of dispossession), is the dissolution, the defeat of the subject in the subject or *as* the subject: the (de)constitution of the subject or the 'loss' of the subject – if indeed one can think the loss of what one has never had . . . (1993: 81–2)

But what is described here in terms of the subject's self-loss is also the community's gain. Nancy takes the delicate 'internal' trembling of the subject and inclines it outwards. The dissociation of the self which I feel most acutely before the other's death becomes something I *share* with the other.

Community begins with the sharing of death that takes me out of myself and positions me in the *in* of being-in-common, the *with* of being-with, and the *and* of you and I. These little words (and others like them) are the mundane linguistic particles that most adequately translate the great existential theme of death. They are place-holders for the outside where you and I are exposed to and share our finitude. Nancy says that this *and* of you and I should not be understood as a social relation that is superimposed on two subjects. Being-in-common should not be confused with intersubjectivity or the ideality of communicative exchange. The *and* must be thought as a *between* which is more originary than the social tie – so originary in fact that the *you* and the *I* can only appear with the prior emergence of the *and*. The *and* says in effect that you and I do not appear to one another – I here and you there – but rather that we co-appear or 'compear' (*com-paraît*) (Nancy 1991, 28). As a thinking oriented towards the outside, the end, the limit and the between, community resists going indoors, retreating to the familiar space of the subject who is one or the subject who contains the many. Nancy writes: 'Community. . .is not a common *being*; it is to be *in* common, or to be *with* each other, or to be together' (1993a, 154). Being-in-common does not take the form of a selfless fusion into a group. Rather, it emerges from the *in*, the syncatagoreme that interrupts my participation in a nominal unit at the same time that it hinges me to others. What we share in common is death – or, in a somewhat less intoxicated idiom – interruption. Without the interruption of the self by others there can be no being-in-common, only the abandonment of relation and the mystical hope of communion.

Perhaps the most difficult thing to grasp in Nancy's thinking of community is that our strange built-in sociality does not provide any groundwork for building a community in any identifiable sense. As Fynsk puts it, '[Being-in-common] is not something that may be produced and instituted or whose essence could be expressed in a work of any kind (including a *polis* or state): it cannot be the object or the telos of a politics' (Nancy 1991, x). Community's absolute resistance to work is indicated in the title of Nancy's texts, *La Communauté désœuvrée*. As a translation, 'The Inoperative Community' emphasizes rightly that community can't be operated or operationalized. But in this translation we miss the crucial conceptual component of work (*œuvre*). In fact, Nancy says explicitly, 'community is made or is formed by the retreat or the subtraction of something: this something . . . is what I call its "work" (1991, xxxviii–ix). Nancy's usage of this word is drawn largely from the writings of Blanchot and, inevitably, the Jena romantics. These sources should alert us to the fact that the defining semantic register here is aesthetic. The work is above all the work of art. The work does not refer to any single object of art, but rather the theoretical work of art – that is, the total or absolute artwork which, thought on the model of organic achievement, becomes itself the working model for all other human projects of self-manifestation (see Lacoue-Labarthe and Nancy 1988). Nancy intends his sense of community to disrupt the work aim and working premise of communitarian thought. Thus, although the term *désœuvrée* means *idle* or *at loose ends*, it should be heard more actively. For *désœuvrement*, instead of *idleness*, which suggests the state that follows from work's absence, Fynsk proposes *unworking* (Nancy 1991, 154, n.23). *La Communauté désœuvrée* is the unworking community. But here too we must press on the translation a little to extract the sense of unworking as an active interrupting or incompleting of some process or product which aims at auto-figuration.

Nancy writes: 'community cannot arise from the domain of *work*. One does not produce it, one experiences or one is constituted by it as the experience of finitude' (1991, 31). Throughout 'The Inoperative Community' the experience of finitude is set to work against work. Not only does finitude unwork the work of community, it also opens the possibility for community as being-in-common. The exceptional difficulty in giving a theoretical account of being-in-common results from the stricture that it cannot be a work, hence cannot be the object of a representation. There is no general theoretical model that can encompass the countless singular experiences of our daily and nightly finitude. Nancy's extended discussion of experiencing the other's death would seem to privilege mortality as the determining paradigm for finitude. But death is just the limit case (as is birth) in an immense phenomenological spectrum of irreducible community experiences. One thing that all these experiences share, however, is the experience of sharing itself. Once again, Nancy does not conceptualize sharing as a selfless melding into a group or as a reciprocal exchange between two subjects. As an experience of the limit, sharing (*le partage*) partitions out my self-identity; in sharing I am exposed to my dissociation, divvied outwards. What we share at the ends of ourselves is neither some commonality nor our separate individualities, but our uncommon *singularity*. For Nancy, singularity names the irreducible particularity of this or that being, *but only in so far as that being is being-with or being-in-common*. In other words, singular beings – we, you, I – cannot appear alone. They or we must appear in common; they, we, must compear. The compearance or sharing of our singularities is so fundamental to our being-in-common, all it takes is a minimal exposure to others. Nancy gives the following example:

> Passengers in the same train compartment are simply seated next to each other in an accidental, arbitrary, and completely exterior manner. They are not linked. But they are also quite together inasmuch as they are travellers on this train, in this same space and for this same period of time. They are between the disintegration of the 'crowd' and the aggregation of the group, both extremes remaining possible, virtual, and near at any moment. (MTC 1991, 9)

Exposure to singularity: that means to be scattered together, like passengers on a train, not quite face-to-face, oscillating between the poles of group fusion and social dispersal, 'solitude and collectivity, attraction and repulsion' (MTC 1991, 9).

The example of strangers on a train illustrates perfectly the banal relation without relation – the exposition of the *with*, the *in*, the *between* and the *and* – in which singularities appear prior to the introduction of identities. However, it strikes me as a rather indifferent example of singularity as such. A better example might be found in the singular relationship of Lacoue-Labarthe *and* Nancy. In his useful introduction to the English volume of Lacoue-Labarthe's *Typography*, Derrida writes:

> What I share with Lacoue-Labarthe, we also both share, though differently, with Jean-Luc Nancy. But I hasten to reiterate that despite so many common paths and so much work done in common, between the two of them and between the three of us, the work of each remains, in its

singular proximity, absolutely different; and this, despite its fatal impurity, is the secret of the idiom. The secret: that is to say, first of all, the *separation*, the non-relation, the interruption. (Lacoue-Labarthe 1989, 6–7)

Earlier Derrida describes Lacoue-Labarthe's 'idiom' in terms of a signature rhythm, a movement of speech that 'multiplies caesuras, asides, parenthetical remarks, cautions, signs of prudence and circumspection, hesitations, warnings, parentheses, quotation marks, italics – dashes above all – or all of these at once ...' (1989, 3). Following Derrida's lead, could we not adduce Lacoue- Labarthe's and Nancy's writing *voice* or *style* as examples of a dissociative relation, a compearance? As markedly different as their voices sound, they seem to share – both writing alone and together – an interrupted or unworking style. By that I mean, in addition to the verbal gestures Derrida compiles, a seemingly endless series of sentences beginning with *on the other hand, on the contrary, more precisely, however, nevertheless* and especially *or, but, yet*. Certainly these words and phrases underscore Lacoue-Labarthe's and Nancy's prudence and circumspection as readers: their patience (but perhaps also their impatience) to get it right. And they may also be read as the mundane markers of collective authorship, rather like stage cues to signal where one voice leaves off and the other takes over. But I would propose we read the *ors* and *buts* which texture their writing as the accents of a shared dissociation – less the signs of a collective authorship than the active unworkings of the very ideas of collectivity and authorship. These endless interruptions make the experience of reading their texts difficult. But it is a difficulty that is absolutely commensurate with their ethico-political intentions – in other words, a pedagogically useful difficulty. Or, from the perspective of re-treating the political, completely useless – that is, unworkable.

Heesok Chang

Further reading and works cited

Agamben, G. *The Coming Community*. Minneapolis, MN, 1993.
Arendt, H. *The Origins of Totalitarianism*. San Diego, CA, 1973.
Blanchot, M. *The Unavowable Community*. Barrytown, NY, 1988.
Cadava, E. et al. (eds) *Who Comes After the Subject?* New York, 1991.
Derrida, J. *Deconstruction in a Nutshell*, ed. J. D. Caputo. New York, 1997.
Eagleton, T. 'Nationalism: Irony and Commitment'. *Nationalism, Colonialism, and Literature*, ed. S. Deane. Minneapolis, MN, 1990.
Farias, V. *Heidegger et le Nazisme*. Paris, 1987.
Heidegger, M. *Being and Time*. New York, 1962.
—. *The Question Concerning Technology and Other Essays*. New York, 1977.
—. 'Overcoming Metaphysics', in *The Heidegger Controversy*, ed. R. Wolin. Cambridge, MA, 1993.
Lacoue-Labarthe, P. *Typography*, ed. Christopher Fynsk. Cambridge, MA, 1989.
—. *Heidegger, Art and Politics*. Oxford, 1990.
—. *The Subject of Philosophy*, ed. Thomas Tresize. Minneapolis, MN, 1993.
—. *Musica Ficta*. Stanford, CA, 1994.
—. *Poetry as Experience*. Stanford, CA, 1999.
— and Nancy, J.-L. *The Literary Absolute*. Albany, NY, 1988.
—. 'The Unconscious Is Destructed like an Affect', *Stanford Literature Review*, 6, 2, Fall 1989.
—. 'The Nazi Myth', *Critical Inquiry*, 16, 2, Winter 1990.
—. 'From Where Is Psychoanalysis Possible?', *Stanford Literature Review*, 8, 1–2, Spring-Fall 1991.

—. *The Title of the Letter*. Albany, NY, 1992.

—. *Retreating the Political*, ed. S. Sparks. London, 1997.

Hamacher, W. 'Working Through Working', *Modernism/Modernity*, 3, 1, January 1996.

Kamuf, P. (ed.) *Paragraph*, 16, 2, 1993.

Keenan, T. *Fables of Responsibility*. Stanford, CA, 1997.

Lyotard, J.-F. *The Postmodern Condition*. Minneapolis, MN, 1984.

—. *Heidegger and 'the Jews'*. Minneapolis, MN, 1990.

Miami Theory Collective (ed.) *Community at Loose Ends*. Minneapolis, MN, 1991.

Nancy, J.-L. *The Inoperative Community*, ed. Peter Connor. Minneapolis, MN, 1991.

—. *The Birth to Presence*. Stanford, CA, 1993a.

—. *The Experience of Freedom*. Stanford, CA, 1993b.

—. *The Sense of the World*. Minneapolis, CA, 1997.

Sheppard, D. et al. *On Jean-Luc Nancy*. London, 1997.

Weber, S. *Mass Mediauras*, ed. A. Cholodenko. Stanford, CA, 1996.

Julia Kristeva (1941–)

Although of Bulgarian origin, Julia Kristeva has long been associated with the French poststructuralists. Arriving in Paris as a doctoral research fellow in the mid-1960s amid what Kristeva describes as the 'theoretical ebullience' surrounding the emergence of structuralism, with its rejection of philosophical humanism and its discovery of the role of language in the constitution of the conscious subject, Kristeva was immediately caught up in the intellectual fervour of the period. Under the tutelage of Lucien Goldmann and Roland Barthes and through her encounter with Philippe Sollers, her future husband and founder of the French literary journal *Tel Quel*, Kristeva came into contact with a number of structuralist and poststructuralist theorists and soon forged a path, along with Foucault, Lacan and Derrida, that diverged from the current structuralist fashion by becoming one of the leading critics of poststructuralist thought. Through her reworking of theoretical concepts borrowed from many different disciplines including structural linguistics, psychoanalysis, literary criticism, marxism, Derridean theory, and Hegelian and Heideggerian philosophy, Kristeva contributed significantly to the advancement of the poststructuralist critique not only of structuralism but also of the rationalist, humanist assumptions structuring the western philosophical and literary tradition as a whole.

That critique provides the basis for the entirety of Kristeva's project from the 1960s to the late 1990s – despite the numerous shifts in focus that occur over the years as she responds to the changes in the social and political context in which her writing takes place. Indeed, given Kristeva's sensitivity to cultural questions, it is surprising that so little attention has been paid by Anglo-American critics to her analysis of contemporary culture. Her reception in the English-speaking world has been largely confined to the questions Kristeva's work raises with regard to feminist issues, questions that have precipitated lively debates as to the usefulness of her theory for a feminist politics, but that have overshadowed any consideration of the highly politicized intellectual and social environment which initially fostered Kristeva's revolutionary project. That environment was characterized not only by the theoretical upheaval wrought by the structuralists' and poststructuralists' interrogation of traditional philosophical and literary precepts but also by the political turmoil that erupted in the 1960s, particularly in the form of the student – worker uprisings of May 1968. Although the revolt was ultimately unsuccessful, the events of May, as Kristeva's recent writings attest, pointed the way toward the possibility of a radical contestation of all forms of authority, including not only that of the state, of the family and of a repressive socio-economic system, but also on a more theoretical level of the exclusionary and ultimately oppressive notions of identity at the very foundations of western thought (Kristeva 1998b, 14–77).

The contestatory spirit that found its expression in the Parisian streets was thus closely echoed in the theoretical and literary work of the period, particularly among those literary writers and theorists associated with *Tel Quel*. Rather than becoming actively involved in the student effort to overturn an oppressive social system, the members of the *Tel Quel* group, which at this point also included Kristeva who began contributing to the journal in 1967, believed that the revolutionary struggle should take place on a more fundamental level, on the level of language itself. Claiming that communicative language is a principal vehicle in the preservation of the ideological structures that dominate western culture and revealing their growing interest in marxist theory, Kristeva and her fellow members attempted to formulate and put into practice a revolutionary materialist theory of language in an effort to work against the traditional concept of the literary text and of language itself as predominantly meaningful structures, and thus to help achieve, by indirection, a transformation of the social order and its oppressive laws as well.

Laying the theoretical groundwork for the *Tel Quel* project in her first work in French, *Séméiotiké* (1969), Kristeva begins by taking up the structural linguists' investigations of language but attempts to counter their tendency to remain within the confines of a strictly linguistic system. Claiming the scientific-positivist approach to semiotics reduces its object of study to a system of verifiable rules or laws while ignoring the productive operations within language that precede signification, Kristeva sets out to formulate an open-ended, self-critical method of analysis, one that she calls *semanalysis* which will account for the heterogeneous elements involved in the process of textual production (27–42; Moi 1986, 74–88). Kristeva's emphasis on 'textual productivity' and her attempt to uncover the multiple, pre-linguistic processes that both constitute but also undermine the unity of meaning are not only central to her own and *Tel Quel*'s critique of traditional notions of language, they are also directly related to their critique of the social order as a whole. By drawing on Marx's analysis of the relations of production within the capitalist system, Kristeva and the *Tel Quel* group conclude that western communicative language and western society are governed by a similar logic, subjected to the very same laws of exchange that structure the capitalist marketplace. For whether the reference is to the exchange of commodities or the exchange of messages, the focus in a capitalist system is always on the goods produced, on the finished and immediately consumable product that hides the processes of production. The communicability of discourse and the self-contained and unified identity of what a capitalist society produces are thus dependent on the exclusion or repression of these processes, Kristeva argues. They must be subordinated to the preservation of a cohesive and productive socio-economic system and to the integrated identity of the principal support of that system, the individual social subject (1969, 34–40).

A concept of the open text which breaks through the boundaries imposed by traditional notions of language by focusing on the process of textual production rather than on the finished product is thus what emerges in the course of Kristeva's analysis. Although its psychoanalytical implications are developed more fully in subsequent texts, Kristeva's concerns in *Séméiotiké* are primarily textual. As opposed, however, to the more formalist approach to the structural linguists who analyse language and the literary text as cut off from their social and historical context, Kristeva elaborates, through the writings of Barthes and especially those of the post-formalist Mikhail Bakhtin, a notion of the text that is not confined to the purely linguistic, written body of literary or non-literary works but that incorporates the unwritten, non-linguistic signifying practices also involved in the process of meaning formation. The text emerges as the intersection of a multiplicity of voices, all of which participate in the production of the text's meaning. Indeed, out of her reading of Bakhtinian dialogism, which sees the text in relation to other texts, or more precisely as a 'dialogue among several writings' including that of the writer, the reader and the socio-historical context, comes her influential concept of intertextuality, a notion that not only poses an important challenge to the objective status of the literary text, but that also deals a serious blow to western notions of the subject as a self-contained, integrated identity (1969, 143–73; Roudiez 1980, 64–91). For the identity of the author who 'creates' the text is called into question. As only one productive voice among many, including those of the non-linguistic social and historical forces that also shape the literary work, the author no longer stands outside the work as the sole source of its language but is drawn into the dynamics of the written text, his activity constituting but also finding itself constituted by its complex operations. The author emerges here not as the unitary subject instituted by a repressive social order but as a subject-in-process/on trial, caught up in the interweaving movement of multiple textual surfaces which at the same time construct themselves as 'the operation of [the subject's] pulverization' (1969, 15; Guberman 1996, 188–203).

Although Kristeva claims that these operations are fundamental to the structure of any text, whether it be traditional or modern, she maintains that it is only in the modern 'literary' work that its intertextual function is rendered explicit. The challenge to what Kristeva calls, following Bakhtin, the traditional monological novel, with its subordination to the Law of One (one author, one meaning, and one legitimate interpretation), does not come from within the traditional novel itself, it comes instead from a radically different text, from the polyphonic novels of Kafka or Joyce, or from the works following the examples of Mallarmé or Lautréamont 'which perceive themselves, in their very structures, as a production irreducible to representation' (1969, 41; Moi 1986, 86, trans. modified). In directing our attention away from the meaning of the text (the *phenotext*) toward the material processes of textual production (the *genotext*), the pluridimensional spaces of these avant-garde literary works form the basis for Kristeva's own revolutionary project, one that is meant to counter western society's 'reifying' logic by preventing the text's emergence as a literary object or 'product' to be consumed by a reading public (1969, 278–317; Moi 1986, 24–33, 120–3).

Whether or not Kristeva is successful in this regard has been subject to debate. For although the emphasis on 'poetic' language is not to be construed, Kristeva argues, as an hypostatization of poetry but rather as a way of describing any discourse in which the material process of its own generation is brought to light, some critics claim that Kristeva's conception does not always avoid the objectifying logic that her semiotic practice is meant to oppose. This criticism has been voiced in particularly strong terms with regard to Kristeva's well-known and much debated distinction between the semiotic and the symbolic in *Revolution in Poetic Language* (1984a) where she extends the more textual aspects of her argument by examining its intrapsychic or psychoanalytical implications. Here, marxist theory is combined with Freudian and Lacanian psychoanalysis in an effort to show that the relations of production, or the economic infrastructure uncovered by Marx, could be equated with the heterogeneous impulses within the individual unconscious that Freud discovered, impulses that have a role in the constitution of the speaking subject but that must be repressed in order for the individual to emerge as an integrated identity. As Kristeva describes the process, the individual establishes himself as an independent and conscious subject (and enters the 'symbolic' order of identity) only after cutting himself off from and repressing the instinctual drives (the 'semiotic *chora*') that lie within his prelinguistic unconscious. This occurs during the earliest 'pulsional' stages of a child's life when his first sounds, rhythms and intonations which are uttered according to the needs of the bodily impulses are repressed in order to establish the discursive function of language and the individual's identity.

The child, at this point, must be weaned from his attachment to the mother so that he may become conscious of his own existence as a distinct and separate identity. This break occurs when the child has mastered normal patterns of speech, and only then is the individual as an integrated being actually formed. Thus the symbolic, as Kristeva describes it, always refers to the logical and syntactical function of language (Roudiez 1980, 133–41). The semiotic, on the other hand, is chronologically prior to the constitution of the linguistic sign and the subject, and although Kristeva maintains that it is also necessary for the acquisition of language in that it provides the foundation out of which language and the subject develop, the integral identities of both can only be constituted after cutting themselves off from this anteriority, by repressing these prelinguisitc 'heterogeneous pulsions'. The task, then, of the revolutionary text is to reactivate these 'repressed drives', to introduce the semiotic in the form of rhythm, intonation and repetition of sounds and rhyme, which becomes the genotext, into the phenotext, so that the unity of the sign and the subject will ultimately be undermined and the differential process of generation itself will be allowed to emerge uncontaminated by its precepts (1984, 19–106; Moi 1986, 89–136).

What Kristeva's critics find objectionable here is that, despite her claim that the two modalities are interdependent and therefore inseparable, the semiotic and the symbolic are often separated by rather clear lines of demarcation. Indeed, a number of Kristeva's detractors have been highly critical of her tendency to define the semiotic and symbolic in essentialist, phallocentric terms. They claim that her view of the semiotic as the 'outside' of language, as an 'archaic, instinctual and maternal territory' that must be repressed or 'sealed off' if the symbolic order of identity is to function, reveals not simply an essentializing celebration of the semiotic's disruptive potential but also, through an uncritical acceptance of the Freudian Oedipal framework, a notion of identity that is paternally grounded, dependent upon both a rejection of the mother as 'abject' and a conception of the paternal order of the symbolic as 'exclusively *prohibitive*' (Butler 1993, 177).

Whether or not one chooses to agree with these critics – and there are many who do not – one can find in Kristeva's next major work, *Powers of Horror* (1982), a continuation of her study of the symbolic's repressive function. Tracing the logic of exclusion operating within primitive societies and throughout biblical history from Judaic monotheism to Christianity, Kristeva calls up disturbing images of the abject. These are the 'horrors' that lie just beneath the surface of civilized society and that are treated as objects of loathing – filth, bodily excretions, the instinctual drives that dwell within the unconscious – indeed, all those elements within our culture that inspire disgust and revulsion and that must be purged or cleansed and purified if the symbolic order of identity is to be instituted. The effort to contest this logic by focusing on those 'borderline practices' that disturb notions of identity, system and order can thus be viewed as a continuation of Kristeva's project to undermine a culture whose social systems are seen as totalizing and repressive. And although the revolutionary rhetoric that often characterized *Séméiotiké* and *Revolution in Poetic Language* has been considerably toned down, she sees in *Powers of Horror* the possibility for a 'great demystification of Power (religious, moral, political, and verbal)' (210) where the 'return of the repressed' in the form of abjection becomes a way to wedge a slight opening in the closures constituted by civilized society, by its 'homogenizing rhetoric' and by its systematized thinking.

If the revolutionary rhetoric appears to have been toned down in *Powers of Horror*, it all but disappears in her work of the 1980s, due in part to the repudiation by the members of *Tel Quel* of their own revolutionary project, following their disillusionment with both Soviet and Chinese marxism, and their loss of faith in the literary avant-garde's utopian objectives. It is attributable also to Kristeva's growing interest in psychoanalysis, which she came to see as a process that 'cuts through political illusions' and thus serves as 'an antidote to political discourse' (Moi 1986, 304). This re-evaluation of her position and the fact that she became a practising psychoanalyst in 1979 bring a change in perspective in Kristeva's work, leading her to focus less on the dynamic of exclusion and more on the inclusive character of the various signifying practices. In *Tales of Love*, for example, which examines western images of love as elaborated in the writings of Plato and certain Christian theologians, as well as in a wide range of literary texts, rather than positing, as she often does in her earlier work, a subjectivity constituted by a radical break with the instinctual heterogeneity of the maternal phase, Kristeva in her analysis of the narcissistic under-pinnings of love in western culture aims to show that drive-dominated narcissistic impulses continue to structure adult relationships to an other. This drive dynamic is indeed what 'feeds' the amatory identifications so essential to subjectivity, according to Kristeva, and it means that, far from repressing instinctuality, the subject in its very essence as a being for another reveals the continuation of the narcissistic economy.

In exposing, however, the problematic of the self that is implied in the narcissistic relation to the other, Kristeva stresses not so much its revolutionary potential as its capacity to support through psychoanalysis the individual's fantasies of wholeness and self-suffi-ciency. In her concern as an analyst for the 'outbreak' of psychic disorders that western society is witnessing today, Kristeva finds in psychoanalysis the possibility for a 'cure'. Recognizing that love is essential to the structuration of the self, she argues that the aim of psychoanalysis today must be to reconstitute the narcissistic relationship through the 'transference love' that inevitably arises between analyst and patient. The goal, however, is not to restore the plenitude that has supposedly been lost, but to allow the subject to construct some measure of subjectivity and thus to function, however tentatively, within the social system. The modern subject thus becomes what Kristeva calls a 'work-in-progess', constantly constructing itself as a necessarily false identity, while recognizing and indeed accepting the inauthenticity of its imaginary constructions (1987, 380–81).

While the stabilizing work of the symbolic is always provisional for Kristeva and should never be understood as a desire to reconstitute its repressive power, there is clearly a change in emphasis here that stems from changes in Kristeva's perception of the social organization and of the place that the individual subject occupies within it. Indeed, it is the very 'insufficiency' of the 'symbolic dimension' that becomes an important issue for Kristeva as she moves into the 1990s. Extending her investigations in psychoanalysis to the cultural sphere in a series of essays appearing in *Nations without Nationalism* (1993) and in *Strangers to Ourselves* (1991), Kristeva responds to a whole range of social problems that, in her view, no longer stem from an oppressive capitalist system but come instead from a society that is in a state of disarray. With the substantial flow of immigrants and the pressures of European economic competition, France, Kristeva writes, is undergoing a crisis in national identity, one that has provoked nationalist, anti-immigrant responses as well as a rise among those who take refuge in their own ethnicity. Turning once again to psychoanalysis as a possible response to growing social conflict and fragmentation, Kristeva calls for a rethinking of our concept of nationhood, for moving our perceptions of national identity beyond their 'regressive, exclusionary . . . or racial pitfalls' (1993, 59) by recognizing the difference of the foreigner 'without ostracism but also without levelling', that is without subsuming diversity under a new homogeneity. This recognition of 'otherness' is made possible, according to Kristeva, through the extension of the Freudian notion of the unconscious to the cultural sphere. As an uncanny strangeness or otherness that inhabits the human psyche, the Freudian unconscious allows for a notion of community that would no longer be assimilated to some national, ethnic or religious identity but would stem instead from a recognition of the difference and foreignness that reside at the core of every being (1991, 185–92).

Kristeva's elaboration of a new ethics of tolerance for today's emerging multinational societies thus restores to psychoanalysis its political dimension and moves her discourse to the point where, in the mid- to late-1990s, it begins to take on some of the political colourations of her work in the late 1960s and 1970s. Indeed, in a series of still untranslated works beginning with *The Sense and Non-Sense of Revolt* and continuing through *La révolte intime*, *Contre la dépression nationale* and *L'avenir d'une révolte*, one finds traces in her writing of the old revolutionary rhetoric, for not only does psychoanalysis function as a '*discours-révolte*', according to Kristeva, but it becomes once again a means of affirming the contestatory spirit of *Tel Quel* and of the generation of May 1968 (1998b, 14–53; Guberman 1996, 172). Kristeva is quick to point out, however, that her call for the revival of the revolutionary 'spirit of '68' should not be understood, as it was in the 1970s, as a simple opposition to repressive social institutions and norms. The old dialectical model of revolt, which assumes a dramatic confrontation between the law and its transgression is no longer operable in the 1990s primarily because the structures of authority against which the protestors rebelled have lost their capacity to exercise power. The disintegration of the family, the replacement of political authority with an amorphous, fluctuating global market, rapid developments in technology and the rise of the mass media with the proliferation of its mind-numbing images have not only rendered contemporary society infinitely more complex but have constituted a power vacuum that deprives individuals of a stabilizing centre. Drawing from Guy Debord's influential work, *The Society of the Spectacle*, Kristeva argues that it is indeed this 'invasion of the spectacle' that is diminishing dramatically our imaginary life. The new technologies of the image threaten to 'abolish the deepest regions of the self [*le "for intérieur"*]' (1997, 127) by transforming individuals into passive, indeed 'robotic', consumers of the products of a commercialized media.

In such a situation as this, however, where the individual suffers from a debilitating lack of constraints, the spirit of revolt is all the more necessary, according to Kristeva. For, not only did Freud's discovery of the unconscious provide the basis for an interrogation of the symbolic (an interrogation that Freud himself never explicitly developed), but his analysis of the process of psychic individuation showed to what extent revolt, whether it be the revolt against Oedipal father, so that the 'I' can come into being, or the revolt of the primal hoard in *Totem and Taboo* that founds the social pact, is an essential condition of both individual and social life. Thus, as a process that allows for the constitution of subjectivity even as it is also accompanied by the forces of dissolution and dispersion, revolt, in the Freudian sense, is seen by Kristeva as a remedy for both the public and private malaise that plagues western culture. Linked to the etymological meaning of *revolvere*, the term, as Kristeva uses it, is understood not as a transgression, as it was during her more militant phase, but as an anamnesis, a movement of 'revolt' that returns to the past, that repeats, interrogates and re-elaborates the most archaic, intimate phases of psychic development (2000, 28–9). Indeed, it is this reconstruction through psychoanalysis of the initial stages of subjectivation that allows for the reinstatement of the limits and prohibitions so essential to our condition as speaking beings and, in so doing, it both rehabilitates the individual subject and gives him 'a capacity for contestation and creation' (1998b, 41).

The rehabilitation of the subject through psychoanalysis should not, however, be understood as a return to the humanist premises of the past. For, if Kristeva's notion of re-volt involves the affirmation of prohibition and the law, it also exposes the subject to an 'unbearable conflictuality', unleashing, in the course of the patient's recounting of his narcissistic and Oedipal dramas, the pulsional forces of the semiotic and the destabilizing relation to an other as well, both of which prevent the subject from closing itself off, from becoming a fixed and unchanging identity. The analytic experience involving the free association of ideas, memories and sensations is not, then, a simple rememoration or repetition, it is also what displaces the past and allows for a 'reformulation of our psychic map' (2000, 50; trans. modified), an 'eternal return' that brings the perpetual deconstruction and renewal of the self. Such an experience has obvious political implications for Kristeva, in that the permanent questioning and restructuring of the individual psyche provides the basis for an interrogation and reshaping of the social structure as well. With its return through psychoanalysis to the archaic imaginary realm, Kristeva's concept of revolt is designed to 'save us' from this 'automation of humanity' (2000, 7), and it does so by giving voice to the heterogeneous processes that lie within the most 'intimate' reaches of the self.

In this context, then, the challenge to 'mediatic' society through an 'appeal to intimacy' can be seen, as Kristeva herself affirms, as a continuation of her earlier work (Guberman 1996, 222, 258–62). It could also be seen as a continuation of a more dialectical notion of revolt as well, one in which the subversive capabilities of a literary and artistic avant-garde come once again into play. Because of their capacity to engage in a fundamentally Proustian exploration of the 'intimacy of the senses' (*l'intimité sensible*), many of the artistic practices of the twentieth century, which include the writings of the surrealists, for example, or those of *Tel Quel* (2000, 112), or even Kristeva's own novel, *Possessions*, can bring us into contact with the very frontiers of thought or, more precisely, of the 'unthought' (*l'a-pensée*) where unconscious pulsions and sensations contest the very possibility of meaning. Returning then to the arguments voiced earlier in *Revolution in Poetic Language*, Kristeva sees the avant-garde literary text as a practice that places the subject, once again, 'in process/on trial', as a confrontation with the 'semiotic *chora*' through which the unity of identity is shattered or destroyed (*se néantise*) (1997, 20).

In walking such a fine line between two contradictory possibilities, involving a concept of revolt that allows for the rehabilitation of the subject (and thus runs the risk of reinstating the humanist or essentialist concept of subjectivity that Kristeva has always opposed) and another that calls for the permanent deconstruction of all notions of identity (and is more in conformity with the contestatory spirit of *Revolution in Poetic Language*, *Tel Quel* and May 1968), Kristeva's recent works will undoubtedly generate a considerable amount of debate. Kristeva's feminist critics might be appeased, however, by the fact that she has now turned to a question that she had previously ignored, to that of the feminine experience and to the influence of women writers on twentieth-century thought. Her most recent work, *Le génie feminin* (1999), devoted to the writings of Hannah Arendt, is only the beginning of a project that takes her through the texts of the psychoanalyst Melanie Klein, as well as those of the early twentieth-century author, Colette (forthcoming). In light of her earliest resistance to the 'self-enclosed category of the "feminine"' (Guberman 1996, 269), which was perceived by Kristeva as inconsistent with her persistent questioning of traditional notions of identity, Kristeva's current explorations of 'feminine genius' represent a significant departure from her earlier position. And although she still avoids any affiliation with an emancipatory, feminist movement, Kristeva affirms the opportunity women present for the 'revalorization of the sensorial experience' and for their capacity to serve as an 'antidote to technological ratiocination' (1997, 11).

Although some of Kristeva's feminist critics might still object to her continued identification of women with the sensorial or instinctual realm, it is this sensitivity to cultural questions and to the place of the subject within the social context that can be considered one of the most compelling aspects of Kristeva's work. Indeed, that sensitivity, which was evident from the very beginning during her association with *Tel Quel*, has led her to produce a body of work that is extraordinarily wide-ranging in scope. Of interest to those who specialize not only in cultural criticism and psychoanalysis but also to those with interests in philosophy, literature (including her own works of fiction), marxist theory and linguistics, her writings should be recognized for the major contributions they have made to poststructuralist thought. Their persistent interrogation of the subject and of its cultural context, their elaboration of such influential concepts as intertextuality, the semiotic and the symbolic, abjection, avant-garde aesthetics and its role in effecting social change, have clearly established Kristeva as one of the most important and provocative theoreticians writing in France today.

Joan Brandt

Further reading and works cited

Brandt, J. *Geopoetics*. Stanford, CA, 1997.
Butler, J. 'The Body Politics of Julia Kristeva', in *Ethics, Politics, and Difference in the Writings of Julia Kristeva*, ed. K. Oliver. New York, 1993.
Fletcher, J. and Benjamin, A. (eds) *Abjection, Melancholia and Love*. New York, 1990.
Fraser, N. 'The Uses of Abuses of French Discourse Theories for Feminist Politics', *Boundary 2*, 17, 2, Summer 1990.
Guberman, R. M. (ed.) *Julia Kristeva Interviews*. New York, 1996.
Jones, A. R. 'Julia Kristeva on Femininity: The Limits of a Semiotic Politics', *Feminist Review*, 18, Winter 1984.
Kristeva, J. *Powers of Horror*. New York, 1982.
—. *Revolution in Poetic Language*. New York, 1984a.
—. 'My Memory's Hyperbole', in *The Female Autograph*, ed. D. C. Stanton. Chicago, 1984b.

—. *Tales of Love*. New York, 1987.
—. *Black Sun*. New York, 1989.
—. *Strangers to Ourselves*. New York, 1991.
—. *Nations without Nationalism*. New York, 1993.
—. *New Maladies of the Soul*. New York, 1995.
—. *Sens et non-sens de la révolte*. Paris, 1996a.
—. *Time and Sense: Proust and the Experience of Literature*. New York, 1996b.
—. *La Révolte intime*. Paris, 1997.
—. *L'Avenir d'une révolte*. Paris, 1998a.
—. *Contre la dépression nationale*, ed. Philippe Petit. Paris, 1998b.
—. 'The Subject in Process', in *Tel Quel Reader*, eds P. ffrench and R.-F. Lack. New York, 1998c.
—. *Le Génie féminin*. I, II. Paris, 1999, 2000.
Lechte, J. *Julia Kristeva*. New York, 1990.
Moi, T. (ed.) *The Kristeva Reader*. New York, 1986.
Oliver, K. *Reading Kristeva*. Bloomington, IN, 1993.
Rose, J. *Sexuality in the Field of Vision*. London, 1986.
Roudiez, L. S. (ed.) *Desire in Language*. New York, 1980.
Smith, A.-M. *Julia Kristeva*. London, 1998.
Stone, J. 'The Horrors of Power: A Critique of Kristeva', in *The Politics of Theory: Proceedings of the Essex Conference on the Sociology of Literature, July 1982*, eds Francis Barker et al. Colchester, 1982.

Slavoj Žižek (1949–)

As recently as 1988, Slavoj Žižek was unpublished in English. Since that date, however, his position as researcher at Ljubljana's Institute for Social Studies has enabled him to produce an average of more than one monograph a year, not to speak of a number of edited collections. At the time of writing, a check of titles forthcoming reveals no fewer than five more books written or co-written or edited by Žižek. Meanwhile, a speaker giving a presentation at a scholarly conference may now find that s/he is giving the second or third Žižekian talk in a row. For sudden full-blown appearance on the intellectual scene, then, Žižek has few rivals. However, one of these few is his principal interlocutor, Jacques Lacan, who had from 1932 to 1966 published only a dissertation and a few stray articles, but then suddenly produced the 924 pages of the *Écrits* and announced as forthcoming the twenty-six volumes of his seminar for the years from 1953 to 1979.

Understand, however, that the groaning shelf of Žižek is informed as much by post-Althusserian marxism and by the whole tradition of German idealism as it is by Lacanian psychoanalysis. Žižek's books are copiously illustrated with discussions of such popular-cultural figures as Raymond Chandler, Patricia Highsmith, Alfred Hitchcock and David Lynch, and are full of asides on *Robocop*, *The Flintstones*, *Forrest Gump* and Michael Jackson. Their principal subject-matter is a rethinking of the problematic of subjectivity and ideology that first emerged in France during the 1960s and made its way into English-speaking criticism during the 1970s. The essential thesis of Žižek is that the 'last Lacan' completes and retroactively restructures a philosophical and theoretical tradition whose main figures are Kant, Hegel, Schelling, Marx, Althusser, Jameson, and Laclau and Mouffe.

In other words, Žižek would have no real quarrel with those intellectual historians for whom modern European thought is a series of French commentaries on German idealism.

By 'the last Lacan', Žižek means the Lacan of Seminars like *Encore* and essays like 'Kant with Sade'. This is the Lacan of the 'obscene shadow of the law', of the interface between the Real and the Symbolic, and of the distinction between reality and the Real, and is understood by Žižek as the last word in an intellectual tradition that reaches back beyond German idealism to Descartes, and perhaps even to Aristotle. This means that Žižek finds his favoured philosophers always more subtle, more prescient and more radical than one would ever gather from the standard histories of philosophy – in fact, one of the most frequent of Žižek's rhetorical moves is the excoriation of the typical reading, the standard reading, the doxa. Thus, in fewer than a dozen pages of *For They Know Not What They Do* (1991a), we find Žižek distancing himself from a 'commonplace opposition' (33), repudiating 'well-known textbook phrases' (33), beginning sentences with 'contrary to the usual conception' (35) and 'contrary to the usual notion' (44), and distinguishing his arguments from the 'everyday' (34) and the 'commonsensical' (44). In principle, this is laudable. Subtle and/or difficult theoretical discriminations do commonly degenerate into an easily applicable received wisdom which deprives them of the forensic value that made them worthwhile to begin with. However, the repudiation of the 'usual conception' is in Žižek a reflex so constant that it begins to seem symptomatic; at the very least, it prepares the way for an outcome in which Žižek's favourites (at first Hegel, then Kant and Descartes, then Schelling) have always-already made the points that later writers imagine they have scored against them. Thus, on the same few pages of the same book, we find first that 'The crucial aspect not to be missed is how Derrida is here thoroughly "Hegelian"' (1991a, 32), then that 'Andrzej Warminski ... falls prey to the error common among perspicacious critics of Hegel and formulates as a reproach to Hegel what is actually a basic feature of Hegel's thought' (40), and finally (à propos of Althusser) that 'Although one usually conceives the category of overdetermination as "anti-Hegelian" ..., it actually designates precisely this inherently Hegelian paradox of a totality which always comprises a particular element embodying its universal structuring principle' (45).

In other words, there's no arguing with a thoroughgoing Hegelian; this is a position that always-already anticipates (or sometimes just 'implies') anything of value that is subsequently voiced. So it is with characteristic relish that Žižek comments after quoting some paragraphs of Hegel: 'Everything is in this marvellous text: from the Foucauldian motif of disciplinary micro-practice as preceding any positive instruction to the Althusserian equation of the free subject with his subjection to the Law' (1999, 36). Žižek's enthusiasm is infectious, so that one feels almost churlish in saying that 'from the Foucauldian motif' to 'the Althusserian equation' can scarcely be described as 'everything', is in fact no great distance – Foucault was Althusser's student, and is cited by his former teacher in the first footnote to *Reading Capital*. This sense of a pre-ordained inevitability is reinforced by Žižek's other favourite formulations, the paradox (*Looking Awry* follows Jean-Claude Milner in reading those of Zeno as psychoanalytic truths), the 'nothing but' ('Lacan's whole point is that the Real is *nothing but* this impossibility of its inscription', 1989, 173) and the rhetorical question – 'Is not the supreme case of a particular feature that sustains the impossible sexual relationship the curling blonde hair in Hitchcock's *Vertigo*?' (1999, 286); 'Do we not find the ultimate example of this impossible Thing ... in the science-fiction theme of the ... Id-Machine?' (1999, 301); 'Is it not clear already in Kant that there is transcendental self-consciousness?' (1999, 304).

Žižek makes much of a concept he derives from Laclau and Mouffe, that of an antagonism fundamental to sexuation, to politics, to ideology, to society and to reality itself. Among other things, this means that his writing has its philosophical antagonists as well as its heroes. But his habit of finding a germinal version of any interesting current perspective in Hegel and Kant turns some of these into straw men. Derrida, chief representative of what Žižek calls the 'postmodern and/or deconstructionist morass' (1999, 232) is a particular problem. Turning once again to *For They Know Not What They Do*, we find that 'the slip unearthed by the hard labour of deconstructive reading is with Hegel the very fundamental and explicit thesis' (1991a, 63), that 'Hegel himself had already "deconstructed" the notion of reflection' (80), and that 'the basic premiss of the Derridean critique of Hegel ... misfires completely' (86). Readers should of course be grateful for Žižek's rubbishing of the facile 'poststructuralism' in which 'everything is language' or 'everything is discourse'. But the 'everything is' kind of statement has long been one of Derrida's favoured targets, and Žižek's repeated attempts to reinscribe Derrida as 'commonsensical' seem at best eccentric. Lacan's Hegelianism, for Derrida such a weakness, is for Žižek a key strength, so one is hardly surprised to find Žižek disdaining Derrida – yet one is still dismayed by Žižek's relegation of Derrida to the philosophical level of Stalin (1999, 133). Similarly debatable is Žižek's Foucault, who is repeatedly assigned positions which seem in fact closer to the antithesis of his arguments. All of this can perhaps be understood as an unfortunate weakness for imaginary combat – Žižek does tend to understand contemporary theory as a struggle for hegemony among Habermas and Derrida, Lacan and Foucault, Lyotard and Deleuze, and clearly sees himself as championing Lacan against these others. Žižek shares with Derrida, Deleuze, Lyotard and Badiou the wish to reassert the importance of philosophy per se, but (as befits a proponent of paradox) takes ideas most frequently from Lacan, the advocate of 'antiphilosophy'.

Žižek is in any case the thinker least likely to agree with Deleuze and Guattari that 'there is no ideology and never has been' (1987, 4). His first book in English is titled *The Sublime Object of Ideology* (1989), and as early as its second page praises Althusser for his 'thesis that the idea of the possible end of ideology is the ideological idea par excellence'. His second book, *For They Know Not What They Do* (1991a), begins similarly, with a discussion of Charles Maurras rallying the right against Dreyfus as an example of the process by which a particular ideological signification gains hegemony. In both books, Žižek is quickly arguing that reality is ideological per se: 'The fundamental level of ideology ... is not that of an illusion masking the real state of things but that of an (unconscious) fantasy structuring our social reality itself. And at this level, we are of course far from being a post-ideological society' (1989, 33). But if reality is ideological by definition, if the end of ideology can never come, how can any statement, including those of Žižek, hope to avoid complicity? One way of escaping this impasse (or at least of complicating it) is to recognize that what Žižek finds in the late Lacan is not only a reality thoroughly permeated with ideology but also something else called the Real.

In Lacan, the Real is by turns the body, birth, death, the unconscious and the pain of the symptom; it is whatever is radically resistant to symbolization, whatever cannot be integrated into our infinite (but never total) universe of signifiers and objects. The idea that the Real cannot be symbolized is the beginning of the difference between the Real and reality, since reality consists of what is symbolized. As Lacan puts it, 'reality is marked from the outset by a symbolic nihilation' (1993, 148); this is to say that the signifier constitutes reality for the subject by negating the Real in favour of objects and symbols. In related formulations, Lacan says that language covers the Real with the network of signifiers (1988a, 262), and that 'the symbolization of the real tends to be equivalent to the universe' (1988b, 322). In other words, reality is un-Real. Reality begins with symbolic opposition, with difference, but the Real is 'without fissure' (1988b, 97), without absence (1988b, 313). This is to say that the Real is an absolute horizon against and out of which reality is constructed; it is encountered as such only exceptionally, only traumatically, when symbolization fails. Death, for example, is Real, and it fully structures the reality of the obsessional, but it can never be experienced as such (Lacan 1988a, 223). The psychotic is close to the Real, but even he or she experiences not the Real itself so much as the signifier in the Real, as in paranoid symptoms that the neighbours are plotting against one or that media voices are addressed to oneself in particular.

In his most stringent formulations, Lacan speaks of the Real as something quite intractable. Not merely something difficult to symbolize, the Real is 'absolutely resistant' to symbolization – we can do nothing with or about it, can never come to terms with it. Thus the notorious dictum that 'the Real is the impossible'. At the same time, a more dialectical Lacan suggests that the Real is the event-horizon against which what we can do and know is defined; thus we will always try to come to terms with it, so that reality represents a determined if doomed attempt to symbolize the Real. There is a definitive sense in which the Real is beyond signification, so that we can never encounter it, but also a sense in which signification works to retrieve a reality from the Real, so that we can never disengage from it. This is by no means to find in Lacan a surprising warrant for returning to an 'objective' reality. As Žižek stresses, 'the Real is not a transcendent positive identity persisting somewhere beyond the symbolic order' (1989, 173). But it is to return to the idea that something defies and limits representation, and thus gives the lie to the easy formula that 'everything is language'. In fact, this traumatic Real with which we cannot come to terms is the reason that we think of any given reality as constructed and partial rather than definitive. As Žižek puts it:

> Our common everyday reality, the reality of the social universe in which we assume our usual roles of kind-hearted, decent people, turns out to be an illusion that rests on a certain 'repression', on overlooking the real of our desire. The social reality is then nothing but a fragile symbolic cobweb that can at any moment be torn aside by an intrusion of the real. (1991, 17)

For Žižek, then, the basic ideological gesture is the symbolization of the 'impossible' Real. This is to say that ideology goes all the way down, since the symbolization of the Real is basic not just to ideology but to thought as such. Why then is the formulation helpful? Because it suggests an understanding true to our experience of ideology as something mutable in practice and yet immutable in principle. Any given instance of ideology is something that, for all our theoretical sophistication, we tend to perceive as just wrong, yet ideology as such is something we recognize as stubbornly insistent in our lives and cultures.

The dialectic of reality and the Real that Žižek derives from Lacan is correlated in *The Plague of Fantasies* (1997) with the idea of a fundamental antagonism mentioned above: 'antagonism, again, is not the ultimate referent which anchors and limits the unending drift of the signifiers ... but the very force of their constant displacement' (216). By the same logic, 'class struggle means that there is no neutral metalanguage allowing us to grasp society as a given objective totality, since we always-already take sides' (216). Meanwhile, sexual difference 'skews the discursive universe, preventing us from grounding its formations in "hard reality"', and 'every symbolization of sexual difference is forever unstable and displaced with regard to itself' (216). Real antagonism is to be understood not as 'the transcendent Beyond which the signifying process tries to grasp in vain' (217), but as something intrinsic to the symbolic, 'the internal stumbling block on account of which the symbolic system can never achieve its self-identity' (217).

Such phrases make clear that the Lacanian–Žižekian Real is quite different from the Kantian thing-in-itself. The main reason is that the Real is not a substance, but instead an 'abyss'. Coterminous with but never available to the Symbolic, the Real is nothing in itself, yet reality is wholly premised on it. But even though the Real is not the thing-in-itself, the distinction between it and reality is inconceivable without the example of Kant. Žižek explains the importance of German idealism as follows: 'the great breakthrough was to outline the precise contours of this pre-ontological Real which precedes and eludes the ontological constitution of reality' (1999, 54). In other words, German idealism is understood as establishing a reality essentially invulnerable to the claims of postmodernism and the tactics of deconstruction. An argument this ambitious is worth delineating in its exact sequence. According to *Tarrying With the Negative* (1993), 'Descartes was the first to introduce a crack into the ontologically consistent universe' (12). That 'crack' is the subject and by extension the whole modern problematic of subjectivity. But Žižek points out that Descartes is quick to plaster over this crack; he 'does not yet conceive of the cogito as correlative to the whole of reality' (13). In other words, Descartes is not properly an idealist, and therefore cannot be reinscribed nearly as effectively as Kant and Hegel under the sign of Lacan. The breakthrough of Kant is that his subject is 'a necessary and simultaneously impossible logical construction' (14) such that 'the inaccessibility of the I to its own "kernel of being" is what makes it an I' (14). In other words, Kant anticipates Jacques Alain-Miller's Lacanian idea of 'extimacy'; this neologism formed by analogy with 'intimacy' proposes that the core of subjectivity must be understood as something 'outside' the experience of the subject. In the simplest sense, this is a restatement of Freud's thesis that the unconscious is primary, that subjectivity is constituted and dominated by an 'otherness'. On a more sophisticated level, the idea becomes a spiralling dialectic that replaces the traditional distinction between subject and object. Thus 'the very notion of self-consciousness implies the subject's self-decenterment' (15), and 'The Kantian subject ... is this very abyss, this void of absolute negativity to whom every ... particular positive content appears as ... ultimately contingent' (27).

Kant's Lacanianism before Lacan may seem to leave little for Hegel to do. However, explains Žižek, Kant's idea of the subject contradicts his own basic principle of a distinction between the unknowable thing-in-itself (the noumenal) and the realm of experience (the phenomenal). This contradiction is for Hegel not a failing, but a clue as to what remains to be thought. The result is that 'Hegel's "absolute idealism" is nothing but the Kantian "criticism" brought to its utmost consequences' (20), so that 'the Hegelian subject ... is nothing but the very gap which separates phenomena from the Thing' (21), or 'a name for the externality of the Substance to itself' (30). The terms 'subject' and 'substance' here may be understood as replacements for the traditional subject and object, necessary to account for the capability of the subject to understand itself as one of the 'objects'. The last (or at any rate latest) word in this sequence belongs to Lacan, for whom the subject 'although nowhere actually present ... nonetheless has to be retroactively constructed, presupposed, if all other elements are to retain their consistency' (33), while the substance too 'is a mirage retroactively invoked' (36). Thus 'what we experience as "reality" discloses itself against the background of the lack ... of the mythical object whose encounter would bring about the full satisfaction of the drive' (37). 'Reality' still denotes everything we can experience and understand, but it is fully premised on the Real, which can never be experienced and understood. In other words, the idealist tradition cannot be written off as a series of delirious involutions of the hard facts of life; on the contrary, we can come to terms with the personal, critical and political questions that most concern us in the material world only by beginning with 'the split separating the accessible, symbolically structured, reality from the void of the Real' (37). It is worth noting that Kant is not unaware of the 'contradiction' in his account of subjectivity, indeed presenting it as a virtue, but it is also worth noting that Žižek elaborates an idea of 'retroactivity' as a way of legitimating a phrase like 'kernel of being', which echoes post-Kantians from Hegel to Lacan more than Kant himself.

All this perhaps begins to explain the importance to Žižek of Lacan's essay 'Kant with Sade' (1989). In that essay, Lacan reads *Philosophy in the Bedroom* alongside *The Critique of Practical Reason*, arguing that both texts urge obedience to a categorical imperative. In Kant, this is the moral law that we find within ourselves; in Sade, the subject is every bit as bound by duty, but in this case is required to do 'the bidding of the Other', to instrumentalize himself in the service of the pleasure of the Other. Where the Kantian subject is unitary, the Freudian–Lacanian–Žižekian subject is constitutively split. Thus the commanding voice of the Other, named by Freud the superego, is another case of 'extimacy', an agency that derives from 'outside' and yet seems to speak from 'inside'. Therefore the superego is not the voice of conscience but the 'obscene imperative' to enjoyment that Žižek discovers in nationalism, in racism, in popular culture and in numerous other contexts.

It is probably fair to say that Žižek's influence on criticism is still formative. Apart from figures like Joan Copjec, whose carefully argued account of Lacan's formulas of sexuation in terms of Kant's antinomies seems more persuasive than Žižek's own efforts, Žižekians tend to fasten onto one or two of Žižek's ideas, to openly imitate his rhetoric, or to proceed directly to textual analysis, frequently dealing with the same figures Žižek himself discusses. Such copycat 'applicationism' is of course typical of the first stage of the reception of any significant thinker. Not so well understood is that the writing of Žižek implies a reorientation of the whole relationship between reality and textuality. This is to say that the calculated outrage to common sense of a distinction between reality and the Real has consequences for the understanding of both the various realisms and the various anti-realisms in every field. Perhaps the most important of these is that representation becomes as much continuous as discontinuous with the everyday conception of reality – both are attempts to come to terms with the impossible Real, and both are polarized against it, since what cannot be symbolized is also what remains to be symbolized, in some cases what most needs to be symbolized. This is a way of thinking quite different from the present critical status quo, which is much better at polemicizing against traditional realist aesthetics than it is at positively rethinking reality and the real. Current criticism is nearly ritual in its quickness to assert that reality is constituted by the signifier; what ensues is typically so much preoccupied with the signifier that reality is effectively ceded to a traditional positivism and/or empiricism. In place of this binary opposition, the work of Žižek suggests a tripartite system (the 'impossible' Real, reality as an attempt to symbolize the Real, and renderings of reality such as fiction and film). In sum, we might propose that the work of any signifying or cultural practice, including those consciously conceived in opposition to realism, is to retrieve a reality from the Real. Only when this begins to sink in will we see Žižekian criticism that passes beyond imitation and/or homage.

When the ideas of Althusser and Lacan first inflected English-speaking criticism in the early 1970s, one of the routine citations of that still politicized period was Lenin on Hegel, to the effect that an intelligent materialism is closer to an intelligent idealism than to an unintelligent materialism. Though the reference has long since fallen into disuse, it remains a virtual template for the analyses of Žižek. This is to touch on the recognition factor, to suggest the extent to which Žižek rethinks an earlier and still influential problematic. Žižek is more Hegelian and (despite his fondness for semiotic rectangles) less semiological than the typical issue of *Screen* from 1975, but is nonetheless asking many of the same questions. Thus the first move of *The Sublime Object of Ideology* is to interrogate 'the sudden eclipse of the Althusserian school', which is best understood not as an intellectual defeat but as a 'theoretical amnesia' (1989, 1). Such a return was always possible insofar as 1970s theory, like so many other intellectual projects of the twentieth century, was not so much surpassed as slowly abandoned when diminishing returns began to set in – that is, when other ideas and approaches began to seem more productive. But a mere return to the thinking of the 1970s would hold little interest. So Žižek is better understood as a renovator, giving distinctly new kinds of answers to previously posed questions.

The theoretical project of the 1970s was at once the continuation of the political project of May 1968, and the beginning of the work of mourning for it. In its utopian, wish-fulfilling dimension, that project thought it possible to combine semiology, psychoanalysis, marxism and feminism into a key to all ideologies. The dream of an all-encompassing, all-purpose theory slowly dissipated, until by the mid-1980s it began to be recalled as something of an embarrassment. Žižek is by no means naive enough to think that one can reanimate an earlier theoretical moment by a effort of sheer will, but he is reminiscent of the utopianism of the earlier project in his sheer exuberance – Janet Bergstom describes the 'high-energy Žižek-effect' as consisting of reference in the course of twenty-five pages to more than four dozen philosophers, novelists, psychoanalysts, political leaders, patients of Freud, fictional characters, films, plays, operas and developments in computer culture.

For Žižek, the personal equivalent of May 1968 must be 1989, the year of both his first English publication and the collapse of the Soviet empire. Žižek is a Slovenian who played a role in the dissident movements which helped bring down Titoist Yugoslavia, and his second book in English is based on a series of lectures given in Ljubljana in winter 1989–90. He describes the dissident movement as a 'vanishing mediator' between state socialism and the new capitalism of Eastern Europe. The vanishing mediator is a notion that Žižek finds in an essay of Fredric Jameson on Weber and applies in literally dozens of contexts. In Jameson, the vanishing mediator is an element essential to a historical and/or intellectual transition that disappears when its work is done. For Žižek, it is an element that is 'nowhere actually present and as such inaccessible to our experience, [but] nonetheless has to be retroactively reconstructed, presupposed, if all other elements are to retain their consistency' (1993, 33). Thus the two books on Schelling value their protagonist as the vanishing mediator between Kant and Marx, Kant himself 'brings to light ... a moment which has to disappear if the Cartesian res cogitans is to appear' (1993, 14). Forrest Gump is a vanishing mediator in that he unwittingly enables a whole series of events in recent American history, and the 'paradoxical relationship of subject and substance, where the subject emerges as the crack in the universal Substance, hinges on the notion of the subject as the "vanishing mediator" in the precise sense of the Freudian–Lacanian Real' (1993, 33). Like the refusal of the usual reading, the paradox and the rhetorical question, the vanishing mediator is an index of Žižek's thinking as a whole; this missing link that must be thought is close to the idea of 'the pre-synthetic Real' as 'a level that must be retroactively presupposed but can never actually be encountered' (1999, 33), and helps to sustain the Hegelian vision of that level as 'already the product, the result, of the imagination's disruptive ability' (1999, 33). With this argument that 'the mythic, inaccessible zero-level of pure multitude not yet affected/fashioned by imagination is nothing but pure imagination itself' (1999, 33), we reach the Žižekian first principle or declaration of faith.

Žižek clearly considers himself quite the card for presenting his difficult philosophical ideas in terms of popular culture; the discussion of subjectivity from Descartes to Lacan summarized above refers throughout to Ridley Scott's 1984 *Blade Runner*. At moments, however, Žižek suggests that he is as much disgusted as enthralled by popular films and fictions, and that Lacan's *jouissance* ('enjoyment') can be understood as precisely this paradox of an element in which one revels despite one's 'better' judgement. At the same time, Žižek's taste in popular culture could not be much more male-professorial – he deals mostly with hard-boiled writers of comparatively established literary value (Hammett, Chandler, Highsmith) and with film directors of auteur status (Chaplin, Hitchcock, Lynch). By the later 1990s, it is true, he does discuss New Age religious books like *The Celestine Prophecy* and mass-audience movies like *The Flintstones*, and (in one of his less persuasive analyses) proposes Mary Kay Letourneau, a 35-year-old schoolteacher who had a compulsive affair with a 14-year-old pupil, as an authentic ethical hero, since she lets us see the distinction between the ethical and the good. But this 'lower' popular culture is dealt with mostly in passing; extended and/or truly philosophical readings are reserved for Conan Doyle rather than Conan the Barbarian. Žižek is in any case just as likely to discuss Joyce and Kafka and Wagner as *Nightmare on Elm Street*. At times, this leads to outright confusion – the works of 'popular literature' listed in the index of *Looking Awry* include *Antigone*, *Un Amour de Swann* and *Finnegans Wake*, as though 'popular' meant the same thing as 'famous'.

Another negative is that Žižek is among the most repetitious of contemporary theorists. The same anecdotes, examples and arguments reappear from text to text, sometimes verbatim and sometimes at length, so much so that it is hard not to think longingly of Lacan's habit of ending the analytic session as soon as the analysand begins to repeat. By *The Ticklish Subject* (1999), Žižek at least begins to seem aware of his habit, offering a self-deprecating footnote to his nth discussion of Hegel's famous paragraph 'the human being is this night'. Yet this does not mean that whole books can be dismissed as rehashes; each of Žižek's titles offers perspectives and analyses not found elsewhere. New readers are best advised to begin at the beginning, with *The Sublime Object of Ideology* and *Looking Awry*, whose problematic is further developed some nine years later in the tour de force that is *The Plague of Fantasies*. A more purely philosophical voice begins to speak in Žižek's *For They Know Not What They Do*; that same voice, as we have seen, discusses Kant and Hegel in *Tarrying With The Negative*, and Heidegger, Alain Badiou and Judith Butler in the encompassing and brilliant *The Ticklish Subject*. Readers more interested in Žižek's Lacan are advised to begin with *Looking Awry* and the edited collection *Everything You Always Wanted to Know About Lacan (But Were Afraid To Ask Hitchcock)*, to look next at *Enjoy Your Symptom!* and finally to consult two anthologies, *Gaze and Voice as Love Objects* and *Cogito and the Unconscious*.

Michael Walsh

Further reading and works cited

Althusser, L. and Balibar, E. *Reading Capital*. London, 1970.

Bergstrom, J. (ed.) *Endless Night*. Berkeley, CA, 1999.

Boynton, R. 'Enjoy Your Žižek', *Lingua Franca*, October 1998.

Copjec, J. 'Sex and the Euthanasia of Reason'. *Supposing the Subject*, ed. J. Copjec. London, 1994.

Deleuze, G. and Guattari, F. *A Thousand Plateaus*. Minneapolis, MN, 1987.

Eagleton, T. 'Enjoy!', *London Review of Books*, 27 November 1997.

Jameson, F. *The Ideologies of Theory. Essays 1971–1986. Volume 2*. Minneapolis, MN, 1988.

Kant, I. *Critique of Practical Reason*. Cambridge, 1997.

Lacan, J. *Ecrits*. Paris, 1966.

—. *The Four Fundamental Concepts of Psychoanalysis*. New York, 1978.

—. *The Seminar of Jacques Lacan. Book I*. New York, 1988a.

—. *The Seminar of Jacques Lacan. Book II*. New York, 1988b.

—. 'Kant with Sade', *October*, 51, 1989.

—. *The Seminar of Jacques Lacan. Book III*. New York, 1993.

—. *The Seminar of Jacques Lacan. Book XX. Encore*. New York, 1998.

Laclau, E. and Mouffe, C. *Hegemony and Socialist Strategy*. London, 1985.

Miklitsch, R. 'Going Through the Fantasy: Screening Slavoj Žižek'. *South Atlantic Quarterly*, 97, 2, Spring 1998.

Miller, J.-A. 'Extimité'. *Prose Studies*, 11, 1991.

Sade, Marquis de. *Philosophy in the Bedroom*. New York, 1966.

Žižek, S. *The Sublime Object of Ideology*. London, 1989.

—. *For They Know Not What They Do*. London, 1991a.

—. *Looking Awry*. Cambridge, MA, 1991b.

—. *Enjoy Your Symptom!* London, 1992a.

—. *Everything You Always Wanted to Know About Lacan (But Were Afraid To Ask Hitchcock)*. London, 1992b.

—. *Tarrying With the Negative*. Durham, NC, 1993.

—. *The Plague of Fantasies*. London, 1997.

— (ed.) *Cogito and the Unconscious*. Durham, NC, 1998.

—. *The Ticklish Subject*. London, 1999.

— and Salecl, R. (eds) *Gaze and Voice as Love Objects*. Durham, NC, 1996.

Cahiers du Cinéma (1951–)

When, in October of 1970, François Truffaut was asked his reasons for leaving the editorial staff of *Cahiers du cinéma*, he replied:

> It was not a disagreement. My name no longer represented the basic tenets of the magazine. When I worked on *Cahiers*, it was another era. We spoke of films only from the angle of their relative beauty. Today at *Cahiers* they do a marxist-leninist analysis of films. Readership of the magazine is limited to university graduates. As for me, I have never read a single line of Marx. (1999)

This statement, coming from a former contributor who had gone on to become a leading participant in the *Nouvelle Vague*, the film-making movement which confirmed *Cahiers du cinéma* in the forefront of French film criticism, clearly indicates the shift the magazine underwent in its first twenty years of publication. However, beginning in the mid-1970s, *Cahiers* returns to alliances with the Nouvelle Vague and a renewed respect for Hollywood, supplanting the most politically engaged phase of *Cahiers'* history. Today, *Cahiers* has come almost full circle, back to the embrace of a critical view that champions popular films of merit, while still trying to broaden filmic tastes. Young French film-makers are championed, but political and theoretical issues are addressed far less frequently. Tracing this history, this essay will look at *Cahiers* in context, examining how the various essayists who wrote for this review brought to film aesthetics a political and theoretical dimension, and how commercial viability and historical shifts affected the life of this influential journal.

The aesthetic viewpoint that gave birth to *Cahiers* and to the Nouvelle Vague is firmly grounded in a school of French film analysis which began in the 1920s. In a theoretical debate on the cinema, leading voices agreed that movies were not vulgar entertainment, but an art form. Canudo held that cinema is a separate and equal art with its own different and specific characteristics. His position was a reaction to the fact that film had so often been judged exclusively by the criteria established for other media, particularly the aesthetics of theatre and literature. But the effect was cyclical. Because it had been assumed that film did the same things as literature and theatre, the movies that were produced in France were often adaptations of works created in other media. These adaptations were often not as expressive as the originals. In other cases, critics who did not allow for the translation of forms of expression did not really understand the specificity of the film medium. As a result, many critics treated the cinema apologetically. Canudo's theory was the beginning of recognition of the validity of cinematic expression. Elie Faure's argument that cinema is a synthesis of the other six arts also added in its own way to the prestige of film and allowed him to think through the spatio-temporal specificity of film. Other theorists who contributed to the development of the Nouvelle Vague include (and this list is still incomplete) Louis Delluc, Jean Epstein, René Clair, Rudolph Arnheim, Marcel L'Herbier, Bela Balàzs and Edgar Morin. Yet the most direct antecedent of the Nouvelle Vague is the theoretical work of André Bazin, and his influence at *Cahiers* was immense.

Bazin's writings (collected in 1958 into a four-volume series called *Qu'est-ce que c'est le cinéma?*) reveal the growth of an aesthetic that concentrated on the cinema's capacity for metaphysical transcendence through realist observation. Behind Bazin's metaphysics is an effort to analyse seriously the way in which films affected him: what filmic devices, what metaphors, and what myths serve as the basis for the transcendental expression achieved. He, too, looked to American films, particularly those of Chaplin, Orson Welles and William Wyler, as the best examples of the development of cinematic language, as well as championing the causes of Jean Renoir and Eric Von Stroheim, whom he felt had not achieved adaquate critical recognition during their careers. Bazin's overwhelming influence on the young men who were to become the 'comité de redaction' of *Cahiers* and later the *Nouvelle Vague* is illustrated by Eric Rohmer:

> Everything had been said by him, we came too late. Now we are left with the difficult duty of pursuing his task; we shall not fail in this, although we are convinced that he pursued it much further than it will be possible for us to do ourselves.... (1999, 113)

In April 1950, the editor of *La Revue du cinéma* was killed in an auto accident. Doniol-Valcroze, Lo Duca and Leontyne Kiegel decided to continue the magazine, publishing articles similar to those in *La Gazette du cinéma*, an erratic broadsheet written and circulated in the Latin Quarter by Jean-Luc Godard, Eric Rohmer and Jacques Rivette. The first issue of the new magazine, *Cahiers du cinéma*, appeared in April of 1951.

Cahiers continued in the direction indicated by Bazin. It was not, however, until January of 1954 that any cohesive definition of the staff's position was enunciated. In an article titled 'Une Certaine tendence du cinéma français', François Truffaut attacked the traditional manner of French cinema and was particularly critical of the role played by screenwriters whom he found unversed in cinematic expression. He sarcastically suggested:

> Why don't we all turn to adapting literary masterpieces of which there are probably a few left … then we'll all be steeped in the 'quality tradition' up to our necks, and the French cinema with its daring 'psychological realism,' its 'harsh truths,' 'its 'ambiguity' will be one great morbid funeral ready to be heaved out of the Billancourt studios and stacked up in the cemetery so appropriately waiting alongside. (1999, 4)

Truffaut called instead for a 'cinéma d'auteur' in which directors would express their personal convictions in their films. *Cahiers'* models were Renoir, Cocteau. Bresson, Hitchcock, Welles, Rosselini and Hawks.

The early success of *Cahiers* might be ascribed in part to the popularity of films, especially the American films the magazine lauded, during a period when many French people still didn't own television sets. However, *Cahiers* critics and editors, Truffaut, Rohmer, Godard, Claude Chabrol and Jacques Rivette, longed to make their own films. They began experimenting in 16 mm, made shorts, and finally graduated to feature length films. By 1959, with the release of Godard's *A Bout de souffle* and Truffaut's *Les Quatre cents coups*, the same year as Alain Resnais' *Hiroshima, Mon Amour*, the Nouvelle Vague had arrived.

There was, however, another important film magazine operating in France at this time which shared few of the aesthetic convictions of the *Cahiers* group, but instead defined its approach to film as marxist-leninist: *Positif*. Many of the *Positif* critics found Bazin and the *Cahiers* staff too liberal and bourgeois in their aesthetic and metaphysical orientation. They could not understand *Cahiers'* respect for certain American directors who produced what they considered right-wing films. Gerard Gozlan, an editor of *Positif*, characterized the Bazinian influence on the *Cahiers* approach by saying,

> It is natural that right-wing critics should welcome a critical system which lies at the crossroads of so many traditions – bourgeois, idealist, liberal, religious, and social democrat. It is natural that rightwing critics should not scorn a 'dialectic' that cleverly combines the prestige of rationalism and the irrational powers of the image, borrowing the linguistic charms from the former and the guiles of faith from the latter. (1997, 132)

The difference between the marxist analysis offered by *Positif* and that which developed in *Cahiers* is emphasized by the fact that the animosity between the two groups never relented. On the contrary, *Positif*'s attacks on *Cahiers* became even more determined as *Cahiers* developed its own form of political criticism. This chasm separating the two schools is understandable in terms of the wide range of ideologies that constitute the French Left, with the Communist Party on one side and the Maoists and anarchists on the other. The 'extreme gauche' called the CP the 'left-wing pillar of order'. It is with this extreme left that the *Cahiers* group eventually aligned. Moreover, the purely aesthetic phase that *Cahiers* criticism went through had an effect on its political criticism; the manner in which films express themselves was always in the forefront of the discussion.

The full-fledged entry of *Cahiers* into the political arena cannot be explained in isolation from the politcal changes occuring in France in the mid and late 1960s. Following two wars of decolonialization, a student and young worker movement emerged. This meant that organized opposition to Gaullism was no longer the exclusive domain of the Communist Party, an anathema to the young for its pro-Soviet line and to the film-makers for its cultural deadness.

As early as 1965, Godard turned a favorable eye to this political movement among youth. In *Masculin-Féminin* the lead character Paul, and his worker friend Robert, paint slogans against American involvement in Vietnam on the side of an American diplomat's limousine. One is reminded of Michel stealing cars in *A bout de souffle*, an earlier form of the same anarchy. While Godard was in the process of becoming an increasingly politically oriented film-maker, the *Cahiers* group began to explore earlier political artistic expression. In 1964 they devoted a section to Bertolt Brecht, arguing that his theories of distanciation should help construct future film practice.

While Brecht's influence on Godard can be seen as early as *Une femme est une femme* (1961), it was never so evident as in *La Chinoise* made in 1967. Not only is one of the characters an actor who forsakes the theatre to become involved in full-time political work and then leaves that work to read Brecht door to door, there are also sequences of pure stylization – a form of filmic guerilla theatre. After Godard left *Cahiers* to devote himself to film-making, he criticized the film-making of others through his own films. He continually suggested new directions for films to take, and his influence on *Cahiers* remained great.

The scholarly studies of Christian Metz on meaning in film began to be published in *Cahiers* in 1965. Metz's investigations, along with those of Roland Barthes and others, represented the French assimilation of and expansion on Russian formalist theorists. Semiotics offered a new methodology with which to study film. The increased academic interest in the study of film corresponded to *Cahiers'* development of longer essays and dossiers on major figures in film history, which would pave the way for the purely theoretical essays that would emerge by the end of the decade. *Cahiers'* collective texts devoted to the analysis of individual films became a prototype for a film semiotics that engaged historical and ideological analysis, on John Ford's *Young Mr Lincoln* in July 1970 followed by analyses of Renoir's *La Vie est à nous*, Von Sternberg's *Morocco* and Cukor's *Sylvia Scarlet*.

The student–worker uprising of May 1968 can be seen as a turning point for the *Cahiers* staff, just as it was for many French people. The Gaullist regime proved more vulnerable than anyone had dreamed and the lines of demarcation between the right wing and the gauchists were so clearly drawn that there remained no comfortable middle ground. The aftermath of this situation for *Cahiers* was that the magazine began to be less concerned with a 'pure' aesthetic and instead pursued a new aesthetic which could be put to concrete political use.

In 1968, the emergence of *Cinéthique*, a film magazine begun by a group formerly associated with the literary review *Tel Quel*, provided a challenge to *Cahiers* just as it was beginning to formulate a political approach. *Cinéthique* had the advantage of a fresh beginning based on a dialectical materialist approach to film. Rejecting any 'cinephile' investigation of film history or any work at documentation such as interviews with film-makers or découpage, *Cinéthique* concentrated instead on a sharply drawn political critique of films. They condemned nearly all films produced up until that point in history, and supported only those films actively engaged in combating traditional bourgeois film expression. All aesthetic considerations were shunned in favour of a critique that considered only a film's ultimate usefulness in breaking down the dominant culture. *Cinéthique* went so far as to praise films for including sequences which were aesthetic failures, arguing that they served revolutionary goals by reducing marketability.

Cahiers' response, a long evaluation of the *Cinéthique* approach, appeared in issue no. 217, November 1969. *Cahiers* criticized *Cinéthique* for the vagueness of its theoretical formulations and for forcing all understanding of cinema into a scientific system which left no allowances for a practicable cinema outside of a role definied as (1) diffusing a knowledge of theoretical science and (2) exposing its own self-conscious nature.

While *Cahiers*' arguments may be seen in part as a defence of its own tradition (including its bourgeois tendencies), they must also be seen as an attempt to salvage a working aesthetic from a purely theoretical approach of negation and rejection. Whatever the internal failings of *Cinéthique*'s the very existence of a cinema magazine taking such a radical position served to stimulate *Cahiers*' own theoretical growth.

Research was begun in 1969 on Russian film-makers and theorists of the 1920s, the fertile period of Soviet cinema before the heavy control of Stalinist social realism. Eisenstein's theories of montage and film language were given exhaustive attention. A fifteen part translation of Eisenstein's 'Non-indifferent Nature' was published in instalments. There was unbounded respect for his scientific analysis of the perception and interpretation of film images as a dialectical process. Dziga-Vertov was rediscovered by *Cahiers* and studied in depth.

Thus the merging of various influences, the changing politics of the country, the research into the work of the early Russian theorists, the challenge of other film magazines and the scientific study of film language combined to give *Cahiers* a decidedly different orientation and style in the last years of the 1960s and early 1970s. In April 1969 Jean Pierre Oudart's 'La Suture' brought to the semiotic focus of film studies an ideological critique of Hollywood continuity editing. Political theoretical analysis also led to a series of articles by Jean-Louis Comolli entitled 'Technique et Idéologie' and another series on 'Politique et La Lutte Idéologique de Classe'.

Comolli's articles are a reaction to Marcel Pleynet's reflections on film technique in *Cinéthique* and Jean Patrick Lebel's book, *Cinéma et Idéologie*. Arguing against Lebel's theory, which tries to distinguish between technical innovations and the use to which they are put, Comolli expands on Pleynet's suggestion that the film image is the perfected form of Renaissance perspective in art and carries with it the advanced form of that historical movement's bourgeois ideology. Comolli argues a materialist history of film would explain the impetus of film innovations. His writing reflects a wide familiarity with film and film history and his theory is made concrete by specific references to films which illustrate his points about deep focus and distortion of perspective.

Cahiers' application of theory to discussion of specific films is also represented by Jean-Pierre Oudart's article in no. 232 called 'L'Idéologie moderniste dans quelques films récents'. Examining first what he terms the 'Bressonian Model' in which a central character refuses communication, and economic and sexual relationships, in order to avoid definition as an object within the social norms, Oudart traces how that 'anti-Hollywood structure' has been treated in films such as Bernardo Bertolucci's *The Conformist* and Louis Malle's *Le Souffle au coeur*.

This intellectual, ideological turn of *Cahiers* met with sharp opposition from its old detractors, the staff of *Positif*. In their November 1970 issue, no. 122, they devoted over a third of their pages to an attack on *Cahiers* which included parenthetically *Cinéthique* and *Tel quel*. The attack called the new form of criticism practised in *Cahiers* 'unreadable, obscure and esoteric' and dismissed *Cahiers*' classification of social realism as a bourgeois art form that should be replaced by dialectical fiction. *Cahiers* responded in its January–Febuary 1971 double issue (which, incidently, was entirely devoted to Eisenstein) with a short sarcastic rebuttal. The staff believed that its own ideology, while complex, was not obscure, and provided the only possible illumination of social conditions. Although they agreed that their theories might not be accessible to everyone, they believed that the ideas would be understood by those who mattered who would then disseminate their understanding through their films.

  Cahiers has consistently held up the work of Godard as an example of the most progressive use of film. *Cahiers* has been Godard's leading critical support in his efforts made in collaboration with Jean-Pierre Gorin and the Dziga-Vertov Collective, and it has devoted much space over the last year to a retrospective view of Godard's and Gorin's political films. In March 1973, they published a long position paper entitled, 'Quelles sont nos taches sur le front culturel?' ['What are our tasks on the cultural front?'] which they worked on after an open meeting with their 'comrades on the ideological front' in August 1972. *Cahiers*' cinephilic endeavours continue throughout even the most ideologically engaged period, but they find new objects to embrace such as the films of Jean-Marie Straub and Danielle Huillet, whose political expression is embedded in formal transformations of cinematic expressions and metaphorical readings of history. The *Cahiers*' appreciation of Japanese film in general gives way to attention to the films of Oshima Nagisa that take various approaches to redefining Brechtian and politically engaged cinema at a formal level.

  One might trace *Cahiers*' history through changes in cover design (yellow covers with photo inserts yielding to the larger format photo covers on glossy paper, then to the plain text 'table of content' covers during the most political period which also saw circulation drop, then the revival of the larger format glossy photo covers). These changes correspond to publisher shifts and economic reorganizations. The revival of the mass circulation cinephilic film review after the glory of the theoretical period turned a near 180 degress on the political denunciation of much of the aesthetics which had built *Cahiers*' early history. The return was a gradual process, with 1978 a transitional year in which Truffaut's *La Chambre Verte* recieved accolades from Pierre Bonitzer and attention to Martin Scorsese marks an interest in new Hollywood films. During the last twenty years, *Cahiers* has repeatedly examined what it calls 'the situation of French film', while bringing critical energy to an increasingly international cinema.

Maureen Turim

Further reading and works cited

Arnaud, P. *Robert Bresson*. Paris, 1986.
Aumont, J. *Du visage au cinéma*. Paris, 1992.
Baecque, A. de. *Les Cahiers du cinéma*. Paris, 1991.
Bazin, A. *Qu'est ce que c'est le cinéma?* Paris, 1958.
— and Narboni, J. *Le cinéma français de la libération à la nouvelle vague (1945–1958)*. Paris, 1983.
Bergala, A. and Narboni, J. *Pasolini cinéaste*. Paris, 1981.

— et al. *Orson Welles*. Paris, 1986.

Bonitzer, P. *Le champ aveugle*. Paris, 1982.

—. *Décadrages*. Paris, 1985.

—. *Eric Rohmer*. Paris, 1991.

Browne, N. (ed.) *Cahiers du cinéma 1969–1972*. Cambridge, MA, 1990.

Godard, J.-L. *Godard on Godard*. New York, 1972.

—. *Godard par Godard*. Paris, 1991.

— and Bergala, A. *Godard par Godard*. Paris, 1989.

—. *Jean-Luc Godard par Jean-Luc Godard*. Paris, 1998.

Gozlan, G. 'In Praise of Andre Bazin'. *The New Wave*, ed. P. Graham. New York, 1997.

Hillier, J. (ed.) *Cahiers du cinéma, the 1950s*. Cambridge, MA, 1985.

Le Berre, C. *François Truffaut*. Paris, 1993.

Lellis, G. *Bertolt Brecht, Cahiers du cinéma and Contemporary Film Theory*. Ann Arbor, MI, 1982.

MacCabe, C. and Godard, J.-L. *Godard*. Bloomington, IN, 1980.

Magny, J. *Claude Chabrol*. Paris, 1987.

Rohmer, E. *Cahiers du cinéma: La nouvelle vague: Claude Chabrol, Jean-Luc Godard, Jacques Rivette, Eric Rohmer, François Truffaut, Petite bibliothèque des Cahiers du cinéma, 27*. Paris, 1999.

Truffaut, F. *Cahiers du cinéma: La nouvelle vague: Claude Chabrol, Jean-Luc Godard, Jacques Rivette, Eric Rohmer, François Truffaut, Petite bibliothèque des Cahiers du cinéma, 27*. Paris, 1999.

Critical Fictions: Experiments in Writing from *Le Nouveau Roman* to the Oulipo

Around 1955 a small number of French authors published – or began publishing – a series of works, mostly novels (later also some short stories, drama and – a typical genre of the 1960s – radio plays), which produced shock among both critics and readers. Thus the New Novel was born and the names of its (unofficial) members became rapidly (in)famous: Alain Robbe-Grillet (*Les Gommes*, 1953; *Le Voyeur*, 1955; *La Jalousie*, 1957); Claude Simon (*Le Vent*, 1957; *L'Herbe*, 1958; *La Route des Flandres*, 1960), Michel Butor (*L'Emploi du temps*, 1956; *La Modification*, 1957) and Nathalie Sarraute (*Martereau*, 1953; *Le Planétarium*, 1959), whose first book (*Tropismes*, 1939) had been published before the Second World War and whose position in the group had always been marginal, not least because she was usually published by Gallimard, the principal mainstream publishing company, instead of by Minuit, the small independent publisher whose name was inseparable with that of the New Novel. Other writers are associated with the movement: Claude Ollier (*La Mise en scène*, 1958), Marguerite Duras (*Moderato Cantabile*, 1958), Robert Pinget (*L'Inquisitoire*, 1962) and Jean Ricardou (*L'Observatoire de Cannes*, 1961), who in fact already belonged to the next literary generation, that of the *Tel Quel* group.

All the aforementioned authors, whose main spokesman was without any doubt Alain Robbe-Grillet (the first to publish a 'post factum' manifesto: *Pour un nouveau roman*, 1963), shaped a new form of writing which was initially despised by most professional critics, largely ignored by the public, enthusiastically supported by an emergent generation of literary scholars such as Roland Barthes and Gérard Genette, and very rapidly discovered and adopted by foreign academics (New Novels appear on reading lists in the US and elsewhere, and scholarly attention is paid to the movement by all the leading institutions). The new 'thing' about the New Novel (a label neither immediately used nor immediately claimed by the authors, who always emphasized their individuality) was something very relative. In France, the plea for an 'objective' literature turned away from the humanist or political message so dominantly present in the fiction of that time (e.g. in the work of Camus, Sartre, Mauriac and many other existential, marxist or Christian authors) but turned towards a more phenomenologically inspired descriptive approach of life, which indeed produced a literary earthquake the force of which can still be compared to the intrusion of Dada and surrealism in the 1920s. The frontal attack against the 'roman à thèse' and the 'Balzacian' model dramatically changed the way the dominant genre of the novel was perceived and opened it to a more writerly vision. Viewed from abroad, however, the New Novel appeared to a certain extent to be nothing more than an overtaking manoeuvre. The New Novelists themselves liked to stress the influence upon their work of great modernist examples: William Faulkner (for Claude Simon), Henry James and Ivy Compton-Burnett (for Sarraute), Franz Kafka (for Robbe-Grillet), James Joyce (for Michel Butor, though not just for him). Nevertheless, even for the foreign public more familiar with modernism in the novel, the French New Novel remained a very innovative and disquieting movement, as it explored in a radically new way the frontier of novelistic *tellability*. New Novels, indeed, focused apparently upon something that in all other types of novel had only a secondary function: objects on the one hand, description on the other. Whereas before, even in very modernist fiction, the object was always viewed in relation to the subject, and description never functioned, except as an auxiliary in plot-making, the New Novel appeared to reject the subject as well as the plot: New Novelists stopped telling, they merely described, and their descriptions were no longer part of a fictional universe ruled by the necessity of putting characters in a meaningful setting. This was at least the way the first readers judged the literary UFOs called New Novels. And although it soon became clear that there was room for the subject, political commitment and narrative, it is important to underline the very difficulties of reading created by the thorough foregrounding of aspects until then under-stressed in novelistic writing, and the apparent censorship of the basic aspects of the novel which Robbe-Grillet called outdated: character, story, diegetic setting and above all message. In its first years, the New Novel was reduced by its enemies to its lust for description and its exclusion of any recognizable story. Its defenders logically emphasized the phenomenological added value of its writing, which can be read as a testimony of the difficulties of being in an alienated society where subjects are replaced by objects. The larger dissatisfaction with the classic rules and stereotypes of the novel was also put forward, but this dissatisfaction was only coded in terms of refusal, not in terms of a change in the hierarchy between content and form. The first labels coined to come to terms with the newness of the movement revealed much of that anxiety: before being labelled New Novel, the group was called 'l'école du regard' (the school of the gaze) and 'l'école du refus' (the school of refusal).

The history of the New Novel is very complex, not only because the New Novelists never constituted a real group and because their work went through different styles and periods, but also and maybe more because no other literary movement had ever been characterized by such a merging of creative work and critical commentary (sometimes of a highly theoretical nature). The New Novel and the theory of the New Novel (either written by the New Novelists themselves or vicariously developed by their enemies as well as their defenders) could not be separated, and the relationship between creative work and critical reflection became so strong that at the point the New Novel aspired to become a kind of writing where the very distinction of fiction and theory no longer held.

During the first period of the New Novel, which ran approximately from 1955 to 1965, creative writing was clearly dominant and theory played only a secondary role. Those were the years of avoidance of traditional plot and story elements, and of insistence on realism and 'objective' style (not fortuitously, those were also the years of New Wave in Cinema and, some years later, New Realism in painting). Slowly, the New Novel started finding its own audience, and its influence in the global cultural debate was undoubtedly growing, at the price of the more radical aspects of its writing. In the mid-1960s, however, a change of tone and style occurred.

Under the influence of radical critics such as Jean Ricardou (related to *Tel Quel* in the 1960s, where he functioned as a kind of bridge between the experiments in the 'novel' and those in 'writing'), the refusal of the *classic* novel became a refusal of the novel *tout court*, whereas the critique of the traditional content and plot elements shifted towards a plea for a formally and linguistically driven type of writing where the critique of the humanist message no longer relied upon the pre-eminence of the object but on that of language (structuralist theory on language and subject now replacing the phenomenological view-point of the 1950s). The New Novel was seen as a verbal architecture that no longer referred to an outside world, the rules and constraints of which were completely internal to the linguistic universe. As Jean Ricardou remarked in one of his many quoted formulas: the New Novel is not 'the story of an adventure' but 'the adventure of a story', a stance by which he meant that the story was no longer the verbal reproduction of something that has been imagined (or even that has really happened), but an invention due to the play of a structure which permanently referred to its own verbal grounding. Reading a New Novel was then no longer reading a plot, but reading the way this plot and its motifs behaved as signals pointing to the underlying verbal layers of the work (a black bird crossing the white sky, for instance, was not a black bird crossing the white sky, but the trajectory of the printed words on the sheet one is reading, and so on). Man in such a context was a useless hypothesis, and the anti-humanism of the first New Novel now turned its arrows against the role and the position of the writer himself, who was considered the mere operator of the instructions launched by the play of the chosen signifiers: the text was not written by the author, but writes itself thanks to the 'productivity' (Kristeva) of the signifier; reading was not reading but writing the text, etc. This stance, which can to a certain degree be compared to the Anglo-Saxon metafiction (but with much less fiction, much less story, much less humour and much less direct dialogue between author and reader), produced a second type of New Novel, sometimes called New New Novel (a neologism rather popular around 1970, but which now has almost completely fallen into oblivion). Contrary to the phenomenological or realist New Novel, the New New Novel was characterized by a shift from the critique of the traditional novel to the more positive affirmation of pure immanent writing. This New New Novel, however, did not go as far as the experiments of *Tel Quel*, where the writing experiments were turned against language itself and explored the domain of frankly 'non-representative' writing, which could no longer be mastered by our traditional ways of thinking but instead aimed to destabilize our very thinking. The acme of this second manner was represented by the incredibly influential conference on the New Novel directed by Jean Ricardou in Cérisy (1971). This conference radicalized the movement (it is, *grosso modo*, the confirmation of the death of the New Novel and the birth of the New New Novel) and initiated its institutionalization in France, but at the same time 'cut' it from the larger audience on the one hand and from the progressive writing community on the other. A group of seven authors were constituted (Robbe-Grillet, Butor, Pinget, Ollier, Ricardou, Sarraute and Butor) and of course immediately contested (even from the inside: Butor, who stopped writing novels after *Degrés*, 1960, withdrew himself very soon and several authors were not willing to accept the way Ricardou tried to transform a group of authors in a real movement with a single doctrine and one single way of writing). At the same time, the public was no longer interested in the audacious and really innovative books written in this period (Claude Simon: *La Bataille de Pharsale*, 1969, *Les corps conducteurs*, 1971, *Triptyque*, 1973, *Leçon de choses*, 1975; Robbe-Grillet: *La Maison de rendez-vous*, 1965, *Projet pour une révolution à New-York*, 1970, *Topologie d'une cité fantôme*, 1975; Robert Pinget: *Le Libera*, 1967, *Passacaille*, 1969, *Fable*, 1971; Ollier; *La vie sur Epsilon*, 1972, *Fuzzy Sets*, 1975).

In the 1980s, postmodernist fiction started penetrating the French market and many authors made a 'come-back' to more classic ways of storytelling. This was the case not only for *Tel Quel*, but also for the (New) New Novel. After having almost disappeared from the literary scene by the end of the 1970s, some of the New Novelists suddenly turned towards a completely different type of New Novel, more in tune with the spirit of the times than all their previous works. Robbe-Grillet, Pinget, Sarraute and maybe most of all Ollier, the most productive author of this period, stopped refusing narrative pleasure, subjective stances and 'fiction-as-worldmaking', and all of them write more or less in the vein of the so-called *autofiction*, a new type of autobiography reusing biographical material in order to create a work of fiction, and vice versa (Robbe-Grillet: *Le Miroir qui revient*, 1984, *Angélique ou l'enchantement*, 1987; Sarraute: *Enfance*, 1985; Pinget: *L'apocryphe*, 1980, *Monsieur Songe*, 1982; Ollier: *Une histoire illisible*, 1986, *Feuilleton*, 1990). Simultaneously, an important shift occurred in the scholarly and critical reception of the New Novel. Lucien Dällenbach replaced Ricardou as the leading theoretician of the New *Novelists* (the New *Novel* as such was no longer an issue) and his studies on Claude Simon clearly showed that times had dramatically changed. Instead of analysing the work as a play of signifiers, Dällenbach did not hesitate to revalorize the signified (either imagined or experienced). The main themes that he underlined were the role of memory, the physical presence of the world, the function of the body, etc. (language becoming once again a tool, not an aim in itself). As a corollary, the rediscovery of the world was also the starting point of the political rereading of the New Novel, whose ideological subtext now appeared more easily at surface level. Postcolonialism made it clear that works such as those of Ollier, to take the most evident example (since many of his fictions are situated outside Western Europe), bear from their very beginnings traces of a direct political commitment. The latest books of Claude Simon, who received the Nobel Prize for Literature in 1985 in a rather hostile environment, proved, however, that the broadening of scope and reorienting towards the world and the subject do not eliminate (as is the case in the work of other New Novelists) the desire to take language seriously and to renew permanently the genre of the novel itself (*Les Géorgiques*, 1982, *L'Acacia*, 1989, *Le Jardin des plantes*, 1998).

The New Novel had enduringly seduced and terrified many writers and critics. Institutionally speaking, the most astonishing accomplishment was perhaps the fact that for many years the traditional novel was no longer taken seriously. Every novel with a message, a story, an author, a *Weltanschauung*, etc. seemed definitely too ridiculous to discuss. Only a small set of authors were strong enough to escape from this doom in the

1960s–1970s, and to create new types of writing that did not fit the canon of the New Novel. Some well known innovative authors continued inventing without being too much influenced by the New Novel. Raymond Queneau, whose first books appeared in the 1930s, is a good example of this (*Zazie dans le métro*, 1959), and also some young authors who tried to innovate in the very fields the New Novel had declared outdated: the sociological description of the world and the psychological analysis of the subject. This was exemplary in the case of Georges Perec, whose first publications were *Les Choses* (1965) and *Un homme qui dort* (1967), which were produced against the grain: the first is the sociological portrait of a young couple whose behaviour is paradigmatic for the emerging consumer society in France; the latter is the report of a psychiatric case narrated in the second person, as if to better mark the difference of this book with the New Novel that most famously launched the success of this narrative technique, Butor's *La Modification*.

Both Perec and Queneau were typical representatives of the Oulipo (Ouvroir de littérature potentielle: workshop for virtual literature), a writers' collective founded by Queneau and François Le Lionnais in 1960, and joined by Perec in 1996 (membership of the Oulipo is only by invitation, and the 'club' now has approximately twenty-five members). Contrary to the New Novel, which was mainly intent on renewing the old-fashioned mainstream genre of the literary system, the Oulipo has a completely different aim: promoting a type of writing which is both absolutely marginal (it breaks with our dominant romantic vision of the inspired writer) and universally acknowledged (in all known literatures there are to be found Oulipian authors or texts *avant-la-lettre*). This writing is the so-called 'writing-under-constraint', a constraint being defined as a rule (or a protocol, an algorithm, a set of instructions, a programme: there is no fixed terminology) the systematic application of which triggers the creative process and is (virtually) susceptible to produce a text. Starting from this very general device, which has not changed since the very foundation of the group, the assignment of the Oulipo workshops is twofold; first, to invent new formulas of writing (and, simultaneously, to list all known examples of 'pre-Oulipian' constraints); second, but without any obligation, to produce texts intended to 'illustrate' the constraints. Most of the constraints are of course strictly formal, such as the lipogram (a text written without a certain letter or without a certain number of letters) or the palindrome (a text that can be read both forwards and backwards). Others are semantic, such as the creation of gender-neutral texts (the characters being described in such a way that the reader cannot know whether they are male or female: an easy thing to do in English (perhaps), but not in French where the nouns are gendered and where adjectives and other forms also vary depending on the gender of the nouns). Often the constraints rely on ancient rhetorical figures, but the first do much more than just radicalize the latter. The major difference is that in writing under constraint these figures were not simply used locally in order to stress from time to time a given textual aspect, but used all over in order to oblige the writer to invent things he would never have thought of without the 'help' of the constraint: Perec's *La disparition*, 1969, for instance, is a 300-page novel that never uses the letter 'e', the most frequently used letter in the French alphabet (on the contrary, the hilarious sequel of this book, *Les revenentes*, 1972, only uses the one vowel censored before: e!).

During its first years, the proceedings of the Oulipo meetings remained very confidential. The authors gathered for fun, their Oulipian activities were more seen as social events of a certain literary inner circle than as a real literary project, there were hardly any publications in the traditional sense of the word, and most attention was paid to the creation and listing of constraints, the production of constrained texts hardly exceeding the creation of some small samples. But slowly, constrained book-length texts began appearing, the group organized public events (the Oulipians also gathered in Cérisy), and some members of the group used more systematically the technique of constrained writing: Georges Perec (*Alphabets*, 1976) and Jacques Roubaud ('E', 1966) in French, Harry Mathews in English, Italo Calvino in Italian, etc. But in spite of all this, the Oulipo was slow to be perceived as a real literary group or even as a real movement. This lack of recognition contrasted strangely with the fact that the group functioned well as a unit, with closely defined rules on membership and activities (the Oulipo was, among many other things, a parody of the Académie française). One of the most important elements which explains the delay in its public recognition was perhaps the fact that not every Oulipian author always writes or publishes Oulipian books (some autobiographical works by Perec, such as the much acclaimed *W ou le souvenir d'enfance*, 1975, was certainly not a 'pure' example of Oulipian writing). Since most of the members were already active at the moment they joined the group, they sometimes acquired a double identity and continued producing two types of books: constrained and not-constrained. (The fact that some of these authors were rather successful in their traditional writing explains perhaps why they consider their Oulipian excursions as nothing more than a game.) And one has to add to this that not every Oulipian text is recognizable as such. Many Oulipian texts create indeed a problem of readability, not in the sense that they are not enjoyable to read (they are often very funny, and are always open to a 'dilettante' reading in the first degree), but in the sense that the constraints used during the production of the text are no longer visible in the final result (see Queneau's metaphor of the scaffold the writer-builder has to eliminate once the text-building has been finished). As a result, the readability issue soon became of one the hottest topics in the discussions concerning Oulipian writing: if the use of constraints is never really questioned, there are those who are in favour of the disclosure of the constraints in the final text, and those who prefer to hide them in order to guarantee the enjoyment of the average reader.

Gradually, the position of the Oulipo in the literary system changed, and although there was certainly no direct relationship with the vanishing influence of the New Novel in the 1970s and the 1980s, it cannot be denied that in many aspects the Oulipo was, more than *Tel Quel*, *Change*, *TXT* or other radical groups of the 1970s, the real inheritor of what constituted the core of the New Novel: not the revolution of the novel itself (it was only after many years that the Oulipo became interested in the novel, and poetry remains still today at the heart of its production, for instance in the work of Michelle Grangaud), but the will to invent new types of writing, a programme which could no longer be realized satisfactorily either by the autofictional versions of the New Novel in the 1980s or by the emerging literary forms of the same decade, all suspected to be a little conservative or mainstream (at least from a strictly literary and formal point of view). Just as the New Novel did twenty or thirty years earlier, the Oulipo now took some very radical stances on the pre-eminent role of language in the literary production. But unlike the New Novel, and in spite of the often thoroughly formalist plays of the group, it also took some very liberating stances on the role of storytelling, on the importance of the subject and the presence of the world outside the text. When comparing the New Novel and the Oulipo in more detail, one becomes rapidly aware of two other differences. First there is the fact that the Oulipo started from a literary theory, but finished with producing fiction that can be read without the help of any theory (of course it's helpful to know more about it, but the previous knowledge of the constraint(s) is not necessarily a condition *sine qua non*), whereas the New Novel, which started from practice and has remained for a very long time 'allergic' to theory, has in a certain sense fallen into the very trap of theory (at one point the fictions produced were simply uninteresting unless one could consider them an answer to problems of literary theory). Second, there was the fact that the Oulipo, even as a select club of often prestigious writers, had succeeded in creating a genuine dynamism in the global field of literature: Oulipian circles were formed throughout the whole Francophone world, the 'ateliers d'écriture' (this very French and most of all very idiosyncratic version of creative writing courses) have widely adopted the technique of writing under constraint and are of invaluable help in the canonization of the group. The way to the use of constraints (instead of inspiration, or spontaneity, or free expression) as a pedagogic tool was certainly prepared by the anti-humanist and formalist devices of the New Novel, but was never fully exploited by the New Novelists who put traditional literary education under attack rather than transforming it as do the Oulipians. (Ricardou, for instance, is possibly the first, conducted many experiments with those 'writing workshops', and was known for the rather authoritarian way in which he controlled the participants' output.) Despite all its theories concerning the necessity of breaking down the frontiers between authors and writers, the New Novel never managed in practice to transform its readers into writers.

It would be an error, however, only to stress the differences between the New Novel and the Oulipo. At the level of their theories and the works produced, the similarities were at least as striking as the disparities. The most basic common element was probably the notion of constraint, although the New Novelist version of the device was without any doubt less systematic than in the case of the Oulipo (but at the level of the global construction of the text, the great novels by Butor can easily compete with the most famous of all Oulipian books: Perec's *La vie mode L'Emploi*, 1978). Recently, young authors and new groups have appeared whose explicit programme is to pursue a kind of synthesis of the several achievements of the modernist innovations à la New Novel and the more playful inventions à la Oulipo. The most interesting of these authors have gathered to the journal *Formules* (subtitled: 'Journal of Literature under Constraint') and they continue the innovative impulses given by the New Novel and the Oulipo, without being seduced to radicalize them, in what has been for so many avant-garde movements of this century an iconoclastic dead end. *Formules* and other related groups and journals are continuing the tradition of modernist writing and thinking and may well breed the New Novelists and the Oulipians of tomorrow.

Jan Baetens

Further reading and works cited

Dällenbach, L. *Claude Simon*. Paris, 1988.
Formules. Paris, 1997–.
Higgins, L. A. *New Novel, New Wave, New Politics*. Lincoln, NE, 1996.
Mathews, H. and Brotchie, A. *The Oulipo Compendium*. London, 1998.
Oulipo. *La littérature potentielle*. Paris, 1973.
—. *Atlas de littérature potentielle*. Paris, 1981.
Ricardou, J. *Pour une théorie du nouveau roman*. Paris, 1971.
—. *Le Nouveau roman*. Paris, 1990.
Robbe-Grillet, A. *Pour un nouveau roman*. Paris, 1963.

Tel Quel (1960–1982)

As most commentators agree, *Tel Quel* has been more than a review, a journal, a simple periodical: if it fell short of creating a cultural 'revolution' or of launching a political movement, as its main contributors would have wished at the turn of the heady 1960s, it managed indeed to embody, sum up or allegorize a whole state of mind, in short to stand for what is now seen with nostalgia and fading awe as 'the age of theory'. In order to overcome endemic intolerance which can lead to sociological reductionism and systematic debunking (Niilo Kauppi), or to avoid at the other extreme a fascinated adulation ready to engage in intellectual contortions so as to justify the most staggering reversals and palinodes (Philippe Forest), it seems the best solution is to remain historical in a broad sense, to steer away from either juvenile enthusiasm or cynical disappointment. These preliminary remarks imply that *Tel Quel* continues to shock today (though not always for the same reasons), while providing one of the best introductions to the French cultural history of the 1960s and 1970s. Historicizing the review, one should neither monumentalize nor systematically deflate; one should, for instance, resist the temptation of reducing *Tel Quel* to having been a mere tool exploited by a clever and unscrupulous literary *arriviste* like Philippe Sollers. Through his identification with the periodical that he more or less dominated (he was the only founding member who always figured on its editorial board), Sollers allows a 're-reader' to perceive the review's rise to fame, its violent contradictions and slow moral collapse as historical and cultural symptoms, compromise formations that condense an entire *Zeitgeist*. Thus, to paraphrase Lacan, one could want to alliterate and speak of 'Sollers the Symptom'; however, even if Philippe Joyaux consciously strove after a Joycean identification, taking as his model a Joyce who for Lacan (then heavily influenced by *Tel Quel*) had become 'the Sinthome', and who for the whole group embodied a radical writing that would, allegedly, provide the best antidote against fascism, one might speak of the irreducible 'saintliness' of the main animator of the periodical – to the point of perversion. Even at the time of the review's latest metamorphosis, when it had finally exchanged Marx and Mao for Pope John Paul II, and replaced dialectical materialism by the mysteries of the true Church, Sollers, tired of being called the 'Pope of the avant-garde', could both announce the 'death of the avant-garde' and claim to belong to the 'avant-garde of the Pope'.

These chiasmic reversals point to the prevalence of forcefully politicized rhetorics in the editorial power games that gave a stamp to the review and lasted for two decades, from 1960 to 1982. The history of the magazine is complex in the sense that it seemed to accelerate as it reflected more and more adequately the acceleration of real history in France after the watershed constituted by May 1968. Let us then go back to the beginnings in order to try and understand how a literary review that originally appeared apolitical in the early 1960s could become ten years later the spearhead of French Maoism, and almost as suddenly, a few years later, begin denouncing Marxism as a repressive and terrorist ideology in the mid and late 1970s.

When a number of young writers united in 1957–9 with the wish to challenge the French literary scene, it was dominated by three rival formations: Sartre's defence of committed literature flirting with marxism coincided with an increased politicization brought about partly by his recent conflict with Camus; then there was what could be considered as a purely literary avant-garde with the practitioners of the *Nouveau Roman* (*New Novel*) that had gathered a number of excellent writers whose ambitions were not identical but who shared a similar dislike for ideological pronouncements: Robbe-Grillet, Nathalie Sarraute, Samuel Beckett and a few others were mainly published by the *éditions de Minuit*. Besides, the official organ of a high culture still under the shadow of Paul Valéry and André Gide was the *Nouvelle Revue Française*, a literary review then dominated by Jean Paulhan, who had imposed his rhetorical sense blended with tact and classical restraint. In a violent political context dominated by decolonization, by the dead-end of military conflicts in Vietnam and Algeria, Sartre remained the main enemy, the successful rival, solidly entrenched with his thriving review *Les Temps Modernes*; Robbe-Grillet's new novel extolled objectivity and intransitivity in the name of a scientific outlook that took objects as objects, and writing as its own medium, never a transparent glass – and it was clear that this was where the original sympathies of *Tel Quel* lay, without endorsing it completely. It was between these ideological formations that Philippe Sollers, Jean-Edern Hallier, Jean-René Huguenin and their friends learned to manoeuvre when they launched their own review in 1960, the very year Camus died. The only acknowledged writer in the group was Philippe Sollers whose first novel had attracted some attention. Sollers had published in 1958 at the age of twenty-two an elegant short autobiographical novel, *Une curieuse solitude*, that had had the distinction of being immediately praised both by François Mauriac, a Catholic and traditionalist writer, and Louis Aragon, a communist, formerly surrealist poet and novelist.

Tel Quel had chosen a different publisher than established literary institutions like Gallimard, the owner of *La Nouvelle Revue Française*, Le Seuil, known for its left-wing Catholic sympathies and its interest for the budding market for human sciences. Earlier in the 1950s, in a depressed context marked by the end of the war, Le Seuil had allowed Jean Cayrol (who was, like Sollers, from Bordeaux) to launch a literary magazine, *Ecrire*, so as to let 'young' and aspiring writers find an outlet. Many of the first contributors to *Tel Quel* had published pieces in *Ecrire* and Cayrol was initially associated with *Tel Quel*. The two main personalities who presided over the birth of the magazine were Jean-Edern Hallier and Philippe Sollers. Hallier was soon to fight with all his other partners, and to discredit himself through dubious political ventures. What had united these young talents was a close friendship with an older writer, a poet essentially, Francis Ponge, still relatively unknown at that time. Originally close to the *New Novel* school of writing, the main inflection brought about by *Tel Quel* as it started was a constant reference to the works of Ponge, whose texts have now ascended to canonical status and are generally thought to dominate French poetics after the war. Indeed, Sartre had already saluted Ponge's groundbreaking *Le Parti Pris des Choses* for its extraordinary closeness to 'things' in 1944, seeing in these minute 'descriptions' of the most banal objects the basis of a new literary 'phenomenology'. But Ponge, who always insisted upon a proud independence, was regretting his isolation (he could only get *Pour un Malherbe*, completed 1957, published in

1965). A fruitful alliance between an older and half-recognized poet and a bunch of very young and enthusiastic young men provided *Tel Quel* with its initial impetus. The very name of the review also called up another poet, Paul Valéry, who had chosen this title when he reprinted 'as such' his critical meditations just a few years before he died (Valéry 1966, 473–781). It was in fact by a more relevant reference to Nietzsche (re-read and filtered through Georges Bataille) that the review opened its first issue. Its epigraph took from Nietzsche a concept of the 'eternal return' underwriting a positive and joyous affirmation of life considered both 'as such' and as a spectacle, which bequeathed a particularly redoubtable hesitation in view of ulterior developments:

> I want the world and I want it AS IS [*Tel Quel*], I want it still, eternally, and I cry out, insatiably: encore! and not only for myself, but for the entire play and for the entire show; and not only for the entire show, but really for me, because I need the show – because the show makes me indispensable – because it needs me and I render it indispensable. (*Tel Quel*, 1, 1960, 1, cit. and trans. Kauppi 1994, 25)

If one has a look at the table of contents of the first issue, certain choices appear clearly: one finds the names of Francis Ponge twice (he opens and closes the issue, as if to insist upon a dominant role), Albert Camus is given a homage, while alongside Virginia Woolf, translated here, only Jean Cayrol and Claude Simon appear as older and recognized writers. In the second issue, Sollers publishes 'Seven propositions on Alain Robbe-Grillet', and in the following issues the names of Claude Ollier, Robert Pinget, Michel Butor, Nathalie Sarraute, Louis-René des Forêts recur. Although the links with the *New Novel* soon become looser, Jean Ricardou who enters in 1962 will soon specialize in rigorous examinations of the formal procedures of this school.

It is the original endorsement of the 'formalism' of the new novel that leads to the first departure: Jean-René Huguenin is forced to leave *Tel Quel* in June 1960, since he embraces a romanticism that radically condemns the 'technological' style of these writers. Mauriac will see in Huguenin a 'new Romantic' who remains traditionalist enough for his tastes, while Sollers and his friends opt for more and more radical departures. Indeed, Sollers's second novel, *Le Parc* – published in 1961 and soon crowned by the coveted Medicis prize – was seen as a not too slavish imitation of Robbe-Grillet. A general uproar greeted the prize, most conservative critics deploring that Sollers should dilapidate obvious literary gifts and fall under the domination of fashion, while a number of well-known writers insisted that this showed the way for a true literary avant-garde: Leiris, Gérard Genette, Louis-René des Forêts all praised the book. What is also noted with various emphasis, is the review's political neutrality at the time of violent protest against the Algerian war. Without qualifying it as a 'right-wing' review, it is clear that the early collusion between the New Novel and *Tel Quel* goes toward a refusal of political commitment. It looks as if this was the original sin that a subsequent radicalization wished to excuse.

New personalities soon were admitted to the committee: Jean-Louis Baudry, Michel Deguy (soon excluded), Marcelin Pleynet, Denis Roche, who all brought strong voices while questioning the very possibility of poetry. Pleynet, an original poet who soon embarked in a career as a successful art critic, remained Sollers's most faithful ally, while Roche played with panache the role of a 'negative poet' who declared that 'poetry is inadmissible and besides does not exist', while working as an astute literary editor at the Seuil. Soon two important critics and philosophers joined the group, Gérard Genette and Jean-Pierre Faye. Their presence contributed to the development of a serious critical outlook, especially when they were relayed by Roland Barthes who signed a number of important essays (as in no. 7, Fall 1961, or no. 16, Winter 1964). A general survey around the use and function of criticism was published in no. 14, Summer 1963, while the names of Bataille – who had just died and was a friend of Sollers – and Ezra Pound, translated and glossed by Roche, marked another type of opening to literary and philosophical experimentation. At the same time, the review was doubled by a series at the Seuil that became rapidly prestigious and issued books by Flaubert, Barthes, Boulez, Sanguinetti, Maurice and Denis Roche, and in 1965 a collection of essays by Russian formalists that became a major element in the global strategy of the review, before publishing Derrida and Kristeva.

In the mid-1960s, *Tel Quel* indeed appeared as a serious and unrivalled magazine aiming at disseminating the theory and practice of literary structuralism. Structuralism was then associated with a revised Russian Formalism, since the Parisian avant-garde had found new bearings when it perceived deep affinities with the Russian avant-garde that had been active in the 1920s. When Tzvetan Todorov presented the texts of the Russian avant-garde poets and critics, the names of Khlebnikov, Brik, Chlovski, Jakobson, Eikhenbaum were launched for the first time in French circles. Todorov, relayed by *Tel Quel*, put an end to the obscurity surrounding these authors and when Julia Kristeva arrived upon the scene just a little later, soon to be captivated by Sollers, she brought a similar expertise to the group: coming like Todorov directly from Bulgaria, she completed the formalist picture by adding new references to the semioticians of the Tartu school and to Mikhail Bakhtin, also totally unknown in France at the time. Not only is the history of the avant-garde sanctioned by reference to an older and very political movement, but also a very concrete proof was given that one could be a 'formalist' (that is, interest oneself in exploring the literariness and literality of poetic and novelistic languages) and a revolutionary at the same time. However, Kristeva did not dispel certain ambiguities, allowing some confusion to float (Medvedev and Bakhtin were not strictly distinguished at first, which created impossible mixtures between literary marxism and anti-Stalinian linguistics of heteroglossia, while Bakhtin's staunch opposition to formalism was never mentioned).

However, from *Théorie de la Littérature* – the collection of Russian formalist essays edited by Todorov in 1965 – to Julia Kristeva's *Séméiotiké* published in 1969 and taking up texts found in *Tel Quel* as early as 1967, a whole revolution had taken place in the field of literary semiotics, a revolution in which *Tel Quel* and its members played a dominant role. Moreover, when the review devoted a special issue to Antonin Artaud in 1965, it included for the first time a ground-breaking essay by a young philosopher, Jacques Derrida. Derrida's impact was immediately and deeply felt, and his name was called upon more and more frequently in the pages of the review. One can say that he introduced yet another revolution through a more philosophical questioning of the main presuppositions that underpinned structuralism. On the other hand, *Tel Quel* provided him with a tribune, a sounding board and a series of exciting invitations to engage with literary issues: the essay Derrida devoted to Mallarmé in 1969 came from a 'double session' at the informal but very successful *Tel Quel* reading groups called *Theoretical Study Groups*, while the entire essay entitled 'Dissemination' presented itself as a jumble of quotations taken from Philippe Sollers's *Nombres* (see Derrida 1991, 173–286, 289–366). Derrida had rightly identified in *Nombres* the utopia of a new 'textual novel' – soon to become the hallmark of *Tel Quel* – that is a series of resolutely 'experimental' texts half-way between poetry and prose, that did not represent anything but the very functioning of language, in the hope that by thus exhibiting its codes, cogs and wheels, the production of a new 'truth' would shatter dominant and repressive ideologies.

The best place to examine how this double revolution was achieved is the volume put together by Sollers and his friends in the Fall of 1968, entitled *Théorie d'ensemble* – a broad title that aims at creating the impression of a group similar to the surrealists, of a collective approach with a scientific slant. However, the volume highlights clearly the importance of three 'masters', Foucault, Barthes and Derrida, whose names are separated from all the other contributors to the review and whose essays appeared elsewhere. Foucault opens the volume with a reading of Robbe-Grillet whom he compares with Faye, Thibaudeau, Pleynet and Sollers. Barthes continues with a piece on *Drame*, Sollers's novel of 1965. Derrida introduces the concept of 'différance' and the unsigned introduction makes it clear that the 'general theory' should not be reduced to either formalism or structuralism. The key words that are proffered as so many new ruptures are *writing, text, the unconscious, history, work, trace, production, scene* (*Tel Quel*, 1968, 7; a good translation of the introductory presentation is to be found in ffrench and Lack, 1998, 21–4). Each of the main theoreticians convoked has brought a new contribution – taken to be a 'definitive' revelation – to the global problematics. Foucault is credited with the idea that texts are not representative but productive; Barthes has demonstrated how writing 'scans history' and decentres it; Derrida has shown that writing can no longer be inscribed within the category of truth (ffrench and Lack 1998, 22–3). Based upon this significant convergence, a fourfold programme posited the need '*to unleash a movement . . .; to elaborate concepts . . .; to unfold a history/histories . . .; to articulate a politics* logically linked to a non-representational dynamics of writing . . .' (ffrench and Lack 1998, 23). The last point concerns the clear admission that the politics of the review is linked with the construction of historical materialism and dialectical materialism, and that two other important 'masters' are Lacan and Althusser. The programme indicates the need to go back to a first 'break' in history, not stopping at the avant-garde of the 1920s (defined by surrealism, formalism, structural linguistics) but rethinking the four emblematic names of Lautréamont, Mallarmé, Marx and Freud – whose main 'discoveries', put together, roughly date from the middle of the nineteenth century. If the writer's names can change from year to year or from issue to issue, for some time this provides the basic formula upon which the review will endlessly improvise. The systematic trope of *Tel Quel* becomes the linking of writers noted for their formal experiments or unorthodox and innovative writing (they may include Dante, Pound, Woolf, Céline, Joyce, Beckett, Bataille, Artaud) with the names of Marx and Freud (for a time complemented by those of Lenin and Mao). 'Theory' understood in this way hesitates between a radical philosophical questioning of literary concepts and a more etymological sense of a 'list' or 'procession' of tutelary figures ritually invoked. Quite often, the references to Althusser and Lacan function as shortcuts for what should read like 'the real thought' of Marx and Freud – Marx 'after' the epistemological break with Hegel and idealism, Freud without the biological naturalism of 'instincts' but in possession of an equation between the Unconscious and language.

The distribution of the contributors reveals a subtle hierarchy: Sollers, Pleynet and Baudry publish four pieces; Houdebine, Kristeva and Ricardou two essays; and Jean-Joseph Goux, Denis Roche, Pierre Rottenberg, Jacqueline Risset, Jean Thibaudeau, only one essay. The overall quality of these pieces is good, and they still make fascinating reading today, if one discards some tics like the recurrent claim of being 'scientific' or the use of 'production' as a generic key term. Some of the best essays are those that link close readings and theories of literature (Ricardou on Poe, Baudry on Freud, Pleynet on Sade or Sue) or those that start from their own texts to provide a key (like Pleynet and Roche about Roche's scandalous and paradoxical anti-poetry and anti-poetics).

The combination of Saussure, re-read by Derrida, of Marx, re-read by Althusser, and of Freud, re-read by Lacan, provides the fundamental trilogy that maps out the world of knowledge and literature. This eventually will lead Goux to a wholesale systematization of the theories of Lacan, Althusser and Derrida when he points out an equivalence between money in capitalism, the phallus in psychoanalysis and the master-signifier in the production and circulation of language. Such syntheses attract to the 'general Telquelian theory' the reproach of hasty assimilation founded upon mere homologies – as if the truth of a capitalism that has yielded the formula of money as the 'general equivalent' had also provided a universal key for the theorization of the avant-garde! However, the need to move beyond a purely structuralist grid forces some authors to look for other names. Thus Kristeva uses a mathematical logic inspired by the Tartu school of semiotics in Estonia, she discusses Saumjan with Chomsky and Greimas, and refers to Peirce, Hegel or Husserl.

Roland Barthes was perhaps the first major critic who publicly acknowledged the fact that Tel Quel had brought about a major change not only to the writing of literary theory but to the very conception of literature – the two tending to blend together more and more. One can witness how in the texts he publishes in the late 1960s, the references to Kristeva (who had been his student) become systematic and deferential. New concepts such as intertextuality, the couple genotext/phenotext, the notion of signifying practice, of 'signifiance' opposed to 'signification', the idea of an infinite productivity identified with a 'text' that is strongly delineated from the 'work' mark for Barthes a shift from a purely 'scientific' (and slightly boring) approach to systems of signs to a new problematic in which dynamism, productivity and infinity are constantly invoked. Barthes's wonderful S/Z (also published in the Tel Quel series in 1970) manages to let the two semiotics coexist side by side. Certain writers would protest, this time less in the name of traditional values than in the name of scientific rigour. Thus in a scathing attack, Jacques Roubaud and Philippe Lusson use their first-hand knowledge of mathematics and logic to demonstrate that most of the logical formulas used by Kristeva in her first book are redundant or contradictory: they either underline decoratively what has been expressed in plain language or mix up incompatible systems of formalization (Roubaud and Lusson 1969, 56–61; 1970, 31–6).

But this attack corresponds to a more troubled period linked with the many splits and struggles that marked the end of the 1960s: the break-up between Sollers and Jean-Pierre Faye, the only intellectual and writer whose stature was equal to Sollers's, in 1967 led Faye to launch the rival magazine Change – also published by Le Seuil! – whose very name intends to contradict Tel Quel and its implied acceptance of things as they are. On the other hand, a review like Poétique founded by three eminent former collaborators of Tel Quel (Genette, Todorov and Cixous) aims less at cultural critique than at prolonging a serious and more academic investigation of the theory and practice of literature. This and the often paradoxical politicization of the review – they became close allies of the French Communist Party just before May 1968, which led most Tel Quel members to keep their distance from a movement considered to be too enthusiastic, dadaist and playful, while the same insistence on radical breaks and dogmatic righteousness led them to become Maoist in 1971 – at a time when pre- and post-68 surrealism is denounced as idealist and Hegelian. Curiously, if the review lost its appeal for many intellectuals upset by its lack of 'seriousness' and its modishness, it increased its publication, and most special issues reached more than

20,000 copies (whereas the usual run would have been between 3,000 and 5,000 before). The fascination for China led Sollers, Kristeva and their friends to a real effort at documentation, but their fatal mistake was to take a group trip to China in the spring of 1974 (Sollers and Kristeva went with Pleynet, Barthes and Wahl) to confront their dream with reality. Even if Kristeva brought back a beautiful book about *Chinese Women*, disillusionment and dissatisfaction with the Chinese utopia was soon to creep in, and the Chinese reference was dropped. In the winter of 1976, Houdebine denounced the dead-end of language in marxism while Sollers accused Maoism of being a mere return to Stalinism (a point that had not escaped earlier observers of the cultural revolution). In spite of its often shrill insistence on the necessary link between politics and literature, the review often evinced a great political naivety, while showing amazing skills at literary tactics of self-promotion.

The year 1976 brought about a last reversal in alliances: the review suddenly opened its pages to a group of writers who called themselves 'new philosophers' and had launched a wholesale attack not just on Stalinism but on Marx, up to then sacrosanct. Marx was suddenly accused of having generated all the subsequent totalitarian deviations produced in his name. Alexander Soljenitsyn, Iossif Brodksi, Andrei Siniaski, André Glucksmann, Bernard-Henri Lévy and Maria-Antonietta Macciocchi appear as main allies in a fight that aims at exposing marxism as the worst alienation of the century. Sollers starts opening each issue with passages from his work-in-progress *Paradis*, an interesting experimental 'text' blending the oral style of the late Céline and an unpunctuated monologue similar to Molly's monologue at the end of *Ulysses*. As if he felt compelled to always espouse the latest trends, Sollers allows himself to be fascinated by the new philosophers' return to religion – either as the Jewish foundation rediscovered by Levy, or as a more 'perverse' or 'baroque' Catholicism that might have been there all the time, after all, in Lacan. The former 'enemy' constituted by the US is now rediscovered as the place of a new utopia in a special issue devoted to the USA (nos. 71–3, Fall 1977). Hoffman, Corso, Ashberry and Roth are selected among the new important influences, while Joyce – to whom many excellent special issues had been devoted – is praised for blending 'obscenity and theology' (Special Joyce issue, no. 83, Spring 1980).

However, around 1980, it became clear that the review had lost its impetus and its impact on French culture. Its main ideas had been fully taken up by academic discourse, while the denunciation of totalitarian ideology seemed more forceful among right-wing magazines. Sollers stood out as the main puppet-master of a moribund avant-garde that had lost all confidence in its master-signifiers, and when he quarrelled with François Wahl, the editor at Seuil, who objected to the publication of *Women* (1983) because it contained a transparent satire of the intellectual milieu they had frequented, with vitriolic portraits of Cixous, Lacan, Althusser, Barthes, Derrida and some famous feminist theoreticians, the review needed to be reinvented. Sollers and Pleynet moved to Gallimard (through Denoeël at first) to found *L'Infini*. Another story had begun for the Parisian avant-garde. Le Seuil, which had intelligently speculated on the rise of the 'human sciences', was to conclude with a new disaffection for high theory. Sartre, Barthes and Lacan had died, soon followed by Althusser and Foucault. In retrospect, facing the work accomplished by *Tel Quel*, it was Sollers himself who meted out both enduring praise and damning accusation. In *Women*, a writer who is a friend of 'S' or Sollers reminisces on the crucial cultural function played by *Tel Quel*. He remembers his difficulties with Boris (an alias for Jean-Edern Hallier) at the time of the foundation of the review during the Algerian war: 'When they started their little avant-garde revue … Which is now, thanks to S'.s grim perseverance, a kind of international institution … It has published the best work of Werth, Lutz, Fals, and many others … Established their reputation' (Sollers 1990, 320). These transparent pseudonyms allude to Barthes, Althusser and Lacan: even if one notes some exaggeration, which after all conforms to the model of a review that indeed became an 'institution', the assessment carries weight. *Tel Quel* managed to change durably the rapport between literature and theory, while allowing a few literary and critical landmarks to be published (besides essays by Barthes and Derrida, one can think of Maurice Roche's *Compact* (1966), subsequently rediscovered by a younger and different avant-garde). On the other hand, the judgement can turn pointedly ambivalent; but here again, the strictest caviller's abuse has been anticipated: when S is asked by Boris to write a puff for his (Boris's) latest book, he replies, in a tongue-in-cheek commendation that can rebound to its originator: '… I've got a good title for an article about you: *In praise of imposture* … In an ultrafalse world, only the height of falsehood can tell the truth about falsehood … You get the idea'. Like most of us who 'get the idea', Boris pretends not to see the irony and just answers: 'Splendid! Write it!' (Sollers 1990, 319).

Jean-Michel Rabaté

Further reading and works cited

Barthes, R. *Writer Sollers*. Minneapolis, MN, 1987.
Benoist, J.-M. *The Structural Revolution*. London, 1978.
Derrida, J. *Writing and Difference*. Chicago, 1978.
—. *Dissemination*. Chicago, 1991.
ffrench, P. *The Time of Theory*. Oxford, 1996.
— (ed.) *From Tel Quel to L'Infini*. London, 1998.
— and Lack, R.-F. (eds) *The Tel Quel Reader*. London, 1998.
Fletcher, J. and Benjamin, A. (eds) *Abjection, Melancholia and Love*. New York, 1990.
Forest, P. *Histoire de Tel Quel*. Paris, 1995.
Goux, J.-J. *The Coiners of Language*. Norman, OK, 1994.
Kauppi, N. *The Making of an Avant-Garde*. Berlin, 1994.
Kristeva, J. *Séméiotiké: Recherches pour une Sémanalyse*. Paris, 1969.
—. *La Révolution du Language poétique*. Paris, 1974.
—. *About Chinese Women*. London, 1977.
Pleynet, M. *Painting and System*. Chicago, 1984.
Reader, K. *Intellectuals and the Left in France since 1968*. Manchester, 1993.
Roche, M. *Compact*. New York, 1988.
Roubaud, J. and Lusson, P. 'Sur la "sémiologie des paragrammes" de Julia Kristeva', *Action Poétique*, 41–2 (1969) and 45 (1970).
Roudinesco, E. *Jacques Lacan and Co*. New York, 1990.
Sollers, P. *Women*. New York, 1990.
Tel Quel. *Théorie d'Ensemble*. Paris, 1968.
Valéry, P. 'Tel Quel', in *Oeuvres vol. 2*, ed. Jean Hytier. Paris, 1966.

Other French Feminisms: Sarah Kofman (1934–1994), Monique Wittig (1935–), Michèle Le Doeuff (1948–)

The 'Mouvement de Libération des Femmes' (MLF), whose name was first coined by the French press and then taken up by French feminists, comprised a shifting array of women's groups that formed in the aftermath of the student and worker movement of May 1968. Almost from its inception, the movement was characterized by fierce differences of opinion, both ideological and pragmatic. Central areas of debate included whether and how to reconcile psychoanalytic and marxist/materialist analyses; the question of sexual difference and women's sexuality; whether and how lesbians and heterosexual women should work together; whether to be 'anonymous, underground, like moles' (cit. Duchen 1986, 17) as the group 'politique and psychanalyse' ('po et psych') wished, or to draw attention via spectacular and witty demonstrations, as the 'Féministes Révolutionnaires' desired; and how to understand the relation between women and language.

The three main currents in the nascent MLF were class-struggle feminism, materialist or radical feminism and psychoanalytic feminism. While marxist/materialist analyses were central to all three approaches, by 1970 many of the women in the MLF were not involved with either socialist or communist party politics; those who were belonged to the 'class-struggle' tendency in the MLF. Class-struggle feminists were active in organized leftist politics but had grown dissatisfied with their parties' stances on women; they strove to reconcile their commitments to feminism and to Leftist politics, as the slogan 'No socialism without women's liberation; no women's liberation without socialism' suggests (Duchen 1986, 27).

Materialist or radical feminists saw women as a class and sexual difference as the effect, not the cause, of women's oppression. Arguing against the idea that sex has a natural or biological essence prior to or outside of culture, they rejected as 'biologism' the notion of an innate feminine specificity or difference. Materialist feminism was closely associated with the 'Féministes Révolutionnaires,' a group that counted Christine Delphy, Colette Guillaumin, Monique Plaza and Monique Wittig among its members; these theorists saw themselves as Simone de Beauvoir's ideological heirs, and the author of *The Second Sex* was one of the founders of the group's journal, *Questions Féministes*.

Psychoanalytic feminists, who made up the third principle tendency in the MLF, drew on Freudian and Lacanian theoretical frameworks and deconstruction. Focusing their analyses on the body, unconscious processes and repression, they theorized feminine specificity and difference by first reversing the male/female hierarchy and then exploding it by calling hierarchical thinking itself into question. Psychoanalytic feminism was popularly affiliated with the group 'politique et psychanalyse'. (Originally named 'Psychanalyse and Politique', the group reversed the order of its concerns and dropped the name's capitals to reflect a shift in its priorities.) Led by analyst Antoinette Fouque, who rejected the term 'feminist' on the grounds that 'feminists are a bourgeois avant-garde that maintains, in an inverted form, the dominant values' (cit. Marks and de Courtivron 1980, 117), the group at one time or another included Hélène Cixous, Luce Irigaray and Julia Kristeva. Another current of psychoanalytic feminism was made up of practitioners of *écriture féminine*, writing grounded in the female body and shaped by women's corporeal specificity: the breasts, the womb, the labia. Writers associated with *écriture féminine* include Chantal Chawaf, Hélène Cixous, Marguerite Duras, Madeleine Gagnon, Xavière Gauthier, Claudine Herrmann and Annie Leclerc.

The fact that some practitioners of *écriture féminine*, like Leclerc, were more concerned to reverse hierarchies that devalued women than to challenge hierarchical thinking, rejecting or ignoring deconstruction, while others, like Cixous, were greatly influenced by deconstruction demonstrates the danger of oversimplifying divisions within French feminist schools of thought. Thus the three broad categories into which I have divided the MLF should not be taken to denote simple or rigid partitions; in actuality, each current comprised multiple groups whose complicated alliances and allegiances render any neat taxonomy misleading. Women frequently belonged to, or attended the meetings of groups belonging to, more than one current, demonstrating that the positions staked out were neither as exclusive nor as comprehensive as some *post hoc* summaries have suggested.

Moreover, the various currents of the MLF shared important ideas and interests. Antoinette Fouque of 'po et psych' asserted that the group's 'top priority was given to making connections between two "discourses": psychoanalytic discourse and historical materialism' (cit. Marks and de Courtivron 1980, 117). Monique Wittig, for a time the spokesperson for 'Féministes Révolutionnaires', argued that materialist feminism 'must undertake the task of defining the individual subject in materialist terms' (1992, 19), and the class-struggle feminists sought to reconcile feminism and socialism.

In spite of these shared concerns and the fact that women moved from group to group and worked simultaneously with more than one group (Duchen 1987, 14), the MLF recorded its share of conflicts. Setting themselves against all 'isms', members of 'po et psych' demonstrated on International Women's Day with signs proclaiming 'Down with feminism!' (Moi 1987, 3) and enraged the rest of the MLF in 1979 by trademarking the name 'MLF' for their publishing house, 'des femmes' and suing those who challenged their exclusive right to the name 'Mouvement de Libération des Femmes.'

A less spectacular but more enduring point of contention has been the question of sexual difference. Annie Leclerc's *Parole de Femme* (*Woman's Word*) was an early celebration of a feminine difference grounded in corporeal specificity: 'I must talk about the pleasures of my body . . . only by talking about it will a new language be born, a woman's word' (cit. Duchen 1987, 60). Leclerc invoked difference to assert women's superiority over men, but other psychoanalytic feminists, influenced by deconstruction, reversed the hierarchy in order to interrogate it. Rather than simply valorizing women, they variously theorized women's exclusion from a monosexual ('hom[m]osexual') economy (Irigaray); posited femininity as a principle of disruption or excess (Kristeva); or postulated a feminine bisexuality that does not fuse masculinity and femininity (cancelling out sexual difference), but oscillates between them (Kofman).

In contrast, the materialist feminist editorial collective of *Questions Féministes* (QF) derided both celebrations of and inquiries into women's difference as 'neo-femininity', arguing that 'it is the patriarchal system which posits that we are "different" in order to justify and conceal our exploitation. It is the patriarchal system which prescribes the idea of a feminine "nature" and "essence"'' (cit. Marks and de Courtivron 1980, 214). Seeing both women and men as classes the former of which is oppressed by the latter, they had no patience with what they saw as neo-feminism's complicity with myths that serve to naturalize cultural oppression. Thus Christine Delphy, one of QF's founders, responded to Leclerc's celebration of the female body by insisting that 'it is essential to recognize that the meaning of periods, for instance, is not *given* with and by the flow of blood, but like *all* meaning, by consciousness and thus by society' (1984, 195). Rather than attending to that which is specific to femininity – that which, 'po et psych' argued, has been repressed – they sought the end of the categories of sex, man and woman, which they saw as the result of oppression. Carefully distinguishing corporeal differences from the meanings with which such differences have been invested, materialist feminists attacked the notion of sexual difference on several fronts: by arguing that to see difference as natural or essential/ biological is to make it appear inevitable and unchangeable, effectively rendering feminists' struggle against oppression moot (Delphy); by insisting on an analysis of difference in its material manifestations, as a historical rather than an essential phenomenon (Delphy, Colette Guillaumin); and by contending that empirical differences grew out of and were synonymous with women's oppression (Guillaumin, Wittig).

Ideological and pragmatic differences not only divided different currents in the MLF from one another but created internal dissension, as well. The majority of the 'class struggle' groups broke up, as some members moved away from organized leftist politics while others retained close ties to party organizations. Many women left 'po et psych', disillusioned with its leader; 'anyone who could no longer accept the group's "line" had to go,' asserted Anne Tristan (cit. Moi 1987, 53). QF and 'Féministes Révolutionnaires' foundered after the publication of two articles, Monique Wittig's 'The Straight Mind' and Emmanuèle de Lesseps' 'Hétérosexualité et Féminisme' ('Heterosexuality and Feminism'). The pieces crystallized the editorial collective's differences by offering opposing answers to the question of whether heterosexuality was compatible with feminism. The ensuing debate prompted the group to separate into the radical feminists and the political (or radical) lesbians.

As the preceding account of common projects and lively disagreements attests, 'French feminism' encompasses more than the work of Cixous, Irigaray and Kristeva. These writers' dominance has tended to obscure other currents of French feminist thought by pre-empting considerations of writers whose work criticizes or differs in its focus from these three women's critical projects; their ubiquity in accounts of French feminist thought has created an incomplete picture of the range of positions taken by feminists in France (among whom I include, albeit with reservations, theorists like Cixous who have disclaimed the name 'feminist' but concern themselves with questions of sexual difference and women's oppression and/or repression). Examining the work of other feminists allows for a more comprehensive understanding of French feminisms in the last quarter of the twentieth century.

Monique Wittig (1935–)

A materialist feminist, Monique Wittig sees women as a class constituted by economic, political and social operations and forcefully negates the notion of women's essential difference, which she argues merely masks the material conditions of women's oppression. Empirical differences between the sexes, in Wittig's analysis, are the result of that oppression, growing out of the hierarchical sex classes that organize and differentiate men and women. Her writings, both literary and critical, seek to distinguish 'woman' the myth from 'women' the social products of a political and economic system based on sex class exploitation. As one of the theorists whose writing gave materialist feminism shape, Wittig helped to define its goal of abolishing sex classes, a goal which grows out of her belief that only then will women cease to be oppressed.

In addition to destroying the categories 'man' and 'woman', Wittig aims to theorize the social basis of 'so-called personal problems' without losing sight of 'the question of the subject of each singular woman – not the myth, but each one of us' (1992, 19). Materialist feminism's task, she argues, is simultaneously to renovate and to conjoin historical materialism and a theory of subjectivity. She faults marxism for effectively naturalizing sexual difference and its categories, man and woman, and thus failing to consider women as a class. At the same time, she rejects psychoanalytic models of the subject as totalizing and ahistorical, deploring a paradigm in which 'human beings are given as invariants, untouched by history and unworked by class conflicts, with identical psyches because genetically programmed' (1992, 22).

In lesbianism, Wittig argued, radical feminism found an ideal strategy; it was both a political choice and the only rational choice for those seeking to destroy a regime of sexual difference governed by the logic of a mandatory heterosexuality whose tenet was 'you-will-be-straight-or-you-will-not-be' (Wittig 1992, 28). Arguing that both lesbianism and heterosexuality were not sexualities but political regimes, Wittig concluded that choosing lesbianism was one way to work towards the destruction of the sex classes that grew out of oppression; perhaps her most famous statement is the claim that 'lesbians are not women' (1992, 32). Rather, for Wittig, lesbians are escapees from their class, existing outside of the mutually dependent categories 'man' and 'woman'. In this sense, Wittig's lesbian is reminiscent of Cixous's or Kristeva's woman, in so far as each is marked by an inability to be contained by her excess.

Language is central to Wittig's analyses, and here she again differentiates herself from psychoanalytic feminism by taking a characteristically materialist approach. Arguing that language enforces gender by requiring those who would be subjects to assume a gender, Wittig argues that our sense of ourselves as subjects depends on our position in language, which is marked by personal pronouns. Uninflected by gender (except in French's third person plural, *ils/elles*), personal pronouns nevertheless 'support the notion of gender while ... seem[ing] to fulfill another function' (1992, 79) because they require past participles and adjectives to reflect a speaker's gender. Thus, when women use language, they are simultaneously empowered and disempowered: 'no woman can say "I" without being for herself a total subject – that is, ungendered, universal, whole ... But gender ... works upon this ontological fact to annul it as far as women are concerned and corresponds to a constant attempt to strip them of the most precious thing for a human being – subjectivity' (1992, 80–1).

Wittig reads the material effects of language on subjectivity as offering opportunity as well as constraint; her fiction is both a meditation and an operation on personal pronouns, which she claimed as 'the subject matter' of her first three books (1992, 82), *The Opoponax*, *Les Guérillères* and *The Lesbian Body*. In each, she recontextualizes a different pronoun ('one', *elles* and 'I' [j/e], respectively) to create a textual universe from which sex classes have been banished. It is her contention that, via such experimentation, literature becomes 'a war machine' (1992, 68) capable of destroying old modes of thought and inaugurating new ones. This capacity, she asserts, is what distinguishes her formal innovations from both conventional literature with a political or social agenda and *écriture féminine*. Although her emphasis on the transformative effects of finding/making a new language is reminiscent of the claims of practitioners of *écriture féminine*, Wittig insists that the two genres against which she defines her literary experimentation remain mired in the myths and stereotypes of heterosexuality, while her work imagines a world unencumbered by sex classes. Wittig's work as a writer of fiction, political theory and social criticism can thus be seen as uniformly marked by her commitment to materialist/lesbian feminism.

Michèle Le Doeuff (1948–)

Michèle Le Doeuff interrogates philosophy's history in order to address some of the discipline's central issues. In readings of Bacon, Descartes, Husserl, Kant, More, de Beauvoir and Sartre, Le Doeuff writes about the nature of the self, the relation between philosophy and ethics, utopianism and the role women – or rather 'woman' – has played in philosophy's conception of itself. Analysing the use philosophers have made of imagery, Le Doeuff investigates a paradox: on the one hand, philosophy dismisses 'thinking in images' (1989, 2) as both incidental to philosophical texts and antithetical to philosophy's commitment to rational thought; on the other hand, philosophical texts depend upon imagery to mask the gaps and inconsistencies in their theoretical projects. In *Recherches sur l'imaginaire philosophique* (translated as *The Philosophical Imaginary*), a collection of seven loosely interrelated essays, Le Doeuff argues for a philosophical discourse that will have relinquished its commitment to the closure of complete knowledge, a discipline more open to the inevitable failure to provide full and final answers and thus less anxious to disguise its inadequacies. Her argument works by first inverting and then calling in question the hierarchical binaries image/knowledge and myth/reason. Showing how imagery which philosophical texts would dismiss as peripheral in fact 'copes with problems posed by the theoretical enterprise itself' (1989, 5), she draws on deconstructive and psychoanalytic techniques to foreground that which has been ignored or elided and insists that thought in images and 'pure' reason are inextricably intertwined.

'The ultimate implication of my conception of the philosophical imaginary', writes Le Doeuff, is that 'it is in the administration of its own legitimacy, the establishment of its own value, that philosophy is drawn into defining and designing its own myths' (1989, 170 fn.4). One myth with which Le Doeuff occupies herself is philosophy's self-proclaimed role as arbiter of knowledge across disciplines. Its claim to this position is grounded in philosophy's endeavour to construct a complete theory of knowledge, an endeavour that also produces the discipline's theoretical bind, for an epistemology that presents itself as all-encompassing will necessarily be haunted by a fear of lacunae. Philosophy's recourse to 'thinking in images', Le Doeuff argues, eases this bind by permitting a text to supplement its rational arguments with imagery that bolsters those claims it cannot otherwise support.

In Le Doeuff's analysis, women's relation to philosophy, like that of thought in images, seems extrinsic but is in fact indispensable to the discipline's self-conception. She examines this relationship in a number of articles, as well as in both *Recherches sur l'imaginaire philosophique* and *L'Étude et le rouet* (translated as *Hipparchia's Choice*), the latter of which also experiments with form, taking the shape of four 'notebooks'. Contending that an iconography of 'woman' is central to philosophy's myths, Le Doeuff asserts that one of its functions is to guarantee philosophy's explanatory status and the philosopher's position as one who knows by relegating women to a domain outside of philosophy's realm of logic. However, in discussing women's access (or lack thereof) to philosophy, Le Doeuff argues that their exclusion has not historically been a matter of simple absence, since there have always been women philosophers; while she does not deny that many women have been prohibited from practising philosophy, she focuses instead on the way in which 'permissiveness is a sly form of prohibition' (1989, 103).

Female philosophers from Heloise to Simone de Beauvoir have approached philosophy via an apprenticeship with a male teacher – an apprenticeship that, Le Doeuff argues, gave these women access only to the school of thought espoused by one teacher, rather than to the field of philosophy as a whole. The difference, she contends, is that between the amateur, whose relation is unmediated by the context of an academic institution, and the professional trained by teachers who are part of an institution. While professional students are not immune to the transference relationship Le Doeuff ascribes to amateur women philosophers, the former enjoy a different relation to philosophy as a field. But if women are not well served by their amateur status, Le Doeuff suggests that their teachers are dependent on it, for the pupils' reverence allows the masters to forget that their theoretical projects are (always, inevitably) incomplete. These students thus serve the function of non-knowers who invest philosophers with the power of those presumed to know, banishing the masters' anxiety and offering a way to negotiate the bind described above.

Le Doeuff's approach to philosophy is in some ways reminiscent of Irigaray's reading of psychoanalysis, in so far as both women use the techniques of their respective disciplines to critique those disciplines ('a practical application of philosophy is necessary in order to oust and unmask the alienating schemas which philosophy has produced' (1989, 101), writes Le Doeuff). But while both writers insist on the need to transform their fields, Le Doeuff promotes pragmatic renovation via traditional scholarly work, steering clear of Irigaray's more revolutionary interest in jamming or disrupting a system of thought (1985, 68–85). Arguing that a feminism of difference is viable only if its practitioners do not dismiss the western philosophical tradition as a masculine mode of thought, Le Doeuff instead seeks to transform philosophy from within.

Sarah Kofman (1934–1994)

Sarah Kofman, a philosopher, has published more than twenty-five books on Comte, Kant, Rousseau, Freud, Nietzsche, Marx, Derrida and Blanchot, among others. Her wide-ranging interests include aesthetics, literary criticism, philosophy, Freudian psychoanalysis and autobiography. Kofman served for more than twenty years as an editor of the *Philosophie en effet* series, along with Derrida, Jean-Luc Nancy and Philippe Lacoue-Labarthe, and deconstruction's influence on her work is manifest. Honing in on moments of contradiction, reduction or aporia, Kofman's readings seek to keep multiple meanings in play at once; her texts eschew the closure of certainty, reversing traditional hierarchies and calling hierarchy itself into question. At the same time, Kofman's critical methodology, with its attention to both the letter of the text and its silences, owes as much to psychoanalysis as to deconstruction.

Reading symptomatically, Kofman positions herself as analyst even as she resists simply diagnosing her subjects. Applying Freud's interpretive techniques to his texts, Kofman presents herself as more faithful to Freud's theories than Freud himself. She attends to what his summaries and interpretations ignore or elide, focuses on moments when Freud short-changes his own critical method, and analyses his sexual economy. The task Kofman set herself was to identify the workings of sexuality and the question of sexual difference in texts that did not always manifest the full measure of their author's convictions – 'pushing', as she put it, 'the Freudian interpretation to its limits, in the most faithful way possible' (1991, 1). In readings of philosophers ranging from Comte to Kant to Rousseau, Kofman adopts a similar strategy. Here, however, Kofman is, as one critic puts it, 'reintroducing sexuality, and thereby the question of sexual difference, in what she calls the "economy" of a thought that claims to remain pure' (Duroux 1999, 138), whereas with Freud there can never have been any question of 'a thought that claims to remain pure.'

If Kofman's debts to psychoanalysis and deconstruction are clear, the influence of feminism in her work is less readily apparent. But while she rejected the notion of a specifically feminine discourse such as *écriture féminine* and neither worked on women philosophers nor participated in the MLF, she herself believed that her status as a woman philosopher and the fact that she wrote made her a feminist. Moreover, both the attention peripheral female figures, especially mothers, receive in her work and her penchant for questioning and analysing binary oppositions such as man/woman, reason/emotion aligns her with deconstructive feminism. Like Le Doeuff, she analyses images of women in the texts of major philosophers, showing how figures of femininity stand for unreason even as such figures expose flaws in the reasoning of the texts in which they appear.

Many critics have read Kofman's second book on Freud, 1980's *The Enigma of Woman*, as a revision of Irigaray's 1974 *Speculum of the Other Woman*, also a rereading of Freud's theory of femininity. The two analyses share both a subject and a deconstructive and psychoanalytic approach to Freud's writing, but Kofman faults Irigaray for misrepresenting Freud, relying on a sloppy translation, and subordinating critical honesty to 'the cause', while maintaining that her criticism does not stem from any wish to 'save' Freud at all costs ('I am no more likely to "save" him than [Irigaray] is' (1985, 14 fn.6), she insists). Kofman's critique of Irigaray is grounded in the notion that faithfulness to the text constitutes 'the minimal intellectual honesty that consists in criticizing an author in terms of what he has said rather than what someone has managed to have him say' (1985, 14 fn.6). But while Irigaray psychoanalyses Freud's texts, Kofman goes further; here as elsewhere in her writing she rejects any rigid distinction between the text and the life, psychoanalysing the author as well as his writings. (In doing so, she parts company with Le Doeuff, who argues that 'where texts are concerned, doubtless the only tenable "psychoanalysis" is that of the reader' (1986, 173 fn.22).)

Although Kofman rejects the notion that writers' lives explain their work in any simple way, she sees an author's life as itself a kind of text and reads her subjects' biographies and their theoretical projects intertextually, deconstructing the opposition between an author's life and work. 'Isn't it an illusion to believe I have any autobiography other than that which emerges from my bibliography?' she asks (1986, 7). Kofman's own biography complicates this question, for in 1994, shortly after publishing the autobiographical *Rue Ordener, rue Labat*, which describes hiding in Paris after her father's deportation and death at Auschwitz, Kofman committed suicide at the age of 65. It seems fitting, then, that Kofman's writing both invites us to analyse her life and work intertextually and warns us against a reductive reading that would purport to 'explain' the latter via the former.

Nicole Fluhr

Further reading and works cited

Berg, E. 'The Third Woman', *diacritics*, 12, 2, Summer 1982.

Delphy, C. *Close to Home*, ed. D. Leonard. London, 1984.

Deutscher, M. (ed.) *Michèle Le Doeuff*. Amherst, MA, 2000.

Deutscher, P. and Oliver, K. (eds) *Enigmas*. Ithaca, NY, 1999.

Duchen, C. *Feminism in France*. London, 1986.

— (ed.) *French Connections*. London, 1987.

Duroux, F. 'How a Woman Philosophizes', in *Enigmas: Essays on Sarah Kofman*, eds P. Deutscher and K. Oliver. Ithaca, NY, 1999.

Gelfand, E. D. and Thorndike Hules, V. (eds) *French Feminist Criticism: Women, Language and Literature, An Annotated Bibliography*. New York, 1985.

Irigaray, L. *This Sex Which Is Not One*. Ithaca, NY, 1985.

Kofman, S. *The Enigma of Woman: Woman in Freud's Writings*. Ithaca, NY, 1985.

—. 'Apprendre aux hommes à tenir parole', interview with R. Jaccard, *Le Monde*, 27–28, April 1986.

—. *The Childhood of Art*. New York, 1988.

—. *Freud and Fiction*. Boston, 1991.

—. *Nietzsche and Metaphor*. London, 1993.

—. *Smothered Words*. Evanston, IL, 1998.

Le Doeuff, M. *The Philosophical Imaginary*. London, 1986.

—. *Hipparchia's Choice*. Oxford, 1991.

Leonard, D. and Adkins L. (eds) *Sex in Question*. London, 1996.

Marks, E. and de Courtivron, I. (eds) *New French Feminisms*. New York, 1981.

Moi, T. (ed.) *French Feminist Thought*. New York, 1987.

Wittig, M. *Les Guérrillères*. New York, 1973.

—. *The Straight Mind and Other Essays*. Boston, 1992.

— and Zeig, S. *Lesbian Peoples*. New York, 1979.

Psychoanalytic Literary Criticism in France

From its inception psychoanalysis has shown a keen regard for literature in whose realm it has often sought to develop its own unique positions on the unconscious motivation of both normal and pathological human behaviour. Freud also created a 'rhetoric' of the unconscious in *The Interpretation of Dreams* (1900), drawing on linguistic and stylistic devices characteristic of western literature since antiquity. Not unlike Freudian theory itself, French criticism of the past sixty years has wavered between two complementary yet also contradictory approaches: the study of depth psychology and the procedures of symptom, text or dream formation. Recent critical developments have issued from discoveries about the mechanism of broken or dismembered signification and have explored the domain of psychological as well as textual secrets.

Early French psychoanalytic criticism followed Freud's dictum: apply the growing body of psychoanalytic knowledge to art and literature. In the 1930s and 1940s, Marie Bonaparte, Charles Baudouin and Rene Laforgue, among others, uncovered psychosexual

turmoil, unconscious fantasies and ambivalent oedipal situations in the lives of authors –
such as Charles Baudelaire, Victor Hugo, Edgar Allan Poe, etc. – through their work. Thus
resulted a type of literary radiography, an X-ray procedure for illuminating the psycho-
pathologies supposedly underlying creative genius. Using bits of biographical information,
the critic transformed the work of art into a clinical document about the author's assumed
neurosis. Creation and neurosis are indeed on the same level as we see critics treating
writers as so many patients on the analytical couch. The method used resembles a word-for-
word translation; the manifest subject matter of the text is converted into a latent content,
the latter being proposed as the unconscious equivalent of the former. Thus Laforgue
equates the 'beauty of evil' in Baudelaire's poetry with the writer's unconscious pull towards
his own demise. Marie Bonaparte sees Poe's dead mother behind Lady Usher and other
female characters given to death. Even though reservations quickly emerged from
philosophical and artistic quarters as to the cogency of applying clinical psychoanalysis
to literature – in a dubious attempt to provide psychiatric accounts of writers – a significant
portion of postwar criticism in France only partially escaped this bias. For example, Jean
Delay, Serge Doubrovsky, Jean Laplanche, Jean-Paul Sartre, etc. continued to emphasize
psycho-biographical objectives even as they sought to address ever so gingerly aesthetic,
poetic and narrative features in a more inclusive approach.

Over a long career, reaching from the 1930s to the 1960s, Charles Mauron developed a
characteristic method of analysis, thematic psychocriticism. He uses the Freudian principle
of free association and searches for latent networks of involuntary ideas that permeate a
multiplicity of texts by the same author. Mauron obtains overlapping associative clusters
that have little to do with a text's apparent subject matter but are helpful in revealing latent
knots of recurring signification. For example, Stéphane Mallarmé's disparate yet frequent
use of 'cradle,' 'musicienne' (female musician), 'pénultième' (the feminine form of the
adjective 'penultimate') throws femininity into relief as an unconscious figure or obsessive
fantasy modulating throughout the poet's work. According to Mauron, the 'obsessive
themes' are steps along the path of 'unconscious self-examination' or involuntary attempts
at self-analysis. Mauron views the involuntary and/or unconscious forms of self-exploration
in literature as the very motor of the creative process. For this reason, his criticism made
strides towards combining classical psychological studies of individual writers with textual
and to some extent formal analysis. In the 1960s and 1970s, other critics such as René
Girard, André Green, Max Milner and Marthe Robert (in part inspired by Mauron) have
examined the latent influence of leading psychoanalytic themes – the Oedipus complex,
fantasies of omnipotence, castration anxiety, the uncanny, etc. – in the emergence of
specific literary genres, for example tragedy, the fantastic novella in romantic literature,
and the novel.

The most innovative theorists have studied the material construction of literary
discourse, the circulation of signification and the mechanism of fractured, dismembered
or secreted meaning. Jacques Lacan in the mid-1950s and Nicolas Abraham in the early
1960s initiated these trends. The two theorists' approaches are convergent in some respects
and widely divergent in others. The common feature of their renewal of psychoanalytic
criticism on an international scale derives from their keen attention to the workings of
language. However, while Lacan studied the vicissitudes of subverted meaning, Abraham
sought to elaborate means whereby signification can be reinstated despite its collapse.

In his 'Seminar on *The Purloined Letter*', Lacan outlines a logical structure of the
unconscious in Poe's tale of the theft by the Minister and the recovery by the detective

Dupin of a compromising letter originally received and read in a public place by the Queen. According to Lacan, the letter – actually the material, written, phonic quality of language or the signifier as such and *not* meaning – stages the dynamics of desire in general. Merely circulating from hand to hand, the letter represents the characters' (and also all humans') inability to master, to fix the object of desire or meaning. Constantly travelling and thus missing from the place where it is supposed to be at any given time, the letter assumes for the characters a delusional or imaginary power of mastery that is yet inexorably undermined by the letter's very displacement of or, formulated otherwise, by the unstoppable flight of signification itself.

Lacan also reignited interest in Freud's research into the unconscious rhetoric of dreams, emphasizing the role of metaphor, metonymy, ellipsis, condensations, semantic displacements, metasemias and the overdetermination and/or juxtaposition of composite verbal elements. Under Lacan's influence a wealth of literary and cinema criticism has developed. Critics have examined the seductive, oblique, elusive, devious and/or ostentatious and flashy course of meaning(s). Roland Barthes, Shoshana Felman, Julia Kristeva and Octave Mannoni have made original contributions to the general field of Lacanian literary criticism – at times combining it with allied approaches such as deconstruction, feminism and semiotics or with more distant disciplines such as marxism. Content and meaning are strictly de-emphasized in favour of the free, even arbitrary, play of signification. Of interest are the verbal or imagistic relations that obtain between truth and error, between manifestation and latency, since, according to Lacan, the unconscious itself is structured like language. This tenet implies that repressed or unconscious desires are transmuted into a passion for the signifier, i.e. into a potentially continuous series of displacements or substitutions along verbal chains that admit of neither a definite starting or end point.

Lacan views meaning as inherently elusive (or barred) because of the structure he confers on desire. More precisely, he equates desire with the structure of language or language with the structure of desire. On account of a putatively constitutive lack (the impossibility to possess or to be the 'phallus'), desire and language function as moving supports or as sheer instruments of purveyance for the unattainable and repressed object. Just as desire never finds more than vicarious satisfaction, language too provides only movement or a procession of (empty) signifiers. In sum, Lacanian and related forms of criticism study the shifting effects of the unconscious, the destabilizing play of language and desire, as opposed to the stability of meaning, associated with the mirage of consciousness, the illusions of power or, in Lacanian terminology, the imaginary. Not surprisingly, the privileged themes or figures of Lacanian criticism are absence, blanks, movement, flight, lack, void, death, etc. These figures serve to point out the deceits of plenitude and display the tricks of the text, played upon unsuspecting and wishful subjects, be they characters, readers or writers.

In 1962 Nicolas Abraham proposed a psychoanalytic approach to the formal aspects of literature in an essay on 'Time, Rhythm, and the Unconscious'. He analysed rhythm as an alternating game of expectations, surprises, fulfilments and disappointments, showing how and why rhythmic incidents constantly enter into or break from patterns. The creation and undoing of temporal patterns correspond to various emotional happenings, such as a narrow escape, an abrupt awakening, a nightmare, the hallucinogenic lulling of a daydream or the creeping imposition of an inexorable reality, etc. On this level of analysis Abraham deliberately disregards semantic content, viewing poems very nearly as musical pieces. He later examines the shifts of rhythmic patterning in relation to the subject matter of the poem at hand. The harmonies and especially the disharmonies between the two realms yield up the unconscious dimension of the text. Though chiefly concerned with poetry, Abraham clearly suggests that studying the dynamic layering, interplay, clashing and/or meshing of expected and unexpected (semantic, prosodic, stylistic, narrative, etc.) features can illuminate all forms of literature.

Abraham introduced the idea of the textual unconscious alongside the contention that each text is strictly speaking a symptom of itself only. In so doing, he outlines several interpretative principles. Literary texts stage fictive conflicts to which they bring solutions or with respect to which they indicate why resolutions are precluded. Literary works give no insight into the psychology of their real authors; instead texts posit a fictive entity (called the 'induced author') as the agent of their creation. Not unlike humans, each and every text is unique: the conflicts, resolutions or impossibilities the text symbolizes are nowhere else to be found. The insistence on singularity places Abraham and his frequent collaborator Maria Torok at odds with the generalizing tendencies of Freudian and some post-Freudian theory; they eschew universal structures, such as the Oedipus complex, castration anxiety, the death drive, etc., viewing them as so many symptomatic modes of expressing as yet undiscovered or undisclosed individual conflicts and traumas.

Given this stance, Abraham and Torok, and later Rand and Torok, have reconsidered the validity of Freud's analyses of literature. Most notably in 'The Phantom of Hamlet or the Sixth Act', Abraham has questioned the Freudian explanation of Prince Hamlet's behaviour (his delay in avenging his father's murder) in terms of his allegedly unresolved Oedipus complex and his unconscious approval of his father's assassin. Abraham claims that the Oedipus complex removes the play's specificity. Hamlet's indecision is the result of events that are literally beyond the Prince's reach because they happened to someone else. Conflicts or a repressed wish of his own do not beset Hamlet; he is unwittingly tormented by the shameful and secret crime of murder his father took to the grave. Interpreting Hamlet's contradictory actions in terms of the haunting influence of someone else's secrets, Abraham places cross-generational group psychology and the disturbing effect of concealed historical events in the forefront of psychoanalysis.

In their work on personal, familial and historical secrets, Abraham and Torok posit the existence of verbal mechanisms whose objective seems to be to disarray, even to destroy the expressive or representational power of language. Appearing under various names (de-signification, anti-metaphor, anti-semantics, cryptonymy, etc.), this psychic aphasia leads to obstructions that prevent linguistic entities from being joined with their potential sources of signification. Abraham and Torok's characteristic method aims at overcoming the resistance to meaning by converting obstacles into guides to understanding. Their theory of readability thus takes full account of the disintegration of meaning, yet only as a preliminary stage in the attempt to recover new forms of coherence even when the very possibility of coherence would appear to be denied.

Nicholas T. Rand

Further reading and works cited

Abraham, N. 'Time, Rhythm, and the Unconscious'. *Rhythms*. Stanford, CA, 1995.
— and Torok, M. *The Shell and the Kernel*, ed. T. Rand. Chicago, 1994.
— and Torok, M. *The Wolf Man's Magic Word*. Minneapolis, MN, 1986.

Anzieu, D. *Le Corps de l'oeuvre*. Paris, 1981.

Barthes, R. *S/Z*. London, 1975.

Baudouin, C. *Psychanalyse de Victor Hugo*. Paris, 1943.

Bellemin-Noël, J. *Vers l'inconscient du texte*. Paris, 1979.

—. *Interlignes: Essais de textanalyse*. Lille, 1988.

Bonaparte, M. *Edgar Poe, Etude psychanalytique*. Paris, 1953.

Bowie, M. *Lacan*. Cambridge, 1991.

Delay, J. *La Jeunesse de Gide*. Paris, 1956/57.

Doubrovsky, S. *La Place de la Madeleine*. Paris, 1974.

—. *Speech and Language in Psychoanalysis*. New York. 1984.

Felman, S. *Writing and Madness*. Ithaca, NY, 1985.

Girard, R. *Mensonge romantique et vérité romanesque*. Paris, 1969.

Green, A. *Un oeil en trop*. Paris, 1979.

Kristeva, J. *Powers of Horror*. New York, 1982.

—. *Sens et non-sens de la révolte*. Paris, 1996.

Lacan, J. 'Seminar on *The Purloined Letter*', *Yale French Studies*, 48, 1972.

Laforgue, R. *L'Echec de Baudelaire*. Geneva, 1964.

Laplanche, J. *Hölderlin et la question du père*. Paris, 1961.

Mannoni, O. *Clefs pour l'imaginaire*. Paris, 1969.

Mauron, C. *Des métaphores obsédantes au mythe personnel*. Paris, 1963.

Milner, M. *On est prié de fermer les yeux*. Paris, 1991.

Rand, N. 'Family Romance or Family History? Psychoanalysis and Dramatic Invention in Nicolas Abraham's *The Phantom of Hamlet*', *diacritics*, 18, 4, Winter 1988.

—. '*The Sandman* Looks at *The Uncanny*', *Speculations After Freud*, eds S. Shamdasani and M. Münchow. London, 1994.

— and Torok, M. *Questions for Freud*. Cambridge, MA, 1997.

Rashkin, E. 'Tools for a New Psychoanalytic Literary Criticism: The Work of Abraham and Torok', *diacritics*, 18, 4, Winter 1988.

Robert, M. *Roman des origines, origines du roman*. Paris, 1972.

Sartre, J.-P. *L'Idiot de la famille*. Paris, 1970/72.

Part II

Theories and Practice of Criticism in North America

Charles Sanders Peirce (1839–1914) and Semiotics

Coined by American philosopher Charles Sanders Peirce, the concept of semiotics involved, at least initially, the examination of various signs and signifiers in relation to one another. Peirce's linguistic theories underscored the significance of social and cultural interaction as fundamental aspects of language. Peirce's discoveries regarding the three classes of signs and the notion of pluralism, moreover, continue to impact the direction of contemporary linguistics and literary criticism.

As a foundational philosopher and exponent of pragmatism, Peirce would seem, at least on the scholarly surface, to be an unlikely proponent of semiotics and its remarkable impact upon twentieth-century linguistics. Nevertheless, he shared in the establishment of several basic principles of modern linguistics. In 1906, Peirce identified the nature and study of signs as a kind of semiosis. Peirce recognized that the emergence of semiotics as a science in its own right required a more dynamic understanding of signification as a linguistic process. As John Deely observes, Peirce realized that 'semiotics could not be merely a response to the question of the being proper to signs ontologically considered'. Rather, 'response must also be made to the further question of the becoming this peculiar type of being enables and sustains itself by. Symbols do not just exist', Deely adds, '[t]hey also grow' (1990, 23). Understanding the social organicism inherent in signs and symbols, Peirce approached semiotics as a distinctive activity in itself and referred to the relationship between such linguistic components as the product of 'brute force' and 'dynamical interaction'. Peirce defined the actions and relationships of signs in terms of their objectivity, while intuitively comprehending the subjectivity that they take on when considered in regard to the present, to the social and cultural forces that exist in the here and now. Simply put, given historical and cultural moments imbue signs and symbols with variant degrees of meaning dependent purely upon the function of time and place.

Having established the interactional and temporal properties of signs, Peirce demonstrated the nature of their action via the concepts of mediation and triadicity. First, signs are invariably mediated by external forces – history, culture, time – and these mediating entities characterize the ways in which we interpret signs and symbols. The second concept, the process of triadicity, finds its origins in the dyadic relationship between the sign itself and the signified, which refers to the idea that constitutes the sign's meaning. Peirce furthered this notion in terms of a more complex, triadic relationship between the sign and the signified, as well as between the sign and the interpretant, which Peirce described as 'all that is explicit in the sign itself apart from its context and circumstances of utterance' (cit. Deely 1990, 26). For Peirce, signs become actualized when they represent something other than themselves. Signs exist as mere objects when standing on their own. In other words, signs always depend upon something other than themselves to establish their uniqueness. In Peirce's philosophy, then, signs are inevitably subordinate to their qualities of representation. As Deely notes, 'the key to understanding what is proper to the sign is the notion of relativity, relation, or relative being. Without this content, the sign ceases to be a sign, whatever else it may happen to be' (35). Essentially, signs can only be recognized in a relational context with something other than themselves; hence, signs take on their unique characteristics of being when interpreted in terms of their historical or cultural antecedents.

The Peircean philosophy of triadicity provided the basis for his postulation of the three classes of signs, which Peirce identified in terms of the relationship between the sign and the signified. The first class of signs, the icon, operates by virtue of its shared features and similarities with that which it signifies. In his work, Peirce referred to the icon rather opaquely as a 'possibility involving a possibility, and thus the possibility of its being represented as a possibility' (cit. Merrell 1997, 53). In *Peirce, Signs, and Meaning* (1997), Floyd Merrell describes icons in regard to their inherent self-referentiality as 'signs of themselves and themselves only' (54). The notion of the index, Peirce's second class of signs, denotes a kind of sign that enjoys a natural relationship with the cause and effect of what it signifies. As Merrell explains, 'Indices, by nature binary in character, ordinarily relate to some *other*' (54). The third class of signs, the symbol or 'sign proper', refers to the unnatural relationship between the sign and its signifier. These symbols ultimately function as the words that constitute the nature of a given language. Peirce described the concept of the symbol as 'a sign which would lose the character which renders it a sign if there were no interpretant' (cit. Lidov 1999, 93). David Lidov usefully recognizes the dependent relationship that exists between Peirce's three classes of signs. While the notion of the symbol has since come to refer to a broader range of textual and linguistic referents in literary studies, Peirce's classification schema continues to impact on the ways in which we understand the interrelationships – indeed, the dependency that exists – between language and the objective reality of a given historical or cultural moment (1999, 93–4).

Peirce's contributions to semiotics also include his expansive philosophies of pragmatism and pluralism, schools of intellectual thought that continue to impact on the course and direction of scholarship in the humanities. Peirce introduced his ground-breaking philosophy of pragmatism during a 1903 lecture at Harvard University. His concept of pragmatism finds its roots, moreover, in our collective understanding of the larger ethical and communal matrix of human behaviour. More than a simple practical approach to life and human discourse, Peirce's pragmatism involves a recognition of the highest form of good, which he describes as the ways in which communities search for forms of higher truth. Peirce ascribes a given person's capacity for accomplishing a higher sense of goodness to their ability to achieve what he refers to as self-control. 'In its higher stages', Peirce writes, 'evolution takes place more and more largely through self-control, and this gives the pragmatist a sort of justification for making the rational purport to be general' (cit. Corrington 1993, 53). By entering into the development and community of the world, then, the pragmatist in Peirce's formulation evolves toward ideal states of being that imbue life with more rational and objective senses of reality. In a 1905 essay on 'Issues of Pragmaticism', Peirce attributes his philosophy of pragmatism to a kind of critical common-sensism, which, in the words of Robert S. Corrington, 'applies evolutionary thinking to the unconscious and foundational propositions of our moral and scientific life' (1993, 54). Honouring the strictures of critical common-sensism affords pragmatists with the capacity for enjoying greater possibilities for self-control and rationalism.

The seemingly logical intellectual result of his notion of a pragmatic philosophy, Peirce's concept of pluralism finds its origins in the multifarious ways in which we perceive the worlds in which we live. In Peirce's philosophical purview, our sensory perceptions of the world are contingent upon the interdependence between our experiences – however divergent they may be – of reality and the facticity inherent in the perceived worlds of our human others. 'The real world is the world of sensible experiences', Peirce writes, and 'the sensory world is but a fragment of the ideal world' (cit. Rosenthal 1994, 3). The notion of possibility – in fact, the very same concept of possibility inherent in the vague spaces of reality that exist between our real worlds and our sensory worlds – operates as the foundation for Peirce's philosophy of pluralism. Sandra B. Rosenthal ascribes the philosopher's ultimate vision of plurality to a comprehension of the power inherent in our creative selves:

> Human creativity can be understood as a uniquely specialized, highly intensified instance of the free creative activity characteristic of the universe within which it functions, and the conditions of possibility of human freedom in general, as self-directedness rooted in rationality, are to be found in the conditions that constitute the universe at large and within which rationality emerges. (Rosenthal 1994, 126)

Clearly, Peirce's ideas of possibility and pluralism – rooted, as they are, in notions of freedom and rationality – offer a fertile intellectual background for the analysis of signs, symbols and signifiers, open-ended concepts that are invariably contingent upon the infinitely more powerful social forces of a given historical and cultural moment.

Kenneth Womack

Further reading and works cited

Chomsky, N. *Aspects of the Theory of Syntax*. Cambridge, MA, 1965.
Colapietro, V. *Peirce's Approach to the Self*. Albany, NY, 1989.
Corrington, R. S. *An Introduction to C. S. Peirce*. Lanham, MA, 1993.
Culler, J. *The Pursuit of Signs*. Ithaca, NY, 1981.
Deely, J. *Basics of Semiotics*. Bloomington, IN, 1990.
Eco, U. *A Theory of Semiotics*. Bloomington, IN, 1976.
Hawkes, T. *Structuralism and Semiotics*. London, 1977.
Holland, N. *The Critical I*. New York, 1992.
Jameson, F. *The Prison-House of Language*. Princeton, NJ, 1972.
Lidov, D. *Elements of Semiotics*. New York, 1999.
Malmberg, B. *Structural Linguistics and Human Communication*. Berlin, 1967.
Merrell, F. *Peirce, Signs, and Meaning*. Toronto, 1997.
Rosenthal, S. B. *Charles Peirce's Pragmatic Pluralism*. Albany, NY, 1994.

The New Criticism

Recent literary theory has had very little good to say about the New Criticism. As Gerald Graff puts it, 'With remarkable speed, the fortunes of the New Criticism in the university had gone from rags to riches to routine' in two decades (Graff 1987, 227). Here I will argue that there is much to learn from both transitions. The New Criticism struck it rich in America because the founding efforts of a few critics – especially John Crowe Ransom, Allen Tate, R. P. Blackmur, Robert Penn Warren and Cleanth Brooks – came to represent two important possibilities for literary education and hence drew many people into loose associations with most of their principles. These critics spoke for many who came to believe it was time to focus on what held individual texts together as distinctive experiences rather than on what bound them to contexts they shared with other aspects of their culture. And they promised that such experiences would foster powers encouraging revolutionary changes in educational practices. The prevailing emphasis on historical and philological scholarship could be replaced by more direct efforts to address the 'dissociation of sensibility' that T. S. Eliot had diagnosed as the fundamental torment for contemporary culture.

But the emerging consensus was made routine because the stress on cultivating powers soon gave way to a transmittable method in which close readings were treated as instruments for producing original interpretations explicating the '*organic unity*' that gave the texts their unique identities. Cognitive claims then typically got reduced to thematic analyses, with the statement of ideas replacing the initial ideal of treating the texts as unique experiences that modified sensibilities rather than addressed ideological frameworks. And, as critics like Frank Lentricchia, Terry Eagleton and John Fekete would later point out, it had also come to seem the case that the basic ideas generating this revolution were in fact very difficult to reconcile. The best way to preserve ideals stressing the organic unity of individual texts is to deal with them as discrete specific contexts whose internal densities continually ironize all efforts at generalization. But this route to individuation seemed to depend on bracketing concerns for intentionality and historical contexts that would in fact prove necessary for any adequate account of how texts confer or contribute to the development of cognitive powers.

Many of the major New Critical essays were written in the 1930s as part of a ferment in critical culture that linked these critics loosely with others like Kenneth Burke and Yvor Winters and William Empson who were trying to develop general interpretive stances attuned to modernist practices. But the movement only took on public identity as a movement with the publication in 1941 of Ransom's *The New Criticism*, with chapters on Eliot, Winters, Richards and 'ontological criticism'. Concentrating on poetry, these early writings defined powers attributable to close reading individual texts by developing sharp contrasts with what were then the two perspectives dominating literary study in America. Because American PhD programmes had been founded in the 1880s on German ideals, the prevailing model for literary study was a positivist historicism concerned with elaborating biographical contexts, tracing the 'evolution' of forms, and establishing the sources and influences for major texts. For the New Critics such work seemed to treat those texts as excuses for studying contexts established by the historian, not by the project of the individual work. The New Critics found some sustenance in neohumanist critiques of that historicism along fundamentally Arnoldian lines. Thinkers like Norman Foerster and Paul Elmer More tried to replace historical frameworks by discourses insisting on the intellectual and moral significance of individual texts. But because these critics treated these texts as offering beliefs that could enter into dialogue with the great philosophers, they seemed no less eager than the historians to sacrifice text to context.

The New Critics' primary task then was to develop a vocabulary and methodology that could foreground what seemed the distinctive concrete experience produced by the words of the text so as to reduce the need for either historical or philosophical contexts. In hindsight it is easy to say that they went too far – clearly, reading is a dialogical relation among what Rene Wellek called 'intrinsic and extrinsic' aspects of a text's presence in the world. But such rapprochement is difficult in practice when one's opponents are no more balanced than oneself and seem a lot more dangerous. More important, rapprochement requires a shared sense of practice. But the New Critics came to power largely because they would not accept the fundamentally academic nature of the discourses carried out by their opponents. Early New Criticism was suffused with the passions of modernist writing. It saw criticism not primarily as scholarship but as an instrument for taking on the cultural project of resisting the *dissociation of sensibility* diagnosed by T. S. Eliot as the basic disease facing modernity. And it therefore concentrated on ways of reading that might actually make a difference in how audiences engaged the blend of market thinking, positivist empiricism and enervated romanticism that seemed to carry public authority in their respective domains.

American New Critical responses to these cultural forces were mostly reactionary. Their roots were Southern agrarian and their sense of manners Mandarin. But resisting modernity was a task that bred strange alliances. We have to imagine those Southern values interacting with a new academic clientele undreamt of in historicist and neohumanist philosophies. Only a few years after Ransom's book, the GI Bill sent millions of Americans to universities and colleges, usually as the first members of their families to enter higher education. And that rush to education soon filtered down into the children of parents who had suffered in the name of freedom and wanted to begin reaping some of its benefits. These new populations had quite practical goals for their educations. But they were curious about the culture that had seemed worth fighting for, and a new age of opportunity made it appealing to imagine remaking psyches through the arts. These new students would not sit long for dry scholarship or pious moralizing, and they could not be expected to bring to their classes the historical education or the trainings in discrimination given to those from families with generations of university attendance. But they were a perfect audience for writers committed to plain prose and practical attention to texts. Guided by New Critical principles popularized in the anthology *Understanding Poetry* (1938), students did not have to bring much learning to literature (and did not have to feel guilty or disqualified by their ignorance of historical contexts). They could work out concrete terms for what brought texts alive for them, and they could imagine themselves participating in the work of cultural reformation largely by recognizing how their reading promised to make their lives quite different from those led by their parents. They could idealize culture as a release from the levelling forces fundamental to modernity without having to idealize the South and its institutions.

After all, these American Southerners themselves learned a good deal from the English psychologist I. A. Richards, whose presence seems to me fundamental to the field of possibilities and struggles that was to constitute New Critical theorizing during the years when it was consolidating power. Richards's *Practical Criticism* (1929) recorded a series of experiments over several years with undergraduates reading for an honours degree in English at Cambridge. Given poems for which the author was not identified, these gifted and privileged students nonetheless proved themselves simply awful readers. They were trained to provide historical backgrounds for identified texts, but they had very weak abilities to interpret and to evaluate work not situated historically for them. Analysing this data led Richards to postulate ten aspects of reading for which teachers and critics had to provide 'educational models more efficient than those we use now in developing discrimination and the power to understand what we hear and read' (1929, 3). Criticism then was not recondite scholarship but the struggle to provide society improved means of making and communicating intricate judgements.

Richards's *Principles of Literary Criticism* (1924) presented his most influential effort to restructure the education enabling such judgements. All the ladders start with a fundamental distinction between science and poetry. Science seeks true propositions by eliminating psychology and developing methods for generating unequivocal, testable statements. Poetry, on the other hand, is not concerned with picturing the world. Its utterances are '*pseudo-statements*' making possible specific *attitudes* affecting how we take up stances towards the world. Where science seeks unequivocal clarity enabling firm decisions between what is to be believed and what rejected, poetry provides textual relations modelling how psyches can compose their energies and form attitudes articulating complex balances for the psyche: 'In describing the poet we laid stress upon. . . the width of the field of stimulation which he can accept, and the completeness of the response that he can make. Compared with him the ordinary man suppresses nine-tenths of his impulses, because he is incapable of managing them without confusion' (1924, 243). Art puts inner impulses into 'equilibrium' and hence 'brings into play far more of our personality than is possible in experiences of more defined emotion' (1924, 251). Close reading is our means of attuning ourselves to such equilibrium, and hence it is fundamental to psychic health. And tragedy's blend of pity, fear and awe offers poetry's richest contribution to composing permanent modifications in readerly sensibilities preparing them to adapt more fully to the world.

The New Critics deeply admired three basic features of Richards's arguments – his emphasis on criticism as oriented towards cultural literacy rather than towards scholarship, his finding cultural roles for modernist emphases on complexity, and his locating that complexity primarily in how texts are read as semantic structures rather than in how they are contextualised. But they were made uneasy by his secular liberal rationalism and his faith in psychological paradigms. So they developed theoretical alternatives for each of his key principles, and in the process they set intellectual currents running that would transform a potentially radical psychology into routine academic exercises.

First and most important, the New Critics could not accept Richards's treating science and poetry as just two distinctive practices, each with its own roles to play in society. The

New Critics had to demonize science because it was the source of dissociated sensibility and the basic instrument for industrial capitalism. Science gave public authority to an inflexible empiricism that could deal with bodies but not with souls, with pleasures but not with the intricate purposiveness of meanings constructed by the imagination. More drastic yet, science gave currency to myths of progress in every domain, so that people were tempted to overlook all that is tragic and unexplainable and probably unchangeable in their lives. Where the populace had once managed to accept their fates, now they would feel entitled to resentment and society would be rife with conflict.

Second, treating the textual density of poetry as if it were mere pseudo-statement simply did not provide a sufficient counterweight to science or to the romantic psychologizing that gave personal resonance to myths of progress and individuality. Poetry had to do more than establish possible attitudes toward the world that were valuable because of the complex states of mind produced. States of mind are useless or dangerous unless they are anchored in actual truths. Only the disciplines associated with pursuing truths beyond the self could free the western psyche from the self-absorption imposed upon it by the nineteenth century. So theory had to show how literature provided cognitive access to some kind of distinctive truth to which science did not have access (a task which required privileging poetry over the novel's embeddedness in social issues). The third dissatisfaction followed naturally. Richards' concern was primarily with how psyches processed different kinds of meanings. But an effective poetics would stress texts, not psyches, since only attention to the text itself could establish objective evidence for the claims that poetry provided a non-discursive knowledge rivalling what science could provide. Stressing texts required minimizing context, and that could best be done by showing how most contextual work depended on what W. K. Wimsatt called the 'intentional fallacy'. There seemed only two choices – either one proposed contexts that limited what the words could be seen as performing or one trusted the complex patterning implicit in the verbal texture as the ultimate arbiter of what texts meant.

Each major New Critic offered a distinctive slant on these topics. Here, I will try to indicate their major differences by concentrating on three different ways they went about approaching the question of poetry's access to truths unavailable to science. Where Richards stressed the overall balancing of affective investments, Ransom locates the balancing in real miraculous integrations of the physical and the metaphorical, Tate turns to what can be known by our experience of the text as itself a real event, and Brooks takes organicism to its logical extreme in a vision of poetry as complex dramatic irony. From there, only routinization can follow because all texts end up sustaining pretty much the same kind of experience.

Ransom's model of poetry is based largely on what he came to call a miraculous fusion of local texture and logical structure. At one pole we find movements like imagism demonstrating the power of a fundamentally physical poetry to make us recognize the sharp edges, the givenness and the density of the material world (1955, 873). But even physical poetry (especially physical poetry) requires rhythm, which is profoundly bodily yet also depends on systemic structures that cannot be made physically visible but appeal to the self-reflexive mind. So poetry is constantly tempted also by a second possibility responding to these transformative mental energies. Ransom calls this orientation that of 'Platonic poetry'. We must feel the energy of an allegorical pull organizing the elements into some kind of overall meaningfulness. But at the same time Ransom constantly reminds us of the danger within this Platonic impulse because it is happiest when it can march images like 'little lambs to the slaughter' (1955, 874). Because this Platonic impulse is so strong within us, we need poetry to provide concrete trials for its ideas (1955, 875), and even to establish a density of experience that does not so much disprove the idea as make it 'look ineffective and therefore foolish' (1955, 876).

Ultimately Ransom denigrates ideas in order to celebrate experiences that can build on reason's energies but thwart its self-confidence. Then even in secular contexts one encounters the fundamental religious awareness of how spirit can live incarnationally in cooperation with the sensuous world rather than as its master. Poetry is cognition in resistance to reason. So where 'science gratifies a rational or practical impulse and exhibits the minimum of perception, Art gratifies a perceptual impulse and exhibits the minimum of reason' (1955, 877). 'Miraculism' is our recognition of how this minimum of reason turns out to be a maximum of spirit, as we see most fully in poetry that is fundamentally metaphysical (that is physical and Platonic). This poetry manifests metaphoric powers capable of making what had seemed mere analogy proceed 'to an identification which is complete' (1955, 880). As a mundane example consider how fully true lovers can make real the figure of exchanging hearts. And as a sublime example think of how Milton's *Paradise Lost* comes to represent for us the entire process of the Fall and the possibilities of redemption that it created. For Ransom poetry takes on the burden of two centuries of seeking substitutes for religion through art, and it almost succeeds in at least keeping alive the possibility that notions like grace and miracle need not be dismissed because of the demise of organized religion.

Allen Tate shared Ransom's sense that the spirit of religion had somehow to be preserved in the face of science. But he wanted to base the claims for poetry on something much more defensible in secular terms than talk of miraculism. So he took on the leading semioticians of his day in order to develop a notion of meaning which did not reduce poetry either to non-sense or to the rhetorical manipulation of feelings (1968, 91). Ransom made a mistake locating the 'reality' of poetry in the image because the image remains a construct, not a perception or proposition. If poetry is to offer a distinctive kind of knowledge, one must be able to characterize it as a distinctive kind of experience in the real world, and one must do that in terms that reach beyond Richards' purely psychological register. Poetry must be the experience of something for which truth claims can be made. Tate faces these challenges by shifting from what poetry says to what poetry does. Its claim for truth depends on the fact that the poem is not merely about the world but in a significant sense 'an object that exists' in its own right (1968, 194). By attending to the work as real object we can show how it provides 'complex wholes which are never in a rigid state of adjustment' so that the experience rendered invites 'infinitely prolonged attention'. And it is this fascinated prolonging of attention which constitutes the major difference between science and poetry. Where 'the half-statement of science arrests our attention at those features of the whole that may be put at the service of the will', poetry presents an object that may be 'known' as a 'qualitative whole' and hence grasped in terms of the intricacy of the internal relations emerging as aspects of the experience that we cannot control but nonetheless find compelling (1968, 194).

Now Tate can provide a theoretical foundation for modernist critiques of views that art is fundamentally a mode of communication, and hence he can show clearly why notions of intention and context based on communication models are inappropriate. Were poetry to seek communication it would have to stress either the extensional or the intentional aspect of its assertions. Either it relies on specific claims to depict actual particulars or it concentrates on mobilizing the range of connotations by which expressions indicate how someone feels. In the one case we have images without cogent purposiveness; in the other we have all too evident purposes without what Ransom called trial by experience (1941, 56–63). But if the poem exists in its own right, then rather than communicating it focuses our infinitely prolonged attention on the conditions by which communications are shaped and modified. The audience is witness to the problematic aspects of communication. Rather than stressing intension or extension, 'the meaning of poetry' consists in 'its "tension", the full organized body of all the intension and extension that we can find in it' (1941, 64). Poetry offers cognition because it organizes experiences of the complex energies running through human actions and interactions. This mode of cognition in turn cannot be judged and tested in scientific terms but depends on the collective body of reflections on experience that constitutes cultural traditions (1941, 63). Poetry's truths depend on previous exposure to poetry's truths – the fundamental circular argument that the humanities cannot escape.

I think it was grappling with this circularity that led to the making routine of New Criticism, along with all those sociological factors set in motion by success within an institution. For critics had to address two contradictory demands: they had to show how works of literature stressed an internal density or organic unity that made them different from typical communicative acts, and they had to show that they could explain the value of this difference by providing some model of cognition that would display the use value of these texts in terms that science could not replicate but had to envy. The distinction of art as experience from art as statement provided a promising beginning. But how could one make distinctive truth claims about experience without reintroducing the very models from science that had to be resisted? One option was to say that the truths involved were manifest only in the audience's enhanced powers for experience. This path, however, led to undemocratic, Nietzschean visions of agency (or radical theological visions of authenticity) incompatible with New Critical Christian humanism, and it undermined struggles against the authority of science in the universities and in politics. If the arts produce little Nietzsches we need science to tell us how to regulate them. So criticism turned instead to simply finding wisdom within the experiences it was characterizing. 'Infinitely prolonged attention' gave way to thematic 'readings' explicating ideas and values which held the unity together (when in fact organic unity must be pervasive, with each element playing its irreducible part). Yet these readings still had to stress the specialness of art, even on the thematic level, so they tended to treat texts as 'about' the power of art or the mystery of metaphor and of love. Thematics suspicious of science and of philosophy has very few ways to avoid becoming routine.

Cleanth Brooks's criticism directly confronted the dilemma of reconciling organic unity claims with cognition claims, but in highly persuasive ways that intensified the pressures on routinization. Where Tate stressed the role of tension at the core of poetic experience Brooks idealized the presentation of paradox resulting from foregrounding that tension. Poetry's terms are 'continually modifying each other and thus violating their dictionary meanings' (Brooks 1947, 9). Consequently, assertions in poetry are always confronted with their opposites, and metaphors continually tilt planes and overlap edges so as to bring contradictory possibilities into play. One could praise the paradox as an end in itself, and hence an analogue to Ransom's miraculism. But Brooks took an overtly more secular tack. Rather than stop with the paradoxical meanings, Brooks insisted that we situate these contradictions in dramatic terms. Then poetry has the immense power of making us aware at every step of the contradictions fundamental to our desires and our practices. Richards' inclusiveness has cognitive force as dramatic irony. Then, probably to dignify that irony and restore a kind of fideism, Brooks adds the unwarranted but powerful insistence that this sense of irony is inseparable from 'the unity of the experience itself'. Here is Brooks summarizing his reading of Randall Jarrell's 'Eighth Air Force': 'In this poem the affirmation. .. seems to me to supply every qualification that is required. The sense of self-guilt, the yearning to believe in man's justness. .. all render accurately and dramatically the total situation' (Brooks 1950, 1048). Irony is poetry's truth, and its organic unity is the privileged means by which this completeness of experience gets embodied.

Brooks was the most influential of the New Critics on academic practice, probably because he offered very full readings of texts and managed to make theory seem practical rather than philosophical. But his success came with a substantial price. There were many possibilities of 'intrinsic criticism' not pursued, especially those offered by Kenneth Burke that stressed authorial action and so were open to a variety of possible projects and ways of organizing materials. More important, the possibilities that were pursued ran the risk of making all readings demonstrate that they have captured the wholeness of the text by revealing how intricately self-cancelling it is. Wholeness could only have cognitive force if it was based on drama – otherwise it was only an aesthetic abstraction. But all one can know through drama is the imposing of positionality on referentiality. Poetry staged personae whose situation dictated what they could assert or even experience.

Burdened by such constraints, the New Criticism had lost most of its intellectual authority by 1960, although vague idealizations of close reading as a cognitive instrument governed most literary practice for at least the next decade. However, this lost intellectual authority served almost as a contrastive springboard against which two new movements could promote themselves. The perspective that would become deconstruction saw itself the eager heir of 'the process of negative totalisation that American criticism discovered when it penetrated more or less unwittingly into the temporal labyrinth of interpretation' (de Man 1971, 35). Where the New Critics tried to domesticate irony by treating it as a form of knowledge subordinate to supple aesthetic and ethical judgements, the spirit of deconstruction required making whatever was positive a direct complement of this absolute negativity. One could not talk of 'cognition' without convicting oneself of terminal naivety. There were no miracles connecting the allegorical to the existential; there was only the tracing or remaking of unjustifiable desires exposed in all their hopeless neediness. Yet as de Man's arrogant prose makes visible, one could find deep pleasure and even full psychological release in the process of continually undermining truth claims in the name of fascination or 'tragic gaiety'. The ethical correlate of art's dense internal patterning was an absolute writerliness committed to treating the real world by analogies with the process of fingering the folds of the text.

There is in all this positioning one irony that de Man apparently did not grasp. At his most arrogant he seems only to repeat one of the most problematic aspects of New Critical theory: 'Considerations of the actual and historical existence of writers are a waste of time from a critical viewpoint' (1971, 35). Perhaps only this insouciant dismissal of history could sustain a belief that there is only *a* critical viewpoint. In any case de Man entirely failed to see that what irony erases as a metaphysical negation, history promises to restore as a field of possible cognitive attachments. For history needs no absolutes and promises not to overcome irony but only to contextualize it in its limitations. So it should be no surprise that the most powerful heir to the New Criticism turned out to be a variety of historicisms, each promising its own versions of Brooks's dramatic view of situations but without the uncomfortable baggage of having to find a place for 'organic unity' or, indeed, for any terms stressing the existential significance of the internal relations writers establish.

It is crucial that we understand how the New Criticism unwittingly set the stage for the success of these historicisms and prepared conditions where a new routinization would soon take hold. It was the New Critics who popularized the demand that literary study pursue cognitive ambitions enabling it to rival the sciences for social and institutional authority. Their particular versions of the cognitive proved impossible to sustain – in part for their quasi-mystical talk about miraculism or just about 'experience', and in part because they could not find a way of making generalizations that was sufficiently responsive to the strong individuality basic to claims about organic unity. But they made literary study very difficult to justify for audiences who had learned to idealize that practice unless the discipline promised some kind of cognitive reward. As the authority of New Criticism waned it became increasingly easy to weaken or bracket the concern for aesthetic unity. That in turn cleared the way to exploring cognitive claims much more closely linked to the kinds of claims made by other disciplines. One could take the particularity of texts as especially dense moments where conjunctions of historical forces become visible. One might even keep principles of close reading but turn them against the aesthetic in order to show how texts worked to conceal ideological interests or to invent ways of grappling with actual historical contradictions. Soon historicist arguments like Terry Eagleton's would analyse the New Critics' evasions of history as itself a historical symptom: these critics were trapped in an aesthetic ideology committed to bourgeois ideals of autonomy, self-sufficiency and independence from demands that might arise from collective interests.

Now the first of these successors to the New Criticism is already in ruins, the second has become routine. Perhaps we have arrived at a time when critics will once again take on the social burden of resisting academicism and exploring the powers that can be developed by focusing on how works of art organize experience and create values. They may well find much in New Criticism that can help them, provided that they learn from its history the costs of ignoring history and of seeking too avidly to attach what geniuses make to what critics can know.

Charles Altieri

Further reading and works cited

Bové, P. *Intellectuals in Power*. New York, 1986.
Brooks, C. *Modern Poetry and the Tradition*. Chapel Hill, NC, 1939.
—. *The Well Wrought Urn*. New York, 1947.
—. 'Irony as a Principle of Structure', in *Literary Opinion in America*, ed. M. D. Zabel. New York, 1951.
— with Warren, R. Penn. *Understanding Poetry*. New York, 1938.
Crane, R. S. 'History vs Criticism in the University Study of Literature'. *The English Journal*, 24, October 1935.
de Man, P. *Blindness and Insight*. New York, 1971.
Eagleton, T. *Literary Theory*. Oxford, 1983.
Fekete, J. *The Critical Twilight*. London, 1978.
Graff, G. *Professing Literature*. Chicago, 1987.
Jancovich, M. *The Cultural Politics of the New Criticism*. Cambridge, 1993.

Janssen, M. *The Kenyon Review 1939–1970*. Baton Rouge, LA, 1990.
Krieger, M. *The New Apologists for Poetry*. Minneapolis, MN, 1956.
Lentricchia, F. *After the New Criticism*. London, 1983.
Ransom, J. Crowe. *God Without Thunder*.
—. *The World's Body*. New York, 1938.
—. *The New Criticism*. Norfolk, 1941.
—. *Poems and Essays*. New York, 1955.
Richards, I. A. *Principles of Literary Criticism*. London, 1924.
—. *Practical Criticism*. London, 1929.
Spurlin, W. J. and Fischer, M. (eds) *The New Criticism and Contemporary Literary Theory*. New York, 1995.
Tate, A. *Essays of Four Decades*. New York, 1968.
Twelve Southerners. *I'll Take my Stand: The South and the Agrarian Tradition*. Baton Rouge, LA, 1980.
Warren, R. Penn. *Selected Essays*. New York, 1958.
Wellek, R. and Warren, A. *Theory of Literature*. New York, 1949.
Winchell, M. R. *Cleanth Brooks and the Rise of Modern Criticism*. Charlottesville, NC, 1996.
Wimsatt, W. K. and Brooks, C. *Literary Criticism*. New York, 1957.
Wimsatt, W. K. *The Verbal Icon*. New York, 1958.

The Chicago School

The Chicago School flourished from the later 1930s into the 1950s. It centred on Ronald Salmon Crane (1886–1967), who taught at Chicago from 1924 to 1951. In 1925, he was made professor, and, ten years later, chair of the English department, holding this position until 1947. Although Crane's early output was largely devoted to the post-Restoration period, this work was not ostensibly concerned with the application of Aristotelian ideas to English literary thought, so important to the shaping of the Chicago School. He was also responsible for a bibliography of journalism from 1620 to 1800, published under the title *A Census of British Newspapers and Periodicals 1620–1800* (1927), and the annual survey of current scholarship in eighteenth-century studies for the *Philological Quarterly*, which he edited from 1930 to 1952. Crane's work was infused with neoclassical ideas and, subsequently, with the awareness of the role that Aristotle had played in the formation of such ideas.

Using Aristotle's *Rhetoric* and *Poetics* as their theoretical base texts, the Chicago School believed, along with T. S. Eliot, that criticism should study 'poetry as poetry and not another thing'. They viewed with suspicion what they regarded as New Criticism's practice of rejecting historical analysis, its penchant for presenting subjective judgements as objective analysis and its emphasis on poetry rather than other genres such as fiction. Crane and others examined other genres, drawing for their 'techniques on a "pluralistic and instrumentalist" basis, from whatever method seemed appropriate to a particular case' (Crane, in Preminger 1974, 22). In *Critics and Criticism* edited by Crane (1952), for example, there are many illustrations of this critical phenomenon including Crane's own essay, 'The Concept of Plot and the Plot of *Tom Jones*', a reading of Fielding's novel.

Becoming chair of Chicago's English department, Crane was instrumental in hiring, over the next decade or so, critics such as Elder Olson, Norman MacLean and W. R. Keast, who were also sympathetic to the application of Aristotelian ideas to the study of literature, and whose work, in retrospect, has become recognized as the Chicago School. A student of Crane's, Wayne C. Booth (1921–), inherited his mantle at Chicago, teaching there from 1962 until well into the 1990s. Booth's *The Rhetoric of Fiction* (1961) was influential in the formation of the study of narratology and its emphasis upon the analysis of how language is used. A major legacy of Booth's work has been narratological analysis of prose carried out by, among others, James Phelan, editor of the journal *Narrative*, whose work is in the same general, neo-Aristotelian tradition as that of Wayne Booth and Sheldon Sacks.

Many of the publications identified with what is regarded as the Chicago School were produced during the 1930s as part of a ferment created by the radical reorganization of undergraduate education at the University of Chicago. Robert Maynard Hutchins re-structured the undergraduate programme. He emphasized the value of interdisciplinary studies and stressed the importance of reading and understanding primary texts. These activities were epitomized by Mortimer Adler's 'Great Books of the Western Tradition' and by philosopher Richard P. McKeon in a course, 'Organizations, Methods and Principles'. The influence of Hutchins, Adler and McKeon directed Crane's focus away from stressing the primary importance of historical criticism to concentrating on a humane liberal arts education for English Department graduates.

In 'History versus Criticism in the Study of Literature', Crane advocated an approach for the teaching of undergraduate literature, not primarily through literature's historical origins, but with a preference for an approach combining textual explication and aesthetics.

Crane's style has been described by Gerald Graff in *Professing Literature* as 'so elephantine and scholastic that it became a target of parody' (1927, 236–7). However, central to Crane's ideas and crucial for the Chicago School was the notion of '*pluralism*', which derives from the work of McKeon, particularly his adherence to the idea of philosophical pluralism. Writing the 1965 entry on the Chicago Critics for Alex Preminger's *Princeton Encyclopedia of Poetry and Poetics*, Crane notes that 'the most explicit statements of . . . "pluralism" are contained in McKeon's "The Philosophic Bases of Art and Criticism", Olson's "An Outline of Poetic Theory"' and his own *The Languages of Criticism and the Structure of Poetry*. Underlying 'pluralism' is a relativist approach that advocates many different forms of literary criticism, each of which has its own interpretive powers and limitations. The Chicago School, in other words, did not advocate one method, but several, to be adopted pragmatically as dictated by the needs of the given text and situation. For Crane, 'the only rational ground for adhering to one of them rather than to any of the others is its superior capacity to give us the special kind of understanding and evaluation of literature we want to get, at least for the time being' (Crane, in Preminger 1974, 117).

Elder Olson observes in his memoir, 'R. S. Crane' (1984), that 'all of us were influenced by McKeon', who 'provided the philosophical foundations for much of our work', although McKeon 'never published anything that could be taken as a formulation of the poetics of the Chicago School' (Olson 1976, 236). McKeon also argues that philosophical systems in history 'were generated by their prior choice of organizations, methods, principles and modes of thought'. In *The Languages of Criticism and the Structure of Poetry*, Crane argues that criticism is unlike other areas of inquiry, such as biochemistry for instance, which has an agreed set of methodological and factual assumptions. Criticism is rather 'a collection of distinct and more or less incommensurable "frameworks" or "languages"'. These critical vocabularies differ radically in 'matters of assumed principle, definition and method'. For Crane, 'we ought to have at our command, collectively at least, as many different critical methods as there are distinguishable major aspects in the construction, appreciation, and use of literary works' (1953, 192). Inasmuch as the Chicago Critics shared the broad acceptance of different critical methods, their approach may be seen to be primarily methodological in nature, rather than ideological, as Paul de Man has correctly asserted (1986, 54). In other words, they concentrated their efforts on the methods of reading literary texts, not on pre-existing political or aesthetic criteria for evaluating such texts.

If McKeon provided a methodological basis for the work of the Chicago School, Crane's personality and vision of literary criticism can be seen to be of equal importance. Crane greatly influenced his students and gathered around him colleagues who developed similar ideas to his own. Olson (1909–1998), for example, gives an account of his initial encounter with Crane, 'one afternoon in 1933', for the start of a new course, 'a survey of English literature from 1660 to 1800'. Crane was, Olson writes, 'a man of immense erudition'. He was 'someone who strained [Olson's] capacities. More than that, he made me realize that I had capacities I had not guessed'. They shared the same concerns: 'criticism should be made into and recognized as an academic discipline'; 'literary history was not really history'; 'the theory of both literary history and history in general must be more closely looked into'; 'that the present condition of critical theory was deplorable'. They also shared a 'distrust of . . . Geistesgeschichte, the "spirit of the age" ' and 'nonsensical classifications as "Classical" or "Romantic" ' (Olson 1976, 232, 234–5). As Gerald Graff has succinctly expressed it, underlying the scepticism towards the history of ideas and historicism was 'the feeling that the power of literature was somehow compromised if it were felt to be rooted in history' (1987, 192).

Writing in what may be taken as the manifesto of the Chicago school of criticism – Critics and Criticism: Ancient and Modern (1952) – Olson makes the now well-known remark that 'criticism in our time is a sort of Tower of Babel'. He adds:

> Moreover, it is not merely a linguistic but also a methodological Babel; yet in the very pursuit of this analogy, it is well to remember that at Babel men did not begin to talk nonsense; they merely began to talk what seemed like nonsense to their fellows. A statement is not false merely because it is unintelligible; though it will have to be made intelligible before we can say whether it is true. (Olson, in Crane 1952, 546)

To make something intelligible needs, according to Crane, 'a general critique of literary criticism . . . such as might yield objective criteria for interpreting the diversities and opposition among critics and for judging the comparative methods of rival critical schools' (546) David Richter indicates that there are inconsistencies in Crane's and Olson's pluralistic position. For Richter, 'there are always going to be reductive theoretical positions we are going to wish to exclude (e.g. 'poetry judged by its suitability for landfill'); secondly, 'there was an ineluctable rhetorical conflict between Crane's position as the chief advocate for the Neo-Aristotelian mode of interpretation, and his meta-critical position as a pluralist' (Olson, in Crane 1952, 92).

Crucial to the Chicago School, already stated, is the idea of 'neo-Aristotelianism' and the Chicago group's 'special interest in the Poetics', as Richter suggests. The reasons for this, as Crane explains in his account of the Chicago School, are 'pragmatic'. The critics were literature teachers concerned with the practical criticism of literary texts and the specifically artistic principles that characterize their construction. These aspects of literary works are 'distinct from their verbal meanings, their historical and biographical back-grounds, or their general qualities'.

But why Aristotle? Crane writes that the

> appeal of Aristotle to the Chicago group lay in the fact that he, more than any other critic they knew, had conceived of literary theory in this *a posteriori* and differential way and had not only formulated some of its necessary distinctions and principles in his brief discussions of ancient tragedy and epic but pointed the way to further inquiries of the same general sort concerning possibilities in these and other literary arts still unrealized at the time he wrote.

Crane adds that the Chicago group has 'attempted to pursue some of these, and with increasing independence of the letter of the *Poetics*, in their writings on the lyric, the drama, and the novel' (1971, 117).

Particularly important to the Chicago critics are the Aristotelian concepts of '*form* and *genre*'. Literary forms include 'species of works, inductively known, and differentiated, more or less sharply, in terms of their artistic elements and principles of construction' (Crane 1967, 2: 59). Important to the idea of 'form' is the concept of 'synolon', or the 'concrete whole', that is 'matter shaped by form, and shaped so as to be coherent, comprehensible, and meaningful in itself. Meaning comes from the inferred sense of the whole, not from the parts' (Richter 1982, 92). Genre is a heuristic concept, conceptual rather than prescriptive; that is, genre is not supposed to be understood as a series of categorical rules, but as a basis which is open to adaptation. Olson writes in *On Value Judgments*: 'The words must be explained in terms of something else, not the poem in terms of the words; and further, a principle must be a principle of something other than itself; hence the words cannot be a principle of their own arrangements' (1976, 13). This 'focus on genre and method does not preclude an interest in historical analysis'. Genre studies by Olson on comedy and tragedy, Crane on the eighteenth century and MacLean writing on the lyric 'are developed around hypotheses of historical change' (Gorman 1994, 145).

The prominent members of the Chicago School include, apart from Crane and Olson, Dryden scholar William R. Keast, Norman MacLean, Richard McKeon and Bernard Weinberg. On the whole, their focus was on poetics. The texts on which they concentrated often came from the eighteenth century, so it is hardly surprising that the University of Chicago produced during the period of Crane's ascendancy many distinguished eighteenth-century scholars. Among these are the editors Donald F. Bond, Arthur Friedman and Shirley Strum Kenny. It also produced scholars such as Gwin J. Kolb, Louis A. Landa, Edward W. Rosenheim and Paul Alkon, as well as historians of ideas such as Philip Harth, James Malek and Howard Weinbrot. The general trend of the second generation, however, has tended to be on rhetoric rather than poetics (Gorman 1994, 145).

The formative voice of the second generation has been Wayne C. Booth. Booth obtained both his graduate degrees at the University of Chicago where he taught from 1947 to 1950. In 1962 he rejoined the English Faculty at Chicago. In a telephone interview with Mary Frances Hopkins (3 December 1981), Booth defined his relationship with the Chicago critics. Hopkins asked him: 'Could you comment on what the Chicago critics are doing now?' Booth replied 'that the school is not at this point a school, even if it ever was one, partly because of a series of tragic deaths'. Booth explains, 'The second generation after Crane and Olson and McKeon, and others who originally met together, there was a kind of second generation school here consisting of Robert Marsh, Sheldon Sachs, [Arthur] Heiserman and me; all three died in their forties' (Hopkins 1982, 58).

Booth also told Hopkins, 'I'm the only one left' in Chicago 'who is even thought of as closely connected with the Chicago critics, and of course I'm always whoring after false gods, like rhetoric, from the point of view of the originators. That's the first point, that there is no Chicago School at Chicago in that narrow sense of a group of Neo-Aristotelian critics'. Booth also suggests that there was neither a 'common mold' nor a unification of focus on subject matters: 'We're different people going different ways', he remarks (Hopkins 1982, 59). What such a statement omits of course is the shared methodological interests, the focus on form, on the eighteenth-century, on 'pluralism', on Aristotle's *Poetics*, which runs as a thread throughout the eclectic writings of the differing generations of the Chicago School. Also, as the direct heir of Crane and the Chicago thinkers, Booth's own preoccupation in *The Rhetoric of Fiction* with communication and the role of readers has in its turn been subsumed into other *reader-oriented* theories, conducted for instance by Norman Holland and Bernard J. Paris among others. But, and this is perhaps more to the point, Booth adds that 'there is a Chicago ethos that I think may be as powerful as ever; the place is permeated with a commitment to reflection about methods – to going twice as deep as anybody else into the assumptions of a text' (Hopkins 1982, 58).

This methodological rigour is exemplified by Booth's own output, which is both complex and prolific. His most influential work remains *The Rhetoric of Fiction* (1961), revised in an augmented edition of 1983. His concern with the ways in which directly and indirectly authors address readers has its roots in Aristotle's *Poetics*. Booth's study is divided into three parts: 'Artistic Purity and the Rhetoric of Fiction', 'The Author's Voice in Fiction' and an investigation of 'Impersonal Narration'. In the Afterword to the second edition, Booth meditates on the changes that two decades have brought on his own thinking and on writing about narrative theory since the first publication of *The Rhetoric of Fiction*. The second edition also contains an additional bibliography compiled by James Phelan of 4,000 writings on narrative theory since the first edition of 1961.

Booth is forced to clarify and modify the central arguments of his rhetorical analysis in the light of the work of Gérard Genette, Mikhail Bakhtin and others, acknowledging their influence. For Booth, the relationship between morality and rhetoric, and our implied moral judgements during the act of reading, are much more complex than he first envisioned. He also refines his ideas of the complex relationships between different kinds of authors, different kinds of readers and different kinds of narrators. Booth's subsequent major work, *A Rhetoric of Irony*, owes more to Longinus than it does to Aristotle. Already in the 1983 revision of the classic *The Rhetoric of Fiction* may be seen the subsuming of the ideas of the Chicago critics.

Other than Booth, of the second generation of critics, Sheldon Sachs' 1964 study *Fiction and the Shape of Belief* is a good illustration of the application of the ideas of the Chicago School applied to fiction and specifically Henry Fielding. Sachs differentiates between the 'comic', the tragic' and the 'serious' in Fielding's writing (1964, 20–4). He argues that Fielding's intention was 'to recommend goodness and innocence'. Fielding the novelist incorporated this into the structure of, for instance, *Tom Jones*, not as a distinct 'theme' or 'vision' but 'through its embodiment in the structure of beliefs by which we are led to evaluate characters and actions' (Richter 1982, 37). Elsewhere, the influence of the Chicago critics is still indirectly refracted through the discourse on narratology conducted by critics such as James Phelan. The Chicago-based journal *Critical Inquiry* also retains the

Chicago concern with the examination of the formal organization of structure and language.

Looked at from a historical perspective, the Chicago critics may be viewed on one level as reflecting a local situation at the University of Chicago. In formulating their theoretical ideas based upon classical principles, Crane and others were reacting to the internal demands of a university dean intent on creating a great school of liberal and humane education. Crane and his colleagues were also trying to place the study of English as a discipline on a sound footing. Indeed, John Crowe Ransom, an influential new critic, writing in 1938 in an essay appropriately entitled 'Criticism, Inc.', refers to Crane as 'the first of the great professors to have advocated [criticism] as a major policy for Departments of English' (1938, 330). These reactions to perceived internal university pressures and threats to English as a legitimate area of study[/help] tended to ignore external events such as the Great Depression and Nazism. Waves of left-wing thought tended to pass Crane and his fellow critics by, although thinkers such as Isaac Rosenfeld and Saul Bellow were Chicago-based. Others, such as George Steiner, who did his undergraduate work at Chicago, left for Europe and were influenced by less insular ideas than those prevalent at the University of Chicago and its English Department. In the late 1930s and during the 1940s Chicago was the centre for the 'Chicago School of Social Thought'. This suggested 'that we go through recurring, even ceaseless cycles of social organization, disorganization, and then social reorganiza-tion, cycles when existing patterns of social interaction and relations, social institutions and forms of life, even forms of individual identity are broken down and dispersed' (Carey 1997, 28). This emphasis on society was not stressed by Crane and his colleagues in the English department who focused instead on form, on the means by which form was expressed, and on reactions to 'New Criticism'.

With the advent of various formalisms in the 1970s, the Chicago School's influence waned further, its approach to analysis even more marginalized. New Criticism, with its emphasis on the word and thematic analysis, could more easily adapt in response to new forms of critical discourse, especially those interested in matters of ideology. Criticism has tended to move away from the focus on the expression of language towards an emphasis on social considerations represented, for instance, by the New Historicists who have been influenced by neo-Marxist thinkers such as Raymond Williams and others. Crane and others were concerned with theory but in a rather insular fashion. Graff indicates in *Professing Literature* that Crane's postwar writings contain 'a critique of the routinization of criticism' reflected in the dominance of the New Criticism (1987, 234). Further, as Graff suggests, Crane's concern in his introduction to the revised edition of *Critics and Criticism* with the 'authority of criticism' and 'the problem of the interpretability of literature' was ahead of its time. The reasons were twofold: first, 'most literary theorists were still preoccupied with the problem of its truth'; second, 'Crane was raising problems few people wanted to hear about at a time when academic literary studies had finally won their institutional autonomy'. For Graff, 'Crane's work looked forward to the later growth of "theory"' (Graff 1987, 236–7, 240).

It is perhaps ironic, then, given their concern for methodological rigour, that the shift of focus in critical study in English departments should be away from the work of the Chicago critics to that of continental thinkers, particularly those from Paris in the late 1950s and 1960s, and represented, for instance, by the import of the thought of Jacques Derrida. In the last decades of the twentieth century, literary criticism in English departments has been profoundly influenced by criticism and philosophy which has emerged from Europe, and the irony exists in the return to concerns with rhetoric, tone and poetics in the work of those who are grouped together under the name 'poststructuralism', while it is forgotten that such were the interests of the Chicago School.

William Baker

Further reading and works cited

Battersby, J. L. 'Elder Olson', in *Modern American Critics since 1965*, ed. I. J. Gregory. Detroit, MI, 1988.

Booth, W. C. *A Rhetoric of Irony*. Chicago, 1974.

—. *The Rhetoric of Fiction*. Chicago, 1983.

Carey, J. *James Carey A Critical Reader*, eds E. Stryker Munson and C. A. Warren. Minneapolis, MN, 1997.

Crane, R. S. 'Imitation of Spenser and Milton in the early Eighteenth Century', *Studies in Philology*, 15, April 1918.

—. 'An Early Eighteenth-Century Enthusiast for Primitive Poetry', *Modern Language Notes*, 37, January 1922.

—. 'Gray's *Elegy* and *Lycidas*'. *Modern Language Notes*, 38, March 1923.

— et al. *English Literature 1660–1800*. Princeton, NJ, 1952.

—. *The Languages of Criticism and the Structure of Poetry*. Toronto, 1953.

— (ed.) *Critics and Criticism*. Chicago, 1952.

—. *The Idea of the Humanities and Other Essays Critical and Historical*. Chicago, 1967.

—. *Critical and Historical Principles of Literary History*. Chicago, 1971.

—. 'The Chicago Critics', in *Princeton Encyclopedia of Poetry and Poetics*, ed. A. Preminger. Princeton, NJ, 1974.

Crane, R. S. and Kaye, F. B. *A Census of British Newspapers and periodicals, 1620–1800*, ed. M. E. Prior. London, 1966.

de Man, P. *The Resistance to Theory*. Minneapolis, MN, 1986.

Gorman, B. 'Chicago Critics'. *The Johns Hopkins Guide to Literary Theory and Criticism*, eds M. Groden and M. Kreiswirth. Baltimore, MD, 1994.

Graff, G. *Professing Literature*. Chicago, 1987.

Gregory, I. J. (ed.) *Modern American Critics since 1965*. Detroit, 1988.

Hopkins, M. F. 'Interview with Wayne C. Booth'. *Literature in Performance*, II, 2, April 1982. *Narrative*, 1, January, 1993.

Olson, E. (ed.) *Aristotle's Poetics and English Literature*. Chicago, 1965.

Olson, E. *On Value Judgments in the Arts and Other Essays*. Chicago, 1976.

—. 'R. S. Crane', *American Scholar*, 53, Spring, 1984.

Phelan, J. 'Wayne C. Booth', in *Modern American Critics since 1965*, ed. I. J. Gregory. Detroit, MI, 1988.

Preminger, A. (ed.) *Princeton Encyclopedia of Poetry and Poetics*. Princeton, NJ, 1974.

Ransom, J. C. 'Criticism, Inc.'. in *The World's Body*. New York, 1938.

Richter, D. H. 'The Second Flight of the Phoenix'. *The Eighteenth Century*, 23, 1, Winter 1982.

—. 'R. S. Crane', in *Modern American Critics since 1965*, ed. I. J. Gregory. Detroit, MI, 1988. April, 1918.

Sachs, S. *Fiction and the Shape of Belief*. Berkeley, CA, 1964.

Selden, R. et al. (eds) *A Reader's Guide to Contemporary Literary Theory*. Hemel Hempstead, 1997.

Northrop Frye (1912–1991)

No single literary critic influenced a period of twentieth-century academic criticism more than Northrop Frye who dominated the 1960s and early 1970s. In his first book, *Fearful Symmetry* (1947), Frye had glimpsed, and demonstrated, an order and a symmetry in the thought of William Blake that nobody had suspected before. Everything in Blake studies since has been affected by it. In his seminal *Anatomy of Criticism* (1957), Frye more or less established the modern field of critical theory as an independent discipline (though it would eventually move in directions that disquieted him). In the 1960s and 1970s, Frye devoted himself to the practical application of his ideas and methods to the central writers of the western tradition: in particular, he made influential contributions to Shakespeare studies, and transformed our understanding of romanticism, providing a catalyst for the 'Romantic revivalism' that marked the earlier careers of Yale critics like Geoffrey Hartman and Harold Bloom. Finally, in the last decade of his life, Frye produced two monumental studies of the Bible and literature – *The Great Code* (1982) and *Words with Power* (1990) – in which his special qualities of unfettered intellectual play, of bringing new shape and structure to previously chaotic subjects, and of being able to appeal to specialist and non-specialist audiences at once, are all still evident.

While Frye brought a great deal to the understanding of criticism and literature, there is almost nothing that he brought that cannot be found, implicit at least, in *Fearful Symmetry*, and hence that cannot be traced back to Blake: indeed, the relationship between Blake and Frye provides as intense an example of identification between a poet and his foremost critic as the English-speaking tradition affords. In particular, *Fearful Symmetry* contains the seeds of Frye's approach to four subjects – the role of the archetype in literature, the function of imagination in art and society, the relation between the religious and artistic visions, and the existence of what he would eventually call the 'literary universe' – that would occupy him for the next four decades, in a 'spiral curriculum' pattern that he described as 'circling around the same issues, though trying to keep them open-ended' (1976b, 100). Several times he described the epiphany that got this movement started. Staying up all night to write an undergraduate paper on Blake's *Milton*, in the early 1930s, he began to ponder the principle that Blake and Milton were connected by their use of the Bible. This seemed both an obvious and an unhelpful fact, since surely it was a likeness that only served to obscure what was 'individual', or really interesting, about each of them:

> Around about three in the morning a different kind of intuition hit me, though it took me twenty years to articulate it. The two poets were connected by the *same* thing, and sameness leads to individual variety, just as likeness leads to monotony. I began dimly to see that the principle pulling me away from the historical period was the principle of

mythological framework. The Bible had provided a frame of mythology for European poets: an immense number of critical problems began to solve themselves as soon as one realized this. (1976b, 17)

Through the attempt to explain the 'private mythology' and 'private symbolism' that critics had always claimed were in Blake, Frye discovered, as he later put it, 'not merely that Blake's mythology was not private, but that the phrase itself made no sense' (1976b, 108). Far from being the eccentric that he was frequently portrayed as, in method at least Blake was an absolutely traditional figure who sought to make explicit the structural connections between his 'prophecies', the epic tradition, myth and folktale – and of course the Bible, which, in a phrase that haunted Frye throughout his life, he called 'the Great Code of Art'. And Blake's characters, Frye argued, weren't failed attempts at realistic representations, but successful attempts to isolate the models, or archetypes, that provide the structure for *all* representations of character (including realistic ones, which are simply, to use Frye's term, 'displaced' from the archetypal models). A fully imaginative vision, for Blake, is one that sees all the works of human genius as contributing to a vast story of loss and redemption; in social terms, this is also a revolutionary vision, one that children possess a natural correspondence with, and that is hence driven out of them so that they may become more docile social subjects. At the close of *Fearful Symmetry*, Frye concludes that Blake's belief in an overarching human vision in which local differences of religion, myth, and doctrine are reconciled 'implies that a study of comparative religion, a morphology of myths, rituals and theologies, will lead us to a single visionary conception which the mind of man is trying to express' (1947, 424). It was to this study that Frye devoted the rest of his life.

Although the feeling in *Fearful Symmetry* is of a productive confrontation between two visionary intellects – Blake's and Frye's – played out before the backdrop of the entire western imaginative tradition, there were more local issues bubbling just beneath the book's surface. It is, after all, a book written during war, and Frye clearly wants to rescue the idea of myth from its perverted use in the rhetoric of fascism. (He was terrified that Blake's mythic heroes could be misread as supermen.) More locally, a suspicion of Blake, and of romanticism generally, had been a spark-plug in T. S. Eliot's canonical arguments, which had in turn strongly influenced the New Critics, whose 'close reading' method had, non-coincidentally perhaps, made little headway with Blake, Milton and other unpopular poets who stressed poetic argument over texture. All of this worked as a challenge and a provocation for Frye, not least because, especially in the Eliot version, it was connected with a broader attack on middle-class Protestants and their values (Frye was a left-liberal, and an ordained minister in the United Church of Canada). Meanwhile the New Critical method, with its obsessive attention to language and its lack of interest in the conventions that create linkages between poems, was already coming under pressure from the Chicago School. While sharing with Crane, Olson and the other neo-Aristotelians an interest in myth, Frye felt that the rigorously inductive procedure with which they sought to oppose the New Critical dissolving of poetry into a kind of language suffered from a similar weakness to the New Criticism itself: it stood so close to the individual poem, in an effort to see how the parts contributed to a successful whole, that there was little possibility of seeing larger connective patterns, of moving towards a genuinely generic criticism.

All of these themes, concerns and undercurrents culminate in *Anatomy of Criticism*, Frye's unquestionable masterpiece, in 1957. Although Frye had not heard of structuralism when he wrote the *Anatomy*, he did at one time consider 'Structural Poetics' as a title for it, and we can see now some remarkable anticipations of the structuralist project: the mythic turn; the architectonic and spatial metaphors; the love of categories and system-building; the dazzling contraries; and, of course, the brimming confidence about the 'human sciences' which smacks of the late 1950s and early 1960s and which has since passed so notably from the whole field of the humanities.

The *Anatomy* may be seen as an attempt to place criticism on a sound intellectual footing within the university, not reliant in any special way upon the disciplines surrounding it, and capable of proceeding in an orderly, non-contentious and progressive manner on the model of the natural sciences. While it is obvious that in this larger aim the book did not succeed, in numerous more specific ways it assuredly did. In the Polemical Introduction, for example, Frye declares famously that the demonstrable value-judgement, anchored in something outside the critic's own preferences, prejudices or social conditioning, is 'the donkey's carrot of literary criticism' (1957, 20). Specific value-judgements he relegates to the 'history of taste', along with 'all the literary chit-chat which makes the reputations of poets boom and crash in an imaginary stock-exchange' (1957, 18). If Eliot's attack on Blake, Milton and the romantics was conventional literary warfare, then Frye's attempt to wipe out evaluation altogether is the nuclear response – and the almost instantaneous disappearance from the academic scene of evaluative literary criticism marks it as one of the rare examples of a definitive clincher in the humanities.

And if value-judgements have no place within a systematic criticism, Frye argues, neither can such a criticism be founded on some externally derived religious or ideological position – here, once again, in his critique of the fallacy of determinism, we feel the barely sublimated animus towards Eliot's Anglo-Catholic polemics. Adapting some of the key terms in the battle between the New Criticism and the Chicago School, which he clearly wishes to transcend, Frye proposes an alternation between an inductive survey of literary experience and the deductive assumption that there is such a subject as criticism, and that it makes or could make complete sense. It is its weakness or hesitancy in the second, conceptual domain that has left criticism so vulnerable to ideology and determinism: 'Criticism seems to be badly in need of a coordinating principle, a central hypothesis which, like the theory of evolution in biology, will see the phenomena it deals with as parts of a whole' (1957, 16).

Of all the passages in the *Anatomy*, perhaps the most startling are those in which Frye outlines this 'central hypothesis' as the 'assumption of total coherence', the belief that the actual works of literature are not haphazard but form a 'literary universe' analogous to the natural universe studied by the sciences, and that, analogous to the order of nature that the natural sciences posit, there is an 'order of words' waiting for critics to uncover its structures and codes: 'We begin to wonder if we cannot see literature, not only as complicating itself in time, but as spread out in conceptual space from some kind of centre that criticism could locate' (1957, 16–17).

The four long essays that make up the body of the *Anatomy* explore the contours of this cardinal assumption about an order of words. The First Essay deals with the historical sequence of 'modes', defined as the literary hero's changing power of action, from ancient myth to contemporary irony; the Second Essay proposes a theory of meaning based on five levels of symbolism; the Third Essay, the central one in the book, is an account of archetype and myth; and the Fourth Essay is an attempt to define the basic genres of literature – drama, epic, fiction and poetry – according to their 'radical of presentation', or the way that they are intended to be consumed by the audience.

The discussion that the book aroused was immediate and enormous, and it centered on the Third Essay, or Theory of Myths. Here Frye proposes four basic narrative myths – comedy, romance, tragedy and irony – all seen as parts of one large story of fall and redemption. Although he draws analogies between these four basic storylines and the seasons of the year, it is not his intention to derive the stories from primitive rites such as fertility rituals. Like these, however, the basic stories told in literature are attempts by the imagination to discover parallels between the human drama and the natural world, attempts to turn a hostile environment into a home and thus part of the larger project of civilization. As he rings the changes upon the typical storylines and characters of each *mythos*, ranging across three thousand years of western literature with extraordinary brio and confidence, Frye comes upon pieces of symmetry that even he concedes are 'forbidding', such as the existence of six 'phases' within each *mythos*, three being parallel to the phases of each neighbouring *mythos*. The *Anatomy* is richly loaded with examples, and one of the things that prevents most readers from feeling that it is as an exercise in empty pigeonholing is the way that Frye's categories and connections can throw a new light on the thousands of texts that he mentions along the way. We are hardly likely to read *Alice in Wonderland* in quite the same way after Frye has described it as a Menippean satire in the tradition of Burton's *Anatomy of Melancholy*.

What was always going to make the *Anatomy* controversial were its correctives, both explicit and implied, to the New Critical methodology that had dominated literary criticism almost since its emergence as a university discipline between the wars. When the Third Essay tells us that we need to 'stand back' from a poem in order to see its archetypal organization (1957, 140), every reader at the time would have sensed a critique of the relentlessly 'close reading' method that defined the New Criticism. Naturally, some of the older New Critics attacked Frye's myths as having no constructive role whatever in practical criticism, since they could not be derived, whole, from any individual work of literature. To this he replied, in 1966:

> The principle that a work of literature should not be related to anything outside itself is sound enough, but I cannot see how the rest of literature can be regarded as outside the work of literature, any more than the human race can be regarded as outside a human being. When I use the metaphor of standing back from a work of literature ... I am trying to give some reality to the word 'literature'. (see Krieger 1966, 3)

For younger critics, the way that Frye's perspective broke out of the New Criticism's claustrophobic attentiveness to the individual poem and suddenly provided lines of sight in new, unexpected directions was a liberation. No less so was the toppling of the anti-romantic literary hierarchy, in particular the denigration of the romantic long poem, that younger critics, many of them inspired by *Fearful Symmetry*, were already bridling against. After all, the *Anatomy* not only had a place for all literary modes and movements: its view of all of these as contributing to one, larger picture seemed to resonate with romanticism itself, specifically with Shelley's vision of 'that great poem, which all poets, like the co-operating thoughts of one great mind, have built up since the beginning of the world' (Shelley 1930, VII: 124). While the New Criticism had run out of steam long before 1957, the *Anatomy* was the final blow. At Yale, which had been a centre of New Critical activity, it was like a burst of oxygen for younger critics like Harold Bloom, who had begun to find the Eliotic atmosphere thin and suffocating. During a personal interview in 1982, Angus Fletcher, a friend of Bloom's and a distinguished follower of Frye himself, told me about a visit to Yale in 1957:

> Harold Bloom came into the room waving this book, shouting at the top of his voice, 'The King is dead!' And the book was the *Anatomy of Criticism*.

The *Anatomy*, then, made Frye famous, and brought him many followers; but he never formed a school, and never sought disciples, which he once told me would only be to invite 'the Judas reaction'. Notoriously introverted by temperament, he resisted numerous invitations to move to the United States after 1957 (though he did teach terms there) and remained for over half a century on the faculty of the University of Toronto, where he had gained his undergraduate degrees.

The 1960s and 1970s were a fertile period for Frye, in which his work moved in two related directions: essays in practical criticism that applied the theories outlined in *Anatomy*, and an increasing emphasis on social criticism, directed at the general public, in which he developed the connections between literature, myth and religion. What links these endeavours is that at their root they are meditations on the same theme, one of Frye's favourites: the survival of romance, particularly in the area of the popular arts, despite all of the apparent gains made against it by realism in the arts specifically and by the scientific worldview in western society generally. In *A Natural Perspective* (1965), his study of Shakespearean romance, Frye takes up Coleridge's distinction between Iliad critics interested in tragedy, realism and irony, and Odyssey critics interested in comedy and romance: 'I have always been temperamentally an Odyssean critic myself, attracted to comedy and romance. But I find myself, apparently, in a minority, in a somewhat furtive and anonymous group who have not much of a theory, implicit or explicit, to hold them together' (1965, 2). In books like *A Natural Perspective* and *The Secular Scripture* (1976), and in essays of practical interpretation like 'Dickens and the Comedy of Humours' (see Frye 1970, 218–40), Frye does much to rectify this situation, suggesting that romance is in fact the core of all storytelling, since it is precisely what reality lacks and only imagination can provide. Even the realist tradition, which Frye sees as a conservative response to romance's anarchic, erotic spirit, can only displace, never avoid, romance patterns and motifs, such as the monster, the questing knight, the descent into an underworld and so on. A writer like Dickens, whose characters are clearly drawn as much from the theory of humours as from 'life', is much better understood as a traditional romancer than as a failed realist. Comedy and romance move from frustration and the blockage of desire towards erotic fulfilment and identity, thus implying 'that what is must never take final precedence over what ought to be' (Frye 1970, 240). It is the fact that, in the last several centuries, this feeling that the realistic world-picture cannot be the whole story has been expressed principally through the arts that causes Frye to call them a 'secular scripture', doing much of the same work in modern societies that religion performed in traditional ones. This connection is more fully sketched in Frye's final two books on the imaginative legacy of the Bible.

Because the vision of identity in comedy, particularly, is a vision of a renewed social identity, Frye's interest in 'Odyssean' forms also allows him to connect his central interests with a social criticism. In books like *The Modern Century* (1967) and *The Critical Path* (1971), we see Frye developing a view of literature as related to a society's 'myth of concern'. While the 'myth of freedom' – essentially, scientific reasoning – has brought modern society many benefits, it is always in a tensely dialectical relationship with the fundamental concerns that unite all human beings in all societies: concerns for things like food, shelter, warmth and love. Literature, says Frye in *The Critical Path*, is not identical with concern, but 'represents the *language* of human concern' and 'displays the imaginative possibilities of concern'. While concern can readily turn into mere tribal will, or ideology, literature contains a more liberal and liberating element, because unlike concern 'it is not to be believed in: there is no "religion of poetry": the whole point about literature is that it has no direct connection with belief' (Frye 1971, 98, 128). In a sense all of Frye's books are following up Blake's point about the imagination's freedom from the constraints of whatever, simply, is, and the way that this freedom enables all visions of a more fully humane world (including, of course, by providing the mythic substratum for revolutionary political stories).

Only criticism, however, can trace these connections, and Frye never departs from the view in *Anatomy* that 'a public that tries to do without criticism, and asserts that it knows what it wants or likes, brutalizes the arts and loses its cultural memory' (Frye 1957, 4). After *Anatomy*, Frye frequently uses the language of the sublime in connection with the destiny of criticism, language that would embarrass most contemporary critics. Literature, he says in his popular 1963 Massey Lectures broadcast on Canadian radio, is 'a human apocalypse, man's revelation to man', and criticism is 'not a body of adjudications, but the awareness of that revelation, the last judgement of mankind' (Frye 1963a, 105). Of course, as critics in the 1980s and 1990s continued to express their preference for combat over cooperation, ideology over myth, Frye's hope that criticism would ever realize the destiny he had posited for it became weaker.

Although the claim that Frye was an arid formalist, a dehistoricizing critic and thus a bourgeois idealist, followed him through most of his career, it is clearer now that only from one, no longer ascendant, perspective, that of historical materialism, is this even remotely plausible. Terry Eagleton, for example, claims that Frye's work 'emphasizes . . . the utopian root of literature because it is marked by a deep fear of the actual social world, a distaste for history itself' (Eagleton 1983, 93); but we may wonder, in response, whether literature is more sequestered from 'the actual social world' by a view that sees it as an ideology masking a deeper reality, or by a view that embraces literature's utopian dreamings and connects them with the mainsprings of social concern, action and vision. Frye subtitled his 1970 collection, *The Stubborn Structure*, 'Essays on Criticism and Society', and he explained the subtitle as follows: 'as some of those who write about me are still asserting that I ignore the social reference of literary criticism, the sub-title calls the attention of those who read me to the fact that I have written about practically nothing else' (Frye 1970, x). Indeed, *Fearful Symmetry* is as good an introduction to the principal currents of eighteenth-century politics, religion, philosophy and aesthetics as one is likely to get, and the cultural context never fades out of Frye's thought; it is simply construed in the very broad terms that characterize other historicist thinkers valued by Frye, like Vico or Spengler. Frye is always aware of the way that specific social formations impose their particular, and necessarily partial, perspectives, their own story-outlines, on the world: that is precisely his subject. But he is also aware that beneath the ideological level of this activity there is a deeper, mythological level that unites rather than divides different societies and periods. Is there a better explanation of why the great artistic works of the past continue to speak to us? For criticism to limit itself to the ideological level is to hand the entire show over to the faculty that Blake called 'corporeal understanding', and which he contrasted with imaginative vision. Critical vision, in Frye, is the fully imaginative response to the creative act that, while it recognizes part of that act as mere historical datum, lifts another part of it clear into the permanent mythological dimension. As he puts it in his last book, *Words with Power*:

> I think of a poet, in relation to his society, as being at the centre of a cross like a plus sign. The horizontal bar forms the social and ideological conditioning that made him intelligible to his contemporaries, and in fact to himself. The vertical bar is the mythological line of descent from previous poets back to Homer. (1990, 47)

On this question of whether there is a level of shared concern more primary than ideology, Frye's humanist optimism, which conceives of the possibility of productive cultural exchange, and which makes imaginative structures like literature central to that exchange, is suddenly starting to look less time-bound than the insistence on irreducible difference that characterized much of the criticism that displaced him in the 1980s and 1990s. With a 'Collected Edition' of Frye's works (which will include his fascinating diaries and notebooks) currently underway with University of Toronto Press, and international meetings on his ideas being held in places as far apart as China, Australia and Canada, there is good reason to subscribe to A. C. Hamilton's view that 'Frye's hope that he may play a role in holding traditional culture together and passing it on to the next generation may well be fulfilled because the multiculturalism characteristic of his criticism will have its place in an increasingly globalized world' (see Boyd and Salvszinsky 1999, 119).

Frye once said that Blake possessed an imagination so large that it was impossible to feel claustrophobic within it: countless readers and students have had a similar experience of Frye's own critical imagination. A scholar and humanist of immense erudition, a brilliantly witty writer and polemicist, and a teacher in the best sense of the word, Northrop Frye was one of the most gifted individuals to devote himself to the theory and practice of literary criticism in the twentieth century.

Imre Salusinszky

Further reading and works cited

Boyd, D. and Salusinszky, I. (eds) *Rereading Frye*. Toronto, 1999.
Denham, R. D. *Northrop Frye*. Toronto, 1987.
—. *Northrop Frye and Critical Method*. University Park, PA, 1978.
Eagleton, T. *Literary Theory*. Oxford, 1983.
Frye, N. *Fearful Symmetry: A Study of William Blake*. Princeton, NJ, 1947.
—. *Anatomy of Criticism*. Princeton, NJ, 1957.
—. *The Educated Imagination*. Bloomington, IN, 1963a.
—. *Fables of Identity*. New York, 1963b.
—. *T. S. Eliot*. Edinburgh, 1963c.
—. *A Natural Perspective*. New York, 1965.
—. *The Modern Century*. Toronto, 1967.
—. *The Stubborn Structure*. Ithaca, NY, 1970.
—. *The Critical Path*. Bloomington, IN, 1971.
—. *The Secular Scripture*. Cambridge, 1976a.
—. *Spiritus Mundi*. Bloomington, IN, 1976b
—. *The Great Code*. New York, 1982.
—. *Words with Power*. New York, 1990.
Hamilton, A. C. *Northrop Frye*. Toronto, 1990.

Krieger, M. *Northrop Frye in Modern Criticism*. New York, 1996.
Lee, A. and Denham, R. D. (eds) *The Legacy of Northrop Frye*. Toronto, 1994.
Shelley, P. B. *The Complete Works of Percy Bysshe Shelley*, eds R. Ingpen and W. E. Peck. London, 1930.

The Encounter with Structuralism and the Invention of Poststructuralism

There is a common perception that poststructuralism arrived in the United States as an import in October 1966, when Derrida read his paper, 'Structure, Sign, and Play in the Discourse of the Human Sciences', at Johns Hopkins University. Bearing in mind that the term *poststructuralism* was not used in Europe until much later, it is important to stress that poststructuralism was not a ready-made object which could be imported, but something that had to be fashioned in the United States, something which emerged, in the 1970s, from a complex set of circumstances in North American criticism, and which was, in particular, deeply bound up with the context of reception of Derrida's work. Poststructuralism was not so much imported as invented in the United States, by a process of decontextualizing and then recontextualizing Derrida. To understand this process it will be necessary to sketch the debates into which Derrida's work intervened, the kind of impact that this intervention entailed, and the reception history of Derrida and other poststructuralist thinkers in the 1970s and 1980s.

Commentators often claim that there was a kind of methodological consensus in North American criticism before 1960. Paul de Man is one who, describing the relationship between American and European criticism, represents the New Criticism as a formalism completely isolated from 'a European sense of history'. It is to be regretted, according to de Man, that the New Criticism 'was never able to overcome the anti-historical bias that presided over its beginnings' and 'that it remained confined within its original boundaries and was allowed to do so without being seriously challenged' (de Man 1983, 20–1). This idea of the New Criticism as an unchallenged, anti-historical formalism is highly influential in accounts of the history of criticism and theory in the United States, but it is not easy to support. There are some hopeful manifestos, such as R. S. Crane's 'History versus Criticism in the Study of Literature' (1935) and John Crowe Ransom's 'Criticism Inc.' (1937), which seek to establish a new criticism explicitly in opposition to a traditional historical scholarship. Commentators have also pointed to the focus on poetry in early New Criticism as a form of anti-historical bias. Eagleton argues that 'poetry is of all the literary genres the one most apparently sealed off from history, the one where "sensibility" may play its purest, least socially tainted role' (Eagleton 1983, 48). Similarly, Norris remarks that 'the New Critics were bent upon preserving [poetry's] uniqueness as an object' (Norris 1982, 8), Culler observes that 'the projects of the New Criticism were linked to the preservation of aesthetic autonomy' (Culler 1983, 20) and Lentricchia describes the New Critical mentality as 'a continuing urge to essentialise literary discourse by making it ... a vast, enclosed textual and semantic preserve' (1980, xiii).

These accounts may be expressing a tendency in some New Criticism, but they do not represent the extent to which historical consciousness continued to thrive within and around the New Critical project. A traditional, positivist model of historicism may have been displaced by the New Criticism, but there is no evidence to suggest that historicism at large ever accepted its demotion, and an impetus for historicist self-renewal became a recurring feature of critical debate throughout the period of supposed New Critical consensus. In the 1920s, Harry Elmer Barnes and James Harvey Robinson were at the forefront of a movement at Columbia University to develop a new historical method that freed itself from the positivist model. In 1940, Matthew Josephson can be found declaring in the *Virginia Quarterly* that 'there seems to be a thirst for history in various forms. Is it because the readers of our time have lived through so much history in the making since 1914 that they are more history-minded than ever before?' (Josephson 1940). Jumping forward to 1952, Cushing Strout argued that Barnes and Robinson's new historicism of the 1920s, marred by its adherence to a linear temporality, nevertheless points the way to new relativist historiography. Six years later the case was still being argued by Roy Harvey Pearce in the *Kenyon Review* (Pearce 1957), this time claiming strong compatibility between New Critical methods and the new historicisms. In 1960, Rene Wellek argued that there has always been a tension within the New Critical movement between criticism and history, and again evidence for this is easy to find. Soon after Ransom's anti-historical manifesto of 1937, Cleanth Brooks published an article in the *Kenyon Review* in which he rejects the conflict between criticism and history as it is represented by his fellow 'Southern Critic' Allen Tate, and Edwin Greenlaw, whose *The Province of Literary History* had sided with historical scholarship in its rivalry with criticism. For Brooks, the question was not 'whether we shall study the history of literature, but rather about what centre this history will be organised?' (Brooks 1940, 412).

The importance of this background is that it is only a very selective, canonical history of theory and criticism that can represent New Criticism in the United States as a serene consensus or a hegemony. From Wimsatt's attempts to define and vindicate the role of history in criticism in *The Verbal Icon* (1954) to Wellek's persistent defence of historicism in literary studies, it is clear that the American universities had no agreed position on history that could be incorporated into their programmes for the study of literature. It is also clear, from Wellek's spat with Gerald Graff in *Critical Inquiry* in 1979, how little agreement there was in retrospective constructions of critical history on the role of history in the period of New Critical influence. Not only is there an apparent war between formalism and historicism running through the journals before 1960, there is also an apparent war between differing interpretations of that period in more recent critical histories. It is in the context of this irreconcilable battle between formalism and historicism that the impact of structuralism and poststructuralism in the United States is best understood. In fact it is hard to say which attitude to this polemic is more influential, those who, like Wellek, seek to stress the ferocity of the debate between criticism and history, or those who, like de Man, aim to reduce the critical past to a stable consensus. In either case, there is a strong sense of continuity between the era of New Critical dominance and the arrival of structuralism in the 1960s. De Man, for example claims that French criticism 'especially in the case of Roland Barthes, appears to be moving in the direction of a formalism that, appearances notwithstanding, is not that different from New Criticism' (de Man 1983, 230–1). This continuity between New Criticism and structuralism is a theme in the work of many critics and commentators. Frank Kermode's *The Romantic Image* suggests, for example, that Frye's *Anatomy of Criticism* extends the New Critical tradition of neo-Coleridgean symbolism into the 1960s despite Frye's explicit repudiation of New Critical aestheticism; Philip Thody's *Roland Barthes: a Conservative Estimate* argues that Barthes's work operates with the same set of assumptions that mobilized New Criticism; Lentricchia finds 'many traces (perhaps "scars" is the word) of New Criticism in the fixed and identifiable positions we have come to know as contemporary theory' (1980, ix); and Wellek's history of criticism describes Richards' view of Jakobson's work as the fulfilment of his own ambitions, and claims an obvious continuity from New Criticism in the structuralist poetics of Tzvetan Todorov. Nor does this sense of continuity stop at structuralism. This is Culler in *On Deconstruction*:

> One can certainly argue that American criticism has found in deconstruction reasons to deem interpretation the supreme task of critical inquiry, and thus to preserve some measure of continuity between the goals of New Criticism and those of the newer criticism. (1983, 220)

Because of the perceived continuity from New Criticism to structuralism and deconstruction, there was always a sense that the encounter with structuralism in the United States was being assimilated into an ongoing conflict between formal and historical approaches to literature.

The exact moment of impact of literary structuralism in the United States is impossible to locate. While the New Criticism grew up in a distinctly Anglo-American context, criticism in the 1960s was moving into a phase of importation and translation of ideas from Continental European thought. The work of Roman Jakobson, for example, had been available from about 1960, but many were not aware of the highly scientific, linguistics-based structuralist project in literary studies until the 1970s, with the publication of *The Structuralist Controversy* and Culler's *Structuralist Poetics*. The 'structuralist controversy' was presented in the United States as a strange concoction of these highly systematic and scientific approaches to literature and the critiques of these systematized linguistic approaches that would later be named as *poststructuralist*. Derrida was, for example, referred to until well into the 1970s as a *structuralist*. Whereas in France there was a slow unfolding of structuralism as a literary critical science followed by a period of mounting critique of the scientism of these approaches (perhaps best represented in the work of Roland Barthes), in the United States, the encounter with scientific structuralism coincided largely with the reception of its critique. It may be that this contemporaneity of classical structuralism and the beginnings of deconstruction was a chronological confusion that necessitated the invention of poststructuralism as a distinct critical tendency.

The reception of Derrida's work in America was also conditioned by the delay between original publication dates in French and the publication of translations. The American academic expert in the reading of French and attentive to French academic journals could have had foreknowledge of the entirety of *L'Écriture et la Différence* by the time of its publication in 1967, eleven years before its translation into English. The publication of *La Voix et le phenomène* and *De la grammatologie* in the same year gave a start of six and nine years over translation-reliant colleagues. The reading of 'Structure, Sign, and Play in the Discourse of the Human Sciences', at Johns Hopkins in October 1966 may be seen as marking the first impact of Derrida in America, but even here there was a complicated time lag. The translation did not appear until its inclusion in *The Languages of Criticism and the Sciences of Man: the Structuralist Controversy* in 1970, and did not reach a wide readership until 1972, when the paperback edition was released under the snappier title *The Structuralist Controversy*. Perhaps the most significant fact about Derrida's reception in the United States was just how little material was available in translation before the process of mediating his work to an English-speaking readership had begun. In 1971, for example, Paul de Man's landmark discussion of Derrida's *De la grammatologie* in *Blindness and Insight* was for many a crucial point of entry, and preceded the translation by five years.

The importance of the translation history and the prominence of mediation is exactly that it provides the opportunity for Derrida's work to be reinvented, refashioned and recontextualized according to the preoccupations, interests and values of the American critical tradition. In the late 1970s and 1980s many commentators held the mediation process responsible for a 'domestication' of Derrida, on the grounds that the original force of his writing had been sacrificed to these distinctly American preoccupations. It could be said that the invention of poststructuralism was structured according to two phases in the reception of Derrida, the first being the initial mediation of his ideas, and the second a revision of his reputation in the early 1980s. I have argued that the principal legacy of the American critical tradition was an ongoing polemic between historicist and formalist approaches, and if we turn for a moment to the critical journals in which the invention of poststructuralism was unfolding, this legacy is overwhelmingly present. Most significant, perhaps, were *New Literary History* and *diacritics*, founded in 1969 and 1970 respectively, in which there was a kind of table tennis being played with the character of poststructuralism between 1970 and 1975. On one hand Derrida can be represented as a kind of arch formalist to be aligned with de Man (see *diacritics*, Winter 1972), who in this period, was perceived above all as the critic who extended the influence of the New Criticism into French studies. He is, for Funt in 1971, 'the avant-garde of the structuralist movement itself', and yet, in early 1972, was contrasted with the structuralists on the grounds of a more historicist orientation:

> One of the characteristics that makes Derrida's work particularly valuable for scholars is that, in contrast to many contemporary Structuralists, he views this formal organisation which in itself has no sense as susceptible to historical delineation. (Gelley 1972, 10)

It would be fair to say, cutting a longer story short, that this kind of uncertainty dominated the early reception of Derrida. It might also be reasonable to see this initial discussion as somewhat more faithful to the character of Derrida's work than the phase which immediately followed, in which he was much more decisively aligned with formalism, and in which deconstruction was consolidated as a critical school in such a way that it was difficult to sustain any notion that Derrida might represent some long awaited return to historicist values. A milestone in this regard was the publication of Jonathan Culler's *Structuralist Poetics*, which stresses Derrida's relation to the language-based paradigms of structuralism. Up to this point, Derrida had been referred to primarily as a structuralist except when being claimed by the historicist camp. The significance of Culler's book is that it emphasizes Derrida's difference form the linguistic analyses of the structuralists, but represents this difference as a deviance in attitude to the linguistic model of analysis in criticism, rather than as a deviation into historicism of any kind. Not for the last time, Culler settled a debate that had been troubling the critical academy, and in so doing, distanced the idea of poststructuralism from the kind of historicism to which it might easily have been linked from the start.

If poststructuralism was invented in the United States, it was invented by these debates which, for contextual reasons, had to decide upon whether it belonged to the formalist or historicist orientation. In the second half of the 1970s, the invented object takes on a distinctly formalist character largely through its heavy association with another invention – deconstructive criticism. One way of telling the story of how deconstruction acquired a formalist character is to look at a debate which arose in *Critical Inquiry* in 1976. Here Wayne Booth argued that Hillis Miller's critique of M. H. Abrams's historicism represented an exhilarating possibility, namely a 'deconstructed history', which would exist in a kind of parasitical relationship to the traditional historicism represented by Abrams. In the same edition of *Critical Inquiry*, Abrams himself develops the question through rumination on the relation between a deconstructed and a traditional criticism. Abrams is clearly talking about the impossibility of writing a literary history when texts in that history are indeterminate (a history of deconstructed texts), without considering the question as Booth had, that the historical analysis is itself a text which tells a story as indeterminate as the texts it analyses. For Booth, an awareness of the textuality of history would constitute a new historical method (a deconstructed history). These two approaches to the question of deconstruction in relation to history might seem identical, since a history of indeterminacy and an indeterminate history might be hard to tell apart. The difference is worth contemplating, however. In Booth's sense there is a theory of history in the work of Miller, Derrida, de Man or Nietzsche, which can be applied to literary history and historicism. In Abrams's sense, there is a prior theory of the indeterminacy of language in general which then leads into historiographical difficulties. These are markedly different ways of assessing the impact of deconstruction and poststructuralism on traditional historicism, since one comes from within historiography and the other from without.

The aftermath of this encounter was of great significance for the invention and impact of poststructuralism in America. At the first meeting of the Modern Language Association's 'Division on Philosophical Approaches to Literature' in 1976, Abrams emphatically endorsed this second conception of the relevance of deconstruction to literary history. He did this by analysing the challenge to his own historicism, and indeed to the 'entire body of traditional inquiries in the human sciences', as one that derives from a theory of language. He then goes on to present what he calls the linguistic premises, in the work of Miller and Derrida, on which the critique of historicism depends. 'It is often said', wrote Abrams, 'that Derrida and those who follow his lead subordinate all inquiries into a prior inquiry into language'. This is one of the clearest incidences of the misrepresentation or reinvention of Derrida in the American context. And Miller's response to Abrams at the symposium is equally revealing (Miller 1977). Miller's 'little example of a deconstructive strategy' focuses on Booth's suggestion that a deconstructive history would be 'plainly and simply parasitical' on traditional history from the point of view of etymology. The use of etymology for Miller is twofold. On the one hand, it resonates with a traditional conception of history, in which earlier meanings are considered more authentic than derived ones, against which he can assert an alternative in which the history of words can be presented as a complex of conflicting senses. Where traditional etymology refers current usage of a word back to the solidity of a prior usage, Miller's discussion of 'parasite' does the opposite, disrupting the secure interpretation of current usage with a complex of prior synonymic and antonymic relations. On the other hand, Miller uses etymology to illustrate just how much indeterminacy a deconstructive reading can produce from a small fragment of text, and therefore affirms Abrams's view that deconstructive strategy entails a view of the language as essentially polysemic and indeterminate. But whereas for Abrams the deconstructive challenge to history was based on prior linguistic premises, Miller's example seems to assert the priority of a historical method upon which the polysemy of language is consequent. In either case, what began as a debate about historical method quickly shifted to a debate about language and interpretation.

There is a discernible process here of polarizing deconstruction as an anti-historicist formalism with linguistic premises which certainly cannot be substantiated with reference to Derrida's writings. But there was a tendency in 1976 and 1977 to represent Derrida, deconstruction and sometimes poststructuralism as a whole in this way. Whereas in 1972, Gelley had argued in *diacritics* that Derrida and Foucault could be distinguished only by the most subtle nuances, it was more common in 1977 to see this nuance presented *as* the opposition between linguistic formalism and political historicism. Edward Said was one who, in *Beginnings* in 1975, had identified the relationship between Derrida and Foucault as a choice, and by 1978 was formulating it as an insistent opposition:

> Whereas Derrida's theory of textuality brings criticism to bear upon a signifier freed from any obligation to a transcendental signified, Foucault's theories move criticism from a consideration of the signifier to a description of the signifier's place, a place rarely innocent, dimensionless, or without the affirmative authority of discursive discipline.

The point here is not that Said is wrong to characterize Derrida in this way, but that this is increasingly common as a representation of Derrida at the end of the 1970s. In both Said's call for a political history and Abrams's defence of a literary history, Derrida's work is represented primarily as an investigation into the signifier, and secondarily as a challenge to historical discourse. Despite the fact that Derrida's engagement with linguistics relentlessly opposes the possibility of linguistic premises, or indeed of linguistic models in criticism, he is repeatedly characterized in this phase as a linguistically orientated theoretician of indeterminacy. But if Miller's debate with Abrams was the place where the idea of deconstruction as a critical approach with linguistic premises was established, it may be that the debate between Derrida and John Searle in *Glyph* in 1977 and 1978 put it to rest. Given the opportunity to represent himself, rather than to be mediated by an American disciple, Derrida used this exchange as a demonstration of the distance between his work and any systematic theory of language. Remembered mainly for what Culler described as Searle's 'egregious misunderstanding of Derrida', the debate between Derrida and Searle illustrated the problems for the academy in the United States of relying too heavily on the mediation of Derrida's work for its understanding of the nature of poststructuralism.

There are three important points to be made here about this history. First, there is a profound theoretical difficulty in any account such as this which seems to imply that Derrida has been misrepresented, misread, domesticated or disrespected by his mediators. Deconstructive reading characteristically rejects the authority of origins and original contexts over translations, misrepresentations, misreadings and errors. Miller, de Man and Bloom have claimed that all readings (including translations) are misreadings. Derrida argues in *Speech and Phenomena* that the relationship between an origin and its supplements is one in which 'a possibility produces that to which it is said to be added on', which is to say that the possibility that a message will go wrong somehow inheres in the original as a possibility. Second, I have been describing a phase of critical history in which the terms poststructuralism and deconstruction (or the name of Derrida) were virtually synonymous, so that the invention of poststructuralism and the reception of Derrida were inseparable processes. Third, the context of polemic opposition between formalism and historicism made it necessary to be able to place a critical approach at one pole or the other. Taken together, these factors began to exert a pressure on the polemical context of American criticism which can be seen to have impelled a revision of the notion of poststructuralism along different lines. The idea, for example, that American poststructuralism represented a domestication of more politicized counterparts in Europe became a commonplace of critical commentary. The extent of this realization at the beginning of the 1980s is striking. At the 'Colloque de Cerisy' in 1980, for example, interventions from American speakers attest to a widespread feeling that the domestication of deconstruction was a function of the institutionalization of Derrida's work in American literary departments. After Rodolphe Gasché's 'Deconstruction as Criticism' in 1979, which sought to retrieve Derrida for a radical philosophy, commentators were lining up to point out the domesticating effects of the American literary critical encounter with poststructuralism. In 1980, Frank Lentricchia's *After the New Criticism* attacked American deconstruction for its fall into ahistoricality, and like Gasché recognized 'traces of New Criticism' in the 'repeated and often extremely subtle denial of history by a variety of contemporary theorists'. In 1983 Wlad Godzich's article 'The Domestication of Derrida' points to some of the marxist semes, and in particular the term *production*, which had held significance for Derrida's original context in the marxist Tel Quel Group, and which had been simply dropped in the American appropriation of Derrida. And in an interview before his death, even Paul de Man recognizes the distortion:

> It is often said – and this is true to some extent – that whatever is audacious, whatever is really subversive and incisive in Derrida's text and in his work is being taken out by academicizing him, by making him just one other method by means of which literature can be taught. (1986, 116)

Perhaps what is most interesting about this realization, recontextualization and revision of the relation of deconstruction and its relation to history and politics is that it allowed the notion of poststructuralism to acquire a wider reference. Lentricchia's *After the New Criticism*, for example, is one of the places where the idea of poststructuralism is cleaved away from American deconstruction to the point where it becomes possible to speak of poststructuralism and history in the same breath. Like Said, Lentricchia depends on Foucault as an uneasy bridge between Derrida and marxism, and blames de Man for all that is wrong with the American invention. But when Lentricchia describes his own project as a 'poststructuralist history', he significantly distances himself from those, like Maria Ruegg and Terry Eagleton, who have condemned poststructuralism as a whole for its ahistoricality. The early 1980s in American criticism can be seen as a period in which it was ensured that, the next time there was a call for a return to history, it could be made in the name of, and not in opposition to, poststructuralism. It is now recognized that the new historicisms that dominated criticism in the 1980s and 1990s represented a more appropriate critical response to Derrida and other poststructuralists than the deconstructive readings in relation to which poststructuralism was initially defined.

Mark Currie

Further reading and works cited

Abrams, M. H. *Natural Supernaturalism*. London, 1971.
—. 'The Deconstructive Angel', *Critical Inquiry*, Spring 1977.
Arac, J. et al. (eds) *The Yale Critics*. Minneapolis, MN, 1983.
Booth, W. 'M. H. Abrams: Historian, Critic, Pluralist', *Critical Inquiry*, Spring 1977.
Brooks, C. 'Literature and the Professors', *Kenyon Review*, 1940.
Crane, R. S. 'History versus Criticism in the Study of Literature', *English Journal*, 24, 1935.
Culler, J. *Structuralist Poetics*. London, 1975.
—. *On Deconstruction*. London, 1983.
de Man, P. *Blindness and Insight*. London, 1983.
—. *The Resistance to Theory*. Manchester, 1986.
Derrida, J. *Speech and Phenomena and Other Essays on Husserl's Theory of Signs*. Evanston, 1973.
—. *Of Grammatology*. Baltimore, 1976.
—. *Writing and Difference*. London, 1978.
Eagleton, T. *Literary Theory*. Oxford, 1983.
Funt, D. 'Piaget and Structuralism', *diacritics*, Winter 1971.
Gasché, R. 'Deconstruction as Criticism', *Glyph*, 6, 1979.
Gelley, A. 'Form as Force', *diacritics*, Spring 1972.
Godzich, W. 'The Domestication of Derrida', in Arac, et al., ed.
Greenlaw, E. *The Province of Literary History*. Baltimore, MD, 1931.
Josephson, M. 'Historians and Mythmakers', *Virginia Quarterly Review*, Summer, 1940.
Kermode, F. *Romantic Image*. London, 1957.
Lentricchia, F. *After the New Criticism*. London, 1980.
Miller, J. H. 'Tradition and Difference', *diacritics*, Winter 1972.
—. 'The Critic as Host', *Critical Inquiry*, Spring 1977.
Norris, C. *Deconstruction*. London, 1982.
Pearce, R. H. 'Historicism Once More', *Kenyon Review*, 1958.
Ransom, J. C. 'Criticism Inc.', *Virginia Quarterly Review*, Fall, 1937.
Said, E. *Beginnings*. Baltimore, MD, 1975.
—. 'The Problem of Textuality', *Critical Inquiry*, Summer 1978.
Thody, P. *Roland Barthes*. London, 1977.
Wellek, R. 'Literary Theory, Criticism and History', *Yale Review*, Spring, 1960.
Wimsatt, W. K. *The Verbal Icon*. London, 1970.

Reception Theory and Reader-Response (II): Norman Holland (1927–), Stanley Fish (1938–) and David Bleich (1940–)

While some commentators (for example, Holub 1984) wish to restrict reception theory to the European tradition embracing both phenomenology and hermeneutics – in shorthand terms, the Geneva and Constance Schools – it is possible and I think valid to extend it – and to use the alternative term 'reader-response', indifferently – to cover a wider and more diverse range of theories of literary effect and response, including the various Anglo-American versions of how literary texts achieve their effects on readers, how readers respond to them, and what the implications of the interaction between reader and text may be. The American scene lacks the apparent homogeneity and orderliness of the European, where the authority of 'schools' of theory has been paramount, at least within the German-speaking arena, and where a culture of collaborative accumulation of theoretical models has been encouraged, in the perhaps delusive hope of establishing an ultimate 'grand theory' of reception. Elements of reader-response criticism are diffused more widely and variously within the American academic and intellectual arena, which has in the postwar period been both more eclectic and more assimilative of a range of theoretical positions, from a still tenacious New Critical stance, various psychoanalytically oriented approaches, through structuralism to poststructuralism (a movement in the history of semiotics given exemplary clarification in the work of Jonathan Culler), and into various broadly socio-logical approaches which stress race or gender or pay particular attention to pedagogy. This multifarious mix no doubt answers to the cultural profusion and the social and ethnic variety of the USA and it has occasioned vigorous critical debate, not to say fractiousness, in some quarters within the academy there in the late twentieth century. However, important though this context is, it is impossible to survey the whole variegated scene in the confines of a brief article (though some indications are given at the end and the bibliography refers to some selected contributions to the wider debate) and I therefore restrict myself largely to discussion of the three critics indicated above.

These major American proponents of reader-response criticism occupy significantly different and individualistic positions within the broad parameters of reception theory, in its general sense – that understanding of literature (and other arts) which stresses the active and formative role of the reader (or audience or spectator) in the constitution of the artwork (primarily the literary text) and which reflects a dissatisisfaction with formalist principles which privilege and prioritize the text over the reader. While Norman Holland and David Bleich share an emphasis on the psychological approach to the activity of reading, their descriptions of that approach are significantly different. Stanley Fish, on the other hand, starting from a more strictly literary-critical position, develops a theoretical model which might be termed, in a specialized and abstract sense, sociological, with a strong rhetorical inflection. All three critics lay varying stress on the pedagogical implications of reader-response theory and practice. All three are also engaged with the overall dialectical pressure that informs reception theory with regard to literature – that is, the tension between reader and text, or subjective and objective principles, the initial affirmation of the former against the latter, and the subsequent 'return of the text', as it might be termed, in the effort to avoid or qualify the subjectivism or impressionism threatened by the stress on the reader's role. Bleich and Holland, true to their emphasis on psychology, each affirm a qualified subjectivism, while Fish, through an ingenious and powerful theoretical strategy, is most successful in overcoming the dualizing pressure of the dialectical model, though this appears to lead him ultimately to a theoretical position which is, to use one of his own celebrated terms, 'self-consuming'.

Norman Holland, engaged in 'constructing a post-Freudian psychoaesthetics' (Freund 1987, 30), gives substantial and predominant force to the conscious personality and unconscious psyche of the reader in the activity of reading, employing concepts taken from American ego psychology to construct a model of the reader as enjoying the psychic pleasures and benefits of engagement with the imaginative work. His starting point is the

Freudian sanctioning of artistic creativity as the therapeutic licence to fantasy which, although grounded in the infantile ego and its unconscious drives, succeeds in transforming these (expressed as either desire or fear) into socially respectable and representable imaginative forms and thereby achieves an adult mediation between fantasizing ego and obdurate reality. Acknowledgement of this creatively mediating activity is developed by Holland into a theory that articulates the secondary operation implicit in it, in his view – that is, the specific mediation between reader as ego and text as object – and involves seeing the process of reading as a dynamic and mutual transaction between the text as artistic form and meaning and the reader as adaptive and defensive ego – what he terms 'the dynamics of literary response' (Holland 1968). He claims that we as readers 'work out through the text our own characteristic patterns of desire and adaptation. We interact with the work, making it part of our own psychic economy and making ourselves part of the literary work – as we interpret it' (Holland 1980, 124). This approach, usually termed transactive (sometimes transactional) criticism, has the merit of recognizing that reading is itself a psychological process and that the reader – any reader – has a subjective reality, but it is perhaps simplifyingly optimistic in its conviction that the dynamic transaction with the text necessarily produces pleasure from the sublimation of traumatic unconscious processes. And although it presents the interaction of reader and text as one that is mutually transformative and explicitly rejects a dualistic Cartesian epistemology, his model retains an implicit dualism with its positing of the imaginative text on the one hand in transaction with the autonomous ego on the other.

For Holland, then, meaning is fundamentally psychological, realized according to a psychoanalytic and indeed Freudian and anti-Jungian prescription, and so he claims a correlation between textual and psychic processes – as the text strives for unity, an eventual thematic harmony, so the individual reader strives for identity, an eventual psychic equilibrium. Text and self are accordingly parallel terms, as are unity and identity, the latter pair seen as abstractions or idealizations of the former, and a sort of isomorphism operates so that textual work (interpretation and understanding leading to thematic unity) and psychic work (expression and control of egoistic drives leading to personal identity) are seen as interinvolved, a mutual process as text and self interactively develop toward the achievement of unity and identity – 'when I arrive at the unity in a literary text or the identity theme of a personality I am studying, I do so in a way that is characteristic for me – for my identity theme' (Holland 1980, 122). Accordingly, 'interpretation is a function of identity' (Holland 1980, 124), an assertion which defines reading as to some degree a common subjective response, in so far as, in Holland's Freudian model, we are all constituted by fundamental psychic drives, passing through the infantile pre-oedipal stages, oral, anal and phallic, into the oedipal crisis – but also as an individual subjective response, in so far as we are all particular persons with our own specific life experiences. The literary text is thus the means for its reader to recreate him or herself through a unifying interpretation, a centripetal movement that brings text and self together in a movement of self-identification on the reader's part. Holland's theory has been criticized for its tendency to subordinate the text to the personality of the reader, making reading a quasi-confessional or autobiographical procedure – the reader ultimately finds only his or her own subjectivity at the core of the text. It has also, predictably, come under attack from a deconstructionist perspective which questions the unitary nature of the identity pre-supposed in Holland's model. Holland has sought to answer some of this criticism, and to take account of his own experimental work with readers (Holland 1973, 1975), by proposing a 'transferential' model, which moderates the emphasis on the reader as personality in favour of a stress on the activity of reading as dialectical, a negotiation between text and reader, although this returns him to the problem of dualism. But overall his theory remains strongly oriented toward a subjectivizing view of the text–reader relationship.

David Bleich, who was associated with Holland and others in the Centre for the Psychological Study of the Arts in New York, also produced a psychological model of reader response, but one that developed away from the ego-based theory of his colleague toward a theory of intersubjectivity based on an epistemology of the reader's initial perception and subsequent interpretation of the text. There is also a recognition of the importance of language as the articulation, both mediating and objectifying, of the self, since language ensures a distancing which enables reflection but also requires the reader as subject for its animation and in consequence cannot claim abstract objectivity. In a quasi-phenomenological spirit, Bleich claims that human attention distinguishes three kinds of entity – people, objects and symbols – and literary works fall into the third category. While the text in its mere physicality is an object, its realization as meaningful work depends on the capacity and desire for symbolization on the reader's part – that is, the reader's initial response – which is followed by a secondary symbolization, or 'a motivated resymbolization' (Bleich 1980, 134), in which an understanding and coherent articulation of the initial response are developed as a process of interpretation. It is the reader as epistemological subject or agent who retains primacy in this process, however, which Bleich terms unapologetically 'subjective criticism' (Bleich 1975, 1978) and it appears that it is the mode of attention, or response, directed by the reader at the object which constitutes the 'perceptual symbolization' (Bleich 1980, 135) of it. This is not, however, a purely individual and arbitrary process because the decision to perceive the object as symbol – as an aesthetic object – both derives from a common immediate experience of seeing the words on the page and leads at once to a confirmation which is collective, that is the agreement of a community which determines the articulation of the resymbolization or interpretation which extends the initial reaction or perception into aesthetic understanding and enjoyment.

However, the basis for discussion of any literary work, for an intersubjective activity related to the text, remains not the text *per se* but the reader's 'symbolization and resymbolization of it' which produce the reader's 'subjective syntheses' (Bleich 1980, 145). For Bleich, then, the text has no efficacy or particular status so far as response is concerned: it is the reader who produces and invests the text-as-work through symbolizations that are grounded in the reader's psychology and therefore inalienably subjective (Bleich 1977). They are not therefore solipsistic and incommunicable, however, because of the intersubjective force of language and the capacity of an interpretive community to mediate responses through an implicit consensus. Bleich locates the origin of these communicative agencies in 'the common social purpose of pedagogy' (Bleich 1980, 158) by which he appears to mean a communal inculcation of responsive knowledge, whether formally instituted in the classroom or not. In the context of the modern developed world, however, 'schools become the regular agency of subjective initiative' (Bleich 1980, 159) and much of Bleich's attention has consequently been devoted to analysing the conditions of subjective response in the framework of pedagogy. As such, his work can be seen as an important contribution to a substantial current of reader-response theory which has been engaged in examining the acquisition and development of reading skills and powers of interpretation.

Bleich's formulations of the roles of both language and community in enabling and controlling subjective response owe a good deal to the thinking of the third of my American representatives of reader-response theory, Stanley Fish. However, Fish's ideas regarding response develop over a period, and he starts out from a position which is in some respects that of the traditional literary critic, examining closely a canonical text. The text in question is Milton's *Paradise Lost*, which Fish subjects to a minutely scrupulous reading that derives from the New Critical tradition, although his arguments from that reading take an importantly different direction. Briefly, he claims that the reader, through the process of reading, realizes an awareness of the parallels between his or her own epistemological situation and the imagined primal human situation articulated through the poem, a tension between reasoned inquiry and analysis on the one hand and faith on the other, and this realization renders the reader not merely an observer of but a participant in the poem (Fish 1967). Although the approach is basically traditional in its centring on the text, the recognition and elaboration of the reader's difficulty and uncertainty of response is a significant first move, for Fish, toward a reader-oriented approach. The insight is developed and extended to treat a wider range of seventeenth-century texts (Fish 1972), again subjected to minute and often brilliant analysis, and a dualizing conception of reading, somewhat similar to the Barthesian division between 'readerly' and 'writerly' text (Barthes 1974), is proposed. The text, or literary representation, is seen as either 'rhetorical', persuasive in its satisfaction of the reader's expectations, or 'dialectical', disturbing expectations and demanding a movement of self-reflection on the reader's part in a recognition of the difficulties of comprehension. The argument opens up but does not resolve, except in a negative way, the problematic of interaction between author, text and reader – the question, that is, of where authority and responsibility for meaning are to lie. The intriguing concept of the 'self-consuming artefact', emphasized in the subtitle, epitomizes the problematic and its negativity, where 'self-consumption' seems indifferently but somewhat obscurely the process to be undergone by author, text and reader in an unresolved play of interpretive and signifying forces. Fish is still holding here to some of the traditional principles of textual objectification and an ambiguity of focus results as he seeks to combine this with an increasingly radical recognition of the dynamic and constructive capacity of the reading process.

However, a little earlier this recognition was generalized and given polemical force in Fish's essay of 1970, 'Literature in the Reader', republished a decade later as the first chapter of *Is There a Text in This Class?* (1980). Here the emphasis shifts decisively toward the reader as the text is reconceived not as object, however problematic in interpretation or dialectical in effect, but as *experience*, and literature understood as *event* rather than content or substance. It opens with a joust against the influential New Critical notion of the 'Affective Fallacy' and claims the text, on the microlevel of the sentence, to be 'no longer an object, a thing-in-itself, but an *event*, something that *happens* to, and with the participation of, the reader' (Fish 1980, 25). Accordingly, *process* is given primacy: as the sentence, and eventually the text, unfolds successively, word following word, it is this temporal flow, the experience of reading, which demands recognition and is not to be subsumed in a result or goal, the determination of a teleology. The text, *a fortiori* the individual sentence (and Fish analyses a selection of sentences from various authors), is not to be viewed as 'a repository of meaning' (Fish 1980, 29) but as a process of making meaning, every part of which remains significant and no part of which is to be relegated by an end-oriented or totalizing interpretative claim. Reading, and the text as reading experience, are kinetic activities not static entities and their qualities of and as movement must be fully realized in any responsible interpretation. The tendency to 'spatialize' and thereby 'freeze' the text formalistically, in Fish's view the besetting sin of New Criticism, must be countered by an emphasis on temporality and flow.

Further questions arise from this fundamental resituating of the relation between text and reader and simultaneous reconstitution of the nature of the text itself. One question concerns language – is the faculty of 'making meaning' in this experiential way peculiar to literary or poetic language a particular kind of semantic and formal strength? Fish answers this in the negative, with a progressively more radical inclusiveness – this faculty belongs as much to the language of literary prose as of poetry, he claims initially, and then, making considerable use of the speech-act theory developed by Austin and Searle (Austin 1962; Searle 1969), widens this to reject any fundamental distinction between literary and non-literary language. All language, he claims (adducing Austin), is performative, and carries illocutionary force (adducing Searle) – that is, it bears with it the intentions and purposes of its speaker, always related to a context, and accordingly demands a corresponding response. Language, in use, is never abstract or neutral, and the meaning of an utterance is never 'pure', fully susceptible to abstract and categorical definition, but always in some sense experientially understood. Another question concerns the nature of the agency responsible for rendering the text-as-experience: who or what is this? Fish introduces the concept of the 'informed reader', which he acknowledges to be 'a construct, an ideal or idealized reader' (1980, 48) but one that he claims is adequately although approximately identifiable with an empirically verifiable reader. The term raises difficulties, however, in its uncertain position between the empirical and the abstract, in its individualizing presumption, and in the degree to which it is understood to be a product or epiphenomenon of the text. Again, Fish revises the concept radically, later situating the reader in the context of what he terms 'interpretive communities', the institutional frameworks which govern individual readings, which he emphasizes in the subtitle of the 1980 collection of essays whose introduction provides an explanation of the term.

Indeed, Fish's contribution to reader-response theory is characterized by a vigorous capacity for self-revision, a willingness to reconsider and reshape his thinking, energized by a considerable capacity for forceful, perhaps occasionally truculent, polemic. First taking issue with New Critical precepts, he moves into an exploration of the complexities and perplexities of reading as process, which leads him to a radical reconsideration of meaning as experience, accompanied by attacks on what are viewed as attempts to re-objectify the text, notably the sophisticated strategies of stylistics (Fish's countering term is 'affective stylistics'), but also by a critique of one-sidedly subjectivizing approaches, and finally to an effort to transcend the dualism of text and reader, object and subject, by means of the concept of 'interpretive communities', understood as ineluctable, given institutions and systemic articulations of meaningfulness, enabling both texts and readers through their power of authorizing and controlling interpretation. Ultimately, as he acknowledges, his theory takes on a kind of implosive force – fulfilled and voided at the same time in its 'truth'. There is no 'grand theory' to be applied to literature *in toto*: there is only the clarification of the conditions of our practice, what we do as readers constrained and enabled by our contexts and capabilities. Clarification of these conditions requires, in a Wittgensteinian way, the removal of false imperatives and directives – the assumed univocal authority of either text or reader, for example. But it also ensures escape from the falsely absolutized assumed consequences, a fall into subjectivism or solipsism on the one hand (the view that only the reader produces meaning) or into objectivism or scientism on the other (the view that only the text does), as well as the, in Fish's view, unproductive dualistic oscillation of the model of text–reader interaction. Nothing is changed by the recognition that Fish argues for: we are still (already) readers, as we were – we have perhaps only the clarification and assurance of the recognition we no longer need.

Holland, Bleich and notably Fish all offer substantial and interesting versions of reception theory – or reader response, as it is more commonly termed in the Anglo-American context – but they are by no means its only proponents. Recognition and investigation of the role of the reader extends back some way in twentieth-century Anglo-American critical history, as the important examples of I. A. Richards and Louise Rosenblatt illustrate, although its appearance is sporadic and it is overwhelmed by the success of the text-based New Criticism until the early 1960s. Thereafter it infiltrates into some of the structuralist models of literary theory, synthesized in Culler, and more broadly, though also contentiously, into linguistics and stylistics, in Chatman and Dillon. It is an aspect of the historical sociology of literature in the work of Ong, as well as more generally of the sociology of reading, notably that current which is concerned with pedagogy – the ways in which reading ability is acquired and the developmental and psychological implications of reading in childhood and adolescence, at home and in school (Purves and Beach 1972; Many and Cox 1992). It also broadens to encompass other media, so that the reading of film in particular (a feature of Holland's work) and of other cultural products may be included – in this it may be seen as true to its roots in reception theory and aesthetics. European reception theory has some influence but this is variable and models are fairly eclectically adopted or engaged with, perhaps because of the vagaries of translation – the major current of German reception theory is only very partially recognized (Holub 1987). The selection of essays edited by Tompkins (1980), by Suleiman and Crosman (1980) and by Bennett (1995) respectively are indicative of the range. Like the European, the American postwar development and efflorescence of reader-response theory and criticism, though beginning a little later, is similarly swift, impressive, but also relatively short-lived – with, again, a lifespan of little more than twenty years. Energized by its often polemical reaction against formalism, reader-response criticism is remarkably extensive in its theoretical exfoliation but also, it appears, determinate in its theoretical implications, although its importance in encouraging a shift of concern toward the pragmatic in literary criticism should not be underestimated.

Jeremy Lane

Further reading and works cited

Austin, J. L. *How to Do Things with Words*. New York, 1962.

Barthes, R. *S/Z*. New York, 1974.

Bennett, A. (ed.) *Readers and Reading*. London, 1995.

—. *Readings and Feelings*. Urbana, IL, 1975.

—. *Literature and Self-Awareness*. New York, 1977.

—. *Subjective Criticism*. Baltimore, MD, 1978.

—. 'Epistemological Assumptions in the Study of Response', in *Reader-Response Criticism*, ed. J. P. Tompkins. Baltimore, MD, 1980.

Chatman, S. *Narrative Structure in Fiction and Film*. Ithaca, NY, 1978.

Culler, J. *Structuralist Poetics*. Ithaca, NY, 1975.

—. *On Deconstruction*. London, 1983.

Dillon, G. *Language Processing and the Reading of Literature*. Bloomington, IN, 1978.

Fish, S. *Surprised by Sin*. London, 1967.

—. *Self-Consuming Artefacts*. Berkeley, CA, 1972.

—. *Is There A Text in This Class?* Cambridge, MA, 1980.

Freund, E. *The Return of the Reader*. London, 1987.

Garvin, H. R. (ed.) *Theories of Reading, Looking, Listening*. Lewisburg, PA, 1981.

Holland, N. *The Dynamics of Literary Response*. New York, 1968.

—. *Poems in Persons*. New York, 1973.

—. *5 Readers Reading*. New Haven, CT, 1975.

—. 'Unity Identity Text Self', in *Reader-Response Criticism*, ed. J. P. Tompkins. Baltimore, MD, 1980.

Holub, R. C. *Reception Theory*. London, 1984.

—. *Crossing Borders*. Madison, WI, 1992.

Mailloux, S. 'Reader-Response Criticism?', *Genre*, 10, 1977.

Many, J. and Cox, C. (eds) *Reader Stance and Literary Understanding*. Norwood, MA, 1992.

Ong, W. J. *Orality and Literacy* [1982]. London, 1988.

Purves, A. C. and Beach, R. *Literature and the Reader*. Urbana, IL, 1972.

Richards, I. A. *Practical Criticism*. New York, 1935.

Rosenblatt, L. *Literature as Exploration*. New York, 1968.

—. *The Reader, the Text, the Poem*. Carbondale, IL, 1978.

Royle, N. *Telepathy and Literature*. Oxford, 1991.

Scholes, R. *Protocols of Reading*. New Haven, CT, 1989.

Searle, J. R. *Speech Acts*. Cambridge, 1969.

Slatoff, W. *With Respect to Readers*. Ithaca, NY, 1970.

Suleiman, S. R. and Crosman, I. (eds) *The Reader in the Text*. Princeton, NJ, 1980.

Tompkins, J. P. (ed.) *Reader-Response Criticism*. Baltimore, MD, 1980.

Weber, S. *Institution and Interpretation*. Minneapolis, MN, 1987.

The Yale Critics? J. Hillis Miller (1928–), Geoffrey Hartman (1929–), Harold Bloom (1930–), Paul de Man (1919–1983)

In 1975, the Algerian-French philosopher Jacques Derrida performed the first of his soon to become famous annual seminars at Yale University. Although Derrida's specialist background was in the critical tradition of Husserl's phenomenology and Heidegger's dismantling of metaphysics, the primary institutional niche he found himself in at Yale was the space of literary studies. Among his prominent colleagues in that location were Harold Bloom and Geoffrey H. Hartman, who both began their academic careers at Yale in 1955, and Paul de Man and J. Hillis Miller, who had both recently (in 1970 and 1972 respectively) moved to Yale from Johns Hopkins University, the venue of the 1966 landmark conference on *The Languages of Criticism and the Sciences of Man* where Derrida delivered his first lecture in the United States. Derrida's arrival at Yale, then, accompanying the gradual emergence, or at least the naming, of the 'Yale Critics', marked an important institutional moment in the establishment of what has come to be known as 'deconstruction in America'. A few years later, in 1979, this moment was half-heartedly monumentalized in the joint publication *Deconstruction and Criticism*, a volume of four essays by Bloom, de Man, Hartman and Miller arranged (even if only by the random order of the alphabet) around an expanded version of one of Derrida's Yale seminars. It was to be the only collective publication of the 'Yale School' – and even that may already be saying too much.

Two obvious but crucial points to be registered in this loose critical constellation are the apparent intent to welcome the 'continental' challenge posed to the Anglo-American humanities, and the determined emphasis on the specific claims of literature in this encounter. Throughout the 1970s, the most visible face of the 'continental' challenge – though by no means the only one – was arguably that of Derridean deconstruction, and for better or worse the American reception and modulation of deconstruction initially took shape primarily in the context of literary scholarship. That this shape should have emerged at all is itself far from self-evident, and it could be argued that its very unlikelihood was an important factor in the impact of its appearance. The constitutive instability of the 'Yale School' simultaneously allowed its members to become members at all (however briefly) and contributed to the Yale Critics' almost implausibly powerful influence on the development of literary studies well into the 1980s.

Paul de Man's immediate response to the 1966 Johns Hopkins symposium mentioned above offers a suggestive illustration of the relative unlikelihood of the Yale Critics' subsequent alliance with Derrida. Addressing what he calls 'the structuralist aberration' as a 'methodologically motivated attack on the notion that a literary or poetic consciousness is in any way a privileged consciousness' (1967, 56), de Man argues that this attack misfires because it mistakenly conceives of the disputed privilege of literary consciousness as a naive belief in the unity of sign and meaning erroneously associated with romanticism. To the contrary, de Man asserts, articulating a position arrived at in the course of reading primarily canonical European romantic and post-romantic authors and their critics since the early 1950s, literary consciousness *is* privileged precisely to the extent that it is 'demystified from the start' (1967, 55): it has always already abandoned this naive myth by presenting itself in the form of radical fiction, as 'pure nothingness, *our* nothingness stated and restated by a subject that is the agent of its own instability' (1967, 56). For this reason, the literary 'self as a constitutive subject' (1967, 47), which structuralism seeks to dismiss, successfully survives the attack of the likes of Lévi-Strauss and, surprisingly, 'Deridda' (*sic*).

The surprise here is not just that de Man misspells Derrida's name, but that he should conceive of him as a structuralist. For Derrida's lecture at the Johns Hopkins symposium de Man alludes to here is pre-eminently a powerful, be it sympathetic, critique of the structuralist project itself. Still, to the extent that Derrida's text does question the 'myth' of 'a subject which would be the absolute origin of its own discourse' (1967, 418), de Man's early misplacement of deconstruction as just another structuralism is perhaps less important than his fundamental reservations concerning what he took Derrida's thought to be, though it is important to underscore de Man's insistence on the critical merits of 'the structuralist aberration' for a 'philosophical criticism ... that takes the critical process itself as its field of inquiry' (1967, 56). For in structuralism at least, and for de Man at the time this includes Derrida's work, 'the problem of the subject', which involves 'the central intent of literature', is mishandled 'on such a vast scale that genuine criticism ensues', while in 'the formalist and narrowly historical methods of literary study' still prevalent at the time, this problem is merely 'bypassed ... in a petty way' (1967, 56). When de Man revised his text for inclusion in his first book, *Blindness and Insight* (1971), which also features a sustained response to Derrida's work as 'one of the places where the future possibility of literary criticism is being decided' (1983, 111), the somewhat anomalous reference to Derrida was erased, but the defence of the literary self as a constitutive subject against all manner of mistaken demystification survived, as did the insistence on the status of literature as 'a primary source of knowledge' (1983, 19). Given the subsequent alliance between de Man and Derrida, it is not entirely surprising that readers of this revised text looking for deconstructive dogma often blatantly misread de Man's sketch of the demystification of literary consciousness as an outline of his own critical project (see Berman 1988, 241 and further instances listed in de Graef 1995, 235). The mistake signals precisely the potential incommensurability between a privileging of literature and what 'true' deconstruction is supposed to be all about, and it is this incongruity which can be read as the signature fissure in the Yale Critical edifice.

   A cursory investigation of the other Yale Critics' publications prior to their establishment as a 'school' reveals a bedrock agreement on the status of literature – and specifically what is received as 'canonical', predominantly romantic and post-romantic literature – as somehow a privileged mode of discourse. More particularly, this privilege involves a recognition of literature as the maximally lucid articulation of what is variously called consciousness, the self, or the subject. In this respect, the Yale Critics' early work participates in a broad resistance to the relative dismissal of consciousness, self or subject that had become codified in the critique of the so-called 'intentional fallacy' at the heart of New Critical orthodoxy, while the historical focus in their readings amounts to a reconsideration of the contemporary as more significantly marked by romanticism than the ideologues of modernism had been willing to admit. In its actual detail, this double emphasis takes on markedly different forms in their writing, yet the general pattern amply succeeds in creating at least the impression of a family resemblance.

   Thus, Harold Bloom's first major works are powerfully idiosyncratic readings of great or, to use Bloom's own favourite term, 'strong' poets in the English romantic and post-romantic tradition. With their unashamed emphasis on the creative struggle of these formidable figures, works like *Shelley's Mythmaking* (1959), *The Visionary Company* (1961), *Blake's Apocalypse* (1963), *Yeats* (1970) and *The Ringers in the Tower* (1971) are so many stages in the antagonistic recovery of a company of extreme and powerful dissident selves from the neglect or even contempt they had suffered at the hands of, especially, the New Critics. Bloom's strong romantic poets are committed to the Stevensian notion that 'the theory of poetry is the theory of life', and just as 'they would not yield the first to historical convention, so they could not surrender the second to religion or philosophy or the tired resignations of society' (1971a, 3). Their 'immense hope' was that 'poetry, by expressing the whole man, could either liberate him from his fallen condition or, more compellingly, make him see that condition as unnecessary, as an unimaginative fiction that an awakened spirit could slough off' (1971a, xxiv). And while Bloom acutely registers the failure of this romantic ambition, he continues to call on the strong selves of true poetry 'to help us in an increasingly bad time' by making 'the dark grow luminous, the void fruitful' (1971b, 11). It is not surprising, therefore, that in the second half of the 1960s, when the New Critical orthodoxy was increasingly becoming a thing of the past, Bloom should have felt the need to measure his distance from the new anti-romantic challenges of the self associated with structuralism much in the same way as did de Man (as witness Bloom's epilogue to the 1971 revised edition of his *The Visionary Company*, 1971a, 463–4) and from 'the anti-humanistic plain dreariness of all those developments in European criticism that have yet to demonstrate that they can aid in reading any one poem by any poet whatsoever' (1973, 12–13). While it is not quite clear who exactly stands accused in this latter blanket judgement (one of Bloom's idiosyncrasies being his cavalier contempt for footnotes and bibliographical references), its implicit indictment of anti-humanism does not seem to augur well for a future alliance with a thinker like Derrida who, in the same seminal essay referred to above, outlined the prospect of a step 'beyond man and humanism' (1967, 427).

It is characteristic of Geoffrey Hartman, whose reluctant articulacy is at least as arresting as Bloom's rhetoric of strength, that he should frame his recognition of the privileged status of literature as an insight brought home to the 'unwilling' company of literary scholars, himself included, who are now, at the time of writing *The Unmediated Vision* (1954), only just 'advanced beyond intellectual naïveté' and find themselves 'forced to consider literature as more than an organic creation, a social pastime, a religious trope, an emotional outlet, a flower of civilization, more even than an exemplary stage for ideal probabilities' (1954, x). More than all of this, literature stands revealed as 'a moral force in its own right, an institution with its own laws, and, incipiently, a distinctive form of knowledge' (1954, x). In the 'hard labor' of pursuing this recognition of 'literature as a distinctive mode of knowledge in which the processes, or, better, the desires of the human mind find their clearest expression' (1954, xi), Hartman envisages the possibility of a universal 'method of interpretation which could reaffirm the radical unity of human knowledge' (1954, x) – a method, in short, which would transcend the parochial status of the mere 'approach' – , though his actual readings here and elsewhere, especially his long and complicated engagement with the workings of the 'consciousness of consciousness' in the poetry of Wordsworth (1971, xii), remain marked by the hesitations and qualifications of the arch(-)interpreter ultimately unwilling to abandon literature to the unity he nonetheless invokes, and of the literary scholar who constantly seeks to retune his reading by confronting it with alternative 'approaches' current at the time. Like Bloom, Hartman registers his reservations concerning the limitations of structuralism, both in its European and in its Anglo-American forms (notably Northrop Frye's archetypal criticism), but, like de Man, he is more usefully ready to recognize the critical potential of these limitations (see, for example, Hartman 1970, 3–23). Similarly, in his strategic play-off between 'formalism' and 'critical intuition', he proposes to rescue formalism from its commodification as 'puerile' 'explication-centred criticism' under the 'dominion of Exegesis' rather than dismiss it altogether (1970, 56–7).

Like his later Yale colleagues, J. Hillis Miller also begins his critical career with predominantly monographical arguments intent on disclosing the characteristic workings of individual literary minds. He differs from them, however, in devoting more attention to narrative fiction and to Victorian authors, pursuing the 'spiritual history' (1965, vii) of a development beyond romanticism through nihilism. His theoretical alliances at that time are primarily with the Geneva School, whose members (Georges Poulet and Jean Starobinski being the pivotal figures) practice a criticism of consciousness based on intimate identification with their literary object. As Miller programmatically states in the Preface to his 1963 study *The Disappearance of God*, 'If literature is a form of consciousness the task of the critic is to identify himself with the subjectivity expressed in the words, to relive that life from the inside, and to constitute it anew in his criticism'

(1965, ix). At a 1965 Yale symposium on literary criticism where de Man and Hartman also delivered papers, Miller found himself called upon to confront this critical principle, which presupposes a maximum access to the presence of consciousness at the heart of literature, with recent alternatives in European criticism challenging this metaphysics of presence (Miller 1966), and by 1970 a clear choice between Poulet and Derrida's interrogation of 'consciousness as the will to language within its presence to itself' seemed inevitable: 'A critic must choose either the tradition of "presence" or the tradition of "difference", for their assumptions about language, about literature, about history, and about the mind cannot be made compatible' (Miller 1970, 223). Except, it seems, in a recognition of the 'failure' of Poulet's criticism (and, by implication, Miller's own earlier work) as itself a partly unwitting exercise in what Derrida calls the 'rigorous reading of metaphysics' (223). The failure of criticism would then be its rigorous recovery of the 'experience of failure' as 'the central movement of literature' itself (224): its naming and renaming of 'the failure of the mind ever to coincide with its point of origin' (225).

The often desperate privilege accorded to literature in the first stages of these four critical careers never disappears from the work of the Yale Critics, though it does undergo considerable modifications in the late 1960s and early 1970s, a period in which the future Yale Critics also begin to emerge as an alliance. This emergence can partly be derived from the fact that they publish alongside each other in new journals like Johns Hopkins's review of contemporary criticism *diacritics*, which features de Man and Miller in its advisory board, but the more decisive formative factors are arguably Miller's repeated attempts throughout the 1970s to articulate the incipient connections between his own work and that of Derrida and de Man in the context of contemporary American criticism. The connections to Bloom and Hartman are less forcefully established, but their work too develops new emphases approaching those highlighted by Miller and de Man.

De Man's retrospective recognition of a movement away from 'the thematic vocabulary of consciousness and of temporality' towards a 'rhetorical terminology' in his seminal 1969 essay 'The Rhetoric of Temporality' (1983, xii) offers a convenient (and therefore admittedly also somewhat insensitive) frame for these emphases. Notwithstanding their lasting differences, Bloom, de Man, Hartman and Miller all articulate more explicitly the problematic linguistic constitution of the literature they continue to uphold as a distinctive discursive mode. One way to investigate that linguistic constitution is by recognizing literature as text, forbiddingly codified by de Man, in a 1975 essay on Nietzsche later republished in his most sustained collection *Allegories of Reading*, as an undecidable construct that 'allows for two incompatible, mutually self-destructive points of view, and therefore puts an insurmountable obstacle in the way of any reading or understanding' (1979, 131). From this perspective, the privilege of literature is bracketed by dint of its unreadability, yet, importantly, the privilege survives, with literature now 'condemned (or privileged) to be forever the most rigorous and, consequently, the most unreliable language in terms of which man names and transforms himself' (1979, 19). This notion of a critically unreliable linguistic naming and transforming effectively brings about a crisis in the earlier emphasis on literary consciousness and (its) history, while at the same time preserving that emphasis in an alternative hermeneutics open to the challenge of Derridean deconstruction, itself fuelled by the recovery of differential unreliability within logocentrism. The practice of reading then becomes the critical tracing of the experience of the undecidable which both informs and unforms interpretation, and the pursuit of language's 'rhetorical, figural potentiality' ('literature itself') (de Man 1979, 10) is one strategy to perform this tracing.

If that, as they say, is the theory, *Deconstruction and Criticism* is a record of the resistance of the practice of reading to the theoretical programme with which it is associated. In his preface to the volume, Hartman seeks to identify the alliance between 'the critics amicably if not quite convincingly held together by the covers of this book' (Bloom et al. 1979, ix) in terms of 'a shared set of problems': the question as to 'what kind of maturer function' criticism 'may claim ... beyond the obviously academic or pedagogical', and the question as to 'the importance – or *force* – of literature' (Bloom et al. 1979, vii). Both questions are clearly related: if the force of literature involves 'the priority of language to meaning', the 'excess' of 'figurative language' over 'any assigned meaning' (Bloom et al. 1979, vii), then the function of the criticism reading this literature will depend on its response to this excess. For Hartman, this appears to generate a distinction between Derrida, de Man and Miller on the one hand, and Bloom and Hartman himself on the other: the former are gently caricatured as 'boa-deconstructors' mercilessly revelling in the repeated disclosure of the 'pathos' of literary language as only ever a thin membrane covering 'the "abysm" of words'; while the latter – 'barely deconstructionists' – retain a special commitment to the 'persistence' and the 'psychological provenance' of this pathos (Bloom et al. 1979, ix).

In Bloom's contribution, this pathos is celebrated as 'the will to utter permanent truths of desire, and to utter these *within* a tradition of utterance' as manifested by 'strong poems' which refuse to be treated 'merely as a formal and linguistic structure', as is the case, according to Bloom, in all rhetorical criticism 'even of the advanced deconstructive kind' (Bloom et al. 1979, 20). The function of criticism is to oppose 'the abysses of Deconstruction's ironies' by championing the strong poetry 'that will not abandon the self to language' (Bloom et al. 1979, 37). Bloom acknowledges an affinity between his conception of texts as the 'interplay of differences' and that of his 'legitimate rival[s]' Derrida and de Man (Bloom et al. 1979, 13–14), but insists on the foundation of that interplay in the 'narcissistic self-regard' (16) of the aggressive and historically situated self articulated in the achieved anxiety of literature which the alert reader must engage in combat. Where Bloom measures his distance from deconstruction as a veritable lord of language properly appreciative of the 'significant difference between Anglo-American poetic tradition, and the much weaker French and German poetic tradition' (Bloom et al. 1979, 13) – a difference he reads as somehow explaining deconstruction's damaging blindness to the strong historical self of literature – Hartman maintains his reserved pose and 'simply' proposes an extremely complex reading of a Wordsworth poem as if nothing much had happened. Yet his subtle unfoldings of the latent undecidability in that genuinely Wordsworthian word 'fit' (Bloom et al. 1979, 209) suggest the workings of his acknowledged awareness of deconstruction's untimely utterances. In Miller's contribution, 'The Critic as Host', that awareness is voiced with an almost apostolic assertiveness matching Bloom's agonistic pathos. An earlier version of the piece had appeared in *Critical Inquiry* in 1977 as one of Miller's fairly regular attempts to explicitly claim ground for the deconstructive company in America, and in *Deconstruction and Criticism* Miller's expanded essay is easily the most programmatic contribution, identifying the 'extreme interpretation' of 'deconstruction' as interpretation itself finally come into its own – 'interpretation as such' – and culminating in the triumphant 'ultimate justification for this mode of criticism' which is 'that it works' (Bloom et al. 1979, 231–2, 252). As Miller also concedes, this is the ultimate justification for *any* conceivable mode of criticism, and in this respect it is instructive to juxtapose his readings in *The Disappearance of God* and its 1965 sequel *Poets of Reality* with the readings collected in his 1985 volume *The Linguistic Moment*: early and late, Miller's reading genuinely works, even to the point that it survives the nagging suspicion that this lasting success must involve a measure of theoretical failure. Miller's slightly shrill and self-consciously serpentine but strategically enabling corporate rhetoric in *Deconstruction and Criticism* stands in sharp contrast to de Man's saturnine reading of Shelley's unfinished long poem *The Triumph of Life*: de Man's is the only piece in the collection that does not explicitly address the shape of deconstruction at all, focusing instead on the 'Shape all light' in Shelley's text whose radical unreadability simultaneously feeds and starves the hermeneutico-archaeological desire to establish meaningful relationships allowing us 'to inhabit the world' (Bloom et al. 1979, 40).

As Hartman points out in the preface, an 'earlier scheme' for the collection had been 'to acknowledge the importance of Romantic poetry directly, by focusing all contributions on [Shelley]', but as it happens only de Man has rigorously observed that scheme. Bloom – the only one of the Yale Critics who frequently engages with contemporary literature – devotes a large part of his piece to John Ashberry; Hartman pursues his admirably interminable interpretation of Wordsworth; Derrida memorably avoids Shelley, primarily by reading him into Blanchot; Miller, as he had promised in the original version of his piece, programmatically uses the 'example' of Shelley's *Triumph of Life* to demonstrate the merits of deconstruction in revealing 'hitherto unidentified meanings and ways of having meaning in major literary texts' (Bloom et al. 1979, 252); de Man stubbornly and single-mindedly *reads* Shelley's 'disfiguration' as a resistance to 'historicism' which, paradoxically, is 'historically more reliable than the products of historical archaeology', but which, frustratingly, is not to be reproduced into 'a *method* of reading', lest we 'regress from the rigor exhibited by Shelley which is exemplary precisely because it refuses to be generalized into a system' (Bloom et al. 1979, 69).

In a somewhat trivial sense, the 'Yale Critics' as a collective may be said to have observed this refusal of systematic methodization inscribed in their non-manifesto, for the Yale School largely remained a phantom formation, randomly held together only by its members' sheer commitment to the task of reading literature as a singularly other mode of discourse. Nonetheless, this commitment proved to be remarkably productive as a point of reference in the institutional developments of literary scholarship, primarily perhaps in the sense that Yale's phantom formation became a privileged target for widely divergent critical objections. Three large groups may be distinguished in this resistance. Proponents of a more traditional conception of the literary humanities grudgingly acknowledged the Yale Critics' commitment to canonical literature but deplored the putative nihilism of this commitment, as well as what was perceived as a perverse blurring of the hierarchical distinction between literature and 'mere' criticism attendant on the self-reflexive scrutiny of the act of reading itself. Politically contestatory representatives of what can loosely be called the left opposed precisely the commitment to the (dead, white, male) canon itself and castigated the Yale School as an essentially conservative or even reactionary body diverting critical challenges to the status quo. In the course of the late 1970s and 1980s, this critique of the Yale School was a rallying issue in the development of feminist and more generally gender-centred reading, postcolonial studies, (post-)marxist scholarship and new historicist research, all of which established various footholds in the newly emerging disciplinary formation of cultural studies. At the same time, however, numerous participants in these alternative critical formations have found considerable support in the Yale Critics' writings and in work produced by scholars associated with or influenced by them such as Gayatri Spivak, Shoshana Felman, Fredric Jameson and Barbara Johnson –

traces of this Yale dissemination are acknowledged in the work of, for instance, Stephen Greenblatt, Judith Butler and Homi Bhabha. A third and sometimes related strand of opposition to the Yale School specifically targeted its alleged abuse of Derridean deconstruction: here, the very preoccupation with literature as such was diagnosed as generating a disabling deflection of the radically political institutional charge of Derrida's thought (Ryan 1982) or as screening an intellectual incompetence or unwillingness to properly appreciate deconstruction's philosophical credentials (Gasché 1979; but see also Attridge 1992 for an excellent reflection on the 'haunting' of literature in Derrida's own work).

The death of de Man in 1983, followed by Miller's move to the University of California at Irvine in 1986, brought the decade or so of Yale Criticism to an appropriately arbitrary end. The heated debate occasioned by the 1987 publicization of de Man's contributions to the German-controlled press during the early years of the occupation of his native Belgium consolidated rather than decisively altered existing critical attitudes, both dismissive and appreciative, towards his later work, though it did lead to a more focused concern for the ethical charges of that work (which had already been foregrounded in Miller's 1986 book *The Ethics of Reading*) and for the historico-ideological thrust of de Manian deconstruction, which he had been articulating more closely in his final years. The essays now published as *Aesthetic Ideology* (1996) by his disciple Andrzej Warminski, together with the essays collected in *The Resistance to Theory* (1992) and *The Rhetoric of Romanticism* (1994) remain impressive testimony to his stubborn but erratic recognition of the literary imperative: literature's demand to be read as a language irreducible to yet of crucial import for the discourses of politics, ethics and philosophy. The critical careers of Bloom, Miller and Hartman have also observed this imperative in their widely different ways. Bloom's 1994 best-selling *The Western Canon* monumentalizes its author as a strong prophet proclaiming the Greatness of Strength in the wilderness wrought by 'the Balkanization of literary studies' (483) at the hands of the members of the 'School of Resentment', including the 'Deconstructionists' (492). Bloom remains a formidable figure in contemporary literary scholarship, partly as a result of his massive self-performances in the rhetoric of the formidable, but also on account of the sheer volume of his output, including his valuable work as editor for Chelsea House's *Modern Critical Interpretations* series. Yet the increasingly under-achieved anxiety of his writing threatens to forfeit the patient reading he does deserve. Doubtlessly, such a reading would have to involve the influence of the figure of patient reading himself, Geoffrey Hartman, whose own reading has gradually become more explicitly preoccupied with the question of culture in the aftermath of the Holocaust (he is a founder and, since 1981, the project director of Yale's Video Archive for Holocaust Testimonies) and in the contemporary context of increasingly aggressive politics of cultural identity, leading him to call for a restoration of 'literature's specificity as a focus for thinking about culture and as a force that challenges a monolithic or complacent culturalism' (1997, 2). An important aspect of that restoration is his at times exorbitant defence of literature as a medium for the representation of trauma, as witness for instance his suggestion that Wordsworth's specific poetic modulation of the traumatic transition from a rural to an industrial society around the turn of the eighteenth century 'saved English politics from the virulence of a nostalgic political ideal centring on rural virtues, which led to serious ravages on the continent' (1997, 7) – a proposal that seems ultimately more productively erratic than Bloom's eccentric tome-thumping thunders. Like Bloom, Hartman has continued to measure his distance from deconstruction, though he remains characteristically unsure about the extent and nature of that distance. Miller, on the other hand, and unsurprisingly, has lived up to his profile as deconstruction's closest advocate, defending its legacy both in his literary-critical writing and in his numerous contributions to debates concerning institutional policy. In 'The Excess of Reading', the coda of *Black Holes*, his 1999 book-length combination of institutional reflection and literary criticism which joins covers with Manuel Asensi's monographic study of Miller's entire work, that defence is still the defence of literature as a discourse rather than anything else, except the reading of literature is 'exemplary' of the encounter with otherness as such: reading 'is exemplary of the aporias of the ethico-political situation in which we all live' (Asensi and Miller 1999, 491). The mechanical extension of this trope into an epitaph for the Yale Critics memorializing their exemplary commitment to the privileged exemplarity of literature remains to be read.

Ortwin de Graef

Further reading and works cited

Arac, J. et al. (eds) *The Yale Critics*. Minneapolis, MN, 1983.

—. *Critical Genealogies*. New York, 1987.

Asensi, M. and Miller, J. Hillis. *J. Hillis Miller or, Boustrophedonic Reading/Black Holes*. Stanford, CA, 1999.

Attridge, D. 'Introduction: Derrida and the Question of Literature', in J. Derrida, *Acts of Literature*, ed. D. Attridge. New York, 1992.

Berman, A. *From the New Criticism to Deconstruction*. Urbana, IL, 1988.

— et al. *Deconstruction and Criticism*. New York, 1979.

— Bloom, H. *The Visionary Company*. Ithaca, NY, 1971a.

—. *The Ringers in the Tower*. Chicago, 1971b.

—. *The Anxiety of Influence*. New York, 1973.

Caruth, C. and Esch, D. (eds) *Critical Encounters*. New Brunswick, NJ, 1995.

Davis, R. C. and Schleifer, R. *Rhetoric and Form*. Norman, OK, 1985.

de Bolla, P. *Harold Bloom*. London, 1988.

de Graef, O. *Titanic Light*. Lincoln, NE, 1995.

de Man, P. 'The Crisis of Contemporary Criticism', *Arion*, 6, 11, 1967.

—. *Allegories of Reading*. New Haven, CT, 1979.

—. *Blindness and Insight*. Minneapolis, MN, 1983.

—. *The Resistance to Theory*. Minneapolis, MN, 1992.

—. *The Rhetoric of Romanticism*. New York, 1994.

—. *Aesthetic Ideology*, ed. and intro. A. Warminski. Minneapolis, MN, 1996.

Derrida, J. *L'écriture et la différence*. Paris, 1967.

Elam, H. R. (ed.) *Essays in Honour of Geoffrey H. Hartman. Studies in Romanticism*, 35, 4, 1996.

Felperin, H. *Beyond Deconstruction*. Oxford, 1985.

Gasché, R. 'Deconstruction as Criticism', *Glyph*, 6, 1979.

Hartman, G. H. *The Unmediated Vision*. New Haven, CT, 1954.

—. *Beyond Formalism*. New Haven, CT, 1970.

—. *Wordsworth's Poetry 1787–1814*. New Haven, CT, 1971.

—. *The Fateful Question of Culture*. New York, 1997.

Miller, J. Hillis. *The Disappearance of God*. New York, 1965.

—. 'The Antitheses of Criticism', *MLN*, 81, 5, 1966.

—. 'Geneva or Paris? The Recent Work of Georges Poulet', *University of Toronto Quarterly*, 39, 3, 1970.

—. *The Ethics of Reading*. New York, 1986.

Ryan, M. *Marxism and Deconstruction*. Baltimore, MD, 1982.

Waters, L. and Godzich, W. (eds) *Reading de Man Reading*. Minneapolis, MN, 1989.

Deconstruction in America

In 1987 Ortwin de Graef announced the discovery of scores of articles written by the young Paul de Man for collaborationist journals in occupied Belgium between 1940 and 1942. This discovery considerably complicated the fortunes of deconstruction in the United States, but also had the virtue of clarifying an intellectual atmosphere that had become somewhat hazy in the previous years, certainly since the death of de Man in 1983. De Man was the principle expositor of deconstruction in the United States, and if Derrida was better known throughout the country, de Man's local presence (at Yale and therefore at schools whose faculty included a substantial number of Yale-trained teachers) guaranteed that his thought and methods would be highly influential to the thinking of a small but elite class of theoretical expositors. De Man was responsible for bringing Derrida to Yale as a yearly visitor, and in large part contributed to the American reception of Derrida's thinking, and in particular to the widespread interest in deconstruction in a literary rather than a philosophical context.

Not that this interest was anti-philosophical. Rather deconstruction in the United States is a strange and interesting hybrid, a kind of imaginary enterprise that made possible an intellectual adventure which could never take place elsewhere. Deconstruction as practised at Yale by de Man and Derrida introduced a philosophical vocabulary to students of literature – especially a vocabulary derived from continental philosophy – that tended to be foreign to the study of literature in the United States. W. K. Wimsatt, it is true, wrote powerfully and penetratingly about Hegel, and Wimsatt's and Monroe Beardesley's seminal article on 'The Intentional Fallacy' set the philosophical tone for one version of the New Criticism, but the European philosophy important to most American students of literature tended in the 1960s to be restricted to somewhat potted versions of Sartre, himself taken to task by Heidegger (one of the centrally proclaimed forerunners of deconstruction) in his polemical 'Letter on Humanism' against Sartre's 'Existentialism is a Humanism'. Deconstruction has tended to be much more interested in Heidegger than in Sartre, but this interest has been largely critical. Heidegger (following Nietzsche, and in a way analogous to Freud who also followed Nietzsche) is regarded as having set the right agenda, as having asked the right questions and probed them deeply but as having become waylaid by an ontology that intensifies and symptomatizes the 'metaphysics of presence' it attempts to dismantle. Heidegger's highly idealizing or metaphysical view of language becomes changed in deconstruction by an emphasis on Saussurean linguistics, and that emphasis, combined with the French critiques of Heidegger by Emmanuel Levinas and by Maurice Blanchot are the major ancestors of deconstruction proper.

Deconstruction came to the United States in the mid-1960s at the beginning of increased attention there to continental, mainly French, interest in the relation of language to psychological and cultural life. That attention has its sources in American interest in Sartre and also Merleau-Ponty (Lacan's teacher), and in New Wave French film-making as well, in particular in Jean-Luc Godard, himself much influenced by contemporary French philosophy: Brice Parain, important to Gilles Deleuze, appears in one of Godard's movies, as himself; it also has sources in New Critical interest in linguistic theory, in particular in Roman Jakobson and the figures who line up with him: in France Ferdinand de Saussure and Emile Benveniste. Saussure's linguistic theory and its expansion and inversion by Lévi-Strauss's structuralist project, and Jacques Lacan's Saussurean reconceptualization of Freudian psychoanalysis, made for an incipient intellectual climate in the United States that was friendly to structuralism and poststructuralism, and deconstruction was received as a similarly vigorous and daring exposition of non-humanistic structures of human thought, agency and subjectivity. Derrida's version of deconstruction was itself profoundly influenced by psychoanalytic ways of thinking, in particular by the idea that repression is constitutive of mental phenomena and mental life, which is to say is constitutive of signifying phenomena and signifying life. The things that the mind thought about, and in particular the things that it regarded as central – subjectivity, being, presence, spirit – were all differentially erected through the repression of the fact and structure of their internal tensions; and this differential constitution was analogous to Saussure's account of the elements of language – difference without positive terms.

De Man was far less interested in psychoanalytic modes of thinking. For him literature provided the unnerving alterity that Derrida and Lacan ascribed to language and to the instabilities of language. De Man here was following in the footsteps of Blanchot, the great French philosopher, critic and novelist (a strong influence on Derrida as well, somewhat less strong on Lacan), who wrote of literary space as the space other to all worlds, strange and proximate but in a proximity without presence: for Blanchot this characterizes love as well, and his fictional work treats love much as his critical work treats literature: as the place of an otherness that haunts all settled nativity in the world. (Geoffrey Hartman had helped introduce Blanchot to an American readership in 1961.) De Man does not write about love, but he does write about the severe power of literature to unsettle system and certitude, and to expose its readers to an experience of power and alienation different from the ordinary business of the world, and not a commentary upon it.

De Man won a fit and fairly large audience through a combination of sheer intellectual power and great personal charisma. In many ways he might be compared to Leo Strauss (although their political views were largely anathema to each other): an extraordinarily charismatic teacher whose pedagogy took the form of discerning hidden meanings in literary and philosophical texts, meanings that were hidden because of the radical danger they presented to dominant ideology. De Man's first book was *Blindness and Insight* (1971), and in that book he offers lucid and powerful critiques not of literary but of critical texts, texts that in various ways are blind to the fact that their own best insights were anticipated and forestalled by the works in relation to which they offer them. De Man is often accused, with his Yale colleagues, of asserting the equality of criticism and the literature that it takes as its object, but where Hartman actually does come close to saying these sorts of things, and Harold Bloom does assert a continuity and partial identity between strong reading or misreading and strong writing, de Man in fact asserts very nearly the opposite doctrine. His canon, though small, is very close to sacred: Shelley, Pascal, Rousseau, Kleist, Kant, Wordsworth, Keats, Mallarmé all challenge their readers with a cognitive power so overwhelming as to force them into evasive strategies of aestheticization (as de Man, following Walter Benjamin, calls it). De Man might seem close to Hartman and Bloom in his sense of the difficulty and rarity of adequate 'reading': the term already sacralized by Bloom becomes in de Man almost apotheosized as the province of an extremely select elite who could confront what was actually going on in a work. And de Man's extreme elitism applies as well to literary works, so that it's not hard to find him condescending to a wide range of literature, from Pope to Schiller, that doesn't meet his cognitive demands. This is the reason he has been mistaken as a relativist as to literary 'standards', whereas in fact he is an absolutist so uncompromising that most canonical literature fails to meet those standards. But those that do are for him beyond praise as they are also beyond argument or subversion. Derridean deconstruction seeks the hidden fault lines and repressions by which a writer or text founds its illusory presence or meaning; de Man is interested not in textual or writerly evasions, but in those practised by readers confronted with literary works. He is concerned not with deconstructing works of literature but with showing how such works deconstruct themselves, or the assumptions readers bring to them, or the wish-fulfilment that characterizes all our relationships with others.

The similarity between Derrida and de Man is in the very high premium that they put on what they variously call 'writing'. But for Derrida writing means a practice of *différance*, something that any particular text struggles to repress in order to come into being and to establish itself as meaning and presence. Texts for Derrida tend to be examples of writing despite themselves, despite their wish and will to function as presence. In de Man the archi-writing that Derrida reads his authors as all evading is what *readers* evade in confrontation with the rare but rigorous works which instantiate it. For this reason de Man is profoundly suspicious of and studiously uninterested in psychoanalytic language or methods of reading which seek to discover anxiety within a work. Derrida is an analyst of constitutive repressions, whereas de Man focuses on the things that works say, not the things they evade or flee.

Both Derrida and de Man derive many of their ideas from Blanchot, so that it is not surprising to see strong affiliations as well as strong differences. The strongest difference would be in the privilege that de Man accords to literature and literary texts (which also embrace a certain order of philosophical work). Derrida reads his central texts as *symptomatic*, de Man his own as *apodictic*. The results of this difference in the adventures of literary theory in the United States are complex, often unexpected and not particularly deterministic, but certain general remarks can be made.

Many of de Man's students and some of his colleagues sought to combine his emphasis on rhetorical criticism with the psychoanalytic proclivities of Derridean deconstruction. The tension between Derrida and de Man is a fruitful one (and their friendship was a deep one), and attempts to resolve that tension remain fruitful. Cynthia Chase, steeped in de Manian ideas, nevertheless is a profound reader of Freud, and exemplifies one virtue of the respect that de Man taught with regard to major textual events (as he called them): unlike Derrida she is less interested in demystifying Freud than in getting the most hidden and unnerving aspects of his writing right, instead of assimilating them to received wisdom. Many of de Man's students and followers remain deeply committed to a psychoanalytic methodology, variously Freudian, Lacanian or Kleinian (as in recent work by Barbara Johnson). Others have stressed his interest in a conceptualization of disruption embodied and represented with and in the other, and have extended these ideas (under the strong influence of Blanchot and his friend Levinas, the French philosopher and Derrida's teacher) to work on trauma and on the witnessing of trauma, for example Cathy Caruth, Shoshana Felman and Thomas Keenan.

The general result of the kinds of psychoanalytic thinking that seems most consistent with de Man was an orientation of this thinking away from the text under analysis to its audience, and the more recent ascendancy of the new historicism, with its talk of cultural anxieties and aesthetic hegemony also finds in de Manian deconstruction an often unacknowledged ancestor, unacknowledged because de Man's philosophical and frankly anti-historical bent is something that the new historicism seeks to counter. But its methods are often de Manian as well as Foucauldian, at least in their origin, particularly to the extent that they overemphasize the political influence and efficacy of literary texts and of ways of reading literary texts. Here the influence might be traced through the arrival of some Yale-educated critics at Berkeley, where they encountered Foucault (also an acolyte of Blanchot's) and combined de Manian sensitivities to literature with a Foucauldian idea of culture. In particular Stephen Greenblatt, D. A. Miller and Walter Benn Michaels, were at the centre of this development, and Greenblatt and Michaels had also been involved with and published in the Johns Hopkins journal *Glyph* which had been (with Cornell's *diacritics*) the central American organs of deconstruction. De Man himself had been a highly influential presence first at Cornell and then at Hopkins before arriving at Yale in 1971, and his influence continued to tell at those institutions. Other figures in whom to trace the movement and cohabitation of a broadly deconstructive orientation to a cultural studies, new historicist, cultural materialist, feminist, queer theoretical or more broadly hegemonic and counter-hegemonic analysis include Alan Liu, in particular his work on Wordsworth, Gayatri Spivak, de Man's student and Derrida's translator, Judith Butler, Eve Kosofsky Sedgwick, Jonathan Goldberg and J. Hillis Miller (de Man's Yale colleague, now at Irvine).

At Cornell, Neil Hertz ought to be singled out as the most important colleague of de Man's in this context. Hertz (who has since gone to Hopkins) has done the most important readings of Freud and of the literature of the sublime central to de Man's later work, as well as of de Man himself. Hertz reads Freud as de Man might have, as operating with an idea about the uncanniness of literary power that he both approaches and avoids but that when applied to Freud himself becomes particularly vivid and powerful and that brings Freud into promising and powerful juxtaposition to Kant's analysis of the sublime. That reading of Freud and of Kant is one in which what has seemed too central a Freudian insight – the fundamental developmental status of the Oedipus complex – turns out in Hertz's reading to be an evasion of a more uncanny, less appropriable agency, which might be inadequately designated as 'the agency of the letter' (Lacan), 'repetition' (Deleuze), 'the sheer arbitrary power of language' (de Man), 'alterity' (Levinas), 'literary space' (Blanchot) or the 'impossible' or 'transgressive' (Georges Bataille). All of these are partial, all of them evasive – just because in one way or another melodramatic, for Hertz, but what he is persistently and indefatigable alert to are echoes of this spookiness in literary works, a spookiness partly spooky because it has no designs on us and yet is not to be put by.

Even the most telling critiques of de Man, by Hertz (who admires him) and by John Guillory, concede the force and power of his writing. Guillory is more interested in the ways that de Man's students and followers have tended to find a doctrine within a set of brilliant readings and aperçus, and he has analysed the academic sociology of this doctrinalism. Guillory is strongly influenced by Max Weber and by Pierre Bourdieu, but that influence itself comes out of interests that de Man was the most imposing teacher of. Guillory's central opposition of Bourdieu to de Man plays out as a critique of the kind of canonicity that de Man (like Strauss) turns out to defend, as we shall remark below.

By an irony that de Man would have relished both his centrality and the evasion of that centrality to American literary theory in the last fifteen years or so has been catalysed by the scandal of his wartime writing. Hertz, Keenan and Werner Hamacher collected that writing in a volume whose companion was a volume of responses to the discovery of that journalism. Those responses range from invective to strong defences of de Man, and as with the notorious Sokal hoax the strongest defences, including Derrida's, had the unfortunate effect of helping to discredit deconstruction in the United States, despite the fact that its ways of thinking continue to be highly influential. (Indeed it also had something of an antithetical effect as well: fair-minded critics like Denis Donoghue who read through de Man's later work in the wake of the scandal were much more impressed by it than they expected to be, and increased attention to that work could only be salutary.)

Perhaps the most pronounced effect overall was the not entirely strange reversal which reduced the small but absolute canon that American deconstruction established to no canon at all in the practice of much of the new historicism. There are two reasons for this: deconstructive scepticism about the value and politics of humanistic culture (a scepticism derivable from Nietzsche through Heidegger) finds an echo in new historicist accounts of how cultural artefacts function in the discursive matrix established by power and the organization of knowledge, but without the deconstructive sense that literature escapes reduction to this matrix; and the discovery that de Man himself had feet of clay (and less invidiously that some of his analyses don't withstand the test of time) means that the canonical figure of de Man himself became an example of the reasons that one ought to be sceptical of canon-formation.

Nevertheless deconstruction, like Foucauldian (and even Bloomian) criticism, continues to have an enormous influence on critical thinking. These modes of criticism have such an effect because the unlikely and somewhat unrigorous ideas they deploy mesh extremely well with the literary vocation that attracts people to the study of literature to begin with. (This may change through its own dialectic: at least in a sardonic introduction to an issue of *Studies in Romanticism* that he edited and which contained essays mainly by his own students, de Man himself suggested, in a tone of elaborate and deadpan praise, that their attraction to literary theory was far less literary than his own had been. On the other hand, critics like Sedgwick, Guillory and Lee Edelman have sought to return the centrality of *pleasure* to the analysis of literature.) As with Strauss, literature turns out in deconstructive (and Foucauldian) analyses to be about things as fantastic and wonderful and strange as we originally believed in our archaic, childhood response to it. Kant, Shelley, Keats were involved with utterly foundational struggles within a Manichean world. Literary and philosophical figures really were heroes of a fundamental and cosmic or at least ontological struggle for the very existence of meaning. When de Man says that Shelley's actual body is inscribed in *The Triumph of Life*, or that texts masquerade as wars, when Derrida reads Lévi-Strauss's anthropology as being itself an actual creation story and not just an account of one, it feels as if we have entered a mythic realm, the place where philosophy and literature, or philosophical literature and literary philosophy, take on mythic stature. Our souls take a proud flight in participating in this story. The new historicism similarly and taking its cue from deconstruction provides a kind of magic realist account of history, so that we're in the realm of Gabriel García Márquez and not of, say, Christopher Hill. As in Strauss, intellectual figures turn out to be engaged in giant struggles that engage us still, that we participate in by reading their work properly. The most explicit and most canny version of this paradigm is in Bloom, who in his accounts of the life and death struggles of strong poets with their precursors makes all poetry into an exciting and mythical agon. But here Bloom is representative of the spirit of his times, and the very resentment he provokes (and encourages) in his fellow-theorists derives from the openness with which he mythologizes a struggle that they wish to believe is real.

I say this not out of the desire to demystify or deflate the pretensions of (broadly speaking) deconstructive literary theory. Its salubrious effects have been far greater than its drawbacks: literary critics are on the whole far more alert, serious, philosophical and intellectually engaged than they have been. That this should come with drawbacks – newer pieties, sloppy thinking, risks of intolerance and resentment, and complacency – is not surprising, and these deficits are no worse than they ever were among critics. And it should be said of deconstruction what is also true of Freud, that it invented a new adventure story, a new and exciting literary experience, which may be judged somewhat harshly as sober analysis, but must be praised highly as a literary enterprise that continues to grip people's imaginations.

William Flesch

Further reading and works cited

Bloom, H. et al. *Deconstruction and Criticism*. New York, 1979.
Caruth, C. *Empirical Truths and Critical Fictions*. Baltimore, MD, 1991.
— and Esch, D. *Critical Encounters*. New Brunswick, NJ, 1995.
Chase, C. *Decomposing Figures*. Baltimore, MD, 1986.
Culler, J. *On Deconstruction*. New York, 1983.
de Man, P. *Allegories of Reading*. New Haven, CT, 1979a.
— (ed. and pref.) *Studies in Romanticism*, 18, Winter 1979b.
—. *Blindness and Insight*. Minneapolis, MN, 1983.
—. *Rhetoric of Romanticism*. New York, 1984.
—. *Resistance to Theory*. Minneapolis, MN, 1986.
—. *Wartime Journalism*. Lincoln, NE, 1989.
—. *Aesthetic Ideology*. Minneapolis, MN, 1996.
Derrida, J. *Memoires: For Paul de Man*, trans. Cecile Lindsay et al. New York, 1986.
Felman, S. *The Literary Speech Act*. Ithaca, NY, 1983.
— and Laub, D. *Testimony*. New York, 1992.
Greenblatt, S. *Learning to Curse*. New York, 1990.
Guillory, J. *Cultural Capital*. New York, 1993.
Hertz, N. *The End of the Line*. New York, 1985.
— et al. *Responses*. Lincoln, NE, 1989
Johnson, B. *The Critical Difference*. Baltimore, MD, 1980.
Keenan, T. *Fables of Responsibility*. Stanford, CA, 1997.
Quinney, L. *Literary Power and the Criteria of Truth*. Gainesville, FL, 1995.
Shaviro, S. *Passion and Excess*. Gainesville, FL, 1990.
Wall, T. *Radical Passivity*. Albany, NY, 1999.
Waters, L. and Godzich, W. (ed.) *Reading de Man Reading*. Minneapolis, MN, 1989.

Fredric Jameson (1934–) and Marxist Literary and Cultural Criticism

More than anything, misreadings of Fredric Jameson's work testify to the remarkable range and variety of elements forming his intellectual background and theoretical method. Variously characterized as a Hegelian, a Lukácsian, an Althusserian, a structuralist and a postmodernist, Jameson in fact draws on all of these thinkers and intellectual traditions without being reducible to any single one of them. Indeed, his work is best represented as an amalgam of marxist and non-marxist thought that exceeds any individual label at the same time that it resists recourse to a moralizing position vis-à-vis its object of study. Perhaps this latter fact more than any other accounts for the numerous misreadings of his work (the debate, for instance, over whether Jameson celebrates or criticizes postmodernism) and simultaneously highlights its singularity. As Jameson himself notes, the tendency to identify him with and/or to position him as either spokesperson or critic of his object of study excludes the possibility of being neither of those things, but obviously 'neither' in a way hard for people to understand (Kellner 1989, 369–70). The possibility of this unusual and complicated 'neither' forms the heart of Jameson's oeuvre; rather than appearing as a fault or defect, Jameson's eclectic and totalizing system of thought can be seen as an important and necessary intervention into both marxian theory generally and literary theory specifically.

Two of Jameson's earliest books, *Marxism and Form* (1971) and *The Prison-House of Language* (1972) established him as a leading marxist literary critic. *Marxism and Form*, in particular, is often cited as the Ur-text of marxist literary criticism in the US academy (Homer 1998, 38). These two works, along with *The Political Unconscious* (1981), not only firmly solidified Jameson's reputation and status but also contain the core components and vocabulary of his intellectual project: the dialectic, utopia, a non-essentialist subject, totality, mediation, the analysis of movements of literary and cultural history (periodization) and the primacy of narrative. As his work has developed and expanded, Jameson has applied and amended these terms in an increasingly diverse set of analyses of texts and cultural objects, from single-author studies of Sartre, Wyndham Lewis, Adorno and Brecht to works on cinema (*Signatures of the Visible* (1990), *The Geopolitical Aesthetic: Cinema and Space in the World System* (1992)), postmodernism (*Postmodernism, or, The Cultural Logic of Late Capitalism* (1991)), and theory (*The Ideologies of Theory*, 2 vols (1988), *The Seeds of Time* (1994), *The Cultural Turn* (1998)). Tracing the lineaments of Jameson's thought throughout this body of work reveals in fitting dialectical form how the sum of Jameson's contributions to contemporary marxism is greater than its parts.

The central concept underlying all of Jameson's intellectual forays – be they into marxist theory, mass culture, third world movements and literature, architecture, film theory or postmodernism – is found in the injunction that opens *The Political Unconscious*: 'Always historicize!' (1981, 9). While on the face of it a fairly straightforward gesture, Jameson's imperative yields surprisingly complex results. First and foremost, it shifts the focus of critical attention away from evaluative judgements (for example, is postmodernism good or bad) towards historical and dialectical analysis (why postmodernism now). The product of such a shift is perhaps most dramatically seen in Jameson's essay 'Reification and Utopia in Mass Culture' (1979). Like *The Political Unconscious*, the essay begins with the need for a 'genuinely historical and dialectical approach', in this case to the opposition between high culture and mass culture. In a reading of theories of mass culture generally and *Jaws* and *The Godfather* I and II specifically, Jameson shows how the high culture/mass culture divide simply represents two sides of the same phenomenon, namely the 'fission of aesthetic production under capitalism' (1979, 14). If high modernist art attempts to resist the commodification of culture in its development of a new language and a new aesthetic, it does so in reaction to the very same processes – capitalist commodification and reification – that produce mass culture. As such, high culture and mass culture are seen to exist in a relationship of structural dependency rather than oppositional independence. This dia-lectical overturning significantly challenges the classic Frankfurt School reading of the 'culture industry' in which traditional high art is valorized over and against the manip-ulative designs of a denigrated mass culture. Instead, both modernism and mass culture are shown to be equally dissociated from group praxis: the former through its very resistance to commodification and its subsequent creation of aesthetic enclaves, and the latter through its absorption into the commodity form.

The exposure of this surprising parallel between modernism and mass culture is but one move, however, in the final dialectical turn of the argument. In his readings of *Jaws* and *The Godfather* I and II, Jameson argues (and this is signature Jameson) that the new model of manipulation he is putting forward contains nothing less than the utopian: 'the hypothesis is that the words of mass culture cannot be ideological without at one and the same time being implicitly or explicitly utopian as well: they cannot manipulate unless they offer some genuine shred of content as a fantasy bribe to the public about to be so manipulated' (Jameson 1979, 29). In other words, these films 'work' only in so far as they tap into deep fantasies about how we wish to live and what sort of social life we want. The simple rejection of mass culture à la the Frankfurt School misses this important move in its emphasis on an evaluative critical stance and therefore too easily dismisses mass culture as mere manipulation. Significantly, the 'content' that is lost is a vision of collectivity, of a desire for a collective form of social life not possible structurally under capitalism (imaged in *The Godfather*, for instance, in the form of the family). This dual move captures Jameson's hermeneutic, or rather 'double hermeneutic' (Kellner 1989, 13): ideological critique coupled with utopian hope, itself a coupling of traditional marxian ideological analysis (Marx et al.) with the utopian marxism of theorists such as Herbert Marcuse and Ernst Bloch.

The need to historicize and the dialectical form through which Jameson's historicism operates marks the nature of his contributions to classical as well as more contemporary marxist and non-marxist thought. On the one hand, as he claims in *The Political Unconscious* (as well as in 'Marxism and Historicism' and the introduction to *The Ideologies of Theory*, vol. 2) marxism is *the* theory of history and thus subsumes all other forms of interpretation (1981, 10, 47; 1979, 149–50, 172–7; Kellner 1989, 14). It is the 'untranscendable horizon', the master narrative that doesn't simply add to other interpretive frameworks but rather (much like the *Aufhebung* of Hegelian dialectics) cancels and preserves them, contains and transcends them. The act of subsumption defines Jameson's method of theoretical incorporation. *The Political Unconscious*, in particular, represents a meeting of marxism and the new continental theoretical work of the 1970s, especially poststructuralism, psychoanalytic criticism and semiotics as well as Althusserian marxism.

Much of the work of continental theorists – Derrida, Foucault, Baudrillard, Deleuze and Guattari, Lyotard, Kristeva and Althusser – share in what Jameson refers to as a Nietzschean and anti-interpretive current: a critique of the hermeneutic act itself as totalizing, reductionist and authoritarian. Against these readings, the premise of *The Political Unconscious* – and one that incorporates these criticisms – is that such a critique is misplaced. The problem isn't interpretation in and of itself but the adequacy of previous hermeneutical models. What is needed and what *The Political Unconscious* as a project offers, then, is a new 'immanent or anti-transcendent hermeneutical model' (1981, 23).

Althusser's model of structural causality provides the framework for a new method of interpretation in which the relationship among different levels within the social system is conceived not in terms of expressive causality (as in Althusser's reading of Hegel) but of semi-autonomy. That is, rather than resting on a notion of expressive identity, in which each part of the system expresses the essence of the whole and thereby exists in a transparent relation to the whole, the notion of various social levels as semi-autonomous allows for the possibility of differentiation among individual parts of the whole – and thus for a more complex and heterogeneous understanding of how the social system functions. Unlike Althusser, however, Jameson conceives of this model of structural causality not as a break with hermeneutics or the dialectical tradition of marxism but as a modification of them. Jameson thus finally situates Althusser (along with the other poststructuralists and theorists he considers) through a 'radical historicizing of their mental operations, such that not only the content of the analysis, but the very method itself, along with the analyst, then comes to be reckoned into the "text" or phenomenon to be explained' (1981, 47). In short, Jameson places them within a dialectical framework, thereby aiming to retain their insights and simultaneously overcome their limits. In the case of Althusser, the result is the development of a hermeneutic derived from the very concept of structural causality, a hermeneutic that accounts both for the totality and for its 'absence'. In the process, Althusser's conception of history as an absent cause is transcoded into a notion of totality: 'Totality is not available for representation, any more than it is accessible in the form of some ultimate truth (or moment of Absolute Spirit)' (1981, 55).

But what is available is narrative itself, which becomes the mode through which a political unconscious works and, in turn, defines the task of the critic: to unmask narratives as socially symbolic acts. Hence the primacy of narrative for Jameson: not only is it the means through which we live history but the means through which history lives. In other words, for Jameson, there is no narrative that is not political. The proper and only critical stance, then, is to apprehend history through its effects, namely in the form of texts or cultural artefacts. The body of *The Political Unconscious* takes up this task by looking at various generic forms (magical narratives, realism and romance) and authors (Balzac, Gissing, Conrad) that progressively mark the increasing commodification of everyday life and of the subject under capitalism.

A certain urgency drives this project given our current historical moment. Just as Jameson comes to terms with contemporary theory, older classical models of marxist criticism (primarily from the 1930s) demand revitalizing because they are unable to account for the complex mediations between cultural artefacts and the socio-economic system. In place of the older base/superstructure formulation (a 'vulgar Marxism'), Jameson turns to a Hegelian marxism for a theory of mediation adequate to the new conditions of monopoly capitalism and its subsequent mutation into late capitalism. As he states in *Marxism and Form*, it is in the context of this historical moment 'that the great themes of Hegel's philosophy – the relationship of part to whole, the opposition between concrete and abstract, the concept of totality, the dialectic of appearance and essence, the interaction between subject and object – are once again the order of the day' (1971, xviii–xix).

In *Marxism and Form*, as well as elsewhere, Georg Lukács and the Frankfurt School provide the prime material for this rethinking. *Marxism and Form* comprises a comprehensive treatment of some of the major figures of western marxism with chapters on Adorno, Benjamin, Bloch, Lukács and Sartre, respectively, and a final chapter entitled 'Towards Dialectical Criticism'. Above all, Lukács's theory of reification underwrites Jameson's approach both to the problems of contemporary capitalist society and to the means toward a solution. Published in 1923, Lukács's *History and Class Consciousness* brought new attention to an aspect of Marx's analysis in *Capital* long neglected, the problem of reification. Lukács develops Marx's ideas about commodity fetishism or reification, arguing that commodity fetishism is a problem specific to the age of modern capitalism (Bottomore 1983, 412). Moreover, he is concerned to show how the 'essence of commodity structure' – so pointedly summed up by Marx as the transformation of the relations between people into the mere relations between things – transforms the 'subject' of the commodity world as much as its objects. So that not only does a qualitative change occur in the world of commodities as a market economy comes to dominate our 'outer life', but this same process penetrates our 'inner life': 'Just as the capitalist system continuously produces and reproduces itself economically on higher levels, the structure of reification progressively sinks more deeply, more fatefully and more definitively into the consciousness of man' (Lukács 1971, 93). For Jameson this translates into an analysis of contemporary capitalism where the reifying logic of capital is precisely that which blocks our ability to see it as a total, now fully global, system. The task of criticism is thus to draw out the very kinds of connections that capital logic denies; to overcome what Max Weber characterized as the process of rationalization (the division of both mental and manual labour, the specialization of skills and the reduction of all social processes to a rational system of calculation) and Lukács argues 'leads to the destruction of every image of the whole' (1971, 103).

For Jameson the concept of 'cognitive mapping' defines this necessary critical function. It is an attempt to map the new space of the postmodern, to conceive the coordinates of the social structure and the totality of class relations on a global scale (1988a, 353). Its spatializing metaphor of the map is meant to capture the new organization of space under late capitalism: the disorientation of saturated space in which any sort of distance itself is suppressed. Central to this characterization of our present social structure is its differentiation from previous modes of production. Each of the three historical stages of capitalism, that is, has generated a space unique to it. Under classical or market capitalism, that space was a grid (and coincided aesthetically with realism); under monopoly capitalism it is best defined as a growing gap between lived experience and structure, a distance defined in terms of irony, and a contradiction which produces, according to Jameson, specific problems of figuration or representation which the various modernisms have at their centre. Within the new complexities of postmodern space and its disorienting effects this problem of figuration becomes especially acute. How to even grasp the system as a whole when the organization of its parts functions to deny anything larger than the fragment and its cognitive effects – of disorientation and fragmentation – prevent any sense of perspectival distance or 'point of view'?

And yet, to cede to this dilemma, to celebrate the fragmentary and the multiplicitous at the expense of the whole, is essentially to abandon a socialist politics altogether. The aesthetic becomes the political and vice versa as culture (the saturated space of the postmodern) gains a certain primacy over economics or politics. The mapping of the cultural logic of late capitalism therefore takes on a political immediacy: 'the incapacity to map socially is as crippling to political experience as the analogous incapacity to map spatially is for urban experience. It follows that an aesthetic of cognitive mapping in this sense is an integral part of any socialist political project' (1988a, 353) – and a project, moreover, that is still yet to be conceived. Cognitive mapping thus attempts, finally, to 'produce the concept of something we cannot imagine' (1988a, 347).

In essence, then, cognitive mapping functions as Jameson's version of what a new realism adequate to the demands and logic of consumer culture would look like, but importantly one that is not 'exactly mimetic in that older sense' given its simultaneously local, national and international coordinates (1991, 51). As such, it is from Lukács' theory of reification rather than his theories of realism that Jameson draws his own analysis of realism. (It is important to note that Jameson distances himself from Lukács' negative pronouncements on modernism, identifying himself much more with Brecht than Lukács when it comes to the question of innovative modernist forms or the creation of new forms of (critical) realism other than classical nineteenth-century realism.) Indeed, as Jameson himself clarifies, ' "cognitive mapping" was in reality nothing but a code word for "class consciousness" . . .: only it proposed the need for class consciousness of a new and hitherto undreamed of kind, while it also inflected the account in the direction of that new spatiality implicit in the postmodern' (Kellner 1989, 387).

The exploration of the new spatiality of postmodernism and its reorganization of politics finds its fullest articulation in Jameson's full-length study *Postmodernism, or, The Cultural Logic of Late Capitalism* (1991), a collection of essays taking its title from the seminal 1984 essay on postmodernism. The same dictum that drives Jameson's earlier work forms the basis of this much later work where the postmodern as a concept is meant to capture the very historicity of historical thinking itself: 'It is safest to grasp the concept of the postmodern as an attempt to think the present historically in an age that has forgotten how to think historically in the first place' (xi). Here Jameson extends his earlier analyses across a wide spectrum of the arts: the visual arts, architecture, video and film. Certainly, the most cited and exemplary of his readings is his analysis of the Bonaventure Hotel in Los Angeles. In his description of its spatial disorientation, of the ways in which it seems designed to cause confusion and an utter inability on the individual's part to map its space, Jameson highlights how both the objects and the subjects of multinational capital are radically altered and transformed from their high modernist counterparts. In contrast to the space of high modernism, the Bonaventure seeks not to differentiate itself from the degraded city fabric around it but rather to replace it altogether. The lack of visible entranceways, the mirroring effects of its glass exterior, and the interior elevators and escalators all conspire to produce a complete hyperspace as a substitute for the city and a totally new built environment that requires the production of new subjects to inhabit it:

'The new architecture ... stands as something like an imperative to grow new organs, to expand our sensorium and our body to some new, yet unimaginable, perhaps ultimately impossible, dimensions' (39). As Jameson argues throughout *Postmodernism, or, The Cultural Logic of Late Capitalism*, these radical changes are not merely stylistic or formal (as many earlier accounts of postmodernism would have it) but structural, linked directly to the social and to the changes in economic production identified by Ernest Mandel in his analysis of contemporary capitalism, *Late Capitalism*. The difficulty and the consequent need to map on a spatial scale figures the need to map on a social scale.

The most controversial of Jameson's work involves his extension of these concerns to so-called third-world literature and culture. Situated as a 'pendant' to the postmodernism essay in its attention to the cognitive aesthetics of third-world literature, his essay 'Third-world Literature in the Era of Multinational Capitalism' provocatively claims that all third-world texts are to be read as national allegories. In the most well-known critique, Aijaz Ahmad (1987) attacks the all-encompassing 'all' in this claim and Jameson's attempt to establish a situation of radical difference between the first and third world. However, the definitiveness of this statement at once draws attention to the standpoint of the dominated in its radically different relationship to multinational capital as well as emphasizes the relative impoverishment of first-world culture. The perspective of the dominated (culled from a combination of Hegel's master–slave dialectic and Lukács' epistemology in *History and Class Consciousness*) reveals certain forms of experience and collectivity no longer available to the first world. Specifically, Jameson finds in representative readings of the Chinese writer Lu Xun and the Senegalese novelist and film-maker Ousmane Sembene wholly different relations between the subjective and the public or political: 'Third-world texts, even those which are seemingly private and invested with a properly libidinal dynamic – necessarily project a political dimension in the form of national allegory: *the story of the private individual destiny is always an allegory of the embattled situation of the public third-world culture and society*' (1991, 69). In a reversal of first-world/third-world relations, Jameson concludes that the first world has much to learn from the third world and its texts – about the reified nature of first-world public and private life, about the libidinal and the political, and about the role of the intellectual and the role of the humanities more broadly in American education. In short, they offer access to a notion of 'cultural revolution' and a vision of community interdependence that has all but disappeared in the first world. In contrast to critiques such as that of Ahmad, then, Jameson's position on third-world culture serves not to subsume everything within a first world perspective (Ahmad accuses Jameson of a form of Orientalism) but to highlight the very processes of first-world cultural imperialism and its 'crippling' effects for the 'masters' or 'we Americans' (1991, 85).

Ahmad's response has its parallel in criticisms of Jameson that equate his emphasis on totality with totalitarianism. In this line of reasoning, the desire to create a totalizing system is described as violent or oppressive in its attempt to incorporate everything. Such a view, when not simply a false equation of two obviously different terms (totality and totalitarianism), mistakes a symptom for a cause: the dissatisfaction with the concept of totality is itself a marker for the increasing difficulties of cognitively mapping contemporary society, a project that, as Jameson underscores, 'stands or falls with the conception of some (unrepresentable, imaginary) social global totality' (Jameson 1988b, 356).

More substantive responses to Fredric Jameson's work often tend paradoxically to centre on his style. Admittedly, Jameson's prose is difficult. It assumes a wide and diverse body of knowledge, from philosophy, to critical theory, semiotics, psychoanalysis, European modernism and popular culture. For anyone who has thought about teaching Jameson to undergraduates, the problem is clear enough. Each text presupposes knowledge of so many other texts that it seems virtually impossible to find a point from which to begin. The breadth of Jameson's references is matched by the sheer bravado (at times) of his dialectical style of writing. In the tradition of the Frankfurt School, his prose is meant to be as difficult as the thought it represents, and because the very processes of dialectical thought are inimical to our reified way of thinking under capitalism, Jameson's style is too. In his own defence, Jameson asks: 'Why should there be any reason to feel that these problems [of culture and aesthetics] are less complex than those of bio-chemistry?' (Jameson 1982, 88).

Responses to Jameson's style range from unqualified admiration of its 'splendour' to serious scepticism about its utility for a properly political or revolutionary criticism. On the positive extreme, Perry Anderson sees in it the perfect embodiment of the multiple texts and multiplicitous signs which it engages, of the melding of form and content (Anderson 1998, 71–2). Style meets content as Anderson glowingly assesses Jameson's contribution to the postmodernism debate and claims that he does what no other theorist of the postmodern does – anchors the aesthetic forms or style of postmodernism in the economic and political alterations of late capitalism. In stark contrast, Terry Eagleton identifies Jameson's style as finally detrimental to an engaged socialist or marxist politics. As he sees it, the very generosity and appropriative nature of Jameson's thought marks the limits of its political bite. Jameson becomes for Eagleton an 'unrepentant *bricoleur*' who too easily absorbs others' ideas and 'leaves everything as it was' (Eagleton 1986, 71). Instead of formulating a sharp relationship between the mystifications of late capitalism or ideology more generally and a practical politics, Jameson, in Eagleton's view, prioritises theory (or ideological critique) over practice. In this sense, his distance from Lukács' *History and Class Consciousness* is marked: 'the dispelling of reification which for that work was an indispensable concomitant and effect of class struggle has become, in Jameson, its theoretical prolegomenon' (Eagleton 1986, 75).

At issue finally is the larger question of institutional marxism and its relationship to the driving force of marxism: class struggle and the overthrow of capitalism. Does Jameson's work suffer from the same limits, for instance, as those of western marxism? If western marxism represents a move away from class struggle and *praxis* towards theory and philosophy, reflective of the political realities post-1968, can the same be said for Jameson's project? According to Perry Anderson, whose *Considerations of Western Marxism* makes this very case about western marxism, the answer is, interestingly, no. He argues that Jameson exceeds the limits of this tradition and provides its 'most complete consummation' by grounding his account of postmodernism in the economic development of late capitalism. Whereas the aesthetic in the western marxist tradition functioned as 'involuntary consolation for impasses of the political and economic' in Jameson no such consolatory function is at work (Anderson 1998, 72). Rather the penetration of culture by capital and capital by culture bespeaks a different political reality and hence the necessity of a different political strategy. The very pervasiveness of 'the cultural' that Jameson analyses in terms of the logic of late capitalism directly confronts the conditions of contemporary life rather than evading them. As a result, Anderson locates Jameson's contribution as central to a properly political intervention into the space of postmodernism: 'So Jameson's resumption of [the] heritage [of western marxism] could yield a much more central and political description of the conditions of contemporary life than the precedents it drew on' (Anderson 1992, 73).

Perhaps, given the conditional nature of Anderson's response, it is simply too soon for any final reckoning of Jameson's theoretical and political contributions. Or, rather, the very provisional nature of such an assessment underscores the necessarily mediated relationship between the theoretical and the political that defines the marxist tradition and Jameson's work within it. In the best tradition of institutional marxism, Jameson harbours no illusions that academic literary marxist criticism is going to topple the capitalist system on its own. At the same time, his work derives its political immediacy from the recognition that in order to even begin to challenge the system we have to first understand how it functions. As with the classical marxist formulation, such theory will only be fully realized when it is put into practice. In the meantime, as Jameson's collection of texts cautions and simultaneously inspires, there is much groundwork yet to be done.

Carolyn Lesjak

Further reading and works cited

Ahmad, A. 'Jameson's Rhetoric of Otherness and the "National Allegory"', *Social Text*, 17, 1987.

Althusser, L. *Lenin and Philosophy, and Other Essays.* London, 1971.

Anderson, P. *The Origins of Postmodernity.* London, 1998.

Bottomore, T. (ed.) *A Dictionary of Marxist Thought.* Cambridge, MA, 1983.

Burnham, C. *The Jamesonian Unconscious.* Durham, NC, 1995.

Eagleton, T. *Against the Grain.* London, 1986.

Hardt, M. and Weeks, K. (eds) *The Jameson Reader.* Oxford, 2000.

Homer, S. *Fredric Jameson.* New York, 1998.

Jameson, F. *Marxism and Form.* Princeton, NJ, 1971.

—. *The Political Unconscious.* Ithaca, NY, 1981.

—. 'Interview' with L. Green, J. Culler and R. Klein. *diacritics*, 12, 3, 1982.

—. 'Third-World Literature in the Era of Multinational Capitalism', *Social Text*, 15, Fall 1986.

—. 'Cognitive Mapping', in *Marxism and the Interpretation of Culture*, ed. D. Kellner. Urbana, IL, 1988a.

—. *The Ideologies of Theory.* Minneapolis, MN, 1988b.

—. 'Afterword: Marxism and Postmodernism', in *Postmodernism/Jameson/Critique*, ed. D. Kellner. Washington, 1989.

—. *Signatures of the Visible.* New York, 1990.

—. *Postmodernism, or, The Cultural Logic of Late Capitalism.* Durham, NC, 1991.

—. *The Geopolitical Aesthetic.* Bloomington, IN, 1992.

—. 'Actually Existing Marxism', in *Marxism Beyond Marxism*, eds S. Makdisi, C. Casarino and R. E. Karl. New York, 1996.

—. *Brecht and Method.* London, 1998.

Jay, M. *Marxism and Totality.* Berkeley, CA, 1984.

Kellner, D. (ed.) *Postmodernism/Jameson/Critique.* Washington, DC, 1989.

LaCapra, D. *Rethinking Intellectual History: Texts, Contexts, Language.* Ithaca, NY, 1983.

Lukács, G. *History and Class Consciousness.* Cambridge, 1971.

Edward W. Said (1935–)

Edward W. Said has not formulated a single, coherent theoretical model of his own – nor has he founded a theoretical school or movement. But he has sketched out a number of important directions for cross-cultural analysis, as well as a unique set of positions within postcolonialist criticism. Said is best known for his work of the 1980s and 1990s, which has established him as a major cultural/political analyst of imperialism – and, more particularly, as a spokesperson for Palestinian rights. Theorizing the cultural implications of power differentials between East and West and commenting on the Middle East situation have brought Said a public stature that is virtually unique among humanistic intellectuals in the US. While his work on imperialism has not had a measurable impact on public policy or discourse, it has had an enormous influence on a number of academic disciplines, including literary theory, Middle East studies, political science, history and anthropology.

Though he has achieved his high public and academic profile primarily as a post-colonialist critic, Said's career, launched in 1966 with the publication of *Joseph Conrad and the Fiction of Autobiography*, has evolved over four decades through a number of theoretical preoccupations. He has moved away from an early grounding in phenomenology and existentialism, through an extremely productive exploration of poststructuralism, and into the profound theoretical scepticism – accompanied by proposals for alternative models of cultural interpretation – that has characterized his more recent postcolonialist work. Appreciating Said's postcolonialist positions, as well as the range of theoretical contributions he has made over the course of his long career, requires an understanding of the persistent problems that have shaped the various stages of his critical development.

Throughout his career, Said has been concerned with the agency of the intellectual, and with his ability to direct and control intellectual progress. At the same time, though, Said has been scrupulously attentive to the power of culture as a limit on intellectual invention. These dual concerns – which, to be sure, characterize much twentieth-century thought – have compelled Said to search for interpretive paradigms adequate to what he sees as the dialectical relationship between such opposing pressures. Said's attempt to develop a dialectical theory of cultural production draws together a number of subsidiary themes in his work: the role of development or transformation within individual texts, over the course of careers or within large cultural movements; the viability of rational forms of knowledge that respect epistemological discontinuities and ruptures; and the complicity of culture with political power. The opposing pressures that have long preoccupied Said – at the most general level: intellectual agency and cultural constraint – also inhabit the very form of his writing. That is to say, Said's writing is often idiosyncratic in its choice of subject and method; but it remains systematically, respectfully focused on canonical writers and dominant intellectual movements. It is both encyclopaedic and oppositional, both learned and iconoclastic. Energized by this unstable dynamism, his writing can appear to be more unclassifiable than that of many other contemporary theorists. It can also seem inherently resistant to discipleship or filiation.

Said's first book extracts a dialectical model for intellectuals and culture from the work of Joseph Conrad, which Said explores as a pre-figuration of phenomenological and existential philosophies. Said claims that Conrad was unable to resolve the tension between intellectual self-consciousness and the agonistic conditions of social existence by positing some authentic identity for the writer; instead, Conrad expresses this tension through dramatic conflicts that perform, without resolving, his own dilemma as an intellectual. Anticipating the emphasis on cross-cultural understanding that marks his later work, Said argues that – unlike many other writers of his time – Conrad welcomed political developments after the First World War, seeing them as a sign that nations had risen to a self-conscious individuality that could, at the same time, still accommodate pan-European cooperation. Conrad's imagined resolution of tensions on an international scale parallel, according to Said, the tensions he perceived between the individual thinker and culture as a whole. At this stage of his career, Said celebrates Conrad's dualistic formulations and, significantly, does not emphasize the link between Conrad's political optimism and his enthusiasm for colonialism – a conjunction that lies at the heart of Said's later work on Conrad, and on other western novelists as well.

In *Beginnings* (1975), Said ambitiously expands his critical horizons to include Western literature over the last two centuries, while he continues to meditate on the possibility of a theoretical 'middle path' between subject-oriented humanism and modernist nightmares of cultural hegemony. *Beginnings* marks a key phase of Said's development in the mid to late–1970s, in which he employs while contesting poststructuralist theory – in particular, Michel Foucault's theories of power – in order to think through problems of cultural production. Said elides the concept of beginning with intentionality, and although he understands intentionality in impersonal terms – as the rules of inclusiveness or pertinence which make the act of beginning a somewhat arbitrary and retrospective one – he understands beginning intentions as a means of reconciling individual agency with the pressures of cultural systems. *Beginnings* risks positing an ahistorical and anti-materialist model of interpretation, by containing the history of beginnings within an opposition of classic to modernist conceptions of intentionality in western writing. Yet by recognizing the persistent emphasis that conflicting philosophies of cultural production have placed on the act of beginning, Said contests the poststructuralist notion that such acts merely disguise 'the perpetual trap of forced continuity' (1975, 43), arguing that they are, in fact, newly generative. Despite late-twentieth-century preoccupations with the hegemony of paradigms and epistemes, then, Said argues that the notion of beginning intention cannot be eradicated from theoretical models, and needs to be theorized comprehensively. Said finds fictions of beginning in poststructuralism, for example, particularly in Foucault's postnarrative methods of knowledge. Bravely celebrating the humanism he finds latent in Foucault's references to effective, if undeniable, pressures for epistemic disruption, Said attempts to undermine from within poststructuralism's goal of separating the construction of knowledge from the individual subject. Nevertheless, Said is very critical – in *Beginnings* and in his other writings from this period – of poststructuralism's collapsing of agency into signification. He is particularly harsh on the 'linguacentricity' (1975, 336) of Derrida, both for failing to account for change and for denying that the discontinuous evolution of knowledge can ever be understood as progressive. Ultimately, Said takes his own preferred model of beginning from Giambattista Vico, the eighteenth-century Italian philosopher who remains a seminal force in much of Said's later work. In Said's view, Vico conceives knowledge as deeply embedded in textual systems, at the same time that he affirms the potency and the unpredictability of intellectual disruption. Significantly, though, Said's dialectical model of beginning largely ignores the role of state power, and its presence within both culture and self-consciousness – an issue that becomes the central concern of his work from the late 1970s on.

Orientalism (1978) is Said's first direct analysis of the relationship between politics and culture, and this book marks a stage in Said's career in which his earlier belief in intellectual agency is sometimes swamped by a monolithic, quasi-Foucauldian conception of power. For the first time in his career, Said formulates a deterministic theory of cultural hegemony, one that continues to appear – though often in more nuanced forms – throughout his later work on imperialism. Starting with Orientalism, the tensions between Said's theories of cultural hegemony and his commitments to intellectual oppositionality break free of his earlier, synthetic models and generate dramatic oscillations – contradictions, some critics would say – within or across Said's own texts. In Orientalism, Said argues that the western discourse of Orientalism – as well as discourses of colonialism more generally – determine the thinking of scholars who set out, whatever their conscious intentions, to acquire 'objective' knowledge about Eastern cultures. Implicitly sceptical of intentionality, Orientalism describes an academic system of knowledge that is static, and that ensnares its adherents in grand misapprehensions. Said's central thesis about Orientalist discourse is that its incapacity for development stems from its founding myth: that Eastern culture is itself a culture of arrested development. He claims that the concept of 'the Orient' is purely a western invention, and that Orientalist discourse conflates knowledge with power in the absence of any real object of such knowledge. Said does historicize developing strategies within Orientalist discourse, but he argues that these strategies did not shift relationships of power or challenge them; rather, they merely enabled the conversion of Orientalism from a contemplative discourse into an administrative and political one. Nevertheless, as James Clifford has pointed out, Said also departs from Foucauldian models of power and contradicts himself by suggesting rather persistently that there is a real Orient which has been distorted and denied the ability to speak (Clifford 1988, 260). Most importantly, though, in Orientalism Said argues for the first time that the fact of political domination is dependent on a legitimating cultural discourse – a cultural reductionism that he will develop much more extensively fifteen years later in Culture and Imperialism (1993).

Orientalism virtually created the academic subdiscipline of colonial discourse analysis. Predictably, it has been vigorously and sometimes abusively attacked by Islamic and Arabist specialists, but it has been well-received by specialists in related fields. It has been ambivalently critiqued by postcolonialist theorists, particularly by those who, like Benita Parry, admire Said's anti-Orientalist stance generally, but find that its totalizing approach suppresses native political voices and makes Said 'indifferent to textual gaps, indeterminacies and contradictions' (Parry 1992, 26) in the dominant discourse as well. Some have argued that Said overestimates the degree to which western scholars have eroticized the Orient (see Spanos 1996). Feminists have attacked him for overlooking questions of gender. He has also been faulted for ignoring the interrelated histories of victimization, particularly in regard to anti-Semitism. In a number of later essays, but particularly in 'Orientalism, an Afterword' (1995), Said strenuously debates these charges – in particular, denying his alleged anti-westernism, his alleged totalizing of the West, and his alleged belief in the Orient as a stable referent – though these criticisms continue to dog his work. Even those who praise Said for his political position and for his scholarship continue to complain that he has presented a history of Orientalism solely from the perspective of the West (though this critique must be seriously qualified in light of Said's work in the 1990s on Arab intellectuals).

Orientalism may be bitingly clear about the insidious aspects of Orientalism, but it largely ignores the very questions about intellectual subversion and oppositionality that dominated Said's first two books and that return to become central aspects of his later work. The dramatic imbalance of Said's thought during this phase of his career is reflected in two books written at roughly the same time which form a kind of trilogy with *Orientalism* – *The Question of Palestine* (1979) and *Covering Islam* (1981). The very existence of these two books seems a refutation of Said's fatalism, in *Orientalism*, about the monolithic relationship of knowledge and power. In *The Question of Palestine*, Said himself takes up the role of oppositional intellectual, as an anti-Orientalist. Said's twin goals are, first, to provide media-misinformed Americans with a general history of the Palestinians, and, second, to defend Palestinian political aspirations in the teeth of Orientalist distortions. In *Covering Islam*, Said shows how Orientalist discourse has contaminated American media depictions of the Arab world. Besides documenting the gross generalizations and cultural clichés that characterize western representations of the Arab world, Said demonstrates how these distortions are embedded in assumptions about American political entitlement – the self-serving belief that world events can and should be reduced to a calculus of American interests. Both these books indict cultural hegemony, while also enacting its subversion by means of historical and political realities – as Said views them – that contradict the dominant discourse.

In the last two books of the Orientalist trilogy, then – both of which eschew the rhetoric of theory and target a mainstream, non-academic readership – Said contradicts the theoretical foundations of *Orientalism* by vigorously calling for what, at the end of *Covering Islam*, he terms 'antithetical knowledge' (1921, 167). Translating his complex thought on the relationship of power and knowledge into ordinary language, he claims that 'any good reader' can go 'a reasonable distance toward overcoming the limitations of orthodox views' (167), and that 'most knowledge about human society is, I think, finally accessible to common sense' (170). This position represents a bold, if unintegrated, return to traditional humanistic values that Said's later work continues to affirm – but in highly qualified ways.

The World, the Text, and the Critic (1983) is an important collection of Said's essays, written between 1968 and 1983, all of which in some way attempt to refine his ideas about the possibilities for antithetical knowledge. These essays revolve around a series of interconnected ideas that could be said to characterize all of Said's major work after his Orientalist trilogy: a strong condemnation of contemporary criticism's obsession with textuality; an even stronger condemnation of what he sees as the over-specialized and professionalized discipline of literary studies; a call for the integration of cultural and political analysis; a systematic analysis of the cultural foundations of imperialism; and an affirmation of alienation, as the necessary starting point for intellectual labour. The importance of the last point cannot be overstated. In his later work, whenever Said affirms the power of the individual intellectual, he discards the humanistic rhetoric that marks early stages of his career by insisting that the awareness of culture as a system of exclusions must ground a genuinely critical consciousness. Yet in Said's later work, that kind of consciousness is never viewed as self-authorizing. Rather, it always negotiates a complex set of relationships between inherited and invented cultural traditions. Said thus reformulates the dialectical models of his early work on Conrad, and in *Beginnings*, by conceiving the intellectual as a kind of cultural bricoleur. Recombining the ideas of selected writers and cultural traditions into an idiosyncratic bulwark against determinative order, the intellectual appropriates and transforms rather than initiating ideas outside of the cultural context – a methodological description that applies to many of Said's own essays on writers he admires, from Vico to Ghassan Kanafani. In 'Secular Criticism', Said distinguishes between inherited order, or what he calls 'filiation', and invented order, or 'affiliation'. In Said's complicated view of these concepts, filiation is said inevitably to produce affiliations, though the latter process can either reproduce filiation or depart radically from it. Imagining the field of culture as a plural and discontinuous repertoire of models for writing and thinking allows Said, in this phase of his career, to rework his earlier, quasi-existential attitudes toward intellectual work within a more complex panorama of strategies for cultural production.

The World, the Text, and the Critic is also a celebration of the essay form. Said is, perhaps quintessentially, a writer of essays. In 'Secular Criticism', he claims that the essay is the privileged form for antithetical thought. Reflecting on his own fundamental dilemma as a critic, Said claims that the book's demands for coherence and totality restrict the writer, while the essay has more affinities with the speculative and the sceptical. The bulk of Said's recent work has come in the form of essays, which have been collected in numerous anthologies, and which have ranged across a great many cultural and political topics – from opera to Arabic fiction to the Balkans. The style of multi-layered thought that his essays, taken as a whole, seem to develop has recently enabled Said to take a more fluid methodological approach in his major projects as well.

The single most important example of this fluid style is *Culture and Imperialism* (1993). On one level, Said's critique of imperialism, and the cultural work that sustains it, seems to return to the totalizing approach of *Orientalism*. Moving beyond his earlier analyses of Orientalist discourse, Said seeks in this book to explore the general relationship between culture and empire. He rectifies one flaw cited by critics of *Orientalism* by tracing the movements of resistance among colonized peoples, rather than describing them simply as the passive recipients of the imperial gaze. Nevertheless, in *Culture and Imperialism*, Said tends to see the formation of both dominant and resistant cultures in a single source: metropolitan self-legitimation. More disturbing, for some of Said's critics, he seems completely to conflate western culture and imperialism, as he argues that culture sustained, legitimated and normalized the imperial project. The British novel comes in for particularly harsh criticism, since Said regards it as the cultural form most responsible for the justification of imperial conquest – one of the realistic novel's 'principle purposes' was to 'almost unnoticeably [sustain] the society's consent in overseas expansion' (12). While he is 'not trying to say that the novel "caused" imperialism', Said does assert that the novel and imperialism 'are unthinkable without each other' (70–1). Said is 'struck by how inexorably integrative' (6) imperial culture was – and, to some extent, still is, since he argues that the western vision of the world is still haunted by imperialism.

This unforgiving, all-encompassing critique has many productive consequences. It allows Said to expose the complicity of contemporary culture with empire in representations of the New World Order and the End of History. It allows him to show how late-nineteenth-century novels of empire were structurally congruent with novels written a century earlier, and to demonstrate how the linkage of domestic and imperial space in the novel grounds British morality in concepts of expansionism. Not just a simple indictment of imperialism, *Culture and Imperialism* provides a thorough diagnosis of imperialist ideology, including its belief in ontological differences between East and West, its codification of ethnological differences, its great creative power and its tendency to construct European subjective autonomy through the subjugation of native peoples.

Oddly incongruent with this central project of *Culture and Imperialism*, however, is Said's celebration of what he terms 'contrapuntal reading' (1993, 66) – a form of analysis he has championed increasingly in the 1990s. Derived in part from his recent studies of music, 'contrapuntal reading', in the context of an analysis of imperialism, means fully taking into account the relationships between dominant and resistant discourses. It also means discovering how complex, hybrid and impure any single text might be – including canonical British novels. Significantly, *Culture and Imperialism* includes a long, useful account of previously neglected colonial responses to the West, and an analysis of the structures of such resistance – an attentiveness to the non-European intellectual that has become central to Said's work since the late-1980s. Said does not reconcile his practice of 'contrapuntal reading' with his uncompromising condemnation of western culture; rather, he weaves these two themes of his work – the totalizing critique of western culture, and his own discovery and appropriation of cultural hybridity – in an elaborate textual score that is finally, in some respects, resistant to theoretical resolution. 'Contrapuntal reading' allows Said to entertain seemingly conflictual approaches to particular issues – for example, he alternates between recognizing the necessity of a homogeneous native identity, including a nationalist one, and the inevitable hybridity of postcolonial identity – a double-voiced reading of postcolonial subjectivity that has brought him into conflict with many postcolonialist critics, notably Homi Bhabha (Bhabha 1983, 200–2). Much of Said's most recent writing has explored, in effect, the dialogics of cross-cultural reading. His lifelong preoccupation with the dialectic of agency and culture has thus taken a productive new form in the shape of a mobile practice of writing and interpretation. Through 'contrapuntal reading', he has been able to discuss disparate texts within multiple social and circum- stantial contexts, and, therefore, to navigate between deterministic and agential perspec- tives. This method drives Said's recent essays on Arabic intellectuals, but it also fuels his essays on Middle East politics, many of which have been collected in *Peace and Its Discontents* (1996) and *The Politics of Dispossession* (1994b).

In the later stages of his career, then, Said recognizes that the tensions between agency and culture that underlie his thought are best handled methodologically, not as a developmental logic but as an 'exfoliating structure of variations' (Buttigieg and Bové 1993, 3). Embracing this style has given Said a unique method, which proceeds by layering analytical projects and positions, building cumulative informational resources and pa- tiently exploring a variety of contextual fields. Said has not attempted to reconcile his method of 'contrapuntal reading' with normative theorizing; instead, he has recently come to identify theoretical enterprises entirely with the privileged conjunction of knowledge and power. Predictably, perhaps, 'contrapuntal reading' has been influential on a wide range of oppositional critics, not all of whom would recognize each other as allies: those who support particular nationalisms as well as those who oppose nationalism in general; those engaged in a critique of various 'universalizing' political discourses, and those defending nativist traditions; those interested in the overdetermination of imperial hegemony as well as those interested in the variable complexity of imperialism. What appeals to all these critics about Said's refusal of orthodox theorizing, more than anything else, is that it prevents him from succumbing to theoretical discourses popular in the wake of poststructuralism that leave no room for the assertion of intellectual will. Said's celebration of intellectual affiliation, or worldliness, as a way for the critic to express oppositional power through alliances with particular cultural systems has generated a great deal of new work by cultural critics from many disciplines who are interested in the political efficacy of cross-cultural and interdisciplinary studies.

John Kucich

Further reading and works cited

Aijaz, A. *In Theory: Classes, Nations, Literatures*. London, 1992.
Bhabha, H. K. 'Difference, Discrimination and the Discourse of Colonialism', in *The Politics of Theory*, eds F. Barker et al. Colchester, 1983.
Buttigieg, J. A. and Bové, P. A. 'An Interview with Edward W. Said', *Boundary*, 2, 20, 1993.
Clifford, J. *The Predicament of Culture*. Cambridge, 1988.
Gandhi, L. *Postcolonial Theory*. New York, 1998.
Loomba, A. *Colonialism/Postcolonialism*. London, 1998.
Lowe, L. *Critical Terrains*. Ithaca, NY, 1991.
Parry, B. 'Overlapping Territories and Intertwined Histories', *Edward Said*, ed. M. Sprinker. Oxford, 1992.
Said, E. W. *Joseph Conrad and the Fiction of Autobiography*. Cambridge, MA, 1966.
—. *Beginnings*. New York, 1975.
—. *Orientalism*. New York, 1978.
—. *The Question of Palestine*. New York, 1979.
— ed. *Literature and Society*. Baltimore, MD, 1980.
—. *Covering Islam*. New York, 1981.
—. 'In the Shadow of the West', *The Arabs*, Channel 4 (London), 1982a.
—. 'Opponents, Audiences, Constituencies, and Community'. *Critical Inquiry*, 9, 1982b.
—. *The World, the Text, and the Critic*. Cambridge, MA, 1983.
—. 'An Ideology of Difference'. *Critical Inquiry*, 12, 1 (Autumn 1985a).
—. 'Orientalism Reconsidered', *Cultural Critique*, 1, 1985b.
—. *After the Last Sky*. New York, 1986.
—. *Musical Elaborations*. New York, 1991.
—. *Culture and Imperialism*. New York, 1993.
—. *Representations of the Intellectual*. New York, 1994a.
—. *The Politics of Dispossession*. New York, 1994b.
—. 'Orientalism, an Afterword', *Raritan*, 14, 1995.
—. *Peace and Its Discontents*. New York, 1996.
—. *Out of Place: A Memoir*. New York, 1999.
Spanos, W. V. 'Culture and Colonization: The Imperial Imperatives of the Centred Circle', *Boundary*, 2, 23, 1996.

American Feminisms: Images of Women and Gynocriticism

In her 1981 essay 'Feminist Criticism in the Wilderness', Elaine Showalter identified three common modes of feminist literary theory which she saw as exemplifying different national tendencies:

> English feminist criticism, essentially Marxist, stresses oppression; French feminist criticism, essentially psychoanalytic, stresses repression; American feminist criticism, essentially textual, stresses expression. All, however, have become gynocentric. All are struggling to find a terminology that can rescue the feminine from its stereotypical associations with inferiority. (1986, 249)

Showalter's separation of the categories of feminism was strategic rather than strictly accurate, though her insistence on the gynocentrism (woman-centredness) of literary feminism is the right and necessary first step towards any feminism worth its name. In the years since the essay was published, however, it has become increasingly clear that feminist literary theories evade national and conceptual boundaries, and that it is perfectly possible to be a marxist-feminist who also takes account of the insights of psychoanalysis in order to make some sense of literary expression.

With the benefit of hindsight, however, it might have been truer to say in 1981 that American feminist literary theory tended to be concerned primarily with issues of representation rather than those of textuality. Representation is used here in its widest sense: the representation of women as characters and images by literary texts whether female- or male-authored; the representation of women writers by literary critics; their representation in the institutional canons of literature departments in universities; their existence on or absence from the lists of publishers, both academic and popular. Some of the effort that went into recuperating and rediscovering women writers from past ages was indeed 'textual' in the sense that it required textual scholarship and original research. But the research itself was motivated by the will of liberal feminism to equalize the representation of the sexes – both in texts and in the world – in the institutions that tend to guard cultural value.

The most significant 1960s text for American feminism was by Betty Friedan, entitled *The Feminine Mystique* (1963). It was not a book about literature, drawing rather on the methodologies of sociology and the language of popular journalism (Friedan herself was a magazine writer while she gathered the material for the book). On the other hand, it did both suggest and exemplify one of the routes that literary feminism would take through its investigation into the discrepancies that existed between the idealized representations women found of themselves in popular magazines aimed directly at them and their own lived experience as American housewives. Friedan examined the lives of women whose material lives could scarcely have been more comfortable – they had enough money, nice houses, husbands and children, and all the labour-saving devices their husband's money could buy. She uncovered, however, an undercurrent of dissatisfaction, neurosis and depression within those lives, in which the women themselves felt empty and insignificant. The women of the 1950s and 1960s appeared to her to be less liberated, less ambitious and far less satisfied than their mothers and grandmothers, the generations of women who had achieved suffrage, higher education and a degree of financial independence for themselves. They were less secure and less contented than the women who had lived through those struggles, and appeared to be objects of a backlash against the liberated women of the immediately preceding generations. Often college-educated and with the vote long achieved, these women had somehow been coerced back into the home, into the joint roles of homemaker and mother. The coercion was linked (though exactly how and why is not clear) to the conservative images fed to women by their own consumer culture.

In the final chapter of *The Feminine Mystique*, Friedan suggested that the solution to the problems encountered by such women was to be found in a serious response to educational opportunity. Women must make themselves a life-plan, and educate themselves to be more than 'just' housewives. This would require a change of heart among women themselves, since too frequently they used their years of education and their early experiences of paid employment merely as time waiting for the right man to come along and 'rescue' them from the ignominy of being a spinster-career-woman. It would also require a change in the educational system, away from training women to be mere homemakers, and towards a more intellectually stimulating curriculum. Finally, for the women already caught up in the feminine mystique, it must be made possible for them to return to education, and to combine their learning with their other duties – so Friedan suggests that part-time undergraduate and graduate courses be administratively tailored to the needs of the housewife student.

Friedan has been criticized for the narrow social focus of her book (with its insistent interest only in middle-class white American women), and it is certainly true to say that *The Feminine Mystique* did not address the needs of those women who suffered acute material deprivation, nor those who were further disadvantaged by a racist society because they were not white. Nonetheless, her example did offer important lessons for feminist literary theory and criticism in the years that followed. The housewives who took Friedan's advice and went back to college to gain an arts education in subjects such as literature or history might well have been disappointed by the curriculum they found there and the methodologies that they were to be taught. History had tended to be the study of the lives of 'great men', and English literature had a rigidly exclusive canon, a great tradition containing, as Terry Eagleton has put it, 'two and a half women, counting Emily Brontë as a marginal case' (1996a, 28). Nonetheless, armed in part with Friedan's insight that the representations of women in literary and cultural forms can have real effects on the lives of women beyond those representations, female critics (they did not usually call themselves feminists because of the hostility such a label often produced) began a process of interrogating the canon, seeking not eternal truths and beauties, but rather investigating the truth status (or otherwise) of the images of women that they found therein. The force of what was essentially a content-based criticism was the presupposition of a woman reader in the pursuit of the woman's image, rather than the previous assumption of a male reader as the norm.

Two of the earliest and most important discussions of the image of woman in literature (mostly in male-authored prose fiction) were Mary Ellmann's *Thinking About Women* (1968) and Kate Millett's *Sexual Politics* (1969), each of which offers a very different response to the material examined.

Ellmann's book takes issue with what she calls the sexual analogy, in which the facts of the superior strength of the male and the prolonged nurturance of offspring by the female are turned into metaphors that govern the representation of every human action, even when these 'facts' have no bearing on the matter in hand. Unlike Friedan, her focus is on the literary text, and on the representation of women within it. She argues that sexual analogy fatally infects literary representation with distortions of the truth. The images that (usually male) writers derive from their belief in the soft feminine woman and the hard warlike man must therefore be stereotypes. Stereotypes undermine both the literary value and the transcendent truth-status of the literary text because of their fundamental untruthfulness and self-evident absurdity. In readings of a wide range of contemporary fiction (largely from the 1940s through to the 1960s) Ellmann gently and wittily demonstrates that the stereotypes are everywhere, and that they are always absurd. In particular, she suggests that female characters are almost always associated with formlessness, instability, confinement, piety, materiality, spirituality, irrationality and compliancy – a list that in itself contains structural oppositions that necessarily render femininity as irrational: how can a woman be at once material and spiritual? And she concludes her discussion with a series of readings of two particularly long-standing types of fictional woman – the witch and the shrew.

Ellmann provides image criticism of a very sophisticated kind. Her arguments proceed through ironic understatements and juxtapositions rather than through strong statement. *Thinking About Women* is a creative performance as well as a critical one, and its poise and irony unsettle the reader's certainties rather than setting out a polemical argument against what she perceives as the wild irrelevance and inaccuracy of most representations of women in fiction. In contrast, Kate Millett's *Sexual Politics*, a much longer book, is also much more forthright in foregrounding its own attitudes and assumptions. It was also a much more immediately successful book, becoming a bestseller in the English-speaking world soon after its publication (*Thinking About Women* has never enjoyed such success). The reasons for the contrasts in fortune are not hard to fathom. Millett wrote a more or less sensationalist book of criticism, focusing as she did on the quasi-pornographic sex scenes in the works of a handful of male authors. And her response to these scenes is unmitigated fury – the message against misogyny is far easier to follow in Millett's text than in Ellmann's.

Millett's first chapter exemplifies her method. She extracts three sexually explicit sex passages from novels by the notoriously misogynistic Norman Mailer and Henry Miller, and from the work of French novelist and playwright Jean Genet. Her comments on each of these scenes demonstrate that there is a relationship in each of the writers between sexual potency and social and/or political power. She argues that the apparently private sexual relationships between men and women reflect the power structures in the world at large, hence her title, *Sexual Politics*, in which the private sphere of the bedroom becomes inescapably entwined with the public sphere of politics. In addition, the representation of sexual relationships at once reflects, and is itself reflected by, the real. The falsity of such images of women matters, argues Millett, because it is to the cultural image that cultured beings turn in order to make their own self-images. What was once the reflection of the real becomes the real, and is then re-reflected in a never-ending interplay between image and reality.

As Toril Moi has noted, images of women criticism became for a while the dominant mode of feminist thought in American institutions. The publication of Susan Coppelman Kornillon's edited collection of essays aimed specifically at college students, *Images of Women in Fiction: Feminist Perspectives* (1972) was influential on a whole generation of American college graduates, for whom it defined what feminist theory might mean. The essays collected in *Images of Women* focused largely on male-authored texts, and discovered, as Ellmann and Millett had done before them, that when men write about women they often write inaccurately. The collection had certain key assumptions that have subsequently been partially dismantled by feminist theory. It took for granted the idea that literature is supposed to be a more or less unmediated reflection of life; that life-experience and fictional representation of experience ought, therefore, to map onto each other; and that for the woman reader, the purpose of fiction is to find her own experience so that she can 'identify' with her fictional counterparts. But, as Moi comments, a naive image critique is a theoretical dead-end. The 'reality test' approach to literature leads to merely repeated critical gestures in which critics seek and find the same inaccuracies over and over again; the reader is led to assume that her own reality is a touchstone for the reality of all readers; and, in certain cases, image criticism fails to account for the persistence of the stereotype, fails to analyse the social context in which the type arises, fails to offer an alternative future – a solution to the problem of representation (see Moi 1985, 42–9).

In a 1979 essay entitled 'Towards a Feminist Poetics', Elaine Showalter, again surveying the field of feminist criticism, identified what she saw as the two most usual modes of feminist practice. The first, which I have called 'images of women' criticism, is named 'feminist critique' by Showalter. She argued that this was a necessary first step in liberating the woman reader from masculine standards of judgement, but she went on to say that there were two fundamental problems with it as it had been practised to date. Firstly, it was 'male-oriented', paying far too much attention to the texts of the male-authored canon; secondly, it had a tendency to 'naturalize women's victimization by making it the inevitable and obsessive topic of discussion' – a tendency, Showalter suggests, that could lead dangerously close to celebrating women's victim-status instead of challenging it (1986, 130–1). To prevent this danger, she suggested that academic feminism might choose as an alternative focus the figure of 'the woman as writer', and she coined the term gynocritics to describe this focus. Gynocritics was to be the study of literary writing by women, its key advantage that it would liberate feminist thought from a dependency on masculine models; in doing so, it would explode the canon by uncovering – or inventing – a separate, but equal, literary tradition in which women had participated. Gynocritics would interest itself in

> woman as the producer of textual meaning, with the history, genres and structures of literature by women. Its subjects include the psychodynamics of female creativity; linguistics and the problem of female language; the trajectory of the individual or collective female literary career; literary history; and, of course, studies of particular writers and works. (1986, 128)

Gynocritics had, in fact, begun to take place, even before there was a word for it. For example, Patricia Meyer Spacks's *The Female Imagination: A Literary and Psychological Investigation of Women's Writing* had been published in 1972. Spacks's argument was that a female tradition did, indeed, exist in literature. There were elements in women's writing that were transhistorical – that remained constant despite the vagaries of time, history, geography and social class – and that could be understood as 'a woman's point of view' (Spacks 1976, 4). Moreover, she discovers not only a female tradition, but also the effects of women's specific problems in literature on female readers of those texts. Using the personal (rather than academically rigorous) responses of her own classes of college students, juxtaposed with her own more measured academic responses, Spacks dramatized the relationships between women as readers and women as writers. Covering quite a range of texts, genres and historical periods, the book argues that femininity (the cultural construction of femaleness) is a double bind, both for writers and for their readers. Passivity, for example, is both attractive and dangerous – attractive because it traditionally affords a technique for getting a man in marriage, dangerous because marriage itself can often be a deceptive state that is not nearly so ideal as romantic fictions portray it. Or, again, she argues that adolescence is felt very differently by women than by men. There is no book she says, that '*celebrates* female adolescence' (158), because adolescence is a time for secrecy and anxiety in women, not for a triumphant entry into the public world, as fiction often portrays it for men. Across history, therefore, women have chosen different solutions from men for the problems they face because the problems themselves are different, given the social set-up that proscribes such different lives for adult females than those it offers to adult males.

In 1976, Ellen Moers also produced a text that performed a gynocritical method. *Literary Women: The Great Writers* consists of chapters made up of essays that Moers had been writing for at least ten years. Moers's focus is also very wide-ranging. She establishes the idea of a female tradition by appealing to writers' biographies, historical contexts and networks of literary influence (which often appear in surprising places); she also considers the significance of finance on women's writing; and she elaborates a theory of the Gothic as a female mode in fiction, a theory that develops very directly out of women's bodies and their material lives. Moers's introduction opens with the bold statement: 'The subject of this book is the major women writers, writers we shall always read, whether interested or not in the fact that they happened to be women' (Moers 1985, ix). The bold assumption is that 'great' women writers do, in fact, exist, and although Moers is careful not to call herself a feminist (the writers she is interested in just 'happened to be women'), she is nonetheless anxious to emphasize that female experience – especially the physical and psychical consequences of femaleness – are a legitimate subject for academic study. And, like Spacks, she is also sure that there are links between women *writers* because they are *women* writers.

For Moers, the female tradition, however, is often indirectly inherited, and is often elusive. Only in her description of the genesis and development of the female Gothic is she convinced of distinct networks of influence and of easily understood patterns of meaning that arise from the woman writer's female body. The Gothic, she says, is a literature of the body: it gets 'to the body itself, its glands, muscles, epidermis, and circulatory system, quickly arousing and quickly allaying the physiological reactions to fear' (1985, 70). It arises because of the suppression in culture of the secrets of the female body (especially the taboos of menstruation, pregnancy and childbirth). And it finds a covert way to speak of the forbidden female. The definition of the female Gothic is important within *Literary Women* as a whole because it points out the ways in which a female tradition will necessarily be the result of both biology and culture – of physiology and the repression of that physiology by different societies at different times. The book argues by implication that there is a commonality in all women's experiences, despite historical, geographical and social variations: and like Spacks, Moers assumes some congruence between the woman writer, the female character and the woman reader. There are problems with this view, to which I will return.

In 1977, Showalter produced her own explicitly gynocritical study, A *Literature of their Own: British Women Novelists from Brontë to Lessing*, in she which set out to place individual women writers and their social, psychological and economic situations into a larger historical picture of literary influence and literary value. Thus, rather than a transhistorical appeal to a female imagination or tradition, Showalter provides a more nearly historicized approach to feminist theory and scholarship. She argues that there are distinctive phases of development in women's writing, phases that are reactions to specific historical and cultural conditions. She declares herself 'uncomfortable with the notion of a "female imagination"' because such a concept risks 'reiterating the familiar stereotypes', and renders the differences between men and women in writing permanent and sex-determined. Instead, her emphasis is on 'not an innate sexual attitude, but [on] the ways in which the self-awareness of the woman writer has translated itself into a literary form in a specific place and time-span'; this enables her to argue that change and development in women's writing are possible (1978, 12). In her description of nineteenth- and twentieth-century women's writing, she proposes that there have been three distinct phases: the feminine phase, roughly from 1840 to 1880, characterized by the choice of male pseudonyms as a strategy for evading a critical double standard, and by the disguise of subversive (feminist) content through displacement and irony; the feminist phase, 1880–1920, the period of women's struggles for suffrage and education, in which women's writing became more overtly politicized and their texts spoke openly of female oppression; and finally, the female phase, from 1920 to the present, in which women's writing eschews the 'dependency' on male models implied by imitation and protest, and turns unapologetically instead to female experience for its raw material (Showalter 1978, 13).

The idea of the differences between women across time is important. For Showalter, women represent a sub-culture within the mainstream, coexisting in an uneasy symbiosis with the dominant, male-authored canon of the time. For women writing in the specific circumstances of Victorian England and its long aftermath, female sub-culture, she argues (as Moers had done before her), was characterized by secrecy, in particular the secrets of women's bodies. Because women could not write directly about their experiences of childbirth or menstruation, they tended to encode them into their texts as displaced images that only other women would notice and understand as shared markers of secret femininity.

But perhaps more important than her commitment to some attempt at historicism is Showalter's commitment to the women writers who have never been classed among the 'great'. Spacks and Moers focused almost entirely on writers who have usually been accepted as writers of literary quality. A *Literature of their Own*, on the other hand, though it does concentrate on Charlotte Brontë, George Eliot, Mrs Gaskell, Dorothy Richardson and Virginia Woolf, also opens its pages to far less well known women writers, women whose names had more or less vanished from the literary canon (at least in 1977). Showalter notes that there has been a tendency for women writers to disappear, and for her, making a female tradition involves historical excavation of the texts that have not survived. It is only by considering even those whose works are 'irreparably minor ... Millicent Grogan as well as Virginia Woolf – that we can begin to record new choices in a new literary history, and to understand why, despite prejudice, despite guilt, despite inhibition, women began to write' (Showalter 1978, 36). And, indeed, attention is accorded to the minor women, as well as the 'great' – though the attention is definitely skewed towards the 'great', and Showalter clearly has some blindspots in relation to issues of literary value when she considers the minor writers.

Two years later, in 1979, Sandra M. Gilbert and Susan Gubar published *The Madwoman in the Attic: The Place of the Woman Writer in the Nineteenth-Century Literary Imagination*. It is clear from their preface that in a relatively short period of time, the idea of a female tradition in literature was pretty well secure. They cite the works of both Moers and Showalter as having established without doubt that 'nineteenth-century literary women *did* have both a literature and a culture of their own – that . . . by the nineteenth century there was a rich and clearly defined female literary sub-culture, a community in which women consciously read and related to each other's works' (1979, xii). Their theoretical and methodological impetus derives not only from the then newly developing feminist tradition of Moers and Showalter, but also from the aggressively masculinist writings of Harold Bloom, in particular his 1973 book *The Anxiety of Influence*. Bloom's argument had been that writers situate themselves in a tradition through violent reaction against their literary forebears. A poet is validated by his (all Bloom's examples are male) hostile rewritings of the texts of the past. The male writer is always engaged in a quasi-Oedipal struggle with his literary father for supremacy. The terms of this argument quite clearly, Gilbert and Gubar suggest, leave no space for the woman writer: poets have no metaphorical mothers, no significant relationships with women as women, or with women as readers and writers to whom their works might be addressed.

Instead of the anxiety of influence, they propose as their model for the woman writer the anxiety of authorship. Women fear to write since in nineteenth-century culture, writing is a masculine activity, and value is only accorded to masculine production. The woman who chooses to write arrogates male power, and will necessarily fail to accrue literary value since she lacks the male gift. Her literary products will be attacked as insignificant or silly, and her person will be attacked as monstrous and aberrantly unfeminine. Gilbert and Gubar then set out to chart how nineteenth-century women writers attempted to evade or confront the hostile literary world. They undertake sustained and impressive readings of the works of Jane Austen, Mary Shelley, Emily Brontë, Charlotte Brontë, George Eliot, Christina Rossetti and Emily Dickinson – an alternative 'great tradition' of women writers. They refer to a massive range of material – from Native American mythology to the poetry of Sylvia Plath in their reading of *Wuthering Heights*, for example – and make connections between female experience and female authorship across vast swathes of time and space. Their approach mixes traditional close readings of the texts with wide citation from critical material and with other more eclectic detail. The book is a *tour de force*; it appears very persuasive and the readings of individual texts remain important and fascinating. But the conclusions Gilbert and Gubar draw about the nature of a female tradition are open to question, and as Nancy Armstrong has argued, they are often dangerously ahistorical because of their will to connect the woman writer to her forebears (see Armstrong 1987, 7–8).

A Literature of their Own and *The Madwoman in the Attic* are very important signpost books that offered both a theory and a method for reading women's writing in its own terms. But like Friedan, Ellmann, Spacks and Moers before them, and for all the apparent inclusivity of their frames of reference, in the end Showalter and Gilbert and Gubar still offered quite a partial view of the woman writer. One criticism has been that their concentration on nineteenth- and twentieth-century literature left earlier periods under-represented, as if there was no such thing as a woman writer in earlier periods. But by far the most serious criticism of all these earlier manifestations of feminist criticism has come from black feminists. Where, in the elaboration of a female tradition, of female representation so far, have been those 'other women'? That is, where are the women who are not white, middle or upper class, straight and relatively privileged? Where are the non-housewives, those for whom work is not a choice or a privilege, but a necessity?

In 1979, novelist, poet and critic Alice Walker spoke at Sarah Lawrence College in honour of Muriel Rukeyser. Her talk, subsequently published in *In Search of Our Mothers' Gardens: Womanist Prose* (1984), was entitled 'One Child of One's Own: A Meaningful Digression Within the Work(s)'. It is a partially autobiographical piece, partly about the experience of maternity, partly about Walker's professional career as a writer and university teacher, and its theme is race and the race-blindness of white people that Walker has encountered. In one passage, she describes how she was, in the early 1970s, working at an upper-class college, teaching a course on black women writers: 'There she shared an office with a white woman feminist scholar who taught poetry and literature. This woman thought literature consisted predominantly of Nikki Giovanni, whom she had, apparently, once seen inadvertently on TV' (1984, 371). Walker, appalled by this ignorance tried to repair it by leaving books on her desks by black women writers such as Gwendolyn Brooks, Margaret Walker, Toni Morrison, Nella Larsen, Paula Marshall and Zora Neale Hurston, believing that this subtle approach would help. Some time passed, and then the white feminist scholar published her most famous book:

> Dozens of imaginative women paraded across its pages. They were all white. Papers of the status quo, like the *Times*, and liberal inquirers like *The New York Review of Books* and the *Village Voice*, and even feminist magazines such as *Ms* ... actually reviewed this work with varying degrees of seriousness. Yet to our young mother, the index alone was sufficient proof that the work could not be really serious scholarship, only serious white female chauvinism. (1984, 371–2)

The scholar was Patricia Meyer Spacks, and the book was *The Female Imagination*. Walker was not unnaturally infuriated to discover that for Spacks, and for many white feminists, the black woman scarcely counted as a woman at all.

In 1977, Barbara Smith had also noticed the yawning gap in feminist scholarship represented by black female experience. In her essay 'Towards a Black Feminist Criticism', she wrote that she did not know where to begin because writing about black women's experiences, and writing specifically about black lesbian experiences, had never been tackled, even by 'white women critics who think of themselves as feminists' (Smith, in Showalter 1986, 168). In many ways, Smith's essay restages some of the battles that white feminist scholars had already fought on their own behalf. First of all she has to establish that a black feminist discourse is necessary. After all, where conditions of severe material deprivation exist, talking about books may not seem very important. But Smith suggests that political and aesthetic theories are one possible vehicle for raising the consciousness of oppressed groups, and knowing the terms of one's oppression is the prerequisite for tackling it. Moreover, because literature itself is a privileged category, claiming some of the value that goes with that privilege for black women writers is a highly charged political act that implies a claim of value for the lives of black women more generally. Black feminist theory necessarily entails a re-evaluation of the status of literary value and works back towards the lives of the women it represents. Smith suggested that black women's writing had to be read in the context of other black women's writing, rather than measured against some pre-existing (white) standard. She advocated a criticism that focused in part on content, on its mediated reflections of lived experience, but she also argued that attention had to be paid to the forms, images, metaphors and plots that this writing expressed. In the examination of the black women's tradition (a tradition that exists, even if it had been buried or forgotten), black feminist critics would be able to see that 'thematically, stylistically, aesthetically and conceptually, black women writers manifest common approaches to the act of creating literature as a direct result of the political, social, and economic experience they have been obliged to share' (Smith, in Showalter 1986, 174). One would also discover a 'specifically black female language' expressing black women's experiences, and an emphasis on the oral tradition. These forms could be celebrated when seen in their proper context, not criticized for being improper, and such language might even then find their way into the discourses of criticism.

Literary feminism, feminism in the academy in the United States, then, has largely been a matter of representation. In whatever guise it appears, it begins by looking at images of women, focusing on content. It then moves to consider the issue of the woman writer, and her representation in the canon, the academic institution and the publishers' lists. But where white feminist criticism was often content to describe what it perceived as the (white) woman problem, black feminist criticism, and the writings of other women of colour, is often much more radical in diagnosing its own problems and seeking change. As well as looking at issues of representation within the text, it also seeks a wider representation in the world beyond the text.

Ruth Robbins

Further reading and works cited

Armstrong, N. *Desire and Domestic Fiction*. Oxford, 1987.
Cornillon, S. Koppelman. *Images of Women in Fiction*. Bowling Green, KY, 1972.
Eagleton, T. *Literary Theory*. Oxford, 1996a.
— (ed.) *Feminist Literary Theory*. Oxford, 1996b.
Ellmann, M. *Thinking About Women*. New York, 1968.
Friedan, B. *The Feminine Mystique*. Harmondsworth, 1992.
Gilbert, S. M. and Gubar, S. *The Madwoman in the Attic*. New Haven, CT, 1979.
hooks, b. *Ain't I a Woman?* London, 1982.
Millett, K. *Sexual Politics*. London, 1977.
Moers, E. *Literary Women*. Oxford, 1985.
Moi, T. *Sexual/Textual Politics*. London, 1985.
Poovey, M. *The Proper Lady and the Woman Writer*. Chicago, 1984.
Showalter, E. *A Literature of their Own*. London, 1978.
— (ed.) *The New Feminist Criticism*. London, 1986.
—. 'Feminist Criticism in the Wilderness' and 'Towards a Feminist Poetics', in *The New Feminist Critic*, ed. E. Showalter. London, 1986.
Smith, B. 'Towards a Black Feminist Criticism', In *The New Feminist Critic*, ed. E. Showalter. London, 1986.
Spacks, P. Meyer. *The Female Imagination*. London, 1976.
Walker, A. 'One Child of One's Own', in *In Search of our Mothers' Gardens*. London, 1984.

Feminisms in the 1980s and 1990s: The Encounter with Poststructuralism and Gender Studies

It is commonplace in historical surveys of American feminism to identify a seismic shift – in both subject matter and modes of inquiry – near the end of the 1970s or beginning of the 1980s. Perhaps the most profound marker of this shift may be situated around the question of 'difference'. As the previous article outlines, the academic feminisms of the 1960s and 1970s urged women to be resistant readers of the male literary canon and to reconsider women writers as part of a distinctly rich, differently established female canon. 'Images of women' criticism (such as Kate Millett's or Judith Fetterley's) and 'gynocriticism' (such as Elaine Showalter's, Sandra Gilbert's and Susan Gubar's) innovatively direct attention to issues of sexual difference within the western literary tradition, laying the important groundwork that has made feminism an undeniable force in academic discourse. Pointing to the ways women are excluded from or subsumed by prevailing concepts of reading, writing, thinking and living, such feminisms follow Simone de Beauvoir's lead and demonstrate that humanism's supposedly universal subject was actually only male all along. For this mode of feminism, the difference between a male subject (or a purportedly ungendered one, which amounts to the same thing) and a female one makes a critical difference. And generally speaking, articulating this *difference between* and analysing what *difference it makes* was the central preoccupation of American feminist criticism prior to 1980. In the next two decades, by contrast, the contribution of feminists of colour, lesbian critiques, deconstruction, psychoanalysis and gender studies all serve to move the question of difference from a *difference between* to a *difference within*.

Much of the energy directing this shift involves feminism's new engagement with poststructuralism's powerful critiques of binary logic, particularly the logic that sanctions the opposition within sexual difference. As such, feminism comes to be increasingly suspicious of the extent to which its own discourse was dependent upon a difference between 'men' and 'women'. Because of this very suspicion towards oppositions, however, easy divisions between feminism 'then' and 'now' also prove unstable. And surveys determined by dates and descriptors calling for aetiologies and definitions become especially hard to provide in discussing feminism's 'encounter with poststructuralism and gender studies' since 1980. In the first place, a number of critics would dispute the notion that earlier feminist work was not concerned with or only naively aware of the theoretical challenges poststructuralism posed for those seeking to define a female literary tradition, or describing the experience of 'reading like a woman', or expressing a unified feminist project. In her own survey, in fact, Naomi Schor emphasizes that feminism of the 1970s itself 'was in fact part of a larger and very powerful critical trend of the early 1970s, the structuralist-poststructuralist critiques of mimetic representation' (1992, 265). In this regard, it might be useful to notice the continuities as well as the break between the two understandings of 'difference' proposed above. For, as Schor implies, both feminist epochs intersect historically and intellectually with poststructuralist theories of representation, and both are concerned with 'laying bare the sexual politics at work in seemingly innocent and authoritative imitations of social reality' (1992, 265).

A further difficulty is that the very gesture of defining poststructuralism as a position, movement or method would be antithetical to those who stress that such an effort is misguided from the start, missing precisely what poststructuralism most has to offer – namely, the critique of foundational 'essence' as such. 'Poststructuralism', asserts Judith Butler, 'is not strictly speaking, a *position*, but rather a critical interrogation of the exclusionary operations by which "positions" [including feminist positions] are established.' Linda Kauffman calls for a similarly rigorous self-consciousness and resistance to objective definition, stressing as well that poststructuralist critique involves a commitment to a continual work in progress: 'I want continually to cast doubt on the status of knowledge – *even as we are in the process of constructing it* – a perpetual project.' Poststructuralism is not grounded in a specific set of methods, except for a commitment to the 'erosion of the very ground on which to take a stand', asserts Peggy Kamuf (all in Friedman 1995, 22). Diane Elam, writing about feminism and deconstruction, highlights the problem of supposing that feminist projects that 'use' deconstruction or other poststructuralist theories simply bring together two discrete methods or movements ('they cannot best be understood as movements') to make a new one. For, more than just historically, 'there is a sense in which feminism already "is" deconstruction, and deconstruction "is" already feminism. And yet, with this said, they also do not collapse into one another and eliminate their differences' (Elam 1994, 9, 21). Such refusals have a strategic efficacy, indeed necessity, as well, for as Barbara Johnson warns, '[a]s soon as any radically innovative thought becomes an *ism*, its specific ground-breaking force diminishes, ... and its disciples tend to become more simplistic, more dogmatic, and ultimately more conservative, at which time its power becomes institutional rather than analytical' (Johnson 1987, 11). Johnson is speaking of 'deconstructionism' in this instance, but her admonition is also in keeping with all of the above statements about feminism and poststructuralism (11).

A similarly self-conscious impulse has brought a key feminist insight to new avenues of inquiry we could place under the larger heading of 'gender studies'. Elam's caution regarding the 'and' in 'feminism and deconstruction' applies equally to the relation between poststructuralism and gender studies as well, for in many ways gender studies 'is' poststructuralist. (The other 'and', however, requires circumspection. Schor cautions that 'feminist and gender studies are not coextensive' and 'cannot simply be collapsed onto each other' (1992, 275, 262).) If there is no category of identity that exists outside of culture, then understanding the construction of femininity must entail studying constructions of masculinity too, as well as the interaction and complicity of those constructs. For instance, Eve Kosofsky Sedgwick's important work on male 'homosociality', in *Between Men* (1985), examines the influence of patriarchal culture upon men's social interactions with other men by means of methods feminists had previously used to study women. While Sedgwick's work is arguably 'feminist' at its core, its focus on male rather than female gender construction also claims new intellectual territory. Her subsequent books, *Episte-mology of the Closet* (1990) and *Tendencies* (1993), have been particularly instrumental in fostering the vitality of gay studies and 'queer theory' of the late twentieth century. Other work one might place under the rubric of 'gender studies' explores the implications of mainstream feminism's 'compulsory heterosexuality', and works with a suspicion towards binary oppositions to promote a specifically lesbian critique of feminism's discourse on 'women'. Naomi Schor points out, however, that it is misleading to assume that gay male gender studies and lesbian studies 'fits neatly into the template of gay-gender studies' (1992, 280). As Sedgwick points out in the specific context of her literary study, it is important not to conflate the two for doing so overlooks 'an asymmetry in our present society between, on the one hand, the relatively continuous relation of female homosocial and homosexual bonds, and, on the other hand, the radically discontinuous relation of male homosocial and homosexual bonds' (1985, 4–5). Schor extends Sedgwick's point to a more general proviso for understanding the projects of contemporary gender studies. '[B]ecause male homosexuality threatens patriarchal society in a way that female homosexuality does not', we must be vigilant about recognizing difference here as well; 'there is no gay continuum' (1992, 281). Such a conflation would obscure as well the challenging role lesbian critique serves within a discourse she would still call 'feminist'. Robyn Wiegman asserts such a role suggestively in a response to Susan Gubar in the pages of *Critical Inquiry*. For Wiegman, an avowedly poststructuralist lesbian critique came about and helped to bring about the epochal shift from a 'difference between' to a 'difference within' feminism, playing the important role of 'the lesbian, [who] threatens to undermine from within the Edenic ... unity' of a heterosexually grounded feminism (1999, 363).

If they disavow definable method or unity of purpose, these assertions do nevertheless suggest a certain critical spirit or disposition we could characterize as specifically 'post-structuralist'. Structural linguistics stressed the arbitrary and differential nature of sig-nification, and poststructural theories brought that insight to bear on issues of psychic formation, gender identity and cultural instantiations of sexual difference in ground-breaking ways. Correspondingly, all of these critics express an intellectual commitment to analytical rigour, scepticism and self-consciousness with regard to their object of study – and in all of these cases, that object is *discourse* and that 'object' includes their own. We could also generalize that most academic feminism of the last two decades regards gender as a construction rather than a natural fact or an essence, produced by a complex set of social, political, psychic, racial, economic, historical, but most emphatically discursive or linguis-tic forces. The particular methodological orientation of a critic tends to be dictated by the privilege she gives to one or a combination of those forces. And in the high-stakes, often divisive intellectual climate that emerges from such a matrix of possibilities, these theoretical choices make all the difference. Though they do so in a vast heterogeneity of ways, arguably all academic feminisms of the last two decades engage in this self-conscious approach and work from these basic premises – or fail to do so at their peril.

In a story many commentators tell, a number of concrete institutional changes also mark the transition between these two periods. Jane Gallop locates this foundational shift rather precisely 'around 1981', a moment in which key incidents of continental drift take place: two major academic journals (*Critical Inquiry* and *Yale French Studies*) devoted entire issues to feminism; poststructuralist theory, much of it imported from France, gained new currency among many American feminists; and feminist inquiries that had largely been the domain of literary critics and members of English departments moved beyond their traditional disciplinary boundaries (Gallop 1992, 1–10). Many note that, more broadly, an institutional rite of passage seems to occur for feminism around this time. Citing Gallop, Naomi Schor adds that 'such leading indicators as the exponentially growing list of feminist publications . . ., the proliferation of feminist sessions at the annual MLA convention, and . . . the tenuring of scholars primarily identified as feminist critics' – including Gallop herself – all point to the fact that 'by the early 1980s feminist criticism and theory were without question no longer marginal activities, practiced by an embattled corps of largely untenured and powerless women' (275). Gubar notes that the last two decades have seen 'some six hundred programs in Women's Studies . . . [develop] since the seventies' and 'prominent feminist scholars serve as the presidents of major professional organizations', along with numerous other gains (2000, 157, 113).

It would be misleading, however, to imply that this is simply a narrative of collective progress and exuberant solidarity. In fact, one of feminism's most suggestive theses is that such narratives are necessarily reductive, that they necessarily efface the incalculable differences within the various categories feminism establishes for study. Though critics like Gubar and Wiegman warn against the seductiveness of casting early feminism as a lost Eden of either singular purpose or harmonious pluralism (whether to celebrate or castigate it), it is fairly safe to say that, in comparison with the body of feminist scholarship produced in the 1960s and 1970s, the subsequent proliferation of theoretical arguments and positions around the question of 'women' and 'gender' have rendered it effectively impossible to speak a 'feminist project' in the singular. This theoretical heterogeneity has also led to new doubts regarding its 'collective' goals and gains. Somewhere 'around 1981', it seems, feminism's very success story becomes the subject of scrutiny for critics who wonder whom this narrative leaves out and at what cost such 'success' might come. Newly challenging assumptions about the insiders and outsiders of feminism, voices emerge with provocative questions. Who has been telling feminism's story? And who gets left out of that telling? Articulated through such questions, crucial concerns are expressed by those who see exclusionary powers at work within the feminist project as well as without.

The discursive self-consciousness of the poststructuralist climate has encouraged scholars to consider the blind spots within the rhetoric and ideology of mainstream feminism itself. Under this lens, the largely white, middle-class, heterosexual bias at work in earlier feminist discourse comes into focus, ushering a new 'generation' of critical work that regards gender as but one variable in the infinitely complex matrix of categories (such as race, class, nationality, religion, sexuality) that establish identity and structure power. bell hooks's pivotal 1981 publication, *Ain't I a Woman: Black Women and Feminism*, to give just one example, posits 'difference within' through the question of race, applying an earlier feminism's method of locating exclusion or occlusion to critique feminism itself. In a similar critical spirit, Gayatri Spivak also examines the difference at work in feminism and critical theory more generally. Her especially heterogeneous theoretical approach works from 'within', both drawing from and critiquing poststructuralist theory to produce her influential 1988 book, *In Other Worlds*. Working with marxist, deconstructive and psychoanalytic theory, Gayatri Spivak expands the black feminist critique of 'white' feminism and grafts it to a critique of 'French' feminism by placing both 'in an international frame' (1988, 134). While offering translations of Indian short stories and literary analyses of texts as varied as Dante, Wordsworth and Woolf, this text also provides extremely influential essays on 'subaltern studies'. Such studies consider the subject formation of the 'subaltern', shaped in complex ways by the intersection of India's 'culture of imperialism', class hierarchies, gender, and recent historical shifts in global politics' (1988, 245). Related to the feminist effort to account for women in a history that has largely left them out, Spivak's project 'attempt[s] to undo a massive historiographic metalepsis and "situate" the effect of the subaltern' by providing a detailed analysis of the existing 'work of Subaltern Studies from within but against the grain' (205). Adumbrating questions of 'difference within' and across race, class, nationality, history and political structures, Spivak's has proved foundational to the burgeoning field of 'postcolonial studies', which has charted significant theoretical territory beyond the bounds of both feminism and gender studies. Her work provides just one illustration of how interdisciplinary and wide-ranging feminisms of the last decades have become, and the extent to which they engage with issues across a broad field of cultural and ethnic studies.

As Gallop and so many others demonstrate, feminisms in the 1980s and 1990s show a similar preoccupation with the political effects of its own historiography. In her essay, 'Making History: Reflections on Feminism, Narrative, and Desire', Susan Stanford Friedman focuses on just such projects, arguing that the strategies at work in feminist historiography have everything to do with the hotly contested question of not only what feminism has been and is, but also what it should be and will become. History, as she defines it, is more something we *do* than something that *is*. To 'make history' is both to engage in a 'heuristic activity' and to stage an 'intervention'. As Spivak stresses the 'interventionist value' and 'strategy' of retelling a history with 'the subaltern as the subject', Friedman considers interventionist strategies in various feminist historiographies (Spivak 1987, 207). She stresses that 'writing the history of feminism functions as an act in the present that can (depending on its influence) contribute to the shape of feminism's future' (13). The purpose of citing Friedman here is, instead, largely heuristic. On the one hand, her project provides a fairly useful – if somewhat arbitrary – example of what premises broadly characterize feminism's 'encounter' with *both* 'poststructuralism and gender studies'. On the other, it also occasions a duly self-conscious acknowledgement of the impossibility of justly synthesizing the voluminously heterogeneous body of work under its heading. In Elam's succinct words, *'her-story is not one story'* (1994, 37).

Primarily, and in the most general sense, Friedman approaches her subject from the premise that history 'is' what we 'make' it. It is a *construction*. Her argument is also informed by the notion that 'the politics of representation' is not simply a *static structure* feminists look at from an intellectual remove, but a profoundly *dynamic process* in which feminists too – including Friedman herself – necessarily participate (1995, 18–19). That underlying distinction – between a criticism that purports to study a static, external representational structure and a criticism that grapples with representation as a dynamic, co-implicating process of construction or 'production' – marks a key shift not only between 'Feminism I' and 'Feminism II', but from structuralism to poststructuralism writ large. In its attention to the way representational dynamics specifically shape feminist narratives, Friedman's approach also indirectly echoes a guiding principle of scholars informed by intersections between deconstruction and post-Freudian psychoanalysis. She directly references Peter Brooks' theory of 'narrative desire', a richly suggestive concept that insists upon a dynamic rather than static understanding of narrative, which Brooks formulates by juxtaposing Freud's drive theory with formalist and structuralist narratology. One could also read in her essay an indirect echo of projects like Johnson's, which bring deconstructive theoretical premises to bear on issues of 'gender, race, literary genre, [and] institutional context' in consistently challenging ways. Johnson's pointed assertion that 'the question of gender is a question of language' issues from the broader aims of a project she describes as 'a critique of the fallacious naturalness and blinkered focus' of institutions and 'articulations of power' that authoritatively claim reference to the 'real world' (Johnson 1987, 37). For Johnson, the 'real world' cannot be referenced except in quotation marks, a theoretical observation many poststructuralist feminists apply to the terms 'woman' or 'women' as well.

Related to such projects are those that examine just how gender comes to be constituted by language, and Friedman's concerns point to another important avenue in feminist and gender studies: the issue of *performativity*. As Friedman's study asserts, accounts that say where we are going and where we have been, to paraphrase the subtitle of the star-studded retrospective on feminist criticism at the December 1994 MLA convention, are, as that panel theatrically demonstrated to a capacity crowd, *performances*. They do not refer to pre-existing categories of knowledge; they are produced and reproduced by being acted out. More simply put, as performances (or 'speech acts'), they do something or make something happen. This emphasis on the performative construction of categories of knowledge we might assume are fixed or 'natural' has especially informed Judith Butler's influential work in gender studies. Butler has taken into provocative new arenas Foucault's insistence on the historically-specific and ideologically-determined discursive construction 'sex' in his land-mark *History of Sexuality* (1976). Butler specifically examines both gender and the presumably 'natural' and more primary category of 'sex', arguing that the two function in a complex interrelationship, and that *both* are indeed constructed rather than essential: 'gender is a performance that *produces* the illusion of an inner sex or essence or psychic gender core' (1991, 28). Gender, for Butler, is a radically unstable category that exists only through repeated performances (iterations) by all of us who live within a sex-gender system (and that is everyone). Like much of the most innovative and challenging feminist theory to emerge in the last two decades, Butler's project both engages with and helps transform poststructuralism's radical critiques of representation, subjectivity and ideology.

As Schor and Wiegman both suggest, the poststructuralist critique of essence and the expanding interdisciplinarity of gender studies has led a number of influential scholars to question the tenability and efficacy of that very adjective ('feminist') for critical theories aimed at examining, even dismantling, the humanist subject they deem irretrievably phallogocentric. The most radical implication of such a critique is one that vexes some feminist orientations and invigorates others, namely that feminism's heuristic privileging of gender, on the word 'women', as a guiding principle might be, in Biddy Martin's bold words, 'plagued from the outset' and even 'may have outlived its usefulness' (Martin 1997, 104, 106). A number of debates over the state of feminist theory at the turn of the century laments such propositions as grievously self-defeating. With a problematic deployment of terms too complex to delineate here, a number of critics lay blame at the feet of 'poststructuralism' itself (arguably by means of poststructuralist premises), charging it with an extreme constructivism that denies any validity to the collective identity categories feminism claims in the service of its 'cause' (see Gubar 2000, 113–34). Gubar complains that feminist discursive self-consciousness too often devolves into *ad feminam* accusations of political bad faith. Similarly, Friedman worries that an unselfconscious commitment to self-consciousness could foster inertia: 'first danger is the problem of paralysis, the kind of infinite regress and fetishization of indeterminacy that can develop out of constant navel-gazing. Perpetual self-reflexivity – particularly with its continual focus on linguistic construction – contains within it the potential of dangerous inaction' (Friedman 1995, 25). The radical and relentless 'differencing' feminist theory demands, however, need not signal defeat, nor imply the job is not still worth doing. And, as Daphne Patai suggests, discursive self-consciousness is not theory's only concern: 'It is a mistake to let ourselves be overwhelmed by these problems. The fact that doing research across race, class, and culture is a messy business is no reason to contemplate only our difficulties and ourselves struggling with them' (in Friedman 1995, 25).

Patai's comment also implicitly points to the possibility that such criticisms misidentify their culprit. Wiegman vehemently responds to Gubar's diagnosis of 'What Ails Feminism?' (a version of an essay originally called 'Who Killed Feminism?') with a Socratic apology, reminding her of a distinction between poststructuralism done badly and poststructuralism as such: 'While it is always the case that critical modes of analysis spawn reductive and predictable scholarship ..., it does not follow that the existence of such scholarship renders illegitimate the intellectual value of the trajectories of analysis being pursued' (1999, 369). Gubar refines her criticism in a response to Wiegman, protesting that what she laments, more precisely, are 'boring, ... routinized default positions [that] inhibit what one would ordinarily call thinking, making it hard for people to risk ideas that do not toe what is assumed to be a morally superior or epistemologically more sophisticated line' (1999, 381). Wiegman's and Gubar's debate is illuminating not just because it stages broader contentions within feminist theory, but also for the unified demand it makes (though each might object to the notion of such a unity). Sparring on the pages of *Critical Inquiry*, both invoke the importance of critical inquiry that proceeds in the face of risk – the risk of bad manners or bad grammar, perhaps, but more profoundly, the risk of genuine *thinking*. Implicitly defending herself against Gubar's charge that her bad grammar is one of the symptoms of what ails feminism, Butler rebuts that it is a 'mistake to think that received grammar is the best vehicle for expressing radical views, given the constraints that grammar imposes upon thought, indeed, upon the thinkable itself' (Butler 1999, xviii–xix). Barbara Johnson, who might remind both Gubar and Wiegman of the theoretical value of 'depersonalization' or 'self-resistance' in their disagreements with one another, acknowledges the pitfalls of a poststructuralism on autodrive: 'It can lead to a kind of infinite regress of demystification, in which ever more sophisticated subtleties are elaborated within an unchanging field of questions' (Johnson 1987, 42–6, 15). More to the point, she demands a rigorous self-consciousness that does not equate with mere 'navel-gazing', but rather remains vigilant against it. Like Butler's commitment to think the unthinkable, Johnson insists that the feminist interrogation of difference demands a commitment to 'what can never be taken for granted' (16). 'The impossible but necessary task of the reader is to set herself up to be surprised' (15).

As such debates and avowals variously demonstrate, no matter how scholarship narrates the development of feminist study throughout the final decades of the twentieth century, a general (if not generalizable) discursive tenor does emerge. Although with widely divergent, variously ominous tones, feminism in the 1980s and 1990s is anything but complacent with – or convinced of – its purported success. Attributed to a great diversity of causes – generational, institutional, political, social, practical and philosophical – the critical mass of critical discourse on feminism of late explicitly locates itself at a particularly pivotal historical moment, at an uneasy crossroads where the work of the past calls for crucial new work to be done in the future. A cursory survey of titles from the period with which this article is concerned provides a telling snapshot of this richly overdetermined moment: *Conflicts in Feminism, Gender Trouble, Feminism Beside Itself, Feminist Contentions, Generations, Critical Condition*. Joan Wallach Scott explains that she named the special issue of *differences* she edited 'Women's Studies on the Edge' – an issue that included essays with such provocative titles as 'The Impossibility of Women's Studies' and 'Success and Its Failures' – to highlight the 'sense of precariousness and uncertain anticipation' that marks this 'time of transition' (Scott 1997, iii, iv). Scott sees troubling irony in the fact that this academic journal comes out just as *Time* magazine asks on its cover, 'Is Feminism Dead?' (accompanied by Ally McBeal's pouty visage silently saying 'yes'), but also recognizes a continued need and promise for feminist discourse in the future. Writes Scott:

> An edge is not only a point of transition, but also a site of contestation, a place where differences become apparent and are erased, where lines divide and converge, and where new configurations emerge – a place of anxiety and irritability, to be sure, but also one of great energy and vitality – a cutting edge, in other words, in the worst and best senses of the term. (Scott 1997, iv)

In this special issue and beyond, the many rich proposals and daring rehearsals of what this project should entail similarly suggest that the 'feminism' of the future will be contentious, multivocal, difficult, even impossible – yet still vital and necessary, a perpetual project.

Megan Becker-Leckrone

Further reading and works cited

Benhabib, S. et al. *Feminist Contentions*. New York, 1995.
Brown, W. 'The Impossibility of Women's Studies', *differences: A Journal of Feminist and Cultural Studies*, 9, 3, 1997.
Butler, J. 'Imitation and Gender Insubordination', in *Inside/Out*, ed. D. Fuss. New York, 1991.
—. *Gender Trouble*. New York, 1999.
Elam, D. *Feminism and Deconstruction*. New York, 1994.
— and Wiegman, R. (eds) *Feminism Beside Itself*. New York, 1995.
Foucault, M. *The History of Sexuality*. New York, 1976.
Friedman, S. Stanford. 'Making History' in *Feminism Beside Itself*, eds D. Elam and R. Wiegman. New York, 1995.
Fuss, D. *Essentially Speaking*. New York, 1989.
Gallop, J. *Around 1981*. New York, 1992.
Gubar, S. 'Notations in Medias Res', *Critical Inquiry*, 25, 1999.
—. *Critical Condition*. New York, 2000.
Hirsch, M. and Keller, E. Fox (eds) *Conflicts in Feminism*. New York, 1990.
hooks, b. *Ain't I a Woman*. Boston, 1981.
Johnson, B. *A World of Difference*. Baltimore, MD, 1987.
—. *The Feminist Difference*. Cambridge, 1998.
Looser, D. and Kaplan, E. Ann *Generations*. Minneapolis, MN, 1997.
Martin, B. 'Success and Its Failures', *differences: A Journal of Feminist and Cultural Studies*, 9, 3, 1997.
Moi, T. *Sexual/Textual Politics*. New York, 1985.
Scott, J. *Gender and the Politics of History*. New York, 1988.
Scott, J. Wallach. 'Women's Studies on the Edge. Introduction', *differences: A Journal of Feminist and Cultural Studies*, 9, 3, 1997.
Schor, N. 'Feminist and Gender Studies', in *Introduction to Scholarship in Modern Languages and Literatures*, ed. J. Gibaldi. New York, 1992.
Seagwick, E. Kosofsky. *Between Men*. New York, 1985.

—. *Epistemology of the Closet*. Berkeley, CA, 1990.

—. *Tendencies*. Dorham, NC, 1993.

Showalter, E. (ed.) *The New Feminist Criticism*. New York, 1985.

Spivak, G. Chakravorty. *In Other Worlds*. New York, 1988.

Weedon, C. *Feminist Practice and Poststructuralist Theory*. Oxford, 1997.

Wiegman, R. 'What Ails Feminist Criticism? A Second Opinion', *Critical Inquiry*, 25, 1999.

Psychoanalysis and Literary Criticism

Surveying the work of Peter Brooks, Barbara Johnson, Shoshana Felman, Neil Hertz, Cynthia Chase or any of the innumerable others who could be added to this list provides ample evidence that some of the most significant contributions to recent psychoanalytic criticism and theory have come from scholars working in the United States. Today, critics at the forefront of this theoretical discourse almost invariably draw from poststructuralist understandings of reading, language, representation and subject formation that were initially 'imported' from Europe in the 1970s. More often with the aid of than to the exclusion of similar discourses in England, France, Germany and elsewhere, the most prominent American efforts to juxtapose psychoanalysis and literature emphasize the complexity involved in the pairing. Some important common aims emerge among these projects: an interest in psychoanalysis as a rich site for exploring the vicissitudes of interpretation and theory as such, including one's own; an emphasis on the fruitful analogy between the workings of language or signification and the workings of the unconscious (often prompted by Jacques Lacan's linguistic 'return to Freud'); an effort to explore not just what psychoanalytic theory can tell us about literature, but also, importantly, what literature or literary study can tell us about psychoanalysis or interpretation as such. Despite the possibility of such a generalization, however, it is also important to point out that recent critics approach these concerns by way of a fairly heterogeneous set of theoretical models, from Freudian to Lacanian vocabularies, from structuralist narratology to deconstructive rhetorical analysis, from feminism to marxism, from psychoanalytic readings of literature to literary readings of psychoanalysis. For these reasons, in fact, it seems specious to speak of *an* American psychoanalytic criticism as such, or an *American* psychoanalytic criticism, or – for that matter – an American *psychoanalytic* criticism. The most suggestive projects we could practically place under such a heading have diverse aims and cross national as well as discursive boundaries. It seems worth pointing out, in this regard, that all of the critics cited above are – in both training and teaching – comparatists.

We might say that this state of the field is as it should be, since the first psychoanalytic literary critic was Sigmund Freud himself, an Austrian whose most famous theoretical formula borrowed from the plot of a Greek drama, and whose 'scientific' study of the unconscious so often took him to the speculative reaches of religion, philosophy and art. Yet despite – or perhaps because of – Freud's formidable precedent, in *The Interpretation of Dreams* and elsewhere, the critical juxtaposition of psychoanalysis and literature has always been a rather anxious exercise. As Brooks himself admits at the outset of a recent essay:

> The enterprise hasn't on the whole made a good name for itself. It's in fact most often been something of an embarrassment ... I find myself resisting the label 'psychoanalytic critic' – though no doubt I am one, in some sense still to be defined – and worrying about the legitimacy and force that psychoanalysis may claim when imported into the study of literary texts. (Brooks 1994, 20)

He speaks here, presumably, of an embarrassment that comes from within, generated by his ambivalent membership in a group whose 'legitimacy and force' he finds questionable. That critical positioning performs a self-consciousness that, because it is a prominent feature of much recent psychoanalytic literary criticism, warrants further consideration. But first, it is instructive to consider the more obvious state of affairs Brooks implicitly glosses. For when he worries that the 'notion of a psychoanalysis applied to literature continues to evoke reductive maneuvers that flatten the richness of creative texts into well-worn categories', he seems to assign blame to both 'reductive' critics and an audience that maintains stereotypical expectations about what psychoanalysis does in the first place.

The ambiguous origin Brooks assigns to this mistaken 'notion' in one sense acknowledges the deep, long-standing and overdetermined popular resistance to psychoanalysis generally and psychoanalytic applications to literature in particular. As Maud Ellmann puts it, 'Freudian literary criticism causes a peculiar form of irritation' uniquely able, it seems, 'to elicit sniggers of embarrassment or snorts of disbelief' (Ellmann 1994, 1). In her lucid introduction to a collection of such essays by prominent continental and Anglo-American critics, Ellmann attributes that reaction in part to the audacious strangeness of Freud's intellectual project and, ultimately, to the profoundly troubling implications of his proposals. Thus, like Brooks' 'embarrassment', this 'visceral' reaction, she suggests, should not necessarily be discounted or lamented. For in a certain sense 'a gut resistance to psychoanalysis often signifie[s] a deeper recognition of its danger than [does] a prompt assimilation of its principles' (1). We could say that much recent criticism privileges the forces of 'resistance' over impulses towards 'assimilation' that occur when psychoanalysis and literature encounter one another, often by finding an inherent, analogous, kind of resistance in Freud's efforts to interpret the unconscious and critics' efforts to interpret literature.

Ellmann argues that the latter reaction – assimilation rather than resistance – more aptly characterizes Freud's initial reception within American intellectual culture, from a medical community that developed from Freud the positivistic 'ego-psychology' Lacan would so virulently attack, to a critical community prone to unsubtle applications of psychoanalysis to study the authors, characters and thematics of literary texts. What proves problematic, however, is that it may still be harder to confront an eager appropriation of psychoanalytic principles for the vocabulary of literary criticism than it is to confront a popular dismissal or resistance to such an approach. The history of Freud's reception in this country bears out this paradoxical truth: the alacrity with which some critics sought to 'apply' psychoanalysis to literature has proven a more onerous legacy than the suspicion with which others greeted it. In this sense, there is no real irony in the fact that the pioneering American psychoanalytic critic Frederick Crews, for instance, would famously come to reject psychoanalysis as a hermeneutic tool, for, as Ellmann wryly observes, he 'seems to have talked himself out of psychoanalysis precisely by applying it too heavyhandedly' (Ellmann 1994, 2). Crews' *Out of My System*, a collection written between 1967 and 1975, gives one notable record of this ambivalence. In it, he offers a reading of Conrad's *Heart of Darkness* – the images of castration and primal horror bespeak Marlow's and perhaps even Conrad's own Oedipal anxieties, he suggests – in the midst of a pervasively anxious meditation on the efficacies and pitfalls of his own critical method. Before and after cataloguing a series of thematic '[d]erivatives of the primal scene' that 'await the hero everywhere' and 'belabor[-ing] the obvious point' that *Heart of Darkness* is deeply autobiographical, Crews concedes that

> Freudian criticism too easily degenerates into a grotesque Easter-egg hunt: find the devouring mother, detect the inevitable castration anxiety, listen … for the bedsprings of the primal scene. A critic who may have been drawn toward Freud by the promise of a heightened sensitivity to conflict in literature may, without ever knowing what has happened to him, become the purveyor of a peculiarly silly kind of allegory. (Crews 1975, 57–8)

But while Crews self-effacingly includes himself among such potentially wayward critics, he also expresses a certain pride in managing to knock literature off the liberal humanist pedestal that he claims, in a questionable hybridization, was kept erect in the twentieth century by 'New-Critical formalism and … Northrop Frye' (167). Arguing that his methods expose the intentional fallacy of a purportedly less self-conscious criticism that supposes its object fully realized by the express motivations of its creator, Crews takes a 'satisfaction in brushing past formal or generic or ironic or (above all) morally uplifting aspects of literature and showing instead that even the sublimist masterpiece traffics in unconscious wishes' (1975, 167).

Throughout his meditation, which includes the imagined protests of 'detractors' and 'nonpsychoanalytic colleagues' (resistance of the common variety), Crews nevertheless sidesteps the more unsparing discursive self-consciousness ('self-resistance', to use Barbara Johnson's term) that a subsequent generation of psychoanalytic literary criticism would insist upon (Johnson 1987, 42–6). The latter generation, indeed, would make it a central aim to account for the motivations of criticism itself, to avoid the condition of an unreflective critic ('without ever knowing what has happened to him …'). For despite the appearance of conscientious reflection, Crews never wavers from nor seeks to ground the operating premise that literary content deserves privilege over literary form or that literature might be in any way resistant to his brand of hermeneutic detective work. 'Using psychoanalytic assumptions', he writes, 'a critic can show how a writer's public intention was evidently deflected by a private obsession … Or again, he can draw biographical inferences on the basis of certain recurrent themes that the author hadn't consciously meant to display' (168). Peter Brooks, working in large part from the formalism Crews considers retrograde, locates much of the embarrassment associated with 'the label "psychoanalytic critic"' in this very assumption; namely, in the notion of psychoanalysis as a stable master discourse that may treat a text as an unmediated record of a particular psyche. Brooks situates that idea in a larger tradition of criticism that has 'over and over again mistaken the object of analysis, with the result that whatever insights it has produced tell us precious little about the structure and rhetoric of literary texts' (1994, 21).

A telling demonstration of the shift in analytical object Brooks effects occurs in his own penetrating reading of *Heart of Darkness*, which stresses that the novel does not simply describe a series of psychic experiences, but presents them within complex frames of narration, so that it proves important to consider how and why Marlow tells the story he tells, and why Conrad might have had him do so (1984, 238–63). Calling for and producing a criticism that avoids the traditional analysis of author, reader or character, Brooks instead emphasizes, so to speak, a psychoanalysis of textuality, acknowledging at the same time the overdetermined textuality of psychoanalysis itself. Whereas Crews considers psychoanalytic criticism a *hermeneutics* (which aims at unveiling the latent meaning of manifest textual content), Brooks considers it a *poetics* (which aims at describing how particular textual elements work to achieve meaning). One central preoccupation for him, in this regard, has been to develop an emphatically *dynamic* poetics of plot he calls 'narrative desire', formulated by putting the relatively static models of formalist narratology together with Freudian drive theory, in order to describe not only how plots tend to be structured but what moves them forward. Rather than unveil 'the meaning' of Marlow's journey into the heart of darkness, Brooks looks at the way Conrad's text, with its ironically framed narration, is itself *about* revelation. The force that moves the narration forward is driven by Marlow's need to retell the story of his search for Kurtz, so that he may construct a meaning – a 'readable report' – out of an initial experience (an 'unreadable report') that disturbingly thwarts his epistemological desire, his desire to know, his need for the end of that journey to be indeed a 'summing-up' (Brooks 1984, 247–8). Throughout, Brooks is careful to align such a 'motor force' with the conventional tendencies of narrative and interpretations as such.

His often-anthologized essay, 'Freud's Masterplot', provides useful illustration of the current interest in reading psychoanalytic texts through the lens of literary study, as well as the reverse. Aristotle's study of reversal and recognition, Tzvetan Todorov's description of 'narrative transformation' and Frank Kermode's 'sense of an ending' are just some of the careful analyses of literary form Brooks incorporates into his reading of Freud's plotting and narrative strategies in *Beyond the Pleasure Principle*. Brooks argues, in turn, that Freud's own discursive style offers a suggestively dynamic 'model' for thinking about 'movement of plot and its motor force in human desire, its peculiar relation to beginnings and ends, its apparent claim to rescue meaning from temporal flux' (Brooks 1984, 90). Exploring the dynamics of beginning and ending at stake not just in Freud's theory of the death drive but also in the very 'plot' Freud's discourse produces, Brooks identifies a complex set of parallels between literary and psychoanalytic textuality – and offers at the same time a provocative statement of purpose that claims to break from the tradition of which Crews was an instrumental part. He writes:

> [W]e can read *Beyond the Pleasure Principle* as a text concerning textuality and conceive that there can be a psychoanalytic criticism of the text that does not become ... a study of the psychogenesis of the text (the author's unconscious), the dynamics of literary response (the reader's unconscious), or the occult motivations of characters (postulating an unconscious for them). It is rather the superimposition of the model of the functioning of the psychic apparatus on the functioning of the text that offers the possibility of a psychoanalytic criticism. (Brooks 1984, 112)

Brooks stresses that his theory does not claim to account for the workings of a particular mind – that of the author, reader or character – but rather, as he states it here, of the 'psychic apparatus' as such. This focus belongs to an explicitly stated premise that '[p]sychoanalysis and literature are mutually illuminating', a premise shared by many recent psychoanalytic critics. Two influential collections of essays devoted to that mutuality emphasize both the potential force of such a pairing and the radical uncertainty it can elicit. Shoshana Felman, in the preface to *Literature and Psychoanalysis: The Question of Reading: Otherwise*, enumerates a new set of questions critics need to ask: 'What does the *and* really mean? What is its conventional sense, its traditional function, in the usual approach to the subject? In what way would we like to displace this function (to reinvent the "and") – what would we like it to mean, how would we like it to work, in this issue?' (Felman 1977, 5). Her response is that the 'traditional function' of this 'and' has been far from neutral, typically 'implying not so much a relation of coordination as one of *subordination* ... in which literature is submitted to the authority, the prestige of psycho-analysis' (5). Felman argues that too often literature is presumed to be a static, passive 'body of *language*' or signs to be interpreted by psychoanalysis' masterful 'body of *knowledge*' – a presupposition, as we have seen, on which Crews' hermeneutical approach depends (5, emphasis Felman's). Underlining the suggestive etymology of her proposed term, she calls instead for a shift from *application* to *implication* ('being folded within'), where the 'interpreter's role would be ... to act as a go-between, to generate implications between literature and psychoanalysis', for instance the fact that literature is 'not simply *outside* psychoanalysis, since it motivates and *inhabits* the very names of its concepts' (9). While 'they are really traversed by each other', literature and psychoanalysis as Felman sees them also contain differences; they are 'other' to one another, each other's 'blind spot' or 'unthought' (10). Thus, Felman's volume raises the stakes. The psychoanalytic project is complicated and fixed on new aims, with the question of reading at the centre.

> [The essays] all reflect upon the textual and theoretical encounter between literature and psychoanalysis not as an answer but as a question, questioning at once its possibilities and limits. They thus suggest ... how the question of the relationship ... might be articulated – *otherwise*: how psychoanalysis and literature might indeed begin to be rethought, both in their otherness and in their common wisdom. (10)

Felman's own critical work – such as the essay on Henry James and Freud, 'Turning the Screw of Interpretation', included in this volume, and *Jacques Lacan and the Adventure of Insight* (1980), which includes important essays on the place of literary examples in the work of Freud and Lacan – demonstrates a commitment to a rigorously self-conscious psychoanalytic criticism and a complicated understanding of literature's 'implication' in it.

The preface and selection of essays in another important collection, *Psychoanalysis and the Question of the Text*, edited by Geoffrey Hartman, states a theoretical purpose similar to those expressed by Brooks and Felman. Hartman begins by somewhat disdainfully distinguishing the psychoanalytic criticism of an earlier period from the efforts of the critics for whom he speaks, echoing the discursive mutuality Felman espouses:

> This volume does not contain something for everyone. It reflects the considerable and, one hopes, fruitful complication of psychoanalytic studies as they accept their mutual rather than masterful relation to language and literature. Those who expect literary case studies will be disappointed ... Every essay included here is, if anything, too conscious of the changing vocabularies and modified models of applied analysis, and particularly of the inadequacy of the applied science model of analysis itself. The emphasis has shifted from producing yet another interpretation, yet another exercise in casuistry, to understanding from within the institutional developments of psychoanalysis, and from the inner development of Freud's writings, what kind of event in the history of interpretation is proving to be. (Hartman 1978, vii)

From that initial provocation, however, Hartman takes a longer view to the past than Felman does, reflecting on Freud's place in a literary critical history that includes romantic and New Critical meditations on character and identity. While he too sees a determined shift in focus and method in the psychoanalytic criticism his collection showcases, he is also careful to acknowledge that the earliest literary critical efforts to engage with Freud did not produce a mere wasteland of naive application, as Brooks, Felman and others sometimes imply. Along with a nod to Kenneth Burke, he favourably cites Lionel Trilling for probing the limits of the ego's unity in literary works, and for 'raising this issue within a perspective that remains literary but assimilates in a highly critical way both Freudian and sociological currents of thought' (Hartman 1978, x). And indeed, Trilling's *The Liberal Imagination* contains a thoughtful meditation on 'Freud and Literature' first published in the *Kenyon Review* in 1940, where he presciently observes that 'it was left to Freud to discover how, in a scientific age, we still feel and think in figurative formations, and to create, what psychoanalysis is, a science of tropes, of metaphor and its variants, synecdoche and metonymy' (Trilling 1947, 51).

Trilling's observation is closer to Brooks' own methodologies than the latter's diagnosis of the criticism's mistaken objects seems to allow, and it suggests, as Ellmann also does, that we would do well to look beyond 'such howlers' as Crews' reading of Conrad in evaluating a diverse, complex critical history (Ellmann 1994, 2). Trilling's description of psychoanalysis as a 'science of tropes' suggests particular continuity with Brooks' explanation for why interest in psychoanalysis and literature persists:

> We continue to dream of a convergence of psychoanalysis and literary criticism because we sense that there ought to be, that there must be, some correspondence between literary and psychic process, that aesthetic structure and form, including literary tropes, must somehow coincide with the psychic structures and operations they both evoke and appeal to. (Brooks 1994, 25)

Even Trilling's otherwise traditional reading of Wordsworth's 'Immortality Ode', in the same book, includes a deeply suggestive moment where he speculates on the striking parallels between Wordsworth's and Freud's intellectual preoccupations – namely, between the poet's idea that the infant's originary state of non-differentiation may be a possible source of our 'intimations of immortality' and Freud's speculation that the 'oceanic feeling', the feeling of 'limitless extension and oneness with the universe', is a vestige of the 'primary ego-feeling' that exists prior to the separation by which the child comes to establish identity (Trilling 1947, 137–8).

Trilling leaves this speculation on Wordsworth and Freud largely undeveloped. But a remarkable number of recent critics who are psychoanalytically predisposed have also given attention to the poetry of Wordsworth in particular and romanticism in general. That common interest seems to reflect a broader theoretical investment: the crucial forbear of these scholars is Paul de Man, a sphere of influence that is somewhat ironic, given de Man's emphatic insistence that language, rhetoric, is radically empty of psychological content and his rare, but rather dismissive, references to psychoanalytic interpretation. (Brooks, it is worth mentioning, dedicates *Reading for the Plot* to de Man.) Regardless of de Man's own assessment of such relevance, critics such as Neil Hertz, Cynthia Chase and Barbara Johnson have offered powerful testimony to the fruitfulness of generating psychoanalytic readings of literature that proceed from the methods de Man's rigorous rhetorical theory – rooted in a radical reading of romanticism – produced. They have, more importantly, demonstrated the compelling resonances between psychoanalytic speculation on the earliest dynamics of significatory identification and de Man's rhetorical or deconstructive account of the materiality of language. Certainly Lacan also provides rich precedent for reading psychic structuration in linguistic terms, and some critics invested in a rhetorically oriented psychoanalytic criticism attest to that influence explicitly. But it is striking, among American critics in particular, that a de Manian model of language so often supersedes a Lacanian one, in spite of these figures' relative theoretical interests.

What de Man offers Cynthia Chase, in her dense but illuminating essay 'The Witty Butcher's Wife: Freud, Lacan, and the Conversion of Resistance to Theory', is an opportunity to read in Freud's and Lacan's theoretical discourse instances of resisting the disturbingly non-referential aspects of language and examples of the necessary disavowal involved in every act of interpretation. Laying out the complex structure of meaning at work in the dream of the 'witty butcher's wife' both Freud and Lacan interpret, Chase argues that the dynamics of mirroring or 'specular rivalry' at work in the woman's story are themselves mirrored in the various analytic treatments of that story – the woman's own, Freud's, Lacan's and Chase's own. She explains the helpfulness of de Man as follows:

> What de Man's essay ['The Resistance to Theory'] describes is a resistance to language, or to the rhetorical nature of language or to the necessity of reading, precisely in theories of language, in 'theory' understood as a reflection on how language is in the first instance about language rather than about the world. (Chase 1987, 991)

Chase demonstrates that each successive, contentious, theory of the dream depends on such a resistance. In a virtuoso demonstration of the self-consciousness and recursiveness recent psychoanalytic theory demands, Chase explores the shadowy ways in which the possibility of meaning ('interpretable and significative') – in a dream, an interpretation, in referential language as such – is predicated on a 'resistance' to the possibility that they are 'essentially non-significative' (999). As one step in this argument, she teases out Freud's contradictory claims about wish-fulfilment, which Lacan also notices: on the one hand, that we sleep in order to dream (and fulfil unconscious wishes), and on the other, that we dream in order to sleep (that is, fulfil a brute need not reducible to 'wish'). Here, Chase is interested in highlighting the 'indeterminably significative status' Freud assigns to the dream, but also of Lacan's own account and of language as such: 'This is the moment in which the mirror wavers, in which the specular symmetry of the structuralist conception about language-about-language breaks down, as language ... seems to mean also that which *does not certainly* signify' (999).

Chase pursues a similar thesis in 'Primary Narcissism and the Giving of Figure: Kristeva with Hertz and de Man' (Fletcher and Benjamin 1990, 124–36). She argues that Julia Kristeva's rhetorically inflected theory of 'primary narcissism', a theory that posits a primordial structure of signification prior to Lacan's mirror stage, has offered Hertz and herself a provocative model for 'mediating between psychoanalysis and non-psychoanalytic discourse, between the discourse to which the concept of primary narcissism would seem to belong, and a practice of rhetorical theory that denies that discourse explanatory authority' (124). Chase sees potent analogies between de Man's rhetorical theory and Kristeva's description of the simultaneously primordial and 'recurrent condition of the speaking subject' Kristeva calls 'abjection' (129). She points out that such a theory 'draws near de Man's considerations' in that Kristeva's specific brand of psychoanalytic theory, like de Man's, 'becomes the analysis of an act of *reading*' (126, emphasis Chase's). The one literary example in this discussion, one which strikingly echoes Kristeva's account and which de Man himself memorably uses, is the 'blessed babe' passage from Book Two of Wordsworth's *Prelude*, which describes the initially intimate, 'indeterminably significative' relation between a mother and infant abruptly thrown into crisis by the mother's death ('the *props* of my affection were removed') (129, 134).

526 THEORIES AND PRACTICE OF CRITICISM IN NORTH AMERICA

As her title suggests, Chase recognizes that Hertz too is interested in such moments, both in an essay on de Man that explores the 'drama of uncertain agency' at work in the figurative logic of his rhetorical theory and, more elaborately, in his excellent book, *The End of the Line: Essays on Psychoanalysis and the Sublime*. In the latter, the subtle rhetorical moves of the first extant theory of sublimity (Longinus' 'On Sublimity'), the notion of blockage in Kant's *Critique of Judgment*, the dynamics of influence in Wordsworth and Milton, as well as readings of George Eliot, Flaubert and Freud, are united by an ambitious, provocative effort to align aesthetic with psychoanalytic discourse. It is in his 'Afterword' that he explains and explores his title. Like Chase, he notably enlists Kristeva's pre-Oedipal theory of abjection to describe a crisis – of signification, but also of subjectivity itself – that is precipitated by differential undecidability, such as the sublimely, unsettlingly 'minimal difference between black and black' in Courbet's painting, *La source de la Loue* or 'the minimal difference between the "Label" on [the] chest and the "fixed face and sightless eyes"' of Wordsworth's famous description of the blind beggar in *The Prelude* (Hertz 1985a, 217). Borrowing from Kenneth Burke, Hertz calls such representations instances of an 'end of the line' structure (218–19). In all such examples (he explores a number of such moments in Wordsworth's poetry), 'what one is drawn to is not a clearly oriented reflection, *a mise en abyme* of the artist's representational project, but an engagement with the act and with the medium of painting or writing condensed almost to the point of nonreflective opacity' (219). Hertz's innovation is to integrate such literary examples and the seemingly felicitous psychoanalytic theory that would account for them with a broader history of discourses on the sublime. He is conscientious, however, to acknowledge Thomas Weiskel's earlier, ground-breaking engagement with just such a juxtaposition in *The Romantic Sublime: Studies in the Structure and Psychology of Transcendence*. Hertz writes: 'It was Weiskel's distinction to have seen that the poetic and philosophical language of the primary sublime texts [Longinus, Kant and especially Edmund Burke] could be made to resonate with two quite different twentieth-century idioms, that of psychoanalysis and that of the semiological writings of Saussure, Jakobson, and Barthes' (Hertz 1985a, 49). Hertz respectfully distinguishes his own efforts to theorize sublimity psychoanalytically from Weiskel's by emphasizing his own debt to recent theories that challenge Freudian, Oedipal model on which Weiskel relies:

> I ... give Weiskel credit for dwelling as long as he did on the puzzles and the anxieties of the pre-Oedipal, while also calling attention to the relief he seemed to have experienced as an interpreter in bringing it all home to the Father. Since 1976 – when *The Romantic Sublime* was published – developments within psychoanalytic practice have converged with the work of feminist and post-structuralist theorists in providing counterirritants to [pre-Oedipal] anxieties and encouraging more, and more varied, exploration of the earliest stages of infancy. In particular, the concept of narcissism has been expanded and generally reworked, both by American psychologists of the 'self' and – more interestingly to my mind – by French writers drawing on Lacan's and Derrida's rereadings of Freud. (Hertz 1985a, 231)

The pressure Hertz puts on Weiskel's recourse to a relatively 'reassuring' Oedipal model and, more remarkably, on the interpretive 'relief' he finds in it recalls the potent critical ma of Barbara Johnson's well-known and widely published essay, 'The Frame of Reference: Poe, Lacan, Derrida' (Hartman 1978, 149–72). Specifically critiquing an exchange between Lacan and Derrida on Poe's 'Purloined Letter' – a detective story about finding a stolen letter hiding in plain sight – Johnson demonstrates that interpretation is inherently prone to 'framing' its object of analysis within an invested theoretical model. Effectively beginning where Crews' reflections on method seemed to stop, Johnson interrogates the very grounds on which meaning is, or may be, asserted in an interpretive act. Looking at Lacan's reading (which claims the story is 'a kind of *allegory of the signifier*') and Derrida's rebuttal to it (which questions Lacan's gesture of fixing meaning on the very thing, the letter, he also claims has no inherent meaning), Johnson argues that Derrida repeats the very 'crime' of which he accuses Lacan (Hartman 1978, 152–3, emphasis Johnson's). Derrida 'frames' Lacan, accusing him of an overbearing faith in the possibility of a psychoanalytic metalanguage, in the same way that Lacan 'frames' Poe's story, to make it readable as an allegory of the signifier. Yet, Johnson argues, 'although the critique of what Derrida calls psychoanalysis is entirely justified, it does not quite apply to what Lacan's text is actually saying' (158). She finds this misreading 'too interesting not to be deliberate' (158). She reads the exchange between these two radically self-conscious writers as performative display of interpretation's tendency – indeed necessity – to read past the *literary* aspect of the text in question, past the *letter* of the text. Johnson subtly demonstrates that, rather than simply blind to this blindness, both Lacan and Derrida self-consciously act it out. The double sense in which she means 'frame' mobilizes the key claim she makes about interpretation and its object, especially with regard to that elusive object of psychoanalysis, the unconscious.

Ultimately, what Johnson reads as the simultaneously inevitable and impossible conditions of psychoanalysis are the conditions of all acts of interpretation, including literary criticism, where 'the theoretical frame of reference that governs recognition is a constitutive element in the blindness of any interpretive insight' (164). In closing, Johnson articulates the multiple connotations of the refrain with which both Lacan and Derrida play: 'a letter always reaches its destination'. Among the things that phrase may indicate is the observation that the resistance of the letter – of literature – to an absolute, decisive reading:

> It is not any one of these readings, but all of them and others in their very incompatibility, that repeat the letter in its way of reading the act of reading. Far from giving us [Lacan's] seminar's final truth, these last words, and Derrida's reading of them, can only enact the impossibility of any ultimate analytical metalanguage, the eternal oscillation between unequivocal undecidability and ambiguous certainty. (170)

What Johnson here describes much of her excellent work performs, exploring encounters between psychoanalytic and literary texts within the force field of this very oscillation. Her most recent publication, *The Feminist Difference: Literature, Psychoanalysis, Race, and Gender*, includes several essays similarly interested in the pitfalls and promise of a psychoanalytic criticism. Here and elsewhere, Johnson approaches the act of reading by means of a 'self-resistant', rhetorically sensitive rigour that characterizes much of the current American work in psychoanalysis. As all of these dynamic studies indicate, psychoanalytic literary criticism – like the 'interminable' enterprise Freud understood his analysis to be – is vitally 'still to be determined' (Brooks 1994, 20).

Megan Becker-Leckrone

Further reading and works cited

Bloom, H. *The Anxiety of Influence*. New York, 1973.
—. *Agon: Towards a Theory of Revisionism*. New York, 1982.
Brooks, P. *Reading for the Plot*. New York, 1984.
—. *Psychoanalysis and Storytelling*. London, 1994.
Chase, C. *Decomposing Figures*. Baltimore, MD, 1986.
—. 'The Witty Butcher's Wife', *MLN*, 102 (1987).
Crews, F. *Out of My System*. New York, 1975.
Davis, R. Con (ed.) *The Fictional Father*. Amherst, MA, 1981.
—. *Lacan and Narration*. Baltimore, MD, 1983.
Ellmann, M. (ed.) *Psychoanalytic Literary Criticism*. London, 1994.
Feldstine, R. and Roof, J. (eds) *Feminism and Psychoanalysis*. Ithaca, NY, 1989.
Felman, S. (ed.) *Literature and Psychoanalysis*. Baltimore, MD, 1982.
Fletcher, J. and Benjamin, A. (eds) *Abjection, Melancholia, and Love*. London, 1990.
Gallop, J. *The Daughter's Seduction*. Ithaca, NY, 1982.
Hartman, G. (ed.) *Psychoanalysis and the Question of the Text*. Baltimore, MD, 1978.
Hertz, N. *The End of the Line*. New York, 1985a.
—. *The End of the Line*. New York, 1985b.
Johnson, B. *The Feminist Difference*. Cambridge, MA, 1998.
Lupton, J. Reinhard and Reinhard, K. *After Oedipus*. Ithaca, NY, 1993.
MacCannell, J. Flower. *Figuring Lacan*. London, 1986.
Muller, J. P. and W. J. Richardson. *The Purloined Poe*. Baltimore, MD, 1988.
Ragland-Sullivan, E. and Bracher, M. (eds) *Lacan and the Subject of Language*. London, 1991.
Schwartz, M. M. and Kahn, C. *Representing Shakespeare*. Baltimore, MD, 1980.
Sedgwick, E. Kosofsky. *Between Men*. New York, 1985.
Skura, M. A. *The Literary Use of the Psychoanalytic Process*. New Haven, CT, 1981.
Trilling, L. *The Liberal Imagination*. New York, 1978.
Weber, S. *The Legend of Freud*. Minneapolis, MN, 1982.
Weiskel, T. *The Romantic Sublime*. Baltimore, MD, 1976.

Feminists of Colour

Feminists of colour in the US have made ground-breaking contributions to feminist thought (scholarship and activism) in general and feminist theory in particular. They have engaged, challenged and reformulated feminist insights from the inception of feminism in the nineteenth century to the present. They have been active participants in the social justice movements (Civil Rights, Latino, Native American, gay and lesbian, and women's liberation) of the past forty years. In the US, African-American women were the first to engage with feminist literary criticism in the early 1970s. Other women of colour followed suit in the late 1970s and early 1980s, calling for coalitions among women of colour as well as for the development of criticism accounting for specific group experiences (Chicana, Asian-American, etc.). These different groups of critics have influenced each other as well as white feminists, male writers of colour and entire academic disciplines. Always at the cutting edge, they have redefined feminism at the levels of nomenclature, theory, methodology and genres or styles of writing.

Nomenclature

Feminists of colour have renamed feminism in order to make it better reflect their concerns. Some have chosen to literally invent a new word, whereas others have opted for retaining the old word (sometimes modifying it) and redefining it to suit their own worldviews.

The most famous renaming is African-American writer Alice Walker's definition of a 'womanist' (1983, xi–xii). Anglicizing the word (from the French etymology of feminist, based on *femme* [woman], to womanist), Walker's definition is grounded first and foremost in African-American cultural and linguistic specificity. Her first definition is 'a black feminist or a feminist of colour', thus placing women of colour at the centre of a concentric definition that expands to include 'a woman who loves other women, sexually or non-sexually' (a direct reference to Jewish-American feminist Adrienne Rich's concept of the 'lesbian continuum', in which all positive woman-to-woman relationships, sexual and non-sexual, are included as a way to bridge the tensions between lesbian and heterosexual feminists). Walker's definition then broadens to a holistic, radical feminist embrace of love of the world and of the self. The fourth and last part of the definition rests on the analogy, 'womanist is to feminist as purple is to lavender'. Reminiscent of Walker's classic novel, *The Colour Purple*, this final definition deconstructs the perception that feminism is a broad category of which feminists of colour are a part, to represent womanist as the standard, deeper colour (purple) and feminist as a variation on purple, a combination of purple and white. Walker's colour symbolism includes the struggle of the gay and lesbian movement, which has chosen the colour lavender (a mixture of pink and blue, the pastel colours typically associated with little girls and little boys in western cultures) as one of its attributes.

Womanist is presented as the more inclusive standard, and feminist as a part of womanist, for two reasons: first, because womanists come out of a historical and social context in which all people of colour, male and female, were and still are subjected to racist domination by a white supremacist order, their worldview includes men as part of the struggle for liberation. Therefore, womanists cannot agree with the gender separatism of some feminist theories. The second reason for womanist being presented as the more inclusive standard is a response to the exclusionary nature of a feminism that focuses solely or mostly on gender issues and refuses to give equal attention to the effects of race, class and other forms of domination. White feminists who are 'committed to the survival of the entire people' can be womanists, white racist feminists cannot. Frances M. Beal was even more direct, as early as 1970: 'Any white woman's group that does not have an anti-imperialist and antiracist ideology has absolutely nothing in common with the black woman's struggle' (1970, 393).

Finally, Walker never uses the form 'womanism', only 'womanist', to indicate that while there are womanists, people of all colours committed to a broad vision of social justice, there is no one way of being a womanist, no one doctrine to follow that would be called womanism. Walker's position is in keeping with that of many other black feminists who insist that there is no such thing as a monolithic black feminist standpoint (Collins), black feminist theory (Christian) or feminist movement (bell hooks). Inspired by Walker's renaming, Latina theologian Ada María Isasi-Díaz coined the term 'mujerista' (from the Spanish word for woman, *mujer*) to refer to Latina feminists who struggle against the oppressive strictures of racism, sexism and economic domination. Similarly, Chicana Ana Castillo has created the word 'Xicanisma' to designate Chicana feminists.

The second way of handling the problem of nomenclature is to continue using the term feminism, qualifying it to redefine its meaning. This is the way that Barbara Smith, among others, has chosen. Smith's redefinition is probably the most famous: 'Feminism is the political theory and practice that struggles to free *all* women: women of colour, working-class women, poor women, disabled women, lesbians, old women – as well as white, economically privileged, heterosexual women. Anything less than this vision of total freedom is not feminism, but merely female self-aggrandizement' (Smith 1990, 25).

Several feminists of colour have modified the term, retaining a connection to it but specifically naming themselves to overcome a history of silencing. For example, Chela Sandoval makes a distinction between 'hegemonic feminism' (a term also used by postcolonial feminist critic Gayatri Chakravorty Spivak to refer to mainstream, white middle-class feminism) and 'US Third World Feminism' (1991, 1). Sandoval's definition makes the link between women of colour in the US and third world women, reminding us that worldwide, women of colour are a majority and that international alliances between women of colour will serve them best. This new formulation bases itself on an analysis of racial domination in the US as a feature of internal colonialism, thus drawing parallels between colonial and neocolonial practices in the Third and the First Worlds. It also points to the class discrimination suffered by many US women of colour, who are disproportionately part of the poorest segments of US society (its 'Third World'). Finally, it is a way to bring together US and foreign-born women of colour in North America in general, and Latinas of diverse nationalities in particular, a group whose interests are of special concern to Sandoval, a Chicana critic. The theorists calling for such alliances are generally part of a migrant or colonial experience (such as Chicanas or Puerto-Rican women) who may have relatives dispersed throughout different countries across North/South borders.

More recently, legal scholars using the methods of close textual analysis and concerned with the intersections of race, class and gender in the law have named themselves critical race feminists. In doing so, they claim their connection to a triple legal tradition: critical legal studies (whose primary focus tends to be class), critical race theory and feminist thought. African-American scholars such as Lani Guinier, Adrien Wing and Kimberlé Crenshaw and Asian-American scholars such as Mari Matsuda have participated in this new and exciting scholarly development.

Theory

From Sojourner Truth in the nineteenth century onwards, women of colour involved in diverse social justice movements have argued that other people's theories about their situation were inadequate: these theories asked them to 'choose' between a focus on race, on class or on gender. Women of colour have been told by white feminists that their insistence on fighting racism was 'divisive' to a movement committed mostly to working against gender oppression. Marxist and labour movements have claimed that a focus on race and gender detracted from the 'real' struggle. Finally, the civil rights leadership tended to replicate patterns of male dominance. Deborah K. King notes that this fundamental difference in conceptualizing oppression (from a monist to a multiplicative analysis) resulted in 'the theoretical invisibility of black women' (1990, 76). She documents how African-American women have historically contributed to developing a multiaxial theory of race, class and gender (and other forms of oppression). For example, the work of Angela Davis has contributed to shaping such a perspective. Similarly, the Combahee River Collective espoused an anti-racist, anti-imperialist, socialist, black lesbian feminist position that theorized all forms of oppression as 'interlocking' in its manifesto (1983, 210).

Lesbian feminists of colour have argued that sexuality, like race, class and gender, is an important part of the system of domination. Audre Lorde, Barbara Smith, Cherríe Moraga and Gloria Anzaldúa were some of the first theorists to analyse the connections between heterosexism and homophobia and other forms of oppression. Perhaps because they often felt rejected by their own communities, lesbian feminists of colour have tirelessly agitated for inclusive spaces and against homophobia within the diverse movements in which they have participated. Mohawk poet and essayist Beth Brant and Laguna Pueblo writer Paula Gunn Allen have called for principled coalitions among people in different liberation struggles. Furthermore, Lorde and Brant have broadened and deepened the definition of sexuality by highlighting the healing and creative power of the erotic and the connections between sexuality and spirituality (Lorde 1984, 53–9; Brant 1994, 55–66).

A fifth element of the system of domination, colonialism, was highlighted in the analyses of two groups of theorists: Native American and postcolonial scholars. Native American women have traditionally had a very vexed relationship with feminism for the following reasons: feminism's general failure to understand the colonial domination of Native peoples, and the discursive colonialism (Mohanty et al. 1991, 51) of much feminist thought. This discursive colonialism is expressed in an unwillingness on the part of most white feminists to acknowledge the impact of US colonialism on the lives of Native Americans, a refusal to support Native claims for sovereignty and self-determination, and a desire to place the blame for Native American women's oppression on the shoulders of Native American men. In terms reminiscent of Frances M. Beal, M. Annette Jaimes and Theresa Halsey state that until feminists start to join the Native American anti-colonial struggle, feminism will bring nothing to Native American women (Jaimes with Halsey 1992, 332). Indeed, few Native women have self-identified as feminists (Paula Gunn Allen, Beth Brant, Janice Gould (Maidu), Wilma Mankiller (Cherokee) and Kate Shanley (Assiniboine) are important exceptions). Critics such as Brant and Gould have highlighted some common themes of Native women's literature: the question of multiple and fragmented identities in a colonial context; the deep sense of connection to the land, the people and other living beings; the question of how to express the centrality of the oral tradition and storytelling through writing; and finally, conveying the pivotal role of humour in the process of healing and survival (Gould 1995; Brant 1994, 5–24). Native writers and theorists have criticized the interlocking forces of colonialism and capitalist destruction of the land (Winona LaDuke), racism, sexism and homophobia (Allen, Brant), as well as the cultural appropriation of their spirituality by New Age religions (Brant, Wendy Rose, Laura Donaldson).

Feminist theorists who migrated to the US from third world countries such as India and Vietnam have also argued for the necessity of including colonialism in a multiaxial analysis of domination and having a more global vision of the struggle to end domination. In particular, US-based South Asians such as Gayatri Chakravorty Spivak and Chandra Talpade Mohanty have argued that western feminists replicated colonialist paradigms when they sought to 'sav[e] brown women from brown men' (Spivak 1994, 93). A monist focus on gender (or gender and sexuality) as the primary source of women's oppression conveniently serves to blind hegemonic feminists to their own participation in third world women's oppression through the neocolonialist and imperialist practices of the US and Europe. The publication of Mohanty's essay 'Under Western Eyes' in 1984 and of Trinh Minh-ha's book, *Woman, Native, Other* in 1989 were landmark events of what came to be known as 'US Third World Feminism'. They sought to promote 'a common context of struggle' between women of colour in the US and women in the third world in order to create broad-based alliances (Mohanty et al. 1991, 7). However, their occasional equation of racism and colonialism is sometimes problematic in so far as it can tend to subsume the concerns of women in the third world to those of US-based women of colour (problems due to colonial or neocolonial practices in the third world are sometimes viewed as being caused by racism by US third world feminists living in the US). In spite of this problem, the call to enlarge feminist issues to transnational ones, which has also been made by ecofeminists, has become a very important aspect of feminist theory. For example, Patricia Hill Collins's revised edition of her classic *Black Feminist Thought* now includes a chapter on 'US black feminism in transnational context' that draws from the work of African women writers and theorists.

Most feminists of colour have built their theoretical frameworks around a recognition of the centrality of self-definition and self-determination. It was crucial to argue for the centrality of women of colour in the theorizing process, especially at a time when their voices were few and silenced. Therefore a majority of criticism written by feminists of colour has focused on the importance of theorizing from experience and placing one's analysis in the appropriate cultural context, in order to avoid common misreadings and oppressive interpretations of the lives and writings of women of colour. Writers such as Patricia Hill Collins and Paula Gunn Allen, Asian-American authors Mitsuye Yamada and Deborah Woo, and Chicana critic Norma Alarcón have forcefully countered and deconstructed stereotypical 'controlling images' (Collins 2000, 69) of women of colour that stand in the way of self-definition. Since the 1970s, literary critics seeking to retrieve the voices of artists have established the existence of literary traditions by women of colour. They have brought back to light forgotten writers of the past, and provided critical attention to the work of contemporary women writers of colour (such literary critics include Barbara Smith, Alice Walker, Amy Ling, María Herrera-Sobek, Mary Helen Washington, Toni Cade Bambara and Yvonne Yarbro-Bejarano). Barbara Christian (1990) has pointed out that she reads and writes about the work of black women writers not as a luxury, but as a life-line, as a way to confirm her own worldview and experiences, in order to survive the theoretical invisibility of black women.

Collins has clearly articulated the concept of a black feminist standpoint. She highlights the fact that black feminist thought not only provides new paradigms, but new epistemological frameworks as well (Collins 2000, 252–74). She sees black female intellectuals as affirming and rearticulating the experiential knowledge of everyday black women into a more specialized form of knowledge (Collins 2000, 32–4). In her view, black feminist thought is produced primarily, but not solely, by black women, who engage in principled coalitions with other groups fighting for and theorizing about social change (Collins 2000, 38). In contrast, theorists of colour who began writing at a time when ethnic literary criticism was blooming are sometimes more critical of the essentialist and overgeneralizing pitfalls that can accompany such positions. Thinkers such as Norma Alarcón, Hazel Carby,

Wahneema Lubiano, Valerie Smith, Hortense J. Spillers, Gayatri Spivak and Trinh T. Minh-ha have countered identity-based or standpoint theories developed by other theorists of colour and argued for a recognition of more postmodern or discursively-based positions. Finally, in the 1990s, feminist theorists of colour such as Rey Chow, bell hooks, Lisa Lowe, Valerie Smith and Michele Wallace have also been important contributors to the growing fields of cultural and film studies.

Methodology and genres of writing

Since what usually counts as theory (including literary theory) originates mostly out of European and Euro-american contexts, feminists of colour have had an ambivalent relationship to the concept of theory itself. Some have argued that theory is inherently oppressive because of its elitist language and disconnection from the actual lives of women. One of the best articulations of this position remains Barbara Christian's essay, 'The Race for Theory', in which she makes a distinction between theory (an obfuscating pursuit that contributes to the theoretical invisibility of black women) and theorizing (a practice that seeks to illuminate the works of black women writers) (Christian 1990, 335–7). Many other thinkers such as Gayatri Spivak, Hortense J. Spillers and Norma Alarcón have refused to disengage from mainstream theory and have thus countered the stereotype of women of colour as untheoretical. Generally speaking, the uncomfortable relationship that feminists of colour have had to theory has contributed to two original developments in the field: methodological innovations and a new use of genres in writing theory.

Since feminists of colour insist on the primary importance of self-definition in any liberatory struggle, many have turned away from western-based theories and sought to establish a theory based on an analysis of the experiences of women of colour. This has contributed to redefining what counts as appropriate disciplinary methods. For example, Patricia Hill Collins explains that the sociological imperative to separate the researcher from her subjects of research is an impediment to black feminist sociological research, which seeks to understand black women's subjugated knowledge, their own interpretations of their experiences (Collins 2000, 254–6). Similarly, because black feminist thought aims to legitimize the voices of black women, Collins, rather than seeking academic credentials through citing authoritative white male sociologists, quotes from the works of black scholars and fiction writers, as well as the testimonies of everyday black women (domestic workers, working women).

Theorizing from experience has also challenged boundaries of genre, as feminists of colour have made ample use of personal narrative as a form suitable to the theoretical enterprise. The work of Cherríe Moraga and Gloria Anzaldúa, in particular, has been central to such reformulations of the genre of theory writing. The form of their books and edited collections, which include theoretical and personal essays, poetry and fiction, as well as texts written in both English and Spanish, reflects the hybridity (*mestizaje*) that they argue is at the heart of their process of identity formation as Chicana lesbians. Similarly, Audre Lorde has argued that 'poetry is not a luxury' but a first step toward articulating one's inchoate thoughts and feelings, a distillation of experience necessary for the process of theorizing (1984, 36–7). Japanese-American poets Mitsuye Yamada and Janice Mirikitani have also theorized and rewritten the silences of history through their magnificent poems. Finally, Barbara Christian points out that the theorizing done by people of colour 'is often in narrative forms, in the stories we create, in riddles and proverbs, in the play with language' rather than in the obfuscating language of high theory (1990, 336).

The use of literary sources in sociological scholarship and the use of personal narrative in much theory by feminists of colour are a testimony to the centrality of literature by women of colour to the process of theorizing. In many ways, theorists of colour are deeply influenced by the work of creative writers such as Toni Morrison, Alice Walker, Maxine Hong Kingston and Leslie Marmon Silko (on whose work Trinh draws heavily to develop her theory of third world women's writing in *Woman, Native, Other*). Conversely, many of these writers (such as Morrison, Silko, Walker, Lorde, Michelle Cliff, Mitsuye Yamada, Paula Gunn Allen, Beth Brant, Wendy Rose and Janice Gould) have also been important theorists and critics.

Conclusion

Because feminists of colour in the US have called for a 'paradigm shift' (Sandoval 1991, 9), not only from feminists, but from other liberation struggles based on monist models of race or class as well as from a variety of academic disciplines, their impact has paradoxically been both immense and modest. Tensions remain between those still subscribing to monist parameters of analysis and those embracing multiaxial paradigms. In other words, the paradigm shift required by US feminists of colour has not yet been achieved in feminist theory and practice today. The work of US feminists of colour has unfortunately often been co-opted through tokenism rather than full integration. The body of literary criticism on women writers of colour has become a field ripe with appropriations and misreadings. Furthermore, the US tendency to think through race issues in Black and White terms still remains strong in women's studies as in other fields. This means that issues of importance to Latinos, Native Americans and Asian-Americans, in particular, are even more vulnerable to tokenism. Finally, while the work of lesbians of colour such as Allen, Anzaldúa, Lorde, Moraga and Barbara Smith has been central to the development of multiaxial theory, homophobia further contributes to their theoretical invisibility as lesbians.

In spite of these continuing problems, however, it is very hard to imagine today the situation in which Barbara Smith found herself in 1977, trying to write one of the first articles ever about a black female literary tradition and black lesbian existence. Similarly, the concerns Barbara Christian expressed over the lack of critical academic attention to the works of Toni Morrison and Alice Walker are no longer an issue (Christian 1990, 344). Today, the study of ethnic and postcolonial literature has become an important part of the women's studies curriculum. Similarly, the study of women writers of colour has become very significant in ethnic studies, and is being incorporated more and more into the study of American literature in English departments. A market for the fiction of women of colour has developed, and academic recruitment in literary and women's studies increasingly demands specialization in, or familiarity with, ethnic literature and theory. Last but not least, the early efforts of scholars such as Smith and Christian have generated a vital, sophisticated tradition of theory and literary criticism analysing the works of women writers of colour through the lens of the interlocking effects of race, class, gender and other forms of domination.

Anne Donadey

Further reading and works cited

Alarcón, N. 'The Theoretical Subject(s) of This Bridge Called My Back and Anglo-American Feminism', in Making Face, Making Soul. Hacienda Caras, ed. G. Anzaldúa. San Francisco, 1990.

Allen, P. Gunn. The Sacred Hoop. Boston, 1986.

Anzaldúa, G. (ed.) Making Face, Making Soul. Haciendo Caras. San Francisco, 1990.

—. Borderlands/La Frontera. San Francisco, 1999.

Bambara, T. Cade (ed.) The Black Woman. New York, 1970.

Beal, F. M. 'Double Jeopardy', in Sisterhood is Powerful, ed. R. Morgan. New York, 1970.

Brant, B. Writing as Witness. Toronto, 1994.

Carby, H. V. Reconstructing Womanhood. New York, 1987.

Castillo, A. Massacre of the Dreamers. Albuquerque, NM, 1994.

Collins, P. Hill. Black Feminist Thought. New York, 2000.

Combahee River Collective. 'A Black Feminist Statement', in This Bridge Called My Back, eds C. Moraga and G. Anzaldúa. New York, 1983.

Christian, B. 'The Race for Theory', in Making Face, Making Soul. Hacienda Caras, ed. G. Anzaldúa. San Francisco, 1990.

Davis, A. Y. Women, Race and Class. New York, 1981.

Gould, J. 'American Indian Women's Poetry', Signs, 20, 4, Summer 1995.

hooks, b. Ain't I a Woman. Boston, 1981.

Isasi-Díaz, A. M. En la Lucha/In the Struggle. Minneapolis, MN, 1993.

Jaimes, M. A. with Halsey, T. 'American Indian Women', in The State of Native America, ed. M. A. Jaimes. Boston, 1992.

King, D. W. 'Multiple Jeopardy, Multiple Consciousness', in Feminist Theory in Practice and Process, eds M. R. Malson et al. Chicago, 1990.

Lorde, A. Sister Outsider. Freedom, 1984.

Minh-ha, T. T. Woman, Native, Other. Bloomington, IN, 1989.

Mohanty, C. Talpade et al. (eds) Third World Women and the Politics of Feminism. Bloomington, IN, 1991.

Moraga, C. Loving in the War Years. Boston, 1983.

— and Anzaldúa, G. (eds) This Bridge Called My Back. New York, 1983.

Sandoval, C. 'U.S. Third World Feminism', Genders, 10, 1991.

Smith, B. 'Racism and Women's Studies', in Making Face, Making Soul. Hacienda Caras, ed. G. Anzaldúa. San Francisco, 1990.

—. The Truth That Never Hurts. New Brunswick, NJ, 1998.

Spivak, G. Chakravorty. 'Can the Subaltern Speak?', in Colonial Discourse and Post-Colonial Theory, eds P. Williams and L. Chrisman. New York, 1994.

Walker, A. In Search of our Mothers' Gardens. San Diego, CA, 1983.

Stephen Greenblatt (1943–) and the New Historicism

'I began with the desire to speak with the dead', wrote Stephen Greenblatt in the introductory essay to Shakespearean Negotiations (1988, 1), speaking of a desire rooted in the political and social upheavals of the 1960s and 1970s. New Criticism dominated

Greenblatt's undergraduate education at Yale University, but during a Fullbright scholarship to Cambridge University he encountered the teachings of Raymond Williams: 'In Williams's lectures all that had been carefully excluded from the literary criticism in which I had been trained – who controlled access to the printing press, who owned the land and the factories, whose voices were being repressed as well as represented in literary texts, what social strategies were being served by the aesthetic values we constructed – came pressing back in upon the act of interpretation' (1990, 2). Greenblatt returned to Yale to finish his PhD with a dissertation on Sir Walter Ralegh's self-presentation (see Greenblatt 1973); then, in his early years at the University of California at Berkeley, he confronted the theories of visiting lecturer Michel Foucault. Such experiences taught Greenblatt that speaking with the dead required better knowledge of the social and political conditions of their lives.

Greenblatt implemented that desire in *Renaissance Self-Fashioning from More to Shake-speare* (1980), a prize-winning analysis of identity formation in early modern England. To describe the situation of individuals caught in a transitional period between the collective economy of medieval feudalism under which a fixed identity was inherited, and the modern world of capitalist individualism, Greenblatt coined the term 'self-fashioning', a logical extension of his earlier examination of Ralegh. Individuals caught between these two models necessarily had to improvise, 'to capitalize on the unforeseen and to transform given materials into one's own scenario' (1980, 227). Sir Thomas More's writings reveal, for example, 'the invention of a disturbingly unfamiliar form of consciousness, tense, ironic, witty, poised between engagement and detachment, and above all, fully aware of its own status as an invention' (1980, 31). Spenser's Red Cross Knight begins *The Faerie Queene* as a 'clown', a rustic who must learn how to play the role of gentleman and knight. Identity is not inherited or stable; it is constructed in the context of political ideologies circulated by and through the state, the church and the family. Thus for Greenblatt, the literary text is not an aesthetic object whose formal qualities set it apart from other texts. Literary works must be situated within the framework of practices, institutions and beliefs that constituted Renaissance culture at large. Greenblatt rejects the strict marxist notion that material conditions control the individual and accepts instead the possibility of agency, however limited; nevertheless, he shows the writer imbricated in social and political currents of which he may not be aware that necessarily shape his or her textual productions.

Greenblatt's critical practice was clearly established before he coined the term 'new historicism' in the introduction to a special issue of *Genre* on 'The Forms of Power and the Power of Forms'; the essays gathered in this volume, he claimed, demonstrate a kind of criticism 'set apart from both the dominant historical scholarship of the past and the formalist criticism that partially displaced this scholarship in the decades after World War Two' (1982, 5). Old historicism, Greenblatt opined, had been monological, finding only one meaning in a text – usually the official ideology of the dominant power structure. In the work of critics such as J. Dover Wilson and E. M. W. Tillyard old historicism described Shakespeare's history plays as literary refractions of the Tudor political ideology articulated in the *Homily Against Disobedience and Willful Rebellion* (1571) or Richard Hooker's *Laws of Ecclesiastical Polity* (1594). In contrast, new historicism situates literary texts, no less than other documents that circulated in the same period, as loci of competing interests and dissenting voices. Shakespeare's histories do, indeed, present spokespersons for Tudor ideology (Richmond, John of Gaunt, *Henry V*'s Archbishop of Canterbury, for example), but usually the plays' most attractive and appealing characters counter that ideology with subversive energies, deeds and actions (Richard III and Falstaff are cases in point). Subversive figures are normally contained by the dominant power structure, but the bulk of the plays' energies are devoted to divisiveness, contestation and debate.

Greenblatt explained his methodology more fully in a 1986 lecture at the University of Western Australia that was later reprinted as 'Towards a Poetics of Culture' (Veeser 1989, 1–14, and Greenblatt 1990, 146–60). Rejecting any totalizing theory, Greenblatt called the 'new historicism' a practice as opposed to a theory or a doctrine. He went on to differentiate new historicism (or cultural poetics, as he prefers to call it) from Fredric Jameson's marxist approach which blames capitalism for separating the private and aesthetic from the public and political; he also differed with Jean-François Lyotard's poststructuralist model of capitalism as a monological system. Instead Greenblatt views capitalism as a complex historical movement that has generated 'regimes in which the drive towards differentiation and the drive towards monological organization operate simultaneously, or at least oscillate so rapidly as to create the impression of simultaneity' (1990, 151). American capitalism in the late twentieth century is characterized, Greenblatt argues, by its effortless 'invocation of two apparently contradictory accounts of art' – 'in the same moment a working distinction between the aesthetic and the real is established and abrogated' (1990, 153). The resulting circulation is generated not just by politics but by 'the whole structure of production and consumption – the systematic organization of ordinary life and consciousness (1990, 154).

Greenblatt's characteristic method is to apply the skilful close reading he learned at Yale to a non-literary text, event or experience and then, in a brilliant intertextual dance, juxtapose that text with a reading of a recognized literary work. The resulting analysis shows how the social energies which circulate between the two texts are, presumably, characteristic of the culture at large. 'Invisible Bullets' works from Thomas Harriot's A Briefe and True Report of the new found Land of Virginia (1588) and its account of the Indians' explanation of their susceptibility to European diseases to Shakespeare's second Henriad; both texts demonstrate the ways in which power allows subversive forces a powerful, if illusory, voice (1988, 21–65). 'Learning to Curse' moves from new world explorers' accounts of Indian languages as defective or uncultured to Caliban's curses in The Tempest (1990, 16–39); 'Shakespeare and the Exorcists' uses Samuel Harsnett's A Declaration of Egregious Popish Imposters (1603) to interrogate King Lear's representation of Edgar as a demonically possessed 'Poor Tom' (1988, 94–128).

The relationship between texts in these analyses is always dynamic; the model is negotiation or exchange. Every text is necessarily embedded in a complex network of social, economic and political practices (similar to Foucault's episteme); literary and non-literary texts circulate inseparably within this network. And because the theatre's intended audience was a community of spectators rather than the individual consciousness, the stage became a fruitful site for such inquiries:

> For the circulation of social energy by and through the stage was not part of a single, coherent, totalizing system. Rather it was partial, fragmentary, conflictual; elements were crossed, torn apart, recombined, set against each other; particular social practices were magnified by the stage, others diminished, exalted, evacuated. (Greenblatt 1988, 19)

Although Greenblatt has often been criticized for opening his essays with an anecdote or petite histoire (sometimes related to Clifford Geertz's concept of thick description), he defends the practice:

> The historical anecdote functions less as explanatory illustration than as disturbance, that which requires explanation, contextualization, interpretation. Anecdotes are the equivalents in the register of the real of what drew me to the study of literature: the encounter with something that I could not stand not understanding, that I could not quite finish with or finish off, that I had to get out of my inner life where it had taken hold, that I could retell and contemplate and struggle with. (1990, 5)

Greenblatt's early work, along with Stephen Orgel's treatments of the Stuart court masque as an instrument of state power (Orgel 1975) and Jonathan Goldberg's analysis of Stuart literature's relationship to James I's court (Goldberg 1983), focuses on the state's power both to license and prohibit acting companies and the subversive energies they represented. In his subsequent work, however, Greenblatt moves away from an emphasis on Foucauldian analyses of power relations to the more aesthetic concepts of wonder and resonance. Wonder occurs during the observer's first encounter with an artefact, natural event or alien other; the viewer stops in his tracks and feels the uniqueness of the experience. Resonance comes as the encounter is repeated; the object, natural event or alien other evokes 'in the viewer the complex, dynamic cultural forces from which it has emerged and for which as metaphor or more simply as metonymy it may be taken by a viewer to stand' (1990, 170). Greenblatt finds the concept of wonder particularly useful in his account of European travel narratives, *Marvelous Possessions: the Wonder of the New World*, because wonder was invariably a 'component of the discourse of discovery, for by definition wonder is an instinctive recognition of difference, the sign of a heightened attention' (1991, 20). At the moment of first contact:

> The seamless and naturalised world of Renaissance Europe is torn apart and dislocated ... The alterity of the indigenous American form of life presents both a fascination and a challenge to the representational economy of the European invaders. The attempts to contain, delimit, order and incorporate the other are figured in the colonialist representation of the native Americans within European imagery. (Colebrook 1997, 216)

As he considers a variety of colonialist representations of the new world and its peoples, Greenblatt shows how Renaissance culture incorporated images of the other into its discourse and how those images evolved in ensuing negotiations.

In the acknowledgements to *Marvelous Possessions* Greenblatt briefly relates his discussion of European dispossession of new world natives to his own Zionist roots, but as he admits in his essay on 'Wonder and Resonance' (1990, 167), because his own interests and values are pervasive, he seldom feels the need to articulate them. Other prominent new historicists are more insistent that the critic reflect on his or her own historical situation.

Louis Adrian Montrose, for example, stresses the importance of recognizing 'the agency of criticism in constructing and delimiting the subject of study' (1986, 7). Thus to Montrose, new historicism's

> collective project is to resituate canonical literary texts among the multiple forms of writing, and in relation to the non-discursive practices and institutions of the social formation in which those texts have been produced – while, at the same time, recognizing that this project of historical resituation is necessarily the textual construction of critics who are themselves historical subjects. (1986, 6)

Like Greenblatt, Montrose locates the objects of his studies within a dynamic and unstable relationship to material conditions of production and circulation.

Montrose's most quoted phrase acknowledges 'the historicity of texts and the textuality of history' (1986, 8 and 1996, 5). The former refers to the 'social and material embedding of all modes of *writing* [and] ... *reading*' (1996, 6); the latter suggests that

> we can have no access to a full and authentic past, to a lived material existence, that is unmediated by the surviving textual traces of the society in question, and furthermore, that the survival of those traces, rather than others, cannot be assumed to be merely fortuitous but must rather be presumed to be at least partially consequent upon complex and subtle social processes of selective preservation and effacement. (1996, 6)

In a move akin to cultural materialism's emphasis on the ways texts become imbricated in the dominant power structure, Montrose cautions the reader to see the text within a continuous process of mediation.

Montrose eschews strict marxist interpretations, seeing the subject as both determined and capable of agency. The process of subjectification, he contends, 'on the one hand, shapes individuals as loci of consciousness and initiators of action'; on the other hand, it also 'positions, motivates, and constrains them within – subjects them to – social networks and cultural codes that exceed their comprehension or control' (1986, 9). Thus Montrose finds a limited space for the individual to shape his world and allows texts a limited ability to shape social and cultural codes.

Montrose's 1996 monograph, *The Purpose of Playing: Shakespeare and the Cultural Politics of the Elizabethan Theatre*, brings together several of his earlier essays in carefully revised form. The first half examines the place of the professional theatre within Elizabethan culture, showing how the emergence of acting companies and the commodification of dramatic impersonation in an entertainment industry 'were consonant with other material and ideological developments – capital accumulation, market calculation, contractual relations, and "possessive individualism" – that manifested the emergence of what we now characterize as merchant capitalism and bourgeois subjectivity' (1996, 92). The stage thus played a major role in the shift from the communal ceremonies of the medieval Catholic church to the nationalization of English culture under the Tudor Protestant state at the same time as it called into question the state's absolutist assumptions. The book's second half examines the relationship between the theatre and the state in A *Midsummer Night's Dream* through its refiguration of popular mythology surrounding Elizabeth, the virgin Queen.

Montrose's concern with 'figurations of gender' is shared by another prominent new historicist, Jean E. Howard. In an early essay outlining new historicism's major tenets, Howard broadened the scope of its inquiries from the power structure of the Elizabethan and Stuart courts to include people of the 'middling sort', among them merchants, apprentices and women.

Even more than Montrose, Howard contends that 'the historical investigator' is a product of her own time and therefore she can never 'recognize otherness in its pure form' but must always see it 'in part through the framework of the present' (1986, 23). The uncertainties of the present moment (late twentieth-century America) explain the selection of the past moment (early modern England): the Renaissance was 'a boundary or liminal space between two or more monolithic periods where one can see acted out a clash of paradigms and ideologies, a playfulness with signifying systems, a self-reflexivity, and a self-consciousness about the tenuous solidity of human identity which resonate with some of the dominant elements of postmodern culture' (1986, 16–17). In the English

Renaissance contemporary critics find fragmentation and dissonance similar to the cacophony of their own world.

Howard stresses that any critical interpretation of the past is an intervention, an attempt to recuperate meaning from the past for the present. Thus her *The Stage and Social Struggle in Early Modern England* (1994) looks at the ways in which a broad range of Renaissance texts – canonical works by Shakespeare and Jonson, anti-theatrical pamphlets and obscure dramas such as *The Whore of Babylon* and *The Wise Woman of Hogsden* – represent theatrical practices through language. She finds that theatrical discourse in the period was contradictory but reflective of social change. True to her self-description as a 'Marxist feminist', Howard focuses on the ways in which servants, rogues, vagabonds, London citizens and women were represented in ways that sometimes supported, but also sometimes challenged, the dominant male, aristocratic power structure. Howard rejects the by-now outmoded model of subversion vs. containment for a more fluid paradigm of social struggle and contestation.

New historicism has had its share of detractors. In the critical ferment of the 1980s, feminists found the movement's founding 'fathers' – Greenblatt, Orgel and Goldberg – negligent for their indifference to the 'woman's part'. Carol Thomas Neely charged that new historicists resorted to the same old 'male, upper class' texts, and continued to marginalize women (1988, 8–10). In a review of studies of the family in Shakespeare, Lynda E. Boose ruefully wondered, 'Since feminism is, by definition, a subversive site of resistance to the dominant discourse, what is to be made out of new historicism's (Foucauldian) premise that any site of subversive resistance is inevitably defeated or co-opted by the dominant institution?' (1987, 741). Peter Erickson surmised that the schism between feminists and new historicists was a result of 'their conflicting attitudes toward the present ... [W]here new historicism regards the present as an influence to be neutralized or escaped, feminist criticism views the present – including the lives we are living or able to imagine now – as a vital resource and a source of strength' (1987, 335).

During the late 1980s and throughout the 1990s, however, the work of materialist feminists such as Jean E. Howard, Karen Newman, Phyllis Rackin, Dympna Callaghan, Valerie Wayne and Catherine Belsey have undermined this binary opposition. Gender in their work, as Steven Mullaney notes, is

> historically situated, not subordinated to an amorphous concept of power (as early versions of new historicism tended to do), but no longer the exclusive or central category of analysis (as early feminist critiques of new historicism insisted it should be); rather, in such work, gender is increasingly inscribed within a complex nexus of class, gender, and race hierarchies. (1996, 34)

The opposition between new historicism and feminism, which was probably exaggerated to begin with, has faded as a new synthesis of approaches develops.

As Lynda E. Boose's critique suggests, new historicism has been particularly vulnerable to criticism for upholding the Foucauldian notion that power ineluctably works to contain and delimit subversion. Greenblatt's conclusion to his most frequently cited essay, 'Invisible Bullets' – 'There is subversion, no end of subversion, only not for us' (1988, 65) – has become a mantra for criticism from both left and right. Academic conservatives see in this doctrine a dangerous shift towards determinism that erases human agency and makes the author a mere conduit of social and political forces. Edward Pechter thus lumped new historicism with marxist criticism because it views 'all history and contemporary political life as determined, wholly or in essence, by struggle, contestation, power relations, *libido dominandi*' (1987, 292).

Critics from the left also attack 'Invisible Bullets' because of its insistence that containment is inevitable, that efforts to effect social change are inevitably doomed. Walter Cohen, for example, charged that 'new historicism describes historical difference, but it does not explain historical change'; he suggested that new historicism was, in effect, a form of 'leftist disillusionment' (1986, 33, 36). Defending new historicism from Pechter's charges of 'Marxism', Carolyn Porter called on its practitioners to examine more carefully their theoretical assumptions: 'new historicists must begin to ask themselves whether and when this kind of analysis becomes complicit in the cultural operations of power it ostensibly wants to analyse and resist' (1988, 781; see also Porter 1989–90). Frank Lentricchia blamed new historicism in general, and Greenblatt in particular, for espousing orthodoxy disguised as radicalism and for suggesting that 'all struggle against a dominant ideology is in vain' (Lentricchia 1989, 239).

Despite this array of critiques – or perhaps because of it – new historicism seems to have blended into the mainstream as the twenty-first century begins. The work of Stephen Greenblatt and other new historicists has opened up new topics for research and new ways of thinking. More important, the multidisciplinary thrust of their work has been widely adopted in literary and cultural studies in the United States. Literary scholars now avidly embrace texts and methodologies that would not have been considered appropriate to the study of literature twenty-five years ago, and they have broadened the canon to include works from a wide array of nationalities and ethnic groups that were previously marginalized.

The new historicist drive to broaden the canon, too, has been subject to criticism. Pechter, for example, decried new historicism's tendency to flatten out all texts, removing great works of literature from a primary place (1987). Paul Cantor echoed this theme: 'New Historicism works to assimilate [masterpieces of literature] to the average and everyday of their era, to diminish their aura, ultimately to strip them of their claims to genius' (1993, 25). But such fears about a total revamp of the canon are clearly unfounded. New historicists continue to proffer Shakespeare pride of place in the literary pantheon: along with Jean E. Howard, Walter Cohen and Katherine Eisaman Maus, Greenblatt edited *The Norton Shakespeare* (1997) for the textbook market, while Bedford editions of Shakespeare's plays provide an abundance of 'Texts and Contexts' that – in accord with new historicist teachings – situate the dramas within the larger framework of early modern political, social and cultural economies.

As early as 1986 Montrose predicted that new historicism was on its way to becoming the newest orthodoxy (1986, 5), a prescient statement that in many ways now seems a reality. No longer a young Turk resisting Yale's formalist father figures, Stephen Greenblatt now holds an endowed chair at Harvard University and, more significantly, he is the new Associate General Editor of the current *Norton Anthology of English Literature* (2000), the two-volume textbook that for decades has set the canon studied by millions of students in the United States.

At the beginning of the twenty-first century, the critical practices grouped together under the rubric 'new historicism' are exercised throughout the United States, not only in university and college English departments, but in the study of foreign literatures, art history, geography, film and culture. One might even say that what in the 1980s seemed to be a strikingly 'new' practice is now simply common practice.

Virginia Mason Vaughan

Further reading and works cited

Boose, L. E. 'The Family in Shakespeare Studies; or – Studies in the Family of Shakespeareans; or – The Politics of Politics', *Renaissance Quarterly*, 40, 1987.

Cantor, P. A. 'Stephen Greenblatt's New Historicist Vision', *Academic Questions*, 6, 1993.

Cohen, W. 'Political Criticism of Shakespeare', in *Shakespeare Reproduced*, eds J. E. Howard and M. F. O'Connor. New York, 1986.

Colebrook, C. *New Literary Histories*. Manchester, 1997.

Erickson, P. 'Rewriting the Renaissance, Rewriting Ourselves', *Shakespeare Quarterly*, 38, 1987.

Foucault, M. *The Order of Things*. New York, 1970.

Goldberg, J. *James I and the Politics of Literature*. Baltimore, MD, 1983.

Greenblatt, S. J. *Sir Walter Ralegh*. New Haven, CT, 1973.

—. *Renaissance Self-Fashioning from More to Shakespeare*. Chicago, 1980.

—. *Shakespearean Negotiations: The Circulation of Social Energy in Renaissance England*, Berkeley, CA, 1988.

—. 'Introduction to the Forms of Power and the Power of Forms', *Genre*, 15, 1982.

—. *Learning to Curse*. New York, 1990.

—. *Marvellous Possessions*. Chicago, 1991.

Howard, J. E. 'The New Historicism in Renaissance Studies', *English Literary Renaissance*, 16, 1986.

—. *The Stage and Social Struggle in Early Modern England*. London, 1994.

Lentricchia, F. 'Foucault's Legacy', in *The New Historicism*, ed. H. Aram Veeser. New York, 1989.

Montrose, L. 'Renaissance Literary Studies and the Subject of History', *English Literary Renaissance*, 16, 1986.

—. *The Purpose of Playing*. Chicago, 1996.

Mullaney, S. 'After the New Historicism', in *Alternative Shakespeares*, ed. T. Hawkes. London, 1996.

Neely, C. T. 'Constructing the Subject', *English Literary Renaissance*, 18, 1988.

Orgel, S. *The Illusion of Power*. Berkeley, CA, 1975.

Pechter, E. 'The New Historicism and its Discontents: Politicizing Renaissance Drama', *PMLA*, 102, 1987.

Porter, C. 'Are We Being Historical Yet?', *South Atlantic Quarterly*, 87, 1988.

—. 'History and Literature', *New Literary History*, 21, 1989–90.

Veeser, H. Aram (ed.) *The New Historicism*. New York, 1989.

Lesbian and Gay Studies/Queer Theory

Queer theory in the United States is opposed to the kind of encyclopaedic categorization of knowledge represented by this volume. At the same time, it is committed to the global dissemination of information also represented by this volume. It is only by acknowledging the difficulty (and perhaps the disingenuousness) of offering a summary overview that any scholar can hope to describe the disruptive critical endeavour undertaken by queer scholars in the United States.

US queer studies is an amalgam of various theoretical methodologies – feminist, marxist, Foucauldian, deconstructive and new historicist (among others). Coming to academic prominence during the last two decades, queer studies offers insight into issues of gender in general and the heterosexual/homosexual nexus in particular. Moreover, like cultural studies, postcolonialism and other nascent disciplines during this period of the so-called 'cultural wars', queer studies stands as a testing ground for a whole range of postmodern attempts to understand 'difference' – both in terms of culturally specific conditions concerning race/ethnicity, class and gender, and as a general category of knowledge.

It is important not to overstate the role of academic critics in the study of gay culture. Homosexuality has, of course, been an object of interest since at least the medico-scientific research of the late nineteenth-century sexologists, most famously Richard von Krafft-Ebing, Karl Heinrich Ulrichs, Magnus Hirschfeld, John Addington Symonds, Havelock Ellis and of course Sigmund Freud. The origins of recent gay scholarship reach beyond academic theory back to the grassroots politics of sexual liberation. As long as there have been homosexuals, there has been interest in defining what constitutes the sub-culture, if only as a means of identifying possible sexual partners without fear of legal prosecution. Quite simply, one has always had to know a fair amount about patterns of homosexual behaviour to know whom to cruise.

The early history of gay academic scholarship is generally comparable to that of other minority disciplines. The haphazard study of homosexuality in America became more systematic after the Second World War, especially as part of Gay Liberation's pursuit of visibility following New York's Stonewall Rebellion in the summer of 1969. In the earliest stage of recent gay studies (the period roughly from the late 1960s to the late 1970s), journalists and scholars offered popular accounts of previously invisible homosexuals. The forerunner of such work was Jeannette H. Foster's pioneering study in 1956 of 'sex variant [lesbian]' women in literature. More than a decade later book-length histories started to appear, often in conjunction with community organizations like San Francisco's Lesbian and Gay History Project or New York's Lesbian Herstory Archives. Jonathan Ned Katz and Martin Greif undertook broad surveys of gay men and women in history. For the popular press, Vito Russo explored the 'closeted' presence of homosexuals in film, while Kenneth Anger tattled on the sexual misdeeds of a Hollywood 'Babylon'. And in the late 1970s, to counteract the soft-core porn of Alex Comfort's heterosexual best-seller *The Joy of Sex*, Edmund White, Charles Silverstein, Emily Sisley and Bertha Harris all proclaimed the more complex sociological 'joy' of gay and lesbian sex. These early commercial efforts were primarily intended to educate straight society and embolden gay readers. Correcting homophobic misconceptions, they offered historical profiles in gay courage to those isolated lesbians and gay men unaware that their sexual preference was shared by approximately one-tenth of America.

Such efforts at consciousness-raising were followed in the late 1970s and early 1980s by more academic social and literary histories. The relocation of the centre of gay studies from the grassroots movements (primarily in urban communities) to the academy entailed certain predictable shifts in form and emphasis. Many of the historical studies addressed specific issues, not all explicitly gay. Making space for sexuality in history was work by (among others): Estelle Freedman on American prison reform; John D'Emilio on pre-Stonewall community groups; Guido Ruggiero on Renaissance Venice; Allan Bérubé on the Second World War; Judith C. Brown on a seventeenth-century Italian nun; B. R. Burg on seventeenth-century Caribbean pirates; and George Chauncey on New York City between 1890 and 1940. Some histories took a broader perspective. John Boswell's encyclopaedic account of Christian tolerance toward homosexuality became the key reference for early Church opinion. In a wide-ranging series of articles, subsequently collected, Martin Bauml Duberman and Carroll Smith-Rosenberg studied same-sex male and female relations respectively in nineteenth-century America. And more recently Freedman and D'Emilio turned from their specialized studies to co-author an overview of the history of American sexuality both gay and straight.

The difference between these histories and their popular predecessors was as much one of method as of meaning, and scholarly work was fully compatible with the popular campaigns for 'gay pride'. In chronicling the social oppression of homosexuals, historians implicitly defended gay civil rights. And in analysing earlier periods to demonstrate the existence of a positive attitude toward homosexuality, they used the precedent of the past to counter contemporary attacks on sexual 'unnaturalness'. The work of professional historians was supplemented somewhat later by comparable studies of gay aspects of literature. Some of these studies – like those of Lillian Faderman on the development of lesbian culture, Martha Vicinus on Victorian working women, G. S. Rousseau on Enlightenment Englishmen or Shari Benstock on the Left Bank female modernists – approached literature with a eye to social history. Others – like Robert K. Martin's survey of a gay male continuum in American poetry – were more traditionally literary in their analysis. Biographers, too, began to pay more attention to the role of sexuality in identity formation, discussing the homosexuality of such writers as Lord Byron, Walt Whitman, Emily Dickinson, Henry James, Willa Cather and even such fellow academics as Ludwig Wittgenstein and Alan Turing.

Although already a substantial body of work, gay and lesbian scholarship did not have much influence on mainstream theory until the 1980s, when an alliance between feminism and gay male studies placed it at the centre of gender debates. The established feminist scholar Elaine Showalter called for a broadening (and renaming) of 'women's studies' as 'gender studies' to signal the greater variety of ways in which one could 'speak of' gender. Readings by D. A. Miller, Craig Owens, Joseph Allen Boone and Lee Edelman responded to (or anticipated) this call, adapting the paradigms of feminist theory to the study of male homosexuality. The central figure in the rapprochement between feminism and gay studies was the trail-blazing theorist Eve Kosofsky Sedgwick. Her 1985 book *Between Men: English Literature and Male Homosocial Discourse* used Gayle Rubin's notion of the 'traffic in women' to explore the misogyny and homophobia behind the representation of male–male 'homosocial' relations in canonical English literature. And *Epistemology of the Closet*, Sedgwick's magisterial 1990 work, placed gay males at the centre of gender theory with its ringing opening statement that 'an understanding of virtually any aspect of modern western culture must be, not merely incomplete, but damaged in its central substance to the degree that it does not incorporate a critical analysis of modern homo/heterosexual definition' (Sedgwick 1990, 1).

In this first stage of academic commodification, gay studies read feminist theory through the postmodern lens of Derridean deconstruction and Foucauldian discourse analysis. Central was Foucault's claim in *History of Sexuality: Volume I* that the history of sexuality is a history not of bodily activities but of 'discursive practices', a history less of 'sex' than of things said about sex. According to Foucault, 'homosexuality' as a concept did not appear until the invention of the medico-scientific discourse of sexuality in 1869. Before that shift in discursive paradigms, homosexuality was understood as a series of related physical acts, but not associated with any sense of a unified sensibility or even of a distinct character type, 'the homosexual'. In Foucault's powerful formulation, 'homosexuality appeared as one of the forms of sexuality when it was transposed from the practice of sodomy onto a kind of interior androgyny, a hermaphrodism of the soul. The sodomite had been a temporary aberration; the homosexual was now a species' (Foucault 1978, 43).

Academic gay intellectuals had always recognized the dangers of identity politics and of the very concept of 'identity' itself. To avoid what Foucault considered the sin of 'transhistoricism', American gay scholarship for the most part insisted that 'homosexuality', along with other categories of minority difference like gender, race and ethnicity, was 'socially constructed'. A debate between this constructionist position and the complementary 'essentialist' reading occupied centre stage throughout the scholarship of the 1980s. Predictably, both positions made valid points, and both were capable of being overstated. Essentialist interpretations began in the attempt to identify the historical and cultural conditions characteristic of a specific sexual subgroup. At their most extreme, however, essentialists treated same-sex love as a timeless entity, leaving themselves open to charges of ahistoricism and even biological determinism. Aiming for greater historiographic and linguistic precision, constructionists demonstrated that the definition of sexual preference as a timeless entity called 'homosexuality' was itself the product of a particular historical moment in nineteenth-century Victorian culture. Coupling Foucault's sense of historical discontinuity with Derrida's theories of linguistic indeterminacy, constructionists insisted that identity categories should be treated as cultural fictions, implicitly within quotation marks. At best the constructionists ably battled presentism and parochialism. The apparent similarity of same-sex object-choice throughout the ages should not obscure how different cultures experience that choice differently: clone lovers in Greenwich Village share little social reality with Sambian adolescents in New Guinea, or with Socrates and Sappho in ancient Greece. When pressed too far, however, this corrective flirted with cultural determinism. It at times represented sexual preference as so wholly imposed from without that same-sex love appeared as merely a social epiphenomenon, with no grounding in desire.

The limitations of the debate were clearest in its treatment of one of the central political issues of the decade – the spread of HIV virus throughout the gay male population of Europe and North America. More than any other single factor, the health crisis made visible the diversity (and disagreements) within western homosexuality. The uneven spread of the virus through gay communities tragically illustrated that differences in gender, race/ethnicity and class (to say nothing of specific sexual practices) could be more important than similarities in sexual object-choice. Just as AIDS problematized definitions of what constitutes 'being gay', it also challenged understanding of the relationship between academic analysis and political activism. The problem was not, as traditionalists occasionally argued, that AIDS was not a proper object for scholarly study. The gaps between biological evidence and scientific interpretation demonstrated that representations of the disease were as fully fictionalized as any literary narrative. Yet there remained questions about what kind of fiction AIDS was and what knowledge could come from analysing it. In the public arena, fiery protests from activist groups like ACTUP combined with acts of civil disobedience profoundly to change governmental policies concerning education and drug distribution. In more purely academic settings, however, comparable deconstructions of 'the AIDS text' seemed less consequential, even smug. It was hard for 'readings' of AIDS not to recycle platitudes about sexism, racism and homophobia, while flirting with the very objectification they deplored. By representing the health crisis in terms of fashionable theoretical paradigms, scholars did not so much use social construction to deconstruct the misconceptions of scientific discourse as use the (easily agreed upon) limitations of AIDS representations to validate Foucauldian and Derridean paradigms as methods of cultural critique.

The problematic relation between deconstructive linguistic theories and practical politics was one played out in many disciplines – race theory, postcolonialism and minority discourse, as well as gay studies. Although continuing to use constructionist language to caution against ahistoricism in sexuality studies, by the 1990s most scholars found the essentialist/social constructionist controversy less interesting than they had five years earlier. The impersonality of some postmodern paradigms simply did not seem to afford a means to discuss subcultural specificity. In the words of the black gay cultural historian Kobena Mercer, 'although romanticist notions of authorial creativity cannot be returned to the central role they once played in criticism and interpretation, the question of agency in cultural practices that contest the canon and its cultural dominance suggests that it really *does* matter who is speaking' (Mercer 1994, 194). And after the banishment of 'the author' and 'the subject' in the 1980s, many minority scholars in the 1990s began to call for a reconsideration of essentialism, whether as 'strategic essentialism' or the 'risk of essentialism'.

Some of the new tone in gay studies undoubtedly resulted from the rise of a parallel but distinct strain of lesbian theory. Both lesbian and gay studies derived considerable intellectual force and professional visibility from their readings in feminist theory. Yet the route by which gay male theory developed out of (and after) feminism was not identical to that by which lesbian theory developed alongside (and contemporaneous with) it. No single model can describe the relation between feminism and lesbian theory. Lesbians played important roles in the rebirth of feminism in the 1960s, and in fact two of modern feminism's founding texts – Kate Millett's *Sexual Politics* (1970) and Robin Morgan's anthology *Sisterhood is Powerful* (1970) – are also early statements in lesbian theory. Straight feminist accounts of homosexuality run the full range of responses, from homophobic to homophilic. The early work of feminist Betty Friedan was explicitly anti-gay and implicitly anti-lesbian. Ellen Moers' early literary history was anti-lesbian, though not anti-gay. Luce Irigaray's theory could be interpreted as anti-gay, though not as anti-lesbian. And most post-Foucauldian theorists – male and female, gay and straight – reproduced their mentor's silence about the role of lesbian desire in the construction of the *fin-de-siècle* homosexual. The very ease with which straight feminists assimilated gay male theory seemed to mask a lingering discomfort with lesbianism. It was at least worrisome, as more than one theorist remarked, that despite numerous accounts of 'gay men in feminism' a parallel history of 'gay women in feminism' remained unwritten, as though the topic were simultaneously redundant and de trop.

Less wedded than gay male theory to Foucauldian or deconstructive paradigms, lesbian theory was more interested in defining what constituted non-traditional sexualities than in attacking those definitions as socially constructed. This difference was apparent in attempts by Bonnie Zimmerman, Julie Abrahams and others to modify the canon by offering an alternative 'history' of lesbian texts, an enterprise that gay male theory regularly rejected as 'essentialist'. The wish to trace lesbian continuities, both across historical periods and among homosexual and heterosexual subjects, resulted in two complementary ways of conceptualizing homosocial relations among women. The historian Carroll Smith-Rosenberg, in her ground-breaking article 'The Female World of Love and Ritual' (first published in 1975), argued that the nineteenth century permitted a ritualized style of romantic, even sentimentalized affection which to modern ears sounds sexualized. She concluded that 'the twentieth-century tendency to view human love and sexuality within a dichotomized universe of deviance and normality, genitality and platonic love, is alien to the emotions and attitudes of the nineteenth century and fundamentally distorts the nature of these women's emotional interaction' (Smith-Rosenberg 1985, 58–9). The poet/critic Adrienne Rich argued for a more 'transhistorical' position five years later in her 'Compulsory Heterosexuality and Lesbian Existence'. Through 'compulsory heterosexuality', the false claim that people are 'naturally' attracted to people of the opposite sex, society institutionalizes behavioural norms like heterosexuality (and by extension domesticity or capitalism) that threaten all forms of feminism gay or straight. To resist covert social attempts to homogenize desire, Rich not only asserted 'lesbian existence'; she imagined female sexual identities positioned along a 'lesbian continuum', a single line that included the full 'range of woman-identified experience, not simply the fact that a woman has had or consciously desired genital sexual experience with another woman' (Abelove et al. 1993, 239).

Much lesbian theory focused on rethinking, even recuperating, cultural stereotypes. Anthropologist Esther Newton praised the usually pejorative notions of camp male 'drag' and of lesbian 'mannishness'. Drama theorist Sue-Ellen Case celebrated the transgressive character of what others had considered the restrictive clichés of the butch–femme relationship and of lesbian vampirism. Especially influential in these recuperations were insights drawn from performance and film theory. Building on Joan Rivière's notion of femaleness as a 'masquerade' and Laura Mulvey's claim that the cinematic gaze was inherently male, theorists like Case, Teresa de Lauretis and Kaja Silverman explored the implications of masquerade and the male gaze for sexuality. One particularly celebrated use of performance theory was that of philosopher Judith Butler. In *Gender Trouble: Feminism and the Subversion of Identity*, Butler argued that 'the identity categories often presumed to be foundational to feminist politics ... simultaneously work to limit and constrain in advance the very cultural possibilities that feminism is supposed to open up'; that 'gender' as a category unwittingly supported gender hierarchy and compulsory heterosexuality (Butler 1990, 147, x). In *Bodies That Matter: On the Discursive Limits of 'Sex'*, Butler explored the interconnections between the 'performativity' of gender and the materiality of the body. Butler conceived performativity both as an authoritarian form of speech, in which power acted *as* discourse, and as a linguistic relation that automatically implicated speakers in the very thing they opposed (Butler 1993, 225, 241). She understood bodily materiality as the effect of a dynamic of power, and construed 'sex' not as a biological fact but as a cultural norm (ibid., 2–3). Her sense that performativity constituted the sex/gender matrix was subsequently taken up by such theorists of male sexuality as Sedgwick, Miller and Edelman, and remains one of the reigning paradigms of contemporary sexuality theory.

The models of performance popularized by Butler and Sedgwick employed an aggressively postmodern notion of 'self', coupling a Derridean focus on iterability with a psychoanalytic (often Lacanian) interest in repetition compulsion, abjection and interpellation to critique as static the more traditional Austinian sense of the linguistic performative. In the early 1990s these high theory paradigms found their notions of transgressive theatricality embodied in a grassroots movement seeking to expose some political limitations of Gay Liberation. At the start of the new decade, a group called 'Queer Nation' extended the political project of ACTUP beyond the specific focus on AIDS reform to decry more generally the conservative, middle-class ethos of 1970s gay activism. Distancing itself from the misogyny and racism of earlier sexual movements, Queer Nation discarded as tainted the adjective 'gay' and adopted instead the self-appellation 'queer'.

Such confrontiveness was not universally admired by older generations, and as a coherent political movement Queer Nation lasted only a few years. Yet scholars saw in its disruptive tactics a model for the transformative potential of language. Judith Butler argued that such a use of 'queer' did not simply redefine a term of derision into one of celebration. Calling into question the very nature of power, queering was 'a linguistic practice whose purpose has been the shaming of the subject it names' (Butler 1993, 226). Others read the movement even more broadly, and influential 'special issues' of *differences* and *Social Text*, edited respectively by Teresa de Lauretis and Michael Warner, used the term 'queer' to call for a coalition among various minority positions – gay and lesbian of course, but also other less clearly defined outcasts. As Warner explained in the introduction to *Fear of a Queer Planet*, 'queer politics brings [together] very differently sexualized and differently politicized people' into a movement that 'rejects a minoritizing logic of toleration or simple political interest-representation in favour of a more thorough resistance to the regime of the normal' (Warner 1993, xvi, xxvi). Or, as he stated in a piece co-authored with Lauren Berlant, 'without assimilating queerness to a familiar minority identity like gay', queer theory 'wants to address the full range of power-ridden normativities of sex': 'the name queer [is not] an umbrella for gays, lesbians, bisexuals, and the transgendered. Queer politics makes available different understandings of membership at different times, and membership in them is more a matter of aspiration than it is the expression of an identity or a history' (Berlant and Warner 1991, 346, 345, 344).

Everyone understood that there were limitations to conceiving of sexuality as oppositional. Leo Bersani long ago remarked that anyone who has ever been to a gay bathhouse understands that homosexuality does not necessary entail open-mindedness. While supporting the principles of 'queeritude', Lauren Berlant cautioned that in its allegiance to the rhetorics of camp and citizenship, Queer Nation might unintentionally have reinforced an American national fantasy of consensus. Moreover, in declaring that 'queer' sexuality does not depend purely on sexual identity, theorists extended minority status to those not systematically discriminated against: people apparently empowered by the mainstream could declare themselves individually 'queered' by their personal deviations from heteronormativity. Doubting the value of any form of institutionalization, queer theory opposed all attempts to map out a 'gay and lesbian' literary canon. The unfortunate result of such an admirable scepticism was that queer theory all too often focused on the already canonical work of Oscar Wilde or Henry James, while ignoring the importance of contemporary work by James Baldwin, John Rechy, Jane Rule, Audre Lorde, Samuel R. Delaney, Thomas Disch, Michael Nava, Dorothy Allison and Jewelle Gomez. Most distressing, however, was the way in which the oppositional strategy was so quickly domesticated by the mainstream. Not offering itself as a new category of knowledge, queer theory meant to challenge the very notion of labelling. When 'queer' became simply the new name for Barnes & Noble shelves formerly labelled 'Gay and Lesbian', the term, evacuated of its political content, lost much of its transformation status.

Queer performativity is still an active, and arguably the dominant, paradigm of contemporary US theory of sexuality, especially as applied to cultural studies and theatre and film theory. Alive to the problems of commodification and co-optation, however, queer theorists have in recent years taken performance paradigms in a range of new directions. While it is too early to generalize comfortably about the shape of these new explorations, two tendencies have emerged. One develops out of ideological criticism in general (and Althusserian accounts of the invisibility of state apparatus in particular) to explore not the minority position but the character of dominant culture. Long ago Richard Dyer deplored the way in which 'whiteness' was 'unmarked', pretending to characterlessness at the same time that it constructed the putative differentiating traits with which to identify racial and ethnic minorities. Dyer and Ruth Frankenberg (among others) have continued to critique this misrepresentation both through delineating the processes by which whiteness manufactures its own invisibility, and by 'marking' whiteness with the traits it represses. Similar critiques of the process by which hegemony renders itself invisible have considered the issues of masculinity and citizenship. Men's studies have for a long time applied feminist paradigms of the sex/gender system to understand maleness. More recently, Judith Halberstam has worked to separate the concept of 'masculinity' from biology to claim that the processes by which masculinity has been constructed are most easily recognized in female masculinity. Similarly Warner, Berlant and a number of other scholars have problematized the notion of American citizenship with quasi-Lacanian critiques of the 'National Symbolic' and 'Queer Symbolic', the linguistic process by which those not actually enfranchised are made to feel as if they have been afforded a voice within national discourse.

Another new direction studies the 'intersectionality' among sexuality and other minority identities, customarily those of gender, race/ethnicity and class. Cultural studies scholars like Stuart Hall had always considered issues of 'double' minoritization, and film-makers – most notably the Sankofa Collective and Isaac Julien in Great Britain and Marlon Riggs and Cheryl Dunye in the US – frequently explored the complexities of black gay identity. Since its institutionalization, lesbian and gay theory has tried to modify its own predominantly white middle-class sensibility, especially along the lines suggested in famous critiques by Kobena Mercer, Tomás Almaguer, Barbara Smith, bell hooks, Gloria Anzaldúa and Cherrie Moraga. Theorists of colour like Kimberlé Crenshaw, Valerie Smith and Norma Alárcon have increasingly focused not on the indeterminacy of individual identities, which are treated as relatively stable, but on the interpretative ambiguities that arise from the intersections (and at times indistinguishability) among those categories. Theorists of sexuality like David Van Leer and Robyn Weigman applied notions of 'intersectionality' to include the sex/gender nexus. They argue that minority identities are traditionally treated as indistinguishable by the dominant culture and cannot really be studied as discrete entities. Such interest in a multi-valent 'minority discourse' rejects the binaries of traditional minority scholarship, emphasizing the conversations among minority identities over the ways in which each is victimized and disciplined by dominant culture.

It is pointless to predict paths for queer theory. Many recent developments in the field cannot be separated from similar impulses to globalization and multiculturalism in related disciplines like women's studies, race/ethnic studies, film studies, postcolonial studies and cultural studies. As a result of these shared impulses, sexuality theory may see less the further development of its own methodologies than an amalgamation with other disciplines. But whether the future of sexuality lies in performativity, multi-ethnicity, or some as-yet undefined interdisciplinary coalition, at the beginning of the new millennium queer theory remains one of the most lively and active of academic enterprises.

David Van Leer

Further reading and works cited

Abelove, H. et al. (eds) *The Lesbian and Gay Studies Reader*. New York, 1993.

Berlant, L. *The Queen of America Goes to Washington City: Essays on Sex and Citizenship*. Durham, NC, 1997.

— and Warner, M. 'What Does Queer Theory Teach Us about X?', *Periodical of Modern Languages Association*, 110, 1991.

Bersani, L. 'Is the Rectum a Grave?', in *AIDS: Cultural Analysis/Cultural Activism*, ed. D. Crimp. Cambridge, MA, 1988.

Boone, J. A. and Cadden, M. (eds) *Engendering Men*. New York, 1990.

Boswell, J. *Christianity, Social Tolerance, and Homosexuality: Gay People in Western Europe from the Beginning of the Christian Era to the Fourteenth Century*. Chicago, 1980.

Butler, J. *Gender Trouble: Feminism and the Subversion of Identity*. New York, 1990.

—. *Bodies that Matter: On the Discursive Limits of 'Sex'*. New York, 1993.

Case, S.-E. (ed.) *Performing Feminisms*. Baltimore, MD, 1990.

Creekmur, C. K. and Doty, A. (eds) *Out in Culture*. Durham, NC, 1995.

de Lauretis, T. *The Practice of Love*. Bloomington, IN, 1994.

Duberman, M. Bauml et al. (eds) *Hidden From History: Reclaiming the Gay and Lesbian Past*. New York, 1989.

Faderman, L. *Surpassing the Love of Men*. New York, 1981.

Foucault, M. *History of Sexuality: Volume I, An Introduction*. New York, 1978.

Frankenberg, R. *White Women, Race Matters*. Minneapolis, MN, 1993.

Fuss, D. *Essentially Speaking*. New York, 1989.

— (ed.) *Inside/Out*. New York, 1991.

Halberstram, J. *Female Masculinity*. Durham, NC, 1998.

Katz, J. N. *Gay American History*. New York, 1976.

Martin, R. K. *The Homosexual Tradition in American Poetry*. Austin, TX, 1979.

Mercer, K. *Welcome to the Jungle: New Positions in Black Cultural Studies*. New York, 1994.

Miller, D. A. *The Novel and the Police*. Berkeley, CA, 1988.

Sedgwick, E. Kosofsky. *Between Men*. New York, 1985.

—. *Epistemology of the Closet*. Berkeley, CA, 1990.

Smith-Rosenberg, C. *Disorderly Conduct: Visions of Gender in Victorian America*. New York, 1985.

Van Leer, D. *The Queening of America: Gay Culture in Straight Society*. New York, 1995.

Warner, M. (ed.) 'Fear of a Queer Planet', *Cultural Politics*, 6, 1993.

Wiegman, R. *American Anatomies: Theorizing Race and Gender*. Durham, NC, 1995.

Zimmerman, B. 'What Has Never Been: An Overview of Lesbian Feminist Criticism', in *The New Feminist Criticism*, ed. E. Showalter. New York, 1985.

Postcolonial Studies

The publication of Edward Said's *Orientalism* in 1978 inaugurated the field of postcolonial studies in the US. Said's demonstration that an enormous number of literary, political, religious and philosophical texts about the Islamic Orient from the eighteenth century to the present functioned as a Foucauldian disciplinary practice linked with British and French colonization, influenced a generation of scholars. Although many, such as Homi

Bhabha, parted company with Said and emphasized the ambivalence rather than the hegemony of colonial discourse, and feminists such as Gayatri Spivak forced a dialogue between western feminism and colonialism, the major areas of inquiry opened up by Said's work – the analysis of western texts as colonial discourse, the investigation of representations of the colonized, the study of forms of resistance to colonization in third world literature – all became important areas of inquiry in literary and cultural studies, and to a lesser extent in history and anthropology. So, too, concerns such as nationalism, decolonization, neocolonialism and imperialism began to be seen as the problems of language itself. More recently, postcolonial studies has concerned itself with the 'internal colonization' of racial minorities in the US and with globalization.

What explains the spectacular growth of postcolonial studies in the US academy in the 1980s? For marxist critics such as Aijaz Ahmad and Arif Dirlik, US postcolonial theory has flourished because of its complicity with global capitalism (Dirlik 1997, 503): its emergence at the beginning of global capitalism; its privileging of the position of the elite migrant intellectual; its attractiveness as a narrative eliding specific inequities of class; and its inbuilt incapacity for praxis because of its critique of grand narratives (Ahmad 1992, 68, 69). To an extent, these critiques are true. There is reason to be vigilant about the politics of postcoloniality because of its production at the metropolitan centre. On the other hand, not all migrant intellectuals are similarly located at the centre. Edward Said's position as a Palestinian activist, which has subjected him to numerous death threats and daily harassment, is not the same as Homi Bhabha's purely western academic positioning, or Spivak's intimacy with historians in India and her precarious status as a feminist in the West, or Partha Chatterjee's split US – India appointments which challenge 'location' itself. Metropolitan location, thus, cannot be homogenized. US postcolonial studies, in fact, includes a diverse variety of interests, having in common an analysis of colonization and its aftermath.

That postcolonial studies are not marxist enough does not go far enough to explain the popularity of this complex field. The reasons for its ascendancy are institutional and cultural and occasion both hope and vigilance. On the positive side, clearly, postcolonial studies has opened up college curricula to third world texts in unprecedented ways. Chinua Achebe's *Things Fall Apart* is probably as well known by undergraduates as Conrad's *Heart of Darkness*. Concerns of colonization and empire have become important in all humanities fields. Postcolonial studies have realized these gains because of the momentum built up by the Civil Rights era, and the formation of African-American and ethnic studies programmes in which prominent intellectuals such as Henry Louis Gates and Ronald Takaki have argued for canon and paradigm expansion. On the more sobering side, one can see two related and troubling issues: (a) the turn toward 'ambivalence' and 'hybridity' as analytic models for colonization and the attractiveness of this turn to both practitioners and observers of postcolonial studies; and (b), the scarcely acknowledged role of postcolonial studies to defuse concerns of race.

When postcolonial studies began, the radical race-based demands for Civil Rights articulated in the 1960s were experiencing a strong backlash, fuelled by the anti-affirmative action policies of the Reagan era. In the social sciences, the paradigm of race (associated with rights and inequalities) was replaced with the safer paradigm of ethnicity (Omi and Winant 1986, 12). African-American studies continued to grow, most significantly in the discovery of nineteenth-century texts and the stature of theorists such as Henry Louis Gates, Houston Baker, bell hooks and Hortense Spillers, but nobody seemed very interested in the Black Panthers. Internationally, most anti-colonial movements had been won and most revolutionary writing had been published at least a decade previously. Postcolonial studies thus entered the academy after the period of active radical politics and has, in some ways, chosen not to be activist. Unlike scholars in fields such as African-American studies, feminist studies and ethnic studies, fields inaugurated to address concerns of domination and exploitation, no postcolonialist has demanded the creation of postcolonial studies programmes. Thus, despite the prestige of a handful of scholars, most postcolonialists could be easily tucked away in departments which could then claim diversity. More importantly, the general movement in postcolonial studies away from Said's model of discourse analysis which, for all its flaws, foregrounded domination and exploitation (seen as too binaristic by some critics) to negotiatory analyses of colonization popularized by Homi Bhabha, has ensured the non-threatening nature of much of the field. Postcolonial studies could thus be seen as a field that, while satisfying marginality, could be used to offset the challenges posed by African-American studies and to neutralize concerns of race. As postcolonial studies grows to cover 'internal colonization', it cannot afford its separatist stance from African-American studies or real concerns of race and domination, concerns currently being addressed by theorists like Lisa Lowe.

Yet, despite its tendency to get co-opted into a liberal pluralism, postcolonial studies have posed significant challenges to our understanding of western modernity, to relations between First and Third Worlds or what is now the North and South, to western feminist theory, to issues of immigration and globalization, and even to the field of American studies. The immediate historical antecedent to the development of postcolonial studies was the decolonization of most of Asia and Africa in the 1950s and 1960s. At the Bandung Conference of 1955, representatives from twenty-nine Asian and African states collectively condemned colonialism and Indian Prime Minister Jawaharlal Nehru used the term third world as a form of identity. The 1950s saw the beginning of the Mau-Mau rebellion in Kenya, the FLN's struggle for liberation in Algeria and the independence of Ghana. By the 1960s and 1970s most of Africa, Asia and the Caribbean was decolonized. The 1950s and 1960s also produced the revolutionary, anti-colonial treatises born of struggle: Aimé Cesaire's *Discourse on Colonialism* (1955), George Lamming's Calibanistic reading of Shakespeare's *The Tempest* in *The Pleasures of Exile* (1960), Frantz Fanon's experiences of racial marginalization in *Black Skin White Masks* (1952), his treatise on the Algerian revolution in 'Algeria Unveiled' (1959) and on the importance of nation in *The Wretched of the Earth* (1961), Tunisian revolutionary Albert Memmi's *The Colonizer and the Colonized*, the numerous works of C. L. R. James, and Roberto Fernandez Retamar's 'Caliban' (1971). The idea of a pan-African identity was begun by revolutionaries in exile in France such as Aimé Cesaire (Martinique) and Leopold Senghor (Senegal) who turned the despised term 'nègre' into a term of pride signified by the term 'negritude', a movement that in turn inspired a generation of African-American activists.

In its most basic sense, the term 'postcolonial' is a temporal marker for the condition after colonialism. Postcolonial theory attempts to understand and interrogate the colonial past, see its effects on the present and, at its best, articulates strategies for cultural survival. The term (first used by Hamza Alavi) has been debated by critics on several grounds. Some claim that the hyphenated term marks a decisive break with the colonial past, while others claim that the non-hyphenated, 'postcolonial' captures more accurately the continuing effects of colonialism. Anthony Appiah describes the 'post' as a 'space-clearing gesture' for producing work which, though marked by colonialism, transcends its modes of knowledge

(Appiah 1997, 432, 440). The term postcolonial is now freely applied to literature being written by the formerly colonized countries and has replaced older terms such as third world literature and imperial terms such as Commonwealth literature. It is also being used as an analytical category in relation to internally colonized cultures such as Native American, Chicana/o, African-American and Asian-American. The prefix 'post' has also generated discussions about postcolonial's connections with other postist terms such as 'poststructuralism' and 'postmodernism'. While hardly identical with these latter terms which do not carry its economic or military weight, postcolonial theory does share with poststructuralism its critique of western master narratives which masked the process of Othering, and with postmodernism its suspicion of historiography as truth. Postcolonial theory also broadly relies on poststructuralism's critique of any sign system as simple representation.

In the US, the major paradigms for postcolonial studies have been offered by Edward Said (colonial discourse analysis), Homi K. Bhabha (psychoanalysis and hybridity) and Gayatri C. Spivak (critiques of western feminism, the sovereign Subject, and attention to the foreclosed subaltern). In *Orientalism* (1978), Said applied Foucault's notion of discourse as that which produces its objects of knowledge and procedures of truth to address an area that Foucault had left out: colonialism. Beginning with the late eighteenth century and up to contemporary anti-Arab sentiment in the US media, Said powerfully demonstrated how Orientalism (including research on the Orient, theories about the Orient, novels, epics, etc. about the Orient, as well as Oriental institutes in the West) was a colonial discourse through which European culture managed and produced the Orient 'politically, sociologically, militarily, ideologically, scientifically, and imaginatively during the post-Enlightenment period' (Said 1978, 3). Despite various writers and genres, Orientalism produced a picture of the Oriental as passive, deviant, feminized and unable to represent itself. In *Culture and Imperialism*, (1993), Said extended his readings to include texts by Conrad, Austen and Camus, as well as resistance literature, and shifted the terms of his analysis to emphasize what he called a contrapuntal reading of the cultural archive with both the metropole and the colony writing with awareness of each other. Nevertheless, Said continued to insist that the division between the 'West and the rest' (Said 1993, 51) ran like a fissure through imperial history. Although Said pays scant attention to issues of gender and class, his work has provided a powerful model for analysing colonial discourse.

If Said stressed the inexorable constructions of the West and the rest in colonial discourse, Homi K. Bhabha has introduced what are probably the most popular terms in postcolonial theory today: hybridity, ambivalence and contradiction. Influenced by Lacanian psychoanalysis, Bhabha emphasized the contradictory motivations of anxiety and defence, mastery and pleasure behind the construction of the stereotype. The stereotype, according to Bhabha, functions as a fetish, at once affirming and disavowing difference (Bhabha 1994, 74–5). Because colonial texts acquire meaning only after being circulated in the colony, difference becomes part of such texts. Consequently, Bhabha writes, 'the colonial presence is always ambivalent, split between its appearance as original and authoritative and its articulation as repetition and difference', producing a mode of authority agonistic rather than antagonistic (1994 107–8). Such split forms of authority, Bhabha argues, are implicit in Said and central to Fanon who evokes the colonial situation through image and fantasy and privileges the psychic dimension of the colonial experience (1994, 42–3).

Does feminism participate as colonial discourse? Gayatri Spivak took up this question in two path-breaking essays: 'French Feminism in an International Frame' (1981) and 'Three

Women's Texts and a Critique of Imperialism' (1985). Spivak employed the techniques of deconstructive reading, marxism and feminism to question the ethnocentrism of French and British feminisms. Spivak demonstrated how French feminists routinely ignored their own emphasis on recognizing the heterogeneity of the concept 'woman' in dealing with third world women; Kristeva spoke for the Chinese women she saw, and analysed them definitively as participants of an unchanging patriarchal culture (Spivak 1988, 137). Spivak also suggested ways in which marxist analysis could help uncover the complicity between domestic womanhood and patriarchal capitalism on the one hand and the repression of the clitoral and the specific oppression of third world women as cheap labour on the other. Throughout her critiques, Spivak has remained strongly Derridean, always suspicious of narratives of origin or totalization. Thus, while Said focused attention on the power of Orientalist representation, and Bhabha on the inevitable ambivalence of this power, Spivak has insistently focused on the situatedness of the speaking position, the problem of representation itself and the inevitable voicelessness of the subaltern. In her most misunderstood and most well known work, 'Can the Subaltern Speak', Spivak critiques Foucault and Deleuze for not recognizing their positions as western intellectuals at the moment at which they suggest the possibility of the oppressed being speaking subjects. For Spivak, the idea of the oppressed being able to speak can too often become a simplified denial of the complex conditions of language and power under which particularly the female subaltern operates. While colonial history homogenizes the subaltern, the attempts of the subaltern studies historians (from India) to retrieve subaltern consciousness is problematic and impossible. 'For the "true" subaltern group, whose identity is its difference, there is no unrepresentable subaltern subject that can know and speak itself' (Spivak 1994, 80). The subaltern, Spivak suggests, can never be adequately represented by intellectuals nor can the subaltern ever have access to what constitutes speech according to the dominant culture. And she will be misrepresented. Thus, Spivak moves to her much criticized statements: 'The subaltern as female cannot be heard or read' and 'The subaltern cannot speak' (Spivak 1994, 104).

In *Outside in the Teaching Machine* (1993), Spivak interrogates what is taken to be third world or marginal writing in the context of the explosion of marginality studies in the US Arguing that the marginal is shaped by the kind of institution (teaching machine) it enters, Spivak critiques the homogenizing imperatives of the US academy as it constructs third world writing as always revolutionary, conscious of marginality and poised against western feminism. Spivak shifts the focus to differences among third world women, and through Bengali writer, Mahasweta Devi, points to a writing outside that of metropolitan post-coloniality. Seemingly reversing her earlier position about the unrepresentability of the subaltern, Spivak suggests that Devi can indeed speak about and write to the subaltern (Spivak 1993, 78). Analyses of the power of western institutions in shaping what is circulated as third world or marginal promise to be an important area in postcolonial studies.

Attention to positionality and to the Derridean deferment of the trace in the figure of the subaltern woman continue to be Spivak's major concerns. In *A Critique of Postcolonial Reason* (1999), Spivak combines these concerns with an increasing attention to native complicity in imperialism and an insistence of the urgency of postcolonial theory to learn from the insights of third world activism. *A Critique* is monumental in its sheer range: four major sections cover Philosophy, Literature, History and Culture; her analysis moves from Kant, Hegel, Marx and the Gita in philosophy to Kipling, Rhys, Mahasweta and Coetzee in literature, to the British management of widow burning in history, to the politics of postmodern fashion in culture. Although derided precisely because of its range by marxist critic Terry Eagleton, *A Critique* emphasizes the responsibility of the postcolonial critic to address precisely those areas deemed separate and unrelated through the epistemic violence of colonialism. Spivak constantly tracks the figure of the native informant, thus emphasizing, for instance, the continuity between the needed and foreclosed figure of the 'raw man' in Kant's construction of the sublime and the contemporary female subaltern who is silenced within a universalist feminist solidarity in which ' "woman" is important, not race, class, and empire' (Spivak 1999, 409). Spivak demonstrates how the native informant is not simply a slight figure within western philosophical and literary narratives, but rather the key on which major concepts rest. Spivak also focuses on uncovering native complicity with imperialism. In a bold move from the politics of resistance broadly accepted by postcolonialists, Spivak writes, 'We cannot merely continue to act out the part of Caliban. One task of deconstruction might be a persistent attempt to displace the reversal, to show the complicity between native hegemony and the axiomatics of imperialism' (Spivak 1999, 37). Thus Spivak demonstrates, for instance, the complicity between Hegel's reading of the Gita as belonging to the unconscious symbolic and the structure of the Gita itself which functions to confirm the social order of the castes, marking the movement away from a tribal social order. In *Critique*, Spivak also suggests a new project intimated by Derrida's more activist phase of affirmative deconstruction in which justice and ethics are undeconstructible terms. Spivak argues for a postcolonial learning of vocabularies *from* (instead of representation of) 'counterglobalist or alternative-development activism' (1999, 429).

Many postcolonial feminists have focused on questions of alterity and identity, on 'authenticity', the status of the diasporic native, and the importance of concrete specificity in feminist analyses of third world women. The issue of authenticity, i.e. what the native woman is 'actually' like or should be represented as, has brought feminists of different races and from different fields together. Thus the highly experimental, postmodern Vietnamese-American film-maker and anthropologist Trinh T. Minh-ha writes, 'Today, planned authenticity is rife … it constitutes an efficacious means of silencing the cry of racial oppression. We no longer wish to erase your difference. We demand on the contrary, that you remember and assert it. At least to a certain extent' (Minh-ha 1989, 89). Similarly, Chandra Mohanty, the Indian-American feminist, critiques the homogenization of diversely classed, sexed and raced women under the singular category, 'third world women' (Mohanty). Rey Chow interrogates the Orientalist lens within China studies that associates the 'authentic' China only with the past, as well as the politics of US academia in which the criticism of Chinese communism by a diasporic Hong Konger can only be seen as retrograde (Chow 1991, 1993). While Minh-ha, Mohanty and Chow focus on sites that can easily be identified as postcolonial (Vietnam, India, Hong Kong), the status of black feminists within postcoloniality has been more vexed. Postcolonial anthologies now include works by black feminists such as Hazel Carby, Audre Lorde and bell hooks (McClintock et al. 1997). This convergence of different feminists under postcolonial studies is, of course, not surprising if we recollect that the third-world movement of the late 1960s was a coalition of African-American, Native American, Asian-American and Chicano/a students who modelled themselves after third world liberation struggles, declaring ghettos to be 'internal colonies'. Conversely, anti-colonial writers such as George Lamming recalled for inspiration the writers of the Harlem Renaissance. Yet the 'inclusion' of black women has not been unproblematic. The postmodern epistemological basis of a lot of postcolonial theory and the historical neglect of black women within the former has been a cause for concern among black feminists. As bell hooks puts it, radical postmodern practice will be politically inept if it fails to incorporate the voices of oppressed blacks. hooks writes, 'third world nationals, elites, and white critics' who 'never notice or look at black people on the streets ... are not likely to produce liberatory theory that will challenge racist domination ...' (hooks 1990, 25). In order for black feminism and postcolonial theory to engage in productive dialogue, postcolonial theorists will have to privilege race more as a category, and to acknowledge the radical insights of early black feminists such as Sojourner Truth. Spivak's dismissal of race as simple chromatism in her most recent work will continue to be problematic (Spivak 1999, 166). It is precisely Lisa Lowe's focus on race as a regulatory mechanism that energizes her study of Asian-Americans as citizens, cultural producers and sweatshop labour (Lowe 1996).

Postcolonial studies has also provided an arena of fierce debate about ideas of nation. While Benedict Anderson claimed 'nation-ness [as] the most universally legitimate value in the political life of our time' (Anderson 1991, 3), demonstrating the inherent democracy of the concept, Partha Chatterjee critiqued Anderson's claims by demonstrating the inherent elitism of third world nationalisms that rested upon western modernity (1993, 11). Globalization and the fast flow of information in the electronic age have added new questions A key argument has been that of Arjun Appadurai who suggests that that the new cultural scene is one of 'global flows' and disjunctures, a 'global culture of the hyperreal' in which many people live in 'imagined worlds' (rather than imagined communities/nations) (1996, 31, 33). Such a world cannot be explained through older centre–periphery models. However, one should note that Appadurai's analysis of globalization through metaphors of movement and disorganization overlooks both the gross economic inequities unleashed by multinational corporations, as well as the one-way movement of American culture to third world countries. While paradigms such as rooted cosmopolitanism have also been posited to address the 'postnational' world, critics of globalization have offered more sobering analyses (Appiah 1998, 91). Aihwa Ong, for instance, suggests that the 'flexible citizenship' of diasporic Chinese from Hong Kong amounts to flexible accumulation of capital (Ong 1998, 138–41).

Many contemporary critics are seeing globalization as an Americanized continuation of colonialism. Within the United States, the idea of examining racially different groups through postcoloniality is increasingly becoming important. The diasporic 'reterritorialization of postcoloniality into ethnicity' has the potential to represent the third world within the First by fundamentally questioning the way dominant regimes dictate questions of identity (Radhakrishnan 1996, xxiv). For Chicano/a and Native American populations within the United States, however, postcoloniality needs no reterritorialization into ethnicity. The colonized, in these cases, is the ethnic. In Borderlands, arguably the most influential Chicana treatise about the colonization of Mexican-Americans, Anzaldúa celebrates the hybrid border cultures formed in the Southwest as a result of US colonization. Following Anzaldúa, Chicano critics such as Jose Saldivar have used the border as a powerful metaphorical challenge to the idea of a dominant, hegemonic nationalism. A similar impetus to Native American studies is being given through the idea of Native Americans as a colonized people (Krupat 1994). Studies of early treaty negotiations, oral narratives and legal battles over forced movement have all energized the study of both contemporary and early US literature.

The examination of early US literary and cultural texts through postcoloniality has the potential to significantly alter the field. Ever since the authors of *The Empire Writes Back* stated that the United States was the first country to produce a postcolonial literature, questions about who can constitute legitimate postcolonial subjects have surfaced. The essays in *The Cultures of United States Imperialism* focus on imperialism as a significant ideology in the culture after US expansion in the 1890s; Malini Schueller's *U.S. Orientalisms* (1998) traces a genealogy of different Orientalist discourses in the US from 1790 to 1890. Edward Watts' *Writing and Postcoloniality in the Early Republic* (1998) argues for a 'Second World' model (appropriate for cultures both colonizing and colonized). As postcolonial studies continue to enjoy academic prestige, its challenge will be to forge a constituency from which minority voices can be articulated without being homogenized and to continue to critique its own emergence from the metropolitan centre of the contemporary world.

Malini Johar Schueller

Further reading and works cited

Ahmad, A. *In Theory*. London, 1992.
Anderson, B. *Imagined Communities*. London, 1991.
Anzaldúa, G. *Borderlands/La Frontera*. San Francisco, 1987.
Appadurai, A. *Modernity at Large*. Minneapolis, MN, 1996.
Appiah, A. 'Is the "Post" in "Postcolonial" the "Post-" in "Postmodern"?, in *Dangerous Liaisons*, eds A. McClintock et al. Minneapolis, MN, 1997.
—. 'Cosmopolitan Patriots', in *Cosmopolitics*, eds P. Cheah and B. Robbins. Minneapolis, MN, 1998.
Ashcroft, B. et al. *The Empire Writes Back*. New York, 1989.
Bhabha, H. K. (ed.) *Nation and Narration*. New York, 1990.
—. *The Location of Culture*. New York, 1994.
Chatterjee, P. *Nationalist Thought and the Colonial World*. Minneapolis, MN, 1993.
Chow, R. *Woman and Chinese Modernity: The Politics of Reading Between East and West*. Minneapolis, MN, 1991.
—. *Writing Diaspora: Tactics of Intervention in Contemporary Cultural Studies*. Bloomington, IN, 1993.
Dirlik, A. 'The Postcolonial Aura', in *Dangerous Liasons*, eds A. McClintock et al. Minneapolis, MN, 1997.
Fanon, F. *The Wretched of the Earth*. New York, 1963.
—. *Black Skin White Masks*. New York, 1967.
Gates Jr, H. L. *'Race', Writing and Difference*. Chicago, 1985.
hooks, b. *Yearning*. Boston, 1990.
JanMohamed, A. *Manichean Aesthetics*. Amherst, 1983.
— and Lloyd, D. (eds) *The Nature and Context of Minority Discourse*. New York, 1990.
Kaplan, A. and Pease, D. (eds) *The Cultures of United States Imperialism*. Durham, 1993.
Krupat, A. 'Postcoloniality and Native American Literature', *Yale Journal of Criticism*. 7, i, 1994.
Lowe, L. *Immigrant Acts*. Durham, NC, 1996.
McClintock, A. *Imperial Leather*. New York, 1995.
— et al. (eds) *Dangerous Liaisons*. Minneapolis, MN, 1997.
Minh-ha, T. T. *Woman, Native, Other*. Bloomington, IN, 1989.
Mohanty, C. 'Under Western Eyes', in *Third World Women and the Politics of Feminism*, eds Mohanty et al. Bloomington, IN, 1991.
Omi, M. and Winant, H. *Racial Formation in The United States*. New York, 1986.

Ong, A. 'Flexible Citizenship among Chinese Cosmopolitans', in *Cosmopolitics*, eds P. Cheah and B. Robbins. Minneapolis, MN, 1998.

Pratt, M. L. *Imperial Eyes*. New York, 1992.

Radhakrishnan, R. *Diasporic Mediations*. Minneapolis, MN, 1996.

Said, E. W. *Orientalism*. New York, 1978.

—. *Culture and Imperialism*. New York, 1993.

Saldivar, J. D. *Border Matters*. Berkeley, CA, 1997.

San Jr, J. E. *Beyond Postcolonial Theory*. New York, 1998.

Shohat, E. 'Notes on the Postcolonial', *Social Text*, 31/32, 1992.

Spivak, G. Chakravorty. *In Other Worlds: Essays in Cultural Politics*. New York, 1988.

—. *Outside in the Teaching Machine*. New York, 1993.

—. 'Can the Subaltern Speak', in *Colonial Discourse and Postcolonial Theory*, eds P. Williams and L. Chrisman. New York, 1994.

—. *A Critique of Postcolonial Reason*. Cambridge, MA, 1999.

Viswanathan, G. *Masks of Conquest*. New York, 1989.

Williams, P. and Chrisman, L. (eds) *Colonial Discourse and Postcolonial Theory*. New York, 1994.

Young, R. *Colonial Desire*. New York, 1995.

Cultural Studies and Multiculturalism

Cultural studies are concerned with the exploration of culture in its multiple forms and of the socio-political contexts within which it manifests itself. As an 'interdisciplinary, transdisciplinary and sometimes counter-disciplinary field' (Grossberg et al. 1992, 4), cultural studies are a relatively new phenomenon in British and American universities. In its current sense, the term was first used by Birmingham's Centre for Contemporary Cultural Studies (CCCS) launched in 1963. As envisioned by Richard Hoggart in his inaugural lecture, cultural studies consist of three domains: 'one is roughly historical and philosophical; another is, again roughly, sociological; the third – which will be the most important – is the literary critical' (1970, 255). The study of English was broadened to include a sociology of literature and the study of non-literary forms (film, television, popular music) previously regarded as 'substandard'. The approach of the CCCS resonated with the incipient American interest in cultural studies that had been prepared by a similar debate about the role of popular culture in the mid-1950s. This debate opposed those who argued the dehumanizing effects of mass culture (a point of view which dominated the anthology *Mass Culture: The Popular Arts in America*, 1957), to emerging postmodern critics like Leslie Fiedler (author of 'The Middle Against both Ends', included in the same anthology, and 'The New Mutants', 1965) and Susan Sontag (*Against Interpretation*, 1960).

The origins of American cultural studies are various and not limited to developments inside academia. The questions of high and mass culture were first articulated and fought outside the academy, media studies emerged from commercial needs as well as from academic concerns, and 'cultural critique was as much the province of the Beat poets and liberal journalists as university intellectuals' (Munns and Rajan 1995, 209). In terms of its academic roots, cultural studies emerged out of structuralist and poststructuralist critical theory, the 'cultural materialism' of the Birmingham Centre, gender and race studies, intellectual history (Foucault, Bourdieu) and cultural anthropology (Geertz, Turner, Clifford). According to Antony Easthope (1991, 140), the two books that initiated modern cultural studies were Raymond Williams's *Culture and Society* (1958) and Barthes's *Mythologies* (1957). Williams's book introduced a social- anthropological approach to culture, understood not only as a conveyor of meanings and values but also as a 'particular way of life' (Storey 1993, 53); Barthes's proposed an approach that unravelled the 'secondary signification' (ideological connotations) of cultural discourses.

An important early boost to American cultural studies came from Hannah Arendt and the members of the Frankfurt School (Max Horkheimer, Theodor W. Adorno and Herbert Marcuse) who moved to New York after Hitler's rise to power to set up a new Institute for Social Research at Columbia University. In 1955 Adorno published *Prisms*, subtitled 'Cultural Criticism and Society', and in 1959 a three-day colloquium organized by the Tamiment Institute in New York brought together philosopher Hannah Arendt, sociologist Edward Shils, historian Arthur Schlessinger and representatives of mass media to debate the effects of the new electronic technologies on culture. Both events helped promote the American interest in cultural studies, articulating some of its later concerns.

Retrieving the best traditions of cultural analysis as articulated by Adorno in the programmatic essay of his 1955 book, American cultural studies have participated in what Henry Giroux, David Shumway, Paul Smith and James Sosnoski have called 'counter-disciplinary' practices: 'fostering forms of resistance' to cultural institutions and modes of production (including those of the academe) and articulating a 'critical pedagogy ... which promote[s] the identification and analysis of the underlying ideological interests at stake in the text and its readings' (1985, 654–5). The inter-/counter-disciplinarity of the field has forced a massive revision of traditional methods of textual and cultural analysis. During the heyday of New Criticism alternative post-formalist approaches to the national literary culture were pioneered by the nascent American studies programmes (the first one established at George Washington University in 1936). These programmes became increasingly interdisciplinary in the 1960s, exploring movements, patterns of thought or the effects of mass communication on culture. Gender became an issue in American studies through the work of feminists like Annette Kolodny who in *The Lay of the Land* (1975) interrogated the recurrent representation of the American land as a female passively awaiting male impregnation. The Vietnam War and the Civil Rights movement also challenged the 'melting pot' paradigm, bringing to the fore issues of race and cultural diversity, as in Angela Davis's *Women, Sex, Race and Class* (1982), which reread American cultural history from a feminist, marxist and ethnic perspective. The growing interest in film and mass communication – or more recently in gay and lesbian studies – upset disciplinary boundaries even further, breaking through some of the last defences of the traditional literary establishment.

As the body of knowledge assembled through empirical, 'ethnographic' methods increased considerably, cultural scholars engaged in a major rethinking of their fields, drawing on a variety of analytic models from linguistics, philosophy, literary theory, rhetoric, semiotics, sociology and anthropology. It is also true that the availability of powerful interpretive tools did not lead to theoretical sophistication across the board. Some scholars continued to resist the methodologies of linguistics, semiotics or literary theory, preferring more empirical approaches. Sociologists, for example, found the 'pan-textualist' approach of cultural studies debilitating, reducing sociality to a matter of discourse. Early mass communication research was similarly divided between a culturalist approach, which applied methods derived from the humanities to the analysis of cultural messages, and an empirical approach that combined quantitative research with a 'behaviouristic' understanding of the process of communication. The integration of the empirical and the theoretical approaches to culture was delayed for at least two decades. The 1980s brought a more profound theoretical restructuring, reflected in the new centres and programmes opened between traditional departments (Duke University's Center for Interdisciplinary Studies in Science and Cultural Studies, Harvard's Center for Literary and Cultural Studies, Georgia Tech's School of Literature, Communication and Culture, the University of Rochester's programme in Visual and Cultural Studies, etc.). The 1990s were witness to the beginning of a new cross-disciplinary collaboration between social and cultural studies. In 1997, for example, Elizabeth Long published under the aegis of the Sociology of Culture Section of the American Sociological Association a collection entitled *From Sociology to Cultural Studies*. Bringing together cultural scholars with sociologists and anthropologists, this collection stressed not only the opportunities for new cross-fertilizations but also cultural studies' need for a firmer sociological grounding.

These ongoing rapprochements make cultural studies difficult to define. Every time a seemingly incompatible theory or practice is brought to bear upon the 'postdiscipline' of cultural studies, a new 'crisis' of adjustment is triggered. The defining collections published since the end of the 1980s (Nelson and Grossberg's *Marxism and the Interpretation of Culture*, 1989; Grossberg, Nelson and Treichler's *Cultural Studies*, 1992; Munns and Rajan's *A Cultural Studies Reader*, 1995; Nelson and Goankar's *Disciplinarity and Dissent in Cultural Studies*, 1996) reflect the ambitious polydimensionality but also the dispersal of the field. As the editors of *Cultural Studies* put it, '[I]t is probably impossible to agree on any essential definition or unique narrative of cultural studies .... Its methodology, ambiguous from the beginning, could best be seen as bricolage' (Grossberg et al. 1992, 2, 3). For Angela McRobbie, who wrote the 'Postscript', cultural studies' 'greater degree of openness' represents a welcome departure from the 'rigidity' imposed by the field's original theoretical models (1992, 724). For Jameson and others, this fragmentation is a matter of serious concern. Responding to the *Cultural Studies* collection, Fredric Jameson chastised the field for failing to clarify its definition and replacing the search for methodology with a fetishistic invocation of precursors such as Raymond Williams whose name 'is taken in vain by virtually everyone and appealed to for moral support in any number of sins (and virtues)' (1993, 615, 618).

Cultural studies can best be defined as a series of interrelated explorations rather than as a single body of theory or methods. Therefore, efforts to synthesize them under one description remain problematic, foregrounding the areas of tension inside cultural studies. Cultural studies have profited from models developed in literary theory, often taking a 'text-based' approach to the exploration of culture. But cultural studies are not reduced to a study of literary texts. Beginning with Barthes's *Mythologies* that effectively applied methods of literary analysis to a potentially limitless range of non-literary products, films, videos, comics, music disks, fashion, computer art and even oral culture have become legitimate objects of study. The work of cultural scholars like Judith Williamson, Richard Ohman, Mas'ud Zavarzadeh, Teresa de Lauretis, John Fiske and Janice Radway has managed to dispel the notion that media texts are transparent bearers of meaning, treating advertisements, film, TV series, or romance novels as 'complex transactions involving not only messages and meanings, but multivalenced media formats and a wide range of audience variables which inflect the ways in which the media text is received and interpreted' (Munns and Rajan 1995, 300). On the other hand these products are difficult to subsume under the traditional category of 'text' because they are not always amenable to an analysis that can identify an author, a stable text or a distinctive genre. Even when a text-oriented approach is taken, the goal in cultural studies is to

> decentre 'the text' as an object of study. 'The text' is no longer studied for its own sake, not even for the social effects it may be thought to produce, but rather for the subjective or cultural forms which it realizes and makes available. The text is only a *means* in cultural studies; [...] it is the raw material from which certain forms (e.g. of narrative, ideological problematic, mode of address, subject position, etc.) may be abstracted. (Johnson 1983, 597)

In spite of this broadening/rethinking of the category of cultural studies, media studies and English continue to have an uncomfortable relationship. Only film has been satisfactorily integrated into English studies, the cinematic work producing a density of interpretation compatible with the kind of critical exegesis expected in literary studies. Other forms of popular culture are still perceived by many literary scholars as unworthy of their attention. Noting this continued crisis of adjustment, John Guillory has contended in *Cultural Capital* that the emergence of cultural studies in American literature departments gives 'more than sufficient evidence of the urgent need to reconceptualize the object of literary study' (1993, 265). According to Guillory, not only literary studies but also literature itself as a 'cultural capital' has entered a terminal phase (x). And yet, while it is true that recent developments in cultural studies have thrown the object of literary scholarship in crisis, English can contribute to cultural studies its sophisticated techniques of analysis and its insights into the processes of cultural creativity. The case for the continued significance of the literary must be made, however, not by returning to some 'neo-New-Critical, antitheoretical, apolitical, exclusive regime of literary study', but rather by valorizing the political and theoretical agendas of cultural studies (DeKoven 1996, 127). As Marianne DeKoven has argued, literary writing remains an important model of discourse because it can act simultaneously as a medium 'of self-assertion and self-construction; an acknowledgment of the division, alienation, and reification of the subject and at the same time an assertion of subjective agency' (128). For cultural critics like Guillory the category of 'literature' simply 'names the cultural capital of the old bourgeoisie' (1993, x). Ironically, this definition ignores the significant contribution made to the literary by the constituencies that cultural studies have been trying to enfranchise. Writers like Toni Morrison, Shirley Anne Williams, Alice Walker, Clarence Major, Leslie Marmon Silko, Audre Lorde, Maxine Hong Kingston, Gloria Anzaldúa, Bharati Mukherjee, Sandra Cisneros, Jonathan Strong and Jamaica Kincaid have retrieved previously marginalized experiences and genres (autobiography, oral storytelling), 'disaggregat[ing] the literary from its conservative uses as a high-cultural gatekeeper and preserve of hegemonic cultural capital' (DeKoven 1996, 137). Following their example, Marianne DeKoven and others have proposed a version of cultural studies that will mix the literary with the non-literary and the canonical with the anti-canonical. This version can be said to already exist in new historicism, regarded by Jameson as the 'basic competition' to cultural studies. While cultural studies often concern themselves with the contemporary represented by mass and popular culture, new historicism (Stephen Greenblatt, Louis Montrose, Jonathan Goldberg, Jean Howard and others) is solidly anchored in history and in literature, pursuing the 'the world's new textuality' (Jameson 1993, 616) from a broad interdisciplinary perpective. Greenblatt originally called his work a 'poetics of culture' (1980, 5), conceiving the work of the critic as an archaeological search for the contextual traces of institutions, values and practices embedded in a text. Cultural poetics relocates literary texts within a web of competing forces, discourses and practices that range from literary to non-literary, aesthetic to political, microstructural to macrostructural.

If the literary component has had a contradictory career in American cultural studies, the political component seems to have fared better. Cultural studies in the US have provided useful frameworks for addressing issues of historical change, cultural diversity and difference. And yet, by comparison to the Birmingham Centre, American cultural studies have tended to be 'less overtly engaged in political critique'.

> While the Marxist heritage has made British cultural studies alert to issues of class, popular culture and sub-cultures, at the expense of issues of race and gender, American forms of cultural studies focused upon the ethnographic approaches, making them more open to questions of gender and race but obscuring issues of class. (Munns and Rajan 1995, 4)

More recently, as cultural studies have begun to be integrated into traditional literature or communication departments, they have raised new questions about their political efficacy. For Jameson, the politics that informs cultural studies is a predictable ' "academic" politics' that operates like 'a kind of United Nations plenary session', giving a 'respectful (and "politically correct") hearing' to each microgroup or social movement but failing to articulate a politics beyond the 'isolationist conception of group identity' (1993, 623).

Such criticisms are overly harsh, ignoring the analytic sophistication and significance of much cultural studies work in the area of 'otherness'. This work is concentrated in several new branches of cultural studies: ethnocriticism, multiculturalism and postcolonial studies. For Arnold Krupat, 'ethnocriticism' or 'multiculturalism' is 'that particular organization of cultural studies which engages and in such a way as to provoke an interrogation of and a challenge to what we ordinarily take as familiar and our own' (1992, 3). This interrogation extends over one's own disenfranchised group ideology, allowing for tensions between group identities, and also to the more general question of why the 'other' has been such a persistent figure in North American society, submitted periodically to discriminatory discourses and policies.

The multicultural movement has developed in response to the charge that traditional American education was focused too narrowly on the dominant Euro-american literary culture and history, ignoring other alternatives. The emphasis on cultural diversity can be traced back to anthropology's interest in non-European cultures, to the civil rights and women's movements, and to postmodernism's attempts to reconceptualize culture from the margins, valorizing the experience of subaltern groups and excluded others. The type of polysystemic and multicultural fiction that has gradually emerged since the mid-1970s (Thomas Pynchon, Toni Morrison, Maxine Hong Kingston, Jamaica Kinkaid, Ishmail Reed, Bharati Mukherjee, Sandra Cisneros, etc.) has provided multiculturalists with a model of reclamation, retelling and refashioning of an experience of previously distorted or marginalized by the dominant culture.

Acknowledging the impact of postmodern theory and practice on multicultural studies, some consider multiculturalism a branch of the postmodern project (Lundquist 1996, 259). But postmodernism's approach to otherness is inevitably limited. Postmodernism has taught us that difference and heterogeneity matter, but did not always tell us how to create that space wherein differences can be negotiated in non-conflictive ways. Stronger models of otherness can be found in new historicism, whose explorations of the richly layered culture of a period are conceived as encounters with the radical 'otherness' of history, its places of dissention and change. Feminism has also explored issues of gendered otherness not only in literary texts, but also in the products of popular culture such as TV and film (Laura Mulvey's influential work on woman as image and man as bearer of the look), formulaic fiction (Tania Modleski, Janice Radway), pop music and fashion (Ros Coward). The very definition of gendered otherness has undergone a radical rethinking: the versions of female identity offered by Gloria Anzaldú's 'mestiza consciousness' or Donna Haraway's cyborg emphasize strange multiplicities and the 'intimate experience of boundaries, their construction and deconstruction' (Haraway 1991, 181). Race studies and, since the 1980s, postcolonial criticism have also played an important role in redefining otherness and exposing the violence done to the body, mind and language of the other by western colonial and postcolonial thought. The works that set the stage for this type of exploration were Frantz Fanon's *Black Skin, White Masks* (1952; trans. 1968), *The Wretched of the Earth* (1963) and Albert Memmi's *The Colonizer and the Colonized* (1965). Building on their insights, Edward Said's *Orientalism* (1978) described the process through which the West constructed the East as a 'colonizable' image. According to Gayatri Chakravorty Spivak, Said's monumental reading of 'orientalism' as an instrument of imperial power made possible the 'study of colonial discourse' and the new discipline of marginality 'where the marginal can speak and be spoken, even spoken for' (1993, 56). Spivak's own work has focused on the double process of 'othering' that produces both the dominant imperial Other that gives the ideological framework for understanding the world, and the small 'others', the colonial subjects (1987, 249). It has also exposed the process of othering that the postcolonial critic inadvertently engages in. *Outside in the Teaching Machine* (1993) describes the institutionalization of marginality studies within the First World metropolitan academy as a 'new Orientalism', a neocolonialist gesture that consolidates the non-West in a position of 'authentic marginality' (1993, 57).

Much of the work in postcolonial studies has been anticipated/supplemented by the analysis of black American culture. African American studies have provided one of the earliest models of cross-cultural analysis for peoples affected by colonization and slavery. As the authors of a recent glossary of postcolonial concepts state, the 'history of the struggle for self-determination by African Americans is historically intertwined with wider movements of diasporic struggles for independence', such as the 'Back to Africa' movement initiated by the Jamaica-born Marcus Garvey (Ashcroft, Griffiths and Triffin, 1998, 7). More recently, efforts have been made to define an interdisciplinary field of 'black cultural studies' that would integrate black literary criticism, black popular culture, critical race theory and film theory. Among its possible contributors are Elizabeth Alexander, Derrick Bell, Barbara Christian, Ann DuCille, Henry Louis Gates, Jr, Paul Gilroy, Stuart Hall, bell hooks, Lawrence W. Hogue, Mae G. Henderson, Valerie Smith, Claudia Tate and Cornell West, whose work has been instrumental in dismantling the 'white supremacist, homophobic, capitalist patriarchy' and offering alternative ways of conceiving race, gender and class that emphasize 'the extraordinary diversity of subject positions, social experiences and cultural identities which compose [such categories]' (Sarup 1996, 61). The critique of the lingering of assumptions these categories is strongest in bell hooks' books that challenge the universal category of 'woman' and redirect the goal of feminism from achieving equal opportunity with men to eliminating sexism and sexist oppression. bell hooks, Henry Louis Gates, Jr, and Barbara Smith have also urged anti-discrimination activists to ally themselves against all forms of 'othering' and oppression. Challenging the persistent homophobia not only in the dominant culture but also in the post-civil rights ethnocentrisms these writers have made clear that all forms of oppression are interconnected and that as long as one discrimination is allowed to stand through ignorance or prejudice, oppression in general is justified. This new awareness has been helped also by the work of queer theorists like Leo Bersani, Teresa de Lauretis, Eve Kosofsky Sedgwick, Gayle Rubin and Jeffrey Weeks, who have argued that sexuality is just as important a category in the configuration of social identities as class and race.

Drawing on these diverse theoretical perspectives, ethnocriticism has focused on the contradictory meanings and political uses of ethnicity, rejecting 'natural' definitions of it. Ethnocriticism offers not only an ethnography but also a critique of 'identities', being concerned with the actual processes of identity formation. Identity, as Charles Taylor reminds us, is 'dialogic', built upon how others see or recognize 'us' (1994, 33). Cultural identity has been experienced very differently on the American continent by the dominant white, heterosexual, Western European immigrants, and by the various non-European minorities or by the Native Americans whose being has been periodically threatened with oversimplification and cancellation. Therefore the work of multiculturalists is needed to redress the balance, reclaiming/reconstructing marginalized experiences and promoting positive representations of minority cultures. But telling positive stories about one's cultural difference or sensitizing the dominant group to the value of the Other is not enough: multicultural writers and theorists are also interested in channelling this differential potential between the dominant and alternative cultures, centres and peripheries, towards 'the mutual revisions of our expressions of reality' (Lundquist 1996, 272–3). Both ethnocritics and multicultural writers believe that listening to the marginalized voice of the Other is essential, but they also seek to activate those forms of cross-cultural communication that submit cultural systems to a process of mutual revision.

Multiculturalism has been defined as 'the reality of the post-melting pot, post-assimilationist era' (Lundquist 1996, 263), but it is by no means an unproblematic perspective. Believers in a unitary conception of society lament the fact that multiculturalism conduces to hermetically sealed ethnic enclaves, anarchy and the lack of an integrating national narrative. Supporters of multiculturalism argue that monocultures need to be converted into polysystemic 'mosaics' in which no group can claim the status of ruling majority and each group enjoys equal rights and respect for its ethnic or gender identity. But they remain aware of the danger of co-option that confronts multiculturalism in the current hyperconsumerist culture, interested in promoting the ethnic flavours of the month, and also of the more subtle reappropriation of otherness by the 'benevolent' discourse of western multiculturalism 'masquerad[ing] as the absent nonrepresenter who lets the oppressed speak for themselves' (Spivak 1988, 292). Marjorie Perloff finds peculiar the fact that, 'despite the lip service currently paid to multiculturalism, one has the sense that the only thing that matters in U.S. culture. .. is U.S. culture. True, that culture is divided up into a dozen of marginalized, disempowered, and minority subsets . . . . But the requisite for all these groups turns out to be U.S. citizenship: the Other, it seems, does not include the literature of other nations or in other languages' (Perloff 1998, 21). Jameson likewise identifies cultural studies with 'an American NATO view of the world' from which whole political geographies (the Pacific rim, China, Japan and sometimes Latin America) are absent (1993, 640).

The fall of the Berlin Wall and the new globalizing impetus of consumer capitalism have posed difficult new questions to multiculturalism. Judging from Stuart Hall's essay 'Culture,

Community, Nation' (1993), multiculturalism and cultural studies in general have not done well on this test. As Saba Mahmood comments, this essay written by a major representative of the Birmingham Centre has difficulty dealing with the social movements (politico-religious and ethnic) that have emerged in Eastern Europe, the Middle East or Central Asia (Mahmood 1996, 2). While noting the parallel development of nationalist movements in post-Cold War Western Europe and the non-western world, Hall carefully divides nationalisms into big and small (or 'good' and 'bad'). He regards the emerging nationalisms of small countries (as a result of the National Liberation Movements of the 1960s and 1970s, or more recently of the collapse of the Soviet Empire) as failed imitations of the big nation-building strategies. Replicating older stereotypical divisions between a Protestant or Catholic Western Europe and an Orthodox or Muslim Central Asia and Eastern Europe, Hall considers the latter cultures by definition ethnically and religiously absolutist, ignoring the fact that the 'othering' violence perpetrated by the secular western states in the last two centuries remains as yet unmatched by the violence committed in the name of non-western religious and ethnic communities.

Cultural studies need to examine the analytical assumptions and stereotypes they have inherited from traditional cultural history, otherwise it is condemned to 'reify boundaries of cultural otherness, political persuasions and objectives' (Mahmood 1996, 10). The concept of multiculturalism itself must be revisited in the postcolonial, post-Cold War world, in order to interrogate its blind spots. One of these blind spots is the unequal treatment of various others (western vs. non-western, diasporic vs. native, etc.). Refusing such polarizations, Ella Shohat and Robert Stam advocate in their recent study of multiculturalism and the media a 'radical *polycentric multiculturalism*' that 'reconceptualizes the power relations between cultural communities', challenging the hierarchical division of communities into 'major' and 'minor' (1994, 47). Polycentric multiculturalism is not about sensitivity towards other groups but about 'dispersing power, about empowering the disempowered, about transforming subordinating institutions and discourses', about deconstructing the 'dominant or narrowly national discourses' and negotiating 'many margins and many centers' (48–9). Taking issue with mainstream multiculturalism that does not offer 'a participatory knowledge of non-European cultures', the authors of *Unthinking Eurocentrism* address the global reach of the contemporary media, offering critiques of imperialist discourses, theorizings of 'Third World' and 'Third Cinema', as well as analyses of African, Asian, Latin American and First World 'minority' and 'diasporic' media.

A similar effort to create a more responsive space for intercultural negotiation can be found in the revamped version of 'culturology' proposed by Ellen E. Berry and Mikhail N. Epstein. Against both deconstruction's cavalier dismissal of firm contours of cultural identity and essentialist multiculturalism's assumption that 'each cultural formation can and should be explained in relation to its racial, sexual or ethnic origin that gives rise to the particular system of social signification' (1999, 80), Berry and Epstein propose a 'transculturalist' approach that acknowledges the 'enduring "physicality" and "essentiality" of existing cultures' but also 'the possibility of their further transcendence, in particular though with other cultures' (84).

> [To be transcultural] means to rise above one's inborn identity, such as 'white, adult male', through a variety of self-deconstructions, self-transformations, and interference with other identities, such as woman, black, child, disabled. For this purpose books, films, and sign systems are created to dissolve the solidity of one's nature, one's identity and to share the experience of 'the other'. (84)

Transculturalism moves us from a 'passive' multicultural perspective that recognizes the 'unqualified multiplicity of cultures without positing any ways for them to interact meaningfully', to a perspective that encourages the interplay of cultures on the surmise that 'each culture has some basic incompleteness that opens it for encounters with other cultures' (97).

While a final assessment of this and other recent projects is not yet possible, it is evident by now that cultural studies have found new resources to respond to the 'disjunctive intersections of global, national, and local cultures' (Berry and Epstein 1999, 129) in the post-Cold War world. Together with women's studies, gay/lesbian studies and postcolonial criticism, cultural studies have contributed substantially to the constitution of the 'new humanities', challenging the accepted practices of knowledge-gathering within the academy, foregrounding the exclusions 'which confirm the privileges and authority of canonic knowledge systems' and recovering those 'marginalized' or 'subjugated knowledges' which have been 'occluded and silenced by the entrenched humanist curriculum' (Gandhi 1998, 42). While many problems remain (cultural studies continue to occupy a peripheral position not only in many English departments, but also in the culture at large; the refiguration of what is studied as 'culture' is far from finished; the battle for the 'soul' of post-Cold War America has not been won by the new culturalist left), the voracious appetite of cultural studies for new intellectual experiences guarantees its future open-endedness and 'need to go on theorizing'.

Marcel Cornis-Pope

Further reading and works cited

Ashcroft, B. et al. *Key Concepts in Post-Colonial Studies*. New York, 1998.
Berry, E. E. and Epstein, M. N. *Transcultural Experiments*. New York, 1999.
DeKoven, M. 'Cultural Dreaming and Cultural Studies', *New Literary History*, 27, 1, 1996.
Easthope, A. *Literary into Cultural Studies*. London, 1991.
Franklin, S. et al. (eds) *Off Center*. New York, 1991.
Gandhi, L. *Postcolonial Theory*. New York, 1998.
Giroux, H. et al. 'The Need for Cultural Studies: Resisting Intellectuals and Oppositional Public Spheres', *Dalhousie Review*, 64 (1985).
Greenblatt, S. *Renaissance Self-Fashioning*. Chicago, 1980.
Grossberg, L. et al. (eds) *Cultural Studies*. New York, 1992.
Guillory, J. *Cultural Capital*. Chicago, 1993.
Hall, S. 'Culture, Community, Nation'. *Cultural Studies*, 7, 3, October 1993.
Haraway, D. 'A Cyborg Manifesto', *Simians, Cyborgs, and Women*. London, 1991.
Hoggart, R. 'Schools of English and Contemporary Society', in *Speaking to Each Other*. Harmondsworth, 1970.
Jameson, F. 'On Cultural Studies', *Social Text*, 34, 1993.
Johnson, R. 'What Is Cultural Studies Anyway?' Stenciled Occasional Paper No. 74 (1983) circulated by the Birmingham Centre for Contemporary Cultural Studies.
Krupat, A. *Ethnocriticism*. Berkeley, CA, 1992.
Lundquist, S. 'Ethnocriticism and Multiculturalism', in *The Critical Experience*, ed. D. Cowles. Dubuque, IA, 1996.
McRobbie, A. 'Post-Marxism and Cultural Studies', in *Cultural Studies*, eds L. Grossberg et al New York, 1992.
Mahmood, S. 'Cultural Studies and Ethnic Absolutism', *Cultural Studies*, 10, 1, 1996.

Munns, J. and Rajan, G. (eds) *A Cultural Studies Reader*. London, 1995.

Nelson, C. and Goankar, D. (eds) *Disciplinarity and Dissent in Cultural Studies*. New York, 1996.

Perloff, M. *Poetry On & Off the Page*. Evanston, IL, 1998.

Said, E. W. *Orientalism*. New York, 1978.

Sardar, Z. and Van Woon, B. *Introducing Cultural Studies*. New York, 1998.

Sarup, M. *Identity, Culture, and the Postmodern World*. Athens, OH, 1996.

Shohat, E. and Stam, R. *Unthinking Eurocentrism*. London, 1994.

Spivak, G. Chakravorty. 'The Rani of Simur'. *History and Theory*, 24, 3, 1987.

—. 'Can the Subaltern Speak?', in *Marxism and the Interpretation of Culture*, eds C. Nelson and L. Grossberg. Urbana, IL, 1988.

—. *Outside in the Teaching Machine*. London, 1993.

Storey, J. *An Introductory Guide to Cultural Theory and Popular Culture*. Athens, GA, 1993.

Taylor, C. 'The Politics of Recognition', in *Multiculturalism*, ed. A. Gutmann. Princeton, NJ, 1994.

Wolin, R. *The Terms of Cultural Criticism*. New York, 1992.

African-American Studies

In a 1985 issue of *Cultural Critique*, Cornel West asserted that the pursuit of academic legitimacy was 'existentially and intellectually stultifying for black intellectuals'. In typically provocative fashion, he claimed further that such a quest

> not only generates anxieties of defensiveness on the part of intellectuals; it also thrives on them. The need for hierarchical ranking and the deep-seated racism shot through bourgeois humanistic scholarship cannot provide black intellectuals with either the proper ethos or conceptual framework to overcome a defensive posture. And charges of intellectual inferiority can never be met upon the opponent's terrain – to try to do so only intensifies one's anxieties. Rather the terrain itself must be viewed as part and parcel of an antiquated form of life unworthy of setting the terms of contemporary discourse. (1985, 116)

Echoing the sentiments of many Black Arts proponents whose criticism of the academy in the 1960s and 1970s had singled out the 'aristocratic' nature of the academy as cause for the black critic's outsider status, West's words describe the bind that the academy creates for black intellectuals. On the one hand, as West implies, the academy beckons as a site of promise: black intellectuals thus turn to the university, seeking in it a place to forge a sense of identity and even community. On the other hand, this existential pursuit for a sense of being in the world – because it is also fraught with a narrative of legitimacy – can for West ultimately have no satisfying end, since the very terms of the intellectual quest are underwritten by the racist assumption that blackness and intellect are incompatible, if not inimical. His critique turns then to counsel: because the academy 'cannot provide either the proper ethos or conceptual framework' that would secure or welcome what it means to be a black intellectual, it can be no institutional home, and therefore must be refused altogether.

The opposition that West sets out between the place and possibility of the black intellectual and the academy marks one way to characterize the problematic history of African-American studies as a discipline. Indeed, if West's account of the difficulties faced by black intellectuals in entering the academy is a useful analogy for the difficulty that African-American studies has encountered in its development as a legitimate discipline, this essay looks to suggest that the inverse holds true as well. That is, just as the presence of black intellectuals in the academy enables for West a critique of the hierarchy and racism that lie at the heart of the institution, so does the emergence of African-American studies pose for the academy the necessity of understanding the mechanisms that drive disciplinarity in the contemporary university. In its own contentious history and debates over theory, practice and teaching, African-American studies, to put it another way, enables a sustained inquiry into the divided nature of disciplinarity.

The significance of such division to African-American studies does not simply begin, however, with the full-blown appearance of the discipline on the academic stage. That is, the complications of making African-American culture an object of study has earlier – or deeper – roots than the disciplinary questions it raises in the late 1960s. Even the quickest of historical glances reveals that investment in such study and the contradictions that accompany it occupied African-American thinkers in the first half of the twentieth-century. For these thinkers, the question of 'African-American-ness' was a necessary inquiry, one driven by the imperative to define and articulate the double-edge of the African-American experience: what W. E. B. Du Bois (1868–1963) famously named the 'veil' of 'double-consciousness'. Thus at the turn of the twentieth century author, magazine editor and journalist Pauline Hopkins (1859–1930) sought to forefront, and thereby create, the beginnings of a written history of African-American individual heroism in 'Famous Men of the Negro Race' (1901) and 'Famous Women of the Negro Race' (1902). W. E. B Du Bois, Arthur Schomburg (1874–1938) and Zora Neale Hurston (1891–1960) complicated this historical perspective by claiming that African-American folklore, religion and material culture, alongside economic and sociological analyses, warranted as much attention as the narratives of history. Du Bois in particular – perhaps the most insistent voice addressing the ways in which the doubleness of the African-American experience constituted its uniqueness – went so far as to argue throughout *The Souls of Black Folk* (1903) that at stake in such close inquiry was nothing less than future progress in race relations. In the meantime writers working during and shortly after the Harlem Renaissance extended this line of thinking through the publication of a number of literary anthologies, including *The Book of American Negro Poetry* (ed. James Weldon Johnson, 1922), *The New Negro* (ed. Alain Locke, 1925), *An Anthology of American Negro Literature* (ed. V. F. Calverton, 1929), *The Negro Caravan* (ed. Sterling A. Brown, 1941) and *The Poetry of the Negro, 1746–1949* (eds Langston Hughes and Arna Bontemps, 1949). The discussions in the introductory pages of these anthologies anticipated the long-standing debate over the canon of African-American literature, whether, for instance, 'Negro literature' should represent literature by and/or about African-Americans, or even whether the use of the term, in its impulse to compartmentalize, might only further marginalize the work. For all that, however, these efforts sought in common to capture, all the while keeping in play, both the distinctiveness *and* American character of the African-American experience. To do so was, as James Weldon Johnson put it, to 'change that mental attitude and raise [the African-American's] status' by demonstrating the 'intellectual parity by the Negro through the production of literature and art' (Johnson 1922, vii).

When the young discipline of black studies (as it was then named) surfaced in the late 1960s, it faced this doubleness in the form of questions concerning its viability, definition and purpose. Student protests and radical activism of the time had produced an atmosphere of academic reform, contributing not simply to the establishment of black studies programmes, but also to the sense that such programmes had a stake in the larger reform of the university (Frye 1976, 1). For many, this meant on the one hand revealing and doing away with assumptions about the homogeneity of culture, the objectivity of scholarly inquiry, including especially the notion that history and historiography embodied realms of pure fact, and the sanctity of any number of traditional liberal arts disciplinary canons (Thelwell 1979, 706–10). Black studies sought, in the words of one activist, 'to correct falsehoods perpetrated by western academia about black people' (Frye 1976, 5). As a result, many black studies proponents insisted that the strength of the discipline would lie in its ability to enact an unprecedented convergence of traditional disciplines – including history, political science, sociology, economics and literature. On the other hand, the development of black studies for scholars also meant the opportunity to make a social and institutional difference vis-à-vis the articulation and expression of, as several put it at the time, a black 'sensibility' that, in embodying an Afrocentric vision, would challenge and revise the assumptions of western intellectual inquiry (one of the missions of the *Negro American Literature Forum*, founded in 1967). This two-handed approach informed the rush of success that black studies experienced in the early 1970s: in 1970, approximately 350 colleges and/or universities had established such programmes, while by 1973, the number had increased to 600 nationwide (Frye 1976, 4). In the meantime, these early years constituted a period of disciplinary self-reflection, a time when workshops, institutes, conferences and 'self-studies' involving administrators, faculty members and students addressed directly the development of black studies (Ford 1973, 88).

Yet in the midst of success, discussions regarding the status, place and future of black studies suggested that, taken together, even these early stages of institutionalization constituted a dilemma for the discipline. While scholars continued to agree that the discipline needed a vision of purpose, methodology, pedagogy and canon, the uniformity of such a vision had no consistent assurance. Around the debate over what 'black studies' entailed, for instance, several questions split scholars into opposing camps. By the late 1970s, when the number of established programmes had declined to 200, proponents found themselves turning to diagnose institutional arrival *itself* as a cause of disciplinary ill health. Responding to increasingly vocal complaints that black studies programmes, paralleling perhaps the radical ideology and aesthetics of the Black Arts movement, sought a separatist – rather than pluralist – agenda, some within the discipline voiced the concern that black studies' political origins, while initially the catalyst for administrative and curricular action, now haunted the discipline precisely by diminishing its institutional legitimacy (Ford 1973, 42). These accusations, however, exposed for other black studies scholars an anxiety on the part of more traditional disciplines that had seen students, courses and funding channelled towards the new and immensely popular field of study. To claim that the discipline was merely the result of political faddishness – and therefore not intellectually serious – was to serve a larger agenda to reclaim territory presumably 'lost' in the fray of institutional competition. That many of these traditional disciplines had begun to add 'black content' to their courses suggested that the old guard was seeking to 'parallel and duplicate Black Studies' (Frye 1976, 37).

To say that more recent developments in African-American studies also indicate this institutional tension is not, however, to argue that the discipline has somehow lost its way. If the discipline has experienced a bumpy ride in its history, this is not because African-American studies possesses at base some inherent flaw. Rather, the impact that African-

American studies has had (and continues to have) on the academy occurs as much through the challenges it has produced and negotiated as through the material it has brought into the academic fold. On the contemporary front, this is perhaps most evident in several areas: in the emergence of the exemplary African-American genre, the slave narrative; in the debates over the place and role of feminism in the discipline; and in the continuing discussion of what constitutes theory in the context of African-American studies.

> In his introduction to *The Classic Slave Narratives*, Henry Louis Gates, Jr. writes that ... one of the most curious aspects of the African person's enslavement in the New World is that he and she wrote about the severe conditions of their bondage ... In the long history of human bondage, it was only the black slaves in the United States who ... created a *genre* of literature that at once testified against their captors and bore witness to the urge of every black slave to be free and literate. (1987, ix, original emphasis)

Writing in 1987, Gates on the one hand extends his earlier claim that slave narratives function as a 'countergenre' (1978, 47) – a genre that, because it does not reside in any one generic category but deploys and mediates between the strategies of other kinds of literature, including conversion narratives, autobiography, sentimental romances, the plantation novel tradition and sermons, demands a rethinking of literary genres. At the same time, he identifies with assurance the fact that slave narratives now constitute a literary genre – that is, a genre so marked and recognizable through certain conventions, thematics and structures that a canon exists by which one can judge and identify specific texts as 'classic'.

In so doing, Gates echoes a statement that Houston A. Baker, Jr had made five years earlier in his introduction to Penguin's edition of the *Narrative of the Life of Frederick Douglass*: 'the appearance of [the *Narrative*] in the Penguin American Library series indicates that a new scholarly paradigm has emerged in our day' (1982, 15). Baker remarks that this recent popularity of slave narratives marks a resurgence of interest, since 'prior to the 1960s, an accepted position in American literary and historical studies was that no distinct, authentic, written Afro-American voice existed in the canons of discourse surrounding American abolitionism' (1982, 7–8). While he does not say so directly, implicit in Baker's statement is the sense that the arrival of the slave narrative as the 'distinct, authentic written Afro-American voice' entails the reinvigoration as well of African-American studies. The certification of generic status and 'a new scholarly paradigm': with such recommendation both Gates and Baker herald the debut of the slave narrative – and therefore the discipline – onto the institutional stage.

The terms of this debut, as Gates' and Baker's comments reveal, mark an interest in the difference of African-American literary expression – and therefore the difference in scholarship that it requires. As a number of commentators have observed, because slave narratives provided source material on the institution of slavery through individual commentary, they mandated and compelled within the discipline a major shift in methodology. Such methodology sought to account for the enormous popularity of slave narratives – within the first four months of its publication in 1845 Douglass' *Narrative* sold five thousand copies; by 1860 the number had topped 30,000 (Gates 1987, xi). To do so meant, for one, to concede and consider the narratives' affective power alongside their rhetorical suasiveness: to read them not simply as political tracts or jeremiads, but as expressions that captured the imagination of the public because, as Margaret Fuller put it in her review of Douglass's *Narrative*, they presented the immediacy of a 'living voice' whose speech could not be ignored (Andrews 1991, 24). At the same time, accounting for the genre's popularity also meant an analysis of the resistance these narratives enacted – whether through their retrospective accounts of escape, their address to abolitionists or even their discussions and advocacy of literacy. Indeed, for many African-American critics the impact of the slave narrative resided most forcefully in their literariness; here, in the wielding of written, published and disseminated language, lay the resistance Gates describes in naming the narratives a 'countergenre'.

Not surprisingly, this sense of the narratives' literary resistance involved reworking the view of literature and literary history that had in the past precisely dismissed slaves' voices as unremarkable or irrelevant. The reintroduction of slave narratives, in other words, enabled African-American critics to take on the notion of canonicity itself. From slave narratives, as Arna Bontemps argued, derived the African-American literary tradition, since they embodied 'the spirit and vitality and the angle of vision responsible for the most effective prose writing by black American writers from William Wells Brown . . . [to] James Baldwin' (Gates 1987, x). The generic legitimacy of the slave narrative confirmed, because it produced, the legitimacy of the African-American literary tradition. What's more, with the emergence of the slave narrative African-American critics turned the American literary canon on its head. Citing nineteenth-century commentary that slave narratives constituted the 'one series of literary productions that could be written by none but Americans', critics claimed in effect that, far from being a marginal subset, African-American literature formed the very basis of American literature (Parker 1976, 245).

Slave narratives, then, turned out to be a weapon on the disciplinary front, a weapon enabling African-American studies both to secure further its academic legitimacy and to trouble long-held assumptions about the history and character of American literary studies. At the same time, slave narratives also proved to be an ongoing occasion for African-American studies to take stock of its own assumptions regarding the work done in its name. When, as part of her ground-breaking *Invented Lives* (an anthology and work of literary criticism), Mary Helen Washington turns to an analysis of the slave woman's narrative, she does so with a larger view of countering a variety of notions about African-American women and their place in the discipline (Washington 1987, 3–12). The difficulties Harriet Jacobs faced in writing *Incidents in the Life of a Slave Girl* – her personal struggle to express a sexuality that nineteenth-century conventions of 'true womanhood' would not allow except to demonize it, the struggle to convince readers that her account possessed validity – have, according to Washington, continued well into the late twentieth century in the form of a literary tradition that refuses to admit, much less acknowledge, the presence of African-American women. Tradition, writes Washington, is 'a word that nags the feminist critic'; for the black feminist critic, it provokes all sorts of angry questions, including those that wonder about the presumption that blackness is male (Washington 1987, xvii).

If in 1987 *Invented Lives* in fact marked an interruption of an African-American literary tradition dominated by male authors and critics, it also was taking part in an ongoing project to found and maintain a literary tradition of writing by African-American women. Washington's earlier books – *Midnight Birds* (1980) and *Black-Eyed Susans* (1975) – both sought to present literature 'by and about black women', and in so doing, had set the stage for critical inquiry addressed to questions of the specific concatenation of difference embodied in and by African-American women *and* the critique of the tradition and the institution that had been unable to imagine how women might have any role but a marginal one in the development of both. The 1970s and 1980s saw, then, the increased institutionalization of such work through the publication of important anthologies – including Washington's, Toni Cade Bambara's *The Black Woman* (1970) and *All the Women are White, All the Blacks are Men, But Some of Us are Brave* (1982), edited by Gloria T. Hull, Patricia Bell Scott and Barbara Smith – as well as the launching of several reprint series – the Beacon Black Women Writers Series, Rutgers' American Women Writers series, and the Oxford-Schomburg Library of nineteenth-century Black Women's Writings. Moreover, this entry into the academy mattered, since, as the editors of *But Some of Us are Brave* put it:

> Merely to use the term 'Black Women's Studies' is an act charged with political significance. At the very least, the combining of these words to name a discipline means taking the stance that Black women exist – and exist positively – a stance that is in direct opposition to most of what passes for culture and thought on the North American continent. To use the term and to act on it in a white-male world is an act of political courage. (1982, 5)

At stake in this statement is the notion that visibility – here in the form of the name 'Black Women's Studies' – means everything: far from simply referring to a group or movement, it wins attention and solidifies support. In that sense, it poses in a nutshell the challenge to and revision of the discipline that black feminist critics were seeking to articulate.

Black feminist scholarship in the meantime experienced a parallel explosion of interest and productivity such that by 1990 the essays in the anthology of criticism *Reading Black, Reading Feminist* could reflect the evenness of pace at which works of criticism and black women's writing were being produced. This, several of the contributors observed, one could say from the perspective of a mere ten years: in the wake of Barbara Smith's 'Toward a Black Feminist Criticism' (1977) followed Christian's *Black Women Novelists: The Development of a Tradition* (1980) and the edited collection *Black Feminist Criticism* (1985), Alice Walker's *In Search of Our Mothers' Gardens* (1983), Marjorie Pryse and Hortense Spiller's *Conjuring: Black Women Writers and Literary Tradition* (1985) and Hazel Carby's *Reconstructing Womanhood* (1987). Much as the literary anthologies had aspired to demonstrate that the preoccupations of black women writers converge on their double experience of oppression, this decade of black feminist criticism turned to theorize the formations that contributed to the literary complex of 'black womanhood', 'black female identity' or 'black feminine sexuality'. Indeed, in so far as Barbara Smith urged fellow critics not to 'try to graft the ideas or methodology of white/male literary thought upon the precious materials of black women's art', black feminist critics privileged experience as the site and source from which the literature emerged (Hull, Scott and Smith 1982, 164).

Still, as the title of Hazel Carby's *Reconstructing Womanhood* implies, the notion that womanhood – black or white, racially 'marked' or 'unmarked' – stood as some uniform, constant and unchanging essence did not go uncontested. By the late 1980s, responding in part to the influx of poststructuralist theory in American literary studies, black feminist criticism sought to reinvigorate the terms of its work, eschewing any naturalness associated either with race or femininity, and positing that the constructed nature of both meant that their entanglements demanded scrutiny of the ways in which literature produced and subverted such ideologies. Not to rely on the 'indigenous' criticism, as Deborah McDowell observes, and to take on 'foreign' theories and methodologies is not so much to capitulate or submit to some interpretative outside (McDowell 1989, 54), nor is it to betray the community of black feminism, the African-American literary tradition or the disciplinary home in which both at times take up residence; rather, to assume the authority of wielding a variety of discourses means – as McDowell, Hortense Spillers, Hazel Carby, Mae Henderson and a number of other black feminists have argued – the possibility of changing 'the contours of Afro-American literary history and of Afro-American critical discourse' (McDowell 1989, 54).

Perhaps the greatest impact that this encounter between black feminist criticism and the thing known as theory has had, however, is on theory itself. Isolating African-American literature or criticism from other discourses is impossible, not only because the encounter already has taken place, but because those encounters have proved meaningful. This fact is nowhere more evident in recent work on the relationships that obtain between feminism, African-American Studies and psychoanalysis. In this context, the work by African-Americanists on the filial configurations imposed by slavery makes the strong argument that the psychoanalytic model of development, underwritten as it is by the figure of the nuclear family, can have no purchase; it is the theory that proves inadequate here, not the families themselves. Such work enables further interrogations of psychoanalysis for its normative presumptions. The knowledge that Freud, for instance, on one occasion figures femininity in terms of Africa – the mysterious 'Dark Continent' that western imperialism would conquer – immediately raises questions about the gendered and radicalized presumptions of Freudian psychoanalysis. In the meantime, as recent work has demonstrated, because these assumptions are not solely the realm of a Victorian past, but continue to occupy contemporary 'white' feminist psychoanalysis, the need for ongoing conversation between African-American studies, feminism and psychoanalysis remains urgent indeed.

The affiliation of change with theory, the contention that theory alone wreaks change, describes only a one-way street of influence. What the 'second generation' of black feminists experienced in their efforts to negotiate the political and ethical implications of taking on 'western' theory – rather than hold strictly onto an Afrocentric vision – amounted to a mediation of the theoretical impulse, a revision, or edition, of what it means to theorize. While this stance is a long way from the statements of Black Arts advocates that the academy bars its doors to African-American critics, it does extend the claims of such writers as Addison Gayle that African-American literature offers a view of the theories that seek to explain it. In this sense, both black feminism and the Black Arts movement converge on a notion that continues to fascinate and vex contemporary African-Americanists: the idea that the relationship between African-American literature and theory, far from being a simple matter of rejection, application or appropriation, is instead a matter of intimate tensions.

That this intimacy takes several forms should be no surprise. One of the earliest occurs in the justification that the criticism of African-American literature needs theory. In *Black Literature and Literary Theory*, one of the first texts to address directly the stakes of theory in African-American literary criticism, Gates offers perhaps the most cited of defences when he asserts that the study of African-American literature *demands* the turn to formalism, structuralism or poststructuralism. 'Who would seek to deny us our complexity?' he asks, implying that one discourse of complexity – literature – requires another (Gates 1984, 4). This justification gains added force when his rhetoric shifts to one of duty: African-American critics, Gates contends, 'owe it to those traditions to bring to bear upon their readings any "tool" which helps us to elucidate [them]' (1984, 10). To perform this duty is to begin to bring these traditions, at this point still on the periphery of the academy, to the centre of the profession.

What critics owe to literature underlies as well the claim that whatever theoretical work African-American literature needs, it generates on its own. When Houston A. Baker and Gates advance this argument in *Blues, Ideology, and Afro-American Literature* (1984) and *The Signifying Monkey* (1988), they in effect call for a view of African-American culture that, while sensitive and responsive to what Madelyn Jablon calls 'extrinsic' theory, is fundamentally derived from its own terms: its vernacular (Jablon 1997, 3). Indeed, through his subtitle, *A Vernacular Theory*, which casts the blues as both an expressive voice of and a theoretical model for the African-American literary tradition, Baker reminds readers that the argument is a 'reorientation', a return. For him, this return to the native sign is motivated by a sense of ethics; it marks 'a minute beginning in the labor of writing/righting American history and literary history' (Baker 1984, 200, emphasis mine). For his part, Gates announces in the preface to *The Signifying Monkey* that Baker 'accomplishes with the blues what I try to accomplish here with Signifyin(g)' (1988, x). Gates, like Baker, enacts a return to the vernacular – here to the African and African-American trickster monkey traditions for which language, interpretation and meta-discourse are fundamental currency – in order to account for the ways in which the African-American literary tradition is based on a dynamic of revising and revisiting. The claim Gates makes in naming this theory 'signifyin(g)' marks a desire to have the tradition 'speak for itself' rather than, as he admits of his earlier work, to have it only spoken by 'the white hermeneutical circle' (1988, 17, 232).

These returns mark an effort to strike a balance between tradition and theory – or better, as the essays from *Afro-American Literary Study in the 1990s* suggest, to strike a balance such that the usual opposition between 'tradition' and 'theory', whatever weight it carries, does not do so invisibly or without scrutiny. In the interstices, African-American literature could be said to do nothing less than read theory, even as theory reads for its nature. Baker in his essay claims for a poetics of African-American women's writing a 'conjure' of phenomenology, feminism and African-American spirituality (Baker and Redmond 1989, 144–50); McDowell urges dialogism not simply as a method of reading texts, but as a figure for the encounters between black feminist criticism and other discourses (Baker and Redmond 1989, 70); Gates, while insisting that the turn inward will mean 'the black critical theory as great as [the] greatest black art', also looks forward to the impact that such a development will have on theory and 'the literary enterprise in general' (Baker and Redmond 1989, 25–9). This, then, is at the heart of what contemporary African-Americanists Michael Awkward, Jr, Henry Louis Gates, Jr, Mae Henderson, Wahneema Lubiano, Deborah McDowell, Hortense Spillers and Cheryl Wall have made evident in their respective works: a commitment to read back and forth between literature, culture and theory, never presuming that one should wholly explain the other, nor expecting from what direction any explanation should derive.

Yun Hsing Wu

Further reading and works cited

Andrews, W. *To Tell a Free Story.* Urbana, IL, 1986.
— (ed.) *Critical Essays on Frederick Douglass.* Boston, 1991.
Baker, Jr, H. A. *Blues, Ideology, and Afro-American Literature.* Chicago, 1984.
—. *Modernism and the Harlem Renaissance.* Chicago, 1991.
—. *Black Studies, Rap, and the Academy.* Chicago, 1993.

— and Redmond, P. (eds) *Afro-American Literary Study in the 1990s*. Chicago, 1989.

Blassingame, J. (ed.) *Slave Testimony*. Baton Rouge, LA, 1977.

Carby, H. *Reconstructing Womanhood*. New York, 1987.

Christian, B. *Black Women Novelists*. Westport, CT, 1980.

—. *Black Feminist Criticism*. New York, 1985.

Douglass, F. *Narrative of the Life of Frederick Douglass, An American Slave, Written by Himself*, ed. H. A. Baker. New York. 1982.

Du Bois, W. E. B. *Souls of Black Folk*. New York, 1961.

Ford, N. A. *Black Studies*. Port Washington, NY, 1973.

Frye, C. A. *Impact of Black Studies on the Curricula of Three Universities*. Washington, DC, 1976.

Gates, Jr, H. L. 'Binary Opposition in Chapter One of Narrative of the Life of Frederick Douglass, an American Slave, Written by Himself', in *Afro-American Literature*, eds R. Stepto and D. Fisher. New York, 1978.

— (ed.) *Black Literature and Literary Theory*. New York, 1984.

— (ed.) *The Classic Slave Narratives*. New York, 1987.

—. *The Signifying Monkey*. New York, 1988.

— (ed.) *Reading Black, Reading Feminist*. New York, 1990.

Gayle, A. (ed.) *The Black Aesthetic*. New York, 1971.

Holloway, K. F. C. *Moorings and Metaphors*. New Brunswick, NJ, 1992.

Hull, G. T., Scott, P. Bell and Smith, B. (eds) *All the Women are White, All the Blacks are Men, But Some of Us are Brave*. Old Westbury, NY, 1982.

Jablon, M. *Black Metafiction*. Iowa City, IA, 1997.

Johnson, J. Weldon (ed.) *The Book of American Negro Poetry*. New York, 1922.

McDowell, D. F. (ed.) *Slavery and the Literary Imagination*. Baltimore, MD, 1989.

Parker (1976) add at proofs.

Stepto, R. *From Behind the Veil*. New York, 1979.

Thelwell, M. 'Black Studies: A Political Perspective', *Massachusetts Review*, Autumn 1979.

Washington, M. H. (ed.) *Black-Eyed Susans*. New York, 1975.

—. *Invented Lives*. New York, 1987.

West, C. 'The Dilemma of the Black Intellectual', *Cultural Critique*, 1, Fall 1985.

Chicano/a Literature

Chicano/a literature is a complex term encompassing political, cultural and gendered historiography dating much earlier than the 1940s. 'Chicano/a' originates from the sixteenth-century name, 'Mexicano/a'. 'Mexicano/a' derives from the Nahuatl 'Mexica', meaning a people who live in the centre of the maguey (cactus plant). Lingually, 'Mexicano/a' in sixteenth-century speech, was articulated as 'Meshicano/a' or 'Mechicano/a' and later altered in the twentieth-century to Chicano/a. Yet the literature belonging under this cultural marker can be traced back to 2 February 1848: the year the Treaty of Guadalupe Hidalgo was signed.

The Mexicans who remained on Mexican-turned-North American lands (as outlined in the Treaty) and those who immigrated 'post-1848' from Mexico and other Latin American countries also chose various names for themselves: Mexican-American, Latino/a and/or

Chicano/a. The term Hispanic (also linked to these identity groupings) has been a controversial name among Latino/a groups in the United States – specifically Chicanos/as. In the 1980s, the US Federal Administration (under Ronald Reagan) instituted a 'Hispanic month' which automatically placed all Latinos (Mexican-Americans, Puerto-Rican Americans, Cuban-Americans, etc.) within a 'Spanish' (denoting Hispania or Spain) historical context. The government also designed census forms and other legal documentation to denote all Latinos as 'Hispanic'. Some groups do claim true lineage from Spain or 'Hispania'. For example, various groups in New Mexico such as communities in Taos or Santa Fe claim Hispanic identity. However, it is important to note that Latino groups should not be considered Hispanic collectively. Chicanos/as especially do not wish to be linked with the term 'Hispanic' because they consider their indigenous roots from Mexico primary, not secondary. 'Hispanic' or 'Hispania' represents a historical marker for indigenous conquest and colonization in Mexico (such as the Spanish conquest of the Aztecs). Chicanos/as then, see their heritage as one of the conquered and the conqueror – the Indian and the Spanish colonizer. The dichotomous intersection of opposing ancestries emphasizes another term linked to the Chicana/o identity: the Mestizo (mixed blood) or Mestizaje (a people of mixed blood). Chicano scholar Rafael Perez-Torres describes Mestizaje:

> Mestizaje cannot be separated from the histories of rape and violation from which it emerges. Simultaneously, it cannot be dismissed in search of an original indigenous identity that is not the condition of Chicano praxis. The cultural products that emerge from Chicano configurations of identity carry with them the conditions of mestizaje: conjunction, enrichment, violation, conquest, fusion, violence. Textualized, mestizaje enables a scrutiny of power and knowledge as these have been enacted or erased through history. (1995, 212)

Mestizaje, then, is an important Chicano/a cultural marker for its signification of Mexican history and most importantly, for its cultural concerns on North American soil. Chicanos/as may see their heritage linked to Mexico, but a Chicano/a is, first and foremost, an immigrant to the United States or born in the United States. Throughout their writings, therefore, the Chicano/a people explore what it means to be an American from a Mexican-American perspective. And the perspectives are multifarious: the Chicano/a farmworker struggling in the fields of such states as California, Nevada, Colorado and Texas, interpersonal relationships which emphasize cultural differences and struggles, religious convictions, cultural traditions and language. Today, the farmworker is also the meatpacker, the factory worker, the sweatshop (maquilladora) worker living either on or near the borders of Mexico or as far as Nebraska, New Jersey, New York. Chicanos/as in Kansas trace their migratory history from those who arrived in Topeka as early as the first decade of the 1900s to work on the railroads. Family units, whose members vary in generation, must contend with symbolic intersections of migration and cultural memory. Religion, as well, is transformed and translated outside and within the family. And of course, cultural traditions and language undergo change. Caló is a good example of a symbolic language migration which appears in Chicano/a literature. According to Chicano scholars Julio Martínez and Francisco Lomelí, Caló is 'an argot common in barrio slang and speech ... filled with metaphoric inventions and creative hybrids of Spanish, English, Spanglish (Spanish mixed with English), and some Nahuatl terms' (474). Chicano scholar Alfred Arteaga writes that Caló is an 'intercultural dynamic', an important ingredient in the construction of 'Chicano identity' (1997, 68). He says:

[B]eing for Chicanos occurs in the interface between Anglo and Latin America, on the border that is not so much a river from the Gulf of Mexico to El Paso and a wire fence from there to the Pacific but, rather, a much broader area where human interchange goes beyond the simple 'American or no' of the border check. It is the space to contest cultural identities more complex than the more facile questions of legal status or images in popular culture ... Mexicans negotiate the border like no others, north and south, south and north, realizing simultaneous cultural fission and fusion. It is this border context that differentiates the styles of linguistic interplay of Chicano poetry from other styles of polyglot poetics. The poetry of Eliot and Pound, for example, incorporates other languages, from the Italian of Dante, to German conversation, to Chinese characters. The poetics of Montoya and Burciaga is similar to Eliot and Pound's in the fact of its linguistic hybridization, but the fact of the border contributes to a different emphasis in the styles of that multilingualism. In Eliot and Pound there is much greater emphasis on quotation and literary allusion; while in Montoya and Burciaga, poetic hybridization tends to replicate the polyglot style of quotidian Chicano discourse. The former often focuses on the content of that form (for example, Dante's Inferno) and interlards 'significant' texts; the latter focuses on the form of that form (for example, caló, hybridization itself) and implements discursive interaction. (Arkeaga 1997, 68–9)

Language is then the vehicle by which hybridization or Mestizaje is created, recreated and laid open. Chicano/a literature explores all of these complexities (history, culture, language) inherent in the formation of identities.

As previously noted, Chicano/a literature began evolving from the moment the Treaty of Guadalupe Hidalgo was signed. In its nascent stage, the literature, by and large, was a literature of *testimonio* (transcribed oral testimonies), history, memoir and protest. By the 1940s, Chicanos/as, colonized and marginalized, were responding to years of oppression in various discursive and performative ways. The Pachuco of the 1930s, 1940s, and 1950s represented a defiance of assimilation. These were young urban Chicanos from El Paso, Los Angeles and surrounding communities who spoke the language of resistance (Caló), wore the *zoot suit* (baggy pant suits, pancake hats, long belt chains) and were involved in petty criminal activities.

While urban Chicanos were creating and proclaiming a resistant identity, a number of Chicanas were focusing upon preserving an identity they did not want to lose. In the southwest, a number of Chicanas were preoccupied with gathering *testimonios* or oral histories of their communities. Chicana scholars Tey Diana Rebolledo and Eliana S. Rivero write:

> In New Mexico, influenced by the New Deal and the Federal Writers' Project, three New Mexican women began to write about their lives and their cultural heritage: they were Cleofas Jaramillo, Fabiola Cabeza de Baca Gilbert and Nina Otero-Warren ... Along with Jovita Gonzales, who was collecting Texas folklore in the 1920s and 1930s, these women felt the need to document what they saw as a vanishing cultural heritage: their sense that their identity was being assimilated through history and cultural domination ... Although their writing presents the perspective of a landed society, they nevertheless cultivate the seeds of cultural resistance to Anglo hegemony ... Close readings of the texts written by these women show that landscape is one symbolic icon for describing the loss of land. In both *We Fed Them Cactus* (Cabeza de Baca) and *Romance of a Little Village Girl* (Jaramillo) the landscape at the beginning of the narration is a verdant paradise and at the end a windswept purgatory. (1993, 17)

From 'verdant paradise' to 'windswept purgatory', the theme of abundance and belonging transformed into disenfranchisement is a constant trope throughout the history of

Chicano/a literature. By collecting these *testimonios*, Chicana writers in the southwest, like Jaramillo and Otero-Warren, were primarily seeking to preserve a heritage for future generations.

Chicanos/as (and this included Pachucos) were also preoccupied with the Second World War as was the rest of the nation. Part of the war effort included inviting new immigrants to join the armed forces. The government offered to speed up the citizenship process in order to allow minorities to join. As a result, many new immigrants from Mexico who sought citizenship in the US enlisted. The war also attracted Chicanos/as who wanted to prove they were patriotic Americans. Their hope was to contribute to the nation and end discrimination. However, their enthusiasm and hopefulness was often met with disappointment upon their return. Felipe de Ortego y Gasca writes:

> The tragedy for Chicanos was that even though they responded patriotically to the colors during the war, they were still considered 'foreigners' by Anglo Americans most of whom had themselves 'recently' arrived from elsewhere, particularly Europe. Ironically, the first draftee of World War II was Pete Aguilar Despart, a Mexican American from Los Angeles. Chicanos were to emerge as the American ethnic group having won more medals of honor than any other group of Americans except Anglos. (1931, 12)

Chicana/o writings during this time of the national war effort also included theatre. Artists such as Daniel Ferreiro Rea and Carlos Villalongín (from Los Angeles and San Antonio respectively) produced shows for free and created *revistas* and *zarzuelas*. A *zarzuela* is a combination of song and recitation within the confines of a dramatic play. *Revistas* are published writings (of plays, poetry or prose writings) in pamphlet or magazine form. Although their efforts were short-lived, Spanish-language theatre remained active due to artists such as Villalongín and Ferreiro Rea. There were Spanish-language vaudeville performers in New York (La Chata Loloesca) and others working in television and Spanish-language radio (Leonardo García Astol) during and after the war. Chicanos/as were not only present in big city theatre venues but also in the agrarian areas of the southwest. These were called 'tent theatres:' makeshift theatres easily constructed for travel. Chicano scholars Julio Martínez and Francisco Lomelí note that '[t]ent theatres also continued their perennial odysseys into the 1950s, often setting up right in the camps of migrant farm laborers to perform their *revistas*. Through these traveling theatres some of the young people who would create a Chicano theater in the 1960s [received] their first exposure to Hispanic theatrical tradition' (1985, 179). These artists and performers were at the forefront of what was to be an important theatrical and literary revival.

> In 1965 the modern Chicano theater movement was born when Luis Miguel Valdez founded El Teatro Campesino in an effort to assist in organizing farmworkers for the grape boycott and the strike in Delano, California. From the humble beginning of dramatizing the plight of farmworkers, the movement grew to include small, agit-prop theater groups in communities and on campuses around the country, and eventually developed into a total theatrical expression that would find resonance on the commercial stage and the screen. By 1968 Valdez and El Teatro Campesino had left the vineyards and lettuce patches in a conscious effort to create a theater for a people which Valdez and other grass roots organizers of the 1960s envisioned as working-class, Spanish-speaking or bilingual, rurally oriented, and with very strong Pre-Columbian cultural ties. By 1970 El Teatro Campesino had pioneered and developed what would come to be known as teatro chicano, a style of agit-prop that incorporated the spirit and presentational style of the commedia dell'arte with the humor, character types, folklore, and popular culture of the

Mexican, especially as articulated earlier in the century by Mexican vaudeville companies that toured the Southwest in tent theaters. (Martínez and Lomelé 1985, 179)

Equally important are the women who were involved with Teatro Campesino from its inception as well as contemporary Chicana artists in theatre today.

Chicana scholar, Yolanda Broyles-González writes that '[w]omen have constituted a distinct force within the Teatro Campesino and, by extension, within the history of Chicana/o theater' (1996, 134). El Teatro Campesino's writing and production work was never solely created by one person but was a collective effort involving bright, vibrant and hard-working women who had to struggle to defend their presence in the theatre due to cultural patriarchal notions. Historically, Latin American and Mexican women have been relegated to the domestic sphere and women in theatre work, especially, are often not considered respectable. In addition to working against these societal attitudes, the women within El Teatro Campesino had to resist stereotyped roles written by the men in the group or work toward the inclusion of complex female characters. Olivia Chumacero, a member, describes the way Teatro Campesino produced plays:

> We used to develop our scripts as we went along, from the improvisations ... Sometimes, like when we were doing La carpa, which was in corrido form [corrido is a popular ballad], we had nights in which people met who wanted to work on writing the versos [verses] for the corrido. Smiley and I would go, along with different other people who were interested in writing. We'd sit down with Luis and work at it that way too. First we would talk ideas, about where we wanted to go in the piece. And then we would write different verses or whatever, and then select from that ... It was a collective way of working. We made our own costumes, we built our own props and sets ... we did all the work collectively. (Broyles-González 1996, 131)

Yet in many historical accounts of El Teatro Campesino, the fact that women and men worked together to write and produce these plays is largely ignored. It is important to highlight the collective nature of this organization to understand Chicano/a theatre at this time because then we can see a logical development of the history of Chicano and Chicana theatre production as well as literary development of all genres. Scholar Broyles-González emphasizes the importance of this understanding:

> The activities of several of the women from El Teatro Campesino – Olivia Chamacero, Socorro Valdez, Diane Rodriguez, Yolanda Parra – and the work of Silvia Wood in Tucson, Arizona; Nita Luna from El Teatro Aguacero in New Mexico; the women and men of El Teatro de la Esperanza; Ruby Nelda Pérez's or María Elena Gaitán's one-woman shows; the plays by Estela Portillo Trambley, Denise Chávez, Cherríe Moraga, and more recently by Josefina López, Edit Villareal, and Evelina Fernández, all mark the entry into a new cycle of theatrical activity for Chicanas ... The history of women's participation in theater history, is of far-reaching significance in and of itself. (1996, 163)

Similarly, the contributions Chicanas have made in fiction and poetry have redefined and repositioned definitions of the Chicano/a within and outside of their respective community. The popularity of Chicano/a theatre which focused upon the human condition and also gave voice to oppressed and impoverished Chicano/a workers prefaced El Movimiento which is also known as the Chicano Movement occurring between the 1960s and 1970s.

The Chicano Movement flourished due to a change in national and international political and economic climates. According to scholar Juan Gómez-Quiñones, 'The civil rights movement of the 1960s focused attention primarily on the problems of Blacks, while devoting some attention to the problems of other minorities. The Kennedy administration's "New Frontier" and Johnson's "Great Society" environment seemed to be willing to consider the increased demands by Mexicans for equal citizenship rights' (1992, 103). As a result, support and available monetary resources increased within community groups who were organizing for equal rights and justice.

> [I]nitiating forces were the Farm Workers Union, the Alianza, the Crusade for Justice, student organizations, and eventually, La Rasa Unida. Workers or persons of working-class origin were key to these forces, and women often provided the organizational backbone. Whatever the particular goals and methods of the political activism, the underlying current was disenchant-ment over the Mexican's political, economic, and social status in an Anglo-dominated capitalist society. Political activists became increasingly concerned with understanding how economic and class exploitation and racism had shaped the Mexican experience in the United States. The struggle to understand the Mexican American experience increasingly focused on questions of alienation, ethnicity, identity, class, gender and chauvinism. An articulation of a historical understanding of the Mexican experience became a paramount motif, a necessity in the struggle to shape a future for La Raza in the United States. (Gómez-Quiñones 1992, 103)

Within this context, the era of the Chicano Literary Renaissance emerged. Although most scholars date the beginning of the Renaissance in 1965, Américo Paredes' important work *With A Pistol in His Hand* (1958) and José Antonio Villarreal's novel *Pocho* (1959) point to a slightly earlier beginning. Chicanas also figured prominently even in this early stage of the Renaissance. Scholar Tey Diana Rebolledo writes that 'Quinto Sol [a Chicano publishing company] published *El Espejo/the Mirror: Selected Chicano Literature* (1969), the first anthology of Chicano literature published by Chicanos. Included among the writers were Estela Portillo, Raquel Moreno, and Georgia Cobos' (21). The Poetry, fiction and non-fiction focused on the perspective of the Mexican-American in the United States just as it had done in the earlier plays of El Teatro Campesino. The Teatro was also still quite active during this marked literary period.

Novelists emerging at this time were Tomás Rivera, ... *Y No Se Lo Tragó La Tierra* (1971); Alurista, *Nationchild Plumaroja* (1972); Rudolfo Anaya, *Bless Me, Ultima* (1972); Oscar Acosta, *The Revolt of the Cockroach People* (1973); and Rolando Hinojosa, *Estampas Del Valle* (1973). In 1975, Chicana novelist Estela Portillo Trambley published *Rain of Scorpions*. It was one of the first Chicana novels during this era. Ten years after *Rain of Scorpions*, the nation would see an explosion of Chicana writing. Between that time (1975–85) scholar Rebolledo notes that publishing was easier for Chicanos than Chicanas:

> [A]lthough some women were included among the first writers to be published, it was the male authors who made the initial inroads, were most easily and frequently published, and were the most recognized
>
> ... These authors became a canonical liturgy for Chicano writing ... Chicanas *were* writing during this early period. They were writing, but, having been silenced for long periods of time, the authors found breaking that silence into a public act difficult. (1995, 22)

Instead, the Chicano perspective was privileged with works such as Alejandro Morales, *La Verdad Sin Voz* (1979); John Rechy, *Rushes* (1979); Richard Vásquez, *Another Land* (1982). After the publication of the first Chicana anthology, *Chicanas en La Literatura y El Arte: El Grito*, which was edited by Estela Portillo Trambley in September of 1973, Chicanas began to publish but activity was slow. Eight years later, Cherríe Moraga and Gloria Anzaldúa published the anthology, *This Bridge Called My Back: Writings by Radical Women of Color* (1981). This anthology not only highlighted Chicana writings, but included women of colour from a variety of backgrounds and prompted an explosion of writings quite different from the earlier writings of the 1970s. This anthology directly addressed what Chicanas felt had always been problematic in the Chicano community (and other communities of colour): women's disenfranchisement, erasure and gendered violence within a male-identified community. The development of the personal essay present in this anthology became a vehicle to express these frustrations. The anthology was a success and also controversial because, as scholar Tey Diana Rebolledo points out, it placed Chicanas in a dilemma:

> 'This dilemma often placed Chicanas in a tenuous position between Anglo-feminists and their male Chicano colleagues. It put an additional strain on the Chicana lesbian feminists who felt, moreover, that their heterosexually oriented sisters did not fully support them. These issues raised in Chicana literature are still in a state of dialogue between the various perspectives as writers struggle with issues of unity versus separation. (Rebolledo and Rivero 1993, 24)

However, it also encouraged communities to begin speaking about these complex privileged and oppressed positions. These writings paved the way for further introspection with Gloria Anzaldúa's work, *Borderlands/La Frontera: The New Mestiza* (1987) and later Ana Castillo's work, *Massacre of the Dreamers: Essays on Xicanisma* (1995). New Chicana novelists emerged in full force during the 1980s and 1990s: Denise Chávez, *Last of the Menu Girls* (1991); Sandra Cisneros, *Woman Hollering Creek* (1992); Helena María Viramontes, *Under the Feet of Jesus* (1996); the aforementioned Ana Castillo, *The Mixquiahuala Letters* (1992) and others. All of these works were ground-breaking for their investigation and perspectives of the Chicana in contemporary society – both within the dominant society and in Chicano communities. Chicano male writers responded by re-investigating their own male identity. Writer Luis J. Rodriguez returns to his childhood in an effort to understand his upbringing in *Always Running: La Vida Loca, Gang Days in L.A.* (1993). In Ray González's anthology, *Muy Macho: Latino Men Confront Their Manhood* (1996) sixteen Chicanos and Latinos re-evaluate their patriarchal social conditioning. As well, Luis Alberto Urrea writes a scathing memoir tracing and critiquing his patriarchal upbringing in *Nobody's Son* (1998). Indeed, Chicano/a literature has certainly experienced much growth in the past forty years: investigating its identity, its place within society politically, economically and personally. In all of these works, it is apparent that Chicanos are moving towards a more inclusive and radical Mestizaje: a consciousness of inclusion and awareness of gendered as well as racial and class-based oppression and privilege. This, above all, is where the Chicano/a acquires her/his power to write.

Amelia María de la Luz Montes

Further reading and works cited

Arteaga, A. *Chicano Poetics*. New York, 1997.
Broyles-González, Y. *El Teatro Campesino*. Austin, TX, 1996.
García, A. M. *Chicana Feminist Thought*. New York, 1997.
Gaspar de Alba, A. *Chicano Art*. Austin, TX, 1998.
Gómez-Quiñones, J. *Chicano Politics*. Albuquerque, NM, 1992.
Gonzales-Berry, E. and Tatum, C. (eds) *Recovering the U.S. Hispanic Literary Heritage*. Houston, TX, 1996.
Gutiérrez, R. and Padilla, G. (eds) *Recovering the U.S. Hispanic Literary Heritage*. Houston, TX, 1993.

Hernández-Gutiérrez, M. de Jesús and Foster, D. W. (eds) *Literatura Chicana, 1965–1995*. New York, 1997.

Herrera-Sobek, M. and Viramontes, H. M. *Chicana Creativity and Criticism*. Albuquerque, NM, 1996.

— and Korrol, V. Sánchez *Recovering the U.S. Hispanic Literary Heritage*. Houston, TX, 2000.

López, T. A. *Growing Up Chicana/o*. New York, 1993.

Mariscal, G. (ed.) *Aztlán and Viet Nam*. Berkeley, CA, 1999.

Martínez, J. A. and Lomelí, F. A. (eds) *Chicano Literature*. Westport, CT, 1985.

Moraga, C. and Anzaldúa, G. *This Bridge Called My Back*. New York, 1983.

Ortego y Gasca, F. de. 'The Quetzal and the Phoenix', *Denver Quarterly*, 16, Fall 1981.

Pérez, E. *The Decolonial Imaginary*. Indianapolis, IN, 1999.

Pérez-Torres, R. *Movements in Chicano Poetry*. New York, 1995.

Rebolledo, T. D. *Women Singing in the Snow*. Tucson, AZ, 1995.

— and Rivero, E. S. (eds) *Infinite Divisions*. Tucson, AZ, 1993.

Sánchez, G. J. *Becoming Mexican American*. New York, 1993.

Trujillo, C. *Living Chicana Theory*. Berkeley, CA, 1998.

Film Studies

We are sometimes told today that film studies has progressed through 'a general movement in approaches to film from a preoccupation with authorship (broadly defined), through a concentration upon the text and textuality, to an investigation of audiences' (Hollows and Jancovich 1995, 8) – a consecutive pursuit of knowledge about film form, then realism, followed by language, and, finally, cultural politics (Braudy and Cohen 1999, xv–xvi). Such accounts forget the hardy perennials of cinema criticism, social and cultural theory and cultural policy: textual analysis of films, identification of directors with movies, and studies of the audience through psychology and psychoanalysis (Worth 1981, 39).

These perennials involve: (a) the identification and promotion of a canon of work that can secure cinema a role as an art form and social text; and (b) anxieties about the impact of the screen on spectators. Under category (a), some film academics separate their work from politics, regarding it as a means of registering and developing aesthetic discrimination 'in a relationship of tutelage, to the more established disciplines' (Bennett et al. 1981, ix). They seek to isolate the 'basic features of film which can constitute it as an art' (Bordwell and Thompson 1997, ix). Textual ranking identifies authors and focuses on form and style. Such old-fashioned disciplinary self-formation, whereby rent-seeking professors define what is art and then instruct others, is a powerful force, as we know from the history of literary studies.

But film always exceeds attempts to institute such New Critical readings, precisely because of its history and currency. As a governmental and business technology that spread with urbanization and colonialism alongside multifarious attempts to comprehend the modernity that it brought into vision (Shohat and Stam 1994, 100–36), film is impossible to delimit in a fetishized manner for long, in all but the most devastatingly intramural cloisters. More political work done under category (a) stresses that the avowed project of elevating cinema to the status of apolitical art is doomed to failure in its attempt to cordon off the social. This is a challenge to the Eurocentrism and universalism of formalist theory, in accord with social movements and Third and Fourth World counter-discourses (Carson and Friedman 1995).

Category (b) – concerns about the audience – includes psychological, sociological, educational, consumer, criminological and political promises and anxieties. These have been prevalent since silent cinema's faith in 'the moving picture man as a local social force ... the mere formula of [whose] activities' keeps the public well-tempered (Lindsay 1970, 243); through 1930s research into the impact of cinema on American youth via the Payne Studies (Blumer 1933); to post-Second World War concerns about Hollywood's intrication of education and entertainment and the need for counter-knowledge among the public (Powdermaker 1950, 12–15).

For the contemporary left, questions of pleasure have been central, as analysts have sought to account for and resist narrative stereotypes and explain 'why socialists and feminists liked things they thought they ought not to' (Dyer 1992, 4). This difficulty over pleasure accounts for film theory being highly critical of prevailing cultural politics, but never reifying itself into the Puritanism or orthodoxy alleged by critics of political correctness. The extraordinary diversity of latter-day film anthologies makes this point clear. A feminist film anthology focuses on issues of representation and production that are shared by many women, but it also attends to differences of race, history, class, sexuality and nation, alongside and as part of theoretical difference (Carson et al. 1994), while a black film anthology divides between spectatorial and aesthetic dimensions (Diawara 1993), and a queer anthology identifies links between social oppression and film and video practice (Holmlund and Fuchs 1997). I shall deal with the discourses of categories (a) and (b) serially, picking up from the latter to suggest a way forward for film studies

Film as an art form

The first move made under category (a) is to uncover directorial authorship (auteurism). There have been three main currents in debates about film authorship. First, authorship has been a category of legal ownership and textual criticism. US law theorizes the producer of a film as its author. But not so US film studies, which seeks directors with an *oeuvre*. In the latter case, the knot that allegedly holds films together across time and space is a recognizable set of concerns and stylistic norms that can be correlated with an individual director's biography and show a capacity to move from denotative storytelling to connotative thematic tropes. Second, a radical alternative argues for the material conditionality of the category, suggesting that authors are constituted through discourses and institutions rather than through personal vision. Third, an argument exists for the social nature of cultural production, the inevitable cross-pollination of signs, genres and codes that sweep across a landscape rather than originating in specific people.

There is something laughably counter-indicative about auteurism. Making films is so obviously collective in its division of labour. Auteurism only makes sense if we consider the medium's claim to art. Authorship is identified and its eminence distributed in synchronization with artistic valorization – once novels, movies, television drama or web pages are held to be of creative significance, a discourse of individual signatures emerges. The effect is a double one – certain authors are named and elevated, and the medium or genre itself receives cross-validation from the process. (This person is an author, he/she is gifted. This medium has authors, it is artistic.) The nice irony, of course, is the use of categories from high-art appreciation to endorse popular culture in a way that acknowledges the audience imagined by film-makers as integral to their creative practice – quite unlike the windswept romantic author pondering the infinite.

Auteur writings covered a broad sweep of politics, and not always from a humanist perspective – structuralists believed that auteurs touched on deeply secreted structures of mythic meaning in a culture, unconsciously opening up lines of fissure. Today arguments are made for auteurism from radical political projects – identifying links between masculinist concerns and directorial surrogates as sites of enunciation within texts, or seeking to promote the work of those marginalized from cinema by virtue of their sex or race.

The second move of category (a) is about film form and style, via narratology. Narratives tell stories through an aetiological chain of cause and effect over time via a linear trajectory from the establishment of questions or problems to their resolution. A film moves from a presumed state of normalcy, or equilibrium, for the characters prior to the text, to a disequilibrium set up in the opening of that text, and then through a series of manoeuvres that results in the achievement of a goal and a new equilibrium. Classical narrative cinema focuses on central characters, whose attitudes to the events going on around them and participation in conflicts and their resolution are critical. The success or otherwise of these moves frequently depends on their ability to engage dual forms of verisimilitude – looking like a film story of a familiar kind, and also resembling the mental processes of ordinary human experience.

Much academic narratology is linked to formalism, which divides narratives in two. The *fabula* or story concerns the chronological unfolding of relations between characters, or actants. This is the immanent structure of the story, the spirit-within that impels a text forward. When that basis becomes orchestrated, it is transformed into a *syuzhet*, or plot (the movement from what is told to how to tell it). The *syuzhet* animates the *fabula* via an array of artistic devices, such as parallelism, retardation, defamiliarization and so on: in short, sources of aesthetic pleasure that do not simply move the narrative forward. Understanding a narrative is more than following the trajectory of a story. It depends on reading the story horizontally as well as vertically – the narrative thread only makes partial sense of a film, along with an attempt to remember, for example, the conduct of a specific character through the text.

The classical Hollywood narrative is about action – a search for an object by a person, and the event that closes the search off. This linear model does not deal particularly well with the atmospheric, processual type of film. A series of emotional engagements and disengagements is entered into, often without obvious motivation in terms of the overall narrative drive of the story. Signs float around in a way that is quite incidental to allowing the hero to find his pot of whatever. Instead, information that is supplementary to the excuse for the film becomes its effective/affective centre, the real template for the action.

Methods of narration are influenced by the use of camera, and here questions of style arise. Subjective narration, which clearly locates the vantage point or enunciation within a character in the diegesis, often involves point-of-view shooting, whereas hidden enunciation is mimetic and favours objective camera. In subjective narration, the camera takes on the function of that character's vision in the text. Conversely, omniscient and objective narration are frequently achieved through a point of view that comes from nowhere, outside the action and seemingly without a particular perspective or form of knowledge. But this narration can be interpreted to bring out the site of enunciation if we examine factors such as the height of the camera. The eye-level shot is taken with the camera horizontal to the ground as if it were in the room in human form but without being seen or reacting to what occurs in front of it. The high-angle shot is taken from above the action. It can emphasize the insignificance of the human actants as opposed to the commercial, natural or architectural features in the frame. Conversely, low-angle shots are tilted up to cover the action, which can inflect it with a certain glow from below as well as highlighting size and speed. This attention to textual detail has been very productive for the aestheticization impulses of category (a).

What of the social and political aspects to category (a)? I shall examine these with particular reference to class. Attempts to do class analysis in film involve a number of moves: literally observing how a class acts on screen – its clothing, gesture, movement, work, leisure, home-life; seeing who controls the means of communication behind a film – technicians, producers, directors, censors, shareholders; analysing the ideological message of stories – personal transcendence versus collective solidarity, the legitimacy of capitalist freedoms, or the compensations in family and community for social inequality; and noting which interests are served by government-sponsored national film industries – local bourgeoisies, men, whites, distributors, the people. In textual terms, those films that foreground class through theme or identification do not exhaust the list of films ready for class readings. Patterns of speech or costume may not only signify the immediate referent of social position, but go beyond that to the trappings, logic and operation of capitalism: how the clothes were made, or the housing conditions that go along with the accent; we might think here of the James Bond series' obsession with small differentiations of social position through food, alcohol and cars, and the way that hotel staff and other employees are easily ordered about. Some of us deem it important that Sean Connery orders the Dom Perignon '52 and George Lazenby the '57.

The price paid for attending a film (exchange-value) takes over from the desires exhibited in the actual practical utility of what is being purchased (use-value). This price expresses the momentary monetary value of that need rather than its lasting utility. That notion of built-in obsolescence and value bestowed via a market is in fact a key to all commodities, popular or otherwise. They elicit desire by wooing consumers, glancing at them sexually, and smelling and looking nice in ways that are borrowed from romantic love but then reverse that relationship: people learn about correct forms of romantic love from commodities, such as love scenes in movies.

This culture industries paradigm has alerted film theory to the fact that organizations train, finance, describe, circulate and reject actors and activities that go under the signs film-maker and film. Governments, trade unions, colleges, social movements, community groups and businesses aid, fund, control, promote, teach and evaluate creative persons. They define and implement criteria that make possible the use of the word 'creative' through law courts that permit erotica on the grounds that they are works of art, schools that require pupils to study film on the grounds that it is improving, film commissions that sponsor scripts on the grounds that they reflect society back to itself, or studios that invite Academy Award voters to parties as promotions for their movies. In turn, these criteria may themselves derive, respectively, from legal doctrine, citizenship or tourism aims, and profit plans. This industrial infrastructure has implications for what it actually means to produce culture:

> '[T]he popular notion of a struggling artist working isolated in a lonely garret is extremely misleading as a representation of the norm. Creators often struggle economically, but in modern

> societies most of them work in organizational settings – either directly in an organization or indirectly dependent upon one or more organizations to distribute or exhibit their work . . . even culture production by individuals occurs in collective contexts . . . networks of functionally interdependent individuals, groups, and organizations. (Zollars and Cantor 1993, 3)

Film and its audience

Testing the relationship between films and their viewers has produced two main forms of analysis: spectatorship theory and audience research. Spectatorship theory speculates about the effects on people of films, but instead of questioning, testing and measuring them, it uses psychoanalysis to explore how supposedly universal internal struggles over the formation of subjectivity are enacted on-screen and in the psyches of watchers. The spectator is understood as a narratively-inscribed concept that can be known via a combination of textual analysis and Freudianism. Audience research is primarily concerned with the number and conduct of people seated before screen texts: where they came from, how many there were and what they did as a consequence of being present. The audience is understood as an empirical concept that can be known via research instruments derived from sociology, demography, social psychology and marketing.

The film spectator is generally understood as the product of two forces: first, psychic struggles for personality that psychoanalytic theory claims are characteristic of maturation and the getting of sexuality; and second how both the texts and the physical apparatus of cinema draw out these conflicts. Psychological battles are in the unconscious, which means that they cannot be known through the thoughts or neurones of people. Instead, they gain expression indirectly, via the repetition of various dramas about power and the self, with sexual identity at their core. Not surprisingly, these narratives find some expression in dreams, and may be sources for fiction as well; hence the similarity between film-going and dreams (the darkness and the abandon in story) is matched by a likeness in the texture of film narrative and the unconscious.

As Dudley Andrew points out, psychoanalysis has been deployed to account for the unconscious of film-makers and spectators, the nature of film as fantasy, the inevitability of identification for fantasy to come into play, and how the unconscious in film may intersect with wider questions of psychoanalysis and culture (1984, 135). Graeme Turner argues that film is friendly towards psychoanalysis because of 'its collapsing of the boundaries of the real'. The cinema occupies the gap between what we see and what we imagine (1988, 113).

Most 1970s psychoanalytic film theory argues that the gaze in film belongs to the heterosexual male and his screen brothers. Feminist theorists and film-makers responded by supporting and making some determinedly unpleasurable films that confronted spectators with their complicity in patriarchy. The cinema is seen as a sexual technology, a site where practices are instantiated that construct sex and desire through such techniques as confession, concealment and the drive for truthful knowledge about motivation, character and occasion. The reproducibility of virtuosic performance provided by electronic technology has produced an era of performativity. Both simultaneity of instant reception and longevity of recorded life come with electronic media. The technology of visual reproduction enables a multiplicity of personalized perspectives inside a world of commodity reproduction. In some cases, this avant-gardisme denied both women's active address and engagement with classical narrative, and crucial social differences within genders that are not about the acquisition of linguistic or familial norms or the getting of sexuality, but are to do with race and class (Pribram 1988, 1–3).

The notion of overturning dominant forms of stitching spectators into the text relates to criticisms of realism. For example, the conventional documentary sets the spectator's gaze up as competent, once it is guided by the knowing hand–eye–technology coordination of the director and editor. Raymond Williams sees the avant-garde as acknowledging the existence of a 'fragmented ego in a fragmented world', defying capitalist neatness and a unilogical realism (1989, 93). There is, of course, intense argument about how different forms of texts can be read. The notion of textually inscribed rules of reading – interpellations of viewers – as a function of naturalism/realism problematized the value of, for example, social realism. It has been an orthodoxy that linear, resolved narratives which compel closure are reactionary in their construction of the possibility of perfect knowledge. Instead, audiences should be confronted with the constructedness of their positioning and the seams of weaving of each text made explicit via self-referentiality. Like psychoanalytic theory, this critique makes symptomatic readings of texts, assuming that spectatorship was less a practice than a by-product of being positioned and attracted by narrative and image that implied perfect knowledge and political orthodoxy in their very essence. Psychoanalytic protocols have proved to be remarkably providential for interrogating questions of masculinity, femininity and postcoloniality. While Freud may be considered outmoded in the social sciences, his doctrine of counter-indicative reading and the centrality of sex remain magnetic to film theory, especially when linked to the apparatus of cinema.

The apparatus in film theory refers to the interaction between spectators, texts and technology. Apparatus theory is concerned with the material circumstances of viewing: the nature of filmic projection (from behind the audience) or video playing (from behind or in front), the darkness of the theatre or the lightness of daytime TV, the textual componentry of what is screened and the psychic mechanisms engaged. In other words, apparatus theory inquires into the impact of the technical and physical specificity of watching films on the processing methods used by their watchers. This goes beyond issues raised in debates over technological innovation (discussed elsewhere) to focus on cinema as a 'social machine'. This machine is more than the obvious machines of the cinema: film, lighting, sound recording systems, camera, make-up, costume, editing devices and projector. A blending of 'narrativity, continuity, point of view, and identification' sees spectators become part of the very apparatus designed for them (Flitterman-Lewis 1990, 3, 12). The apparatus takes the spectatorial illusion of seeming to experience film as real life and makes it a combination of power and yet relaxation, of engagement coupled with leisure.

Apparatus theory has basically operated at the level of speculation, apart from a brief flurry of writing on technological history and meaning that looked at those moments when the very technology of cinema was highlighted to audiences, or that retrieved cinema's prehistory via studies of panoramas, magic lanterns, dioramas and cineramas (de Lauretis and Heath 1985). This is because the principal interest of apparatus theorists never diverged from how subjectivity is constituted via the imaginary and the symbolic and their dance around the real. The interest in the specific technical apparatus of cinema is inextricably intertwined with an interest in marxist theorization of prevailing ideological norms plus psychoanalytic theorization of fantasies and complexes.

The subject is presented with what looks like unveiled, transparent truth, whereby the camera substitutes for the eyes. Spectatorship is like being there, but with intriguingly radical transformations of time and perspective: the distant grows near, the past becomes present and points of view shift. The spectator's loss of mobility is compensated by this promiscuous look, which travels to the most dangerous or painful as well as exhilarating places, and with impunity, as classical narrative ensures the ultimate restoration of equilibrium through perfect knowledge. The eye transcends the body to roam across multiple viewpoints and scenes. Just as ideology is the means whereby social subjects have their conditions of existence represented back to them in everyday life, masquerading as an unvarnished, transcendent truth, so film is a key mechanism for encapsulating such cultural messages (Allen 1997, 19).

Initial contributions and ripostes to apparatus theory came from feminist scholars for its failure to distinguish the different experiences and psychic mechanisms of men and women – that male viewers were principally involved in fetishizing women on screen and identifying with men on screen, which apparatus theorists had ignored. That engagement, by such writers as Constance Penley (1989), Sandy Flitterman-Lewis (1990) and Teresa de Lauretis (de Lauretis and Heath 1985), enlivened apparatus theory by showing the centrality of difference to spectacle and the need for feminist film-making and feminist critical practice to account for and disrupt the association of the apparatus with the male gaze.

A further critique of apparatus theory is that it has no mechanism for predicting or investigating how spectators in fact process information. It cannot establish whether disavowal occurs or does not. In short, symptomatic theories have no means of being falsified, because they know the answers from the theoretical baggage that poses the questions. Any interest in the concrete meaning-making of audiences, their ability to engage actively with texts and the apparatus via personal and collective cultural history and systems of interpretation, would displace the assumption that the unconscious is automatically and universally engaged by technologies of viewing. Such conflictual and manifold processes may see a proliferation of cross-identifications that go far beyond not just the limits of the body, but beyond the norms of psychic training and bodily awareness into entirely new territory (men identifying with women in melodramas, women identifying with male action heroes, Native Americans identifying with western pioneers – in short, the theatre as a site of carnival as much as machine, where viewers transcend the dross of their ordinary social and psychological lives [Stam 1989, 224]). At the same time, this interest in the ability of audiences to make meaning has seen another, seemingly conflictual paradigm emerging under the sign of Michel Foucault that considers the contemporary moment as an electronic transformation of a long history of surveillance under modernity, from the panoptic prison designs of Jeremy Bentham to the all-seeing gaze and internalization of today's mall security and virtual home cinema (Denzin 1995). Between them, these two moves pull apart, replicate and make empirical many of the concerns that apparatus theory sought to synthesize.

In short, symptomatic theory valuably problematized the exclusive concentration on representation, demonstrating that materiality and perception, too, had their place. This emphasis on ideology and the interplay of machine, text, culture and person guaranteed that film theory would not be caught in the formalism of much literary criticism. At the same time, its very mechanistic mode of inquiry, strangely redolent of the very metaphors it so disparaged, limited its utility as a paradigm for research.

The second discourse of category (b) shifts to the empirical audience. There are three primary sites for defining this audience: the film industry, the state and criticism. In this sense, the audience is artificial, the creature of various agencies that then act upon their creation. Many discussions of the audience are signs of anxiety: laments for civic culture in the US correlate an increase in violence and a decline in membership of parent-teacher associations with heavy film viewing – as true today as it was when the Payne Fund Studies of the 1930s inaugurated mass social-science panic about young people, driven by academic, religious and familial iconophobia and the sense that large groups of people were engaged with popular culture beyond the control of the state and ruling classes. Before even that, films were connected to gambling and horse racing in various forms of social criticism – the arts of popular commerce forever threatening an orderly conduct of urban life – or were lunged for as raw material by the emergent discipline of psychology, where obsessions with eyesight and the cinema gave professors something to do. At the same time, social reformers looked at the cinema as a potential forum for moral uplift; if film could drive the young to madness it might also provoke a sense of social responsibility (Austin 1989, 33–5).

But unlike such institutions, the cultural audience is not so much a specifiable group *within* the social order as the principal site *of* that order. Audiences participate in the most global (but local), communal (yet individual) and time-consuming practice of making meaning in the history of the world. The concept and the occasion of being an audience are textual links between society and person, at the same time as viewing involves solitary interpretation as well as collective behaviour. Production executives invoke the audience to measure success and claim knowledge of what people want. But this focus on the audience is not theirs alone. Regulators do it to organize administration, psychologists to produce proofs and lobby-groups to change content, hence the link to panics about education, violence and apathy supposedly engendered by the screen and routinely investigated by the state, psychology, marxism, neoconservatism, the church, liberal feminism and others. The audience as consumer, student, felon, voter and idiot engages such groups. This is Harold Garfinkel's notion of the 'cultural dope', a mythic figure 'who produces the stable features of the society by acting in compliance with preestablished and legitimate alternatives of action that the common culture provides.' The 'common sense rationalities ... of here and now situations' used by people are obscured by this condescending categorization (1992, 68). When the audience is invoked as a category by the industry or its critics and regulators, it immediately becomes such a 'dope'. Much non-Hollywood film wants to turn such supposed dopes into a public of thinkers beyond the home – civic-minded participants in a political and social system as well as an economy of purchasing. National cinemas in Europe, Asia, the Pacific, Latin America and Africa are expected to win viewers and train them in a way that complements the profit-driven sector. The entertainment function is secondary to providing programmes the commercial market would not deliver. Audiences are encouraged not just to watch and consume, but to act, to be better people.

Future developments

Perhaps the most significant innovation in recent film theory has been a radical historicization of context, such that the analysis of textual properties and spectatorial processes must now be supplemented by an account of occasionality that details the conditions under which a text is made, circulated, received, interpreted and criticized. The life of any popular or praised film is a passage across space and time, a life remade again and again by institutions, discourses and practices of distribution and reception – in short, all the shifts and shocks that characterize the existence of cultural commodities, their ongoing renewal as the temporary property of varied, productive workers and publics and their stasis as the abiding property of businesspeople.

The crucial link between theories of the text and spectatorship – one that abjures the idea of the dope – may come from a specification of occasionality, that moment when a spectator moves from being 'the hypothetical point of address of filmic discourse' to membership in 'a plural, social audience'; for that moment can produce surprises (Hansen 1994, 2). Jacqueline Bobo's analysis of black women viewers of *The Color Purple* shows how their process of watching the film, discussing it and reading the novel drew them back to Alice Walker's writing, with all three processes invoking their historical experience in ways quite unparalleled in dominant culture – a far cry from the dismissal of the film by critics. These women 'sifted through the incongruent parts of the film and reacted favorably to elements with which they could identify' (1995, 3). Similarly, gay Asian-Caribbean-Canadian video-maker Richard Fung (1991) talks about searching for Asian genitals in the much-demonized genre of pornography, an account not available in conventional denunciations of porn and its impact on minorities. Again, this type of historicized specificity is a valuable antidote to any purely textual or symptomatic reading.

This is the abiding lesson of film theory: the medium's promiscuity points every day and in every way towards the social. It is three things, all at once: a *recorder* of reality (the unstaged pro-filmic event); a *manufacturer* of reality (the staged and edited event); and *part of* reality (watching film as a social event on a Saturday night, or a protest event over sexual, racial or religious stereotyping).

Toby Miller

Further reading and works cited

Allen, R. *Projecting Illusion*. Cambridge, 1997.
Andrew, J. D. *Concepts in Film Theory*. Oxford, 1984.
Austin, B. A. *Immediate Seating*. Belmont, CA, 1989.
Bennett, T. et al. 'Preface', in *Popular Television and Film*, eds T. Bennett et al. London, 1981.
Blumer, H. *Movies and Conduct*. New York, 1933.
Bobo, J. *Black Women as Cultural Readers*. New York, 1995.
Bordwell, D. and Thompson, K. *Film Art*. New York, 1997.
Braudy, L. and Cohen, M. 'Preface', in *Film Theory and Criticism*, eds L. Braudy and M. Cohen. New York, 1999.
Carson, D. and Friedman, L. D. (eds) *Shared differences*. Urbana, IL, 1995.
— et al. (eds) *Multiple voices in Feminist Film Criticism*. Minneapolis, MN, 1994.
Cook, P. and Bernink, M. (eds) *The Cinema Book*. London, 1999.
de Lauretis, T. and Heath, S. (eds) *The Cinematic Apparatus*. London, 1985.
Denzin, N. 'The Birth of the Cinematic, Surveillance Society', *Current Perspectives in Social Theory*, 15, 1995.
Diawara, M. (ed.) *Black American Cinema*. New York, 1993.
Dyer, R. *Only Entertainment*. London, 1992.
Flitterman-Lewis, S. *To Desire Differently*. Urbana, IL, 1990.
Fung, R. 'Looking for my Penis: The Eroticized Asian in Gay Video Porn', in *How Do I look?*, ed. Bad Object-Choices. Seattle, WA, 1991.
Garfinkel, H. *Studies in Ethnomethodology*. Cambridge, 1992.
Hansen, M. *Babel and Babylon*. Cambridge, MA, 1994.

Hill, J. and Church Gibson, P. (eds) *The Oxford Guide to Film Studies*. Oxford, 1998.

Hollows, J. and Jancovich, M. 'Popular Film and Cultural Distinctions', in *Approaches to Popular Film*, eds J. Hollows and M. Jancovich. Manchester, 1995.

Holmlund, C. and Fuchs, C. (eds) *Between the Sheets, in the Streets*. Minneapolis, MN, 1997.

Lindsay, V. *The Art of the Moving Picture*. New York, 1970.

Miller, T. and Stam, R. (eds) *A Companion to Film Theory*. Oxford, 1999.

Penley, C. *The Future of an Illusion*. Minneapolis, MN, 1989.

Powdermaker, H. *Hollywood: The Dream Factory*. Boston, 1950.

Pribram, E. D. 'Introduction', in *Female Spectators*, ed. E. D. Pribram. London, 1988.

Shohat, E. and Stam, R. *Unthinking Eurocentrism*. New York, 1994.

Stam, R. *Subversive Pleasures*. Baltimore, MD, 1989.

— and Miller, T. (eds) *Film and Theory*. Oxford, 2000.

Turner, G. *Film as Social Practice*. London, 1988.

Williams, R. *The Politics of Modernism*. London, 1989.

Worth, S. *Studying Visual Communication*, ed. L. Gross. Philadelphia, 1981.

Zollars, C. L. and Cantor, M. G. 'The Sociology of Culture Producing Occupations', *Current Research on Occupations and Professions*, 8, 1993.

Feminist Film Studies and Film Theory

Strictly speaking, it is impossible to talk of a single feminist film theory, if by this title we assume a coherent, unified, intellectual, academic and political project. Indeed, that feminist film theory, in whatever guise, is, and has always been, avowedly political in its agendas and interests, implies fracture and contest, heterogeneity, difference and diversity in the various interests and perspectives which may be considered to belong to the identity of 'feminist film theory'. Thus, this essay, in recognizing the question of political engagement as necessary to any feminist project concerned with the analysis of filmic modes of gendered identity construction and representation within various historical and cultural contexts, will seek to address various aspects of feminist film theory, without assuming any simple coherence or consonance in the guise of a unified area of study.

Furthermore, while this essay addresses a range of feminist interventions in the area of film studies in the broader context of the North American university, this is not to say that feminist interventions in film study or theory are not restricted, on the one hand, to the university exclusively, or, on the other hand, to North America during the last three decades, roughly speaking. Of course, no discourse evolves in isolation from other discourses, and the history of feminist film theory in all its guises is marked by debate, appropriation, intervention and dissent from other theoretical, philosophically inflected, and political languages and processes. However reformulated, and however self-reformulating, so-called feminist film theory is, in part, an epistemo-political project engaging not only with feminist politics obviously, but also with semiotics, psychoanalysis, the discourses of race and gender, questions of culturally determined aesthetics, matters of mimesis and historically informed and mediated processes of identity construction, among a number of intellectual and social frameworks

Moreover, this essay does not assume that, in addressing feminist film theory in the US, the subject of this essay has evolved without the influence of work pursued in film studies and related areas from outside the US. The work of French theorist Christian Metz and British critics Laura Mulvey and Jacqueline Rose on matters of the gaze and sexuality has been of crucial importance in the field. However, as far as is possible, while acknowledging the impossibility and undesirability of containing any discourse artificially according to national or continental boundaries, this article will speak to particular strategic moments in the study of film as though there were a specifically North American history.

Polemical beginnings

While there is no absolutely justifiable beginning to which we can turn, it is provisionally possible to identify as one initiating moment in the history of feminist film theory the establishment of the relatively short-lived journal *Women and Film*, the first issue of which appeared in 1972, at the same time as the emergence of women's film festivals, notably those in New York and Edinburgh. The goal of *Women and Film* was to address filmic images of women as these represented and reflected the oppressed, stereotyped and marginalized position of women in society as brought into focus by the women's movement of the 1960s. Part of the polemic of the journal was to envision through critical intervention the, in retrospect, perhaps somewhat utopian ideal of transforming the representation of women in film so as to reflect more accurately the reality of female experience.

Drawing in part on and responding to the work of, among others, Kate Millett and Germaine Greer, as well as Simone de Beauvoir, *Women and Film* thus may be seen in retrospect as speaking to and exemplifying a sociological approach (as distinct from the perception of feminist film theory in Great Britain, specifically through articles published in *Screen*, as primarily theoretical). Such an approach (however reductive this identification may be) sought, in the words of the editors, to take 'up the struggle with women's image in film and women's roles in the film industry' (1972, 5) as part of a necessary corrective to the 'political, psychological, social and economic oppression of women' (1972, 5). As Sue Thornham points out, the journal had a threefold goal: to transform film-making practice, to end ideological oppression, and to establish a 'feminist critical aesthetics' (1999, 9–10).

Sharon Smith's article, 'The Image of Women in Film: Some Suggestions for Future Research', which was published in the first issue in 1972, typifies the political stance and goals of the journal. Smith aims to establish how the range of representations of women in film is limited and stereotyped in both limiting and negative ways which reproduce the experience of lived oppression, thereby perpetuating social marginalization. Film, Smith argues, needs to be transformed so as to represent a greater variety of women's roles and experiences. As Smith suggests, '[t]he role of a woman in film almost always revolves around her physical attraction and the mating games she plays with the male characters', while representations of men extend beyond the physical and biological, to the social and historical worlds (1999, 14–15). Films thereby 'express the fantasies and subconscious needs of their (mostly male) creators' (15). For Smith there is a direct correlation between the representation of women and the access to positions of power in the film industry, including writing, editing and production (19). But, as Smith argues in conclusion, things can only change when cultural perceptions of women outside filmic representation have changed.

A significant moment in the early years of feminist film study which built on the work of *Women and Film* and the kinds of arguments presented by Smith was the publication in 1974 of Molly Haskell's *From Reverence to Rape*. (Haskell's is, of course, not the only text of significance, but due to lack of space we can only gesture towards other titles such as Marjorie Rosen's *Popcorn Venus* and Joan Mellon's *Women and Sexuality in the New Film*). Part of Haskell's significance is in her recognition of film as not merely a mimetic mode of representation but as a complex textual process of encoding and registration around matters of gender and social roles. Haskell's position is similar to Smith's but is significantly more complex in its comprehension of representations of women. Identifying a range of positions and images for women in film across the history of film, Haskell locates what might be termed a typology of restrictive representation. However, where Haskell diverges from Smith is in her reading of film for the possibilities it contains for the encoding of heterogeneous and possibly subversive modes of address. In support of this thesis, she turns to the 'woman's film' of the 1930s and 1940s. While women may well be punished frequently in such films (*Dark Victory* with Bette Davis is a significant example) as a means of reaching closure whereby women are, finally, recuperated within a male-centred vision, yet, for a while, Haskell argues, the woman dominates and controls the narrative, and it is this temporary control which may be read as implicitly, if not explicitly, subversive, because it presents an equally temporary strong, positive image of woman. (*Mildred Pierce* is one such cautionary tale; ambivalent and complex, it traces Joan Crawford's rise to economic and social importance; she, however, ultimately is chastened and 'punished' because her resistance to being subservient to men, it is implied, leads to her youngest daughter's death and her eldest daughter's arrest for murder.)

Theoretical interventions

Feminist film theory, while developing in North America in the 1970s, did not remain unaffected by the theoretical explorations of critics in Britain such as Claire Johnston and Laura Mulvey. Indeed, by the late 1970s, the signs of a sea change in favour of a turn to theory are marked by the establishment, in 1976, of the journal *Camera Obscura*, and an article by B. Ruby Rich, 'The Crisis of Naming in Feminist Film Criticism', first published in the journal *Jump Cut* (1978), which took a retrospective glance at the history of feminist film studies up to that point. Rich addresses the need to theorize as a way of providing a language of analysis where previously silence existed. Drawing on the silencing of the female voice in western culture, Rich argues for an understanding of the female spectator as an active creator of meaning, rather than being merely a passive consumer of stereotyped images.

Claire Johnston (1973) argued, as Sue Thornham puts it, that 'the figure of "woman" functions within film as a sign within patriarchal discourse' (Thornham 1999, 53), rather than being simply a reflection of some unmediated reality. Laura Mulvey, drawing on psychoanalysis, the film work of Christian Metz and Jean-Louis Baudry, and addressing adjunct concerns to those of Johnston, formulated the idea of cinema as an apparatus which situates the spectator (Thornham 1999, 53), aligning the spectator with the gaze of the camera. As Robert Stam summarizes Mulvey's position, '[v]isual pleasure on the cinema thus reproduced a structure of male looking and female-to-be-looked-at-ness, a binary structure which mirrored the asymmetrical power relations operative in the real social world' (2000, 174). More specifically, the spectator's pleasure is intrinsically interwoven with the gaze, in fetishized processes of voyeurism and scopophilia. At the same time, as Mulvey makes plain and echoing Metz, the spectator, whether male or female, is situated in a gendered position: the spectator is assumed to be male, the gaze that of a male spectator and the code 'woman', constituted within the filmic text, an eroticized and fragmented, and therefore fetishized, figure.

Such psychoanalytically inflected analysis is exemplified in North American feminist film studies by the work of Mary Ann Doane, Teresa de Lauretis and Kaja Silverman, whose publications punctuate film theory's interrogations in the 1980s. Doane's essay, 'Caught and Rebecca: The Inscription of Femininity as Absence' (1981) and a number of other essays subsequently collected in Femmes Fatales (1991) move beyond Mulvey in their analysis of the role and construction of the female spectator. Through examination of the 'woman's film', 'weepies' and the figure of the 'femme fatale', Doane questions psychic processes of identification and alignment between the female spectator and the images of women, whereby the female spectator comes to terms with herself as object of desire. At the same time, however, 'the "woman's film" centres both our narrative identification and its structures of looking on a female protagonist, so that its narratives claim, at least, to place female subjectivity, desire and agency at their centre' (Thornham 1999, 55). Such processes come at a cost for the female spectator, however, the cost being that, for being momentarily privileged, situated as the agent rather than the object of desire, such female characters are finally silenced, constituted through narrative as ultimately silent or absent. The essays of Femmes Fatales extend such analysis to examine how the forms and technologies of cinema are employed so as to reinforce the instability of 'woman' as signifier. In the figure of 'femme fatale', woman is shown to be constituted through dissimulation, masquerade and duplicity. Female sexuality is perceived as threatening because both emphasized and fetishized (through close-up, lighting, focus and so on), and maintained as a site which troubles epistemological assumptions concerning what can and cannot be known (Doane 1991, 1). Doane thus presents a reading of a variety of films where the woman is unveiled, psychically, the threat explored through the mechanics of the gaze.

Silverman and de Lauretis both explore the process of cinematic and psychic identification, while complicating Mulvey's comprehension of the gaze as being always aligned with masculinity. In different ways, both examine how the structures of identification can involve a double, and sometimes paradoxical, engagement on the part of female spectators, whereby they identify with both the 'positions of both desired object and desiring subject' (Thornham 1999, 56). Identification for de Lauretis, the engagement of female subjectivity in narrative movement, is inextricably involved with the pleasures of narrative. However, this is never neutral, for as de Lauretis argues, narratives are always in some manner Oedipal. Thus, '[t]he cinematic apparatus, in the totality of its operations and effects, produces not merely images but imaging. It binds affect and meaning to images by establishing terms of identification, orienting the movement of desire, and positioning the spectator in relation to them' (de Lauretis 1999, 85). As de Lauretis comments, '[i]f governed by an Oedipal logic, it is because it is situated within the system of exchange ... where woman functions as both a sign (representation) and a value (object) for that exchange' (1999, 88).

Silverman comprehends cinema as figuring a psychic plenitude, its range of signifiers seducing the viewer with the paradoxically impossible possibility of psychic completion, from which the subject has been separated since infancy. For Silverman, cinema therefore re-enacts the primary displacement identified by Freud, by which the human subject comes to be constituted through separation and lack. Woman in film, in Silverman's reading, stands in as both mirror and screen of male lack (Thornham 1999, 56), in a complex reconfiguration of the signs of absence belonging to a Freudian lexical triangulation of castration, disavowal and fetishism (Silverman 1988, 6ff.). 'Always on display', woman, Silverman concludes, has so little resistance to the male gaze, 'that she often seems no more than an extension of it' (Silverman 1988, 32).

Spectatorship

Clearly, the discussion opened between feminism and psychoanalysis in the field of film theory opens up the problematic of the gaze as both assumed locus in the constitution of subjectivity and in its practical-ideological positioning of the female spectator. As psycho-analytic work reveals, the spectator is not simply the person sitting in the cinema but is also the imagined subject constituted by a range of textual effects, not confined to diegesis but extending to framing, editing, lighting, sound and so on. The technology of cinematic representation and projection, in extending its powers of imaginary and phantasmatic constitution beyond the immediate matters of narrative and representation, has arguably greater control over subjectification for its 'invisibility' (most members of film audiences do not, arguably, distance themselves from the narrative so as to observe the processes by which those narratives create their effects – at least, not during a screening).

However, it can be argued that the psychoanalytic focus on psychic positioning of the subject and the objectification of woman leaves the female spectator with only a passive role, wherein, constituted always as object of desire and as lack or absence, there is little or no position which runs counter to the structures that psychoanalytically inflected analysis imposes as much as it interprets. Moreover, as B. Ruby Rich appositely summarizes, the political problematic inherent in the psychoanalytic project, inasmuch as 'sexuality and psychoanalysis are considered ahistorical, eternal, outside ideology', so analytical proce-dures addressing sexuality and situated by psychoanalytic reading reproduce in theory the traditional positioning of women (Citron et al. 1999, 117). The feminist focus on the female spectator seeks to redress the balance, by analysing female figures which trouble, albeit momentarily, the effects of containment and closure effected by mainstream Hollywood or narrative cinema. Reading those subversive or excessive representations and their effects against the ideological grain extends the possibility of power and resistance for the female spectator. It has thus been a necessary project of feminist film analysis to articulate difference, dissonance and resistance within the mainstream, rather than simply reading displacement and the maintenance of passivity or in seeking to create a purely oppositional filmic discourse.

A striking example of analysis which situates the dissident within mainstream cinema with regard to the female spectator is that of Mary Ann Doane, already mentioned, in *Femmes Fatales*. In the first chapter, 'Film and the Masquerade: Theorizing the Female Spectator' (Doane 1991, 17–32; first published in *Screen* in 1982), Doane develops her arguments concerning a different spectatorship through a reading of Joan Riviere's essay 'Womanliness as a Masquerade', first published in *The International Journal of Psychoanalysis* (1929). Doane therefore draws on psychoanalytic theory, and yet provides a more active, participatory role for the female spectator. Drawing on Riviere's argument that 'womanli-ness' is not essential but a mask or role to be performed, Doane suggests that the masquerade, 'in flaunting femininity, holds it at a distance. Womanliness is a mask which can be worn or removed. The masquerade's resistance to patriarchal positioning would therefore lie in its denial of the production of femininity ... Masquerade ... involves a realignment of femininity' (1991, 25–6). There is thus a destabilization in the truth of the image, which is resistant to patriarchal assumptions concerning woman's 'truth', and which, therefore, has an affirmative potential for dissident identification on the part of the female spectator. Such identification on the part of the female spectator with the fact that femininity is performed (and can thus be changed, denied, abandoned, in favour of other performative masks or affects), leads Doane to the conclusion that '[f]emininity is produced very precisely as a position within a network of power relations ... the elaboration of a theory of female spectatorship is indicative of the crucial necessity of understanding that position in order to dislocate it' (1991, 32).

Matters of difference

We have seen above that psychoanalytic feminist film critique is available to criticism in that its concerns reproduce the implicitly patriarchal ideologies of universalism and ahistoricism. In addition, there is a sense in which the woman, whether as spectator or film image, has been analysed or otherwise addressed without due attention to matters of class. While feminist film studies 'began' in the United States with specifically sociological and ideological critiques of patriarchal and capitalist structures of aesthetic representation in mind, the transformation of film analysis by the intervention of theory (specifically psychoanalysis) can be read, in retrospect, as a retreat from the political, for all its apparent radicality. While the work of the critics already cited is undeniably of great significance and marks, moreover, a series of urgent interventions, what the various debates between film theorists have revealed are a number of limits to aspects of the theoretically driven project. The binarisms 'male-active/female-passive' on which certain theoretical assumptions in feminist film studies rest (Mulvey's essay has been extensively criticized for this static model) do not account for matters of class, race and sexual orientation. In recent years, critics such as Jane Gaines have drawn attention to the blindness in film theory to the possible theorization of a lesbian gaze or to the 'elision of the specificity of black women's positioning', to which Lola Young has drawn our attention.

    Young has remarked, in the context of Freud's metaphor of woman as 'the dark continent', as follows: 'There has been white feminist overinvestment in the gender component of the "dark continent", which has resulted in the virtual elimination of the racial and colonial implications. Thus this most racialized of sexual metaphors has become synonymous with the concerns of white women' (1996, 177). Jane Gaines has also spoken to the inability of a 'high-theoretical' discourse to speak to the historical and cultural specificities of race experience, while also considering the relative silence on lesbian spectatorship. In an essay from 1988, 'White Privilege and Looking Relations: Race and Gender in Feminist Film Theory', first published in *Screen*, Gaines begins by suggesting that '[p]ositing a lesbian spectator would significantly change the trajectory of the gaze' (in Thornham 1999, 293). She continues, '[i]t might even lead us to see how the eroticised star body might be not just the object, but what I would term the visual objective of another female gaze within the film's diegesis – a gaze with which the viewer might identify' (293). As an example of such a situation for the gaze, Gaines locates the reciprocal, subversive gaze between Marilyn Monroe and Jane Russell in *Gentlemen Prefer Blondes*, which, as

Gaines goes on to suggest, can be read as excluding both the straight and the male perspective and location, and effectively erasing the 'male/female opposition' (294).

On the question of race, Gaines points out that the 'dominant feminist paradigm actually encourages us not to think in terms of any oppression other than male dominance and female subordination'; however, 'it is clear that Afro-American women have historically formulated identity and political allegiance in terms of race rather than gender or class ... Even more difficult for feminist theory to digest is black female identification with the black male. On this point, black feminists diverge from white feminists, in repeatedly reminding us that they do not necessarily see the black male as patriarchal antagonist, but feel instead that their racial oppression is "shared" with men' (294–5). Thus, what Gaines brings into focus is the urgent necessity of not sealing off the subject as an idealized category, however much that categorization may appear to be based on questions concerning gender, from the subject's historicity and her real historical experience. A theorization of position which forgets to account for cultural and historical specificity ultimately undoes its political potential in being structured from its initiating moments around unread assumptions which amount to a retreat from political engagement.

bell hooks addresses the question of black female spectators in her *Black Looks: Race and Representation* (1992). Importantly, in analysing the power of the look, she argues, from a reading of Frantz Fanon, that '[s]paces of agency exist for black people, wherein we can both interrogate the gaze of the Other but also look back, and at one another, naming what we see'. She continues, '[t]he "gaze" has been and is the site of resistance for colonized black people globally. Subordinates in relations of power learn experientially that there is a critical gaze, one that "looks" to document, one that is oppositional ... one learns to look a certain way in order to resist' (1992, 116). Criticizing the psychoanalytic paradigm as hegemonic within film studies, hooks resituates the question of resistance in specifically political ways, drawing on models of analysis taken from cultural studies in presenting an argument that the gaze is materially constructed.

The work of bell hooks, Jane Gaines and Lola Young has been of vital significance in opening the field of feminist film theory to itself, in order to articulate the various blind spots which have historically developed as a result of, on the one hand, ahistorical and formalist theorization, and, on the other, the institutionalization of radical theorization and the often all too inevitable concomitant effect of depoliticization. Other critics, such as Tania Modleski and Judith Butler, have also sought to redress the balance in addressing matters of race and gender in filmic representation. Modleski (1991) has turned to the psychoanalytic/deconstructive work of Homi Bhabha in the field of postcolonial studies, particularly his powerful articulation of the functions of mimicry and ambivalence as resistances to racial and cultural stereotyping. Butler's own work (1991), informed by deconstruction, has also sought to destabilize heterosexist assumptions concerning the authenticity and essentialist truth of gender, addressing gender and sexual identity in terms of impersonation and performativity, as a series of supplements without origin.

This is not, of course, to suggest that feminist film theory has arrived at a point where the political problematic has been effectively and comprehensively countered, or that feminist film theories have reached some cosy or facile consensus with regard to matters of methodology, analysis or concern. (Nor, indeed, should they necessarily, for to do so would be, finally, to announce that film theory's time had come and that there were no more political questions to be asked, thereby negating the very premise on which the very idea of feminist film analysis arose.) As Barbara Christian has remarked, with regard to the question of addressing race in relation to gender: 'if defined as black, her woman nature was often denied; if defined as woman, her blackness was often ignored; if defined as working class, her gender and race were muted' (cit. in Young-Bruehl 1996, 514). Yet we should not rush, as some have done, to say that so-called feminist film theories, have lost impetus or direction because of what might appear to be 'internal' debates. What remains vital is the political condition of feminist film analysis, as a politics irreducible to institutional theoretical or academic concerns. As Sue Thornham has so cogently summarized the position, '[i]f that politics has had more recently to recognise divisions and fragmentations in subjectivity ... and histories and experiences other than those of the white woman under western patriarchy, such recognitions of the differences between women may be seen to signal the further development of and not, as some have suggested, a loss of direction in feminist film theory'.

Julian Wolfreys

Further reading and works cited

Butler, J. *Bodies that Matter: On the Discursive Limits of 'Sex'*. London, 1993.
Citron, M. et al. 'Women and Film', in *Feminist Film Theory*, ed. S. Thornham. Edinburgh 1999.
de Lauretis, T. *Alice Doesn't*. Basingstoke, 1984.
—. 'Oedipus Interruptus', in *Feminist Film Theory*, ed. S. Thornham. Edinburgh 1996.
Doane, M. A. *The Desire to Desire*. Basingstoke, 1987.
—. *Femmes Fatales* New York, 1991.
Erens, P. (ed.) *Issues in Feminist Film Criticism*. Bloomington, IN, 1990.
Gaines, J. 'White Privilege and Looking Relations: Race and Gender in Feminist Film Theory', in *Feminist Film Theory*, ed. S. Thornham. Edinburgh, 1999.
Haskell, M. *From Reverence to Rape*. Chicago, 1974.
hooks, b. *Black Looks*. London, 1992.
Johnston, C. 'Women's Cinema as Counter-Cinema', in *Notes on Women's Cinema*, ed. C. Johnston. London, 1973.
Kaplan, E. A. *Women and Film*. New York, 1983.
Mayne, J. *Woman at the Keyhole*. Bloomington, IN, 1990.
Modleski, T. *The Woman who Knew Too Much*. New York, 1988.
—. *Feminism without Women: Culture and Criticism in a 'Postfeminist' Age*. London, 1991.
Mulvey, L. 'Visual Pleasure and Narrative Cinema', *Screen*, 16, 3, 1975.
Pietropaolo, L. and Testafarri, A. (eds) *Feminisms in the Cinema*. Bloomington, IN, 1995.
Rich, B. R. 'The Crisis of Naming in Feminist Film Criticism', *Jump Cut*, 19, 1978.
Silverman, K. *The Acoustic Mirror*. Bloomington, IN, 1988.
—. *The Threshold of the Visible World*. New York, 1996.
Smith, B. 'Toward a Black Feminist Criticism', in *The New Feminist Criticism*, ed. E. Showalter. London, 1986.
Smith, S. 'The Image of Women in Film', in *Feminist Film Theory*, ed. S. Thornham. Edinburgh, 1999.
Stam, R. *Film Theory*. Oxford, 2000.
Thornham, S. (ed.) *Feminist Film Theory*. Edinburgh, 1999.
Women and Film, Editorial, 1, 1972.
Young, L. *Fear of the Dark*. London, 1996.
Young-Bruehl, E. *The Anatomy of Prejudices*. Cambridge, MA, 1996.

Ethical Criticism

The recent incarnation of ethical criticism in literary studies functions both as a response to the alleged nihilism of poststructuralist theoretical concerns such as deconstruction and postmodernism, as well as to the return to humanistic interpretation. By the mid-1980s, deconstructionist, marxist and postmodernist methodologies appeared to reach their influential apex, prompting a critical backlash from a variety of quarters. As David Parker remarks: 'The irresistible expansive moment of post-structuralism in the 1970s and early 1980s has suppressed some discursive possibilities which, constituted as we partly are by various religious and humanistic traditions, we stand in abiding need of, and are poorer without. The possibilities I mean are evaluative, and especially ethical ones' (1994, 3–4). With the evolution of a number of new, socially challenging and culturally relevant modes of critical thought – including, for example, gender studies, historical criticism and other forms of cultural criticism – poststructuralist schools of interpretation, deconstruction in particular, increasingly endured charges of 'anti-humanism' and the development of 'anti-theory' movements that persist in the present. The emergence of these movements accounts for the revival of ethical criticism, an interpretive paradigm that explores the nature of ethical issues and their considerable roles in the creation and interpretation of literary works.

The recent apotheosis of ethical criticism finds its origins in the North American academy – and particularly as a result of the institutionalization of English studies and literary theory in the United States. In European circles, ethical criticism has taken on entirely different theoretical dimensions. While some British critics – Christopher Ricks, for example – have sporadically challenged the place of theory in literary studies, many European scholars opt to examine ethical issues in terms of their philosophical possibilities rather than through the interpretive lens of cultural studies. The current North American re-evaluation of poststructuralism's theoretical hegemony finds its roots in the initial critical responses that often accompanied the promulgation of the trend's various sub-movements. This is, of course, not at all unusual, for new critical paradigms inevitably blossom amid a fury of debate. Jean-François Lyotard's widely acknowledged postmodernist manifesto *The Postmodern Condition* (1979), for example, enjoyed its publication almost concomitantly with the appearance of Gerald Graff's *Literature against Itself* (1979), a volume that problematizes 'the myth of the postmodern breakthrough' as a literary and critical movement destined to implode because of postmodernism's dependence upon its own extreme elements of scepticism, alienation and self-parody. As a historical response to modernist conceptions of art as a panacea for the chaos of the early twentieth century, postmodernism posits that art lacks the required faculties of consolation to assuage the human condition in the post-industrial world. 'Postmodernism signifies that the nightmare of history, as modernist aesthetic and philosophical traditions have defined history, has overtaken modernism itself', Graff writes. 'If history lacks value, pattern, and rationally intelligible meaning', he continues, 'then no exertions of the shaping, ordering imagination can be anything but a refuge from truth' (1979, 32, 55). Rather than asserting its utter impossibility in the postmodern world, Graff's search for truth in literature and criticism underscores one of the principal arguments emanating from the practitioners of ethical criticism: that literature and its interpretation *do* offer readers the possibilities for locating truth and defining value despite the persistence of a contemporary landscape that seems to rest upon a sceptical and chaotic social foundation. 'Postmodern literature', Graff remarks, 'poses in an especially acute fashion the critical problem raised by all experimental art: does this art represent a criticism of the distorted aspects of modern life or a mere addition to it?' (1979, 55). The criticism that postmodernist literature evokes likewise subverts the normative roles of meaning and value in literary interpretation.

In *Truth and the Ethics of Criticism*, Christopher Norris examines the ways in which literary theory has redefined itself in a contemporary hermeneutic circle concerned with epistemological rigour and cultural critique. Norris argues that literary theorists can implement a series of correctives that may yet infuse the theoretical project with much needed doses of pragmatism and social relevance. Norris characterizes this paradigmatic shift as 'the retreat from high theory', as an era in which 'a great deal depends on where one happens to be in terms of the wider socio-political culture and the local opportunities for linking theory and practice in a meaningful way' (1994, 1, 5). By providing readers with the means to establish vital interconnections between texts and the divergent, heterogeneous community in which we live, ethical criticism attempts to empower the theoretical project with the capacity to produce socially and culturally relevant critiques. This way of reading, Norris writes, allows critics to look to 'the prospect of a better, more enlightened alternative where the difference *within* each and every subject is envisaged as providing the common ground, the measure of shared humanity, whereby to transcend such differences *between* ethnic and national ties' (1994, 94). In this way, Norris posits an ethics of criticism that self-consciously assesses the theoretical presuppositions under-girding the moral character of contemporary hermeneutics.

In one of the more forceful ethical critiques of literary theory, Tobin Siebers identifies the crisis that confronts modern criticism – an interpretive dilemma that 'derives in part from an ethical reaction to the perceived violence of the critical act' (1988, 15). He further argues that an ethical approach to literary study requires critics to engage their subjects self-consciously with sustained attention to the potential consequences of their interpretive choices: 'The ethics of criticism involves critics in the process of making decisions and of studying how these choices affect the lives of fellow critics, writers, students, and readers as well as our ways of defining literature and human nature.' Siebers ascribes the aforementioned crisis in criticism to a linguistic paradox that inevitably problematizes critical practice. 'Modern literature has its own cast of characters', he writes. 'It speaks in a discourse largely concerned with issues of language, but behind its definitions of language lie ideals of human character' (1988, 10). Siebers argues that acknowledging the place of ethics in critical theory affords practitioners of the discipline the autonomy to offer relevant conclusions about literary texts and their considerable social and ideological import. 'Literary criticism cannot endure without the freedom to make judgements', Siebers notes, 'and modern theory urgently needs to regain the capacity to decide' (1988, 41). The ability to render sound, moral interpretations, then, provides the foundation for an ethical criticism that fully engages the remarkably human nature of literary study. Such a reading methodology allows for the self-conscious reassessment of our evaluative procedures and their potential for the production of meaningful critiques. As Siebers concludes: 'To criticize ethically brings the critic into a special field of action: the field of human conduct and belief concerning the human' (1988, 1).

Volumes such as Wayne C. Booth's *The Company We Keep* (1988) and Martha C. Nussbaum's *Love's Knowledge* (1990) demonstrate the interpretive power of ethical criticism, as well as the value of its critical machinery to scholarly investigations regarding the nature of literary character, the cultural landscapes of fiction, and the ethical motivations of satire – the narrative manoeuvres that Booth ascribes to our desire to 'make and remake ourselves' (1988, 14). Critics such as Booth and Nussbaum avoid the textual violence of censorship to advocate instead a form of criticism that explores the moral sensibilities that inform works of art. In *Love's Knowledge*, Nussbaum illustrates the nature of ethical criticism's recent emergence as a viable interpretive paradigm: 'Questions about justice, about well-being and social distribution, about moral realism and relativism, about the nature of rationality, about the concept of the person, about the emotions and desires, about the role of luck in human life – all these and others are debated from many sides with considerable excitement and even urgency', she writes (1990, 169–70). In its desire to examine the ethical nature of these artistic works, ethical criticism seeks to create a meaningful bond between the life of the narrative and the life of the reader. Although ethical criticism hardly functions as a conventional interpretive paradigm in the tradition of marxist, Lacanian or gender textual readings, it serves effectively nevertheless as a self-reflexive means for critics to explain the contradictory emotions and problematic moral stances that often mask complex and fully realized literary characters. Ethical criticism provides its practitioners, moreover, with the capacity to posit socially relevant inter-pretations by celebrating the Aristotelian qualities of living well and flourishing. In this way, ethical criticism evokes the particularly 'human character' of literature that Siebers extols the merits of in *The Ethics of Criticism*.

In *The Reader, the Text, the Poem* (1978), Louise M. Rosenblatt supplies ethical critics with an interpretational matrix for explaining the motives of readers and their 'transac-tions' with literary texts. Rosenblatt identifies two different types of reading strategies – aesthetic reading, in which the reader devotes particular attention to what occurs *during* the actual reading event, and non-aesthetic reading, a reading strategy in which the reader focuses attention upon the traces of knowledge and data that will remain *after* the event. Rosenblatt designates the latter strategy as a kind of 'efferent' reading in which readers primarily interest themselves in what will be derived materially from the experience (1978, 23–5). Efferent readers reflect upon the verbal symbols in literature, 'what the symbols designate, what they may be contributing to the end result that [the reader] seeks – the information, the concepts, the guides to action, that will be left with [the reader] when the reading is over' (1978, 27). Booth argues that ethical criticism functions as a methodology for distinguishing the 'efferent freight' that results from this reading strategy (1983, 14). Rosenblatt describes the act of reading itself – whether aesthetic or non-aesthetic – as a transaction that derives from the peculiar array of experiences that define the reader's persona: 'Each reader brings to the transaction not only a specific past life and literary history, not only a repertory of internalised "codes", but also a very active present, with all its preoccupations, anxieties, questions, and aspirations', she writes (1978, 144). This

recognition of the complexity of the reading transaction underscores the deep interconnections between readers and the human communities in which they live and seek
personal fulfilment.

Rosenblatt argues that the transaction of reading involves 'laying bare the assumptions
about human beings and society and the hierarchy of values that govern the world derived
from the text' (1978, 149–50), a conclusion regarding the ethical value of art in the human
community that John Gardner illuminates in his influential volume, *On Moral Fiction*
(1978). He argues that literary art should offer readers the opportunity for receiving
knowledge from its pages, the possibility – rather than the didactic requirement – of
emerging from a reading experience with a heightened sense of communal awareness.
Gardner writes:

> We recognize art by its careful, thoroughly honest search for and analysis of values. It is not
> didactic because, instead of teaching by authority and force, it explores, open-mindedly, to learn
> what it should teach. It clarifies, like an experiment in a chemistry lab, and confirms. As a
> chemist's experiment tests the laws of nature and dramatically reveals the truth or falsity of
> scientific hypotheses, moral art tests values and rouses trustworthy feelings about the better and
> the worse in human action. (1978, 19)

The role of the ethical critic, then, involves the articulation of a given text's ability to
convey notions of knowledge and universal good to its readers, whether through the
auspices of allegory, satire, morality plays, haiku or any other fictive means of representation. In Gardner's estimation, ethical critics can only accomplish this end through the
fomentation of understanding in their readership. 'Knowledge may or may not lead to
belief', he writes. But 'understanding always does, since to believe one understands a
complex situation is to form at least a tentative theory of how one ought to behave in it'
(1978, 139). Thus, ethical criticism examines the ways in which literary characters respond
to the divergent forces they encounter in the fictional landscapes that they occupy. Their
human behaviours and actions provide the interpretive basis for moral reflection and
conclusion.

As Gardner notes in *On Moral Fiction*, however, practitioners of ethical criticism must
invariably confront the spectre of censorship, a dangerous commodity rooted in the human
tendency to instruct without regard for the plurality of competing value systems at work in
both the theoretical realm of literary criticism and the larger world of humankind.
'Didacticism', he cautions, 'inevitably simplifies morality and thus misses it' (1978,
137). Similarly, critics must avoid the perils of attempting to establish models of behaviour
and codified moral standards of acceptability, for such practices inevitably lead to the
textual injustice of censorship. Gardner writes: 'I would not claim that even the worst bad
art should be outlawed, since morality by compulsion is a fool's morality' (1978, 106).
Despite his own admonitions to the contrary in *On Moral Fiction* – and because of the
dearth of genuine scholarly wisdom inherent in his study of moral criticism – Gardner
himself nevertheless trolls dangerously close to the shores of censorship when he speaks of
carrying out 'art's proper work': art 'destroys only evil', he argues. 'If art destroys good,
mistaking it for evil, then that art is false, an error; it requires denunciation' (1978, 15).
Such a proposition inevitably leads to the establishment of singular standards of good and
evil in the heterogeneous, pluralistic spheres of criticism and human reality. Can *ethical*
critics, in good conscience, operate from superior positions of moral privilege and arrogant
didacticism?

Understanding the place of moral philosophy in the latest incarnation of ethical criticism offers a means for exploring this dilemma. Bernard Williams's *Ethics and the Limits of Philosophy* (1985), for instance, discusses the ways in which the tenets of moral philosophy provide a context for us 'to recreate ethical life' in the sceptical world of contemporary western culture (1985, vii). In addition to examining the Johnsonian question of how to live, Williams devotes particular attention to assessing the role of the ethical critic. 'Given people who are in some general sense committed to thinking in ethical terms, how should they think?' he asks. 'Are their ethical thoughts sound?' (1985, 71). The issue of a valid ethical criticism itself poses a spurious philosophical quandary, for it requires the critic to define standards of moral correctness, or, as Williams concludes, to dispense with establishing them altogether. 'An ethical theory is a theoretical account of what ethical thought and practice are', he writes, which 'either implies a general test for the correctness of basic ethical beliefs and principles or else implies that there cannot be such a test' (1985, 72). Williams suggests that critics can only surmount this dilemma by interpreting a given set of events from an empathetic position, and, moreover, through their 'ability to arrive at shared ethical judgements' (1985, 97). In this way, ethical critics and moral philosophers alike engage in a form of ethical practice that allows for the reflexive process of critical contemplation, a self-conscious methodology for critically articulating the pluralistic nuances of that which constitutes a shared sense of moral correctness.

In addition to questioning the nature of our communal sense of ethical propriety, moral philosophers such as Williams attempt to account for the motives of those critics who dare to engage in the interpretation of human values. Such critics must assume the risks – whether or not they employ an equitable and pluralistic system of evaluation – of impinging upon the current direction of the philosophical conversation regarding human ethics. 'Critical reflection should seek for as much shared understanding as it can find on any issue, and use any ethical material that, in the context of the reflective discussion, makes some sense and commands some loyalty', Williams notes, although 'the only serious enterprise is living, and we have to live after the reflection' (1985, 117). For this reason, the principles of moral philosophy charge ethical critics with the maintenance of a sense of free intellectual discourse, in addition to obliging them to render sound moral conclusions. 'We should not try to seal determinate values into future society', he warns, for 'to try to transmit free inquiry and the reflective consciousness is to transmit something more than nothing, and something that demands some forms of life more rather than others' (1985, 173).

Ethical criticism endeavours, as a matter of course, to communicate the meaning of this 'something' and its greater social relevance through the interpretation of literary works. In *The Company We Keep*, Booth offers an expansive account of ethical criticism and its potential for literary study, while also attempting to allay any fears that his heuristic rests upon dogmatic foundations. Booth affords particular attention to the range of hermeneutic functions that ethical criticism performs, as well as to its unfortunate lack of clarity as an interpretive paradigm:

> We can no longer pretend that ethical criticism is passé. It is practised everywhere, often surreptitiously, often guiltily, and often badly, partly because it is the most difficult of all critical modes, but partly because we have so little serious talk about why it is important, what purposes it serves, and how it might be done well. (1988, 19)

Booth notes that ethical criticism's opponents often misread the paradigm's intent as didactic in nature. Instead, Booth argues, 'ethical criticism attempts to describe the encounters of a storyteller's ethos with that of the reader or listener. Ethical critics need not begin with the intent to evaluate, but their descriptions will always entail appraisals of the value of what is being described.' In this way, Booth supports a reflexive interpretational methodology, an ethical criticism that allows for the recognition of the interconnections between the reading experience and the life of the reader. Ethical criticism acknowledges, moreover, the powerful factors of language and ideology in its textual assessments. 'There are no neutral ethical terms', Booth writes, 'and a fully responsible ethical criticism will make explicit those appraisals that are implicit whenever a reader or listener reports on stories about human beings in action' (1988, 8–9).

Booth defines these instances of appraisal – these practical applications of ethical criticism – as acts of 'coduction', referential moments in which critics compare their reading experiences with the conclusions of others. Like Siebers, who argues that 'the heart of ethics is the desire for community' (1988, 202), Booth notes that the act of 'judgement requires a community' of trustworthy friends and colleagues (1988, 72). Coduction, in Booth's schema, valorizes the reflexive relationship that develops between texts and their readers, as well as the equally reflexive manner in which texts postulate meaning. 'The question of whether value is in the poem or in the reader is radically and permanently ambiguous, requiring two answers', Booth writes. 'Of course the value is not in there, *actually*, until it is actualized, by the reader. But of course it could not be actualized if it were not there, *in potential*, in the poem' (1988, 89). Booth also notes ethical criticism's pluralistic imperatives and their value to the understanding and operation of ideological paradigms. In his analysis of feminist criticism, for example, Booth discusses the ways in which 'the feminist challenge' derives from fundamental ethical dilemmas inherent in the construction of literary texts: 'Every literary work implies either that women can enter its imaginative world as equals or that they cannot – that instead they must, in reading, decide whether or not to enter a world in which men are a privileged center' (1988, 387). As Booth reveals, feminist criticism itself functions as a type of ethical criticism, a means of literary interpretation that seeks to repair an abiding social injustice that, through its misogyny, problematizes the lives of the larger community of readers.

In *The Ethics of Reading*, J. Hillis Miller posits an 'ethics of reading' that seeks to explain the reflexive process that occurs between the text and the reader, in addition to offering testimony to the ethical possibilities of poststructuralism, particularly deconstruction. Miller argues that the act of reading ethically transpires when 'an author turns back on himself, so to speak, turns back on a text he or she has written, re-reads it' (1987, 15). For Miller, such a process allows readers – the *de facto* authors of the texts that they appraise – to offer relevant conclusions about the moral properties of literary works and the ethical sensibilities of the readers' theoretical premises, whether they be deconstructive or otherwise. In *Versions of Pygmalion* (1990), Miller proffers a similar argument regarding the 'ethics of narration' and the shifting, performative aspects of reading experiences. Miller derives the title of his volume from the story of Pygmalion in Book 10 of the *Metamorphoses* – a narrative in which something inanimate comes alive, just as reading ethically creates a vital, living relationship between the text and the reader. Miller devotes special attention to the ways in which reading defies stasis, as well as to the manner in which reading ethically, moreover, evolves during successive readings of a given text: 'Reading occurs in a certain spot to a certain person in a certain historical, personal, institutional, and political situation, but it always exceeds what was predictable from those circumstances', he observes. 'It makes something happen that is a deviation from its context, and what happens demands a new definition each time' (1990, 22). In his paradigm for the ethics of reading, Miller allows for the negative possibilities of reading, aspects that Booth, in his effort to celebrate ethical criticism and its myriad of affirmative outcomes, prefers to ignore: 'A theory of the ethics of reading that takes seriously the possibility that reading might lead to other morally good or valuable actions would also have to allow for the possibility that the reading even of a morally exemplary book might cause something morally deplorable to occur', Miller writes (21). In this manner, Miller postulates a valuable corollary to the reflexive properties of ethical criticism and the ways in which context and temporality possess the propensity to alter the quality of reading experiences.

Like Williams, Nussbaum advocates an ethical criticism with tenable foundations in moral philosophy, as well as an interpretive mechanism that functions as an impetus for sustaining moral discourse and social interconnection. In addition to her enthusiastic subscription to many of the arguments inherent in Booth's ontology for an ethical criticism, Nussbaum proffers a series of essays in *Love's Knowledge* that sharpen the ethical paradigm's focus through her discussion about the interrelations between philosophy and literature, as well as through her close, ethical readings of a diversity of writers, including Henry James, Proust, Ann Beattie and Samuel Beckett, among others. Drawing upon selected works by these figures, Nussbaum examines the ways in which style and content impinge upon ethical issues, while also deliberating about the manner in which the ethical interpretation of literary works offers readers a means for exploring the moral import of emotions and locating paths to self-knowledge. Nussbaum affords particular attention to the roles that stylistics, linguistics and structure play in articulating the moral essence of a given narrative:

> Form and style are not incidental features. A view of life is *told*. The telling itself – the selection of genre, formal structures, sentences, vocabulary, of the whole manner of addressing the reader's sense of life – all of this expresses a sense of life and of value, a sense of what matters and what does not, of what learning and communicating are, of life's relations and connections. Life is never simply *presented* by a text; it is always *represented as* something. (1990, 5)

In Nussbaum's schema, then, the literary artist bears the responsibility for honourably positing narratives that allow readers the opportunity to discover their own paths to self-understanding and meaning, to formulate their own strategies for living well. Like Booth, Nussbaum equates the quality of life with the ethical dimensions of literature. 'The novel is itself a moral achievement', she writes, 'and the well-lived life is a work of literary art' (1990, 148).

In addition to advancing the ethical notion of community in her work, Nussbaum argues for the place of love as a subject in the evolving discourse of ethical criticism. 'The subject of romantic and erotic love is not often treated in works on moral philosophy', she admits (1990, 336). For this reason, Nussbaum differentiates between the Kantian notions of 'pathological' and 'practical' love in her analysis. Pathological love, she notes, signifies the often irrational emotions of romantic love in sharp contrast to the more enduring qualities of practical love, an emotion that Nussbaum defines as 'an attitude of concern that one can will oneself to have toward another human being, and which is, for that reason, a part of morality'. The moral dimensions of practical love, therefore, merit considerable attention as a methodology for understanding the many ways in which readers respond ethically to literary texts. Moreover, 'if one believes, in addition, that the realm of morality is of special and perhaps of supreme importance in human life ... one will be likely, having once made that distinction, to ascribe high *human* worth to practical love' (1990, 336–7). In this way, the acknowledgement of practical love provides additional insight into human conceptions of living well and the manner in which literary texts depict love's capacity to produce personal fulfilment. Nussbaum also refines the communal aspects that mark the ethical paradigm. She extends the metaphor that ethical criticism forges a type of community between text and reader to allow for not only the possibility of living well as an individual, but living together well in a much larger sense of the word. 'A community is formed by author and readers', she writes. 'In this community separateness and qualitative difference are not neglected; the privacy and the imagining of each is nourished and encouraged. But at the same time it is stressed that living together is the object of our ethical interest' (1990, 48). In *Poetic Justice* (1995), Nussbaum advances this concept through her exploration of the value of ethical reading as a means for influencing political theory and public discourse: 'If we think of reading in this way, as combining one's own absorbed imagining with periods of more detached (and interactive) critical scrutiny, we can already begin to see why we might find in it an activity well suited to public reasoning in a democratic society' (1995, 9). By widening the scope of the ethical paradigm to account for a range of emotional states, as well as a variety of public and private modes of discourse, Nussbaum shares in the creation of an ethical criticism that provides for the relevant interpretation of the social, political and cultural nuances of the human community.

In *Getting It Right*, Geoffrey Galt Harpham continues Booth's and Nussbaum's efforts to elaborate the ethical paradigm as an interdisciplinary means of interpretation. Ethical criticism should 'be considered a matrix, a hub from which the various discourses and disciplines fan out and at which they meet, crossing out of themselves to encounter each other', he writes. 'Ethics is perhaps best conceived as a 'conceptual base' – neither as organic drive nor as properly conceptual superstructure, but rather as a necessary, and necessarily impure and unsystematic, mediation between unconscious and instinctual life and its cognitive and cultural transformation' (1992, 17–18). Harpham supports this endeavour through his examinations of such 'ethical terms' as 'obligation', '*ought*', 'ethical duty' and 'ethicity'. Through their delineation, he seeks to establish meaningful interconnections between ethical criticism and other means of textual inquiry. Harpham argues that the issue of choice lies at the heart of obligation. 'One can – one must – choose which principle to be governed by', he observes. 'Ethics in general is a species of risk that affords no rigorous way to tell ethical reasons from other reasons, choices from obligations' (1992, 37). Harpham further asserts that 'at the dead center of ethics lies the *ought*', or the ethical obligation. This notion of an *ought* – the moral obligations of an ethical person – reveals that person's 'commitments, values, character. To be ethical, an *ought* must not refer itself to threats or desires, coercion or self-ends' (1992, 18). Harpham defines 'ethical duty' as a form of critical reflection: 'One must always reflect', Harpham writes. 'This is the law that ethical discourse virtually presumes as well as teaches' (1992, 42). Finally, in Harpham's conception of an ethical terminology, 'ethicity' refers to the interpretive moment in ethical criticism: 'the most dramatic of narrative turnings, the climactic point just between the knitting and unravelling of the action, the *fort* and the *da*, the moment when the rising line of complication peaks, pauses, and begins its descent into the dénouement'. Addressing the narratological and characterological essences of this evaluative instance – what Harpham calls the 'macro-turn' – enables ethical critics, through their obligations to their own sets of values and commitments, to reflect upon and interpret the moral choices depicted in narratives (1992, 171).

Despite the publication in recent years of a number of volumes devoted to the humanistic study of literary works, ethical criticism must still successfully contend with several issues of historical and contemporary import in order to authenticate itself as a viable interpretive paradigm. Apart from continuing to underscore its usefulness to literary study, ethical criticism must effectively differentiate itself from the contemporary critical prejudice associated with the 'traditional humanism' previously associated with such figures as F. R. Leavis and Northrop Frye. Practitioners of ethical criticism are succeeding in this regard in a variety of ways, including their critical alliance with the ethical philosophies of Emmanuel Levinas and via the recent emergence of the law and literature movement. By also demonstrating its significant pedagogical value, as well as establishing itself as a meaningful component in the future of the theoretical project, the ethical paradigm may yet realize Booth's vision in *The Company We Keep* of a reading methodology that shuns theoretical dogma in favour of 'critical pluralism' and highlights the ethical interconnections between the lives of readers and their textual experiences (1988, 489).

Kenneth Womack

Further reading and works cited

Booth, W. C. *The Company We Keep*. Berkeley, CA, 1988.
Clausen, C. *The Moral Imagination*. Iowa City, IA, 1986.
Davis, T. F. and Womack, K. (eds) *Mapping the Ethical Turn*. Charlottesville, VA, 2001.
Eaglestone, R. *Ethical Criticism*. Edinburgh, 1997.
Gardner, J. *On Moral Fiction*. New York, 1978.
Goldberg. S. L. *Agents and Lives*. Cambridge, 1993.
Graff, G. *Literature against Itself*. Chicago, 1979.
Harpham, G. Galt. *Getting It Right*. Chicago, 1992.
Lyotard, J.-F. *The Postmodern Condition*. Minneapolis, MN, 1984.
Miller, J. Hillis. *The Ethics of Reading*. New York, 1987.
—. 'Is There an Ethics of Reading?', in *Reading Narrative*, ed. J. Phelan. Columbus, OH, 1988.
—. *Versions of Pygmalion*. Cambridge, 1990.
Newton, A. Z. *Narrative Ethics*. Cambridge, MA, 1995.
Norris, C. *Truth and the Ethics of Criticism*. New York, 1994.
Nussbaum, M. C. *The Fragility of Goodness*. Cambridge, 1986.
—. *Love's Knowledge*. New York, 1990.
—. *Poetic Justice*. Boston, 1995.
Parker, D. *Ethics, Theory, and the Novel*. Cambridge, 1994.
Parr, S. Resneck. *The Moral of the Story*. New York, 1982.
PMLA, Special Issue, 'Ethics and Literary Criticism', 114, 1, January 1999.
Posner, R. A. 'Against Ethical Criticism', *Philosophy and Literature*, 21, 1997.
Rosenblatt, L. M. *The Reader, the Text, the Poem*. Carbondale, 1978.
Salmagundi, Special Issue, 'Art and Ethics: A Symposium', 111, Summer 1996.
Siebers, T. *The Ethics of Criticism*. Ithaca, NY, 1988.
Spacks, P. Meyer. 'The Novel as Ethical Paradigm', in *Why the Novel Matters*, eds M. Spilka and C. McCracken-Flesher. Bloomington, IN, 1990.
Tirrell, L. 'Storytelling and Moral Agency', *Journal of Aesthetics and Art Criticism*, 48, Spring 1990.
Williams, B. *Ethics and the Limits of Philosophy*. Cambridge, 1985.
Worthington, K. L. *Self as Narrative*. Oxford, 1996.

Postmodernism

Any discussion of postmodernism in the USA must adopt an interdisciplinary and comparative perspective. The intellectual history of postmodernism can only be understood in its intricate interconnections that straddle cultures, fields and practices. The literary criticism we associate with postmodernism is for the most part theoretical, concerned not only with 'literature as a question' (Lucy 1997, 141) but also with questions of language, representation, identity, origin and truth. At the same time, the 'global' features of postmodernism can be studied more efficiently in their specific 'local' manifestations. Despite its increasing globalization, postmodernism has continued to encourage cultural differentiation and local solutions. The evolution of American postmodernism is a case in point. Many innovative practices in poetry, fiction, architecture, the visual and the performing arts were developed beginning in the mid-1950s in direct response to the economic and political environment of post-Fordist, Cold War America. These practices have benefited from an interaction with the emerging poststructuralist theories of France (deconstruction, Lacanian psychoanalysis, French feminism) and Germany (reader-oriented theory), or with the literature of the European avant-gardes and the Latin American boom, but they cannot be seen as derivative. Theo D'haen and Hans Bertens's recent book (1997) on the reception of postmodern American fiction in four West European countries demonstrates not only the impact of American postmodernism abroad but also the extent to which the dialogue with other literary experiences has helped expand the definition of American postmodernism to include alternative experiences and issues of gender, ethnicity or subjectivity.

The earliest American uses of the term 'post-Modern' to describe tendencies in postwar literature can be found in Charles Olson's essays beginning with 'Projected Verse' (1950). Olson reserved the term for the anti-modernist and anti-rationalist aesthetics pursued by the poets and artists associated with the Black Mountain College. Limited originally to discussions of poetry and architecture, the term was gradually expanded to other artistic and cultural endeavours that reacted against modernism's emphasis on transcendent reason and its separation of art from history and mass culture. The early postmodern theorizings (William Van O'Connor, Leslie Fiedler, Susan Sontag) encouraged an anti-elitist, experiential approach to art. This approach was subsequently developed along two lines: one *existential-phenomenological*, emphasizing performative immediacy, process art and ontological pluralization (Richard Wasson, William Spanos, Richard Palmer, Charles Altieri, Richard Pearce); the other *structural-epistemological*, highlighting a range of 'doubly-coded', dislocating and reconfiguring procedures in literature (Jerome Klinkowitz, Larry McCaffery, Marjorie Perloff, Linda Hutcheon), architecture (Robert Venturi, Charles Jencks, Kenneth Frampton), the visual arts (Leonard B. Meyer, Hal Foster,

Rosalind Krauss, Craig Owens), photography (Douglas Crimp, Linda Andre), theatre (Herbert Blau), film (Noël Carroll) and dance (Sally Banes). Ihab Hassan was the first to pull these directions together into a comprehensive definition of postmodernism as an epistemic mutation in the 'Western mind', a vast 'unmaking' of the 'tyranny of wholes' and their replacement with 'fragments or fractures, and a corresponding ideological commitment to minorities in politics, sex, and language' (1977, 55). Hassan mapped this mutation in binary oppositions: abstraction, metaphor, depth, transcendence, technologism, elitism, the genital and the phallic are modern; new concreteness, metonymy, surface, immanence, runaway technology, anti-authoritarianism, the polymorphous and the androgynous are postmodern. First introduced in *The Dismemberment of Orpheus* (1971), Hassan's lists of contrastive features were amplified and revised in *Paracriticisms* (1975), *The Right Promethean Fire* (1979) and the retrospective collection *The Postmodern Turn* (1987), according a non-linear, 'paracritical' style that imitated the experimental nature of postmodernism itself.

The break with modernism was viewed from the outset in contradictory ways. For critics formed at the school of modernist and New Critical principles, postmodernism was a retrograde assault on the values of Enlightenment rationalism and an 'anti-intellectual' abandonment of aesthetic and cultural standards (Irving Howe, 'Mass Society and Post-Fiction', 1959; Harry Levin, 'What Was Modernism', 1960). For supporters, postmodernism was 'everything that is radical, innovative, forward-looking' (Perloff 1998, 6); it was a 'new sensibility' that attempted to 'close the gap' between highbrow literature and mass culture, art and life (Susan Sontag, 'One Culture and the New Sensibility', 1965; Leslie Fiedler, 'The New Mutants', 1965, 'Cross the Border – Close that Gap: Postmodernism', 1969; Ihab Hassan, 'POSTmodernISM: A Paracritical Bibliography', 1971). This divided way of thinking about postmodernism has continued unchanged until today. Many critics still oppose a reproductive, 'neoconservative' postmodernism to an emancipatory or 'resistant' one. For example, Charles Russell has typically distinguished an academic form of postmodernism, that has led to the 'embourgeoisement' of the old avant-garde (1982, 54), from a socially-conscious form 'which attempts to combat the reigning discourse and substitute alternate codes' (57). More recently, Paul Maltby has contrasted the 'introverted' self-reflection of Nabokov, Barth and Gass, which exposes 'the operation of its narrative codes or rhetorical strategies' (1991, 1, 5, 15), with the 'dissident' self-reflection of Acker, Barthelme, Burroughs, Coover, DeLillo, Pynchon or Reed, that engages more directly the 'surrounding or contemporaneous discourses (including literary narrative forms and the meaning-systems they embody') (17). This division has been replicated in the social sciences where one can identify an 'affirmative social discourse (Drucker, Etzione, Ferre and theorists of the post-industrial society) [which] reproduced the 1950s optimism ... that technology and modernization were making possible the break with an obsolete past' (Best and Kellner 1991, 14), and a negative discourse 'that reflected a pessimistic take on the trajectories of [post]modern societies' (Toynbee, Mills, Bell, Steiner, Baudrillard).

Despite persistent disagreements regarding its definition and applications, postmodernism became an established term in literary and art criticism by the mid–1970s. About the same time it began to be acclimatized in the discourses of social and physical sciences as a catch-all designation for a new cultural-scientific episteme (Ferré 1976; Spanos 1982; Rorty 1983; Prigogine and Stengers 1984). Postmodernism was drawn in this phase into a 'poststructuralist orbit' (Bertens 1995, 5), being associated at first with the textualist-deconstructive practices inspired by Roland Barthes and Jacques Derrida, then with the ideas of Michel Foucault, Jacques Lacan and Gilles Deleuze who anchored textuality in relations of power, knowledge and subjectivity. The translation of Lyotard's *La condition postmoderne* (1984), in which a prominent poststructuralist adopted the term 'postmodern', acknowledging his indebtedness to Hassan, 'seemed to many to signal a full-fledged merger between an originally American postmodernism and French poststructuralism' (Bertens 1995, 6). In the comprehensive definition supplied by Lyotard and other cultural critics of a poststructuralist or neo-marxist ilk (Jameson, Foster, Harvey, Lash) postmodernism was the 'cultural logic' of a new phase in the development of western societies: the phase of post-industrial consumerism, informational glut, and multinational capitalism. In a few years, postmodernism 'became an indispensable concept in theories of the contemporary' (Bertens 1995, 111), especially through Jameson's contributions beginning with 'Post-modernism and Consumer Society' (1983) that turned postmodernism into a global paradigm and brought home the theoretical debate between Lyotard and Habermas concerning the limits of this episteme. Another contributor to the rethinking of post-modernism along systematic sociocultural lines was William V. Spanos, founder of the first American journal of postmodern theory, *boundary 2* (1972). Spanos's essays through the 1970s and early 1980s reoriented the discussion of postmodernism from a Heidegger-inspired phenomenology (Spanos's 1972 essay, 'The Detective and the Boundary', praised postmodernism's 'existential imagination' and gave the poetry of Robert Creeley and Charles Olson a neo-Heideggerian reading) to an emphasis on cultural revision that reconciled Heidegger's critique of the onto-theo-logical tradition with Foucault's prosecu-tion of modernity's totalizing modes of thought. As Spanos put it in his most recent reassessment, the emergence of oppositional postmodernism in the 1960s and 1970s contributed to the break up of the 'anthropological structure privileged by the post-Enlightenment' and the '(neo-)imperial structure of American/European modernity', foregrounding possibilities 'utterly precluded . . . by the instrumental logic of the dominant discourse' (Spanos 1996, 67, 68).

The turn of postmodern discourse to (poststructuralist) theory and cultural analysis has been questioned by practical critics interested in preserving the idiosyncratic open-endedness of the movement. Marjorie Perloff has thus deplored the shift from a literary-utopian postmodernism prevalent in the early 1970s, that 'involved a romantic faith in the . . . ability of [the literary and artistic discourses] to transform themselves', to a theoretical-prescriptive postmodernism in the 1980s which hardened art 'into a set of norms' (1998, 9). As she notes, in spite of 'all the talk of rupture, transgression, antiformalism, the breaking of vessels – in Lyotardian terms, the delegitimation of the great metanarratives – there seem to be more rules and prescriptions around than ever' (10). The conflation of postmodernism with poststructuralism is problematic from another point of view. French poststructuralism has focused primarily on modern and premodern literary phenomena, with rare sallies into postmodern popular culture. Its chief contribu-tion, according to Andreas Huyssen, is 'an *archeology of modernity*, a theory of modernism at the stage of exhaustion' (1984, 39). The application of poststructuralist theories to the analysis of postmodern discourses has often resulted in an overrating of their deconstructive features at the expense of the transformative ones. The emphasis on disruptive, anti-representational aspects of postmodernism predominated in the criticism of the late 1970s and 1980s (Federman's *Surfiction* (1975), Klinkowitz's *Literary Disruptions* (1980), Allen Thiher's *Words in Reflection* (1984), Cristopher Nash's *World-Games* (1987)), even though one can identify also the beginning of a counter-trend which argued for a socially-conscious definition of postmodernism (Jonathan Arac's collection *Postmodernism and Politics* (1986), Brian McHale's *Postmodern Fiction* (1987), Tom LeClair's *The Art of Excess* (1989), Hutcheon's *The Politics of Postmodernism* (1989) and Jerry A. Varsava's *Contingent Meanings* (1990)).

But criticism was not alone in emphasizing the disruptive, self-referential side of the project. Innovative writers and artists share with their critics the responsibility for their misrepresentation, overstating initially the playful, self-cancelling aspects of their work. Ronald Sukenick's 1970s 'digressions on the act of fiction' called for a radical version of 'nonrepresentational' fiction whose 'main qualities are abstraction, improvisation, and opacity' (Sukenick 1985, 211). By making its language opaque, innovative fiction resists the game of make-believe, calling attention to the structure and 'truth of the page' (212). This reorientation toward the materiality of the novel was regarded by unsympathetic critics as an act of ideological 'recoiling', creating 'a new kind of flatness or depthlessness, a new kind of superficiality in the most literal sense' (Jameson 1991, 9). Yet it is clear from other more considered statements made by Sukenick and his colleagues that the point innovative writers were trying to put across was not that the world exists solely within the word, but that our versions of reality depend on perceptual and discursive systems that offer biased representations under the guise of a 'natural' order. Therefore, it is the writer's duty to challenge naturalized conventions of representation, imagining better aesthetic and sociocultural syntheses. On an experiential level, postmodern literature disrupts the consensual boundaries of 'reality' through improvisation and 'invention' in order to allow more experience to slip through. On a cultural level postmodern literature interrogates the 'great system of constraints by which the West compelled the everyday to bring itself into discourse' (Foucault 1979, 91), rearticulating our narrative and cultural options.

Criticism has often dissociated the disruptive and rearticulative sides of innovation, describing the postmodern project alternatively as overly critical and socially destabilizing, or as non-implicated and self-fetishizing. Underlying both descriptions is a nostalgic concept of literary discourse as an effective integrating machine. Within this model, epistemological and compositional concerns are ignored or subordinated to the representational function of literature. What the contemporary novel needs, according to Charles Newman, is not poetic self-interrogation but comprehensive acts of order-making that reinforce 'the positive socializing function of literature' (1985, 5–6). Critiques of postmodernism on the left have not been more helpful. The prevailing view among theorists like Jean Baudrillard, Alex Callinicos, Terry Eagleton, Hal Foster, Fredric Jameson and Christopher Norris is that postmodernism is an art of pastiche and simulation that renders history 'reified, fragmented, fabricated – both imploded and depleted' (Foster 1985, 123). In Jameson's critique, postmodernism confines itself to a narrow textual and ideological circuit that reinforces 'the logic of consumer capitalism'. But Jameson's own argument suffers from circularity, focusing on forms of art that give support to his deterministic view that postmodernism is complicit with late multinational capitalism: the fiction of E. L. Doctorow, that 'epic poet of the disappearance of the American radical past' (1991, 24), nostalgic-parodic architecture and film, or the science fiction of Philip K. Dick. On the other hand, he ignores the political polysystemic novel of Coover and Pynchon, surfiction, L=A=N=G=U=A=G=E poetry, feminist literature and film, and oppositional uses of video that have successfully tested some of the methods envisioned by him, such as 'global cognitive mapping' and 'transcoding' (1991, 54).

Critical terminology has also prevented a more balanced understanding of postmodern innovation. Used all too often to describe experimental forms of narrative, concepts such as 'metafiction', 'anti-narrative', 'pure fiction', 'parody', 'pastiche' have reduced postmodernism to an 'either-or' logic that opposes invention to imitation. A prevailing trend in the criticism of the 1970s and 1980s has been to regard innovative literature as a heterogeneous collection of anti-referential procedures (self-reflection, digression, distortion, decomposition, displacement, cancellation, pla[y]giarism, arbitrary formal patterning, collage, cutups), estranging narration from reality. More recent criticism has re-evaluated the postmodern agenda through finer theoretical tools (feminist, new historicist, postcolonial), amending its earlier view of experimentation as politically uninvolved. For example, Hutcheon's *Politics of Postmodernism* (1989) found self-reflection compatible with a politically significant stance interested in revising the culture's power systems. Likewise, Brian McHale's *Constructing Postmodernism* acknowledged the 'double-coded', culture-conscious nature of postmodern fiction (1992, 2). In lieu of the inventory of structural-thematic features which undergirded the 'descriptive poetics' of *Postmodern Fiction* (1987), McHale's new book proposes 'a plurality of constructions' that valorize postmodernism's bifurcating options: ontological construction vs. political destabilizing, centring micro-worlds vs. living in the 'zone', paranoid reading vs. reading 'otherwise' (2–3).

While appropriately rehistoricizing innovative literature, inscribing literary aesthetics within the framework of a cultural politics, such re-evaluations continue to waver between two theoretical descriptions of postmodern innovation: one explains the writer's task as a 'purification' of language by 'rendering [it] seemingly incoherent, irrational, illogical, and even meaningless' (Federman 1993, 33); the other emphasizes the socially relevant task of reformulation, arguing that 'the techniques of parody, irony, introspection, self-reflexiveness directly challenge the oppressive forces of social and literary authorities' (32). At the root of this conceptual hesitation is a simplified application of Jacques Derrida's deconstruction and of Michel Foucault's and Jean-François Lyotard's critiques of the universalizing discourses of modernity. The role of postmodern writing, as Lyotard saw it, is to undercut the powerful metanarratives that societies resort to in order to minimize risk and unpredictability. When it does not simply suggest an economy of the 'unpresentable' (1984, 82), Lyotard's theory of resisting writing translates into 'discontinuous, catastrophic, nonrectifiable, and paradoxical *petits récits*' (66). These local stories recognize 'the heteromorphous nature of the language games' (66), but also prevent a comprehensive view of the cultural system as a whole.

Against Lyotard's agonistic theory of postmodern signification, other writers and theorists have sought a transactive model that would valorize the mediating-transformative role of literary imagination. One such model has been found in (poly)system theory, applied to postmodern literature by Tom LeClair, Joseph Natoli, William Paulson, Molly Hite, David Porush and Marcel Cornis-Pope. As a radical development of the 'dynamic functionalism' proposed by the Russian formalists, polysystem theory describes 'system[s] of various systems, which intersect with each other and partly overlap, using concurrently different options, yet functioning as one structured whole, whose members are interdependent' (Even-Zohar 1990, 11). Itamar Even-Zohar urges us to think of polysystems not 'in terms of *one* center and *one* periphery, since several such positions are hypothesized' (14), but as dynamic stratifications that incessantly redefine centre and periphery. This theoretical perspective is particularly useful in rethinking the functions of postmodern innovation. We can argue that postmodernism employs strategies of decentring and frame-breaking as part of a transformative agenda that converts closed hierarchical systems into dynamic polysystems that acknowledge 'multiple forms of otherness as they emerge from differences in subjectivity, gender, sexuality, class, and "race"' (Sarup 1996, 101). While traditional literature tried for the most part to mask the 'difference of disorder' within a system (Natoli 1992, 203), postmodern literature exploits the subversive potential of boundary-crossing and intersystemic interference. The '"motley" society macroimage' that Joseph Natoli recognizes in Acker, Barth, Pynchon or Sorrentino allows us to see 'what a social order cannot see but has already been made "see-able" by the "dissident" acts of narration' (124).

The task of delineating a cooperative rather competitive model of signification that would reconcile the disruptive with the rearticulative side of postmodernism has been pursued more vigorously by postcolonial and postmodern feminist theorists. Feminism's challenge, according to Sandra Harding, has been to articulate a gender-specific episte-mology as a defence against male claims of 'objectivism/universalism', on the one hand, and self-denying relativism on the other (1990, 87). For this particular task Lyotard's 'agonistic theory of language and paralogistic theory of legitimation cannot serve as basis' (Benhabib 1990, 122). The tendency of Lyotard's version of postmodernism to put everything 'under erasure' pre-empts important cultural concepts such as those of knowing subject, gendered agent and female experience. As Nancy Fraser and Linda J. Nicholson insist, feminism still requires these concepts or 'at minimum large narratives about changes in social organization and ideology' (1990, 26). And yet, in spite of their mutual mistrust and different discursive paths, the two 'most important political-cultural currents of the last decade' (19) have had reasons to cooperate, correcting/enhancing each other's critiques of the master narratives of modernity. Feminism has called into question the excessive fragmentation of the postmodern sociocultural vision and the marginalization of female issues in the male avant-gardes. In turn, the postmodern perspective has been useful in challenging the separatism characteristic of some versions of cultural feminism, and the feminist recourse to conventional narrative forms or to essentialist categories like 'sexu-ality, mothering, reproduction, and sex-affective production [that] group together phe-nomena which are not necessarily conjoined in all societies' (Fraser and Nicholson 1990, 31). From the blend of a feminist standpoint epistemology (Harding) and a revisionistic literary poetics has resulted a stronger, politically oriented version of postmodernism.

The concept of difference itself has been re-evaluated in recent postmodern feminism and certain postcolonial projects, being removed from the earlier emphasis on a 'single concept of "otherness" [that] has associations of binarity, hierarchy, and supplementarity ... in favor of a more plural and disprivileging concept of difference and the ex-centric' (Hutcheon 1989, 65). Navigating between a 'politics of difference' focused on 'building new political groupings with categories neglected in previous modern politics such as race, gender, sexual preference, and ethnicity' and a 'politics of identity' that attempts to construct 'identities through political struggle and commitment' (Best and Kellner 1991, 205), postmodernism has managed to develop diversified strategies that avoid the reification of difference. The play of cultural differences has been evoked in recent postmodern/postcolonial literature (Charles Johnson, Toni Morrison, Bharati Mukherjee, Thomas Pynchon) and theory (Gloria Anzaldúa, Zygmund Bauman, Homi Bhabha, Rey Chow, Susan Stanford Friedman) not in order to enhance divisions based on race, class, gender or sexual preference, but rather to create a more responsive framework for intercultural translation.

Much of this work of rethinking and mediation has been carried out by the writers themselves in the oblique, self-questioning forms of postmodern theorizing that shares Richard Rorty's aversion for context-transcendent claims to truth. Theoretical reflections can be found in the most unlikely places, such as in the story of the cyborg Abhor in Kathy Acker's *Empire of the Senseless* (1988), in the debate between two philosophic dogs in Robert Coover's *Pinocchio in Venice* (1991), or in the adventures of an electric bulb called Byron in Pynchon's *Gravity's Rainbow* (1973). The very distinction between fiction and criticism, analysis and performance, breaks down in Hassan's *Paracriticisms* (1975) or Federman's *Critifiction* (1993), two leading compendiums of postmodern poetics that emphasize the 'extemporaneous', open-ended nature of narrative and theoretical articulation. Sukenick's own critical 'digressions on the act of fiction' follow a 'questioning' rather than 'answering' mode, being carefully dissociated from the 'hierophantic complications' of 'formal thinking' (1985, 4). Like Sukenick's 'surfiction', his 'working theory' depends on a revisionistic type of 'experiential thinking' that seeks to 'undercut official versions of reality in favour of our individual sense experience' (67). Sukenick thus shares with other recent reformulative projects (postcolonial literature, L=A=N=G=U=A=G=E poetry, innovative feminist fiction and film) a basic principle of narrative and cultural rewriting. Rewriting devises 'new sets of rules by which the familiar pieces could be rearranged' (Federman 1993, 125); it also 're-invents what [has] been banished, hidden, or expelled from individual or collective memory' (128). As defined further by postmodern feminism, rewriting is both an 'act of looking back, of seeing with fresh eyes' – hence an 'act of survival' for those who have been misrepresented – and an act of looking forward, 'seeing difference differently' (Rich 1979, 35). In this sense, 'rewriting' covers a broad range of possibilities from mere parody to cultural intertextuality wherein a text engages and transforms not only previous texts but also an old discursive system.

An important object of rewriting in postmodern literature and theory has been history. Taking its cue from the philosophies of history developed during and after the Second World War (the 'negative dialectic' of the Frankfurt School, Heidegger's emphasis on the gap between 'historicity' and 'real history', Sartre's questioning of history's intelligibility in terms of the individual's aspiration to freedom, or Foucault's critique of unified notions of historical agency and memory), postmodern fiction has foregrounded the problematic nature of all historical representation. Coming of age in the 'decade after Hiroshima', John Barth, Donald Barthelme, Richard Brautigan, Robert Coover, Thomas Pynchon, Ishmael Reed and Kurt Vonnegut denounced the ideological myths on which official representations relied, retelling history in a satirical key. Other writers emerging after 1968 and associated with the trend of surfiction (Walter Abish, Russell Banks, George Chambers, Raymond Federman, Madeline Gins, Steve Katz, Clarence Major, Ursule Molinaro, Gilbert Sorrentino, Ronald Sukenick) rejected mimetic realism altogether, denouncing its 'silent agreement with the official discourse of the State' (Federman 1993, 28–9). Their 'critifictional discourse' attacked 'the vehicle that expressed and represented that reality: discursive language and the traditional form of the novel' (32).

Innovative literature and criticism share with postmodern historiography (Fernand Braudel, the Annales School, Michel Foucault, Jean-François Lyotard, Hayden White, Gianni Vattimo, Michael Rogin) a suspicion of linear evolutionary models, regarding them as verbal fictions. But while subverting history's metanarratives, postmodernism has also tried to retrieve those details of everyday life that do not fit into easy patterns. The fiction of Coover, DeLillo, McElroy and Pynchon illustrates a dialogic vision of narrative that accommodates alternative histories and voices. Resorting to what Morrison has called acts of 're-memory' in *Beloved*, postmodern feminist fiction has also tried to '*intervene* in history rather than *chronicle* it' (Marshall 1992, 150), retrieving ignored events and shifting attention from 'winners' to 'ordinary people' or the 'historically displaced'.

Significant work of rewriting/revision has been carried out also in the area of cultural identities. To the extent the current geopolitical scene is more hospitable to intercultural understanding, some credit is due to the revisionistic imagination of postmodernism that has deconstructed the polarized ideology of the Cold War era, replacing it with poly-systemic mappings. As Rorty put it, human beings come together when imaginative descriptions of Us and the Other are available (1989, xvi). The work of previously marginalized minority and women writers has been particularly useful in rethinking questions of identity. Charles Johnson, Clarence Major, Maxine Hong Kingston, Toni Morrison, Leslie Silko, or Alice Walker have radicalized the novel thematically and poetically, taking it out of its traditional patriarchal, rationalistic and monocultural moorings. Their re-creative impulse bears out Barbara Christian's observation that '[P]eople of color have always theorized – but in forms quite different from the Western form of abstract logic. ... [O]ur theorizing ... is often in narrative forms, in the stories we create, in riddles and proverbs, in the play with language' (1987, 52). Drawing on their work, Henry Louis Gates Jr, Hortense Spillers, Robert B. Stepto, Mae G. Henderson, David Cowart and W. Lawrence Hogue have articulated a new poetics for African-American and multicultural literature, one that problematizes received ideas about identity, gender, race and history.

It is also true that postmodernism has raised at times unrealistic expectations about the emancipatory potential of its rewritings. The events of 1989 have brought some of these limitations into focus. While the collapse of the Cold War system may be regarded as a success story of the type of experimental thinking that postmodernism itself has been deploying for two decades, it has also raised questions about the role that literary experimentation can play in the 'new world order'. Are the idioms of cultural 'resistance' and artistic innovation viable strategies in the age of globalized capitalism and the dominance of market culture that renders the work of intellectuals all but superfluous? Can literary discourse mediate between the ethnocentric concepts of culture that have re-emerged in many places? As Susan Suleiman put it, in the post-1989 world 'Things are [no longer] so simple; the idea of a postmodern paradise in which one can try on identities like costumes in a shopping mall ... appears ... not only naive, but intolerably thoughtless in a world where – once again – whole populations are murdered in the name of (ethnic) identity' (1996, 54). But Suleiman is first to admit that a revamped form of 'ethical postmodernism', without 'universal values, but also without the innocent thoughtlessness of the "happy cosmopolitan"' (55), is needed today to interrogate 'the unitary and essentialist conception of self' (56) that informs ethnocentric conflicts. Building on Lyotard's post-totalitarian ethic of discourse but strengthening its mediating function, this ethical postmodernism would emphasize multicultural translation, making the world 'safe for dialogue' again (63).

In order to better respond to these new solicitations, postmodernism has undergone a slow process of reconstruction in the 1990s, both in literary studies (McHale, Hutcheon, Maltby, Suleiman, Gates Jr) and in social theory and philosophic/religious thought (Laclau and Mouffe, Best and Kellner, Michael Walzer, Vincent Leitch, Charles Taylor). As William Spanos has argued recently, this revamped postmodernism can participate in the 'urgent project of interrogating the post-Cold War discourse of the New World Order'

(Spanos 1996, 69), breaking the dualities of self and other, First World and Third World, global and local, that still haunt this emergent order. Susan Stanford Friedman has likewise highlighted in *Mappings: Feminism and the Cultural Geographies of Encounter* (1998) the contribution postmodernism can make to the articulation of a post-Cold War epistemology, 'specify[ing] a liminal space in between [self and other, western and non-western], the interstitial sight of interaction, interconnection, and exchange' (3).

The theorists' guarded optimism about literature's potential for renewal in the post-Cold War age is shared by experimental poets and writers. A 1990 collection of essays on *The Politics of Poetic Form* made bold claims for literature as a form of cultural 'resistance', 'provocation', 'remaking', active historical 'recovery' and subversive 'public plasma'. In response to the contemporary 'crisis of expression', this collection rallied innovative writers around an oppositional poetics meant to re-empower art. Innovative writing was credited with the capacity to reconfigure the larger sociocultural situation, offering its innovations 'not only as alternative aesthetic conventions but also as alternative social formations' (Bernstein 1990, 243).

This liberationist project may appear utopian in the rapidly shrinking space that literary discourse occupies in the current high-tech mediascape. But postmodern writers have discovered new possibilities at the intersection of literature and the electronic media. The 'postlinear' poetry of Clark Coolidge, Steve McCaffery, Karen MacCormack, Charles Bernstein, Susan Howe and Bruce Andrews has explored the possibilities of intertextual and mediatic crossovers. The new cyberpunk and avant-pop fiction of Mark Leyner, Mark Amerika, William Vollman, Eurudice or Criss Mazza has tried to reconcile narrative innovation with techno-pop, using a range of recycling/rewriting strategies to expose the 'hyperreality' of consumer culture.

The literary and theoretical work produced since 1989 demonstrates postmodernism's capacity to refashion itself in response to the challenges of the post-Cold war transition. The series of novels published in the 1990s – Coover's *Pinocchio in Venice* (1991), Federman's *To Whom It May Concern* (1990), Morrison's *Jazz* (1992) and *Paradise* (1998), Pynchon's *Vineland* (1990) and *Mason & Dixon* (1997), or Sukenick's *Doggy Bag* (1994) and *Mosaic Man* (1999) – give ample proof that contemporary innovative writing has not surrendered its commitment to transformative thinking. The input of their narrative imagination that emphasizes counter-hegemonic mappings – fluid, multiplex, interactive – can play a significant corrective role in the current ideological restructuring. The kaleidoscopic range of definitions and agendas that we continue to associate with postmodernism also testifies to its 'discursive centrality'. For 'only those signifiers around which important social practices take place are subject to this systematic effect of ambiguity' (Laclau 1988, 80).

Marcel Cornis-Pope

Further reading and works cited

Benhabib, S. 'Epistemologies of Postmodernism', in *Feminism/Postmodernism*, ed. L. J. Nicholson. New York, 1990.
Bernstein, C. 'Comedy and the Poetics of Political Form', in *The Politics of Poetic Form*, ed. C. Bernstein. New York, 1990.
Bertens, H. *The Idea of the Postmodern*. London, 1995.

Best, S. and Kellner, D. *Postmodern Theory*. New York, 1991.

Calinescu, M. *Five Faces of Modernity*. Durham, NC, 1987.

Callinicos, A. *Against Postmodernism*. New York, 1989.

Christian, B. 'The Race for Theory', *Cultural Critique*, 6, 1987.

D'haen, T. and Bertens, H. (eds) 'Closing the Gap': *American Postmodern Fiction in Germany, Italy, Spain, and the Netherlands*. Amsterdam, 1997.

Even-Zohar, I. 'Polysystem Theory', *Poetics Today*, 11, 1, Spring, 1990.

Federman, R. *Critifiction*. Albany, NY, 1993.

Feroé, F. *Shaping the Future*. New York, 19

Foster, H, *Recodings*. Port Townsend, NY, 1985.

Foucault, M. *Power, Truth, Strategy*, eds M. Morris and P. Patton. Sydney, 1979.

Fraser, N. and Nicholson, L. J. 'Social Criticism without Philosophy', *Feminism/Postmodernism*, in *Feminism/Postmodernism*, ed. L. J. Nicholson, New York, 1990.

Friedman, S. Stanford. *Mappings*. Princeton, NJ, 1998.

Harding, S. 'Feminism, Science, and the Anti-Enlightenment Critiques', in *Feminism/Postmodernism*, ed. L. J. Nicholson. New York, 1990.

Hassan, I. 'The Critic as Innovator', *Amerikastudien*, 22, 1977.

Hogue, L. W. *Race, Modernity, Postmodernity*. Albany, NY, 1996.

Hutcheon, L. *The Politics of Postmodernism*. New York, 1989.

Huyssen, A. 'Mapping the Postmodern', *New German Critique*, 33, 1984.

Jameson, F. 'Postmodernism and Consumer Society', in *The Anti-Aesthetic*, ed. H Foster. Port Townsend, NY, 1983.

—. *Postmodernism, or, the Cultural Logic of Late Capitalism*. Durham, NC, 1991.

Klinkowitz, J. *Literary Disruptions*. Urbana, IL, 1980.

Laclau, E. 'Politics and the Limits of Modernity', in *Universal Abandon*, ed. A. Ross. Minneapolis, MN, 1988.

Leitch, V. B. *Postmodernism*. Albany, NY, 1996.

Lucy, N. *Postmodern Literary Theory*. Oxford, 1997.

Lyotard, J.-F. *The Postmodern Condition*. Minneapolis, MN, 1984.

McHale, B. *Postmodern Fiction*. New York, 1987.

—. *Constructing Postmodernism*. New York, 1992.

Maltby, P. *Dissident Postmodernists*. Philadelphia, 1991.

Marshall, B. K. *Teaching the Postmodern*. New York, 1992.

Natoli, J. *Mots d'Ordre*. Albany, NY, 1992.

Newman, C. *The Post-Modern Aura*. Evanston, IL, 1985.

Perloff, M. *Poetry On & Off the Page*. Evanston, IL, 1998.

Rich, A. *On Lies, Secrets, and Silence*. New York, 1979.

Rorty, R. *The Consequences of Pragmatism*. Minneapolis, MN, 1983.

—. *Contingency, Irony, and Solidarity*. New York, 1989.

Russell, C. 'Subversion and Legitimation', *Chicago Review*, 33, 2, 1982.

Sarup, M. *Identity, Culture, and the Postmodern World*. Athens, OH, 1996.

Spanos, W. et al. (eds) *The Question of Textuality*. Bloomington, IN, 1982.

—. 'Rethinking the Postmodernity of the Discourse of Postmodernism', in *International Postmodernism*, eds H. Bertens and D. Fokkema. Amsterdam, 1996.

Sukenick, R. *In Form*. Carbondale, 1985.

Suleiman, S. Rubin. 'The Politics of Postmodernism after the Wall', in *International Postmodernism*, eds H. Bertens and D. Fokkema. Amsterdam, 1996.

The Role of Journals in Theoretical Debate

The place of literary theory within journals is necessarily tied in with the development of the literary journal, and the literary essay, as a whole. All literary criticism is at some level a contribution to the field of theory in that it contains a range of aesthetic, ideological and philosophical assumptions. Sometimes these assumptions are heavily veiled, but nonetheless the reviews and more general literary articles contained within nineteenth-century forerunners – notably the *Atlantic Monthly*, which was founded in 1857 by a group of literary-minded Republicans at the time that their party was developing its pro-abolition stance – may be regarded as contributions to the theoretical debates of their day. Some of the issues raised – about literary value and what we would now term canonicity, about the relationship between texts and morality/ethics, about the effects of reading, and about literatures and national identity – are still very much with us.

Although literary theory may be defined as that which focuses on the conceptual and abstract, on form and structure, effect and ideology – rather than, say, on content or the biographical aspects of an individual author – the dividing line between literary theory and literary criticism remains a necessarily blurred one. This has been true from the inception of the subject-dedicated journal, which may be dated to the foundation of *PMLA* – the *Publications of the Modern Language Association of America* – in 1884. As an organ of association, it has, in addition to its role as a generalist journal publishing scholarly articles relating to modern languages (in an Anglo-and-euro-centric understanding of the term), had an important role in diffusing information about the profession, especially in North America. Thus its advertisements valuably highlight coming publications, and both the requests for conference papers and for articles for edited volumes, and the programme of papers to be delivered at the annual MLA conference, when taken together with its annual bibliography, function as a symptomatic index of the state of literary studies, including trends in theoretical work. In recent times, special issues have highlighted areas of particular relevance to literary theory, such as reader-response criticism (1991), colonialism and the post-colonial condition (1995), queer theory (1995) and ethnicity (1998). The *South Atlantic Quarterly*, founded in 1901, has changed even more conspicuously with the times, having no obligation to fulfil the utilitarian requirements of a profession's journal. Now published exclusively in special issues, it both debates the work of individual intellectuals and creative writers (Bakhtin 1998; Deleuze 1997; Walcott 1997) and analyses particular issues (domestic tragedy, 1998; psycho-marxism, 1998; nations, identities, cultures, 1995).

Other long-established journals, such as *Modern Philology* (founded 1903), while rarely containing articles of direct interest to literary theorists, nevertheless bring their readers into dialogue with theoretical issues through the generous number and length of their book reviews. But the most notable decade in the first half of the twentieth century for literary theory's development within the periodical was the 1930s. The *Southern Review* (founded 1935) and the *Kenyon Review* (1939, under the editorship of John Crowe Ransom), as well as the *Sewanee Review* (1892), were all instrumental in disseminating the close reading which was beginning to take hold as a dominant critical method in universities. This stressed formal and aesthetic values, de-emphasized both textual scholarship and regionalism, and was quite distinct from the far more cultural and political criticism published by the *New Republic* (founded 1914), *The New Masses* (1926–48) and the *Partisan Review* (founded 1936). It was sharply differentiated, too, from *English Literary History* (founded 1934), which, with its continuing commitment to publish studies that interpret the conditions affecting the production and dissemination of English and American literary texts, has been flexibly receptive to the historio-graphic shifts and ideological self-interrogation in recent literary-historical scholarship, as well as to issues of gender and race. *Modern Language Quarterly* has even more conspicuously adapted to changes within the field. Founded in 1940, its original stance was philological (the opening article, by J. D. M. Ford, was on 'Some Principles of Linguistic Change in Romance'). But from March 1993, an issue devoted to 'The State of Literary History', it added 'A Journal of Literary History' to its masthead. As the editorial matter explains, when it was launched, 'literary study often meant a quest for origins – in sources and influences, in authorial intention, in the history of ideas, and in the fixing of texts'. Subsequent critical movements have sought to disrupt such efforts, but a constant undercurrent has been provided by calls for a new literary history – prompted in particular by, but not limited to, 'new historicism'. The journal now seeks out contributions on all aspects of literary change, whether these encompass influence, reception, or dissemination of texts themselves, or the historical dimensions of semiotics, hermeneutics and deconstruction, or the poetics of history, the history of the profession or the history of literary history. Claiming 'we particularly welcome theoretical reflections on these topics, and on historicism in relation to feminism, ethnic studies, cultural materialism, discourse analysis, and all other forms of cultural representation and cultural critique', one can see very clearly how the turn towards historicism, and cultural history above all, in the 1990s has enabled new life, informed by critical theory, to be breathed into old journals without them rupturing entirely with their former identities.

John Fisher, in an article surveying a century of *PMLA*, notes how the decade of social and academic ferment between 1960 and 1970 witnessed a leap in the MLA's membership from 12,000 to 30,000, and simultaneously saw the inception of over two thousand periodicals in fields once largely served by *PMLA*. Specialization, and to some extent fragmentation, of the discipline had arrived. As will be seen, the specialization on the page was often symbiotically linked to the development of a particular critical emphasis within a university department. Many of the period-specific journals founded at this time, like *Victorian Studies* (1957) and *Modern Fiction Studies* (1955), which actively encourages a dialogue between literature and theory, pioneered the inter-disciplinarity which has become a notable feature of contemporary literary studies. The publication history of others provides an indicative pointer to broader developments within social and ideolo-gical conceptualizing. Shifts in racial nomenclature and self-perception, for example, lie behind the retitling of the *Negro American Literature Forum* (founded 1967) to the *Black American Literature Forum* in 1976, to *African American Review* in 1992. What remains constant, however, is this publication's commitment to diversity within its particular ambit: thus in 1992 alone it produced special issues on the black church and black theatre, film, the literature of jazz and fiction.

Many of the journals which have made the biggest impact in terms of literary theory were founded at the very end of the 1960s, or during the 1970s. When Ralph Cohen, *New Literary History*'s long-standing editor, established this highly influential quarterly in 1969, he wrote that he envisaged it becoming 'a challenge to the profession of letters', and it has sought to maintain this role ever since, through interrogating the relationship between works from the past and current critical and theoretical needs. Focusing on the reasons for literary change, the definitions of periods and the evolution of styles, conventions and ideologies, it has been notable for introducing writing from some of the most significant European theorists of the last quarter-century, starting, in the very first issue, with Georges Poulet, on 'Phenomenology of Reading', and Robert Weimann, on 'Past Significance and Present Meaning in Literary History'. On occasion – as with the translation of Roland Barthes' 'An Introduction to the Structural Analysis of Narrative' which appeared in 1975 – the journal has been responsible for disseminating through translation work which had been available for some time in its original tongue (Barthes' piece first appeared in the French periodical *Communications* in 1966) but which subsequently, and dramatically, found a whole new Anglophone audience. It has always been open to experimental presentation, whether in the form of Ihab Hassan's 'POSTmodernISM' (1971) or Hélène Cixous's introspective 'Without End/no/State of Drawingness/no, rather:/The Executioner's Taking off' (1993). More recently, the journal has manifested a self-awareness of its own Euro-and-American centricity: the 1998 issue entitled 'Theoretical Explorations', for example, contains an interview with Fredric Jameson, a stalwart contributor to the journal, conducted by Xudong Zhang, which from a Chinese perspective interrogates the relationship between western scholarship and critical theory during the past fifty years.

New Literary History's emphasis has, more than that of most other journals, been on 'pure' theory – on hermeneutics, phenomenology, formalism and concepts of history and ideology. *SubStance* (founded 1971) which explicitly devotes itself to issues concerning the perception of contemporary culture, be these humanistic or scientific in their emphasis, ranges through literary theory, philosophy, psychoanalysis, art criticism and film studies. *diacritics*, launched the same year from the Department of Romance Studies at Cornell (again indicative of the impact of European continental thought on the discipline) has similarly always stressed interdisciplinarity in that it is interested in films and drama as well as the written word. From the start it has been deliberately polemical. From 1978, it has quite explicitly stated in its editorial policy that it is 'concerned primarily with the problems of criticism', its diacritical discussion – typically taking the form of a review, and a response to the issues raised in the review – setting out to distinguish 'the methodological and ideological issues which critics encounter and setting forth a critical position in relation to them'. *boundary 2*, originating in 1972 from the English Department of the State University of New York at Binghampton under the editorship of William V. Spanos (and in 1990, when its publication was taken over by Duke University Press, coming under the guidance of an editorial collective under the overall leadership of Paul Bové), began as 'an international journal of postmodern literature' and now announces itself as 'extending beyond the postmodern'. Throughout its history, it has been especially valuable for the political, historical and theoretically informed analysis its contributors have brought to bear on a range of topics and problems within literature and culture, such as Poetry and

Politics (spring 1999), Aesthetics (summer 1998), Edward Said (spring 1998) and Feminism and Postmodernism (summer 1992). The two issues edited by Donald Pease, in spring 1990 and spring 1992, importantly focused on the redefinition of what may be said to constitute 'American' culture in contemporary critical approaches.

Critical Inquiry, probably as influential as *New Literary History*, albeit, again, in a more interdisciplinary way, was inaugurated in 1974. On its original title page – a proclamation almost instantly dropped – it glossed itself as 'A voice for reasoned inquiry into significant creations of the human spirit', and in its first editorial statement, Sheldon Sacks wrote that its instigators were 'interested in criticism that aspires to be a special kind of "learning" – not in any sense dispassionate or impersonal but something akin to that fusion of human commitment'. This emphasis was reflected in its first pair of articles, Wayne C. Booth on 'Kenneth Burke's Way of Knowing' and a somewhat pained response by Burke himself, and has been continued in *Critical Inquiry*'s willingness to publish articles which, while maintaining scholarly and philosophical rigour, nonetheless find space for the personal voice, the speculative, and the stylistically daring, whether these include Marjorie Garber's speculations concerning ' " " ' (1999), or Michael Taussig's meditations on 'the beach' (2000), or some of the contributions of the 'Intimacy' issue of 1997, with its investigations of the interplay of privacy and public in the intimate sphere. *Critical Inquiry* has a particular knack for spotting current trends and then interrogating the particular assumptions that are in danger of becoming ossified by them. Thus Homi Bhabha, in his introduction to the 'FRONT LINES/BORDER POSTS' number of 1997, writes of how the crossing of cultures, and the hybridity of knowledges and identifications thus produced, have become 'the *activity* of a theoretical enterprise that negotiates a range of critical conditions with the *post* mark – poststructuralist, postfeminist, postcolonial, postmodern'. But why, he asks, 'never post-*the other?*'

Certain articles, even if subsequently published in volume form, may be isolated not just for their intrinsic importance, but for their role as setting down pointers for the direction in which subsequent critical trends were to develop. French feminism's introduction into the United States, for example, owes a good deal to the publication in translation of Luce Irigaray's 'Et l'une ne bouge pas sans l'autre' in a 1981 issue of *Signs*. Or one might cite Stephen Greenblatt's formulation of 'new historicism' in his introduction to 'The Forms of Power and the Forms of Power in the Renaissance', which appeared in a special issue of *Genre* in 1982; or Donna Haraway's launching of the post-gender concept of the cyborg – that utopian notion of what humans might just possibly become – in 'A Manifesto for Cyborgs: science, technology, and socialist feminism in the 1980s', in *Socialist Review*, 1985; or Homi Bhabha's 'Signs Taken for Wonders: questions of ambivalence and authority under a tree outside Delhi, May 1817', in *Critical Inquiry*, 1985. In each of these cases, the authors subsequently published these pieces as part of fuller, single-authored volumes, but the ideas they contain received their earliest airings, and established their influence, through journal publication. The journal, too, provides a site for graduate students and others early in their career paths to make an impact before they bring out a whole book. In certain areas, and postcolonial study is perhaps notable here, the publication of a well-received article can carry at least as much weight as a longer volume.

On occasion, particular issues of periodicals have taken on a seminal importance, something reinforced by their subsequent publication in separate volume form. In 1992, Kwame Anthony Appiah and Henry Louis Gates edited the 'identity issue' of *Critical Theory*, which shifted the issue of identity from the terrain of personhood (whether this be understood in terms of the individual or community) and resituated it as a question of historical and geographical positioning. Or, to take an earlier example, in 1981 *Yale French Studies* published a rare – for this journal – feminist issue, edited by a collective of seven Dartmouth faculty women, and combining feminist analysis with psychoanalytic theory: a timely conjunction with the appearance of Irigaray in *Signs*. *Signs* was not, however, the earliest major journal fostering an analytical response to feminist issues. *Feminist Issues* was started in 1969, early in the contemporary women's movement, by Ann Calderwood, who, as a note from the editors in February 1978 informs us, for years ran it 'as an out-of-pocket, out-of-apartment operation. She not only helped to solicit manuscripts and scrupulously edited them, she also set the type, handled the subscriptions, and addressed the envelopes' – a significantly different enterprise from the scholarly journal with its departmental backing. The journal went mainstream in 1973: while a barometer of changing trends in feminist theory and criticism, it has maintained its explicitly politicized, and optimistic aims of not just interpreting women's experiences, but of changing women's condition, through looking to alter consciousness, social forms and modes of action. *Signs*, which began in 1975 under the editorship of Catherine Stimpson, has consistently published articles which have employed philosophical and conceptual formulations to interrogate the material conditions of women's' lives, and which have, likewise, used concrete practices and examples to challenge theoretical assumptions. Its very first issue, on the theme of power, included Julia Kristeva's 'On the Women of China': the first English translation of Kristeva, 'among the most provocative and respected contemporary French intellectuals', and its focus has been global ever since, contributing to discussions, within its own pages and elsewhere, of the consistent factors and the necessary variables that must be taken into account in assessing the methodology of feminist theories. A number of other journals devoted to feminist studies have ranged somewhat less widely in their foci. *Tulsa Studies in Women's Literature* (founded in 1982) has a strong tradition of publishing feminist literary analyses and articles on women's literary history. *Hypatia*, which first appeared in 1986, has its roots in the Society for Women in Philosophy: intended to encourage and communicate many different kinds of feminist philosophy, it debates issues of knowledge and identity, particularly at the intersection of gender, race and nation, and discusses the nature of love, desire and the emotions, as well as manifesting an increasing interest in ecofeminism. *camera obscura* (1976) has offered innovative (in presentation as well as in critical methodology) feminist perspectives on film, television and visual media.

The boundaries of feminist criticism became very fluid from the late 1980s onwards, transforming not just in dialogue with other critical categories, especially those of race (and earlier, class), but under the influence of gender studies. The direction taken by *differences*, founded in 1989 as 'a journal of feminist cultural studies' and affiliated with the Pembroke Centre for Teaching and Research on Women at Brown University, is symptomatic of these developments, both in its desire to interrogate how concepts and categories of difference – notably but not exclusively gender – operate within culture. The Fall 1997 number, guest edited by Joan Wallach Scott, epitomizes the anxious self-questioning of the entire field: her own introduction is called 'Women's Studies on the Edge', and others are entitled 'The "Women" in Women's Studies', 'The Impossibility of Women's Studies' and 'Do Women's + Feminist + Men's + Lesbian and Gay + Queer Studies = Gender Studies?' Having helped to create a field and to disseminate debate within it, the proliferation of sub-fields bring into question the very identity of the originating field itself. *GLQ* (founded 1993) has explicitly taken on board the task of offering queer perspectives on all issues touching on sex and sexuality, whether these are within law, science, religion, political science or literary studies. From the early 1980s, the direction taken by established periodicals, and, in particular, the character of new journals, has reflected the degree to which cultural studies – originally, an import from Britain – has supplanted post-structuralist theory as a dominant force within the US academy. *Representations* was founded in 1983 with an editorial board co-chaired by Svetlana Alpers and Stephen Greenblatt: the first issue, featuring articles by each of them, also published pieces by D. A. Miller (English literature), Thomas Laqueur (history) and Jean-Joseph Goux (French literature). While its opening number contains no explicit editorial statement – the approach which was to become labelled 'new historicist' is left to speak for itself – the order form which it contains carried the endorsement of the historian Natalie Zemon Davis, explaining that the periodical will provide 'intellectual discovery and delight to the many readers who want to understand how cultural forms are made', and it has continued to provide leadership in the practice of materialist cultural history. *American Literary History* (founded 1989) has notably concerned itself with how one thinks *about* America, and has played a very influential role in shaping the agenda for what constitutes American cultural studies. It has given especial weight not just to the social, economic and political aims of American literature, and to such issues as the reading process, reception and the institution of American criticism, but it has foregrounded the problematics of canon formation, and has emphasized ethnic and native American issues. Likewise, *American Quarterly* (1949), especially under the editorship of Lucy Maddox, has broadened the standard understanding of what constitutes 'American studies', and has also started to investigate the role of hypertext scholarship in the field. In broader terms, *Social Text* (founded 1979) was an early leader in the area of cultural studies and cultural theory, consistently focusing on gender, sexuality, race, the environment and labour relations: it has been especially notable for the range of provocative interviews it carries. Launched in 1987, the *Yale Journal of Criticism* has published a range of polemical work in the humanities, including not just scholarly articles and review essays, but original artwork, and experimental and performative material, developing the possibilities of such critical genres as memoir, confession and fable. More recently still, a number of journals dedicated to analysing cultural practice among specific ethnic groups from theoretically inflected viewpoints have been established, such as the *Journal of Asian American Studies* (1998), and *Hopscotch* (1999), which looks at a whole range of material from past and present Hispanic cultures, from African slaves to later waves of immigration, covering art, literature, cinema and politics. The 1990s, too, has seen a growth of journals dedicated to specific areas of cross-disciplinarity, bringing critical theory to bear on the intersections between disciplines. *Configurations*, for example, was launched in 1993, and is dedicated to the study of discourse pertaining to the theories and practices of science, technology and medicine, exploring the relationship of literature and the arts to these areas. The next year, *modernism/modernity* was founded, focusing systematically on the methodological, archival and theoretical exigencies particular to modernist – i.e. post-1860 – studies, whether in music or architecture, the visual arts or intellectual and literary history.

The interest in globalization which one finds within journals, particularly in connection with postcolonial theory, is also reflected in the mobile publishing contexts and histories of some publications. For example, the twice-yearly *History and Memory* (founded 1989) is based in both Tel Aviv and Los Angeles. Unsurprisingly, its emphasis is on historical consciousness, the area in which collective memory, the writing of history and other modes of shaping images of the past continually returns to the example of the Holocaust, thus both drawing from and helping to establish the centrality of this atrocity within memory studies, a prominent area of 1990s theoretical investigation. *Transition* was founded in Uganda by Rajat Neogy in 1961 (suspended 1968–71 and 1977–90): now published in the US as an official publication of the W. E. B. Du Bois Institute under the editorship of Appiah and Gates, it retains a strong African link, not least by having Wole Soyinka as chair of its editorial board. It is particularly striking both for its imaginative use of photography and its incorporation of creative writing, and for its broad-based investigation of ethnic diversities, whether concerning itself with Romanian street children or the legacy of James Baldwin, contemporary Indian fiction or French identity politics. *Callaloo*, started in 1976 as an offshoot of the creative writing workshops conducted by its editor Charles H. Rowell at Southern University, Baton Rouge, initially fostered the writings of the African-American Southern writing community that had emerged in the 1960s and 1970s, but soon became more internationalist in scope, featuring a combination of scholarly and creative writing and visual art from throughout Africa and the African diaspora: as it approached its twenty-fifth anniversary in 2001, the redirection of its mission to 'discovering, nurturing, and publishing new and young writers from marginalized communities' was announced.

The trend towards globalization – and the speed of dissemination of ideas which is a key factor in periodicals' power of influence – has been yet further accentuated by the development of the on-line journal, whether this puts material from the printed publication onto the web, or whether it exists solely as an e-journal. The latter tend to have irregular postings, and, at least in the realm of literary theory, are less remarkable than individuals' postings on their own websites or one-off projects (the theory sections of the on-line resource, Alan Liu's *Voice of the Shuttle*, at http://vos.ucsb.edu/shuttle/english.html, provide quick links to such resources). CTHEORY, however (at http://ctheory.com) provides an exception: in existence since 1993, this on-line journal of theory, technology and culture contains a combination of analytical thinking (a series of articles by Jean Baudrillard from 1994 is notable here) and more meditative and creative pieces concerning contemporary culture.

Journals invite their own mode of reading, which differs from single-authored volumes. The juxtaposition of articles both engages the conceptual imagination of the browsing reader, who may, among the heterogenous offerings, serendipitously encounter new ideas that they would not otherwise have been let to read. Undoubtedly, the energetic enthusiasm shown by American university presses (who derive a considerable percentage of their profits from journal publication) to launch and devote journals dedicated wholly or largely to theoretical matters has had an enormous effect on the spread and popularization of theory throughout the American academy and, indeed, further afield. The economic advantages to college libraries of an annual journal subscription, as opposed to buying a handful of books, are obvious: both a range of viewpoints, and information and opinion about volume publications, are placed into rapid circulation, and an atmosphere of debate, even urgency, created. In turn, this generates discussion about the degree to which American concerns translate, or fail to be readily adaptable, to other localized sites.

Kate Flint

Further reading and works cited

Association of American University Presses. http://aaup.princeton.edu/journals/subjects/
Chielens, E. E. (ed.) *American Literary Magazines*. Westport, CT, 1986.
CTHEORY, however. http://ctheory.com
Fisher, J. H. 'Remembrance and Reflection: *PMLA* 1884–1982', *PMLA*, 99, 1984.
Gallop, J. *Around 1981: Academic Feminist Literary Theory*. London, 1992.
Liu, A. *Voice of the Shuttle*. http://vos.ucsb.edu/shuttle/english.html
Project Muse. http://muse.jhu.edu/journals/index.html

Whiteness Studies

Whiteness studies investigates the parameters of white racial identity, locating its scope and function in systems of representation. This field of study takes as its founding premise the constructed nature of identity, a poststructuralist concept heralded by race theorists who argue that race itself is not a natural or biological category but rather a social construction given meaning through historical contexts. Whiteness studies gained academic prominence in the 1990s after minority theorists such as Toni Morrison and bell hooks challenged white critics to examine their own 'racial' speaking position instead of solely focusing on the 'Other'. The rise of multiculturalism and the pluralization of 'the canon' did much to further whiteness studies; as ethnic traditions gained visibility and strength, many critics questioned why texts written predominantly by white male authors had never been treated as 'white' texts but rather as 'universal' texts representing all people. This tendency of whiteness to occlude or erase markers of particularity is now recognized as one of its characteristics. Investigations in the field have spread from feminism, labour history and literary studies to cultural studies, psychoanalysis and beyond.

Whiteness studies owes it origins in part to all of those who have agitated against the privileges of 'white skin', who have sought to unsettle social, political and economic hierarchies based upon categories of race. While movements against social injustice have occurred across disciplines and beyond the academy, whiteness studies in its current sense finds articulation primarily through academic theorists who focus on upsetting 'white privilege' and power through the analysis of whiteness. This critical project finds its antecedents in the works of writers of colour who have examined the characteristics of white identity. Most germane for contemporary studies is the work of Langston Hughes and W. E. B. Du Bois. In 1926, Hughes published 'The Negro Artist and the Racial Mountain' that outlined the attributes of '"white" culture', a culture distinguished by rigid 'manners, morals and Puritan standards' (694). For him, whiteness operates as a set of oppressive beliefs and values which could be adopted at will; he describes 'this urge within the [black] race towards whiteness, the desire to pour racial individuality into the mold of American standardization, and to be as little Negro and as much American as possible' (692). Hughes' assimilation theory finds voice in later sociological renderings of Americanization and contemporary theories on whiteness. As a historian and race theorist, W. E. B. Du Bois explores the labour arena, defining whiteness as a set of benefits white workers accrue which offset any economic disadvantages they may experience in a classed society. In his study *Black Reconstruction in America*, he argued that white workers received a 'public and psychological wage' which included 'public deference', access to public facilities, judgement in a court of law by peers of one's racial group, better schools, etc. to compensate for economic inequities (1975, 700–1). Instead of fighting for all workers to forward the cause of democracy, white workers turned to racism for social and political gain (30). Labour historians rely on Du Bois's constructs to understand white working-class identity today.

Research in the history of white racism also serves as a backdrop for contemporary whiteness studies whose critics rely on a range of analytic tools borrowed from a number of disciplines – psychoanalysis, cultural studies, marxism among others – to understand the persistence of 'white skin privilege'. Early psycho-cultural studies locate a combination of cultural and psychological forces as the source of white identity. Winthrop Jordan's *White Over Black* serves as a case in point. Jordan outlines the ways Elizabethan concepts of blackness and darkness, whiteness and light (to symbolize evil and good respectively) informed the imaginary constructs of colonizing Europeans who perceived African-Americans as sexualized primitives and Native Americans as errant savages. Like others who followed, Jordan relies on psychoanalytic theory to show how a certain psychic splitting and projection occurs, an interpretative process which remains in vogue even if the psychological explanations for such projections vary. Jordan's approach garners criticism for being ahistorical and dependent on the concept of a collective psyche whose existence cannot be supported (Saxton 1990, 11–12). Many historians turn instead to a socio-economic approach, one which finds its most well regarded and comprehensive example in Edmund S. Morgan's *American Slavery/American Freedom: The Ordeal of Colonial Virginia*. According to Morgan, racism did not originate overseas but rather found root on American soil among legislators who sought to control the labour force through racial division. Fearing the combined uprising of African-American slaves and European-American bond-labourers following Bacon's Rebellion of 1676, the Virginia Assembly passed a series of acts meant to 'foster the contempt of whites for blacks and Indians' (1975, 331). Sounding much like Du Bois, Morgan argues that such laws provided 'social, psychological, and political advantages' to white labourers to encourage them to align their loyalties with Anglo slave holders (1975, 344). While Morgan's work retains wide currency, he fails to consider the persistence of racism and white identifications under other economic and social circumstances. Contemporary theorists such as David Roediger and Alexander Saxton instead rely on ideological arguments to more completely explain the existence of racism, strategies now widely adopted by whiteness critics. Saxton, for example, argues that racism is not simply economically driven but rather constitutes a system of beliefs and values which shape 'reality'. Like Morgan, Saxton gives weight to economic benefits but, turning to the theories of Italian Communist Antonio Gramsci, stresses more completely the manner in which social identities are constructed through scientific, historical, religious and economic discourses intended to sustain class hegemony (1990, 13–15). In *The Rise and Fall of the White Republic*, he points to the origins of racism in the mid-fourteen hundreds when Western Europeans sought to expand and conquer in their desire to accumulate capital. He writes, 'Since Europeans were generally white-skinned, while the peoples they encountered are generally dark, for three and a half centuries basic human relationships centered on the domination of whites over people of color' (14). Racism became a series of discourses which supported such hierarchies, expressed through the religious and scientific theories of the nineteenth and twentieth centuries (15).

Whiteness studies also locates its historical origins in the first and second wave of Anglo-American feminism which, with its failure to attend to racial identity, enacted its own racial ideology. Instead of locating themselves as middle-class white women, activists and academics tended to focus on gender as the only significant axis of identity. In the early 1980s, women of colour such as bell hooks, Barbara Christian and Norma Alarcón among others protested widely, showing how racism pervaded the (white) women's movement that took as its primary subject, in its early years, the oppression and plight of (white) domestic housewives. Adrienne Rich suggests that early white feminists suffered from a type of 'white solipsism – not the consciously held *belief* that one race is inherently superior to all others, but a tunnel-vision which simply does not see non-white experience or existence as precious or significant' (1979, 306). French feminists, of course, were guilty of the same oversight. The privileging of gender as the initial site of oppression found its way into feminist psychoanalysis in which white feminist theorists argued that all other oppressions, such as race and class, find their origins in the recognition of sexual difference.

In the mid to late 1980s, white academic feminists responded in part by trying to build coalitions with women of colour or by shifting their attention from texts written by white women to those authored by minority writers. Such moves unfortunately left unexamined whiteness as a speaking position and inadvertently reactivated traditional hierarchies in which the 'Other' either became responsible for educating whites about the nature of her oppression or once again became the object of investigation. The real work on whiteness did not take place until writers such as Marilyn Frye and Peggy McIntosh sought to give voice to the nature of whiteness and white privilege. Frye offered what is now considered common sense to whiteness theorists. She writes, referring to herself and other white feminists, '[I]t never occurred to us to modify our nouns . . .; to our minds the people we were writing about were *people*. We don't think of ourselves as *white*. It is an important breakthrough for a member of a dominant group to come to know s/he is a member of a *group*, . . . only *a part* of humanity' (1983, 117). McIntosh outlined the contents of an 'invisible knapsack' of 'skin-colour privileges' benefiting those phenotypically white – again reminiscent of Du Bois's wage – including varied images in greeting cards, dolls, toys, etc. to curriculum materials, welcoming attitudes in middle- to upper-class neighbourhoods, wide representation in courts of law and police forces, and easy access to simple items appropriate for one's group such as hair care products and 'flesh' colour bandages (1990, 33–4).

Such observations corresponded with the work of Richard Dyer, a film critic, whose ideas now form the bedrock of the field. In his study of US and British popular films, he compares the way whiteness functions representationally in US and British culture to colour theory:

> Black is always marked as a colour (as the term 'coloured' egregiously acknowledges), and is always particularizing; whereas white is not anything really, not an identity, not a particularising quality, because it is everything – white is no colour because it is all colours. This property of whiteness, to be everything and nothing, is the source of its representational power. (1988, 45)

Whiteness tends to be 'subsumed into other identities' (45), much like Hughes' equation of whiteness with 'American standardization'; whites tend to identify themselves according to nation, region, gender or class, etc. rather then race so that the explicit characteristics of whiteness disappear behind the definitions of the 'norm' (46). As Dyer notes, 'Power in contemporary society habitually passes itself off as embodied in the normal as opposed to the superior' (45). Such a sense of invisibility makes it difficult to name the ways white domination operates; whites tend to experience their identities more as a case of 'historical accident, rather than a characteristic cultural/historical construction, achieved through white domination' (46).

Dyer's advances in film study found reflection in the scholarship of Toni Morrison who in a 1989 article in the *Michigan Quarterly Review* articulated the premises of her more widely known study *Playing in the Dark: Whiteness and the Literary Imagination*. She brings whiteness to the forefront of the literary arena, asking readers to consider ways American literature is shaped by white imaginations responding to an African-American presence and more inclusively to 'Africanism', 'the denotative and connotative blackness that African peoples have come to signify' (1992, 6). Her work fundamentally shifted the focus for many literary critics from the conceptualization of American literature as representing 'universal' themes to a literature in which race functions as a founding marker of identity. Morrison writes, 'Africanism is inextricable from the definition of Americanness' (65): '[I]ndividualism is foregrounded (and believed in) when its background is stereotypified, enforced dependency. Freedom (to move, to earn, to learn, to be allied with a powerful centre, to narrate the world) can be relished more deeply in a cheek-by-jowl existence with the bound and unfree, the economically oppressed, the marginalized, the silenced' (64). Huck's freedom and individuality becomes visible in light of Jim's enslavement. Morrison's critique centres not only on the books themselves but also on critics who historically have ignored figurations of race. Her work has revolutionized American literary studies and has spawned countless investigations, from rereadings of American 'classics' such as Melville's *Moby Dick* (racing the white whale) and Edgar Allan Poe's *The Voyage of Arthur Gordon Pym*, to surveys of whiteness in early American literature, regional literature, modernist drama and poetry, and contemporary fiction by writers of all ethnic backgrounds.

Coincident with Morrison's breakthrough in literary analysis was David Roediger's innovations in labour history. While Roediger's *The Wages of Whiteness* followed Alexander Saxton's *The Rise and Fall of the White Republic*, it made a more lasting impact on the field. Roediger refuses traditional marxist tendencies to privilege class over race, an act which erases the relational and integrated nature of the terms. He rejects the simplicity of earlier split-market labour theories which located fault with the ruling class for the promotion of racism. Such theories position workers, Roediger argues, as innocent 'dupes' instead of participants in their own ideological becoming, constructing their identities in response to a range of economic and social pressures (1999, 9). He turns to Du Bois's concept of the 'public and psychological wage' and the linguistic theories of Mikhail Bakhtin who, in Roediger's words, reveals the ways meaning is 'socially contested ... neither absent nor unconnected with social relations' (15). Roediger traces the way white workers linguistically registered racial identity in the urban North in the early nineteenth century. For example, white labourers adopted the signifier 'help' and 'hired man' to replace the word 'servant' (synonymous with 'slave' at the time) (47–8) and 'boss' to replace 'master' (54). Such assertions signalled their membership in a free republic and difference from the bound, servile black population of the South (49). Roediger also makes a considerable contribution to interpretations of black minstrelsy. He argues that the popularity of minstrelsy in Northern cities in the early 1800s signalled a desire for a 'preindustrial past' which blacks represented (97). Driven by a capitalist regime that required more and more regimentation in daily living, white labourers turned to blacks to express their own desire for spontaneity. Roedigger's work finds later comment in texts which more completely address the changing face of minstrelsy and the anxieties which surround white working-class masculinity.

Such early work on whiteness has resulted in a burgeoning of whiteness studies such that critics no longer separate race from gender or class. Advances have been made across the spectrum, most notably in gender and cultural studies. The meanings of white femininity have found critical comment, from histories on the construction of white womanhood during the suffrage, abolitionist and women's movements to contemporary investigations into the meaning of whiteness for white women in today's world. To a far greater extent, however, white straight masculinity has attracted critical attention, with particular emphasis placed on a culture of white male victimhood which has emerged in response to advances in feminism, civil rights and economic changes that have disempowered the working-class white male since the 1950s. Reactions against affirmative action and gay rights legislation have helped fuel an image of white heterosexual manhood as under siege. Critics have tracked this image through the popular press, film and the predominately white men's movement of the 1980s, unpacking the ways in which white masculinity is constructed as multivalent and contested. For example, in his inaugural study *White Guys: Studies in Postmodern Domination and Difference*, Fred Pfeil challenges the belief that white straight masculinity is a 'single, monolithic category ... shot through with violence, megalomania, instrumental rationality, and the obsessive desire for recognition and definition through conquest' (1995, viii). He suggests it functions as a 'dialectical co-construction whose on-going identity is at least partially dependent on the very forms and modalities of femininity it seeks to dominate and control' (ix). He argues that like other identities, 'the modalities of white straight masculinity are multiple, and/or riven by contradictions and fissures, and and/or subject to flux and change' (x). Such advances in gender and race theory throw in question any easy opposition between races or genders and highlight the limits of multiculturalism. If all identities result from historical change, varying according to social context, it becomes difficult to maintain the oppositions that gave birth to whiteness studies as an area of academic study.

As the field reaches the end of its first decade of study, it wobbles on its ontological moorings. Some regard it as a form of 'vulgar multiculturalism' in which whiteness becomes essentialized as evil (Wray and Newitz 1997, 12, note 7). Repeated characteristics attached to the category create a form of cultural racism, replacing earlier biological forms. Matt Wray and Annalee Newitz argue that not all forms of whiteness function oppressively. In their anthology *White Trash: Race and Class in America*, the authors, paraphrasing the words of John Waters, write, ' "white" trash' is not just a classic slur – it's also a racial epithet that marks out certain whites as a breed apart, a dysgenic race unto themselves' (1997, 2). Pointing to the eugenic studies of the early twentieth century which labelled poor whites as inferior, Wray and Newitz suggest that the category of white trash resists what one might call the 'invisibility' argument of Dyer in favour of a certain visibility – in scientific studies and more recently in the media and popular culture. Elvis becomes the white trash king and pornographic movies are analysed as a form of 'social and moral protest' (10). The anthology usefully draws attention to the ways 'white trash' as a signifier alleviates middle- and upper-class anxiety about class inequities in a democratic yet capitalist culture. Yet simultaneously it seeks to claim a place for 'white trash' alongside other ethnic groups. The authors write: '[W]hite trash is one place multiculturalism might look for a white identity which does not view itself as the norm from which all other races and ethnicities deviate' (5). While Wray and Newitz argue that '[p]erhaps white trash can also provide a corrective to what has been called a "vulgar multiculturalist" assumption that whiteness must always equal terror and racism' (5), they veer towards creating the very dynamics they seek to avoid. Lower-class whites become stripped of racial privileges to be located as 'victims', a position that belies work to date on working-class whiteness. The authors' comments bespeak a certain desire to locate whiteness outside of its historical constructions as dominating in ways that throw the goals of the larger critical project into disarray.

Similarly, while anthologies, panels, special issues and articles reveal an ardent enthusiasm to eradicate 'white skin privilege', their very existence may have the opposite effect in the academy. In 1997, Howard Winant charged that studies that aim to 'abolish whiteness' may actually preserve the category in order to transcend it. Most representative of such studies was Noel Ignatiev and John Garvey's activist/academic journal *Race Traitor*, an early 1990s series republished as an anthology in 1996. The authors sought to move beyond academic meditations on whiteness to actions individuals could take to 'abolish' the 'white club', 'which grants privileges to certain people in return for obedience to its rules' (1996, 35). Winant's charge find its echo in criticism of the rise of whiteness studies which suffers, many argue, from a certain narcissism, or willingness to dwell on racial subjectivity by those who are 'white', redirecting academic attention once again from margin to centre. Such an appropriation of margins offers white critics a new opportunity to enter the multicultural fray, having found a sanctioned enterprise for hawking academic wares on the marketable topic of race.

Despite such criticism and epistemological dangers, the future of whiteness studies remains hopeful. While many critics have investigated the ways whiteness depends on blackness for definition (either through contrast or appropriation of cultural forms), several now acknowledge the ways whiteness functions antithetically or multiply in relation to a range of other ethnic identities. The cultural studies arena has exploded with varied interrogations of whiteness in the popular media, from Rush Limbaugh talk shows to country music. In addition, critics working within gay and lesbian studies are helping shed the light on the long association of white maleness with heterosexuality. Finally, interesting work has emerged which looks at whiteness as a series of performative acts, whether that be in ethnographies, in which women of colour assume a white masculinist gaze in order to critique it, to the performance of whiteness on stage as a deconstructive act. The inventiveness of such strategies for 'seeing' whiteness bodes well for a future that may be textured and rich, one which moves beyond analyses of United States culture as vested completely within black and white dualities.

Betsy Nies

Further reading and works cited

Allen, T. *The Invention of the White Race*. London, 1994.
Babb, V. *Whiteness Visible*. New York, 1998.
Delgado, R. and Stefanic, J. (eds) *Critical Whiteness Studies*. Philadelphia, 1997.
Du Bois, W. E. B. *Black Reconstruction in America*. New York, 1975.
Dyer, R. 'White', *Screen*, 29, 4, Autumn 1988.
Frankenberg, R. *White Women, Race Matters*. Minneapolis, MN, 1993.

— (ed.) *Displacing Whiteness*. Durham, NC, 1997.

Frye, M. *The Politics of Reality*. New York, 1983.

Hill, M. (ed.) *Whiteness*. New York, 1997.

Hughes, L. 'The Negro Artist and the Racial Mountain', *The Nation*, 122, 3181, 23 June 1926.

Ignatiev, N. *How the Irish Became White*. New York, 1995.

— and Garvey, J. *Race Traitor*. New York, 1996.

Jordan, W. D. *White Over Black*. Chapel Hill, NC, 1968.

Lopez, I. F. Haney. *White by Law*. New York, 1996.

Lott, E. *Love and Theft*. New York, 1993.

McIntosh, P. 'White Privilege', *Independent School*, 31–6, Winter, 1990.

Morgan, E. S. *American Slavery/American Freedom*. New York, 1975.

Morrison, T. *Playing in the Dark*. New York, 1992.

Nelson, D. D. *National Manhood*. Durham, NC, 1998.

Pfeil, F. *White Guys*. London, 1995.

Rich, A. *On Lies, Secrets, and Silence*. New York, 1979.

Roedigger, D. *Towards the Abolition of Whiteness*. London, 1994.

—. *Wages of Whiteness*, afterword D. Roedigger. London, 1999.

Savran, D. 'The Sadomasochist in the Closet', *differences: A Journal of Feminist Cultural Studies*, 8, 2, 1996.

Saxton, A. *The Rise and Fall of the White Republic*. London, 1990.

Ware V. *Beyond the Pale*. London, 1992.

Winant, H. 'Behind Blue Eyes', in *Off White*, eds Michele Fine et al. New York, 1997.

Wray, M. and Newitz, A. (eds) *White Trash*. New York, 1997.

Masculinity and Cultural Studies

What does it mean to be a man? One response to this question is fairly straightforward: one might define being a man in terms of biology, the possession of a male anatomy, and in particular, of course, the possession of the principal sign of sexual difference, the penis. But being is, of course, not merely a biological fact, since we exist and become conscious of ourselves and others within culture, within, that is, a system or systems of values. It is through culture, then, that we begin to attribute and internalize a certain significance to being one sex or another, so that being a man is as much about the consequences attendant on the possession of a particular anatomy as it is about the mere possession of it. Hence, the familiar distinction made in gender studies between sex and gender, where sex denotes biology, and gender those cultural norms conventionally attributed to biological sex. Masculinity, then, is the gender associated with maleness, and in essentialist thinking is considered the natural expression of this biological condition, whereas in cultural studies, which broadly challenges the conservatism of such forms of essentialism, masculinity is regarded as a construction grounded in nothing more than social discourses and practices. Consequently, this cultural studies perspective promotes the view that the qualities associated with masculinity are open to challenge and change. In more recent work, as we will see, the 'necessity' of viewing masculinity as an expression of maleness – whether culturally conditioned or otherwise – has even been called into question.

This approach to masculinity within cultural studies is largely a product of feminist thinking from the late 1960s and 1970s which interrogated the relationship between female and feminine, arguing that the assumed 'naturalness' of the relationship between these was one of the crucial means by which women were oppressed. Indeed, it is possible to see the contemporary interest in masculinity as arising from this period, specifically as a response to feminist concerns and the issues that these raised for men, since men, in patriarchal society, were the problem, the ones who exercised, or were at least invested with, power. Andrew Tolson's book, *The Limits of Masculinity*, for instance, emerged from his involvement with a men's group formed in response to feminist challenges to the privileges and powers accorded to men, though that experience was the reverse of the kind of empowerment which women's groups emphasized at that time:

> In all our practical activities, we faced an immediate contradiction. As men, as the agents of a patriarchal culture, we remained the dominant gender. In a certain sense, we were imperialists in a rebellion of slaves – concerned, defensively, about the threat to our privilege. The very notion of 'men's politics' was paradoxical. We had no experience of sexual oppression, violence, jokes at our expense. There were no issues to unite us – no basis for action against a system that already operates in our favour. (Tolson 1977, 143)

Tolson therefore highlights one of the problems with studies of masculinity and what has become known in some quarters as 'men's studies', and some feminists have remained suspicious of this increasingly common focus. In her critique of Kaja Silverman's book *Male Subjectivity at the Margins*, for instance, Abigail Solomon-Godeau writes that 'It is all very well and good for male scholars and theorists to problematize their penises, or their relations to them, but is this so very different from a postmodern mal de siècle . . . in which, once again, it is male subjectivity that becomes the privileged term' (1995, 76).

Whether or not the growth in studies of masculinity is itself a manifestation of the male ego's typical absorption in self-pity at a time of emotional change, it does appear to be the case that the contemporary interest in masculinity – and not just in the academy – is related to social changes in men's roles. Lynne Segal, writing in 1997, points out that the 'ineluctable rise in men's studies and the accompanying glut of books on masculinity (over 400 new texts in the last 10 years alone), register a topic newly fraught with personal doubts, social anxieties and conceptual fragmentation' (1997, xii), and this surge in interest in masculinity is characteristic of literary and cultural studies on both sides of the Atlantic (I will be discussing both British and US work here). It has even become conventional to talk about a 'crisis in masculinity'. But if there is such a crisis it is not only bound up with the impact of feminism – though we shouldn't minimize feminism's social gains in challenging, for instance, men's leadership in the workplace, or the automatic assumption that the heterosexual male should be a family's breadwinner, or the conviction that women's sexual role is primarily to service the requirements of men. Men's sense of diminishing power is also related to other, economic changes; principally, the erosion of job security as a consequence of the economic policies which have dominated government policies in Britain and the US since the 1980s (on this see, for instance, Rutherford 1996, 4–5). Of course, no one – other than, possibly, the CBI and other such employers' representatives – would want to celebrate the economic disempowerment of male workers, but one problem with the resistance to, or dissatisfaction with, such transformations is that it is often expressed in gendered terms and in ways which result in women bearing the brunt of the anger that is generated.

Consequently, while the academic world has seen the rise of studies of masculinity in response to the changes outlined above, outside it we have witnessed the emergence of anti-feminist movements and spokespersons, as well as other less explicitly reactionary, but nonetheless problematic, social phenomena which betoken a resistance to change. We have seen in the US in the early 1990s, for instance, the emergence of the men's movement inspired by the mythopoetic writings of Robert Bly, encouraging men to separate themselves from women in order to commune with their inner masculinity (see Schwalbe 1996). In Britain, we have witnessed the New Laddism associated with various men's magazines, representing a transmutation, rather than a transformation, of masculinity in its combination of a self-consciousness – possibly even an ironic consciousness – of aspects of masculinity with a reluctance to abandon its privileges, reflecting in this way a disjuncture between traditionally defined roles and changing realities.

But even though I've begun to touch here on the historically variable nature of masculinity, there has still been a tendency in my account so far to write about it as if it were a coherent and easily recognizable phenomenon. When we start to consider the qualities associated with the term, however, what should strike us is the diversity, even contradictoriness, of its connotations. In certain contexts, for instance, masculinity connotes rationality and self-control. Jonathan Rutherford argues that 'A history of masculinity is the struggle to tame and subdue the emotional and sexual self and to recognise the ascendant and superior nature of reason and thought' (Rutherford 1996, 26). Yet often masculinity is associated with an uncontainable aggression or (threatening) sexual virility. Indeed, such is the diversity of ways in which masculinity has been constructed, enacted or even embodied, that it has become usual to talk in the plural of masculinities, rather than of a singular masculinity (though we might also want to consider the limits to such fashionable pluralizing since masculinity cannot be endlessly variable without ceasing to be recognizable as a phenomenon, and it is surely at least as important to develop some sense of those overarching features which render different forms of masculinity still discernibly masculine).

Herbert Sussman has pointed out that 'the emphasis on the constructed rather than the innate, and on the multiple rather than the unitary view of the masculine calls attention to the historical contingency of such formations of manliness and of male power itself, thus questioning male dominance and supporting the possibility of altering the configuration of what is marked as masculine' (Sussman 1995, 9), and, indeed, one of the features of studies of masculinity has been to emphasize its historically variant features. In the twentieth century, for instance, masculinity has tended to be defined against homosexuality since homosexuality has tended to connote effeminacy (even though there are masculine, even macho, styles of homosexuality, it is a common feature of gay personal ads that an individual will describe himself as 'straight acting', thus confirming the elision between homosexuality and effeminacy). Eve Sedgwick has famously noted that in the spectrum of different forms of male homosociality, or male bonding, ranging from business contacts to sports camaraderie to sexual relations between men, there is a 'prohibitive structural obstacle' (Sedgwick 1985, 3) in the form of homophobia which renders that spectrum discontinuous. Yet, as Alan Sinfield has recently argued, prior to the Oscar Wilde trials in 1895 the effeminacy of the dandy tended to be associated with a generalized libertinism, and only after this watershed was the specific cultural link established between homosexuality and effeminacy (Sinfield 1994). The change signalled by the Wilde trial is a particularly dramatic one, whereas typically changes in gender formations tend to take rather longer and may be uneven, but nonetheless it is indicative of the extent to which constructions of gender are subject to historical forces.

Masculinity and history

In the short space available here, it would be impossibly reductive to attempt a survey of the extensive historicist work on masculinity. What I intend to do, therefore, is to provide some sense of the work that has been carried out in one particular historical period which has seen a significant increase in the number of texts on this subject – the Victorian period – while at the same time using this work to signal certain broader themes in the treatment of masculinity.

One of the classic texts in the discussion of masculinity in the Victorian period is that of Leonore Davidoff and Catherine Hall, *Family Fortunes*. This charts the ways in which both masculinity and femininity were constructed by the economically, and therefore culturally, increasingly important middle class. Davidoff and Hall's approach to the study of gender, in itself, alerts us to the ways in which particular expressions of gender have been bound up with other forms of difference (in this case, class, but other studies have focused on the determining forces of 'race' and nation). They argue that a religious, and especially Pauline, discourse of male dominance was reinforced by an increasing physical segregation of work and domestic space in the spatial organization of nineteenth-century industrial cities, as businesses and factories were located away from suburban living areas, thus consolidating and intensifying the distinctions between public and private, masculine and feminine, and helping to constitute the Victorian 'separate spheres' ideology (Davidoff and Hall 1987).

But Davidoff and Hall's account does not represent an exhaustive discussion of the multiple determinants of gendered identity in the Victorian period. Medical discourse is also crucial to Victorian perceptions of masculinity and femininity, though in ways which connect Victorian perceptions with more persistent attitudes. Simone de Beauvoir has pointed out that man 'thinks of his body as a direct and normal connection with the world, which he believes he apprehends objectively, whereas he regards the body of woman as a hindrance' (Beauvoir 1972, 15). The status of women's perceptions as bound up with an overwhelming *subjectivity* in the Victorian period was a consequence of their supposed greater susceptibility to nervous instability, ultimately to hysteria, something confirmed by the medical discourses about the nervous system which developed in the late eighteenth century (see Logan 1997). The consequences of this discourse were particularly important, not merely in terms of specific relations between men and women, but in terms of consolidating the conservatism of Victorian attitudes, since, as I have argued elsewhere, revolutionary politics in the period following the French Revolution were perceived as hysterical in contrast to the 'rational', gradualist and therefore manly character of British politics (Alderson 1998, esp. 34–9). In this sense, manliness was at the heart of an English – and, by extension, British – national character.

That same stable, manly sensibility which was considered definitive of British constitutional politics, though, was also considered to be a specifically Anglo-Saxon trait (Alderson 1998, 32–4), and this further reflects the way in which gender has been bound up with race and colonialism. Other races – notably, among European races, the Celts (Cairns and Richards 1988, 42–57; Alderson 1998, 98–119), and beyond Europe, Asians (see, for instance, Sinha 1995) – were feminized, at least in part because imperial ideology attributed to these groups an incapacity for autonomous government. Indeed, the relationship between gender and imperialism has been the focus of numerous studies (see, for instance, Bristow 1991; Dawson 1994; McClintock 1995; Midgley 1998; Phillips 1997), not least since one of the characteristic tropes for colonial or imperial conquest, from late sixteenth-century Ireland to late nineteenth-century Africa, has been one of sexual conquest, often of a virgin territory awaiting, even inviting, masculine penetration. Elaine Showalter has further discussed the late nineteenth-century context and the perceived remasculinization of the novel in relation to the Scramble for Africa of the late nineteenth century. She discerns a shift in fictional themes and genres away from the domestic novel towards the 'male quest romance', typically centred on Africa and 'represent[ing] a yearning for escape from a confining society, rigidly structured in terms of gender, class, and race, to a mythologized place elsewhere where men can be freed from the constraints of Victorian morality' (Showalter 1991, 81; on the male quest romance more generally, see Fraser 1999). Showalter's argument is problematic in that she goes on to suggest that this flight from feminine domesticity is bound up with homosexual desire, thus eliding the homosocial and the homosexual in ways which Sedgwick's distinction between the two hoped to avert, but it nonetheless indicates the ways in which the imperial context was structured by gender.

There has perhaps been a tendency to dwell too heavily on the consequences of imperialism for those white men who dominated empires, though, whereas an awareness of empire – and of the slave trade and racism which were integral to it – behoves us to consider its damaging effects and legacies on those who were subject to it.

Masculinity and race

Black men's relationships to masculinity, in particular, have been deeply influenced by racist social structures and by those anxieties of white men which have their roots in the most powerful structuring oppositions of western culture. As Daniel P. Black points out, 'black men have wrestled with the concept and the attainment of manhood since the days of their enslavement by Europeans' (Black 1997, 4). Frantz Fanon has famously written that 'For the majority of white men the Negro represents the sexual instinct (in its raw state). The Negro is the incarnation of a genital potency beyond all moralities and prohibitions' (Fanon 1986, 177). Further, this essentially biological condition attributed to black men is in opposition to the cerebral, since there are 'Two realms: the intellectual and the sexual. An erection on Rodin's Thinker is a shocking thought' (Fanon 1986, 165). This opposition has been both tenacious – infecting even black self-images – and pernicious. Historically – and let us not forget that history is far from finished – it has determined the most brutal manifestations of racism: in the American South the widely practised lynchings of the nineteenth and twentieth centuries, for instance, commonly culminated in the castration of the black man. Indeed, one of the common justifications of such acts was the 'need' to protect white women, and the association between black men and rape has been a persistent one. Lynne Segal records that 'To this day, although 50 per cent of men convicted of rape in the Southern states are white, over 90 per cent of men executed for rape are black (mostly accused of raping white women). No white man has ever been executed for raping a black woman' (Segal 1997, 179). Moreover, the significance of recent high-profile cases, involving figures such as Clarence Thomas, Mike Tyson and O. J. Simpson, has been overdetermined by issues raised by this history – which is not to say that issues of guilt or innocence are insignificant – and often black activists have been set against feminists. In this sense, in so far as masculinity connotes sexual potency, black men have been defined as excessively so, but in so far as masculinity connotes greater rationality and self-control, the black man has been viewed as insufficiently so.

Moreover, racism has affected the material construction of black masculinity. Crucially, there is 'a close connection between the disproportionate representation of black male youth in unemployment data and their over-representation in crime statistics' (Mercer and Julien 1996, 113–14). Hence black males have been denied the role of wage earner which, in western societies, has been a principal source of male dignity, and at the same time and partly in consequence of this, they have been associated with a malevolent hostility to those societies they inhabit, reinforcing the well established link between white–black oppositions and metaphysical concepts of good and evil. The legacies of all this are profound and consequently raise profoundly sensitive matters. Crucially, the black struggle not merely for political rights, but for a recognition of human dignity has frequently been gendered, taking on the form of a struggle for black *male* dignity which has involved a corresponding high investment in forms of black masculinity, and causing problems for those – for instance, women and black gay men – who may be stigmatized or disempowered by it. The most obvious recent expression of this tendency took the form of the Million Man March of 1995 which explicitly excluded women's participation – prompting protests from black feminists – and which encouraged black men to embrace their patriarchal responsibilities for themselves, their families and their communities. As Segal points out, this message was 'fully in line with conservative attacks upon affirmative action, welfare and public resources generally' (1997, xvii).

These are some of the principal questions which have been interrogated by the substantial rise in studies of black masculinity. Respect for the complexity – not least the *political* complexity – of the subject matter, especially given the limitations of space here, lead me to foreclose discussion at this point and to point readers in the direction of some of this material (Blount and Cunningham 1996; Gilroy 2000; Majors and Billson 1992; Marriott 2000).

Masculinity and sexual difference

I began this piece by stating the conventional wisdom that masculinity is the set of culturally defined norms attributed to maleness. That is a definition whose adequacy has been increasingly challenged, though, since if masculinity is a cultural norm rather than a biological given we should not expect the relationship between masculinity and maleness to be automatic: men may demonstrate feminine traits and might even, in the face of stigmatization, consciously adopt feminine identifications, and women may assume or adopt masculine identifications. Indeed, this (in)appropriation of gender norms has become celebrated as a mode of subversiveness following Judith Butler's *Gender Trouble*. Butler's argument revisits the sex/gender division so influential on feminist thinking in order to argue that the body too is constructed in and through discourse, and is therefore itself a cultural, rather than straightforwardly biological phenomenon. Instead, the relationship between gender and sex is a performative one, that is, dependent on certain modes of (imitated or learnt) behaviour:

> That the gendered body is performative suggests that it has no ontological status apart from the various acts which constitute its reality ... acts and gestures, articulated and enacted desires

create the illusion of an interior and organizing gender core, an illusion discursively maintained for the purposes of the regulation of sexuality within the obligatory frame of reproductive heterosexuality. (Butler 1990, 136)

Hence, Butler argues for the importance of those forms of gender performance which suggest a radical dislocation of gender and sex, seeing in drag in particular an erosion of the assumed connection between the two by highlighting precisely the performative element involved in that relationship. More recently, Eve Sedgwick has argued that 'it is important to drive a wedge in, early and often and if possible conclusively, between the two topics, masculinity and men, whose relation to one another it is so difficult not to presume' (Sedgwick 1985, 12). Judith Halberstam's recent book-length study, *Female Masculinity*, attempts to assert alternative forms of masculinity to those hegemonic forms embodied in, or performed by, white men, since 'transsexuality and transgenderism ... afford opportunities to track explicit performances of nondominant masculinity' (1998, 40).

Such emphases are also characteristic of recent cultural production. In Jeanette Winterson's *Written on the Body*, for instance, the gender of the sexually 'promiscuous' narrator is never specified, leaving us to speculate on whether s/he is a 'womanizing' heterosexual or a lesbian who challenges the 'proper', sexually restrained behaviour of women. Jackie Kay's *Trumpet* deals with the aftermath of the death of an apparently male jazz trumpeter, Joss Moody, who is discovered by the coroner – representative, perhaps, of the normalizing institutional forces in our society – to have been (biologically) a woman. Just to complicate matters, Joss was married – his 'widow' lives on – and has an adopted son. Significantly, at one point in the novel, he denies that he is a lesbian – as does Brandon Teena, the central character in the film *Boys Don't Cry* (Peirce 1999) which presents the true story of a woman, Teena, who dressed as a man in order to have relationships with women, and who was raped and ultimately murdered by two men as a punishment for her 'perversion'. It is not at all clear in either *Trumpet* or *Boys Don't Cry* that these characters' rejection of lesbianism is a form of self-denial or false consciousness – as it might have been treated in lesbian cultural productions of, say, the 1970s or 1980s – so that in both cases we are forced to confront the question of whether gender identity, rather than sexuality, is the primary organizing category for such characters and in such relationships (for further commentary on this issue, see Sinfield 2000).

But these narratives also raise questions about the tenacity of what Sinfield calls the 'cross-sex grid' (1994, 161–75) and the effectiveness of attempts to transgress them. One of the significant features of Kay's novel, for instance, is the pursuit of Joss Moody's story by an opportunistic journalist who clearly wants to frame the narrative in a populist way, treating it as a form of perversion and a betrayal of the son's relationship with his father, and, while ultimately the journalist is thwarted by the son's refusal to co-operate, the novel makes us aware that dominant discourses have their own ways of constructing transgendered identities. This reminds us therefore that, as Butler herself recognizes (1990, 137), the efficacy of 'parody' as a form of subversion is dependent substantially on how its message is received (though it should be noted too that, according to the narrative, Moody succeeded in passing as a man, and in this respect his masculinity did *not* point up the performative aspects of gender; it simply fooled people).

This emphasis on gender as performance, pose or style has probably become the dominant one in contemporary studies of masculinity (and femininity, for that matter), and, in this respect, there is a discernible if subtle shift in the direction of such studies: from an emphasis on the denaturalization of masculinity as a privileged term in male–female and other relations to an emphasis on masculinity as a depthless style or performance on the part of persons of either sex. This latter emphasis need not necessarily exclude a sense of the former, of course, but it does seem to me that there is at least the risk that the emphasis on masculinity as a 'performance' might obscure our sense of it as bound up with the possession of power and the desire to retain that power. Clearly, overtly performative versions of masculinity, such as those by drag kings, may dislocate the relationship between masculinity as a set of signifiers and the male body, but the further relationship between that masculinity and the power that is attendant on its 'authentic' relation to the body is surely another thing. *That* relationship is beyond individual stylistic choices or identifications, and one of the problems with the emphasis on 'performance' – at least in some invocations of it – is that it tends towards an emphasis on voluntarism and choice, on gender as a commodity.

I will end this survey of recent work with a few observations which may not be particularly original but which seem to me to bear repetition. First, it may be that there are problems attendant on regarding masculinity as an identity – whether ironized or not – in the first place, on talking about it as a kind of possession – that is, as 'my' or 'his' or 'her' masculinity. Speaking for myself – and self-reflexiveness is a significant feature of many studies of masculinity – my sense of my own gender is a variable one, bound up with specific contexts and with roles which are expected of me which I might adopt or – possibly in the face of strong pressure and involving the refusal of certain rewards for 'good' conduct – decline. This leads me to an attendant observation, that in talking about gender we are dealing with the body, its socialization and its social meaning and value, and indeed our relations to our bodies will always be culturally mediated in one way or another. But to say this is not to say that the body is simply a product of discourse: bodies have needs and are characterized by differences which may themselves have social significance. For instance, the capacity to bear children, whether exercised or not, has consequences in terms of people's relationship to their work and the rights which they might want to claim, though whether or not our current distinctions between male and female are helpful or adequate may well be a matter for debate. The ultimate political challenge implicit in these debates about gender is to create social values and relations which do not assign power and privileges on the basis of particular configurations of the body.

David Alderson

Further reading and works cited

Alderson, D. *Mansex Fine*. Manchester, 1998.
— and Anderson, L. (eds) *Territories of Desire in Queer Culture*. Manchester, 2000.
Beauvoir, S. de. *The Second Sex*. Harmondsworth, 1972.
Berger, M. et al. (eds) *Constructing Masculinity*. London, 1995.
Black, D. P. *Dismantling Black Manhood*. New York, 1997.
Blount, M. and Cunningham, G. P. *Representing Black Men*. London, 1996.
Bristow, J. *Empire Boys*. London, 1991.
Butler, J. *Gender Trouble*. New York, 1990.
Cairns, D. and Richards, S. *Writing Ireland*. Manchester, 1988.
Chapman, R. and Rutherford, J. *Male Order*. London, 1996.
Davidoff, L. and Hall, C. *Family Fortunes*. London, 1987.

Dawson, G. *Soldier Heroes*. London, 1994.

Fanon, F. *Black Skin, White Masks*. London, 1996.

Fraser, R. *Victorian Quest Romance*. Plymouth, 1999.

Gilroy, P. *Between Camps*. Harmondsworth, 2000.

Halberstam, J. *Female Masculinity*. Durham, NC, 1998.

Kay, J. *Trumpet*. London, 1998.

Logan, P. *Nerves and Narratives*. Berkeley, CA, 1997.

McClintock, A. *Imperial Leather*. New York, 1995.

Majors, R. and Billson, J. Mancini *Cool Pose*. New York, 1992.

Marriott, D. *On Black Men*. Edinburgh, 2000.

Mercer, K. and Julien, I. 'Race, Sexual Politics and Black Masculinity: A Dossier', *Male Order*, eds R. Chapman and J. Rutherford. London, 1996.

Midgley, C. (ed.) *Gender and Imperialism*. Manchester, 1998.

Phillips, R. *Mapping Men and Empire*. London, 1997.

Schwalbe, M. *Unlocking the Iron Cage*. Oxford, 1996.

Sedgwick, E. Kosofsky. *Between Men*. New York, 1985.

—. '"Gosh, Boy George, You must be Awfully Secure in Your Masculinity!"', in *Constructing Masculinity*, eds Berger M. et al. London, 1995.

Segal, L. *Slow Motion*. London, 1997.

Sinfield, A. *The Wilde Century*. London, 1994.

Showalter, E. *Sexual Anarchy*. London, 1991.

Silverman, K. *Male Subjectivity at the Margins*. New York, 1992.

—. 'Transgendered identities', in *Territories of Desire in Queer Culture*, eds D. Alderson and L. Anderson. Manchester, 2000.

Sinha, M. *Colonial Masculinity*. Manchester, 1995.

Solomon-Godeau, A. 'Male Trouble', in *Constructing Masculinity*, eds M. Berger et al. London, 1995.

Sussman, H. *Victorian Masculinities*. Cambridge, 1995.

Tolson, A. *The Limits of Masculinity*. London, 1977.

Winterson, J. *Written on the Body*. London, 1992.

Part III

Criticism, Literary and Cultural Studies in England, Ireland, Scotland and Wales

Samuel Taylor Coleridge (1772–1834) and Matthew Arnold (1822–1888)

In 'The Perfect Critic' (1920), T. S. Eliot performs an early critical variation on the commonplace recognition of Samuel Taylor Coleridge and Matthew Arnold as foundational figures in the history of modern criticism in English: 'Coleridge was perhaps the greatest of English critics, and in a sense the last. After Coleridge we have Matthew Arnold; but Arnold – I think it will be conceded – was rather a propagandist for criticism than a critic, a popularizer rather than a creator of ideas' (Eliot 1957, 1). If this characterization of Arnold does not quite inspire confidence, the tell-tale 'perhaps' in the praise for his predecessor suggests that Coleridge, too, somehow fails to satisfy Eliot's requirements. A remark later on in the same essay confirms this suspicion:

> Coleridge is apt to take leave of the data of criticism, and arouse the suspicion that he has been diverted into a metaphysical hare-and-hounds. His end does not always appear to be the return to the work of art with improved perception and intensified, because more conscious, enjoyment; his centre of interest changes, his feelings are impure. (Eliot 1957, 13)

In the 'Introduction' to The Sacred Wood, Arnold's failure to live up to Eliot's definition of a true critic is diagnosed in remarkably similar terms as a swerving from 'the centre of interest and activity of the critical intelligence' (1957, xii) in pursuit of 'game outside of the literary preserve altogether, much of it political game untouched and inviolable by ideas' (1957, xiii). In hindsight, Eliot's observation that both Coleridge and Arnold had trouble keeping the 'centre of interest' of criticism proper firmly in focus would seem to strengthen rather than diminish their claim to foundational status for twentieth-century criticism. For diversions into philosophical hare-and-hounds and the pursuit of political game are hardly exceptional features of contemporary criticism – if anything, they figure prominently among criticism's multiple centres of interest today.

It is tempting to celebrate this apparent decentring of critical practice deplored by Eliot as a welcome turn to impurity, away from what appears as a rigid obsession with the canonical literary artefact as an object of disinterested aesthetic contemplation. Yet such celebration is in danger of repeating the purist obsession it decries. It risks foreclosing the double challenge of literature's constitutive impurity: its resistance not only to the confinement of 'Literature' (or, worse, 'Poetry') to itself as its own self-sufficient 'centre of interest', but also to the programmatic release of literature into the healthy outdoors of philosophico-political relevance. The task of criticism is to monitor this double resistance by allowing for a radical displacement of its centres of interest, including its currently central interest in the displacement of literature itself. The well-founded suspicion that neither Coleridge nor Arnold would recognize themselves in this plea for radical displacement does not in the least disqualify them from ranking among its prime precursors.

Coleridge's early activities were decisively shaped by the reformist energy associated with the French Revolution. In 1794, he developed a scheme, in tandem with Robert Southey, to found a commune in New England on the principles of what Coleridge called 'Pantisocracy': the rule of all as equals. The scheme never materialized but Coleridge continued to divulge his democratic views on religion, politics and education in numerous lectures and in articles in the periodical press, including his own weekly *The Watchman*. He meanwhile published religious and philosophical poetry and began to develop a life-long interest in German metaphysical thought. His greatest poetical works were written around the turn of the century, at a time when his association with William Wordsworth laid the foundations of what was to become British romanticism. Intent on a solid philosophical frame for the proper pursuit of poetry, Coleridge increasingly turned to the construction of ambitious but abortive blueprints for a future comprehensive metaphysics, which were meant to culminate in his projected but never completed magnum opus, the 'Logosophia'. Arguably the most lasting groundwork for this 'total and undivided philosophy' (Coleridge 1983, I, 282) is the *Biographia Literaria* (1817), a sprawling account of his 'literary life and opinions' which, together with his numerous public lectures on literature and criticism, was to become the basis for Coleridge's massive reputation as a literary critic and theorist. His more directly socio-political and moral preoccupations were developed in his *Lay Sermons* (1816–17), the first of which was significantly entitled *The Statesman's Manual* (meaning the Bible but also, in some measure, itself), and in the two most substantial products of his last decade, *Aids to Reflection* (1824) and *On the Constitution of Church and State* (1830). In these last works, Coleridge emerges as a formidable conservative authority calling for the proper establishment of a corporate intelligentsia, a 'permanent, nationalized, learned order, a national clerisy or church' (Coleridge 1976, 69) whose task it is 'to form and train up the people of the country to obedient, free, useful, organizable subjects, citizens and patriots, living to the benefit of the state, and prepared to die for its defence' (54).

On the Constitution of the Church and State was probably Coleridge's most influential contribution to nineteenth-century public thought. Among those 'profoundly influenced by the idea it presented of a Christian society' (Colmer 1959, 165) was Thomas Arnold, Headmaster of Rugby, a powerful figure in the field of public school education and father of Matthew Arnold. Matthew Arnold's early records, however, appear at odds with this missionary ethos of high public purpose. In his first decade as a writer, he produces his most significant poetical works, an arresting body of writing uncomfortably strung between celebrations of nature and melancholy introspection. At the start of that same decade, in 1851, Arnold became an Inspector of Schools, a taxing position he would hold for some thirty-five years and which demanded frequent travelling in England and Europe as well as considerable administrative labour, including the production of educational policy reports. In 1857 he was elected Professor of Poetry at Oxford, the first non-clergyman ever to hold this position, and the first to lecture not in Latin but in English. The lectures he delivered were often published and some found their way into his first series of *Essays in Criticism* (1865), a volume which established his reputation as a critic. This reputation was further consolidated for posterity with his influential collection of essays in political and social criticism, *Culture and Anarchy* (1869), in which he champions the cultivation of culture as an indispensable cohesive agent properly positioning the individual in a state intent on harmonious perfection: true culture, the ongoing encounter with the 'sweetness and light' of 'the best that has been said and thought in the world', is the only defensible centre of authority in a society otherwise doomed to dissolution as a result of the incommensurable interests of its class components – the Barbarians (the aristocracy), the Philistines (the middle class) and the Populace. In the 1870s Arnold addresses the condition of religion and its institutions in modern society in a number of books of which the controversial *Literature and Dogma* (1873) was and remains the most widely read. Subtitled 'An Essay towards a Better Apprehension of the Bible', *Literature and Dogma* calls for a reading of the Bible which would release it from the straitjackets of dogmatic orthodoxy and sectarian dissent and thereby re-establish it as an effective instrument of culture. Such a reading would have to be informed by the critical 'tact' trained in the study of literature. Arnold's last years as an author were devoted to further exercises of this critical tact, collected in a second series of *Essays in Criticism,* published soon after his death.

A first curious similarity between these two critical trajectories is that they both take shape in the aftermath of a relatively short-lived poetic career: Coleridge wrote his major poetry before he turned 35, Arnold before he turned 40, and both suffered from an acute sense of disappointment at what they regarded as an unfulfilled promise. Yet the all too readily available inference that their later critical work is to some extent a second-best exercise in compensation for personal poetic failure – a sad shift away from a centre of interest they could not hold – threatens to obscure the seriousness of their critical commitment. Caught up as they were in the massive reorganization of the universe of discourse accompanying the relatively rapid transition from a largely rural-agrarian to an urban-industrial culture, involving unprecedented demographic expansion and redistribu- tion and the emergence of new social and political entities, Coleridge and Arnold addressed questions whose urgency is not to be trivialized as a function of their own self-assessed shortcomings in the province of poetry. Nor was their continued critical concern with literature merely a form of corporate escapism on the part of a putative literary establishment. The fact that both authors did reserve a crucial role for literature in the attempt to address the pressing issues of the modern condition is all too frequently glibly demystified as an overdetermined escape from these issues in the serene spheres of aesthetic unworldliness. If the hopes they invested in literature seem extravagant, that is because they are: powered by the conviction that literature at its best has a potential for alteration that must be allowed to wander outside the narrow discursive formation to which it is confined. The critical question, however, is whether this alternative extravagance itself can be contained.

Coleridge and Arnold share the twin assumption that theirs is a culture profoundly marked by a disabling imbalance. Their further diagnostic assessments of the nature and history of this imbalance, however, are quite distinct, as are the remedies they advance in order to redress it. Coleridge's is ultimately a profoundly theological cultural ideology, while Arnold resolutely (although not therefore whole-heartedly) advances a secular perspective on culture and its discontents. Reading them in sequence is to follow an important strand in the history of secularization.

In 1800 Coleridge announced his intention to write 'an Essay on the Elements of Poetry' which 'would in reality be a *disguised* system of Morals & Politics' (cit. Coleridge 1983, I, xxxii). When he eventually composed the *Biographia Literaria* some fifteen years later, he proposed a definition of the central faculty without which this disguise could only ever be a wilful travesty. The question whether Coleridge's proposal ultimately succeeds in warding off charges of wilful – and potentially sinister – imposition can be responsibly addressed only in the larger context of what has been called the 'aesthetic ideology' (de Man 1996), of which it is a forceful representative. Here, we are primarily concerned with the internal logic of Coleridge's argument.

The faculty which allows for a transfer from the realm of poetry to that of morals and politics is the Imagination, and an expansive reading of Coleridge's definition of it reveals the principal features of his theological ideology. The imagination in general is 'the living Power and prime Agent of all human Perception' (Coleridge 1983, I, 304). The critical context of this thesis is Coleridge's opposition to the then (at least in Britain) dominant empiricist doctrine, hailing back to John Locke and David Hume, which conferred absolute primacy to sensory experience and thereby, according to Coleridge, reduced the universe to a dead wasteland of determinist materialism, and human society in particular to a mere laboratory for mechanistic utilitarian experiments. Coleridge's resistance to this system found a foothold in the critical philosophy of Immanuel Kant, who took on board Hume's empiricism but developed an alternative perspective leaving room for a dimension transcending the empirical. Most crucial to Coleridge – who, liberally borrowing from contemporary post-Kantian German philosophers, modified Kant's extremely sophisticated system to his own ends – Kant distinguished between two faculties of the mind: the Understanding, the cognitive faculty strictly speaking, concerned with determined certainty derived from sensory experience; and Reason, the faculty of volition and desire concerned with supra-sensory Ideas, chief among them the final purpose of freedom. In order to ensure a proper connection between these two faculties, Kant introduced the mediating faculty of judgement – in Coleridge, this 'intermediate faculty' (Coleridge 1983, I, 125) is the Imagination, which alone can furnish a synthetic view of the universe as a living organic purposive whole in which the human subject participates to the full, as opposed to a mere material aggregate of objects which '(as objects) are essentially fixed and dead'. (Coleridge 1983, I, 304). To perceive the world imaginatively is to see it as a living, organic whole with a distinct final purpose. Coleridge leaves little doubt as to the nature of that purpose: the imagination is 'a repetition in the finite mind of the eternal act of creation in the infinite I AM' (Coleridge 1983, I, 304).

The bottom line of Coleridge's ideology, then, is his conviction that to construe the world properly, i.e. imaginatively, is to recognize its ultimate foundation in God. At the close of the *Biographia Literaria*, Coleridge drives the point home by asserting that his true goal has always been 'to kindle young minds, and to guard them against the temptation of Scorners, by shewing that the Scheme of Christianity, as taught in the Liturgy and Homilies of our Church, though not discoverable by human Reason, is yet in accordance with it', ending on an image of 'the Soul steady and collected in its pure *Act* of inward Adoration to the Great I AM, and to the filial WORD that re-affirmeth it from Eternity to Eternity, whose choral Echo is the Universe. Glory to God alone' (Coleridge 1983, II, 248). The implication of this didactic intent is clearly that, although the imagination is taken to be 'the living Power and prime Agent of *all* human Perception', it is under constant threat and in need of cultivation.

Indeed, this was already suggested in the initial definition, where Coleridge distinguishes between the 'primary' imagination (the imagination in general) and the 'secondary' imagination. This latter Coleridge considers as an echo of the former, co-existing with the conscious will, yet still as identical with the primary in the *kind* of its agency, and differing only in *degree*, and in the *mode* of its operation. It dissolves, diffuses, dissipates, in order to re-create; or where this process is rendered impossible, yet still at all events it struggles to idealize and to unify. (Coleridge 1983, I, 304)

Although Coleridge does not develop the point at this juncture, the distinction between the primary and the secondary imagination amounts to a fundamentally hierarchical conception of human society which can either be seen as an uncomfortable supplement to his initially 'broadly "Jacobin" or Democratic' outlook, or indeed as a confirmation of what was in fact from the very outset 'a conservative political philosophy, not greatly different from that of *Church and State*' (Gravil 1990, 6). It is clear, at any rate, that Coleridge considers those endowed with the truly creative secondary imagination as exemplary human beings, and to the extent that poets are indeed endowed with the imagination to this degree, a critical investigation of the elements of poetry could legitimately lay claim to the status of 'a *disguised* system of Morals & Politics'.

The bulk of Volume II of the *Biographia Literature* constitutes Coleridge's concerted attempt to properly pursue this investigation, primarily through the critical assessment of the poetry of Wordsworth, intent on measuring his achievement against the theoretical definition of '[t]he poet, described in *ideal* perfection', as one who 'brings the whole soul of man into activity, with the subordination of its faculties to each other, according to their relative worth and dignity' and who 'diffuses a tone, and spirit of unity, that blends, and (as it were) *fuses*, each into each, by that synthetic and magical power, to which we have exclusively appropriated the name of imagination' (Coleridge 1983, II, 15–16). In its actual execution, Coleridge's 'practical criticism' here and elsewhere remains a model of acute attention to the technical detail of poetics, as witness, for instance, the constant critical reconstruction and deconstruction in the course of the last century of his definition of the symbol as the pre-eminent product of the creative imagination, vastly superior to the mechanical artifices of allegory (see Day 1996, 105–25). Moreover, Coleridge's emphatic commitment to an articulate reflection on the very premises of criticism has made his work an extremely valuable point of reference in the development of literary theory as such. Yet whether his criticism indeed lives up to his stated intention to develop 'a *disguised* system of Morals & Politics' is questionable. For the 'disguise' is never quite dropped. More precisely: inasmuch as the *Biographia Literature* contributes to Coleridge's ideological institution of the imagination, it functions as an 'attempt to ground, formalize, and institute (Tory) politics through philosophy' (Pyle 1995, 54) by establishing it as 'a governing social principle in the interests of the nation' to be developed 'through the national clerisy, through the pedagogical and administrative offices organized in the "civil service"'. (Pyle 1995, 55). And to the extent that poetry can be seen as essentially a performance of this imagination, the disguise would be effective and could therefore eventually be dropped. The fact, however, that Coleridge does not proceed to champion poets as the acknowledged legislators of the state and in his programme for the national clerisy does not even, strictly speaking, mention poetry a single time (a vague reference to 'the Literae Humaniores, the products of genial power' hidden in a footnote is the closest he gets (Coleridge 1976, 54)) suggests that literature ultimately does not live up to the prescriptive demands of Coleridge's theological ideology of the imagination and consequently fails to adequately cover his conception of the system of morals and politics. What must continue to exercise contemporary criticism, however, is the nature, or rather the culture, of this failed synthesis, and to this end Coleridge's criticism, precisely because it is informed by a frustrated totalizing desire to erase the difference between literature and its others, remains a formidable test case.

After his second lecture as Professor of Poetry in May 1858, Matthew Arnold reported in a letter to his mother on the relative dwindling of his audience – 'the theatre was, to me, depressingly too big for us' – and suggested that the very project of his lectures might have been to blame: 'the attempt to form general ideas is one which the Englishman generally sets himself against: and the one grand'-idée of these introductory lectures is to establish a formula which shall *suit* all literature: an attempt which so far as I know has not yet even been made in England' (1996, 389). Placed in its immediate context, Arnold's remark can be read as an ironic gloss on his entire critical career. There is the powerful critical ambition to suitably represent the essence of literature which is necessary for a proper perception of the literary object 'as in itself it really is' (1964, 9) which will, in turn, enable a solid evaluative classification of the entirety of literature and, eventually, of all culture in the *'disinterested endeavour to learn and propagate the best that is known and thought in the world'* (1964, 33). Unfortunately, however, this project took its most influential shape as the mere establishment of a sequence of indiscriminately repeated formulas, soundbites censoriously celebrating the virtues of 'tact' and 'taste' in discrimination but typically divorced from systematic critical analysis. And there is the characteristic blend of arrogance and melancholy in the conviction that the project of criticism is alien to English thought – a conviction condemning Arnold to a lifetime of urbane opposition from the margins of his culture in the name of the centrality of culture, trying 'to pull out a few more stops in that powerful but at present somewhat narrow-toned organ, the modern Englishman' (1964, 4), in a theatre which has become 'depressingly too big'.

It is in his oppositional mode that Arnold is at his most intriguing – not so much in his blanket condemnation of the lack of 'sanity' he diagnoses in his modernity (1979, 673), but in his 'vivacious' attacks on Victorian complacency. A justly celebrated example from 'The Function of Criticism at the Present Time' (1864) is his juxtaposition of contemporary eulogies of the Anglo-Saxon race as 'the best breed in the world' (1964, 22) with a harrowing newspaper account of a workhouse girl called Wragg who strangled her illegitimate child and was placed in custody. As Arnold puts it, 'There is profit for the spirit in such contrasts as this; criticism serves the cause of perfection by establishing them' (1964, 24). Importantly, however, Arnold does not develop the contrast as an object lesson in social iniquity, but instead focuses on the fact that the girl's Christian name and the reference to her sex have been 'lopped off' in the article – 'Wragg is in custody' – and further abuses the name 'Wragg' to call attention to 'what a touch of grossness in our race, what an original shortcoming in the more delicate spiritual perceptions, is shown by the natural growth amongst us of such hideous names, – Higginbottom, Stiggins, Bugg!' (23). The social criticism is implied in the very introduction of the case as one of those 'inconvenient facts' which Max Weber considered it the duty of intellectuals to force on the attention of the dominant ideology; it is rehearsed in the indignant observation of the newspaper's callous clipping of the girl's name; but Arnold's idiosyncratic signature consists in his framing of the fact in a general aesthetic judgement no less aberrant for being ironical. The example captures the stark logic of Arnold's salvational critical programme: the task of criticism is to teach the English to properly recognize the imperfection of their culture, incongruously exemplified in the hideousness of their names, by introducing them to the best that has been thought and said in the world – the rest will follow, including, presumably, a better future for the children of girls like Wragg. The task of the critic is to defy the 'defiant songs of triumph' of the present 'only by murmuring under his breath, *Wragg is in custody*', 'in no other way will these songs of triumph be induced gradually to moderate themselves, to get rid of what in them is excessive and offensive, and to fall into a softer an truer key' (24).

For Arnold, that 'softer and truer key' is essentially the key of poetry, and its perplexing introduction at this point in 'The Function of Criticism' amounts to an ambivalent recognition of the sheer unlikeliness of his critical enterprise. It is this ambivalence which makes Arnold's writing still a powerful and disturbing precedent for literary studies in search of self-legitimation. When this ironical reservation all but disappears, as in his preaching promotion of poetry to the status of religion in his influential late essay on 'The Study of Poetry' (1880), with its dispiriting propagation of 'the high seriousness of the great classics' (1964, 250) as 'an infallible touchstone for detecting the presence or absence of high poetic quality' (242), the function of criticism is to refute him by kicking his touchstones back into the long grass – or into the wilderness of 'that most Arnoldian of fields, Cultural Studies' (Bell 1997, 217).

In Coleridge there is an unmistakable gravitation towards the final foundation in God, but his writing seems almost perversely driven to avoid that centre by losing itself in magnificent digressions that have saved his criticism from the fate of his theological ideology. In Arnold, the central point is invoked on almost every page, perhaps because it no longer bears the self-evidently authoritative name of God but is simply, or rather merely, called 'the best' – and in his worst moments, all he accomplishes is a tedious liturgy of Literature as the High Point of High Culture. The blatant absence of a secular notion of excellence comparable in authority to the notion of God and, perhaps more importantly, the disastrous consequences of some attempts to found such a notion in the course of the last century, still make Arnold something of a suspicious figure today. It has seemed easier to bracket Coleridge's solid theological commitment than to forgive Arnold for his ultimately far less fundamentalist commitment to the centrality of a true culture whose core is poetry. Yet as recent reinvestigations suggest, Arnold's actual criticism of culture is itself a powerful ally in the displacement of culture as the position of a stable centre of authority, towards culture as 'always already culture critique', a 'dis-position' that 'severs any attachment to the particularization and positionality of cultural identity' (Walters 1997, 364–5). Instead of forgiveness, Arnold deserves the critical reading he practised rather than preached.

Ortwin de Graef

Further reading and works cited

Appleyard, J. A. *Coleridge's Philosophy of Literature*. Cambridge, 1965.
Arnold, M. *Essays in Criticism, First and Second Series*, intro. G. K. Chesterton. London, 1964.
—. 'The Critical Prefaces of 1853 and 1854', in *The Poems of Matthew Arnold*, ed. K. Allott, 2nd edn M. Allott. London, 1979.
—. *Culture and Anarchy*, ed. Samuel Lipman. New Haven, CT, 1994.
—. *The Letters of Matthew Arnold. Volume 1: 1829–1859*, ed. C. Y. Lang. Charlottesville, VA, 1996.
Ashton, R. *The Life of Samuel Taylor Coleridge*. Oxford, 1997.
Bell, B. 'The Function of Arnold at the Present Time', *Essays in Criticism*, 47, 3, July 1997.
Butler, M. *Romantics, Rebels and Reactionaries*. Oxford, 1981.

Coleridge, S. T. *On the Constitution of the Church and State*, ed. J. Colmer. Princeton, NJ, 1976.
—. *Biographia Literaria, or, Biographical Sketches of My Literary Life and Opinions*, eds J. Engell and W. Jackson Bate, 2 vols. Princeton, NJ, 1983.
Collini, S. 'Arnold', in *Victorian Thinkers*, eds A. L. Le Quesne et al. Oxford, 1993.
Colmer, J. *Coleridge: Critic of Society*. Oxford, 1959.
Day, A. *Romanticism*. London, 1996.
de Graef, O. 'Congestion of the Brain in an Age of Unpoetrylessness: Matthew Arnold's Digestive Tracts for the Times'. *Victorian Literature and Culture*, 26, 2, 1998.
de Man, P. *Aesthetic Ideology*, ed. and intro. A. Warminski. Minneapolis, MN, 1996.
Eliot, T. S. *The Sacred Wood*. London, 1957.
Fulford, T. and Paley, M. D. (eds) *Coleridge's Visionary Languages*. Rochester, NY, 1993.
Gallant, C. *Coleridge's Theory of Imagination Today*. New York, 1989.
Gravil, R. *The Coleridge Connection*. London, 1990.
Hawkes, T. 'The Heimlich Manoeuvre', *Textual Practice*, 8, 2, 1994.
Levine, G. 'Matthew Arnold: The Artist in the Wilderness', *Critical Inquiry*, 9, 3, March 1983.
Orr, L. (ed.) *Critical Essays on S. T. Coleridge*. New York, 1994.
Pyle, F. *The Ideology of Imagination*. Stanford, CA, 1995.
Trilling, L. *Matthew Arnold*. London, 1963.
Tucker, H. F. *A Companion to Victorian Literature and Culture*. Oxford, 1999.
Walters, T. 'The Question of Culture (and Anarchy)', *Modern Language Notes*, 112, 3, 1997.

John Ruskin (1819–1900) and Walter Pater (1839–1894): Aesthetics and the State

Although John Ruskin and Walter Pater made their contemporaneous reputations as critics and theorists of art and are indeed virtually the only two British aesthetic (as opposed to literary) theorists of note in the nineteenth century, twentieth-century critics have read them primarily in the tradition of nineteenth-century prose, along with Coleridge, Carlyle and Arnold. From this perspective, Ruskin has had considerable importance in extending the Coleridgean idea of organic form into an organic critique of British society that influenced William Morris's socialism and through him the British labour party (Rosenberg 1961, 131). Along with Coleridge and Arnold, Ruskin continued to influence the British Cambridge critics' organicist social views (he had less influence on American New Critics and Ruskin specialists in the United States, following Rosenberg, discuss his organicism generally in connection with his social and economic theories). Both Ruskin's political heirs and his academic critics have then construed Pater's writings as an aesthetic narrowing of Ruskin, a concern for aesthetics that deliberately drained it of moral and political significance, as indeed Ruskin saw it (see Ruskin 1903–12, IV, 35). Although the view of Pater as an ahistorical relativist and quietist has been increasingly contested (see Williams 1989 and Loesberg 1991), the view of Ruskin as having turned his earlier Evangelical art theory into a secular, mostly left critique of capitalism and of Pater as resisting Ruskin's absolutist theorizing and moralist preference for the Gothic over the Renaissance (see Hill's notes to *The Renaissance*, in Pater 1980, 294 and Bloom 1974, xvi) remains standard.

The view of Ruskin through the lens of William Morris's socialist reading of him certainly captures an aspect of his later economic theories and there is no question that his theories of both art and society are deeply and explicitly organicist. But this version of Ruskin ignores or writes off as marginal his extremely authoritarian view of how organic relations should work in society, as well as the precise nature of his turn from art to politics and economy. It also not only falsifies the general tenor of Pater's theories but also reduces our view of Ruskin's and Pater's dialogue to one about Gothic and Renaissance or to whether art is a matter of perception or theoretical apprehension, while leaving Pater's larger social, historical and critical views to be influenced mainly by Arnold (for this influence see DeLaura (1969) and Dowling (1984)). As a corrective to these perspectives, I will look at Ruskin's and Pater's dialogue over the political significance of art in terms of the decidedly un-British idea of the aesthetic state. The idea of the aesthetic state begins with the Jena German romantics and particularly with Friedrich Schiller. Ruskin read little Schiller, barely mentions him and then only to misinterpret him (see Wilkinson and Willoughby 1967, clviii) and although Pater had read as much in Schiller as in German romanticism (see Inman 1981, 100–2), he does not seem to have particularly attended to this concept. Still, by using the idea that art, rather than being relevant as a moral activity or as a taste analogous to a moral sentiment (these are the eighteenth-century British ideas about the relevance of art to morality, as most significantly formulated by Shaftesbury and Hutcheson, and they remain largely definitive of how Anglo-American critics make the connection), is a model pattern for how a state may be formed (the best history of the idea of the aesthetic state is in Chytry 1989), we will be able to see the line from Ruskin's early aesthetic theories to his critique of laissez-faire capitalism as both insufficiently benevolent and insufficiently authoritarian. The relevance of Pater's critique of organicism, and his views on art and society from his earliest published works through *Plato and Platonism* to Ruskin's theories and the anti-statist political significance of Pater's aesthetics will also emerge.

Ruskin's theory of beauty, in its earliest articulation, attributes our sense of beauty to a recognition of God's ordering of the universe as a gift to us. Although Ruskin formulated this theory as part of an early Evangelical project to prove the divinity of art and beauty, that early articulation is already ready to be stripped of its religious elements and to serve as a general model of value for Ruskin. He starts by distinguishing between aesthesis and theoria, defining aesthesis as the pleasure afforded by the senses alone and theoria as 'the moral perception and appreciation of the ideas of beauty' (Ruskin 1903–12, IV, 35). Despite his use of the word 'moral' and his late footnote directing this passage at aestheticism, his target in this distinction necessitating an extra-sensual apprehension to appreciate beauty seems not to be theories of art that do not recognize its moral elements (as Landow 1971, 90, seems to suggest) but rather the eighteenth-century British theorists who saw the appreciation of art in terms of sense-apprehension and argued its moral relevance in terms of analogy between a moral and an aesthetic apprehension. Ruskin, in contrast, asserts an identity between moral and aesthetic apprehension.

Having set up the distinction between aesthesis and theoria, Ruskin then defines the workings of beauty on the theoretic apprehension:

> Now in whatever is an object of life, in whatever may be infinitely and for itself desired, we may
> be sure there is something of the divine, for God will not make anything an object of life to his
> creatures which does not point to or partake of Himself . . . But when instead of being scattered,

> interrupted, or chance-distributed, [pleasures of the sight] are gathered together, and so arranged
> to enhance each other as by chance they could not be, there is caused by them not only a feeling
> of strong affection towards the object in which they exist but a perception of purpose and
> adaptation of it to our desires; a perception therefore, of the immediate operation of the
> Intelligence which so formed us, and so feeds us. Now the mere animal consciousness of the
> pleasantness I call aesthesis; but the exulting, reverent, and grateful perception of it I call
> theoria. (Ruskin 1903–12, IV, 46–7)

The first thing to notice is that though this passage seems to indicate that the designed
arrangement is instrumental to producing a gratification that we desire, in fact this
distinction between instrument and end cannot be the case since Ruskin insists on a
difference between objects that instrumentally gratify us (food to satisfy our hunger) and
objects that are intrinsically gratifying in themselves. This design leads to no purpose
outside itself and it gratifies us inherently. The value of design making unity out of
scattered variety is fundamental and objective (Landow 1971, 92 and Hewison 1976, 55
note Ruskin's contestation of subjectivist theories of beauty), there in objects and thus
universally apprehensible. Even the gratitude to an external, designing intelligence cannot
really be a consequence of the perception of design since that would suggest a distinction
between purpose and object (although in this case between the divine designer's purpose
and its object) that Ruskin's theory denies. Apprehension of design contains simultaneously as equivalent elements gratification and gratitude.

As Ruskin moved from an Evangelical to a more and more explicitly humanist
justification of this theory of the intrinsic and fundamental value of mere design, he
moved increasingly to a political and economic theory from an internal necessity that made
that later political theory essentially still an aesthetic one and that also had as a
consequence the authoritarianism so many of Ruskin's critics want to downplay as an
idiosyncrasy. The first step in the movement from aesthetics to politics occurs famously in
The Stones of Venice, when he uses his qualities of beauty to judge the ethics of the society
that produced the beauty. While still tying this value to Christianity, Ruskin praises the
Gothic arrangement of labour for what amounts to an aesthetic arrangement that respects
the freedom of its labourers:

> Therefore to every spirit which Christianity summons to her service, her exhortation is: Do
> what you can, and confess frankly what you are unable to do; neither let your efforts be
> shortened for fear of failure, nor your confession silenced for fear of shame. And it is, perhaps the
> principal admirableness of the Gothic schools of architecture, that they thus receive the results
> of the labour of inferior minds; and out of fragments full of imperfection in every touch,
> indulgently raise up a stately and unaccusable whole. (Ruskin 1903–12, X, 190)

Critics have long noted the incipient social theory in this passage (see Spear 1984, 123).
The great Gothic cathedrals, using imperfect workers and finding a place for all of them
within a more perfect whole, are models of just societies. Further, if Gothic beauty
manifests this social arrangement, then the relevance of art to society is only too clear: that
which produces beauty is also just.

The problem is that, at first glance, the relationship between mode of production and
designed object seems less than perfect. Although Ruskin famously argued in *The Crown of
Wild Olives* that you could not really have Gothic architecture without living in a Gothic
society and that great works of art could only be produced by a properly organized society,
the truth of that assertion is not self-evident. Not only can one imagine justly organized

systems producing less than beautiful works of art, if only as a result of technical failure, but, precisely because beauty is an objective quality of things, its mode of production is logically irrelevant to it. Only if it is, by some natural law as rigorous as the law of gravity, impossible to produce beautiful works except through just organization will Ruskin's equivalence between Gothic labour systems and beauty hold as more than an analogy.

The answer to this problem lies in the equivalence outlined above between the apprehension of design and the experiences of gratification and gratitude. For Ruskin, the capturing of variety within unity has, as an objective part of its pattern, the recognition that the pattern was designed and the gratitude that that recognition elicits. In the discussion of aesthesis and theoria, the designed object recognized as beautiful was in the first instance natural and the designer was the divine intelligence that Ruskin, in his Evangelical period, wanted to prove necessarily connected to the appreciation of beauty. When one moves to an artificed object, a cathedral in *The Stones of Venice*, however, because human beings do the designing, the apprehension of design will equivalently include the designing system to which an experience of beauty entails a gratitude. In other words, one perceives as beautiful those objects designed by justly organized systems, where justly organized means organized to contain variety within unity (the stonecutter's freedom and imperfection within the larger purpose of the cathedral). As one can see, a justly organized society will be perceived as aesthetically valuable, then, not by a separate, non-moral judgement, but precisely by an aesthetic judgement that appraises moral arrangement.

As Ruskin secularizes his definition of aesthetic design, he must also, because of his sense of what it then means to call that design objective, both depart from nature as the model of its working and insist on authoritarian control. To understand how this change works, one must note the difference between Coleridgean organicism and explications of productive design and design in objects in both *Modern Painters II* and in *The Stones of Venice*. Coleridge's highly influential definition distinguishes natural order from artificial order in terms of the immanence of natural order and its absence of any impress of an external stamp. The extension of this definition to art is by loose analogy since art is by definition externally authored. Moreover, this argument is not friendly to the idea that natural objects show evidence of being divinely designed, since such evidence would be precisely the mark of external stamping. For Ruskin, as an evangelical, though the recognition of divine design is immanent in the design, indeed a part of it, it is still at least intellectually separable enough to mark it out as part of the definition. When Ruskin loses his belief in a divine designer, because design for him always entails gratitude to a designer, he must also give up nature as the model from which to explain design. He continues to believe in an order to the appearance of nature and he continues to describe it in terms of achieving purposes, for instance in *Modern Painters V* (published in 1860, two years after what Ruskin describes as his un-conversion and clearly with his turn to political and economic writing already in mind), but he no longer insists that nature was ordered by God for our appreciation and he constantly describes natural order with social and political analogies: 'And in the arrangement of these concessions there is an exquisite sensibility among the leaves. They do not grow each to his own liking, till they run against one another, and then turn back sulkily; but by the watchful instinct, far apart, they anticipate their companions' courses, as ships at sea' (Ruskin 1903–12, VII, 48).

But as artificed ordering replaces natural order as the model for design that both art and society share, the ramifications of its objective status shift. When Ruskin believed that natural order was the first model of beauty and that art created beauty by being true to that natural order, he also believed that all human beings were naturally disposed to appreciate that beauty (see Landow 1971, 93–4 for a discussion of this issue). Those who did not appreciate the beauty of Turner simply did not understand how nature really worked or appeared. When they were fully instructed on how storms or light worked, the beauty of both nature and Turner automatically became manifest. When humanly artificed order replaces divinely patterned nature as simultaneously artistic beauty and proper social arrangement, though, the import of the fact that evidently all humans do not perceive either beauty or social justice in the same way changes. Although Ruskin regularly claims that anyone who simply looks at the evidence straightforwardly or reads what the Bible says will understand that his claims about society or his interpretation of a text are obviously and irrefutably right, his experience of being constantly contested also clearly meant that not all humans would by themselves see beautiful art as beautiful or a just society as just. Our taste for beauty is now part of our moral make-up and cannot be easily improved by the kind of education the first two volumes of *Modern Painters* imagined. Thus Ruskin now argues that

> . . . a picture of Titian's, or a Greek statue, or a Greek coin, or a Turner landscape, expresses delight in the perpetual contemplation of a good and perfect thing. That is an entirely moral quality – it is the taste of the angels . . . it is not an indifferent nor optional thing whether we love this or that; but it is just the vital function of all our being. (Ruskin 1903–12, XVIII, 436)

Saying that taste is a moral quality is not new for Ruskin. Since he describes moral and aesthetic order with the same language throughout *Modern Painters*, taste has always been a moral quality. But since it is now so deeply imbedded in us, good taste cannot be taught in any easy way: thus Ruskin immediately goes on to say that a scavenger or a costermonger could not be taught to enjoy Dante or Beethoven without entirely changing his nature. In other words, beauty and equitable order are still equivalent and objective, but they are not dependably and universally apprehensible.

This article opened by arguing the value of the concept of the aesthetic state for explaining Ruskin's political and economic theories. We are now ready quickly to go through the features of those theories that indicate he aimed at an aesthetic order and neither a welfare state (as Rosenberg 1961, 139 argued) nor some form of organic socialism, as those following from William Morris's interpretation have argued. First, although *Unto this Last* quite famously argues for replacing competition with affection as the basis for social relation, Ruskin also states quite explicitly that he does not espouse affection as a matter of abstract justice but as a reality of organization: 'Observe, I am here considering the affections wholly as a motive power; not at all as things in themselves desirable or noble' (XVII, 30). If one takes this claim seriously and puts it in the context of the theory of artistic composition in *Modern Painters V*, the aesthetic basis of Ruskin's concept of social organization becomes clear: 'Now invention in art signifies an arrangement in which everything in the work is thus consistent with all things else, and helpful to all else . . . Also in true composition, everything not only helps everything else a *little*, but helps it with its utmost power' (Ruskin 1903–12, VII, 208–9). In other words, Ruskin argues against political economy with what he takes to be a basic law of composition, though it is also an aspect of human relationship. Moreover, although Ruskin does describe what he calls here the Law of Help as the basis of organic life, the difference between organic life and art is that if the parts do not help each other in a plant, the plant will die – the law is inescapable. In art, one can disobey the law but one will create flawed works of art. In society, one can disobey the law at least in the short run by choosing competition, but the rules of artistic composition show the ultimate mistake of doing so. Ruskin's key claim, then, 'Government and co-operation are in all things and eternally the law of life' (Ruskin 1903–12, VII, 207), literally true of organic life, becomes true of social order (and the terms 'government' and 'co-operation' have their primary meaning there and not in organic life) through the lens of artistic composition.

Although the theory of the aesthetic state has frequently had as part of its vision an ordered whole comprised of individual human actions freely chosen and Schiller, at least, was suspicious of any easy analogy between the artist and the teacher or the politician (see Wilkinson and Willoughby 1967, clxii and cxci as well as Chytry 1989, 82), the concept of an ordering and controlling artist as a model for a state leader has frequently forced its way through. In Ruskin's case, as we have seen, his theory's secularization forced the replacement of a divine designer with an artist. And his recognition that human beings did not inevitably perceive beauty or accept proper social organization meant a strong stress on authority. In *Unto this Last*, that stress is at its weakest, though one can still find him insisting on the necessity of teaching people what to desire (Ruskin 1903–12, XVII, 83). In *A Joy For Ever*, though, on a note to the need for fatherly authority in the state, Ruskin makes clear how little he values 'liberty': 'I will tell you beforehand what I really do think about this same liberty of action, namely, that whenever we can make a perfectly equitable law about any matter, or even a law securing, on the whole, more just conduct than unjust, we ought to make that law (XVI, 109). And, in an inflammatory defence of slavery that gives a dark context to his reading of Turner's painting of the slave-ship and to his statement about a worker's freedom under medieval Christianity, Ruskin makes clear his sense of the absolute necessity of compulsion: 'The fact is that slavery is not a political institution at all, *but an inherent, natural, and eternal inheritance* of a large portion of the human race – to whom the more you give of their own free will, the more slaves they will make themselves' (Ruskin 1903–12, XVII, 256). When Ruskin moved from art to society then, the model he used remained aesthetic in the sense that the state would follow rules of composition, those rules being simultaneously moral and artistic, and that that composition would come from a designing authority, the ends of whose designs would assuredly be a just and equitable ordering, but whose means would be the artist's control of the elements of his or her work.

Although Pater read Ruskin as early as 1859 (Gosse, cit. Inman 1981, 62), if he was as influenced as many argue (Bloom 1974, xvi, calls Ruskin, improbably, Pater's 'only begetter'), he buried that influence deeply. Even the seemingly obvious connections – the opening of *The Renaissance* and its rejections of abstract theory in favour of concrete experience (Pater 1980, xix), the general reversal of Ruskin's evaluations of the Gothic and the Renaissance – are at best reliable guesses since Pater almost never mentions Ruskin. In discussing Pater's response to Ruskin in terms of the latter's view of art and the state, one can hardly be sure that Pater thought he was responding directly to Ruskin, since the writers he discusses in outlining his alternative are William Morris, Coleridge, Winckelmann and Plato, among others. Still at key moments in various texts, Pater took direct aim at the idea of a state organized on organicist, or aesthetic principles, at its valuing of ideal order, at its authoritarian principles. Moreover his view of art's value and its relation to issues of moral judgement constitute one of the primary oppositions in aesthetic literature to the notion of the aesthetic state.

Pater's first three published essays, 'Coleridge's Writings', 'The Poems of William Morris' and 'Winckelmann' (in 1866, 1867 and 1868), read together rather than in their reprinted versions in *The Renaissance* and *Appreciations*, seem more like the first works of a social critic than of an art critic. Both 'The Poems of William Morris' and 'Winckelmann' end

with visions of an overarching value of art that has led to the usual view of Pater as a
hedonist who tries to separate art from moral significance. But what the essays share most
clearly with each other is a sense that the kinds of objectivist theories we have seen Ruskin
trying to formulate amount to an escape from the realities of modern life. In the case of
Coleridge, Pater is at his least sympathetic, and thus most directly refutes the idealized view
of nature and art as unifying forces that we have seen Ruskin articulating (he refutes
Coleridge's organicism first – 1866, 55, and then his notion of a natural order that shows
itself by the way it holds together disparate parts, 1866, 57). But precisely because it is more
sympathetic with what we frequently take as the Ruskinian ideal of the earthly paradise, in
Ruskin's clearest immediate inheritor, the opening of 'The Poems of William Morris' is
more striking:

> Greek poetry, medieval or modern poetry, projects above the realities of its time a world in
> which the forms of things are transfigured. Of that world this new poetry takes possession and
> sublimates beyond it another still fainter and more spectral, which is literally an artificial or
> 'earthly paradise'. It is a finer ideal, extracted from what in relation to any actual world is already
> an ideal . . . The secret of enjoyment of it is that inversion of home-sickness known to some, that
> incurable thirst for the sense of escape, which no actual form of life satisfies, no poetry even, if it
> be merely simple and spontaneous. (1868, 144)

Pater opens here an article that praises this transfiguration in Morris's poetry in the highest
terms. But the passage quite clearly describes the transfiguration as an escape and the
earthly paradise as the artifice of someone who cannot deal with the world before him. The
first problem with an aesthetics of order proposed as a social model, then, is that it is really
an escape from the demands of the world before us rather than a mode of dealing with it. In
this context, the theory of art's value that closes the essay, and that became the notorious
'Conclusion' to *The Renaissance*, posits a form of aesthetic apprehension that will accept
rather than turn from the world science shows us, that will learn how to value experience
rather than idealize it away.

   Moreover, Pater does have a view of a moral vision contained in this form of aesthetic
apprehension, and again it seems to contrast almost deliberately with what Ruskin thinks
art has to tell us about morality. Pater suggests that view in 'Coleridge's Writings' and in
The Renaissance, but there he seems mainly concerned to challenge abstract and absolute
codes of morality, offering the basis for the view of him as a moral relativist. In an essay on
Measure for Measure, however, he concludes with a more positive articulation of the ethics
of art:

> It is for this finer justice, a justice based on a more delicate appreciation of the true conditions of
> men and things, a true respect of persons in our estimate of actions, that the people in *Measure
> for Measure* cry out as they pass before us . . . It is not always that poetry can be the exponent of
> morality; but it is this aspect of morals which it represents most naturally, for this true justice is
> dependent on just those finer appreciations which poetry cultivates in us the power of making,
> those peculiar valuations of action and its effect which poetry actually requires. (1910a, 183–4)

Like Ruskin, Pater here claims a morality implicit within the working of art. And their moral
imperatives contrast just as do their views of art. For Ruskin, art modelled a unifying order
that contained variety and led to a cohering Law of Help. For Pater, far from offering
overarching orders, art shows us how to attend to our experiences in all their individual
intensity, giving 'the highest quality to your moments as they pass, and simply for those
moments' sake' (1980, 190). The morality that follows entails a recognition of the

irreducible individuality of situations and, more significantly, human beings. This recognition does not imply that no moral judgements can be made, but that moral judgements to be just to individual human beings cannot follow abstract laws or orders.

A suspicion of social order might seem to follow naturally enough from this view and, indeed, Pater's justification of Winckelmann's insincere conversion to Roman Catholicism in terms of Winckelmann's private needs is based on the claim that 'the aim of our culture should be to attain not only as intense but as complete a life as possible' (1980, 150). Although culture here means self-cultivation, the passage also suggests that a culture in the sense of a social order also must be aimed at the development of its individuals. But Pater's explicit treatment of the concept of a state modelled on aesthetic principles is in fact more ambiguous. An aesthetic order, as opposed to other orders, after all, has an element of self-undercutting in it that always endangers its own authority. Pater can discuss Morris's earthly paradise as an aesthetic achievement precisely because his evaluation of its effectiveness as a vision entails a recognition of its artifice and its escape.

In *Plato and Platonism*, Pater carries out to the limit this sympathetic appraisal of the concept of the aesthetic state that undercuts by its very sympathy. In the discussion of Plato's *Republic*, he specifies that Platonic justice rests on 'a unity or harmony enforced on disparate elements' (1910d, 242–3). This sounds very much like Ruskin's vision at various points. But then, in the most astonishing chapter of that book on 'Plato's Aesthetics', while mentioning hardly at all and only in the most indirect way Plato's most famous and notorious ideas about art's insufficiencies, Pater finds Plato's real aesthetics precisely in his design of his state: 'We are to become – like little pieces in a machine! you may complain. – No, like performers rather, individually, it may be, of more or less importance, but each with a necessary and inalienable part, in a perfect musical exercise which is well worth while' (1910d, 273). Although this may sound like a defence of Plato's state in terms of its aesthetic order, in fact the finding of Plato's aesthetics in his statecraft soon changes the value of that theory into one that attunes us to what we find attractive in the concept of a number of ordered states – notably a Ruskinian gothic that shares with Plato's republic only its Ruskinian ordering (1910d, 279). By the end of that chapter, aesthetics becomes the central force of Plato's thinking, though, since it is an aesthetics of askesis and self-resistance, it controls its own aesthetic temperament. In becoming an aesthetics, though, Plato's state can no longer function as overarching order, but only as an order, an artifice that continues to work out Pater's aesthetic of individuation.

Pater's aestheticization of Plato's republic may seem the kind of reduction that has led to the view – held by Ruskin as well as numbers of contemporary critics – that Pater's formalism denied art any moral or intellectual content. But, in fact, it drained Ruskin's aesthetics of its moral content to use it to delineate a different moral evaluation, one that Pater wanted to find in all art – even the aesthetic states of Ruskin's gothic and Plato's republic. Bloom locates Ruskin's most threatening influence on Pater in his valuing of the ability above all to see clearly (1974, xi). If Pater did indeed see this as what he learned from Ruskin, he absorbed it so completely that he made it seem far more his own than Ruskin's dictum, so completely, finally, that he could turn Ruskin's aesthetic state into a Paterian moral moment. In so doing, he opposes to the view of the aesthetic state in both its harmony and its oppression neither a deliberately anti-aesthetic politics nor an amoral aesthetic but the opposing position always potential in any aesthetic, a scepticism about the naturalness of order.

Jonathan Loesberg

Further reading and works cited

Bloom, H. 'The Crystal Man', in *Selected Writings of Walter Pater*, ed. H. Bloom. New York, 1974.
Chytry, J. *The Aesthetic State*. Berkeley, CA, 1989.
Dale, P. A. *The Victorian Critic and the Idea of History*. Cambridge, MA, 1977.
DeLaura, D. *Hebrew and Hellene in Victorian England*. Austin, TX, 1969.
Dowling, L. *Language and Decadence in the Victorian Fin de Siècle*. Princeton, NJ, 1986.
—. *Hellenism and Homosexuality in Victorian Oxford*. Ithaca, NY, 1994.
Helsinger, E. *Ruskin and the Art of the Beholder*. Cambridge, MA, 1982.
Hewison, R. *John Ruskin and the Argument of the Eye*. Princeton, NJ, 1976.
Hunt, J. D. *The Wider Sea: A Life of John Ruskin*. New York, 1982.
Hutcheson, F. *An Inquiry Concerning Beauty, Order, Harmony, Design*, ed. P. Kung. The Hague, 1973.
Inman, B. A. *Walter Pater's Reading, 1858–1873*. New York, 1981.
Landow, G. *The Aesthetic and Critical Theories of John Ruskin*. Princeton, NJ, 1971.
Levey, M. *The Case of Walter Pater*. London, 1978.
Loesberg, J. *Aestheticism and Deconstruction: Pater, Derrida, and De Man*. Princeton, NJ, 1991.
Pater, W. 'Coleridge's Writings', *Westminster Review*, January 1866.
—. 'Poems of William Morris', *Westminster Review*, October 1868.
—. *Appreciations*. London, 1910a.
—. *Greek Studies*. London, 1910b.
—. *Marius the Epicurean*, 2 vols. London, 1910c.
—. *Plato and Platonism*. London, 1910d.
—. *The Renaissance: Studies in Art and Poetry*, ed. D. L. Hill. Berkeley, CA, 1980.
Rosenberg, J. D. *The Darkening Glass: A Portrait of Ruskin's Social Genius*. New York, 1961.
Ruskin, J. *Works*, eds E. T. Cook and A. Wedderburn, 39 vols. London, 1903–12.
Sawyer, P. *Ruskin's Poetic Argument: The Design of the Major Works*. Ithaca, NY, 1985.
Shaftesbury, A. Cooper, Third Earl of. *Characteristics of Men, Manners, Opinions, Times, Etc.* ed. J. Robertson, 2 vols. London, 1900.
Spear, J. *Dreams of an English Eden: Ruskin and His Tradition in Social Criticism*. New York, 1984.
Wilkinson, E. and Willoughby, L. A. 'Introduction' to F. Schiller, *On the Aesthetic Education of Man*, eds E. Wilkinson and L. A. Willoughby. Oxford, 1967.
Williams, C. *Transfigured World: Walter Pater's Aestheticist Historicism*. Ithaca, NY, 1989.

Oscar Wilde (1854–1900): Aesthetics and Criticism

Devoting most of his career to poetry, prose fiction and drama, Oscar Wilde wrote the bulk of his critical work between 1885 and 1891. Along with a number of book reviews and brief articles, this corpus consists chiefly of just six major essays: 'The Truth of Masks' (1885), 'The Decay of Lying' (1889), 'Pen, Pencil and Poison' (1889), 'The Portrait of Mr. W. H.' (1889), 'The Soul of Man Under Socialism' (1890) and 'The Critic as Artist' (1890). In May 1891, four of these six essays were published together in a volume suggestively entitled *Intentions*, although each of the six was at one time or another considered for inclusion in the book (Danson 1997, 7–8). Wilde also published in 1891 the well-known 'Preface' to his only novel, *The Picture of Dorian Gray*; a brief series of aphorisms on beauty and art, the 'Preface' serves as a pithy distillation of the paradoxical, subtly equivocal theoretical framework the essays collectively establish. In 1895, Wilde's own words would be interpreted, ironically, as utterly unequivocal evidence against him in the scandalous libel and criminal suits that eventually sent him to jail and effectively ended his career.

This tragic conclusion did not extinguish Wilde's legacy. In fact, it is safe to say that his words have graced more greeting cards and bookbags than any other author featured in this encyclopaedia – all testaments to the prominent place Wilde holds in our cultural landscape to this day. Yet such a distinction does more than indicate a unique literary and critical influence. Most obviously, it attests to the witty, epigrammatic memorability of his declarations and, moreover, acknowledges that when many people speak of Oscar Wilde, they often refer to a personality and a life as much as a collection of ideas and texts. Indeed, for a writer who famously explores the question of art's relation to life, and whose life and work together offer an uncommonly rich site for examining the overdetermined sexual and social culture of late-Victorian England, such a focus is in many ways warranted. For despite his avowed artistic detachment from the age in which he lived, Wilde was a keen social critic. In 'The Soul of Man Under Socialism', to name just one example, his description of the public's despotic potential to quash – like Mill's 'tyranny of the majority' – independently thinking, creative individuals provides an eerily prescient analysis of the fate which would befall him. Recent Wilde scholars have explored such issues in ground-breaking ways. But noting his status as cultural icon also points to a peculiar challenge his critics face, that of diffusing the still popular idea of Wilde as just a stereotype or a sloganeer.

Beyond the mannered eccentricities Wilde exhibited in his deliberate cultivation of a public persona, beyond the famous utterances that seem to serve as captions to it, lies a largely coherent and complex aesthetic theory of 'art for art's sake', derived from the aestheticism of Walter Pater, though not merely derivative of it. Morality and immorality, art and life, truth and lies – throughout his work, each of these categories garner their very particular meaning by way of Wilde's paradoxical rhetoric and self-consciously performative style. In a generically diverse body of criticism – which includes lists of cryptic or ambiguously referential aphorisms, a story of a fatally wayward critic, an appreciation of a forging and murdering artist, and two dialogues involving voices that are not merely transparent representations of Wilde's own theoretical 'intentions' – *how* he makes his arguments often matters just as much as *what*, at isolated moments, they assert. Separated from their intellectual or discursive context – on bookbags or greeting cards – these statements amuse, convey a personality and perhaps seem cleverly apt. In their discursive context, they do much more. Wilde's response to important critical thinkers who preceded him, his critique of the prevailing wisdom of his time and his relevance to theoretical debates that continue to this day are considerable and warrant serious consideration.

Wilde's insistence on the separation between art and life, and his claim for art's priority in that pairing, point significantly to questions of aesthetic representation and reception that span the history of critical discourse from the classical age to the present. The privilege he gives to the imaginative, rather than mimetic, function of art recalls the ancient poetic dispute between Plato and Aristotle and also situates him in a tradition of poetic apologies from Sidney to the romantics. As Hazard Adams explains, Wilde recognizes in his own era that 'the theory of imitation was undergoing a crucial change. The trend, at least since Kant and Coleridge, had been to emphasize art's power to *make*, not to *copy*' (Adams 1992,

657). Like Pater's, Wilde's concept of aesthetic autonomy belongs to and raises the stakes of this intellectual current. If art does not primarily 'copy' life or nature, then what does it do? Wilde's provocative response to this question at once *severs* and *reverses* this mimetic relationship, proposing instead that 'Life imitates Art' (Wilde 1989, 985). Although it is the second effect – the reversal – in Wilde's proposal that has gained the status of truism, both of the gestures have significant implications within the history of critical theory.

In the first sense, the separation Wilde imposes upon the mimetic formula, upon 'natural' order from life to art, elaborates a chief tenet of Pater's aesthetic criticism: art in its highest form is something more and other than a mere reflection of the natural world. This emphatic distinction underwrites aestheticism's notorious insistence that, in Pater's words, '[t]he office of the poet is not that of the moralist' (Pater 1986, 427). For Pater, the true source of art – its 'active principle' – corresponds to what Wilde also privileges – 'imagination' (Pater 1986, 428). What it generates, for both of them, is 'beauty' and 'pleasure'. Wilde's at times outlandish preference for the artificial over the natural – his protagonist's refusal, for instance, to go outside in 'The Decay of Lying' – are best read within this specific context. As Pater explains in his essay, 'Wordsworth' (1874), the active principle in art is not entirely natural – not 'rooted in the ground' or 'tethered down to a world' – but rather 'something very different from this' (Pater 1986, 428). In the 'Preface' to *The Renaissance*, Pater calls this 'something' Wordsworth's 'unique, incommunicable faculty, that strange, mystical sense of a life in natural things', but he implies that this 'strange ... sense' might *itself* be of another order (Pater 1980, xxii). Even this quintessential nature poet, Pater audaciously suggests, produces his greatest work not in mirroring the world around him, but in 'moments of profound, *imaginative* power, in which the outward object appears to take colour and expression, *a new nature* almost, from the prompting of the observant mind' (Pater 1986, 424, emphasis mine). In such moments, 'the actual world would, as it were, dissolve and detach itself, flake by flake, and he himself seemed to be the creator ... of the world in which he lived' (424). In Pater's figuration here, the visiting light of the imagination upon the natural object decisively transforms it. The result is a 'new nature' and a different world.

The true task of the aesthetic critic, correspondingly, consists of discovering the elemental traces of such moments in the work of art – and again, aesthetic *separation* proves a key dynamic. Pater outlines this project in the 'Preface', where he characterizes the critic's work as a subliming process of elemental 'refinement'. The 'function of the aesthetic critic' – like that of a 'chemist' – 'is to distinguish, to analyse, and separate from its adjuncts' precisely what generates beauty from what does not. Reading Wordsworth's poetry, in particular, Pater argues the aesthetic critic must 'disengage this virtue from the commoner elements with which it may be found in combination ... [and leave] only what the heat of their imagination has wholly fused and transformed', thus subtly dismissing in the domestic, earth-bound aspects of Wordsworth's poetry nineteenth-century readers typically privileged (what Paul de Man calls the 'Victorian Wordsworth') (Pater 1980, xx–xxi). Though often by exaggerating it to the point of seeming elitism, translating it into impertinent solipsism or playing it up as the stereotypical dandy's hot-house cult of artifice, Wilde adheres closely to Pater's aesthetic vision.

The effective reversal in Wilde's life-and-art formula draws less directly from Pater and has, perhaps fittingly, become Wilde's signature claim. Yet it does not just describe the uncanny way in which real events seem to offer types or act out scenarios prefigured by artistic media, as it is popularly interpreted. Nor does it simply 'refer ... to the fact that fashionable ladies in the 1880s tried to dress and look like the beautiful figures in the paintings of Rossetti or Burne-Jones' (Zhang 1988, 90–1). Rather, Wilde argues we perceive the world by means of the conceptual models provided for us by art. 'Things are because we see them, and what we see and how we see it, depends on the arts that have influenced us', explains Vivian in 'The Decay of Lying' (Wilde 1989a, 986). No perception is immediate. What *is* is culturally constructed, and in a sense interpreted for us, already, by existing forms of understanding. While by no means original to Wilde, this observation highlights a significant post-romantic intellectual undercurrent to the prevailing realism and positivism of Victorian culture; namely, a growing scepticism in the possibility of objective perception, aesthetic or otherwise. In 'The Critic as Artist' and 'The Portrait of Mr. W. H.', his insistence on implicating critical discourse itself in this constructivist condition aligns him suggestively with Nietzsche and even Freud.

For this reason and others, Wilde's reversal resonates unmistakably with concerns central to contemporary theory. If, as Jonathan Culler has recently suggested, theory characteristically involves a critique of common sense and an interrogation of what we assume is 'natural', then Wilde's work is theoretical through and through (Culler 1997, 4). The aestheticism or decadence Wilde espouses declares itself overtly 'against nature' in its emphasis both on art's autonomy and on the constructedness of 'life'. As Linda Dowling argues, the aestheticist proposal announces a specifically late-Victorian state of affairs: a linguistic and epistemological condition wherein 'nature', 'reality' and 'truth' cannot be sustained as self-evident, stable or authoritative categories, if indeed they ever could be. Both Wilde's theory of art and his often affected stylistic self-consciousness, according to Dowling, 'emerge . . . from a linguistic crisis, a crisis in Victorian attitudes towards language brought about by the new comparative philology earlier imported from the continent' and largely inherited from romanticism (Dowling 1986, xi–xii).

One benefit of Dowling's reading is that it obviates the need to reconcile the seeming inconsistency between the gravity of Wilde's ideas and the levity of their presentation. In this light, we can see the relentless play of Wilde's texts – his dizzying use of paradox, the witty exaggerations, carefully staged dialogues and complex narrative frameworks – not as the frivolous camouflage for serious ideas, but as performative demonstrations of them. What Wilde's essays so often ironically present are occasions that raise, in Dowling's words, the 'spectre of autonomous language' – that is, adumbrations that our words might not correspond to our world or, more ominously, our 'intentions' in a harmoniously referential way (xii). In this sense, there is a profound consistency between the content of Wilde's aesthetic theory and his performative style. Dowling considers the latter a strategically formulated 'counterpoetics of disruption and parody and stylistic derangement, a critique not so much of Wordsworthian nature as of the metaphysics involved in any sentimental notion of a simple world of grass and trees and flowers' (x). For this reason, Dowling suggests that aestheticism and key poststructuralist projects – Foucault's, Derrida's – share a common critical lineage, albeit on separate sides of the 'metaphysical rupture brought about by Saussurean linguistics' (xiii).

A close look at Wilde's notorious use of paradox serves as an instructive illustration of the 'counterpoetics' Dowling describes. In all of his paradoxical assertions, Wilde takes the common-sense, apparently natural order of things (the *doxa*) and reverses it, goes against it (*para*) in a way that seems initially wittily absurd, but which comes to make a certain sense upon reflection. To cite just one example, we can look at the concluding sentences of Wilde's 'Preface' to *The Picture of Dorian Gray*, written in part to counter the moral opprobrium the novel's serial appearance first precipitated. Here, Wilde offers three declarations that, taken together, form a kind of skewed syllogism:

> We can forgive a man for making a useful thing as long as he does not admire it. The only excuse for making a useless thing is that one admires it intensely.
>   All art is quite useless. (Wilde 1989, 17)

In a text purportedly defending Wilde's own work of art, it seems absurd to declare such a work 'useless'. But the paradoxical logic draws out a key cultural assumption – in this case, the presumed connection between utility and value, especially with regard to art. He also glosses the seemingly obvious truth that what is 'useful' would also have more value than what is 'useless'. Wilde's apparently self-defeating defence, that '[a]ll art is quite useless', in fact, both articulates a long-standing bias – at least since Plato – that art is not socially or morally 'useful' and thus not valuable (or conversely, that it is useful, but only to the extent that it *does* serve society or morality) and turns it on its head. In the process, Wilde dislocates utility and value, makes them opposites and then reorders them, so that what is 'useful' becomes, paradoxically, what is *not* to be 'admire[d]'. And art's 'uselessness', in turn and inextricably within these terms, becomes its unique, lofty essence. Danson stresses the importance of context, both textual and intellectual, in understanding the force of such utterances: 'In Wildean paradox ... the ironized new meanings of words are only realizable in relation to their old meanings, which the paradox, for its subversive purpose, keeps in circulation' (Danson 1997, 150). Thus, the word 'useless' becomes a kind of portmanteau in which we may read a long history of aesthetic theory. His paradox glosses at once Plato's banishment of poetry from the republic, Kant's description of the aesthetic object's 'purposive purposelessness', the 'intense' aesthetic admiration Pater advocates, as well as the contemporary popular sentiment Wilde means to subvert.

The longer essays employ this strategy and others to enact a similar theoretical engagement. 'The Decay of Lying', the first and most anthologized essay in *Intentions*, is a not-quite Platonic dialogue considering the mimetic relationship between art and nature. The dialogue's title refers to an article Vivian (the parlour-room Socrates) reads to Cyril (his unequal foil) in the course of their discussion: 'The Decay of Lying: A Protest'. Vivian's 'protest' most pointedly objects to realism's dominance as an artistic method and aesthetic ideal in nineteenth-century art. But the protest is embedded in a larger discussion that both articulates aestheticism's central argument and situates it in long history of discourse on mimesis.

'[W]hat I am pleading for is lying in art', *not*, Vivian emphasizes, in spheres where lying merely serves venal interests – in politics, for instance. Vivian instead values the 'fine lie', informed purely by the imagination, and created solely for its own sake (Wilde 1989a, 971). This differentiation points to the first of his four 'doctrines of the new aesthetics', namely that 'Art never expresses anything but itself. It has an independent life ... and develops purely on its own lines' (991). As does the 'uselessness' argument in the 'Preface', Vivian's doctrine calls art a distinct enterprise not properly judged according to normative, rational standards of truth. In both instances, Wilde draws on the Kantian argument that 'to judge an art object in terms of use' – or truth value – 'is not to make an aesthetic judgement' (Adams 1992, 659). Kant's separation of aesthetic from rational or practical judgement also recalls Aristotle's rescue of poetry from Plato's banishment. Wilde's dialogue subtly restages the ancient poetic debate between Plato and Aristotle, echoing Aristotle's insistence that poetry – in medium and manner – operates differently than other forms of representation and should be judged accordingly. In characteristically paradoxical fashion, Wilde has Vivian explicitly enlist Plato himself in support of this argument as much as he does Aristotle. Adopting Plato's mimetic formula – wherein poetry, at two removes from 'truth', is a 'lie' – Wilde also turns it on its head. What Plato declares poetry's ultimate weakness Wilde celebrates as its unique strength.

Vivian's second doctrine argues that realism strays from art's distinct *raison d'être*. 'As a method, realism is a complete failure [for] it forgets that when art surrenders her imaginative medium she surrenders everything' (979). His supporting argument recalls Aristotle's own mode of defence. He offers an aetiological history of aesthetic development that sees imaginative instinct as its 'first stage': 'Art begins with . . . purely imaginative and pleasurable work dealing with what is unreal and nonexistent' (978). Like Aristotle, Vivian too claims that this primal instinct is 'natural'. But even more so, Vivian's 'first stage' is self-generated, 'natural' in that it stems from human nature, from within. We 'start . . . in life with a natural gift for exaggeration', and so too does art begin with this essential element (973). The second stage in this history might surprise those who read Wilde's separation of art and life absolutely, for here Vivian makes clear that there is indeed a connection – but a very particular one: 'Art takes life as part of her rough material, recreates it, and refashions it in fresh forms' (978). Like Pater's Wordsworth, who throws the light of his imagination on nature and produces 'a new nature', Vivian's vision of art relies on nature ('life') as well, but secondarily. Realism's crucial error is to reverse this proper order, to present a 'third stage' in which 'life gets the upper hand, and drives art into the wilderness'. By Wilde's subtle redefinition of the very label his critics used to condemn his aesthetic, realism's late aberration becomes art's 'true decadence, and it is from this that we are now suffering' (978).

Mistaking the proper relation between life and art, elevating life as an 'artistic method' instead of using it as 'rough material', stems from a more comprehensive misreading of the mimetic formula. This 'third doctrine' is the familiar suggestion that 'Life imitates Art far more than Art imitates Life' (985). In its service, Wilde provides Vivian with some of his most outrageous claims: that London fogs 'did not exist till art had invented them', that 'the whole of Japan is a pure invention. There is no such country, there are no such people' (986, 988). But of course, Vivian is not negating what 'exists' and what 'is', but placing them within a specific theory of perception. The outlandishness of the examples may stem from the fact that Cyril reminds Vivian that he needs these proofs to make his theory 'complete' and challenges him to do so. Vivian's flourish demonstrates that he confidently accepts the challenge: 'My dear fellow, I am prepared to prove anything' (986).

That Vivian indeed manages to show that what seems so patently false may possess a certain kind of truth underscores a further implication of 'The Decay of Lying', as well as its fourth doctrine. The aesthetic theory Vivian proposes does not sophistically devote itself to what is merely *false*. And the 'lying' Vivian values, ultimately, does not merely oppose truth, but rather a narrow understanding of it: 'not simple truth but complex beauty' (978). Perhaps recalling Keats, Vivian supplants 'simple truth' with 'complex beauty' and thus implicitly equates the latter with some higher, 'truer' object. The paradoxical, equivocal valence of 'truth' and 'lies' throughout the essay are contained in the essay's 'final revelation', that 'lying, the telling of beautiful untrue things, is the proper aim of art' (992).

'The Critic as Artist', also a dialogue, pursues many of these same assertions. Aestheticism's spokesman here is Gilbert, who corrects a number of 'gross popular error[s]' regarding criticism's proper relation to its aesthetic object. In typical Wildean style, Gilbert presents this hypothesis by means of counter-intuitive paradoxes that Ernest, more pugnaciously than Cyril, earnestly resists. 'The creative faculty is higher than the critical. There is really no comparison between them', intones Ernest, Wilde's voice of orthodox opinion (1020). Gilbert counters that we are wrong to consider criticism merely secondary to the work of art it interprets and never creative in its own right. He argues instead that this hierarchy is unstable, indeed 'entirely arbitrary' (1020). 'Criticism is itself an art', and conversely genuinely 'fine imaginative work' is actually critical (1026, 1020). For 'there is no fine art without self-consciousness, and self-consciousness and the critical spirit are one' (1020). Like poetry, criticism too involves a working with existing materials and putting them into a new form (1027). And here Gilbert insists that not only do poets work with words and generic conventions, they draw from existing works of art as well. Like Vivian, Gilbert argues that art imitates other art more often than life: Homer retells existing myths, Keats writes poems about a translation of Homer's retelling, and so on. The work of the critic is yet one more extension of that same process, its own retelling of what has been told before. The argument glosses Arnold's claim that 'the proper aim of Criticism is to see the object as in itself it really is' and rehearses Pater's response to it (1028). Like Pater, Gilbert believes instead that the critic's 'sole aim is to chronicle his own impressions' (1028). The critic deludes himself if he believes objectivity or 'discovering the real intention of the artist' is possible (1029). Gilbert's supporting example – in which he claims 'the work of art [is] simply ... the starting-point for a new creation' – subtly suggests that Pater's much criticized, idiosyncratic reading of the *Mona Lisa* might be remarkable not for how wilfully wrong it seems, but rather for how dramatically it demonstrates this discursive and epistemological condition (1029).

In fact, one may fruitfully read Wilde's 'Pen, Pencil and Poison' by the light of this proposal as well. Written in the style of Pater's *Appreciations* and *Imaginary Portraits*, the essay studies the 'artistic temperament' of Thomas Griffiths Wainewright, a minor nineteenth-century artist who was also a notorious forger and murderer. In 'The Critic as Artist', Gilbert tells Ernest that Pater's 'imaginative insight ... and poetic aim' – indeed his very words – suffuse his own impressions of the *Mona Lisa*. 'Pen, Pencil and Poison' makes such a tongue-in-cheek avowal of influence its guiding principle. Along with details from Wainewright's life and work (which Wilde liberally embellishes), the essay is strategically laced with plagiarisms from Pater's critical work. Wilde's 'new creation' from this raw material is at once a rehearsal of the critical ideal expressed in 'The Critic as Artist' and an ingenious parody of it. Taking aestheticism's purported separation between aesthetic and moral judgements, Wilde offers hyperbolic enthusiasm for Wainewright's work, impertinently insisting that '[t]he fact of a man being a poisoner is nothing against his prose' (1007). By giving his detractors such an outrageous version of aestheticism's ills – its flirtation with danger, its complicity with violence and amorality – Wilde satirizes their censorious objections and, in the process, offers his own subtle commentary on where the real force of Pater's critical project might lie. 'The Portrait of Mr. W. H.', Wilde's story of a wayward critic, explores similar ground. Obsessed with the personally overdetermined belief that he knows the 'true secret' of Shakespeare's sonnets, Cyril Graham wanders down the garden path from creative criticism to outright forgery, manufacturing evidence when he cannot find it. The story shrewdly outlines just how much epistemological desire, perhaps at the heart of creativity, necessarily drives the critical impulse. Our own critical projects, variously aimed at uncovering Wilde's true 'intentions', would do well to remember that lesson.

Megan Becker-Leckrone

Further reading and works cited

Adams, H. (ed.) *Critical Theory Since Plato*. Fort Worth, TX, 1992.

Beckson, K. (ed.) *Oscar Wilde: The Critical Heritage*. London, 1970.

Brown, J. Prewitt. *Cosmopolitan Criticism*. Charlottesville, VA, 1997.

Culler, J. *Literary Theory: A Very Short Introduction*. Oxford, 1997.

Danson, L. *Wilde's Intentions: The Artist in His Criticism*. Oxford, 1997.

Dellamora, R. *Masculine Desire*. Chapel Hill, NC, 1990.

Dollimore, J. *Sexual Dissidence*. Oxford, 1991.

Dowling, L. *Language and Decadence in the Victorian Fin de Siècle*. Princeton, NJ, 1986.

—. *Hellenism and Homosexuality in Victorian England*. Ithaca, NY, 1994.

Ellmann, R. *Oscar Wilde*. New York, 1988.

Gagnier, R. *Idylls of the Marketplace*. Stanford, CA, 1986.

— (ed.) *Critical Essays on Oscar Wilde*. New York, 1991.

Gillespie, M. P. *Oscar Wilde and the Poetics of Ambiguity*. Gainesville, FL, 1996.

Knox, M. *Oscar Wilde: A Long and Lovely Suicide*. New Haven, CT, 1994.

Kohl, N. *Oscar Wilde: The Works of a Conformist Rebel*. Cambridge, 1989.

Pater, W. *The Renaissance: Studies in Art and Poetry, The 1893 Text*, ed. D. L. Hill. Berkeley, CA, 1980.

—. *Three Major Texts: The Renaissance, Appreciations, and Imaginary Portraits*, ed. W. E. Buckler. New York, 1986.

Raby, P. *Oscar Wilde*. Cambridge, 1988.

— (ed.) *The Cambridge Companion to Oscar Wilde*. Cambridge, 1997.

Rieff, P. 'The Impossible Culture: Wilde as Modern Prophet', *Salmagundi*, 58, 1983.

Schmidgall, G. *The Stranger Wilde*. New York, 1994.

Showalter, E. *Sexual Anarchy*. London, 1991.

Sinfield, A. *The Wilde Century*. New York, 1994.

Small, I. *Conditions for Criticism*. Oxford, 1991.

—. *Oscar Wilde Revalued*. Greensboro, NC, 1993.

Stokes, J. *Oscar Wilde: Myths, Miracles, and Imitations*. Cambridge, 1996.

Wilde, O. *The Artist as Critic: Critical Writings of Oscar Wilde*, ed. R. Ellmann. New York, 1969.

—. *The Complete Works of Oscar Wilde*. New York, 1989a.

—. *Oscar Wilde's Oxford Notebooks*, eds P. E. Smith and M. S. Helfand. Oxford, 1989b.

Willoughby, G. *Art and Christhood: The Aesthetics of Oscar Wilde*. London, 1993.

Zhang, L. 'The Critical Legacy of Oscar Wilde'. *Texas Studies in Literature and Language*, 30, 1988.

The Cambridge School: Sir Arthur Quiller-Couch (1863–1944), I. A. Richards (1893–1979) and William Empson (1906–1984)

In 1910, Sir Harold Harmsworth (Lord Rothermere) donated money to Cambridge for a new Chair in honour of the late Edward VII to deliver courses on English literature from the age of Chaucer onwards, and to 'treat this subject on literary and critical rather than on philological and linguistic lines' (Brittain 1947, 57). After the death of the first classicist in post, Arthur Verrall (1912), when Prime Minister Asquith wanted the Donne scholar H. J. Grierson in post, Lloyd George persuaded him to make a political appointment of a Liberal (Tillyard 1958, 39). Hence Sir Arthur Quiller-Couch ('Q'), who had been knighted in 1910, became Professor. English was then not a separate subject, but part of the Medieval and Modern Languages Tripos, founded in 1883. In association with H. F. Stewart and H. M. Chadwick, Professor of Anglo-Saxon, 'Q' aimed at making English its own full subject. Philology, Anglo-Saxon and Middle English would be optional. The English Tripos was established in 1917, within the patriotic atmosphere that the war engendered (the Germanic associations of philology soured this discipline). 'Q', an Oxford classicist, writer and novelist, anthologist, and editor of fourteen of Shakespeare's Comedies for Cambridge between 1921 and 1931, who divided his time between Cambridge and Fowey in Cornwall, held that 'Literature cannot be divorced from life, that Literature cannot be understood apart from the men who have made it, that Literature is a living art, to be practised as well as admired' (Brittain 1947, 92). The genteel amateurism is worked into the study of literature from the beginning. Oxford had begun its English School in 1893, and had appointed Sir Walter Raleigh (1861–1922) in 1904 as Professor, but the differences that Cambridge English implied were soon to be noticed. The context of the new school fitted with the Newbolt Report, 'The Teaching of English in England' (1921, commissioned 1919) which urged the teaching of the national literature at all levels of schooling and at universities as a means of uniting divided classes after the war. Whereas Oxford and London, which had begun the study of English in 1859, placed Anglo-Saxon, philology and the history of the language near the centre of their English schools, and Oxford had until recently finished its syllabus at 1830, Chadwick moved Anglo-Saxon out of English, making it a cultural field of study in itself, so that Cambridge's syllabus, beginning with Chaucer, extended to the then present and responded to the modernism of the 1920s. Early lecturers in English at Cambridge included Mansfield D. Forbes, E. M. W. Tillyard, G. R. Coulton and H. S. Bennett (Medievalists) and F. L. Lucas; after 1924, when women were allowed to lecture, Hilda Murray and Enid Welsford. Basil Willey, T. R. Henn and F. R. Leavis followed.

Perhaps the most considerable voice was I. A. Richards, who, from an undergraduate degree in Moral Sciences (i.e. Philosophy), began lecturing in 1919 on the theory of criticism. Richards collaborated with C. F. Ogden (1889–1957) to produce *The Meaning of Meaning* which worked from the arguments about language then being made current by Peirce and Saussure, and paralleled by Wittgenstein in the *Tractatus Logico-Philosophicus* which aimed at identifying a foundation in semantics for linguistic statements. Richards and Ogden, borrowing from Jamesian pragmatism and behaviourism, held that meaning was dependent upon context, that words do not correspond to things. Yet this does not imply acceptance of the Saussurian arbitrariness of the signifier, and the relativity, therefore, of all systems of meaning: instead *The Meaning of Meaning* sees 'the relationship between words and things as *the* modern problem of knowledge, judgement and culture' but which can be solved by 'not making conceptual mistakes' (Bove 1986, 51). Attention to context will make mistakes avoidable, which is the positivism in Richards' thought, and his commitment to a belief in unitary truth. Insisting on the autonomy of science, in a way which made his thought hospitable to American pragmatism, Richards's position, from a marxist perspective, still the most influential one in reading Cambridge English, 'ends up obscuring the contexts in which questions regarding purpose and human meaning, deep moving forces of human life, can be given historical, non-metaphysical answers referring to the production and reproduction of the totality of human existence. In consequence he subverts the argument that problems of meaning can be resolved only through or in relation to human praxis. He himself will seek the solution in questions of mental organization' (Fekete 1977, 271). Whereas the progress of science was advanced and unquestionable, Ogden and Richards held that language uses in other areas were held back by the hold of mystical, superstitious attitudes towards language which prevented users of language from seeing its instrumentality.

With such a sense of the possibility of controlling language-use, which would eventually find its destiny in the project for Basic English, the authors divided language-uses up into the referential and emotive, keeping the first category for science and the latter for poetry. The symbolic use of words was statement, communication, while the emotive use of words expressed or excited feelings or attitudes. Poetry did not 'mean' something objective, but it worked upon feelings, and it was this which Richards followed up in later writings. Richards took from Coleridge and John Stuart Mill and Matthew Arnold the importance of nurturing feelings, and regarded poetry as a means of providing homeostasis, equipoise (as opposed to satisfaction), a calming of subjective feelings – on the principle that 'anything is valuable which will satisfy an appetency without involving the frustration of some equal or *more important* appentency' (Richards 1924, 48). The echo of the language of Jeremy Bentham and the Utilitarian implications of this are plain and can be contextualized through Richards's adoption for himself of John Stuart Mill's challenge of 1840: 'whoever could master the premises and combine the methods of [Bentham and Coleridge] would possess the entire English philosophy of his age' (Richards 1962, 18). Mill had been brought up as a Benthamite, and had found emotional stability through reading Words- worth: his essays on Bentham and Coleridge reflected his sense of the impossibility of putting together these two opposing voices and philosophies. Richards in the twentieth century hoped to combine Bentham's materialism and psychological determinism (he calls himself a Benthamite) with Coleridge's idealism and belief in the imagination as an integrative, unifying tendency, reconciling opposites. It will be recalled how, in Coleridge's *Biographia Literaria*, the 'secondary imagination' 'dissolves, diffuses, dissipates, in order to re- create; or, where this process is rendered impossible, yet still at all events it struggles to idealize and to unify' (Richards 1950, 516). According to Pamela McCallum, Richards 'wished to introduce to literary theory the apex of the early liberal tradition' (McCallum 1983, 88) – i.e. the moment when bourgeois ideology was not obviously wholly inflected by capitalism and its powers of destabilization – and he hoped also to incarnate a specific Englishness, identified with that liberalism. In this thinking, the limits of social, political and economic theory were defined through Bentham and the limits of thought about the individual or about imagination and the work of art were set through Coleridge. Poetry in the modern world could be justified for its contribution to feelings, but poetry in itself said nothing, its statements were 'pseudo-statements' (see Rosso 1989, 239). It had less to do with cognition than the ordering of attitudes. The crisis to do with the dominance of alienated science in modernity 'like every other problem in Richards, is interpreted as a problem of misunderstanding and hence is accessible to resolution on the level of consciousness' (Fekete 1977, 28).

At the same time, an Arnoldian stress appears in Richards in *Science and Poetry*, when he says that 'our protection [from the authority of science], as Matthew Arnold ... insisted, is in poetry. It is capable of saving us, or, since some have found a scandal in this word, of preserving us or rescuing us from confusion and frustration' (Richards 1970, 78). Salvation does not come from some act of the individual, even though the poet is 'the man who is most likely to have experiences of value to record. He is at the point where the growth of the mind shows itself ... his work is the ordering of what in most minds is disordered' (Richards 1924, 61). The modernism implicit in the sentence accounted for his essay on *The Waste Land*, just after its appearance in 1922 (Richards 1924, 289–96). The attempt to equate emotional education (ordering) with something scientific accounted for Richards's method of 'practical criticism' (Richards 1929), in *Practical Criticism*, the book which his biographer, John Paul Rosso, takes to be his 'masterpiece' (Rosso 1989, 294). The title Richards took from the opening of Coleridge's *Biographia Literaria*, chapter 15 (1950, 525). The book, comprising an examination of students and contemporaries' responses to poems including those by Leavis and Mansfield Forbes, contained approaches to thirteen undated and unsigned poems, including ones by Donne, Hopkins and Lawrence, and reads the students' responses to them. Cambridge English thus became identified with an empirical approach – in Richards's case, an empirical observation of other people working their way through the poems he had set – which presupposes an implicit refusal of theory, while not recognizing that the empirical approach was itself premised on theory. It involves a regulation of emotions, and a sense that a poem – or any literature – could be pronounced on for its worth outside of context.

In 'practical criticism', whose Benthamism is heard in Richards's will, as he puts it, to 'prepare the way for educational methods more efficient than those we use now in developing discrimination and the power to understand what we hear and read' (1929, 3) readers, whose power to respond to what they heard and read in, say, politics, was to be formed, defined and delimited on the basis of their response to the literary – had to respond to the sense of the poem and to its feeling, to its tone and to the author's intention, distinguished by Richards as 'the four kinds of meaning' (1929, 179–88). Judgement as to the worth of a poem came from attention to its details: from the idea of a union of sound and sense, the poem's aural patterning (e.g. in alliteration and assonance) corresponding to and amplifying its meaning which was immanent, immediately available and visible in the text's 'minute particulars' (Richards 1929, 302), and so ahistorical, not requiring any hermeneutic approach. By requiring the poem's rhythms and patterns of speech – matters of a reader's 'sensuous apprehension' – to follow the rhythms of everyday speech, the text allowed no space to notions of *ostranenie* (estrangement) such as Russian formalism allowed for. The result was the text's tendency towards conservatism, replicating the dominant ideology, the norms of present-day society, with no sense, for instance, of the power of alienation – this even though Richards offered the work as a study of 'comparative ideology' (1929, 6) and dwelt on the need to avoid the 'stock response' (1929, 15–16), where the reader's predisposition towards the sentiments expressed in the poem prevented a reading of what the text actually said – the phrase belonged to behaviourism and to the notion of a 'conditioned reflex'. Richards also used Freud to discuss inhibition, which he defined as a blocking off of necessary emotions, and sentimentality, which he saw as the opposite, squandering mental energy (1929, 255–70). Yet he employed psychoanalytic concepts 'without recognising their subversive, interrogative potential' (McCallum 1983, 73, compare Richards 1926, 29–30, where psychoanalytic criticism is accused of being 'unverifiable') and in doing so, implied his own delimiting of allowable emotions, whose class and gender bases and whose history were never examined.

Criticism is then an act of responding relevantly to the 'words on the page', giving an account of what the poem is doing, so that criticism becomes a means of saying more fully what the poem already said, and being passive before it requires a position on the reader's part. It is such a position which Raymond Williams finds to be a form of servility, as he also accuses Richards's position as servility to the literary establishment (Williams 1963 245; compare Fekete 1977 30). It produces, further, a pessimistic conclusion: that 'if poetry remains inscrutably impenetrable to the most suitable readers, it will be inaccessible to the majority of the population' (McCallum 1983, 74). In this sense of the near impossibility of changing the course of 'mass' culture, which in the work of Leavis and *Scrutiny*, became a full-scale cultural despair, passivity and pessimism were inseparable from a conservatism or reaction which was expressed literally, in suggesting that 'the arts are our storehouse of recorded values' (Richards 1924, 32), which means that education means passing on a received 'tradition', a term given new currency by T. S. Eliot. More subtly, the reactionary agenda appeared in that new, postwar undergraduates were being regimented towards 'right' feelings – which are also class-feelings – in a process of self-discipline, the passivity of reading being a form of depoliticization, and the intention being 'normalization' (Bove 1986, 61). On this reading, Cambridge English with Richards as its inspiration put in position a powerful set of tools to produce a new hegemonic subject, which, unlike Oxford English, would have the power of directly moulding thought through the nurture of sensibility and right feelings, and preserve a liberalism and humanism that concealed its own relationship to power. It is revealing to note how the opposition to Cambridge English from Oxford was characteristically expressed in terms of the Cambridge school's 'Puritanism' which was 'reluctant to regard literature simply as a matter for enjoyment' (Rosso 1989, 529). The Cambridge school in contrast to the Oxford – and class-distinctions are implicit in the use of the concept of the Puritan – looks to English as a means of critique, even critique of ideology. While this contains something positive, especially in its attention to 'literary language' and metaphor, its most obvious limitation is that it does not go outside the terms of the English liberal tradition in order to make that critique.

The tendency in Cambridge in the 1920s was modernist, and practical criticism may be seen as a strategy belonging to that ethos: 'practical criticism believes it can be successful if it can establish that reality is like a modernist poem: complex, ambiguous, interrelated but 'orderly' and finally 'static' in its 'organic' relationships. The poem and reality are both systems whose workings can be understood only on the model of the sublime intellectual's complex sensibility or reading skills' (Bove 1986, 54–5).

After 1929, Richards's rationalist tendencies increased in his attempts to give a utilitarian reading of Coleridge, in his attempts to classify metaphor in terms of tenor (the idea) and vehicle (what the principal subject is being compared to) in *The Philosophy of Rhetoric* (1936) and in his collaboration with Ogden on Basic English, carrying his critical belief in precise language to an experimentally reduced version of English with a vocabulary of 850 words, and intended for places where English might be a second language, especially China. In 1939 he became director of the Commission of English Language Studies at Harvard, and remained in America until 1974, returning then to Cambridge.

The Cambridge English Richards dominated through the 1920s had moved towards 'difficult' and 'strenuous' or 'muscular' poetry. The decade coincided with Cambridge's emphasis on Metaphysical poetry (and the diminution of Milton on account of his classicism): in 1926, T. S. Eliot gave the Clark lectures on 'The Metaphysical Poets' and the culmination of the decade, which saw the graduation of Muriel Bradbrook, the Cambridge Shakespeare scholar, and William Empson set its seal upon the importance of poetry held to be tough, rational, not plangent, anti-romantic, anti-Victorian and certainly anti-Georgian. Empson, who had read Mathematics before turning to English, was supervised by Richards in his final year, and produced *Seven Types of Ambiguity* the year following, as a culmination of work done with Richards (see Richards 1929, 340–5 on ambiguity as basic to language). Empson's poetry, which was praised by Leavis in *New Bearings in English Poetry* (1932) similarly showed the impact of Metaphysical poetry, its conceits, its wit, its rapid association of idea with idea.

Seven Types of Ambiguity took assorted passages of drama and poetry for analysis, and for its first six types located 'ambiguity' as a point of complexity in a text, and indicative of richness of thought in it, though even the first had the potential to explode Richards's neat sense of metaphor, for it implied that 'far from referring back to an object that would be its cause, the poetic sign sets in motion an imaging activity that refers to no object in particular. The "meaning" of the metaphor is that it does not "mean" in any definite manner' (de Man 1983, 235). It found ambiguity in Shakespeare and seventeenth-century poetry, but, predictably, given the temper of 1920s Cambridge English, much less in Victorian verse, with the exception of Hopkins. Eliot, too, as a modern displayed ambiguity. The seventh type of ambiguity, introduced by a reference to Freud's essay 'The Antithetical Meanings of Primal Words', showed 'a fundamental division in the writer's mind' (Empson 1930, 192) – ambivalence, rather than ambiguity, a contradiction that could not be resolved. Discussing Hopkins's poem 'The Windhover', a poem given some attention by Richards in 1926 (Richards 1976, 139–47) – Hopkins's verse had first appeared in volume form in 1918, and it was read as distinctively modern – Empson found in its use of the word 'Buckle', 'a clear case of the Freudian use of opposites, where two things thought of as incompatible, but desired intensely by different systems of judgements, are spoken of simultaneously by words applying to both' (Empson 1930, 226). Paul de Man, in 'The Dead-end of Formalist Criticism' (1954), writes of this seventh type in a piece on New Criticism which contrasts Empson with Richards. He finds Empson more interesting, and accuses Richards's criticism of being premised on 'the adequation of the object itself with the language that names it' (de Man 1983, 244). This, of course, harks back to the issues that haunt *The Meaning of Meaning*. Thus, de Man says, whereas Richards 'did recognise the existence of conflicts [in poetry] ... he invoked Coleridge, not without some simplification, to appeal to the reassuring notion of art as the reconciliation of opposites'. But in Empson's reading, 'the text does not resolve the conflict, it *names* it' (de Man 1983, 237). This reading of Empson has made him seem like a precursor of deconstruction (Norris 1985), and antagonistic to the strains in American New Criticism which see contradiction as subsumable under the formal headings of paradox, or tension or irony, an integral part of the poem's organisation: this is how de Man takes Empson. In relation to the ideology of Cambridge criticism, it will be seen that *Seven Types of Ambiguity* has the potential to undo the integrative tendencies of liberal thought, whose organicist images, in striving to idealize and unify, have the effect of insinuating the irrelevance of class difference, and impose an imaginary unity within the nation.

Empson followed *Seven Types of Ambiguity* with *Some Versions of Pastoral*, whose topic is not a separate genre called 'pastoral', since he says that the formula which applies to pastoral poetry – that of 'putting the complex into the simple' might include all literature (1965, 25). Literature here is thought of as ideology, whose pretension is that the complex – which may be indescribable, even sublime (in either the traditional or postmodern, Lyotard-derived sense of this term) may be thought of in terms of the unifying, whole terms of the text which itself may be criticized or appreciated. Richards's view of the relation of thought to expression, as de Man criticizes this, will come to mind. The consciousness in its split state invents at that stage of recognizing its condition as split (i.e. as complex) the notion of some natural, originary condition. De Man (1983, 238–45) picks on Empson's point that marxism itself is a form of pastoral to argue that the split Empson identifies is inherent to the state of Being (the Heideggerian tendency in de Man's thought), like the contradictoriness implied in the seventh type of ambiguity. By doing so, he depoliticizes and dehistoricizes Empson's text (for there is no moment when alienation has historically occurred: there is no development of a split within modern literature). The project of Richards-inspired criticism is 'to expect a reconciliation from poetry; to see in it a possibility of filling the gap that cleaves Being' (de Man 1983, 245); but Empson's criticism has the potential of showing the impossibility of doing this. Claiming Empson for deconstruction opposes one element in his thought to rationalism, but to date, the comparable project, of linking Empson's approach to language with Bakhtin on the dialogic, and thus showing how Empson's work is open to the presence of otherness, has not been undertaken.

Paul de Man comments on Empson's third book, *The Structure of Complex Words* in a later essay, 'Wordsworth and the Victorians' via Empson's essay 'Sense in [Wordsworth's] *The Prelude*' to argue that 'Empson shows that, if one follows the trace of a recurrent word in a given corpus, the emerging confusion cannot be reduced to any known model of trope that would control an identifiable semantic field; it is impossible, in other words, to make sense out of Wordsworth's "sense"' (de Man 1984, 88). 'Complex' in Empson's title derives from his definition of pastoral, and with Freud on antithetical meanings behind it contains his conviction that words are nodal points of contradictory senses which have been overdetermined historically. Empson reads literary history in words such as 'wit', 'fool' and 'folly' and 'honest' and 'sense' – terms which often enough presuppose clear distinctions between the clear and the non-clear, and finds ambiguity and complexity not at the level of a text's context, which is where Richards had started from, but in the buried history of apparently simple words. De Man reads Empson in a radical way, and derives a Wordsworth from him who is the opposite of the integrative Coleridge of Richards's arguments (and thus suggesting the possibility of rereading English romanticism) but it also as an argument runs counter to the rationalism in Empson (Fry 1991, 79) which impels a belief that 'you can decide what a piece of language conveys' (Empson 1951, 437), which allowed Empson to support Basic English (Empson 1987, 191–238), and which, more positively, structured his further study, *Milton's God*, whose target is the irrationalism of the 'neo-Christian', defined as 'those recent critics, some of whom believe in Christianity and some not, who interpret any literary work they admire by finding in it a supposed Christian tradition' (Empson 1985, 229).

Empson's direct targets are, in Milton studies, C. S. Lewis and E. M. W. Tillyard, and in the United States, Hugh Kenner's Catholic readings of Joyce (in contrast to Richard Ellmann's), Dorothy Sayers on Dante, and American New Criticism and T. S. Eliot, the argument being that English literature has become a way of presenting pseudo-metaphysics, occluding rationalism. Such a covert message in English studies promotes, for example, the pessimism of Orwell's *1984* – against which Empson contends that 'the human mind, that is, the public human mind as expressed in a language, is not irredeemably lunatic, and cannot be made so' (Empson 1951, 83). Empson's rationalism is repeated in Milton's Satan – 'a very argufying character' (1985, 62; i.e. not like a romantic poet, as in Blake) and

Empson's argument about Milton's *Paradise Lost* is that 'Milton ... positively denied [the] importance of blind obedience, and ... expressed anxiety verging upon horror lest God be found unjust' (1985, 286–7). Milton's God is not the Christian God, but an invention of Milton's, justifying an 'appalling' theology, and to read *Paradise Lost* adequately means not 'sinking [the] mind into the mental world of the author' on the assumption that such a mental world would be simply Christian. Instead, Empson assumes that Milton himself thought outside the terms of that mental world (1985, 204). The rationalism dehistoricizes, makes claims to be outside the relativity of historical systems of thought. The importance given to the story the epic tells (Empson, 1951, 36) is an example of how Empson implicitly rejects Richards's arguments for poetry as 'pseudo statements' in the sense that these in their apparent permission of illogic have allowed literature to become susceptible to religious readings (1951, 13).

Empson's rationalism means that he holds on to notions of intention, and to the author, and remains hostile to the theory with which Norris tried to identify him (1985, 20–1). Negatively it seems that Empson's agenda, by being focused on the English literature that he felt had been commandeered by neo-Christians, remained both too committed to identifying its form of rationalism with Englishness, and delimited its sense of religion in relation to middle-class views of Christianity. The paganism of Empson's thought did not extend as far as to, say, Bataille on the sacred, nor towards the transgressive. A fine reading of Cowper's poem 'The Castaway', whose theme is the subject's madness, goes through verse by verse, with detailed attention to the story, but has nothing at all to say about madness, or its existence as a limit-state; in this way, Empson, though madness had been a topic in his poetry, as in 'Let It Go' (1955, 81), and a topic for *The Structure of Complex Words*, turns away from exploring a state which would pull him away from certain conventionalities (1987, 289–96). He was caught, in his Milton discussions, by the common-sense terms with which more conventional critics than himself – such as C. S. Lewis – set the debate, and in this it seems that Empson's own thinking was more conventional than it should have been and necessarily more obsessed with issues that showed his entrapment in a subject too small for his talent. The Cambridge with which he sparred – though he never taught there – showed its continuing resistance to theory in the 'structuralist' arguments of 1979: in so doing it perpetuated its tendency to reify its institutionalized genteel amateurism in policing the bounds of the subject: a tendency which had been there from the beginning, and which played a sizeable role in limiting Empson's achievement to a certain provincialism of thought.

Jeremy Tambling

Further reading and works cited

Baldick, C. *The Social Mission of English Criticism, 1848–1932*. Oxford, 1983.
Bove, P. *Intellectuals in Power*. New York, 1986.
Brittain, F. *Arthur Quiller Couch: A Biographical Study of Q*. Cambridge, 1947.
Culler, J. *Framing the Sign*. Oxford, 1988.
de Man, P. *Blindness and Insight*. Oxford, 1983.
—. *The Rhetoric of Romanticism*. New York, 1984.
Eagleton, T. *Against the Grain*. London, 1986.
Empson, W. *The Structure of Complex Words*. London, 1951.

—. *Collected Poems*. London, 1955.

—. *Seven Types of Ambiguity*. Harmondsworth, 1961.

—. *Some Versions of Pastoral*. Harmondsworth, 1965.

—. *Milton's God*. Cambridge, 1985.

—. *Argufying*, ed. J. Haffenden. London, 1987.

Fekete, J. *The Critical Twilight*. London, 1977.

Fry, Paul H. *William Empson*. London, 1991.

Hawkes, T. *That Shakespeherian Rag*. London, 1986.

McCallum, P. *Literature and Method*. Dublin, 1983.

Norris, C. 'Some Versions of Rhetoric: Empson and de Man', in *Rhetoric and Form: Deconstruction at Yale*, eds R. Con Davis and R. Schliefer. Norman, OK, 1985.

— and Mapp, N. (eds) *William Empson: The Critical Achievement*. Cambridge, 1993.

Richards, I. A. *The Philosophy of Rhetoric*. Oxford, 1936.

— (ed.) *The Portable Coleridge*. New York, 1950.

—. *Principles of Literary Criticism*. London, 1960.

—. *Coleridge on Imagination*. London, 1962.

—. *Practical Criticism*. London, 1964.

—. *Poetries and Sciences*. New York, 1970.

—. *Complementarities*, ed. J. P. Russo. Manchester, 1976.

— with Ogden, C. K. *The Meaning of Meaning*. London, 1923.

Rosso, J. P. *I. A. Richards: His Life and Work*. London, 1989.

Tillyard, E. M. W. *The Muse Unchained*. London, 1958.

Williams, R. *Culture and Society: 1780–1950*. Harmondsworth, 1963.

James Joyce (1882–1941): Theories of Literature

If Joyce's central place in high modernism is undisputed today, the relationship between a masterpiece such as *Ulysses* and the literary or aesthetic theories developed in the novel and employed in its very construction is more complex, even contested. Besides, James Joyce, after a number of early experiments collected in his *Critical Writings*, soon decided not to write any self-contained aesthetic treatise and even more decidedly refused to engage at any length in the kind of critical writing that marked the works of immediate modernist contemporaries like Woolf, Pound, Lewis or Eliot.

If most readers of Joyce sense that there is something like an aesthetic theory that would be specific to his works, it is unlikely that two readers will agree as to what the term exactly covers. Rather than starting with an abstract definition of these terms, it might be more helpful to begin by surveying the available corpus. A good place to start might be Joyce's perception of his own canon in the making, as evinced by the proud assertion made to his mother (from his first Parisian 'exile') that among his projects, an aesthetic theory would have to figure prominently. In a juvenile manner, he outlines a work schedule filling up the two next decades: 'Synge says I have a mind like Spinoza! . . . I am at present up to the neck in Aristotle's Metaphysics . . . My book of songs will be published in the Spring of 1907. My first comedy about five years later. My "Esthetic" about five years later again. (This *must* interest you!)' (*L*, IV, 19) Surprisingly Joyce was in fact quite right about the first date: *Chamber Music* was actually published in 1907, while *Exiles* (if it can be called a 'comedy') was only started in 1914. But no 'Esthetic' was ever published or written – unless we count the few reviews and odd essays collected under the title of *Critical Writings* and add to them a few theoretical passages in *Ulysses* (1922), mostly culled from Stephen Dedalus's ruminations on art, paternity, creation and rhythm. Indeed, one could easily realize with Joyce's writings what Meschonnic had done with Mallarmé when he edited his 'Writings about the Book' and produced a careful selection of theoretical fragments from letters, reviews and essays that, put together, provide a strikingly coherent aesthetic. It might be harder to find a workable title in Joyce's case, although one could easily settle for a conservative subtitle such as 'post-Aristotelian poetics'. I will have to return to the philosophical lineage that Joyce had chosen for himself, and the fact that when he was supposed to follow medical studies in Paris, he spent most of his time in the Sainte Geneviève library opposite the Panthéon – not just contemplating his own inevitable immortality but reading Aristotle. This brief survey will find a focus in two main concepts that are not arranged historically but map out the entire field of what can be called a Joycean aesthetic theory: the epiphanies and mimesis.

Epiphanies

This is probably the term most lay readers will immediately associate with Joyce's aesthetics. Despite its familiarity and systematic occurrence in various contexts, its meaning and use are nevertheless quite tricky. The most detailed description is provided by Joyce in the unfinished manuscript called *Stephen Hero*. He begins with a famous example of a 'triviality' overheard as he passes through Eccles Street (the very street in which Molly and Leopold Bloom live in *Ulysses*):

> A young lady was standing on the steps of one of these brown brick houses which seem the very incarnation of Irish paralysis. A young gentleman was leaning on the rusty railings of the area. Stephen as he passed on his quest heard the following fragment of colloquy out of which he received an impression keen enough to afflict his sensitiveness very severely.
>
>   The Young Lady – (drawling discreetly) ... O, yes ... I was ... at the ... cha ... pel...
>   The Young Gentleman – (inaudibly) ... I ... (again inaudibly) ... I...
>   The Young Lady – (softly) ... O ... but you're ... ve ... ry ... wick ... ed.
>
>   The triviality made him think of collecting many such moments together in a book of epiphanies. By an epiphany he meant a sudden spiritual manifestation, whether in the vulgarity of speech or of gesture or in a memorable phase of the mind itself. He believed that it was for the man of letters to record these epiphanies with extreme care, seeing that they themselves are the most delicate and evanescent moments. (*SH*, 210–11)

What may puzzle one is the almost total lack of content in the actual words of a vignette that allegorizes a fascinating mixture of Irish paralysis and sexual banter. Moreover, this curious emptiness generates a serial concept: having captured one epiphany, Stephen decides to compose a whole book of them, showing concretely the link between two meanings of 'aesthetic *theory*': first, capturing a moment of revelation in a privileged glimpse or audition, then, through a 'procession' of these moments, the emergence of some sort of order or process underpinned by a new sense of authority. We know – and this complicates the picture – from archival evidence and the testimony of several friends and relatives that Joyce made no secret about his collecting these 'moments' in a book of epiphanies. The epiphanies appear thus as urban snapshots caught at unforeseen intersections, 'trivial' indeed from being generated by chance encounters with anonymous strangers seen or heard at crossroads rather than suggested by bucolic scenes remembered in romantic tranquillity.

When Robert Scholes edited all the extant epiphanies (forty short vignettes survive out of at least seventy-one according to Joyce's own numbering), he pointed out the variety of genres and scenes evoked: the short texts range between dream transcriptions and fragments of dialogues, between first drafts of relatively objective narrative passages and very autobiographical confessions. The impression left by them upon Joyce must have been very strong since these pre-written passages reappear systematically in the later fiction: *A Portrait of the Artist as a Young Man* seems to have been structured by at least twelve important epiphanies, from the first scene evoking castrating eagles (already in epiphany no. 1) to the last page with one of Stephen's diary entries saluting the 'spell of arms and voices' (which quotes epiphany no. 30). Some epiphanies recur with a curious and inexplicable insistence in all of Joyce's works, as the scene overheard at the corner of Connaught Street in epiphany no. 38 in which a male child only answers '. . . Na . . . o' to a young lady who asks him who his sweetheart may be, which is then reintroduced into the scene with Gerty MacDowell and the children who play on the beach in the 'Nausicaa' episode of *Ulysses*, to be finally reused in the Mime section of *Finnegans Wake* – this time, it is Glugg who tries to guess the name of a flower, answering negatively with a crescendo of 'Nao', 'Naoho' and finally 'Naohaohao' (FW, 233.21–6; see also 225.23–7).

Enigmatic as they may be, these recurrences should not veil another factor: as these pre-written fragments are reinscribed in the narrative texture, they lose their own appellation as 'epiphanies'. This is why the term is not even mentioned in *A Portrait of the Artist as a Young Man* whereas it has clearly become derogatory in *Ulysses*. (Stephen muses in ironic retrospection on his juvenile fantasy of sending copies of his 'epiphanies on green oval leaves' to 'all the great libraries of the world, including Alexandria'.) Critics like Scholes have speculated that this should be taken as a clear sign that by the late 1910s, Joyce did not believe in a theory of the epiphany any longer: the term can be employed to define a certain genre of writing, closer to his later systematic note-taking process (more recently, David Hayman has coined the category of 'epiphanoids' in *The 'Wake' in Transit* to describe the fragments collected in notebooks that cover all the personal vignettes, memories, dream fragments, bits of dialogue, passages from conversations that, till a very late stage, continue to find their way into the crowded and rather illegible pages of the archive, often to be reworked and introduced into the Wake.

One can notice that the epiphany does not aim at defining a type of object but a dialectical and temporal process linking an object and a subject in such a way that one will keep on hesitating between an objective pole (let us not forget that for the Stephen of *Stephen Hero*, 'the clock of the Ballast office was capable of an epiphany' (SH, 216), a fortiori, any object will be 'capable' of a similar process of inner and outer illumination) and a subjective pole (since it becomes a 'task' for the artist to 'record' these). Aesthetic pleasure might well consist in prolonging this hesitation, even more as we also hesitate between a religious and a profane sense of the term. Let us return to that famous Dublin clock in Stephen's optical and almost technological version of the theory of the epiphany – one can almost imagine a gigantic spiritual camera at work: 'Imagine my glimpses at that clock as the gropings of a spiritual eye which seeks to adjust its vision to an exact focus. The moment the focus is reached the object is epiphanised. It is just in this epiphany that I find the third, the supreme quality of beauty' (SH, 216–17). Here, the subjective pole is downplayed, a shift that is accounted for by the need for a general theory of aesthetic. Stephen follows suit with an attack on the idea of 'tradition' – 'No esthetic theory ... is of any value which investigates with the aid of the lantern of tradition' (SH, 217) – which allows him paradoxically to quote (and distort) Aquinas's three main concepts of 'integrity', 'wholeness' and 'radiance' in support of his theory:

> For a long time I couldn't make out what Aquinas meant. He uses a figurative word ... but I have solved it. *Claritas* is *quidditas*. After the analysis which discovers the second quality the mind takes the only logical possible synthesis and discovers the third quality. This is the moment which I call epiphany. First we recognise that the object is *one* integral thing, then we recognise that it is an organised composite structure, a *thing* in fact: finally, when the relation of the parts is exquisite, when the parts are adjusted to the special point, we recognise that it is *that* thing which it is. Its soul, its whatness, leaps at us from the vestment of its appearance. The soul of the commonest object, the structure of which is so adjusted, seems to us radiant. The object achieves its epiphany. (SH, 218)

If the epiphany is a manifestation of the very soul of any object chosen at random, it organizes a principle of individuation comparable to Duns Scotus's 'haecceitas' revisited by Hopkins: the absolute singularity shines forth and somehow proves the existence of a God who loves 'dappled' things. Joyce chooses Aquinas as a guide, although it has often been noted that he does this at the price of major distortions – for instance Stephen replaces the 'good' by the 'true' in his discussions of beauty, and he is very careful, as Noon has noted, to disentangle his line of reasoning from a theological system based upon the notion of divine and human love. One might say that the earlier formulations use a post-romantic opposition between the imagination and the intellect to steer away from ethical concerns, while the later rearrangements of aesthetic fragments in *A Portrait of the Artist as a Young Man* combine insights garnered from post-Hegelian philosophers of aesthetics like Bosanquet.

Joyce was not Hopkins, although he was a student in the same university – and he soon abandons the Platonician and romantic echoes of the theory when he rewrites *Stephen Hero*. In *A Portrait of the Artist as a Young Man*, all this phraseology recurs but without being underpinned by the momentous term of 'epiphany' so as to make the reader follow Stephen's 'curve of an emotion' while seeing the elaboration of the theory of epiphanies as a mere stage, a progression through juvenile neo-Shelleyian aesthetics. This seems to be confirmed by the fact that if the scene of the novella 'The Dead' in *Dubliners* takes place around the Epiphany, the usual associations of a 'manifestation' showing forth the divine nature of the divine child lead in this case to a final disclosure that appears much more negative. Gabriel does not bring any 'good news' to either the Virgin or himself, but confronts his own blindness, his selfishness and limitations. Like Stephen who brags about his new 'theory' concocted through an Aquinas he does not understand very well, Gabriel forces us to understand that there is a narrative process at work that is more crucial than the perception of the radiance of the thing qua thing. In that sense, one may say that the subjective pole has not been forgotten, it has simply been eclipsed for a while by the 'aesthetic theory' in order to return with a vengeance like the repressed of Freudian theory.

While showing us all the radiance of its manifestation, the epiphany has not concealed its part of blindness; it conveys an important connotation of 'betraying' or revealing something that had been concealed and in that sense should be connected with the loaded geometrical term of 'gnomon' offered as a hermeneutic key to the first story of *Dubliners*: a parallelogram with one corner missing. In that sense, Joyce's epiphany is never far either from the Freudian symptom or from the political drama of an Ireland systematically abused and betrayed from within and without. In Stanislaus Joyce's useful account, the 'manifestations or revelations' in which the epiphanies consist undo the very process of ideological concealment while exhibiting ironically the type of repression at work: 'Jim always had a contempt for secrecy, and these notes were in the beginning ironical observations of slips, and little errors and gestures – mere straws in the wind – by which people betrayed the very things they were most careful to conceal ... The revelation and importance of the subconscious had caught his interest' (Joyce, S. 1958, 134–5). A good exemplification would be epiphany no. 12 in which we see Hanna Sheehy, asked who might be her favourite German poet, reply sententiously after a pause and a hush: 'I think ... Goethe ...' Here, all the irony comes from the multiplication of the dots. This is an 'epiphany' because the pretensions of a shallow culture that takes itself too seriously have been caught in a moment of revelation that condenses an entire social symptom. In brief, the epiphany is not the key (given too soon in earlier drafts and then withheld for obscure reasons) of a theory of aesthetics but a bridge to a mimetic practice of language. It is therefore important to understand precisely what Joyce meant by mimesis.

Mimesis

In the Paris notebook (1903) one entry famously states: '*e tekhne mimeitaiten physin* – This phrase is falsely rendered as 'Art is an imitation of Nature'. Aristotle does not here define art; he says only, 'Art imitates Nature' and means here that the artistic process is like the natural process ...' (CW, 145). The replacement of the noun (*mimesis*) by a verb implies that mimesis is a process connecting art with life, and more precisely actively refusing any divorce between art and life. This seems to be a constant feature of Joyce's aesthetic theories, from the very early essay 'Drama and Life' (1900) that urges us to follow the model of Ibsen who has 'let fresh air in' (CW, 46) and shown us how to accept Life 'as we see it before our eyes, men and women as we meet in the real world, not as we apprehend them in the world of faery' (CW, 45), to a relatively late declaration made to an Irish friend, Arthur Power, a few years after *Ulysses* had been published: '... that is now what interests me most, to get to the residuum of truth about life, instead of puffing it up with romanticism, which is a fundamentally false attitude' (CW, 36). Here lies the source of the well-known 'classicism' of Joyce and of his resistance to a romanticism which he always associates with idealization and lyrical delusion (symptomatically, Power professed being a romantic himself). Ibsen, whom Joyce took as a literary example very early on, or Maupassant and Zola are thus superior to older models because they try to grapple with 'real life' in all its aspects.

This posture is in fact based upon Joyce's aesthetic tenets, and there again he finds Aristotle as a principal source of inspiration. If the *Poetics* define tragic drama as the 'imitation of an action' that produces pity and terror, it is because the playwright's aim is not the creation of a resembling picture of this or that man, but wishes to create emotions similar to those inspired by suffering characters like Oedipus. As Butcher's commentary on Aristotle's *Poetics* (a book upon which Joyce based his remarks, as Aubert (1992) and Schork (1998) have both demonstrated) insists, mimesis is the imitation of an action, of real 'men in action' (1895, 123). This is why music and dancing can be said to 'imitate' passions. Butcher concludes that 'imitation' is synonymous with 'producing' or 'creating according to a true idea' (1895, 153) which suggests a dynamic theory of an imitation linked with a living process and completely divorced from any preconception of the beautiful. Joyce's itinerary from Aristotle to Vico appears thus relatively direct, since both philosophers share the belief that imitation is a fundamentally human process and not based upon any notion of the beautiful or even limited to categories of aesthetics.

The concept of 'imitation' based on Aristotelian theories thus defines a psychological realism that has important consequences. As Stephen explains to a friend, 'Aristotle's entire system of philosophy rests upon his book of psychology' (APAM, 208). This position justifies an effort aiming at paralleling formal structures of the work of art with the stages of the mind's apprehension of it. Psychology and aesthetics are both underwritten by a more fundamental genetic and mimetic rationality since aesthetics cannot become a 'science of the particular' without accounting for its own genesis. Here lies the main quandary of A Portrait of the Artist as a Young Man, a Bildungsroman in which the description of aesthetic experience explains how any subject is bound to follow Stephen and apprehend the three stages of the individuating beauty in an object, and also lays the foundations of a quasi biographical narrative.

In Stephen Hero, the youthful Stephen Dedalus had been presented as a 'hero' when he managed to link the production of an aesthetic theory with an attitude of refusal or subversion of dominant values. This is accompanied by an attendant fetishization of the word 'theory', the term being a short-cut for 'aesthetic theory' but brandished in a repeated gesture of distanciation and negation, but also of ecstatic contemplation leading to a heightened sense of revelation – as when Stephen is described as exultant, under the shock of the vision of a young girl wading in the sea at the end of chapter IV in A Portrait. We have seen that the Aristotelian heritage claimed by Joyce leads him to refuse any notion of beauty as a guiding principle or Platonician essence. Does this for all that push him closer to a concept of the sublime? This is what Ginette Verstraete (1998) has argued about a Joycean 'feminine sublime' based less on Kant or Hegel than on Schlegelian aesthetics (possibly mediated by Croce). If a new 'feminine sublime' can be described, it would fundamentally encompass ugliness and ridicule. And even if Joyce was not aware of Schlegel's theses, he shares his basic insight into the duplicity, irony and reversibility of any gendered version of the Sublime.

Joyce thus soon felt the need to move beyond the confines of German romanticism, whether it be under its neo-Hegelian aspect with Bosanquet, or under a more Schlegelian guise, to engage less with offshoots of Hegelianism than with earlier forms of 'philosophy of history'. History had to embody the very site of a mimesis that did not wish to be measured by subjective psychological categories alone, or of a sublime that tended to overthrow all the older 'forms' determined by previous representations. This is why in philosophical and aesthetic terms, Joyce deliberately 'regresses' from Hegelianized theories of History to Vico's ricorsi storici in the New Science. Vico becomes his favourite source of inspiration because his aesthetics (like the investigations into the 'true Homer', or the theories of a 'poetic language' full of bodily metaphors) cannot be distinguished from his theory of the cyclical return of cultures and civilizations.

In Vico's New Science, however, Joyce also found another version of the Aristotelian notion of mimesis as a congenital property of men's activities in the world. The concept of mimesis was then be reinterpreted in the terms of what Vico calls the world of 'civil society', which is in fact (according to Vico) the only world that we can ever know since we cannot fathom the world of absolute truths that would reside in God only. It is the world of historical and social artefacts kept for us in monuments and language. For instance, in Vico's account of the genesis of language, some archaic giants who had thus far been sporting in the open evolved a mimetic response to the noise of the thunder which they took for God's angry rebuke at their sexual licence. These primitive beings then took refuge in caves where they invented marriage ceremonies, then added funerary rituals and started using language to distinguish relations of parenthood. The basic institutions of social life were thus invented: religion, marriage and burial. These first men who acted like children who imitate everything around them also gave birth to our distinctively human world – and it is the epic of this slow historical process that is being narrated in *Finnegans Wake*.

Joyce's mimetic theory – in a somewhat unexpected derivation – finally generates a theory of a universal language. As Joyce was toiling on his 'Work in Progress', a book he took seventeen years to complete and whose concept was based on the combined theories of Giordano Bruno and Giambattista Vico, he found an unforeseen help in the work of a French Jesuit, father Jousse. Jousse, who had started by investigating what he called the 'rhythmico-motric' style of a historicized Jesus whom he saw primarily as a Rabbi who wished to teach in such a way that his words would never be forgotten, and for that aim exploited all the resources of an embodied memory, must have looked to Joyce as a belated confirmation of his earlier theories about rhythm and language. Indeed, in the 1907 'Trieste Notebook', one finds under the heading of 'Esthetic' several entries that bear on this issue. The last of them is 'The skeleton conditions the esthetic image' and it comes just after: 'Art has the gift of tongues' and 'Pornography fails because whores are bad conductors of emotion'. This is echoed by Stephen in *Ulysses* where he is seen in 'Circe' entering the red light district of Dublin and exclaiming drunkenly: 'So that gesture, not music not odours, would be a universal language, the gift of tongues rendering visible not the lay sense but the first entelechy, the structural rhythm', to which his companion Lynch replies: 'Pornosophical philotheology'. We are thus sent back to much earlier discussions of the 'static' nature of beauty as opposed to a negative dynamism of desire in pornography in the Paris notebook and *Stephen Hero*. Here, Joyce reaches a satisfactory conclusion through Stephen's divagations, which also provides him with a basis for the construction of the 'tower of Babel' of the Wake. Jousse's idea of a rhythmic verbo-motricity based on the bilateral nature of the body and the brain confirms earlier speculations on the silent language of gesture and the principle of basic rhythm that would underpin Universal History. This is why one can assert that the language of the Wake is mimetic throughout (it is easy to provide examples of lisping 'baby talk' with Issy or of male Freudian symptoms betraying lust or hunger in Shaun's absurdly greedy speeches). Jousse and Vico agree with Joyce on one central point: it is the human body that becomes the foundation not only for the creation of poetic metaphors but also for the rhythmic reception of the structural 'music of time' thus produced. This is why *Finnegans Wake* avoids falling into the trap of Jungian universal archetypes, while working through bodily music and literary stereotypes based upon a synthetic universal language.

Jean-Michel Rabaté

Further reading and works cited

Aubert, J. *The Aesthetics of James Joyce*. Baltimore, MD, 1992.
Bosanquet, B. *A History of Aesthetics*. London, 1982.
Butcher, S. H. *Aristotle's Theory of Poetry and the Fine Arts*. London, 1895.
Eco, U. *The Aesthetics of Chaosmos: The Middle Ages of James Joyce*. Tulsa, OK, 1982.
Hayman, D. *The 'Wake' in Transit*. Ithaca, NY, 1990.
Jaurretche, C. *The Sensual Philosophy: Joyce and the Aesthetics of Mysticism*. Madison, WI, 1997.
Jousse, M. *The Oral Style*. New York, 1990.
Joyce, J. *Finnegans Wake* [FW]. London, 1939.
—. *Stephen Hero* [SH] London, 1956.
—. *Critical Writings* [CW] eds E. Mason and R. Ellmann. New York, 1964.
—. *A Portrait of the Artist as a Young Man* [APAM] ed. C. Anderson. New York, 1968.
—. *Selected Letters* [L, IV], ed. R. Ellmann. London, 1975.
—. *Ulysses*, ed. H. W. Gabler. London, 1986.
—. *Dubliners*, ed. T. Brown. London, 1992.
Joyce, S. *My Brother's Keeper*. New York, 1958.
McGrath, F. C. *The Sensible Spirit: Walter Pater and the Modernist Paradigm*. Tampa, FL, 1986.
Mahaffey, V. 'Joyce's Shorter Works', in *Cambridge Companion to James Joyce*, ed. D. Attridge. Cambridge, 1990.
Mallarmé, S. *Ecrits sur le Livre*, ed. H. Meschonnic. Paris, 1985.
Noon, W. T. *Joyce and Aquinas*. New Haven, CT, 1957.
Power, A. *Conversations with James Joyce*. London, 1974.
Scholes, R. (ed.) *The Workshop of Daedalus*. Evanston, IL, 1965.
— and Corcoran, M. G. 'The Aesthetic Theory and the Critical Writings', in *A Companion to Joyce Studies*, eds Z. Bowen and J. F. Carens. Westport, CT, 1984.
Schork, R. J. *Greek and Hellenic Culture in Joyce*. Gainesville, FL, 1998.
Tysdahl, B. J. *Joyce and Ibsen*. Oslo, 1968.
Verene, D. P. (ed.) *Vico and Joyce*. Albany, NY, 1987.
Verstraete, G. *Fragments of the Feminine Sublime in Friedrich Schlegel and James Joyce*. Albany, NY, 1998.
Walton Litz, A. *The Art of James Joyce*. New York, 1961.
Weir, L. *Writing Joyce*. Bloomington, IN, 1989.

Virginia Woolf (1882–1941): Aesthetics

Many of the fundamental ideas and debates of literary criticism and theory concerned with modernism, feminism and even postmodernism have been shaped by and with reference to the work of Virginia Woolf. Although she did not write in the style of high theoretical discourse, Woolf has been recognized for her experimentalism with, and transformation of, critical writing itself. Her avant-garde novels, essays and short stories have been read with one eye on her notoriety as a leading member of what later was called the Bloomsbury Group. Other members of this liberal, pacifist and at times libertine intellectual enclave of Cambridge-based privilege included art critics Roger Fry and Clive Bell, artists Vanessa

Bell (Woolf's sister) and Duncan Grant, economist Maynard Keynes, critic Lytton Strachey, novelist E. M. Forster and political journalist and publisher Leonard Woolf (Woolf's husband). Virginia Woolf's aesthetic understanding was in part shaped by, and at first primarily interpreted in terms of, (male) Bloomsbury's dominant aesthetic and philosophical preoccupations, rooted in the work of G. E. Moore, and culminating in a pioneering aesthetic formalism. But, increasing awareness of Woolf's feminism and of the influence on her work of other women artists, writers and thinkers has meant that these points of reference, though of importance, are no longer considered adequate in approaching Woolf's aesthetic. Woolf's writing has been of central interest to the major shifts in feminist critical debates concerning, in the 1970s, marxism, materialism and androgyny, in the 1980s subjectivity and textuality, and more recently historicist, cultural materialist and postcolonialist theories.

Woolf was not only a writer of experimental fiction but also (from a young age) a professional reviewer, publishing many anonymous reviews, for example, in the *Times Literary Supplement*; a biographer (*Roger Fry* (1940)); an accomplished and innovative essayist – she published two collections of essays as *The Common Reader* (1925 and 1932), and several collections have appeared since her death; an impressive polemicist (*A Room of One's Own* (1929) and *Three Guineas* (1938)); and not least, along with her husband, a successful and influential publisher. The Hogarth Press was responsible, for example, for the first major works of Freud in English, and published significant works by key modernist writers such as T. S. Eliot and Gertrude Stein. Since her death the publication of Woolf's private and personal writings has provided a rich and controversial literary and critical resource, which is often cited in commentaries on Woolf's fiction and on modernist writing more generally, and which has also been influential in recent theorizing on autobiography.

While her fiction has always been central to canonical high modernism, some of her work in other genres has come to dominance more recently, not least because of its transgeneric qualities (although a number of Woolf's novels also push the boundaries of genre, experimenting, for example, with elegy, journalese and academic biography). The (draft) essay-novel, *The Pargiters* (published posthumously, 1978), was an ambitious project conceived to combine critical and political argument with fictional narrative, which Woolf eventually divided for publication into two works, the epistolary anti-fascist, pacifist polemic, *Three Guineas*, and the conventional novel, *The Years* (1937). Her feminist tract, *A Room of One's Own*, undoubtedly her most important contribution to literary criticism and theory, notoriously blurs the boundaries between critical and fictional discourses. It is regarded as a founding text for feminist aesthetics, not least because it is also a source of many, often conflicting, theoretical positions. *A Room of One's Own* is cited as *locus classicus* for a number of important modern feminist debates concerning: gender, sexuality, materialism, education, patriarchy, androgyny, subjectivity, the feminine sentence, the notion of 'Shakespeare's sister', the canon, the body, race, class, and so on. Woolf's other texts of significance to literary theory include: the essays 'Modern Fiction' (1919), 'Mr Bennett and Mrs Brown' (1924) and the short story 'The Moment: Summer's Night' (c.1929), all of which have been influential in the theorizing of modernism; the essays 'Memories of a Working Women's Guild' (1930), 'Professions for Women' (1931) and the 'The Leaning Tower' (1940), which have influenced theories of feminism, class and fiction; and the posthumously published collection of autobiographical writings *Moments of Being*, which includes the memoir, 'A Sketch of the Past' (c.1939), where Woolf explains her 'philosophy' in terms of epiphanic moments. Her critical writing is discussed below in terms of modernism and feminism.

Modernism

'Modern Fiction', first published in April 1919 (as 'Modern Novels') and revised for the first *Common Reader* (it is the revised, 1925, version – often dated 1919 – that is commonly anthologized and cited here), is perhaps Woolf's most well known and most frequently quoted essay. Woolf here distinguishes between the outmoded 'materialism' of the Edwardian novelists, H. G. Wells, John Galsworthy, and Arnold Bennett, and the more 'spiritual' and experimental writing of her Georgian contemporaries. The tyranny of plot and characterization afflicts Bennett's work, she contends, along with the obligation 'to provide comedy, tragedy, love interest, and an air of probability embalming the whole so impeccable that if all his figures were to come to life they would find themselves dressed down to the last button of their coats in the fashion of the hour' (*Essays*, 4, 160). Such writing fails to capture 'life', as Woolf's most famous and most quoted passages of criticism explains:

> Look within and life, it seems, is very far from being 'like this'. Examine for a moment an ordinary mind on an ordinary day. The mind receives a myriad impressions – trivial, fantastic, evanescent, or engraved with the sharpness of steel. From all sides they come, an incessant shower of innumerable atoms; and as they fall, as they shape themselves into the life of Monday or Tuesday, the accent falls differently from of old; the moment of importance came not here but there; so that, if a writer were a free man and not a slave, if he could write what he chose, not what he must, if he could base his work not upon convention, there would be no plot, no comedy, no love interest or catastrophe in the accepted style, and perhaps not a single button sewn on as the Bond Street tailors would have it. Life is not a series of gig lamps symmetrically arranged; life is a luminous halo, a semi-transparent envelope surrounding us from the beginning of consciousness to the end. Is it not the task of the novelist to convey this varying, this unknown and uncircumscribed spirit, whatever aberration or complexity it may display, with as little mixture of the alien and external as possible? (160–1)

Woolf's story, 'The Moment: Summer's Night', offers a closer, equally lyrical, account of a luminous moment, and is often cited in conjunction with this passage, which, in advocating subjective, fleeting, interior, experience as the proper stuff of fiction along with the abandonment of conventional plot, genre and narrative structure, has become one of the standard critical sources in the discussion of modernist literary qualities – particularly 'stream-of-consciousness' – not least because it is followed by a (not uncritical) defence of James Joyce's work. Woolf cites his *Portrait of the Artist as a Young Man* (1916) and the extracts from *Ulysses* (1922) recently published in the *Little Review* (1918) to exemplify the new 'spiritual' writing. Joyce, she argues, is 'concerned at all costs to reveal the flickerings of that inmost flame which flashes its messages through the brain' (*Essays*, 4, 161). Woolf's alchemical imagery here owes much to Walter Pater's aesthetics, and her concern with subjective temporality – the epiphanic 'moment' – to the philosophy of Henri Bergson. Although Woolf identifies, in 'Modern Fiction', a fragment of *Ulysses* ('Hades') as a 'masterpiece' for 'its brilliancy, its sordidity, its incoherence, its sudden lightning flashes of significance', she nevertheless finds that it 'fails to compare' with the work of Joseph Conrad or Thomas Hardy 'because of the comparative poverty of the writer's mind' (161). Woolf is less generous to Joyce in private. On reading *Ulysses*, she notoriously captures him in her diary as 'a queasy undergraduate scratching his pimples' (*Diary*, 2, 188). 'Modern Fiction' nevertheless stands as an early and significant defence of his work, and as a manifesto of modernism.

'Mr Bennett and Mrs Brown', like many of Woolf's essays, evolved from a speech (in this instance to the Cambridge Heretics Society), and many of its rhetorical features survive into the published text. Here Woolf continues her assault on the Edwardians, Wells, Galsworthy and Bennett, for their materialist conventions, and her uneven defence of the Georgians, Joyce, Eliot, Forster, Lytton Strachey and D. H. Lawrence, whose work, she declares, must make us 'reconcile ourselves to a season of failures and fragments' (Essays, 3, 435). The essay's title is derived from its central, virtuoso, conceit whereby Woolf illustrates the inadequacies of the Edwardian novelists as she makes a number of attempts, using their 'tools', to construct a fictional narrative about the character of 'Mrs Brown', a stranger encountered on a train. The essay also contains one of Woolf's most famous, and most quoted, assertions: 'on or about December 1910 human character changed' (421). This has come to represent for many cultural commentators the cataclysmic moment of modernity, the inception of the avant-garde, the shock of the new. In the context of the essay, it marks the shift from the Edwardian to the Georgian era, when 'all human relations have shifted – those between masters and servants, husbands and wives, parents and children. And when human relations change there is at the same time a change in religion, conduct, politics, and literature' (422). But Woolf is not arguing that literature merely changes in terms of subject matter to reflect new, modern, experience, but that literary form itself undergoes radical and turbulent, transformation: 'And so the smashing and the crashing began ... Grammar is violated; syntax disintegrated' (434). The work of Joyce, Eliot and Strachey illustrate the point that modern literature has necessarily become caught up in the business of finding new form. Readers must 'tolerate the spasmodic, the obscure, the fragmentary, the failure' (436). The self-reflexive, fragmentary, subjective and momentary qualities of modernist writing are, of course, acknowledged and celebrated by Woolf's avant-garde contemporaries, but her own particular aesthetic was anathema to some. Woolf's 'luminous halo' metaphors, for instance, 'imply an art that rejects precise statement and moral certainty', according to M. H. Levenson, 'in favour of the suggestiveness and imprecision usually associated with symbolism or Impressionism. [Ezra] Pound on the other hand, opposed all "mushy technique" and "emotional slither", preferring a poetry "as much like granite as it could possibly be"' (1989, 154–5). In quoting from Pound's essay, 'The Hard and the Soft in French Poetry', and reflecting T. E. Hulme's taste for 'hard' poetry, Levenson alerts us to the critical ruptures of the period. Yet there is common ground between Woolf and Pound. Eliot, who owed much to Pound, for example, was also championed by Woolf.

Feminism

It was not only her choice of metaphor that could distance Woolf from her male contemporaries, but her feminism. 'There are spots of it all over her work,' according to her friend Forster, 'and it was constantly in her mind' (1997, 34). But even he acknowledged A Room of One's Own as 'brilliant' (34). The title alone has had enormous impact as cultural shorthand for a modern feminist agenda, while the book itself is widely regarded as 'the first book of feminist literary criticism' and 'the founding text of Anglo-American feminist literary theory' (Gallop 1992, 77, 145). Woolf developed the text from two lectures to Cambridge women students and an essay version on 'Women and Fiction', and although much revised and expanded, the final version significantly retains the original's sense of a woman speaking to women. Woolf again adopts fictional narrative strategies and shifting narrative personae to present her argument. She anticipates postmodernist, post-Lacanian, theoretical concerns with the constitution of gender and subjectivity in language when she begins by declaring that ' "I" is only a convenient term for somebody who has no real being ... (call me Mary Beton, Mary Seton, Mary Carmichael or by any name you please – it is not a matter of any importance)' (1992a, 5). Woolf here invokes the Scottish ballad 'The Four Marys', and ventriloquizes much of her argument through the voice of her own 'Mary Beton' (Marcus 1987a, 197). In the course of the book she encounters the other Marys – Mary Seton has become a student at 'Fernham' college and Mary Carmichael an aspiring novelist – and it has been suggested that Woolf's opening and closing remarks may be in the voice of Mary Hamilton (the narrator of the ballad). This multivocal strategy, along with the text's multitude of other citations, has encouraged later feminists to celebrate A Room of One's Own as a dialogical text. The intertext with the Scottish ballad feeds a subtext in Woolf's argument concerning the suppression of the role of motherhood – Mary Hamilton sings the ballad from the gallows where she is to be hung for infanticide. (Marie Carmichael, furthermore, is the nom de plume of contraceptive activist Marie Stopes who published a novel, Love's Creation, in 1928.) Woolf further insists, in her later essay, 'Professions for Women', on the woman writer's necessary suppression of a traditionally submissive – and domestic – feminine role, encapsulated in Coventry Patmore's 'Angel in the House': 'Had I not killed her she would have killed me. She would have plucked the heart out of my writing. . . . Killing the Angel in the House was part of the occupation of a woman writer' (153).

Woolf's main subject in A Room of One's Own is, as her earlier title indicates, 'Women and Fiction', and her main argument is that 'a woman must have money and a room of her own if she is to write fiction' (1992a, 4). Woolf's contempt for the 'materialism' of the Edwardian novelists seems forgotten here, as the narrator begins by recounting her experience at Oxbridge where she was refused access to the library, and compares in some detail the splendid opulence of her lunch at a men's college with the austerity of her dinner at a more recently established women's college (Fernham). This account is the foundation for the book's main, materialist, argument: 'intellectual freedom depends upon material things' (141). Woolf extends this line of argument in her later essay, 'The Leaning Tower', a paper she read to the Workers' Educational Association, to discuss the class alignments of writing. She claims that 'all writers from Chaucer to the present day . . . come from the middle class' and 'were educated at public schools and universities' (165). D. H. Lawrence is her only exception. She rallies her working-class audience by insisting 'we are not going to leave writing to be done for us by a small class of well-to-do young men who have only a pinch, a thimbleful of experience to give us. We are going to add our own experience, to make our own contribution' (178). If the categorization of middle-class women like herself with the working classes seems problematic here, Woolf has already proposed, in A Room of One's Own, that women be understood as a separate class altogether. Here is the nub of contention in feminism's encounters with marxism. Yet the alignment of women and the working class is hardly exclusive to Woolf. A Room of One's Own was published in the year after the full enfranchisement of women, ten years after the enfranchisement of working-class men along with middle-class, propertied women over 30 years of age. Woolf's point concerns the exclusion of women and the working classes from material resources and education. In 'Memories of a Working Women's Guild' she explores the complexities of her position as an educated and privileged middle-class woman aligned with working-class women in organized feminist politics. In Three Guineas,

Woolf's counterblast to fascism (which she aligns with patriarchy), she more radically separates off the category of women as, paradoxically, transcending all boundaries, including national ones: 'As a woman, I have no country. As a woman I want no country. As a woman my country is the whole world' (1992a, 313).

Woolf puts forward, in *A Room of One's Own*, a sophisticated and much-quoted simile for the material basis of literary production when she begins to consider the apparent dearth of literature by women in the Elizabethan period:

> For it is a perennial puzzle why no woman wrote a word of that extraordinary literature when every other man, it seemed, was capable of song or sonnet. What were the conditions in which women lived, I asked myself; for fiction, imaginative work that is, is not dropped like a pebble upon the ground, as science may be; fiction is like a spider's web, attached ever so lightly perhaps, but still attached to life at all four corners. Often the attachment is scarcely perceptible; Shakespeare's plays, for instance, seem to hang there complete by themselves. But when the web is pulled askew, hooked up at the edge, torn in the middle, one remembers that these webs are not spun in mid-air by incorporeal creatures, but are the work of suffering human beings, and are attached to grossly material things, like health and money and the houses we live in.

Feminist scholarship has since corrected the view of a singularly male Elizabethan literary canon, while feminist literary theory has claimed 'Virginia's web' as a defining figure for writing by women. The passage offers a number of different ways of understanding literary materialism. Firstly, it suggests that writing itself is physically made, and not divinely given or unearthly and transcendent. Woolf seems to be attempting to demystify the romantic figure of the (male) poet or author as mystically singled out, or divinely elected; but this idea is also connected to a strand of modernist aesthetics concerned with writing as a self-reflexive object and to a more general sense of the materiality of the text, the concreteness of words, spoken or printed. Secondly, the passage suggests writing as somatic process or bodily production. The material status of the body is far from stable here, and the figure of the spider suggests a gendered somatic model of writing. Thirdly, writing as 'the work of suffering human beings' suggests that literature is produced as compensation for, or in protest against, existential pain and material lack. Finally, moving from this general sense of connection with human lived experience to a more specific one, in proposing writing as 'attached to grossly material things, like health and money and the houses we live in', Woolf is delineating a model of literature as grounded in the 'real world', that is in the realms of historical, political and social experience. This latter position may be broadly associated with marxist literary theory, but Woolf's work cannot very readily be reconciled to this category *per se*, and it is possible to understand, in any case, this sense of materialism as not strictly speaking marxist. It should be noted that *A Room of One's Own*, experimental in form, appeared before the Soviet and marxist anti-modernist strictures of the 1930s after which social(ist) realism was the dominant marxist aesthetic; and this has some bearing on later feminist debate, in the 1980s, centring on this work (see Moi 1985). It is not merely Woolf's avant-garde aesthetic, however, that problematizes this work's relationship to marxism, but – more significantly – her feminism. Attempts to 'marry' marxism and feminism, in short, arose from the desire to correct and supplement a historical and class-based analysis of literature with a gender-based one, and vice versa. Materialist feminism, although sometimes a more polite term for marxist-feminism, may also be understood as the issue borne of that well documented 'unhappy marriage'. Woolf's work remains an important focus for both marxist and materialist feminist literary theory.

Interestingly, Jane Marcus has argued (with Woolf's nephew and biographer, Quentin Bell, who insisted 'Woolf wasn't a feminist and wasn't political') that Woolf's work is in fact marxist (See Homan 1993, 7). Whereas Michèle Barrett, while acknowledging in the introduction to *Virginia Woolf, Women and Writing*, that 'Woolf's writings on women and fiction constitute a sustained analysis of the historical determinants of women's literary production [which] might gladden the heart of a contemporary Marxist feminist critic' (1979, 17), nevertheless refutes the idea that 'her general "materialist" argument [in *A Room of One's Own*] could under any circumstances be regarded as a Marxist argument', but not on the grounds of her feminism. Woolf, she explains, 'explores the extent to which, under adverse conditions, art may be restrained and distorted by social conditions, but she retains the notion that in the correct conditions art may be totally divorced from economic, political or ideological constraints' (23). Woolf's theory of androgynous art, and her vision of a transcendent poetics, 'resists the materialist position she advances in *A Room of One's Own*' (22).

The narrator shifts scene, in *A Room of One's Own*, to the British Museum where she researches 'Women and Poverty' under an edifice of patriarchal texts, concluding that women 'have served all these centuries as looking glasses . . . reflecting the figure of man at twice his natural size' (1992a, 45). Here Woolf touches upon the forced, subordinate complicity of women in the construction of the patriarchal subject. Later in the book, Woolf offers a more explicit model of this when she describes the difficulties for a woman reader encountering the first person pronoun in the novels of 'Mr A': 'a shadow seemed to lie across the page. It was a straight dark bar, a shadow shaped something like the letter "I". . . . Back one was always hailed to the letter "I". One began to tire of "I" . . . In the shadow of the letter "I" all is shapeless as mist. Is that a tree? No it is a woman' (130). This displacement of the feminine in the representation and construction of subjectivity not only points up the alienation experienced by women readers of male-authored texts but also the linguistic difficulties for women writers in trying to express feminine subjectivity. It certainly explains Woolf's sliding and elliptical use of the first person throughout her argument. But Woolf's idiosyncratic narrative strategies in *A Room of One's Own* have been regarded as detracting from her feminist message. The American feminist Elaine Showalter notably takes Woolf to task for the book's 'playfulness [and] conversational surface' (1977, 282). Toril Moi, in her introduction to *Sexual/Textual Politics* (1985), claims to 'rescue' Woolf's text from such criticism by showing how its very playfulness is in fact a feminist strategy that anticipates the deconstructive and post-Lacanian work of the French feminists, Julia Kristeva, Hélène Cixous and Luce Irigaray (broadly associated with the idea of '*écriture feminine*'). Moi's reading of Woolf's writing as radically feminist by virtue of its textuality, although helpful to her basic introduction to French feminism, is dismissive of the latent humanism and marxism in much 'Anglo-American' feminist criticism and makes no account of such aspects in the argument, however circumlocutionary or playful, of *A Room of One's Own*, which nevertheless puts forward a strong materialist and historicist approach to women's writing.

In trying to discover the conditions of women's lives in, for example, the Elizabethan period, the narrator discovers a significant discrepancy between women in the real world and 'woman' in the symbolic order:

> Imaginatively she is of the highest importance; practically she is completely insignificant. She pervades poetry from cover to cover; she is all but absent from history. She dominates the lives of kings and conquerors in fiction; in fact she was the slave of any boy whose parents forced a

ring upon her finger. Some of the most inspired words, some of the most profound thoughts in literature fall from her lips; in real life she could scarcely spell, and was the property of her husband. (1992a, 56)

Woolf here points up not only the relatively sparse representation of women's experience in historical records, but also the more complicated business of how the feminine is already caught up in the conventions of representation itself; how women may be represented at all when 'woman', in poetry and fiction, is already a signifier in patriarchal discourse, functioning as part of the symbolic order: 'It was certainly an odd monster that one made up by reading the historians first and the poets afterwards – a worm winged like an eagle; the spirit of life and beauty in a kitchen chopping suet. But these monsters, however amusing to the imagination, have no existence in fact' (56).

Woolf converts this dual image to a positive emblem for a feminist writing:

> What one must do to bring her to life was to think poetically and prosaically at one and the same moment, thus keeping in touch with fact – that she is Mrs Martin, aged thirty-six, dressed in blue, wearing a black hat and brown shoes; but not losing sight of fiction either – that she is a vessel in which all sorts of spirits and forces are coursing and flashing perpetually. (56–7)

This dualistic model, contrasting prose and poetry, is of central importance to Woolf's modernist aesthetic and is encapsulated in the term, 'granite and rainbow' (*Essays*, 4, 478), which she elsewhere ('The New Biography' (1927)) uses to describe innovations in the art of biography. In the essay, 'Poetry, Fiction and the Future' (1927; also known as 'The Narrow Bridge of Art'), Woolf acknowledges the different tasks each traditionally performs, but is interested in creating a new form of writing that marries prose and poetry:

> [Poetry] has always insisted on certain rights, such as rhyme, metre, poetic diction. She has never been used for the common purpose of life. Prose has taken all the dirty work on to her own shoulders; has answered letters, paid bills, written articles, made speeches, served the needs of business men shopkeepers, lawyers, soldiers, peasants. (*Essays*, 4, 434)

She anticipates a new form of writing in a 'prose which has many of the characteristics of poetry', asking whether prose can 'chant the elegy, or hymn the love, or shriek in terror, or praise the rose' (436) and so on. This is a celebration of the new lyrical prose of modernism – and indeed of her own novel, *To the Lighthouse*, which she famously christened an elegy (see *Diary*, 3, 34). But, *A Room Of One's Own* explores the gender implications of this new form of writing and puts it forward as a feminist tool – just as *To the Lighthouse*, in exploring the social politics surrounding the execution of a painting by a woman artist, is simultaneously a high modernist and a feminist text.

Yet it is still considered controversial, in some quarters, to talk of Woolf's writing as feminist. The source of the confusion may well be the much cited passage in *A Room of One's Own* where it is declared that 'it is fatal for anyone who writes to think of their sex' (136) and a model of writerly androgyny is put forward, derived from Samuel Taylor Coleridge's work:

> It is fatal to be a man or woman pure and simple; one must be woman-manly or man-womanly. It is fatal for a woman to lay the least stress on any grievance; to plead even with justice any cause; in any way to speak consciously as a woman. And fatal is no figure of speech; for anything written with that conscious bias is doomed to death. It ceases to be fertilized ... Some collaboration has to take place in the mind between the woman and the man before the art of creation can be accomplished. Some marriage of opposites has to be accomplished. (136)

Woolf's theory of androgyny has been interpreted as positioning her argument beyond feminist concerns, yet it is conceived in the context of her analysis of women and fiction, and is proposed as a goal not yet attained by most of her contemporaries because of inequalities between men and women. Shakespeare, the poet playwright, is Woolf's ideal androgynous writer. She lists others – all men – who have also achieved androgyny (Keats, Sterne, Cowper, Lamb and Proust – the only contemporary). Carolyn G. Heilbrun (1973) and Nancy Topping Bazin (1973) were the first critics to explore Woolf's theory of androgyny. Showalter's (1977) attack on it, in her famous chapter, 'Virginia Woolf and the Flight into Androgyny', marks the start of continuing ferocious theoretical debate on the subject. For critics like Moi, Woolf's theory of androgyny anticipates the French feminist concept of '*différance*'.

A Room of One's Own culminates in the prophesy of a woman poet to equal or rival Shakespeare – 'Shakespeare's sister'. But in collectively preparing for her appearance, women writers need to develop in several respects. In predicting that the aspiring novelist, Mary Carmichael, 'will be a poet ... in another hundred years' time' (1992a, 123), Mary Beton seems to be suggesting that prose must be explored and exploited in certain ways by women writers before they can be poets. She also finds fault with contemporary male writers – such as Mr A who is 'protesting against the equality of the other sex by asserting his own superiority' (132). She sees this as the direct result of women's political agitation for equality: 'The Suffrage campaign was no doubt to blame' (129). She raises further concerns about politics and aesthetics when she comments on the aspirations of the Italian fascists for a poet worthy of fascism: 'We may well join in that pious hope, but it is doubtful whether poetry can come out of an incubator. Poetry ought to have a mother as well as a father. The Fascist poem, one may fear, will be a horrid little abortion such as one sees in a glass jar in the museum of some county town' (134). Yet if the extreme patriarchy of fascism cannot produce poetry because it denies a maternal line, Woolf argues that women cannot write poetry either until the historical canon of women's writing has been uncovered and acknowledged. Nineteenth-century women writers experienced great difficulty because they lacked a female tradition: 'For we think back through our mothers if we are women' (99). They therefore lacked literary tools suitable for expressing women's experience. The dominant sentence at the start of the nineteenth century was 'a man's sentence ... It was a sentence that was unsuited for women's use' (99–100).

Woolf's assertion here, through Mary Beton, of gendered syntax, and that 'the book has somehow to be adapted to the body' (101) (again anticipating the libidinal writing projects of French feminism), seems to contradict the declaration that 'it is fatal for anyone who writes to think of their sex'. She identifies the novel as 'young enough' to be of use to the woman writer:

> No doubt we shall find her knocking that into shape for herself when she has the free use of her limbs; and providing some new vehicle, not necessarily in verse, for the poetry in her. For it is the poetry that is still the denied outlet. And I went on to ponder how a woman nowadays would write a poetic tragedy in five acts. Would she use verse? – would she not use prose rather? (100–1)

Woolf seems to confirm this theory of gendered aesthetic form in her earlier review (1923) of Dorothy Richardson's novel, *Revolving Lights*: 'She has invented, or, if she has not invented, developed and applied to her own uses, a sentence which we might call the psychological sentence of the feminine gender. It is of a more elastic fibre than the old, capable of stretching to the extreme, of suspending the frailest particles, of enveloping the vaguest shapes' (*Essays*, 3, 367). But, acknowledging that men also have constructed similar sentences, she points out that the difference lies with content rather than form:

> Miss Richardson has fashioned her sentence consciously, in order that it may descend to the depths and investigate the crannies of Miriam Henderson's consciousness. It is a woman's sentence only in the sense that it is used to describe a woman's mind by a writer who is neither proud nor afraid of anything that she may discover in the psychology of her sex. (367)

This assertion of woman as both the writing subject and its object is reinforced in *A Room of One's Own*: 'above all, you must illumine your own soul' (1992a, 117), Mary Beton advises. The 'obscure lives' (116) of women must be recorded by women.

Mary Carmichael's novel in fact explores women's relationships with each other. *A Room of One's Own* was published shortly after the obscenity trial of Radclyffe Hall's *The Well of Loneliness* (1928), and Woolf flaunts in the face of this a blatantly lesbian narrative: 'if Chloe likes Olivia and Mary Carmichael knows how to express it she will light a torch in that vast chamber where nobody has yet been' (109). Her refrain, 'Chloe likes Olivia', has become a critical slogan for lesbian writing. Woolf's own fictive celebration of her lesbian lover, Vita Sackville-West, in the satirical novel *Orlando* (1928) escaped the censure directed at Hall's work. In *A Room of One's Own*, she calls for women's writing to more openly explore lesbianism and for the narrative tools to make this possible. Lesbian writing has certainly been widely published in the decades following, but it is only recently that lesbian criticism of Woolf's own work has flourished.

A Room of One's Own has not always been regarded positively by feminists, as Showalter's work has shown, but it has become a touchstone for most feminist debates. One of the most controversial passages, for example, concerns Woolf's positioning of black women. Commenting on the sexual and colonial appetites of men, the narrator concludes: 'It is one of the great advantages of being a woman that one can pass even a very fine negress without wishing to make an Englishwoman of her' (1992a, 65). In seeking to distance women from colonial practices, Woolf disturbingly excludes black women here from the very category of woman. This has become the crux of much contemporary feminist debate concerning the politics of identity. The category of women both unites and divides feminists: white middle-class feminists, it has been shown, cannot speak for the experience of all women, and reconciliation of universalism and difference remains a key issue. 'Women – but are you not sick to death of the word?' Woolf retorts in the closing pages of *A Room of One's Own*, 'I can assure you I am' (145). The category of women is not chosen by women, it represents the space in patriarchy from which women must speak and which they struggle to redefine. Woolf's ambition for the coming of Shakespeare's sister has been taken up by feminist critics and anthologisers. 'Judith Shakespeare' stands for the silenced woman writer or artist. But to seek to mimic *the* model of the individual masculine writing subject may also be considered part of a conservative feminist agenda. On the other hand, Woolf seems to defer the arrival of Shakespeare's sister in a celebration of women's collective literary achievement: '– I am talking of the common life which is the real life and not of the little separate lives which we live as individuals' (148–9). Shakespeare's sister is a messianic figure who 'lives in you and in me' (148) and who will draw 'her life from the lives of the unknown who were her forerunners' (149), but has yet to appear. She may be the common writer to Woolf's 'common reader' (a term she borrows from Samuel Johnson), but she has yet to 'put on the body which she has so often laid down'

(149). The sense of a collective authorial voice, here, along with the multivocal narrative of *A Room of One's Own*, has been seen to anticipate Woolf's more formally stylized and poetic, multivocal novel, *The Waves* (1931). But while writing *The Waves*, Woolf was also composing her introduction to another, more prosaic perhaps, multivocal text, *Life as We Have Known It*, a collection of letters by members of the Working Women's Guild (see Goldman 1998, 192).

Woolf puts forward a collective and non-transcendent sense of the writing subject in her memoir, 'A Sketch of the Past', where she maintains

> that behind the cotton wool is hidden a pattern; that we – I mean all human beings – are connected with this; that the whole world is a work of art; that we are parts of the work of art. *Hamlet* or a Beethoven quartet is the truth about this vast mass that we call the world. But there is no Shakespeare, there is no Beethoven; certainly and emphatically there is no God; we are the words; we are the music; we are the thing itself. And I see this when I have a shock. (72)

This epiphanic vision, more radical than Eliot's theory of impersonality, and anticipating in some respects Roland Barthes' idea of 'death of the author', seems to move beyond questions of gender and feminism to a sense of an ungendered collective aesthetic. Yet it appears in the context of Woolf's account of her experience of childhood sexual abuse by her brother and of the domestic tyranny of her father. Having recalled these unhappy autobiographical details, she goes on to consider how memory operates, and to record three particular 'moments of being'. She explains that such moments are triggered by physical shocks. Woolf's 'moments of being' have been likened to Henri Bergson's idea of the *durée* – subjective, non-spatial temporality – but they are also rooted in, record and resonate with the historical and material. Her aesthetic attempts both to record the real, including the interior, lives of women and to imagine life and art beyond such concerns.

Jane Goldman

Further reading and works cited

Auerbach, E. *Mimesis*. Princeton, NJ, 1953.
Barrett, M. (ed.) *Virginia Woolf, Women and Writing*. New York, 1979.
Bazin, N. Topping. *Virginia Woolf and the Androgynous Vision*. New Brunswick, NJ, 1973.
Beer, G. *Virginia Woolf*. Edinburgh, 1996.
Bowlby, R. *Feminist Destinations and Other Essays*. Edinburgh, 1996.
Brosnan, L. *Reading Virginia Woolf's Essays and Journalism*. Edinburgh, 1997.
Dowling, D. *Bloomsbury Aesthetics and the Novels of Forster and Woolf*. London, 1985.
Ezell, M. J. M. 'The Myth of Judith Shakespeare', *New Literary History*, 21, Spring 1990.
Forster, E. M. 'Virginia Woolf', in *Icon Critical Guide: Virginia Woolf*. ed. J. Goldman. London, 1997.
Gallop, J. *Around 1981: Academic Feminist Literary Theory*. New York, 1992.
Goldman, J. *The Feminist Aesthetics of Virginia Woolf*. Cambridge, 1998.
Heilbrun, C. *Towards Androgyny*. London, 1973.
Homans, M. (ed.) *Virginia Woolf*. Englewood Cliffs, NJ, 1993.
Hulme, T. E. *Speculations*, ed. H. Read. London, 1924.
Hussey, M. *The Singing of the Real World*. Columbus, OH, 1986.
— (ed.) *Virginia Woolf A–Z*. Oxford, 1995.
Kamuf, P. 'Penelope at Work'. *Novel*, 16, 1982.
Levenson, M. H. *A Genealogy of Modernism*. Cambridge. 1989.
Marcus, J. (ed.) *New Feminist Essays on Virginia Woolf*. Lincoln, NE, 1981.

— (ed.) *Virginia Woolf*. Lincoln, NE, 1983.

— (ed.) *Virginia Woolf and the Languages of Patriarchy*. Bloomington, 1987a.

— (ed.) *Virginia Woolf and Bloomsbury*. Bloomington, IN, 1987b.

—. *Art and Anger*. Columbus, OH, 1988.

Minow-Pinkney, M. *Virginia Woolf and the Problem of the Subject*. Brighton, 1987.

Modleski, T. 'Some Functions of Feminist Criticism, or The Scandal of the Mute Body', *October*, 49, Summer 1989.

Moi, T. *Sexual/Textual Politics*. London, 1985.

Pound, E. *Literary Essays of Ezra Pound*, ed. T.S. Eliot. London, 1954.

Showalter, E. *A Literature of Their Own*. Princeton, NJ, 1977.

Smith, S. Bennett. 'Gender and the Canon', in *Virginia Woolf: Themes and Variations*, eds V. Nevarow-Turk and M. Hussey. New York, 1993.

Woolf, V. 'Memories of a Working Women's Guild', in *Life As We Have Known It*, by Co-Operative Working Women, ed. M. Llewelyn Davies. London, 1931.

—. *The Death of the Moth and Other Essays*. London, 1942.

—. *The Diary of Virginia Woolf*, 5 vols, eds A. Olivier Bell and A. McNeillie. London, 1977–84.

—. *Moments of Being*, ed. J. Schulkind. London, 1985.

—. *The Essays of Virginia Woolf*, 4 vols. ed. A. McNeillie. London, 1986–92.

—. *The Complete Shorter Fiction of Virginia Woolf*, ed. S. Dick. London, 1989.

—. *A Room of One's Own & Three Guineas*, ed. M. Shiach. Oxford, 1992a.

—. *A Woman's Essays*, ed. R. Bowlby. Harmondsworth, 1992b.

T. S. Eliot (1888–1965)

From the 1920s until his death T. S. Eliot had a massive influence on literature and literary criticism in the English-speaking world. Though Eliot's modernist contemporaries – such as Ezra Pound, Wyndham Lewis, Virginia Woolf, D. H. Lawrence – also wrote criticism, they were not taken seriously as critics in the way that Eliot was. Eliot's criticism was seen as being almost equal in importance to his poetry whereas the criticism of Pound and the others was seen as very much secondary to their creative output. Eliot was also the most respected of Modernist writers – with the possible exception of Joyce, who had no aspiration to be a critic – and this gave his criticism a special status. Modernist writing had created a crisis for traditional forms of criticism since it seemed to demand a new critical approach that would be appropriate to the literary innovations ushered in by modernism. The fact that Eliot was both a high priest of modernism and a critic who seemed to take his criticism as seriously as his poetry gave him authority as a critic unmatched in the twentieth century. Over the past thirty years or so a reaction has set in and Eliot has been attacked on a number of fronts: for example, a marxist critic such as Terry Eagleton describes his criticism as a response to a 'world imperialist crisis' which led him 'to adopt the aesthetics of a late phase of Romanticism (symbolism), with its view of the individual artefact as organic, impersonal and autonomous, and then project this doctrine into an authoritarian cultural ideology' (1976, 147); it has also been suggested that his criticism as well as his poetry is contaminated by anti-Semitism (Julius 1995), and that it devalues 'minor' cultures by denying them any possibility of producing significant literature since '[n]o writer can achieve real significance, "maturity", unless he has the weight of a developed tradition on which to draw' (Craig 1996, 14). But despite such attacks, just as it is impossible to discuss twentieth-century poetry without taking account of Eliot's work, likewise the foundational force of his criticism cannot be denied even by those who may be in basic disagreement with its premises.

Though Eliot was a major innovator in literary form, in some respects his criticism is old fashioned. If one compares it with the writings of the Russian formalists or with the work of I. A. Richards or William Empson it seems to belong to a previous tradition: that of the critical essayist. He does not explore fundamental concepts in the manner of Richards, nor was he a close reader in the manner of Empson or the New Critics. Indeed, Eliot rejected the idea that there could be critical laws or even a critical method: 'there is no method except to be very intelligent' (1960, 11). However, though Eliot was not a theorist in the orthodox sense, significant theoretical assumptions and implications clearly emerge from his criticism.

Eliot's most important and influential critical study is his collection of essays, *The Sacred Wood*, first published in 1920, and the most highly regarded essay in the collection was 'Tradition and the Individual Talent' which has been reprinted in virtually every anthology of twentieth-century criticism. A major reason for Eliot's authority as a critic was that unlike major literary innovators of the past who tended to see themselves as rebels in both social and artistic terms, Eliot was a strong defender of conservative values. He had no interest in striking bohemian attitudes *pour épater le bourgeois* in the manner of such poetic predecessors as Shelley or Baudelaire or Rimbaud, and even more important: though associated with literary innovation in his poetry, in his criticism he defended tradition and regarded himself as a traditionalist. 'Tradition and the Individual Talent' is a crucial essay because it confronts this paradox and explains how Eliot can be both a practitioner of and advocate for the new while apparently being faithful to what has gone before.

T. E. Hulme in *Speculations* (1924) saw classicism and romanticism as being in fundamental conflict and Eliot's allegiance in this conflict, like Hulme's, was to classicism. Eliot's detestation of romantic subjectivism and individualism is clear all through his criticism. Instead of art being a matter of individual self-expression on the part of the artist, he claims in 'Tradition and the Individual Talent' that 'The progress of an artist is a continual self-sacrifice, a continual extinction of personality' (1960, 53). He goes on to declare that 'The emotion of art is impersonal', with the poet achieving such impersonality by 'surrendering himself wholly to the work to be done' (1960, 59). Moreover, he argues 'that not only the best, but the most individual parts of [the poet's] work may be those in which the dead poets, his ancestors, assert their immortality most vigorously', and he goes on to say that 'No poet, no artist of any art, has his complete meaning alone' (1960, 48, 49). Tradition is a force in poetry precisely because it is not inert, something passively inherited; the poet must 'obtain it by great labour' (1960, 49). The poet must acquire a historical sense so that he writes not only for readers in the present 'but with a feeling that the whole of the literature of Europe from Homer and within it the whole of the literature of his own country has a simultaneous existence and composes a simultaneous order' (1960, 49). What follows from this is the paradox that the present is as much an influence on the past as the reverse: 'what happens when a new work of art is created is something that happens simultaneously to all the works of art which preceded it. The existing monuments form an ideal order among themselves, which is modified by the introduction of the new (the really new) work of art among them' (1960, 49–50). A radical theory of intertextuality, therefore, underlies Eliot's discussion of tradition.

Eliot's concept of tradition had consequences for both literary practice and critical judgement. To make a significant literary contribution it was not enough merely to be an innovator: innovation should not ignore tradition but must seek out a relationship with it. Thus for Eliot a poet such as Blake could not be a major figure as his work was too individual. In an essay on Blake in *The Sacred Wood* he writes: 'His philosophy, like his visions, like his insight, like his technique, was his own' (1960, 155). The consequence was that Blake was 'eccentric' and his poetry 'inclined to formlessness'. In contrast, writers such as Dante or Lucretius who did not create original philosophies avoid formlessness: 'Blake did not have that more Mediterranean gift of form which knows how to borrow as Dante borrowed his theory of the soul; he must needs create a philosophy as well as a poetry' (1960, 156) This is not merely a problem for Blake but 'frequently affects writers outside of the Latin traditions' (1960, 157). Eliot asserts that 'What [Blake's] genius required, and what it sadly lacked, was a framework of accepted and traditional ideas' (1960, 157–8), and given this situation he was inevitably limited, a kind of do-it-yourself poet whom one might admire in the same way as one might admire someone who creates 'an ingenious piece of home-made furniture' (1960, 156) to which Eliot compares Blake's philosophy.

Blake could be seen as a romantic in the broad sense since he rebelled against tradition in terms both of art and of ideas. However, the modern writer could not merely emulate Dante and identify easily with tradition. The problem for the modern writer was that such a relationship with tradition no longer seemed possible. Here we see Eliot's critical concerns coming together with his concerns as a poet. It has often been pointed out that Eliot's criticism should be seen as part of a strategy to justify his own poetic practice and what is clear from that practice, especially in a poem such as *The Waste Land*, is that the modern writer must connect with tradition in new ways and this means that modern writing must adopt very different forms from those that had been dominant in the past. It seemed clear to modernists like Eliot that western culture had been fragmented by various cultural developments so that traditions based on classicism and Christianity had broken down. There was no obvious way in which such fragmentation could be overcome and some sort of unity restored; rather the modern writer had to try to construct a tradition out of fragmentation. As Eliot famously put it at the end of *The Waste Land*: 'These fragments I have shored against my ruins.' Whereas poets of the past and their readership had shared traditions, this no longer obtained for modern poets. Yet since Eliot believed that great poetry could only be written in relation to tradition, his only option was to forge the tradition necessary for himself as poet. An added incentive for doing this was that Eliot regarded the English poetic tradition as conventionally perceived, one in which Milton was a dominant figure, as an unfortunate development in the history of English poetry. Since Eliot the poet needed a tradition for himself as a modern poet and believed that a poet could achieve major status only within one of the major literary traditions, Eliot the critic set about adapting this tradition to suit his purposes.

As an American, Eliot felt he had not been born into a major poetic tradition but he believed that he and other writers in a similar situation were not necessarily at a disadvantage since it was open to writers to make a commitment to such a tradition, Eliot himself choosing to identify with an English tradition within the wider European tradition. For him, great literature could only emerge from such a tradition. In a discussion of Scottish literature, questioning whether Scottish writing could ever have major literary status, he wrote: '. . . when we assume that a literature exists we assume a great deal: we suppose that there is one of the five or six (at most) great organic formations of history' (Craig 1996, 14). And in *Notes towards the Definition of Culture* he claimed that 'the benefits which Scottish, Welsh and Irish writers have conferred upon English literature are far in excess of what the contribution of all these individual men of genius would have been had they, let us say, all been adopted in early infancy by English foster-parents' (Craig 1996, 15–16). In other words, writers from 'minority' cultures have to identify with the literary tradition of a major culture if they are to have any chance of achieving significant literary status, but once such identification has taken place, as with Eliot himself, the writer who comes from outside the culture may have much greater influence than native-born writers. There is reciprocity: the outsider is absorbed but in compensation may bring new life to an existing major tradition. The influence of Eliot's ideas about tradition are apparent in the work of F. R. Leavis who in *The Great Tradition* included the American Henry James and the Pole Joseph Conrad along with George Eliot in his triumvirate of the greatest of English novelists, James and Conrad in Leavis's view having chosen to situate their fiction within the tradition of the English novel.

One of the most significant elements of Eliot's critical project arising out of his belief both in tradition and in the need continually to renew it is canon formation. At the time he began writing Milton and the major romantics were seen as central to the tradition of English poetry, whereas writers he admired more and who were more useful to him as a poet were seen as marginal: the Metaphysical poets and Elizabethan and Jacobean dramatists. Tradition must therefore be reconstructed (or perhaps deconstructed) to marginalize Milton and Shelley and place Donne and Webster closer to the centre as well as being widened to take account of European literature. Even Shakespeare's status could be questioned in this reconstruction of tradition. In *The Sacred Wood*, Eliot questions whether the play generally regarded as Shakespeare's greatest, *Hamlet* – and perhaps significantly the play most revered by the romantics – could be regarded as artistically successful: 'So far from being Shakespeare's masterpiece, the play is most certainly an artistic failure' (1960, 98).

It is in 'Hamlet and his Problems' that Eliot introduces a critical concept that was to be extremely influential: the 'objective correlative'. Eliot's critique of *Hamlet* is indirectly an attack on the romantic approach to writing. The elevation of *Hamlet*, Eliot claims, is the result of critics who were also artists, such as Goethe and Coleridge, 'find[ing] in Hamlet a vicarious existence for their own artistic realization' (1960, 95). For Eliot this is artistic heresy since the critic's 'first business was to study a work of art' and to resist such subjective indulgence as identifying with characters. The problem with *Hamlet* is that it encourages this kind of subjectivist criticism because of Shakespeare's artistic failure, since '*Hamlet*, like the sonnets, is full of some stuff that the writer could not drag to light, contemplate, or manipulate into art' (1960, 100). This leads Eliot to formulate an alternative to the idea that art arises out of the self-expression of emotion:

> The only way of expressing emotion in the form of art is by finding an 'objective correlative'; in other words, a set of objects, a situation, a chain of events which shall be the formula of that *particular* emotion; such that when the external facts, which must terminate in sensory experience, are given, the emotion is immediately evoked. (1960, 100)

It is clear that this can be equated with Eliot's impersonal view of art: there is no need to discuss the artist or the artist's state of mind since the work itself, if it is successfully realized, embodies emotion dramatically, and such emotion does not necessarily need to have been experienced directly by the artist. It is also clear that the concept of the 'objective correlative' reflects the idea that the image was seen as overwhelmingly the dominant element in modernist writing. In such writing interpretation was also superfluous because one could not adequately paraphrase an image. As Eliot writes earlier in 'Hamlet and his Problems': '*Qua* work of art, the work of art cannot be interpreted; there is nothing to interpret; we can only criticize it according to standards, in comparison to other works of art' (1960, 96).

By implication, therefore, the problem for the modern artist was how to achieve form given the emphasis on the image and the loss of a coherent sense of tradition that existed for earlier poets such as Dante. One of the reasons why Eliot admired Joyce's *Ulysses* was that he saw it as offering a solution to the problem of form for the modern artist living in a contemporary reality that seemed fragmentary or chaotic. Joyce's use of myth Eliot asserts – in '*Ulysses*, Order and Myth' (1923) – 'is simply a way of controlling, ordering, of giving a shape and a significance to the immense panorama of futility and anarchy which is contemporary history' (Eliot 1997, 22). Eliot believes this 'mythical method' has general application to modern writing and can provide the superstructure, as it were, within which modern writing can establish a relation to tradition. But since the writer has to reformulate tradition rather than sharing one with the reader, tradition can enter modern writing only in a fragmentary and allusive way. It has also to be accommodated to the dominance of the image which has a further fragmentary effect. The inevitable consequence of this is a form of writing that may seem wilfully obscure. Whereas writers in the past in alluding to tradition in the form of allusions or citations from classical or Biblical texts would assume that their ideal reader would share this knowledge, modern writers could assume no such ideal reader. They wrote in the knowledge that their works might appear to be wilfully obscure not only because tradition could only exist within works in a fragmentary form but also because many works that a writer such as Eliot regarded as central to his sense of tradition, such as plays by minor – at least by conventional literary standards – Jacobean dramatists, would not have been familiar to even a well-educated readership.

Eliot's belief that conventional notions of poetic tradition needed to be undermined and that modern writing needed to relate itself to what he regarded as a more authentic tradition was based on one of his most influential critical ideas: his claim that feeling and intellect had become split off from each other because of a 'dissociation of sensibility' that took place in the middle of the seventeenth century. This idea was first put forward in Eliot's essay on the Metaphysical poets, published in 1921. He refers to the presence in Chapman of 'a direct sensuous apprehension of thought, or a recreation of thought into feeling, which is exactly what we find in Donne' (1951, 286). In contrast nineteenth-century poets such as Tennyson and Browning 'do not feel their thought as immediately as the odour of a rose' (1951, 287). They are the victims of a dissociation of sensibility, one from which, Eliot claimed, 'we have never recovered', and which 'was aggravated by the influence of the most powerful poets of the [seventeenth] century, Milton and Dryden' (Eliot 1951, 288). In later writings Eliot modified his position somewhat, absolving Milton and Dryden from responsibility and seeing it as a consequence of the English Civil War and even having wider European origins.

The historical basis of Eliot's claim has been attacked, notably by Frank Kermode in *Romantic Image*, first published in 1957. For Kermode, 'The theory of the dissociation of sensibility is, in fact, the most successful version of a Symbolist attempt to explain why the modern world resists works of art that testify to the poet's special, anti-intellectual way of knowing truth' (1966, 143). However, the idea not only allowed Eliot to discard writers who embodied a tradition that was antagonistic to his own poetic purposes – such as Milton, romantic and Victorian poetry – but to justify this in critical terms and thus deflect the claim that his preferences merely reflected his own poetic prejudices. Attacks on the 'dissociation of sensibility' on the grounds that it lacks historical objectivity are perhaps beside the point despite Eliot's attempts to argue that it did have a historical basis. It should perhaps be seen as similar to such concepts as Freud's 'Oedipus complex' or Lacan's 'mirror phase' which are beyond confirmation in empirical terms. The value of such concepts lies in their explanatory power, and the influence of Eliot's notion of a 'dissociation of sensibility' over several decades indicates that for many people it did have an exceptional explanatory power. Of course, the culture has moved on since and arguably the idea of a 'dissociation of sensibility' may now have outlived its usefulness, but it is undeniable that the concept has played a major role in twentieth-century culture.

Eliot's key critical concepts: tradition, artistic impersonality, the objective correlative, the dissociation of sensibility have had a crucial effect on twentieth-century criticism. The work of the critics and theorists who came after him: I. A. Richards and especially F. R. Leavis and the American New Critics, were fundamentally affected by these concepts. For a while the literary status of Milton and romantics such as Shelley was seriously undermined; Donne ascended the poetic hierarchy almost to the level of Shakespeare; the fusion of feeling and thought through images that could not be paraphrased became a criterion of literary value, together with its corollary that literature was a force in itself separate from history or philosophy. Even when advocates of a different critical philosophy emerged, such as Northrop Frye and Harold Bloom, one can feel the power of Eliot's thought in the background as something to be resisted. His influence has only been seriously weakened by the emergence of forms of literary criticism that have been shaped by critical and cultural theories influenced to a considerable extent by continental philosophy. Many critical questions that were not addressed for several decades during the ascendancy of Eliot and Eliot-influenced criticism have now come back onto the agenda.

Perhaps one of the most crucial of these questions is whether art and literature can be separated from the political. One of Eliot's fundamental assumptions is that the poem is a work of art and is autotelic, that is it has no purpose or end beyond itself. In the introduction to the 1928 edition of *The Sacred Wood* Eliot declared that 'the problem appearing in these essays, which gives them what coherence they have, is the problem of the integrity of poetry, with the repeated assertion that when we are considering poetry we must consider it primarily as poetry and not another thing' (1960, viii). He dismisses the definitions of great predecessors such as Wordsworth or Arnold, denying that poetry is 'emotion recollected in tranquillity' or a 'criticism of life', nor can it be reduced to morals, politics, religion or to 'a collection of psychological data about the minds of poets, or about the history of an epoch' (1960, ix). His conclusion is 'that a poem, in some sense, has its own life ... that the feeling, or emotion, or vision, resulting from the poem is something different from the feeling or emotion or vision in the mind of the poet' (1960, x).

The issues raised here are perhaps highlighted most powerfully in relation to Eliot's own poetry. The extent to which Eliot succeeded in dominating critical thinking up until the 1960s is indicated by the fact that certain aspects of his own poetry were hardly ever mentioned or discussed, notably the apparent anti-Semitism of certain of the earlier poems. A subject such as anti-Semitism in its twentieth-century context does powerfully raise the question as to whether Eliot's view that poetry can be discussed legitimately only as poetry and not in terms of other discourses is sustainable. If one adopts Eliot's critical philosophy there seems no way of confronting directly anti-Semitism in his poetry yet these poems are clearly embroiled in the cultural matrix that created the conditions for mass murder. During the ascendancy of Eliot and those critics influenced by him this kind of problem was ignored because Eliot had created a critical discourse that defined literature in very narrow terms and endeavoured to preserve literature from any contamination by non-literary considerations. To discuss questions of meaning was anti-literary as the literary text was a special form of discourse: in Archibald MacLeish's celebrated formulation: 'A poem must not mean / But be.' Though this view now seems highly questionable what one should put in its place still remains problematic as going to the opposite extreme and judging poetry by its content seems equally unsatisfactory. Does 'great poetry' somehow transform anti-Semitism and if so in what way, or should poetic value be simply denied to any poetry embodying such an ideology, or does the issue need to be discussed in quite different terms? These are questions that still need to be debated and perhaps the emergence recently of a theoretically sophisticated 'ethical criticism' which has redirected critical attention to the responsibility of both author and reader in the production of meaning in literary texts indicates an awareness that these sorts of questions need to be discussed.

Other related developments in contemporary criticism that have undermined Eliot's critical philosophy are the claims by feminist and gay critics that gender and sexual orientation cannot be excluded in any discussion of a literary text, and as a result of their work the textualism and anti-intentionalism of the Eliot-influenced New Critics have been seriously undermined. Although textualism still remains powerful in contemporary criticism in the work of deconstructive critics, it takes its cue not so much from Eliot as from a theorist like Derrida who comes from a quite different tradition. Also Eliot's claim that significant writers must belong to a major literary tradition can be questioned on the grounds that many of the most significant writers of the twentieth century were born outside the dominant culture and resisted identification with it, writers such as Yeats, Joyce, Beckett, MacDiarmid, Rilke, Kafka. It has been argued that, contrary to Eliot's cultural philosophy, 'peripheries' have refused to accept the dominance of the 'cultural core' as this unequal relationship between centre and margins is founded on 'a system of cultural exchange designed to enhance the core and impoverish the periphery and thereby to maintain the power relations between them' (Craig 1996, 29), and that in this changed cultural context Eliot's identification of tradition with the dominant culture has lost its force.

K. M. *Newton*

Further reading and works cited

Austin, A. T. S. Eliot: The Literary and Social Criticism. London, 1974.
Baldick, C. Criticism and Literary Theory from 1890 to the Present. Oxford, 1996.
Craig, C. Out of History. London, 1996.
Eagleton, T. Criticism and Ideology. London, 1976.
Eliot, T. S. The Use of Poetry and the Use of Criticism. London, 1933.
—. After Strange Gods. London, 1934.
—. Selected Essays. London, 1951.
—. The Sacred Wood. London, 1960.

—. *To Criticize the Critic and Other Writings*. London, 1965.

—. 'Ulysses, Order and Myth', in *James Joyce: Ulysses; A Portrait of the Artist as a Young Man*, ed. J. Coyle. Basingstoke, 1997.

Gray, P. *T. S. Eliot's Intellectual and Poetic Development, 1909–1922*. London, 1982.

Jay, G. S. *T. S. Eliot and the Poetics of Literary History*. Oxford, 1983.

Julius, A. *T. S. Eliot: Anti-Semitism and Literary Form*. Oxford, 1995.

Kermode, F. *Romantic Image*. [1957]. Oxford, 1966.

Leavis, F. R. *Anna Karenina and Other Essays*. Harmondsworth, 1967.

Lee, B. *Theory and Personality*. Cambridge, 1979.

Lobb, E. *T. S. Eliot and the Romantic Literary Tradition*. London, 1981.

Newton-de Molina, D. (ed.) *The Literary Criticism of T. S. Eliot*. London, 1977.

Ricks, C. *T. S. Eliot and Prejudice*. London, 1988.

Shusterman, R. *T. S. Eliot and the Philosophy of Criticism*. Oxford, 1988.

Wellek, R. *A History of Modern Criticism*. New York, 1986.

After the 'Cambridge School': F. R. Leavis (1895–1978), *Scrutiny* (1932–1952) and Literary Studies in Britain

Whether there is or was a recognizable 'Cambridge School' of English literature criticism is debatable, because the justification for recognizing such a thing would probably necessitate accepting the centrality to Cambridge of F. R. Leavis, who while fervent in support of an 'English school' at the centre of the ideal university, throughout his life polarized opinion in Cambridge, making more enemies than friends, and who now has few people speaking from something like his standpoint either in Cambridge or other universities. From the time of his first publications in 1930 and the founding of the quarterly journal *Scrutiny*, Leavis, with his students, friends and, above all, with his wife, Queenie Dorothy Leavis (who wrote powerful novel-criticism, some of which has attracted some feminist attention), in writing for *Scrutiny*, set a course for the study of English literature in the twentieth century. This was given some official backing when he took up a full-time position at Downing College, Cambridge, in 1936. Leavis retired from Cambridge in 1962, and he never held a Professorship there, though he was to go and take a Chair at York for the rest of the 1960s.

Leavis's impact worked in schools (English public schools and grammar schools: it is arguable that the timbre of his work could not work in comprehensive schools), in syllabuses and in educational theory which placed 'English' and English literature at the centre of the curriculum. It was disseminated through the employment of his ex-students in universities throughout the UK and Commonwealth countries in the 1950s and 1960s, and through such popularizations of his work as Boris Ford's edited *Penguin Guide to English Literature* (1953–62), written, mostly, by Leavis's ex-pupils. The most important influence was the writing: the books of Leavis himself, Q. D. Leavis, and such other *Scrutiny* associates as Marius Bewley, D. J. Enright, D. W. Harding, L. C. Knights, Wilfrid Mellers, H. A. Mason, John Speirs, Denys Thompson, E. W. F. Tomlin, Derek Traversi, Martin Turnell, and then by others who were too young to have contributed to *Scrutiny*, such as David Holbrook and Ian Robinson. Such books, many using *Scrutiny*-derived material, have become formative of an approach which is perhaps lamely called 'Cambridge English', as have many others on literature published by Cambridge University Press in the 1960s and 1970s, which at that stage had a pro-Leavis editor in Michael Black. Two journals at least have derived from Leavis: *Essays in Criticism*, which was begun by F. W. Bateson at Oxford in 1951 in response to *Scrutiny*, and the *Cambridge Quarterly*, begun by Leavis's ex-pupils in 1966, is similarly still recognizable in character: local judgements may be different, but the emphasis continues. The journal *New Universities Quarterly* also showed much influence from Leavis. On the Left, the work of Richard Hoggart, Raymond Williams and Terry Eagleton shows further derivations, while also remaining independent. In America, Leavis's influence has been in significant relation to 'New Criticism', and been found in such journals as *The Kenyon Review* and *The Sewanee Review*.

Influences on Leavis came from the criticism of Matthew Arnold, Henry James, T. S. Eliot and D. H. Lawrence; from Edgell Rickword and his journal *The Calendar of Modern Letters* (1925–7), from John Middleton Murray, whose *The Problem of Style* (1921) showed some Oxford competition to Cambridge, from G. Wilson Knight on Shakespeare, for an approach that was anti-A. C. Bradley, and in an immediate and important sense from I. A. Richards, with whom all his work might be seen to be in dialogue. Leavis took 'practical criticism' from him and focused on the texts he studied an intense concentration. In the belief that great writers responded to the English language as to something which created them and which survived in ordinary speech acts, and in pre-capitalist popular culture, he argued that great writing responds to speech and in it 'we read as we read the living' (1936, 18). The demonstrable features of writing that follows the creativity of the language can be pointed to in a poem or novel, or play (Leavis referred to Shakespeare's plays, and to novels, as 'dramatic poems') in a form where the critic says 'This is so, isn't it?' and gets the response 'Yes, but ...' – thus making criticism collaborative, and – based on T. S. Eliot's 'the common pursuit of true judgment' (1953, 18) – directed towards greater sensitivity, creativity and closer response to the 'life' of the poem. Leavis argued that great writers showed a sensitivity and reverence for 'life' as this surfaced within language, and their 'impersonality' demonstrated itself as they set aside their own impositions of order or rationality in favour of the life welling up in the text. Creative writing was heuristic, driven by a 'nisus' or need, and with an intuitive *ahnung* prompting it (1975, 62–3). Thus great writing had a moral import, but it would not be possible to specify the morality, nor would the writer's local allegiances (e.g. to Christianity, or to marxism) be relevant in the face of such 'impersonality' (a word taken from Eliot's 'Tradition and the Individual Talent' (1953, 21–30) but given a much stronger reading by Leavis). The enemies throughout were triviality, grossness of response and dullness, or Milton's artificiality adopted towards the language (and Leavis continued the Cambridge distancing from the classics, from histories of the language, and from Anglo-Saxon in the English curriculum).

Such readings of literary texts, religious in their intensity – Leavis frequently quoted the line from *The Rainbow* 'he knew he did not belong to himself' (1970, 270) to indicate his commitment to an individual's connectedness – though without conforming to any religion, imposed as strong inclusions as exclusions. Leavis wrote enthusiastically, and path-breakingly, on Shakespeare, Donne, Wordsworth, Blake, Hopkins, Eliot and Pound's

Hugh Selwyn Mauberley, and among novelists, on Austen, Dickens, George Eliot, James, Conrad and D. H. Lawrence, the last of whom continued to assume greater and greater importance for him. The 'essence' of Leavis's positions may be found in his essay on *Hard Times* (1948). In this essay, which specifically alludes to John Stuart Mill and which refers to his utilitarian background as crippling, Leavis attacks Benthamism, and so, implicitly, Richards, and Richards's desire to restate the romantic stress on the imagination and creativity in terms of Bentham. The heart of Leavis's position will also be found in his essay on *Macbeth* in 'Tragedy and the Medium' (1952), in the essay on *Women in Love* (1955) and in the essay on Wordsworth (1936). Examples of his close readings will be found in Leavis (1943, 1975). Negatively, Leavis rejected Milton, Sterne and Joyce (*Finnegans Wake* especially), for their playing with the language, treating it as a thing in itself, Shelley for his displays of emotion that were never criticized or distanced (likewise Swinburne and much other Victorian verse), Fielding, Thackeray and Trollope for their lack of 'serious-ness' and the Bloomsbury group likewise (so that Virginia Woolf never received recogni-tion), and the Pound of the *Cantos*. None of these rejections was innocent: all implied a hostility to the social attitudes these writers represented. A position assumed with regard to language presumed a position with regard to life.

René Wellek (see Leavis 1952, 211–22; Mulhern 1979, 163–6) addressed Leavis's readings of English poetry with the demand that he state his assumptions explicitly. Leavis's response formulated a distinction between philosophic statement and poetry which decidedly gave the edge to poetry; the point returns in a discussion of Quentin Anderson's work on the Swedenborgian influences on Henry James, where Leavis contends that 'extraneous knowledge about the writer's intentions' cannot replace 'the tests of realization' (i.e. making real – a crucial term for Leavis). The tests are 'a matter of his sense . . . of what the living thing looks like – of the difference between that which has been willed and put there, or represents no profound integration, and that which grows from a deep centre of life . . . the deep animating intention [may be] something very different from the intention the author would declare' (1952, 225). A marxist critique, such as Eagleton's, would see Leavis's refusal to see that his 'petty bourgeois non-conformist humanism' (1976, 13) was passing itself off as a source of potentially universal judgement as to what is 'the real', and refusing to notice its partiality and relativity. The implied reference to the unity of the work in the word 'integration' is non-Freudian, non-Machereyan, and distinct from deconstruc-tion, since it has no sense of texts being marked by absences, or by the symptoms of something else not present: Leavis insists on significance (rather than meaning – a word he regards as reductive) being present in the text, even if, as in D. H. Lawrence's phrase, 'Never trust the artist. Trust the tale' (1956, 297) he does not regard intention as a final decider, and so admits the complexity of the text, its disagreement with its own stated positions. Nonetheless the sense of the importance of the word 'presence' – see his essay on Wordsworth (Leavis 1936) – makes for a comparison with Paul de Man on Wordsworth (1984). It indicates why marxist, rather than deconstructive, criticism has engaged with Leavis's positions – on account of the commitment to the text making a difference, existing in a world where 'meanings still exist' (Eliot 1953, 57). Yet Leavis's 'real' is outside ideology, it is neither engendered by Lukács's 'realism', nor hospitable to the idea that all language uses may be constructed, artificial, so that no language use can be closer to the real (see MacCabe 1978). Attacks on Leavis on these lines in the 1970s and 1980s became frequent and have necessitated the question of how he may be reread after them: a task not yet addressed.

Marxist readings of Leavis have had also to face Leavis's analyses of social history. Here, reinforced by Q. D. Leavis's PhD thesis, published as *Fiction and the Reading Public* (1932), *Scrutiny* increasingly, and Leavis especially in his later writings (1969, 1970, 1972, 1975, 1976), presented a social history of cultural decline owing something to Eliot's theory of a 'dissociation of sensibility' setting in in the seventeenth century (1953, 117) and entailing the current triumph of 'technologico-Benthamitism' (Leavis 1969, 109). Inflected by the marxism of R. H. Tawney's *Religion and the Rise of Capitalism* (1926), which influenced one of the most considerable ventures into literature and sociology and social history, L. C. Knights' *Drama and Society in the Age of Jonson* (1937), Leavis tried the same with the nineteenth century, and the results were simplistic. He read the modern in terms of loss of *Gemeinschaft* (the 'organic society') and replacement by a substitute culture formed by mass-circulation newspapers, market-driven popular fiction and loss of contact with the past. Though he could have received support from Adorno on the 'culture industry', the argument ignored any marxist analysis, conveying rather an impression of hostility to industrialism (as opposed to capitalism) and to the modern. Unnuanced as far as its response to present-day popular culture was concerned (in that it hardly listened to that culture), it gave the impression that the writers Leavis praised were elitist and that education meant the education of elites. By linking arguments about literary texts to a banal sociology, conducted in the face of sociologists, Leavis became in the 1970s and 1980s a prisoner of the Right (e.g. Roger Scruton in *The Salisbury Review*) and an apparent reactionary in speaking for a 'great tradition' which must be taught, or civilization would be lost.

Critical theory of the late 1970s onwards, then, has been explicitly or implicitly anti-Leavis, from varying degrees of awareness of his work. While Leavis was of the wrong generation to respond to Barthes, Foucault or Derrida, post-Leavis writers have avoided such a confrontation, taking refuge in the general lack of responsiveness in Britain to new theory, and thereby becoming the more reactionary. The implicit drive in Leavis's work towards an assertion of the power of English could not survive Britain's multi-racialism, any more than Lawrence's reputation (and hence Leavis's) could quite survive undented the feminism of Kate Millett's *Sexual Politics*. There is no need to align Leavis with conservatism, even though the tradition within which he worked and helped produce has remained bourgeois, humanist, Arnoldian in its appeal to 'culture' as 'the best that is thought and known in the world' (Leavis 1943, 141). It could not be simply that, as his enthusiasm for Dickens's inwardness with his own popular culture indicated to him. Nonetheless, in his own time, Leavis, for all his astonishing inwardness with regard to poetry, was also guilty of parochialism with regard to Cambridge, whose importance he inflated (the importance of teaching there) as much as it has inflated its own. If he had accepted a career outside Cambridge, he might have done something to lessen that university's grip in terms of alliance of class and culture. In accepting Cambridge, he silently underwrote its exclusiveness. While cultivated in other literatures himself, he gave the impression of seeing English literature as unique, which not only implied a cultural imperialism and developing anti-Americanism – so much that he would not even recognize the work of Lionel Trilling and Edmund Wilson with regard to Dickens (Leavis 1970) – but also an anti-marginality (see his contempt for Wilde and put-down of Proust, 1948). It produced cut-off points in his own thinking, which disappointing in him were death-dealing in some of his followers, and productive of a reaction against him. He never said much which implied attention to Freud – and so to the unconscious of the text, in a suspicion that such attention would prove reductive or predictable; nonetheless, such a refusal weakened his sense of how the text might differ from the intention behind it. Despite the evident possibility of a dialogue, and the point that there has been a whole left-Leavisism engendered by his approach, he had little to say on Marx, beyond giving a sense that the marxist stress on the economic entailed a reduction of attention to the values of the 'human world' (Leavis 1972, 61). He had even less to say on Nietzsche. *Scrutiny* never attended to European modernism (Flaubert, Kafka, Beckett, Mann). Leavis's insistence on thought being embodied in creative uses of the language might have led him to Heidegger (see Bell 1988), but instead impelled him towards the comparatively minor: Michael Polanyi, Marjorie Grene, A. N. Whitehead and R. G. Collingwood, from whom he took his philosophy. While he knew Wittgenstein, Leavis's 'anti-philosopher' stance meant that he never became a challenge to his thought. The social historians and economists he relied on in his later books tended to be narrowly anti-modern and of the Right, while the targets he selected for attack – for instance C. P. Snow, in Leavis's famous lecture of 1962 rejecting the idea that there were 'two cultures's, scientific and literary, contending only for one, that based on literature (Leavis 1972) – again now hardly make a ripple intellectually.

In the 'two cultures' debate may also be seen something of Leavis's ongoing critique of Richards, never fully articulated (see Leavis 1952, 134–5; 1975, 31). Richards's bracketing off of meaning from poetry's 'pseudo-statements', like Empson's continual finding of ambiguities, Leavis finds a form of trivialization of poetry's claims to relevance and to its discovery of 'the real'. This informs Leavis's anti-philosopher stand, and makes what he finds in 'practical criticism' different from Richards. It is here that Leavis is most vulnerable, and also, perhaps, most sensitive and interesting, in his demand that the text should become a form of cognition, and English 'a discipline of thought'. That said, the greatest criticism of Leavis would not be that his work needs rereading under the impact of critical theory, as do the writers he spoke for, because in a sense that work is clearly antagonistic to what it would see as the reductiveness implied in the very premises of such theory before the theory has begun its work. The critique would be that he fought a battle he could win too easily against English intellectual mediocrity and Cambridge parochialism, and never perceived that there were more interesting challenges to his own position. While the debates about culture that he in the twentieth century did much to initiate in Britain, and that have generated British cultural studies, have gone beyond his concern with the literary and poetic uses of language, his work there, while remaining definitive in some instances, is also end-stopped. The criticism, in its self-justifications and rebukes, comes across often as paranoid and self-protective, so that the critic's call to openness to 'life' shows also the traces of being closed-off and filled with the impulse to dominate, which itself asks to be read psychoanalytically.

Jeremy Tambling

Further reading and works cited

Anderson, P. 'Components of the National Culture', *New Left Review*, 50, May–June 1968.
Bell, M. *F. R. Leavis*. London, 1988.
de Man, P. *The Rhetoric of Romanticism*. New York, 1984.
Eagleton, T. *Criticism and Ideology*. London, 1976.
—. *The Function of Criticism From The Spectator to Post-Structuralism*. London, 1984.

Eliot, T. S. *Selected Prose*, ed. John Hayward. Harmondsworth, 1953.

Lawrence, D. H. *Selected Literary Criticism*, ed. A. Beal. London, 1956.

Leavis, F. R. *New Bearings in English Poetry*. London, 1932.

—. *Revaluation*. London, 1936.

—. *Education and the University*. London, 1943.

—. *The Great Tradition*. London, 1948.

—. *The Common Pursuit*. London, 1952.

—. *D. H. Lawrence*. London, 1955.

—. *Anna Karenina and Other Essays*. London, 1966.

— (ed.) *A Selection From 'Scrutiny'*. Cambridge, 1968.

—. *English Literature in Our Time and the University*. London, 1969.

— with Leavis, Q. D. *Dickens the Novelist*. London, 1970.

—. *Nor Shall My Sword*. London, 1972.

—. *The Living Principle*. London, 1975.

—. *Thought, Words and Creativity*. London, 1976.

—. *Collected Essays*, ed. G. Singh. Cambridge, 1983–89.

— with Leavis, Q. D. *Lectures in America*. London, 1969.

Leavis, Q. D. *Fiction and the Reading Public*. London, 1932.

MacCabe, C. *James Joyce and the Revolution of the Word*. London, 1978.

MacKillop, I. *F. R. Leavis*. Harmondsworth, 1995.

Millett, K. *Sexual Politics*. New York, 1970.

Mulhern, F. *The Moment of 'Scrutiny'*. London, 1979.

Nairn, T. 'The English Literary Intelligentsia', in *Bananas*, ed. E. Tennant. London, 1977.

Samson, A. *F. R. Leavis*. London, 1992.

Strickland, G. *Structuralism or Criticism?* Cambridge, 1981.

Thompson, D. (ed.) *The Leavises*. Cambridge, 1984.

Williams, R. *Politics and Letters*. London, 1979.

J. L. Austin (1911–1960) and Speech-Act Theory

Austin and the ordinary language philosophy he invented loomed large on the philosophical scene from about 1948 on; Austin was felt to be Oxford's answer to Cambridge's Wittgenstein, and one of the leaders of the movement to deny that a vast number of apparent philosophical problems had a general and coherent meaning. Roughly speaking, Austin belonged to a movement that found its earliest expositions in William James's pragmatism, a movement that included not only the later Wittgenstein but also G. E. Moore and W. V. Quine, and that opposed the high metaphysical idealism not only of Kant and Hegel, but also of Bertrand Russell, A. J. Ayer and the early Wittgenstein. This broad statement needs considerable qualification, since the arguments among the more pragmatist philosophers are as intense as their arguments with their metaphysical opponents (Austin sharply distinguishes himself from pragmatism, but it is notable that he felt he had to do so); and also because the modern metaphysics of Russell and Frege is itself based on the same kind of attentive consideration of sentences or propositions paid by the ordinary language movement Austin led. The apposition of sentence and proposition I have just made is one place to summarize the differences, however. The metaphysicians, as they might be abbreviated, sought to find the propositions named or expressed by sentences (the same proposition would be expressed by 'Snow is white' and 'Der Schnee ist weiss'), whereas Austin, Quine and the later Wittgenstein denied the reality of that abstract entity, the 'proposition' (and therefore as well the reality of that abstract entity, its 'meaning'), and concentrated instead on sentences.

In doing so, they might be said to have identified one of the great projects – and great errors – of the philosophical tradition as that of canonical paraphrase. Ever since Platonic dialectic, philosophical discourse has aimed at a clarified translation of what people say and what people think. Such translation would then have the virtue of making manifest the hidden assumptions, contradictions and begged questions of ordinary thinking, and allow for a perspicuous presentation of justified claims, possible truths and clear falsehoods. Socrates' incessant demand for definition inaugurates this sceptical demand for clarity. Get clear on the claims that people tend to make (as to what piety is, for example, or that I really am sitting at my desk writing) or the questions that they tend to ask (e.g. what is time? am I dreaming? are universals real?) and then you can begin analysing those claims and questions.

This through-line in the history of philosophy might be said to find its culmination in the attempts of Frege and his followers to invent a formalism – codified in the modern logic Frege invented – which would allow for the derivation of all true consequences from true premises. Such a project would naturally affect conceptions of truth and knowledge, and the strengths and limitations of the latter. All philosophical claims worth analysis or debate might then be paraphrased in this canonical notation for readier analysis. Unfortunately logic, at least any logic with the power to analyse general statements, itself runs up against inherent and insoluble structural difficulties, mainly through paradoxes of self-reference that cannot be avoided. The early Wittgenstein attempted to deal with these by regarding all self-reference as nonsense, although necessary nonsense, and in so doing he implicitly opened the way to his later philosophy of language, which no longer sought to purge language of what the logicians regarded as its vagueness, heterogeneity or arbitrariness.

The anti-metaphysicians (including the later Wittgenstein) might all be said to share the idea that canonical paraphrase, far from clarifying, falsifies. Its simplifications are all deceptively plausible but false renderings of the things that it claims to be setting forth. Austin was regarded by legal theorist H. L. A. Hart as having the makings of a great lawyer or judge, especially at common law, and like a lawyer Austin knew that in cross-examination (Socrates' method) skilful paraphrase could make any witness seem to be saying what a cross-examiner wanted him or her to say, and even to agree to. Resisting the force of such paraphrase as more fitted to forensics than to philosophical investigation, Austin bases his method on the idea that human language, as it has evolved down the centuries, is far more supple, fertile of distinction and expressive of subtlety than any artificial substitute:

> Our common stock of words embodies all the distinctions men have found worth drawing, and the connexions they have found worth marking, in the lifetimes of many generations: these surely are likely to be more numerous, more sound, since they have stood up to the long text of the survival of the fittest, and more subtle, at least in all ordinary and reasonably practical matters, than any that you or I are likely to think up in our arm-chairs of an afternoon – the most favoured alternative method. (1979, 182)

The relevance to literature and post-romantic literary theory should become at once evident if this passage is juxtaposed with Wordsworth's account of his own poetic ambition, in the Preface to *Lyrical Ballads*, in which he says that he wishes to write the natural language of natural men. Austin is as radical as Wordsworth in his sense of what we can learn by paying attention to the way people actually use language and what they use it for. To put the point as succinctly as possible, what people tend to use language for is something other than designating true propositions.

Austin shows that the central role of language in human life is what he calls 'performative'. To say something is always to do something. It is to do something within a social situation, in which the hearers of what you say also participate, more or less actively. Followers of Austin take promising as the paradigmatic example of what Austin called 'performative utterances' and sometimes 'speech acts' (a phrase that he seems first to have published in 1953, in 'How to Talk'). When I promise (or bet, or take in marriage, or christen, or congratulate, or bequeath) I am not saying something true or false; I am doing something and *not* describing what I am doing. Not that my act necessarily succeeds: my bet may fail to find a taker; my promise might not be heard; the person I would espouse might already be married, etc. Failures of performative utterance, however, are not failures in point of truth or falsity (I don't *lie* when I make a bet), but in point of achievement; my speech act may turn out to be unhappy in various ways. Two major rubrics group a large number of these ways: it can be void – the act can be purported but misfire, as for example if I christen the wrong ship, one which already has a name; or it can be hollow – the act can be professed but abusive, as when I promise what I do not intend to fulfil. (These are not mutually exclusive categories of infelicity: I may bequeath what I know not to be mine to give, and in that my bequest would be both hollow and void.)

These considerations have philosophical as well as sociological interest. Austin approaches the traditional philosophical questions without accepting the insidious paraphrase that goes into formulating them. A short list of those questions might include: what is knowledge? what is willing? what is the self? what is matter (or what is the world made of)? does the external world exist? do other minds exist? what are possibility, actuality, and necessity? what is truth (or by virtue of what is a proposition true)? All of these questions, for Austin, have something wrong with them, or at least very quickly give rise to misleading ways of thinking and speaking.

Consider some examples of how attention to ordinary language can make a difference here. In 'Other Minds' (1946) Austin considers the claim that there are some things that we can know with certainty and others that we can never claim to *know* at all (as, for example, what another person is feeling), and that there are very grave limitations on the extent of our possible knowledge. Austin considers the variety of contexts and of situations in which we do in fact claim to know something and suggests that in each case, or in most cases, such a claim tends to answer the question or more or less friendly challenge, 'How do you know?'

Suppose I have said 'There's a bittern at the bottom of the garden', and you ask 'How do you know?' my reply may take very different forms:

(*a*) I was brought up in the fens
(*b*) I heard it
(*c*) The keeper reported it
(*d*) By its booming
(*e*) From the booming noise
(*f*) Because it is booming. (1979, 79)

Each reply answers a different possible doubt or inquiry: how do I come to be in a position to know about bitterns? or how do I come to be in a position to say that there's a bittern here and now? or how can I tell bitterns, or how do I tell them? or how can I or do I tell the thing here and now as a bittern? Austin's partial list of 'ordinary' answers to the question does not contemplate the idea that someone might ask me what theory of epistemology allows me to assert ideal knowledge about an empirical fact. For I am talking about bitterns and *not* about empirical facts. We rarely talk about empirical facts: we talk about goldfinches or bitterns or elections or money or restaurants or parents.

This account of how we answer the question 'How do you know?' denies the relevance of the philosophical claim that if I *know* something I can't be wrong. What if it turns out that what I heard was a recording of a bittern, or that the keeper lied to me, or was wrong, or that I had misheard? Would such events shake my theory of knowledge? Not at all: rather I would apologise for or explain my mistake. And this then leads to Austin's most characteristically important claim: when I say that 'I know' I am doing something like making a promise. I am assuring you that you can rely on my statement. My answer to the question 'How do you know?' tells you why you can rely on me. I am giving you my word that I am not merely guessing, or hoping, or betting: that I'm not merely pretty sure, nor even that I am absolutely certain. If I say I'm certain, I am telling you that *I* would act on my belief without hesitation, but I am not actually guaranteeing it. In saying 'I know' I could of course be attempting to mislead, just as I can give a false or hollow promise, and I would be open to the same opprobrium if I did so. What is important is that the use of the verb 'I know' has nothing to do with some theory of unmediated access to truth; it belongs to a social situation and refers to various issues that might arise in the context in which it is said.

In 'A Plea for Excuses' (1956–57) Austin takes on the philosophical chestnuts of selfhood and action by considering the various ways that we *explain* our actions when we feel called upon to explain them. We may apologize for them, or seek to excuse ourselves, or justify them; we may modify our descriptions of them by calling them unintentional, or accidental, or inadvertent, or clumsy, and in each case we are thinking about them differently, or explaining different kinds of actions.

Thus Austin treats explanations of action or assurances of knowledge as performative utterances or speech-acts, and in so doing he dislodges knowledge and action as the central philosophical enigmas and makes them rather counters or props within the speech act, things invoked in response to various human or social situations. Like the later Wittgenstein, Austin's method is to see the solution of philosophical problems consist in the vanishing of the problem. But he nonetheless has positive doctrine to assert as well: the doctrine of speech-acts and how they function, put forth most strenuously in *How to Do Things with Words*, the William James lectures given at Harvard in 1955, and published posthumously in 1961.

In this little book Austin catalogues a variety of speech acts and the different sorts of effects they might aim at as well as have. The most important single conclusion of the book is that all utterances are in some central way performative, that is all speech is social action, and sentences are not names or pointers to truth or falsity but parts of social interaction (something like what Wittgenstein called language-games). Austin describes himself as being inclined to 'play Old Harry with two fetishes ... viz. (1) the true/false fetish, (2) the value/fact fetish' (1975, 151). These are the fetishes of the metaphysician whose philosophy falsifies by paraphrase that might have analogous truth-value, or designate a synonymous fact, but that misses the point of utterances and their uptake:

It is essential to realize that 'true' and 'false'. like 'free' and 'unfree', do not stand for anything simple at all; but only for a general dimension of being a right or proper thing to say as opposed to a wrong thing, in these circumstances, to this audience, for these purposes and with these intentions. (1975, 145)

How to Do Things with Words inaugurated a project followed up by John Searle to come up with a kind of taxonomy of speech-acts. From a philosophical point of view, the taxonomy is wonderful and illuminating fun, but Austin's goal isn't so much a new grammar as a critique of the older philosophical one. His project is in many ways very close to William Empson's in *The Structure of Complex Words*: critical and not philological, but the criticism relies on great philological sensitivity and dexterity.

Austin has also reminded readers with a continental background of Nietzsche and the ways he derives philosophy from grammatical categories, especially in *The Genealogy of Morals*. Indeed Judith Butler makes the connection explicit in an article on hate speech, 'Burning acts, injurious speech'. She relies on another terminology established by Austin in *How to Do Things with Words*, between the locutionary, illocutionary and perlocutionary aspects of a speech act. These formidable terms are easily sketched: the locutionary aspect is something close to a statement of fact, what the utterance says. The illocutionary aspect names what act the utterer was performing *in* (in- = il-) uttering it. The perlocutionary aspect is one of effect: what the utterer did *by* (per) uttering it. I tell you 'The toast is on fire.' The locutionary aspect states a fact. The illocutionary force is to warn or admonish you to do something about it. The perlocutionary effect is to alarm you (the effect I may aim at) or to exasperate you (which I may not be aiming at).

Unfortunately Butler, like most literary theorists who make use of Austin, tends not to pay attention to his distinctions, nor to his warning that 'Our interest . . . is essentially to fasten on the second, illocutionary act and contrast it with the other two. There is a constant tendency in philosophy to elide this in favour of one or other of the other two' (1975, 103). Most literary-theoretical uses of Austin, because they attempt to relate him to a continental or Nietzschean version of the philosophical matrix he is subverting, tend to fall into this elision. Even the best of them – Shoshana Felman – assimilates Austin to Nietzsche and thereby assimilates also the illocutionary to the locutionary or constative: she wants what Austin calls a happy performative to be true in virtue of the fact that it is self-describing. 'I beg you to believe me' would be a successful instance of begging, and therefore a true statement, even as its perlocutionary effect might be an implicit but false promise. But Austin firmly declines to make the happy performative into an instance of, say, analytic or tautologous truth. And he also firmly declines to make the perlocutionary effect the same thing as the utterer's independent action, as Butler would have it. The logic of her argument would allow injury to be an illocutionary aspect of the utterance (as though one could say, 'I hereby injure you') and not its perlocutionary effect (as one may indeed say, 'Your words injured me').

This misreading of Austin probably results from the fact that literary theorists have tended to come to Austin through Derrida's 'Signature Event Context' (1988) which Butler cites approvingly, an essay in which Derrida himself calls Austin's procedure 'nothing less than Nietzschean' (1988, 13). His most telling critique of Austin is that Austin tends to describe literary uses of language as *aetiliolated, non-serious, parasitic* (1975, 104, for example). As Stanley Cavell points out, in the most important critical account of Derrida's essay (in *A Pitch of Philosophy*, 1994), Austin's view of ordinary language effectively excludes such deeply human and characteristic uses of language as writing poetry and telling jokes (104); both of these feature on Wittgenstein's list of language-games in *Philosophical Investigations*, a list Austin took to task in his unscripted 1956 radio talk 'Performative Utterances', where he rebukes 'philosophers' but quotes Wittgenstein for talking 'about the *infinite* uses of language' (1975, 234: cf *Philosophical Investigations*, 1972, part I, section 23: where he says there are '*unzählige*' – 'countless' different kinds of use of what we call 'symbols', 'words', 'sentences'). In general, however, Derrida's critique of Austin is misguided, since he imagines that Austin's theory of performative utterance relies on some relic of the correspondence theory of truth, namely an *adequation* between performance and a conspectual system guiding that performance. But like Wittgenstein, Austin is deeply sceptical of the notion of 'rule-following' as involving correspondence or reference to the rule being followed, and thirty years later it is Derrida who seems to have been caught in a metaphysical trap in 'Signature Event Context'. Derrida there insists on the iterability of the sign as its shimmering foundation, but Austin and Wittgenstein are not interested in the semiotic questions of signification or representation at all, but in what people do.

Nevertheless, Derrida's generally high praise of Austin had the effect of introducing him to a broad range of literary theorists. That praise is not surprising since Austin too tends to have a bracing view of binary opposition; see, for example, his 1947 account of the way binary oppositions distort the phenomena they are meant to clarify:

> One of the most important points to grasp is that these two terms, 'sense-data' and 'material things', live by taking in each other's washing – what is spurious is not one term of the pair, but the antithesis itself. The case of 'universal' and 'particular', or 'individual', is similar in some respects though of course not in all. In philosophy it is often good policy, where one member of a putative pair falls under suspicion, to view the more innocent-seeming party suspiciously as well. (1964, 4; the last two sentences footnote the first)

Austin's policy of inversion leads to his demonstration that the things metaphysicians take as the real puzzle – direct perception, or knowledge, or intention – are actually only terms that would come up to name a contrast that might be relevant to a real situation: seeing your shadow, and so perceiving you, but *not* directly, or hearing a recording and so being wrong when I said that I knew a bittern was there because I heard it booming, or shooting your donkey *un*intentionally, because I was aiming at my own. Direct perception, knowledge, intention: Austin calls it glib to make these into philosophical problems as though they name some central issues about our relation to the world or to being, when in their usage down the generations what they really *do* is act as assurances in some case where there might be a reason to wonder about how something happened.

Paul de Man also helped interest American theorists in Austin, since he used the distinction between performative and constative as a parallel or at least homology to his distinction between grammatical and rhetorical structures of language. Like Derrida, de Man saw that a writer of fiction might suffer some interesting anxiety about whether a fictional sentence were performative or cognitive (as he called it), and if performative in what way. De Man's students (including Felman) extended his interest in Austin, and made one received version of him a kind of staple in deconstructively oriented literary theory in America. But there is some irony in the fact that American readers of Austin have tended to come to him through Derrida and de Man, since Derrida himself was reading Cavell's essay on Austin in 1970. Cavell is the literary theorist who understands Austin best, or who has thought about Austin most clearly and profoundly in a literary context (and thereby in a philosophical context as well). Not the least of Derrida's contributions will have been the fact that he has sent readers back to Austin, and onwards to Cavell.

William Flesch

Further reading and works cited

Austin, J. L. *Sense and Sensibilia.* New York, 1964.
—. *How to Do Things With Words.* Cambridge, MA, 1975.
—. *Philosophical Papers.* Oxford, 1979.
Benveniste, E. *Problems in General Linguistics.* Coral Gables, FL, 1971.
Butler, J. 'Burning Acts, Injurious Speech', in *Performativity and Performance*, eds A. Parker and E. Kosofsky Sedgwick. New York, 1995.
Cavell, S. *Must We Mean What We Say?* Cambridge, 1976.
—. *The Claim of Reason.* Cambridge, MA, 1979.
—. *A Pitch of Philosophy.* Cambridge, MA, 1994.
de Man, P. *Allegories of Reading.* New Haven, CT, 1979.
Derrida, J. *Limited Inc.,* ed. Gerald Graff. Evanston, IL, 1988.
Felman, S. *The Literary Speech Act.* Ithaca, NY, 1983.
Gould, T. 'The Unhappy Performative', in *Performativity and Performance*, eds A. Parker and E. Kosofsky Sedgwick. New York, 1995.
Parker, A. and Sedgwick, E. Kosofsky (eds) *Performativity and Performance.* New York, 1995.
Searle, J. *Speech Acts.* London, 1969.
Wittgenstein, L. *Philosophical Investigations.* Oxford, 1972.

Richard Hoggart (1918–), Raymond Williams (1921–1988) and the Emergence of Cultural Studies

The term 'culture' has become virtually ubiquitous in our society. In certain circumstances and on certain occasions it still retains some of its elitist and exclusive connotations, and yet we also talk frequently enough of popular culture, of black or gay cultures – even of business or management cultures – terms which might once have been considered antithetical. All such phenomena might – indeed have – come within the purview of contemporary cultural studies. Yet, in Britain, the emergence of cultural studies as a project or discipline was very much bound up with the work of figures such as Richard Hoggart and Raymond Williams, and therefore with a fairly specific history and debate which requires us to understand the significance of the term 'culture' as it circulated during the nineteenth and early twentieth centuries. Indeed, a great deal of Williams's work in particular is explicitly concerned with the genealogy and connotations of the term 'culture', culminating in a particular theoretical position, cultural materialism, which emerged out of this lengthy engagement.

As Williams argues in his important early work, *Culture and Society*, the term becomes increasingly important in the nineteenth century, denoting a broadly humanistic rather than merely formal education. This sense of the term is most closely associated, though it did not originate with Matthew Arnold for whom the dissemination of culture represented the best hope for achieving national unity in the face of contemporary class divisions between barbarians (the dissolute gentry and aristocracy), philistines (the puritanical and determinedly uncultured bourgeoisie) and a potentially unruly populace (the working class). Arnold's was therefore an organic ideal, as indeed is implied by the term's origins in an analogy with the development of the land, 'cultivation'. In his supposed class neutrality and undogmatic appeal to 'the best that has been thought and said' Arnold believed he was promoting a form of education which would develop our essential *humanity* – in the sense that humanity is not merely another species but one characterized by intellectual, imaginative and, crucially, moral faculties which are capable of various degrees of development: the value of culture was therefore potentially universal. Moreover, the principal opposition which culture formed for Arnold was with 'machinery', in its literal and metaphorical senses. Machinery was, of course, the vehicle of economic power for the dominant class of the period, the bourgeoisie, but Arnold expanded the term's significance, using it to refer to those institutions, laws and principles in which the bourgeoisie placed its faith for the improvement of civilization. By contrast, culture was 'a study of perfection and of harmonious perfection, general perfection, and perfection which consists in becoming something rather than in having something, in an inward condition of the mind and spirit, not in an outward set of circumstances' (Arnold 1966, 48). It is significant—and a feature of the conservatism of Arnold's thought – that he did not provide a precise definition of culture, and his sense of what constitutes culture is based on supposedly self-evident criteria. His strategy was rather to say 'look at this particular product of philistine civilization and compare it with this example of true culture'. But Arnold's lack of specificity in this respect emerges with an ideological consistency from his own ideals, since to provide a definition of culture would be to establish a new set of machinery, an 'external' set of guidelines akin to the rule-bound thinking of the middle classes which so offended Arnold's humanism.

The most prominent twentieth-century advocate of Arnoldian ideals was F. R. Leavis, and the timing of his writing in defence of a culture which he perceived to be under threat from the forces of modernity also serves to highlight one of the conditions for the emergence of cultural studies: Leavis polemicized against the effects of a developing 'mass culture', including, crucially, an expansion of the various media and new levels of popular consumerism. In his famous, perhaps notorious, essay 'Mass Civilization and Minority Culture', Leavis focuses his attack on the standardization and mass production which characterized modern capitalism – once again, machinery acts as a metonym for dehumanization – and which were increasingly setting the values by which things other and more sacrosanct than commodities were to be judged. Leavis argued for a renewed defence of culture against the encroachment of such values. This, he claimed, would necessarily be the task of an elite which would include, most prominently, university lecturers such as himself. Again, as with Arnold, nowhere does he make explicit the values he is defending, but merely holds up for ridicule the judgements and values of those who typify contemporary degenerate principles (Leavis's chief instance in this respect is Arnold Bennett, whom Leavis derides in rather patrician fashion for being both provincial and middle class and therefore an enemy of the supposedly universal culture Leavis aims to restore).

We need to note two things in particular about this version of 'culture', since, for those who still give voice to Arnoldian and Leavisite principles, 'cultural studies' is anathema. First, despite its supposed universalism, what counted as 'culture' was clearly informed by educational traditions which, though not specifically 'aristocratic', were certainly the province of an elite centred on Oxbridge. Second, 'culture' was a specifically untheorized and, for ideological reasons, untheorizable phenomenon, since to theorize culture – that is, to take it as an object of study, rather than as a means of transmitting desirable qualities – would be to betray its essentially humanistic, non-mechanistic and unstandardizable values. These are key features of older ideas of 'culture', then, and it is instructive to contrast them with certain typical features of cultural studies. Hoggart's work – and also that of the historian E. P. Thompson, whose *The Making of the English Working Class* played a significant role in the discipline's emergence – took as their object the lived values – the *cultures*, in a different sense, that is – of the English working class, ascribing to them a significance and validity which the Arnoldian tradition would deny. The work of Williams, while less descriptive of particular class lifestyles, nonetheless explicitly repudiates Leavisite elitism and is informed by socialist convictions. The trajectory of cultural studies, moreover, has largely been to focus on popular culture: it is more likely to consider *Coronation St* than *Coriolanus*, and therefore to 'collude' with that standardization so despised by Leavis. Finally, cultural studies has been keenly receptive to what we tend to refer to rather homogenizingly as 'theory', and in this respect also offends against the Arnoldian distrust of 'machinery'.

Richard Hoggart

Richard Hoggart's principal contributions to the development of cultural studies are twofold: his publication of an innovative analysis of the changing patterns of working class life, *The Uses of Literacy*, and his role in the development of the School for Contemporary Cultural Studies at Birmingham University in the 1960s.

The significance of *The Uses of Literacy* is that it was probably the first book written from a 'cultured' – in the Leavisite sense – perspective which sought to analyse in a serious way not merely the publications which were then being consumed in working-class circles, but also the ways in which these related to the dominant values of working-class life. Hoggart's intimacy with the context he describes results from his own working-class background in Leeds, though, as was the case with Raymond Williams, he was educated at grammar school and university in ways which produced a sense of separation, even alienation, from that background. This is something which is self-consciously dealt with in the book's description of 'the scholarship boy' who 'has left his class, at least in spirit, by being in certain ways unusual; and he is still unusual in another class, too tense and over-wound' (1992, 302). The consequence of this is that in his analyses Hoggart tends to combine an insider's knowingness with an outsider's judgements, and, in this respect, it would be easy to accuse him of developing a merely snobbish relationship to working-class life, most notably in his disdain for the vulgarity of modern developments (notoriously, for instance, in his characterization of 'juke-box boys' who frequent 'milk-bars [which] indicate at once, in the nastiness of their modernistic knick-knacks, their glaring showiness, an aesthetic breakdown so complete that, in comparison with them, the layout of the living-rooms in some of the poor homes from which the customers come seems to speak of a tradition as balanced and civilized as an eighteenth-century town house' (1992, 247–8)). However, there is a critical emphasis in his work which, though it often incorporates disdain, is arguably not reducible to this.

Leavis's attack on modernity was, as we have seen, directed at machinery and mass standardization and focused in particular on the development of a mass media. Hoggart was influenced by Leavis's critique and is also concerned with this phenomenon and with the effects of mass consumerism in disrupting, transmuting or corrupting working-class attitudes. Invariably, change is for the worse. The 'popular publicists' he denounces disseminate an unquestioning belief in progress which is more or less synonymous with the spread of materialism (in its pejorative sense). I want to focus here on the four general tendencies Hoggart discerns since these are perhaps more important than any specific manifestation of them as described in the book:

1. Principles of tolerance and freedom rooted in the pragmatic working-class senti- ment of 'live and let live' have acquired a different inflection, enabled by – or perhaps the consequence of – the sensationalism of contemporary publications: the unwillingness to admit that freedom should have its limits. For Hoggart, 'The tolerant phrases have been joined by others in similar dress; the new depreciate the old, and together they become the ritual uniform of a shared unwillingness to admit that freedom can have its punishments. Anything goes and there is no scale' (1992, 178).

2. Similarly, Hoggart discerns a shift in the established principle of working-class solidarity – which enjoins a suspicion of outsiders ('them and us') – since this has been debased and transformed into a form of intolerance. The popular press, in identifying themselves with 'the people', promote the sense that the people's ideas are not only as good as anyone else's, but are even superior because they are more representative. Hoggart illustrates this with a still recognizable pseudo-democratic phenomenon: 'The popular press ... conduct polls on this matter and question- naires on that matter among their readers, and so elevate the counting of heads into a substitute for judgement' (1992, 179–80).

3. Materialism goes together with, and is encouraged by, an unquestioning belief in progress, which is partly bound up with the kudos of science. The consequence of this is a historical amnesia and 'glorification of youth' (Hoggart 1992, 193). Hoggart's image of this process invokes explicitly Arnoldian language: 'the wagon, loaded with its barbarians in wonderland, moves irresistibly forward: not forward to anywhere, but simply forward for forwardness's sake' (1992, 193–4).

4. Finally, all of these processes together have produced an 'indifferentism' (another Arnoldian term) and relativism by contributing 'to an endless flux of the undistinguished and the valueless, to a world in which every kind of activity is finally made meaningless by being reduced to a counting of heads' (1992, 194–5). Moreover, this process is paradoxically accompanied by an abdication of respon- sibility and a pervasive surrendering to authority on the part of the working class.

Though Hoggart's account of these developments involves some perceptive commentary on the transformations being wrought by mass consumerism, it is manifestly the case that his work is tinged with nostalgia and conservatism. His role in the institutionalization of cultural studies, however, was of more radical and lasting significance. Some years after being appointed Chair of English at Birmingham University, Hoggart decided to continue the work he had begun with *The Uses of Literacy* by setting up a Centre for Contemporary Cultural Studies in 1964, the first of its kind, though subsequently there were to be numerous university centres in related fields. Stuart Hall, who took up the directorship following Hoggart's departure in 1968, records that it was regarded contemptuously by other cognate disciplines who considered themselves under threat, and this is indicative of the status of cultural studies as neither 'science' (sociology) – a status it would be even more keen to repudiate in these poststructuralist times – nor belletristic humanism (literature):

> On the day of our opening, we received letters from the English department saying that they couldn't really welcome us; they knew we were there, but they hoped we'd keep out of their way while they got on with the work they had to do. We received another, rather sharper letter from the sociologists saying, in effect, 'We have read *The Uses of Literacy* and we hope you don't think you're doing sociology, because that's not what you're doing at all.' (1990, 13)

As Hall also points out, though, the CCCS was not bound by any particular consensus about what it was its staff were up to, and, in political terms, Hall was significantly to the left of Hoggart in his thinking. Hall's directorship of the Centre saw a change in orientation away from the focus on working-class lived experience towards the study of 'the relations between media and ideology ... through the analysis of signifying systems in texts' (Turner 1996, 72). Indeed, Hall is more of a representative figure than Hoggart in terms of the contemporary practice of cultural studies, and his work has largely eclipsed the outdated approach of Hoggart himself. The same, however, cannot be said of Raymond Williams, whose influence remains considerable.

Raymond Williams

Williams's relationship to the English tradition of thinking about 'culture' is both more sustained and, ultimately, more critical than that of Hoggart. As a statement of his early position, we might consider his 1958 essay 'Culture is Ordinary'. Here he acknowledges two intellectual debts in particular, marxism and Leavis, which perhaps inevitably produce tensions and contradictions in the essay which remain characteristic of his work up to his elaboration of cultural materialism in the 1970s. But even in this essay, we find a discernibly leftist version of the organicism which is integral to the Arnoldian ideal of a common culture, and also a recognition of the disdain which has characterized other versions of that ideal of culture. Williams, for instance, refuses simply to indulge in any blanket condemnation of modernity, citing the real improvements to working-class life which have been made by mechanization and industrialization. More to the point here, he is also contemptuous of the minoritizing, elitist view of culture, of culture as 'the outward and emphatically visible sign of a special kind of people, cultivated people'. But if Williams wants to rescue culture from the minority, he also wants to defend it against those who, because of its elitist aura, would make it 'a dirty word' (1958, 5). Implicitly, he is referring to marxists at this point, those who have argued that the cultural ideal was ultimately 'bourgeois'. Williams rejects this, claiming not only that there is 'a distinct working-class way of life, which I for one value', but also that 'the arts and learning. .. are in a real sense a national inheritance, which is, or should be, available to everyone' (1958, 8). In this sense, while Williams is clearly writing with the grain of postwar democratization – and, indeed, much of his work in texts such as *The Long Revolution* has been directed not merely at analysing culture, but in arguing for an expansion of democracy, even to those areas of our lives dominated by the undemocratic writ of the market – there is still an acceptance of culture's organic credentials as rooted in essentially human values (see especially Eagleton 1976, 21–42). Only much later, and after a rapprochement with marxist thinking, did Williams fully recognize that culture can be marked by relations of conflict.

Williams's trajectory through the 1960s led him away from an engagement simply with literature to a consideration of other media, including television. This, indeed, represented the logical extension of his concern that the study of culture should not be rooted in an idealization of the pre-industrial past or in a disdain for its popular forms, including those governed by capitalist organization and directed towards 'the masses' (who, crucially, Williams consistently argues, only have an existence in the constructions of them made by those who disdain them while actually having a design on them – newspaper proprietors and the like). The first movement in this direction was with *Communications* in 1962 which, though now outdated in its approach, is significant precisely because of its attempt seriously to analyse modern media, rather than reject them as part of the dehumanizing tendency of modernity. Williams's later book *Television: Technology and Cultural Form*, published in 1975, once his theoretical orientation had moved significantly leftwards, is a much more sophisticated work while maintaining his established emphasis on cultural *production*, that is with culture as something which is bound up both with material processes and broader values. It is impossible to do justice here to the reach of Williams's argument which involves consideration of the historical development of television technology as a consequence of specific social and commercial pressures as well as a consideration of the specific forms television adopts. It ends, characteristically, with speculation on the possibility of democratizing televisual technology.

This final point is also indicative of another aspect of Williams's career as an intellectual, since he was not the kind of academic figure so familiar today whose academic work is merely coterminous with their political interventions. He was, for instance, an activist in the Labour Party up to 1966 – when he rejected it because of its lack of radicalism on key issues and because of 'the ruling-class style of the Wilson government' (O'Connor 1989, 21) – as well as in CND and the anti-Vietnam war movement. His later intellectual development emerged out of a re-engagement with marxist thought after the revolutionary protests of 1968 and following the translation and promotion of Western European marxist thought – particularly that of Gramsci – by the New Left. His key theoretical statement, an elaboration of what he called 'cultural materialism', came with the publication of the somewhat misleadingly named *Marxism and Literature* in 1977, a work which elaborates and extends the arguments made in an earlier essay originally published in *New Left Review*, 'Base and Superstructure in Marxist Cultural Theory', which, for reasons of space, I will focus on here. The essay is very much concerned with theorizing possibilities for change.

Most marxist cultural theory has concentrated on refining and complicating the determining relationship between base and superstructure in the classical model in which the base refers to the forces and relations of production and the superstructure to just about everything else – law, philosophy, religion, art, for instance. Williams, though, argues for a reconsideration of the whole set up:

> We have to revalue 'determination' towards the setting of limits and the exertion of pressure, and away from a predicted, prefigured and controlled content. We have to revalue 'super-structure' towards a related range of cultural practices, and away from a reflected, reproduced or specifically dependent content. And, crucially, we have to revalue 'the base' away from the notion of a fixed economic or technological abstraction, and towards the specific activities of men [sic] in real social and economic relationships, containing fundamental contradictions and therefore always in a state of dynamic process. (1980, 34)

In this respect, while recognizing the fundamental importance in our society of specifically capitalist economic production – the production of commodities – Williams argues for a recognition that cultural productivity is itself part of 'the material production and reproduction of real life' (1980, 35), hence the term 'cultural materialism'.

Not that Williams wants to do away with the concept of determinism; hence his resort to the Gramscian concept of hegemony. But here again, Williams is keen to emphasize the complexity of this term which he takes to refer to 'the central, effective and dominant system of meanings and values, which are not merely abstract but which are organized and lived' (1980, 38). Crucially, though, to say that these meanings and values are dominant is to imply nothing about their *value*. However, for Williams, hegemony is also to be considered as a dynamic *process*, always in need of renewal in one way or another, hence the complex relations between these *dominant* meanings and values and those which are either *residual* or *emergent*, that is bound up with a prior or developing historical moment. The crucial point is that residual or emergent meanings and values are rarely treated with indifference by those who seek to defend dominant ones – unless those residual or emergent values are simply *alternative*, or content to remain marginal, rather than truly *oppositional* – hence the importance, even urgency, for the dominant order of *incorporating* these areas of experience. In this way, Williams is able to suggest a more sophisticated, more historically nuanced form of marxist cultural analysis which moves beyond those abstract epochal designations such as 'feudal' or 'capitalist' – invaluable, but unwieldy – which have characterized marxist cultural analysis.

The development of Cultural Studies

Williams's recognition that conflict, rather than consensus, was characteristic of culture is *the* important break in his thought, and the terms dominant, residual and emergent have continued to be invoked in literary and cultural analysis. However, cultural studies have also been increasingly influenced by other traditions, both within and external to western marxism: while retaining its leftist leanings, cultural studies has arguably increasingly privileged analyses emerging out of what used to be known as the 'new social movements' – feminism, racial politics, the lesbian and gay movements, for instance – over the kinds of class and economic concerns which dominate Williams's thinking (though it should also be said that Williams's political engagements both in his work and in practice were not bound up with the labour movement in any narrow sense).

In some cases the shift of focus has been the consequence of explicit disagreement with the work of Williams, as in Paul Gilroy's critique of the impression given by Williams that the culture and society tradition was one which was generated through purely indigenous English processes. Gilroy argues that 'the New Left heirs to the aesthetic and cultural tradition in which Turner and Ruskin stand. .. reproduced its nationalism and its ethnocentrism by denying imaginary, invented Englishness any external references whatsoever. England ceaselessly gives birth to itself, seemingly from Britannia's head' (1993, 14). The force of Gilroy's argument is that Williams's work itself constitutes a selective tradition – a term originally invoked by Williams in *The Long Revolution* and reinvoked in 'Base and Superstructure' to describe 'that which, within the terms of an effective dominant culture, is always passed off as "*the* tradition", "*the* significant past"' (1980, 39) – in occluding the influence of colonial matters in the development of the culture and society tradition as well as the contributions which black writers and activists have made to supposedly indigenous radical traditions. Gilroy's critique, then, is both a contribution to and symptomatic of the broadening of cultural studies. Indeed, cultural materialism has itself evolved and integrated such concerns into its purview, with one of its most prominent contemporary advocates providing the following gloss (albeit principally in relation to literary analysis): 'Cultural materialists say that canonical texts have political projects, and should not be allowed to circulate in the world today on the assumption that their representations of class, race, ethnicity, gender and sexuality are simply authoritative' (Sinfield 1994, 38).

Moreover, the impression should not be given that cultural studies has remained in thrall to the theoretical approach elaborated by Williams. As with modern literary studies, or indeed most disciplines which have opened up to the influence of 'theory', cultural studies routinely engages with a number of other theoretical models, from the Frankfurt School to the ideologically liberal influences of postmodernism and poststructuralism. Nonetheless, given that, in Britain at least, the term 'culture' remains peculiarly bound up with a specific and politically charged history of debate about education, class and value, Williams's contribution will remain central.

David Alderson

Further reading and works cited

Arnold, M. *Culture and Anarchy*. Cambridge, 1966.
Eagleton, T. *Criticism and Ideology*. London, 1976.
Gilroy, P. *The Black Atlantic*. London, 1993.
Hall, S. 'The Emergence of Cultural Studies and the Crisis of the Humanities', *October*, 53, 1990.
— et al. *Policing the Crisis: Mugging, the State, and Law and Order*. London, 1978.
Hoggart, R. *The Uses of Literacy*. Harmondsworth, 1992.
Hebdige, D. *Subculture: The Meaning of Style*. London, 1979.
Inglis, F. *Cultural Studies*. Oxford, 1993.
Leavis, F. R. 'Mass Civilization and Minority Culture', *Education and the University*. London, 1948.
O'Connor, A. *Raymond Williams*. Oxford, 1989.
Sinfield, A. *Cultural Politics – Queer Reading*. London, 1994.
Thompson, E. P. *The Making of the English Working Class*. Harmondsworth, 1968.
Turner, G. *British Cultural Studies*. London, 1996.
Williams, R. *Culture and Society 1780–1950*. London, 1958.
—. *The Long Revolution*. London, 1961.
—. *Communications*. Harmondsworth, 1962.
—. *Television*. New York, 1975.
—. *Marxism and Literature*. Oxford, 1977.
—. *Problems in Materialism and Culture*. London, 1980.
—. *Towards 2000*. London, 1983.
—. *Resources of Hope*. London, 1989.

Raymond Williams (1921–1988)

Raymond Williams is widely regarded as the most significant 'left-wing' figure in late twentieth-century British intellectual life, or in Cornell West's forgivable hyperbole 'the last of the great European male revolutionary socialist intellectuals' (1995, ix). His various contributions, as a creative writer, as a central source of inspiration for the proto-discipline of cultural studies, as a key figure in the New Left intelligentsia, have all been variously acknowledged. Much less common, however, is a serious acknowledgement of his role as a critical theorist. Yet Williams himself increasingly came to characterize his work as a distinctive kind of theory, that is as a kind of 'cultural materialism'. He had first used this term in a short essay published in the hundredth issue of the journal New Left Review, to which he had been a long-standing contributor. Cultural materialism, he explained, 'is a theory of culture as a (social and material) productive process and of specific practices, of "arts", as social uses of material means of production'. He added that the position would be 'spelled out more fully' in Marxism and Literature and in the book that would eventually be published as Culture (1980d, 243). There is an important sense in which these two books do indeed 'spell out' the theory, and they will therefore command our attention here. But we should note also Williams's own insistence, in the 'Introduction' to Marxism and Literature, that cultural materialism had been 'a position which, as a matter of theory, I have arrived at over the years' (1977, 5). Its pre-history, as part of a much longer intellectual evolution, demands our attention also.

Trained in English at Cambridge, Williams derived much of his initial critical vocabulary from the Leavises and Scrutiny. Formed by the biographical experience of Welsh working-class life, he was also a lifelong socialist, with an enduring interest in marxist and quasi-marxist cultural theory. At one point in his 1977 interviews with the New Left Review, he recalls the establishment of Politics and Letters, which he had co-edited at Cambridge during 1947 and 1948: 'Our intention was to produce a review that would . . . unite radical left politics with Leavisite literary criticism. We were to be to the left of the Labour party, but at a distance from the CP. Our affiliation to Scrutiny was guarded, but . . . nevertheless quite a strong one' (1979a, 65). An understanding of Williams's intellectual evolution will require some appreciation of how he variously negotiated this doubly ambivalent relationship to Leavisism on the one hand, marxism on the other. From Leavis, he inherited organicist and holistic conceptions of culture and methods of analysis, a strong sense of the importance of the particular, whether in art or in 'life', and an insistence on the absolute centrality of culture. But he rejected Scrutiny's cultural elitism, especially as displayed in the mass civilization versus minority culture topos. From marxism, he inherited both a radically socialistic critique of ruling class political, economic and cultural power and a strong sense of 'materiality'. But he rejected the economic determinism of the so-called 'base/superstructure' formula and the structural determinism of later Althusserian and quasi-Althusserian theories of ideology.

It is possible to identify three main 'phases' in Williams's thought, each explicable in terms of its own differentially negotiated settlement between Leavisism and marxism, and each characterizable, in perhaps overly political terms, in relation to a relatively distinct, consecutive moment in the history of the British New Left. In the first such phase, that of the moment of '1956' and the foundation of the first New Left, Williams addressed himself very directly to the definition of a third position, simultaneously dependent upon but in contradictory relation to Leavisite criticism and orthodox marxism. He thus played a central role in the development of a peculiarly 'culturalist' post-Communist marxism, a kind of indigenously British 'Western Marxism'. The key texts from this period are without doubt *Culture and Society* and *The Long Revolution*. The central procedure of *Culture and Society* could not be more Leavisite: to move by way of a series of close readings of particular texts to the account of a distinctively 'English' national 'tradition'. Moreover, Williams's sense of the intellectual content of this tradition had much in common with Leavis and Eliot. And for Williams, as for Leavis, the tradition developed in more or less explicit antagonism to utilitarianism (though this remained in many respects a surprisingly underdeveloped theme). Williams's strategic purpose was nonetheless radically opposed to the explicit cultural and political conservatism displayed by Eliot and increasingly by the Leavises. To the contrary, he sought to demonstrate that, in its very complexity, the 'culture and society' tradition remained, not only finally unassimilable to any obvious conservatism, but also often openly amenable to radical, indeed socialistic, interpretation. Quite fundamentally, Williams rejected the Leavisite notion of 'mass civilization', and with it the notion of 'masses': 'There are in fact no masses; there are only ways of seeing people as masses' (1963, 289) He rejected also the notion of a distinctively valuable minority culture, but did so nonetheless in distinctly Leavisite terms. A culture, Williams wrote, 'is not only a body of intellectual and imaginative work; it is also and essentially a whole way of life' (1963, 311). In principle, this is little different from Eliot or Leavis. But in the practical application of the principle, Williams so expanded its range as to include within 'culture' the 'collective democratic institution', by which he meant, primarily, the trade union, the cooperative, and the working-class political party (1963, 313).

Thus redefined, the notion of a common culture became supplemented, and importantly qualified, by that of a plurality of class cultures. Yet, despite such qualification, the normative ideal remained central: 'We need a common culture, not for the sake of an abstraction, but because we shall not survive without it' (Williams 1963, 304). This ideal provided Williams, as it had Leavis, with the ground from which to mount an organicist critique of utilitarian individualism. But a common culture could never be properly such, he argued, if established on the basis of the merely vicarious participation Eliot and Leavis had sanctioned. 'The distinction of a culture in common', he wrote, 'is that ... selection is freely and commonly made and remade. The tending is a common process, based on a common decision' (1963, 322). In a characteristically leftist move, Williams thus relocated the common culture from the idealized historical past it occupied in Eliot and Leavis, to the not too distant, still to be made, democratically socialist future. If the common culture was not yet fully common, then it followed that the literary and cultural tradition should be seen, not so much as the unfolding of a group mind, as in Eliot, but as the outcome, in part at least, of a set of interested selections made in the present. A 'tradition is always selective,' wrote Williams, 'and ... there will always be a tendency for this process of selection to be related to and even governed by the interests of the class that is dominant' (1963, 307–8). Where Leavis had revered a 'Great Tradition', Williams would thus detect a selective tradition. But even as he insisted on the importance of class cultures, he was careful also to note the extent to which distinctions of class are complicated, especially in the field of intellectual and imaginative work, by 'the common elements resting on a common language' (1963, 311). For Williams, any direct reduction of art to class, such as is canvassed in many versions of marxism, remained unacceptable. 'The area of culture', he observed, 'is usually proportionate to the area of a language rather than to the area of a class' (1963, 307). This argument is repeated and significantly elaborated upon in the opening theoretical chapters of *The Long Revolution*:

> The selective tradition creates, at one level, a general human culture; at another level, the historical record of a particular society; at a third level ... a rejection of considerable areas of what was once a living culture ... selection will be governed by many kinds of special interest, including class interest ... The traditional culture of a society will always tend to correspond to its *contemporary* system of interests and values ... (1965, 68)

Once again the stress falls on selection according to class-specific criteria, but once again also on the reality of a truly general human culture.

It is here too that Williams proposed an initial theorization of the concept of structure of feeling, a term actually coined in the much earlier *Preface to Film* (Williams and Orrom 1954), but not hitherto given any extensive theoretical articulation. 'In one sense', he wrote, 'this structure of feeling is the culture of a period: it is the particular living result of all the elements in the general organization' (1965, 64). He continues: 'in this respect ... the arts of a period ... are of major importance ... here ... the actual living sense, the deep community that makes the communication possible, is naturally drawn upon' (1965, 64– 5). A structure of feeling, Williams makes clear, is neither universal nor class specific, though it is 'a very deep and very wide possession' (1965, 65). Nor is it formally learned, he speculates, and thence follows its often peculiarly generational character: 'the new generation will have its own structure of feeling, which will not appear to have come "from" anywhere' (1965, 65). This concept of 'structure of feeling' was to prove quite extraordinarily fruitful. In *The English Novel*, for example, Williams would attempt to show how, from Dickens to Lawrence, the novel became one medium among many by which people sought to master and absorb new experience through the articulation of a structure of feeling the key problem of which was that of the 'knowable community' (1974a, 14–15). In *Drama from Ibsen to Brecht* he would produce an account of the development of naturalism and of expressionism in the modern theatre organized around precisely 'the history and significance of the main dramatic forms – the conventions and structures of feeling' (1973a, 14). The concept would also occupy a commanding position in his later cultural materialism.

In *The Long Revolution* Williams sought to chart the long history of the emergence of modernity and of the interrelationships within British society between the democratic revolution, the industrial revolution and the 'cultural revolution' embodied in the extension and democratization of communications (1965, 10–12). The book's central novelty lies in its form, in its peculiar combination of theoretical discussion, substantive 'sociological' analysis and expressly political argument. The opening theoretical discussions, in which the concept of a structure of feeling is elaborated, are both dense and original. The book's second part moves to supplement the more conventional procedures of Leavisite textual criticism with a sociological account of the historical development of a number of major British cultural institutions: there are pioneering analyses of the education system and the growth of the reading public, the popular press and the development of 'Standard English'; followed, in turn, by chapters on the social backgrounds of a selection of canonical English writers and on the social histories of dramatic forms and the contemporary novel. The concluding third part, in effect an exploratory inquiry into the structure of feeling of the early 1960s, critically addresses the politico-cultural problems of the apparent moral decline of the labour movement (1965, 328–9). The combination of a sharply analytical intelligence and an at times near-utopian radical vision, which informs much of this last essay, spoke powerfully and provocatively to a society slowly shrugging off the moral and political conservatism of the 1950s.

What holds the book together, however, is its very strong underlying sense of the materiality of culture, at once a restatement and a transcendence of the position originally outlined in *Culture and Society*. 'It was certainly an error', Williams wrote against Leavisite humanism, 'to suppose that values or art-works could be adequately studied without reference to the particular society within which they were expressed' (1965, 61). But, 'it is equally an error', he wrote against marxism, 'to suppose that the social explanation is determining, or that the values and works are mere by-products' (1965, 61). He moves thence to what might well be the book's central set of propositions:

> If the art is part of the society, there is no solid whole, outside it, to which ... we concede priority. The art is there, as an activity, with the production, the trading, the politics, the raising of families ... It is ... not a question of relating the art to the society, but of studying all the activities and their interrelations, without any concession of priority to any one of them we may choose to abstract ... I would define the theory of culture as the study of relationships between elements in a whole way of life. (1965, 61–3)

Here, then, was the prospectus for what would become a thoroughgoing cultural materialism.

In the interim between the first publication of *The Long Revolution* in 1961 and that of *Marxism and Literature* in 1977, Williams's work proceeded by way of a series of often radically innovative encounters with an extremely diverse set of substantive issues, ranging across the whole field of literary and cultural studies: the mass media (Williams 1974b, 1976a), the novel (Williams 1974a), the drama (Williams 1973a, 1979b) and the pastoral (Williams 1973b). In the work on theatre and on television a new awareness of the social conventionality of form and of the interrelationship between technology and form is increasingly brought to bear. Williams's coupling of the problem of cultural form to that of cultural technology clearly drew attention in each case to the materiality of what were in orthodoxly marxist terms 'ideal' superstructures. This led him, in turn, to a simultaneous rejection of both technological determinism and the notion of a determined technology (1974b, 12–13), and thence to a much more complex understanding of the notion of determination itself. The chronological overlap between Williams's work in theatre studies and that on the mass media is thus by no means merely 'coincidental'. Disparate though the work might appear, it proceeds along clearly connected lines of inquiry. And these connections are empirical and substantive as well as theoretical and methodological. As Williams had noted in the 'Conclusion' to his *Drama from Ibsen to Brecht*: 'drama is no longer coexistent with theatre ... The largest audience for drama, in our own world, is in the cinema and on television' (1973a, 399).

The cumulative effect of these apparently diverse lines of inquiry would finally be registered in *Marxism and Literature*. In Williams's earlier 'left culturalist' writings the 'deep community' that is culture had been understood as simultaneously transcendent of class and yet irredeemably marked by it. For all the eloquence with which this position had been argued, it remained quite fundamentally incoherent: the competing claims of commonality and difference, culture and class, Leavisism and marxism, formed a circle which stubbornly refused to be squared. But in the second phase of his work, that of the moment of '1968' and the emergence of a second New Left, it finally became possible for Williams to explain, to his own satisfaction at least, how it could be that structures of feeling are common to different classes, and yet nonetheless represent the interests of some particular class. In this second phase, his engagement with a series of continental European western marxisms, each only very recently translated into English (Lukács, Goldmann, Althusser, Gramsci), and with various forms of Third Worldist political radicalism, clearly paralleled, but nonetheless neither reduplicated nor inspired, that of the younger generation of radical intellectuals associated with Perry Anderson's *New Left Review*. The radicalism is readily apparent in *The Country and the City*, where a developing critique of various mythological accounts of rural life (including Marx's own dismissal of 'rural idiocy') eventually culminated in a defence of Third World insurrectionism (Williams 1973b, 304). The theoretical encounter with western marxism initially entailed little more than a recognition that not all marxisms were necessarily economically determinist and a corollary discovery of preoccupations similar to his own in the work of individual western marxist writers. Williams's response to Goldmann, for example, had centred on the recognition that they were 'exploring many of the same areas with many of the same concepts' (1980b, 20). The response to Gramsci, however, was of an altogether different order, precipitating a much more positive redefinition of Williams's own theoretical stance. As he would insist in *Marxism and Literature*: 'Gramsci's ... work is one of the major turning-points in Marxist cultural theory' (1977, 108).

Williams was impressed both by Gramsci's work on intellectuals, which seemed to him an 'encouraging' and 'experimental' model for work in the sociology of culture (1977, 138), and by the wider implications of the theory of hegemony. The significance of the latter had registered initially in an essay written in 1973, entitled 'Base and Superstructure in Marxist Cultural Theory' (1980c, 37). But in *Marxism and Literature* the argument is elaborated upon at much greater length. Here, as before, Williams argued against the base/super-structure model for cultural analysis, on the grounds that culture is both real and material: 'From castles and palaces and churches to prisons and workhouses and schools; from weapons of war to a controlled press ... These are never superstructural activities. They are necessarily material production within which an apparently self-subsistent mode of production can alone be carried on' (1977, 93). Here, though, this more general materialism is decisively articulated to the theory of hegemony. The first and last chapters respectively of the book's first part are devoted to two key concepts and two keywords, deriving respectively from Leavisism and marxism, 'Culture' and 'Ideology'. In a subsequent chapter, Williams argues for the theoretical superiority over each of these of the Gramscian notion of hegemony:

> 'Hegemony' goes beyond 'culture' ... in its insistence on relating the 'whole social process' to specific distributions of power and influence ... Gramsci therefore introduces the necessary recognition of dominance and subordination in what has still, however, to be recognized as a whole process. It is in just this recognition of the *wholeness* of the process that the concept of 'hegemony' goes beyond 'ideology'. (1977, 108–9)

For Williams, Gramsci's central achievement consisted in the articulation of a culturalist sense of the wholeness of culture with a more typically marxist sense of the interestedness of ideology. Thus, hegemony is 'in the strongest sense a "culture", but a culture which has also to be seen as the lived dominance and subordination of particular classes' (1977, 110). Understood thus, culture is no longer either 'superstructural', as the term had been defined in the marxist tradition, or 'ideological', in either the more generally marxist or the more specifically Althusserian definition. On the contrary, 'cultural tradition and practice ... are among the basic processes', which need to be seen 'as they are ... without the characteristic straining to fit them ... to other and determining ... economic and political relationships' (1977, 111). Whether all of this remains exactly faithful to Gramsci's own intent seems open to some doubt. But whatever the original authorial intention (and this is by no means at all self-evident), Williams's appropriation of Gramsci finally delivered that resolution of Leavisite and marxist thematics hitherto denied him.

In one respect, Williams's reading of Gramsci remains clearly faithful to its object: for both, the counter-hegemonic moment is what truly matters, hence Williams's own attempt to distinguish between practices, experiences, meanings and values that are part of the effectively dominant culture and those that are not. The dominant or hegemonic culture, he reminds us, 'is always an active process', an organization of often quite disparate meanings, 'which it specifically incorporates in a significant culture' (1977, 115). Rehearsing an argument first broached in *Culture and Society*, he points once again to the decisive importance of 'selective tradition' in the effective operation of such processes of incorporation (1977, 115). In *Marxism and Literature*, however, the selective tradition is also seen as necessarily dependent both upon identifiable institutions and what Williams terms 'formations', that is intellectual or artistic movements and tendencies (1977, 117–120). This double stress is explored at greater length in *Culture*, where he advanced a preliminary historical typology of institutions and formations (Williams 1981, 35–86). For all this attention to the hegemonic, however, Williams remained insistent that, at the level of 'historical' as distinct from 'epochal' analysis, that is at the level of movement rather than system, there is much in any lived culture that cannot be reduced to the dominant (1977, 121). Here, he dissents sharply from the implied consensualism of Althusserian theories of ideology: '*no mode and therefore no dominant social order*', he wrote, '*and therefore no dominant culture ever in reality includes or exhausts all human practice, human energy, and human intention*' (1977, 125, emphasis in original).

Williams's initial theorization of the alternatives to hegemony had been broached in the 'Base and Superstructure' essay, where he had sought to distinguish between 'alternative' and 'oppositional', 'residual' and 'emergent' cultural elements (1980c, 39–42). The terminology recurs both in *Marxism and Literature* and in *Culture*. By 'residual' Williams means, not the simply 'archaic', defined as 'that which is wholly recognized as an element of the past', but rather those cultural elements external to the dominant culture which nonetheless continue to be lived and practised as an active part of the present 'on the basis of the residue ... of some previous social and cultural institution or formation' (1977, 122). Unlike the archaic, the residual may be oppositional or at least alternative in character. Thus he distinguishes organized religion and the idea of rural community, which are each predominantly residual, from monarchy, which is merely archaic. But it is the properly 'emergent', that is those genuinely new meanings and values, practices, relationships and kinds of relationship, which are substantially alternative or oppositional to the dominant culture (1977, 123), that most interest him. For Williams, as for Gramsci, the primary source of an emergent culture is likely to be the formation of a new social class. But there is also a second source of emergence: 'alternative perceptions of others, in immediate relationships; new perceptions and practices of the material world' (1977, 126). For Williams, as for Gramsci, the exemplary contemporary instance of a new social class is that of the development of the modern working class. At the second level, however, which Williams termed 'the excluded social [human] area' (1977, 126), a level often peculiarly pertinent to the analysis of artistic and intellectual movements, the situation is much less clear. As Williams writes in *Culture*: 'No analysis is more difficult than that which, faced by new forms, has to try to determine whether these are new forms of the dominant or are genuinely emergent' (1980d, 205). This testimony to complexity is no mere rhetorical gesture on Williams's part. Quite the contrary: his work both in drama studies and in media studies had made him all too aware of the difficulties entailed in distinguishing the properly emergent from the merely novel.

In *Marxism and Literature*, Williams was able to offer an unusually interesting formulation of this problem, if not necessarily of the ways in which it might be resolved. Here he redeployed and significantly redefined the concept of 'structure of feeling'. An emergent culture, he argued, unlike either the dominant or the residual, requires not only distinct kinds of immediate cultural practice but also and crucially 'new forms or adaptations of forms'. Such innovation at the level of form, he continued, 'is in effect a *pre-emergence*, active and pressing but not yet fully articulated, rather than the evident emergence which could be more confidently named' (1977, 126). It is at this level of the pre-emergent, then, that the concept of structure of feeling is brought back into play. From *The Long Revolution* onwards, Williams had used the term to denote both the immediately experiential and the generationally specific aspects of artistic process. In *Marxism and Literature* both emphases are retained, but are conjoined to a quite new stress on cultural pre-emergence. In this reformulation the experiential remains at odds with official, 'formal' culture precisely in so far as it is indeed genuinely new: 'practical consciousness is what is actually being lived, ... not only what it is thought is being lived' (1977, 130–1). And similarly the generationally-specific remains different from the experience of previous generations precisely in so far as it too is indeed genuinely new. Structures of feeling writes Williams in an unusually arresting formulation

> can be defined as social experiences *in solution*, as distinct from other social semantic formations which have been *precipitated* and are more evidently and more immediately available ... The effective formations of most actual art relate to already manifest social formations, dominant or residual, and it is primarily to emergent formations ... that the structure of feeling, *as solution*, relates. (1977, 133–4)

Structures of feeling are no longer, then, in any simple sense 'the culture' of a period: they are, rather, precisely those particular elements within the more general culture that most actively anticipate subsequent mutations in the general culture itself; in short, they are quite specifically counter-hegemonic.

At one level, this distinctly Gramscian reformulation merely recaptures something of what Williams had all along intended: the problem of the knowable community in the English novel and the naturalistic revolution in the modern theatre each delimit a distinct structure of feeling only in so far as they are indeed genuinely innovatory. But in each case these respectively pre-emergent qualities are never fully theorized. It is as if the concept itself was still pre-emergent and required the encounter with Gramsci for precipitation. Moreover, the substantive question of the precise interplay between the emergent or pre-emergent on the one hand, and novelty within the dominant on the other, in both mass media and modernist avant-garde forms, was to become especially pressing in Williams's later work. In the third and final phase of his work, that produced during the 1980s, the developing globalization of corporate capitalism and the promise of a postmodern radicalism centred around the new social movements each obliged Williams to think through the theoretical and practical implications of an apparent decentring of the British nation state on the one hand, class politics on the other. The key texts here are the 1983 reworking of the long revolution analysis, *Towards 2000*, and the posthumously published and sadly unfinished *The Politics of Modernism*. Both books attempt to reformulate the earlier aspiration to community and to culture as a whole way of life by way of a critique of 'postmodern' appropriations both of modernism and of the popular mass media.

In *Culture and Society* and *The Long Revolution*, Williams had respectfully but determinedly aired his differences with the guardians of Leavis's minority culture. In *Towards 2000*, however, he set out to show how late capitalism had itself effectively collapsed the distinction between minority and mass arts: 'There are very few absolute contrasts left between a "minority culture" and "mass communications"', he wrote; 'many minority institutions and forms have adapted, ... with enthusiasm, to modern corporate capitalist culture' (1983, 134, 140). The older modernisms, which had once threatened to destabilize the certainties of bourgeois life, have been transformed, he argued, into a new ' "postmodernist" establishment' which 'takes human inadequacy ... as self-evident' (1983, 141). The deep structures of this now dominant postmodernism are present, moreover, in effectively popular cultural forms like film, television and fiction: 'these debased forms of an anguished sense of human debasement ... have become a widely distributed "popular" culture that is meant to confirm both its own and the world's destructive inevitabilities' (1983, 141–2). The 'pseudo-radicalism' of 'the negative structures of post-modernist art' (1983, 145) is thus neither pre-emergent nor emergent, but rather a moment of novelty, indeed perhaps the institutionalization of novelty itself, within the already dominant culture. As Williams would observe in *The Politics of Modernism*, the dominant institutions 'now incorporate or impose' such 'easy labels of radicalism' (1989, 176). But if the dominant culture had indeed so mutated, then Williams was also able to detect a more properly innovatory, pre-emergent 'structure of feeling' (though the term itself is not actually used) in the politics of the new social movements. He would thus seek to claim the peace movement, the ecology movement, the feminist movement and what he termed the movement of 'oppositional culture' as 'resources of hope' for a journey beyond capitalism (Williams 1983, 250). Yet, even as he invoked the new movements, he would insist that only a 'misinterpretation' could see them as 'getting beyond class politics'. Rather, these 'new' issues, followed through, 'lead us into the central systems of the industrial-capitalist mode of production and ... into its system of classes' (1983, 172–3). The specifically 'cultural' corollaries of this analysis are quite explicitly anti-postmodern:

> If we are to break out of the non-historical fixity of *post*-modernism, 'then we must search out and counterpose an alternative tradition taken from the neglected works left in the wide margin of the century, a tradition which may address itself not to this by now exploitable because quite inhuman rewriting of the past but, for all our sakes, to a modern *future* in which community may be imagined again. (1989, 35)

If Williams's early 'left Leavisism' was in the most obvious of senses a 'culturalism', then the later cultural materialism might best be understood as a kind of 'post-culturalism'. This is so in more than a simple chronological sense. Before Williams, the culturalist tradition had typically subscribed to a kind of 'objective idealism' in which truth is seen as inhering in the cultural tradition itself. Williams's deconstruction of this notion, through the idea of the selective tradition, effects a relativizing turn similar to that of poststructuralism in relation to structuralism. It does so by virtue of an appeal to the role of the (collective) reader. It more than gestures in the direction of a recognition of the intrication of power within discourse such as the later Foucault acknowledged, and of the materiality, historicity and arbitrary variability of the linguistic sign similar to that in both Derrida and Foucault. And all this remained coupled to a sense of genuinely free communicative action – a truly common culture – as normative, of which even Habermas might approve. Hence, perhaps, Terry Eagleton's judgement that: 'Williams's work has prefigured and pre-empted the development of parallel left positions by, so to speak, apparently standing still' (1984, 109).

Andrew Milner

Further reading and works cited

Dworkin, D. L. and Roman, L. G. (eds) *Views Beyond the Border Country*. London, 1993.
Eagleton, T. *The Function of Criticism*. London, 1984.
— (ed.) *Raymond Williams: Critical Perspectives*. Cambridge, 1989.
Eldridge, J. and Eldridge, L. *Raymond Williams*. London, 1994.
Higgins, J. *Raymond Williams*. London, 1999.
— (ed.) *The Raymond Williams Reader*. Oxford, 2000.
Inglis, F. *Raymond Williams*. London, 1995.
Milner, A. *Cultural Materialism*. Melbourne, 1993.
O'Connor, A. *Raymond Williams*. Oxford, 1989.
Pinkney, T. *Raymond Williams*. Bridgend, 1991.
West, C. 'In Memoriam: The Legacy of Raymond Williams', in *Cultural Materialism*, ed. C. Prendergast. Minneapolis, MN, 1995.
Williams, R. *Culture and Society 1780–1950*. Harmondsworth, 1963.
—. *The Long Revolution*. Harmondsworth, 1965.
—. *Drama from Ibsen to Brecht*. Harmondsworth, 1973a.
—. *The Country and the City*. New York, 1973b.
—. *The English Novel*. St Albans, 1974a.
—. *Television*. Glasgow, 1974b.
—. *Communications*. Harmondsworth, 1976a.
—. *Keywords*. Glasgow, 1976b.
—. *Marxism and Literature*. Oxford, 1977.
—. *Politics and Letters*. London, 1979a.
—. *Modern Tragedy*. London, 1979b.
—. 'Notes on Marxism in Britain Since 1945', in *Problems in Materialism and Culture: Selected Essays*. London, 1980a.
—. 'Literature and Sociology: In Memory of Lucien Goldmann', in *Problems in Materialism and Culture: Selected Essays*. London, 1980b.
—. 'Base and Superstructure in Marxist Cultural Theory', in *Problems in Materialism and Culture: Selected Essays*. London, 1980c.
—. *Culture*. Glasgow, 1980d.
—. *Towards 2000*. London, 1983.
—. *The Politics of Modernism*, ed. T. Pinkney. London, 1989.
— and Orrom, M. *Preface to Film*. London, 1954.

Stuart Hall (1932–)

Stuart Hall is a central figure in the history and the continuing evolution of cultural studies and marxist intellectual thought in Britain. He came to Britain from Jamaica as a Rhodes scholar in the early 1950s, and since then he has played a key role in the development of 'New Left' political thinking, in the foundation and institutionalization of the discipline of cultural studies, and in contributing to, and promoting, marxist cultural and sociological analyses of contemporary Britain. His work since the 1950s has been engaged chiefly in marxist debates about the role of ideology in popular culture, but this has taken a wide variety of forms, from his neo-Leavisite examination of popular cultural forms in the book he co-authored with Paddy Whannel, *The Popular Arts* (1964), to his Althusserian studies of the ways in which 'Thatcherism' had become embedded as an ideology in media and cultural forms in the 1980s. His most important achievement is to have successfully engineered a central place for cultural studies in the academy in Britain, and to have demonstrated its usefulness as a discipline for investigating a broad range of sociological, political and economic issues, as well as the more obvious cultural expressions, such as the jazz and rock 'n' roll music which he wrote about in *The Popular Arts*. Alongside Raymond Williams and E. P. Thompson, Hall is also the most prominent marxist academic in Britain of the postwar period, and his work is central to debates about the relevance and function of marxist and post-marxist thought in contemporary British culture.

Hall became part of the intellectual left in Britain at a time of profound change in left-wing politics. Prior to the Second World War British marxists tended to look towards Russia as a model for Marxist social and economic revolution, but in the 1950s Russia's aggressive interventions in East Germany (1953) and particularly in crushing the popular uprising in Hungary (1956) led many British marxists to criticize the forms which marxism had taken in Russia. Hall writes that he was not a marxist prior to the Hungarian uprising: 'I came into marxism backwards: against the Soviet tanks in Budapest, as it were' (Morley and Chen 1996, 264). For British marxists, the events in Hungary effected a dramatic shift away from the notion that marxism need only transfer the economic means of production to the proletariat in order for a revolution to succeed. The fact that a post-revolutionary state could become as imperialist as the capitalism which it had defeated signalled to intellectuals such as Williams and Hall that marxism had to counter the ideology of capitalism much more effectively. The New Left which emerged in the 1950s thus emphasized the role played by ideological forms – culture, media, education, religion – in bolstering the power of capitalism, and in harnessing the working class within capitalist hegemony.

Hall pioneered marxist analyses of culture, firstly in his role as editor of the *Universities and Left Review* (*New Left Review* after 1959) between 1957 and 1961, and later when he played a central role in the evolution of cultural studies. Initially, Hall's conceptions of culture owed much to the work of F. R. Leavis, even though he disagreed with Leavis's politics. Hall believed that Leavis's discussions of the nineteenth-century novel in particular could be appropriated for a socialist-humanist criticism, especially in the way in which Leavis believed that literature could represent 'experience', morality and 'a whole way of life'. Hall understood from Leavis that literature had much to offer a political study of society 'as a whole', as he argued in 1958:

> The political intellectual is concerned with the institutional life of the society: the creative artist with the attitudes, the manners, the moral and emotional life which the individual consummates within that social framework. It seems to me that the beginning of a common socialist humanism is the realisation that these are not two distinct areas of interest, but the complementary parts of a complex, common experience. (1958b, 87)

In the *Universities and Left Review*, Hall promoted the study of 'lifestyles' with a view to integrating insights into culture with a broad-based socialist political analysis, and thus shared in common with the emerging generation of working-class writers an interest in the ways in which literature and politics intersected. Hall persevered with this interest when he co-authored a book with Paddy Whannel, *The Popular Arts*, which took as its subject the cultural politics of mass culture. The book distinguished between 'popular' and 'mass' culture in useful ways, but it also entailed a Leavisite focus on the 'quality' of popular culture. Hall and Whannel replicated the Leavisite bias towards 'complexity' and 'richness', arguing that jazz was preferable to rock 'n' roll because it was as creative as classical music, just as film was preferable to television. The criteria by which Hall and Whannel judged popular music – such as rhythmic variety, musical diversity, personal expression and imagination – borrowed heavily from Leavis, and ultimately failed to analyse the possible relationships between popular culture and social struggle, partly because it did not extend its analyses sufficiently far to take into account the ways in which popular music was appropriated and used by its audiences. Hall's first book-length study of popular culture thus replicated the terms of Leavisite analysis, and contained little of the political engagement which a marxist cultural studies seemed to promise.

This changed radically in the course of Hall's career, however. After lecturing at Chelsea College, University of London, for three years, Hall was appointed a Research Fellow at Richard Hoggart's Centre for Contemporary Cultural Studies at the University of Birmingham in 1964, and he became its Acting Director in 1968. The Centre was first formed as an annex to the English department at Birmingham university and its original goal, outlined and defended by Hoggart in his inaugural address in 1964, was to apply the traditional methods of literary criticism to the new domains of popular and mass culture. Admittedly, this also entailed a recognition that new criteria would have to be found for the evaluation of specific texts, but their early judgements tended to parallel normative standards, those standards which were always already set by high culture. Hall became the Centre's Director from 1972 to 1979, and, as Andrew Milner argues, 'displayed a remarkable flair for academic entrepreneurship' (Milner 1993, 76). He founded a house journal, *Working Papers in Cultural Studies*, and published several volumes of collected work on culture, society and politics in Britain. Under Hall's influence, the work of the Centre increasingly moved away from the influence of Leavis towards marxist analysis of the role of culture in ideology, and in the 1970s the work of the Centre in general attempted to fuse the socialist humanism of the early writings of Raymond Williams and Richard Hoggart with the influential structuralism of continental marxism. Hall's own writings also moved from the essentially culturalist analysis of Leavis to studies which were focused more specifically on ethnographic issues and which increasingly borrowed from the work of Gramsci and Althusser. Thus, Hall's work made the paradigm shift in cultural studies which he himself described as moving between culturalism and structuralism (Hall 1980).

If in *The Popular Arts* Hall had attempted to locate cultural forms which might be resistant to capitalism *per se*, such as jazz, and thus recapitulated culturalist solutions to the problem of ideology, in *Resistance Through Rituals*, the book he edited with Tony Jefferson, he and his co-authors explored the ways in which youth subcultures emerged as structural effects of capitalism, and yet embodied some degree of oppositional content. For Hall and the Centre for Contemporary Cultural Studies in general, the study of youth subcultures was a way of focusing on the relationship between class and culture without returning to absolute distinctions between the proletariat and the bourgeoisie. The emergence of teenage subcultures in the 1950s and 1960s was a product of market capitalism in the sense that teenagers were created for the first time as a specific section of consumers with their own tastes and spending habits, but they also symbolized a threat to the social order by identifying with radical subcultural elements. This threat was represented throughout the postwar period in a series of moral panics and crises which revolved around notions of delinquency, mugging, drugs, sexual licence and deviancy. *Resistance Through Rituals* included studies of skinheads, teds, mods, rockers, junkies, Rastafarians and hippies, and there lurked a series of assumptions throughout the anthology that these subcultures existed within a parent culture defined by class. As Robert Hewison has argued, however, 'the issue that remained unresolved ... was to what extent the "magical" resolutions that these different ritualistic assertions of identity represented were truly capable of resisting domination' (1994, 190). Hall argued that such subcultures were the products of specific socio-economic circumstances, and therefore were determined by capitalist structures of power, but so too the structural position of subcultures enabled them to expose the contradictions of the parent culture. Hall thus located the agency for exposing ideological contradictions in contemporary society in youth subcultures, even if their capacity for developing effective forms of resistance remained underexamined.

But Hall's work was increasingly turning away from a 'simple' search for agencies of resistance to a thorough examination of forms of domination. *Policing the Crisis*, which he co-wrote with Chas Critcher, Tony Jefferson, John Clarke and Brian Roberts, was a study of 'mugging' as a social phenomenon in contemporary British society. Hall and his co-authors were not interested particularly in 'mugging' from criminological perspectives, nor were they interested in the 'revolutionary' aspects of mugging. Instead, the book was a study both of the 'social causes' of mugging and 'why British society reacts to mugging in the extreme way it does'. Mugging had become 'an index of the disintegration of the social order' in political and media discourses:

> The book is ... about a society slipping into a certain kind of *crisis*. It tries to examine why and how the themes of *race*, *crime* and *youth* – condensed into the image of 'mugging' – come to serve as the articulator of the crisis, as its ideological conductor. It is also about how these themes have functioned as a mechanism for the construction of an authoritarian consensus, a conservative backlash. (Hall et al. 1978, viii)

Policing the Crisis is almost Foucauldian in its analysis of 'mugging' as a discursive formation which is produced within political and media discourse as 'panics' and 'crises' in order to entrench further the authoritarian values of law and order. It borrowed extensively from marxist studies of ideology, specifically from Althusser's 'ideological state apparatus' and Gramsci's hegemony, but also developed earlier anthropological work, such as Stan Cohen's *Folk Devils and Moral Panic* (1972). As such, it is as much an examination of the rising 'new right' ideologies in the 1970s as it is an attempt to grapple with the complex and ambiguous relationship between mugging and forms of class resistance.

The next phase of Hall's work developed the former strand more than the latter. It became clear to him that the election to government of the Conservative party under Mrs Thatcher's leadership in 1979 was the obvious manifestation of a political and cultural shift which had been taking place in Britain throughout the 1970s. 'Thatcherism', as Hall termed it in 1983, was a new development in right-wing ideology in Britain, which significantly departed from the establishment conservatism of the early postwar decades. Hall examined the phenomenon of Thatcherism in three books in the 1980s: *The Politics of Thatcherism* (1983), *The Hard Road to Renewal* (1988) and *New Times* (1989). Hall sought to explain and understand why Thatcher's policies were so popular among the working classes in Britain in the 1980s, and recognized that the attraction of her particular brand of politics – what Hall called 'authoritarian populism' – could not be explained only in economic terms. Thatcher's populism was based on ideologies of patriotism and national identity (the Falklands War in particular), 'family values', 'traditionalism', 'authority' (standing up to the miners), all of which are consonant with traditional 'one nation' Toryism. But it coupled these with 'the aggressive themes of neoliberalism – self-interest, competitive individualism, anti-statism' (Hall 1988, 48) and material social relations, including the use of new media forms (such as the marketing strategies of Saatchi & Saatchi and the dominance of the tabloids). Initially, Hall's overtly Gramscian conclusions on the success of Thatcherism as an ideology found its marxist detractors. In a famous series of articles in the *New Left Review*, Jessop and others argued that Hall's analysis of Thatcherism failed to grasp the real economic shifts and social reconstructions it effected (Jessop et al. 1984, 1985, 1990). As Thatcherism continued without serious ideological challenge, however, Jessop and his colleagues began to admit the importance of ideology in securing the support of the working class within a conservative economic and social politics.

Hall became an important critic and analyst of the new right ideologies which dominated Britain in the 1980s, but while his publications and research focused largely on Thatcherism, he was also busily engaged in consolidating cultural studies in his new post as Professor of Sociology at the Open University, which he took up in 1979. He was a key contributor to the module on 'Popular Culture' which ran at the Open University between 1982 and 1987, which Antony Easthope has described as 'the most ambitious, serious and comprehensive intervention in cultural studies in Britain and, apart from the work of the Birmingham Centre, the most important' (1991, 74). In addition, he has continued to publish important essays which have defined and delimited the values, methods and problems of cultural studies through the 1980s and 1990s. He remains committed to marxist analyses of culture and society, but Hall's marxism is one which registers the interplay between many competing, shifting ideologies and cultural differences. Thus Hall characterized the relationship between marxism and cultural studies not in terms of a theory or an application, but as a struggle. Cultural studies, for Hall, was 'working within shouting distance of marxism, working on marxism, working against marxism, working with it, working to try to develop marxism' (Morley and Chen 1996, 265), never quite inside it or produced by it. Hall's concerns with race, ethnicity, feminism and youth subcultures throughout his work prompted a number of speculations that Hall was indeed more a post-marxist than a marxist proper, but this is to ignore the ways in which Hall has himself insisted on marxism as a shifting set of questions and concerns, not as an orthodox theory or doctrine:

> I am a 'post-marxist' only in the sense that I recognize the necessity to move beyond orthodox marxism, beyond the notion of marxism guaranteed by the laws of history. But I still operate somewhere within what I understand to be the discursive limits of a marxist position ... So 'post' means, for me, going on thinking on the ground of a set of *established problems*, a problematic. It doesn't mean deserting that terrain but rather, using it as one's *reference point*. (Hall, in Morley and Chen 1996, 148–9)

Stuart Hall remains active in writing and thinking about the politics of contemporary Britain, and in contributing to debates about the evolution and current practices of cultural studies. Although it could be argued that cultural studies as a discipline has moved away from the marxism of Hall and its other founders, it has remained closer to Hall's persistent concern with the politics of identity and difference, and to the methodological combination of ethnographic study with discursive analysis. The establishment of the discipline of cultural studies, and his contributions to its methods and modes of analysis, is Hall's most important achievement to date, but, as Morley and Chen argue, he has also attracted the admiration of his peers as a role model of intellectual practice:

> Hall has demonstrated his commitment to living out the contradictions of the role of the 'organic intellectual' identified by Gramsci – the commitment to being at the very forefront of intellectual, theoretical work and, simultaneously, the commitment to the attempt to transmit the ideas thus generated, well beyond the confines of the 'intellectual class'. (1996, 20)

John Brannigan

Further reading and works cited

Cohen, S. *Folk Devils and Moral Panic*. London, 1972.
Dworkin, D. *Cultural Marxism in Postwar Britain*. Durham, NC, 1997.
Easthope, A. *British Post-Structuralism since 1968*. London, 1991.
Hall, S. 'A Sense of Classlessness', *Universities and Left Review*, Autumn 1958a.
—. 'In the No Man's Land', *Universities and Left Review*, Winter 1958b.
—. 'Cultural Studies: Two Paradigms', *Media, Culture and Society*, 2, 1980.
—. *The Hard Road to Renewal*. London, 1988.
—. 'The Emergence of Cultural Studies and the Crisis of the Humanities', *October*, 53, 1990.
— and du Gay, P. (eds) *Questions of Cultural Identity*. London, 1996.
— and Jefferson, T. (eds) *Resistance Through Rituals*. London, 1976.
— and Jacques, M. (eds) *The Politics of Thatcherism*. London, 1983.
— and Jacques, M. (eds) *New Times*. London, 1989.
— and Whannel, P. *The Popular Arts*. London, 1964.
— et al. *Policing the Crisis*. London, 1978.
— et al. (eds) *Culture, Media, Language*. London, 1980.
— et al. (eds) *State and Society in Contemporary Britain*. Cambridge, 1984.
Hewison, R. *Culture and Consensus*. London, 1994.

Jessop, B. et al. 'Authoritarian Populism: Two Nations and Thatcherism', *New Left Review*, 147, 1984.

— et al. 'Thatcherism and the Politics of Hegemony', *New Left Review*, 165, 1985.

— et al. 'Farewell to Thatcherism?', *New Left Review*, 179, 1990.

Milner, A. *Cultural Materialism*. Victoria, 1993.

Morley, D. and Chen, K.-H. (eds) *Stuart Hall*. London, 1996.

Storey, J. (ed.) *Cultural Theory and Popular Culture*. Hemel Hempstead, 1994.

— (ed.) *What is Cultural Studies?* London, 1996.

Terry Eagleton (1943–)

> If criticism is no more than a knack, like being able to whistle and hum different tunes simultaneously, then it is at once rare enough to be preserved in the hands of an elite, while 'ordinary' enough to require no stringent theoretical justification. (Eagleton 1983, 214)

The greatest part of Terry Eagleton's career has been devoted to attacking the 'genteel amateurism' of literary criticism in English departments, by which literary study was only ever a form of 'appreciation'. His publication of *Literary Theory: An Introduction*, first published in 1983 and reprinted thirteen times between then and its second edition in 1996, reflected the increasing interest in theory among literary critics, but it also popularized theory for a generation of subsequent students and teachers. That for Eagleton this was always a political manoeuvre is evident in the quotation above, for behind this comment lie the debates concerning how we might define culture and the literary canon, and how we might explode the idea that aesthetics is a matter of fine, refined feeling, with all the class bias which such feeling invokes. The connections between Eagleton's introductory guide of literary theory and his marxism are, of course, obvious. *Literary Theory* was never going to be an explanatory book in the sense of an impartial consideration of the theories discussed. In describing and explaining New Critical, hermeneutic, structuralist, poststructuralist and psychoanalytical theories, Eagleton was also intervening in the debates about theory and from an explicitly marxist position. Rather than a neutral survey of literary theories, the book's aim is to reveal the ideological underpinnings of modern literary theories. Eagleton himself calls for a new 'rhetorical' practice, a theory which would acknowledge its own interested status, its own political commitment. Marxism and feminism, then, are celebrated as theoretical practices which do not hide behind the pretence of theoretical and political neutrality. Many teachers now refuse *Literary Theory* because of its obviously polemical stance. But Eagleton is fair to the strengths of the approaches he discusses, while admitting his own dissension from them. And this dissension is seen as inevitable. Eagleton refuses the idea that such issues could be adjudicated with 'impartiality'. Such thinking is a part of the very liberal humanism which his work so strenuously resists.

To begin thus is to suggest that Eagleton's significance as a theorist is as a popularizer and a polemicist. But the opening quotation also suggests a third, equally important aspect of Eagleton's work: the way in which Eagleton's own style is intrinsically a part of his theoretical work. Lucid, witty and combative, Eagleton's writing style is frequently a provocation as well as entertainment. Theoretical excurses are discussed through frequently extravagant hyperbole, comic irony (what Stephen Regan has described as 'deflationary humour') and the use of such rhetorical devices as alliteration, parallelism, zeugma (as, for example, in saying 'language lies at the root of human identity and to tamper with that is either poetry or treason'; Regan 1998, 149). His is an anecdotal, epigrammatic wit ('Shakespeare still embodies timeless value; it's just that you can't produce his stuff without the sponsorship of Prudential Insurance', Regan 1998, 147), whose literary antecedents might be Wilde or Swift, as Stephen Regan has noted:

> A favourite Swiftian technique is to construct some plausible, sophisticated argument with meticulous care, only to knock the skids from under it and watch it topple to oblivion. Conversely, we are just as likely to be presented with a set of seemingly ridiculous, far-fetched assumptions, and then discover in the course of argument how just and reasonable they are. (1998, viii)

Eagleton himself cites Benjamin's comment that 'there is no better starting point for thought than laughter' (1990, 337). Although this kind of flippant wit often means that Eagleton raises more hostages to fortune than he can afford to, it also illuminates a real desire to communicate. Many readers have been introduced to the finer details of aesthetic philosophy through the use of exactly such humour.

While the examples of Eagleton's style given above are to be found in the transcript of his inaugural lecture as Warton Professor of English at Oxford, entitled 'The Crisis of Contemporary Culture' (1992; rpt. Regan 1998), this kind of mordant wit is also to be found in Eagleton's most difficult, but arguably also his best, work – The Ideology of the Aesthetic (1990). In this work, as in Literary Theory, the ideological motivation of that which is apparently 'ideology-free' is revealed: here, the aesthetic in place of literary criticism or theory. Eagleton demonstrates how the aesthetic has been appropriated as 'Culture' to serve bourgeois individualism, but counters this orthodoxy by reading the aesthetic through the figure of the oxymoron and by insisting on the intrinsically contradictory nature of the aesthetic, as of other things. Embedded in the tradition of the aesthetic is a contradictory clash between an impulse to freedom and a complicity with power, which only a dialectical thought can both trace and interrogate. Such rhetorical strategies as comic irony and serious flippancy are then related to Eagleton's commitment to dialectical thinking, or the attempt to hold oppositions in a productive tension.

This kind of attention to dialectical thinking is the most frequently overlooked aspect of Eagleton's work. The most frequent criticism of Eagleton's marxism, usually from non- or anti-marxist critics, is that of a determinism in his theoretical thinking which any close reading would show is just not there. Instead, I would argue, Eagleton's theoretical marxisms have been thoroughly self-reflexive and revisionary. Indeed, the very course of marxist literary theory in Britain might be traced through Eagleton's publishing career. After The New Left Church (1966), the closest we get to a 'vulgar' deterministic marxism, Eagleton proceeds through such successive influences as Raymond Williams (Shakespeare and Society, 1967), Lucien Goldmann and an emerging Althusserianism (Myths of Power, 1975), Pierre Macherey (Criticism and Ideology, 1976), Benjamin and Brecht (Walter Benjamin, 1981), strands of feminism, psychoanalysis and poststructuralism (The Rape of Clarissa, 1982) and, in the insistence on contradiction in The Ideology of the Aesthetic (1990), Adorno. These studies have introduced the work of other theorists to new audiences but they have also reflected critically upon that work. Eagleton's absorption of Machereyan ideas in *Criticism and Ideology*, for example, is also a critique of their latent aestheticism, their continuing allegiance to 'Literature' as an ideological construction. And Eagleton's debt to Lucien Goldmann's theory of 'categorial structures' as key mediations between literary form, textual ideology and social relations is criticized in the later edition of *Myths of Power* as a kind of theoretical 'over-totalisation' (1988, xiii).

His own work has also been open to this kind of revisionary analysis, with much of Eagleton's later career commenting obliquely on earlier work. The most significant turn comes with the publication of *Walter Benjamin* (1981), when Eagleton leaves the more theoreticist models of Althusserianism behind. Such high theoreticism was most acutely evident in the schemas of *Criticism and Ideology* (1976a), with its 'science of the text'. Here the literary text is situated within a range of contexts: the general mode of production (the dominant form, such as late capitalism); the literary mode of production (such as print-capitalism, or distributing cheap broadsides in the street); authorial ideology (not an 'expression' of the author's beliefs, but that which is produced by a combination of the general ideology and biographical factors); and aesthetic ideology (the specific, aesthetic region of the general ideology). The literary text is then seen as produced by an interaction of these structures, but it is not the passive product of such formations, since the text also 'determines its own determinants' (1976a, 63). Eagleton's attention to the specificity of different formations, and the many individual examples cited in support, are more nuanced than might be anticipated from such a scheme. The relationship between the literary text and ideology is not a determined one: not all texts, for example, work 'against' ideology, in being able to reveal it just by their 'literariness' (1976a, 68). And the relationship between literary text and ideology can be dialectical once the 'literary' is itself analysed as ideological. (The later work on the aesthetic sketched one such philosophical context for this kind of approach.)

However, this kind of explicitly marxist science is abandoned thereafter. In retrospect, then, *Walter Benjamin* (1981) marks the moment at which Eagleton turns to Brechtian praxis rather than some kind of pure marxist theory. This is reflected too in *Literary Theory: An Introduction*, in which the concluding chapter 'Political Criticism' intentionally disappoints expectations in providing no account of 'Marxist literary theory'. Instead throughout the book, and in later work too, other theoretical ideas are shamelessly appropriated for marxist ends. Derrida, Kristeva, Lacan – all are used as tools for political analysis. In *Walter Benjamin*, the practice of the socialist worker is defined not only as 'projective', in its gestures towards an alternative, and 'polemical', in its challenge to inequality, but also 'appropriative' (1981, 113). Such work might include 'encouraging others to reap pleasure from the beauty of religious imagery, encouraging the production of works with no overt political content whatsoever, and arguing in particular times and places for the "greatness", "truth", "profoundly moving", "joyful", "wonderful" qualities of particular works ...' (1981, 113). These literary qualities are, of course, also those celebrated by liberal humanism and defenders of traditional canonicity, but liberal humanist ideas of 'Literature' are called upon here in ways which democratize while also questioning these values. Similarly, while deconstruction is one of the many theoretical influences at work in *The Rape of Clarissa* (1982) and in *William Shakespeare* (1986a), other work in this period argues that deconstruction unallied with political feminism or marxism cannot fulfil its radical claims. (Such work would include the chapter 'Marxism and Deconstruction' in *Walter Benjamin*, 1981 and the essays on poststructuralism in *Against the*

Grain, 1986, originally published in 1984.) The consequence of a deconstructive style divorced from a politicized historicism is read into William Warner's masculinist celebration of Richardson's Lovelace (1979):

> Clarissa ... holds to a severely representational ideology of writing, trusts in the stable sign and the unitary self, and subscribes to the values of truth, coherence and causality; Lovelace, by contrast, is a proto-Nietzschean who celebrates plurality, groundlessness and *jouissance*. It seems logical, then, that a contemporary deconstructionist should find Lovelace the hero and Clarissa the villain, without allowing a little matter like rape to modify his judgement. (Eagleton 1982, 65–6)

Eagleton's engagement here is to defend a materialist feminism, but this does not mean that poststructuralist ideas are not part of his own writing. There is a recognition here that Clarissa and Lovelace embody different attitudes towards textuality, but Eagleton's own reading of the novel is alert to the kinds of indeterminacies which Lovelace exploits, and in the distinction between awareness and political misuse lies Eagleton's frustration with much contemporary poststructuralist theory. Two years later, *The Function of Criticism* (1984) returns to the eighteenth century, a time which Eagleton argues preceded the separation of literature from its culture, when literature was 'foregrounded as the medium of vital concerns deeply rooted in the general, intellectual, cultural and political life of an epoch' (107). The eighteenth century then becomes a surprisingly traditionalist model for contemporary criticism. But it is also a return to the kinds of Enlightenment values which Eagleton would come to defend in his attacks on postmodernism in the 1990s: the stubborn insistence on our need for truth, reason, justice, without the fastidious distancing of scare quotes.

Eagleton's immensely prolific career, then, illustrates the changes within marxist approaches to literature over the past thirty years as it is also a continuing engagement and revision of his own practice as critic and theorist. Indeed, in more recent writings, Eagleton appears to be increasingly aware of criticism in advance. For example, in the final essay of *Crazy John and the Bishop* (1998a), there is an attempt to disarm criticism by anticipating it. There is a strength here, in so far as it recognizes that one's own work is inevitably a part of other debates and even suggests an ability to see from other positions. But there is also a tendency to caricature such criticisms, which comes to take the place of an engagement with them.

Many perceived a turn to Irish Studies in Eagleton's career with the publication of *Heathcliff and the Great Hunger* (1995), *Crazy John and the Bishop* (1998a) and *Scholars and Rebels* (1999). But Eagleton's interest in Ireland had certainly been apparent not only in such works of the later 1980s as the Field Day pamphlet on 'Nationalism: Irony and Commitment' (1988) and his own creative writing (*Saints and Scholars*, 1987; *Saint Oscar*, 1989), but in an interest in Yeats and Joyce evident as early as *Criticism and Ideology* (1976a, 151–7). While it is easy to deride Eagleton's gestures towards his own 'Irishness', more potent is the argument that Irish culture is and has been politicized in a more overt way than is the case in Britain. When thought of in these terms, Eagleton's turn to Irish studies is hardly surprising.

Concurrent with these works have been continuing attacks on theoretical postmodernism (*The Illusions of Postmodernism*, 1996 and *The Idea of Culture*, 2000), but there are important ways in which these interests overlap. If the pressing political issue is now that of an international conflict between advanced capitalism and postcolonial emergent economies, then for Eagleton, Ireland is particularly situated, 'cusped ... between modernity and postmodernity', poised at the moment at which it decides whether to 'continue to cast its fortunes with a global capitalism' or to 'draw upon the resources of its own history of dispossession in order to align itself with the coming epoch' (Regan 1998, 327). But the specific economic conditions of contemporary Ireland, which resemble the high-tech and service-sector economies of advanced capitalism, are absent from Eagleton's account, where contemporary Ireland is primarily the site of continued ethnic conflict. There's a sense here in which Eagleton's argument is ill served by the specificities of his example, and this is a more general problem in Eagleton's career overall.

Eagleton's polemical stances are crucial in that they bring a lively and honest engagement to debates which are often arcane and politically unaware (perhaps deliberately so). But what Eagleton gains in wit and force, he often loses in subtlety. His is not the work of the miniaturist. Instead there's a kind of deliberate ham-fistedness throughout all his work, an almost inevitable tendency for wit and provocation to become forms of reductiveness. Eagleton's work raises the temperature of literary and cultural analysis with its provocation, its frequent sarcasm and combative manoeuvres. The example from *The Rape of Clarissa* above is, then, an important one. In discussing the 'rape' of Clarissa, Eagleton chooses a topic where the ethical responsibility is high indeed, and unavoidable. Eagleton's cultural work insists that textual interpretation matters, that we have a responsibility to connect our political aspirations with our reading practices.

Eagleton's significance on literary theory, the philosophy of aesthetics and cultural politics in Britain has been immense, his work already equalling that of Raymond Williams in its influence. He has been, and continues to be, an immensely prolific and wide-ranging writer, whose interests have included Shakespeare, Yeats, 1890s Britain, Samuel Richardson and so on. Indeed, the bibliography included here can only cite major monographs. As the most distinguished British writer working within marxist cultural politics, he has continued to provoke and inspire in equal measure. Through the growing acceptance of theory within British universities, Eagleton's interventions have maintained a marxist dimension – often adapting, often refusing and always engaging with contemporary and competing theories.

Moyra Haslett

Further reading and works cited

Eagleton, T. *The New Left Church*. London, 1966.
—. *Shakespeare and Society*. London, 1967.
—. *Exiles and Émigrés: Studies in Modern Literature*. London, 1970.
—. *Criticism and Ideology*. London, 1976a.
—. *Marxism and Literary Criticism*. London, 1976b.
—. *Walter Benjamin, or Towards a Revolutionary Criticism*. London, 1981.
—. *The Rape of Clarissa*. Oxford, 1982.
—. *Literary Theory*. Oxford, 1983.
—. *The Function of Criticism*. London, 1984.
—. *William Shakespeare*. Oxford, 1986a.
—. *Against the Grain*. London, 1986b.
—. *Saints and Scholars*. London, 1987.
—. *Myths of Power*. London, 1988a.

—. *Nationalism*. Derry, 1988b.

—. *Saint Oscar*. Derry, 1989.

—. *The Ideology of the Aesthetic*. Oxford, 1990.

—. *Ideology: An Introduction*. London, 1991.

—. *The Crisis of Contemporary Culture*. Oxford, 1993.

— (ed.) *Ideology*. London, 1994.

—. *Heathcliff and the Great Hunger*. London, 1995.

—. *The Illusions of Postmodernism*. Oxford, 1996.

—. *Crazy John and the Bishop and other Essays on Irish Culture*. Cork, 1998a.

—. *Scholars and Rebels in Nineteenth-Century Ireland*. Oxford, 1999.

—. *The Idea of Culture*. Oxford, 2000.

— and Milne, D. (eds) *Marxist Literary Theory*. Oxford, 1996.

Regan, S. (ed.) *The Eagleton Reader*. Oxford, 1998.

Warner, W. B. *Reading Clarissa*. New Haven, CT, 1979.

Screen (1971–)

During the 1960s a strange outbreak of Francophilia associated with the journal, *New Left Review*, took off from Louis Althusser's marxist ideas. Although the immediate consequences were mainly political, the long-term effect, one still working its way through English culture, was to inject an almost unprecedented form of rationalism into the pervasively empiricist tradition.

In 1964, for example, Tom Nairn argued that the history of the English working class, cut off from the Enlightenment, could be explained by the degree to which it was 'immunized against theory' yet needed it 'like no other' comparable proletariat. Nairn's essay concludes, 'It still does' (1964, 57). Around 1970 a small group linked with the New Left was encouraged to develop work in the area of art and aesthetic practice. Since at that time literary study was hermetically sealed in a concern with 'authors' and 'imagination' they decided to attempt theoretical work in a relatively untheorized domain, cinema. The vehicle chosen for this intervention was the film journal *Screen*, published from 1971 by the Society for Education in Film and Television funded by the British Film Institute. Following an idea taken up from the Left Book Club in the 1930s *Screen* sponsored reading groups throughout the country. At one point in 1977 *Screen* had nearly 1,200 subscribers. Two other factors shaped its trajectory. One was the degree to which, like the contemporary *Tel Quel* group in France, *Screen* succeeded as a collective endeavour with a number of people learning from and playing off each other. A second spur was the seemingly endless stream of new names that arrived across the Channel each month. Moving out from a basis in Russian formalism, Brecht and Althusser, *Screen* progressively took on board Metz, Bellour, Lacan, Kristeva, Foucault (but not, significantly, Derrida: see Easthope 1996).

In distinction to the other arts, cinema seems to have a particular relation to the real. Film is both caused by the real (light rays reflected from an object being recorded on light-sensitive material) and resembles the real by looking like it. From its origins in the 1920s film theory could be divided into two contrasted positions, those of 'realists' (typified by André Bazin) and 'creationists' (Rudolf Arnheim). While the realist view valued cinema because of its purchase on the real, creationists insisted that cinema did not just record but was *also*, in addition, artistically significant. Both positions share the view that cinema has a privileged relation to the real. *Screen* broke with any such 'naturalist' or 'reflectionist' assumptions. It was helped along the path because film theory in the 1960s had already developed from *auteur* theory into a formalism concerned with genre and iconography. *Screen* developed this approach by joining it to structuralism, largely retrieved from French sources, which supported a general assumption that any form of meaning must be understood as the effect of a system producing it. In the place of a notion of film as reflection of the real, *Screen* asserted in 1976 that 'no one has yet seen a signified without a signifier' (Heath 1981a, 44), and that 'a text is structured primarily at the level of the signifier' since 'it is the order of the signifiers which determines the production of the signifieds' (Wollen 1976, 19). It was consistently argued that film, including documentary film, should be approached as an act of representation and not as a record of the real, an achievement of culture, not nature.

This premise was powerfully confirmed by Christian Metz. He had already claimed that in a film 'the image of a house does not signify "house", but rather "Here is a house"'' (1974, 116). His 'The Imaginary Signifier' was published in Paris in May 1975 and translated for *Screen* later that summer. It draws on psychoanalysis and the theory of the fetish to argue that in cinema, the more vividly present the image seems to make its object, the more it insists the object is actually lacking, 'made present', as Metz says, 'in the mode of absence' (1982, 44).

Starting from this basis the *Screen* project came to be defined in an essay of 1976 as the attempt to theorize 'the encounter of Marxism and psychoanalysis on the terrain of semiotics' (Heath 1981b, 201). The aim was to think together cinema overdetermined semiologically, ideologically, subjectively. In concluding I shall offer some comments on the limitations of this endeavour; here I need say no more about the diachronic construction of the project except that just at the point when the hoped-for synthesis trembled on the edge of dissolution, after the mid-1970s it found a new impetus in relation to feminist theorizations of film.

Dovetailed with Althusserian marxism *Screen's* formalist emphasis imported a striking novelty. Most traditional marxist analysis of art and literature shared with conventional criticism a main concern with 'content' though differed in thinking of this as an expression of ideology. *Screen* was determined to understand film not just in terms of thematic content and ideology at the level of the signified – what was referred to dismissively as 'the province of a traditional "content analysis"'' – but on the basis of its 'ideological *operation*' (Heath 1981b, 201). That concern is taken over from the work of the Russian formalists who directed attention towards the *differentia specifica* of literature, its particular 'literariness'. With close attention to the formal properties of cinema *Screen* undertook a detailed and thorough investigation of deep focus, lighting, the point of view shot. These constituted its 'ideological operation', at the level of the signifier. Film was to be understood as 'a *specific signifying practice*':

> 'Signifying' is the recognition of a language as a systematic articulation of meanings; 'practice' refers to the process of this articulation, to the work of the production of meanings, and in so doing it brings into the argument the problem of the relations of the subject within that work; 'specific' gives the necessity for the analysis of a particular signifying practice in its specific formations. (Heath 1974, 128)

This needs a little unpacking. The concept of a 'signifying practice' picks up the claim that film makes rather than reflects meanings; 'specificity' refers back to the Russian used by Sklovsky and the others but has acquired a decisive connotation from Althusser's analysis of 'practice'.

The concepts Screen borrowed from Althusser were the political, the economic and the ideological. Marx can be accused of thinking that the structure of society was mechanically determined as a fixed shape, with the economic structure forming 'the real foundation' on which rises a 'political superstructure' and to which correspond forms of ideology (Marx and Engels 1950, I, 328). It's not hard to spot here that Marx's thinking is spatial. Althusser rethinks structure as temporal, a process of transformation, and therefore a practice. Accordingly, each practice has a relative autonomy in relation to the others; it operates as itself, not something else, but it is simultaneously determined by its place in a totality. This account underpinned Screen's conception of cinema as a signifying practice. The New Left took great encouragement from this view because it made it possible to argue that marxism did not entail a mechanical sense of determination but rather recognized the 'specific effectivity' of each practice. It was left for others later to ask if a practice is autonomous, exactly how can it be relative? if relative, how can it be autonomous?

Given his commitment to thinking of society as a 'social formation' constantly in process, Althusser was compelled to rethink inherited ideas about science. He would not consider it as a static knowledge, achieved once and for all, but rather as a form of practice, theoretical practice. In doing so, he contrived to maintain a traditional marxist contrast between 'science' and 'ideology' since theoretical practice was defined as a transformation and refinement of ideology. These ideas empowered the Screen project. If as an object cinema was ideological practice, the theoretical work of the journal could construct a knowledge of it. Moreover, Althusser's willingness to think of practices in terms of 'different times' (Althusser and Balibar 1975, 96) lets him embrace the possibility that subjectivity unfolds according to its own temporality. Althusser contends that the subject of ideology is constructed through a process of interpellation, that is ideology 'hails' the subject into position, rather as someone in the street calls 'Hey, you there!' and you have to recognize that it is really you who is being addressed.

In a recent revitalization of the concept Judith Butler suggests that for Althusser interpellation 'precedes and forms the subject' and 'appears to constitute the prior condition' of 'subject-centred speech acts' (1997, 24). I think Althusser indeed supposes that the subject is exclusively constituted by interpellation, of which subjectivity is an effect. But here Althusser's understanding departs from that of Jacques Lacan (on whom he initially drew in his formulation of subjectivity) which defines the signifier as that which 'represents a subject not for another subject but for another signifier' (1972, 194); subjectivity and desire always exceed any position into which the subject is hailed. A rather formal distinction but, as we shall see, this bad weld leads to a fissure that runs through the whole project. Screen follows Althusser in treating the subject as only the effect of interpellation. Interpellation constitutes or produces the subject to imagine itself as constitutive, a free agent (a duality deriving from Lacan's theory of the mirror stage). Interpellation therefore comprehends both the opposed accounts of the subject traditional in philosophy, '(1) a free subjectivity, a centre of initiatives, author of and responsible for its actions; (2) a subjected being, who submits to a higher authority' (Althusser 1977, 169). In this view ideology functions through a pervasive naturalization. Developing from Althusser Screen works out a number of propositions for the analysis of film.

Mainstream cinema is, in Althusser's terms, an ideological state apparatus (the fact that Hollywood is an extreme expression of private capital is not thought to damage the argument that it nevertheless serves the state). As such it constructs forms of subjectivity, as Metz described: 'the cinematic institution is not just the cinema industry (which works to fill cinemas, not to empty them), it is also the mental machinery – another industry – which spectators "accustomed to the cinema" have internalized historically' (1975, 18). *Screen* proceeded, though with a certain unease, on the assumption that cinema as a 'mental institution' produced a position for the reader. This was 'inscribed in the film' (MacCabe 1975, 61), bringing about an 'implicit reader', one who 'conforms to the supposed intentions of the text' (Brewster 1977, 162).

Over the question of position *Screen* leans on the work of Julia Kristeva and her concept of the subject (*Screen* also borrowed the idea of 'signifying practice' from her, see: 1976, 60–75). In *Revolution in Poetic Language*, Kristeva affirmed that the 'realm of signification' is always 'a realm of *positions* ... establishing the identification of the subject' (1984, 44). The avant-garde work of Mallarmé, Lautréamont and others is potentially radical because it threatens to break the unity of the subject. Yet there is a difference here. Kristeva offers a history of literary texts analysed in terms of subject and position while *Screen* sees position as an effect of the text on its reader.

A characteristic of what I have been calling 'the *Screen* problematic' is its readiness to incorporate a range of theorizations, some of which have already been addressed. *Screen* contrasted two forms of subject position as afforded by the conventional realist text on the one hand and the modernist or experimental text on the other. In working this out *Screen* referred back to the 1930s and Brecht's critique of theatrical form. Brecht argued that realist theatre produced empathy in the spectator. Non-naturalist theatre, using 'alienation-effects', brought about a critical attitude. Thus realism led to passive identification, non-realism to active criticism.

After 1968 *Cahiers du Cinéma* amplified Brecht's formal account of spectator reactions by linking it with Althusserian analysis. In addition to the intervention between the work of Brecht and that of Althusser, Russian formalism, the *Cahiers* manifesto and the work of Kristeva were fed into the *Screen* problematic. The novel move, however, was to rethink cinema within the framework of psychoanalysis. Since cinema is a visual signifying practice *Screen* turned to Lacan's theory of vision. The topic needs some care.

In *Seminar 11* of 1964 Lacan discusses the development of modern 'perspective' representation in the art of the Quattrocento (see 1977b, 65–119). He was out fishing when a small boy in the group pointed to a sardine tin on the surface, glittering in the sun: '*You see that can? Do you see it? Well, it doesn't see you*' (95, emphasis in original). The can does not see you but someone situated there might, since whatever I can see constitutes a point from which I could be seen. Lacan says 'That which is light looks at me' (96): I think I see the sardine tin but the same light is the grounding condition of possibility for someone else to look at me from there. In supposing I see – as though I alone could see – I disavow the point of view I myself can never see from since it belongs to the Other, the order of the symbolic. Next issue: 'I see only from one point, but in my existence I am looked at from all sides' (72); to look and 'see the world' comes within the dominion of the conscious I and what Lacan terms 'the imaginary'. To 'be the object of the gaze' represents the operation of the unconscious, the domain of the Other on which I depend for my being but which I can never lay claim to. In Quattrocento painting the aim has been for the look to overcome the gaze in *dompte-regard*, 'a taming of the gaze' (109), the imaginary to appear fully present to itself by containing the symbolic. Perspective would ensure that I see and possess the represented image while the inescapable possibility of the gaze, looking back, is controlled and effaced. By rendering the image as an object for my eye Quattrocento painting techniques try to exclude the gaze of another.

In its engagement of marxism and psychoanalysis *Screen* was willing to map the gaze and the look, the gaps and fissures introduced by the symbolic and the seeming plenitude fantasized by the imaginary onto Althusser's account of the process of ideology as operating to produce 'a subjected being' who imagines itself as 'a free subjectivity, a centre of initiatives', and these in turn onto modernist and realist cinema and the positions into which each interpellated the viewer. Thus the textual operation of modernist and avant-garde film, exhibiting the signifiers it relied on, had a radical force because it would confront the reader with his or her construction within ideology, denaturalizing, opening up the possibility of social change. The operation of the signifiers in the realist text produce a position for the viewer but deny the fact of that production. In situating the viewer as a subject for the look, outside, as it were, and looking on, realism tends to confirm the subject as self-sufficient, a 'transcendental ego', a master, not wanting a world different from the one there appears to be.

In an essay on 'Narrative Space', Stephen Heath analyses 'classical', that is conventional, realist cinema. Film depends upon photography, which in turn depends on the Quattrocento tradition developed to depict three-dimensional objects on a flat surface. Quattrocento space relies not only on linear perspective but various strategies for placing the viewer at the centre of an apparently all-embracing view. But cinema consists of 'moving pictures'. This process constantly threatens the fixity and centring aimed for by the tradition of the still image. Figures and objects constantly move, moving in and out of frame, likely therefore to remind the spectator of the blank absence which surrounds the screen. Classical cinema would make good this dangerous instability through a narrativization which 'contains the mobility that could threaten the clarity of vision' (Easthope 1992, 76); its narrative constantly renews a centred perspective for the spectator. Heath cites the procedures advised by the film manuals – use of master-shot, the 180-degree rule, matching on action, eyeline matching, avoidance of 'impossible angles' and so on – and affirms these are designed to ensure that 'the spectator's illusion of seeing a continuous piece of action is not interrupted' (Heath 1977a, 80).

An example of 'narrative space' is the beginning of *Jaws*:

> a beach party with the camera tracking slowly right along the line of faces of the participants until it stops on a young man looking off; eyeline cut to a young woman who is thus revealed as the object of his gaze; cut to a high-angle shot onto the party that shows its general space, its situation before the start of the action with the run down to the ocean and the first shark attack. (Heath 1981b, 80)

Classical cinema always operates like this: 'in its movement, its framings, its cuts, its intermittences, the film ceaselessly poses an absence, a lack, which is ceaselessly recaptured for – one needs to be able to say "for in" – the film, that process binding the spectator in the realisation of the film's space' (88). Through such narrativization conventional cinema seeks to transform process into fixity in an ideological operation which promotes the imaginary over the symbolic.

It is just here, when the *Screen* project achieves what is probably its most complete statement, that the attempted totalization begins to fall into crisis. In the mid-1970s the air round the journal was thick with epistemological anxiety: by trying to make its theoretical project work in practice *Screen* inadvertently articulated doubts about the conception of knowledge as 'theoretical practice'. However, *Screen* adroitly changed position, propelled by an article published in 1975.

While many feminists had written against psychoanalysis, Juliet Mitchell's *Psychoanalysis and Feminism* argued that a theorization of the unconscious was necessary to understand why so many women seem to submit to patriarchy. Laura Mulvey followed this lead in 'Visual Pleasure and Narrative Cinema' by appropriating psychoanalysis 'as a political weapon' (1992, 111), extending the *Screen* analysis of the reader as an effect of the text to show that in mainstream cinema gender positions are assigned according to the principle '*Woman as image, man as bearer of the look*' (116, emphasis in original). Through this, cinema gives pleasure and that pleasure must be contested. What pleasure though? Early in the *Three Essays on the Theory of Sexuality* Freud introduced *Schaulust* or 'looking pleasure' ('scopophilia') as one expression of desire. Looking is obviously central to the pleasures of cinema. Taking up Freud's distinction between object libido and ego libido, Mulvey argues that scopophilia has both a sexual component, which Freud describes, but also a narcissistic aspect, investigated by Lacan in his analysis of the mirror stage. The first leads to looking at someone as an erotic object, the second to identification with an image seen. In principle one might expect these two contradictory forms to find equal expression in culture; in practice, they do not.

Mainstream cinema invites men to imagine identifying with men on the screen and, with them, look at women; women to identify with the women looked at:

> In a world ordered by sexual imbalance, pleasure in looking has been split between active/male and passive/female. The determining male gaze projects its fantasy onto the female figure, which is styled accordingly. In their traditional exhibitionist role women are simultaneously looked at and displayed, with their appearance coded for strong visual and erotic impact so that they can be said to connote *to-be-looked-at-ness*. (Mulvey 1992, 116)

The visual regime promotes men as active instigators of narrative while women are more often placed in a static position as an object of the look.

The same organization also mobilizes male homophobia: if in present society men in the audience do not look with desire at male objects on the screen it is because a man, says Mulvey, 'is reluctant to gaze at his exhibitionist like' (117). Elsewhere she suggests that for women 'trans-sex identification is a *habit* that easily becomes *second nature*' (129). If a woman enjoys conventional films it is because they revive a memory of her early 'masculine' or phallic phase (133).

Lacan speculates that having the phallus is masculine, being the phallus feminine (see 1977b, 289). Mulvey takes this up as an analysis of phallocentric society. The image of woman is bound into the structure twice over, both exciting the threat of castration and becoming fixed in place of that lack. She opens the wound her passivity is meant to close. On this basis, reintroducing the distinction between ego and object libido, Mulvey typifies two different kinds of film narrative. One offers mastery when a woman's mystery is investigated and she is punished or saved; in the other her imputed castration is disavowed as she is turned into a fetish. All these procedures depend upon classic realism and coherent narrative in order to establish identification as well as hold objects for the look (the public images in a modern city – advertisements and so on – provide overwhelming empirical support for Mulvey's discussion). Mulvey avoids the problem of an essentialist definition of gender by moving from signified to signifier, from the obvious maleness represented by on-screen heroes to formal operations of the 'look' of the camera and point-of-view shots. Problems remain, which I shall come back to.

The closer the *Screen* project approached to a worked-out synthesis between marxism, psychoanalysis and semiotics, the more the joints began to leak. When Stephen Heath asserted that the two processes of history and the unconscious form a 'necessary simultaneity – like the recto and verso of a piece of paper' (1976, 62) he implicitly concedes that they cannot be theoretically integrated. If so, it would not be possible to amalgamate an Althusserian theory of ideology with Lacan's account of the subject constructed in discourse. Associated doubts spilled onto *Screen*'s claim that its study of cinema was historical. At best its perspective on history was epochal, the history of the Quattrocento and realist visual representation, the capitalist institution of cinema and the 'mental machinery' that went with it. This provoked Terry Eagleton's charge against *Screen* that its formalism evaporated history so 'the historical specificity of the ideological codes' examined was merely a 'gesture' (1978, 23).

More troubles presented themselves. A major worry for *Screen* grew over Althusser's opposition between science and ideology. Sympathizers began to doubt that theory could produce a knowledge of cinema and this led to a more general failure of nerve, a situation exacerbated when Althusser himself conceded that the science/ideology opposition could not be regarded as absolute (see 1976, 106). Much more than a local difficulty peculiar to *Screen* the misgiving was part of a widespread intellectual phenomenon ensuing from Derrida's critique of logocentrism.

In 1978 an article in *Screen* pointed out what had always been disavowed:

> There remains an unbridgeable gap between 'real' readers/authors and inscribed ones ... Real readers are subject in history, living in given social formations, rather than mere subjects of a single text. The two types of subject are not commensurate. But for the purposes of formalism real readers are supposed to coincide with constructed readers. (Willemen 1978, 48)

There are all kinds of problems with 'real readers', mainly that analysis of them is only as good or bad as the theoretical model according to which their reality is interpreted. Willemen's brutal frankness demonstrates how far the *Screen* theory had been a structuralism all along. For Althusser, subjects are the effect of interpellation; for *Screen*, readers are the effect of the position provided by a textual organization. The problem extends to Mulvey's analysis as well. She assumes that the process of desire means that neither men nor women ever overshoot any fixity assigned to them. Adequately grasped, Lacan's teaching shows they always do. Nevertheless, Mulvey's classic article has led to a shelf of books concerned with the question of gender and the cinema, and particularly the issue of the feminine look at film, and it is not an exaggeration to say that today the prevailing though certainly not exclusive mode for feminist analysis of cinema has become psychoanalytic.

The importance of an attempted theoretical totalization is not measured by its theoretical cohesion. *Screen* has had a lasting effect on English intellectual life, and this is explicitly acknowledged in innovative versions of cultural studies, social psychology, art history and literary criticism the were published during the 1980s (see Easthope 1988). The subsequent influence of a generation of teachers on the students they taught is hard to calculate. Although few people today would give the same answers as *Screen* to the questions it posed, the debate resulting from them remains fully active or is overlooked only at a price.

Antony Easthope

Further reading and works cited

Althusser, L. *Essays in Self-Criticism*. London, 1976.
— 'Ideology and Ideological State Apparatuses', in *Lenin and Philosophy*. London, 1977.
— and Balibar, E. *Reading Capital*. London, 1975.
Brecht, B. *Brecht on Theatre*, ed. John Willett. London, 1964.
Brewster, B. 'Notes on the Text of John Ford's *Young Mr Lincoln* by the Editors of Cahiers du Cinéma',
    Screen Reader I, ed. J. Ellis. London, 1977.
Butler, J. *Excitable Speech*. London, 1997.
Eagleton, T. 'Aesthetics and Politics', *New Left Review*, 107, January/February 1978.
Easthope, A. *British Post-Structuralism since 1968*. London, 1988.
— (ed.) *Contemporary Film Theory*. London, 1992.
Heath, S. 'Lessons from Brecht', *Screen*, 15, 2, Summer 1974.
—. 'Anata mo', *Screen*, 17, 4, Winter 1976.
—. *Questions of Cinema*. London, 1981a.
—. 'Jaws, Ideology and Film Theory'. *Popular Film and Television*, eds A. Bennett et al. London,
    1981b.
—. *Revolution in Poetic Language*. New York, 1984.
Kristeva, J. 'Signifying Practice and Mode of Production'. *Edinburgh Magazine*, 76, 1976.
Lacan, J. 'Of Structure as an Inmixing of an Otherness Prerequisite to Any Subject Whatever', in *The
    Structuralist Controversy*, eds R. Macksey and E. Donato. Baltimore, MD, 1972.
—. *The Four Fundamental Concepts of Psycho-Analysis*. London, 1977a.
—. *Ecrits, A Selection*. London, 1977b.
MacCabe, C. 'The Politics of Separation', *Screen*, 16, 4, Winter, 1975.
Marx, K. *Capital*. London, 1970.
— and Engels, F. *Selected Works*. London, 1950.
Metz, C. *Film Language*. Oxford, 1974.
—. 'The Imaginary Signifier', *Screen*, 16, 2, Summer 1975.
—. *Psychoanalysis and Cinema*. London, 1982.
Mulvey, L. 'Visual Pleasure and Narrative Cinema', in *Contemporary Film Theory*, ed. A. Easthope.
    London, 1992.
Nairn, T. 'The English Working Class', *New Left Review*, 24, March/April 1964.
Willemen, P. 'Notes on Subjectivity', *Screen*, 19, 1, Spring 1978.
Wollen, P. ' "Ontology" and "Materialism" in Film', *Screen*, 17, 1, Spring 1976.
—. 'Derrida and British Film Theory', *Applying: to Derrida*, eds J. Brannigan, R. Robbins and J.
    Wolfreys. London, 1996.

Structuralism and the Structuralist Controversy

Imagine if cultural phenomena could be broken down and analysed with all the precision of a chemistry experiment – this was the structuralist dream. Its most intense phase (in the English-speaking West) was a ten-year period from towards the end of the 1960s to the late-1970s, when the study of culture was felt by many to have been transformed from an art into a science. That feeling did not, of course, go unchallenged, and for a brief while all hell broke loose.

However much they may have since mutated, the reverberations emanating from the controversy – indeed the scandal – structuralism caused in the 1970s, especially although not exclusively in the UK, are ongoing. At their heart lies a dispute (no doubt an incommensurable disputation) over competing concepts of culture. But no less important – now as then – is a certain Anglo-American suspicion, if not hostility, towards continental thought.

For literary studies, the controversy took the form of criticism versus theory. By the end of the 1970s, literary theory had attained 'quite suddenly', in the words of British literary critic and essayist Frank Kermode, 'a central importance it had not possessed since Aristotle' (1983, 1). At that time literary theory was dominated by a structuralist approach to the study of narrative; hence the resistance to theory was in large measure a reaction against the perceived threat to literary studies posed by the scientific presumptions of structuralism. Yet it would be wrong to see it only as a professional demarcation dispute, for the resistance to theory – so often vehement if not violent in expression – was also energized by a culturally patrician attitude on the part of many English-speaking literary critics towards what they saw as the philosophical and scientific pretensions of European theorists.

We will come back to that controversy in a moment. But for now we need to ask, what are some of the key concepts and principles of structuralism? As would be expected, the importance of a certain concept of *structure* underpins the dream of a science of culture: just as the objects of scientific investigation are understood to be explicable in terms of chemical, mathematical and other measurable relations, so too, for structuralism, cultural phenomena are taken to be reducible to the hidden structures that generate and sustain them. Here the work of Ferdinand de Saussure is of crucial importance. Indeed it was Saussure himself who first projected (or dreamt of) a new mega-discipline he proposed to call semiology (or semiotics), based on his radical overturning of received ideas on language, whose proper object of study would be no less than the social life of signs in general (Saussure 1974, 16). Saussurean linguistics, then, was but a branch of the much larger, if not all-encompassing, discipline of semiotics whose object was to be the whole field of cultural practices and meanings, the totality, as it were, of sign usage in every conceivable occurrence and context.

As the inheritor of that dream, or the realization of the promised science of culture in general, structuralism has to be seen as having thought big! Consistent with that ambition, its objects of analysis are typically macrological in scale (not, for example, individual works of literature but literature as a *system*), where the aim is to identify the underlying rules and constraints that form the structural basis of particular meanings. Following Saussure, structuralism is concerned with *langue* (a rule-governing system, like language) rather than *parole* (particular cases of a general type: individual speech acts, for example, which are made possible by language as a system). In the extreme, this can lead to grandiose generalizations that overlook all manner of stubborn details; in practice, though, a good deal of structuralist work is concerned not to locate meanings as effects of universal conditions but as the property of particular sign-using communities. These communities may of course exist within the 'same' culture; hence the meanings and values accorded, say, to a Primal Scream CD will vary, often quite dramatically, from the contemporary dance scene to the hip hop crowd to fans of Guns n' Roses, and so on.

This is to encounter a key structuralist principle, once again deriving from Saussure: meanings are effects of differential relations; 'in language [or any system] there are only differences *without positive terms*' (1974, 120). The meanings attributed to a Primal Scream CD are produced therefore out of differences between communities (and not only music-based communities) as well as being an effect of internal differences from and affinities to other forms of music (by the Rolling Stones, the Chemical Brothers, the Stone Roses, etc.) within the system of popular music at large. On its own – outside these differences or sets of differential relations – there could be no sense in which, for structuralism, the music of Primal Scream could be said to mean in any positive or meaningful way at all.

Structuralism, then, goes looking for these sets or, as the French structural anthropologist Claude Lévi-Strauss called them, 'bundles' of relations, which it takes for the base units of meaning in any system. Lévi-Strauss's analysis of the structure of the Oedipus myth is the most famous case in point (1968, 213–18; Lucy 1997, 7–11). Here we must be brief: the analysis proceeds according to the method of laying out the myth's constituent elements (in the form of bundles of relations or 'mythemes') along horizontal (diachronic) and vertical (synchronic) axes. The story of the myth is read off from the horizontal axis, the structure from the vertical axis. Arranged as four columns, the mythemes encapsulate (1) excessive blood relations, (2) undervalued blood relations, (3) monster slaying and (4) problems in walking upright. Columns one and two are inversions of each other (Oedipus marries his mother; Oedipus kills his father), but the relation between the second pair of columns is not as seemingly straightforward. According to Lévi-Strauss, though, Oedipus's name (meaning 'swollen foot') recalls the story of our rising out of the primordial mud, laming ourselves in the process; column four refers then to the myth of auto-generation. Column three denies the myth, because monsters like the Sphinx would keep us from being born. Hence the relation between these columns is one of a tension between origin myths: are we born of one (sameness) or two (difference)? Can I, in other words, be wholly at one with myself (self-same) if who I am depends on an originary and ineluctable difference from myself, in the form of the two others (who are not me but not not-me) who brought about my conception?

From this we can see that binary relations (between pairs of columns, in the present case) are crucial to a structuralist method of analysis. Once again *difference*, in the form of these binary relations or oppositions, is seen to *structure* meaning. Rather than inhering in 'positive terms', meaning is produced out of *structures of difference*. Yet – and this is to raise a serious question for structuralism – are not these very structures of difference themselves required to function as if in fact they were positive terms? What price, after all, the scientific credibility of Lévi-Strauss's analysis of the Oedipus myth if the structures of difference he identifies as underpinning it (in all its manifold forms) were open to endless disagreement or simply to counter-claims? This amounts to saying that the structure of 'structure', as it were, has to be seen as positive – the abstract equivalent of a natural or found object, over whose identity and constitution nothing has to be decided – or the whole structuralist enterprise would be in danger of collapsing back from 'science' into a simplified and familiar hermeneutics.

This point has been made most famously by Derrida (1978). In a nutshell, it accounts for the poststructuralist critique of structuralism, which is not the concern of the present essay. Nevertheless it should be noted that poststructuralism is not in a relation of *opposition* to structuralism, as might be said to characterize the response of many Anglo-American literary critics in the 1970s to what they saw as structuralism's scandalous affront to prevailing views on literature. The principal 'enemy' was not so much, however, Lévi-Strauss as a younger generation of European theorists associated with the Parisian journals *Communications* and especially *Tel Quel* in the 1960s. Of the many key figures – including Italian semiotician Umberto Eco, French narratologists A. J. Greimas, Claude Bremond and Gérard Genette, Bulgarian feminist psychoanalyst Julia Kristeva and French film theorist Christian Metz – whose work appeared in those journals, helping to refine and also (via Marx's influence on some of them) to politicize the nature of the structuralist enterprise, we will look briefly here at some of the ideas of Tzvetan Todorov and Roland Barthes.

For Todorov, a deep 'universal grammar' underlies all languages and indeed all signifying systems of every description across cultures. 'This universal grammar is the source of all universals and it gives definition even to man himself. Not only all languages but all signifying systems obey the same grammar' (cit. Scholes 1974, 111). Like Lévi-Strauss, then, whose structural anthropology dared to dream of revealing the deep structure of 'the' human mind, Todorov believed that cultural and historical phenomena could be made to give up the transcendental laws of structuration underpinning all signifying systems and defining 'our' very being as a species. While this can be seen as hubris, nevertheless it is an ambition that promotes a radical concept of 'man himself' as the product of a transcendental grammar (or *langue*) of structuration, as opposed to the conservative idea of individual men and women of genius whose special talent for creatively manipulating a particular grammar (or *parole*) justifies the hermeneutic and appreciative tasks of literary criticism.

Since the all but infinite grammatical possibilities enabled by a language render almost impossible the work of analysing the universal grammar of all languages, Todorov turns instead to the linguistic subset of narrative fiction for evidence of who 'we' are (albeit 'our' identity turns out to be inseparable from the political and cultural histories that shape it). His most famous case study is of the *Decameron* by the fourteenth-century Italian poet Giovanni Boccaccio. Not surprisingly, given that in 1965 he had produced a French translation of many of the key texts of Russian formalism from the 1920s, Todorov's analysis is strongly influenced by a formalist approach and elaborates especially on methods developed by Vladimir Propp whose *Morphology of the Folktale*, first published in 1928 but virtually unknown outside the former Soviet Union until much later, represents one of the earliest extended attempts to find a *langue* of narrative. Briefly, Propp maintained that behind the confusing mass of *parole* forms of Russian fairy tales lay a systematic organizing principle in the form of characters' *functions*. Variables such as age, height, hair colour and the like aside, each character performs one or more of a total of 31 functions (the hero leaves home, the villain is punished, etc.) and, although Propp found no tale to contain all of these at once, he argued that the order by which functions appear in any tale is always the same. From this he drew four laws, the most striking being that 'All fairy tales are of one type in regard to their structure' (1968, 63).

Building on Propp's method, Todorov saw in the one hundred tales of the *Decameron* the manifestation of a set of underlying grammatical rules, of which the two most important concern *propositions* and *sequences*. As syntactical units equivalent to a sentence, propositions consist of irreducible actions (X does Y); sequences then are strings or micro-systems of propositions equivalent to a paragraph. More structurally basic still, however, are the *parts of speech* that Todorov identifies in every tale as follows: characters function as proper nouns; actions as verbs; attributes as adjectives. Hence each proposition (or sentence) comprises a noun in juxtaposition with either a verb or adjective. The complexity of Todorov's analysis cannot be fully accounted for here; what needs to be stressed, though, is that he draws from it not a lesson in literary style or genre, but a lesson in political economy. Noting that the text privileges a 'daring personal initiate', Todorov sees this as expressing extra-textual values in support of an emerging 'ideology of the new bourgeoisie' that fostered an ideal of individualism as a liberating triumph over the 'restrictive' forces of an older, more apparently interventive political and economic system (cit. Scholes 1974, 116). In celebrating individuals' 'free action', then, the *Decameron* is consistent with the new 'liberal' ideology of the time, 'which could make believe, at the beginning at least, that it amounted to the total disappearance of system' (116).

The suggestion, by Todorov and other European structuralists of the 1960s who were broadly marxist in outlook, that literature could be understood as an ideological expression of political and economic interests rankled with many Anglo-American critics in the following decade, by which time a significant body of so-called 'French' theory had been translated into English. What rankled most, it seemed, was the structuralist insistence on regarding those liberal attitudes, which Todorov and others saw as having begun to reshape European cultural codes and values in the fourteenth century, as a formation born of ideology instead of nature.

There were several consequences of this new and (from an Anglo-American view) provocative approach to literature, but none more controversial than – to give the English title of a famous essay by Barthes that appeared in 1968 in the journal *Mantéie* – 'the death of the author'. Challenging the humanist belief in the self-expressive individual, Barthes argued that in works of literature 'it is language which speaks, not the author' (1977, 143) – a variation on the structuralist idea of man himself as a *subject* of semiotic systems. For literary criticism, every instance of writing is understood as the expression of an authorial 'voice'; for Barthes, though, 'writing is the destruction of every voice, of every point of origin' (142). This is to say that no instance of writing can be separated from the general structure of writing as a system, or indeed from the entire field of signifying systems at large. On this radical view, a work of literature is not an inspirational but a structural or (con)textual phenomenon: as writing, it cannot be said to 'speak' at all (hence 'the destruction of every voice') and cannot be seen as the exclusive property of an individual or era (hence 'the destruction ... of every point of origin'). Set loose from the tyranny of the author-centred model, Barthes' theory of literature acknowledges the creative work of reading as the only condition by which a semblance of 'unity' might be said to hold for any text: 'a text's unity lies not in its origin [the author] but in its destination [the reader]' (148). It must be stressed, however, that this is not to affirm the biological fact of the reader (in substitution for the humanist author), especially given Barthes' insistence that 'the reader is without history, biography, psychology; he is simply that *someone* who holds together in a single field all the traces by which the written text is constituted' (148). Far more radically, Barthes approaches writing as an affirmation of *the semiotic act of reading*. Hence it is only in the process of being read that a work of literature can be said to signify, and to do so over and over again across 'the space of writing' (147). From this it follows that, instead of saying *literature*, 'it would be better from now on to say *writing*' (147) because this concept remains relatively unaffected by a theological (and ideological) notion of literary works as repositories of 'secret' or 'ultimate' meanings put there by authors, according to which the task of criticism is to find them. The effect of such a task is 'to close the writing' (147). But the task of reading is to keep the writing open, on the understanding that, '[i]n the multiplicity of writing, everything is to be *disentangled*, nothing *deciphered*' (147).

In granting such privilege to the reader (as a structural function of texts and not, to repeat, as an embodied subject sitting in an armchair reading a book), Barthes threatened the very enterprise of literary criticism by challenging the commonsensical or natural – in a word, the 'disinterested' – status of its assumptions. At first, in books such as *Mythologies* (1957), *On Racine* (1963) and *Elements of Semiology* (1964), his critique of common sense keeps faith with the structuralist dream of creating a science of forms. Its fullest expression is realized in the essay 'Introduction to the Structural Analysis of Narratives', published in *Communications* in 1966, which had some impress on North American structuralism in the 1970s through its influence on Jonathan Culler's *Structuralist Poetics* (1975), a book, albeit, that was written while Culler was teaching at Oxford and Cambridge. Representing what might be called his 'high' structuralist moment, Barthes' essay on narrative draws on the work of Propp, Lévi-Strauss, Todorov, Roman Jakobson (a leading light of the Prague Circle of linguists in the 1950s), Russian formalism and of course Saussure. Hence it develops an analytical method which is classical in its reliance on language as the model *par excellence* of all signifying systems and its declaration of 'structuralism's constant aim to master the infinity of utterances [*parole* forms] by describing the "language" [the *langue* or deep structure] of which they are the products and from which they can be generated' (Barthes 1977, 80).

If, however, Barthes still holds to an ideal of scientific observation in the 1966 essay, his methods aimed only at better *description*, his thinking can be seen to shift by 1968 with the 'The Death of the Author'. What marks the shift (aside from flashes of a certain speculative and stylistic bravura that came to 'tag' his later work as poststructuralist) is a more open or less positive concept of structure than the dream of a science of culture relies on. Instead of functioning as the bedrock of signification, structure comes to be conceived as a kind of groundless ground of signifying effects which are *produced* in acts of reading; hence the attention in his later work to the 'space' or 'surface' of writing in contrast to the idea of particular works of literature having an essential 'core' or 'depth' of meaning, whether thought to originate authorially or structurally. By 1970, in his widely read and much debated *S/Z*, this formative affirmation of the signifier develops into Barthes' distinctive theory of literature as an ongoing process of reading rather than a finished product of writing: 'the goal of literary work (of literature as work) is to make the reader no longer a consumer, but a producer of the text' (1974, 4; see also Eagleton 1996, 116–23, and Lucy 1997, 75–7). Rather than what has been written, literature is what always remains *to be read*. All the properties of writing (in the standard sense of a creative practice associated with genius authors) are given over therefore to this new sense of reading conceived as productive activity rather than passive reception. This, for Barthes, is the condition of literature in general, and it is precisely this condition to which literary criticism remains blind. For literary criticism, works of literature are always (as Barthes terms it) 'readerly': they are always already unified in advance of any act of reading them, having to be conceived as finished (albeit complex) products waiting to be read in the sense of being passively consumed. But understood as demanding and defining *work* in the sense of interpretative activity, literature can be reconceived in terms of the 'writerly' text which always remains to be written (and rewritten) in acts of reading (and rereading) because its semiotic potential is always in excess of literary criticism's delimiting concepts of genre, authorship, unity, style and the like. Hence the writerly is 'the novelistic without the novel

..., writing without style, production without product, structuration without structure' (Barthes 1974, 5). Although for Barthes all literature is writerly (as his brilliantly destabilizing reading of a classical readerly text, 'Sarrasine' by Honoré de Balzac, shows in S/Z), writerliness seems more pertinent to some forms of literature than others. This is true especially of the *nouveau roman* in France (the 'new novel' associated most famously with the work of Allain Robbe-Grillet in the 1950s and 1960s) and what came to be known as 'metafiction' in the US, or a kind of writing practised by the likes of John Barth, Donald Bartheleme and Robert Coover in the 1960s that draws attention to itself *as writing* rather than attempting to represent 'reality' as prior and external to it. Even so, while writerliness is arguably a conspicuous feature of so-called avant-garde literature, it is important to stress that the writerly text is irreducible to a style or genre: it is rather *an effect of reading* understood in terms of a theoretical approach to writing as a dynamic process, a process which cannot be contained or explained by what Barthes calls 'the law of the Signified' (1974, 8) that sets the limits and determines the goal of literary criticism both as a professional enterprise and an ideology.

This point was not always well taken by Barthes' earliest admirers and critics in the UK. Much of the controversy over structuralism in the 1970s – its newsworthiness deemed to be important enough for coverage in such outlets as *The Times Literary Supplement*, *The Times Higher Education Supplement* and *The London Review of Books* – concerned the mistaken belief that Barthes and other continental thinkers were calling for a kind of 'anything goes' approach to the evaluation of culture generally, but especially to the interpretation and appreciation of literature. Somewhat later, this belief would come to be associated (mistakenly again) with poststructuralism, but at that time 'structuralism' was the preferred term of the British press and tended to be used as the marker both of 'ideological' and 'relativistic' approaches to literature and culture. Since it enflamed so much passion at the time, British literary theorist Colin MacCabe's work is central to the controversy surrounding 'structuralism' in the UK. As late as 1983, indeed, in an essay by the conservative British critic Iain Wright, MacCabe was still being scolded (albeit by inference) for espousing a so-called 'doctrinaire a-historical relativism' associated with 'doctrinaire anti-realists' whom Wright chose not to name (1983, 60, 66). A year earlier, the British philosopher Roger Scruton had put the case against structuralism and its reliance on 'Saussurean jargon' in no uncertain terms: acknowledging that structuralist studies were 'by now widely accepted as part of the academic repertoire', Scruton himself chose not to imitate them 'out of respect for a concept – that of truth – which many of those studies seem to overlook' (1982, 86)!

Simply for daring to want to find, or to dream of finding, what Culler called 'a poetics which strives to define the conditions of meaning' (1975, viii), structuralism was unfairly hectored by many conservative critics in the UK in the 1970s and beyond. While the case against it could, however, have been put more graciously, that does not mean that structuralism has no case to answer at all. But its problem is not the patrician accusation that it ignores 'truth'; the problem for structuralism, rather, is that it thinks truth can be found in a stable concept of structure.

Niall Lucy

Further reading and works cited

Barthes, R. *On Racine*. New York, 1964.
—. *Elements of Semiology*. New York, 1968.
—. *Mythologies*. New York, 1973.
—. *S/Z*. New York, 1974.
—. *Image Music Text*. London, 1977.
Culler, J. *Structuralist Poetics*. London, 1975.
—. *Saussure*. London, 1976.
Derrida, J. *Writing and Difference*. London, 1978.
Eagleton, T. *Literary Theory*. Oxford, 1983.
Eco, U. *A Theory of Semiotics*. Bloomington, IN, 1976.
Genette, G. *Narrative Discourse*. Oxford, 1980.
Greimas, A. J. *Sémantique structurale*. Paris, 1966.
Hawkes, T. *Structuralism and Semiotics*. London, 1977.
Jameson, F. *The Prison-House of Language*. Princeton, NJ, 1972.
Kermode, F. *Essays on Fiction*. London, 1983.
Lévi-Strauss, C. *The Savage Mind*. London, 1966.
—. *Structural Anthropology 1*. Harmondsworth, 1968.
Lucy, N. *Postmodern Literary Theory*. Oxford, 1997.
MacCabe, C. *James Joyce and the Revolution of the Word*. London, 1978.
Macksey, R. and Donato, E. (eds) *The Structuralist Controversy*. Baltimore, MD, 1972.
Propp, V. *Morphology of the Folktale*. Austin, TX, 1968.
Robey, D. (ed.) *Structuralism*. Oxford, 1973.
Saussure, F. de. *Course in General Linguistics*. London, 1974.
Scholes, R. *Structuralism in Literature*. New Haven, CT, 1974.
Scruton, R. 'Public Text and Common Reader', *Comparative Criticism*, 4, 1982.
Todorov, T. *Grammaire du Décaméron*. Paris, 1969.
Wright, I. ' "What Matter Who's Speaking?": Beckett, the Authorial Subject and Contemporary Critical Theory', *Comparative Criticism*, 5, 1983.

The Spread of Literary Theory in Britain

By the late 1990s literary theory had become the most compulsory topic on English degree courses in Britain. Of the seventy-six university institutions which responded to a questionnaire on the syllabus sent out in 1998 by 'CCUE' (the Council for College and University English) forty listed it as an obligatory topic of study. (The study of Victorian fiction – the second most compulsory topic on the syllabus – is obligatory at thirty of the responding institutions.) How did this spectacular rise come about? What follows is a kind of ethnographic 'thick description' of the institutional assimilation of literary theory (hereafter referred to just as 'theory') into English studies in Britain.

It is usually suggested that before the outbreak of continental theory in the 1970s an unbroken liberal-humanist quietus completely dominated literary studies in Britain, but it should be emphasized that there already existed currents of 'native' dissent from the

Leavisite consensus, and that these provided fertile ground in which imported theories could later take root. In the late 1950s, for instance, Richard Hoggart's *The Uses of Literacy* (1957) and Raymond Williams's *Culture and Society* (1958) offered broader notions of culture than Leavisite approaches allowed, and these concerns became the focus of the influential Centre for Contemporary Cultural Studies at Birmingham University, which had been founded by Hoggart in 1963 and was directed by him till 1968, and then by Stuart Hall from 1968 to 1979. Perry Anderson's 'Components of the National Culture' (1968, 3–57), was an influential full-frontal attack on the residual dominance of Leavis, and this was broadly aligned in spirit with that of several other prominent UK critics of the time, including Alan Swingewood (of the LSE), whose book *The Sociology of Literature* (written with Diana Laurenson) was published in 1972 by Paladin (an imprint which would become an important progressive force in the 1970s), and David Craig (of Lancaster University), author of *The Real Foundations: Literature and Social Change*, another key work which challenged Leavis's resistance to the broader social contextualization of literature. This kind of material overlaps chronologically with the arrival of the work of continental theorists in the early 1970s, and the Birmingham CCCS under Stuart Hall increasingly made use of these newly available perspectives. Theory, then, did not take root by magic in a liberal-humanist desert, but in ground which was ready to nourish such a crop.

The growth of 'theory' proper in the UK falls into four distinct phases, each of about five years' duration. Phase one covers the first half of the 1970s, roughly 1970 to 1975. The Oxbridge–London University triangle was the early centre of 'theory' in the UK. The Cambridge wing included Stephen Heath and his student Colin MacCabe, both of whom had studied structuralism in Paris. An important early text, from Oxford, was David Robey's edited collection *Structuralism: An Introduction*. Roland Barthes' work was promulgated by the London Graduate Seminar started by Frank Kermode after he became Professor of English at University College, London. This seminar was a significant moment in the importation of structuralism into Britain, briefly described by Bernard Bergonzi in his 1990 book *Exploding English*: the seminar, he says, 'discussed the literary implications of structuralism, semiotics, and emergent poststructuralism ... establish[ing] a useful informal link with the work going on at Cambridge, and participants included Stephen Heath, Jonathan Culler ... Veronica Forrest-Thomson ... Christine Brooke-Rose, Christopher Norris, and Shlomith Rimmon' (99). 'Theory', then, was well under way by 1973, when the *TLS* devoted the major part of two issues to a 'Survey of Semiotics', with articles by Eco, Todorov and Kristeva, and others, and in the same year a translation of *Mythologies* appeared, also in the trend-setting Paladin imprint, this being the work which established the popularity of Roland Barthes in Britain. (A little later Stephen Heath edited and translated a selection of Barthes's essays under the title *Image-Music-Text*. This became the standard 'portable Barthes' for British readers, and was published by Fontana – another important progressive paperback imprint – in 1977, in the 'Communications' series which had Raymond Williams as its general editor.) The culmination of the first phase of theory is marked by Jonathan Culler's *Structuralist Poetics*, based on his Oxford doctoral dissertation, a book which was one of the crucial mediating texts of theory. Culler had substantial Oxbridge affiliations, having taken a doctorate at Oxford and then taught for four years at Cambridge. It should be added that the 'mediatory' books mentioned here (Heath/MacCabe, Robey and Culler) which were the keystone of the first phase of 'theory' in Britain, were often obliged to discuss and summarize 'primary' theoretical (mainly French) texts which had not yet been translated into English.

The uncompromising central point of Culler's book is its insistence that the proper object of literary study is not the appreciation and enjoyment of individual works of literature, but the quest for an understanding of what constitutes 'literariness'. He writes:

> The type of literary study which structuralism helps one to envisage would not be primarily interpretive; it would not offer a method which, when applied to literary works, produced new and hitherto unexpected meanings. Rather than a criticism which discovers or assigns meanings, it would be a poetics which strives to define the conditions of meaning. (1975, viii)

On the face of it, this proposal for a change of direction in literary studies did not seem terribly promising, for it is difficult to imagine undergraduates enrolling in large numbers on a course which 'strives to define the conditions of meaning'. But the appeal of such an approach to postgraduates and to younger academics was considerable, for in Britain, to a great extent (and more so than in America), general ideas had been artificially suppressed in English studies for a long time, thereby inevitably creating a strong appetite for them. Thus a whole range of questions were never touched upon at all, questions, for instance, concerning the purpose and potential of literature itself, the nature of literary language and literary representation, the role of the reader and of the academy in the creation of literary canons, and so on. Theory offered to release this hidden, repressed subconscious of English studies, to break the taboo on ideas and generalizations which many decades of practical criticism had effectively imposed.

The characteristics of this first phase of theory in Britain, then, are, firstly, that there is relatively little availability of the primary texts of theory, and consequently a high degree of dependency on works like those just mentioned which are 'summative' or 'mediatory' in character: where primary materials were available it was mostly in the form of single chapters or articles only, like those in Jacques Ehrmann's *Structuralism*. Secondly, 'theory' at this stage was more genuinely cross-disciplinary than it later became – Culler, for instance, taught in a French department, not an English department, and there was as much interest in linguistics as in structuralism. Thirdly, theory at this time had very little impact on the undergraduate syllabus; it was the concern of 'faculty' and of graduate-school members, and finally, it had a markedly restricted geographical and 'social-academic' spread, being confined mainly to the most privileged university centres in southern England.

The second phase of theory covers the latter half of the 1970s (roughly 1976–80), when its influence spread to English departments across the whole higher education system, but still predominantly at graduate level. The definitive milestone of this phase was the founding in 1977 of Methuen's 'New Accents' series of introductory books on aspects of theory, beginning with *Structuralism and Semiotics* in that year by Terence Hawkes, the General Editor. At this stage there was still a prominent belief (characteristic of the time, and now somewhat dated) in the radicalizing potential of linguistics: the General Editor's Preface to 'New Accents' remarks that modern linguistics has 'provided a basis for the study of the totality of human communication, and so ultimately for an analysis of the human role in the world at large'. The prominence of linguistics reflected the prestige of Noam Chomsky's theories of generative grammar, and the widespread reverence for the work of Roman Jakobson and the Prague Linguistic Circle, but it also drew on the fact that literary linguistics (later called 'stylistics') had in the 1960s offered an overt challenge to the 'liberal humanist' consensus in literary studies (albeit from a very different starting point from that of the emergent New Left critics), as instanced by the polemical exchanges between F. W.

Bateson and the linguist Roger Fowler in Bateson's journal *Essays in Criticism* (see 1967, 332–47, and 1968, 164–82). Unsurprisingly, therefore, the second 'New Accents' volume was Fowler's *Linguistics and the Novel*. This second phase of theory in Britain ends with the publication of Catherine Belsey's highly successful and influential New Accents book *Critical Practice* in 1980. 'Critical practice' became the catchphrase denoting a newly theorized way of reading literature which would replace the old consensus method of practical criticism. The book insisted that there is a single system of representation, with no privileged literary realm (an assertion directly analogous to Fowler's view that there is, in effect, no such thing as literary language, no distinct linguistic entity working to different rules from language in general). Thus high literary works like *Middlemarch*, on the one hand, and advertisements for cosmetics, on the other, use the same signifying system, and draw on similar images, archetypes and signifying systems. It is, for Belsey, merely bourgeois mystification to suggest that language and representation work in a special way in literature. All the same, a particular kind of writing, literary realism, is especially to be condemned since it is of its very nature an act of collusion with a conservative status quo in society. In reading such realist works, which fraudulently attempt to efface their own status as representation, the task of the reader is constantly to resist the illusion of reality they create, avoiding, for instance, any discussion of 'characters', imagined as if they were real people. Instead, the book urges us to concentrate on the techniques and structures of representation which are seen at work in the text under consideration. Thus, *Critical Practice* reflects the strong influence of Althusser on key British theorists during this phase, for the book expresses the view that as soon as a novelist signs the realist 'contract', providing characters who are presented through the medium of psychological realism, set within a detailed and recognizable social setting, then inevitably there is a fatal collusion with the reader's 'common sense' expectations and beliefs about the world. As she puts it: '[The realist text] however critical of the world it describes, offers the reader a position, an attitude which is given as non-contradictory, fixed in "knowing" subjectivity.' Hence, the realist literary text inevitably becomes an aspect of what Althusser called the 'ISA', the ideological state apparatus by which we are rendered subject.

As this second stage progresses, theory begins to popularize its basic beliefs, starting to establish them as the taken-for-granted postulates on which further argument can be built. At this stage, therefore, the balance of pedagogical interest within theory began to shift from graduate schools to the undergraduate literature courses which would become the next frontier for the dissemination of theory. The other distinctive point about the end of this second phase is that already interest was shifting from structuralism to poststructuralism, from Barthes to Derrida, from linguistics to philosophy. Thus, if phases one and two of theory are mainly about structuralism, then the next two phases centre on poststructuralism. Deconstruction and poststructuralism became a major force in Britain with the publication of another key book, *Deconstruction and Criticism* in 1979, a book with five authors, the so-called 'Yale Mafia' of Harold Bloom, Paul de Man, Jacques Derrida, Geoffrey Hartman and J. Hillis Miller. It was harshly reviewed in both the *New York Review of Books* and the *London Review of Books*. In the former, Denis Donoghue, using the title 'Deconstructing Deconstruction', wrote that it had 'more to do with the rhetoric of power in American universities than with its ostensible subject'. These hostile reviews, however, were but a foretaste of the polarization and acrimony which are the dominant characteristic of phase three, the period of the 'theory wars in English'.

This third phase, then, comprising the first half of the 1980s, is that of head-on conflict between theory and 'liberal humanism'. This is the period of the 'theory wars', of bad-tempered semi-private rows at department meetings and graduate papers, and of more public ones at conferences, on television and radio programmes, and in the columns of national newspapers and academic journals. It was a strangely fraught time, with the frustrations induced by what was happening on the national political scene spilling over into the academic sphere. The Labour Party had collapsed into seemingly terminal in-fighting and the long ascendancy of Thatcherism began in 1979 with the first of four successive Tory election victories. The crude Thatcherite extremism encapsulated in the slogan 'There is no such thing as society' generated its reversed counter-image in English studies, which, in its high Althusserian phase, increasingly seemed to maintain that 'there is no such thing as the individual'. The cultural situation was rendered even more unstable because for over a year, from 1979, the *Times* newspapers, having moved to a new high-tech plant in Wapping, fought to the death with the print unions. For that period the *TLS* and the *THES* disappeared, leaving a spate of new journals – Richard Boston's *Quarto*, Ann Smith's *The Literary Review* and the *London Review of Books* under Karl Miller – to debate structuralism and poststructuralism. All these were sceptical, at best, about the new theories, but they were willing to devote a great deal of space to them, and for a time there seemed to be polemical pieces in almost every issue. These were days when the review of a new work of literary theory could be followed by up to two years of irate correspondence, sometimes with complaints and accusations spilling over into the correspondence sections of other journals. The effect of these new journals, then, was to heat up the temperature by breaking away from the residual politeness and gentility of the *TLS* and giving overt expression to the internal tensions which many English departments suffered in the 1980s between traditionalists and theorists. On the return of the *Times* and its stable, the *TLS* caught up by publishing a symposium entitled 'Professing Literature' (December 1982) and the *THES* had a similar 'Perspective' compilation on 11 February 1983, as indeed did the journal *PN Review* (1985). These symposia, each with its train of embattled correspondence, give a powerful insight into the polarized opinions of the time.

One of the most notorious of these public controversies followed the publication in 1982 of a New Accents book called *Re-Reading English*, edited by Peter Widdowson. Roger Poole was commissioned by the *TLS* to review the book, but his broadly favourable review was rejected by the editor, Jeremy Treglown (on grounds of 'style'), and another and highly critical one commissioned (from Claude Rawson). Here, allegedly, was proof of the Establishment's ruthless hold on the channels of cultural dissemination. The matter came to light in a letter to *PN Review* (1984, 40, 4) by Antony Easthope, responding to a piece in issue 37 earlier in the year on 'The Politicisation of English'. Treglown was invited to respond to the accusation of cultural bias in the same issue (40), and did so. Poole put his side of the case (42, 6), and Rawson his (43, 5), to which Poole responded (1985, 44, 7), and Rawson added a riposte (45, 4). In the *London Review of Books* the reviewer of the same book was the poet and critic Tom Paulin (17–30 June 1982). Paulin was even more scathing than Rawson had been, and his article generated a vicious and bitterly divided correspondence which ran – in this fortnightly journal – until February 1983, under the appropriate title 'Faculty at War'. (Paulin's piece was reprinted in his collection *Ireland and the English Crisis*, 1984.) The crisis in English studies was, he said, partly a reflection of 'that futureless and pastless sense of blankness which distinguishes the present generation of students'. Partly, too, it was the result of the vacuum left by the period of critical exhaustion which followed the overthrow of the revolution brought about by 'that sour puritan' F. R.

Leavis and his disciples many years before. English ought to be happy enough to let everybody get on with doing their own thing, since its characteristic quality as a subject is that it is 'about everything and nothing, and so is endlessly plastic'. It seemed difficult for Paulin to understand why the subject was suddenly riven with schism, since unlike a religion, or even a social club, it had never had a set of agreed aims and principles and had always been only the loosest of coalitions. Paulin did not attempt to explain why the non-aggression pacts had suddenly broken down, but his wrath was directed against *Re-Reading English* which he saw as attempting to exploit the looseness of the subject's boundaries, demystifying the notion of literary value, developing instead a 'politics of reading' and extending the word 'text' so that it could include newspaper reports, popular songs, political speeches and so on. Paulin feared that English was becoming 'a nightmare of subsidized nonsense, an arid wilderness of combative attitudes, deconstructed texts, abolished authors and demonic critical technicians'. These technicians, he said, could make the experience of reading the poetry of Philip Sydney sound like 'a spell in a forced labour camp'. These quotations illustrate the extreme heat generated in these polemical exchanges. One such – a later flare-up in the *London Review of Books* between Graham Hough and Terence Hawkes – ended with the latter inviting the former to 'piss off' (21 November 1985).

Aside from broader political considerations, the great rancour of these exchanges is partly the result of frustration at the fact that during phase three, theorists were still usually in a minority in their own departments, unable to take a decisive grasp on the reins of power (this was the lesson of the so-called 'MacCabe Affair' at Cambridge in February 1981) so that the public sphere became (in the much-used phrase) a 'site of contestation'. But a strong counter-network of conferences, organizations and sympathetic journals had grown up, which was in effect a government-in-exile which would come into its own when the theory revolution had run its course later in the decade. The network included the Sociology of Literature conferences at the University of Essex, organized by Francis Barker and Peter Hulme from 1977 to 1981 (and later the 'Essex Symposia'). Also significant was the Literature, Teaching, Politics group ('LTP'), which met annually at different venues. Between 1980 and 1986 there were annual meetings at Cardiff, Cambridge, Birmingham, Sunderland, Ilkley, Bristol and Glasgow, attracting well over a hundred delegates at their height. There were also regional 'LTP' groups, each taking responsibility for the printing, publication and distribution of an issue of the journal *Literature Teaching Politics*, including Cardiff (1980), Sussex (1981), Cambridge (1982), Leeds (1983), Birmingham (1984), Bristol Polytechnic (1985) and Glasgow (1986). Another such group set up the 'UTE' conferences (University Teachers of English), later 'HETE' (Higher Education Teachers of English), which went on throughout the 1980s, meeting at Reading (1984), Liverpool (1985), Sussex (1986), Kent (1987), Glasgow (1988), Birkbeck College (1989) and Strathclyde (1990). Events like these were attended by commissioning editors and new titles were commissioned in the several series of books which were now spreading the message of theory. In this troubled and excited climate a new left-wing theoretical/cultural consensus had begun to take shape, led by a number of vigorous and prolific academic writers and polemicists: these included Terry Eagleton, at Wadham College, Oxford; Jonathan Dollimore and Alan Sinfield at Sussex University; Catherine Belsey, Christopher Norris and Terence Hawkes at the University of Wales, Cardiff; Isobel Armstrong, Maud Ellmann and Robert Young at Southampton University; Peter Widdowson at Thames Polytechnic; John Drakakis at Stirling University; Antony Easthope at Manchester

Polytechnic; and Colin MacCabe, now at the University of Strathclyde, after his much-publicized 'Last Exit' from Cambridge.

The great success of the pioneer 'New Accents' series continued: Christopher Norris's *Deconstruction: Theory and Practice* (1982) was the definitive phase-three title, doing for poststructuralism what Culler's *Structuralist Poetics* had earlier done for structuralism. Two other key publishing events of this phase were the publication of ground-breaking general accounts of the whole field of modern literary theory, both making a serious attempt to 'package' theory for an undergraduate rather than a graduate audience, namely Terry Eagleton's *Literary Theory: An Introduction* (1983) and Raman Selden's *A Reader's Guide to Contemporary Literary Theory* (1985). The characteristics of phase three of theory, then, are firstly, prolonged and bitter hostilities between traditional approaches to literary study (usually called 'liberal humanism') and 'theory'; secondly, the continuation of the shift from structuralism to poststructuralism; thirdly the growing confidence of theorists through a vigorous culture of conferences and dedicated journals, leading to the spread of theory across the whole range of traditional universities, and throughout the so-called 'public sector' of polytechnics and colleges of higher education; and finally, its shift from being a mainly postgraduate preoccupation to its becoming established at the heart of the undergraduate syllabus.

Phase four, roughly 1985 to 1990, is marked by an abrupt and at first puzzling outbreak of peace, for the theory wars seemed suddenly to disappear. On reflection. however, the marked change in the academic climate is readily understood. *Firstly,* the attempt to teach theory at undergraduate level threw up a major problem, which was the challenge of showing that theory could be *used* in the practical study of literature. Wherever it was taught, students wanted to know what they could *do* with theory, and it was always implausible to pretend (aping the high disdain of Paul de Man for any descent from the lofty plateau of Ivy League Graduate School debate) that making such a demand was simply a form of 'resistance to theory'. Trying to meet the demand from students for clear exposition and plausible applications absorbed much of the energy which would otherwise have been available for peer-group polemic. The pioneer book of 'applied theory' was Douglas Tallack's edited collection *Literary Theory at Work: Three Texts* (1987). New series of books aimed at undergraduates also began to appear, like Blackwell's 'ReReading Literature', under the general editorship of Terry Eagleton. Extracts from the primary texts of theory were packaged into 'readers' for undergraduate courses, including Rick Rylance's *Debating Texts* (1987), David Lodge's *Modern Criticism and Theory: A Reader* (1988), K. M. Newton's *Twentieth Century Literary Theory: A Reader* (1989) and Philip Rice and Patricia Waugh's *Modern Literary Theory: A Reader* (1989). The pattern of coursebook provision in phase four is that the three different kinds of book – the discursive general account of the field (like Eagleton's and Selden's), the 'reader' of primary materials (like Lodge's and Rylance's) and the 'applied theory' text (like Tallack's) – existed as separate entities. Later on, in the 1990s and beyond, the trend would be to combine two or three of these into a single integrated theory coursebook.

As this implies, another reason for the ending of the theory wars in phase four is that theory had made such sweeping gains. Theory books sold extremely well, and commissioning editors attended the theory-based conferences, eager to sign up new authors to fill these series, and the balance of power began to tip very rapidly in theory's favour as many young academics quickly built up the kind of publication lists which lead to promotions and professorships. The shift of power away from the more conservative forces in the discipline was further accelerated by the arrival, in 1986, of Research Assessment, which is the system whereby the research and publication output of university-level departments is formally assessed and graded by quasi-governmental bodies. The grade attained determines the amount of research funding received from the public purse. The exercise was repeated in 1988, 1992, 1996 and 2001, becoming a major part of institutional and disciplinary culture. Consequently, prolific theorists became highly desirable properties. Suddenly, theory had landed and theorists were in charge, and by 1990 it had become the norm for undergraduate degrees to include compulsory literary theory.

In the 1990s and beyond, the major task of theory was to make up its 'pedagogical deficit', so that progressive teaching methods appropriate to progressive content could be developed. Hitherto, as Ben Knights had put it, 'the change of mind-set at the level of theory ha[d] grafted itself upon a very traditional pedagogy, and one which reproduce[d] the hierarchical model of transmission which theory might have been supposed to subvert or replace' (1995, 64–5). Making up the deficit may well have been accelerated by another of the new forms of assessment to which universities are subject, for since 1994 English departments, like all others, have undergone 'TQA', Teaching Quality Assessment, in which each department's teaching is assessed and given a public rating. Since theory now forms a major part of the syllabus, teaching it effectively has become a vital matter, of major importance, not just to postgraduates and young lecturers, as it was during the 'theory wars' of the early 1980s, but to heads of department, faculty deans and vice-chancellors. Theory in Britain has not just come of age, then, it has entered middle age, and carries with it the cares and responsibilities of office. Indeed, the 'Copernican revolution' of theory (to use Catherine Belsey's term) may already have passed its perihelion, for there are now likely to be younger members in most departments who question the need for and the usefulness of theory. Again, too, this shift is partly driven by changing patterns of funding, for the sabbatical leave, fellowships, research readerships and research professorships which are offered each year by governmental and charitable bodies (and which carry greater personal and institutional prestige even than publication itself) seem more likely to be awarded for traditional archival research and for major labour-intensive scholarly projects than for the production of new deconstructive or postcolonial readings of literary texts. As theory itself would tell us, theory is socially and politically constructed, and is 'always already' part of some such broader institutional picture. Inevitably so.

Peter Barry

Further reading and works cited

Anderson, P. 'Components of the National Culture'. *New Left Review*, 50, 1968.
Barry, P. *Beginning Theory*. Manchester, 1995.
Barthes, R. *Image-Music-Text*, ed. S. Health. London, 1977.
Belsey, C. *Critical Practice*. London, 1980.
Bergonzi, B. *Exploding English: Criticism, Theory, Culture*. Oxford, 1990.
Bloom, H. et al. *Deconstruction and Criticism*. London, 1979.
Bradford, R. (ed.) *The State of Theory*. London, 1993.
Craig, D. *The Real Foundations*. London, 1973.
Culler, J. *Structuralist Poetics*. London, 1975.
Eagleton, T. *Literary Theory: An Introduction*. Oxford, 1996.
Ellis, J. M. *Against Deconstruction*. Princeton, NJ, 1989.

Essays in Criticism, 16, 1967.
Essays in Criticism, 17, 1968.
Evans, C. *English People*. Buckingham, 1993.
— (ed.) *Developing University English Teaching*. Lampeter, 1995.
Hawkes, T. *Structuralism and Semiotics*. London, 1977.
Knights, B. 'The Text and the Group', *Developing University, English Teaching*. London, 1995.
Lodge, D. *Modern Criticism and Theory*. London, 1988.
Newton, K. M. *Twentieth Century Literary Theory*. Basingstoke, 1997.
Norris, C. *Deconstruction: Theory and Practice*. London, 1982.
Parrinder, P. *The Failure of Theory*. Brighton, 1987.
Pope, R. *The English Studies Book*. London, 1998.
Rylance, R. *Debating Texts*. Milton Keynes, 1987.
Selden, R. et al. *A Reader's Guide to Contemporary Literary Theory*. Prentice Hall, 1996.
Sim, S. (ed.) *The A to Z Guide to Modern Literary and Cultural Theorists*. Hemel Hempstead, 1995.
Tallack, D. (ed.) *Literary Theory at Work: Three Texts*. London, 1987.
Tredell, N. *The Critical Decade*. Manchester, 1993.
Widdowson, P. (ed.) *Re-Reading English*. London, 1982.
Wolfreys, J. (ed.) *Literary Theories*. Edinburgh, 1999.

Feminism and Poststructuralism

In their introduction to the recent anthology of *Feminisms*, the editors consider the current trend in feminist academic practice to 'denounce totalizing theories, to celebrate difference, recognize "otherness", and acknowledge the multiplicity of feminisms' as directly undermining any attempt to define or represent 'feminism' itself as a coherent discipline (Kemp and Squires 1997, 4). At the same time, Second Wave feminism has a long pre-academic history and originated in grass-roots activism by women's campaigning groups and consciousness-raising techniques. I understand British and American academic (and hence largely theoretical) feminism to be a development of the practice(s) and impetus of the Second Wave Women's Movement in the context of academic conditions. So rather than bewailing a severance of academic and grass-roots feminisms, we might understand academic/theoretical feminism as simply what happens to feminism when it enters the academy, or indeed what happens to the academy/theory when feminist academics enter the scene.

Poststructuralism is a composite term drawing on a number of influential theoretical methodologies developed in late 1960s and 1970s France. While a comprehensive list of theorists contributing to poststructuralist ideas is too long for the purposes of this study, in the context of encounters between feminism and poststructuralism three figures in particular seem to have attracted significant and enduring attention (Derrida, Foucault and Lacan). So while Chris Weedon identifies Althusser at the centre of the feminist-poststructuralist project, his name does not feature at all in the index to the recent *Feminisms* anthology which charts pretty comprehensively contemporary academic feminist concerns (1987, 13). The most influential French feminist-poststructuralists (Cixous,

Irigaray, Kristeva, et al.) have been drawn on in a variety of ways in the development of what has come to be called 'Sexual Difference' feminism, active mostly outside the UK in the work of Moira Gatens, Rosi Braidotti, Michelle Boulous Walker, Elizabeth Grosz as well as current in Italian feminist theory more generally. British feminism, on the other hand, with its history of engagement with a tradition of British socialism, tends to be turned off by ideas of 'Sexual Difference', but has taken up aspects of poststructuralist methodologies as conducive to an extended materialist analysis of gender, power and representation. However, the British feminist encounter with poststructuralism is largely – if not exclusively – the result of an ongoing feminist critique of the implications and pitfalls of poststructuralist methodologies for women inside and outside the academy, a response to poststructuralism that is a direct result of British feminism's largely socialist roots. At one extreme of the range of views in play poststructuralism is considered to be a threat to the very terms in which a feminist politics is grounded, characterized by Kate Soper's announcement that 'feminism as theory has pulled the rug from under feminism as politics' (Soper, in Squire and Kemp 1997, 289). At the other extreme we can find feminist-oriented theoretical work in the British journal *m/f* intent on deconstructing gender in a way that calls feminist politics *as a practice* into question. This essay will offer a frame in which to consider what is at stake in the feminist-poststructuralist affair at large, and how it has developed in British academia more specifically.

Patricia Waugh identifies the core issue in any discussion of feminism and poststructuralism when she writes:

> Those excluded from or marginalized by the dominant culture – for reasons of class, gender, race, belief, appearance, or whatever – . . . may *never* have experienced a sense of full subjectivity in the first place. They may never have identified with that stable presence mediated through the naturalizing conventions of fictional tradition. Such Others may, indeed, *already* have sensed the extent to which subjectivity is constructed through institutional dispositions of relations of power, as well as those of fictional conventions. (1989, 2)

Waugh's comment highlights the degree to which the affair which has developed between feminism and poststructuralism since their meeting in the mid–1970s has been marked by a simultaneous convergence and breach. Both positions share a general concern with, and critical undermining of, the dominant 'Subject' of Euro-western culture since the Enlightenment. Yet the specificity of the feminist position is characterized by the degree to which this 'Subject' is understood to map onto an inherently male/masculine model, as well as the consequences and implications of its/his destabilization in theory and practice.

Whereas classical (European) poststructuralists 'deconstructed' the Enlightenment 'Subject' through a series of radical theoretical displacements (Lacanian emphasis on the structure of unconscious processes producing an illusion of conscious subjectivity; Derridean decentring of the unitary and coherent 'subject' of philosophy; Foucault's emphasis on the discursive and disciplinary practices producing the experience of subjectivity; and Barthes' displacement of the authorial control of meaning in writing), feminists begin from the radical displacement of dominant subjectivity put in motion by their embodied existence as women (the feminine Other embodied). Hence feminism arises in the first instance from an experiential (rather than theoretical) context of the common ground of the female-embodied subject's situation as *already* fragmented, dispersed, self-contradictory, etc., and the history of feminism has hitherto been dominated by women's struggle to overcome this marginalized, fragmented and Othered status. Feminism, then, recognizes that the 'Subject' under deconstruction by poststructuralist meth-odologies was never more than an epistemic fiction, but brings to the debate the understanding (largely absent elsewhere) that its/his erection was (and continues to be) established on the grounds of their/her exclusion, containment, marginalization, fragmentation and Othering. Hence feminism generally, and British feminism particularly, responds to poststructuralism with dismay (because women have never had the chance to experience the kind of stable subject position currently being theoretically dismantled) as well as familiarity (because the conclusions reached by poststructuralist methodologies echo something of the status of female-embodied subjectivity). We must also consider, following Morris (1993), to what extent we misrepresent and/or overdetermine feminism as a purely academic-theoretical practice when we consider it analogous to poststructuralism, as this encyclopaedia invites us to. For this reason I have tried in the following discussion to offer a historical as well as theoretical situating of the feminism/poststructuralism affair in British universities over the last twenty years or so.

The questions raised by the coincidence in academic practice of feminist and post-structuralist methodologies have produced a heated and productive international and interdisciplinary debate (Weedon 1987; Alcoff 1988; Adams 1978; Nicholson 1990; Riley 1988 – to name but a few). While this debate spans the western academic world, the burden of discussion has been carried by feminist theorists. Poststructuralism is a key issue in feminist theory, but feminism tends to be avoided by poststructuralist theory not self-identified as feminist. Much of the ongoing debate concerns an inherent tension within the feminist movement between praxis and principle, or between grass-roots activism and academic argument, or between experience and theory. Feminism has a long and varied history preceding the incorporation of poststructuralist theory, yet it often appears that only since feminism began to think in and through the diction of 'theory' has it been noticed outside its own domains and integrated within academic disciplines more generally. Feminism over the last 20 years has become of the order of things to be included in an encyclopaedia of criticism and theory, but – perhaps – only as an 'and' category (see Spivak 1993, 188).

To make sense of the persistent but explosive relationship between feminism and poststructuralism (by which I understand the bearing of poststructuralism on feminism *and* the bearing of feminism on poststructuralism as well as the critical area in which these become integral and mutually-informing practices) we need to understand something of the history of feminism in Britain and in particular its entry into the academy in the 1970s. This is the story of the political evolution of feminism as much as of the politicizing of the academy since the late 1960s. Prior to its engagement with feminism, poststructuralist theory was sex-blind in the sense that, whatever their theoretical sophistication, the core figures associated with this term appeared to feminist academics in the familiar guise of a new – but all too familiar – 'male pantheon' (Morris 1993, 380). The work of the poststructuralist triumvirate in particular might be characterized by a general gender aphasia: Lacan's inability/refusal to see agency beyond the phallic (Irigaray 1985; Grosz and Probyn 1995; Fraser 1997); Foucault's inability/refusal to see sexed embodiment as a factor in the production/experience of subjectivity (Sawicki 1991; McNay 1992); Derrida's claim to the disembodied 'feminine' as if female-embodment (being a woman rather than writing like a woman) remained irrelevant to the question (Whitford 1991, 50; Morris 1993, 379). Yet feminism and poststructuralism maintain an important and active symbiosis of concerns and strategies including: recognition of the partial nature of Enlightenment claims to the universal; a desire to find ways of describing the world that aim to recreate the world; a concern over difference and the politicization of the personal (local, interior, marginal); radical attention to the determinacy of structure and process in the making of meaning; a willingness to take seriously the aesthetic/semiotic realm as a site of massive political and social stakes, and so forth. But the differences and arguments remain. Feminism as understood by poststructuralist purists stands accused of essentialism in its claims to the significance of sexual difference, and of clinging to the fictional metanarrative of patriarchy (Adams 1979; Walby 1990, 33). Conversely, poststructuralism is suspected by much of feminism to have de-essentialized sexual difference to the point of absurdity and political redundancy (Braidotti 1991; Spivak 1988; Alcoff 1988). There is the added, but important, complication that 'theory' only perceives 'feminism' as 'feminist theory (the structuralist/poststructuralist variety)' (Smith 1987, 34 and 267 n. 2, cit. Morris 1993, 374). Somewhere in the (con)fusion committed feminists/poststructuralists continue to adapt, develop and subvert the poststructuralist canon in the ongoing struggle to undermine patriarchy/phallocentrism in the name of 'woman'. The slippage between patriarchy and phallocentrism marks the feminist/poststructuralist exchange: the former indicates an analysis of a network of social and economic institutions while the latter focuses on the symbolic as the privileged locus of power and sexed identities. The two terms are neither entirely analogous nor exclusive (phallocentrism can be understood as the symptoms of patriarchy in processes of symbolization, patriarchy as phallocentrism materialized). As Sadie Plant observes: 'the text itself is patriarchy' (1997, 503). Perhaps the most radical and potent feminist theory today is that which has integrated, but significantly problematized, poststructuralist methodologies and which then makes use of these to analyse the phallocentric tendencies at the heart of poststructuralism itself. More recent British poststructuralist-feminist work tends to draw from and develop the insights of the first-generation French poststructuralist-feminists (Irigaray, Cixous, Kristeva) as well as developing Foucauldian, Derridean, Barthesian and/or Lacanian problematics (for example Whitford 1991; Waugh 1989; Battersby 1998). French poststructuralist-feminism, however, remains a highly charged area for British feminism, due to the ongoing and heated essentialism argument. It is argued (by Felski 1989 among others) that the biologism inherent in theoretical claims to a 'feminine' writing (for example Cixous's *écriture féminine* or Irigaray's *parler-femme*) returns women to the 'anatomy as destiny' conundrum feminism has for so long been struggling to overcome. But see also Margaret Whitford's shrewd and fruitful analysis of Irigaray's work, or Elizabeth Grosz's feminist philosophy for less defensive and more strategically minded accounts which perceive a strong political manoeuvre in the reiteration of otherwise essentialist arguments by feminist theorists.

Feminism entered the British academy as a serious critical position in the 1970s, almost simultaneously with the advent of French poststructuralism. British women's desire for access to the academy is enshrined in the history of feminist writing and activism (as documented in Virginia Woolf's *Room of One's Own* in 1929), and included as one of the four original demands of the Women's Liberation Movement in Britain agreed by the first national Women's Conference held – significantly – at Ruskin College, Oxford in 1970. Since then feminist academic activism has taken root in every discipline of British academia, as well as establishing at least one of its own in 'women's studies'. While branches in the humanities have flourished and born fruit, some in the sciences (particularly the 'masculinist' disciplines of mathematics and chemistry) have yet to bud. As arguments continue in Britain regarding the demise of grass-roots feminist activism in the face of an increasing professionalization of feminism, the development of a self-conscious and active (as well as funded, resourced and globally networked) feminist practice in academic theory, research and teaching continues apace (Radstone, in Squire and Kemp 1997, 105). Academic feminism, which is driven by but not reducible to feminist theory, remains informed by feminist academics' (as well as students') extra-curricular as well as professional struggles, and can be understood as an 'unobtrusive mobilization' of the political Women's Movement at the heart of the institutions through which our culture produces, maintains and transmits 'Truth' and 'Knowledge' (Katzenstein 1990, 27; Morris 1993, 374–5). Feminist theory is not reducible to poststructuralist-feminism (see, for example, materialist feminism), but one of the key questions engaging feminist theory over the last twenty years has been the 'equality or difference' debate sparked by poststructuralism's apparent 'deconstruction' of the term 'woman' in whose name feminism had been claiming equality. Linda Alcoff summarizes what is at stake in this debate in her question: 'How can we ground a feminist politics that deconstructs the female subject?' (1988, 419). Partly the debate rests on the notion that pre-poststructuralist – or at least liberal feminist – claims to 'equality' simply reinforced the primacy of male-masculine cultural positions, by demanding access without considering the need fundamentally and irreversibly to transform the institutions and models at which these claims were aimed. Academia itself offers a strong example: women have achieved access to universities at every level, although in relatively small numbers and against institutional resistance (women academics are still 550 per cent less likely to become professors according to the latest HESA statistics, collected by the government about British universities). To achieve this level of access and promotion women have to show they can do the job as it stands, 'passing' as normative academic subjects. In the process women become homo-genized in the institution, and are no longer in a position to notice, let alone critique and undermine, its masculinist assumptions. Equality in this instance might be understood as integration: the incorporation of the (feminine) Other which answers her critique, but only at the expense of neutralizing her in the process. 'Sexual difference' feminist theory tends to raise immediately the question of the phallocentrism of dominant cultural institutions and models (including writing/consciousness/subjectivity), and has developed a number of textual and representational strategies for undermining the inherent mascu-linism at play in these processes. The academic-theoretical wing of feminist activism, then, largely associated with poststructuralist methodologies, is perhaps best understood as a strategic and adaptive response to, or counter-colonization of, the context in which arguments concerning sex, gender and power are increasingly conducted: between aca-demic disciplines, between colleagues within academic disciplines, between teaching staff and students, and between feminists working in interdisciplinary research and women's studies generally. We might like to think of feminist-poststructuralist theory generally as consciousness-raising writ very large indeed.

British academic feminism's first encounter with poststructuralism appeared in Juliet Mitchell's *Psychoanalysis and Feminism* (1974) and almost simultaneously via the *Screen* phenomenon of radical film theory which made full use of post-Lacanian tools (described by Mulvey as 'political weapons') and feminist methodologies when Sam Rhodie retitled and reconceived the journal in 1971 (Mulvey 1975). Mulvey's paradigm for considering cinema as constitutive of gendered subjectivity (the 'male gaze' and the woman's 'to-be-looked-at-ness') has had a particularly wide and international influence on subsequent feminist work in cinema and representation generally (see *Screen*, 1992), although she has subsequently revised the argument established in her *Screen* debut in a later reflective piece

(Mulvey 1989). Mitchell's work was largely a response to Kate Millett's influential rejection of (particularly Freudian) psychoanalytic methodologies in feminist work as inherently reactionary and patriarchal constructs, originally published in 1969 (Millett 1977). Mitchell's book reclaimed a post-Lacanian psychoanalysis for feminist critical methodology: 'However it may have been used, psychoanalysis is not a recommendation *for* a patriarchal society, but an analysis *of* one. If we are interested in understanding and challenging the oppression of women, we cannot afford to neglect it' (Mitchell 1975, xv). Both Mulvey and Mitchell were influenced by radical French feminist theory which was aiming to bring psychoanalytical analysis to a marxist framework, particularly in the 'Psych et Po' (Pyschoanalysis and Politics) collective. After Mitchell and Mulvey, poststructuralist-feminist film theory and (particularly psychoanalytic) poststructuralist-feminist theory in general began to dominate feminist theoretical and philosophical work, if not in the form of an agreed and coherent methodological frame then in the form of a preoccupation with arguments over 'equality or difference' the deconstructive tendency in poststructuralist thought had provoked.

There are, broadly, two quite distinct ways to consider the enduring and evolving association between British academic feminism and poststructuralist theory since Mitchell's and Mulvey's ground-breaking studies appeared. To consider feminism's appropriation and revision of poststructuralist thought we might follow the popular understanding set out by Michèle Barrett in terms of a poststructuralist-led theoretical exposure of the essentialist and universalist bias hidden in the pre-poststructuralist feminist position (Barrett, in Barrett and Phillips 1992, 201–2). In this version the poststructuralist revolution produces a feminist fragmentation into what Moi has characterized as 'Anglo-American' and 'French' schools (all sophisticated word-play with the latter and all naive socio-politics with the former) (1985; see Todd 1988; Caine 1997, 255–71). This fragmentation, while sparked by the catalyst of poststructuralist theory, was heralded by – and answered – deep criticisms of the class, race and sexuality biases embedded in 1970s feminist thought. Black and lesbian feminists argued convincingly throughout the 1970s that 'feminist' definitions of the 'woman' in whose name the feminist agenda was developing was a fiction, and a racist and homophobic one at that (Carby 1982; *Women's Liberation Newsletter*, 1974). Poststructuralism – in this version – comes to the rescue of an untheorized feminism petrified by the horror of internal racism and homophobia. The convenient ready-made analytical tools provided by the poststructuralist canon offered the means to 'deconstruct' the reified notion of 'woman' that had been the (mis)leading light in the feminist project, with the concomitant effect of destabilizing and fragmenting the project itself. The journal *m/f* was established in 1978 to address precisely these concerns through a development of poststructuralist-feminist theory.

Conversely we might consider the *affinities between* feminism and poststructuralism in such a way as to understand the latter as symptomatic of a defence mechanism on the part of the patriarchal British academy to the influx of feminist activism in its midst, such that feminist-poststructuralist theory constitutes a counter-colonization of the newly arising dominant discourse by ever-inventive feminist academic activists. The first narrative, while historically accurate, seriously misrepresents pre-poststructuralist feminist thought through the theoretical grid of poststructuralism, and results in the perception of a 'gulf between 1970s and 1990s' feminisms (Barrett and Phillips 1992, 2) – a gulf hollowed out by poststructuralism's scornful judgement of the 'naive' feminist demand for explanations of origins and causes to the oppression of women (i.e. pre-poststructuralist feminism's investment in questions of the diachronic as well as the synchronic) (Fraser 1997). I'd like to propose and develop the second understanding here – by approaching poststructuralism from the perspective of a poststructuralist-feminist analysis of institutions of power (of which the academy we must always remember is a less than shining example) which function through the exclusion and/or containment of the feminine (Irigaray 1985). This narrative might go something as follows. Academia had been a privileged arena in which the ever-more-detailed but never-changing story of the history and significance of a universalized 'Man' was formalized, documented and perpetuated for so many hundreds of years. The Women's Liberation Movement impacted that institution in Britain via student politicization and the emergence of a new generation of politically astute and academically armed feminist activists (see Jardine on the two waves of feminist academic generations since 1968, in Squire and Kemp 1997, 80–1). Exclusion of the female-embodied Other was no longer an overt institutional option, particularly since the newly educated feminism achieved sexual discrimination legislation through parliament in 1975 (although we might wonder at the slow pace of change, given that women still constitute only a third of lecturers in the UK). Furthermore, the female-embodied Other now in the midst of the academy rapidly made use of – and developed for her own uses – the new-found institutional facilities and networks (not to mention policy-making power, budgets, research funding, archives, equipment and pedagogical processes) to question fundamentally and on its own terms the universal status of the ontological subject in whose name the entire edifice has been running since anyone cared to remember. At this moment (mid–1970s) there emerged from France into the very disciplines in which these questions are raised the loudest (humanities, sociology, philosophy, literature) a 'new' approach to knowledge that: (a) appropriated the (disembodied) feminine as a key theoretical tool; (b) hastily announced the 'death' of the subject and the agentic position to which feminist-inspired legal reform was beginning to make a powerful claim; (c) decreed that all metanarratives (including that of the 'oppression of women') are naive and unsustainable; (d) resulted in a witch-hunt on 'essentialism' which – at its purest – rules out any claim made by feminist academics to speak in the name of women (Walby 1990, 35–6). The fragmentation of the term 'woman' that is the key to poststructuralist engagements with feminism, however, does not necessarily result in a weakening of the feminist position. As Squire and Kemp remind us in their anthology, '[t]he development of multiple feminist theoretical perspectives and the painful splintering of the women's movement occurred almost simultaneously with the growth of second-wave feminism, despite its oft-presumed unity. Today such fragmentation is largely viewed as symptomatic of, rather than problematic for, feminist endeavours' (Squire and Kemp 1997, 4).

Morris considers the self-perpetuating theoretical machinery of a subsequent postmodernism which continues to exclude and marginalize women theorists as 'a twilight of the gods [. . .] the last ruse of the patriarchal University trying for power to fix the meaning, and contain the damage, of its own decline' (Morris 1993, 380). Poststructuralism, in this rather simplified narrative, offered a lateral theoretical defence formation against the feminist challenge to a self-perpetuating male-masculine ontology in all its manifestations. Hence poststructuralist theoretical tools have been deployed to argue 'that the categories of men and women have no use in a social analysis' because these constitute 'essentialist' concepts, thereby removing the ground of a feminist critique just at the moment that it was beginning to gather steam (Walby 1990, 35; see Adams 1979). Feminist-poststructuralist work has subsequently developed modes of argument and analysis which reintroduce sexed embodiment and sexual difference to the debate with full consciousness of the heavy charges of essentialism at risk in such a project, producing subtle and increasingly adept interventions in the discussions that have come to dominate British academic research in the humanities since the 1980s (see especially Coward 1984; Rose 1986; Walby 1990; Whitford 1991; Barrett and Phillips 1992; Morris 1993; Radstone 1997; Battersby 1998).

It is probably worth distinguishing here between feminist theory which takes up the methodological questions of poststructuralism and their effectiveness for feminist politics, from feminist work which applies poststructuralist theory within the terms of a given discipline. Catherine Belsey's *The Subject of Tragedy* was an important instance of applied poststructuralist literary criticism (Belsey 1985), whereas Rosalind Coward's *Female Desire* (1984) was a theoretical analysis of women in popular culture which made use of poststructuralist theory without making a great fuss of it, and Walby's *Theorizing Patriarchy* (1990) deploys the problematics of feminist-poststructuralist methodologies to articulate an account of patriarchal forms which answers adeptly the criticism of an untheorized metanarrative at the heart of feminist thought. Jacqueline Rose's work on psychoanalysis, sexuality and visuality (Rose 1986) makes a strong case for poststructuralist psychoanalytic theory in critical and theoretical feminist practice, while Whitford's highly engaging and intelligent critical encounter with Irigaray (Whitford 1991) offers both a serious and challenging account of Irigaray's work, and an argument for the strategic deployment of feminist-poststructuralist methodologies more generally. Barrett's turn from marxism to poststructuralism has produced some of the clearest expositions of the questions posed by poststructuralism to feminist thought, as well as arguing for a new materialism which avoids an excessive mechanistic simplicity and reintroduces female experience as a critical category. Barrett's essay on 'Words and Things' (in Barrett and Phillips 1992) strikes me as the best place to start in any attempt to understand what is at stake in British feminism's encounter with, and transformation by, poststructuralist methodologies. It offers a full and thoughtful account of her own 'turn to theory' in the context of a more general 'turn to culture' in feminism during the 1980s.

Barrett notes that feminist theory's incorporation of poststructuralism tends to cluster around identifiable areas and has resulted in a general 'turn to culture' as the primary site of contestation. The 'turn to culture' signals a heightened concern with representation in reaction to some of the mechanistic excesses of a materialist methodology (Barrett, in Barrett and Phillips 1992, 208–11). The feminist debate, then, has shifted from a sociological focus towards the semiotic (cultural feminism). In this context Foucault's 'analysis of the exclusions and prohibitions of discourse' is easily assimilable to 'a feminism that has pioneered understanding of the power of naming and the efficacy of language' (211). Derridean deconstruction, Lacanian psychoanalysis and Foucauldian discourse analysis and foregrounding of the body as a critical locus are the favoured poststructuralist tendencies of feminist work, offering as they do a means to address 'sexuality, subjectivity and textuality' – themes already high on the pre-poststructuralist agenda (215). However, it remains a mistake to consider poststructuralism as the theoretical arm of an otherwise largely untheorized feminism – as Weedon's influential study of *Feminist Practice and Poststructuralist Theory* tends to do (Weedon 1987) – and there remain serious theoretical feminist concerns with the implications of poststructuralism, especially as this tends towards a postmodernist emphasis. As Rita Felski has argued strongly: 'the question of the politics of feminist reading or writing is not a question which can be resolved at an aesthetic level alone; it is inextricably linked to the fate of the women's movement as a whole' (Felski, in Squire and Kemp 1997, 429). In other words, the British feminist encounter with poststructuralism remains consistently anxious about poststructuralism's elision of the marxist concern with materiality. Similarly Linda Alcoff has argued that the tendency in poststructuralism to designate particularities as subjective and fictional constructs alongside a destabilization of the authority of the subjective position 'coincides neatly with the classical liberal's view that human peculiarities are irrelevant' (1988, 420). As Soper reminds us:

> The paradox of the poststructuralist collapse of the 'feminine' and the move to 'in-difference' is that it reintroduces – though in the disguised form of an aspiration to no-gender – something not entirely dissimilar from the old humanistic goal of sexual parity and reconciliation. And while one can welcome the reintroduction of the goal, it may still require some of the scepticism which inspired its original deconstruction. (1990, 243)

Perhaps the most compelling and distinctive aspect of British feminist-poststructuralist work derives from British feminism's long history of and investment in a committed socialism and a related cultural materialism. Mitchell's work was steeped in a British marxist tradition, and her argument was challenging in its appropriation of psychoanalytic critical tools in this context. Hence poststructuralist critical apparatus tends to have been subjected to a rigorous and highly critical scepticism in British academic feminism, rather than ingested whole and unaltered. The resulting arguments have a refreshing absence of jargonese, tend towards a careful self-examination of concepts and position, and are usually successful in avoiding narcissistic theoretical loops. The British encounter between feminism and poststructuralism, then, has resulted in recent years in an internalization by feminist theorists and practitioners of the serious questions raised by poststructuralist methodologies, and these questions in themselves have become integral to – rather than undermining of – the larger feminist academic project. So while Radstone identifies 'insecurities and doubts which currently shake feminist theory to its core, producing a range of questions concerning the status of the category "woman"' leading to the fundamental question: 'is a politics grounded in women's *collective* experience still desirable, given poststructuralism's deconstruction of binary oppositions?', feminist theory continues to produce a range of committed feminist theoretical and pedagogic practices which incorporate poststructuralist questions and methodologies without conceding the political efficacy and importance of the notional 'woman' in whose name the feminist project acts (Radstone, in Squire and Kemp 1997, 106–7). Elizabeth Grosz understands this process well at the level of political intervention when she notes that some anti-poststructuralist critics radically miss the point when they assume that 'feminists take on essentialist or universalist assumptions … in the same way as patriarchs, instead of attempting to understand the ways in which essentialism and its cognates function as unavoidable and therefore possibly strategically useful terms'. For Grosz, the anti-poststructuralist-feminist position 'silences and neutralises the most powerful of feminist theoretical weapons, the ability to use patriarchy and phallocratism against themselves, to take up positions ostensibly opposed to feminism and to use them for feminist goals' (Grosz and Probyn 1995, 57). Feminism remains undeniably – and some might say gloriously – parasitic on the academy in British universities, surviving and in some areas flourishing by its radical and unsettling mimeticism, a transmuting ability to reproduce itself in forms ostensibly designed or appropriated to undermine it (poststructuralism included).

Ashley Tauchert

Further reading and works cited

Adams, P. 'The Subject of Feminism', m/f, 2, 1978.

—. 'A Note on Sexual Divisions and Sexual Differences', m/f, 3, 1979.

Alcoff, L. 'Cultural Feminism Versus Post-Structuralism: The Identity Crisis in Feminist Theory', Signs, 13, 1988.

Barrett, M. and Phillips, A. (eds) Destabilizing Theory. Cambridge, 1992.

Battersby, C. The Phenomenal Woman. Cambridge, 1998.

Belsey, C. The Subject of Tragedy. London, 1985.

Braidotti, R. Patterns of Dissonance. Oxford, 1991.

Brennan, T. (ed.) Between Feminism and Psychoanalysis. London, 1989.

Caine, B. English Feminism 1780–1980. Oxford, 1997.

Carby, H. 'White Woman Listen! Black Feminism and the Boundaries of Sisterhood', in The Empire Strikes Back. London, 1982.

Coward, R. Female Desire. London, 1984.

Docherty, T. (ed.) Postmodernism. London, 1993.

Felski, R. Beyond Feminist Aesthetics. London, 1989.

Fraser, N. 'Structuralism or Pragmatism? On Discursive Theory and Feminist Politics', in The Second Wave, ed. L. Nicholson. London, 1997.

— and Nicholson, L. 'Social Criticism Without Philosophy: An Encounter Between Feminism and Postmodernism', in The Second Wave, ed. L. Nicholson. London, 1997.

Gatens, M. Imaginary Bodies. London, 1996.

Grosz, E. and Probyn, E. (eds) Sexy Bodies. London, 1995.

Irigaray, L. Speculum of the Other Woman, trans. G. C. Gill. Ithaca, NY, 1985.

Jardine, A. 'The Demise of Experience', In The Second Wave, ed. L. Nicholson. London, 1997.

Katzenstein, M. 'Feminism Within American Institutions: Unobtrusive Mobilization in the 1980s', Signs, 16, 1, 1990.

Kemp, S. and Squires, J. (eds) Feminisms. Oxford, 1997.

McNay, L. Foucault and Feminism. Cambridge, 1992.

Millett, K. Sexual Politics. London, 1977.

Mitchell, J. Psychoanalysis and Feminism. Harmondsworth, 1975.

Moi, T. Sexual/Textual Politics. London, 1985.

Morris, M. The Pirate's Fiancée. London, 1993.

—. 'Feminism, Reading, Postmodernism', in The Second Wave, ed. L. Nicholson. London, 1997.

Mulvey, L. 'Visual Pleasure and Narrative Cinema', Screen, 16, 3, 1975.

—. Visual and Other Pleasures. Bloomington, IN, 1989.

Nicholson, L. (ed.) Feminism/Postmodernism. New York, 1990.

Nicholson, L. (ed.) The Second Wave. London, 1997.

Plant, S. ' "Beyond the Screens": Film, Cyberpunk and Cyberfeminism', in The Second Wave, ed. L. Nicholson. London, 1997.

Radstone, S. 'Postcard From the Edge: Thoughts on the "Feminist Theory: An International Debate" Conference Held at Glasgow University, Scotland, 12–15 July 1991'.

Riley, D. Am I That Name? Basingstoke, 1988.

Rose, J. Sexuality in the Field of Vision. London, 1986.

Sawicki, J. Disciplining Foucault. New York, 1991.

Screen. The Sexual Subject, ed. Mandy Merck. London, 1992.

Smith, P. and Jardine, A. (eds) Men in Feminism. New York, 1987.

Soper, K. Troubled Pleasures. London, 1990.

Spivak, G. C. In Other Worlds. New York, 1988.

—. Outside in the Teaching Machine. New York, 1993.

'Straight Women', Women's Liberation Newsletter, 63, 1974.

Todd, J. *Feminist Literary History*. Cambridge, 1988.
Walby, S. *Theorizing Patriarchy*. Oxford, 1990.
Waugh, P. *Feminine Fictions*. London, 1989.
Weedon, C. *Feminist Practice and Poststructuralist Theory*. Oxford, 1987.
Whitford, M. 'Introduction', *The Irigaray Reader*, ed. M. Whitford. New York, 1991.
Woolf, V. *A Room of One's Own*. London, 1929.

Cultural Studies

Originating with a series of 1950s investigations of the 'commonality' and 'ordinariness' of culture, and gradually institutionalized as a key element of British academic and intellectual life, the set of postwar scholarly practices identified as British cultural studies has passed through two major subsequent phases: a 1960s and 1970s moment primarily concerned with the ideological structuring of the public media, mass cultural communicative forms and working-class culture, and a post-1980s investigation of the significance of racial, gender and imperial histories to contemporary British cultural life.

Marx writes that 'Men make their own history, but they do not make it just as they please; they do not make it under circumstances chosen by themselves, but under circumstances directly encountered, given, and transmitted from the past' (1977, 15). Substitute the word 'culture' for the word 'history' in this sentence and you will have a fair outline of the history of British cultural studies from its mid-1950s 'founding' in the works of Richard Hoggart, Raymond Williams, and E. P. Thompson, to its quasi-institutionalization in the 1960s, 1970s and 1980s (in both a series of university spaces – most prominently the Centre for Contemporary Cultural Studies at Birmingham University (CCCS) – and a range of academic journals and enterprises, including the *New Left Review, Screen, Cultural Studies, New Formations* and the Open University's Course 'Mass Communication and Society'), to its internal post-1980s interrogation by an assortment of scholars who, while indebted to cultural studies and working within its general paradigms, have questioned its initial blindness to questions of race, gender and a range of other problems haunting the contemporary circumstances of British cultural life.

To suggest a rough analogy between Marx's dictum and the history of British cultural studies is, as this tripartite history implies, to suggest that British cultural studies may be loosely periodized into three 'moments' – each characterized by a dominant logic or problem – in much the fashion that Marx's statement may be divided into three primary claims. Thus, by this paraphrase, the key problem of the first, 1950s, moment of British cultural studies was the problem of coming to understand what it meant to conceive of culture as something 'made' rather than something simply 'found' or 'revered'. In the 1960s and 1970s, the problem was coming to understand what it meant for culture to be the product not of the autonomous will of its agents and artisans but of a range of enveloping, ideological 'circumstances' within which the subjects of culture 'find' themselves and by whose constraining force they discover themselves limited or determined. And the problem of the post-1980s immanent critique of British cultural studies has been that of demonstrating that the contemporary circumstances of British life are circumstances the nation 'inherits' from its imperial and patriarchal past, circumstances carried over into the present from a 'past' that is not, after all, past.

To gloss a complex history so is of course to oversimplify, and to exclude developments of research and thought and trajectories of inquiry that cannot be so neatly contained by a single descriptive framework. While this is, then, a framework that I think has some value, developing it also implies attending to at least some of what it leaves out. But before doing either of those things, the very terms of this history of British cultural studies require some interrogation. For whatever else they have been and whatever else they have accomplished, the set of postwar intellectual enterprises contained within the rubric of British cultural studies have demonstrated a persistent questioning of the status of the concept with which I began, a persistent investigation of just what we mean by 'culture', a questioning that has, indeed, been so constant that the history of British cultural studies might equally well be said to be the history of the attempt to unlock the riddle of this word.

Raymond Williams' *Culture and Society, 1780–1950* (1958; which, together with Richard Hoggart's *The Uses of Literacy* and E. P. Thompson's *The Making of the English Working Class*, is regularly identified as one of the founding texts of British cultural studies), provides the first key to the logic by which that riddle has been unlocked. Playing itself off Matthew Arnold's *Culture and Anarchy* – which had insisted on an essentially aestheticist conception of culture, on a notion of culture as a high sphere set apart from the ordinary transactions of life, as 'the best that has been thought and known' – Williams's text argued both for a massive expansion of those forms of human activity and production that we think of as cultural and a consequent abandonment of the notion that 'culture' names the rarefied, the exceptional, the exquisite. 'Culture', Williams insisted in one of the most famous formulations of this earliest phase of cultural studies, 'is ordinary', a suggestion whose implications Stuart Hall glosses so:

> The conception of 'culture' is itself democratized and socialized. It no longer consists of the sum of the 'best that has been thought and said', regarded as the summits of an achieved civilization – that ideal of perfection to which, in earlier usage, all aspired. Even 'art' ... is now redefined as only one, special, form of a general social process: the giving and taking of meanings, and the slow development of 'common' meanings – a common culture: 'culture', in this special sense, 'is ordinary' ... If even the highest, most refined of descriptions offered in works of literature, are also 'part of the general process which creates conventions and institutions, through which the meanings that are valued by the community are shared and made active', then there is no way in which this process can be hived off or distinguished or set apart from the other practices of the historical process. (1986, 35)

As Hall's reading of Williams's argument indicates, to conceive of culture as 'ordinary' is simultaneously to think of it as 'common' (in both senses of the word, i.e. as everyday and as a shared possession rather than the exclusive property of a privileged few); as eternally unfixed, constantly caught in the give and take of its collective making; and, perhaps most significantly for the consequent development of a cultural studies epistemology, as something not 'set apart', something not identical with an exclusive set of aesthetic, idealizing practices, but, rather, something fully present within that 'social' domain no longer conceivable as distinct from the cultural sphere.

This last suggestion – by which Williams not only 'democratizes and socializes' culture but also, it is frequently remarked, 'anthropologizes' it, correlates it, as another of his well-known formulations has it, with 'lived experience' – was to have major implications for the consequent study of culture and the development of a cultural studies methodology. Detached from an exclusive association with the museum, the opera house and the 'literary' canon, 'culture' was freed to name a massively proliferating array of sites and of texts. For the cultural studies methodologies that emerged in the wake of Williams's intervention, the study of culture was to imply as fully the study of television, fashion, educational curricula, mechanisms of policing, habits of working-class life and the ritualized practices of 'youth' subcultures, as it was the close analysis of painting, ballet or the romantic lyric. Hoggart's *The Uses of Literacy* (1958) demonstrated what this new kind of study might look like as Hoggart applied his Leavisite training in literary study (his 'literacy' in textual analysis) to a broad range of working-class 'texts'. In doing so, Hoggart was able not only to apply 'the analytical protocols of literary study to a wider range of cultural products: music, newspapers, magazines, and popular fiction in particular', but, as significantly, and much like Williams, to demonstrate 'the interconnections among various aspects of public culture – pubs, working-men's clubs, magazines, and sports – and the structures of an individual's private, everyday life – family roles, gender relations, language patterns, the community's "common sense" … a complex whole in which public values and private practices are tightly intertwined' (Turner 1990, 44).

If 'culture', for Hoggart, as for Williams, is thus democratic, social, common, ordinary, then it is equally important to note that as culture is thus 'anthropologized', the anthropological is simultaneously 'textualized', treated as that which can be read much as a literary text can be read, as that which can be decoded by readerly protocols developed for the analysis of the 'literary'. Cultural studies, from its earliest moment, thus names not so much the absolute abandonment of the literary, or a simple substitution of an anthropological for an aesthetic conception of culture, as a re-deployment of textual literacy to a massively expanded field of inquiry. Cultural studies, then, is at its heart a double-order procedure, one which simultaneously 'anthropologizes' culture and textualizes the field of study it has thus enlarged. In the process, the literary is not so much overthrown as distributed across the entire social and historical terrain. Through this act of double expansion cultural studies not only reveals its debts to the institutional history of literary study but offers less to abolish this earlier mode of study (as is so often claimed) than to establish its readerly protocols at the centre of an expanded universe of inquiry.

'Expanded', may, however, not be the most precise word with which to characterize cultural studies' re-understanding of the domains of the literary, the cultural and the anthropological and its new mode of studying its renovated objects of inquiry. In his influential essay on the development and fundamental paradigms of British cultural studies, Stuart Hall indicates that 'convergence', 'conjunction' and 'intersection' may be better terms for both the new, post-Williamsite, conception of culture and the new methods of critique this reconceptualization has demanded. On this understanding it is not so much that 'culture' has expanded to become coextensive with the entire field of lived human experience as that culture names a new practice of study by identifying the site where the historical, the political, the social, the aesthetic, the economic, et al. intersect or converge. Hoggart's densely particular, concrete study of some aspects of working-class culture and Thompson's historical reconstruction of the formation of a class culture and popular traditions in the 1790–1830 period formed, between them, the break and defined the space from which a new area of study and a new practice opened. Culture was the site of the convergence (Hall 1986, 34–5). Hall's point, though plainly stated, is a complex one. For there are at least three 'convergences' at work here, all named by, and complicatedly contained within, the notion of culture.

The first convergence is between the work of Williams, Hoggart and Thompson whose writings are connected by their common interest in something called culture. The second convergence is that articulated by the concept of culture itself, or, somewhat tautologically, by the rearticulation of culture as the site of the convergence of what had previously been held to be separate (economic, historical, aesthetic) phenomena. Cultural studies' new 'area of study' is thus an area constituted by, and as, the conjunction of all the (no longer) disparate materials of a total 'historical process'. If such convergences are, thus, *what* 'cultural studies' studies then the third convergence pertains to *how* this 'new practice' articulates a method by which to examine this new field of study. As 'culture' itself is seen to be the site of complex convergences, so its study demands the conjunction of previously separate methodologies, not just the conjunction of methodologies developed by the disciplines of literature and anthropology but, increasingly, as this new practice invented itself, the convergence of methods derived from the fields of politics, economics, philosophy, media-studies, semiotics and ideological analysis. A revolution in the conception of 'culture', cultural studies thus equally announces a revolution in critical method, a revolution in which the new, hybrid, method developed for the study of 'culture' imitates the hybrid form of the culture it studies by making itself out of a broad array of interpretive protocols which can no longer be 'set apart' from one another.

This brief outline of some of the problems and possibilities opened by a critical interrogation of the concept of 'culture' summarizes much of the work of the first phase, the 1950s, of British cultural studies, a phase commonly, and unsurprisingly, referred to as the 'culturalist' moment of British cultural studies – generally in contradistinction to the 'structuralist' moment that was to follow in the 1960s and 1970s as various cultural studies practioners, Stuart Hall prominent among them, began the work of consolidating Williams's insights, developing institutional centres for a cultural studies practice and, fairly rapidly, reversing one of the claims central to the work of Williams, Hoggart and Thompson. But to get some sense of what was at stake in this 'structuralist' critique of Williams, Hoggart and Thompson's 'culturalism', one last thing needs to be said about this first phase.

I have suggested that the 1950s moment of cultural studies might be typified as a moment in which a range of scholars began to consider what it meant to say that 'men make their own culture', and thus far I have concentrated on what this has implied for a reconceptualization of culture as a collective, complex work, as something collaboratively fashioned by the everyday subjects of history. The phrase implies more, however, than a notion of collectivity more than an understanding of culture as a 'commonly' fabricated work. It also suggests a fairly substantial exercise of agency on the part of those making this common culture, a relatively high degree of freedom to, in fact, fashion a collective 'lived experience'. As such, this understanding of culture-making sits rather uneasily with both a classical marxist 'base and superstructure' paradigm and with marxian readings of the relatively high degree to which human activity is not autonomous or free but largely constrained or determined by the material conditions of worldly existence (the 'circumstances' not of our 'own choosing' in the second clause of Marx's formula).

The first problem could be fairly easily resolved by suggesting, as Williams and Thompson in different ways did, that 'culture' does not belong to some 'ideal' domain 'superstructural' to the material 'base' of society but is itself an element of our phenomenological materiality. The critique of Matthew Arnold's aestheticist, and separatist, notion of culture is thus, equally, a critique of the base/superstructure paradigm and indicates why cultural studies is also often referred to as a form of 'cultural materialism'. The second problem (one commonly glossed as the problem of 'agency and determinism') was not so easily resolved. Indeed, at the last, it was not resolved. Instead, Williams, Thompson, and to a lesser extent Hoggart, implicitly defined their projects as resistant to a strong theory of determinism, as something like one or other species of marxist humanism. For Thompson this implied, as *The Making of the English Working Class* makes clear, that 'class consciousness' is not the automatic and inevitable by-product of economic conditions but is something a human collectivity fashions ('makes') for itself from the brute materials of experience, indeed something out of whose making this collectivity 'makes' itself. For Williams this marxist humanism finds perhaps its most crystalline, and its most enigmatic, form in his concept of the 'structure of feeling', a phrase which admits the idea that experience is to some extent structured by an array of determinants (rather than purely self-fashioned) but limits the determining power of such structuration by suggesting that structure must work its way through, and find itself reworked by, 'feeling': a word which, in this context seems to imply the affective consciousness, desire, will and disposition of a collection of human actors.

The structuralist critique of culturalism (the critique which I am suggesting loosely corresponds to Marx's interest in the ways in which historical and cultural 'making' occurs within, and is determined by, circumstances not of our own choosing) coincided, ironically enough, with a proto-institutionalization of cultural studies within British university and intellectual life. That institutionalization took a variety of forms, perhaps the most significant of which were the establishment of the Centre for Contemporary Cultural Studies (CCCS) at Birmingham University (first directed by Richard Hoggart and then, beginning in 1970, by Stuart Hall), the emergence of a series of cultural studies journals, and, as the name of the Birmingham Centre indicates, a turn from the sort of long histories of British life that had occupied much of Williams and Thompson's attention to a primary interest in the contemporary, particularly the contemporaneous nature of British education, media and urban culture. With both a field and a method of study roughly in place, British cultural studies began, with these steps, to define a project for itself, and it seems fair to say that while this second phase of cultural studies derived its field and its method from Williams and Thompson, it inherited its project from Hoggart.

For all its methodological originality, Hoggart's *The Uses of Literacy* was, as has been widely remarked, a deeply nostalgic text, an elegy of sorts to a working-class culture Hoggart took to be vanishing under the assault of a new, commercialized, homogenized, hyper-mediated social order. Hoggart saw the rich particularities of working-class culture giving way to a generalized mass culture disseminated by television, radio and the magazines. While Hoggart's nostalgia was not a marked feature of the second moment of British cultural studies, his interest in the power of the media to penetrate and shape a social order was. Indeed this interest in the power of the media to order and construct social and cultural life and, somewhat later, in the means by which media consumers adopt, interpret or resist media representations of their 'realities', was, to a large extent, to define the 1960s and 1970s project of British cultural studies. Unsurprisingly, then, many of the more influential works of this period took an analysis of television and film as their central objects of inquiry (though, it must be noted, a cultural studies analysis of the 'media' does not imply simply an attention to such technologies of communication; education, among other things, certainly falls within the field of media studies, one perhaps more accurately identified as communication studies). Raymond Williams, still an active participant in the unfolding history of cultural studies, published *Television* (1974); Stuart Hall wrote a number of important essays on television and the media; John Fiske and John Hartley's *Reading Television* (1978), Judith Williamson's *Decoding Advertisements* (1978) and Terence Hawkes' *Structuralism and Semiotics* (1977) were among the field-defining works of the new media-oriented cultural studies; and the film journal *Screen*, established itself as a major influence in British intellectual life.

Screen was more than a journal, it became the byword for a form of theory and the central exponent of the structuralist critique of some of cultural studies' founding assumptions. The structuralist 'turn' was not, however, just a turn against Williams and Thompson's marxist humanism, it was also a turn to a body of philosophical and critical writings on semiotics, post-Freudian psychoanalysis and structuralist marxism and anthropology that had become widely influential on the European continent in the postwar years. Hall, in his years as director of the CCCS, and, through him, the Centre itself, were enormously important in introducing many of the strands of postwar continental theory to the British cultural studies debates. (Graeme Turner (1990) identifies Hall's two 1971 essays on 'Television' and the 'Media' as watershed moments in this process). But it was *Screen* that most insistently 'structuralized' a cultural studies epistemology. And the major influence on *Screen*, and the major force behind 'Screen theory', was undoubtedly Louis Althusser, his theory of 'ideology' and his notion of 'interpellation'.

Through the 1970s, *Screen* became something like the party organ of an Althusserian structuralism, the hard centre of a bleakly determinist reading of film, television and the other media's power to order cultural life. The *Screen* writers were not alone in pursuing such theories, but their Althusserian orthodoxy inspired resistance among other scholars who, while wanting to take such 'ideology critique' seriously, also sought a more flexible solution to the general problem of agency and determinism. The key to that solution came via the work of another continental thinker, Antonio Gramsci, whose theories entered the British cultural studies debate through the writings of scholars at the Birmingham Centre, centrally, once more, Stuart Hall. The Gramscian response to Althusser (and, in effect, the CCCS critique of 'Screen theory') was developed around the Italian philosopher's notion of hegemony. For Gramsci 'hegemony' defined the means by which state apparatuses of power maintain themselves in all those ordinary moments in which entrenched power formations cannot secure their existence through the direct application of violent force but must, much as Althusser suggested, convince a subordinate or subaltern group of the rightness of their oppression. The difference between this reading of hegemony and an Althusserian reading of ideology is, to simplify matters entirely, that while for Althusser ideology is largely irresistible (and the possibilities and realities of historical change thus inexplicable), for Gramsci 'hegemony' defines a set of limits and pressures, a series of dominant representations of the real, but, crucially, also a set of occasions for contestation, an array of representations not so much to be passively 'consumed' as decoded, resisted, subverted. For Gramsci, then, ideology is less an irresistible than an invitation: to resistance, to critique, to a reimagining of our relation to the 'real'.

The Althusserian and Gramscian poles of ideology critique defined the limits within which much of the 1970s cultural studies work in Britain operated, thus effecting a displacement whereby 'ideology' took the place of 'culture' as the central term on which British cultural studies went to work. The writings to emerge from this period were rich and varied, too various to catalogue. I will therefore mention just two works which, while representative of this moment, also anticipated crucial elements of the phase that was to follow. Stuart Hall and Tony Jefferson's edited collection of essays *Resistance through Ritual* was emblematic in this regard. If the Althusser/Gramsci opposition is understood as a contest of sorts, then *Resistance*, through its very title, signals its Gramscian partisanship and also the eventual outcome of that contest. While Gramsci has clearly outlasted Althusser as a central influence on British cultural studies it has partially been because in texts such as *Resistance*, Hall, Jefferson, and others were able to discover in the 'subculture' (the minor, antagonistic, counter-culture within a larger cultural formation) a series of localized, individuated practices of cultural re-invention by which minoritarian collectivities refashion inherited cultural codes. Subcultural 'resistance' is thus not simply a possibility, a standing invitation to contestation latent within the master texts of hegemonic cultural formations, but an alternative or oppositional cultural ensemble, a coherent and specific set of cultural practices, active within a social totality. The attention paid to particularized, realized, subcultural 'practices' of contestation in texts such as Hall Jefferson's *Resistance* and Hebdige's *Subculture* was eventually to develop into a more general theoretical interest in 'practices' most influentially worked out in the writings of the French philosopher Michel de Certeau. As de Certeau suggests, to speak of practices is to speak of a theory of 'consumer reproduction', a theory of the ways in which subordinate groups productively consume 'legitimate culture', making of the 'rituals, representations, and laws imposed on them something quite different from what their conquerors had in mind ... using them with respect to ends and references foreign to the system they had no choice but to accept' (de Certeau 1984, xiii).

The second text to mention from this 1970s moment is another co-edited by Hall, *Policing the Crisis* (1978), less significant for its methodological originality than for its introduction of a hermeneutics of race to the ongoing cultural studies enterprise. In this respect, *Policing the Crisis* anticipates the shift to a third moment of cultural studies work in Britain but it does not quite define it. It addresses the construction of a criminalized concept of race but does so largely within the by now dominant paradigms of a communications-theoretical cultural studies project. To put things another way, *Policing the Crisis* poses race as a problem for the British state and British society, it does not yet think race as a crisis within and a problem for cultural studies. That critical move (and with that move the shift to a third phase moment willing, once again, to subject some of the governing assumptions of British cultural studies to a thorough going critique) was to come a few years later and was most notably signalled by *The Empire Strikes Back* (1982).

By 1982, the British empire, while not quite dead, was largely, or so many Britons had taken to believing, a thing of the past. *The Empire Strikes Back* suggested otherwise, suggested, in effect, that the empire had less collapsed than collapsed inward, returned 'home' to the scene of its founding. In the decades since the end of the Second World War, ex-colonial subjects from India, Pakistan, Africa and the Caribbean had emigrated to Britain in significant numbers, at first encouraged by 1950s governments in search of labour power to reconstruct the immediate postwar economy, but then, increasingly, as a black British community expanded and consolidated itself, treated with bureaucratic and juridical hostility by the British state. Many of the authors of *The Empire Strikes Back* were members of that black British community and the letter their text returned to Britain signalled not only the arrival of an increasingly active generation of black British intellectuals and the persistence of an imperial 'past' in the nation's putatively 'post-imperial' present, but a strong rejoinder to a 'British' cultural studies enterprise that had never quite detached itself from a quasi-nationalist investment in the logics of a 'common' culture whose bonds of commonality were geographically and racially exclusive.

The problem with British cultural studies, Paul Gilroy indicated in the introduction to *The Empire Strikes Back*, was, in a word, its Britishness or, somewhat more complexly, its closet identification of 'Britishness' with 'Englishness', its exclusive interest and investment in an English national culture that constitutes only one element of a far more diverse, and entangled, national and imperial cultural formation. Even when produced as an oppositional intellectual practice, politically committed to articulating a working-class critique of the nation's dominant culture, British cultural studies, Gilroy and his co-authors suggested, implicitly confirmed the centrality of English culture to British national and imperial history. The very notions of a 'common culture' and of a 'lived' and 'long' experience functioned, they suggest, as codes that effectively defined the 'field' of cultural studies as insular, nationalist and white. If, as the title of Gilory's subsequent book *There Ain't No Black in the Union Jack* (1987) indicated, the conservative guardians of the British state had envisioned themselves as the wardens of a racially homogeneous polity, then so too had the leftist critics of that polity constructed a 'radical' cultural studies project unable to address the 'lived experience' of those British subjects whose most common experience of a 'common' culture was the experience of being told that this was a culture to which they did not belong. Two main strands of work have followed from this field-altering critique: one, typified perhaps by Kobena Mercer's *Welcome to the Jungle* (1994), has retained an interest in 'British' cultural life as its prime object of inquiry but has done so in order to examine the ways in which black cultures are constitutive of a hybrid British cultural ensemble; the other, for which Gilroy's *The Black Atlantic* (1993) is undoubtedly the central text, has sought to reposition cultural analysis outside the defining parameters of the nation, in Gilroy's case by mapping the counters of a cross-Atlantic black cultural ensemble.

The racial critique of contemporary British culture and British cultural studies was not, however, unique. Four years before the publication of *The Empire Strikes Back*, the Women's Studies Group at the CCCS had published *Women Take Issue* (1978), a collection which launched a similar critique of British cultural studies, though here, as the title of the volume suggests, it was the ways in which cultural studies work had systematically excluded women's histories from its accounts of British cultural life, indeed the implicit masculinization of both a 'common culture' and a common field of cultural study, that is at stake. Like *The Empire Strikes Back*, which helped generate a great deal of subsequent work in black British cultural studies, *Women Take Issue* introduced an ongoing feminist critique, and reinvention, of cultural studies that has helped define the third phase of the British cultural studies enterprise.

At the heart of that third moment, as I have suggested, is something like a theory of the cultural uncanny, an analysis of the ways in which 'prior' modes and experiences of repression return to assert their priority in any account or critique of the contemporary, an examination of the ways in which the current 'circumstances' of British cultural life *and* the circumstances from which British cultural studies 'makes' its project are directly encountered, given or transmitted from an imperial and patriarchal 'past' that is not, in fact, past. A moment of critique, reorientation and redefinition, this third phase should, however, be understood less as a moment of departure than as a moment of re-creation. Like the stages that have preceded it, this third moment of cultural studies has not so much dissolved the field of study from which it originates as expanded the parameters of that field, redeployed its strategies and practices of reading to an enlarged field of investigation, multiplied both its sites of analysis and its modes of enquiry. Perhaps, to conclude, it is best to say that what this third 'phase' demonstrates is that the history of British cultural studies has been not simply a dialectical history but, as Stuart Hall has it, the history of a series of convergences, the history of an ever more complex mode of studying an ever more complex object, the history, indeed, of a collective project that has proven itself capable of conjoining an ever more various range of discourses, experiences, practices, representational codes and histories under the sign of that *not* after all 'common' word, 'culture'.

Ian Baucom

Further reading and works cited

Arnold, M. 'Culture and Anarchy', in *Poetry and Criticism of Matthew Arnold*, ed. A. Dwight Culler. Boston, 1961.

Ashcroft, B. et al. (eds) *The Empire Writes Back*. London, 1995.

Brantlinger, P. *Crusoe's Footprints*. London, 1990.

Davies, I. *Cultural Studies and Beyond*. London, 1995.

de Certeau, M. *The Practice of Everyday Life*. Berkeley, CA, 1984.

Dworkin, D. *Cultural Marxism in Postwar Britain*. Durham, NC, 1997.

Fiske, J. and Hartley, J. *Reading Television*. London, 1978.

Franklin, S. et al. (eds) *Off-Centre*. London, 1991.

Gilroy, P. *There Ain't No Black in the Union Jack*. London, 1987.

—. *The Black Atlantic*. Cambridge, MA, 1993.

Hall, S. 'Deviancy, Politics and the Media', CCCS Stencilled Paper 11, 1971

—. 'Television as a Medium and its Relation to Culture', CCCS Stencilled Paper 34, 1975.

—. 'Cultural Studies: Two Paradigms', in *Media, Culture and Society*, eds R. Collins et al. London, 1986.

— and Jefferson, T. (eds) *Resistance Through Rituals*. London, 1976.

— et al. (eds) *Policing the Crisis*. London, 1978.

Hawkes, T. *Structuralism and Semiotics*. London, 1977.

Hebdige, D. *Subculture*. London, 1979.

Hoggart, R. *The Uses of Literacy*. London, 1958.

Marx, K. *The Eighteenth Brumaire of Louis Bonaparte*. New York, 1977.

Mercer, K. *Welcome to the Jungle*. London, 1994.

Rose, J. *Sexuality in the Field of Vision*. London, 1986.

Thompson, E. P. *The Making of the English Working Class*. London, 1963.

Turner, G. *British Cultural Studies*. London, 1990.

Williams, R. *Culture and Society, 1780–1950*. London, 1958.

—. *The Long Revolution*. London, 1961.

—. *Television*. London, 1974.

Williamson, J. *Decoding Advertisements*. London, 1978.

Women's Studies Group, Centre for Contemporary Cultural Studies, University of Birmingham. *Women Take Issue*. London, 1978.

Cultural Materialism

Cultural materialism emerged in Britain in the 1980s as a critical approach to literature which understood and read literary texts as the material products of specific historical and political conditions. Its central concerns are in the ways in which literature relates to history, and what interpretations of a literary text might result from analyses which privileged historical contexts as the key to understanding the meanings and functions of literature. An important realization of cultural materialism is that texts produce different meanings and interpretations when read in different times and in different locations. Shakespeare's *The Tempest* might have been understood in very different ways in late sixteenth-century England than it has been read and performed in the Caribbean in the twentieth century, for example. The most prominent practitioners of cultural materialism – Alan Sinfield, Jonathan Dollimore, Catherine Belsey – share much in common with new historicists in the USA, particularly in treating literary texts as agents in making sense of a culture to itself. They also share with new historicists a common preoccupation with the Renaissance period, and with the roles which literature and theatre played in interpreting and explaining Renaissance society to itself. Cultural materialists participated with new historicist critics in the radical reinterpretation of Shakespeare and his contemporaries, shifting the focus of Shakespeare studies away from traditional emphases on the bard's universalism and humanism and towards a study of how Shakespeare's texts functioned in Elizabethan society to articulate specific cultural, gender or sexual identities, or indeed to highlight the ways in which power was deployed, distributed and manipulated in sixteenth-century England. But cultural materialists have also gone further than new historicists in emphasizing the political functions of literary texts in our own time, and in critiquing the ways in which literature is often appropriated in conservative political discourses to shore up notions of national heritage or cultural superiority. Accordingly, cultural materialists tend to read literary texts in ways which frustrate conservative interpretations, either by interpreting texts as the vehicles of radical critiques of conservative politics, or by exposing the means by which texts do serve the interests of conservatism.

The roots of cultural materialism lie in the work of prominent left-wing academics of the 1960s and 1970s who challenged 'traditional' approaches to literature by, firstly, contesting the ways in which certain kinds of texts were privileged as 'literary' and others dismissed as 'popular', and secondly, debating the validity of the idea of literature as embodying timeless, universal human values. The work, for example, of Stuart Hall, Raymond Williams and Richard Hoggart in extending literary analyses to the broader domain of 'culture' exposed the ways in which literary criticism had conventionally scorned the value of popular forms of entertainment and reading as tasteless, mass consumption and privileged the reading of a select canon of 'literary' texts as an index of sophistication.

Hall, Williams and Hoggart, each in their own ways, suspected that what lay behind such distinctions between the popular and the literary was a class distinction whereby the working classes were conveniently represented as slavishly following mass-market trends while the middle and upper classes were seen to be improving their minds and morals by reading 'high' literature. Culture was, however, shown to be more complex than this in the work of these left-wing critics, for whom examples abounded of the ways in which popular expressions could mean as much, and function in similar ways, as a literary text. 'We cannot separate literature and art from other kinds of social practice', wrote Raymond Williams, because those who enjoyed classical music and Shakespeare's plays were no more sophisticated, privileged or special than those who preferred The Beatles or Mills & Boon novels (Williams 1980, 43). Cultural studies was not so interested in making the icons and fashions of popular culture equivalent to high art and literature, however, as it was preoccupied with studying the ways in which cultures told stories about themselves through all forms of media and artistic representation. It was predominantly marxist in its critique of the ideological functions of 'culture', and suggested that culture was inseparable from politics. Walter Benjamin had argued in his definition of *historical* materialism that since history was written by the rulers and conquerors, accordingly the 'cultural treasures' of the world were the spoils of conquest and oppression, remarking: 'There is no document of civilization which is not at the same time a document of barbarism' (1992, 248), which in practice means that we must take care when we encounter stories of genius writers and great art to analyse the material circumstances which enable art and literature to be so highly acclaimed. Thus, in cultural materialist terms, the claim that Shakespeare is a universal writer is also a claim that English literature can make sense of and explain the world to itself, a claim which is then uncomfortably close to the boast of English imperialism. That Shakespeare's reputation as a universal genius gained considerable ground in the eighteenth and nineteenth centuries, when English imperialism reached its height, should alert us to the historical circumstances in which 'greatness' is celebrated and promoted.

Implicit in Benjamin's explanation of historical materialism is a radical reversal of the assumption of progressive humanism that the road to civilization leads away from the barbarism of the past. Benjamin proposes instead that civilization depends on barbarism, that in order for the middle classes to become civilized the working classes must be made barbaric, or in order for the English to be civilized, there must be a barbaric 'other' in the colonies against whom the English can define themselves. One can see in Benjamin's thinking the significance which he attributes to 'representation'. Conventional marxist analyses emphasized the economic means of control which the middle classes exerted over the working classes, but for Benjamin, as for Antonio Gramsci, the ideological or representational means of control were even more important. The 'bourgeois' class may dominate the workers by economic means, but their dominance is made plausible and is perpetuated at the level of representation. For Gramsci the task of marxist criticism is then to engage with capitalism on an ideological level, representing the interests of the working and peasant classes and exposing the contradictions and 'false consciousness' of the bourgeoisie. Indeed the possibility of all social and political change relies upon the outcome of this ideological struggle; as Gramsci explains in his *Prison Notebooks*, 'men acquire consciousness of structural conflicts on the level of ideologies' (Gramsci 1971, 365). According to the view which sees economics as the sole determining factor, ideology is a delusion which conceals the real, and therefore need only be dismissed as false while the real task of transferring the means of economic production to the proletariat is conducted. But this is to miss the point that bourgeois ideology succeeds in holding the captive attention and support of all classes. Gramsci referred to this condition as hegemony.

The influence of marxist ideas and approaches is one of the key factors in distinguishing between the practices of cultural materialism and those of new historicism, for new historicists were more influenced by Michel Foucault's historicist model of power relations than by marxist cultural studies. For Sinfield, Dollimore and other cultural materialists, however, the emphases which marxists such as Gramsci, Benjamin and Williams placed on the function of literature as an agent of bourgeois ideology and power suggested the need for an interpretative approach to literature which could accommodate marxist analyses of the politics of representation. Dollimore and Sinfield published what amounted in effect to a manifesto of cultural materialism as a foreword to an edited collection of essays entitled *Political Shakespeare* in 1985, a collection which represented and celebrated the arrival of radical new historicist perspectives in Renaissance studies. In their preface, the editors acknowledged a debt to Raymond Williams for the term 'cultural materialism' which he had used to describe his own work in *Marxism and Literature*:

> It is a position which can be briefly described as cultural materialism: a theory of the specificities of material cultural and literary production within historical materialism ... it is, in my view, a Marxist theory, and indeed ... part of what I at least see as the central thinking of Marxism. (1977, 5–6)

In acknowledging the debt to Williams, Dollimore and Sinfield were declaring that cultural materialism was in many senses the progeny of marxist literary and cultural studies. It shared with marxism the notion of history as perpetual struggle between social and cultural factions, and it shared too the idea that representations of all kinds played a part in the cultural politics of their time. Dollimore and Sinfield set out the key principles of cultural materialism in the foreword to *Political Shakespeare*:

> Our belief is that a combination of historical context, theoretical method, political commitment and textual analysis offers the strongest challenge and has already contributed substantial work. Historical context undermines the transcendent significance traditionally accorded to the literary text and allows us to recover its histories; theoretical method detaches the text from immanent criticism which seeks only to reproduce it in its own terms; socialist and feminist commitment confronts the conservative categories in which most criticism has hitherto been conducted; textual analysis locates the critique of traditional approaches where it cannot be ignored. We call this 'cultural materialism'. (1985, vii)

The four key principles in this statement are not particularly descriptive of the method or critical practice of cultural materialism, but they are general indications of the conditions in which cultural materialists see themselves operating. The principles proposed by Dollimore and Sinfield are designed to displace what they call 'traditional' approaches, the main features of which are implied in the definition of each of the principles. Cultural materialism, accordingly, is defined as a reaction against criticism which treats texts as possessing 'transcendent significance', which interprets a text 'in its own terms' and within 'conservative categories', and which grounds its understanding of a text solely within close textual analysis. In contrast to the liberal and conservative critical approaches suggested in this foreword, cultural materialists registered a new phase of political and ideological conflict, in which literary criticism could not remain neutral. While the liberal political beliefs and practices of postwar Britain, realized in the form of the welfare state, the NHS (National Health Service), scholarships, nationalized industries and local government, were steadily, often swiftly, eroded by the new right-wing ideologies of Thatcherism, literary critics like Dollimore, Sinfield, Belsey, Barker and Holderness scrutinized how literary texts played their part in sustaining and perpetuating conservative ideologies. Sinfield, for example, has shown how Shakespeare has been pressed into service to teach reactionary social norms, to justify imperialist ideology, even to sell military weapons, but in reply Sinfield has offered dissident readings of Shakespeare's texts which challenge traditional conservative and humanist readings. Cultural materialists have sought to change the terms in which writers such as Shakespeare are read and interpreted. Instead of the humanist focus on issues of character, morality and 'timeless' human values, cultural materialists have asked questions of texts which are concerned with power and resistance, race and gender, ideology and history.

Jonathan Dollimore's *Radical Tragedy* is exemplary of cultural materialist approaches. Dollimore analyses Jacobean tragedies for the ways in which they relate specifically to two major ideological constructs – establishment providentialism (which held sway in Renaissance times as the explanation of monarchical power as the product of divine will, therefore justifying the union of church and state, and discouraging possible rebellions or criticisms of either institution), and the autonomous, essential individual (which posits the idea of an unchanging human nature, symbolized in the individual soul). Dollimore's study is partly recovering the ideological contexts in which Jacobean texts were produced and read, but partly also a self-consciously twentieth-century return to those contexts to challenge humanists ways of reading them. So, for example, in the case of providentialism, Dollimore shows how texts such as Marlowe's *Dr Faustus* and Jonson's *Sejanus* not only foreground providentialist explanations of Renaissance politics and society but also provoke disquieting and challenging questions about the limits and contradictions of providentialism. At stake in his analyses is not just a concern to discover how such texts interacted with their own historical contexts, but Dollimore is also keen to show that literature acts in subversive as well as conservative ways, that literary texts can expose the limitations and faults of conservative political orthodoxies as it can reinforce them. Thus Dollimore's book demonstrates the value of analyses of historical context, as well as highlighting the political commitment of cultural materialism to discovering the ways in which texts go against the grain of conservative interpretations and values.

In *Political Shakespeare*, Dollimore and Sinfield brought together the work of new historicist critics like Leonard Tennenhouse and Stephen Greenblatt and the work of cultural materialists, largely, although not exclusively, represented by themselves. The title is polemical to begin with, advertising the commitment to politicizing literature which has become characteristic of cultural materialism. In the foreword the editors articulated their dislike of criticism which disguises its political agenda and which pretends to be politically neutral:

> Cultural materialism does not, like much established literary criticism, attempt to mystify its perspective as the natural, obvious or right interpretation of an allegedly given textual fact. On the contrary, it registers its commitment to the transformation of a social order which exploits people on grounds of race, gender and class. (Dollimore and Sinfield 1985, viii)

This is quite different to the work of new historicism, almost invariably focused on the past as belonging to a different epoch, ideologically and politically, to our own. Cultural materialists are committed to interpretations and investigations which have overt political ends in the contemporary world. Perhaps the best example of this commitment is Sinfield's synthesis of literary analysis, historical investigation and political engagement in *Literature, Politics and Culture in Postwar Britain*, in which he traces the emergence of consensus politics in postwar England, with its promises of full employment, comprehensive free education, and welfare and healthcare for all, and charts also the destruction of the welfare state under Mrs Thatcher's governments in the 1980s. Sinfield studies the ways in which the literature of the period foregrounds and contributes to these historical shifts, finding in the working-class writing of the 1960s, for example, that such writers as Alan Sillitoe, John Braine and John Osborne did not represent the genuine interests and aspirations of the working class, but instead reflected the process of embourgeoisement which the consensus politics of the 1950s and 1960s seemed to effect. The emergence of working-class writing does not indicate for Sinfield an improvement in the lot of the working class, merely that the working class have become the object of closer cultural scrutiny, in which service a handful of writers came to prominence. However authentic the class credentials of the writers, the fate of the working class cannot be changed, according to Sinfield, if the oppressed social position of the writers has no effect on the form in which they are working. Sinfield argues that writing itself was an inherently conservative act: 'There were writers of lower-class origin, it was acknowledged, but in the very act of becoming writers they were co-opted to middle-class forms' (Sinfield 1989, 40). The premise of Sinfield's argument is that the act of writing itself in the 1950s was a middle-class act, and that the readers and audiences for literature in the 1950s were largely middle class. The representation of working-class life apparently achieves no dramatically radical position when performed to a middle-class audience already hungry for representations of 'the other' anyway. Such an analysis of the conservative cultural politics of working-class writing is offered up in Sinfield's study as part of an explanation for the state of Britain in the 1980s, which for left-wing intellectuals was a dramatic shift away from the promises of the Labour government of 1945 to provide for the poor and disenfranchised of British society. Sinfield has been the most prominent cultural materialist to engage so actively in diagnosing contemporary political problems in the course of interpreting and explaining literary texts and their functions within society. Reading literature for cultural materialists is a political activity. It reflects and shapes the meanings which we as a society assign to texts and cultural practices, and it is therefore also a site of contest between competing political ideologies.

This sense of reading as political conflict can also be seen in Sinfield's *Faultlines*, in which he states that his intention is 'to check the tendency of *Julius Caesar* to add Shakespearean authority to reactionary discourses' (1992, 21). Literary texts acquire and are assigned cultural authority to different degrees and at different times in each society, and can be appropriated and co-opted to speak for one or more political ideologies. The meanings of these texts will always be contested, but what cultural materialists are interested in showing is that where meanings are contested there is almost always more at stake than insular aesthetic or artistic principles. Sinfield summarizes his argument in *Faultlines* as the following: 'dissident potential derives ultimately not from essential qualities in individuals (though they have qualities) but from conflict and contradiction that the social order inevitably produces within itself, even as it attempts to sustain itself' (1992, 41). In new historicist accounts of the operations of power, power seems to function as a flawless, perfectly efficient and effective machine. Sinfield disputes this, however, and offers a reading of power which reveals its faults, or more correctly, the conflicts and contradictions within power which may reveal dissident perspectives and which Sinfield calls 'faultlines'. It is through these 'faultlines', Sinfield claims, that we can read the alternative identities and values, and dissident ideas, of a given society.

In *Faultlines* Sinfield argued that the motivation for cultural materialist readings lay in the conservative and reactionary uses to which literary texts had been put. Cultural materialism as a practice necessarily reacts against the appropriation of literature in conservative political discourses:

> Conservative criticism has generally deployed three ways of making literature politically agreeable: selecting the canon to feature suitable texts, interpreting these texts strenuously so that awkward aspects are explained away, and insinuating political implications as alleged formal properties (such as irony and balance). (1992, 21)

In order to counter these conservative readings, and in order to make texts politically *dis*agreeable, cultural materialists can adopt the same strategies, or turn them against traditional or reactionary texts. If, as cultural materialist critics assert, Shakespeare is a powerful ideological tool in our society, there are ways of reading which can counter the authority which Shakespeare lends to reactionary discourses.

In an essay published in 1983 Sinfield explained that there were four principal ways of dealing with a reactionary text:

> [1. Rejection] of a respected text for its reactionary implications ... can shake normally unquestioned assumptions ... [2.] Interpretation ... so as to yield acceptable meanings ... is, of course, available to the socialist critic ... [3.] Deflect into Form(alism): One may sidestep altogether ... the version of human relations propounded by the text by shifting attention from its supposed truth to the mechanism of its construction ... [4.] Deflect into History: The literary text may be understood not as a privileged mode of insight, nor as a privileged formal construction. Initially, it is a project devised within a certain set of practices (the institutions and forms of writing as currently operative), and producing a version of reality which is promulgated as meaningful and persuasive at a certain historical conjuncture. And then, subsequently, it is re-used – reproduced – in terms of other practices and other historical conditions. (Sinfield 1983, 48)

The last method is a preferred method of cultural materialists in general, of putting the text in its contexts, whether the contexts of production or the contexts of reception, so as to expose the process by which it has been rendered in support of the dominant culture. Once this process has been exposed then the text can be interpreted by dissident critics 'against the grain'. Examining literary texts in their historical contexts is, for cultural materialists, a process of estranging those texts from the naturalized conservative readings to which they have been routinely treated. To show that Shakespeare's plays were inseparable from the ideological struggles of their time is, firstly, to dismiss the idea that his plays are timeless and universal, but it is also to alert us to the ways in which Shakespeare serves ideological functions in our own time too. In this case, historically situated and contextualized readings taught cultural materialists that the past could lend radically different meanings to canonical literary texts.

In the 1980s both new historicism and cultural materialism were interested in stressing the extent to which the past differs from contemporary uses of the past, the extent to which the past is alien or 'other' to our own modern epistemé, and, borrowing from Michel Foucault and Clifford Geertz, they were at the same time aware of the structural similarities between this historical difference and the cultural differences being emphasized by postcolonial critics, feminists, gay theorists and race theorists. Increasingly in the late 1980s and throughout the 1990s, cultural materialist critics extended their analyses into the domains of 'queer' theory, postcolonialism and feminism. Jonathan Dollimore published *Sexual Dissidence* in 1991, while Alan Sinfield examined the representations and figures of effeminacy in twentieth-century culture in *The Wilde Century* in 1994. Both studies extended and deepened the ways in which cultural materialist critics read literature and culture through concepts of 'difference', focusing in particular on the cultural politics of sexual difference. Do gay and lesbian sexualities pose a radical challenge to the prevailing norms and values of our societies, or are they merely the same as 'straight' sexualities? This is a question which concerns both Sinfield and Dollimore in their respective studies, and it indicates the extent to which their recent work builds on their early work as cultural materialists. Both critics have extended the analyses of earlier concepts of dissidence, faultlines and deviance by focusing more particularly on the specific cases of sexual dissidence, and the dissident strategies of lesbian and gay subcultures.

Cultural materialism, like new historicism, has succeeded in literary studies in displacing earlier formalist concerns with textual unity and humanist concerns with character and authorship, and changing the ways in which we approach literary texts and their meanings. Although there are very few critics who identify themselves explicitly as 'cultural materialist', the influence of cultural materialism on literary studies in Britain has been pervasive, most notably in the current centrality of historicist approaches, the suspicion of texts with 'canonical' or cultural authority, and the importance of concepts of 'difference' in analyses of the cultural politics of texts. Arguably too, cultural materialism has been instrumental in encouraging self-reflexivity in our critical practices, and a wider concern for the way in which literary studies interacts with, and learns from, the study of culture, society, history, politics and other disciplines. Cultural materialism has enriched literary studies by probing the relationship between literature and social, cultural, political and sexual power, and giving literary criticism a sharper political focus on the present as well as the past.

John Brannigan

Further reading and works cited

Barker, F. *The Tremulous Private Body*. London, 1984.
Belsey, C. *The Subject of Tragedy*. London, 1985.
Benjamin, W. *Illuminations*, ed. H. Arendt. London, 1992.
Brannigan, J. *New Historicism and Cultural Materialism*. Basingstoke, 1998.
Dollimore. J. *Radical Tragedy*. Hemel Hempstead, 1984.
—. *Sexual Dissidence*. Oxford, 1991.
— and Sinfield, A. (eds) *Political Shakespeare*. Manchester, 1985.
Drakakis, J. (ed.) *Alternative Shakespeares*. London, 1985.
Gramsci, A. *Selections from the Prison Notebooks*. London, 1971.
Hawkes, T. (ed.) *Alternative Shakespeares Vol. 2*. London, 1996.
Hawthorn, J. *Cunning Passages*. London, 1996.
Holderness, G. (ed.) *The Shakespeare Myth*. Manchester, 1988.
Milner, A. *Cultural Materialism*. Carlton, Victoria, 1993.
Prendergast, C. *Cultural Materialism*. Minneapolis, MN, 1995.
Ryan, K. (ed.) *New Historicism and Cultural Materialism*. London, 1996.

Sinfield, A. *Literature in Protestant England 1560–1660*. London, 1982.
—. 'Four Ways with a Reactionary Text', *Journal of Literature Teaching Politics*, 2, 1983a.
— (ed.) *Society and Literature 1945–1970*. London, 1983b.
—. *Alfred Tennyson*. Oxford, 1986.
—. *Literature, Politics and Culture in Postwar Britain*. Oxford, 1989.
—. *Faultlines*. Oxford, 1992.
—. *The Wilde Century: Effeminacy, Oscar Wilde and the Queer Moment*. London, 1994a.
—. *Cultural Politic – Queer Reading*. London, 1994b.
Williams, R. *Marxism and Literature*. Oxford, 1977.
—. *Problems in Materialism and Culture*. London, 1980.
Wilson, S. *Cultural Materialism*. Oxford, 1995.

Postcolonial Studies

In his critique of postcolonial theory in the 1980s, Arif Dirlik answers Ella Shohat's question 'When exactly . . . does the "post-colonial" begin?' with the barbed comment that the discipline is in part to do with the arrival of 'Third World intellectuals' into the 'First World academe'. Although this should not lead to a knee-jerk dismissal of the subject on grounds of complicity and elitism, postcolonial critical discourses, perhaps more than most academic discourses, crosses national boundaries; they are products of transnational intellectual activity within the institutional framework of the academy, although not entirely in the way Dirlik imagines. Historically, this is particularly true of a context where the emergence and development of discipline is bound up with Empire, and the anti-colonial and nationalist movements that have ensued its demise; for postcolonial studies is, above all, concerned with the historical, political, cultural, social, aesthetic and philosophical structures of colonial and neocolonial power. Postcolonial studies in Britain is shaped firstly by the movement of peoples and theory that is the result of the educational, literary and cultural links that are formed firstly between Britain and the newly independent colonies, and then latterly as part of a network of transnational academic links. Individuals from different parts of the globe such as Wole Soyinka, Ngũgĩ Wa Thiong'o, Edward Brathwaite, George Lamming, Homi Bhabha, Gayatri Spivak, Stuart Hall, Benita Parry and David Dabydeen have been – or are – based in the UK, moving between metropolitan 'centre' and colonial 'periphery'. But in tackling diverse topics like the legacy of empire, colonial historiography and literature, global capitalism and neocolonialism, nationalism, cultural identity, diaspora, aesthetics, language and the place of literature in society, their contributions have shaped the very contours of modern literary studies in Britain.

The history of 'British' postcolonial studies can perhaps be divided into distinct but overlapping periods and movements. Postcolonial studies is often spoken of as having been inaugurated with Edward Said's *Orientalism* (1978) and the methodological innovations that came in the wake of a discourse theory model of representation and power. Yet critics like Bart Moore-Gilbert, Stephen Slemon, Alan Lawson and Helen Tiffin have also made a case for an alternative genealogy in relation to the UK – one which is indebted to stronger creative and literary affiliations. Hence, Moore-Gilbert speaks of 'postcolonial literary criticism' while Tiffin, Lawson, Leigh Dale and Shane Rowlands, write of early 'Commonwealth post-colonial critics' who wrote initially within a discipline that was deeply moulded by the assumptions, values and precepts of English studies. Yet these early works on colonial writing and the literatures of the British Commonwealth also register critical resistance to, and a 'guerrilla war' against, the Anglo-centric domain of English literature. Among the early works here, one can list Susan Howe's *Novels of Empire* (1949), which looks not only at the colonial literature of Empire but also settler fiction of Australia and New Zealand, and John Matthews' *Tradition in Exile* (1962), which offers a comparative approach to Australian and Canadian poetry. Matthews' preoccupations with a common imperial legacy, the impact of location and environment on creating new different national literatures will be taken up by a succeeding generation of literary critics that work under the umbrella term of 'Commonwealth literature'. A. L. McLeod's *The Commonwealth Pen* (1961), John Press's edited conference proceedings taken from the 1964 inaugural conference on Commonwealth literature at Leeds in Britain, *Commonwealth Literature: Unity and Diversity in a Common Culture* (1965), and introductory companions such as William Walsh's *Commonwealth Literature* (1973) and Bruce King's *Literatures of the World in English* (1974) fall into this category. Here the creation of the disciplinary term 'Commonwealth literature' is somewhat ambivalently located within the paradigm of English that would reinscribe a network of exchanges which would still underscore the importance of the English literature model. But ambivalence should be stressed even in this early period, for the centrality of British literature and educational establishments in the developing empire of literary studies is assumed by some and actively contested by others. 'Commonwealth literature' as a disciplinary field is recognized as problematic even in the disciplinary standard bearer for the 1960s, the *Journal of Commonwealth Literature*. Interestingly, Press's proceedings also echo some of the basic concerns of contemporary postcolonial studies like identity, nationality, language, space/place, the relationship between literature, politics and history, interdisciplinary approaches to literary/textual study, the difficulties of reading texts from other cultures and so on. The volume includes Chinua Achebe's much cited lecture 'The Novelist as Teacher' on education and the need for the regeneration of African literature; Achebe was at this point already serving as Editorial Advisor to the newly formed African Writers Series produced by Heinemann Educational Books, whose subsidiary companies in Africa and the Caribbean did much to nurture indigenous publications. The African Writers Series, and later the Caribbean Writers Series, did much during the succeeding decades to make diverse African and Caribbean writers such as Ngũgi Wa Thiong'o, Cyprian Ekwensi, Bessie Head, Michael Anthony, Beryl Gilroy among others widely available nationally and internationally. The educational connections between the University of London and its external colleges, especially in Africa and the Caribbean, the programmes of exchanges funded by the British Council and the contacts made by its overseas branches, and the curriculum innovations at Universities of Leeds and Kent in the 1960 and 1970s have also facilitated the movement of writers and intellectuals between Britain and the (then) developing world. Reminders of such mundane traffic between 'centre(s)' and 'peripher(ies)' are necessary for they offer a materialist dimension to literary study and highlight the institutional dimensions of postcolonial intellectual activity.

The freedom of movement between the Commonwealth and Britain and labour shortages in Britain coupled with economic depression in the West Indies were factors that led to the recruitment of West Indian labour in the postwar period. The arrival of the *Empire Windrush* in 1948 heralded a generation of West Indian migration into Britain; a number of Caribbean novelists, poets and critics who came to live and work in Britain, notably George Lamming, Andrew Salkey, Wilson Harris, Sam Selvon and – as students – V. S. Naipaul, Edward Kamau Brathwaite and Stuart Hall, made a significant impact on the cultural and literary scene. George Lamming's *The Pleasures of Exile* (1960) explores diverse issues, notably what it means to be a writer from the Caribbean, racism, the state of literacy and publishing, the links between Africa and the Caribbean. *Exile* is an early productive example of using the Prospero–Caliban coupling from Shakespeare's *The Tempest* as a political metaphor for colonial relations, power and representation, although the trope is present as early as Octave Mannoni's *Prospero and Caliban: The Psychology of Colonialism* (1950). Brathwaite's importance as a founding member of the Caribbean Artist Movement cannot be overstated. CAM, formed in 1966, provided a London-based forum (especially in its early years) for debates on the nature of a Caribbean aesthetic, the role of the intellectual, the problems of writing and publishing in the Caribbean and the oral and literary traditions in Caribbean writing. CAM's members comprise not only writers, artists and critics who were concerned with the independent islands of the Caribbean but also student activists concerned with a more assertive grass-roots politics and a Black British identity in a country that had already seen the 1958–9 race riots, the 1962 Commonwealth Immigration Act and Enoch Powell's infamous 1968 incitement to racial hatred, the 'rivers of blood' speech. These CAM student activists were influenced by the Civil Rights campaigns in the US and the Black Power movements that followed in its wake. Brathwaite's distinctive contributions have been to explore the specific African (and Amerindian) ancestry of Caribbean identity, and the use of folk and performative elements in Caribbean poetry which has its roots in black musical rhythms. His concern with creolization (*The Development of Creole Society*, 1971) explores not only the poetics but also the politics of Caribbean hybrid artistic forms. He calls creole English 'nation language'; it is the 'language of the slaves and labourers' with African and Amerindian rhythms, syllables and idioms that by-pass the English pentameter in verse forms (*History of the Voice: the Development of Nation Language in Anglophone Caribbean Poetry*, 1984). Brathwaite's theorization of folk is continued by David Dabydeen's more recent interventions on the use of dialect in poetry, 'On Not Being Milton', which raises important questions about language and audience. Wilson Harris's famous *Tradition and the West Indian Novel* (1964) was given as a lecture to the West Indian Student Union in London; he argues against the widespread generic use of realism in terms of plot, characters and theme prevalent in a number of Caribbean novels, a form that stems from the legacy of nineteenth-century European novels. Harris offers instead a transformative and changing mytho-poetic 'vision of consciousness' (*History, Fable and Myth in the Caribbean and Guianas*, 1970); he argues for a radical openness to a creolization of an intuitive and buried archive of folk beliefs, rituals, superstition, myths and practices. These provide a unique and rich resource for the native writer that moves the novel along very different avenues. As both Andrew Bundy and Bart Moore-Gilbert note, there are strong similarities between Harris's work and that of more contemporary poststructuralist and postcolonial theorists of hybridity and difference such as Homi Bhabha. Derek Walcott's later Nobel prize acceptance speech also picks up the theme of the Antillean experience as a unique 'shipwreck of fragments' of histories, languages and 'remembered customs'. Orlando Patterson was a founding member of CAM and his history of slavery, *The Sociology of Slavery* (1967), complements the literary, sociological and philosophical texts that were produced from these productive exchanges. Although C. L. R. James was not part of the active CAM network, he represents a towering figure for these generation of writers and for Caribbean writing in general; his seminal history of the slave revolt that led to the founding of Haiti, *The Black Jacobins* (1938), is still an influential text.

Chinua Achebe's collected essays, *Morning Yet on Creation Day* (1975), posed fundamental questions about eurocentric criticism, colonialist discourse, universalism, the function of art, the responsibilities of the artist and the use of English language, and addresses literature and the curriculum in newly independent nations. These debates were continued by Wole Soyinka's *Myth, Literature and the African World* (1976), the *bolekaja* critics, Chinweizu and Madubuike's, *Towards the Decolonization of African Literature* (1983) and also Ngũgĩ Wa Thiong'o's *Homecoming* (1972), and *Decolonising the Mind: the Politics of Language in Africa* (1986). In particular, the desire to reclaim African art and writing for Africa triggered debates about what was authentically African, and how literary criticism was to come to terms with the difference of African oral performative traditions. Chinweizu, Jemie and Madubuike argued against comparing African writers against a European literate tradition and complaining about their differences; such 'pseudo' universalism is nothing but European ethnocentrism in disguise. Yet the *bolekaja* critics' talk of a separate and autonomous development of the African novel based on indigenous oral antecedents, 'African reality', traditions and 'authentic African imagery' is problematic given the historical experience and legacy of colonialism. Soyinka contests the claims of Negritude and rejects any prescriptive approach to literature, especially those that do not take into account the complexities of modern Africa; *Myth, Literature and the African World* attempts to forge a distinctive Africanist literary discourse that takes seriously the aesthetic, philosophical, religious and cultural basis of African art. Concern about the reach and penetration of global capitalism, neocolonialism and elitism led Ngugi to argue passionately, *pace* Fanon, that the task of decolonization has yet to be accomplished despite the political transition to independence. In *Decolonising the Mind*, he tackles the issue of continued European hegemony in Africa especially in relation to expressive forms of art and culture, and addresses – pointedly – the issue of African writing in European languages (an issue first broached by Achebe). His interventions reminds us that the politics of national and international publishing remains unresolved, and issues concerning audiences, literacy, uneven development and access are still very much alive today.

In the late 1970s and 1980s, postcolonial theory was dominated on both sides of the Atlantic by three major figures – Edward Said and Gayatri Spivak, based in the US but also giving important lectures in Britain, and Homi Bhabha, based initially at the University of Sussex in the UK. The publication of Edward Said's *Orientalism* (1978) represented a real watershed for postcolonial studies. *Orientalism* sought to fuse two distinctive sets of interests – a poststructuralist interest in textuality and rhetoric, and a humanist, ethical and marxist interest in the workings of power and domination. In discourse theory, Said found a way to recognize and address the network of power that is articulated through a particular way of seeing the world, the geopolitical division of the West and the East, the Occident and the Orient. The expression, sedimentation, reinforcement and overdetermination of this division across history, culture and politics is the focus of a somewhat sweeping, Foucauldian and Gramscian influenced reading of colonial power and representation. Said's later *Culture and Imperialism* (1993) attempts to think 'contrapuntally' and opens out into an ambitious study of an 'intertwined' global history of imperialism for both colonizer and colonized, metropolis and periphery, that is missing from *Orientalism*'s focus on colonial discourse. If his utopian investment in the idea of the (cosmopolitan) secular intellectual goes against the grain of an at times modern cynicism about the function and significance of the academy, it cannot be easily dismissed. His commitment to theory is matched by equal attention to the worldly question of politics in volumes such as *After the Last Sky, The Question of Palestine*.

Gayatri Spivak's work has been immensely influential in the field of colonial histor-iography, feminist studies, cultural studies and postcolonial studies. Her writing has always sought to bring together the insights of poststructuralism, deconstruction, marxism, psychoanalysis, feminism and colonial discourse theory, pointing out not only their usefulness but also their limitations. In 'The Rani of Simur', originally given as a lecture to the 1984 Essex Sociology of Literature conference, 'Europe and its Others', Spivak extends Said's investigations into colonial discourse and its contributions to the shaping of the modern world. She argues that Europe consolidated its sovereignty and subjectivity through the epistemic violence of othering. This 'worlding' forces the 'native' to see himself as 'other'; colonial discourse obliges 'the native to cathect the space of the Other on his home ground' (Barker et al. 1985, 133). Spivak's concern with the epistemic violence has also led her to (re)consider the role of elites, intellectuals, institutional power and privilege that have always haunted the project of speaking for/to oppressed groups ('Subaltern Studies: Deconstructing Historiography', 1985; 'Can the Subaltern Speak?', 1988; *Outside in the Teaching Machine*, 1993). Critical of western feminism's humanist credentials, she poses the question of what it means to address woman (femininity, sexual difference) as a unifying universal analytic category, given that different cultures, histories, mythologies, political and legal contexts have produced very different notions of the 'sexed subject' ('French Feminism in an International Frame', 1981; 'Three Women's Texts and a Critique of Imperialism', 1985; *In Other Worlds*, 1988; 'The Political Economy of Women as seen by a Literary Critic', 1989).

Homi Bhabha's work is informed by psychoanalysis, enunciation theory, poststructur-alism, deconstruction and also postmodernism. 'The Other Question' (1983) emerged initially to redress Said's emphasis on knowledge and information production, by suggest-ing that Orientalism is also a site of fantasy, desires and anxieties. The essay explores racism and racial stereotyping though a psychoanalytic lens; here the dynamics of sexual fetishism in Freud are used to understand racism as a kind of fetishistic disavowal of (racial rather than sexual) difference. Because fetishistic disavowal is based both on a recognition and a negation that must be repeatedly re-enacted, Bhabha can claim that colonial discourse is split, ambivalent and vacillates between control and paranoia. In 'Of Mimicry and Man' (1984), and the influential and widely reproduced 'Signs Taken for Wonders' (1985), he extends the idea of ambivalence by suggesting that colonial authority should not be reified as totalizing in its effectivity and reach. Instead, colonial discourse can be read as more fractured and contradictory, seen especially in its troping on mimicry (attempts to reproduce a reformed Other mirrors or mimics the colonial self). Here colonial discourse can produce an Other that mocks or menaces precisely through its resemblance – 'almost the same but not quite', 'almost the same but not white'. It is this ambivalence, hybridity, indeterminacy and self-contradiction that unsettles or disturbs the presence of colonial authority. Bhabha's later essay 'Dissemination' develops the implicit conceptual critique of origins in the direction of national identities and narratives of the nation. Others like 'The Postcolonial and the Post-modern' propose a problematic, unstable, intersubjective poststructuralist theory of agency away from consciousness, individuation, intentionality, simple causality and control.

The Essex Sociology of Literature conference proceedings, *Europe and its Others* (1985), can be situated in the conceptual paradigm opened up by the expanded notion of rhetoric, textuality and 'worlding' initiated by Said, Spivak and Bhabha. Diverse essays on orientalist painting, Islam and the idea of Europe, travel writing, multiculturalism in Australia, Indian historiography and European and American literature from a variety of disciplines address the textual weave of European (and American) subject formation through its many socio-political, historical cultural and psychosexual strands. The influence of European theory (epitomized by the intellectual exchanges at the Essex conference) made for a flowering of literary theoretical activity particularly in the area of colonial history and literature, for example Peter Hulme's *Colonial Encounters* (1986) which addresses the discovery and settlement of the New World through different generic texts (from poetry to memoirs, log books and official documents). Hulme's exploration of historical and mythical encounters such as that between Columbus and the indigenous peoples of the Caribbean, John Smith and Pocahontas, and fictive encounters such as those between Prospero and Caliban, Crusoe and Friday, Inkle and Yarico, unearth the language of savagery and cannibalism that was used to manage the dispossession of the Amerindians and to justify the exploitation of the Americas. The *Oxford Literary Review's* special issue on colonialism in 1988 included work by Gauri Viswanathan on the political uses of English in India (later published in her *Masks of Conquest*) and Benita Parry's important critique of Spivak and Bhabha. Parry's turn to the revolutionary Fanon, as opposed to Bhabha's turn to the psychoanalytic Fanon, is part of the debate over the legacy of the revolutionary theorist, activist and psychoanalyst, Frantz Fanon. Such debates reflect the intense contestation over the Fanon who wrote *Black Skins/White Masks* and the Fanon who wrote *The Wretched of the Earth*.

Robert Young's *White Mythologies* (1990) explores postwar theories of history in relation to imperialism but is perhaps more noted for its lucid exposition of the difficult and complex work of Spivak and Bhabha. Young's commentary signals a moment in which postcolonial theory reaches a critical mass and marks its institutionalization in the teaching machine. A number of anthologies follow in quick succession, notably *Colonial Discourse and Post-colonial Theory* (1993), *The Post-Colonial Studies Reader* (1995) and *Contemporary Postcolonial Theory: A Reader* (1996). Bill Ashcroft, Gareth Griffiths and Helen Tiffin's *The Empire Writes Back* (1989) offers a survey of postcolonial literatures (and theories) in English and, with such a synoptic introduction, a user-friendly, teachable text for the higher educational curriculum. The increasing attention to what seems a veritable industry in postcolonial intellectual commodities sounds a necessary note of caution. Parry's recuperation of nationalism, 'Resistance Theory/Theorising Resistance or Two Cheers for Nativism', Neil Lazarus' 'National Consciousness and the Specificity of (Post)colonial intellectuals' and Anne McClintock's much cited critique of 'postcolonialism' collected in *Colonial Discourse/Postcolonial Theory* (1994) are early essays that mark a disenchantment with the drift of postcolonial theory. Vijay Mishra and Bob Hodges's 'What is Post-colonialism?' on the significance of the hyphen in post-colonial (1991), Ella Shohat's 'Notes on the Post-colonial' (1992), the *Oxford Literary Review's* 1991 issue on neocolonialism, Spivak's continuing interventions on the role of intellectuals, Aijaz Ahmad's *In Theory* (1992) and Arif Dirlik's *The Postcolonial Aura* (1997) are critical interventions against the complacency which sometimes characterizes the celebratory assumption of ethical and political effectivity that accompanies such academic discourses. More recently, Bart Moore-Gilbert's excellent stock-taking survey and critical assessment of postcolonial theory, *Postcolonial Theory* (1997), and Ato Quayson's *Postcolonialism* (2000), mark a point whereby postcolonial studies have (ironically) come of age. If the debates surrounding effectivity show no sign of going away, and the issues surrounding the global capitalism and neocolonialism are still as prevalent today as they were decades ago, the battles over their place in the curriculum have mostly receded. But this only begs the question not only of what is postcolonialism, but who and what postcolonial studies are for.

With the interventions of Ashcroft, Tiffin and Griffiths (academics based in Australia) and Moore-Gilbert, Said, Bhabha and Spivak's later work, there is a diminishing sense of the divide between theory and (untheorized) literary criticism. The division is perhaps artificially created with the predominance of European theory and the almost exclusive focus on colonial literature and documents (hence the term colonial discourse) in the early years following *Orientalism*. As Alan Lawson, Leigh Dale, Helen Tiffin and Shane Rowlands point out, the suspicion with which the study of Commonwealth literatures was held related to its potential for 'imperial sentimentality' and its English literary focus. Furthermore, creative writers were 'ignored' for their 'collusion' with a 'Euro-modernist project' and their determined production of 'realist', anti-colonial and nationalist narratives. But over the last two decades there has been a willingness to read literature informed by the developments of theory and to consider creative writers and their work as interventions in theoretical debates. Just as Helen Tiffin and Stephen Slemon's *After Europe* (1989), Ian Adam and Helen Tiffin's *Past the Last Post* (1991) and Bruce King's *New National and Post-Colonial Literatures* (1996) show the distance travelled from the early days of *Commonwealth Literature* (1973) and *Literatures of the World in English* (1974), 'theorized' studies like *Culture and Imperialism* (1993) consider creative writers and thinkers from the developing world. In the meantime, the dividing line between creative and conceptual/theoretical work and theory fades with writers like Wilson Harris, Amitav Gosh, Salman Rushdie and David Dabydeen.

Crossover with the field of cultural studies and cultural theory, particularly with regard to diasporic culture and Black British identity in the work of Stuart Hall and Paul Gilroy, has also been enormously productive. Hall's much anthologized essays, 'Cultural Identity and Diaspora' (1990) and 'New Ethnicities' (1989), have paved the way for a more complex understanding of cultural identity as a shifting and ongoing process of identification rather than a finished product that is inherited, and a theorized black British cultural politics that 'engages rather than suppresses difference'. Hall's earlier collection of essays *Policing the Crisis* (1978) examined the media's management of race relations in the wake of racial disturbances and *The Empire Strikes Back* (1982), produced by the Centre for Contemporary Cultural Studies, is equally critical of 'race relations' sociology in Britain. Paul Gilroy's influential *There Ain't No Black in the Union Jack* (1987) looks at the cultural politics of race and nation beyond ethnic absolutism and explores urban black expressive culture and community. His recent study of the African diasporic connections between Europe and America, *The Black Atlantic* (1993), argues for an ethnohistorical approach to modernity. His charting of the transnational and intercultural flow of ideas that are present in black vernacular culture and nationalist thought develops the trope of the ship as one of the key figures of the history of black migration. Such a trope is also part of Gilroy's general attempts to forge a new language of cultural identity that is non-organic, hybrid and non-essentialist. Hall and Gilroy's work on black British cultural politics must also be read in conjunction with feminist work on the area, particularly Pratibha Parmar's cinematic and conceptual work on gender and cultural identity and Avtar Brah's reassessment of Asian diasporic identities in the light of contemporary theories of diaspora, locations and borders, *Cartographies of Desire* (1996). One should also not forget the three important early collections of essays, stories, interviews and creative work by black and third world women, *Watchers and Seekers* (1987), *Charting the Journey* (1988) and *Let it be Told: Black Women Writers in Britain* (1988), that made such communities visible. The enduring challenge and rewards for postcolonial intellectuals is to 'think concretely and sympathetically, contrapuntually, about others' (Said 1993, 408).

Gail Ching-Liang Low

Further reading and works cited

Achebe, C. *Morning Yet on Creation Day*. London, 1975.
Ashcroft, B. et al. (eds) *The Empire Writes Back*. London, 1995a.
— et al. (eds) *The Post-colonial Studies Reader*. London, 1995b.
Barker, F. et al. (eds) *Europe and its Others*, 2 vols. Colchester, 1985.
— et al. (eds) *Colonial Discourse/Postcolonial Theory*. Manchester, 1994.
Bhabha, H. *The Location of Culture*. London, 1994.
Brathwaite, E. *History of the Voice*. London, 1984.
Bundy, A. (ed.) *Selected Essays of Wilson Harris*. London, 1999.
Chinweizu, O. J. and Madubuike, I. *Towards the Decolonisation of African Literature*. Washington, DC, 1983.
Dirlik, A. *The Postcolonial Aura*. Boulder, CO, 1997.
Fanon, F. *The Wretched of the Earth*. Harmondsworth, 1983.
—. *Black Skins, White Masks*. London, 1986.
Gilroy, P. *There Ain't No Black in the Union Jack*. London, 1987.
—. *The Black Atlantic*. London, 1993.
Hulme, P. *Colonial Encounters*. London, 1992.
King, B. *New National and Post-Colonial Literatures*. Oxford, 1996.
Lamming, G. *The Pleasures of Exile*. London, 1960.
Lawson, A. et al. (eds) *Post-Colonial Literatures in English*. New York, 1997.
Moore-Gilbert, B. *Postcolonial Theory*. London, 1997.
Quayson, A. *Postcolonialism*. Oxford, 2000.
Rutherford, J. *Identities*. London, 1990.
Said, E. *Orientalism*. London, 1978.
—. *Culture and Imperialism*. New York, 1993.
Slemon, S. 'The Scramble for Post-colonialism', in *De-Scribing Empire*. eds C. Tiffin and A. Lawson. London, 1994.
Soyinka, W. *Myth, Literature and the African World*. Cambridge, 1976.
Spivak, G. Chakravorty. 'Three Women's Text and a Critique of Imperialism', *Critical Inquiry*, 12, 1, 1985a.
—. 'Can the Subaltern Speak?', *Wedge*, 7/8, 1985b.
—. *Outside in the Teaching Machine*. London, 1993.
Wa Thiong'o, N. *Decolonising the Mind*. London, 1986.

Gay/Queer and Lesbian Studies, Criticism and Theory

One could chart the beginning of British queer literary criticism in the 1890s with Edward Carpenter's celebration of the writings of Walt Whitman, offering a model of masculine love and classless affiliation as a counter to the Oscar Wilde model of the indolent, upper-class, dandified, effeminate homosexual. The diaries and writings of twentieth-century writers like Siegfried Sassoon, J. P. Ackerley, E. M. Forster, even T. E. Lawrence, show that there was some notion of a gay literary canon, shared by an intellectual subculture, even if there was no openly gay critical writing (much like the contrast between the private and public writings of American critic F. O. Matthiessen). However, what can be called a body of gay and lesbian literary criticism and theory began in Britain in the 1970s.

Two crucial but radically different works were published in 1977, Jeffrey Meyers's *Homosexuality in Literature*, and Jeffrey Weeks's *Coming Out*. Though limiting himself to non-dramatic prose, Meyers's work demonstrates one of the important tactics of early gay criticism, canon formation. His first footnote lists 'the most important homosexual writers of the last hundred years', and the volume itself focuses on the prose works Meyers thinks are most indicative of the homosexual aesthetic he describes and celebrates. Unfortunately what Meyers admires are the tactics of subterfuge of an earlier, more repressive era separate from any critique of the social policing of homosexuality and homosexual discourse.

> Homosexual novels are characteristically subtle, allusive and symbolic – the very qualities we now admire in Yeats and Eliot, and the novels of Flaubert and Henry James – and form an eighth kind of literary ambiguity. For the ambiguous expression of the repressed, the hidden and the sometimes secret theme suggests a moral ambiguity as well. If a specifically homosexual tone, sensibility, vision or mode of apprehension exists, then it would be characterized by these cautious and covert qualities, and by the use of art to conceal rather than to reveal the theme of the novel ... (1977, 1–2)

The converse of Meyers's fascination with the subterfuges of the closet is his distaste for the new generation of openly gay writers. For him, 'the emancipation of the homosexual has led to the decline of his art' (Meyers 1977, 3). Though Meyers claims that he has 'no desire to praise or condemn homosexuality', he ends his long introductory essay with James Baldwin's negative vision of the gay subculture of his time. Meyers's study was the sort of work gay readers once accepted as affirming in merely taking up the subject, but actually negative in its view of homosexuality.

Jeffrey Weeks's work is another matter altogether. Though neither literary criticism or theory, his first volume, which offers a careful history of the emergence of gay self-consciousness and politics, would be important to later critics. *Coming Out: Homosexual Politics in Britain from the Nineteenth Century to the Present* begins from the premise established by Michel Foucault, that the word 'homosexual' 'is itself a product of history, a cultural artefact designed to express a particular concept' (Weeks 1977, 3). For Weeks, the concurrent rise in hostility toward homosexuality with emerging new definitions of homosexuality found in the late nineteenth century 'can only be understood as part of the restructuring of the family and sexual relations consequent upon the triumph of urbaniza-tion and industrial capitalism' (Weeks 1977, 2). Like much of the major work in British queer studies that followed, Weeks's first major volume is a work of cultural materialism, which Alan Sinfield, building on the pioneering work of Raymond Williams, concisely describes as

> analytic work which sees texts as inseparable from the conditions of their production and reception in history; as involved, necessarily, in the making of meanings which are always, finally, political. (Sinfield 1994b, vii)

Within this framework, our sense of homosexuality becomes historically shaped and ever changing. As Weeks puts it:

> There is no *essence* of homosexuality whose historical unfolding can be illuminated. There are only changing patterns in the organization of desire, whose specific configuration can be decoded. This, of course, propels us into a whirlwind of deconstruction. (Weeks 1985, 6)

This is the primary assumption of Week's work and much of what follows in British queer studies – the careful historicizing of a dynamic subject, considered static and unnatural – which historians, psychoanalysts, sexologists, queer historians and critics resist. If homo-sexuality is itself a contingent cultural construction, what of supposedly 'natural' hetero-sexuality, or of any essentialist gender definitions? On that question rests the wider claims of queer studies to be central to current critical discourse beyond its own anti-homophobic agenda.

Weeks's three major volumes were written between the enactment of legislation legalizing same-sex acts, and Margaret Thatcher's attempt to silence anti-homophobic education and art through Clause 28. His first volume, a history of British lesbians and gay men's acceptance, evasion and resistance of definitions imposed by their society from the supposedly scientifically neutral 'homosexual' to the more self-affirmative 'gay', *Sex, Politics and Society* (1981) elaborates on the relationship of regulation of sex in general and homosexual acts in particular with the growth of industrial capitalism. *Sexuality and Its Discontents* (1985) is a close investigation of the literature on sex, sexology and homo-sexuality from the nineteenth century to the present. While Weeks's work is historical, it is also focused on the power of language to regulate and resist. For some, Weeks's work may seem more in the realm of social sciences than literary studies, but in Britain, the two were linked as what was called gay studies was, as Alan Sinfield puts it, 'unthinkable outside a general left-wing orientation' (Sinfield 1995b, 73).

Weeks distilled his ideas in an essay which appears in the volume *The Making of the Modern Homosexual*, edited by Kenneth Plummer (1981), which is a kind of prolegomena for further research in the social sciences. This collection of essays by sociologists and anthropologists includes Mary McIntosh's classic 1968 essay, 'The Homosexual Role'. McIntosh's assertion, now taken for granted, is that 'it is not until he sees homosexuals as a social category, rather than a medical or psychiatric one, that the sociologist can begin to ask the right questions about the specific content of the homosexual role and about the organization and functions of homosexual groups' (McIntosh, in Plummer 1981, 43), and a social role is dynamic, not static. In an afterword included in the volume, McIntosh in essence critiques and updates her essay, asserting as Weeks had done that 'you can't understand homosexuality without locating it in sexuality in general' (McIntosh, in Plummer 1981, 46). In the same volume, Annabel Faraday, in 'Liberating Lesbian Research', attacks the notion that one can study lesbianism and male homosexuality as if they were the same phenomena: 'heterosexuality itself is a power relation of men over women; what gay men and lesbians are rejecting are essentially polar experiences' (Faraday, in Plummer 1981, 113). Faraday's essay, the only one to address lesbian issues in Plummer's volume, introduces a problem in early British queer studies, the relative absence of the lesbian voice.

Few books have had as much impact on gay literary studies as Alan Bray's *Homosexuality in Renaissance England* (1982). At the time a high-ranking civil servant and an independent scholar (a category more respected in England than in the US), Bray took the work of Foucault and Weeks and applied it to the English Renaissance. More importantly, he raised questions regarding the proper historical methodology for gay scholars. What interested Bray was the fact that 'there was an immense disparity in this society between what people said – and apparently believed – about homosexuality and what in truth they did' (Bray 1982, 9). Bray deals with this disparity in three related essays. The first deals with the way sodomy and buggery (the word homosexuality, of course, did not exist, nor the assumptions about identity it defines) were symbolized in literature as symptoms of 'the disorder in sexual relations that could, in theory at least, break out anywhere' (Bray 1982, 25). If the worldview suggested a tenuous cosmic order that could be shaken by any individual disorderly act, sodomy could have catastrophic consequences. Yet it is clear from court records that homosexual activity took place and was not always punished when it was discovered. More importantly, given the close knit social structure, such activity usually transpired between people who knew each other, often members of the same household. As in earlier societies, those relations were determined 'by the prevailing distribution of power, economic power and social power, not the fact of homosexuality itself' (Bray 1982, 56). Bray's main question is how, given the universal excoriation of homosexual acts, there could be what he calls a 'cleavage between an individual's behaviour and his awareness of its social significance' (Bray 1982, 68). The answer, in short, is that there was little or no social pressure for one to define one's sexuality, to connect one's actions with the state described in the anti-sodomy literature. So there was a reluctance on the part of the actors and of society at large to see specific actions as examples of the 'fearful sin of sodomy' (Bray 1982, 76). Bray characteristically frames his most succinct response as a question: 'Was society any more likely than the individual to recognize in the everyday reality of homosexuality the figure of the sodomite when this figure was spoken of in imagery so divorced from the social forms homosexuality actually took?' (Bray 1982, 77). Bray's final chapter moves to the eighteenth century and the institution of Molly houses to contrast the incoherences of homosexuality in the previous two centuries with a social context (London in the eighteenth century) in which there was clearly an organized homosexual subculture. The success of Bray's book on both continents (it was one of the most influential British works of gay studies in the United States) is due not only to the material and convincing argument, but to the authorial voice. The reader is aware of a constantly questioning presence, realizing that every question leads to another and that every conclusion is provisional. For some, Bray became a model of the postmodern gay scholar. It is not surprising that his next essay on homosexuality and male friendship in the English Renaissance took issue with some of his own previous conclusions as it analysed documents of same-sex affection.

Because of the British investment in cultural studies, some of the ground-breaking gay work was in film rather than literature. *Gays and Film* (1977, rev. edn 1984), edited by Richard Dyer, was a crucial starting point. Dyer's own essay, 'Stereotyping', categorizes modes of representation of gay men in mainstream gay cinema. Caroline Sheldon's 'Lesbians and Film: Some Thoughts' begins with what appears now as a theoretically simplistic description of the 'lesbianfeminist' point of view ('lesbianfeminism implies a certain analysis of the power structure in which sexism is the primary oppression and lesbianism is defined as a political and emotional choice' (Sheldon, in Dyer 1984, 5), and moves on to a consideration of lesbian representations in film. For Sheldon, 'films are often tools to maintain depoliticization' (Sheldon, in Dyer 1984, 5). Like Weeks, she sees capitalism and the modern bourgeois family as the forces both shaping and opposing homosexuality. Jack Babuscio's seminal 'Camp and the Gay Sensibility' is a fundamental attempt to move beyond Susan Sontag's classic essay on camp and create a stronger link between gayness and camp, which describes 'those elements in a person, situation or activity which express, or are expressed by, a gay sensibility' (Babuscio, in Dyer 1984, 40). While Babuscio's essentialist view of 'the gay sensibility' seems outmoded, the essay has been a crucial starting point for further inquiry.

Dyer has gone on to write some of the most important gay-oriented film criticism. Particularly important is his book-length analysis of gay-oriented film, *Now You See It* (1990). For Dyer, these films, from Germany in the 1920s through Genet to independent film of the 1970s, represent 'what could be done within actual social and historical reality' (Dyer 1990, 1):

> It is this interaction, this within and against, of historically specific lesbian/gay subcultures and particular filmic traditions, as worked through in the texts of the films, that is the subject of this book. (Dyer 1990, 2)

In the 1990s, the two major figures in queer criticism in Britain were Jonathan Dollimore and Alan Sinfield, co-founders of the graduate programme in Sexual Dissidence and Cultural Change at the University of Sussex.

Dollimore's *Sexual Dissidence: Augustine to Wilde, Freud to Foucault* (1991) is nothing if not ambitious. Dollimore begins with the meeting of André Gide and Oscar Wilde who become representatives of essentialist and constructionist attitudes toward homosexuality. Both became avatars of sexual transgression, but saw their transgressiveness in diametrically different ways:

> For Gide, transgression is in the name of a desire rooted in the natural, the sincere, and the authentic; Wilde's transgressive aesthetic is the reverse: insincerity, inauthenticity, and unnaturalness become the liberating attributes of decentred identity and desire ... (Dollimore 1991, 14)

As he does for other British queer critics (Neil Bartlett, Alan Sinfield, Joseph Bristow), Wilde becomes the postmodern queer, reversing false binaries (nature/culture, depth/surface). For Dollimore, the prerequisite to admitting transgressive desire is 'an erasure of self, a decentring' (Dollimore 1991, 17). Gide foolishly and stubbornly maintained his belief in the centred, essential self. While Gide, who survived Wilde by over half a century, has been relegated to minor status as an artist, 'decentred' Wilde is still central to literary studies and is the true father of queer theory. He understood that 'there is no freedom outside of history, no freedom within deluded notions of autonomous selfhood' (Dollimore 1991, 33).

Dollimore's principal project is a history of sexual dissidence, which unsettles the opposition between dominant and subordinate cultures. That opposition is fought through 'those conceptions of self, desire, and transgression which figure in the language, ideologies and cultures of domination and in the diverse kinds of resistance to it' (Dollimore 1991, 21). The form of sexual dissidence of most interest is, of course, homosexuality: 'It is perhaps as something under erasure, even in its emergence, that homosexuality provides a history remarkably illuminating for the issues of marginality and power upon which contemporary debates, cultural, psychoanalytical and literary, have been converging' (Dollimore 1991, 32). Two terms are of particular importance in Dollimore's argument: the 'perverse dynamic' ('that fearful interconnectedness whereby the antithetical inheres within, and is partly produced by, what it opposes' (Dollimore 1991, 33)), and 'transgressive reinscription'. If homosexuality is not actually the 'other' to heterosexuality, but rather its 'proximate', related temporally and spatially, then what is called the other can easily 'track back' into the dominant. Transgressive reinscription, then, is 'the return of the repressed and/or the suppressed and/or the displaced via the proximate' (Dollimore 1991, 33).

These terms become the foundation for Dollimore's survey of dissidence from early Christianity through psychoanalysis and literary criticism to postmodernism. Ultimately the book celebrates the perverse dynamic, which 'reidentifies and exploits the inextricable connections between perversity, proximity, paradox, and desire'(Dollimore 1991, 230). *Sexual Dissidence* provides a merger of British cultural materialism with the work of the central figures in United States queer theory, particularly Eve Kosofsky Sedgwick.

Alan Sinfield's volumes written during the 1990s (*The Wilde Century, Cultural Politics – Queer Reading, Gay and After*), while remaining firmly entrenched in cultural materialism, demonstrate three different approaches to queer studies.

In *The Wilde Century* (1994), Sinfield explores the ways in which the persona of Oscar Wilde came to link the new notion of homosexuality with effeminacy, aestheticism and aristocratic decadence, states which heretofore had no association with homosexuality. For Sinfield, 'Wilde and his writings look queer because our stereotypical notion of male homosexuality derives from Wilde and our ideas about him' (Sinfield 1994a, vii). Wilde's person and writings comprise what Sinfield calls a 'faultline story', a narrative that exposes a culture's 'unresolved issues'. Given a society's desire to silence homosexuality, one needs to examine secrets and silences as carefully as speech. It is through understanding those silences that we come to better understand a society's ideological project, which is crucial since it is ideology that shapes us: 'it is hard to be gay until you have some kind of slot, however ambiguously defined, in the current framework of ideas' (Sinfield 1994a, 17). Wilde's exposure gave homosexuality a definition, a narrative: the leisured, effeminate, aesthetic dandy having sex for money with lower class boys. Such an image showed the homosexual as disruptive of all forms of Victorian social order. It also created a stereotype, a recognizable picture of the homosexual which men who were so inclined could model themselves after or rebel against. Central to this picture is effeminacy, which ties the homosexual to a rigid, fictional masculine-feminine binary, but at the same time gave many twentieth-century homosexuals a mode of affirmation: 'Effeminacy has over manliness the advantage of being a central gay cultural tradition which we may proudly assert' (Sinfield 1994a, 196).

The Wilde Century joins Dollimore's *Sexual Dissidence* and other volumes devoted to Wilde's centrality in the creation of a gay persona that was both limiting and liberating. Neil Bartlett's 'personal meditation' *Who Was That Man* analyses the historical and symbolic Wildes: the writer who became a scandalous sexual criminal and the supposed father of the modern gay community. Bartlett accumulates historical and literary details to demonstrate that the historical Wilde was not an anomaly: 'the gay culture of London was there. It was organized in a variety of forms, spoke both private and public languages, inhabited both private and public spaces, was both terrified and courageous' (1988, 127–8). Wilde, then, was not intolerable to his society because he was homosexual: 'he was intolerable because he was a public man who was homosexual' (Bartlett 1988, 148). Bartlett scans historical writing and Wilde's *oeuvre* to discover what homosexuality meant to Wilde and what Wilde meant to a gay man in the 1980s:

> There was no real Oscar Wilde, if by real we mean homosexual. He did not, like us, have the alibi of 'being like that'. London in 1895 had no conception of a man being 'naturally homosexual'. A man who loved other men could only be described as an invert, an inversion of something else, a pervert, an exotic, a disease, a victim, a variation. Wilde was an artist as well. He was entirely uninterested in authenticity. (1988, 163–4)

Joseph Bristow's *Effeminate England* (1995) begins with the same idea asserted in Sinfield's *The Wilde Century* – that effeminacy only became a stereotype of homosexuality after the Wilde scandal. Given this taint of effeminacy and the Uranian notion that a homosexual was some sort of hermaphrodite caught in the middle of the gender binary, Bristow asserts that 'homoerotic writing after 1885 constantly defines itself against the predominant assumption that to be a man-loving man necessarily meant that one was weakened, morally and physically, by the taint of effeminacy' (Bristow 1995, 10), which informed the writer's presentation of male-male desire and their often contemptuous treatment of women. Sinfield's *The Wilde Century* asserts that 'the villain of the piece is the masculine/feminine binary structure as it circulates in our cultures' (Sinfield 1994a, vii). Bristow's work is also built on this assumption.

Most of Alan Sinfield's recent work focuses on gay culture and discourse. *Cultural Politics – Queer Reading*, published the same year as *The Wilde Century*, contains lectures Sinfield gave at the University of Pennsylvania critiquing the relationship of what he calls 'Englit' the profession of literary criticism as it is practised in English departments, and homosexuality and queer studies. In essence, he is writing a clear, articulate argument for his cultural materialist approach. Sinfield is particularly interested in the dynamics of subcultures, particularly the gay subculture: 'the advantage of subculture as an interpretive tool is that it designates a distinctive framework of understanding that is neither determined by the dominant nor immune to it' (Sinfield 1994b, 68). For him, gayness is a mode of categorizing, not a property of individuals.

Sinfield is always concerned with the ways in which his ideas affect the political reality of present-day queers and how we can effect social change, how we realize the possibility of 'subcultural strategies'. *Gay and After* (1998), Sinfield's contribution to what is called 'post-gay' writing, begins from the notion that ' "gay" as we have produced it and lived it, and perhaps "lesbian" also, are historical phenomena and now may be hindering us more than they help us' (Sinfield 1998, 5). Post-gay, for Sinfield, is a time 'when it will not seem so necessary to define, and hence to limit, our sexualities' (1998, 14). There is not one monolithic homosexuality, but a variety of homosexualities shaped by different circumstances of class, education, race and ethnicity. Gay readers neither live nor read the same way. The only condition those defined as gay share is that of being not heterosexual. Therefore the term 'gay' neither reflects this variety nor allows for changes in the sex-gender system.

A sense of the ways in which queer studies were influencing literary studies can be found in a collection of essays edited by Joseph Bristow (1992). A central concern of the volume is the elimination of the notion of gay and lesbian identity and readership. In his introduction, Bristow begins challenging the monolithic notion of homosexuality which 'denies the gendered difference between men and women who desire their own sex. It produces sameness where there is not necessarily any at all' (1992, 3). In her essay 'What Is Not Said', Diana Colecott elaborates Bristow's argument: 'The male body dominates current discussion in gay studies, while the female body is doubly deleted: is deleted as maternal body, and as both subject and object of lesbian desire' (Colecott, in Bristow 1992, 93). Even more than in the writings of gay men, the key words in lesbian criticism are 'silence' and 'erasure': silence about the desire and experience of lesbians and erasure of their difference. 'This situation leaves the lesbian conscious of herself as an absence from discourse, and the lesbian writer, teacher, or theorist is in an historical position that does not synchronize with the relative recognition and the relative freedom of gay men to write, teach, and theorize' (Colecott, in Bristow 1992, 93).

The first British collection of essays by lesbians on literature was not published until 1991. *What Lesbians Do in Books*, edited by Elaine Hobby and Chris White, reinforces what might be called the lesbian canon (Sappho, Radycliffe Hall, Virginia Woolf, Audre Lorde, Adrienne Rich), but expands into areas like the lesbian detective story. What is most provocative about the essays are their rethinking of accepted ideas of queer theory. Chris White offers a rebuttal to both Michel Foucault and Jeffrey Weeks's account of the history of sexology. For White, Foucault's 'one way' power dynamic between society and the individual does not take into account the fact that much of the change in discourse about homosexuals that took place in the nineteenth century was instigated by homosexuals trying to find neutral, if not positive, definitions. Katherine Phillips asserts that the accounts she has found of female–female desire before the nineteenth century raise doubts about Foucault's primary thesis that there could not be a homosexual without the language to define her. More important to the writers of this volume are feminist theorists like Luce Irigaray and the psychoanalytic theories of Jacques Lacan. As the essays in the volume make clear, lesbian writers, critics and theorists draw their ideas and empowerment more from the body of feminist criticism than the work of gay male writers.

John M. Clum

Further reading and works cited

Bartlett, N. *Who Was That Man*. London, 1988.
Bray, A. *Homosexuality in Renaissance England*. London, 1982.
Bristow, J. *Sexual Sameness*. London, 1992.
—. *Effeminate England*. New York, 1995.

Dollimore, J. *Sexual Dissidence*. Oxford, 1991.

Dyer, R. *Gays and Film*. New York, 1984.

—. *Now You See It*. London, 1990.

Hobby, E. and White, C. (eds) *What Lesbians Do in Books*. London, 1991.

Meyers, J. *Homosexuality and Literature*. London, 1977.

Plummer, K. (ed.) *The Making of the Modern Homosexual*. Totowa, 1981.

— (ed.) *Modern Homosexualities*. London, 1992.

Shepherd, S. *Because We're Queers*. London, 1989.

Simpson, M. (ed.) *Anti-gay*. London, 1996.

Sinfield, A. *The Wilde Century*. New York, 1994a.

—. *Cultural Politics – Queer Reading*. Philadelphia, 1994b.

—. *Gay and After*. London, 1998.

Smith, A. M. *New Right Discourse on Race and Sexuality*. Cambridge, 1994.

Smyth, C. *Lesbians Talk Queer Notions*. London, 1992.

Still, J. and Worten, M. (eds) *Textuality and Sexuality*. Manchester, 1993.

Weeks, J. *Coming Out*. London, 1977.

—. *Sex, Politics and Society*. London, 1981.

—. *Sexuality and Its Discontents*. London, 1985.

—. *Against Nature*. London, 1991.

Ernesto Laclau (1935–), Chantal Mouffe (1948–) and Post-Marxism

The suggestion that there could be an intimate link between literary theory and political philosophy might come as something of a surprise in certain circles, not least perhaps in those of literary theory and political philosophy themselves. Yet it was precisely by applying literary theoretical, psychoanalytic and semiotic concepts and techniques to the analysis of the political that Ernesto Laclau and Chantal Mouffe developed a radical version of marxist political theory. This new theory, which they termed 'post-marxism', found its first thoroughgoing articulation in their co-authored work, *Hegemony and Socialist Strategy: Towards a Radical Democratic Politics* (1985). This work carries out a methodical historical critique and conceptual deconstruction of 'classical Marxism' (1985, 3), which enables them to identify why classical marxist theory could not predict, account for, or adequately explain the behaviour of political struggles and socio-political or economic 'classes'. This 'failure' became increasingly apparent throughout the nineteenth and twentieth centuries, and represented a severe challenge to the validity of marxism, threatening its credibility, while also initiating a 'crisis' *within* marxism itself. For this 'failure' ran entirely contrary to the claims that marxism could be the *objective science* of historical processes (1985, 2). As such, Laclau and Mouffe begin their analysis by identifying an antagonism, between marxism's claims about the socio-political world on the one hand, and the 'reality' or observable development of actual societies on the other (1985, 122).

As 'objective science', marxism aimed to predict the course history must *necessarily* take, culminating in the revolution of a 'universal class' of workers. But, in the face of the failure of this prediction, marxism could most readily survive by switching the emphasis of its claims, away from being the *declarations* of an *objective science* (of the order: 'This *will* happen'), and changing to those of *injunctions* made in the name of an *ethical programme* (of the order: 'This *should* (be made to) happen') (Derrida 1994; Laclau 1996, 66). However, for Laclau and Mouffe, any move which entails abandoning the idea of marxism's objective and scientific aspirations, and the subsequent – and supplementary (Laclau and Mouffe 1985, 51; Derrida 1974, 141) – adoption of a position in which marxism would be considered merely *ethical*, was simply unsatisfactory – academically and politically.

Although they would not disagree that marxism entails an *ethical dimension*, especially regarding the primary question of *justice*, which is always in some measure at the heart of democratic struggles (1985, 174), their analysis does not remove itself from the matter of the *mechanisms* governing social and political 'reality'. However, where classical marxism concerned itself with *objective* 'reality', Laclau and Mouffe see objectivity itself as only one part of 'reality'. So, as 'objectivity' is only one part of a social totality, it is not, therefore, coterminous or coextensive with 'reality' as such, and any analysis of the *totality* should not therefore concern itself with only that one *part* (1985, 111). Accordingly, their emphasis moves from the objectivity of that which exists, 'is', or has being or presence (Spivak, in Derrida 1974, xiv ff.), and focuses instead upon the 'logic' of the social and political – the *logic* of socio-political mechanisms. They do not ignore the status of the 'objective' and objectivity, but in their analysis the focus is more upon the logical mechanisms through which 'objective reality' actually gains that status of being – or what they term 'the *conditions of possibility* of any objectivity' (Žižek 1989, xiii). But this logic is far from being a logic organized by 'identity' and the law of 'non-contradiction' (Laclau and Mouffe 1985, 124). It is rather a deconstructive logic, which is intelligible most readily in terms of the Saussurean semiotic notion in which the identity of any sign (or, in Laclau and Mouffe, any *entity* at all) is constituted on the basis of defining and asserting itself in terms of *that which it is not* – that is, on the basis of difference (de Man 1978, 22).

Their revaluation and overhaul of marxist theory in *Hegemony and Socialist Strategy* constituted a concerted attempt to 'save' the project of marxism from obsolescence, while not abandoning the aspirations, aims and objectives (*telos*) of marxism: namely, the hope of egalitarian emancipation for all from the exploitation and subjection attendant to capitalist production. Hence the term 'post-marxism': the reference to the *telos* of marxism remains in place, as a guiding idea, but the 'post' signifies 'after', 'more than', 'other than' marxism. In addition, of course, the term 'post-marxism' carries more than a passing allusion to 'post-modernism': in a sense, post-marxism is marxism reformulated in light of profound changes in the topography of what has become a postmodern world (Laclau 1993, 329). The 'post-' of post-marxism thereby signifies the abandonment of those axioms that Laclau and Mouffe call 'essentialist' (1985, 47). Their deconstruction of these essentialisms has caused much controversy among other marxist theoreticians (Geras 1985), and in a sense this con-troversy exists actually *because* their analysis of the social, political, ideological and economic takes the form of a *deconstruction*.

For, deconstruction itself is controversial. Often, it is not generally recognized as being 'political' at all, or of any use to political analysis – especially not before Laclau and Mouffe's intervention (Bennington 1994, 6). As a tool for literary analysis, and occa-sionally for drawing out philosophical themes within texts, deconstruction is often construed as being something worthwhile only in so far as it constitutes a radical form of *reading* (Weber 1987). But Laclau and Mouffe use deconstruction to read the texts of classical marxism, and to reassess and reformulate them according to this peculiar reading practice.

Already it is possible to see that 'post-marxism' is far from being *proper* marxism: the way that it denies some of the central tenets of marxism and applies a form of analysis, often deemed anarchic and even irrational, to political texts, has led 'post-marxism' to be received as a *transgression* of marxism, or even as *not marxist at all*. But, Laclau and Mouffe argue, their critical analysis of marxist categories and their subsequent construction of a deconstructed and deconstructive post-marxist paradigm (1985, 14; Mowitt 1992, 17), constitutes a necessary reinvigoration and radicalization of the tradition, which is the only way to keep open the possibility of the marxist project, as a valid and viable political force. Let us trace the outline of their argument, as presented in *Hegemony and Socialist Strategy*, and indicate its subsequent development, and the ways it has contributed to contemporary understanding of the nature of 'the political' (Beardsworth 1996, xi), before suggesting its limitations.

In the opening movement of the book, Laclau and Mouffe focus on the social conditions characterizing 'revolutionary situations'. Reading Rosa Luxemburg's analysis of these situations, they argue that

> in a revolutionary situation, it is impossible *to fix the literal sense* of each isolated struggle, because each struggle overflows its own literality and comes to represent, in the consciousness of the masses, a simple moment of a more global struggle against the system. And so it is that while in a period of stability the class consciousness of the worker … is 'latent' and 'theoretical', in a revolutionary situation the *meaning* of every mobilization appears, so to speak, as split: aside from its specific literal demands, each mobilization represents the revolutionary process as a whole; and these totalizing effects are visible in the overdetermination of some struggles by others. This is, however, nothing other than the defining characteristic of the symbol: the overflowing of the signifier by the signified. *The unity of the class is therefore a symbolic unity.* (1985, 10–11)

Here, the 'literal meaning' of an event is shown to depend on the context in which it occurs, or in which it is interpreted and given meaning. The literal meaning of anything – what semiotics calls 'denotation' – cannot be divorced from its 'connotation' (Hall 1980, 133), and both the connotation and denotation of a signifier (whether a word, image or historical event) will always be established within the confines of a certain context: the same signifier will connote and denote very different things (signifieds or referents) in different contexts, depending on the context in which it occurs (as well as the infinite range of possible contexts in which it could thereafter be interpreted) (Derrida 1977, 1–25). In the case of a revolutionary political situation, as Laclau and Mouffe argue, any particular event in that struggle will attain a meaning in which it is 'equivalent' to all other events in that struggle, no matter how 'different' it might *literally* be. The *meaning* of any event (what it 'stands for', what it 'symbolizes') will arise as a result of the 'overdetermina-tion' (Laplanche and Pontalis 1988, 292) of the context in which it occurs, or the context in which it is interpreted.

In the revolutionary situation described by Laclau and Mouffe, the 'event' and its 'interpretation' take place in the same 'context' – that of the 'revolutionary situation' itself. But it is important to note that the meaning of an event is open to the possibility of being renarrated in different contexts, so that it will *mean* – and even '*be*' – something entirely different. In this example, though, Laclau and Mouffe are concerned with the meaning of an event within the interpretive context of a 'revolutionary situation', and not with its meaning 'outside' or 'after' that situation. Later on, they consider the importance of the reiteration of an event's meaning *into* different discursive contexts, as a key moment of articulating (connecting, constructing, saying, representing) a certain desired *meaning* to *any* event, so that its meaning becomes *relatively fixed* within the socio-political imaginary, thus enabling it to work (or, to *tend* to work) for the purposes of a certain political project.

That is to say, in a revolutionary situation, the meaning of all events will be over-determined by the revolutionary factors bearing on their significance or status as events. So, in a non-revolutionary situation, were a group of workers to strike for better pay or better working conditions, then that strike would not *necessarily* symbolize any general cause or struggle. In a revolutionary situation, in which an entire society has become polarized into two opposing camps (say, the 'people' versus the 'aristocracy' or *'ancien régime'*, in the manner of the French Revolution), then when a particular group strikes, it will symbolize the entire struggle, the entire plight of 'the people'. In Laclau and Mouffe's terms, in such a situation, or context, whatever 'the people' do – however *different* each act is – it will be *equivalent* in status and meaning when considered in terms of the general struggle: it will be a symbol of and for it. For as long as the struggle persists, it will be immensely important to each side of the struggle to *reiterate* a certain meaning for these events, in order that, over time, and through the 'regularity in dispersion' of these reiterations, the meaning which best serves the cause will become consolidated and sedimented as 'true' in the minds, or imaginary, of as many people as possible. The meanings which *tend* to become dominant in the social-political imaginary, and which work to strengthen a particular cause, political position or power structure, will, in Laclau and Mouffe's terms, have become hegemonic, working to constitute, represent and perpetuate the dominant hegemony or dominant hegemonic political position.

Another way to put this would be to say that, in such a situation, certain acts or events would have a *synonymous meaning*. In a revolutionary situation, then events as ostensibly *different* as strikes, graffiti, petitions, pamphlets, the formation of unions and other social bonds, even terrorism, violence, conflict, law-breaking and refusals to conform to certain tasks (taxpaying, voting, etc.), would all be synonymous with and symbols *of and for* 'the cause'. On the other hand, in a non-revolutionary situation, then such events would not necessarily be interpreted as *equivalent* symbols of a unified struggle against the dominant hegemony in the popular imaginary (the 'hearts and minds' and practices of the populace). They would perhaps *tend* to be interpreted as unique 'differences' *within* the hegemony, or differences (classified, say, as differences of personal opinion) that could be resolved without changing the established institutional dynamics of society (the *status quo* of a social hegemony).

The example of the synonym is helpful. For, whereas in conventional usage, any given word will have a certain set of general synonyms – for example 'truth' is conventionally synonymous with 'fact', 'reality', 'certainty', 'accuracy', 'genuineness', 'precision', and so on – in a precise discursive context, for example that of a novel, poem (or literary genre, generally), a political manifesto or philosophical treatise, it might become synonymous with very different words (note that none of the synonyms of 'truth' listed above actually name a concrete or tangible *referent* themselves). Staying with our hypothetical revolutionary situation, 'truth' might become synonymous with 'the cause', 'the plight of the people', 'emancipation from exploitation and oppression'. That is because, in that situation, the context is highly overdetermined. But, it is important to note, the same process of *the overdetermination of meaning takes place in all contexts*. In fact, the *tendency* to establish (articulate) certain meanings in certain ways can be viewed as one of the ways of defining or delimiting the notion of 'context' itself. So, where, in existentialist philosophy, 'truth' will be constructed in such a way as to be read as 'absurdity', perhaps, elsewhere, as in romantic poetry, it will be constructed so as to be synonymous with 'nature', or, in religious contexts, it will mean 'God' or 'the Divine', and so on.

In this way it can be seen that 'truth' itself is a 'floating signifier' (Laclau and Mouffe 1985, 171; Laclau 1996, 36). That is, as semiotics has shown, it is not *necessarily* attached to any final signified, or precise referent. It all depends, in Laclau and Mouffe's terms, on 'precise discursive conditions of emergence'. In the discourse of classical marxism, the 'truth' of social 'reality' lies with the economic base of any given society. This means that, for such marxists, the *real, fundamental* situation of human societies is that there are, first and foremost, *material economic factors* which determine everything about that society. For instance, the location of a source of raw materials, along with the viability, presence or possible presence of the other factors of production (land, labour, capital) will govern the decision (Mouffe 1996, 54) to locate (or not to locate) a factory thereabouts. As such, it is by way of the dictates of the economic base that the presence and form of *any* social activity is determined. So, for classical marxism, it is true to say that *the economy is determinant in the first and last instance of social relations*. In marxist terms, the effects of the determination of all aspects of society by the economy are felt nowhere more profoundly than in a society operating under a capitalist economy, where the population is displaced and located according to the dictates of profitability, and where the fate of nations is determined according to decisions made by capitalists. In terms of this 'truth', then, classical marxism sees a distinction between the constitutive factor of the 'economic base', and the subordinate element of the 'ideological superstructure'. This second term, the 'super-structure', names the lived relations of a society: its beliefs, practices and relationships – the family structure, the educational apparatus, religious institutions, the whole infrastructure and its attendant systems of values, truths or 'ideology'. (But, immediately, post-marxism points out, it is really quite impossible to maintain the distinction between base and superstructure, as they are symbiotic, overlapping and non-separable, which is why they offer the more Foucauldian term of 'discourse', to indicate the entire structure, rather than maintain the impossible *essentialist* distinction (1985, 174).)

For marxism, this base/superstructure relationship is held in place and operates success-fully (for capitalists, who hold power and extract excess profit) only on the basis of 'false consciousness' or 'ideology'. 'False consciousness' is anything which prevents 'the masses' from perceiving the 'truth' of their situation: namely, anything which blocks their 'knowledge' of the 'fact' that they are exploited, in so far as the fruits of their labour ('profit': 'surplus value') are being illegitimately extracted from their work (alienation) and are going to those who do not, *by rights* or *justifiably*, deserve it, i.e. the capitalists who own the factors of production, including, actually, *the workers themselves*.

In the terms of classical marxism, then, it is the blinkers of 'false consciousness' instituted by 'capitalist ideology' that need to be overcome, overthrown: the classical argument therefore emphasizes that the workers of the world need consciously to realize their own economic exploitation (Marx and Engels 1967). But before this can happen, they must realize that their beliefs as to what is 'natural' and 'true' about society and social relations are all part and parcel of capitalist ideology. This is the realm of the ideological super-structure: the lived beliefs and practices of everyone's everyday lives. Louis Althusser's statements about the 'ideological state apparatuses' in 'Ideology and Ideological State Apparatuses' exemplify this position (Althusser 1971).

However, as Laclau and Mouffe argue, the base/superstructure argument of marxism is flawed by a certain essentialism. This essentialism, they argue, takes the form of a belief in the simple fixed identity of notions like 'individual', 'class' and 'society'. Instead of preserving the kind of thinking which takes an 'individual' to be a member of a 'class' a class which is itself a coherent part of a coherent 'society', Laclau and Mouffe focus on these terms themselves. What is an 'individual'? What is a 'class'? And what is 'society'? They subject such notions to a rigorous deconstruction, by way of inquiring into the relationship between the *concept* (for example, the concept of 'working class') and the *referent* which is thought to be signified by that term (in this example, the concept or signifier of 'working-class subject' would be tied necessarily to some specific living person, exemplifying and representing *the* 'working class').

The first essentialism that Laclau and Mouffe point to is this kind of referential thinking: namely, *that* someone who occupies at certain times a 'working-class subject position' *is therefore* 'a member of the working class', purely, simply and entirely. They argue that while it is true that at certain times in certain people's lives, they will quite literally occupy what are deemed to be working-class subject positions, it is equally likely that such a person who at times qualifies as being 'working class', will at other times occupy a contradictory 'subject position', one not consistent with being a 'working-class subject'. They argue that this referential essentialism has led to theoretical 'confusion' in marxist theory (1985, 119), as it has led thinkers to either the 'logically illegitimate conclusion . . . that the other positions occupied by these agents are also "working-class positions" ' or, alternatively, to argue that these contradictions in the variety and inconsistency of 'subject positions' occupied by 'working-class' subjects has come about as the result of some 'separating' power of capitalism, working in the 'superstructure'. That is to say, Laclau and Mouffe disagree with much marxist theory in the sense that they deny it is ever simply the case that there is an essential unity to the 'working class', a unity extending to all the possible subject positions occupied by all the 'individuals' who make up the 'class'. Whereas earlier marxist theory would consider ideological contradictions to be the result of the divisive power of capitalism, used in order to perpetuate the mystification and delusion of subjects who would otherwise be able to see the truth of their situation as the exploited working class, Laclau and Mouffe disagree. They argue that many of the problems of theoretical marxism have been brought on by their own manner of theorizing: marxism they argue, theorizes the 'individual' as being a referent, 'individuals' as the being 'origin and basis of social relations' (1985, 115), and 'society' itself as actually *being a* '*thing*', a referent.

However, as the passage cited above reveals, Laclau and Mouffe argue that any 'class unity' that might occur – a unity in which individuals see themselves as part of a class, and act as a class, in unity – will only by a *symbolic identification*. It is the work of symbolic signification which has the power to make or break the notion of 'class' as a valid political force. But what this means is that, in stark distinction to traditional marxist theories of political action and transformation, it is quite possible that members of many different classes could identify with the symbol of a political struggle, and become identifiable as a *consciously unified* group, struggling for a particular political transformation.

The key point here is that political groups need not essentially consist of members of the same class: the traditional conception of 'class' is 'essentialist' and 'confused'. Nor are 'political groups' total and complete – they are rather *partial and provisional identifications* with a cause. Unity will not be complete, total or permanent. As soon as the cause is lost, won or dissipates, the group will effectively cease to exist. The *identity* of the group has no *essence* outside of the *antagonism*, around, against and in terms of which it constructed itself. Thus, they argue, one should not *identify* political agents with named or real *referents*. A political identity will be formed in relation to a political issue (an antagonism); that identity is not the whole or entire identity of the person or persons who hold it, even though some political antagonisms persist to such an extent that the identities of certain people and groups will be dominated and overdetermined to a massive extent by these political antagonisms. One need only mention those political antagonisms that can be expressed under the headings of racism, sexism, homophobia, xenophobia, ethnocentrism, anti-Semitism, imperialism, exploitation, oppression and discrimination on many other grounds in order to appreciate this possibility – and also to see the implication of very many contextual factors in the determination and establishment of all 'individual' subjectivity.

Thus a theory of the political cannot theorize in terms of 'individuals'. For the 'identity' if an individual will depend on contextual factors in precisely the same way that, in Saussurean linguistics and semiotics, the identity of a signifier will depend on the position it occupies within a signifying structure – it will be overdetermined by a context. This application of semiotic insights to the theory of the identity of 'individuals' or 'subjects' constitutes a radical contribution to political theory. But, Laclau and Mouffe also bring psychoanalytic considerations to bear on political analysis (especially since Slavoj Žižek's involvement with their project), exploring the roles played by the imaginary and fantasy within the political domain (Žižek 1989). All of these perspectives expand the field of the political and transform the nature of any consideration of the political from the simplicity of thinking about 'individuals' *in* 'society'.

For, just as looking at 'individuals' will miss profound *discursive* or *structural* elements relevant to the study of political issues – especially the political issues related to the construction of an 'individual' subjectivity itself (for the notion of the 'individual' implicitly takes the identity of that 'individual' to be set and already established, while Laclau and Mouffe show how any 'individual identity' will be constituted by factors such as the very fact of their involvement in a struggle) – they also point out that the object of political analysis termed 'society', 'the social' or 'socius', is not only *not* pre-given, already-existing, established, unified and 'objectively real' (which it is often assumed to be), but that, in actual fact, *society does not exist* (Žižek, in Laclau 1990, 249).

This point deserves further clarification. The point is that 'society' or 'the social' is not a *thing* (or *referent*). It is a 'construct', or a 'figure', without a final signified. You cannot put your finger on any object and declare that *it is* society. There is no object which objectively *is* society. Laclau and Mouffe proceed broadly in accordance with semiotics, in arguing that 'society' functions as a signifier, but it has no final signified. Everyone 'knows' what it 'means' (although this meaning will differ in its representation, from context to context), but no one could put their finger on some*thing* that 'is' the '*essence*' of the social. Semiotically speaking, 'society' or 'the social' has no denotative signified of itself, 'essentially', there being no *thing* which *is* the social. There are *figures* of and for the social/society (metonymies, metaphors, symbols, etc.), but 'society' is itself already a 'figuration' or a 'construct' for something which, Laclau and Mouffe argue, is *constitutively absent* (Laclau and Mouffe 1985, 125). It is in this sense that they can argue that 'society' does not exist.

But, of course, 'society' or 'the social' *does exist*. It is just that our thinking of what it means to say that something exists has to be reassessed (Spivak, in Derrida 1974, xiv).

'Society' does not exist as an *essence* residing somewhere, fully present and intelligible in any way. It is rather a construct, or as Slavoj Žižek says, it exists as 'ideological fantasy'. It is a signifier that has no adequate signified, but only partial, provisional and insufficient signifiers of 'itself'. Indeed, whenever a signifier of 'society' or 'the social' is presented as being *the* signifier *of* 'society' – examples might range from the figure of the monarch (or a rebel) to the results of a census or a table of statistics about a society – it is immediately obvious that this representation is not that society *itself*, that it in no way captures the 'essence' of the society, that there would seem to be so much more to it than that. This is because, as Laclau and Mouffe point out, 'the totality is not a datum but a construction' (1985, 144), and always both less and more than any given signifier of it. They refer to this effect as that of the 'surplus of meaning', an effect which is the result of the semiotic fact that because 'identities are purely relational ... there is no identity which can be fully constituted' (1985, 111).

This formulation of the relational character of identities here means not only the identity of linguistic or discursive terms, but also even what we tend to think of as the 'identity' of 'individuals', the identity of institutions and even those of historical events. None of these identities are 'fixed', but rather all identities are the effect or result of their relationships with other identities, and the relationships between identities (it being the *relationship* in which an identity is placed or articulated that determines the meaning and being of that identity) are established in what Laclau and Mouffe term 'discourse'.

To stay with the concept of 'the social' or 'society', we can say that, because it is intelligible, or because we all know what it is, even though 'it' is a construct with no ultimate referent, this intelligibility has been constructed by *discourse*: discourses of value, which assert what society *is like* or *should be like*, using the term rhetorically (through analogy), and empirical discourses, using statistical constructs which take parts as indicators of the whole (metonymically). The features of rhetorical or value-based discourses and those of empirical discourses mark the coordinates of all discourses of the social. Historical, literary, anthropological, governmental and bureaucratic discourses and so on, all incorporate the *evaluatory* and the ostensibly *referential* in order to suture the meaning of 'society'.

Sutured means stitched together, weaved or fabricated. It is a textile and textual metaphor, as is the notion or concept of 'text' itself. The suturing of the notion of 'society', so that it means something whole, complete, knowable, etc., implies what Laclau and Mouffe call (using a Foucauldian expression) the 'regularity in dispersion' of its reiteration in many and varied discursive contexts (1985, 142): the signification of 'society' (or any term) becomes partially fixed (yet always open to the polysemy of many possible meanings) only on the basis of its regular deployment as a signifier, in familiar ways, in everyday discourses (educational, governmental, familial, media and so on), throughout time and space. Laclau and Mouffe invoke the Lacanian concept of the *point de capiton*, or 'quilting point', to explain the way that meaning becomes relatively fixed within different discursive contexts. These quilting points are overdetermined by their status within discourses (examples might include the idea of 'Man', the 'individual' or 'God'), and they prevent the slippages of meaning that would occur in interpretation were there no relatively stable terms to refer to in communicating or interpreting. Their stability is a result of the work of their 'regularity in dispersion' throughout dominant discourses. But a deconstructive analysis of the situations in which they are used to structure meaning reveals that, despite their 'obvious' intelligibility or their transparency of meaning, it remains impossible to identify a concrete signified or referent for them other than through connotation, metaphor, metonymy, symbol and other such literary or poetic techniques. This leads to the peculiarity in which even the ostensible literality of speaking about the 'individual' reveals itself to be figurative language! Thus it can be shown that even the objectivity of objective language is itself a construction which relies on rhetorical, textual, poetic, and otherwise literary techniques, or, as Laclau and Mouffe say, 'all discourse of fixation becomes metaphorical: literality is, in actual fact, the first of all metaphors' (1985, 111).

In a sense, all of this runs contrary to all discourses that claim to be objective. It goes against them, and it implicitly rejects all claims made in the name of *neutral* objectivity. Even objectivity, in post-marxism, is *not neutral*, but is rather *contestable* and, hence, *political*. This reading of objectivity as a non-neutral (hence, political) construct subverts the notion of objectivity and the authority of discourses claiming to be objective. As such, for 'objective discourses', what we have just asserted will always be inadmissible – for, were it to be accepted, then it would enable the contestation of the authority of authoritative discourses and authoritative structures of power and knowledge. In Laclau and Mouffe's terms, we have just located a site of antagonism (1985, 122). Antagonism cannot be objective, as it will arise by virtue of an experience of objective relations that are experienced as being *unjust* or *wrong* (1985, 125). They explore the example of the development of feminism (1985, 154), in which the claims for the equal rights of women were *articulated* with reference to the *ethos* and *telos* of equality and democracy. But, they point out, 'in order to be mobilized in this way, the democratic principle of liberty and equality had first to impose itself as the new matrix of the social imaginary; or, in our terminology, to constitute a fundamental nodal point in the construction of the political' (1985, 154–5).

Thus it was the institution of 'democracy' as a *point de capiton* which paved the way for the possibility of the birth of feminism. In their terms, it was the democratic revolution which constituted the conditions of possibility for the emergence of feminist/sexist antagonisms *as* antagonisms and for the construction of a democratic feminist struggle. In fact, Laclau and Mouffe locate, in the democratic revolution, or in the concept of democracy itself, a profound transformation of the range of possibilities for 'politics', in a radical extension of the entire political terrain, moving *the political* into every relation and institution which has a place (or does not yet have a place) in every aspect of every sense that can be signified by the notion of 'society'. As they argue:

> The 'democratic revolution', as a new terrain which supposes a profound mutation at the symbolic level, implies a new form of institution of the social. In earlier societies, organized in accordance with a theological-political logic, power was incorporated in the person of the prince ... the radical difference which democratic society introduces is that the site of power becomes an empty space ... The possibility is thus opened up of an unending process of questioning ... (1985, 186)

When society is no longer considered to be organized according to some theological hierarchy based on 'divine right', then the members of that society must bear the responsibility for *its* (*their own*) organization. If society's hierarchies and institutions are deemed to be unjust, then democratic principles enable the contestation of that situation on the basis of appeals to justice and equality. In post-marxism, then, democracy promises to be the best means of assuring that any injustice, exploitation and oppression can be countered, and that *all* power be accountable, precisely because democratic principles contain within themselves the basis of their own critique and contestation. The advent of this new kind of politics, Laclau and Mouffe argue, initiated a political logic that they term 'hegemony'.

Their theory of hegemony and hegemonic politics takes its inspiration from the work of Antonio Gramsci, who theorized hegemony as the name of a mechanism of socio-political organization in which:

> previously germinated ideologies become 'party', come into confrontation and conflict, until one of them or at least a combination of them tends to prevail, to gain the upper hand, to propagate itself throughout society – bringing about not only a unison of economic and political aims, but also intellectual and moral unity, posing all the questions around which the struggle rages, not on a corporate but on a 'universal' plane, and thus creating the hegemony of a fundamental group over a series of subordinate groups. (Gramsci 1971, 181–2)

The key difference between Gramsci's model and that of Laclau and Mouffe lies in the latter's emphasis on the discursive construction of every political identity, in that identities do not exist *before* their construction around antagonisms. This is the reason why the post-marxists talk of 'subject positions' as opposed to 'subjects', as political identities are partial, provisional and constantly in a state of flux. Accordingly, Laclau and Mouffe emphasize the prime importance of the '*tendency*': the *tendency* to represent certain issues or figures in a certain way, the *tendencies* by which certain issues are articulated as equivalent or different, related or separate, and so on. For it is the 'regularity in dispersion' of manners of representation and modes of articulation that governs the character of a political hegemony, and so any changes at the point of representation or articulation will affect changes throughout an entire hegemonic structure – a structure that encompasses all areas of the social, political and institutional make-up of a society.

Strong criticisms of post-marxism have come from within marxist political theory itself, and these have been widely detailed elsewhere (Lechte 1994, 191). But perhaps the most interesting, challenging and *widely unacknowledged* critique of post-marxism actually comes from within the very field of literary and cultural studies from which post-marxism took its formative analyses of the symbol and other 'literary' tools. As you will recall, post-marxist political theory developed by way of recourse to literary theoretical and deconstructive techniques of textual analysis. Yet, in reading Laclau and Mouffe, the *debt* (Derrida 1994) they owe to the theory of the text, as developed by Barthes, Derrida, Kristeva and so on, is given little attention. John Mowitt has argued that both this oversight, as well as their use of the Foucauldian notion of 'discourse' in preference to that of 'text' (even though they actually use 'text' to define 'discourse' (Mowitt 1992, 15)), constitutes *a limitation of the radical implications of the theory of the text – a theory that was already, from the outset, profoundly political and subversive*. Mowitt urges 'political' academia not to forget the 'textual paradigm' by accepting the 'discourse paradigm' of the post-marxists, because, in his sense, the concept of 'discourse' is a lot less radical and political than that of 'text' in the work of Barthes, Derrida and Kristeva (Mowitt 1992). Indeed, there would be a certain compelling logic at play – a deconstructive logic, at least – were we to *return* to the 'literary' theory that *supplemented* the genesis of post-marxism, in order to look once again at that ostensibly purely '*literary* theory', and to examine how profoundly political it already is, *or could be – were it read accordingly*. The relationship between the 'literary' and the 'political' is intimate, and perhaps it would be a political error to subordinate the one to the other, as is the *tendency* of many modes and manners of *articulation* and *representation* within the *hegemony* of political or literary study.

Paul Bowman

Further reading and works cited

Althusser, L. *Lenin and Philosophy.* New York, 1971.
Arditi, B. and Valentine, J. *Polemicization.* Edinburgh, 1999.
Beardsworth, R. *Derrida and the Political.* London and New York, 1996.
Bennington, G. *Legislations.* London, 1994.
de Man, P. 'The Epistemology of Metaphor', in *On Metaphor*, ed. S. Sacks. Chicago, 1978.
Derrida, J. *Of Grammatology*, intro. G. Chakravorty Spivak. Baltimore, MD, 1974.
—. *Limited Inc.* Evanston, IL, 1977.
—. *Specters of Marx.* London, 1994.
Geras, N. 'Post-Marxism?', *New Left Review*, 163, 1985.
Gramsci, A. *Selections from the Prison Notebooks of Antonio Gramsci*, eds Q. Hoare and G. Nowell
    Smith. New York, 1971.
Hall, S. *Culture, Media, Language.* London, 1980.
Laclau, E. *New Reflections on the Revolution of Our Time.* London, 1990.
—. 'Politics and the Limits of Modernity', in *Postmodernism.* London, 1993.
—. *The Making of Political Identities.* London, 1994.
—. *Emancipation(s).* London, 1996.
— et al. *Contingency, Hegemony, Universality.* London, 2000.
—. 'Politics, Polemics and Academics: An Interview by Paul Bowman', *parallax*, 11, 1999.
— and Mouffe, C. *Hegemony and Socialist Strategy.* London, 1985.
Laplanche, J. and Pontalis, J.-B. *The Language of Psychoanalysis.* London, 1988.
Lechte, J. *Fifty Key Contemporary Theorists.* London, 1994.
Marx, K. and Engels, F. *The Communist Manifesto.* St Ives, 1967.
Mouffe, C. *The Return of The Political.* London, 1993.
— (ed.) *Deconstruction and Pragmatism.* London, 1996.
—. *The Challenge of Carl Schmitt.* London, 1999.
Mowitt, J. *Text: The Genealogy of an Antidisciplinary Object.* Durham, NC, 1992.
Smith, A. M. *Laclau and Mouffe.* London, 1998.
Torfing, J. *New Theories of Discourse.* London, 1999.
Weber, S. *Institution and interpretation.* Minneapolis, MN, 1987.
Žižek, S. *The Sublime Object of Ideology.* London, 1989.

Psychoanalysis in Literary and Cultural Studies

In 'In Memory of Sigmund Freud', W. H. Auden expresses the challenge represented by Freud to entrenched powers, to systems and structures that satisfied some by oppressing others, evidenced by the burning of Freud's books by the Nazi regime and by his death in exile. While it is by no means unique, this explicitly political reading of the significance of psychoanalysis is useful as the starting point for an exploration of the relationship between psychoanalysis and literary and cultural studies over the last sixty years. The poem reveals that which constitutes the core of the relationship. Auden celebrates Freud's lifework in part because he sees its effects – 'the fall of princes' – as analogous to those of poetry. Psychoanalysis, like poetry, has effects beyond its own boundaries as theory and practice. Indeed, for Auden, both poetry and psychoanalysis challenge the very boundaries that keep in place the political status quo. It is this analogy, its interactions, enmeshments and various consequences, that has come to dominate the current cultural use of psycho-analysis. In the contemporary life of the humanities in Britain, the relationship between psychoanalysis and cultural criticism is not that of a couple, but rather of a *ménage à trois*. To put this another way, if ideally the relationship between literary and cultural studies and psychoanalysis is that of a dialogue (Donald 1991, 3), what they speak to each other about is politics.

The difficulty with this *ménage*, however, is that none of the participants holds one position for very long. If literature and psychoanalysis occupy analogous positions in their relationships to politics, it can also be said that literary studies came to need psychoanalysis because of the revelation of its own political implications. As postwar Britain experienced a shift in terms of established loyalties, an expanding educational sector and the beginnings of a consumer culture, so an English studies dominated by Leavisite definitions of cultural value seemed less and less viable. Leavis had eschewed all approaches to literature, psychoanalytic criticism included, which privileged a pre-existing agenda over the literary work itself. In contrast, the work, among others, of Raymond Williams and Richard Hoggart in the 1950s concerned itself with making 'the experiences of ordinary people and the texture of everyday life... a legitimate and necessary focus of concern' (Donald 1991, 4) for explicitly political purposes. Rather than something to be defended against or 'cured' by Leavis's 'minority culture', working-class *culture* became itself an object of critical interest and a site of potential political change. As part of this challenge, traditional definitions of literary value were revealed as complicit with the operation of self-interest on the part of the powerful. 'Great' literature was that which upheld the status quo, which reconfirmed the validity of bourgeois privilege, which mystified economic determinacy. It is in these marxist critiques that British cultural studies originates and consequently so too does the problem of talking about a specifically 'literary' studies. Just as the position of English studies became established within the British academy, Williams and others began its undoing. It is less the texts themselves that come under scrutiny, rather the methods and values of the literary critical establishment.

The desire of critics such as Williams and Hoggart to focus on the 'everyday' and 'lived' experiences of 'ordinary people', both as individuals and collectively, would seem to overlap with psychoanalysis's concentration on the quotidian. The marxist critics of the 1950s too began to question orthodox explanations for the relationship between the individual and the social, between consciousness and history, between inside and outside. Their focus on working-class culture and identity forced a rereading and reinterpretation of literary and cultural production and of historical events. What they also did, however, was to assume that 'working-class identity', however sophisticated its critical construction, fitted neatly with individual consciousness; that indeed 'identity' as such was what was being observed. Here, rather than mirroring it, psychoanalysis, with its central concept of the unconscious, 'explodes the very idea of complete or achieved identity to which [the marxist critics] ascribe such critical and political importance' (Donald 1991, 5). The unconscious as theorized by psychoanalysis is that which does not fit, which exceeds our control, our reason, our ability to know. It is that which intrudes when it is least wanted, which undoes our mastery, which challenges the whole notion of identity. In his analysis of the Rat Man, Freud uses the concept of ambivalence to explain his patient's symptoms, in particular his habit of constructing long prayers to cover his unconscious wishes.

> This became clearly evident in our patient on one occasion, for the disturbing element did not remain unconscious but made its appearance openly. The words he wanted to use in his prayers were, '*May God protect her*', but a hostile '*not*' suddenly darted out of his unconscious and inserted itself into the sentence. (*SE*, 10, 242)

It is the presence of that 'not' wherein lies the 'not enough' of Williams's matching of politics with literary and cultural criticism; it is the explanation of that 'not' that constitutes the significance of psychoanalysis as a theory. While for later political positions it is precisely for this reason that use is made of psychoanalysis, what the application of psychoanalysis to such marxist analyses demonstrates is something that is repeated over and over in its conjunction with politics and cultural criticism. First, it is the place and definition of the unconscious that is of the essence (Rustin 1995, 241); second, any position that is predicated on the notion of the unconscious contains the seeds of its own undoing, of the revelation of its own 'not enough'. In the historical survey which follows, the relations between the participants in our *ménage à trois* are effects of the unconscious as much as of any theoretical choice, and as such undo, reform, regroup and shout 'not' at awkward moments. What is significant, though, is that each case, each position, each relation resists stasis, and, in its contradictions and paradoxes, points beyond. It is the theoretical possibilities and problematics of going 'beyond' in which the significance of psychoanalysis for literary and cultural studies in the British academy originated and by which it is still constituted – beyond common-sense ways of reading, beyond conventional categories, beyond the either/or of traditional debate. Further, it is this question of a going 'beyond' which forms psychoanalytic criticism's debates with other theoretical and critical positions, most significantly those with deconstruction.

The origins of the current importance of psychoanalysis in British literary and cultural studies can be found in the wider political and intellectual change of the 1960s. In part because of the expansion of higher education, the academy began to be seen as complicit with the establishment, and this cosy consensus was challenged from a number of positions. The belief that intellectual life produced 'objective knowledge' was revealed as a powerful fantasy by those who were not white or male or from a privileged class. Identity and its political implications began to move to the centre of debates in the humanities. Interest began to focus on its construction, its meaning, its place in continuing traditional divisions of privilege and power. Two things marked this as different from both earlier left-wing political analyses and from early marxist cultural criticism. First, analysis moved from a focus on economics, the 'base' in traditional marxist terms, to a consideration of culture, the 'superstructure', as also a determinant in the construction of the social world. Second, identity was no longer defined just as a matter of class, but of ethnicity, gender and sexuality, and an awareness grew that class-based methods could not simply be transferred unchanged to these. The question became: what part does culture play in constructing or challenging identities which perpetuate the status quo? As suggested above, however, previous attempts to unite cultural criticism and an explicit left-wing position had come unstuck around the very concept of identity. In the 1960s, the work of two structuralist analyses provided frameworks within which the question could begin to be answered; this work, taken together, suggested possibilities for the coming together of political and cultural analyses via a renewed psychoanalysis.

Jacques Lacan had begun his 'return to Freud', first within and then outside the French psychoanalytic institution, during the 1930s. His work only began to be more widely disseminated outside psychoanalytic training circles, however, in the 1960s, with the publication of *Écrits* in Paris (1966). Lacan reread Freud as a radical challenge to conventional assumptions about the stability of identity, the primacy of the conscious and the autonomy of the individual that had come to dominate the psychoanalytic institution, particularly in the United States. In the notions of, most particularly, the imaginary, the symbolic and the 'mirror stage', Lacanian psychoanalysis provided cogent readings of the self-deceiving properties of language and culture. Identity is acquired and constantly renewed, not only through the oppressive operations of an external force, but because it affirms the human subject. 'Identity', however seemingly negative or oppressive, is a product of fantasy. Moreover, identity is acquired through the subject's insertion into and subjection to the determining systems of the symbolic, pre-eminently that of language.

At around the same time the work of Louis Althusser, who had long been a significant presence in French intellectual life, became more widely known with the publication of *For Marx* (1965), an attempt to retrieve marxism from the, for Althusser, distorting grasp of Christianity, humanism and economic determinacy. From Freud's *The Interpretation of Dreams*, and via Lacan's rereading of Freud, Althusser took the concept of 'overdetermination' to explain the relation between the economic level and ideology, that is the cultural, the social, the linguistic. For Freud, the relation between the latent content and the manifest content of a dream is one of overdetermination, carried out through, principally, condensation and displacement. Further, this relation exists between unconscious wishes and each place where, in a disguised form, they force their way into the conscious – slips of the tongue, jokes, day dreams, hysterical symptoms. For Althusser, although the modes of production are determining in 'the last instance', their effects are not self-evident at the level of ideology, but rather have to be read symptomatically, that is to say, they must be *analysed*. Ideology functions, then, as a disguise; it

> represents in its necessarily imaginary distortion not the existing relations of production (and the other relations that derive from them), but above all the (imaginary) relationship of individuals to the relations of production and the relations that derive from them. (Althusser 1971, 155)

Crucially, what both Lacan and Althusser focus on in their structuralist rereadings of Freud and Marx is the determining function of language in the creation of the subject. Whereas previous cultural criticism from the left struggled with the notion of subjectivity, a renewed psychoanalysis and a renewed marxism seemed to offer a coherent theory of the relation between the individual and the social.

While some literary and cultural critics have made use of psychoanalytic traditions other than the Lacanian, such as Klein, Winnicott and Hanna Segal, which can be broadly described as humanist, this has occurred mainly in the American academy (see Holland 1990). It is Lacanian psychoanalysis that dominates intellectual life in Britain. More particularly, the pattern of engagement between literary and cultural studies and psycho-analysis in the last three decades of the twentieth century is incomprehensible without an understanding of the intellectual history of feminism. It is largely feminist politics that has driven forward psychoanalytic engagement with cultural criticism. Indeed, this situation can be seen in part as a result of the problems inherent in the left's appropriation of psychoanalysis. Althusser had taken from Freud an account of subjectivity that he saw as useful for his explication of ideology. However, of course, psychoanalysis is an account of the construction of a *gendered* identity, not a class-based one. Increasingly, the use of psychoanalysis in cultural criticism became dominated by feminism. In his introduction to a series of talks given at the ICA in 1987 on psychoanalysis and cultural theory, James Donald admits that 'psychoanalysis' in British intellectual debate means 'psychoanalysis after the feminist rereading of Lacan's rereading of Freud' (Donald 1991, 2).

The significance of this in a British intellectual life increasingly concerned with a political reading of identity and its relation to the social and cultural can be seen in *Feminism and Psychoanalysis* (1974) by Juliet Mitchell. During the late 1960s she was closely associated with the British journal *New Left Review* and with its importation of Althusser. As Mitchell makes clear in her introduction, the feminists of the early second wave, particularly in the United States, were almost unanimous in seeing Freud and psychoanalysis as the enemy. For Germaine Greer, for example, psychoanalysis may accurately describe femininity as constructed within patriarchy, but it does nothing to undermine, critique or dismantle it. Rather, the theories of Freud and his followers are 'a farrago of moralism and fantasy unillumined by any shaft of commonsense' (Greer 1981, 95). For Mitchell, however, to continue this rejection would be 'fatal' for feminism precisely because psychoanalysis provides a theoretical model at odds with commonsense. An analysis that asserts things as self-evident will inevitably find itself re-enmeshed with the operations of oppression. While Freud's practice may or may not have been conservative, his 'discovery' of the unconscious provides a radical *theory* which is vital as the basis of a truly radical politics. Without it, any political theory or activism will inevitably collapse back into oppressive notions of identity and self, ultimately oppressive because reliant on an essence rather than seeing identity as constructed. Significantly, Mitchell makes clear both the influence of Lacan's theories and the absolute necessity of using it in tandem with Althusserian marxism.

> So where Marxist theory explains the historical and economic situation, psychoanalysis, in conjunction with the notions of ideology already gained by dialectical materialism, is the way into understanding ideology and sexuality. (Mitchell 1974, xxii)

What is particularly significant about Mitchell's reading of the situation is her assertion of a positive correlation between an openness to psychoanalytic theory and feminism as a radical political agenda (1974, 297–9). Psychoanalysis is paired, then, not with bourgeois orthodoxy, but with radical critiques concerned to reveal at the deepest level the workings of capitalism and patriarchy.

Although Mitchell does not foreground language, a general outcome of this position for cultural criticism can be seen by comparing two feminist readings of the same novel. In *Sexual Politics*, Kate Millett sees psychoanalysis as merely 'cloth[ing] the old doctrine of the separate spheres in the fashionable language of science' (1985, 178). In her reading of Charlotte Brontë's *Villette* (1853) she is concerned to read the novel as subversive, as radical in its critique of patriarchy. However, without a notion of the unconscious, Millett is forced to do this, not only by a problematic reading of the main character, Lucy Snowe, as if she were a real woman, but more problematically still, by assuming that both Brontë and Lucy Snowe are in control, that they know what they are doing, that their actions and behaviour are the results of conscious choice. Anything that contradicts this reading is dismissed by Millett as Brontë's necessary compromise with orthodox Victorian sensibility, what she describes as 'mawkish nonsense' (1985, 147). In comparison, Mary Jacobus' reading of the novel, which sees both it and literature in general as the reserve of both the repressed and its uncanny return, finds that it is at these very moments of 'nonsense' that the subversive, destabilizing effects of the novel are located (Jacobus 1987, 41–2). Significantly, what is being analysed is neither character nor writer, but *language*; *Villette* is 'a text formally fissured by its own repressions' (41). Psychoanalysis shows how, because of the effects of repression, things both say and do not say at the same time. Without this, criticism will merely repeat the obfuscations of ideology – in this case that reasoned choice is the foundation of political subversion. What this comparison makes clear then is the centrality of the unconscious for political readings of cultural products.

> The force of the psychoanalytic metaphor in this discourse derived from the idea that ideology was most effective when its distortions, its one-sidedness, its silences, and omissions became implicit and taken-for-granted routines, not depending on overt prohibition. (Rustin 1995, 229–30)

Interestingly, despite Mitchell's very early use of Lacan, it was American feminist writers that produced the first full-length attempts to work together Lacanian psychoanalysis, feminism and literary and cultural criticism. Shoshana Felman and Jane Gallop, in particular, developed sophisticated critical positions aware of the relationships *between* the three discourses, rather than taking for granted the usefulness of one as a meta-discourse. However, the feminism of Felman and Gallop lacks the materialist base of the dominant strands of British feminism, and as a result their use of psychoanalysis can seem a matter of hermeneutics rather than politics. So, for example, in her *Feminism and Psychoanalysis* (1982), Gallop criticizes Mitchell for her implicit assumption that together feminism and psychoanalysis point the way unproblematically to a political *practice*. In Mitchell's final claims for psychoanalysis, then, it would seem that she has forgotten the very thing which began her assertion of its necessity – the unconscious. In Gallop's own work, then, rather than making claims for psychoanalytic models of social change, she instead suggests 'attending to the odd truths revealed in the accidental material of language' (Gallop 1982, 29). For Gallop and Felman, Lacan's importance is as a theorist of language, and it is as a hermeneutics that it is potentially radical.

In Britain in the 1970s and early 1980s, feminist analyses using Lacanian psychoanalysis were most visible in politically radical interventions into and critiques of culture which went beyond the traditional focus of British literary criticism. The feminist journal *m/f*, co-founded by Parveen Adams and Elizabeth Cowie and published between 1978 and 1986, was the forum for many of the central debates, in particular the continued friction between the role of subjectivity and the place of materialist, class-based critiques. What the work published in *m/f* makes clear, though, is that this relation, however fraught, had come to occupy a pre-eminent place in intellectual critical debate. A 'pure' psychoanalytic criticism had become impossible in the British context.

The tensions and debates generated by this can be seen very clearly in another journal, *Screen* (which included Elizabeth Cowie on its editorial board, and published the work of, among others, Juliet Mitchell, Jacqueline Rose, Stephen Heath and Colin MacCabe), in particular the way in which a feminist political position sharpens the focus of a more general relation between psychoanalysis and cultural criticism. So, for example, in Laura Mulvey's seminal 'Visual Pleasure and Narrative Cinema', which first appeared in *Screen* in 1975, Lacanian psychoanalysis is explicitly used as a 'political weapon' to challenge the reproduction of the status quo through the 'magic' of the cinema (6). At the same time, however, Mulvey challenges *Screen* itself for ignoring 'the importance of the representation of the female form' and at the end suggests the implications of her analysis for feminist and other sorts of radical film-making (see essay on *Screen* for more detailed discussion of this). What Mulvey's intervention suggests, though, is that 'total', stable critical position is likely somewhere to be covering up its partial, self-interested position. Of course, it is this insight into and theorization of the non-rational in rational thought for which psychoanalysis is primarily responsible. What can be seen in the history of its use in the humanities in Britain is an acting out of this very insight.

A further inflection of this jostling for position can be seen in Lola Young's *Fear of the Dark: 'Race', Gender and Sexuality in the Cinema* (1996). Citing Mulvey's article, Young suggests how 'race' has been left out of feminist debates *because* of the latter's relation with psychoanalysis and its privileging of gender. Mulvey, she argues, in attempting to work out this relation ignores historical perspectives, does not differentiate between women and is oblivious to the extent to which her essay is about *white* people (16–17). Despite this, Young herself makes use of psychoanalysis in her theoretical framework because, she argues, materialist explanations of racial oppression privilege class over race and are unable to explain 'how the power relations embedded in textual systems and forms of representation may be unconsciously sustained' (17). On the other hand, she argues, critics who use psychoanalysis to unpick the construction of 'race' in cultural representation have ignored the difference that gender makes. Young criticizes the work of Homi K. Bhabha for this, and for precisely the absence of a materialist analysis.

> Bhabha does not express reservations about the use of psychoanalysis as a cultural theory: neither does he refer to any difficulty or tension which might exist because of what might be characterized as the cultural and temporal specificity of psychoanalytic theory or its lack of an historical and materialist base. (Young 1996, 29)

What is significant is that Young argues that the absence of a gender-based analysis *allows* Bhabha's other theoretical and methodological failings. To put it another way, it is the repression of one aspect that makes possible a supposedly water-tight theoretical position. Again, we see the insights of psychoanalysis being acted out in the very discourses that use psychoanalytic methods.

In the British context, the attempt to create a politically engaged critical position which uses psychoanalysis to investigate cultural representation without covering over these problematics finds its exemplar in the work of Jacqueline Rose. Situated at the intersection of psychoanalysis, feminist theory and literary studies, it attempts to use the insights of each to interrogate each from an explicitly political position and resists the use of any one discourse as a 'meta-discourse' (Rose 1993, 242–3). In 1982 Rose co-edited and, with Juliet Mitchell, translated and provided one of the introductions for a collection of articles by Lacan and other members of the *école freudienne*, most of which had not appeared in English before (Mitchell and Rose 1982). As well as contributing practically to the debate around Lacan's work in British intellectual life, what both introductions insist upon is that, rather than being just one aspect, debates about feminine sexuality have constructed psychoanalytic theory and psychoanalytic traditions as we know them. Its significance for feminist theory and practice is, then, incontrovertible. In her subsequent work, though, what is clear is that, while the concept of the unconscious is absolutely central, and is used, as in Lacan, to resist any normalizing focus on the ego, she resists any idealization of it as an 'outside' of oppressive political structures, as some feminist engagements with psychoanalysis have done, 'whether as writing or pre-oedipally or both' (Rose 1993, 42). In this way, Rose's work can be seen as different from and critiquing aspects of French feminism, for example *écriture féminine*. Rose's use of Melanie Klein in the 1990s has been a way of countering this idealization through an investigation of aggression and violence that does not just place it at the door of an 'external' patriarchy (1993, 41–71). While critiquing the position that sees 'woman's writing' as inherently subversive, though, Rose allows the language of the literary text its own interpretative status, its own strangeness and difficulty. Rose's *The Haunting of Sylvia Plath* (1991) is a celebrated example of this type of reading, and its exemplary position is shown by selections from it being included in a number of anthologies on psychoanalysis and literary criticism.

> In Rose's work, poetry and theory, feminism and psychoanalysis, politics and fantasy meet without either identifying with the other or affirming identity against the other. The assurance of stable identity that forgets the aberrant ways of sexuality, the fantasies of culture, or the autocracy of patriarchy has in her work been subjected to a sustained and eloquent critique. (Rose 1993, 12)

She is keen, though, not to privilege the literary sphere, for which she again criticizes a number of French theoretical positions (1993, 238), in particular that of Kristeva, and her work includes analysis of the visual, popular culture and contemporary political culture. It shows a nuanced and delicate balance between the critical discourses with which she engages.

However, the problem for feminism and indeed all politically engaged critical positions is that the psychoanalytic questioning of the constructions of identity lessens the possibility of the assertion of autonomous identity, and points to an impossibility in organizing politically around such claims. For example, Rose's claim that '[t]he question of identity is ... the central issue through which psychoanalysis enters the political field' (1986, 5) partly informs her critique of Derrida's critique of psychoanalysis and of deconstruction generally (1986, 19–23). For example, deconstruction cannot answer the question of 'how we can begin to think the question of violence and fantasy as something that implicates us as women' (Rose 1993, 106). However, on the other hand, her answer to the charge from cultural materialist feminists (Rose 1986, 11–12) that psychoanalysis does not provide adequate models of social change insists that it is vital for feminism because of its very questioning of the limits of subjectivity. A rejection of this would mean that oppression is sent out 'wholesale into the real from which it can only return as an inevitable and hallucinatory event' (1993, 106).

If politically radical critical positions have been responsible for the primacy of Lacanian psychoanalysis in literary and cultural studies over the last three decades, then in this relation can also be seen their discomfort. The question of whether anti-humanist positions can really inform radical political praxis remains. In Terry Eagleton's chapter on Freud in *The Ideology of the Aesthetic*, after a cogent analysis of the political implications of the superego and of the Freudian notion of desire, and of Freud's challenge to a separate realm of the aesthetic, the argument strangely retreats to an assertion of the transformative possibilities of morality or love. Freud is criticized for concentrating too much on Eros and not enough on Agape (Eagleton 1990, 284). In the end, as a resolution, Eagleton implies a distinction between Freud's theories and psychoanalysis as a practice. Freud provides no political solution to the problems of authority and aggression, but '[t]o acquire a more reciprocal, egalitarian style of loving is thus one of the goals of psychoanalysis as it is of revolutionary politics' (1990, 285). The problem here is that psychoanalysis is being forced to answer something, to solve something.

> Both Marxism and feminism, then, in incorporating psychoanalysis, have tried to use it as a way of articulating the individual with the social, or subjectivity with society. But they then tend to get caught up in acting out the conflict between the psychic and the social, rather than, as psychoanalysis itself does, producing a theory of that incompatibility. The lesson of psychoanalysis is that they have to be lived simultaneously as two irreconcilable positions – which is why we have an unconscious. (Donald 1991, 142)

It may be, however, that some kind of re-engagement with psychoanalysis as a practice will be the next set of repositionings in our ménage, indeed that it has already begun (Rose 1993, 255; Shamdasani 1994). British psychoanalysis has remained mostly impervious to the debates within the humanities. Any therapy cannot but retain some connection to the idea of cure, and since the structuralist and marxist challenges of the 1960s, the questioning of literary value, of the 'healing' possibilities of aesthetics and of a stabilizing identity has made crossover between the two unlikely. It may be that the feminist questioning and reformulation of psychoanalytic orthodoxies is located in the academy because of the inflexibility of psychoanalytic institutions themselves. However, what this survey has shown is that the profound importance of psychoanalytic theory is due to its ability to contain and explain contradictions, impossibilities, the presence and not-presence of that 'not' discussed above, and to describe a 'place' between two seemingly bounded positions, thereby unsettling them both. The poles of the ultimate failure of interpretation and of interpretation as cure are present indeed in Freud's work; it is perhaps time for a renegotiation of their mutual impossibility.

Leigh Wilson

Further reading and works cited

Adams, P. and Cowie, E. (eds) *The Woman in Question*. Cambridge, MA, 1990.
Althusser, L. *Lenin and Philosophy and Other Essays*. London, 1971.
Auden, W. H. *Collected Poems*. London, 1976.
Brennan, T. (ed.) *Between Feminism and Psychoanalysis*. London, 1989.
Donald, J. (ed.) *Psychoanalysis and Cultural Theory: Thresholds*. London, 1991.
Eagleton, T. *The Ideology of the Aesthetic*. Oxford, 1990.
Easthope, A. *Literary into Cultural Studies*. London, 1991.
—. *The Unconscious*. London, 1999.
Elliott, A. and Frosh, S. (eds) *Psychoanalysis in Contexts*. London, 1995.
Ellman, M. (ed.) *Psychoanalytic Literary Criticism*. London, 1994.
Freud, S. *The Standard Edition of the Complete Psychological Works of Sigmund Freud*, eds J. Strachey and A. Freud, 24 vols. London.
—. 'Notes upon a case of obsessional neurosis', *Standard Edition*, vol. 10, 1909.
Gallop, J. *Feminism and Psychoanalysis*. Basingstoke, 1982.
Greer, G. *The Female Eunuch*. London, 1981.
Holland, N. N. *Holland's Guide to Psychoanalytic Psychology and Literature-and-Psychology*. New York, 1990.
Jacobus, M. *Reading Women*. London, 1987.
Lacan, J. *Ecrits: A Selection*. London, 1977a.
—. *The Four Fundamental Concepts of Psycho-analysis*. London, 1977b.

—. 'Desire and the Interpretation of Desire in Hamlet', in *Literature and Psychoanalysis*, ed. S. Felman. Baltimore, MD, 1982.

—. 'Seminar on "The Purloined Letter"', in *The Purloined Poe*, eds J. P. Muller and W. J. Richardson. Baltimore, MD, 1988.

Lechte, J. (ed.) *Writing and Psychoanalysis*. London, 1996.

Millett, K. *Sexual Politics*. London, 1985.

Mitchell, J. *Psychoanalysis and Feminism*. London, 1974.

— and Rose, J. (eds) *Feminine Sexuality*. London, 1982.

Mulvey, L. *Visual Pleasure and Narrative Cinema*. London, 1989.

Rose, J. *Sexuality in the Field of Vision*. London, 1986.

—. *The Haunting of Sylvia Plath*. London, 1991.

—. *Why War?* Oxford, 1993.

Rustin, M. 'Lacan, Klein and Politics: The Positve and Negative in Psychoanalytic Thought', in *Psychoanalysis in Contexts*, eds A. Elliott and S. Frosh. London, 1995.

Shamdasani, S. 'Introduction', in *Speculations After Freud*, eds S. Shamdasani and M. Münchow. London, 1994.

Wright, E. *Psychoanalytic Criticism*. Cambridge, 1998.

Young, L. *Fear of the Dark*. London, 1996.

Young, R. 'Psychoanalysis and Political Literary Theories', in *Psychoanalysis and Cultural Theory: Thresholds*. London, 1991.

Feminism, Materialism and the Debate on Postmodernism in British Universities

While there are obvious dangers in classifying a number of theoretical endeavours in terms of national boundaries, we can probably safely agree with the American feminist Alice Jardine that there is a delicate '*pas-de-deux*' of current American and French feminist, or post-feminist, theory and also agree with Toril Moi that this dance excludes certain strands of materialist feminist theory, more often associated with British feminism. Yet both 'transatlantic' and British feminism are informed by radical feminism and radical feminism has itself been described as Anglo-American. Interestingly, each theory has, for a variety of reasons, claimed to be materialist. There are three main meanings of the term 'materialism' that concern us in this essay: realism, physicalism and historical or dialectical materialism. Toril Moi once said that 'a feminist intellectual is one who seeks to stress her own politics, not one who seeks to replace it with geography'. This essay will aim to keep these materialisms conceptually distinct while showing that the exclusion from the dance of the type of materialism, linked not only with British feminist theory but also socialist feminism, leads to a form of postmodernism which aims to be one of resistance but which must end up being merely concerned with the mechanics of signification.

The first form of materialism (M1) can be identified as a realism about the existence of a mind-independent world. A materialist, in this sense, need not believe that there is direct access to that world nor need they dismiss the existence of consciousness. We should not confuse materialism with empiricism. The term empirical usually denotes the belief that a proposition can be confirmed or denied by immediate sense experience. Empiricism attempts to tie knowledge to experience in such a way that anything that cannot be immediately before the senses, or inferred from the class of things observed to be true, is not considered to be a legitimate road of inquiry. This means that we must distinguish between empiricism and scientific analysis.

The second form of materialism that concerns us is often linked with physicalism (M2) and is prevalent in the philosophy of mind and cognitive sciences. It is the theory that because cognition is a matter of computational data processing, the best way to approach the human mind is as though it were a computer. Behaviour is understood as being caused by internal mental states and these mental states are thought to be reducible to physical processes or brain states. Within the philosophy of mind there is a tendency towards reductionism, the belief that one science can be better explained by a more general, lower level, science but this is not unproblematic.

Dialectical or historical materialism (M3) is the final form of materialism that is of interest to us and its most famous exponents were Marx and Engels. It was first fashioned as a response to Hegel's idealism. This is basically the doctrine that the world is essentially a mental construct or image and is contrasted with the common-sense realist view that there is something 'out there', mind-independent and distinct from the perceiver. Marx, though, does concede that the human world is fashioned from human activity but makes a sharp distinction between this sort of production and the 'production' of concepts or thinking. Consciousness, ideas and concepts, according to Marx, result from the social experience of production. Production itself takes various forms and changes over time and therefore our social experience must also alter.

The second aspect of Marx's materialism relates to his methodology and can be referred to as a 'context principle'. Taking from Hegel the idea that each thing needs to be understood in its relationships with other things, Marx 'turned Hegel on his head' and argued that the relations between things are not conceptual but are historical and social. To grasp what a thing is we must first place it in its context which is at once social, political and historical. Any attempt to analyse a thing abstracted from its context will lead to erroneous, and often ideological, judgement. Historical materialism is thus a theory of relations such that individual identity can be seen to be a consequence of antecedent social processes.

Lastly, the term 'materialism' in historical materialism conveys a commitment to a scientific method of inquiry. This brings the two previous points together. It is the belief that there is a 'mind-independent' world, that events in that world can only be understood in context and that the situation of the knower might well effect knowledge claims. The scientific hypothesis includes within its explanatory framework abstract entities such as 'the family', 'state' and 'culture' and these entities are taken to designate something actual. Economic, social and psychological processes are presumed to be open to scientific assessment, but because they are processes only a method which can accommodate change, non-conformity and difference has sufficient explanatory potential. The appropriate scientific method is dialectical and the underlying epistemic position fallibilist; we can make truth claims with the understanding that what counts as true now might well alter over time.

Materialist feminism has been defined as a synthesis of postmodern, Anglo-French, feminism and socialist, British, feminism. For any synthesis to be even possible we must allow that postmodernism and marxism are not incommensurable theories. 'Postmodernism' has been defined as a historical era corresponding to a new mode of production, post-fordism, and as an 'attitude', a new way of thinking about, and experiencing, modernity. The point of contention is whether or not it is possible to adopt a new attitude, to break from specific patterns of thought, while our social and political context remains the same, if, indeed, it does. Benhabib encourages us to separate postmodernisms into 'strong' and 'weak'. The former postmodernists, with the exception of Derrida, tend to believe that it is possible to adopt a 'postmodern' attitude even if our socio-economic climate is still modernist. Strong postmodernism is a response to specific philosophies of language and tends to extreme relativism. According to Benhabib, feminist theory can ally itself with it only at the risk of incoherence and self-contradictoriness. Weak postmodernism is an attempt to combine realism with a number of postmodern insights, specifically the relevance of the context principle to questions of epistemology (1992, 213–30). I shall be arguing that unless we take the softest form of postmodernism then the theories are indeed incommensurable, due to disagreements over what counts as 'materialism' and thus to divergent accounts of 'the real context'. The *pas-de-deux* is necessarily an exclusive dance.

Kristeva, in her now seminal essay 'Women's Time', argues that the feminist movement can be divided into three distinct phases (1982, 31–53). The first phase is associated with liberal and existentialist feminism, the second with radical and socialist feminism and the third with postmodernism. Liberal and existentialist theorists have shared a surprising number of political assumptions and political aspirations. They believed that the political demands for rights and inclusion in the decision-making processes ought to be central to a feminist politics. Because they shared a philosophical lineage, liberal and existentialist feminists, such as Wollstonecraft, Taylor, de Beauvoir and, more recently, Radcliffe Richards, agreed that there is no relevant difference between the two sexes and that the human subject is essentially rational. Any marked differences between men and women can thus be explained as the consequence of education or the general cultural milieu. Because they considered the property of rationality to be the only quality relevant for participation in political decision-making processes, they also believed that there could be no plausible argument for the exclusion of women. For this reason, the first phase of feminism has been described as one which promoted the moral equality of autonomous rational agents.

British materialist feminism is associated with the second wave of feminism. The symbolic beginning of the second wave has often been assumed to be 1968. In Britain it is coupled with the first national conference of the Women's Liberation Movement at Ruskin College in 1970. The four simple demands, adopted at Ruskin, were equal pay, equal education and opportunity, twenty-four-hour nurseries, free contraception and abortion on demand. Later conferences added demands for financial and legal independence, an end to discrimination against lesbians, a woman's right to choose her own sexuality and freedom from intimidation and violence (1974, 1978). From the 1970s we can detect a change in emphasis from the liberal or existentialist political agenda to a much broader set of political goals and strategies. This can, in part, be explained by the influence of left politics from the 1960s onwards. Liberal, socialist and radical politics coexisted, within the women's movement of the 1970s, with ecofeminism, peace campaigns and anarchism. Underlying the change was a general acceptance that women had never been simply excluded from the social contract. Modern social structures, it was agreed, managed to include women in the political order in such a way that formal demands could be met without the substantial changes that it had been thought would necessarily follow.

The second wave of feminism began with an analysis of these structures. Influenced by

American feminist theorists such as Friedan, Millett and Firestone, radical feminists began to analyse the family, sexuality and forms of cultural representations. They concluded that the political gains of the first wave had been quite empty because traditional structures and values had been left in place and it was these very structures which defined the roles of men and women and gave femininity and masculinity different values. Radical feminists can be divided into two broad camps: essentialists and anti-essentialists. Men and women, it was agreed, are allocated different categories of activities, considered useful or socially necessary for social production or reproduction. A generally held rationale for this was that certain types of work can be identified with certain behavioural characteristics or dispositions (gender). The argument was whether or not these traits can be thought to be caused by primary or secondary sexual characteristics (sex) or whether sex and gender were brought together through various social processes, including educational and religious practices, family, labour and the learning of conceptual schemes. This was, therefore, a disagreement as to the role and type of causal processes involved in the oppression of women.

Radical feminism is characteristically concerned with the differences between men and women, differences in power and authority as well as different dispositions and character-istics. Essentialists and anti-essentialists agreed that the liberal political slogan 'equal but different' obviously mystifies the base fact that masculinity is valued over femininity and men are guaranteed sanctioned domination over women. The structures themselves would need to be revised and revised according to different values. Some argued that the appropriate values were those associated with femininity. Others argued that characteristics associated with femininity were a product of the very system to be replaced, hence a 'revaluation of all values' was required. But connecting these arguments was a real belief in the moral equality and value of men and women. This belief in the 'metaphysical' equality of all human beings existed side by side with the belief that the two sexes are biologically different and the belief that because social systems change over time, the type of human subject who is a result of such social processes, their abilities and characteristics, also changes. This theory of the changing human subject inaugurated a break from the 'abstract individualism' of the liberal and existentialist project and this would, in the end, remove from the feminist project its ability to sustain a defensible moral position.

We can see that a number of questions concerning the nature of patriarchy and the causal origins of oppression perplexed second wave feminists during the 1970s. Socialist and marxist feminists were not inured from such arguments raging within the women's movement. Fundamentally they wished to analyse the material structures of patriarchy and capitalism but had to first decide whether or not patriarchy should be analysed as a set of social institutions distinct from capitalism, with its own history and its own causal origins. Dual systems theorists argued that patriarchy and capitalism are two distinct systems that may, or may not, intersect. Unified systems theorists argued that capitalism and patriarchy can be seen as a set of social relations and that therefore one conceptual scheme ought to be adequate. In a nutshell, the problem was how to explain the relation of production to reproduction: whether women's subordination to men is an effect of economic depen-dency, a dependency that is the result of women's role in sexual reproduction, a role that is required by capitalism or whether economic dependency is another facet of a more general system of male power and that this might or might not coincide with a specific organization of labour defined as capitalism. This discussion came to a head in the domestic labour debate of the 1970s. The argument concerned the function of domestic labour and its role in the reproduction of capitalism.

The initial argument was between those who drew on Engel's speculative comments about the pre-capitalist sexual division of labour and those who argued that sex-based labour roles were brought about by capitalism. Within the marxist frame of reference, this argument was significant for only those involved in productive labour; those producing commodities and surplus labour were considered to be part of the revolutionary class. The Wages for Housework Campaigners argued that domestic labour indeed produces a commodity which is central to capitalism – labour power. For this reason, Selma James, Dalla Costa and others proposed a domestic wage. Apart from signalling the productive nature of domestic labour, the proposal was also designed to cut at the heart of the assumption that the principal, or male, wage earner was paid a family wage. This point intersected with arguments being made by various dual systems theorists such as Juliet Mitchell and Mary McIntosh. Not only had no man ever been paid a 'family wage', it was argued, but also the very idea of the family wage hid the fact that many women were either primary or important, if supplementary, earners and that women were paid less than men for work 'of the same value'. Inevitably these views threw the socialist and marxist feminist movement into conflict with the trade union and labour movement. As Bea Cambell and Val Charlton wrote in 1979: 'the labour movement has managed to combine a commitment to equal pay with a commitment to the family wage, you can't have both'.

Marxist feminists recognized that the categories of economic analysis tended to reduce questions of power to the simple matter of who owned and controlled the means of production and who had surplus labour extracted. Setting themselves the task of redressing this, marxist feminists tried to identify the operation of gender relations as and where they may be distinct from, or connected with, the process of production and reproduction, understood by historical materialism. The marxist concepts of exploitation, alienation and the labour theory of value, with the implied exchange principle, were worked through theoretical explanations to clarify just how the intricate relationship between 'the private' and 'the public' was entwined through, and dependent upon, material conditions. The term 'material conditions' refers to a mind-independent set of practices which can be analysed scientifically but which, in turn, affect our ideas and beliefs. The analysis provoked heated debate due to the obvious inclination to separate the base, economic structures, from the superstructural beliefs, the family, forms of cultural representations, but, at the same time, to think of the two in a continual process of (dialectical) interaction.

As pointed out by Shelia Rowbotham and Veronica Beechey, dual systems theorists, often referred to as socialist feminists, had a tendency to be softer on marxism. This was because they could accommodate gender analysis within an exposition of patriarchy, rather than forcing the economic analysis of marxism to answer the questions outlined above. Mitchell contended that the two systems are theoretically irreducible and argued that there had been a tendency in marxism towards reductionism, such that the function and role of reproduction, sexuality and socialization were taken to be determined by the economic base (Mitchell 1971). The merits of this particular interpretation of marxism aside, it is instructive to see a number of questions being posed concerning the acquisition of mature subject identity. If we accept that an adult subject will actually desire things that will, in effect, maintain the current social organization and if we believe that the congruence of sex, gender and sexual orientation is the result of various processes that secure desires and that our sense of who we are depends on these beliefs, desires and behaviours then it makes sense to look for a theory which describes ways in which the individual is assigned a place in the social order. By extending and developing Marx's account of ideology it seemed possible to make some sense of women's 'false consciousness' (Barrett 1988). For this reason various dual systems theorists looked to Althusserian marxism and hoped to find in his theory of 'interpellation' an account of ideology which would be able to explain the exigencies but force of patriarchal ideology. Mitchell herself tried to combine insights of structural linguistics with psychoanalysis, to flesh out an analysis of the development of subject identity. Her argument is that women's relation to production, low pay, part-time work and economic dependency is a cause of oppression but that this operates in tandem with biosocial considerations and more general ideas circulating in society concerning masculinity and femininity (Mitchell 1974). Her psychoanalytic analysis of patriarchy, the supposed transition from monocausal to polyvalent analyses, has been called non-materialist because it is concerned with ideas, feelings and the unconscious. But this is to mistake, rather than to criticize, the Freudian insistence on psychoanalysis as a science and is a simplistic understanding of the meaning of the term 'materialism'.

Radical feminist ideas about the complex nature of subject identity, and the ways in which heterosexuality functions to maintain social stability, influenced the arguments between dual and unified systems theorists (Keohane, in Kristeva 1982, 1–30). Issues relating to sexuality were brought to the fore of the political agenda by work in women's refuges and rape crisis centres and around pornography, and culminated in the separatist and political lesbianism debates of the middle 1970s to early 1980s (Evans 1995, 54–74). These arguments, centring on subject identity and sexuality, occurred as the British left, most notably the *New Left Review*, moved onto a philosophical terrain that could accommodate psychoanalysis and theories concerning the cultural significance of various forms of representation. This move, especially that of Juliet Mitchell and Jacqueline Rose into Lacanian psychoanalysis, was not uncontested, for example by Parveen Adams in *m/f*, but from it rose a curious hybrid of literary and cultural studies. Although two schools of literary criticism are often distinguished, the French and the Anglo-American, it has been suggested that this is to overplay the part of British feminist theory. Instead, and unsurprisingly given the history of feminist theory, what we find is that British feminist theory contributes to the international debate mainly through its sociologists and cultural theorists. The development of cultural theory in Britain was largely guided by Hoggart and Hall, who founded and ran the Centre for Contemporary Cultural Studies (CCCS) at Birmingham University. Lovell suggests that the convergence of textual with socio-historical analysis made cultural studies a natural habitat for feminist theory.

Cultural studies has a tendency towards eclecticism and humanist and economist readings of Marx were replaced by an interest in 'marxian' theorists such as Gramsci, Althusser, Lacan, Barthes and Foucault. Perhaps the most important question at the time was whether or not a socialist history could incorporate a historicized notion of human subjectivity. Those such as Cora Kaplan warned that unless semioticians and psycho-analytic theorists retained their materialist and class analyses they would end up producing no more than 'an anti-humanist avant-garde version of romance'. Thus, the critique of the subject, the idea that apparent unified subject identity is actually a consequence of antecedent linguistic and psychosexual processes, led to a series of arguments about the nature of psychoanalysis. Marxism and psychoanalysis share three basic characteristics. They present themselves as scientific and materialist, they question the viability of the idea of value-free scientific method and they are interested in the socialized human subject. However, although marxism and psychoanalysis are concerned with processes of change, conflict and resolution, there is fundamental disagreement as to the nature of the processes in question. Those influenced by psychoanalytic theory argued that marxists socialized structures which caused conflict and aggression and that their explanations of commodity fetishism and ideology were profoundly one dimensional. Marxists argued that psychoanalysis naturalized human motivation and posited invariant and universal psychic structures. In effect, marxists argued that psychoanalysis was an individualized response to the misery of alienation and that the abstraction of the experience of alienation from its context resulted in a theory of individual reconciliation to the status quo.

The philosophical argument over the 'principle of identity' was a fairly natural consequence of, or at least a fellow traveller with, 'identity politics' and signalled a move from psychoanalytically influenced cultural theory into postmodernism: Kristeva's third wave. The philosophical argument was that the belief in subject identity, the autonomous rational agent of liberalism, the proletariat of marxism or the individual of radical feminism was premised on a prior commitment to an ontology of natural kinds underlying certain forms of materialism or to principles of rational, logical identity, underlying forms of rationalism. Individuals, postmoderns argued, are subsumed under general concepts according to features which they supposedly share. These concepts become organizational categories, according to which bodies are subjected to various regimes of power. Influenced by Derrida, Kristeva, Cixous and Irigaray poststructuralist feminists argued that radical and marxist feminists used this principle of identity and this explained how they suppressed varieties of experiences and silenced the women who did not conform to their cognitive framework: black women, lesbian women and working-class women. The critique of the subject hence led to an investigation of the differences between men and women, differences within the group 'women' and differences embodied in 'one' woman. Feminist theory became aligned with a method of reading, a way to uncover the hidden or suppressed Other in texts. This, in turn, became a matter of looking at the ways in which meaning is constructed and values percolated through language and texts. Thus we have a radical break from realism (M1) and a separation of the term 'materialism' from 'scientific analysis'. Questions concerning representation became questions about 'reality' itself.

Identity theory made its appearance in the 1980s, theoretically prefigured by the pivotal role of experience, almost an extreme form of empiricism, in radical feminism, the left turn to psychoanalytic marxism in the 1970s and French literary criticism. At the same time 'identity politics' was making its appearance felt on the national political stage. The 1980s saw a tremendous change in the political culture of Britain. There was an intricate and complicated relationship between the rise of Thatcherism, 'free market' fiscal policy, left disunity and the demise of feminism as a political force. It has been suggested that what distinguishes and shapes British feminism is its roots in the high levels of working-class action in the 1960s and 1970s (Rowbotham 1990). And during the 1980s, with a number of extremely important exceptions, including the Miner's Strike and anti-Section 28 demonstrations, there was a general decline in trade union and labour activity. However, a contributory factor in the demise of feminism as a political force were the tensions within the Women's Liberation Movement that had been brewing for over a decade. Conflicts between radical and socialist feminists, between middle-class and working-class feminists, between black feminists and white feminists, heterosexual and lesbian feminists were played out in local organizations, at conferences and through the editorial boards of *Spare Rib*, *Trouble and Strife* and the *Feminist Review*. These conflicts forced feminists into recognizing their own location and acknowledging the universalizing tendencies within feminist thought itself. Suddenly, it was no longer feasible to argue that just because an individual had a certain sexed body s/he ought to align with a particular political movement, and the goals of feminism as a political movement became hard to justify. This recognition occurred as divisions concerning the appropriate place for feminist activity became entrenched. Some, such as Sheila Rowbotham and Hilary Wainwright, attempted to transform labour politics from within, while others argued that a more open and democratic political movement was incompatible with old-style labour or workers' political groups.

Corresponding to this demise of feminism as a political force was a consolidation of academic feminism (Oakley and Mitchell 1986). Academic feminism has, in turn, been described as a deradicalization of feminist theory and this has been linked to the rise of 'municipal feminism', the filtering through of women and feminist theory into public institutions, including, but not exclusively, those of Higher Education (Lovenduski and Randall 1993). There are two main reasons why an increase in the mass of women in Higher Educational Institutions could be causally related to a deradicalization of feminist theory. The first refers us to the ways in which the institutional body manages to exert a determining influence on the type of work done. The second refers us to the type of academic theory which became prevalent. To take the first. An institution can be defined as a form of physical organization which includes sedimented relations of power and lines of funding management. A certain 'norm' of academic practice and an image of an 'ideal' academic practitioner filter through. The rules of academic practice constrain and inform the content of the subject matter itself (Garry and Pearsall 1989, 1–46). In addition to these problems which are endemic to all forms of academic inquiry, as women's studies courses were gaining ground, the vicious spending cuts and actualization programmes of the 1980s and 1990s took place. There is a prima facie case for arguing that the type of academic work which was done was the type which could be safely funded and published.

The second explanation for the deradicalization of theory concerns the nature of the theory itself. Identity politics and theory have provided strategic and theoretical problems. It has been argued that feminist discourses of difference pulled the rug from under feminism as politics (Soper 1990). This is for two main reasons. Firstly, once the diversity of women is recognized and privileged over community, any sort of collective and goal-directed action becomes problematic. Secondly, the substance of feminist theory became itself and the purpose of theory became the reflection upon and the interrogation of internal divisions and conflicting subject positions (Whelehen 1995). The type of feminist theory inhabiting cultural and media and English departments was directly influenced by psychoanalytic literary theory, which, in effect, amounted to a rejection of realism (M1). Various arguments blossomed. If feminist theory could be reduced to a way of reading then women could no longer claim a privileged standpoint and men could justifiably call themselves 'feminist' (Jardine and Smith 1987). If feminism was still a political practice what were its goals? Due to its rejection of the values of modernity and to its anti-realism in ethics, feminist strategy had to be limited to the demonstration of the vagueness or fluidity of conceptual discrimination. The only aim left was to experience, perhaps desire, outside the parameters of western logic. This return to the 'body' or 'embodiedness' had every claim to materialism but without any sort of realist purchase.

If we abandon our realist commitments in epistemology, it becomes extremely difficult to argue, with any conviction, about the causal origins, effects and even nature of material practices. Against the grain, some, such as Liz Stanley, Michèle Barrett and Alison Assiter, have attempted to revise traditional epistemology, in light of feminist criticisms, and to take subjectivity into account while retaining a form of realism. Along with Benhabib, we can call this a form of 'soft' postmodernism. Others have responded by using 'discourse analysis' as proposed by Foucault, in the belief that he successfully keeps an idea of material social conditions but manages to marry this with the recognition of the located and social nature of knowledge claims and an anti-essentialism (Shildrick 1997). This appears to be materialist (M3) but due to its rejection of realism (M1) is actually unable to justify its own descriptions.

In conclusion, it is clear that feminism is fundamentally a modern project and this can be seen in the fact that the political goal of feminism has been, in various guises, to end the oppression of morally valuable human subjects. Where 'hard' postmoderns insist on being post-humanist, they are in fact arguing for an anti-realism in epistemology and in ethics (Weedon 1987). This makes it virtually impossible not only to talk meaningfully about material conditions, but also to argue against the current form of social organization and to consider alternatives. There have been three main solutions proposed to this. The first, following Donna Haraway, replaces the concept of the moral agent with the concept of the (unnatural) body and attempts to give content to the term 'oppression' by referring to 'negative and positive' physical effects. The second is a revision of identity politics as 'queer theory', where images and representations are deployed in a way which is supposed to force a renegotiation of basic political categories and a reappraisal of purposes of political action. But, again, this tends to mean that the arena of political struggle is that of cultural representation, cloistered conferences and textual exchange. The last, more honestly, eliminates all talk of the human subject, moral agency and consciousness by reducing the mind to the brain and the brain to a computational data processing organ (Kemp and Squires 1997, 468–529). But the idea of 'cyberfeminism' must be recognized to be an oxymoron. Physicalists eliminate the very gender categories on which feminism bases its politics and then they reduce subjectivity to causally determined physical laws (M2). Indeed, I would argue that we are left with a perfect coincidence of a certain form of global capitalism, a 1990s backlash against feminism and a deradicalization of theory masked as radical postmodern chic. This would be to return to my original point. There are certain versions of postmodernist feminism which a marxist feminist would describe as the cultural logic of developed capitalism and the graceful *pas-de-deux* as a dance to the death.

Gillian Howie

Further reading and works cited

Assiter, A. *Enlightened Women*. London, 1996.
Barrett, M. *Women's Oppression Today*. London, 1988.
—. *The Politics of Truth*. Cambridge, 1991.
Benhabib S. *Situating the Self*. Cambridge, 1992.
Bock, G. and James, S. (eds) *Beyond Equality and Difference*. London, 1992.
Brennan, T. (ed.) *Between Feminism and Psychoanalysis*. London, 1989.
Bryson, V. *Feminist Political Theory*. London, 1992.
Evans, J. (ed.) *Feminist Theory Today*. London, 1995.
Garry, A. and Pearsall, M. (eds) *Women, Knowledge and Reality*. London, 1989.
Hennessy, R. *Materialist Feminism and the Politics of Discourse*. New York, 1993.
Jardine, A. and Smith, P. (eds) *Men in Feminism*. New York, 1987.
Jeffreys S. 'Creating the Sexual Future', in *Feminist Theory Today*, ed. J. Evans. London, 1995.

Kemp, S. and Squires, J. (eds) *Feminisms*. Oxford, 1997.

Kristeva, J. 'Women's Time', in *Feminist Theory*, ed. N. O. Keohane, M. Z. Rosaldo and B. C. Gelpi. Brighton, 1982.

Lovell, T. (ed.) *British Feminist Thought*. Oxford, 1990.

Lovenduski, J. and Randall, V. *Contemporary Feminist Politics*. Oxford, 1993.

MacKinnon, C. 'Feminism, Marxism, Method and the State: An Agenda for Theory', *Feminist Theory*, eds N. O. Keohane, M. Z. Rosaldo and B. C. Gelpi. Brighton, 1982.

McNay, L. *Foucault and Feminism*. Cambridge, 1992.

Mitchell, J. *Woman's Estate*. Harmondsworth, 1971.

—. *Psychoanalysis and Feminism*. London, 1974.

Mitchell, J. and Oakley, A. (eds) *What is Feminism?* Oxford, 1986.

Moi, T. *Sexual/Textual Politics*. London, 1985

Nicholson, L. *Feminism/Postmodernism*. New York, 1990.

Oakley, A. and Mitchell, J. (eds) *Who's Afraid of Feminism?* New York, 1997.

Rowbotham, S. *The Past is Before Us*. Harmondsworth, 1990.

Shildrick, M. *Leaky Bodies and Boundaries*. London, 1997.

Soper, K. *Humanism and Anti-Humanism*. London, 1986.

—. *Troubled Pleasures*. London, 1990.

Stanley, L. *Feminist Praxis*. London, 1990.

Tong, R. *Feminist Thought*. Sydney, 1989.

Weedon, C. *Feminist Practice and Poststructuralist Theory*. Oxford, 1987.

Whelehen, I. *Modern Feminist Thought*. Edinburgh, 1995.

British Poststructuralism since 1968

There are several ironies involved in the title 'British poststructuralism since 1968'. At first glance the phrase 'British poststructuralism' may seem something of a contradiction in terms. 'Poststructuralism' is characteristically French, the common noun designating a heterogeneous collection of texts by Jacques Derrida, Hélène Cixous, Julia Kristeva, Michel Foucault, Jacques Lacan, Roland Barthes, Louis Althusser *et al*. However, 'poststructuralism' is not a French word, nor is it a translation of a French word. The later neologism in French, 'poststructuralisme', is a translation of the English to describe an experience of appropriation and translation. Poststructuralism is what happens to a certain strand of French thought in the Anglo-American academy. For example, in France the work of Jacques Derrida and those associated with him, colleagues or students, has been met with resolute resistance by the academic institution. In 1980 when it appeared likely that Derrida would succeed Paul Ricoeur's chair of philosophy the then education minister Alain Saulnier-Seite abolished the post. When another professorship was set up as a replacement, with certain preconditions, the university colleagues who had invited Derrida to apply voted against him. Meanwhile in America, Derrida has occupied chairs in the most prestigious institutions, including Yale and Irvine. As director of studies at the Centre Études Féminines in Paris, Hélène Cixous faces annual threats of closure for the only interdisciplinary and only 'women's studies' programme in France. In 1980 the conservative Barre government abolished the doctorate in Études Féminines; it was re-established in

1982 by the new socialist government. Meanwhile in America, Cixous has occupied chairs in the most prestigious institutions, including Northwestern and Virginia. Such stories seem anathema to the easy understanding of 'poststructuralism' often invoked in the English-speaking world, the '1968 and all that' version of critical theory.

Indeed it could be argued that far from being a contradiction, 'British poststructuralism' is a tautology. 'Poststructuralism' designates a history of reception of certain French philosophers and literary critics, originally in the Anglo-American academy and later in all its colonial satellites, including France. In this respect 'poststructuralism' is made in Britain. Claims can be made for the American origins of 'poststructuralism'. In many respects the 'Structuralist Debate' conference at Johns Hopkins University, Baltimore, at which Derrida met Lacan and de Man for the first time in 1966, was already 'post-structuralist' in character. However, to attempt any such historicization of this term would be to adopt an idea of history which has been thoroughly 'deconstructed' by poststructuralism itself. It would be a mistake to think it possible that one might identify an origin of poststructuralism, a moment when this intellectual interest in the Anglo-American academy began. Indeed, if we take deconstruction as a metonym for poststructuralism, as it so often was in the 1980s (see, for example, Eagleton on 'Poststructuralism' (1983) or the 1987 collection of essays on deconstruction *Poststructuralism and the Question of History*) then how can we speak of something like 'British deconstruction'? Such a phenomenon would certainly resist the temporal limits implied by the qualifying phrase 'since 1968'. Deconstruction will have been a situation in Britain and British writing for as long as the idea of Britain has existed. Perhaps one might say that Britain has been in/under deconstruction for a long time. It might also be possible to identify a tradition of deconstruction in Britain prior to, and in ignorance of, Jacques Derrida. Here one could identify the texts of Oscar Wilde, James Joyce, Lewis Carroll, Mary Shelley, Tom Paine, Jonathan Swift and so on. In this respect, the question of Britishness also comes into question.

'British poststructuralism' is in fact a contradiction because the first word in this coupling presupposes an idea of continuity, stability and exclusion which the second word works to undo. In order to ask what is 'British poststructuralism' one must ask the prior question of what is 'Britain'? Britain is a concept. It involves the ideological union of heterogeneous identities (English, Scottish, Welsh, Irish, protectorates) around an idea of sovereignty derived from a colonial history. As such the question of 'British poststructuralism' is a complicated arrangement of competing interests. For example, one might think of English scholars such as Christopher Norris and Catherine Belsey working in the Centre for Critical and Cultural Theory at Cardiff, a Scottish scholar like Thomas Docherty working at the University of Kent, English scholars such as Nicholas Royle and David Punter working at the University of Stirling. The only identity that such people share might be the nomadic internationalism of the professional academic. While Scotland and Wales have always had a strained relationship with England, recent constitutional reform has redefined that relation and so rewritten the concept of Britain. Furthermore, an understanding of 'British poststructuralism' will have to negotiate the double problematic of Ireland and black Britain. This would be a matter of examining the displacement of 'Britain', as both a concept and a political entity, by postcolonial theory. In the case of Ireland, poststructuralist analysis by Seamus Deane, David Lloyd and Luc Gibbons (among others) has questioned the geographical certainty of the term 'British' in relation to Britain's historical occupation of Ireland and continued governance of Ulster. In the case of black Britain, the poststructuralism of Paul Gilroy, Homi Bhabha and Angela MacRobbie (among others) has disrupted the stability of 'Britishness' by proposing that this term is constructed in opposition to and exclusive of 'blackness'. If there is a form of 'poststructuralism' which is characteristically 'British' then it is one that has persistently questioned the term 'British'.

The formulation 'since 1968' will also have to be interrogated. The adverb 'since' both presupposes a historical point of origin for 'British poststructuralism', namely 1968, and implies the non-originary nature of such a starting point, 'British poststructuralism before 1968' would be another entry in this encyclopaedia. Perhaps, in the sense outlined above, it suggests that poststructuralism became British after 1968. The date 1968 refers to the events in May of that year in which student protest for academic reforms combined with nationwide trade union action to precipitate a general strike in France. Momentarily it seemed that revolution was possible but disputes between the various factions on the left resulted in the dissipation of the protests. It would seem odd then that 'British post-structuralism' should be defined by events in another country. For the British 1968 is perhaps more significantly marked by the rise of the civil rights movement in Northern Ireland and the beginnings of what has been euphemistically called 'the Troubles'. In this sense, 'British poststructuralism' might be more accurately situated within a sustained encounter with the dissolution of Britishness than with the appropriation of the exoticism of Paris in 1968.

May 1968 retains a talismanic quality for the Left (another term that would require to be unpacked with care) as a metonym for both the possibility of revolution in an advanced liberal democracy and the failures of revolutionary practice. It is most often described as a 'lost historic opportunity'. Accordingly, if poststructuralism can be characterized as a rethinking of the aporias of the marxist project after the experience of the inadequacy of its programme then 1968 seemingly stands as a significant moment in this task of revaluation. However, even though the principle players of poststructuralism participated in les événements they certainly did not direct them – Derrida, for example, retained a certain distance from them – and they have never been the explicit topic of any prolonged analysis by these theorists. If the emergence of 'poststructuralism' can be tied to a specific historical conjunction there are more convincing candidates than 1968. Derrida cites the importance of 1958:

> What we had known or what some of us for quite some time no longer hid from concerning totalitarian terror in all the Eastern countries, all the socio-economic disasters of Soviet bureaucracy, the Stalinism of the past and the neo-Stalinism in process (roughly speaking from the Moscow trials to the repression in Hungary, to take only these minimal indices). Such was no doubt the element in which what is called deconstruction developed – and one can understand nothing of this period of deconstruction, notably in France, unless one takes this historical entanglement into account. (1994, 15)

For Derrida the influences of French thought lie elsewhere. Similarly, Robert Young, a British poststructuralist, cites a moment in which the idea of 'Frenchness' is called into question:

> If so-called 'so-called poststructuralism' is the product of a single historical moment, then that moment is probably not May 1968 but rather the Algerian War of Independence – no doubt itself both a symptom and a product. In this respect it is significant that Sartre, Althusser, Derrida and Lyotard, among others [add here Cixous and Deleuze], were all either born in Algeria or personally involved with the events of the war. (1990, 1)

As such the tropes and interests of poststructuralism (history, marginality, origins, authority, etc.) may be the result of a colonial rather than a revolutionary experience.

In this sense the 'post' in 'poststructuralism' may be the same 'post' in 'postcolonialism'. However, such an assertion would merely beg the question of the nature of the 'post' itself. Certainly, the 'post' here does not imply a simple idea of 'after', 'poststructuralism' coming after structuralism. 'Post' as a temporal marker is implied at least twice in the phrase 'British poststructuralism since 1968', with 'since' suggesting 'after' 1968. However, while 'post' in a temporal sense means 'coming after' in its spatial sense it means 'behind'. We might think here of the ambiguities implied by the word 'posterior'. Robert Young writes:

> 'Poststructuralism' suggests that structuralism itself can only exist as always already inhabited by poststructuralism, which comes both behind and after. It is always already unfolding as a repetition not of the same but as a kind of *Nachträglichkeit*, or deferred action. In this sense, poststructuralism becomes structuralism's primal scene. (1982, 4)

If we take this logic of *Nachträglichkeit* [deferral] seriously then something like 1968 as a 'symptom and product' of poststructuralism, or poststructuralism as a symptom and product of 1968, looks more like an experience of repetition than a point of origin – a primal scene that is never primal enough. Thus, the question of 'poststructuralism' becomes a question of the meaning of structuralism and vice versa. If the difference between the two signifiers cannot be resolved in terms of a historical break this is because the conceptual difference between the two remains elusive. At what point does structuralist narratology become poststructuralist narrative theory? When does Lacan's 'structuralist' rereading of Freud in the 1950s become 'poststructuralist' psychoanalytic theory? How can we characterize Derrida's essay 'Structure, Sign and Play in the Discourse of the Human Sciences', given at the 'Structuralist Debate' conference in Baltimore in 1966, as anything other than 'poststructuralist'? The very term 'poststructuralism' seems to contain within itself the impossibility of a clean break from structuralism. Rather than 'poststructuralism since 1968' one may as well speak of the continued operation of structuralism since 1968, but again this would be to imagine that structuralism was somehow less resistant to the holistic demands of historicism than 'poststructuralism'.

The phrase 'British poststructuralism since 1968' is taken from Antony Easthope's seminal study of the same name. Professor Easthope died a few months before this entry was written and the encyclopaedia is dedicated to his memory. In his preface to that book he rehearses similar reservations as those outlined above to his own title, noting that the 'book should be called 'English poststructuralism' (Easthope 1988, xiv), and starts its historical analysis in 1965 as an important year for British (English) marxism. However, despite his preliminary worries Easthope goes on to offer a historical overview of so-called 'British poststructuralism' between 1965 and 1988. His aim in the book, as he told me on a separate occasion, was to commit to print important facts before they were lost to distant memory for all time. In this respect, his study provides a wealth of information on the origins of critical theory in England during the 1970s and 1980s, from the politics of the founder members of the film journal *Screen* to the development of the Open University module on popular culture. The value of Easthope's book is that it views 'British poststructuralism' as a consequence of inter-disciplinary research rather than a product of, say, literary studies. He provides us with accounts of the emergence of theoretical inquiry in film studies, the social sciences, art history and philosophy, among others. In short, the argument runs that an indigenous British marxism had come to a moment of conceptual impasse in the 1960s and found a revitalizing force in the spaces opened up by certain French philosophers at that time. 'British poststructuralism' began with the translation of Althusser and Lacan in *Screen* and blossomed out into a full-blown paradigm-shift in the humanities. This may explain the autobiographical path of the author of *British Poststructuralism since 1968* but I am not sure that it will do as an account of the complexity and heterogeneity hinted at by Robert Young when he talks of 'so-called "so-called poststructuralism" ', in which the 'so-called' is indicative of histories of misunderstanding and institutional contest. 'British marxism' – there is not enough time to unpack this phrase – has always been suspicious of 'poststructuralism' and remains today the primary reactionary force against it in the British academy. Even now after more than thirty years of theoretical inquiry in British universities, it is still more acceptable to the majority of British academics to be a 'marxist' than a reader of Derrida.

However, Easthope's book lacks insight as an account of 'poststructuralism' because, as a matter of choice, it adheres to a historicist account of origins, causes and effects which 'poststructuralism' itself rejects. It cannot historicize theory because it does not sufficiently theorize history. Undoubtedly, 'poststructuralism', if such a thing exists and it is one, has a history and this history remains to be written. However, such a history will first have to think through the question of history itself as a precondition of telling the story of 'poststructuralism'. When it is finally told this story will be inseparable from the history of something like 'deconstruction in America' (see Derrida 1989, 18, 122–3) and the history of France *per se*. Since it has been a minimum requirement of this entry to provide a number of basic facts and events which would make up the story of 'British Poststructuralism since 1968', on reflection, this essay may prove as arbitrary as the date from which it is obliged to commence.

Martin McQuillan

Further reading and works cited

Attridge, D. et al. (eds) *Poststructuralism and the Question of History*. Cambridge, 1987.

Barker, F. et al. (eds) *Literature, Politics and Theory: Papers from the Essex Conference 1976–1984*. London, 1986.

Barthes, R. *Image-Music-Text*. London, 1977.

Belsey, C. *Critical Practice*. London, 1980.

Bennett, T. *Formalism and Marxism*. London, 1979.

Bennington, G. *Legislations*. London, 1994.

Bhabha, H. K. (ed.) *Nation and Narration*. London, 1990.

Brennan, T. (ed.) *Between Feminism and Psychoanalysis*. London, 1989.

Culler, J. *Structuralist Poetics*. London, 1975.

—. *On Deconstruction: Theory and Criticism after Structuralism*. London, 1983.

Derrida, J. *Of Grammatology*, trans. G. Chakravorty Spivak. Baltimore, MD, 1976.

—. *Memoirs for Paul de Man*. New York, 1989.

—. *Specters of Marx*. London, 1994.

—. 'Honoris Causa: "This is *also* extremely funny" ', *Points: Interviews, 1974–1994*, ed. Elisabeth Weber. Stanford, CA, 1995.

Dews, P. *Logics of Disintegration*. London, 1987.

Dollimore, J. *Sexual Dissidence: Augustine to Wilde, Freud to Foucault*. Oxford, 1991.

Drakakis, J. (ed.) *Alternative Shakespeares*. London, 1985.

Eagleton, T. *Literary Theory: an Introduction*. Oxford, 1983.

Easthope, A. *British Poststructuralism since 1968*. London, 1988.

Foucault, M. *The Order of Things*. New York, 1970.

Gilroy, P. *There Ain't no Black in the Union Jack*. London, 1987.

Hawkes, T. *Structuralism and Semiotics*. London, 1977.

Lacan, J. *Ecrits: A Selection*. London, 1977.

Laclau, E. and Mouffe, C. *Hegemony and Socialist Strategy*. London, 1985.

Lyotard, J.-F. *The Postmodern Condition*. Manchester, 1984.

McQuillan, M. et al. (eds) *Post-Theory*. Edinburgh, 1999.

Mitchell, J. *Psychoanalysis and Feminism*. London, 1974.

Mulvey, L. 'Visual Pleasure and Narrative Cinema'. *Screen*, Autumn 1975.

Norris, C. *What's Wrong with Postmodernism*. Baltimore, MD, 1994.

Readings, B. *The University in Ruins*. Cambridge, MA, 1993.

Royle, N. *After Derrida*. Manchester, 1995.

Salusinsky, I. *Criticism in Society: Interviews*. London, 1987.

Sinfield, A. *Cultural Politics – Queer Readings*. London, 1994.

Young, R. (ed.) *Untying the Text*. London, 1981.

—. 'Poststructuralism: The End of Theory', *Oxford Literary Review*, 5, 1982.

—. *White Mythologies*. London, 1990.

— (ed.) '(Neocolonialism)', *Oxford Literary Review*, 13, 1991.

—. *Torn Halves*. Manchester, 1996.

Glossary

Abject/Abjection – Term used by Julia Kristeva as an attempt to undo the **binary** logic of much psychoanalytic thought, where the concepts of (desiring) **subject** and object (of **desire**) often represent a co-dependent opposition. The abject, says Kristeva, is 'neither subject nor object'; instead it opposes the ego by 'draw[ing] me to the place where meaning collapses'. While the subject/object structure makes logical meaning possible, the abject is an **uncanny** effect of horror, threatening the logical certainty of subject/object binary. Absolutely essential to all cultures, the abject is, among other things, the forbidden **desires** and ideas whose radical exclusion is the basis of cultural development.

Absence/Presence – Example of **binary opposition**, whereby, according to structuralist linguistics and, subsequently, structuralist critical analysis, neither term or, in fact, the concept articulated by such a term generates its meaning without implicit acknowledgement of its opposite term and the necessary implication of one in the other. Jacques Lacan draws on the linguistic work of Roman Jakobson to explore the dynamic of absence/presence in the **symbolic** order.

Aesthetic/Aesthetic Theory – From Greek *aistetikos*, meaning perceptible to the senses, aesthetic approaches to literature are ones which concern themselves primarily with the work's beauty and form, rather than with extra-textual issues such as politics or **context**. Aesthetics, which involves the exploration of beauty and nature in literature and the fine arts, involves two theoretical approaches: (a) the philosophical study of the nature and definition of beauty; and (b) the psychological examination of the perceptions, origins and performative effects of beauty.

Aetiology – From Greek words *aitita* meaning cause, and *logos* meaning rational discourse, aetiology is the philosophical or scientific pursuit of laws of cause and effect.

Affective Fallacy – Term coined by W. K. Wimsatt and M. C. Beardsley in Wimsatt's *The Verbal Icon*, which identifies the mistaken analysis of a text in terms of its emotional or 'affective' results, thereby misunderstanding the difference between what a text is and what it does (see *intentional fallacy*).

Agency – Literally 'activeness'; more usually used to suggest one's ability to act on the world on one's own behalf or the extent to which one is empowered to act by the various **ideological** frameworks within which one operates.

Alienation – In marxist theories, alienation is the experience of being distanced or **estranged** from the products of one's labour, and by extension from one's own sense of **self**, because of the effects of **capitalism**.

Alterity – Condition of **otherness** in critical and philosophical discourse to signal a state of **being** apprehended as absolutely, radically other. In *Time and the Other* (1987) and other works Emmanuel Levinas addresses the absolute exteriority of alterity, as opposed to the **binary, dialectic** or reciprocal structure implied in the idea of the other. For Levinas, the face of the other is the concrete figure for alterity. My sense of **self** is interrupted in my encounter with the face of the other, and thus the self, the I as Levinas puts it, knows itself no longer in its self-sameness but in its own alterity, in coming face to face with the face of the other.

Ambiguity – The condition of an utterance having more than one meaning, thereby producing uncertainty. The term is given detailed attention by William Empson in his *Seven Types of Ambiguity* which denotes the richness and variety of verbal speech. Empson's conception of ambiguity includes seven categories: (a) a given or word or syntax can connote several effective meanings at once; (b) two or more meanings may comprise a writer's single intended meaning; (c) a pun can offer two simultaneous ideas; (d) a writer can employ different meanings in order to establish a clear, albeit complicated, state of mind; (e) an image may exist halfway between two ideas; (f) readers may be forced to concoct their own interpretations when confronted with contradictory statements by the writer; and (g) two contradictory meanings may signal an intellectual division in the writer's state of mind.

Ambivalence – Employed in particular strands of postcolonial critical discourse, and developed specifically from the work of Homi Bhabha, ambivalence in this **context** signifies the condition produced through the discourse of **mimicry**, whereby in the process of imposing on the colonial subject the desire to render that **subject** the same as the colonizer (for example, through the colonizer's language), there is produced, says Bhabha, a **difference**, slippage or excess. Thus, the colonial **other** is produced as almost, but not quite, the same, thereby producing disquiet in the colonialist, and thus a renewal of the fear of the other.

Analogy – From the Greek, *ana*, according to, and *logos*, rational discourse: an analogy is a comparison made between one word, object, story or concept and another for purposes of comparison and explanation.

Analytical Criticism – Type of criticism which assumes the text or other work of art as an organic or autonomous whole, the meaning of which can be discerned without reference to features supposedly external to the text (e.g. **context**, history, **ideology**) through close consideration of its various features and their formal relationships within the work.

Anastomosis – Originally a biological term indicating interconnection between blood vessels, but given a literary application by J. Hillis Miller, in his *Ariadne's Thread: Story Lines*, who points out a contradiction within the etymology and definition of anastomosis: it suggests an intercommunication between, on the one hand, 'two vessels' and, on the other, 'two channels'. Furthermore, the figure of anastomosis is doubly contradictory, in that it figures, as Miller puts it, both 'container and thing contained'. As preface to a lengthy critical analysis of Goethe's *Elective Affinities*, Miller examines James Joyce's own use of the word. Joyce employs the term three times, once in *Ulysses* and twice in *Finnegans Wake*. As Miller shows, anastomosis for Joyce marks (a) the interconnection between past, present and future; (b) the interconnection of 'each person to all the previous generations back to Adam and Eve; (c) the 'intercommunication' of sexual intercourse; and (d) the intercommunication imagined in the passing of 'the genetic message on to future generations'.

Anthropologism – From the Greek *anthropos*, human, and *logos*, rational discourse: anthropology is the science of humanity; by extension, anthropologism is the application of anthropological insights, methods and practices to other fields of intellectual engagement.

Anthropomorphism – The transformation of a non-human **subject** through an analysis which imbues it with qualities peculiar to human beings and thereby makes familiar or 'quasi-human' the subject in question.

Anti-foundationalism – Term that refers to the rejection of the philosophy of the existence of a single, unified whole in which everything is ultimately interrelated. Divided into three principal subcategories – sophism, pragmatism and scepticism – anti-foundationalism underscores the notion that knowledge is transient and is commonly derived from personal experience.

Anti-intentionalism – A critical position in which the intentions of the author are regarded as immaterial to the interpretation of the work.

Anti-materialist – Any critical or theoretical stance which opposes a materialist viewpoint; that is, any stance that refuses the conditions of material life as the basis of its interpretation. Anti-materialism can be mystical or religious, or it can simply be a depoliticized position.

Anxiety of Influence – Concept developed by Harold Bloom in his book of the same name. Bloom's phrase signals a theory of poetic influence and indebtedness. Specifically, Bloom's theory addresses the way in which the work of major or what Bloom calls 'strong' poets persists as an influence on poets of later ages, and how later poets, in developing and struggling with their strong precursors, effectively 'misread' their influences so as to produce their own 'strong' poetry. The process of struggling with one's major influences, Bloom argues, involves inescapable 'anxieties of indebtedness'.

Aporia/Aporetic – Deriving from the Greek for 'unpassable path' or 'impasse', aporia has been used by Jacques Derrida to describe the effects of *différance*: the aporetic and the experience of its excess is figured in the **undecidable** in meaning; irreducible to a limited semantic horizon, language announces its radical undecideability, whereby contrary to the limits of logic, a concept is shown to be identifiable as being disturbed internally, on the one hand, as *neither* this *nor* that, while, on the other hand, as *both* this *and that*.

Archaeology – Term used by Michel Foucault which indicates a mode of analysis or methodology of discursive formations and statements without assigning or seeking origins in the human sciences (e.g. psychiatry, political economy). For Foucault, such discursive strata distinguish the human sciences from any 'pure' scientificity.

Arche-écriture – From the Greek, *arche* means a founding, original or governing, controlling principle; Jacques Derrida coins the term, translatable as archi- or arche-writing, to indicate how the very idea of an origin or founding principle is not self-sufficient, full or undifferentiated but, at its origin, is always already traced by the work of **différance** or **writing** in order for it to be articulated. Sense or meaning is never originary or fully present but always spaced and structured temporally.

Architectonic – Referring to construction or structure, and, as Aristotle employs it, having control over structure, the term is used critically as addressing the systematization of knowledge.

Aristotelian – Ideas deriving from the writings of the Aristotle, whose *Poetics* in particular is an early example of literary criticism. The *Poetics* is an analysis of the elements of tragedy that make one example of the genre more or less successful than another example. His focus is on the structure of the plot, especially as it connects to the moral lesson of the play. He isolated the features that have since come to be known as the unities: the unities of time (the action takes place in one day), place (it takes place in one location) and action (it is concerned with one significant action). The highest shape of the tragic plot in Aristotle's terms was one which focused on elements of reversal in the fortunes of the protagonists, recognitions of moral lessons and catharsis in the audience, whereby the viewer is purged by his/her experience of seeing the action played out. The emphasis is thereby on structure and the audience's moral response to structure.

Aura – The 'aura' of a work of art is what Walter Benjamin calls the 'unique phenomenon of distance' that is to be found in high cultural forms. The work's aura appears to be threatened by 'mechanical reproduction' which theoretically dissipates the work's uniqueness and brings it into the grasp of everyone. The unique artefact is distanced by its uniqueness – its unattainability. Benjamin argues, however, that though dissipated by modern technologies of reproduction, a work's 'aura' continues to give it **authority** and mystery.

Author/Authorship – The notion of authorship refers to the concept of the individual who employs his or her imaginative and intellectual powers in the construction of a given literary text, while, historically, concepts of authorship have been tied to the legal status of creative works and the rights of the author. In the poststructuralist era, the idea of authorship has become dispersed. Many literary theorists, for example, subscribe to the concept of authorship as the product of multiple cultural, historical and social forces that impact the act of textual production. Hence, Roland Barthes announced the '**death of the author**' in 1968 in an effort to challenge our existing, traditional notions of authorship and textual authority.

Authorial Intention – The idea that, through the close reading of a literary text, the reader can discern or in some manner gain access to the author's intentions, or what the author really means to say.

Authority – The power that comes from the assumption of being unique or originary, or the significance invested in the cultural status of an originator or author (from which the word derives) of a given work; the assumption of power invested in signs, practices, laws or discursive practices. Thus, the limits placed on meaning when interpreters turn to the biographies or the known **authorial intentions**.

Autonomy of Art – The view that art/literature is autonomous – that is, that it has no function beyond itself, that it is politically, socially, economically and personally disengaged; a view of literature favoured, implicitly or explicitly, by the New Critics in the US, and by F. R. Leavis and the other contributors to *Scrutiny*.

Avant-garde – From the French for 'vanguard', avant-garde in art or literature means artistic practices that deviate daringly from conventional practice: the art of the new.

Base/Superstructure – Concepts derived from Marx's Preface to *A Contribution to the Critique of Political Economy*. Marx argued that the economic organization of any given society (what he called the relations of production or base) was the foundation of all other social relations and cultural production: that is, the economic base makes possible or determines the kinds of legal, political, religious and general cultural life of the world – what Marx termed the superstructure. The relationship between base and superstructure has variously been understood as absolutely determining (the base is like the foundations for a superstructure like a house), or as mutually dependent (with the base acting like railway tracks and the superstructure as rolling stock).

Becoming – In the work of Mikhail Bakhtin, **being** is both spatial and temporal, perceived as an event implying relationship to others and as a process of continuity or becoming. The concept of becoming is articulated in the work of Gilles Deleuze and Félix Guattari in relation to the economics and **flow** of **desire**. Because the flow of desire precedes the **subject**, such flow is neither restricted to nor defined in relation to the psyche of the individual. Traversing subjectivity, flows open onto potential becomings. Because the notion of becoming is indicative in the work of Deleuze and Guattari of an oceanic, radical destabilization of discrete or finite meaning or identity (see **deterritorialization**), it cannot be thought as merely being a liberatory transformation which, once achieved, comes to rest in an alternative identity (such transformation would merely reside within a general process of economic exchange). Indeed, it is because of the radically utopian conceptualization of becoming as resistant to the very idea of meaning or identity that it becomes problematic in the extreme to provide a definition. Deleuze and Guattari describe a series of different becomings – becoming-animal, becoming-woman, becoming-imperceptible, becoming-minoritarian, **becoming-other** – all of which are examples of the multiplicity of flows termed **desiring machines**. None of these implies a conscious imitation or identification but, in the words of Tamsin Lorraine (from *Irigaray and Deleuze: Experiments in Visceral Philosophy*), 'becomings are encounters that engage the subject at the limits of corporeal and conceptual logics already formed and so bring on the destabilization of conscious awareness that forces the subject to a genuinely creative response'. Becoming is thus for Deleuze and Guattari (as they put it in *Kafka: Toward a Minor Literature*), 'absolute deterritorializations'. 'To become animal', they write (to take one example of the envisioning of becoming), 'is to participate in movement, to stake out a path of escape in all its positivity, to cross a threshold, to reach a continuum of intensities that are valuable only in themselves, to find a world of pure intensities where all forms come undone, as do all the significations, signifiers and signifieds, to the benefit of an unformed matter of deterritorialized flux, of nonsignifying signs' (see **empty signifier**).

Being – In philosophical discourse, the term is applicable to all objects of sense or thought, material or immaterial. In continental philosophy, aspects of being are distinguished in the following ways: (a) as *being-for-(it)self*, which names conscious being or being as actuality; (b) *being-in-(it)self*, this phrase identifying being either which lacks conscious awareness or which otherwise determines being as mere potentiality; (c) *being-itself*, which determines the idea of pure being, regarded as infinite and uncharacterizable, also usually signified as *Being*; (d) *being-with*, which names human existence as part of a shared community of beings. Martin Heidegger has provided the most sustained and radical reorientation of the question of Being in twentieth-century philosophy, employing the term *Dasein* (lit. *there-being*) to indicate the condition of beings within Being. One's being is a *there-being* in that one only comprehends one's being as 'thrown', to use Heidegger's term. This suggests that being is never experienced in the abstract but only ever in the experience of *being-in-the-world*. Heidegger employs the term *Dasein* in order to move beyond discourses of being rooted in notions of an originary being from which first principle we might then comprehend our being. Furthermore, the thinking of *Dasein* therefore does not assume intrinsic or essential qualities to being but, instead, conceives being in its temporal existence in relation to others in order to examine the experience of being and how existence is possible. *Dasein* is thus not the expression of a self-reflexive entity reflecting on the world, but is always already immersed in the world, our existence determined through specific historical and cultural locations.

Binary Opposition – Any pair of terms which appear diametrically opposed; therefore: good/evil, day/night, man/woman, centre/margin. First considered by Aristotle in his *Poetics* and subsequently given attention much later among structuralist and poststructuralist thinkers. In literary theoretical discourse, neither term in a binary opposition or pair is considered absolute. Rather, one term defines and is, in turn, defined by what appears to be its opposite. As the work of Jacques Derrida shows, any pair of terms, far from maintaining their absolute semantic value, slide endlessly along a semantic chain, the one into the other through the effect of **difference**. Also, Derrida makes clear how the apparent equivalence of terms is not in fact true: instead, in all binary oppositions, one term, usually the former of the two, is privileged hierarchically over the other in western thought.

Black/White – The terms refer to the racial **binaries** that continue to have an impact on the course of western culture, particularly in terms of identity politics and regarding existing ethnic biases and prejudice.

Bourgeois – French for middle class. By extension, it has come to mean a set of conventional attitudes which tend to support a conservative status quo.

Bourgeois Individualism – A key term in Ian Watt's proto-marxist study *The Rise of the Novel*, used to define one of the conditions for the novel's appearance. The bourgeois individual exhibited a new kind of (middle-class) **consciousness** and new sensibility in relation to his/her relations with God, other people generally and servants in particular, and the market, consisting primarily in a view that the individual is significant in his/her own right, rather than having his/her significance subsumed by the general needs of society.

Camp – Camp is notoriously difficult to define but critical considerations such as those of Jonathan Dollimore and Alan Sinfield agree that the question of camp involves an act or performance which, while remaining elusive, nonetheless destabilizes the perception of stable gender identity. There is little consensus among critics as to a definition of camp and this it might be suggested is camp's strength. What can be said, albeit cautiously, is that camp appears to be a performative play which engages with flirtation, comedy and flippancy, occasionally, if not frequently, for the purpose of pointed critical attack. There is in camp a glib, self-reflexive admission that what Jonathan Dollimore terms the 'masquerade of camp' shows up the lack of substance in any normative construction of identity. While camp, strictly speaking, is concerned with codes concerning the reading and performance of gender and sexually-orientated identities, the performative condition of camp masquerade allows for a form of dis-identification within identity – the deliberate staging of a gendered identity announces that all gendered positions are, to some extent, perfomances without essence – which refuses both to allow itself to be taken seriously and to be pinned down. One cannot fix an identity-in-common for the idea of camp. Moving between normative and transgressive gendered identities, transgressing the very idea of gender, camp announces the paradoxical power *and* powerlessness instituted in the politics of gender identities.

Canon/canonical/canonicity – Originally, the term *canon* referred to those books of the Bible that had been accepted by Church authorities as containing the word of God. More recently, in literary studies, it has come to mean the 'great books' or 'great tradition' of texts that everyone should study or know in order to be considered educated in literature – that is, works called 'canonical'. The means by which the canon has been constructed, however, have been radically exclusionary – leaving out, for example, works written by those in marginal or excluded groups. Contemporary focus on canonicity, therefore, has tended to move to broadening the category of what 'counts' as **literature**.

Capitalism – Any system of economic relations which is driven by the profit motive; capitalism depends on the investment by private individuals and companies of their own funds to provide the economic means of production, distribution and exchange in return for profits from their investment.

Carnival/Carnivalesque – Terms drawn from the work of Mikhail Bakhtin on the novel. The carnivalesque is that in **narrative** forms where social hierarchies and **power** structures oriented around positions of 'high' and 'low' are temporarily inverted, often through forms of parody, in order to destabilize in order to make comic that which is taken seriously within social order.

Cataleptic impression – Term often associated with Stoic **epistemology** and moral philosophy that refers to a cognitive, philosophical phenomenon that has the power to impact on an individual or culture and hence alter that individual or culture's belief system. Such a moment transforms a person's soul with absolute certainty, perhaps even more profoundly or suddenly than an epiphany.

Chora – Originally deriving from Plato's *Timaeus*, where the word is a figure of multiple **ambiguity**, meaning 'the receptacle of meaning, invisible and formless, which contains intelligibility but cannot itself be understood'. Jacques Derrida, spelling the term *khora*, provides a telling analysis of Plato's text, in which he aims to demonstrate how *khora* can be defined in ways pertaining neither to the sensible (having to do with feeling and emotion) nor the intelligible (having to do with rationality and intellect), and thus names that which is resistant to naming, which cannot be gathered by any name, and yet which is neither negative nor positive; *khora* thus 'names', if we can put it this way, the **aporetic** beyond, in excess of, any defining paradigm, while being irreducible to a definition as either just this experience of the aporetic or the idea of the **aporia**. Julia Kristeva has adapted the term to describe a pre-linguistic realm which underpins language and meaning, but which cannot itself be pinned down. In the process of language development the chora is split to enable words (defined by limitation – by what they leave out) to come into meaning. The chora represents endless possibility but no single significance – single significance being what defines language itself.

Chronotope – Concept developed by Mikhail Bakhtin, which refers to the **aesthetic** or envisioning of the human **subject** as situated materially within a specific geotemporal location or spatial/temporal structure which determines the shape of a **narrative**; thus, protagonists of epic narratives can be described as defined by, as well as inhabiting, a particular chronotopic space.

Clinamen – A trope, signifying a swerve. The figure is employed by Harold Bloom in his *Anxiety of Influence* to describe the act of poetic misprision by which poets of later generations produce their strong readings of the earlier poets who influence them (see *anxiety of influence*).

Close Reading – Formal analysis of the recurrent figures, motifs, tropes of a text so as to suggest a greater unity or organic whole to the work; a term usually associated with New Criticism or the work of F. R. Leavis and other critics associated with Leavis and the journal *Scrutiny*. In this sense, close reading is implicitly assumed to be an act of reading divorced from any matters supposedly extraneous to the text, such as matters of history or **context**, questions of politics, issues of gender and race, and so on.

Code – The signification system that allows for the comprehension of a text or event.

Codification – The process of establishing rules and procedures that are apparently consistent and coherent for any intellectual practice. In structuralism, the process of unravelling and interpreting codes of signification – for example, the codes that tell you that this is a detective novel and that that is an advert for pizza.

Colonial/Colonialism – Terms denoting the manner in which one culture appropriates the land, people and resources of another to further its **imperialist** ends. Edward Said defines colonialism as the necessary consequence of imperialist practices and attitudes, thereby suggesting a causal relationship. The idea of colonialism may also be said to designate the attributes of the specific political and **epistemological** discourses by which the colonizing power defines those who are subjected to its rule. Postcolonialism refers in literary studies to literary texts produced in countries and cultures that have come under the control of European powers at some point in their history.

Commodification – The process by which an object or a person becomes viewed primarily as an article for economic exchange – or a commodity. Also the translation of the **aesthetic** and cultural objects into principally economic terms. The term is used in feminist theory to describe the objectification of women by patriarchal cultures. Through the processes of commodification, the work of art lacks any significance unless it can be transformed by economic value.

Commodity fetishism – Term used by marxist critics after Marx's discussion in Volume One of *Capital* to describe the ways in which products within capitalist economies become objects of veneration in their own right, and are valued way beyond what Marx called their 'use-value'. Commodity fetishism is understood as an example of the ways in which social relations are hidden within economic forms of **capitalism**.

Condensation – A psychoanalytic, specifically Freudian, term referring to the psychic process whereby phantasmatic images assumed to have a common affect are condensed into a single image. Drawing on the linguistic work of Roman Jakobson, Jacques Lacan compares the Freudian notion of condensation to the work of metaphor.

Connotation/Denotation – A word's connotations are those feelings, undertones, associations, etc. that are not precisely what the word means but are conventionally related to it, especially in poetic language such as metaphor. The word gained popular currency in relation to structuralist theories of language and literature, where connotation is opposed to denotation – the precise meaning of a word, what it means exactly as opposed to what it might mean by association. Denotation is the act or process of implying or connoting meaning or ideas.

Consciousness – In Freudian discourse, one of the principal manifestations of the psychic apparatus, the others being the **unconscious** and preconscious.

Constellation – The idea of the constellation names for Walter Benjamin the critical observation of **heterogeneous** yet not absolutely dissimilar images and figures of thought gathered from both present experience and other historical moments. Benjamin seeks to maintain the **difference** of the historial condition of thought, rather than troping figures, concepts and ideas from the past in terms of present conceptualization by some transhistorical critical gesture.

Consumer culture – A description of postwar western-type economies in which the consumption of commodities – and of cultural artefacts as commodities – is a principal determining feature of a specific society.

Context – Usually used simply to describe all the extra-textual features (conditions of production and reception, historical events, general cultural milieu, biography, etc.) which may have a bearing on the interpretation of a literary text. The term has also been co-opted and adapted by Luce Irigaray to describe a kind of *écriture féminine* in which the **analogy** between pen and penis derived from Freudian thought is rewritten to an analogy between cunt (in French *con*) and writing, hence *con-texte*.

Co-optation – The process of borrowing from one discourse the methods and theoretical models of another, often with radical effects. Politically, the appropriation of an individual or group, or the ideas of an opposition, and put to work willingly or otherwise in the service of those who effect the appropriation.

Counter-history/Counter-memory – Terms employed by Michel Foucault in his critique of psychology's official account of the history of madness as it is socially and institutionally conceived. Conventional historical models of **narrative** are grounded in psychological terms of continuity and identity. In contradistinction to such models, Foucault seeks through various reading strategies and the deployment of various concepts to resist any monolithic history of mental illness. Treating the various modalities of discourse at different historical moments, Foucault offers a discontinuous counter-history. In arguing for a disjunctive and polyvocal counter-history which in its consideration of discourse, modes of confinement, surveillance and the psychiatric gaze, for example, gives access to a critical perspective on present views of mental illness through a critical history disruptive of progressivist models, Foucault seeks to constitute a counter-memory, that which is forgotten in the official and institutional 'memory' expressed as the history of psychology or psychiatry.

Countertransference – Psychoanalytic term, coined by Freud but employed to a far greater extent after his death by other analysts, to indicate the analyst's unconscious emotions towards the analysand. Lacan reformulates the idea of countertransference in terms of resistance, a structural dynamic typical of the analytic experience and grounded in a fundamental incommensurability between **desire** and speech.

Criticism – The act of analysing and evaluating literary texts, films and images, cultural forms and phenomena. The varieties of criticism are numerous and extend at least as far back as Aristotle's *Poetics*.

Cultural Capital – A phrase used by Pierre Bourdieu to describe the hidden value attached to learning and education in otherwise apparently ruthlessly capitalist western societies; also, the dissemination of literary knowledge for the express purpose of enhancing the moral sensibilities of a given nation or culture's readership.

Cultural Materialism – A term first associated with marxist critic Raymond Williams that refers to the manner in which economic forces and modes of production inevitably impinge upon cultural products such as literary works. Movement in British literary theory that insistently pursues the materialist basis of cultural phenomena. Alongside textual evidence, cultural materialists pursue all kinds of contextual evidence in order to try to explain the text as a material object – both an object produced at a particular time and an object being consumed in the present.

Cultural Poetics – Term first employed by Stephen Greenblatt in 1988 to signify a mode of critical analysis developed along the premises of new historicism but distinct from it. The analytical praxis of a cultural poetics concerns the identification of historically and culturally distinct cultural practices as these arise in particular historical moments, and the relations between the practices and the discourses by which they are articulated.

Culture – The patterns of human knowledge that refer to the customary beliefs, social formations and traits of racial, religious or social groups. Culture similarly denotes an acquaintance with the humanities, fine arts and other intellectual or scientific pursuits. The term culture is applied to assemblages of social practices defined periodically and in terms of race, belief and class.

Cyberwar – Term often associated with Paul Virilio that refers to the **commodification** of information and its nearly invisible dispersal within technological culture. Cyberwar entails virtual enemies inflicting virtual casualties among their invisible foes.

Cyborg – Term which has been used by feminist theorist Donna Haraway to posit an alternative mode of **being** in which a hybrid of human and mechanical elements would be beyond the constraints of biological sex and culturally stereotyped gender.

Death of the author – From Roland Barthes's essay of the same title, the phrase has come to mean the resistance to using information derived from the writer's life or known **authorial intentions** as part of the process of interpretation since this presumes that the author imposes the final limit on meaning and attributes to him (or her) self a godlike status.

Deconstruction – Commonly, though mistakenly, assumed to be a school of criticism, critical methodology or mode of analysis, deconstruction is an old term in both French and English with legal connotations, which has been reintroduced to critical language through the work of Jacques Derrida. Derrida employed the term initially as a French translation for the terms 'Destruktion' and 'Abbau' in the text of Martin Heidegger. Derrida's choice was governed by the need for a word which could operate in French in a manner similar to Heidegger's terms in the German philosopher's critique of metaphysics, but without the negative implications of the German. Deconstruction, if it can be defined at all, is that within any system or structure, whether one is speaking of linguistic, grammatical, conceptual, institutional or political structures, which makes possible the articulation of the structure, and yet which escapes or is in excess of the systematic logic or economy of the structure in question. In Derrida's words, it is an 'economic concept designating the production of differing/deferring'.

Defamiliarization – A concept employed by Russian formalists, defamiliarization signifies the attribute of some kinds of writing or other works of art which communicates in non-transparent ways that make the world seem strange. The point of defamiliarization is that it shakes up reading and writing habits, undercuts conventional propriety in language and literature, and thus prevents the reader from making merely habitual or conventional responses.

Demystification – Term often associated with philosophies of cultural materialism that maintain that only social contradictions and economic conditions, rather than literary criticism and theory, possess the capacity for altering the course of reality; hence, materialist philosophy attempts to 'demystify' **bourgeois** pretensions toward totality and completeness.

Desire – An ineluctable force in the human psyche distinguished from need, desire holds a crucially central position in Lacanian psychoanalysis and, subsequently, in psychoanalytically inflected critical discourses. Desire for Lacan is always an unconscious drive, conscious articulations of desire being merely symptomatic of this unstoppable force. Need is seen as a purely biological instinct, while desire, a purely psychic phenomenon, is a surplus or excess beyond all articulation of demand. Desire, writes Lacan, comes always from the unconscious, and is thus unlocatable as such, while being, equally, 'desire for something else' (as it is expressed in *Écrits*), by which formula Lacan indicates that one cannot desire what one has, while what is desired is always displaced, deferred.

Desiring Machine – Rethinking the processes of desire as these have been defined within psychoanalytic discourse as a function of the human **subject**, Deleuze and Guattari describe desire as machinic. In doing so, they are not seeking to supply an estranging metaphor. Instead, they see the **flow** of **desire** as simply an endless and unstoppable 'flight'. It has no organizing or generative organic centre or origin. Nor does desire arise as some function of the **self**. Desire is subject to no law and the comprehension of the desiring machine serves to **deterritorialize** those forms of thinking which apply to some law or identity. The subject does not produce desire but the flow of desire plays a role in the constitution of the subject.

Determinism – Doctrine maintaining that acts of will, natural occurrences or social phenomena find their origins in preceding events or the laws of nature.

Deterritorialization – Term often associated with Gilles Deleuze and Félix Guattari that refers to a simultaneous process of fictionalization, escape from stable states, contiguity and bifurcation. This process is marked by an eschewing of monolithic ideologies in favour of 'disjunctive syntheses' that allow for genuine interconnection. Moreover, the purpose of deterritorialization as the pursuit or liberation of what Deleuze and Guattari call **flows** or 'lines of flight' is to destabilize the finite idea of corporeality, the **subject** or the state in potential processes of constant becoming.

Diachronic/Synchronic – Terms often associated with Ferdinand de Saussure that account for the relationships that exist between phonemes, which he explained in terms of their synchronic and diachronic structures. A phoneme exists in a diachronic, or horizontal, relationship with other phonemes that precede and follow it. Synchronic relationships refer to a phoneme's vertical associations with the entire system of language from which individual utterances derive their meaning.

Dialectic – Broadly speaking, argument or debate; systematic analysis. A term associated with marxism, derived from the work of G. W. F. Hegel, indicating both a scientific method and the rules of antagonism governing the historical transformations of reality. The Hegelian dialectic is defined, at its simplest, as *thesis – antithesis – synthesis*.

Dialectical Materialism – Marxist theory that postulates that material reality exists in a constant state of struggle and transformation, prioritizing matter over mind. The three laws of dialectical materialism stress: (a) the transformation from quantity to quality making possible revolutionary change; (b) the constitution of material reality as a unity composed of opposites; (c) the negation of the two oppositions in the condition of material reality as a result of their antagonism, out of which historical development takes place which, however, still retains traces of the negated elements.

Dialogism – Term derived from the work of Mikhail Bakhtin, indicating the polyphonic play of different voices or discourses in a text, without the assumption of a dominant, monolithic authorial position or voice.

Diaspora – Settling of various peoples away from their homelands; often associated with the notion of the Jewish diaspora in modern Israel, but extended in cultural studies, postcolonial studies and race theory to consider the displacement of peoples by means of force such as slavery.

Diegesis – A long disused term, brought back into use by film theorists, and subsequently used by Roland Barthes and Gérard Genette, among others, denoting narration or description presented without judgement or analysis.

Différance – Neologism coined by Jacques Derrida. Derrida makes the term differ from the more conventional 'difference' by spelling it with an 'a'. The purpose is to point out that there is that in writing which escapes aural comprehension ('a' in the French pronunciation of 'difference' sounding the same as 'e' in 'différence'). Thus, the difference in 'différance' is purely graphic. In this manner, Derrida signifies the graphic element in the production of meaning, whereby writing silently inscribes the spacing, the deferral and differentiation (both terms implied in 'différance'), spatial and temporal, without which no writing or reading is possible.

Difference – A concept deriving from the political necessity to recognize that different groupings (female people, black people, gay and lesbian people) differ not only from the white heterosexual norm favoured by Enlightenment thought, but also differ among themselves: women, for example, may be middle-class or working-class, black or chicana, straight or gay or bi, and/or any combination of any set of attributes. Also, the understanding in Saussurian linguistics and structuralist criticism of the way meaning is neither intrinsic to a word nor produced solely through reference to a **signified** or object, but in and through the differential relation to other **signifiers**.

Differenciation – Term often associated with Gilles Deleuze that refers to the increasingly diffuse boundaries between art, technology, industry and society. No longer functioning as obvious demarcations, these boundaries endlessly merge with one another in mass culture. Deleuze develops the term in *Difference and Repetition* to signify the process of **becoming**-different (which is signalled in the 'c' in the spelling) as the possibility of diversity.

Digitality – Term often associated with Jean Baudrillard that refers to the transformation of human **consciousness** via mass culture's dissemination in a digital format, otherwise referred to by Baudrillard as the digital logic of the code. When images, thoughts and ideas become disembodied from their creative sources, traditional conceptions such as authorship become diffuse. As Baudrillard suggests in *Symbolic Exchange and Death*, with the ever-increasing destabilization, loss of reference and semantic finality, resemblance and designation in modes of communication, signs, becoming digital and programmatic in their functions, have only 'tactical' value in relation to other signs.

Discourse – Defined by Michel Foucault as language practice: that is, language as it is used by various constituencies (the law, medicine, the church, for example) for purposes to do with **power** relationships between people.

Displacement – Freudian term for psychic process whereby one psychic figure is relocated in another manifestation or image. Lacan likens the work of metonymy to displacement.

Dissemination – Term employed by Jacques Derrida. Derrida points up the homophonic similarity between the Latin *semen* and the Greek *sema*, the former signifying 'seed', the latter 'sign', and accords a certain equivalence between the concept of *dissemination* and his radical extension of the notion of writing. This is exemplified in the graphic *sem* of *dissemination*. While there is no necessary relation between the Greek or Latin words, and while utterance supposedly helps determine through **context** the appropriate signification in writing and as the effect of writing, it is impossible to keep in place or otherwise limit the graphic play. Derrida employs the figure of dissemination in opposition to ideas of communication or polysemy. Far from being either fully, unequivocally communicative in a stable, fixed fashion, or being determined by an agreed multiplicity of signification, the effects of writing are to displace decidable signification through excess and overflow ungovernable, as Derrida makes clear in the essay 'Signature Event Context', by any concept of communication.

Dominant/Residual/Emergent – Marxist terms derived from the writings of Raymond Williams to describe the ways in which there are competing discourses, beliefs and practices in any given culture. Roughly speaking, the dominant discourses are those to which the majority subscribe at a particular historical moment; the residual are those to which an older generation continues to subscribe; and the emergent are those discourses which are emerging in a culture, but which have yet to achieve consensus across the majority of the population.

Dromology – Term associated with the work of urbanist and architect, Paul Virilio, from the Greek, *dromos*, for *race*, relating to speed. The term is methodological in orientation, coined by Virilio within a discourse of urban, cultural analysis, which, in being a neologism, serves the strategic purpose of disrupting the commonsensical, while being applied as an analytical methodology to explore and express cultural, and particularly urban, matters of flow and speed, whether by this Virilio means the speed and acceleration of information transferral through the various modes of tele-technologies, or the question of the accelerated flow of living brought about by transport systems.

Écriture/écrivance – In Roland Barthes's conception, the former is the term for literary writing, that is language which draws attention to its artificiality; the latter term, Barthes contends, signifies that kind of writing, as in realist **narrative**, which strives for transparency, thereby being complicit with the prevailing dominant **ideology**.

Écriture Féminine – 'Feminine/female writing' (French). Term derived from the writings of Hélène Cixous to describe a mode of textual production that resists dominant **phallic** models of communication. It is not necessarily written by women, but is produced instead by those who occupy what might be called a 'feminine' space in culture – which will often be women, but might also include certain kinds of excluded men.

Ego – The fundamental, conscious component of the **self**, particularly in terms of the way in which humans contrast themselves with the world. In psychoanalytic theory, the ego functions as one of the three divisions of the psyche and refers to the manner in which people **mediate**, perceive or adapt to reality.

Embodiment – The state of giving body to or becoming incarnate.

Empiricism – Philosophical approach to knowledge which puts forward the idea that all knowledge is derived from experience and not derived from reason or logic.

Empty Signifier – Term often associated with Félix Guattari, also given as 'a-signifying' or 'non-signifying', that denotes a signifier with a vague, unspecifiable or non-existent signified. In such instances, the signifier has endured a form of radical disconnection from its signified.

Epic theatre – A style of dramaturgy developed primarily in both practice and theory by Bertolt Brecht from the 1920s onwards. Epic theatre is episodic rather than dramatically unified; it intersperses action with songs, poetry and dance; and it focuses the audience's attention on the fictionality of what they are observing.

Epistemology – Branch of philosophy which addresses the grounds and forms of knowledge. Michel Foucault employs the idea of the episteme to indicate a particular group of knowledges and discourses which operate in concert as the dominant discourses in any given historical period. He also identifies epistemic breaks, radical shifts in the varieties and deployments of knowledge for ideological purposes, which take place from period to period.

Erasure – The gesture of erasure, or placing a term under erasure, refers graphically to the act of crossing out a word but retaining the word and the crossing through. Martin Heidegger employs this practice in *The Question of Being*, in which the word **Being** is crossed through. Heidegger's purpose is to show how the term can no longer be employed, given that the concept as it is used has slipped away from, and thereby forgotten, the question of Being. For Heidegger, the very idea of Being is always presupposed. Any question asking 'what is "Being" ' is only articulable to the extent that the very idea of Being makes it possible to consider the being of Being. But it is this idea which has been occluded in the consideration of Being. Crossing through the word releases it, both from the assumptions that the term is known or that the meaning of Being is somehow understood and the idea that, in asking the question, 'what is "Being" ', there is somehow the presumption of an answer. Moreover, as Derrida points out in *Of Grammatology*, with regard to Heidegger's practice, the crossing through is not a negative gesture but one which indicates how, while signification is necessary, the thought of the idea of Being as a 'transcendental signified' has reached a particular limit in the text of Heidegger. Derrida also places particular terms *sous rature* (under erasure) because their conventional function within metaphysical and logical discourse is exhausted. Such terms no longer retain their full sense; neither do they signify a presence or origin, for which the signifier stands, but only other structural traces, such as themselves.

Essentialism/Essentialist – An essentialist belief is one that mistakenly confuses the effects of biology with the effects of culture; in particular it refers to the belief that biology is more significant than culture in **subject** formation. It is used as a term of disapproval by critics whose interests are in race and gender.

Estrangement – Like **defamiliarization**, estrangement is a process of making one's experience of text or artwork strange or, more particularly, distant. Its aim is usually to subvert the reading experience (or viewing experience in the visual arts, theatre and film) away from conventions and habits. Sometimes given as translation for the Brechtian term *Verfremdung*, which is more commonly translated as *alienation*. In the context of Brechtian theatre, estrangement names the theatrical practices by which the audience are encouraged to engage intellectually and ideologically with the political and philosophical issues of a play by the deliberate foregrounding of theatrical artifice, thereby seeking to prohibit the audience's engaging empathetically with the subject material or the characters.

Ethics – A set of moral principles or values, as well as an understanding of moral duty and obligation. Ethics also refers to accepted standards of conduct. In literary theory, ethical critics address the moral properties inherent in literary works in an effort to understand their social, cultural or **aesthetic** implications for readers and texts alike.

Ethnicity – Refers to a given individual's racial, national, cultural, religious, tribal or linguistic background, classification or affiliation.

Ethnography – Systematic and organized recording and classification of human cultures.

Existentialism – A philosophical movement that involves the study of individual existence in an infinite, unfathomable universe. Existentialism devotes particular attention to the individual's notion of free will and interpersonal responsibility without any concrete knowledge of what constitutes right and wrong. A variety of twentieth-century thinkers and writers have explored the possibilities of existentialism, including Jean-Paul Sartre, Martin Heidegger and Simone de Beauvoir, among others.

False consciousness – Illusory or mistaken beliefs, usually used in marxist theories to designate the beliefs of groups with whom one disagrees or who are in need of liberation and enlightenment.

Fantasy – In everyday language, fantasy refers simply to the workings of the imagination, but in different theoretical models it has more force. In psychoanalysis, for example, fantasies are often compensatory dreams of wish-fulfilment that allow the dreamer to cope with disappointment – and the dreamer may even convince him/herself that the fantasy is real. In structuralist writings, fantasy in literature (or the fantastic), as defined by Tzvetan Todorov, refers to stories or events within them whose status is left unclear to the reader: is it real or not? The term has also been used to describe any **narrative** mode that is set in an imagined world that echoes an imagined past – especially one of dwarves and fairies (as opposed to science fiction/cyberpunk which look to the future and to technology for fantastic effects).

Fascism – A political philosophy, movement or regime that elevates conceptions of race and nationhood over the individual. Such groups often involve a centralized, autocratic governmental structure led by a dictator. In addition to regimenting social and economic policies, fascist regimes frequently engage in the forcible suppression of their political or cultural opposition.

Fetish/ism – Sexual excitement, in Freudian discourse, brought about by the **subject**'s focus on a specific object or body part. Further employed in postcolonial discourse by Homi Bhabha in relation to the processes of racial stereotyping.

Fetishization – Marxist term that refers to the manner in which mass culture **commodifies** various socio-cultural concepts, ideologies or traditions.

Fiction – An imaginative story or **narrative** (including prose and verse) that offers an invented account of events.

Flow – Also 'flux', a term from the work of Gilles Deleuze and Félix Guattari, signifying material and **semiotic** flows (such as **desire**) which, it is argued, are not essential to human **subjectivity**, but precede the subject. Pursuing such flows, Deleuze and Guattari maintain, offers potential lines of flight and thus the **deterritorialization** of the sovereign subject.

Formalism – Refers to the critical tendency that emerged during the first half of the twentieth century and devoted its attention to concentrating on literature's formal structures in an objective manner.

Gaze – Psychoanalytic concept, developed by Lacan following Jean-Paul Sartre's analysis of 'the look' and subsequently adopted in feminist film studies, which theorizes the ways in which one sees another **subject** and also comprehends how one is seen. In understanding how one is looked at, the human subject comprehends that the **other** is also a subject. Lacan develops a theory of the gaze distinct from Sartrean conceptualization along with the concept of *objet petit a*. In this theorization, the gaze names the object of a scopic drive, impersonal and irreducible to the sight of the subject.

Geist – German for *spirit* or *ghost*. Term that denotes the manner in which we imagine or conceive of nationhood, culture and social or political movements, in the form of a shared 'spirit' which constitutes our identity as English, German, American, Liberal, Democrat, Socialist, and so on. Hence, *geist* refers to our shared assumptions – often unarticulated except as the idea of national identity, for example – cultural **ideology**, by which sameness is asserted at the expense of that which is different or **other** within the constitution of identity. However, because the term is doubled and divided 'internally' by its different meanings and is therefore haunted by the condition of **undecideability**, there is, as Jacques Derrida argues, always something 'invisible' within the idea of *geist* which disturbs the very premise of the shared assumption which is grounded on the notion of undifferentiated identity and what that seeks to exclude but which returns nonetheless.

Gender – Term denoting the cultural constitution of notions concerning femininity or masculinity and the ways in which these serve ideologically to maintain gendered identities. In much sociological and feminist thought, gender is defined against biological sex. It represents the socially acceptable, and socially acquired, forms of being either male or female. Gender might then include everything a person does, from the clothes s/he wears, to choices of leisure activity, and from career and education to tone of voice. The concept of gender argues that a person may have male sex, but may have feminine attributes in relation to the cultural norms of his society, and vice versa, a female person may exhibit masculine traits. It provides grounds for arguing against essentialist concepts of selfhood and sex. Gender therefore describes the ways in which masculinity and femininity (the performance of gender, as opposed to the biology of sex) serve ideologically to maintain a particular status quo in society at large. More recently, the **binary opposition** underlying this kind of definition (the opposition between biology and performance) has been attacked and deconstructed by critics working in queer theory, particularly by Judith Butler who argues against the priority given to biology as essence that underpins even the concept that gender is performative.

Gender Parody – Term often associated with Judith Butler that refers to the manner in which transvestism or drag can expose the inevitably artificial and restrictive nature of gender identity.

Genealogy – Modelled on Friedrich Nietzsche's genealogies, Michel Foucault conceives of genealogy as a method for searching for hidden structures of regulation and association, of tracing etymological, psychological and ideological ancestors of modern social, cultural or political practices. Genealogical methodology is interested in ruptures as well as continuities, contradiction as well as coherence. The genealogist, moreover, is aware of the provisional nature of her/his own **subject** position in relation to inter-pretations of the past, in contrast to the historian's pretence of neutrality.

Generalized Communication – Term often associated with Gianni Vattimo that refers to an increasing pluralization of groups and identities. This often media-spawned rapid proliferation results in new and disorienting social possibilities, new myths, hybrid tribes and multiple dialects and subcultures among people.

Genotext/Phenotext – Corresponding terms often associated with Julia Kristeva that refer to a set of horizontal and vertical axes establishing an organizing principle structured on the repetition and displacement of language.

Globalization – The transnational and multinational tendency toward a new world order in which economic, cultural, social and political issues become increasingly driven on a global, as opposed to localized, basis.

Gothic – Originally referring to certain Germanic tribes and their languages, and subsequently signifying, on the one hand, a style of handwriting or typefaces from the thirteenth century, or, on the other hand, a style of European architecture (twelfth–sixteenth centuries), *gothic* came in the latter half of the eighteenth century and the early years of the nineteenth to be associated with a literary genre, the **narratives** of which dealt with supernatural, mysterious or ghastly events and the apprehension or production of terror, and which were usually situated in wild, stormy landscapes, eerie manors or castles. Recent studies of the gothic have emphasized the role of the reader, questions of **gender**, the gothic interest in the **abject** body and corporealization in general, and the inner feelings or phenomenological perceptions of the gothic terrain on the part of its principal protagonists. Distinctions have been made between gothic narratives of the eighteenth century, with their emphasis on mystery, and those of the nineteenth century, exemplified by the novels of Charlotte Brontë, which explore the inner condition of the protagonist.

Grand Narrative – Discourses of science, religion, politics and philosophy which are supposed to explain the world in its totality, and to produce histories of the world as **narratives** of progress. Jean-François Lyotard has, however, defined postmodernism, in part, as the collapse of such totalizing explanatory frameworks.

Gynesis – Beginning with some discomfort with the term 'feminism' because the term is 'semantically tortuous and conceptually hazardous', Alice A. Jardine (in *Gynesis: Configurations of Woman and Modernity*, 1985) coins the term gynesis in order to be attentive to the methodological, political and conceptual differences within feminist thought. In particular, her concern arises out of the arguments between US and French feminisms in the early to mid 1980s. She suggests that Anglophone and Francophone feminisms have each tended to caricature the other mode of feminist practice as flawed. French feminisms were presented by the US feminist academy as both uncritically essentialist, and yet simultaneously wedded to masculist models of theoretical knowledge, especially to the writings of Marx, Lacan and Freud. American feminists on the other hand were accused by their French counterparts of wilful theoretical and political blindness in relation to the intersections that exist between sexual politics and the patriarchal bias of economics (Marx) and psychoanalytical models of human development (Lacan and Freud). Jardine's aim, therefore, was to think through the consequences of situating American experiential models of feminist activism and critical practice (what real women have politically done in the real world, what real women have experienced) within the scope of the allegedly masculist, objectivist, theoretical models then being developed in France and elsewhere in Western Europe. For Jardine, then, gynesis means 'the putting into discourse of "woman" ' – placing both 'woman' and real women into the theoretical languages that have tended to exclude femininity. Her aim is thereby to permit thinkers to see in new ways. She argues that gynesis produces and reproduces neither mere representation (images of the eternal feminine, for example), nor **unmediated** reality (the experience of real women, whoever they may be). Rather, gynesis is a reading effect – a woman-effect in reading – which destabilizes old versions of femininity, and undoes the **binary** of masculine ideals of femininity versus the reality of women who live in a material, not an idealized, state. It is a reading practice, and especially a creative critical practice, in which (masculine) objectivism is parodied and punctured as well as attacked on the grounds of its own illogicality (it cannot claim universality if it does not address 'woman' or women). Thus both real experience and the theoretical interventions of academic feminism conspire together in gynesis for both political (real or experiential) and academic (philosophical and theoretical) ends.

Gynocentrism – Literally, woman-centred. In critical practice, it refers to the presumption that the reader and the writer of a literary work are both female, and that the critical act is also aimed towards the woman reader.

Gynocritics – Literally, criticism of women. The term was coined in English by Elaine Showalter to describe a literary-critical presumption that feminist criticism would focus its attention on the works of women writers.

Hegemony – Term associated with Italian marxist Antonio Gramsci that refers to the cultural or intellectual domination of one school of thought or **ideology** over another (or others).

Hermeneutic circle – The phrase is used to describe the impossibility of knowing anything except through what is already known. The phrase thus embodies a paradox: while a reader may be assumed to comprehend the entirety of a text fully only after all the component parts are understood, the various parts of the text cannot be understood until the text as a whole is discerned in its totality.

Hermeneutics – Originally a term associated with biblical exegesis and the interpretation of religious texts and especially their allegorical aspects; now more commonly employed as a defining term for a branch of interpretation developed from modern linguistics and philosophy which addresses modes of interpretation.

Heterogeneity – Those elements or aspects of texts or other subjects of analysis which are dissimilar and incongruous, or which cannot be incorporated by analysis into an organic whole.

Heteroglossia – Term often associated with Mikhail Bakhtin that refers to the many discourses that occur within a given language on a microlinguistic scale; 'raznorechie' in Russian, heteroglossia literally signifies as 'different-speech-ness'. Bakhtin employed the term as a means for explaining the hybrid nature of the modern novel and its many competing utterances.

Heuristic – A heuristic argument is one that depends on assumptions garnered from past experience, or from trial and error.

History/Historicism – History designates, broadly, the study or record of a series of chronological events. In addition to denoting a sphere of knowledge that explores past events, history refers to the events or phenomena that affect a given nation or institution. A somewhat vague term, historicism in critical discourse suggests either that human thought is historically grounded and undergoes **epistemological** transformations during the course of history (so that what constitutes the idea of beauty in **aesthetic** thought does not remain static but changes, for example), or that history is understood as a teleological process, whereby transformations occur as part of a general and necessary series of developments. More generally, historicism connotes an aspect of literary criticism that studies literary works within their **heterogeneous** or interrelated historical **contexts**. In addition to exploring the social or cultural forces at work in a given literary text, historical critics attempt to account for the reception and literary significance of that work in the past and the present. Historical critics recognize that literary works function as the product of the social, historical and cultural forces inherent in the era of their composition.

Homophobia – Fear and hatred of homosexuals.

Homosocial – Term coined by Eve Kosofsky Sedgwick to describe the networks of male-male relationships in literature and in culture at large. Homosociality covers a spectrum of male relationships from father and son, buddies, love rivals, sports opponents and team-mates, club members and so on – which might all be undertaken by strictly 'straight men' – through to entirely homosexual relationships at the other end of the spectrum.

Humanism/Humanist – Western European philosophical discourse, the first signs of which emerged in the Early Modern Period, and, subsequently, critical mode that argues for the centrality of man (or more broadly, humanity) as a critical category; often, though not always, implicitly or explicitly secular.

Hybridity – Originally naming something or someone of mixed ancestry or derived from **heterogeneous** sources, the term has been employed in postcolonialism, particularly in the work of Homi Bhabha, to signify a reading of identities which foregrounds the work of **difference** in identity resistant to the imposition of fixed, unitary identification which is, in turn, a hierarchical location of the colonial or **subaltern subject**.

Hyperreality – Term associated with the work of Jean Baudrillard, defined succinctly by him as 'the meticulous reduplication of the real, preferably through another, reproductive medium, such as photography'. The representation of the real assumes a reality of its own, achieving a **fetishistic** condition no longer simply being the sign of the concrete real.

Icon – Identified in modern **semiotics** as a particular type of sign, wherein there is a resemblance, rather than an arbitrary relationship, between the **signifier** and **signified**.

Idealism – Belief in a transcendent or metaphysical truth beyond reality.

Identity Politics – Refers to the ideologies of **difference** that characterize politically motivated movements and schools of literary criticism such as multiculturalism, in which diversity or ethnicity functions as the principal issue of political debate.

Ideological State Apparatus – Term coined by Louis Althusser, in his essay, 'Ideology and Ideological State Apparatuses'. Althusser argues that ideology is not only a matter of ideas or mechanisms of representation but of material practices which exist in the form of apparatuses and institutions, such as schools, the church and so on. Literature is not simply a text but a production of legal, educational and cultural institutions.

Ideology – Systems of cultural assumptions, or the discursive concatenation of beliefs or values which uphold or oppose social order, or which otherwise provide a coherent structure of thought that hides or silences the contradictory elements in social and economic formations.

Imaginary/Symbolic/Real – Jacques Lacan's version of psychoanalytic thought posits three psychic realms. The aim of the 'healthy' adult is to achieve a certain mastery within the Symbolic realm: that is, the realm of ordered, structured paraphrasable language, the realm of Law. However, the Symbolic realm is not ideal because language itself is, following Saussure, conventional, and only arbitrarily connected to the objects its describes. Indeed, language in Lacan's definition describes what is not there. He argues that a child learns to speak in response to the absence of his object of **desire** (the mother, or her breast); he learns to say 'I want' and thus becomes initiated into the beginnings of his necessary if painful accommodation with the Symbolic. This process of 'joining' the Symbolic order begins with the **mirror phase** which initiates the child into the beginnings of language after he catches sight of himself – or rather of a reflection of himself – in a mirror, and recognizes himself for the first time as a separate and distinct **being**, not one with either the world or with his mother. Lacan calls this very early beginning of acculturation 'Imaginary' because the mirror image that reveals the child to himself is, in fact, merely an image – or a signifier. His recognition of himself is therefore a misrecognition of an image, not a fact. No one, Lacan argues, no matter how well adjusted, ever leaves the Imaginary realm completely; there are always Imaginary residues (misrecognitions) even in the most powerful Symbolic forms. The Real, Lacan's third realm, is by far the least important. He uses the term to refer to the merely contingent accidents of everyday life that impinge on our **subjectivity**, but which have no fundamental psychic causes or meanings: trapping your hand in the car door might hurt, but it doesn't signify, and it belongs to the realm of the Real.

Imperialism – Refers to the ways in which one culture or nation appropriates the land, people and resources of another to further its colonial ends; also, the practices and discourses which promote and maintain the cultural, economic and ideological assumptions underpinning the dominance of one nation by another. In *Culture and Imperialism* (1993), Edward Said argues that imperialism names the practices, attitudes, and theories 'of a dominating metropolitan centre ruling a distant territory', and that colonialism, defined by Said as the occupation of that territory, is the consequence of imperialism.

Implied Author – Term associated with Wayne Booth, who in his *The Rhetoric of Fiction* distinguishes between the *real* and *implied* author. The latter is an idealized figure, distinct from the narrator. The implied author, defined by Booth as the 'core of norms and choices' which dominate a given text, is discernible through the reader's assumptions about the moral, political and other values which are expressed by the text as a whole, regardless of the real author's statements on such matters outside the text (in interviews and so forth). The three formal aspects of a text which serve to define the implied author are *style*, *tone* and *technique*.

Implied Reader – Wolfgang Iser defines the *implied reader* in his *The Act of Reading: A Theory of Aesthetic Response* as a hypothetical figure or concept produced through the assumptions, beliefs, historical knowledge, and philosophical and political positions, embedded in and constituting the structure of a given text.

Intentional Fallacy – Term coined by W. K. Wimsatt and Monroe C. Beardsley to describe critical methods that seek to interpret a literary work by reference to the **author's intentions**. Wimsatt and Beardsley argued that this position was necessarily untenable since (a) the author's intentions could never be satisfactorily recovered; and (b) the work could only be read and judged in its own terms, without reference to extra-textual information.

Intersubjectivity – Denotes the concept of intercommunication between separate, conscious minds. Intersubjectivity also connotes the capacity for becoming accessible to multiple subjects.

Intertextuality – Term coined originally by Julia Kristeva, intertextuality refers to the ways in which all utterances (whether written or spoken) necessarily refer to other utterances, since words and linguistic/grammatical structures pre-exist the individual speaker and the individual speech. Intertextuality can take place consciously, as when a writer sets out to quote from or allude to the works of another. But it always, in some sense, takes place in all utterance.

Intervention – Term often associated with theorist Gayatri Chakravorty Spivak that refers to the political act or strategy of entering into, or 'intervening' in, a given debate or historical moment so as to have a voice on a particular subject.

Irony – The contradiction, incongruity or discrepancy between appearance or expectation and reality. Irony can be understood in terms of events, situations and the structural components of literature. Dramatic irony involves a situation in which a given character's statements come back to haunt him or her, while tragic irony refers to situations in which the protagonist's tragic end is foreshadowed by a sense of foreboding and misinformation. Structural irony reflects a given author's attempt to establish an ironic layer of meaning throughout a text, often by virtue of the ironic distance provided by the narration of a literary work.

Isotopy – A semantic strategy that allows for a uniform reading of a story.

Iterability/Iteration – Idea, formalized in the work of Jacques Derrida, specifically in *Limited Inc*, which, as a quasi-concept, challenges the very idea of the stability of concepts and conceptuality in general. Iterability does not signify repetition simply; it signifies an alterability within the repetition of the same: a novel is a novel, generically, but every novel will inevitably differ from every other. Thus the concept of the novel is destabilized by our experience of every novel we read and, argues Derrida, we have to deal with the paradox of the simultaneity of sameness *and* **difference**.

Jouissance – Literally, in French, 'pleasure, enjoyment' but with legal connotations relating to property and rights, lost in translation, referring to the right to enjoy. The word has come to be used in psychoanalytic and feminist theories to mean more especially pleasures associated with sensuous and sexual gratification, or orgasm. As such, it refers to a fulfilment that is necessarily merely temporary, and that must therefore always be sought anew.

Kenosis – Greek, for 'emptying', traditionally employed within Christian theology referring the idea of Christ's renunciation of the power of incarnation. Harold Bloom employs the term in *The Anxiety of Influence* to suggest the revisionary process by which a poet 'empties' or 'isolates' himself from his or her poetic influences so as to create a poetry which is not simply a repetition of the precursor's influence in other words. The term is also associated with the work of Gianni Vattimo which refers, particularly in feminist theology, to the notion of 'self-emptying', or giving oneself to the world.

Labour theory of value – Tendency of the value (or price) of goods produced and sold under competitive conditions to be in proportion to the labour costs incurred during production.

Language – Refers to words, their pronunciation and their syntactical combination in order to be understood by a community. Language similarly denotes a given system for communicating ideas or feelings via the use of signs, sounds, gestures or marks.

Langue/Parole – In Saussurean linguistics, *langue* refers to the whole system of a given language (its grammar, vocabulary and syntax); *parole* refers to the individual instance of utterance that takes place under the framework of the *langue*. Saussure's interest was primarily in the study of the system or *langue*.

Law of the Father (*Le nom du père*) – Phrase used by Jacques Lacan in relation to the Oedipus complex, which signals the **subject's** comprehension of paternal or authoritative prohibition, a prohibition constitutive of **authority**. Lacan plays on the homophonic quality of the French for name (*nom*), which sounds like the French for 'no' (*non*).

Liberal Humanism – Often used as a pejorative term, the values of liberal humanism have to do with democracy, decency, tolerance, rationality, the belief in human progress and a whole-hearted support of the individual against the machinations of 'inhuman' political systems. The problem of liberal humanism is that it frequently lapses into **universalism** or **idealism**, and has no proper responses to totalitarianism where the individual is frankly powerless. It is a belief system that also disguises the very profound inequities and horrors of even western democratic societies. It is a rejection of systematized thought in return for a generalized belief in the essential goodness of most people most of the time.

Libidinal economy – By positing the libidinal as an 'economy', Jean-François Lyotard reads **desire** as a material, rather than simply psychic, process. He is less concerned with what desire 'is' than in how it functions. He sees desire as the energy of society, but an unstable energy, unpredictably connecting the psychological to the economical in a type of feeling and desire Lyotard calls an 'intensity'. **Narrative**, broadly defined as a poem or an advertisement, binds these moments of intensities into an apparently coherent pattern in order to exploit the power residing there.

Liminality – From the Latin, *limen*, meaning threshold, liminality signifies a condition of being at a threshold or limit, spatially or temporally. Textual analysis of liminality draws attention to the passage across limits, boundaries or thresholds in **narratives**, where the limit being crossed is constituted as an assemblage of culturally significant values.

Lisible/Scriptible – Used by Roland Barthes in the definition of types of text, the terms are translatable as 'readable' and 'writerly' respectively. The readerly text does all the work for the reader, leaving the reader in the role of passive consumer. The writerly text makes the reader work and resists the conventions of readerly or realist textuality, principally the assumptions of linguistic transparency and the self-evidence of meaning.

Literature – At its most neutral, and broadest, *literature* signifies textual manifestations of **writing**. The term also refers to the production of literary works and to specific bodies of poetry or prose. *Literature* has been used to designate any 'imaginative', 'creative' or 'fictional' writing, whether in poetry, drama or prose. There is, furthermore, in the use of the term an implicit **aesthetic** or other form of **value** judgement, so that some works are considered literary while others are not. Another determination of *literature* is in a recognition of the use of language in particular ways which transform so-called ordinary or everyday speech, through **tropological** estrangement or intensification, for example. One perspective is that literary language, or certain aspects of it and the way in which it functions, is noticeable in that it draws attention to its departures from everyday utterances. Another perspective is that **context** can determine the definition of literature, whether this is a matter of institutional **authority** or a marketing device which announces a book as a 'novel'. The question of the literary therefore comes down not necessarily to any perceivable intrinsic qualities as it does to acts of **reading** and the ways in which reading directs itself to particular aspects of a text rather than others.

Logocentrism – Term ascribed to French philosopher Jacques Derrida that refers to the nature of western thought, language and culture since Plato's era. The Greek signifier for 'word,' 'speech' and 'reason', logos possesses connotations in western culture for law and truth. Hence, logocentrism refers to a culture that revolves around a central set of universal principles or beliefs.

Machine Subjectivity – Term associated with Félix Guattari that refers to '**semiotic** productions of the mass media, of computers, of telecommunications, robotics, etc., outside of psychological subjectivity'. For Guattari, the technologies of information and communication serve to reorient and transform the thinking of subjectivity in terms of **heterogeneous** semiotic flows. Machinic subjectivity is productive, 'polyphonic' and irreducibly multiform rather than unifying. However, while it may be productive in hitherto undreamed of ways, Guattari warns that machine subjectivity has the potential for a 'mind-numbing mass mediatization'.

Manicheanism – Belief in a kind of philosophical or religious dualism.

Masculinity/Femininity – **Binary opposition** which refers to the construction of attributes of identity associated with or based on a given individual's **sexuality** or

gender-ascribed perspectives and/or culturally encoded value systems concerning behaviour.

Masquerade – In contemporary gender theory, the concept of masquerade, derived from the writings of Joan Rivière, is central, particularly her essay 'Womanliness as a Masquerade' (1929). It argues that gender is a performance rather than a natural phenomenon with which one is born; it has to be acquired, learned and polished and is in no sense natural.

Mass culture – Term often associated with British cultural theorist Richard Hoggart that refers to a new commercialized social order that finds its roots in the mass dissemination of television, radio, magazines and a variety of other media; in Hoggart's view, mass culture shapes and reconstructs cultural, social and intellectual life in its image and via its **mediated** depiction of artificial levels of reality.

Master/slave dialectic – Hegel's model for understanding the interaction between two self-consciousnesses and the manner in which each entity considers the **other** in terms of the **self**. Hegel argues that this admittedly 'primitive' model reveals the ways in which each figure functions as a 'mirror' for the **other** and ultimately eschews co-operation because of their inherently subordinate relationship.

Materialism – Doctrine or system of beliefs that maintains that economic or social change occurs via material well-being rather than intellectual or spiritual phenomena.

Mediation – The manner in which various conflicting parties either intervene or promote reconciliation or settlement on behalf of others. Concept of textual transformation, often employed in marxist and other materialist criticisms, which supersedes reductive or crude models of reflection which assume that any given text simply reflects the world, instead of mediating that image and thereby shaping or influencing the reader's comprehension in a particular way. Also, the notion of mediation is employed to suggest that the text is itself not a simple recording or representation but is influenced in its shaping by a number of factors including matters of historical, cultural and ideological relation.

Metacriticism – Critical mode which takes the act of criticism, its principles, processes, concerns and interests, as its principal subject. Works such as Terry Eagleton's *Literary Theory: An Introduction* or Jonathan Culler's *Structuralist Poetics* are, typically, works definable as metacritical.

Metafiction – A fictional mode that takes fictionality – the conventions of writing fiction – as part of its own subject matter.

Metalanguage – Roman Jakobson defines metalanguage as any form of language which defines linguistic properties. Following the work of Alfred Tarski, Colin MacCabe describes metalanguage which announces its object languages as material, and signals them so through the conventions of the imposition of quotation marks and other diacritical markers, while assuming an implicit transparency for itself. Thus, for MacCabe, the 'narrator' or '**narrative** voice' in a realist novel assumes the role of a metalanguage, in that it appears to 'observe' rather than to interpret or analyse.

Metaphysics – A division of philosophy that explores the fundamental nature of reality or **being**; includes such disciplines as **ontology**, cosmology and **epistemology**, among others.

Mimesis – Can be used in two distinct ways. Firstly, mimesis (from the Greek *mimos*, a mime) refers to the imitation or representation of reality in art. Mimesis can also be used to describe the process by which one writing mimics another kind: for example, a fiction might pretend to be a historical document in order to gain **authority** for its account.

Mimicry – Generally, the practice, act or art of imitation, often for the purpose of ridicule. Homi Bhabha uses the term to identify a form of colonial control of its **subjects**. The colonizer seeks to impose on the colonial subject the forms and values of the colonial master, so the Anglicization of Indians and Africans during British colonial rule. However, as Bhabha identifies, there remains a gap between the desire to erase **difference**, indicated by Bhabha in the phrase 'not white/not quite', from which emerges **ambivalence**.

Mirror Phase – Jacques Lacan posited that a baby, at first an oceanic bundle of undifferentiated **desire** who believes himself to be continuous with the larger world and his mother, first comes to a realization of himself as a unitary and separate **being** when, at age six to eighteen months, he first sees his own reflection in a mirror. For Lacan, this is the beginning of the **ego's** development, but it is significantly founded on a misapprehension, since the image in the mirror is a signified – a substitute image of the **self**, not the self itself. Hence, the mirror phase implies that the ego is founded on highly unstable grounds rather than in any essential personality.

Mise en abyme – From the French for 'placed into the abyss', *mise en abyme* has come to mean **narrative** or philosophical moments of infinite regression. Although Chinese boxes or other infinite regressive features are often used for comic effect, the French term emphasizes the terror of emptiness that is also part of the free play of language where language has only the most tangential, arbitrary and conventionalized relationships with reality.

Mnemotechnic – Literally, the work of memory or that which memory causes to appear. The concept of mnemotechnic combines the idea of involuntary memory, the idea that memory is not passively stored in the mind but is, instead, an active force which can return without conscious effort, with that of impersonal memory through the effects of chance association and signification. Thus a literary text may be said to be produced out of, while actively producing, preserving and remembering personal, social and cultural pasts beyond the immediate **intentions of the author**.

Modernism – Term referring to the literary, artistic and general culture of the first half of the twentieth century. Modernism is distinguished by its general rejection of previous literary traditions, particularly those of the late nineteenth century and of **bourgeois** society. In addition to involving an existentialist view of the universe, modernists explore myth as a device of formal organization.

Modernity – From one perspective, modernity may be defined as the condition of embracing or reflecting the value systems inherent in modernism's intellectual value systems, as 'modernism' signifies a project identifiable with intellectual and artistic projects of the early twentieth century. However, the idea of modernity is a vexed one, not least because there is little agreement as to where the moment of modernity, in **epistemological** terms, emerges historically. There are arguments that initial instances of modernity or 'early' modernity are coterminous with the development of notions of **subjectivity**, corporeality and autonomy in the Renaissance or, as it is alternatively described, the Early Modern Period. On the other hand, modernity is also identified as a specifically 'Enlightenment' project, related in particular to the thinking of the inevitability of progress. Whichever cultural, intellectual and historical set of circumstances one identifies with or as the idea of the modern, what is consistent in these arguments is the idea that modernity emerges as a struggle, critical tension or even break with its forebears. At the same time, it is argued that that which is comprehended as modern, while opening a gap between its own instance and the past, still bears traces of that past in its own thinking. Another aspect of the conceptualization of modernity, drawn chiefly from the work of Martin Heidegger and Walter Benjamin, is a transformation in the relationships between society and technology, relationships which are examined extensively in the work of, for example, Paul Virilio, Giorgio Agamben and Gianni Vattimo.

Molar/Molecular – Terms employed in the work of Gilles Deleuze and Félix Guattari, to describe the processes constituting the organization of the human **subject**. The molar signifies the territorially defined stability of conscious awareness (see **deterritorialization**). The molecular are those unconscious elements in their multiplicities which constitute the **flows** of **desiring machines**, which are brought to a halt and thereby stabilized or otherwise excluded within the molar organization of **consciousness**. It is the function of **schizoanalysis** to destabilize and **deterritorialize** the flows and their molar organization, so as to accommodate without limiting the processes of molecular **becoming**.

Monist – A person who reduces all phenomena to a single viewpoint or principle; also, a given individual who views reality as the product of a singular, unified vision, rather than as the sum of a series of component parts. Monist analysis – analysis that focuses solely or primarily on one form of domination (for example, gender, or race, or class).

Monologism – Term coined by Mikhail Bakhtin to describe characters representing multiple points of view while being clearly dominated by a single voice or **ideology**.

Morpheme – The smallest linguistic or structural unit of language.

Multiculturalism – Refers to the social and political movement and/or position that views **differences** between individuals and groups to be a potential venue of cultural strength and renewal; multiculturalism celebrates and explores different varieties of experience stemming from racial, ethnic, gender, sexual and/or class differences.

Multiplicative analysis – Analysis developed by feminists of colour. It seeks to account for the experiences of people who have been subordinated to several forms of domination. Whereas an additive approach would see (for example) race, class and gender as three discrete systems that accumulate oppressions on poor women of colour, a multiplicative approach analyses how race and class change the meanings of gender, how race and gender change the meanings of class, and how class and gender change the meanings of race. A multiplicative approach highlights the differential experiences of women of colour rather than their 'double' or 'triple' oppression. Finally, a multiplicative approach is contextual and historically informed. It recognizes that in certain cases, one of the features (race, gender, class, sexuality, etc.) may be more salient than the others. Also called multiaxial analysis, or intersectionality.

Myth – The traditional story of pseudo-historical events that functions as a fundamental element within the worldview of a given people or nation. Myths are similarly employed by human communities to attempt to explain the nature of various practices, beliefs, or natural phenomena.

Narrative – At its most fundamental, a narrative is an account of events, whether real or fictional. However, narrative differs from a simple account or report of events which are not shaped or reordered (supposing such a thing to be possible). Gérard Genette offers a sustained account of narrative structure and form in his *Narrative Discourse* ([1972] 1980), which addresses five principal aspects of narrative: (a) order of events; (b) duration of events and the time it takes to tell incidents; (c) frequency or repetition of events and how such recurrences shape the narrative form from the basic **diegesis**; (d) mood, by which Genette indicates the narrator's point of view, perspective, distance or proximity to the events narrated; (e) narrative voice. For Genette, the analysis of narrative concerns itself and implies the study of a series of relationships which make up narrative, these being (a) the relationship between a particular discourse and the events which are retold through that discourse, and (b) the relationship between the discourse and the act of narration. Thus there is for Genette a tripartite structure at its most basic to any narrative: discourse, narration, event, or, as he formulates it, analysis of narrative is 'a study of the relationships between narrative and story, between narrative and narrating, and. . .story and narrating'. Studying narrative is therefore not simply comprehending it as an account but also an analytical understanding of how a narrative is given the shape it has, why certain events have greater significance than others, in relation to the totality of the narrative, and how events retold are shaped by the act of narration or the role of the narrator.

Narratology – Theory and systematic study of **narrative**, and especially the study of the structural, formal and temporal elements of narrative and the relationships between them. Narratology will address the functions of duration, repetition, the chronological or anachronic reordering of events out of a progressive temporal linear sequence, the role of the narrator and the various levels of discourse, along with their hierarchical or **architectonic** relationships, which constitute narrative structure.

Neoimperialism – Relating to the manner in which nations, policies or practices extend their dominion or **authority** over other, often less economically or culturally viable others.

Nomad/ism/Nomadology – Term associated with the work of Gilles Deleuze and Félix Guattari which figurally stresses the possibility of thinking differently, and which is given extended consideration in their *A Thousand Plateaus*. Deleuze and Guattari's concern in employing this term is not with a particular content of thought so much as with the utopian expression of an other modality of thought beyond dominant philosophical models. Deleuze does not propose an absolute model of nomadic thinking but merely suggests, idealistically and as a hope, its possibility. Nomadic thinking would be *just* thinking which does not remain within **epistemological** territories. Indeed, a feature of nomadism in thought would be its **flow** and, with that, its **deterritorialization** of structured models or disciplines of thought. Concomitant on that flow of nomadic thinking would be its strategic 'weakness', that is to say the abandonment of the aggressiveness typical of territorial modes of thought. Furthermore, nomadic thinking *is* nomadic, it drifts, often from itself, in that it is not centred on any authoritative, governing or originary principal, by which it might ground itself (and thereby defend its 'territory') and to which it might return.

Nominalism – A theory that argues against the notion of universal essences in reality and maintains that only individual perspectives, rather than abstract generalities, exist.

Normativity – The postulation of **hegemonic**, culturally prescribed norms or standards such as heterosexuality.

Objectification – The manner in which various individuals or social groups treat others as objects and expressions of their own senses of reality; reducing an **other**'s sense of **being** into a form that can be experienced universally by other individuals and social groups.

Objet petit a – A complex term from Lacanian psychoanalysis. Lacan suggested that objects of **desire** are always changing because the desiring **subject** is always changing too. He wanted to find a term to describe the mutability and mortality of the desired object, and to describe it in a way that disrupted what he saw as the stability of the **binary** 'desiring subject/desired object' in Freudian thought. The term he came up with is 'objet petit a', where 'a' stands for 'autre' (French for **other**), distinguished from the Other elsewhere in his writing by the lower case initial letter. *Objet petit a* can be anything at all that is touched by desire. Desire is fleeting and mutable hence the object of desire is always in flux and is always just out of reach or just beyond the field of vision. In many ways, then, the term stands for desire, always understood by Lacan as absent and unattainable, but always equally constitutive of the subject (who is what s/he desires or lacks).

Oedipus Complex – In Freudian psychoanalysis the Oedipus Complex refers to the whole complex of both loving and hostile feeling experienced by a child towards its parents in the process of achieving acculturated maturity. The Oedipus Complex manifests itself as an intense rivalry, including the horrifying wish for his/her death, with the parent of the same sex for the love of the parent of the opposite sex (which is to be understood as a libidinal or sexualized **desire**). Negotiation of this complex, the relinquishing of forbidden (incestuous) desire and its displacement onto suitable substitute objects (a boy must love not his mother, but a woman *like* his mother; a girl must love not her father, but a baby given to her by a man *like* her father) is required to achieve healthy adulthood. The complex is never completely successfully negotiated, however, and there are always residual Oedipal problems in even the healthiest of adults.

Ontic – Relating to **epistemological** inquiry concerning the real rather than the phenomenal **being**, existence or structure of entities.

Ontology – Branch of philosophy addressing the meaning or essence of **being**.

Ontotheology – Any form of **ontological** or, in general, metaphysical determination, modelled on theology, in terms of a uniquely superior **being**, concept or word, such as the divine of theology.

Organic unity – A term employed to define a conceptual framework offering a coherent model for the mind–body duality derived from Cartesian thought. Organic unity has three significant strands: (a) identity, that which is understood as relationship mental perception of external events and the materiality of those events; (b) continuity, which describes the linguistic-conceptual system that incorporates mental and physical terms; (c) finally, there is **dialectic**. The final term signifies the relationship between empirical and **hermeneutic epistemologies**, the former indicating the physical domain, the latter the mental realm of the subject. Each of these perspectives on the dualism is itself an integrated form providing the mind–body dualism a consistent unity. Most generally the notion of organic unity indicates a unity comprising different systems that function independently of, and yet which are coterminous with one another.

Orientalism – Term coined by Edward Said naming the ensemble of western, usually though not exclusively European discourses and other forms of representation of non-western cultures. Said traces the history of Orientalist discourses in literature, the arts and other documents from the eighteenth century onwards.

Other/otherness – Term employed throughout critical discourse in differing ways, otherness names the quality or state of existence of **being** other or different from established norms and social groups; the distinction that one makes between one's self and others, particularly in terms of sexual, ethnic and relational senses of **difference**; in Lacanian psychoanalysis, there is the other and the Other: the former signifies that which is not really other but is a reflection and projection of the **ego**; the latter signifies a radical **alterity** irreducible to any imaginary or subjective identification. In the texts of Luce Irigaray, the other indicates the position always occupied by woman within patriarchal culture and other masculinist cultures which privileges masculinity as self-sameness, or otherwise a signifier of presence, origin or centrality.

Overdetermination – The act or practice of overemphasizing, or resolving in an excessive fashion, a given conclusion of psychological factors. Alternatively, a text which is said to be overdetermined is available for multiple readings from various, **heterogeneous**, if not theoretically or polemically incompatible, positions.

Parapraxis – Freudian term, denoting inadvertent slips of the tongue or pen as revealed symptoms of psychic disturbance; the **subject** or analysand, intending to say or write one thing, says or writes something else which has been repressed.

Parody – A written imitation of an author's work, following closely the tone or style of the original, but reworked so as to produce comic or inappropriate effect.

Pathetic Fallacy – Term coined by John Ruskin to signify the attribution of nature with human emotions and qualities, or the **displacement** of a psychic condition onto natural phenomena such as atmospherics.

Patriarchy – Literally 'the rule of the father'. Patriarchy is the name given to the whole complex systems of male dominance by which most societies are run now and in the past. Patriarchy includes the systematic exclusion of women from rights of inheritance, to education, the vote, equal pay, equal rights before the law; it also includes the ways in which even more liberal regimes tend to leave women out of structures of **power** even when they claim to be regimes based on equality.

Performance/Performative – The act of public exhibition that results in a transaction between performer and audience; an utterance that, via its public display, causes a linguistic interaction with the exhibition's object. The condition of performative articulation is given particular consideration by Jacques Derrida in the context of the instability of speech acts. Derrida's analysis of the performative in 'Signature Event Context' comes as a response to the work of speech act theorist J. L. Austin, who distinguishes between constative and performative or illocutionary utterances, the former being an 'assertion' or 'description', the latter being an 'utterance which allows us to do something by means of speech itself'. In *Bodies that Matter: On the Discursive Limits of Sex*, Judith Butler identifies performative speech acts as 'forms of authoritative speech: most performatives, for instance, are statements that, in the uttering, also perform a certain action and exercise a binding power'. Derrida's critique, on which Butler draws, is built on his understanding that an utterance is never stable but always available for citation and iterability and, indeed, only aspires to communicability in being transmissible, repeatable, beyond its supposedly 'original' **context** (which itself is never self-sufficient). Thus the idea of a speech act as act is already troubled by the iterable condition of the sign.

Phallic – Relating to or resembling the phallus, a symbol of generative power; refers to an interest in the phallus or a masculinist point of view; in psychoanalysis, a reference to particular stage in male development when the **subject** is preoccupied with the genitals.

Phallic Primacy – Concept often associated with Freud's castration complex, phallic primacy refers to the presence of male genitalia and its impact upon psychosocial relations.

Phallocentrism – Privileging of a masculinist, specifically unitary, singular, point of view in terms of individuals, institutions or cultures.

Phallocratism – The institutionalization and **hegemony** of a masculinist perspective; in the parlance of French feminist Luce Irigaray, phallocratism refers to the often masculinized division of labour that exists between the sexes.

Phallogocentric – Term coined by Jacques Derrida to describe the privileging of the masculine gender in western culture, language and thought. Derrida's neologism combines the ideas of phallocentrism and **logocentrism** (the idea that all ideas are centred on certain key concepts, such as truth, beauty, reason, goodness, God).

Phantasm – A mental image, the product of **fantasy**, the imagination, or delusion; imaginary projections or visualizations, images arising from the unconscious. Louis Althusser observes in his reading of the Freudian concept of the phantasm that, inasmuch as the phantasm is a figure for **desire**, it thus operates metaphorically.

Phenomenology – School of thought founded by German philosopher Edmund Husserl that maintains that objects attain meaning through their perception in a given person's **consciousness**.

Phoneme – The basic sound unit of pronunciation in language; English, for example, includes forty-five phonemes.

Pleasure/Pleasure principle – Pleasure refers to a state of gratification, particularly in terms of delight or sensual fulfilment. Freud names the pleasure principle the psychic drive after gratification which has to be repressed in order that humans can function in the social world. Jacques Lacan develops a distinction between pleasure and *jouissance*, with the pleasure principle naming a symbolic law which, in Lacan's words, 'regulates the whole functioning of the psychic apparatus'. *Jouissance*, on the other hand, is disruptive rather than regulatory.

Pluralism – Variety of approach and assumption. A pluralist approach to criticism is one that has many different methods and assumptions at its disposal, rather than an approach that imposes a single model on all texts, no matter what the circumstances. What is significant about critical pluralism is that the various positions which any pluralist discourse brings together are not significantly at odds with one another, and that pluralism often signals an implicit, if not explicit, consensus.

Point de capiton – Phrase employed by Jacques Lacan, usually translated as 'quilting' 'anchoring' or 'suturing' point. Taken from embroidery, the phrase indicates for Lacan moments in the psyche where signifier and signified are gathered, or stitched together, thereby momentarily bringing to a halt the slippage of signification by which **subjectivity** is constituted.

Polysemy – Relating to the possibility of a simultaneous multiplicity of meaning encoded within a single phrase or text.

Positivism – Philosophical theory, formulated by Auguste Comte, which privileges observable facts and phenomena over modes of knowledge such as theology and metaphysics.

'Post' – The notion – as signalled in terms such as postmodernism, post-marxism, poststructuralism or post-theory – of an intellectual moment that ensues after the occurrence of a paradigm shift or **epistemological** transition of sorts. In addition to denoting the pastness of a given intellectual or cultural epoch, 'post' suggests the persistence of enduring philosophical quandaries and discoveries associated with such historical or theoretical moments, which the notion of 'postism' hints are not, in fact, over, but which haunt or disturb the progressivist sense of having apparently moved beyond particular modes of inquiry.

Postmodernity – Term referring to the era, state of being or literary arts associated with postmodernism. Jean-François Lyotard defines postmodernity as being marked by a suspicion of **grand narratives**. The idea of a postmodern era is also one provisionally defined by the advent of **tele-technologies**, the emergence of globalization and post-industrial society, and the power of the image and **simulacrum** within consumer culture, where images such as the Coke or Nike logos assume greater significance in themselves than any real product or reality to which they might refer.

Power – In the work of Michel Foucault, power constitutes one of the three axes constitutive of **subjectification**, the other two being **ethics** and truth. For Foucault, power implies knowledge and vice versa. However, power is causal, it is constitutive of knowledge, even while knowledge is, concomitantly, constitutive of power: knowledge gives one power, but one has the power in given circumstances to constitute bodies of knowledge, discourses, and so on, as valid or invalid, truthful or untruthful. Power serves in making the world both knowable and controllable. Yet, the nature of power, as Foucault suggests in the first volume of his *History of Sexuality*, is essentially proscriptive, concerned more with imposing limits on its subjects.

Presentism – Refers to a radical overemphasis or privileging of the present over what is perceived to be a less culturally and technologically effectual past.

Primal/horde/scene – That which is primal refers in Freudian psychoanalysis to the **desires**, fears, needs and anxieties, constitutive of the origins of the **subject's** psyche. The idea of the primal horde signifies an originary human social collective. The primal scene is that moment in Freudianism when the infant subject becomes aware of sexual relations between its parents.

Projection – In psychoanalytic discourse, the transference of **desire** or **fantasy** onto another person, object or situation, in order to avoid the recognition of the **subject's** responsibility for his or her behaviour or actions.

Queer – Term often associated with the contemporary gay and lesbian studies movement – i.e. queer theory (this identification, it should be noted, registering a significant development from, or even, in some cases, break with, the idea of gay and lesbian studies). Queer denotes a sense of **otherness**, as well as a means for breaking with convention and theorizing about sexuality and its significant place in the construction of transcultural models of homosexuality. 'Queer' has been deployed as an affirmative and performative term which resists becoming a fixed category and thus gives voice to those elided or marginalized by 'gay' and 'lesbian' studies: bisexuals, transexuals, sado-masochists, for example. It is thus the very identificatory slipperiness in the term which maintains its political potential. *In Bodies that Matter: On the Discursive Limits of Sex*, Judith Butler argues that it is in the **iterable** mutability of *queer*'s semantic operation that it can operate most effectively. Only while the term resists being domesticated, Butler argues, will it remain strategically, critically and, most importantly, politically efficacious.

Race – Refers to a family, tribe, people or nation that shares a set of common interests, beliefs, habits or characteristics.

Rationalism – Refers to the reliance upon reason as the basis for establishing religious or philosophical truth. In addition, philosophical notion, deriving from the work of Descartes, which emphasizes the constitution of knowledge based on reason rather than observation or sense perception.

Reader/Reading – A reader can be provisionally defined as a person who evaluates intellectually a given manuscript or image in an effort to comprehend or interpret its contents or form for a range of reasons, whether these reasons are defined as 'entertainment', 'education', 'enlightenment', 'pleasure', or a combination of these and other purposes. What we call reading is an active participation with a piece of writing or an image for the purpose of producing meaning, or, more generally, to 'translate' the book or image (or, indeed, the world) from its condition as a perceived ensemble of potential signs to a text on which the process of interpretation is brought to bear. It is important, if seemingly obvious, to note that reading takes time; the analysis of signs does not occur immediately, even if the object of reading is a poster or advertisement in a magazine. Reading is thus engaged in and as a temporal experience, an experience which is not limited to the time of holding the book open, standing in front of an image or watching a film (whether in the cinema or on a video). Moreover, reading is never simple or innocent, even when one reads 'for pleasure', as the phrase has it, because the reader, any reader, is always positioned through culture, history, education, **ideology** and so on. Thus the possibility of reading is constituted in various ways prior to any individual act of reading. At the same time, every text has a **singularity** for which the act of reading should be responsible and to which the act of reading should respond. One should therefore avoid producing a reading which, on the one hand, is neither simply a passive consumption nor, on the other, the active imposition of a particular meaning which suppresses or excludes other elements. Such a reading might be a 'politicized' reading which in its address of matters of class representation ignores issues of gender or race. Or there is the formal reading which, in discussing the **aesthetic** aspects of the writing, ignores or downplays the roles of history or ideology, or the function of **epistemological** assumptions behind the value judgements which the text appears to advance or which we, as readers, bring to the text. How one reads is therefore irreducible to a prescription or formula because of singularity and the responsibility to that singularity which reading entails. In the light of the question of singularity, some critics have suggested that to impose a 'reading' along certain lines (the political, the purely formal) is to avoid the complex negotiation that reading involves; it is the imposition of a reading within limits and towards a limit or horizon (this being the 'political', 'philosophical' or 'historical' meaning which is sought), and is, therefore, not a reading at all, but the avoidance of reading. At the same time, however, the responsibility of reading is such that one cannot simply read as one likes; one has to be attentive to the ways in which the text is articulated, the ways in which it appears to articulate itself and the ways in which it appears to be silent on matters. There is, furthermore in the act of reading the experience of the **undecidable**. For these reasons, properly speaking, the act of reading cannot come to an end. Reading always remains to come, not as a future moment or horizon in itself at which textual explication will arrive eventually and therefore have done with reading, but as the responsibility of the encounter with **singularity, undecideability** and **otherness**.

Realism/Realist – Realism has many meanings and is potentially an unusable word since people differ over what they mean by reality. In literature and the arts, however, it describes a common tendency from the early nineteenth century onwards to represent real life in fiction and painting, and to do so using common conventions of representation. One of the key problems with the term, though, is that nineteenth-century realist writers were generally ruthlessly selective in their materials, presenting no so much real life in the raw, but reality filtered and purged. Realism is often associated with representing average experience – the lives of middle-class characters who do little that is unusual or exciting; it prefers an objective standpoint, and is illusionist in that it asks its readers to forget that they are reading fiction. Readers are meant to 'identify' with characters as if they were real people. Events should be probable (or at the very least, possible); narrators should on the whole maintain a third-person distance and perspective; judgement should be easy for the reader. These conventions have become naturalized in many people's reading habits so that it is often difficult to disentangle reality from its representation. Nonetheless, many critics have attacked **bourgeois** realism for its narrow focus, moral certainties and social exclusivity.

Reality principle/effect – Term often associated with Jean Baudrillard that relates to the ways in which reality is often established and becomes represented for some individuals and cultures through hyperreal media such as photography, film and other media.

Referent – In Saussurean linguistics, the referent is that to which the word or sign refers: the real object in the real world for which the word or sign is an arbitrary and conventional signal.

Referential – A text that is referential is one that disguises its status as a work or text by making extended reference to the conditions of real life. The reader, that is, is encouraged to forget that what s/he is reading is *merely* a text.

Reification – The process or result of rendering some idea or philosophy into a material or concrete entity. The process by which philosophical or ideological concepts disappear to the extent that they become incorporated into the everyday. Concept employed in marxist discourse, which emphasizes the depersonalization of the **subject** as a result of capitalist modes of production and the **alienation** of labour.

Repetition compulsion – The neurotic and often harmful psychological condition in which the afflicted continue to engage in patterns of self-destructive and dangerous behaviour.

Repression – In psychoanalytic thought, repression is the process by which **subjects** try to get rid of **desires**, linked to instincts and imaged in thoughts and memory, that are somehow known to be forbidden by the wider culture. The forbidden thoughts are consigned to the unconscious; but they do not disappear, and may manifest themselves in symptomatic behaviours, in dreams, slips of the tongue and physical tics. Such symptoms are examples of what Freud called 'the return of the repressed'.

Rhetoric – The study of the art of speaking or writing effectively, as well as a skill involving the correct usage of speech. Rhetoric similarly refers to a given mode of language or aspect of verbal communication.

Rhizome – The figure of the rhizome, which is taken from a form of continuous, underground plant stem growth consisting of lateral shoots, is adapted strategically by Gilles Deleuze and Félix Guattari in A *Thousand Plateaus*. It suggests for Deleuze and Guattari a non-formalizable figure for thinking differently so as to affirm and potentialize the constant **becoming** of a thinking which **deterritorializes** the boundaries of conventional thinking within disciplines.

Romanticism – The literary term that refers to the literary, artistic and general culture of the first half of the nineteenth century. Romanticism is distinguished by its general embrace of the emotions and nature, particularly in response to a growing sense of materialism and to such moments of violence and upheaval as the French Revolution of 1789. In addition to rejecting the forms and conventions often associated with classicism and neoclassicism, romanticists sought value in spontaneity, subjective experience and original expression.

Saussurian Linguistics – A linguistic model deriving from the lectures of Ferdinand de Saussure. Saussure argued that the meanings that we give to words are not intrinsic but arbitrary; there is no connection between a word and its meaning except the one that we choose to give it. He further suggested that meanings are also relational. If a word has no inherent connection with its meaning, then its meaning derives from relations to do with **context** and syntax. Thirdly, Saussure also argued that language constitutes our reality since our only access to meaning is through language, so language itself must form us and our thoughts, not the other way around. However, if language is only ever arbitrary and relational, then reality is also contingent. His interest in language was to study the linguistic system (or langue) rather than the individual utterance (or *parole*) in order to understand the complete picture of human language, an approach taken up by structuralist theory which concentrates on larger structures.

Schizoanalysis – Term associated with the work of Gilles Deleuze and Félix Guattari. Schizoanalysis is opposed to the normative imperative in psychoanalysis embodied in the idea of the cure. As an analytical discourse, it aims to **deterritorialize** the discourses of the individual within an Oedipal schema, and to read various flows of **desire** irreducible to the imposition of limiting structures on the **self**. Schizoanalysis announces such flows as lines of escape, Deleuze and Guattari seeking to construct a critical discourse which itself escapes such limiting notions as the 'human=', and the situation of the 'proper' human **subject** within economic frameworks such as the Oedipal. Schizoanalysis is described in *Anti-Oedipus: Capitalism and Schizophrenia* ([1972] 1985) as a radical political and social form of psychoanalysis which extends beyond the traditional territory of psychoanalysis, the family. Through this Deleuze and Guattari propose to connect desire to **capitalism's** effects in particular ways, defining so-called human drives as the work of **desiring machines** while also proposing, in their words, 'to demonstrate the existence of an unconscious libidinal investment of sociohistorical production, distinct from the conscious investments coexisting with it'.

Scopophilia – The (often sexualized) pleasure in looking. Feminist critics in particular have criticized Freud's theories of infantile sexuality for their scopophilic emphasis on 'looking' and seeing the (**absence or presence** of the) sexual organs of the other sex. Feminist film theory, following the work of Laura Mulvey and influenced by Lacanian psychoanalysis, has theorized the **gaze** – that of both the camera and the audience – in terms of a scopophilic drive.

Selective tradition – Term coined by Raymond Williams to denote how a cultural heritage, apparently bequeathed to the present by the past, is in fact constructed in the present through processes of active selection.

Self – The psychological or cultural conception of a given individual's identity or sense of human particularity.

Self-referentiality – A self-referential text is one that refers to its own processes of production – a text that talks about its textuality. Unlike the referential text, it encourages its readers continually to recall that what is being read is fictive or illusory, not real at all.

Semiology – Analysis of linguistic signs; coined by Swiss linguist Ferdinand de Saussure in the early twentieth century as the linguistic study of socially and culturally inscribed codes of human interaction.

Semiotic/s – In the plural, semiotics refers to the 'science of signs' – systematic codes of representation. Julia Kristeva, however, has coined the term 'the semiotic' to refer to a mode in language. Language, she says, consists of the symbolic (derived from Lacan), the linguistic realm of transparency, paraphrasability, conformity and power. The semiotic is the pre-linguistic residue of language, made up of sounds, rhythms, the babbling incoherence of the child, the language of poetry and the language of psychosis. It is not precisely meaningless, but it cannot be subsumed in the symbolic. The semiotic pulses against symbolic language, making it mean both more and less than it intends.

Sexual difference – The differences between the sexes that derive from their different biological sex organs; by extension, sexual difference in psychoanalysis and other theories, is also shown to have cultural and psychic effects beyond the merely bodily.

Sexuality – A mobile concept, not easily contained through definition. If we follow the work of Elizabeth Grosz (in *Volatile Bodies: Towards A Corporeal Feminism*), it is possible to define sexuality in four different ways: (a) as a psychoanalytic drive; (b) as a constellation of practices 'involving bodies, organs and pleasures'; (c) as an identity which is culturally and psychically assumed and projected, and closely related to concepts and constructions of **gender**; (d) as a 'set of orientations, positions, and desires'. To this schema we can add that, in ordinary language, sexuality simply refers to sexual practice, to the performance in various ways of desire. In literary and cultural theory, however, the word is much more complex and contested. For Freud, sexuality refers to the attempts to achieve desired objects, whether or not these desires are self-evidently sexual or not. In Freudian terms, **masculine** sexuality is defined by competitiveness and aggression; **feminine** sexuality by lack (of the phallus) and passivity. The achievement of gendered sexuality is the prerequisite for the achievement of maturity. For other writers, most notably Michel Foucault, sexuality is the placing of sexual practice into the realm of discourse; sexuality is not so much 'what we do' as 'how we describe what we do', and the conditions culturally and socially by which the ways in which we describe become shaped and so determine our articulations (the types of words we use, in what **contexts**, how the terms change according to context, the associations of pleasure or guilt with the discourse). Furthermore, Foucault argues that such descriptions are always necessarily implicated in the formation and use of **power**. In much feminist writing, there has been a revision of Freudian analysis, especially in relation to feminine sexuality. Writers such as Luce Irigaray and Hélène Cixous have argued that feminine sexuality is not reducible to a series of simple formulae (lack and passivity); instead feminine sexuality is to be understood as multiple, flowing and unlimitable. This model is proposed partly in order to re-evaluate the question of female creativity against male-ordained versions of a femininity that cannot be active in its own behalf, and which is not defined by pleasure (or *jouissance*).

Sexuate – Term associated with French feminist Luce Irigaray's notion of suppressed maternal womanhood.

Sign – According to C. S. Peirce, a sign, or *representamen*, is 'something that stands to somebody for something in some respect or capacity'. Peirce demonstrated the nature of a given sign's attributes via such concepts as mediation and triadicity. Peirce argues that signs are invariably **mediated** by the external forces of history, culture and time, and these mediating entities characterize the ways in which we interpret signs and symbols. The process of triadicity finds its origins in the dyadic relationship between the sign itself and the signified, which refers to the idea that constitutes the sign's meaning. Peirce furthered this notion in terms of a more complex, triadic relationship between the sign and the signified, as well as between the sign and the interpretant, which Peirce described as 'all that is explicit in the sign itself apart from its context and circumstances of utterance'. For Peirce, signs become actualized when they represent something other than themselves. Signs exist as mere objects when standing on their own. In other words, signs always depend upon something other than themselves to establish their uniqueness. In Peirce's philosophy, then, signs are inevitably subordinate to their qualities of representation. Essentially, signs can only be recognized in a relational **context** with something other than themselves; hence, signs take on their unique characteristics of being when interpreted in terms of their historical or cultural antecedents. According to Saussure, a sign comprises a sound image, or signifier, and a concept, or signified. The signifier refers to a set of speech sounds in language, while the signified functions as the meaning that undergirds the sign itself. Eschewing Peirce's theories regarding the objectivity and subjectivity of language, Saussure's semiology contends that the senses of identity or uniqueness of all aspects of language emerge via the **differences** inherent in that language's network of linguistic relationships, rather than through a given language's objective features. This concept demonstrates Saussure's paradoxical argument that in a given language system meaning is generated only through difference between signifiers. There are no positive terms or signs the meaning of which is self-sufficient.

Signification – Relates generally to Ferdinand de Saussure's conception of the sign, which consists of two inseparable aspects, the signifier and the signified. The signifier refers to a set of speech sounds in language, while the signified functions as the meaning that undergirds the sign itself.

Signifier/Signified – Saussure argues that a word or image (the sign) comes in two parts. There is the sound it makes (or its graphic equivalent) which he terms the 'signifier'; and there is the mental image that the sound or graphic equivalent produces in the reader/viewer – the signified. The relationship between signifier and signified is entirely arbitrary and conventional; it is, however, also impossible to separate the two. Furthermore the relationship between the sign in its constituent parts of signifier/signified and its referent (the real object to which it refers) is also arbitrary. In other words, signified and referent are not interchangeable terms for Saussure.

Simulacra/Simulacrum/Simulation – Term often associated with Jean Baudrillard's notion of the reality effect, which relates to the ways in which reality is often established and becomes replaced for some individuals and cultures through hyperreal media such as photography, film and other media; hence, simulacrum refers to the image, representation or reproduction of a concrete other in which the very idea of the real is no longer the signified of which the simulacrum is the signified. Simulation, the process whereby simulacra assume their function, belongs to what Baudrillard terms the 'second order': there is no anterior 'real', the idea of the 'real' only comes into being through the cultural dissemination of images (such as those of advertising) or simulacra.

Singularity – Jacques Derrida postulates that our understanding of every sign involves an assumption of the absolute singularity, the uniqueness of that sign or mark, that is to say, its singularity. However, for it to be possible for the sign to communicate or have meaning, it has to be transmissible, reiterable. It therefore cannot be absolutely singular. Yet, paradoxically, the possibility of inscription outside of any finite or determinable **context** – in order to function properly as my name, my proper name must be able to be transmissible outside my presence – while denying absolute singularity, also suggests the singularity which apparently gives the sign its **authority**. The term is employed by Jean-

Luc Nancy to describe a given individual's particularity, or the essence that establishes and maintains their irreducible sense of **self**, with the proviso that any sense of self, subjectivity or **being** is also, always, a being-with, or being-in-common.

Sinthome – Lacanian term meaning symptom; the spelling of the word is archaic. For Lacan, the symptom is a radical signifier of the unconscious irreducible to any interpretation or meaning.

Social construction – Concept that explains the ways in which ideas, identities and texts result from the interaction amongst socialized norms of existence, cultural politics and individualized senses of identity.

Solipsism – The belief that one can only ever have proper evidence of one's own existence; an absolute egotism which depends on refusing to admit the existence, demands and needs of others.

Speaking (as) woman **(parler-femme)** – Term employed by Luce Irigaray indicative of experimental modalities of writing, implicitly stressing Irigaray's understanding of relation between writing and female sexuality and disruptive of univocal syntaxes and logic.

Speech-Act Theory – A theory of language established by British philosopher John L. Austin, who believed in contextualizing language study. Austin's theories rejected the prevailing notions that all possible sentences are basic or *kernel* sentences and that such sentences declare something that can be determined to be either true or false. Austin defined verbal utterances as either constatives or performatives. According to Austin, constatives refer to something that can be determined to be either true or false, while performatives denote sentences that engage in such activities as questioning, admonishing or pleading.

Structure of Feeling – Term coined by Raymond Williams as a mediating concept between 'art' and 'culture' to denote the 'deep community' that makes communication possible. A structure of feeling is neither universal nor class specific, but 'a very deep and wide possession'. The term was meant to embrace both the immediately experiential and the generationally-specific aspects of artistic process.

Subaltern – Term, taken from the work of Antonio Gramsci and used initially to define proletarian and other working-class groups, *subaltern* is employed in postcolonial studies after Gayatri Spivak to address dominated and marginalized groups.

Subject position – The location in a text identified as that belonging to the human **subject**, or the assumed position within a text that is identified as its 'voice'.

Subject/Subjectivity – The concept of selfhood that is developed in and articulated through the acquisition of language. A subject is a **self** in language; subjectivity is the process of attaining and expressing selfhood in and through language or the location of the self situated and subjectified by cultural, **epistemological, ideological** and other social discourses and institutions.

Sublimation – A Freudian term, sublimation signifies the ways in which sexual drives are rerouted into other creative and intellectual areas of activity which are socially acceptable.

Sublime – An **aesthetic** category, that which in a work of art which produces responses of awe and strong emotion. Most if not all of the current discourses of the sublime in critical thinking are inherited or developed, directly or otherwise, from commentaries of the concept of the sublime in the eighteenth century, as that concept came to be elaborated in relation to matters of taste, **empirical** psychology, the discourse of the landscape and related philosophical considerations. While it is the work of Edmund Burke which has traditionally been considered as constituting the principal consideration of the sublime, this is by no means the only discussion to be taken into account. Much recent theoretical work which addresses the question of the sublime, and the ways in which analysis of aesthetic effect is tied to human perception and the constitution of the **subject**, has returned to Immanuel Kant's profound analysis of the sublime.

Supplement/Supplementarity – Quasi-concept which, as Jacques Derrida points out, means both an addition and a replacement, developed in response to Rousseau's understanding of writing as a supplement to speech. The idea of supplementarity puts into play the disruption of a full presence of a sign in making possible signification, indicating the work of **difference** within the self-same. The supplement is supposed to act as an addition or complement which completes. In so doing, the supplement is meant to cover up a lack, but, in being a supplement, in producing the meaning of the 'original', it disrupts the very idea of the original as self-sufficient.

Suture – Term in Lacanian psychoanalysis describing the moment that a given **subject** enters into language; hence, the suture denotes the linguistic gap that the subject subsumes within a given language.

Symbolic Institution – Term often associated with Slavoj Žižek that refers to the ways in which individuals or cultures attempt to manipulate their conventional, more socially or politically relevant others by enacting artificial systems of thought or organization in their places.

Symbolism – The usage of symbols in order to represent other things, ideas or concepts. In literary works, symbolism refers to an author's attempt to create a series of associations and incremental or applied meanings. Symbolism also refers to the late nineteenth-century French literary movement that rejected literary realism in favour of subjective symbols that evoke emotional reactions among readers.

Symptomatic Reading – Refers to a kind of reading practice that accounts for the **power**/knowledge relations that exist when the notion of meaning is in intellectual or ideological conflict; symptomatic readers reconstruct a given text's discursive conditions in order to treat the text as a symptom, understand its internal relations, and comprehend – by challenging the text's intellectual properties – the ways in which it ultimately produces (or fails to produce) meaning.

Syntagm – Term often associated with Roman Jakobson that refers to an orderly combination of interacting signifiers that establish a meaningful whole; in language, for example, a sentence functions as a syntagm of words.

Technoscience – Term often associated with Paul Virilio that refers to the ubiquitous ways in which technological culture and the information world dominate social, political and economic spheres of influence.

Tekhne – From the Greek for 'making', but also defined by Heidegger as a 'bringing forth'; Heidegger argues that *tekhne* is most appropriately understood not as or in the act of manual production so much as what is revealed by the act of making. A general term pertaining to any technical rather than essential determination in the broadest sense of technique, relating to technology, writing (in Derrida's sense), artistic technique and so forth, in opposition to essence or substance, to which technique is traditionally or metaphysically subordinated as at best an auxiliary means. The term is usually used, primarily following Heidegger and Derrida, to indicate, by contrast, the equally constitutive rather than subordinate role of *tekhne* and, by so doing, to enable a more general deconstruction of the metaphysics of presence.

Tele·technology – Refers to all electronic media such as the Internet, video, e-mail, television, telephony and the general thought of the system to which these belong, by which images, messages, signals and signs, discourses, etc. are transmitted and circulated.

Telos/Teleology – Telos refers to any form of ultimate end or conclusion; teleology denotes the study of the role of design in nature and an attempt to explain the existence of natural phenomena.

Text/Textuality – Since the work of Roland Barthes and other critics who are associated with the terms structuralism and poststructuralism, the term *text* has taken on the sense of a process rather than a finished product, of which books and other literary forms are examples. A novel may be a text, but textuality is not confined by the idea of the book. Textuality thus names the interwoven discourses, phenomena or other grouping of signs, images and so forth by which we perceive the world and by which we, as **subjects**, are situated.

Theory – A very loosely wielded term which has become somewhat vacuous, at least potentially so, 'theory' refers, in the field of literary studies, to the critical movement which has emerged in the Anglo-American university since the 1960s, as a response in large part to interest within the English-speaking academic world in particular strands of continental linguistics, **narratology**, psychoanalysis, **semiotics** and philosophy. What is termed theory is often associated with equally diffuse terms such as poststructuralism in which literary theorists have attempted to establish new spheres of learning and new approaches to canonical and non-canonical texts alike. Such approaches might best be defined, albeit warily, as certain momentary hybrid coalitions or assemblages of **epistemological** and **ontological** interests, a rethinking of the historical, the constitution of **subjectivity** and sexuality, and the political and philosophical grounds of **narrative** and representation.

Trace – Jacques Derrida formulates the idea of the trace as what remains when an instance of **singularity**, such as a signature, has erased the possibility of its absolute singularity in having been inscribed. The trace is the mark of that which has never been presentable as such. The trace makes meaning possible by being, for Derrida, the *différance* which disrupts any notion of absolute origin. Jean Baudrillard's use of the term refers to the trace of meaning that the reality effect fosters; arguing that postmodernity has resulted in an artificial era of hyperreality, Baudrillard explains the notion of trace as a kind of nostalgia via which we establish meaning in our lives.

Tradition – A socially or culturally established, inherited or customary pattern of thought, action or behaviour. Tradition also refers to a characteristic manner, method or style of organization or conduct.

Transference – Psychoanalytic term indicating the process by which the analysand transfers and thereby repeats the psychic dynamic developed in early childhood pertaining to **desire** of the other onto the analyst.

Transgression – Generally, the act of breaking a law, or of overstepping, crossing, a boundary or limit, one which is usually socially, institutionally or conventionally defined and applied. Michel Foucault develops the concept and thinking of transgression as practical critique of the limits of forms of knowledge in specific ways relating to the **subject's** freedom. Foucault points out the interdependency of the concepts of the limit and transgression. There could be no idea of the limit unless it were crossable, at least in principle. However, the duration of transgression in relation to the limit is very brief: for, as Foucault argues, once the act of transgression crosses the limit, the transgression is no longer a transgression, strictly speaking. The importance of the idea of transgression for Foucault is in the fact that, as he puts it, 'transgression forces the limit to face the fact of its imminent disappearance'. The relationship of transgression to the limit thus comprehended is not one of simple **binary opposition** but is, instead, a radically destabilizing relationship. For Foucault transgression does not simply oppose, nor is it a negative. Rather, it affirms in a neutral fashion an instance of freedom and limitlessness.

Transparency – The idea that the **narrative** voice in realist fiction does not **mediate** or interpret the world it presents but that it allows direct access to that world in neutral terms.

Trope – A word or figure of speech used so as to suggest a sense other than that which is commonly assumed; otherwise the figurative use of language.

Typology – A system or scheme of classification based upon a set of principles, concepts or types.

Uncanny – Most often associated with the work of Freud but also found in Heidegger's discussion of **Being** as a fundamental experience of one's being in the world and one's relationship to existence, *uncanny* is the somewhat inaccurate translation in the text of Freud for the German *unheimlich* (lit. unhomely). Freud employs the term in the essay of the same name (1919) to signify the feeling of discomfort and strangeness which arises in the **self** without warning. As Freud suggests, the feeling of the uncanny *is* uncanny precisely to the extent that the sensation comes about in places where one should feel most secure or with which one is most familiar. Freud's use of the German demonstrates how the experience of the uncanny is structural, that is to say how the sense of being 'not-at-home' or 'unhomely' occurs within the idea of the home.

Unconscious – In psychoanalysis, the unconscious is the mental realm into which those aspects of mental life that are related to forbidden **desires** and instincts are consigned through the process of repression. The unconscious is absolutely unknown to the **subject** except where it exerts pressures on conscious life, as when repressed objects refuse to remain repressed. The instincts and desires it contains are usually disguised through a repressive censorship that turns forbidden ideas into different images by the processes of **condensation** and **displacement** (Freud's terms), where they become metonymies and metaphors (Lacan's terms). These censored images seek to re-enter **consciousness** through dreams, symptoms and verbal and physical tics. The subject is unable to interpret the new images him/herself and must submit to analysis to 'read' the pulsions of his own unconscious realm.

Undecidability – A term associated with the work of Jacques Derrida, often confused with the idea of indeterminacy. Undecidability persists within structures of meaning, even within particular words, such as the Greek *pharmakon*, which signifies both cure *and* poison, and thereby resists translation into either cure *or* poison. However, undecide-ability is not simply a matter of equivocation in the etymology of words, even though the doubling and division which inhabits, which spaces and which makes possible **writing** is seen to belong to the structure of a supposedly originary word. As Derrida shows in his essay 'Psyche: Inventions of the Other' ([1987] 1991), the undecidable haunts, and thereby makes impossible, any possible distinction between performative and constative speech acts. For, as Derrida puts it in 'The Double Session', undecideability 'is not caused by some enigmatic equivocality'. If the undecidable *is* anything, that is to say, if we can risk an **ontic** proposition, it is that which marks the movement between ontic or **ontological** definitions and which, in so marking (as the effect of **difference** or writing, or through the strategic use of terms such as *hymen* in 'The Double Session') any attempted articulation of meaning grounded on the structural separation – and thus, stabilisation – of terms, undermines the very process by which the stable identity or meaning is read. Thus, because of this movement within language and as what remains in language, one cannot complete a 'reading' or make the break with a text that the idea of a reading implies.

Universalism – Refers to the practice of perceiving generalization in all aspects of human life or intellectual discourse; the **ideology** of making universal assumptions (e.g. concerning 'humanity') which ignores culturally or historically specific or determined aspects of societies, cultures and individuals.

Value – The estimation, appraisal or interpretation of a given commodity's worth, significance or utility. Value also refers to a moral principle established by a given individual or community.

Writing – Though a familiar enough term indicative of the inscribed marks representing speech, Jacques Derrida explores and expands the term in ways which destabilize the conventional notion of writing as a more or less unproblematic mode of communication or otherwise as the idea of the graphic approximation of speech. In the essay 'Signature Event Context', Derrida schematizes how what he calls the classical concept of writing is usually understood: (a) as a mark which can be reiterated, the function of which is not 'exhausted' in any single inscription. Such a mark, whether in the form of a statement, a signature or proper name, or, indeed, a literary text such as a novel, is in principal communicable *as* a writing in that it can communicate beyond and, indeed, before, without, the presence of any living **subject**, such as the author; (b) at the same time, what we call writing may be cited outside its immediate **context** and its meaning therefore transformed, again beyond the control of any author or the notion of authorial intent. Derrida points out that, because the written sign (qua writing) is iterable, and can be extracted from any context, its function or meaning cannot be contained by, or reduced to any finite context; (c) the break with what we call context indicates for Derrida the spacing of which any writing partakes in the first place in order to be meaningful. A written sign, in order to be meaningful, has to function not only through its immediate presence but, importantly, in its spatial **difference** from other signs. The spacing by which meaning emerges and is in fact possible at all is not a simple blank space or 'negative' for Derrida but is, instead, that which makes the mark or inscription possible. In pursuing these aspects of writing by giving attention initially to the written sign, narrowly conceived as the written or printed words on a page, Derrida demonstrates how all language, including spoken language and images, is in fact a writing, available only through spacing, through difference (and more significantly, *différance*). Thus not only is there no immediacy or plenitude in any sign, but writing, far from being the secondary, debased supplement to the spoken word and to the idea of language in general (and with that the promise of presence for which the vocable apparently acts as guarantor), is, in fact, that which makes any communication possible, even while, as writing, all signs can only refer to other signs, without ever attaining semantic or syntagmatic stability.

Contributors

Amir Ahmadi, University of Sydney
David Alderson, Manchester University
Charles Altieri, University of California, Berkeley
Jan Baetens, Katholieke universiteit, Leuven
William Baker, Northern Illinois University
Peter Barry, University of Wales, Aberystwyth
Ian Baucom, Duke University
Megan Becker-Leckrone, University of Nevada, Las Vegas
Paul Bowman, Leeds University
Joan Brandt, Claremont Colleges
John Brannigan, Queen's University, Belfast
Marcia Butzel, Clark University
Heesok Chang, Vassar College
John M. Clum, Duke University
Claire Colebrook, Stirling University
Elizabeth Constable, University of California, Davis
Marcel Cornis-Pope, Virginia Commonwealth University
Mark Currie, Anglia Polytechnic University
Dirk de Geest, Katholieke universiteit, Leuven
Ortwin de Graef, Katholieke universiteit, Leuven
Anne Donadey, San Diego State University
Antony Easthope, Manchester Metropolitan University
Luke Ferretter, Wolfson College, Cambridge
William Flesch, Brandeis University
Kate Flint, Linacre College, Oxford University
Nicole Fluhr, University of Michigan
Véronique M. Foti, Pennsylvania State University
SunHee Kim Gertz, Clark University
Jane Goldman, University of Dundee
Karen Green, Monash University
Ullrich Michael Haase, Manchester Metropolitan University
Kevin Hart, Monash University
Moyra Haslett, Queen's University Belfast
Lynn A. Higgins, Dartmouth College

Robert C. Holub, University of California, Berkeley
Gillian Howie, University of Liverpool
R. Brandon Kershner, University of Florida
Loren Kruger, University of Chicago
John Kucich, University of Michigan
Jeremy Lane, University of Sussex
Garry Leonard, University of Toronto
Carolyn Lesjak, Swarthmore College
Mitchell R. Lewis, Oklahoma University
Jacques Lezra, University of Wisconsin-Madison
Jonathan Loesberg, American University
Gail Ching-Liang Low, University of Dundee
Niall Lucy, Murdoch University
Juliet Flower MacCannell, University of California, Irvine
Martin McQuillan, Leeds University
Nick Mansfield, University of Melbourne
Toby Miller, New York University
Andrew Milner, Monash University
Warren Montag, Occidental College
Amelia Mariá de la Luz Montes, University of Nebraska, Lincoln
K. M. Newton, University of Dundee
Betsy Nies, University of North Florida
Brian Niro, De Paul University
Arkady Plotnitsky, Purdue University
David Punter, Bristol University
Jean-Michel Rabaté, University of Pennsylvania
Nicholas T. Rand, University of Wisconsin-Madison
Ruth Robbins, University College, Northampton
Alain-Michel Rocheleau, University of British Columbia
Alison Ross, Monash University
Imre Salusinszky, University of Newcastle, Australia
Malini Johar Schueller, University of Florida
Stephen Shapiro, University of Warwick
Kenneth Surin, Duke University
Jeremy Tambling, Hong Kong University
Ashley Tauchert, Exeter University
Maureen Turim, University of Florida
David Van Leer, University of California, Davis
Virginia Mason Vaughan, Clark University
Michael Walsh, University of Hartford
Leigh Wilson, University of Westminster
Boris Wiseman, Durham University
Julian Wolfreys, University of Florida
Kenneth Womack, Pennsylvania State University, Altoona
Yun Hsing Wu, Indiana University
Ewa Ziarek, Notre Dame University

Index

Bold page references refer to terms in the glossary.